MANAGEMENT: A BOOK OF READINGS

McGRAW-HILL SERIES IN MANAGEMENT
KEITH DAVIS, CONSULTING EDITOR

MANAGEMENT:
A BOOK OF READINGS

HAROLD KOONTZ
Graduate School of Business Administration
University of California, Los Angeles

CYRIL O'DONNELL
Graduate School of Business Administration
University of California, Los Angeles

McGRAW-HILL BOOK COMPANY, NEW YORK • SAN FRANCISCO • TORONTO • LONDON

PREFACE

One of the difficulties encountered by all who read or teach in the area of management theory and policy is that much of the best thought and experience in the field is in widely scattered sources. Moreover, the great interest in management in recent years has led to a deluge of materials on the subject. The reader who wades through this mass of information finds difficulty in selecting the most pertinent and representative selections. And even guided by a well-compiled bibliography, he has to cope with the limitations of libraries and his understandable desire to have the material conveniently at hand.

Particularly for students, but also for the practicing manager who would like to have some of this material readily available, a book of selected readings in management has seemed to us especially worthwhile. None of the books devoted to an analysis of managerial functions can do much more than refer to some of the more significant literature. The tendency for such books to be rather narrow in approach and to deal with the subject matter summarily, rather than broadly, is unavoidable. This is not the choice or the fault of those who write such books; rather, it naturally results from the restrictions of space imposed by the publishers and the size limitations of such a book from the standpoint of the reader.

This situation appears to be especially serious in the area of general management. It is compounded because the source material is widely scattered, in books and journals devoted to the social sciences, in business and management association publications, and in journals concerned with business activities.

The authors, in attempting to collect the more significant writings on general management, have found that the problem of selecting appropriate material from hundreds of sources is monumental. It was so when an earlier version was published in 1959. It is even more true now that the volume and quality of writing in the field has increased so tremendously. Fortunately, the publisher has found it possible to again include nearly half the volume of readings included in the earlier version. Some of the classics from the old book appear in the new, but some items, even with the increased space, simply had to be dropped. The reader will find that the emphasis here is on presenting adequate material on both the theory of management and on modern practical applications. The book has changed so greatly that the old title Readings in Management has been dropped.

The materials have been grouped according to a very widely accepted theory of management. That is, the book has a general introductory part and, subsequently, five parts on the principal management functions: planning, organization, staffing, direction, and control. This framework is flexible and inclusive enough so that it permits presentation of a wide variety of selections, written from many different points of view. Users will find these selections effective in almost any classroom situation (the "principles" course, graduate courses, seminars, management development groups) as well as in the practicing manager's office.

In making the selections, we thought it best to cover most subjects in as thorough a way as the originals, rather than to give brief excerpts as is often done. While, in some cases, we have omitted sentences and even paragraphs, the material is essentially as it was when originally published.

We are indebted to the authors of these selections and to their publishers for permission to reprint. Their cooperation has been both prompt and courteous, and we trust that our readers will appreciate having such a wide selection of the best management literature available in one volume.

Harold Koontz • Cyril O'Donnell

CONTENTS

PART SIX.   CONTROL   423

PART ONE

THE BASIS
OF A THEORY OF
MANAGEMENT

This introductory section contains a selection of readings which indicate why a theory of management is necessary, what makes for a systematic theory, the central thesis of management theory, and the various approaches that have been made toward developing a theory. Because most pioneers in management thinking viewed theory primarily as a means for effectively teaching the practice of management, the comments of the great Henri Fayol, generally regarded as the father of modern management theory, are reproduced. It is interesting to note that Fayol's central thesis was that principles, or theory, become the means by which light is shed on the understanding and improvement of management practice.

In order to develop understanding and distill fundamental truths of use to practitioners in any field, one must recognize what a theory is, how it contributes to the development of science, and how it must be based on a conceptual scheme that "makes sense." The authors have selected for this purpose an excerpt from the writings of Prof. Talcott Parsons, the social theorist.

To show the various approaches that have been made toward study and research in management, particularly in recent years, the editors have included Harold Koontz's provocative article "The Management Theory Jungle." In this article, the author attempts to distill, from the recent deluge of writings, research, and statements of philosophy on this subject, a classification of approaches or "schools" of management theory. In doing so, he outlines the differences among these schools and suggests that the various approaches can be integrated into a useful and systematic theory of management.

The article by Professor Cooper, "Newer Analytic Approaches to Management," illustrates the application of the methodologies of the physical sciences to the area of management. As Professor Cooper aptly points out, these newer techniques are primarily ones of analysis and, as such, fit into the framework of management planning. He depicts them as techniques which can improve the quality of management decision making and not as functions of the manager.

1

The Need for and Possibility of Management Teaching*

HENRI FAYOL

The real reason for the absence of management teaching in our vocational schools is absence of theory; without theory no teaching is possible. Now there exists no generally accepted theory of management emanating from general discussion. There is no shortage of personal theorizing, but failing any accepted theory each one thinks that he has the best methods and everywhere there may be observed—in industry, the army, the home, the State—the most contradictory practices under the aegis of the same principle. Whereas in the technical sphere a head would not dare to infringe certain established rules without risking total loss of prestige, in the managerial one the most undesirable practices may be indulged in with impunity. The methods used are judged not on their own merits but on their results, which often are very remote and mostly difficult to relate to their causes. The situation might be quite otherwise were there an accepted theory, that is to say, a collection of principles, rules, methods, procedures, tried and checked by general experience. It is not principles which are lacking: were it sufficient to proclaim them to have them prevail we should enjoy the best possible management everywhere. Who has not heard proclaimed a hundred times the need for the grand principles of authority, discipline, subordination of individual interest to the common good, unity of direction, co-ordination of effort, foresight, etc.? It must be admitted that proclamation is not enough. The fact is that the light of principles, like that of lighthouses, guides only those who already know the way into port, and a principle bereft of the means of putting it into practice is of no avail.

Nor is there any lack of methods: their name is legion, but good and bad are to be found side by side at the same time in the home, workshop and State, with a persistence only to be explained by lack of theory. The general public is not in a position to pass judgment on managerial activity, hence the importance of establishing a theory of management as soon as possible. It would be neither lengthy nor difficult if a few industrial leaders decided to set forth their personal views on the general principles which they consider most calculated to promote smooth running and on the means most conducive to the realization of such principles. Light would soon be thrown on the subject as the result of comparison and discussion. But the majority of higher managers have neither time nor inclination for writing and most often depart without leaving either doctrine or disciples. Hence too much reliance must not be placed on help from this quarter.

Fortunately there is no need to be concerned with the running of a large-scale undertaking or to proffer a masterly treatise in order to make useful contribution to the building up of theory. The slightest comment appropriately made is of value, and since there is no limit to the possible number of commentators it is to be hoped that once the stream has started to flow it will not be stemmed. It is a case of setting it going, starting general discussion— that is what I am trying to do by publishing this survey, and I hope that a theory will emanate from it. This done, there is the question of teaching to be solved. Everyone needs some concepts of management; in the home, in affairs of State, the need for managerial ability is in keeping with the importance of the undertaking, and for individual people the need is everywhere greater in accordance with the position occupied. Hence there should be some

* Reprinted by permission of the publisher from Henri Fayol, *General and Industrial Management*, Pitman Publishing Corporation, New York, 1949, pp. 14–16. Mr. Fayol was a highly successful French industrialist who perceived the universality of management and the need for management principles. This excerpt was originally published in 1916 and was based, in part, on lectures delivered in 1908.

generalized teaching of management; elementary in the primary schools, somewhat wider in the post-primary schools, and quite advanced in higher educational establishments. This teaching will no more make good managers out of all its pupils than technical teaching makes excellent technicians out of its trainees. All that would be asked of it would be services analogous to those rendered by technical education. And why not? It is chiefly a matter of putting young people in the way of understanding and using the lessons of experience. At present the beginner has neither management theory nor method, and in this respect some remain beginners all their lives. Hence

an effort must be made to spread management ideas throughout all ranks of the population. Obviously school has a large part to play in this teaching. In establishments for higher education teachers will be well able to work out their courses the day when management forms part of their teaching. It is more difficult to conceive what primary school teaching of management should be. On this point I have made an attempt which I shall set out, without claiming anything for it, in the conviction that a good primary teacher will be better able than I am to select from theory and put within his pupils' reach what is suitable to teach them.

2

*The General Nature and Functions of Systematic Theory**

TALCOTT PARSONS

It is scarcely too much to say that the most important single index of the state of maturity of a science is the state of its systematic theory. This includes the character of the generalized conceptual scheme in use in the field, the kinds and degrees of logical integration of the different elements which make it up, and the ways in which it is actually being used in empirical research. On this basis the thesis may be advanced that sociology is just in the process of emerging into the status of a mature science. Heretofore it has not enjoyed the kind of integration and directed activity which only the availability and common acceptance and employment of a well-articulated generalized theoretical system can give to a science. The main framework of such a system is, however, now available, though this fact

* Reprinted by permission of the publisher from Talcott Parsons, *Essays in Sociological Theory,* The Free Press of Glencoe, New York, 1954, pp. 212–219. Mr. Parsons is professor of sociology, Harvard University.

is not as yet very generally appreciated and much in the way of development and refinement remains to be done on the purely theoretical level, as well as its systematic use and revision in actual research. It may therefore be held that we stand on the threshold of a definitely new era in sociology and the neighboring social science fields.

"Theory" is a term which covers a wide variety of different things which have in common only the element of generalized conceptualization. The theory of concern to the present paper in the first place constitutes a "system" and thereby differs from discrete "theories," that is, particular generalizations about particular phenomena or classes of them. A theoretical system in the present sense is a body of logically interdependent generalized concepts of empirical reference. Such a system tends, ideally, to become "logically closed," to reach such a state of logical integration that every logical implication of any combination of propositions in the system is explicitly stated in some other proposition in the same system.[1]

In a highly developed system of theory there may be a wide variety of different types of generalized concepts and functions which they may serve. A thorough discussion of the possibilities cannot be undertaken here, so attention will be confined to those most vital to the general status of the scientific field. The two most general functions of theory are the facilitation of description and analysis. The two are most intimately connected since it is only when the essential facts about a phenomenon have been described in a carefully systematic and orderly manner that accurate analysis becomes possible at all.

The basic category of all scientific description seems to be that of empirical system. The empirical references of statements of fact cannot be isolated from each other, but each describes one aspect or feature of an interconnected whole which, taken as a whole, has some measure of independent significance as an entity. Apart from theoretical conceptualization there would appear to be no method of selecting among the indefinite number of varying kinds of factual observation which can be made about a concrete phenomenon or field so that the various descriptive statements about it articulate into a coherent whole, which constitutes an "adequate," a "determinate" description. Adequacy in description is secured in so far as determinate and verifiable answers can be given to all the scientifically *important* questions involved. What questions are important is largely determined by the logical structure of the generalized conceptual scheme which implicitly or explicitly, is employed.

Specific descriptive propositions often refer to particular aspects or properties of an empirically existent set of phenomena. Such propositions are, however, empirically meaningless unless the "what" which they qualify is clearly and determinately conceived and defined. This "what," the interconnected empirically existent phenomena which constitute the field of description and analysis for a scientific investigation, is what is meant by an empirical "system." It is that which can, for scientific purposes, be treated at the same time as a body of phenomena sufficiently extensive, complex and diversified so that the results of their study are significant and not merely truistic, and sufficiently limited and simplified so that the problems involved are manageable

and the investigator does not get lost in the maze.

The functions of a generalized conceptual scheme on the descriptive level seem to be performed mainly in terms of two types of conceptual elements. The first consists in what is called the "frame of reference." This is the most general framework of categories in terms of which empirical scientific work "makes sense." Thus, in classical mechanics, three-dimensional rectilinear space, time, mass, location, motion are the essential elements of the frame of reference. Every descriptive statement, to be applicable to a mechanical system must be referable to one or more "particles" each with a given mass, capable of location in space, changing its location in time through motion, etc. Besides providing the specific categories in terms of which a system is described, the function of the frame of reference is above all to provide a test of the determinacy of the description of a system. It is a logical implication of the structure of the conceptual system that there is a limited number of essential categories, specific values for which must be obtained before the description can be determinate. Its use is the only way of locating the important gaps in available knowledge.

The second level is that of the structure of systems as such. Phenomena which are significantly interrelated, which constitute a system, are intrinsically interrelated on the structural level. This fact seems to be inherent in the most general frame of reference of empirical knowledge itself, which implies the fundamental significance of the concept of system as that is taken for granted here. Structure is the "static" aspect of the descriptive mode of treatment of a system. From the structural point of view a system is composed of "units," of subsystems which potentially exist independently, and their structural interrelations. Thus a system in mechanics is "made up" of particles as its units. The structure of the system consists in the number of particles, their properties, such as mass, and their interrelations, such as relative locations, velocities and directions of motion.

The functions of the frame of reference and of structural categories in their descriptive use are to state the necessary facts, and the setting for solving problems of dynamic analysis, the ultimate goal of scientific investigation. Besides the immense possibilities of variation in the scope of analysis, there are two aspects of the goal itself; first the "causal explanation" of past specific phenomena or processes and the prediction of future events; second, the attainment of generalized analytical knowledge, of

[1] For a fuller development of this view of theory, see the author's *The Structure of Social Action,* McGraw-Hill Book Company, New York, 1937, especially chaps. 1 and 19.

"laws" which can be applied to an indefinite number of specific cases with the use of the appropriate factual data. The attainment of the two goals, or aspects of the same goal, go hand in hand. On the one hand specific causal explanation is attainable only through the application of some generalized analytical knowledge; on the other, the extension of analytical generalization is only possible by generalization from empirical cases and verification in terms of them.

3

The Coordinative Principle*

JAMES D. MOONEY

Organization begins when people combine their efforts for a given purpose. We have shown this by the simple illustration of two people uniting their efforts to lift and move some weighty object. This combination, however, is not the first principle of organization. It is only an illustration of organization itself.

To find the first principle, let us carry the illustration a step further. The efforts of these two lifters must be coordinated, which means that they must act together. If first one lifted, and then the other, there would be no unity of action, and hence no true organization of effort. Coordination first appeared in organization when one of those hairy slow-witted ancestors of ours assumed authority and gave the guttural equivalent of "heave ho!" *Here, then, we find the first principle of organization.*

Coordination, therefore, is the orderly arrangement of group effort, to provide unity of action in the pursuit of a common purpose.

When we call *coordination* the first principle, we mean that this term expresses the principles of organization *in toto;* nothing less. This does not mean that there are no subordinated principles; it simply means that all the others are contained in this one of coordination. The others are simply the principles through which coordination operates and thus becomes effective.

As coordination contains all the principles

of organization, it likewise expresses all the purposes of organization, in so far as these purposes relate to its internal structure. To avoid confusion we must keep in mind that there are always two objectives of organization, the *internal* and the *external*. The latter may be anything, according to the purpose or interest that calls the group together, but the internal objective is coordinative always.

AUTHORITY

In some spheres of organization the external objective is not continuous. This is true of army organizations in peacetime, when all external objectives are in abeyance, and the army merely waits for mobilization day, for the day of action. In every form of organization, however, the internal objective must be constant. This internal objective is organized efficiency, and everything that is essential to such efficiency is expressed in the single word "coordination." There can be no waiting for "M-day" in coordination. It is a constant necessity in organization, essential to the existence of the organization itself.

As coordination is the all-inclusive principle of organization, it must have its own principle and foundation in *authority,* or the supreme coordinating power. Always, in every form of organization, this supreme authority must rest somewhere, else there would be no directive for any coordinated effort.

The term "authority," as here used, need not imply autocracy. Where true democracy prevails, this authority rests with the group as

---

* Reprinted by permission of the publisher from James D. Mooney, *The Principles of Organization,* Harper & Row, Publishers, Incorporated, New York, 1947, pp. 5–13. Mr. Mooney was an industrialist and a director on numerous corporate boards.

a whole, as it rests in our government with the people of the United States. In the simplest and most compact forms of democratic organization it is represented in the entire group, assembled at one time, in one place. Examples in secular government are separated as widely in time as the ecclesia of ancient Athens and the present New England town meeting.

In whatever form it may appear, this supreme coordinating authority must be conceived simply as the source of all coordination, and not necessarily as the coordinating directive that runs through the entire organization. In a democracy like our own this authority rests with the people, who exercise it through the leaders of their choice.

The distinction between authority and leadership is such a vital one that it will in due course be considered at greater length. It is sufficient here to observe that the supreme coordinating authority must be prior to leadership in logical order, for it is this coordinating force that makes the organization. Leadership, on the other hand, always presupposes the organization. There can be no leader without something to lead. Leadership, of course, must exercise a derived authority. In absolutist forms of government the supreme coordinating authority usually exercises its own leadership, but this fact does not alter their essential difference.

Just as vital as the distinction between authority and leadership is that between authority and power, two terms so often confused. Power in the psychic sense—that is ability to do things—is distinctly an individual possession. When we speak of the power of an organization we mean that this power has become collective through coordinated effort.

Authority, on the other hand, is a right. Hence we use the expression "moral authority," and may say of some great teacher, as was said of Jesus, the greatest of all teachers, that he speaks "as one having authority," which means that he has a moral right to speak as he does. In organization, authority is likewise a right, because it inheres legitimately in the structure of the organization. The distinction in the political sphere between de jure and de facto governments is based on the difference between the right of authority, acquired through some procedure recognized as legitimate, and the mere possession of power, however obtained.

The same observations apply to the exercise of authority, a truth that is not altered by the fact that authority rests on *moral right*. Rights cannot be divorced from duties, and if authority does not use its rights with due solicitude relative to these duties, it is sooner or later bound to fall. No organization has any prospect of stability if moral factors are not its basis.

MUTUAL SERVICE

Community of interest is the legitimate basis of every organization. In searching for its psychic fundaments we find that it can mean only *mutuality of interest*. This in turn implies mutual duties, which means the obligation to *mutual service*. This obligation is universal, transcending, therefore, the sphere of organization. As expressed in the ancient Roman juridical maxim *do ut des* (I give that thou mayest give), it is the manifest basis of all human relations.

In a special sense, however, it has an application within the sphere of organization. Here it is the moral phase of the principle of coordination. It is for this reason that organizations of all kinds, whether governmental, religious, military, or industrial, furnish our best human examples of the spirit of mutual service.

Although the formal technique of organization has, until recent years, received but scant attention, the humanistic phases of organization have an extensive literature. In this literature the obligation to mutual service is called by various names, among them cooperation, integration, functional relating, and integrated functioning. All these terms suggest the formal as well as the human side of coordination, which shows how impossible it is to separate them. We must keep in mind that organizations are the creations of people, and hence that everything that is formal in organized forms must rest on psychic fundaments.

A true coordination must be based on a real community of interest in the attainment of the desired object. It is equally true that a community of interest that is real, not only in the objective sense but likewise in everybody's consciousness, can come only through a real community of understanding. This means not merely that administration and members must understand each other, but that each and all must understand what the real purpose is and, furthermore, that every group represented in the organization must understand how and why the attainment of this purpose is essential to the welfare of all.

The reason, we think, is obvious. Mutuality of interest or, let us say, a common interest, does not, so far as human consciousness is concerned, constitute an *identity* of interest. The only conceivable means of attaining a true integration of all group interests in organization is through administrative policies that will make this community of interest a more tangible reality to every member of the group.

It is evident that every element of psychic coordination is a necessity in the establishment of harmony in all internal relations. Even this statement, however, does not include everything necessary in a truly coordinated efficiency. Before we leave this subject of coordination, therefore, let us consider one more element, especially conspicuous in church and military organization, which has its lessons for organizers in every sphere.

DOCTRINE

Coordination implies an aim or objective. But it does not follow, even where there is a true mutual interest, a mutual understanding, and a degree of mutual participation, that each and every member of the organization does in fact carry in his mind a deep understanding of the objective and how it may be attained. Among the higher officials, those who are responsible for results, this understanding should be ever present. They should know, furthermore, that the more this understanding seeps down through all ranks and grades, until all are permeated with it, the greater will be the coordinated effort and the greater the strength of the organization for the accomplishment of its purpose. It is the necessary means to this end that brings us in contact with the significant word "doctrine."

To most people this word has a religious flavor, and well it may, for, of all forms of organization, religious associations are the ones that are most deeply imbued with its spirit. But the word itself has a broader meaning. We see this illustrated in the various applications of the title "doctor," which means simply the teacher, representative, or practitioner of a doctrine. There is, indeed, a doctrine for every conceivable form of collective human effort.

Doctrine in the primary sense means the *definition of the objective*. In religious associations this doctrine is based on faith, as formally stated in the *creed*. In industrial organizations it is the attainment of a *surplus through service*. In governmental organization we find different and constantly changing doctrines, but always a doctrine of some sort, however varied its interpretations by the leaders and statesmen of history. In this primary sense doctrine is synonymous with the objective.

When we consider, however, the *procedure necessary to attain the objective* we encounter the secondary meaning of the word, which it seems a misnomer to call secondary, for it often transcends the primary meaning in practical importance. This fact the following examples will show.

With a physician or surgeon the doctrine of the objective is obvious. It is to make the patient well. But the doctrine of procedure and its application call for a thorough training and wide experience. Likewise, the doctrine of the military objective is simple. According to the school of Foch and Napoleon, it is the forcing of a decision through the overthrow of the adversary. The necessary procedure, however, constitutes a highly technical art, in which all the principles of military strategy and tactics are involved.

This point is vital in all forms of coordinated effort. Always there is sure to be a doctrine of procedure of some kind, but it is not enough to have such a doctrine, nor is it sufficient for the doctrine to be a sound one. Above all, is is essential that this doctrine shall, in the popular phrase, be "sold" to everyone concerned. Every member of an organization should not only know its doctrine, but he should feel it and absorb it until he lives in its atmosphere and makes it the guide of all his acts.

A doctrine of procedure does not mean a body of set rules that must be accepted as though they were articles of faith. We shall presently discuss more broadly the distinction between rules and principles in organization. "Indoctrination" in the military sense means simply the inculcation of those principles which serve as the guide of the military man, whatever the situation he is compelled to face.

To find a simpler illustration of unity of doctrine, and its necessity in the attainment of any group objective, we may turn to the field of sports, such as our national games of baseball and football, where groups are competing and where success in the attainment of the purpose depends on coordinated effort. In these sports there is a real functional differentiation of duties. In the formal sense, however, the problems of organization are all predetermined by the rules of the game. The primary objection also is so simple that the shortest word will state it. It is to *win*.

When we come, however, to procedure, in other words, to the means necessary to win, we find emerging in each case a real doctrine which accounts for the high importance of the baseball manager and the football coach. Tracing each doctrine through all the intricacies of baseball and football strategy we find that it rests, as it must, on the first principle of organization, namely, coordination of effort. This coordination, so essential to victory in any sport where a number of players combine their efforts for a common purpose, has given us the splendid word "teamwork."

Another illustration in a different sphere is the coordination of a symphony orchestra. Here the purpose is the production of a collective harmony, not as a means to an end but as an end in itself. To attain this end each individual musician merges himself in the common purpose. Functionalism in an orchestra is as varied as the nature of the different instruments. In the orchestra these individual functions derive their importance solely from their contribution to the common purpose, and the relation of each musician's function to this purpose is ever present in the instant result. This fact of the objective resulting instantly from the initial coordination makes the orchestra the supreme symbol and the simplest illustration of a coordinated effort.

DISCIPLINE

One other factor essential to organized efficiency must not be overlooked. Organized efficiency in the pursuit of any objective demands a doctrine, but the efficient application,

even of the soundest doctrine, demands in turn an organized *discipline*. By this we mean something more vital than the discipline imposed by command. That is essential, but even more vital is the discipline which command must impose on itself, for such is the first necessity to ensure a truly organized efficiency. Without such self-discipline at the top it would be useless to expect it anywhere else down the line. The commander of a battleship is subjected to a greater degree of discipline than a bluejacket. Even the pope must every year wash the feet of a beggar and must go to confession twice a week. Discipline by example we may call it, but such examples are essential to the discipline of any organization.

The sum of these observations is that the strength of an organization is determined by its spirit, that the spirit must be determined by the purpose and the means necessary to its attainment, and that these means imply a doctrine out of which the spirit of an organization grows and on which it lives. On the other hand, no organization can live on its spirit alone. Coordination must have its formalism, which means its technique or method by which its power is directed to the attainment of the purpose.

4

*The Management Theory Jungle**

HAROLD KOONTZ

Although students of management would readily agree that there have been problems of management since the dawn of organized life, most would also agree that systematic examination of management, with few exceptions, is the product of the present century and more especially of the past two decades. Moreover,

* Reprinted by permission of the publisher from the *Journal of the Academy of Management*, vol. 4, no. 3, pp. 174–188, December, 1961. Mr. Koontz is Mead Johnson Professor of Management in the Graduate School of Business, University of California, Los Angeles.

until recent years almost all of those who have attempted to analyze the management process and look for some theoretical underpinnings to help improve research, teaching, and practice were alert and perceptive practitioners of the art who reflected on many years of experience. Thus, at least in looking at *general* management as an intellectually based art, the earliest meaningful writing came from such experienced practitioners as Fayol, Mooney, Alvin Brown, Sheldon, Barnard, and Urwick. Certainly not even the most academic worshipper of empirical research can overlook the empiricism involved in distilling fundamentals from decades of experience by such discerning practitioners as these. Admittedly done without questionnaires, controlled interviews, or mathematics, observations by such men can hardly be accurately regarded as *a priori* or "armchair."

The noteworthy absence of academic writing and research in the formative years of modern management theory is now more than atoned for by a deluge of research and writing from the academic halls. What is interesting and perhaps nothing more than a sign of the unsophisticated adolescence of management theory is how the current flood has brought with it a wave of great differences and apparent confusion. From the orderly analysis of management at the shop-room level by Frederick Taylor and the reflective distillation of experience from the general management point of view of Henri Fayol, we now see these and other early beginnings overgrown and entangled by a jungle of approaches and approachers to management theory.

There are the behavioralists, born of the Hawthorne experiments and the awakened interest in human relations during the 1930's and 1940's, who see management as a complex of interpersonal relationships and the basis of management theory the tentative tenets of the new and undeveloped science of psychology. There are also those who see management theory as simply a manifestation of the institutional and cultural aspects of sociology. Still others, observing that the central core of management is decision-making, branch in all directions from this core to encompass everything in organization life. Then, there are mathematicians who think of management primarily as an exercise in logical relationships expressed in symbols and the omnipresent and ever revered model. But the entanglement of growth reaches its ultimate when the study of management is regarded as a study of one of a number of systems and subsystems, with an understandable tendency for the researcher to be dissatisfied until he has encompassed the entire physical and cultural universe as a management system.

With the recent discovery of an ages-old problem area by social, physical, and biological scientists, and with the supersonic increase in interest by all types of enterprise managers, the apparent impenetrability of the present thicket which we call management theory is not difficult to comprehend. One can hardly be surprised that psychologists, sociologists, anthropologists, sociometricists, economists, mathematicians, physicists, biologists, political

scientists, business administration scholars, and even practicing managers, should hop on this interesting, challenging, and profitable band wagon.

This welling of interest from every academic and practicing corner should not upset anyone concerned with seeing the frontiers of knowledge pushed back and the intellectual base of practice broadened. But what is rather upsetting to the practitioner and the observer, who sees great social potential from improved management, is that the variety of approaches to management theory has led to a kind of confused and destructive jungle warfare. Particularly among academic disciplines and their disciples, the primary interests of many would-be cult leaders seem to be to carve out a distinct (and hence "original") approach to management. And to defend this originality, and thereby gain a place in posterity (or at least to gain a publication which will justify academic status or promotion), it seems to have become too much the current style to downgrade, and sometimes misrepresent, what anyone else has said, or thought, or done.

In order to cut through this jungle and bring to light some of the issues and problems involved in the present management theory area so that the tremendous interest, intelligence, and research results may become more meaningful, it is my purpose here to classify the various "schools" of management theory, to identify briefly what I believe to be the major source of differences, and to offer some suggestions for disentangling the jungle. It is hoped that a movement for clarification can be started so at least we in the field will not be a group of blind men identifying the same elephant with our widely varying and sometimes viciously argumentative theses.

THE MAJOR "SCHOOLS" OF MANAGEMENT THEORY

In attempting to classify the major schools of management theory into six main groups, I am aware that I may overlook certain approaches and cannot deal with all the nuances of each approach. But it does seem that most of the approaches to management theory can be classified in one of these so-called "schools."

The Management Process School This approach to management theory perceives management as a process of getting things done through and with people operating in organized groups. It aims to analyze the process, to establish a conceptual framework for it, to identify principles underlying it, and to build up a theory of management from them. It regards management as a universal process, regardless of the type of enterprise, or the level in a given enterprise, although recognizing, obviously, that the environment of management differs widely between enterprises and levels. It looks upon management theory as a way of organizing experience so that practice can be improved through research, empirical testing of principles, and teaching of fundamentals involved in the management process.[1]

Often referred to, especially by its critics, as the "traditional" or "universalist" school, this school can be said to have been fathered by Henri Fayol, although many of his offspring did not know of their parent, since Fayol's work was eclipsed by the bright light of his contemporary, Frederick Taylor, and clouded by the lack of a widely available English translation until 1949. Other than Fayol, most of the early contributors to this school dealt only with the organization portion of the management process, largely because of their greater experience with this facet of management and the simple fact that planning and control, as well as the function of staffing, were given little attention by managers before 1940.

This school bases its approach to management theory on several fundamental beliefs:

1. that managing is a process and can best be dissected intellectually by analyzing the functions of the manager;
2. that long experience with management in a variety of enterprise situations can be grounds for distillation of certain fundamental truths or generalizations—usually referred to as principles—which have a clarifying and predictive value in the understanding and improvement of managing;
3. that these fundamental truths can become focal points for useful research both to ascertain their validity and to improve their meaning and applicability in practice;
4. that such truths can furnish elements, at least until disproved, and certainly until sharpened, of a useful theory of management;

5. that managing is an art, but one like medicine or engineering, which can be improved by reliance on the light and understanding of principles;
6. that principles in management, like principles in the biological and physical sciences, are nonetheless true even if a prescribed treatment or design by a practitioner in a given case situation chooses to ignore a principle and the costs involved, or attempts to do something else to offset the costs incurred (this is, of course, not new in medicine, engineering, or any other art, for art is the creative task of compromising fundamentals to attain a desired result); and
7. that, while the totality of culture and of the physical and biological universe has varying effects on the manager's environment and subjects, as indeed they do in every other field of science and art, the theory of management does not need to encompass the field of all knowledge in order for it to serve as a scientific or theoretical foundation.

The basic approach of this school, then, is to look, first, to the functions of managers. As a second step in this approach, many of us have taken the functions of managers and further dissected them by distilling what we see as fundamental truths in the understandably complicated practice of management. I have found it useful to classify my analysis of these functions around the essentials involved in the following questions:

1. What is the nature of the function?
2. What is the purpose of the function?
3. What explains the structure of the function?
4. What explains the process of the function?

Perhaps there are other more useful approaches, but I have found that I can place everything pertaining to management (even some of the rather remote research and concepts) in this framework.

Also, purely to make the area of management theory intellectually manageable, those who subscribe to this school do not usually attempt to include in the theory the entire areas of sociology, economics, biology, psychology, physics, chemistry, or others. This is done not because these other areas of knowledge are unimportant and have no bearing on management, but merely because no real progress has ever been made in science or art without significant partitioning of knowledge. Yet, anyone would be foolish not to realize that a function which deals with people in their various activities of producing and marketing

---

[1] It is interesting that one of the scholars strongly oriented to human relations and behavioral approaches to management has recently noted that "theory can be viewed as a way of organizing experience" and that "once initial sense is made out of experienced environment, the way is cleared for an even more adequate organization of this experience." See Robert Dubin in "Psyche, Sensitivity, and Social Structure," critical comment in Robert Tannenbaum, I. R. Weschler, and Fred Massarik, *Leadership and Organization: A Behavioral Science Approach,* McGraw-Hill Book Company, New York, 1961, p. 401.

anything from money to religion and education is completely independent of the physical, biological, and cultural universe in which we live. And, are there not such relationships in other "compartments" of knowledge and theory?

The Empirical School   A second approach to management I refer to as the "empirical" school. In this, I include those scholars who identify management as a study of experience, sometimes with intent to draw generalizations but usually merely as a means of teaching experience and transferring it to the practitioner or student. Typical of this school are those who see management or "policy" as the study and analysis of cases and those with such approaches as Ernest Dale's "comparative approach."[2]

This approach seems to be based upon the premise that, if we study the experience of successful managers, or the mistakes made in management, or if we attempt to solve management problems, we will somehow understand and learn to apply the most effective kinds of management techniques. This approach, as often applied, assumes that, by finding out what worked or did not work in individual circumstances, the student or the practitioner will be able to do the same in comparable situations.

No one can deny the importance of studying experience through such study, or of analyzing the "how-it-was-done" of management. But management, unlike law, is not a science based on precedent, and situations in the future exactly comparable to the past are exceedingly unlikely to occur. Indeed, there is a positive danger of relying too much on past experience and on undistilled history of managerial problem-solving for the simple reason that a technique or approach found "right" in the past may not fit a situation of the future.

Those advocating the empirical approach are likely to say that what they really do in analyzing cases or history is to draw from certain generalizations which can be applied as useful guides to thought or action in future case situations. As a matter of fact, Ernest Dale, after claiming to find "so little practical value" from the principles enunciated by the "universalists," curiously drew certain "generalizations" or "criteria" from his valuable study of a number of great practitioners of management.[3] There is some question as to whether

Dale's "comparative" approach is not really the same as the "universalist" approach he decries, except with a different distiller of basic truths.

By the emphasis of the empirical school on study of experience, it does appear that the research and thought so engendered may assist in hastening the day for verification of principles. It is also possible that the proponents of this school may come up with a more useful framework of principles than that of the management process school. But, to the extent that the empirical school draws generalizations from its research, and it would seem to be a necessity to do so unless its members are satisfied to exchange meaningless and structureless experience, this approach tends to be and do the same as the management process school.

The Human Behavior School   This approach to the analysis of management is based on the central thesis that, since managing involves getting things done with and through people, the study of management must be centered on interpersonal relations. Variously called the "human relations," "leadership," or "behavioral sciences" approach, this school brings to bear "existing and newly developed theories, methods, and techniques of the relevant social sciences upon the study of inter- and intrapersonal phenomena, ranging fully from the personality dynamics of individuals at one extreme to the relations of cultures at the other."[4] In other words, this school concentrates on the "people" part of management and rests on the principle that, where people work together as groups in order to accomplish objectives, "people should understand people."

The scholars in this school have a heavy orientation to psychology and social psychology. Their primary focus is the individual as a socio-psychological being and what motivates him. The members of this school vary from those who see it as a portion of the manager's job, a tool to help him understand and get the best from people by meeting their needs and responding to their motivations, to those who see the psychological behavior of individuals and groups as the total of management.

In this school are those who emphasize human relations as an art that the manager should advantageously understand and practice. There are those who focus attention on the manager as a leader and sometimes equate management to leadership, thus, in effect, tending to treat all group activities as "managed" situations. There are those who see the study

[2] Ernest Dale, *The Great Organizers: Theory and Practice of Organization,* McGraw-Hill Book Company, New York, 1960, pp. 11–28.
[3] *Ibid.,* pp. 11, 26–28, 62–66.

[4] Tannenbaum, Weschler, and Massarik, *op. cit.,* p. 9.

of group dynamics and interpersonal relationships as simply a study of socio-psychological relationships and seem, therefore, merely to be attaching the term "management" to the field of social psychology.

That management must deal with human behavior can hardly be denied. That the study of human interactions, whether in the environment of management or in unmanaged situations, is important and useful one could not dispute. And it would be a serious mistake to regard good leadership as unimportant to good managership. But whether the field of human behavior is the equivalent of the field of management is quite another thing. Perhaps it is like calling the study of the human body the field of cardiology.

The Social System School   Closely related to the human behavior school and often confused or intertwined with it is one which might be labeled the social system school. This includes those researchers who look upon management as a social system, that is, a system of cultural interrelationships. Sometimes, as in the case of March and Simon,[5] the system is limited to formal organizations, using the term "organization" as equivalent to enterprise, rather than the authority-activity concept used most often in management. In other cases, the approach is not to distinguish the formal organization, but rather to encompass any kind of system of human relationships.

Heavily sociological in flavor, this approach to management does essentially what any study of sociology does. It identifies the nature of the cultural relationships of various social groups and attempts to show these as a related, and usually an integrated, system.

Perhaps the spiritual father of this ardent and vocal school of management theorists is Chester Barnard.[6] In searching for an answer to fundamental explanations underlying the managing process, this thoughtful business executive developed a theory of cooperation grounded in the needs of the individual to solve, through cooperation, the biological, physical, and social limitations of himself and his environment. Barnard then carved from the total of cooperative systems so engendered one set of interrelationships which he defines as "formal organization." His formal organization concept, quite unlike that usually held by management practitioners, is any cooperative

system in which there are persons able to communicate with each other and who are willing to contribute action toward a conscious common purpose.

The Barnard concept of cooperative systems pervades the work of many contributors to the social system school of management. For example, Herbert Simon at one time defined the subject of organization theory and the nature of human organizations as "systems of interdependent activity, encompassing at least several primary groups and usually characterized, at the level of consciousness of participants, by a high degree of rational direction of behavior toward ends that are objects of common knowledge."[7] Simon and others have subsequently seemed to have expanded this concept of social systems to include any cooperative and purposeful group interrelationship or behavior.

This school has made many noteworthy contributions to management. The recognition of organized enterprise as a social organism, subject to all the pressures and conflicts of the cultural environment, has been helpful to the management theorist and the practitioner alike. Among some of the more helpful aspects are the awareness of the institutional foundations of organization authority, the influence of informal organization, and such social factors as those Wight Bakke has called the "bonds of organization."[8] Likewise, many of Barnard's helpful insights, such as his economy of incentives and his theory of opportunism, have brought the power of sociological understanding into the realm of management practice.

Basic sociology, analysis of concepts of social behavior, and the study of group behavior in the framework of social systems do have great value in the field of management. But one may well ask the question whether this *is* management. Is the field of management coterminous with the field of sociology? Or is sociology an important underpinning like language, psychology, physiology, mathematics, and other fields of knowledge? Must management be defined in terms of the universe of knowledge?

[7] "Comments on the Theory of Organizations," *American Political Science Review, vol.* 46, no. 4, p. 1130, December, 1952.
[8] Wight Bakke, *Bonds of Organization,* Harper & Row, Publishers, Incorporated, New York, 1950. These "bonds" or "devices" of organization are identified by Bakke as (1) the functional specifications system (a system of teamwork arising from job specifications and arrangements for association); (2) the status system (a vertical hierarchy of authority); (3) the communications system; (4) the reward and penalty system; and (5) the organization charter (ideas and means which give character and individuality to the organization, or enterprise).

[5] J. G. March and H. A. Simon, *Organizations,* John Wiley & Sons, Inc., New York, 1958.
[6] Chester Barnard, *The Functions of the Executive,* Harvard University Press, Cambridge, Mass., 1938.

The Decision Theory School Another approach to management theory, undertaken by a growing and scholarly group, might be referred to as the decision theory school. This group concentrates on rational approach to decision—the selection from among possible alternatives of a course of action or of an idea. The approach of this school may be to deal with the decision itself, or to the persons or organizational group making the decision, or to an analysis of the decision process. Some limit themselves fairly much to the economic rationale of the decision, while others regard anything which happens in an enterprise the subject of their analysis, and still others expand decision theory to cover the psychological and sociological aspect and environment of decisions and decision-makers.

The decision-making school is apparently an outgrowth of the theory of consumer's choice with which economists have been concerned since the days of Jeremy Bentham early in the nineteenth century. It has arisen out of such economic problems and analyses as utility maximization, indifference curves, marginal utility, and economic behavior under risks and uncertainties. It is, therefore, no surprise that one finds most of the members of this school to be economic theorists. It is likewise no surprise to find the content of this school to be heavily oriented to model construction and mathematics.

The decision theory school has tended to expand its horizon considerably beyond the process of evaluating alternatives. That point has become for many only a springboard for examination of the entire sphere of human activity, including the nature of the organization structure, psychological and social reactions of individuals and groups, the development of basic information for decisions, an analysis of values and particularly value considerations with respect to goals, communications networks, and incentives. As one would expect, when the decision theorists study the small, but central, area of decision *making,* they are led by this keyhole look at management to consider the entire field of enterprise operation and its environment. The result is that decision theory becomes no longer a neat and narrow concentration on decision, but rather a broad view of the enterprise as a social system.

There are those who believe that, since management is characterized by its concentration on decisions, the future development of management theory will tend to use the decision as its central focus and the rest of management theory will be hung on this structural center.

This may occur and certainly the study of the decision, the decision process, and the decision maker can be extended to cover the entire field of management as anyone might conceive it. Nevertheless, one wonders whether this focus cannot also be used to build around it the entire area of human knowledge. For, as most decision theorists recognize, the problem of choice is individual, as well as organizational, and most of what has been said that is pure decision theory can be applied to the existence and thinking of a Robinson Crusoe.

The Mathematical School Although mathematical methods can be used by any school of management theory, and have been, I have chosen to group under a school those theorists who see management as a system of mathematical models and processes. Perhaps the most widely known group I arbitrarily so lump are the operations researchers or operations analysts, who have sometimes anointed themselves with the rather pretentious name of "management scientists." The abiding belief of this group is that, if management, or organization, or planning, or decision making is a logical process, it can be expressed in terms of mathematical symbols and relationships. The central approach of this school is the model, for it is through these devices that the problem is expressed in its basic relationships and in terms of selected goals or objectives.

There can be no doubt of the great usefulness of mathematical approaches to any field of inquiry. It forces upon the researcher the definition of a problem or problem area, it conveniently allows the insertion of symbols for unknown data, and its logical methodology, developed by years of scientific application and abstraction, furnishes a powerful tool for solving or simplifying complex phenomena.

But it is hard to see mathematics as a truly separate school of management theory, any more than it is a separate "school" in physics, chemistry, engineering, or medicine. I only deal with it here as such because there has appeared to have developed a kind of cult around mathematical analysts who have subsumed to themselves the area of management.

In pointing out that mathematics is a tool, rather than a school, it is not my intention to underestimate the impact of mathematics on the science and practice of management. By bringing to this immensely important and complex field the tools and techniques of the physical sciences, the mathematicians have already made an immense contribution to orderly thinking. They have forced on people in management the means and desirability of seeing many problems more clearly, they have pressed on scholars and practitioners the need for establishing goals and measures of effectiveness, they have been extremely helpful in getting the management area seen as a logical system of relationships, and they have caused people in management to review and occasionally reorganize information sources and systems so that mathematics can be given sensible quantitative meaning. But with all this meaningful contribution and the greater sharpness and sophistication of planning which is resulting, I cannot see that mathematics is management theory any more than it is astronomy.

THE MAJOR SOURCES OF MENTAL ENTANGLEMENT IN THE JUNGLE

In outlining the various schools, or approaches, of management theory, it becomes clear that these intellectual cults are not drawing greatly different inferences from the physical and cultural environment surrounding us. Why, then, have there been so many differences between them and why such a struggle, particularly among our academic brethren to obtain a place in the sun by denying the approaches of others? Like the widely differing and often contentious denominations of the Christian religion, all have essentially the same goals and deal with essentially the same world.

While there are many sources of the mental entanglement in the management theory jungle, the major ones are the following:

The Semantics Jungle   As is so often true when intelligent men argue about basic problems, some of the trouble lies in the meaning of key words. The semantics problem is particularly severe in the field of management. There is even a difference in the meaning of the word "management." Most people would agree that it means getting things done through and with people, but is it people in formal organizations, or in all group activities? Is it governing, leading, or teaching?

Perhaps the greatest single semantics confusion lies in the word "organization." Most members of the management process school use it to define the activity-authority structure of an enterprise and certainly most practitioners believe that they are "organizing" when they establish a framework of activity groupings and authority relationships. In this case, organization represents the formal framework within an enterprise that furnishes the environment in which people perform. Yet a large number of "organization" theorists conceive of organization as the sum total of human relationships in any group activity; they thus seem to make it equivalent to *social* structure. And some use "organization" to mean "enterprise."

If the meaning of organization cannot be clarified and a standard use of the term adopted by management theorists, understanding and criticism should not be based on this difference. It hardly seems to me to be accurate for March and Simon, for example, to criticize the organization theories of the management process, or "universalist," school for not considering the management planning function as part of organizing, when they have chosen to treat it separately. Nor should those who choose to treat the training, selecting, guiding or leading of people under staffing and direction be criticized for a tendency to "view the employee as an inert instrument" or a "given rather than a variable."[9] Such accusations, proceeding from false premises, are clearly erroneous.

Other semantic entanglements might be mentioned. By some, decision-making is regarded as a process of choosing from among alternatives; by others, the total managerial task and environment. Leadership is often made synonymous with managership and is analytically separated by others. Communications may mean everything from a written or oral report to a vast network of formal and informal relationships. Human relations to some implies a psychiatric manipulation of people, but to others the study and art of understanding people and interpersonal relationships.

Differences in Definition of Management as a Body of Knowledge   As was indicated in the discussion of semantics, "management" has far from a standard meaning, although most agree that it at least involves getting things done through and with people. But, does it mean the dealing with all human relationships? Is a street peddler a manager? Is a parent a manager? Is a leader of a disorganized mob a manager? Does the field of management equal the fields of sociology and social psychology combined? Is it the equivalent of the entire system of social relationships?

While I recognize that sharp lines cannot be drawn in management any more than they are in medicine or engineering, there surely can be a sharper distinction drawn than at present. With the plethora of management writing and experts, calling almost everything under the sun "management," can one expect management theory to be regarded as very useful or scientific to the practitioner?

[9] March and Simon, *op. cit.*, pp. 29–33.

The *a priori* Assumption Confusion in management theory has also been heightened by the tendency for many newcomers in the field to cast aside significant observations and analyses of the past on the grounds that they are *a priori* in nature. This is an often-met accusation made by those who wish to cast aside the work of Fayol, Mooney, Brown, Urwick, Gulick, and others who are branded as "universalists." To make the assumption that the distilled experiences of men such as these represent *a priori* reasoning is to forget that experience in and with managing *is* empirical. While the conclusions that perceptive and experienced practitioners of the art of management are not infallible, they represent an experience which is certainly real and not "armchair." No one could deny, I feel sure, that the ultimate test of accuracy of management theory must be practice and management theory and science must be developed from reality.

The Misunderstanding of Principles
Those who feel that they gain caste or a clean slate for advancing a particular notion or approach often delight in casting away anything which smacks of management principles. Some have referred to them as platitudes, forgetting that a platitude is still a truism and a truth does not become worthless because it is familiar. (As Robert Frost has written, "Most of the changes we think we see in life are merely truths going in or out of favor.") Others cast away principles of Fayol and other practitioners, only to draw apparently different generalizations from their study of management; but many of the generalizations so discovered are often the same fundamental truths in different words that certain criticized "universalists" have discovered.

One of the favorite tricks of the managerial theory trade is to disprove a whole framework of principles by reference to one principle which the observer sees disregarded in practice. Thus, many critics of the universalists point to the well-known cases of dual subordination in organized enterprise, coming to the erroneous conclusion that there is no substance to the principle of unity of command. But this does not prove that there is no cost to the enterprise by designing around, or disregarding, the principle of unity of command; nor does it prove that there were not other advantages which offset the costs, as there often are in cases of establishing functional authorities in organization.

Perhaps the almost hackneyed stand-by for those who would disprove the validity of all principles by referring to a single one is the misunderstanding around the principle of span of management (or span of control). The usual source of authority quoted by those who criticize is Sir Ian Hamilton, who never intended to state a universal principle, but rather to make a personal observation in a book of reflections on his Army experience, and who did say, offhand, that he found it wise to limit his span to 3 to 6 subordinates. No modern universalist relies on this single observation, and, indeed, few can or will state an absolute or universal numerical ceiling. Since Sir Ian was not a management theorist and did not intend to be, let us hope that the ghost of his innocent remark may be laid to deserved rest!

What concerns those who feel that a recognition of fundamental truths, or generalizations, may help in the diagnosis and study of management, and who know from managerial experience that such truths or principles do serve an extremely valuable use, is the tendency for some researchers to prove the wrong things through either misstatement or misapplication of principles. A classic case of such misunderstanding and misapplication is in Chris Argyris' interesting book on *Personality and Organization*.[10] This author, who in this book and his other works has made many noteworthy contributions to management, concludes that "formal organization principles make demands on relatively healthy individuals that are incongruent with their needs," and that "frustration, conflict, failure, and short-time perspective are predicted as results of this basic incongruency."[11] This startling conclusion—the exact opposite of what "good" formal organization based on "sound" organization principles should cause, is explained when one notes that, of four "principles" Argyris quotes, one is not an organization principle at all but the economic principle of specialization and three other "principles" are quoted incorrectly.[12] With such a postulate, and with no attempt to recognize, correctly or incorrectly, any other organization and management principles, Argyris has simply proved that wrong principles badly applied will lead to frustration; and every management practitioner knows this to be true!

The Inability or Unwillingness of Management Theorists to Understand Each Other
What has been said above leads one to the conclusion that much of the management

[10] Chris Argyris, *Personality and Organization*, Harper & Row, Publishers, Incorporated, New York, 1957.
[11] *Ibid.*, p. 74.
[12] *Ibid.*, pp. 58–66.

theory jungle is caused by the unwillingness or inability of the management theorists to understand each other. Doubting that it is inability, because one must assume that a person interested in management theory is able to comprehend, at least in concept and framework, the approaches of the various "schools," I can only come to the conclusion that the roadblock to understanding is unwillingness.

Perhaps this unwillingness comes from the professional "walls" developed by learned disciplines. Perhaps the unwillingness stems from a fear that someone or some new discovery will encroach on professional and academic status. Perhaps it is fear of professional or intellectual obsolescence. But whatever the cause, it seems that these walls will not be torn down until it is realized that they exist, until all cultists are willing to look at the approach and content of other schools, and until, through exchange and understanding of ideas some order may be brought from the present chaos.

DISENTANGLING THE MANAGEMENT THEORY JUNGLE

It is important that steps be taken to disentangle the management theory jungle. Perhaps, it is too soon and we must expect more years of wandering through a thicket of approaches, semantics, thrusts, and counterthrusts. But in any field as important to society where the many blunders of an unscientifically based managerial art can be so costly, I hope that this will not be long.

There do appear to be some things that can be done. Clearly, meeting what I see to be the major sources of the entanglement should remove much of it. The following considerations are important:

1. *The need for definition of a body of knowledge.* Certainly, if a field of knowledge is not to get bogged down in a quagmire of misunderstandings, the first need is for definition of the field. Not that it need be defined in sharp, detailed, and inflexible lines, but rather along lines which will give it fairly specific content. Because management is reality, life, practice, my suggestion would be that it be defined in the light of the able and discerning practitioner's frame of reference. A science unrelated to the art for which it is to serve is not likely to be a very productive one.

Although the study of managements in various enterprises, in various countries, and at various levels made by many persons, including myself, may neither be representative nor adequate, I have come to the conclusion that management is the art of getting things done through and with people in *formally organized groups,* the art of creating an environment in such an organized group where people can perform as individuals and yet cooperate toward attainment of group goals, the art of removing blocks to such performance, the art of optimizing efficiency in effectively reaching goals. If this kind of definition of the field is unsatisfactory, I suggest at least an agreement that the area should be defined to reflect the field of the practitioner and that further research and study of practice be done to this end.

In defining the field, too, it seems to me imperative to draw some limits for purposes of analysis and research. If we are to call the entire cultural, biological, and physical universe the field of management, we can no more make progress than could have been done if chemistry or geology had not carved out a fairly specific area and had, instead studied all knowledge.

In defining the body of knowledge, too, care must be taken to distinguish between tools and content. Thus mathematics, operations research, accounting, economic theory, sociometry, and psychology, to mention a few, are significant *tools* of management but are not, in themselves, a part of the *content* of the field. This is not to mean that they are unimportant or that the practicing manager should not have them available to him, nor does it mean that they may not be the means of pushing back the frontiers of knowledge of management. But they should not be confused with the basic content of the field.

This is not to say that fruitful study should not continue on the underlying disciplines affecting management. Certainly knowledge of sociology, social systems, psychology, economics, political science, mathematics, and other areas, pointed toward contributing to the field of management, should be continued and encouraged. And significant findings in these and other fields of knowledge might well cast important light on, or change concepts in, the field of management. This has certainly happened in other sciences and in every other art based upon significant science.

2. *Integration of management and other disciplines.* If recognition of the proper content of the field were made, I believe that the present crossfire of misunderstanding might tend to disappear. Management would be regarded as a specific discipline and other disciplines would be looked upon as important bases of the field. Under these circumstances, the allied and underlying disciplines would be welcomed

by the business and public administration schools, as well as by practitioners, as loyal and helpful associates. Integration of management and other disciplines would then not be difficult.

3. *The clarification of management semantics.* While I would expect the need for clarification and uniformity of management semantics would largely be satisfied by definition of the field as a body of knowledge, semantics problems might require more special attention. There are not too many places where semantics are important enough to cause difficulty. Here again, I would suggest the adoption of the semantics of the intelligent practitioners, unless words are used by them so inexactly as to require special clarification. At least, we should not complicate an already complex field by developing a scientific or academic jargon which would build a language barrier between the theorist and the practitioner.

Perhaps the most expeditious way out of this problem is to establish a commission representing academic societies immediately concerned and associations of practicing managers. This would not seem to be difficult to do. And even if it were, the results would be worth the efforts.

4. *Willingness to distill and test fundamentals.* Certainly, the test of maturity and usefulness of a science is the sharpness and validity of the principles underlying it. No science, now regarded as mature, started out with a complete statement of incontrovertibly valid principles. Even the oldest sciences, such as physics, keep revising their underlying laws and discovering new principles. Yet any science has proceeded, and more than that has been useful, for centuries on the basis of generalizations, some laws, some principles, and some hypotheses.

One of the understandable sources of inferiority of the social sciences is the recognition that they are inexact sciences. On the other hand, even the so-called exact sciences are subject to a great deal of inexactness, have principles which are not completely proved, and use art in the design of practical systems and components. The often-encountered defeatist attitude of the social sciences, of which management is one, overlooks the fact that

management may be explained, practice may be improved, and the goals of research may be more meaningful if we encourage attempts at perceptive distillation of experience by stating principles (or generalizations) and placing them in a logical framework. As two scientists recently said on this subject:

> The reason for this defeatist point of view regarding the social sciences may be traceable to a basic misunderstanding of the nature of scientific endeavor. What matters is not whether or to what extent inexactitudes in procedures and predictive capability can eventually be removed . . . : rather it is *objectivity,* i.e., the intersubjectivity of findings independent of any one person's intuitive judgment, which distinguishes science from intuitive guesswork however brilliant. . . . But once a new fact or a new idea has been conjectured, no matter how intuitive a foundation, it must be capable of objective test and confirmation by anyone. And it is this crucial standard of scientific objectivity rather than any purported criterion of exactitude to which the social sciences must conform.[13]

In approaching the clarification of management theory, then, we should not forget a few criteria:

1. The theory should deal with an area of knowledge and inquiry that is "manageable"; no great advances in knowledge were made so long as man contemplated the whole universe;
2. The theory should be *useful* in improving practice and the task and person of the practitioner should not be overlooked;
3. The theory should not be lost in semantics, especially useless jargon not understandable to the practitioner;
4. The theory should give direction and efficiency to research and teaching; and
5. The theory must recognize that it is a part of a larger universe of knowledge and theory.

---

[13] O. Helmer and N. Rescher, "On the Epistemology of the Inexact Sciences," The Rand Corporation, P-1513, Santa Monica, Calif., pp. 4–5.

5

Some Implications of the Newer Analytic Approaches to Management*

W. W. COOPER

Linear programming, game theory, queuing theory and statistical decision theory and statistical decision theory, these are some of the newer analytical techniques. Others are: simulation, gaming and Monte Carlo analyses which, in company with high speed electronic computers, have expanded to include systems analyses of adaptive systems, heuristic programming and, more generally, artificial intelligences.

Most of us are familiar with some or all of these—at least as they have been embodied in "operations research," "management science," "automation" and related to, or applied in, management. Numerous companies have now utilized some or all of these approaches. In some cases they now even have available, and on their full time staffs, persons who are qualified experts in one or more of these activities.

We may remind ourselves that only a decade or so ago these words were alien and unknown to most managements. Many of them, in fact, had not even been invented or developed to a point where, even in science, they could easily be isolated and identified as "separate" and important activities. Equally important, and also interesting, is the change in our outlook towards the underlying causes from which these developments have sprung: I think that we now expect, for instance, that still further changes and new developments will henceforth be the normal state of affairs. In fact, I suspect (like most of you) that the trend of these developments is likely to be one of accelera-

tion and proliferation rather than one where retardation, contraction or leveling off will occur.

It is possible, of course, that these subsequent developments will displace or transform existing managerial practices, including even some of the newer analytical techniques that we have just mentioned. But this is less important to us than another variation.

MANAGEMENT PROBLEMS AID SCIENCE

It is the liaison that has now been effected between management and science. The use of received scientific knowledge and methodology by management was demonstrated, of course, as far back as F. W. Taylor and his associates and followers. There is therefore no great need to dwell on this so let us refer, instead, to another aspect of the liaison by means of which the problems and processes of management are used as a stimulus (and even a guide) for research which is designed to push back the boundaries of science itself.

This has naturally attracted some of the best and most distinguished scientific talent. The efforts of these scientists have been intense and sustained so that, apparently, they find the problem materials here both scientifically satisfying and rewarding. That is, they have been satisfied in terms of the depth associated with the challenges here; they have also found their endeavors rewarded by fruitful contributions to science as well as management.

I do not mean to suggest that the liaison is one in which this kind of talent is available at the beck and call of management. It is represented rather better as a broad spectrum in which the practicing manager and his staff specialist or consultant lie at one end, and the abstract scientific theorizer and methodologist lies at another end. These two ends of the spectrum are related through a series of intermediate links all of which now appear to

* Reprinted by permission of the publisher from *California Management Review*, vol. 4, no. 1, pp. 51–64, Fall, 1961. Mr. Cooper is professor of economics and industrial administration in the Graduate School of Industrial Administration at the Carnegie Institute of Technology.

This article is based upon a talk given by the author at a meeting of the Pittsburgh Chapter of the Society for the Advancement of Management.

be on the way towards being adequately manned and attended to.

Furthermore, provision is also now being made at major centers of learning for the educational developments that are needed to provide a continuing supply of persons with the necessary prerequisites and abilities to continue in the traditions of scientific research that have now been initiated, and to translate the results of this research into practical applications, on the one hand, and communicate new problems and other materials to the instant sciences on another hand.

U.S.S.R. EMPLOYS
MATHEMATICAL APPROACH

To underscore these points, and to indicate the scope of the events referred to, I shall now quote from a report on related developments from the other side of the Iron Curtain.[1]

> From the 4th–8th of April 1960, at the Academy of Science there was held the first scientific conference for the use of mathematical methods for economic research and planning. It was brought together by the initiative of the Departments of Economics, philosophy, and law, and the Siberian Department of the Academy of Science of the USSR.
>
> At this conference for the first time there met for joint work representatives of two independent branches of knowledge—economics and mathematics. There were also a large number of representatives from economic practice—production men, planners, statisticians and teachers. They met to discuss the first results of economic-mathematic research, and to plan the further course of the introduction of new methodology into economic science and into production planning practice.

It is of interest to note that this same article refers to 56 reports which were distributed at this conference, and covered in 6 sessions organized according to the following divisions: Mathematical analysis of expansion of productivity, Interdepartmental balances, Linear programming, Mathematical methods for the solution of transportation and technical-economic problems, Mathematical statistics.

The attendees at this conference included high officialdom (such as the President of the Academy) and many of Russia's outstanding scientists. After noting the resistances that had been encountered—e.g., from the practicing bureaucracy—the conference concluded on a positive note, which I quote in some detail as follows:

> (New Council and Institute) Among the decisions of the conference were noted concrete measures directed to the wider introduction of new mathematical methodology. It is to be used in practical economic research and planning in our country.
>
> Given present trends, there was felt a need for a single coordination center which could direct, in a planned manner, the theoretical and practical work in this field. Without having single unified guidance, without mutual agreement in the work of scientific search and experiment, departmental efforts will get lost in the usual narrow channels. Subsequently it will require more, unjustified, effort to bring them together in a comprehensive overall complex of mathematics in economics.
>
> The first step for the creation of such a center was made through the decision to create at the Academy of Science an interdepartmental scientific Council. It is to deal with questions of use of mathematics in economics.
>
> Representatives on the council were drawn from economic and mathematical sciences, as well as planners, production men, statisticians and engineers.
>
> For the solution of scientific problems of economic-mathematical methodology, the conference recommended to the Directorate of the Academy of Science, USSR, the creation of a special Laboratory, and in the future, an Institute.
>
> (New Publications) At the same time the conference emphasized the need to organize a means of spreading information in this field. It recommended that journals regularly carry relevant articles. Also, books should be published on the given theme, as well as translations of foreign materials.
>
> (Education) Further, the conference considered existing regulations for the training of personnel capable of independently preparing decisions on economic mathematical tasks. It was felt that the present training was not satisfactory. Broadened teaching programs are needed in higher institutes of economics. Mathematics, linear and dynamic programming, and so on, are required. Also it is necessary to create courses to raise the mathematical qualifications of economists.
>
> The carrying out of these measures will guarantee the availability of trained personnel endowed with the newest methods. They will be capable of fighting for the solution of production and planning tasks.
>
> The introduction of mathematics and the use of computers in economic research and planning in a substantial fashion will enrich economic

science. It will raise the level of planning guidance of the national economy. This will serve as one of the factors which will hasten the transition of our society on the path to communism.

This concludes the report referred to, as well as my quotations from the cited translation of it. The main point to be made is that the activities we have been discussing are now represented on a broad base that is not confined to one political-economic system in one country.

MANAGEMENT FUNCTIONS AND MATHEMATICS

Bearing this, and related, points in mind, we may now turn to another variation of our theme and inquire as to the nature of the concepts and applications that have been made. This will then provide a point of departure for prognostications later about some possible future courses in these developments.

For this purpose we may think of managerial activities and problems as being classified into three broad groups: (1) planning (2) operations, and (3) control. The *planning* phase of management, as here conceived, is primarily concerned with the procedures for delineating and assessing alternative courses of action.

PLANNING

Generally, this involves forming some sort of image, mental or otherwise, in terms of which data are assembled and likely consequences are traced. The "planning decisions" do not usually involve actual commitments of resources and, in this respect, we can distinguish between "planning" and "operations" in that decisions to commit resources are made in the latter rather than the former of these two divisions that we are discussing.

The intended distinctions can perhaps be made sufficiently clear by referring to, say, a budgeted inventory level for a certain item as a planning decision while the actual issuance of a purchase order represents an operating decision when it is intended as a *bona fide* commitment to pay for an item which will then be supplied by a specified vendor.

CONTROL

With these examples and distinctions in mind we may then refer to a third managerial activity, "control," which is concerned with conformance between plans and operations.

The control area is, as we shall see, somewhat more subtle in its connotations than are the activities and associated constructs in planning or operations. For the moment, however, the usual accounting characterization of a variance (red or black) from a standard may be thought of as an immediately simple example in the control area.

To date, most applications of the newer analytical techniques have occurred in the area that we have characterized as planning. More specifically the bulk of these have been directed to functional (rather than organizational) planning.

Examples are: linear programming allocations in machine loading schedules and financial studies of capital facilities alteration proposals; queuing analyses of maintenance forces; game theoretic studies of advertising budgets; and so on. By contrast, studies directed towards prescribing staffing qualities and organization relations are in a more backward state —perhaps because these topics quickly merge into the more subtle field of control problems as represented by, say, the kinds of issues which attend auditing examinations of internal-control and check systems.

In summary, then, the bulk of the applications and the bulk of the research has occurred in the area of functional planning. More recently, work has begun to be initiated in the area of organization planning, too, mainly in the form of computer and simulation studies. These are still largely embryonic or programmatic in character, however, and so I think we can leave them aside in order to focus on some of the newer analytic approaches that have been associated with recent mathematical applications in functional planning.

We might now find it useful to distinguish, with Warren Weaver,[2] various divisions of mathematics according to whether the main advantages offered are in the ability to deal with (i) subtlety, (ii) complexity and (iii) disorder. Representative specimens in each division are (i) calculus, (ii) algebra and (iii) statistics.

STATISTICS

Consider the area of statistics as a first example. Quality control and acceptance sampling represent adaptations of an underlying mathematics which has enabled managements to apply statistical principles to such diverse areas as production, procurement, accounting, control of clerical operations, and so forth. Here the ideas of randomness are systematically applied to the numerous combinations in which variations can occur (in a process or product) as a result of chance alone, and these are then distinguished from other variations that can also occur when more orderly causes are operating.

As the name suggests, these applications are directly pertinent to the control area of management, and the statistical quality control literature is indeed replete with discussions of problems arising because of lack of conformance between plans (e.g., blueprinted product specifications) and operations (e.g., products produced by an ongoing process).

On the other hand, these are applications only to rather simple parts of the control process. While (to date at least) attempts to extend them to the more significant multidimensional problems of an organizational or accounting variety have not been wholly successful,[3] it must also be remembered that the subject matter of statistics is vast. It is backed by an established and growing literature which is rooted in a long and continuing tradition of scientific research whose possibilities are far from exhausted by such managerial applications as have been essayed.

The history of major developments in statistics may be traced through the original "theory of errors" in the natural sciences to the revolutionary developments of the 1920's and 1930's which occurred in conjunction with an extension of these ideas to biological (including agricultural) phenomena and problems where rigorous and efficient principles of experimental design were finally evolved by reference to statistical considerations.

STATISTICAL DECISION THEORY

This is, of course, only a thumbnail sketch which supremely oversimplifies a rich and varied history. It will help us, however, to distinguish these preceding developments in statistical mathematics from those that are currently embodied in the name "statistical decision theory."

The latter, as its name suggests, has more of a managerial orientation than is usually to be found in the preceding developments. In fact, R. A. Fisher, the chief architect of the statistical revolution of the 1930's has criticized rather strongly the ideas with which A. Wald introduced the topic of statistical decision theory—because, he contends, the relevant cost-and-benefit matching relations that are needed for the decision functions have neither meaning nor relevance for purely scientific work.[4]

The same kinds of relations (costs and benefits) are, of course, immediately pertinent to the problems of management where statistical-mathematical ideas are beginning to exert an influence which either modifies some of the preceding applications, as in quality control, or indicates further areas of potential use, as in rational investment planning.[5]

For our present purposes, we need only note two things: One, the suggested extensions in management are almost entirely directed to planning activities. Two, statistical decision theory has, in fact, provided a new unifying viewpoint and a stimulus to further scientific research in statistical theory, as witness, for example, the following quotation from the opening of a recent text by two well known statisticians:[6]

> Statistics is a body of methods for making wise decisions in the face of uncertainty. This modern conception of the subject is a far cry from that usually held by laymen. Indeed, even the pioneers in statistical research have adopted it only within the past decade or so.

The algebra that is associated with linear programming in management planning, will help us to indicate rather quickly what we mean by complexity. Consider, for instance, the loading of products onto a sequence of machines. The products are numerous and so are the machine possibilities. The data consist of machine processing times and capacities, customer orders, market potentials, and so on.

At least to the level of understanding that is now needed for applied work, each datum is simple enough. The solution variables also yield reasonably straightforward interpretations —at least if one does not ask too many questions—and this is all to the good.

On the other hand, the number of variables and the number of conditions (or equations) that need to be considered can easily run into thousands in many applications. Thus if one tries to ensure that, say, a minimum total cost will be achieved for the planned loads he quickly finds himself enmeshed in a huge— hence complicated—problem where efficient analytical guidance is welcome when it is available.

BUSINESS MATHEMATICS NOT HARD

This kind of complexity offers an example of a situation where the recently developed mathematics that is associated with linear programming may be useful. I do not wish to argue that all of this mathematics is obvious or easy. This is not the case. But I do wish to contrast it with the calculus, or analysis, kind of mathematics that many of us have been exposed to and used at one time or another.

As you know, the expressions that are typical in this kind of mathematics refer only to a relatively small number of variables: A time rate of change of one variable, an acceleration of still another variable and possibly a few connecting relations between them may be all that is apparent in an explicit statement of such a problem. On the other hand, implicit relations may be encountered at various levels of an analysis and these subtleties may then require recourse to recondite and advanced mathematical techniques.

Indeed, it is often the case that no solution is possible in terms of elementary algebraic relations. The end of an analysis then still yields an expression whose meaning is not wholly evident without recourse to strong bodies of supplementary theory—e.g., the theories of physics—and rather careful interpretations of such purely mathematical ideas as "infinitesimals" and the "infinitely large" or "infinitely numerous."

These three examples of mathematics and their usage will at least help to suggest, I hope, that the field is capable of division according to the problem needs and the state of knowledge which prevails in management. Thus, the most striking developments of the newer analytic approaches have, in recent years, occurred in the areas of disorder and complexity—rather than in the area of subtlety where mathematical aids have proved indispensable in dealing with the more subtle problems in the developed sciences.

Although the areas of disorder and complexity, separately and in combination, have received most of the attention to date, it is possible that the accumulation of substantive knowledge via these channels will open other areas at a later date where the mathematics of subtlety will be needed in management, as in other sciences.

If this does occur, we will find, then, I think, that the progress of this mathematics in its relation to the natural sciences will already provide results that are in a position to accommodate many of our requirements—at least initially.

THE AREA OF CONTROL

The control problems of management are now beginning to receive increasing research attention and here, as we shall see, the phenomena are likely to involve varying degrees of subtlety as well as complexity and disorder. Computer simulations involving so-called man-machine systems and "live" organization units have provided one avenue of attack. Another is represented by combined analytic and laboratory approaches in the study of such phenomena as auditing (in both its supervisory and accounting senses)[7] and budgeting (in the sense of a control instrument).

A. Stedry's recently released book, *Budget Control and Cost Behavior*,[8] is illustrative of the latter kind of development. To isolate Stedry's topic, we may use the distinctions that we previously introduced and relegate the forecasting and coordination aspects of budgetary preparation into the area of planning activity. Then we can note that such problems as points of budgetary initiation and the designation of participants in the process of adjusting the initial—or subsequent—budgetary levels are a part of the problem of securing effective budgetary control. These problems and the subsequent accounting reports are then judged by reference to their effects on behavior.

Thus, in Stedry's own words,[9]

> A "good" *control* budget is one which produces "good" results. If it is desired to minimize cost in a given department, and if a budget of $1,000 produces a cost of $1,001, and a budget of $300 produces a cost of $1,000, the latter is a better budget. The magnitude of the budget figure is unimportant other than in terms of its impact on cost.

Of course, Stedry does not deny that the $1,000 budget provides the better forecast and, possibly, the better basis for coordinating the plans of various divisions within a firm. But he does suggest—and adduces direct laboratory evidence in his support—that this does not settle the control question.

By means of his experiments, Stedry was able to state and test a variety of circumstances in which so-called tight and loose budgets might be made to apply, as well as a variety of circumstances in which the person to be controlled might better initiate (or participate) in the process of budgetary formation and also to delineate circumstances in which this same participative procedure might have an wholly adverse effect on behavior.

There are still other aspects of this study that are worthy of attention, but here I shall mention only that Stedry's approach to cost (and performance) reporting suggests the introduction of a category that might be called "motivational costs" because they are tailored to produce, in each individual case, the kinds of motivation which will lead to desired patterns of behavior.

In this view the now common standards of "accurate" and "timely" cost reporting might be replaced with an alternate approach wherein personal characteristics and the job that is attended to by specific persons need to be considered before deciding upon the information that is to be supplied on, say, variances from standard according to one uniform and unvarying set of reporting rules. Extended still further, one might think even of supplying information to different individuals which will lead them to take corrective action in advance of the errors that they might otherwise make.

Stating the matter in the technical jargon of one of the newer analytic approaches, we may imagine a person who tends to assess the "pay-off matrix" of a certain "game" in a way that leads him to play it rather badly. But then we might replace the true matrix with another (artificially contrived) one in terms of which this same person will, by his own assessments, play the true game rather well.[10]

These possibilities are certainly ones that are managerially conceivable in terms of twin duties which management must ultimately assume: (1) to inspire people to want to do what they ought to do and (2) to make it possible for them to do this notably better than they could without the aid of management.

You will note that I have deliberately avoided any implication that the "oughts" are those that a particular management—or that whole group of top managers—happen to cherish. We are still far from having exploited all the conceivable managerial forms for bringing the correct "oughts" into existence.

The area of control is intimately connected with organization design and analysis. These are, in turn, intimately connected with individual character formation and behavior and, ultimately, with the whole fabric of society. Hence, I propose consideration of this topic as still another variation on our theme, since it was implicitly introduced in preceding paragraphs. I shall do so, however, in a somewhat different way.

Research in this area is at best embryonic, as I have already suggested. So let us turn to certain criticisms now being made of management practice (and education) in this area. In particular, I shall make a topical selection from William H. Whyte's *Organization Man*[11] and try to discuss these in a way that will help advance our analysis of possible implications from the science-management liaison described earlier in this paper.

Consider, first, the way in which Mr. Whyte indicts management in the form of what he calls "the administrator":[12] "The creative individual he does not understand, nor does he understand the conditions of creativity."

This indictment certainly carries force with anyone who has witnessed the common and constant frustrations of creative individuals in the type of organizations Whyte describes. One must be careful, however, to distinguish between "the administrator" and the managerial instruments he employs. For our purposes, at least, it is also necessary to distinguish between currently available managerial forms and the kinds that might be invented or developed in the future.

Mr. Whyte has examined and savagely described some of these modes of management and "scientism." I would suggest, however, that neither management nor science is as static or as stable as Whyte's discussion implies. I would also suggest that the same idea may have quite different consequences when it is coupled with different ways of managing it.

Personnel testing and selection may be used as a case in point if only because Mr. Whyte has seized upon these as major symbols of current managerial (and "scientism") shortcomings.[13] Let us therefore imagine how ideas of personnel testing and selection might be used with improved modes of managerial implementation.

Suppose, for instance, that we are able to develop the means that are needed to deal with the subtlety, complexity, and disorder that would be involved if we were to undertake any large-scale and continuous matching of a multiplicity of individuals with all of their relevant relational possibilities.

With such instruments at hand, we might then be able to manage arrangements whereby organizations were accommodated to the relevant individuals and to the tasks that should be performed. All of this might then be done in a notably more flexible manner than is now, apparently, possible. This, in turn, would probably lead to different social fabrics and it might also produce a different "Social Ethic."[14]

I have just supposed that a different "Social Ethic" might emerge from continued progress in managerial instrumentation and organization. But we might also be led to a different view of even this same Social Ethic—i.e., the one that Whyte inveighs against—if it were to prevail under an altered series of managerial arrangements. Note, for instance, that the present managerial practice (or custom) of fixing each individual in a particular geographic locus and organization hierarchy for his work need not be regarded as a permanent and unchanging feature of managing.

Historical and contemporary data (here, and in the Soviet Union and elsewhere) suggest, to be sure, that the habits and expectations engendered by repeated relations of propinquity and positioning of individuals in relatively fixed, or static, hierarchical arrays are, at present, a necessity for many of the current modes of managing. But these are data that antecede the kinds of developments we are discussing, and hence are neither practicably decisive nor scientifically compelling. In certain kinds of large-scale, scientific development and research contracts, for example, there have already appeared cases in which it has been possible to shift persons across the boundaries of established legal entities, as personal talents and interests have suggested and as the circumstances of the task have demanded.

Such shifting has been accompanied, of course, by awkwardness and organization straining.[15] But I would suppose that we might ultimately develop better instruments for such accommodations. I also see no reason why a boundary should be established around the scientists in an organization. Automation, when it has been pushed far enough, may well take a form in which individuals operate across a variety of organizations in order to perform their services to best advantage.[16]

I do not wish to convey the impression that these developments will come either easily or rapidly. I am simply using the illustration of possibly more fluid organization relations in order to supply some perspective on the topics of personnel testing and selection and the Social Ethic with which Mr. Whyte associates them.

The point is that these alterations in managing could bring about a situation in which these same management (or "scientism") ideas and this same ethic might then be used to unlock rather than repress the creative "individuality" which is a main concern for Whyte in his studies.

Something more than an examination of the current "facts" of management is evidently required if we are to finish our assessment of the difficulties and the dangers that Mr. Whyte has called to our attention. Unfortunately, he does not provide us with an explicit prognosis on the future course of managerial developments. Hence we cannot examine his ideas on this subject and so, perforce, I shall turn to another topic that has been suggested by his concern.

It is "business education." I select the topic, not merely because of its interest per se, but also because it will help highlight the shortcomings of a purely "factual" approach to the topic that we are examining. For, under the impact of some of the newer analytic approaches, there are already strong signs of an alteration in this education which may well negate most of Mr. Whyte's main thrusts against it.

Noting the large, and rapidly rising, enrollment in business and commerce curricula, Mr. Whyte proceeds as follows in his discussion of the training they provide for the organization man: "These figures bring out a very important point. The conflict is not, as some embattled humanists believe, between the sciences and the liberal arts. *The conflict is between the fundamental and the applied."*[17] [Italics supplied.] He then, shortly thereafter, quotes from *The Daily Pennsylvanian* (of the University of Pennsylvania body).[18] I now excerpt from his cited quotation as follows:

> The first and most important destructive influence at Pennsylvania . . . is the Wharton School of Finance and Commerce. Justly famed for the excellent business training which it offers, and for which it grants an academic degree, the Wharton School by the sheer force of its reputation and undergraduate appeal has given to undergraduate social and extracurricular life an atmosphere which, while it is seldom anti-intellectual, is usually nonintellectual, and which tends to discourage the popularity of those interests which ordinarily occupy the time of the students of other universities where the school of liberal arts is the main impetus for student activity.

DISCIPLINE AND IMAGINATION

I am myself a product of a school of business and can therefore attest to the verisimilitude of Mr. Whyte's descriptions, at least in my own case. But I do not agree with either his analysis or his statement of conflict. The earlier writings of Professor A. N. Whitehead[19] were, I think, closer to the mark when (in his discussion of the business school) he becomes preoccupied, inter alia, with the coupling of discipline and imagination as a main feature of this part of the educational (and research) process.

If the discipline referred to is scientific or analytical in a sense akin to, say, that in engineering, then Professor Whitehead may have been premature. But this prematurity may also have to be accorded the status of prescience since the kinds of developments that we are discussing now make it possible to undertake this approach in large and important areas of business education. They most certainly make it possible, in any event, for business schools to undertake research in this vein, as some of them are now beginning to do, and this itself augurs well for the educational process.

The recent Ford[20] and Carnegie[21] Foundation reports have developed these topics both constructively and in detail.[22] Hence, we can lay them aside here in order to follow out another of the ideas that is suggested by the following quotation from Whitehead's essay:[23]

> The universities have trained the intellectual pioneers of our civilization—the priests, the lawyers, the statesmen, the doctors, the men of science, and the men of letters. They have been the home of those ideals which lead men to confront the confusion of their present times. . . . The conduct of business now requires intellectual imagination of the same type as that which in former times has mainly passed into those other occupations; and the universities are the organizations which have supplied this type of mentality for the service of the progress of the European races.

Up to this time, the schools of business have tended to take the existing states of knowledge and methodology in *both* management *and* science as given. They now have an opportunity to vault over both of these states, as they now exist, and thereby contribute to science and to management.

In the process of doing this they will help to equip their students to be intellectual—i.e., educated[24]—pioneers in the innovation of social institutions. This is something that society can rightfully expect of them (as well as their students) in addition to their other duties such as discovering and evaluating new knowledge and established practices.

Insofar as their own research and teaching acts as a prod, or a stimulus, for other schools that are gathered on the same campus, the schools of business will also then implicitly justify their presence as members in an academic world which is concerned with advancing our higher learning. This will not, however, be gained, at least as far as the management schools are concerned, by joining in Whyte's distinction between "the fundamental and the applied." The two should rather, here, be joined—as they will be when schools of management learn how to adjust the sciences to their applications and their applications to the sciences—in both their research and educating activities. These schools will then have come closer, in their social setting, to the goal that Whitehead ascribes to all technical education[25] ". . . a commonwealth in which work is play and play is life. This is the ideal of technical education. . . ."

CONCLUSION

These variations on the theme, some implications of the newer analytic approaches to management, may provide some general guides for the reader's imaginings. I now conclude by reminding you of the significance that we have been attaching to the recently established liaison between science and management. We might in this manuscript have varied this theme in order to explore some of the dangers that could conceivably emerge from such a liaison, as well as dangers that might emanate from other quarters to frustrate or subvert some of the developments that we have suggested as likely candidates for examination.

In any event, recent years have witnessed an evolution of new methods and instruments of analysis which have enabled the scientist to come forth from his laboratory into the world of management. The resulting situation may be as pregnant as the one described by Max Weber in *The Protestant Ethic and the Spirit of Capitalism*:[26]

> The great Protestant reformers managed to bring forth the monk from his monastery. There then resulted an invasion that infused into management a spirit of sustained "rational-economic" dedication to the tasks of enterprise.
>
> This, together with a developing set of methods and discoveries, in the hard sciences and technology, ultimately transformed an existing feudalism into a modern capitalist and industrial society. This transformation may have made the individual less secure in some ways, but it provided him with other benefits (and dangers) greater than any that he had previously known.

REFERENCES

(This paper was written as part of the contract, "Planning and Control of Industrial Operations," with the Office of Naval Research and the Bureau of Ships, at the Graduate School of Industrial Administration; Carnegie Institute of Technology—W. W. C.)

1. V. Dadayan and U. Chernyak, "Mathematical Methods in Economics," *Economic Science*

(*Ekonomicheski Nauki*), no. 3, pp. 140–151, 1960. Translation, by P. Kircher and G. Ginsburgs, to appear soon in *Management Science*.

2. Quoted, but with considerable liberties taken, from G. L. Thompson, "Computers and the Undergraduate Mathematical Training of Engineers," *Conference on Electrical Engineering Education*, Syracuse University, N.Y., 1960. See also A. Charnes and W. W. Cooper, "Management Models and Industrial Applications of Linear Programming," *Management Science*, vol. 4, no. 1, October, 1957.

3. See, e.g., R. M. Trueblood and R. M. Cyert, *Sampling Techniques in Accounting*, Prentice-Hall, Inc., Englewood Cliffs, N.J., 1957.

4. See R. A. Fisher, "Statistical Methods and Scientific Induction," *Journal of the Royal Statistical Society*, Series B (Methodological), vol. 17, no. 1, pp. 69–77, 1955. See also J. W. Tukey, "Conclusions vs. Decisions," *Technometrics*, vol. 2, no. 4, pp. 423–433, November, 1960.

5. For examples, see e.g., R. Schlaifer, *Probability and Statistics for Business Decisions: An Introduction to Managerial Economics under Uncertainty*, McGraw-Hill Book Company, New York, 1959.

6. From W. A. Wallis and H. V. Roberts, *Statistics: A New Approach*, The Free Press of Glencoe, New York, 1956.

7. See N. Churchill and L. Teitelbaum, "The Effects of an Audit," Office of Naval Research —Carnegie Institute of Technology Research Report, Carnegie Institute of Technology, Graduate School of Industrial Administration, Pittsburgh, Pa., May, 1960; N. Churchill and W. W. Cooper, "An Experiment for Measuring the Effects of an Audit," Office of Naval Research—Carnegie Institute of Technology Research Report, Carnegie Institute of Technology, Graduate School of Industrial Administration, Pittsburgh, Pa., December, 1960.

8. A. Stedry, *Budget Control and Cost Behavior*, Prentice-Hall, Inc., Englewood Cliffs, N.J., 1960.

9. *Ibid.*, p. 17.

10. See A. Charnes and W. W. Cooper, "Management Models and Industrial Applications of Linear Programming," *Management Science*, vol. 4, no. 1, October, 1957.

11. William H. Whyte, *Organization Man*, Doubleday & Company, Inc., Garden City, N.Y., 1957.

12. *Ibid.*, p. 57.

13. *Ibid.*, e.g., his Appendix, "How to Cheat on Personality Testing."

14. This term is used by Mr. Whyte to characterize ". . . the contemporary body of thought which makes morally legitimate the pressures of society against the individual. Its major propositions are three: a belief in the group as the source of creativity; a belief in 'belongingness' as the ultimate need of the individual; and a belief in the application of science to achieve the belongingness." (*Ibid.*, p. 7.). Mr. Whyte, it should be noted, proceeds to qualify such terms as "individual" and "societal"— but neither so adequately nor so succinctly as Aristotle's ancient, "He who is unable to live in society, or who has no need because he is sufficient for himself, must be either a beast or a god." (Cf. *The Basic Works of Aristotle*, R. P. McKeon (ed.), Random House, Inc., New York, 1941, p. 1130.)

15. I do not mean to suggest that the "facts" of inter-organization assignment are new or are even now confined only to scientists. I choose this example partly because Mr. Whyte has himself noted the exceptional status accorded to certain scientists and creative workers in some companies (cf. Whyte *op. cit.*, pp. 446ff.) and partly because some of the organization strains resulting from the need to effect these accommodations are of a relatively novel or revealing sort—as when, say, under the promptings of some of their scientists, company managements have been willing to permit these persons to remain on the payroll while servicing, or being serviced by, other organizations (e.g., universities) which sometimes do not even reimburse either these scientists or their parent companies.

16. See Appendix 5 in *Automation*, Her Majesty's Stationery Office, London, 1956, for references to research on management structures under automation that is being conducted in England and the USSR. See also W. W. Cooper, "Management Science and Management," Carnegie Institute of Technology, Graduate School of Industrial Administration, Pittsburgh, Pa., 1956. (Ditto report.)

17. Whyte, *op. cit.*, pp. 88ff.

18. Cf. *ibid.*, pp. 93ff.

19. A. N. Whitehead, *The Aims of Education*, The Macmillan Company, New York, 1929. Republished as a Mentor Book in July, 1949.

20. R. A. Gordon and J. E. Howell, *Higher Education for Business*, Columbia University Press, New York, 1959.

21. F. C. Pierson and others, *The Education of*

American Businessmen, McGraw-Hill Book Company, New York, 1959.

22. See also L. S. Silk, *The Education of Businessmen,* Supplementary Paper of the Committee for Economic Development, no. 11, December, 1960; B. D. Finberg, *A Summary of the Education of Businessmen,* Carnegie Corporation of New York, 1960.

23. Whitehead, *op. cit.,* p. 99.

24. I am dealing here with only their technical education, in Whitehead's sense, and hence ought to warn the readers of this paper that there are issues of wisdom, self satisfaction and culture that also need attention. Cf. *ibid., passim,* on the subjects of liberal and technical education.

25. *Ibid.,* pp. 53ff.

26. Max Weber, *The Protestant Ethic and the Spirit of Capitalism,* trans. Talcott Parsons, with a foreword by R. H. Tawney, Charles Scribner's Sons, New York. See also R. H. Tawney, *Religion and the Rise of Capitalism,* Penguin Books, Inc., Baltimore, 1947.

PART TWO $\mathcal{P}$LANNING *Except for Part 1, on Theory,*
this book of readings is divided into sections on planning, organization,
staffing, directing, and control, since these are seen by the editors as the basic
functions of managers. In Part 2, we present readings which cast light on
the function of planning, the most basic of these five functions. Planning,
defined as the selection, from among alternatives, of courses of future ac-
tion, is the function by which the manager determines (within the area of
his authority) what goals are to be accomplished and how and when they
will be reached. Consequently, the readings for this part have been grouped
under the headings "Nature and Purpose of Planning," "Objectives," "Fore-
casting for Planning," "Operations Research and Decision Making," "Policy
Formulation," and "Making Plans Operational."

Of particular importance in the development of thought about the nature
and purpose of planning are two classics: the extraordinarily perceptive de-
scription of this function by Henri Fayol, a description which, although
written over fifty years ago, is as up to date as today; and the original contri-
bution of Billy E. Goetz, who crisply and accurately codified the types of
basic plans and pointed to their interdependence. To this is added an ex-
cerpt from the recent research by Stewart Thompson into how representative
well-managed companies actually undertake planning.

It is recognized that objectives lie at the base of management planning,
simply because we must *plan toward something. Despite the recent interest*
of scholars and practitioners in this subject, management literature on ob-
jectives is still scarce. Among the best and most discerning writing is that
of John F. Mee and Peter F. Drucker and the scholarly treatment of objec-
tives found in a book by D. W. Miller and M. K. Starr, excerpts from which
are presented.

Because the planner must be able to estimate the future in which his
planning must necessarily operate, forecasting is essential. Two articles on
this subject are included. One, J. W. Redfield's "The Elements of Forecast-
ing," is still one of the finest summaries of forecasting that has been written.
The second is a more recent article on the specialized area of sales fore-
casting by William Lazer, who deals succinctly with the nature of the sales
forecast and its role in integrated management action.

Decision making has generally been regarded as central to planning and,
indeed, to all management. There are even those who view it as the total
task of managers. However, the editors look upon decision making as play-
ing a more limited, but still immensely important, role—that of rational
selection of the optimum alternative in the light of goals sought and against
the background of future environment to be encountered. In the view of the
editors, the excerpt from the late Chester I. Barnard's classic The Functions
of the Executive *in which he deals with the occasion and the environment*
of the decision, is still the best writing on this subject. The more recent
article by Charles Z. Wilson and Marcus Alexis, "Basic Frameworks for
Decisions," is selected as an excellent summary of the central concepts of
the decision theorists who have contributed so much to the understanding
of the decision process.

Closely related to decision making, in that it is a useful scientific tool of
orderly analysis of alternatives, is the technique generally known as opera-
tions research. Still one of the best summaries of the nature of this manage-
ment technique is the article by C. C. Herrmann and J. F. Magee. This arti-
cle describes what operations research is and comments on its limitations and

potentialities. Supplementing this paper is a more recent article by Robert A. Hammond, "Making OR Effective for Management," an interesting analysis of how this valuable tool, which really has not lived up to its expectations and potential in practice, can be made more useful in actual managing.

Policies are guides to thinking in decision making. They therefore furnish the framework for management planning. Although policies are as legion as the levels of management and the subjects of management planning, a single area—product policy—is treated briefly, to give the reader some understanding of policy development. The major considerations that must be kept in mind in arriving at a product policy are outlined in "Product Planning for Future Profits," by Richard D. Crisp. An analysis of what product policy should reflect is contained in the article by Charles H. Kline.

No plan, of course, is more than a mental exercise unless means are available and steps taken to make it operational. In this important area, four examples of helpful analyses are included. One is the excerpt from a presentation, by George A. Peck, of how a plan for new production may be implemented. Another is from a presentation, by Robert I. Phemister, showing how a program of cash forecasting works in a major company and emphasizing the importance of translating plans into cash requirements. It is placed here to draw the reader's attention to the great significance of foreseeing and meeting future cash requirements, since no company can make plans operational unless it has the necessary cash available.

A third article emphasizes the importance of integrating planning and control in order to make planning effective. That this is necessary is apparent from the fundamental truth that we cannot control except against the standard of a plan, nor should we plan without the means of doing all possible to make sure that plans are successful in practice. Such a message is the essence of John O. Tomb's article "A New Way to Manage: Integrated Planning and Control."

The final article in this area is George A. Steiner's "Making Long-range Planning Pay Off." Dr. Steiner's article deals with the important, and recently widely fashionable, area of long-range planning, analyzing what it is and making valuable suggestions to assure that long-range planning is done, is done well, and contributes to effective operations.

Planning*

HENRI FAYOL

The maxim, "managing means looking ahead," gives some idea of the importance attached to planning in the business world, and it is true that if foresight is not the whole of management at least it is an essential part of it. To foresee, in this context, means both to assess the future and make provision for it; that is, foreseeing is itself action already. Planning is manifested on a variety of occasions and in a variety of ways, its chief manifestation, apparent sign and most effective instrument being the plan of action. The plan of action is, at one and the same time, the result envisaged, the line of action to be followed, the stages to go through, and methods to use. It is a kind of future picture wherein proximate events are outlined with some distinctness, whilst remote events appear progressively less distinct, and it entails the running of the business as foreseen and provided against over a definite period.

The plan of action rests: (1) On the firm's resources (buildings, tools, raw materials, personnel, productive capacity, sales outlets, public relations, etc.). (2) On the nature and importance of work in progress. (3) On future trends which depend partly on technical, commercial, financial and other conditions, all subject to change, whose importance and occurrence cannot be pre-determined. The preparation of the plan of action is one of the most difficult and most important matters of every business and brings into play all departments and all functions, especially the management function. It is, in effect, in order to carry out his managerial function that the manager takes the initiative for the plan of action, that he indicates its objective and scope, fixes the share of each department in the communal task, co-ordinates the parts and harmonizes the whole; that he decides, in fine, the line of conduct to be followed. In this line of conduct it is not only imperative that nothing should clash with principles and rules of good management, but also that the arrangement adopted should facilitate application of these principles and rules. Therefore, to the divers technical, commercial, financial and other abilities necessary on the part of a business head and his assistants, there must be added considerable managerial ability.

GENERAL FEATURES OF A GOOD PLAN OF ACTION

No one disputes the usefulness of a plan of action. Before taking action it is most necessary to know what is possible and what is wanted. It is known that absence of plan entails hesitation, false steps, untimely changes of direction, which are so many causes of weakness, if not of disaster, in business. The question of and necessity for a plan of action, then, does not arise and I think that I am voicing the general opinion in saying that a plan of action is indispensable. But there are plans and plans, there are simple ones, complex ones, concise ones, detailed ones, long- or short-term ones; there are those studied with meticulous attention, those treated lightly; there are good, bad, and indifferent ones. How are the good ones to be singled out from among the others? Experience is the only thing that finally determines the true value of a plan, i.e., on the services it can render to the firm, and even then the manner of its application must be taken into account. There is both instrument and player. Nevertheless, there are certain broad characteristics on which general agreement may be reached beforehand without waiting for the verdict of experience.

Unity of plan is an instance. Only one plan can be put into operation at a time; two different plans would mean duality, confusion, disorder. But a plan may be divided into several parts. In large concerns, there is found alongside the general plan a technical, commercial,

* Reprinted by permission of the publisher from Henri Fayol, *General and Industrial Administration*, Pitman Publishing Corporation, New York, 1949, pp. 43–52. Henri Fayol was a French industrialist who probably earlier than anyone else saw management as a universal, pervasive task based upon principles. His book, based largely on lectures delivered in 1900 and 1908, first appeared in French in 1916.

and a financial one, or else an overall one with a specific one for each department. But all these plans are linked, welded, so as to make up one only, and every modification brought to bear on any one of them is given expression in the whole plan. The guiding action of the plan must be continuous. Now the limitations of human foresight necessarily set bounds to the duration of plans, so, in order to have no break in the guiding action, a second plan must follow immediately upon the first, a third upon the second, and so on. In large businesses the annual plan is more or less in current use. Other plans of shorter or longer term, always in close accord with the annual plan, operate simultaneously with this latter. The plan should be flexible enough to bend before such adjustments, as it is considered well to introduce, whether from pressure or circumstances or from any other reason. First as last, it is the law to which one bows. Another good point about a plan is to have as much accuracy as is compatible with the unknown factors bearing on the fate of the concern. Usually it is possible to mark out the line of proximate action fairly accurately, while a simple general indication does for remote activities, for before the moment for their execution has arrived sufficient enlightenment will have been forthcoming to settle the line of action more precisely. When the unknown factor occupies a relatively very large place there can be no preciseness in the plan, and then the concern takes on the name of venture.

Unity, continuity, flexibility, precision: such are the broad features of a good plan of action.

As for other specific points which it should have, and which turn on the nature, importance and condition of the business for which the plan is drawn up, there could be no possibility of settling them beforehand save by comparison with other plans already recognized as effective in similar businesses. In each case, then, comparable elements and models must be sought in business practice, after the fashion of the architect with a building to construct. But the architect, better served than the manager, can call upon books, courses in architecture, whereas there are no books on plans of action, no lessons in foresight, for management theory has yet to be formulated.

There is no lack of good plans, they can be guessed at from the externals of a business but not seen at sufficiently close quarters to be known and judged. Nevertheless, it would be most useful for those whose concern is management to know how experienced managers go about drawing up their plans. By way of information or sample, I am going to set out

the method which has long been followed in a great mining and metallurgical concern with which I am well acquainted.

Method of Drawing up the Plan of Action in a Large Mining and Metallurgical Firm

This company includes several separate establishments and employs about ten thousand personnel. The entire plan is made up of a series of separate plans called forecasts; and there are yearly forecasts, ten-yearly forecasts, monthly, weekly, daily forecasts, long-term forecasts, special forecasts, and all merge into a single programme which operates as a guide for the whole concern.

(i) *Yearly Forecasts.* Each year, two months after the end of the budgetary period, a general report is drawn up of the work and results of this period. The report deals especially with production, sales, technical, commercial, financial position, personnel, economic consequences, etc. The report is accompanied by forecasts dealing with those same matters, the forecasts being a kind of anticipatory summary of the activities and results of the new budgetary period. The two months of the new plan which have elapsed are not left without plan, because of provisional forecasts drawn up fifteen days before the end of the previous period. In a large mining and metallurgical firm not many activities are quite completed during the course of one year. Co-operative projects of a technical, commercial, and financial nature, which provide the business with its activities, need more time for their preparation and execution. From another aspect, account must be taken of the repercussions which proximate activities must have on ultimate ones and of the obligation to prepare far ahead sometimes for a requisite state of affairs.

Finally, thought must be given to constant modifications operating on the technical, commercial, financial and social condition of the industrial world in general and of the business in particular, to avoid being overtaken by circumstances. These various circumstances come outside the framework of yearly forecasts and lead on to longer-term ones.

(ii) *Ten-yearly Forecasts.* Ten-yearly forecasts deal with the same matters as yearly ones. At the outset these two types of forecast are identical, the yearly forecast merging into the first year of the ten-yearly one, but from the second year onwards notable divergences make their appearance. To maintain unity of plan each year the ten-yearly forecasts must be reconciled with annual ones so that at the end of some years the ten-yearly forecasts are generally so modified and transformed as to be

Yearly and Ten-yearly Forecasts

CONTENTS

Technical Section

Mining rights. Premises. Plant.
Extraction. Manufacture. Output.
New workings. Improvements.
Maintenance of plant and buildings.
Production costs.

Commercial Section

Sales outlets.
Marketable goods.
Agencies. Contracts.
Customer importance. Credit standing.
Selling price.

Financial Section

Capital. Loans. Deposits.

Circulating assets $\begin{cases} \text{Supplies in hand.} \\ \text{Finished goods.} \\ \text{Debtors.} \\ \text{Liquid assets.} \end{cases}$

Available assets.
Reserves and sundry appropriations.

Creditors $\begin{cases} \text{Wages.} \\ \text{Suppliers.} \\ \text{Sundry.} \end{cases}$

Sinking funds. Dividends. Bankers.

Accounting

Balance sheet. Profit and Loss account. Statistics.

Security

Accident precautions.
Works police. Claims. Health service.
Insurance.

Management

Plan of action.
Organization of personnel. Selection.
Command.
Co-ordination. Conferences.
Control.

no longer clear and need re-drafting. In effect the custom of re-drafting every five years has become established. It is the rule that ten-yearly forecasts always embrace a decade, and that they are revised every five years. Thus there is always a line of action marked out in advance for five years at least.

(iii) *Special Forecasts.* There are some activities whose full cycle exceeds one or even several ten-yearly periods, there are others which, occurring suddenly, must sensibly affect the conditions of the business. Both the one and the other are the object of special forecasts whose findings necessarily have a place in the yearly and ten-yearly forecasts. But it must never be lost sight of that there is one plan only.

These three sorts of forecasts, yearly, ten-yearly, and special, merged and harmonized, constitute the firm's general plan.

So, having been prepared with meticulous care by each regional management, with the help of departmental management, and then revised, modified, and completed by general management and then submitted for scrutiny and approval to the Board of Directors, these forecasts become the plan which, so long as no other has been put in its place, shall serve as guide, directive, and law for the whole staff.

Fifty years ago I began to use this system of forecasts, when I was engaged in managing a colliery, and it rendered me such good service that I had no hesitation in subsequently applying it to various industries whose running was entrusted to me. I look upon it as a precious managerial instrument and have no hesitation in recommending its use to those who have no better instrument available. It has necessarily some shortcomings, but its shortcomings are very slight compared with the advantages it offers. Let us glance at these advantages and shortcomings.

ADVANTAGES AND SHORTCOMINGS OF FORECASTS

(a) The study of resources, future possibilities, and means to be used for attaining the objective call for contributions from all departmental heads within the framework of their mandate, each one brings to this study the contribution of his experience together with recognition of the responsibility which will fall upon him in executing the plan.

Those are excellent conditions for ensuring that no resource shall be neglected and that future possibilities shall be prudently and courageously assessed and that means shall be appropriate to ends. Knowing what are its capabilities and its intentions, the concern goes boldly on, confidently tackles current problems and is prepared to align all its forces against accidents and surprises of all kinds which may occur.

(b) Compiling the annual plan is always a delicate operation and especially lengthy and laborious when done for the first time, but each repetition brings some simplification and when the plan has become a habit the toil and difficulties are largely reduced. Conversely, the interest it offers increases. The attention demanded for executing the plan, the indispensable comparison between predicted and actual facts, the recognition of mistakes made and successes attained, the search for means of repeating the one and avoiding the other—all go to make the new plan a work of increasing interest and increasing usefulness.

Also, by doing this work the personnel increases in usefulness from year to year, and at the end is considerably superior to what it was in the beginning. In truth, this result is not due solely to the use of planning but everything goes together; a well-thought-out plan is rarely found apart from sound organizational, command, co-ordination, and control practices. This management element exerts an influence on all the rest.

(c) Lack of sequence in activity and unwarranted changes of course are dangers constantly threatening businesses without a plan. The slightest contrary wind can turn from its course a boat which is unfitted to resist. When serious happenings occur, regrettable changes of course may be decided upon under the influence of profound but transitory disturbance. Only a programme carefully pondered at an undisturbed time permits of maintaining a clear view of the future and of concentrating maximum possible intellectual ability and material resources upon the danger.

It is in difficult moments above all that a plan is necessary. The best of plans cannot anticipate all unexpected occurrences which may arise, but it does include a place for these events and prepare the weapons which may be needed at the moment of being surprised. The plan protects the business not only against undesirable changes of course which may be produced by grave events, but also against those arising simply from changes on the part of higher authority. Also, it protects against deviations, imperceptible at first, which end by deflecting it from its objective.

CONDITIONS AND QUALITIES ESSENTIAL FOR DRAWING UP A GOOD PLAN OF ACTION

To sum up: the plan of action facilitates the utilization of the firm's resources and the choice of best methods to use for attaining the objective. It suppresses or reduces hesitancy, false steps, unwarranted changes of course, and helps to improve personnel. It is a precious managerial instrument.

The question may be asked as to why such an instrument is not in general use and everywhere developed to the farthest extent. The reason is that its compilation demands of managerial personnel a certain number of qualities and conditions rarely to be found in combination. The compilation of a good plan demands for the personnel in charge—

1. The art of handling men.
2. Considerable energy.
3. A measure of moral courage.
4. Some continuity of tenure.
5. A given degree of competence in the specialized requirements of the business.
6. A certain general business experience.

(i) *The Art of Handling Men.* In a large firm the majority of departmental managers take part in the compiling of the working arrangements. The execution of this task from time to time is in addition to ordinary everyday work and includes a certain responsibility and does not normally carry any special remuneration. So, to have in such conditions loyal and active co-operation from departmental heads an able manager of men is needed who fears neither trouble nor responsibility. The art of handling men is apparent from keenness of subordinates and confidence of superiors.

(ii) *Energy.* Yearly and ten-yearly forecasts and special forecasts demand constant vigilance on the part of management.

(iii) *Moral Courage.* It is well known that the best-thought-out plan is never exactly carried out. Forecasts are not prophecies, their function is to minimize the unknown factor. Nevertheless, the public generally, and even shareholders best informed about the running of a business, are not kindly disposed towards a manager who has raised unfulfilled hopes, or allowed them to be raised. Whence the need for a certain prudence which has to be reconciled with the obligation of making every preparation and seeking out optimum possible results.

The timid are tempted to suppress the plan

or else whittle it down to nothing in order not to expose themselves to criticism, but it is a bad policy even from the point of view of self-interest. Lack of plan, which compromises smooth running, also exposes the manager to infinitely graver charges than that of having to explain away imperfectly executed forecasts.

(iv) *Continuity of Tenure.* Some time goes by before a new manager is able to take sufficient cognizance of the course of affairs, its general set-up and future possibilities, so as usefully to undertake the compiling of the plan. If, at such a moment, he feels that he will not have enough time to complete the work or only enough to start putting it into execution, or if, on the other hand, he is convinced that such work, condemned to bear no fruit, will only draw criticism upon him, is it to be thought that he will carry it out enthusiastically or even undertake it unless obliged? Human nature must be reckoned with. Without continuity of tenure on the part of management personnel there can be no good plan of action.

(v and vi) *Professional Competence and*

General Business Knowledge. These are abilities just as necessary for drawing up a plan as for carrying it out.

Such are the conditions essential for compiling a good plan. They presuppose intelligent and experienced management. Lack of plan or a bad plan is a sign of managerial incompetence. To safeguard business against such incompetence—

1. A plan must be compulsory.

2. Good specimen plans must be made generally available. (Successful businesses could be asked to furnish such specimens. Experience and general discussion would single out the best.)

3. Planning (as a subject) must be introduced into education. Thus could general opinion be better informed and react upon management personnel, so that the latter's inefficiency would be less to be feared—a state of affairs which would in no wise detract from the importance of men of proven worth.

7

*Managerial Planning**

BILLY E. GOETZ

Plans alone cannot make an enterprise successful. Action is required; the enterprise must operate. Plans can, however, focus action on purposes. They can forecast which actions will tend toward the ultimate objective of economic efficiency, which tend away, which will likely offset one another, and which are merely irrelevant. Managerial planning attempts to achieve a consistent, coordinated structure of operations focused on desired ends. Without plans, action must become merely random activity, producing nothing but chaos.

* Reprinted by permission of the publisher from *Managerial Planning and Control: A Managerial Approach to Industrial Accounting,* McGraw-Hill Book Company, New York, 1949, pp. 63–68, 83–89. Mr. Goetz is professor of management at the Massachusetts Institute of Technology.

Various segments of an enterprise have repeated contacts with the same other economic and social units. Each of these other units also has managers who plan its operations in terms of its environment. These managers are inconvenienced and antagonized and their cooperation lost if the enterprise's contacts lack consistency, either through lack of coordination among its personnel or through vacillation. All points of contact should be coordinated; e.g., advertising, salesmen, product design and quality, packaging, credit arrangements, repair service, and delivery should all be fused into a team conveying a unified impression of quality and service.

The sequence and timing of events are parts of the master plan formulated by management. Failure in timing may mean congested shop departments, shutdowns, delayed deliveries, excessive carrying charges. Even the managerial activity of planning is itself subject to planning in which sequence and timing are important. For example, a company decided to formalize its compensation structure. Its management analyzed each position as to job content and as to knowledge, skill, responsibility, judgment, and experience required of the job incumbent. The study incidentally revealed much duplication of effort and some activities directed at cross-purposes. A complete procedural analysis was undertaken, which resulted in major changes in assignment of duties to departments and persons. Many job descriptions and analyses were rendered obsolete, and the job analysis and evaluation study has to be repeated.

The broader and more permanent plans, i.e., policies and procedures, reduce management cost by eliminating recurrent decisions. Once a policy or procedure is adopted, recurrent problems are met by automatic, routine application of the rule adopted. For example, a company may work out the economic lot to purchase for each separate item needed. It may later discover that economic purchase lots for castings tend strongly to be approximately 3 months' usage while those for screw machine parts approximate a 6 months' supply. Starting from these facts, investigation may show that the cost of calculating each purchase lot separately is not justified by the minor savings resulting from the precision of separate calculations. A policy of buying 3 months' supply of castings and 6 of screw machine parts loses the minor savings of precision but avoids the costs of recurrent analyses and decisions.

Interdependence of Plans   The plans of an enterprise should constitute an integrated program. Necessarily all current plans of a single management share a common environment. They should all be directed toward a single consistent pattern of objectives. The plans should reinforce one another; they should mesh in an articulated sequence.

Perhaps the best illustration of a complete program of plans, internally consistent and properly articulated, is the budget produced by a well-conceived budgetary procedure. Typically, the sales department furnishes estimates of sales volumes and selling expenses, both broken down to show component elements. On the basis of these sales estimates, the planning department plans inventories and production. These plans serve as a basis for estimates of purchases of materials, of employment of labor, and of needs for machinery and equipment.

These estimates, in turn, supply a basis for forecasting purchasing and employment department activities and thus for estimating the expenses of these two departments. Data concerning machinery needs and aggregate personnel requirements furnish the starting point for calculations of floor space, locker- and washroom facilities, heating, electricity, etc., required to maintain over-all operations. All these plans are reduced to anticipated cash revenues and expenditures, leads and lags are estimated, and a cash budget calculated. Finally, estimated financial statements are prepared. The whole procedure provides a complete, internally consistent, integrated program of enterprise operations.

Structure of Managerial Plans   We have assumed that the ultimate objective of management is economic efficiency, i.e., maximization of the ratio of output to input. This objective is implemented by major policies formulated by stockholders or board of directors. These major policies largely determine the general form of the operating organization, i.e., the division of the enterprise into major departments. Each department head, with some collaboration by his colleagues, with some assistance from his subordinates, and subject to review by president and board of directors, formulates departmental policies directed at carrying out the major policies imposed from above. These departmental policies largely determine departmental organization. Both the processes of policy formulation and of organizational design are repeated on the division level and so on down to the terminal operational level.[1] The number, elaborateness, and specific detail of these plans increase rapidly as the operation level is approached. This terminus is represented by a mass of specifications, drawings, dimensions, and standard-practice instructions. Perhaps the penultimate is reached in motion studies, such as those of surgical operations wherein every motion of each finger is planned and prescribed.

In a large enterprise, the activities of thousands of employees are directed and coordinated by this elaborate hierarchy of plans. A few broad plans are implemented by policies of several levels, and these are supported by a multitude of almost as permanent procedures.

---

[1] In a sense, policies are sometimes generated at the operating and first-line supervisory levels and imposed upward. If certain matters are not recognized or provided for by the set of policies adopted, or if regularly adopted policies are not enforced, customs may gradually emerge and achieve the generality, permanence, and authority of true policies.

The whole governs almost numberless specific detailed decisions. For example, a company is formed to manufacture and sell road machinery (stockholder-level decision). Policies are formulated by the board of directors as to the scope to be given this general plan: Will the company manufacture road scrapers, steam shovels, ditchers, pavement finishers, rollers, snowplows, or sweepers? These decisions are implemented at the departmental level by policies governing the sizes and styles of each line included in the program, materials to be purchased, processes to be performed, and items to be subcontracted. Many procedures for handling customers' orders, for routing and scheduling production, for keeping the score of the profit-seeking game. Finally, a multitude of detailed decisions are made within the permanent general frame: should a specific customer order be accepted? Should a particular part be a casting or a forging? Should the company buy a turret lathe or an engine lathe?

POLICIES

Major Policies   Some policies are considered important enough to be imbedded in the corporate charter or in its by-laws. These can be changed only by vote of its stockholders and are the broadest and most fundamental of corporate policies. Typically, the choice of industry is stated in the purpose clause, and the scale of operations vaguely fixed by the authorized capital structure. The composition and organization of the board of directors is usually stated in the by-laws. Many companies refer other matters to annual stockholders' meetings, e.g., pension plans, plans for major financing operations, and profit-sharing plans.

Somewhat less significant (or more urgent) plans and choices are made by the board of directors. These policies tend to be company-wide in scope, crossing departmental lines, although a few departmental matters may reach the board through financial importance alone. Choice of industry is perhaps the most fundamental of company policies, underlying and limiting all departmental policies. In its broadest sense, this choice is usually written into the corporate charter and thereby reserved to the stockholders' discretion. However, within these broad limits the board may decide to take on a new line or to discontinue an old one. For example, the board of directors of a manufacturer of plastic firebrick may decide to bring out a line of air-setting materials or a manufacturer of thermostatic controls may add a line of recording thermometers. The new line presents new problems to sales, production, and finance departments. Prospect lists must be revised with the new products in mind; new sales stories must sing the praises of the new line; perhaps additional sales force will have to be recruited and trained to give the new line effective representation. The engineering department will have to prepare new formulas or designs. The factory will have to buy new tools, dies, and fixtures and possibly new machinery; radical changes may become necessary in the system of production scheduling and cost control. New financing may be necessary, and credit policies may need revising, as the new line is sold to new types of customers. Both the importance and the interdepartmental character of the change make it a subject for consideration by the board of directors. After its decision is made, all departments will have to revise their policies to conform.

Selection of the competitive level is a similarly all-pervasive issue, properly the prerogative of the board. If the board decides to seek the quality market, the engineering department must specify close tolerances and fine finishes, the purchasing department must buy good materials from dependable sources, the personnel department must hire and train workmen able to produce the desired quality product, the production department must acquire high-grade equipment and provide adequate inspection, the sales department must stress a quality appeal in its advertising copy and in the type of salesperson employed, and the financial department should arrange credit terms appropriate for the quality trade. Every department must orientate its plans and operations with regard to this major policy imposed by the board of directors.

A third all-pervasive basic set of decisions fixes the company's policy as to venturesomeness, aggressiveness, and expansion. Closely related are policies regarding dilution of stockholders' equity and disposition of earnings. Aggressive expansion suggests extensive borrowing and plowing back of profits. Implications of these policies with respect to departmental plans are too obvious to require detailed comment.

In addition to formulating such fundamental policies, the board coordinates departmental plans through review and approval of the master budgets. This gives the board an opportunity to review departmental plans and ascertain that such plans are designed to implement the broader policies set by the board. Also, the board reviews and approves major expenditures before departments are allowed to proceed with their plans. Later the board compares performance with plans and passes on explanations and new plans growing out of experience with the old.

Within the frame imposed by the board of directors, all departments of whatever type formulate more specific policies to give effect to those set by the board. This will be true whether the major departments follow commodity or functional lines. Thus Chevrolet policies may differ substantially from Cadillac, and both will necessarily differ widely from Frigidaire or Electromotive: the variety of styles and sizes offered, the financing of sales, the channels of distribution will all differ profoundly. General Foods can appeal to coffee lovers with Maxwell House, to coffee haters with Postum, and to limbo with Sanka. Since no two enterprises have the same commodity divisions, commodity departmental policies must be discussed with reference to a specific company. However, many enterprises are divided into substantially similar functional departments, and commodity departments themselves are divided into similar patterns of functional divisions. This affords opportunity to investigate and partially catalogue the wide range of policies formulated by functional departments.

PROCEDURES

Nature of Procedures Procedures are a species of managerial planning. As such, they share with policies and organizational configuration the objectives and techniques of managerial planning. Procedures, in common with other forms of planning, seek to avoid the chaos of random activity by directing, co-ordinating, and articulating the operations of an enterprise. They help direct all enterprise activities toward common goals, they help impose consistency across the organization and through time, and they seek economy by enabling management to avoid the costs of recurrent investigations and to delegate authority to subordinates to make decisions within a frame of policies and procedures devised by management.

Procedures also share the techniques of managerial planning. Many alternate procedures may implement the same policy complex. The managerial technique for devising procedures, as for all other planning, is one of analysis of alternate possibilities and selection of the most desirable. For example, professional firms are jealous of the accuracy of their reports. The final copy must be carefully checked to eliminate errors of typing. Columns of figures may

be checked by reading back, figure by figure, to check against the original, or they may be checked by footing and comparing the total with that of the original column. The two procedures can be checked for effectiveness in catching errors and for cost.

Policies are relatively general, reasonably permanent managerial plans. Procedures are less general but comparably permanent. A policy maps out a field of action. It determines objectives and limits the area of action. Procedures are stipulated sequences of definite acts. Procedures mark a path through the area of policy. They may fork, generally with adequate clues to determine clerical choice of path; they may contain trivial gaps to be filled in at the discretion of a clerk; but there is little that resembles the extension of a policy. Procedures are not multidimensional; they do not cover areas of behavior; they have only chronological sequence.

Procedures implement policies. Specific routings of salesmen embody a policy concerning territories within which sales shall be sought. Scheduling of work through the shop gives effect to policies regarding size of inventories and balancing of load factors. As already noted production planning procedures may, as a matter of policy, be based on estimated shipping requirements, on stock limits, or on customer orders. Similarly, purchasing procedures may implement a policy of shopping the market for bargains or one of selecting a few reliable sources. Policy always sets an objective or delimits an area of action, while procedures fix a path toward the objective or through the area. Sequence is the *sine qua non* of procedure.

Structure of Procedures Since a great objective can be analyzed into partial objectives or a large area divided into smaller areas, a major policy can be sub-divided into a number of minor policies. Thus policy has structure —usually paralleling the organizational configuration. Procedures also have structure. Many important procedures cross departmental lines, binding the activities of all into a common effort. Thus, a typical sales order procedure is initiated by receipt of an order from a customer. The sales department interprets the order and prepares multiple copies on the company's own standard forms. One copy may be sent to the engineering department as instructions covering necessary designs and estimates. Another may later be sent to the factory as an order directing the factory to produce the articles required for shipment to the customer. A third may be sent to the shipping department directing it to make shipment of the goods when received from the factory. A fourth may be sent to the bookkeeping department as an original evidence to be journalized and posted. A fifth may be sent to the customer as an invoice. These procedures obviously supply an important part of the connective tissue that holds the enterprise together.

Such all-pervasive procedures are main arteries tying together a great many branch paths. Many of these subordinate procedures are intradepartmental in character, but not necessarily so. Thus a complete sequence of cues and acts touched off by receipt of a customer's order could include all details of interpretation and write-up of the order by the sales department, origin and issuance of a series of shop orders with all their supporting documents and posting of production control records by the planning department, origin and return of reports of shop performance with more posting of production control and cost records, and all billing and collection procedures in the accounting department. Automatically instigated ramifications may lead through virtually all purchasing and disbursing procedures, into all pay-roll procedures, etc.

There are also a large number of relatively independent procedures tending to be largely intradepartmental in nature. Among these are procedures governing assignment and payment of second or swing shifts, employee bidding on job vacancies, the settling of employee grievances, seniority rights, handling of customer complaints, taking physical inventory counts, and many more. Though adding little to the coordinative machinery of the enterprise, these procedures are of great importance in achieving the objectives of consistency and economy.

All these procedures are implemented by a great mass of detailed procedures pertaining to single operations—often called "standard-practice instructions." For example, the operation sheet charts a series of acts by a number of employees necessary to production of articles ordered by a customer or needed for stock. Each operation listed is defined and described by blueprints and standard-practice instructions detailing setup, tooling, fixtures, feeds and speeds, and motion patterns. Standard-practice instructions govern such activities as issuance of new telephone directories, the routes of plant messengers, follow-up of delayed purchase orders, the posting of journal entries to the ledgers. Some companies produce "manuals of style" to govern preparation of letters, reports, and other written documents used by the company.[2] Similar manuals may regulate various accounting or tabulating procedures.

Recurrent Procedural Problems   A number of problems recur persistently in the course of procedural design. Among the most common are (1) relevance of the procedure, (2) duplication of effort, and (3) use of clerical substitutes.

Relevance of Procedure.   Perhaps most frequent and most important of recurrent procedural problems is the problem of relevance. Does the procedure do a useful job? Is it worth what it costs? There are several major sources of useless procedures. Clerks and minor supervisors may attempt to build up their prestige and bolster their security by devising intricate and obscure rituals. Or procedures may become obsolete without being discontinued. For example, material shortages may plague a company. Reports may be instituted to inform a number of executives as to condition of inventories and probable delivery dates on outstanding purchase orders. Later the supply situation eases. One by one the executives no longer need or use the report. None orders it discontinued, as each believes that others use it. But the law of clerical procedures inexorably produces and submits the report until positive orders are issued to discontinue it.

Many procedures are traditional or copied from other enterprises where they may or may not be useful. Perhaps many cost procedures illustrate this possibility. Some costs are computed because "all businesses should figure costs," not because someone is going to use the figures obtained. It is customary for cost accounts to "tie in" with general ledger controls, but many cost systems have gradually been converted to standard cost systems in which clerical errors and deviations of performance from standard are merged in the variance accounts. Yet extra clerical costs are incurred to figure costs on trivial nonrepetitive jobs or to obtain redundant data on repetitive work to secure the tie-in that no longer serves its prime purpose of proving arithmetic accuracy.

Procedures may lose relevancy by getting hopelessly behind. Data produced may be altogether obsolete, and yet reports continue. For example, one cost department was reporting

---

[2] For example, among a multiplicity of other procedures governing its educational processes, e.g., matriculation, registration, the University of Chicago issues a 61-page booklet of detailed rules governing the physical appearance of dissertations submitted by candidates for higher degrees. A typical detail is the insistence on the use of Roman numerals to designate chapters.

costs of producing tools some 9 months after tools were completed and in use. By the time facts regarding excessive costs of tool production became known, it was much too late for the superintendent to take remedial action. Finally, the superintendent issued instructions to skip 9 months of figuring tool costs and so got on a current and useful basis. Had he worshipped the tie-in with general ledger controls, he would have put on extra clerical help to produce useless cost data at an accelerated rate until the data were brought to a current basis.

Duplication of Effort. Many procedures are heedlessly duplicated because of a desire for secrecy or through ignorance. Foremen often keep private records of departmental production because they have no access to or knowledge of duplicate records kept by the planning department. The cost department may keep records of material prices charged by different vendors that duplicate records kept by the purchasing department. Stock-room records, cost records, and planning department records may maintain a useless triple watch over inventory balances. Avoidance of such duplication is one major reason for centralizing responsibility for design of forms and procedures and for conducting periodic reviews of procedural configurations.

Duplication often stems from a desire for "protection." Private, duplicate records are maintained to protect individuals rather than through mere ignorance of existing similar records. Forms may be routed to a long succession of persons or duplicate copies sent each for the legitimate purpose of informing each of certain activities or to provide each with expensive but useless protection. The game may be played to the extent of requiring virtually every person touching a form to initial it to prove he has seen it. He may be required to date his initials to protect himself from a charge of delaying vital procedures.

Skillful design of procedures may eliminate clerical copy work by provision of duplicate forms. For example, copies of sales invoices filed chronologically may serve as the sales journal, eliminating traditional methods of journalizing. In some instances, another copy filed alphabetically may serve as customer's ledger, substituting filing for more expensive forms of posting. Such multiple use has resulted in many companies producing tens or even hundreds of copies of basic documents. So many companies are requesting duplicate or triplicate copies of invoices that provision of such copies is becoming standard practice. Some procurement divisions of the federal government require as many as 21 copies of invoices. The principle

involved is sound. Why should clerks in one company copy documents prepared by clerks in another if the first can produce the required number of forms with little or no extra effort?

Sometimes accuracy is sought through verification by duplication. Thus, extensions may be computed on the customer's order and recomputed on the sales invoice to prove the accuracy of the original computation and of the subsequent typing. When possible, it is usually cheaper and better to verify by juncture rather than by duplication. An illustration is the checking of total hours reported on job time tickets against the total shown on employees' gate cards. Another illustration is verification of detail carried in subsidiary ledgers by comparison of trial balances of such ledgers with the balances of corresponding general ledger controls.

Use of Clerical Substitutes. Taylor and his disciples revolted against the rule of tradition. Trade mysteries, long carried in the memories of skilled craftsmen, were subjected to scientific test, standardized, and made a matter of record. Policies and procedures were reviewed and reduced to writing. Routing and scheduling were taken from foremen and made subjects of elaborate clerical rituals. Taylor's functional foremen became whole departments: planning, personnel, cost, toolroom, maintenance, stock room, and materials handling. The ratio of indirect to direct labor rose spectacularly.

In general, the new technique proved amazingly effective. Clerical work became important and hence the subject of inventive activity and intensive development. Clerical aids of all kinds were vastly improved. Duplicating devices, calculating machines, visible records, and tabulating equipment were invented or improved to conserve clerical time and reduce clerical errors. Today, determination of the extent to which clerical procedures should be mechanized and selection of the most effective types of equipment are major problems of the procedural analyst.

At times, paper work has been overelaborated. Too many managers at all levels have attempted to use reports to the exclusion of direct observation. For example, a shop superintendent attempted to install planning procedures that would virtually be automatic. Provision was made for reporting all irregularities. There appeared to be no remaining reasons why the man should ever leave his comfortable office. Two disadvantages gradually emerged. The superintendent lost all feeling for intangibles, which resulted in foolish decisions and the antagonism of all foremen, and several clerks were required to keep all records posted currently and to originate the multitude of required reports. A successor superintendent found that one planning clerk armed with a simple memorandum record of shop orders could visit every machine in the shop and ascertain progress of every order in less than 2 hours. The simple memorandum served adequately both as progress record and as report to the superintendent.

Dependence on paper work and the accounting fetish of a tie-in with general ledger controls often produce needlessly elaborate inventory records. There is seldom sufficient reason for carrying extensions and dollar values in such records. Receipts and withdrawals can be entered in physical units, and balances priced and extended whenever financial statements are to be prepared. Furthermore, trivial items can be controlled by physical means rather than by paper procedures. Stock limits can be set, and minimum quantities separately packaged. Each minimum package is thrown into the corresponding bin of parts. When the bin is emptied, the minimum package is broken, and an attached tag bearing the part number is sent to the purchasing or planning department as an indication that a new order should be released for the part.

8

What Planning Involves*

STEWART THOMPSON

The contribution of the business planner is this: Despite the impossibility of accurately forecasting the future, he identifies a range of possibilities and prepares for them. Once this is understood, the difference between planning and forecasting becomes clearer. "Forecasting" is the attempt to find the most probable course of events or a range of probabilities. "Planning" is deciding what one will do about them.

Specialists in market research and economic forecasting can be useful in gathering information on which plans for the business can be based. But decisions on what is to be achieved, and why, are business decisions, to be made by top management. This view was generally supported by the managers who participated in this research project. Most of those interviewed in firms which have staff planning departments emphasized that the work of these departments is not that of making business decisions. Instead, they declared, these departments help top management by gathering information, by identifying problems, by recommend-ing procedures to be followed in formulating and reviewing plans. It is top management that decides the kinds of work to be performed, the kinds of material to be used, and the needs of specific customers to be satisfied. Top management decides the risks the company is willing to take and states whether the future of the firm is to be staked on one or more products, on one or more markets. Top management decides what things the company will do as a side line and what things it will do as a life-or-death commitment.

CHARACTERISTICS OF A BUSINESS PLAN

Even though the future is largely unknown, work in the present takes on added significance when it is performed in contemplation of future results. A business plan states what results are to be achieved and states things that people actually can and should do to achieve them. It also provides for the evaluation and measurement of results.

Underlying the use of planning in business is the insight that management is not only "feel" or experience, but also choice of a rational course of action. The decisions and actions of business men are based on certain

* Reprinted by permission of the publisher from *How Companies Plan*, American Management Association, Research Study, no. 54, New York, 1962. Mr. Thompson is manager of research projects for the American Management Association.

ideas regarding the kind of business they manage, the market and economy in which they operate, the resources at their disposal, and the effect of their actions upon the business and upon persons outside the business.

Objectives, assumptions, and risks are always present in the thoughts, decisions, and acts of a manager. Even though these elements may not be always clear to him, he must act on the basis of some ideas about the character of his business: its environment, its resources, its potential. No matter how important intuition and experience may be, business decisions and actions can be rational. A major purpose and contribution of a business plan is to bring out and sharpen this rationality.

A business plan is a preparation for action. It involves making decisions and scheduling results.

Scheduling takes into account the magnitude of the problems in bringing about a result. Scheduling tests the feasibility of a plan. For example, it may show that results needed "immediately" would, in fact, require three years of preparation. Thoughtful scheduling extends the possibility of making business decisions effective. Without schedules, business plans may be only unrealistic dreams. Scheduling has to do with such questions as these: "What must I have completed on what date?" "What stages can be accelerated?" "What stages can be got under way concurrently with other stages?" Scheduling starts with the knowledge of what is desired and works backward.

By tying business decisions to specific times and results, a plan for management can be formulated which, when used imaginatively, can aid in maintaining and augmenting the value of a business to the society of which it is a part.

THREE KINDS OF BUSINESS PLANNING

In different ways, the experience of managers reported here shows three kinds of business plans: (1) plans for doing current business, (2) plans for continuing in business, and (3) plans for business development and growth. The major emphasis of this study is on business plans of the kinds listed as (2) and (3).

Plans for doing current business are related to creating today's business and to scheduling today's work in accordance with time and quality standards. These are the operating plans of the manager and the supervisor and the worker, piece by piece, order by order. Since they concern customer service and operating efficiency in an immediate way, effective planning and scheduling of today's business are essential to future survival and growth. The importance of this point has been emphasized by David Packard, President of Hewlett-Packard Company, in these words:

> The keystone of our entire program at Hewlett-Packard Company can be summarized in the statement that we believe tomorrow's success is based on today's performance. In our opinion, this is so obvious a statement as hardly to require repetition, but we often see other firms which are so busy worrying about tomorrow that they never quite seem to do otherwise, and the first order of business is almost always to make sure that current operations are on a sound and profitable basis. It is true that this approach is fairly conservative and that our rate of progress has probably been somewhat limited by our desire to avoid overcommitments to the future, but on the other hand we find that, when we have our current situation under firm control, all our key people seem to have a little more time to look constructively toward the future.[1]

Plans for continuing in business are those that deal with the changing character of the customer's business, with the changing habits and expectations of workers and society at large. These plans do not deal specifically with only one order or one customer. Rather, they are plans reasoned from the manager's assumptions on long-term trends and the changes in those trends. These are plans to build the changing values of the customer into the products and services of the business.

In addition to—or instead of—plans made to perpetuate a business in the markets it already serves, the chief executive may see opportunities his business could logically exploit in other areas. Plans made by the top management of Harris-Intertype Corporation to move into electronics are of this kind, in part at least. Plans for business development and growth sometimes involve preparation to open markets different from those traditionally served by the business, with products different from those the business itself makes. Or, the plans may be to serve essentially the same customers with different or more expanded products and services.

For many companies, business planning is the act of making decisions in one or more of these areas. By thinking of plans to meet needs

[1] David Packard, "Assuring the Company's Future," American Management Association, General Management Series, no. 175, New York, 1955, p. 27.

in each of these three areas, a manager can identify the areas in his own company in which planning ought to be accelerated.

PLANNING AS PRACTICED BY MOST COMPANIES

An analysis of the remarks of the business men who participated in this study shows that their business planning usually involves the following steps:

- Gathering information on both the external environment and the company internally, in order to see the major problems facing the business.
- Identifying and studying the factors which may limit the company's efficiency and growth in the future.
- Formulating basic assumptions (such as, for example, "No major war within the next five years," or "A continuation of the present economic trends for the planning period"). It may also involve determination of several plans for the future, based on a set of markedly different assumptions.
- Laying down the objectives or the goals of the business, based on information gathered, assumptions, predictions, and a study of major problems.
- Determining the actions which must be taken to achieve the objectives.
- Setting up a timetable for these actions. . . .

THE CONCEPT OF THE BUSINESS BOUNDARY

Through planning, a manager creates a strategy for the survival and growth of his business. What must he do to assure the health of his firm as a growing enterprise? His answer commits money, knowledge, and skills to specific tasks in order to accomplish specific results. These results change the circumstances of the business, change its problems and its opportunities, and may create the need for changes in its character and its plans for the future.

The manager plans his business by defining a particular relationship of work-product-customer to highlight those factors that are of greatest importance to his business. In effect, the manager defines boundaries within which his business will operate. The effectiveness of a business plan depends largely upon the ability of the manager to select appropriate boundaries. A clear statement of business boundaries has the value of concentrating thought on the problems that are vital to the business.

Mason Smith, Vice President and Treasurer of Whirlpool Corporation, emphasized this point when he spoke of the manager's need for a frame of reference for his business:

A frame of reference is essential for long-range planning—and by "frame of reference" I mean, specifically, the definition and statement of the company's broad objectives and policies in such a way that they are understood clearly by all personnel. I am convinced that any attempt to initiate and maintain a long-range planning program without some general, company-wide understanding of the kind of business that the management is attempting to build will yield very few tangible benefits. In addition to a cold, clear acknowledgment of the company's financial limitations, these objectives and policies should provide some indication of whether the company will intensify within one industry or diversify; whether or not it will integrate; whether it will attempt only to maintain the Number One position in its industry or try to balance size with other considerations; whether it will assume a posture of statesmanship in its industry or operate under short-run principles. Decisions regarding such matters are, of course, subject to review and revision by the board and by management at any time. When they are revised, however, management should be sure that the long-range planning program is following whatever new statement of policy is laid down.[2]

In solving operating problems, the manager reasons from agreed-on boundaries to implications for the particular problem. If seemingly promising lines of action conflict with accepted boundaries, there are two solutions: change the boundaries or drop the action. So it may be said that business planning covers (1) exploration and improvement within boundaries that have been laid down, and (2) the questioning, evaluation, and restructuring of the boundaries themselves.

This testing and correcting of the boundaries is a vital part of business planning. "Who are our customers?" "Why?" "Under what circumstances does a customer become a noncustomer?" "To our customers Jackson, Jones, and Johnson, what is the function and value of our product?" "What consulting services does our special competence enable us to provide that our competitors cannot provide?" "Is our main strength in making the product, or

[2] Mason Smith, "How to Initiate Effective Long-range Planning," *The Dynamics of Management*, American Management Association, Management Report, no. 14, New York, 1958, p. 70.

in our methods of selling it, or in our company image, or in our knowledge supplied to the customer on how to use, store, and maintain the product?" These are some of the questions that the participants in this study have answered or tried to answer.

THE NEED FOR BOUNDARIES

According to a statement by one of its executives, the top management of one company which took part in this research had no clear idea of the boundaries of the business. Eventually, a situation arose that sharply pointed up the need for well-defined boundaries. Although some aspects of the situation have been altered in the telling, in order to comply with this firm's desire for anonymity, the problem was essentially as reported here.

A researcher came up with a device to aid surgeons by measuring the oxygen content of blood continuously while surgery was in progress. When a vice president discovered that almost $100,000 had been spent on the instrument he ordered the work to be discontinued. Recalled an official of the firm:

> We stopped work on that project, but we did not know why. Nobody, not even the president or the officer who issued the order, seemed to know why. I raised the question: "O.K.," I said, "let's stop work on the project, but let's be sure we know why. Do we not want to do medical research? Do we not have the money to finish the project? Do we want to make only radio and TV sets?" Nobody was prepared to get down to some careful thinking on the issue. We just stopped. The researcher left us, taking his ideas with him. In time, the failure to examine the possibilities the researcher was opening up for us may prove to be one of the greatest fumbles we ever made. As I see it, the fumble was not so much the decision to stop the project, unfortunate as that may have been, but the larger issue of failing to thoroughly consider the areas in which the competence of those in the firm can best be applied. We still lack a central concept about our business. It is badly needed here.

THE SYSTEM BOUNDARY

There are two concepts of business boundaries. The one just discussed involves the choice of objectives and behavior for the firm. In this case the boundary marks off the area of business purpose and conduct selected by the top management for present or future operations of the company.

The other concept relates to changes in the dynamic structure or climate within which the managerial decisions and plans must be made. This dynamic structure, or "system," consists of the variables affecting and affected by the business. The system includes the interaction of individuals within the firm, the interaction of the firm with its customers and with other businesses, and influences within the society of which the firm is a part. In this context the boundary—more specifically, the system boundary—is the moment of significant change in the variables of the system.

Let us assume that at some point in the operation of a particular business one of its essential variables (for example, its most important customer) does not continue as before. This discontinuity can be described as a system boundary. The business might have to dissolve, or at least its managers would be faced with a grave problem. The business could perhaps establish a new relationship with another type of customer in order to survive. If this were done, a new climate or business system would operate and new variables would govern the company. There would be new factors (or a re-weighting of old factors) to be considered in the new business plan. Business planning seeks to identify such points of major change and to enable the manager to make preparations in case of need. In some cases, proper response may require very significant changes in company concepts, with such results as adding new products, hiring a new president, or selling a division of the company.

A COMPANY EXPERIENCE

The following case illustrates an evolution of a business and a change in the boundaries within which it operated. This firm's experience points out that changes in the way the firm did business created a new business system. These changes were subtle, not easy to recognize, not easy to define precisely. The president did not call them "boundaries," but he did recognize that at different points in time an isolated change created new stages in his firm's growth and gave rise to new kinds of opportunities and problems and a need for new plans. The firm made storage racks, hand trucks, and other equipment used in handling and storing materials.

> The owners of the firm hired a new president to help achieve higher profits. As the president examined sales records and visited customers, he found that his competitors gained considerable business from the use of attractively pre-

pared and well-illustrated catalogues. It seemed to him highly desirable to have such catalogues, but he felt that his company could not afford them.

The president proceeded to expand his product line to some extent and redesigned much of it to approximate closely the products of one of his principal competitors, a much larger company. In the course of soliciting business, particularly from those firms he knew well, he used his competitor's catalogue, sometimes offering lower prices and usually providing earlier delivery. In addition, he studied the utilization of his equipment in the customer's plants. As his profits increased, he later brought out his own descriptive catalogue, added some especially designed devices, and concentrated on the technical training of his firm's salesmen. His sales proceeded to match and then outstrip the business of even his largest competitors. Salesmen of the competitor sold from the catalogue in a routine way ("Order by number, please"), but this president had his salesmen bring special problem-solving skills to his customers' operations. Incidentally, for many of his salesmen this change in the character of their work launched them on a new career in the firm.

Recognizing an opportunity to depart still further from the traditional marketing methods of "the industry" and to publicize the unique character of his company, the president offered his own help and that of his salesmen to aid customers solve problems of layout and utilization in their plants. Some of the customers began to request his aid in training members of their own staffs in his techniques of analysis. These requests came with such frequency that for a time he seriously considered setting up another business to deal with the consultations. However, he decided against this idea.

Hearing of his success in his own line, manufacturers of other related products sought to have his firm distribute all or some of their lines. The directors of the firm, well pleased with operations under their president, recommended diversification into other businesses.

A major problem became that of planning and controlling the growth of the business in order to utilize effectively the evolving skills and growing reputation of the firm while avoiding, as far as possible, an uncontrolled dissipation of energy.

COMPANY CHARACTER

Business decisions that clarify the boundaries within which the business will operate, and a timetable of results, imply as well as a plan a

particular conception of "management." The way in which this conception is defined by the individual manager gives "planned character" to his firm. The president's concept of the firm he is managing, for example, largely defines the kind of planning he will do.

There is a difference between financial manipulation and business management. There is a difference between a corporation and its individual components. Sometimes confusion exists as to what kind of planning the managers should do, because the kind of business the chief executive is managing or creating is not clear.

Some managers believe their company operates as a federalized enterprise with a central office and various decentralized divisions, when in actual fact the characteristics of the company are more those of a financial trust. As a financial trust, the primary concern of the central management is the investment of shareholders' capital in various businesses. These investments may be, for the most part, in minority interests. Buying and selling of interests in various firms is done for appreciation of capital rather than for building an enterprise with a logic of its own. Planning in a financial trust type of operation requires different knowledge and skills and addresses itself to kinds of problems which are different from those in a decentralized company.

A "federalized company," as the term is used here, is a firm which has a headquarters office for two or more enterprises, each of which has its unique products, processes, and markets and complements the others. In an enterprise of this type, planning within the divisions applies to the exploration of markets and improved efficiency, within the boundaries laid down. Plans would also include means for clarifying the boundaries of the divisions and of the total enterprise in the light of new problems and opportunities. Problems relating to new product ideas and new markets that do not fall clearly within the scope of one or more of the divisions would have to be resolved. Headquarters as well as divisional management may have parts to play in planning for action to be taken by two or more divisions that may form together a single unit in order to achieve a specific purpose. Business planning at headquarters may involve the raising of capital and the strengthening of management competence in the subsidiary and affiliated businesses, as well as provision for assuring that continuous development of managerial competence is energized within the divisions by themselves. The orientation of management at headquarters may aim to do less and less in the way of managing the divisions, so that top management can concentrate on identifying and planning for those events that most affect the whole firm.

Another form of business that has special planning needs of its own is the holding company. Such firms own either a substantial minority interest or a controlling interest in various enterprises, no single one of which may relate to the markets, products, or processes of the others. The central concern of management of a holding company often is to acquire capital at the most favorable terms. The capital is utilized by the subsidiary enterprises for their growth and expansion and may represent funds which the subsidiaries could not have acquired had they not had affiliation with the holding company. Planning at headquarters may emphasize the appropriation of acquired capital (and regular profits) among the affiliated businesses. Very often, management at headquarters is skilled in dealing with the financial problems of the business but incompetent to deal with the more specialized plans of individual affiliated businesses. To distinguish the areas of competence of headquarters management and to define the kinds of contributions headquarters can make to the profit-producing end of the enterprise (the divisions) is a matter for careful planning and of large consequence.

In addition to the federalized corporation and the holding company, there is the business that does not have a relationship to a central headquarters. This is the one-plant, one-management business. It may or may not be owned by its managers. It may or may not be a large corporation. With regard to planning for this kind of business—as for the others—difference in size is not in itself so major a consideration as is the difference in the kind of problems with which top management must deal. Even a small company, like its larger counterparts, may have many circles of affiliation with other businesses, and these should be recognized in the business plan. There are many forms of affiliation that are becoming increasingly common.[3]

It is most unlikely that any enterprise will fit neatly into such arbitrary classifications as

those given here. Nonetheless, managers of individual companies must continually think of their businesses according to some structure of ideas in order to know what they are really doing and whether they are doing the essential things. A manager—of whatever business—cannot do everything. He needs some rational framework for determining which kinds of decisions he will leave for others and which ones he is to decide for himself. In clarifying the definition of this framework, top managers must carefully examine the nature of their relationship to the operating executives. The classification just listed, while oversimplified, may enable managers to question their assumptions regarding the main issues they habitually retain—perhaps without conscious examination—for their own attention.

INADEQUACIES OF PLANNING

The objective of this report is to describe the kinds of business planning done, and the methods followed, in a selected group of companies. This implies differences in personal preference, from one company to another (or even within the same company), on how planning ought to be done. It implies as well that examples of both good and not-so-good planning are to be found in this report.

Some companies, for example, are currently enamored of change, accelerating change, and innovations and new developments. The intoxicating enthusiasm for change and "new frontiers" sometimes leads to neglect of the stable elements which do not change. Anticipation of and planning for change is fruitless unless it is coupled with anticipation of and planning for factors which will be stable. It is probably a matter of individual emphasis, but the examples in this study weigh heavily on the side of managements' concern for change. They do not express equal awareness of the stable elements of the businesses.

Along the same line is the emphasis on new developments and acquisitions, as contrasted with improved efficiency within existing markets. Commented an official of one firm, "Farming the same farm more efficiently usually has a better chance, I'll wager, than new products or other expansion." He was right in going on to suggest that many companies do not seem to study the possibility of becoming more efficient within the current boundaries of the business with the same thoroughness that characterizes plans for diversification into other fields—which often prove later to be beyond their competence.

Clarifying boundaries and areas of compe-

---

[3] In this regard the following articles are worthy of note: Robert Hershey, "No Job Is Too Big . . . The Multiple Organization: Management's Answer to Complexity," *The Management Review*, February, 1959, p. 9; John J. Corson, "Government and Business: Partners in the Space Age," *The Management Review*, September, 1959, p. 9; and Robert G. Sproul, Jr., "Developing Profitable Partnerships in Overseas Operations," *The Management Review*, October, 1960, p. 4.

tence is a pressing need in many companies, including some of those represented in this study. . . . [One company's] "Ten-Year Forward-planning Program" . . . does not meet the definition of a plan as proposed in the text. It is a rather vague declaration of intention. A plan stipulates courses of action to produce measurable results. This document does not. A plan must be operational in the sense that it describes actions in terms of things people actually can do. This document does not. The document does speak of improved results. But it will be a plan only when the desired improvement is stated as a recognized standard. A plan states that certain results must be obtained (for example, reduced costs) and states specifically what those results are and what will be done to achieve them.

This is not to say that a document of intention is of no value; such a document may be the precursor of specific and realistic plans. It is sometimes essential to think through, in broad terms, what one intends to do. Good intentions can lead to sound and effective action. (In fact, all action ought to be based on "good intentions.") Still, the manager ought to distinguish a business plan from a statement limited to the expression of good intentions.

In other situations, top management participation in business planning is entirely lacking. Plans are called for from various division and department heads and "coordinated" (a word which is often used but seldom defines clearly the work performed) at the top. A clear view of what the division and department heads must contribute is often lacking. Asking department heads or even senior officers in a firm what it is they would like to do in the coming year or in ten years may be one way to attempt to capture their interest. But it is not business planning. To limit the formulation of a business plan to this kind of procedure is to do little more than make an opportunity for people to do what they want to do, undisciplined by clear purposes and concrete objectives vital to the whole. In such a case, planning is in the nature of recreation or play, where people plan to do the things they enjoy. It is the task of top management to provide the purpose and to set the boundaries, using as directly as possible the best brains in the business (and outside it, too) to do so. But it is correct to view the interests and skills of its people as the company's special strengths. A business plan should include thinking on the numbers and levels of skills required and how they can best be related to each other in order to get the vital work of the business done. Presidents and

managers interviewed spoke also of a number of other problems and inadequacies associated with making plans for a business—for example, the following:

- The manager may confine his thinking to largely obsolete or contemporary ideas.

- The manager may be unwilling or unable to see that this plan was either ill-conceived or well-conceived but, in any case, not feasible. He won't believe he is headed for failure until his business is liquidated.

- There is danger of "throwing good money after bad." One may be inclined to invest another $100,000 to try to save a $50,000 investment that is not producing. More thought might bring to mind a more profitable avenue in which to direct the $100,000.

- It is often difficult to stop work on a planned project, even when instructions to do so have been given. In one company a project had been officially stopped because the results planned were not being realized. But it took an additional (and unplanned) $250,000 to bring the works finally to a halt.

- To plan to make something out of a company, if it cannot possibly be made, can be extremely costly if the plan is followed.

- A business plan in itself is no guarantee that desired results will be realized. While deliberate planning is one aspect of good management, it is not a substitute for it.

HOW FAR INTO THE FUTURE?

Certain characteristics of every business must be identified in order to determine what needs to be planned and for what period of time. The reader will find that many companies that participated in this research study state they plan five years into the future and make annual or half-yearly reviews of accomplishments, with an eye to altering the plan if necessary. Thus each year (or each six months) an entirely new five-year plan may be devised. Other firms establish a five-year plan but make no changes in it except as changes of great magnitude may require, such as unforeseen opportunities and drastic changes in the nation's economy.

A public utility which plans as far as 25 years in advance in order to provide future sites for its system may be exercising no more foresight than another firm, manufacturing consumer products, which plans six months in advance. Both companies have needs to be met in the future which must be prepared for in the present. The wisdom of a lumber business in providing now for wood to be available 100 years hence does not mean that its managers are gifted with some special talent; the fact that they embark on a reforestation program to assure (insofar as possible) that there will be trees does not prove that they are clairvoyant. To be sure, in such cases, the managers would be exercising good judgment. At the same time, it would not be good judgment to lay elaborate plans for an advertising or sales-training program 100 years in advance.

A few managers in this study mention plans for the next ten years. A number of firms have very long-range plans in addition to their basic five- or ten-year plans, but these are more often in the nature of statements of ultimate objectives than of detailed plans.

Insofar as a norm could be discerned among all the company statements, five years seems to be the planning period for many of the participating firms. This does not mean that plans for all aspects of the business are made for a five-year period. Rather, it means that when certain managers spoke of their "long-range plan" they had in mind marketing and product plans (sometimes, other kinds of plans as well) that looked to certain results in five years or intermediate periods. This does not indicate that every business should have a five-year plan. Two of the reasons why some managers think of planning in terms of five years may be that (1) this period is as far in the future as they can or need to anticipate; and (2) constant repetition of the phrase "five-year plan" by commentators speaking and writing about the U.S.S.R. and certain other countries may have had its influence.

Deciding on a range of time for planning is associated with the problems of evaluating the success of a manager. If one evaluates a man's work today, the result may be different than the result of an evaluation in five, ten, or 25 years. In formulating objectives, the manager must visualize the results as he expects them to be in the future. The range of time to be considered is a decision of large consequence in formulating a plan. Planning has to do with identifying what Peter Drucker calls "the futurity of today's decisions." There are some guides to be followed in deciding the "length of futurity" appropriate for the plans of a particular business or special unit within a business.

There are certain characteristics of the operations of each firm that lead to the selection of a particular span of time for planning. Long-range planning for a manufacturer of women's wear may be practically yesterday for the capital goods producer or the large public utility. Factors which lead to a selection of the proper planning time span are the following:

1. Lead time. This is the length of time it takes from the realization that major new products are needed to the completion of their design, production, and distribution, plus a major period of utilization before the product is obsoleted.

2. The length of time required to recover the capital funds invested in plant and equipment and in training skilled personnel. A plan should provide for recovery of the capital funds invested in the actual physical construction of the plant and equipment and in hiring and training managers and skilled personnel. For example, a firm with a heavy investment in manufacturing and other facilities would have to base some of its plans on a period of time during which the machines would remain useful. Often this time span would be well in excess of the time required to manufacture one line of products.

3. The expected future availability of customers. For manufacturers of machinery and equipment used by other manufacturers, this is the time period up to the expected obsolescence of the customers' products.

4. The expected future availability of raw materials and components. If it takes 99 years to grow a forest to replace the trees the company uses in its manufacture of wood products, someone has to think about planting seedlings now. In this area, the planning span would be 99 years. Research may possibly shorten such long planning spans by providing entirely new raw materials.

As previously stated, one useful concept in determining the planning span is lead time. If one is driving a car, for example, and decides to turn a corner, there is either enough time to do it or there is not. If a firm is supplying a foreign market by sea, the manager must make the decision to ship the goods well before the material is at dockside and ready to be loaded.

Lead time should be defined in relation to the kind of action one is willing to take. In situations where the process of production or transportation is familiar, lead time is readily determined. If a ship takes five days to cross the Atlantic and five days are needed to load and unload, the lead time is ten days. This can be shortened, if necessary, by using air express. As another example, a driver can stop an automobile by exerting ordinary pressure on the brakes, or he can come to an emergency stop. Normally, when driving one does not want to make a series of emergency stops; he allows for routine stops. "Lead time," therefore, may be best defined as the period between decision and arrival at the final results. If routine methods are used, the period or range of time would be considered normal lead time.

With respect to planning, the appropriate ranges of time may also be described in terms of lead time. If, for instance, the building of facilities is being considered, one could thus express the relevant lead time required to decide what to build and where to build, plus the time needed to complete the construction.

In planning within the basic direction and limits of company growth, however, a lead time of even 20 to 30 years for facilities construction is not long enough. There is the additional time which represents the useful life of the building or facility. A firm does not normally plan to put up a building and scrap it shortly thereafter. The planning span might well be the total time the facilities are expected to be of use to the firm.

In some cases the time span of the business plan may end with the discontinuation of the business as it is presently conceived. A plan should provide for discontinuing work and jobs that do not need to be done, just as it should provide for discontinuing products and divisions that fail to advance the firm toward its goals. A business plan may have to include an estimate of the date on which the design of products, method of production, and kind of customer to be served will be altered to such a degree that the manager will need to reconceive his aims in terms of being in a new business.

It is evident, then, that the study of lead-time requirements can help in determining the planning span. But a carefully laid plan with a lengthy lead time may become a short-term expedient—if not altogether useless—if the actions of competitors (or of customers or others) create new situations not provided for in the plan. One manufacturer of tacks and nails suddenly found large segments of his market vanishing because of new kinds of adhesives being produced by firms he had never before thought of as competitors. An economic recession may cause the managers of a business to restudy their business plan and the span of time it covers. Vital decisions need to be made: Should the managers cut back on growth plans, thereby keeping outgo commensurate with income? Should they go ahead, with faith in the company, pursuing long-range goals established at a time of abundance? These are questions to be answered by business men who have large areas of responsibility for shaping the future of their businesses and of society as a whole.

9   B. OBJECTIVES

The Essential Nature of Objectives*

JOHN F. MEE

Interest in management philosophy and practice has steadily increased during the present century. Since World War II, students of business and public administration have joined efforts with administrators in business and government to formulate an acceptable philosophy of management as a guide both for modern management practice and for the education of those who aspire to a career in the field. Professor Ralph C. Davis[1] offers the following comment concerning the problem of management philosophy.

The problem of greatest importance in the field of management is and probably will continue

* Reprinted by permission of the publisher from "Management Philosophy for Professional Executives," *Business Horizons*, December, 1956, pp. 5–7. Mr. Mee is Mead Johnson Professor of Management and head of the Department of Management of the School of Business at the University of Indiana.

[1] Dr. R. C. Davis is professor of management at Ohio State University.

to be the further development of the philosophy of management. A philosophy is a system of thought. It is based on some orderly, logical statements of objectives, principles, policies and general methods of approach to the solution of some set of problems. . . .

Business objectives involve the public interest as well as the interests of customers, dealers, bankers, owners and employees. They affect everyone in an industrial economy. A managerial philosophy cannot supply a basis of effective thinking for the solution of business problems, if it is satisfactory only to owners and employees. A managerial philosophy that is commonly accepted is a requisite for a common scale of values in an economy. It is necessary, therefore, for unity of thought and action in the accomplishment of economic objectives. We cannot have an effective industrial economy without effective industrial leadership. We cannot have an effective leadership without a sound managerial philosophy.

Industrial leaders without such a philosophy are business mechanics rather than professional executives. . . .[2]

The main reasons for the continued interest in management philosophy among educators, public administrators, and progressive businessmen are:

1. The increasing trend toward decentralization of operating responsibilities and decision-making in business and governmental organizations.

2. The increasing numbers of professional executives required in business and government for growth and decentralization of operations.

3. The necessity for a logical framework of management philosophy and practice as a basis for training in executive-development programs and college curricula.

OBJECTIVES

In current thinking and writing, the starting point for either a philosophy or the practice of management seems to center around predetermined objectives. The entire management process concerns itself with ways and means to realize predetermined results and with the intelligent use of people whose efforts must be properly motivated and guided. Objectives may

be general or specific; they may concern the organization as a whole, a segment of it within a decentralized unit, or even a particular function such as production, sales, or personnel.

What are or should be the objectives of management in our industrial economy? A study of current management literature and the published objectives of business firms provides some revealing and interesting concepts from recognized authorities. Here are some selected statements:

- The goal of the organization must be this—to make a better and better product to be sold at a lower and lower price. Profit cannot be the goal. Profit must be a by-product. This is a state of mind and a philosophy. Actually an organization doing this job as it can be done will make large profits which must be properly divided between user, worker and stockholder. This takes ability and character.[3]

- If we were to isolate the one factor, above all others, that transformed the tiny company of 1902 into the industrial giant of 1952, while hundreds of competitors failed and are forgotten, I should say that it has been Texaco's settled policy of thinking first of quality of product and service to the customer, and only second to the size of its profit. To some of you, this may sound somewhat trite. But it is the starkest kind of business realism. In a highly competitive industry such as ours, the highest rewards are reserved for those who render the greatest service.[4]

- To make and sell quality products competitively and to perform those functions at the lowest attainable cost consistent with sound management policies, so as to return an adequate profit after taxes for services rendered. As a corollary objective, the corporation must be the low-cost producer of the product it offers for sale. (United States Steel Corporation statement of general company objectives.)

- The mission of the business organization is to acquire, produce and distribute certain values. The business objective, therefore, is the starting point for business thinking. The primary objectives of a business organization are always those economic values with which we serve the customer. The principal

2 Ralph C. Davis, "Research in Management During the '50's," in Arthur E. Warner (ed.), *Research Needs in Business during the '50s,* School of Business, Indiana University, Indiana Business Report, no. 13, Bloomington, Ind., 1950, p. 32.

3 James F. Lincoln, *Intelligent Selfishness and Manufacturing,* Lincoln Electric Co., Bulletin, no. 434, New York.
4 Harry T. Klein, *The Way Ahead,* The Texas Co., New York, 1952, p. 14.

objective of a businessman, naturally, is a profit. And a profit is merely an academic consideration, nevertheless, until we get the customer's dollar.[5]

Numerous further examples of published and stated objectives of modern business management could be presented. However, all of them could be summarized with the conclusion that: (1) *Profit* is the motivating force for managers. (2) *Service* to customers by the provision of desired economic values (goods and services) justifies the existence of the business. (3) *Social responsibilities* do exist for managers in accordance with ethical and moral codes established by the society in which the industry resides. The economic values with which customers are served include increased

[5] Ralph C. Davis, "What the Staff Function Actually Is," *Advanced Management*, vol. 19, p. 13, May, 1954.

values at lower costs through innovation and creativity over a period of time.

In formulating and developing a modern management philosophy for successful practice, a combination of the above objectives in the correct proportion is required. Every decentralized organization unit and essential function must contribute to the realization of the general objectives by attaining the organizational, functional, and operational objectives. Unless predetermined objectives are set and accepted, little or no basis exists for measuring the success and effectiveness of those who perform the management functions.

The importance of predetermining the objectives desired has resulted in the formulation of the management principle of the objective. This principle may be stated as follows: Before initiating any course of action, the objectives in view must be clearly determined, understood, and stated.

10

The Objectives of a Business*

PETER F. DRUCKER

Most of today's lively discussion of management by objectives is concerned with the search for the one right objective. This search is not only likely to be as unproductive as the quest for the philosopher's stone; it is certain to do harm and to misdirect.

To emphasize only profit, for instance, misdirects managers to the point where they may endanger the survival of the business. To obtain profit today they tend to undermine the future. They may push the most easily saleable product lines and slight those that are the market of tomorrow. They tend to short-change research, promotion and other postponable investments. Above all, they shy away from any

* Reprinted by permission of the publisher from Peter F. Drucker, *The Practice of Management,* Harper & Row, Publishers, Incorporated, New York, 1954, pp. 62–65, 126–129. Copyright 1954 by Peter F. Drucker. (Also published by William Heinemann, Ltd., London.) Mr. Drucker is a well-known management consultant, lecturer, teacher, and author.

capital expenditure that may increase the invested-capital base against which profits are measured; and the result is dangerous obsolescence of equipment. In other words, they are directed into the worst practices of management.

To manage a business is to balance a variety of needs and goals. This requires judgment. The search for the one objective is essentially a search for a magic formula that will make judgment unnecessary. But the attempt to replace judgment by formula is always irrational; all that can be done is to make judgment possible by narrowing its range and the available alternatives, giving it clear focus, a sound foundation in facts and reliable measurements of the effects and validity of actions and decisions. And this, by the very nature of business enterprise, requires multiple objectives.

What should these objectives be, then? There is only one answer: *Objectives are needed in every area where performance and results directly and vitally affect the survival and prosperity of the business.* These are the areas which are affected by every management decision and which therefore have to be considered in every management decision. They decide what it means concretely to manage the business. They spell out what results the business must aim at and what is needed to work effectively toward these targets.

Objectives in these key areas should enable us to do five things: to organize and explain the whole range of business phenomena in a small number of general statements; to test these statements in actual experience; to predict behavior; to appraise the soundness of decisions when they are still being made; and to enable practicing businessmen to analyze their own experience and, as a result, improve their performance. It is precisely because the traditional theorem of the maximization of profits cannot meet any of these tests—let alone all of them—that it has to be discarded.

At first sight it might seem that different businesses would have entirely different key areas—so different as to make impossible any general theory. It is indeed true that different key areas require different emphasis in different businesses—and different emphasis at different stages of the development of each business. But the areas are the same, whatever the business, whatever the economic conditions, whatever the business's size or stage of growth.

There are eight areas in which objectives of performance and results have to be set:

Market standing; innovation; productivity; physical and financial resources; profitability; manager performance and development; worker performance and attitude; public responsibility.

There should be little dispute over the first five objectives. But there will be real protest against the inclusion of the intangibles: manager performance and development; worker performance and attitude; and public responsibility.

Yet, even if managing were merely the application of economics, we would have to include these three areas and would have to demand that objectives be set for them. They belong in the most purely formal economic theory of the business enterprise. For neglect of manager performance and development, worker performance and public responsibility soon results in the most practical and tangible loss of market standing, technological leadership, productivity and profit—and ultimately in the loss of business life. That they look so different from anything the economist—especially the modern economic analyst—is wont to deal with, that they do not readily submit to quantification and mathematical treatment, is the economist's bad luck; but it is no argument against their consideration.

The very reason for which economist and accountant consider these areas impractical—that they deal with principles and values rather than solely with dollars and cents—makes them central to the management of the enterprise, as tangible, as practical—and indeed as measurable—as dollars and cents.

For the enterprise is a community of human beings. Its performance is the performance of human beings. And a human community must be founded on common beliefs, must symbolize its cohesion in common principles. Otherwise it becomes paralyzed, unable to act, unable to demand and to obtain effort and performance from its members.

If such considerations are intangible, it is management's job to make them tangible by its deeds. To neglect them is to risk not only business incompetence but labor trouble or at least loss of worker productivity, and public restrictions on business provoked by irresponsible business conduct. It also means risking lackluster, mediocre, time-serving managers—managers who are being conditioned to "look out for themselves" instead of for the common good of the enterprise, managers who become mean, narrow and blind for lack of challenge, leadership and vision.

HOW TO SET OBJECTIVES

The real difficulty lies indeed not in determining what objectives we need, but in deciding how to set them.

There is only one fruitful way to make this decision: by determining what shall be measured in each area and what the yardstick of measurement should be. For the measurement used determines what one pays attention to. It makes things visible and tangible. The things included in the measurement become relevant; the things omitted are out of sight and out of mind. "Intelligence is what the Intelligence Test measures"—that well worn quip is used by the psychologist to disclaim omniscience and infallibility for his gadget. Parents or teachers, however, including those well aware of the shakiness of its theory and its mode of calculation, sometimes tend to see that precise-looking measurement of the "I.Q." every time they look at little Susie—to the point where they may no longer see little Susie at all.

Unfortunately the measurements available to us in the key area of business enterprise are, by and large, even shakier than the I.Q. We have adequate concepts only for measuring market standing. For something as obvious as profitability we have only a rubber yardstick, and we have no real tools at all to determine how much profitability is necessary. In respect to innovation and, even more, to productivity, we hardly know more than what ought to be done. And in the other areas—including physical and financial resources—we are reduced to statements of intentions rather than goals and measurements for their attainment.

For the subject is brand new. It is one of the most active frontiers of thought, research and invention in American business today. Company after company is working on the definition of the key areas, on thinking through what should be measured and on fashioning the tools of measurement.

Within a few years our knowledge of what to measure and our ability to do so should therefore be greatly increased. After all, twenty-five years ago we knew less about the basic problems in market standing than we know today about productivity or even about the efficiency and attitudes of workers. Today's relative clarity concerning market standing is the result not of anything inherent in the field, but of hard, concentrated and imaginative work.

WHAT SHOULD THE OBJECTIVES OF A MANAGER BE?

Each manager, from the "big boss" down to the production foreman or the chief clerk, needs clearly spelled-out objectives. These objectives should lay out what performance the man's own managerial unit is supposed to produce. They should lay out what contribution he and his unit are expected to make to help other units obtain their objectives. Finally, they should spell out what contribution the manager can expect from other units toward the attainment of his own objectives. Right from the start, in other words, emphasis should be on teamwork and team results.

These objectives should always derive from the goals of the business enterprise. In one company, I have found it practicable and effective to provide even a foreman with a detailed statement of not only his own objectives but those of the company and of the manufacturing department. Even though the company is so large as to make the distance between the individual foreman's production and the company's total output all but astronomical, the result has been a significant increase in production. Indeed, this must follow if we mean it when we say that the foreman is "part of management." For it is the definition of a manager that in what he does he takes responsibility for the whole—that, in cutting stone, he "builds the cathedral."

The objectives of every manager should spell out his contribution to the attainment of company goals in *all areas* of the business. Obviously, not every manager has a direct contribution to make in every area. The contribution which marketing makes to productivity, for example, may be very small. But if a manager and his unit are not expected to contribute toward any one of the areas that significantly affect prosperity and survival of the business, this fact should be clearly brought out. For managers must understand that business results depend on a balance of efforts and results in a number of areas. This is necessary both to give full scope to the craftsmanship of each function and specialty, and to prevent the empire-building and clannish jealousies of the various functions and specialties. It is necessary also to avoid overemphasis on any one key area.

To obtain balanced efforts the objectives of all managers on all levels and in all areas should also be keyed to both short-range and long-range considerations. And, of course, all objectives should always contain both the tangible business objectives and the intangible objectives for manager organization and development, worker performance and attitude and public responsibility. Anything else is shortsighted and impractical.

MANAGEMENT BY "DRIVES"

Proper management requires balanced stress on objectives, especially by top management. It rules out the common and pernicious business malpractice: management by "crisis" and "drives."

There may be companies in which management people do not say: "The only way we ever get anything done around here is by making a drive on it." Yet, "management by drive" is the rule rather than the exception. That things always collapse into the *status quo ante* three weeks after the drive is over, everybody knows and apparently expects. The only result of an "economy drive" is likely to be that messengers and typists get fired, and that $15,000 executives are forced to do $50-a-week work typing their own letters. And yet many managements have not drawn the obvious conclusion that drives are, after all, not the way to get things done.

But over and above its ineffectiveness, management by drive misdirects. It puts all emphasis on one phase of the job to the inevitable detriment of everything else. "For four weeks we cut inventories," a case-hardened veteran of management by crisis once summed it up. "Then we have four weeks of cost-cutting, followed by four weeks of human relations. We have just time to push customer service and courtesy for a month. And then the inventory is back where it was when we started. We don't even try to do our job. All management talks about, thinks about, preaches about, is last week's inventory figure or this week's customer complaints. How we do the rest of the job they don't even want to know."

In an organization which manages by drives people either neglect their job to get on with the current drive, or silently organize for collective sabotage of the drive to get their work done. In either event they become deaf to the cry of "wolf." And when the real crisis comes, when all hands should drop everything and pitch in, they treat it as just another case of management-created hysteria.

Management by drive, like management by "bellows and meat ax," is a sure sign of confusion. It is an admission of incompetence. It is a sign that management does not know how to plan. But above all, it is a sign that the company does not know what to expect of its managers—that, not knowing how to direct them, it misdirects them.

HOW SHOULD MANAGERS' OBJECTIVES BE SET AND BY WHOM?

By definition, a manager is responsible for the contribution that his component makes to the larger unit above him and eventually to the enterprise. His performance aims upward rather than downward. This means that the goals of each manager's job must be defined by the contribution he has to make to the suc- cess of the larger unit of which he is a part. The objectives of the district sales manager's job should be defined by the contribution he and his district sales force have to make to the sales department, the objectives of the project engineer's job by the contribution he, his engineers and draftsmen make to the engineering department. The objectives of the general manager of a decentralized division should be defined by the contribution his division has to make to the objectives of the parent company.

This requires each manager to develop and set the objectives of his unit himself. Higher management must, of course, reserve the power to approve or disapprove these objectives. But their development is part of a manager's responsibility; indeed, it is his first responsibility. It means, too, that every manager should responsibly participate in the development of the objectives of the higher unit of which his is a part. To "give him a sense of participation" (to use a neat phrase of the "human relations" jargon) is not enough. Being a manager demands the assumption of a genuine responsibility. Precisely because his aims should reflect the objective needs of the business, rather than merely what the individual manager wants, he must commit himself to them with a positive act of assent. He must know and understand the ultimate business goals, what is expected of him and why, what he will be measured against and how. There must be a "meeting of minds" within the entire management of each unit. This can be achieved only when each of the contributing managers is expected to think through what the unit objectives are, is led, in other words, to participate actively and responsibly in the work of defining them. And only if his lower managers participate in this way can the higher manager know what to expect of them and can make exacting demands.

11

Executive Objectives*

D. W. MILLER and M. K. STARR

GOALS, PURPOSES, AND RATIONAL BEHAVIOR

The question of the formulation of objectives is very closely related to some of the major ethical questions. This might be expected since, after all, the classical philosophers were interested in discovering the steps that an individual should take in order to achieve the good life. And what is the idea of the good life if not an objective to be achieved?

As a matter of fact, the classical conception of rationality was defined in terms of the ability to select means to achieve goals or objectives. In other words, rationality was construed to be the same thing as the ability to pursue objectives. This line of reasoning was subsequently subjected to serious questioning.

First, the extension of this definition of rationality led to the interpretation of everything in terms of the purpose it fulfilled. Thus, the argument ran, if one saw a watch one could infer the existence of a watch-maker. Similarly, if one sees an ear one must infer the existence of a designer of that ear so that it could achieve its purpose of hearing. Reasoning of this sort is called teleological reasoning. The interpretation of events in these terms was what Aristotle called the "final causes" of the things. Such arguments have their place in religion and philosophy but are likely to impede scientific analysis. Thus, one of Darwin's major contributions was the demonstration of the fact that a remarkable adaption to environment could result from the interplay of a great number of essentially random factors. In short, he showed that it was unnecessary to assume final causes in order to understand the adaptation of living things to their environments.

A second argument against this kind of approach arose from the positivistic movement in science. A human being can introspect and believe that he has purposefully selected means to achieve his objectives. It is an easy step, then, to assume a similar purposefulness in the behavior of a white rat that is hungry. However, it is clearly not necessarily the same with a white rat as it is with a human being. As a matter of fact, modern psychology throws some doubt on human purposefulness in at least some situations where humans think they are being purposeful. In any event, positivism in science led to a desire to base scientific conclusions only on observable evidence. In psychology this took the form of the ruthless elimination of introspection as a source of valid scientific information. The school of psychology that carried this out to the fullest extreme is known as *behaviorism,* from the fact that only the observable behavior of the subject is studied. The net effect of the positivistic movement was to strongly prejudice scientists against ascribing rationality to goal-seeking or objective-seeking behavior.

OPEN SYSTEMS

Recent developments in science serve to confirm the fact that rationality cannot be identified with purposeful selection of means to achieve desired ends. A biologist, Ludwig von Bertalanffy, has introduced and extensively analyzed a new concept of a system, which he calls open systems. There are a number of highly interesting characteristics of such systems. For our purposes the most interesting characteristic is the fact that such a system will seem to seek objectives without being, in any possible sense of the word, "rational." A number of examples of such systems can be found in various kinds of chemical solutions but von Bertalanffy has found more interesting examples in living creatures and, possibly, even in higher systems which are composed of living creatures—for example, human society. The reason that the system appears to be goal-seeking, although there is no rationality behind

* Reprinted by permission of the publisher from D. W. Miller and M. K. Starr, *Executive Decisions and Operations Research,* Prentice-Hall, Inc., Englewood Cliffs, N.J., 1960, pp. 33–47, 51–53. Mr. Miller and Mr. Starr are on the staff of Columbia University and are consultants in operations research and management science.

it, is that the system is so set up that it has an equilibrium among its component parts. Any disturbance of this equilibrium initiates compensating reactions which immediately lead to the establishment of a new equilibrium. In other words, the system will search for equilibrium or stasis every time its equilibrium is disturbed. Now, since a great many human objectives can be easily redefined in terms of equilibrium it becomes very interesting to discover to what degree the search by humans for objectives (equilibrium) can be understood in terms of the dynamic process of open systems.

That this reasoning about open systems is not purely theoretical was demonstrated nicely by W. Ross Ashby, who designed and built an electrical device which he named the Homeostat. This is a complicated piece of electrical circuity which will hunt for equilibrium whenever it is disturbed. Further, it will find a new equilibrium which was not intentionally built into the device by its maker. Therefore, when the device has achieved a new equilibrium no one, including the designer, will know what circuits it has completed in order to achieve the equilibrium. Other similar devices have now been constructed by many different people. Some of them show the most disconcertingly "lifelike" behavior when in pursuit of their objective. And yet there is simply no rationality in any of them. It has become quite clear, in short, that the existence of seemingly rational searches for some kinds of objectives by no means implies that rational choice dictated the selection of means used to attempt to achieve the given objective.

These remarks may seem singularly irrelevant to any study of organizational objectives. However, they are not really so far-fetched. The conclusion that one could reach from the arguments about open systems is that an open system will find equilibrium by itself. If the process by which the system achieves equilibrium is continually disturbed by "rational" efforts it may well produce an inherent instability and the equilibrium may never be achieved. For example, the United States national economy is an enormously complex organization which may well have many of the characteristics of open systems. A national economic objective is frequently stated as being the achievement of prosperity without inflation. Since the quantity of money in circulation plays a fundamental role in the national economy, the Federal Reserve system uses its control over the money supply to attempt to achieve the national objective. The means it uses, such as changes in the discount rate, are

given wide publicity and are well known. It is therefore interesting that a number of economists maintain that the rational efforts of the Federal Reserve system are of no avail and perhaps worse than useless. One point of view holds that a policy which is fixed in advance should be adhered to by the Federal Reserve system and that no changes should be made in this policy because of the changing economic situation. If, indeed, the national economy is an open system, then it would adapt itself to the new policy, maintaining the national objectives as part of its own search for equilibrium. Consequently, our national objectives would have a better chance of being achieved. Similar possibilities exist in the case of business organizations.

It will be worthwhile to present a brief illustration of a business system that regains equilibrium after it has been disturbed. Consider the case of a mail-order company which solicits new customers by means of direct mail. (For the sake of clarity and to avoid obscuring the main point of this example we have not introduced random variation in the hypothetical data.) The company mails 800 letters each week and obtains orders from 1 per cent of the mailing. The repeat-order rate is constant. One-half of each week's new customers reorder in the second week, one-fourth reorder in the third week, one-eighth reorder in the fourth week, and so on. Table 3.1 shows how the generation of orders, composed of new-customer orders and repeat orders, reaches an equilibrium value of 15 orders per day. In the eighth and ninth weeks the company experiences an unusually heavy response. This raises the total orders for a period of six weeks. At the end of that time, by the fourteenth week, total orders have returned to equilibrium. Figure 3.1 shows how the system gradually returns to equilibrium.

In actuality, a system of this type is always being disturbed by random variation in both the number of new customers and the reorder rates. However, if the random variation comes from a stable process, then the system is always hunting for its equilibrium value. If a basic change takes place then the system adopts a new equilibrium value and continues to return to this new value after all random disturbances. An attempt by management to maintain total orders at 15 per week by controlling the number of letters mailed or by providing incentives to increase the repeat-order-rate can result in far greater fluctuation than would occur if the system were left alone. Only when management fully understands the nature of the system with which it is dealing can it

TABLE 3.1   Generation of Orders of a Mail-Order House

Week number	1	2	3	4	5	6	7	8	9	10	11	12	13	14	15	16
Number of new customers	8	8	8	8	8	8	8	20	20	8	8	8	8	8	8	8
First repeat order		4	4	4	4	4	4	4	10	10	4	4	4	4	4	4
Second repeat order			2	2	2	2	2	2	2	5	5	2	2	2	2	2
Third repeat order				1	1	1	1	1	1	1	2	2	1	1	1	1
Fourth repeat order				—	—	—	—	—	—	—	—	1	1	—	—	—
Total orders	8	12	14	15	15	15	15	27	33	24	19	17	16	15	15	15

provide rational decisions that might improve the performance of the system.

From examples such as the one given above, we learn that it is not necessarily the case that all objectives can be, or should be, achieved by rational selection of means to a given end. If we cannot identify rational behavior by observing the means that are chosen to achieve a specific end, can we recognize rationality in terms of objectives themselves?

GOALS OF THE INDIVIDUAL AND OPERATIONALISM

Organizational objectives coexist with the objectives of the individuals who compose the organization. They are not the same. Our intention is to analyze the way in which objectives at different levels in the organization interact with each other. Therefore, we must begin with the individual's role, which is the smallest entity in the organization.

The goals of individuals have been the subject of discussion and debate for many centuries. To say that happiness is the goal of the individual, which is a frequent suggestion, does not solve any problem. We cannot define happiness in operational terms. Operationalism is an important concept for the understanding of operations research. It implies concreteness, the ability to observe, measure, and analyze. Since an analysis of the operations that must

FIGURE 3.1   The System Returns to Equilibrium after Disturbance

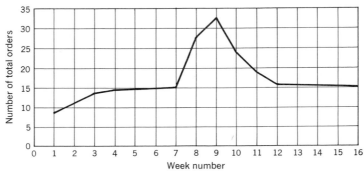

be performed in order to be happy cannot be obtained, we cannot treat happiness as an operational term. Measurements cannot be made to distinguish degree of happiness. Although each of us can testify to the fact that happiness exists, we cannot reduce our awareness to concrete terms. Similar problems result from any other suggested choice for the fundamental objective of individuals. Since life is too short to follow the arguments of philosophers in a book which is intended to be operationally useful, we must consider other ways of examining the goals of individuals.

GOALS OF THE ROLE

People play many roles. Each role can be associated with its own objectives. Individuals simplify their decision problems by establishing for themselves these multiple objectives instead of just one basic objective. Most people, for example, will establish some kind of objective for themselves in the area of their professional activities. They will usually have other objectives relating to their interpersonal relationships; e.g., father, husband, son. They will also have objectives regarding their relationship to society as a whole, e.g., political activity or public-spirited work. They will often have some objectives regarding their leisure activities. And, of course, we can continue and obtain quite a catalogue of the different areas in which people are likely to set themselves some kind of objectives. It appears that most people handle their decision problems in a particular field of activity by ignoring the objectives of other fields of activity. Thus, a business executive will solve his decision problems in business—for example, what position he will accept—in terms of his professional objective.

Even within a single field of activity an individual has many different roles. An executive reports to his boss and in turn has people reporting to him. His position in the organization determines the extent of his responsibility and the importance of decisions he must make. The goal of the executive is strongly tied to the complex image he has of his role. Although no two executives have the same situations, the similarity of goals which they share as a group causes us to speak about executive goals. However, similarity should not blind us to the differences. In the same way, for convenience, we group employee goals, ownership goals, salesmen's goals, and so on. There is a certain relevant pattern of goal-seeking within each of these groups. It is hardly necessary to expand on what these might be. On the other hand, it

is an observable fact that sometimes there is a conflict between the objectives of several groups to which the individual belongs.

CONFLICT BETWEEN GOALS

The individual has various roles and each role has its objectives. The groups and subgroups to which the individual belongs have organizational objectives. Conflicts between goals can occur in a number of ways. There can be: (1) conflicts between roles, (2) conflicts between group objectives, and (3) conflicts between the individual's role and the group objective. Looking at conflicts of the first type, the individual cannot confine his attention to the objective of one field of activities and ignore the other parts of his life. Thus, a new position may entail relocation and possible stresses and strains on the individual's family relationships. In this event he must attempt to weigh his different objectives, one against the other. Now, this is difficult to do because there is no underlying single objective that suffices as a means of measuring the importance of the different subobjectives. Nevertheless, people do it many times in their lives. Generally, they convert the decision problem into some estimates of the amounts of happiness involved— even though there are serious difficulties and even contradictions involved in this notion of happiness.

Considering the second kind of conflict, the individual who participates in two groups that have conflicting objectives may not even be aware of this fact. The reason is that his roles may not come into conflict. This point is intended to emphasize the fact that an individual cannot entirely identify with and share the objectives of an organization. Furthermore, the individual does not weigh the groups to which he belongs as being of equal importance. For example, an employee who participates in a stock-purchasing plan is also a part owner of the company to which he belongs. When this employee demands higher wages, he is, in effect, reducing the dividend which he could receive as a stockholder. It is clear that the employee does not consider his role in the ownership group to be as important as his role as an employee. Whenever the individual's role objectives strongly coincide with the objectives of the groups that are in conflict, the result is either conflict between roles or between the individual and at least one of the groups. In the latter case, which is the third type of conflict, the individual withdraws from the organization that he feels he is in conflict with, or else he tries to change that group's objectives.

SUBOPTIMIZATION

Whenever there is no conflict between objectives, the individual can proceed to solve his decision problems separately. As long as the action taken to achieve either objective is independent of the other, he can do this. However, when objectives are dependent, the optimization of one can result in a lower degree of attainment for all the others. This condition is known as *suboptimization*. For example, an executive may decide to take a new position on the basis of his professional objectives. The new job, however, entails extremely long hours and much traveling. Assume that the new job is optimal in terms of the executive's professional objective. The fact that the time he can now spend with his family is sharply reduced may have such adverse effects that he will find that his optimization in terms of one objective has produced a result which is very much less than optimal in terms of all his objectives.

This same notion of suboptimization is involved in the effects on the decision problem of the fact that we lead our lives through time and that we have only very imperfect ability to foresee the future. This means that any decision problem can be solved only in terms of the knowledge and situation obtaining currently. But the action chosen may, and probably will, have effects on the decision-maker's situation for a considerable period in the future. An optimal action at one time may, therefore, turn out to have been a very inferior suboptimization in terms of a longer period of time.

Consider, for example, the decision problem of selection of courses as electives which faces an engineering student. In terms of his professional objective he wants to become as good an engineer as he possibly can so he decides to use all his electives to take additional engineering courses. This decision may appear to be an optimization in terms of his professional objectives at that time. But some years later this engineer may discover that the stultification which results from too narrow specialization has had serious consequences on his ability to achieve satisfactory interpersonal relationships or on his desire to have a well-rounded life or even on his objective of achieving professional advancement. His decision, in short, may have resulted in distinctly less than an optimal situation with regard to subsequent decision problems, even in the same field of activity.

It is quite clear that we can never really achieve optimization. Over time, unexpected events can change what had appeared to be an optimal decision into an inferior decision. There is almost no reversibility in decision systems. Generally speaking, by the time we find out that a decision was not a good one, we cannot return to the state which prevailed before the decision had been made. Consequently, decision systems should provide the best possible predictions of future expectations. And in addition, decision systems should not commit us to irrevocable action for very long periods of time. And so we reach the conclusion that a *sequential decision process* permits maximum flexibility with respect to both objectives and actions.

BOUNDED RATIONALITY

We have been using the word "optimum," and some other forms of the same word, rather loosely. In fact, it is important to note that people rarely make a prolonged effort to achieve the optimum action in any realistic decision problem facing them. To paraphrase John Maurice Clark, people simply don't have such an irrational passion for dispassionate rationality. Furthermore, there are good reasons why they shouldn't. All of the reasons have reference to the exorbitant complexity of any realistic decision problem. Three main aspects of this complexity should be noted.

First, consider the point just made, that an optimum decision made at one point in time is only suboptimum in terms of subsequent times. Since we are very limited in our ability to foresee the future it follows that it would be useless to go to extreme lengths in order to achieve an optimum solution to any decision problem.

Second, there are an enormous number of possible choices of action (strategies, as we have called them) and any attempt to obtain information on all of them would be self-defeating. Consider the decision problem of the executive looking for a new job. Should he attempt to catalogue every available position in the world in order to select the best one? Obviously, if he tried he would die of old age before he got the necessary information. People simply don't behave this way, and if they did it is unlikely that humanity would have survived this long.

Third, there are virtually innumerable factors outside the control of the decision-maker (we call them states of nature) which may affect the outcome of his decision. It would be simply impossible to list them all and determine the effects they might have in order to discover the optimum action. Often the necessary information isn't even available. The umbrella manufacturer does not attempt to determine the effect of war, nuclear holocausts, prolonged depression, or explosion of the sun on the outcome of his decision regarding the number of umbrellas to make. He simply assumes some reasonable kind of stability and acts accordingly.

The net effects of these limitations on human decision-making procedures have been observed and neatly summarized by Herbert Simon in his "principle of bounded rationality." Accordingly to this principle human beings seldom make any effort to find the optimum action in a decision problem. Instead, they select a number of possible outcomes of their available strategies which would be good enough. Then they select a strategy (choose an action) that is likely to achieve one of the good-enough outcomes. Thus, the executive looking for a new job makes no effort to discover all possible jobs from which he can then select the best (optimum) one. Instead, he decides what he wants from a job in terms of his various objectives. Then he searches for a job that will provide him with the things he wants, e.g., certain income, satisfactory working conditions, chances for advancement. He does not try to find that one job somewhere in the world which might give him the optimum. The principle of bounded rationality is a neat way to describe the actual procedure of human beings involved in the decision problems of life, and it succinctly reminds us not to assume any irrational extremes of rationality.

PRINCIPLES AND MAXIMS

The difficulties involved in these everyday decision problems appear to be enormous. Yet introspection and observation would indicate that people do attempt to be rational in their selection of actions despite all the problems. In short, they do as well as they can. Fortunately, everyone has available an important source of help. No one of us is the first to have to face any specific decision problem. More usually, millions of people have been faced with the same problem in times past and society has accumulated an immense store of information concerning possible solutions and approaches to solutions. This wisdom is stored up in the form of a great number of ethical and other principles and maxims which warn us to consider certain factors or proceed at our own peril.

These principles are no guarantee of success. Often there are contradictory maxims: "Look before you leap" but "He who hesitates is lost." Yet both of these maxims serve to re-

mind us that the speed with which we reach a decision may be an important factor. Kant's dictum that we should always treat other individuals as ends in themselves rather than as means to our own ends suggests that we consider whether any action on our part may not subsequently redound to our disadvantage, i.e., turn out to have been a suboptimization. The Golden Rule is another codification of considerations which should govern our choice of actions lest we end by suboptimizing in terms of our interpersonal objectives. Finally, these ethical maxims provide a necessary and powerful pressure on us to consider whether our objectives themselves are reasonable. The eight-year-old boy can have as his major objective the eating of a maximum number of chocolates. Indeed, if one speaks to him of the pleasures of marriage he may ask if it is like eating chocolates. It is fortunate that society offers us a great deal of advice to the effect that we should not commit ourselves too wholly to the pleasures of eating chocolates because we may subsequently find that it was not a satisfactory objective.

SUMMARY OF THE GOAL-SEEKING CHARACTERISTICS OF INDIVIDUALS

Let us examine what we have discovered by considering the decision procedures of people involved in the business of living.

1. Being unable to satisfactorily describe their goals in terms of any one objective, people customarily maintain a number of different objectives. Each objective is relevant to some phase of their life activities.

2. The existence of multiple objectives leads to the problem of possible conflict between objectives. We have called this a *suboptimization problem*.

3. A particularly important aspect of the suboptimization problem is that we can only optimize in terms of the time when the decision is made, and this may be a suboptimization in terms of subsequent times.

4. The typical decision problem is so complex that any attempt to discover the optimal action is useless. Instead, people find outcomes that are good enough and attempt to achieve them (Simon's principle of bounded rationality).

5. Granted all the difficulties, human beings do try to be rational in their decision problems. As help, they have a great store of past human experience codified for them in the form of ethical principles. These principles and maxims are not such that adhering

to them is any guarantee of success but they do afford some guides to the avoidance of error.

ORGANIZATIONAL OBJECTIVES

When we turn to consider organizational objectives we find the same difficulties and similar resolutions of them. Certainly an organization differs from an individual with regard to rationality, suboptimization problems, and the principles that help in guiding it. Nevertheless, in essentials we will find that the organization's problems of formulation of objectives are just the same as those of the individual.

First, what is an organization? Most business organizations take the form of corporations, which are legally created persons. But these fictitious persons are markedly different from real persons in several major respects. They have no appointed number of years and for all practical purposes they can be considered to be eternal. Obviously, such qualities as happiness have no relationship to organizations. Nonetheless, the usefulness of having a basic overriding objective remains, as well as the impossibility of formulating one that covers all cases. Probably the best that can be done in this context is to affirm the fundamental assumption of accounting: that the business is a going, continuing concern. Phrased in terms of objectives we can state that the fundamental objective of every business organization is to continue its existence. If we return for a moment to the case of the individual we see that the analog to this corporate objective would be the individual's object of continuing his life. Survival is not the all-important objective of most individuals, notwithstanding the fact that it is a singularly important subobjective. This is demonstrated by the historical fact that literally millions of individuals have given up their lives, reluctantly or cheerfully, for the sake of values and objectives which they held more dear. This fact should give us pause in the case of corporations. Perhaps they, too, have more deeply held objectives than merely continuing their existence.

Fortunately we do not need to enter into any analysis of this question. For corporations, as for individuals, the search for any single underlying objective is likely to prove a fruitless one. Further, even if the above-stated objective were accepted it would provide little help in solving decision problems. The question would still remain to be answered: What state of affairs ensures a continued existence? The problem of suboptimization over time would be one of many which would arise to haunt

us when we tried to deal with this question. No, for corporations, as for individuals, we find that the maintenance of multiple objectives is an analytical, as well as practical necessity.

MULTIPLE OBJECTIVES

Just as in the case of the individual, the organization is likely to maintain objectives in in the different areas of its activities. Peter Drucker lists eight areas in which objectives have to be maintained:

> Market standing; innovation; productivity; physical and financial resources; profitability; manager performance and development; worker performance and attitude; public responsibility.[1]

Now, the areas could be classified differently or arranged in a different way but it does appear that most businesses do, in fact, maintain these kinds of objectives. A specific business entity can ignore any one of the areas only at the risk of its future performance in any of the others. And as soon as we recognize the existence of multiple objectives we are immediately faced with the problem of suboptimization. How does this work out in the case of the business organization? Let us follow Peter Drucker in his discussion of what may happen if a business devotes its attention exclusively to profit.

> To obtain profit today they tend to undermine the future. They may push the most easily saleable product lines and slight those that are the market of tomorrow. They tend to short-change research, promotion, and the other postponable investments. Above all, they shy away from any capital expenditures that may increase the invested-capital base against which profits are measured; and the result is dangerous obsolescence of equipment. In other words, they are directed into the worst practices of management.[2]

Any one of the objectives, emphasized to the exclusion of the rest, can lead to equally unpleasant consequences.

ORGANIZATIONAL PROBLEMS OF SUBOPTIMIZATION

Under what conditions does suboptimization arise in business? Of course we can answer

[1] Peter Drucker, *The Practice of Management,* Harper & Row, Publishers, Incorporated, New York, 1954, p. 63.
[2] *Ibid.,* p. 62.

that it arises whenever an action has an effect on several different objectives simultaneously. But this is merely to state the same thing in different words. In fact, there is no general answer to this question. The best that can be done in any specific decision problem is to utilize intuition, experience, and all available methodology to endeavor to see whether actions intended for one purpose have any probable effects on other objectives. If they do then it follows that the problem is one that involves a possible conflict of objectives and it must be handled with this fact in mind.

It should be explicitly noted that no genuine problem of a conflict of objectives can be reconciled by expressing all the possible outcomes in terms of the utility measure for one of the objectives. Now, it is fortunate that many decision problems of business can be framed in terms such that the possible outcomes can be measured in dollars. But it is by no means the case that all business objectives can be expressed in dollars. If, to take an instance, workers' attitudes could be measured in dollars, then it would follow that all possible outcomes in the area of workers' attitudes could be expressed in dollars. The total objective need only be stated as the maximization of profit. We would not require a special description of workers' attitudes. No such easy solution to the problem of conflicting objectives is usually available. Fortunately, we do have some resources and procedures with which to attempt to deal with this problem. . . .

Looking at the bright side, there are a great number of important decision problems that do not involve any conflict of objectives. For any one of these we can attempt to optimize with no fear of difficulties arising from suboptimization. In particular, we can state that, at the minimum, a business must attempt to optimize its situation with regard to each specific objective as long as it does not affect adversely its situation with regard to any other objective. This construction is a variant of an idea introduced in a different context by the Italian economist and sociologist, Vilfredo Pareto. Pareto was concerned with the problem of what should govern the actions of society if it is assumed that the utilities of the various individuals composing the society cannot be compared. By utility we mean the subjective value that each individual subscribes for the various goods and services available. Under these circumstances society cannot act to achieve the greatest total utility because this idea has no meaning for the stated conditions. Pareto suggested that society should then try to achieve at least an optimum such that each individual

had the maximum utility possible without subtracting anything from anyone else's utility. In other words, if society can act so as to increase one individual's total utility without taking anything away from anyone else, then it should do so. A condition where this has been accomplished is known as *Paretian optimality*.

The problem with which Pareto was dealing arises because there is no common standard or measure of value between individuals. And this is precisely analogous to the problem of multiple objectives with which we are dealing. Our problem arises because there is no common measure of value for the various objectives. If there were one common measure we could formulate one objective rather than several. Therefore we can state, along with Pareto, that any business should always attempt to achieve a condition of Paretian optimality with regard to its various objectives.

As we saw above, the problem of suboptimization also arises for individuals with reference to time. This is obviously true of organizations and for precisely the same reason: the very limited ability of human beings to foretell the future. It must be emphasized that the ability is limited but nevertheless existent. The decision to build a new factory requires knowledge of sales trends, economic trends, costs of land, costs of building, and so on. The location chosen, the design of the building, the dates of construction, and many other factors represent opportunities to optimize if we could only predict the future. However, with imperfect predictions we must suboptimize. As another illustration, many companies manufacture products that must be on the drawing boards years in advance. As much as possible, they would like to reserve judgment on design commitments that would inexorably fix the nature of the product. As far as possible, decisions are made that permit a broad range of eventualities. In this way, suboptimization can be improved over time, permitting them to gradually approach an over-all optimization. The same reasoning applies to short- and long-range company planning. If a decision made in a short-range plan does not permit several eventualities in the long-range plan, then it creates a suboptimization that cannot be improved upon.

Business organizations are subject to still another kind of suboptimization problem. Whereas a real person is a unit that is more or less indecomposable, the fictitious person of the business corporation is usually made up of a number of different departments or divisions. The successful functioning of the business demands the integration of the efforts of the various departments that compose it. The achievement of any of the business objectives requires that the various departments should each achieve some departmental objectives. But, by the very nature of things, departments are likely to have considerable autonomy and it can happen that the objectives they set are not in accord with the over-all business objectives. It can also happen that the actions of one department have an effect on the situation of other departments such that an optimal strategy for one department in terms of its own objectives deleteriously affects other departments and, hence, the entire business. Both of these kinds of situations represent other variants of the suboptimization problem.

BOUNDED RATIONALITY OF THE ORGANIZATION

Simon's idea of bounded rationality holds for corporations just as much as and perhaps even more than it does for individuals. First, the suboptimization difficulties force some boundaries on the various possibilities taken into account. For many decision problems it is necessary and reasonable to assume that the action taken in one department will have no significant effect on another department. Yet we know full well that a business entity is a functioning whole and that adjustments in one area will almost always have at least some slight effect on other areas of the business. In spite of this, the assumption of independence is usually made, and successfully. Not every factor can be considered in every problem precisely because of the limitations of human rationality.

Second, there are sharp limitations on the availability, at least at a reasonable cost, of information that is obviously needed in order to resolve a decision problem. For example, many decision problems on sales promotion and advertising would have better solutions if detailed information were available about the sales of competitors by regions. Yet this information is rarely available with any degree of accuracy. So we do as well as we can without it.

Third, sometimes there are enormous excesses of information which simply cannot be sorted, classified, and processed. Consider the promotional problems of a large mail-order house. Such an organization typically will have huge masses of information in its files concerning the location of its past customers, what they bought, how they paid, and various other items of information. It is quite possible that accurate formulation of promotional decision problems would benefit from an analysis of all this information. Yet even the modern large-scale computers may well be insufficient for the task, assuming that someone was willing to take responsibility for the expense. And even so, who would have the time to study the many thousands of results? So, instead, we take bits and pieces of the information, using informed judgment, and more or less hope for the best.

Fourth, there are an incredibly huge number of possible states of nature, to say nothing of competitors' actions, and no decision problem could be even formulated if the attempt were made to include all these possibilities. Business is dependent on the national economy. Almost any change in the economy is reflected in the business and, hence, may affect the decision problem in question.

These and other difficulties mean that an optimum solution of any specific decision problem in terms of its formulation will probably be less than optimum in terms of the factors left out of account. Therefore, the realistic decision-maker is not likely to strive for any optimum in this sense. Instead, he will select a group of situations that are good enough and he will be satisfied with a reasonable degree of suboptimization.

PRINCIPLES AND POLICIES

Fortunately, the business executive has, just like the individual in his life problems, a vast store of knowledge abstracted from the good and bad experiences of his innumerable predecessors. These generalizations and rules of thumb function for the executive in the way ethical principles function for the individual. And, similarly, they are not laws that can be disproved by a contrary instance. Rather, they are means of calling the attention of the decision-maker to things he might overlook and to risks he might be running.

Consider, for example, the policy that the current liquid assets should be at least equal to the current liabilities. This policy is not falsified by the case of a corporation that ignored it and went on to achieve success and affluence. It simply codifies the fact that many businesses have run into difficulties when they have ignored this ratio. As another example, consider the frequently stated policy of large department stores: "The customer is always right." Do they really think that this is true? Far from it. Do they always act as if it were true? Certainly not. It serves only to call the attention of the clerks and department managers to the fact that the objectives of the store demand careful attention to customer relations.

In short, it is the exceptions that must be justified, not the principles or policies that traditionally guide the executive of a business organization.

SUMMARY OF THE GOAL-SEEKING CHARACTERISTICS OF ORGANIZATIONS

We can now attempt to summarize the important aspects of organizational objectives that we have considered.

1. Organizational goals cannot be described by one simple objective. Therefore organizations are credited with multiple objectives.

2. Multiple objectives are required to understand the organization's relationship with the outside world. Conflicts between these objectives lead to one type of organizational suboptimization.

3. Multiple objectives also exist within the organization. The fictitious entity which is the organization is built of many groups and sub-groups which are in themselves entities. The individual is the basic building block of the structure. Conflicts of two basic kinds occur, but it is quite clear that many variations can appear. Conflicts between the organization and any lesser group are one cause of suboptimization. Conflicts between components of the organization can also result in suboptimization.

4. As was the case for the individual, suboptimization occurs in time. The relationship of short-range to long-range planning requires that short-range planning should not destroy the possibilities contemplated by the long-range plan. Short-range planning is certainly suboptimization, but it is decision-making in a framework that is ex-pected to include the opportunity for optimization. Moving in steps, the sub-optimization approaches optimization in the long run.

5. Organizational decision problems are admittedly very complex. But organizational objectives do not have the entirely tenuous nature of many individual objectives. Frequently it is possible to find measurable quantities that represent utility to the organization. The discovery of "true" optimality is no more available to the organization than it is to the individual; nevertheless, it is frequently possible to determine a suitable or allowable degree of suboptimization.

6. The executives of organizations make every effort to be rational in their decisions. They are, of course, affected by bounded rationality as are all individuals. However, they have a vast body of past experience, part of which is codified in the form of policy to guide them.

Despite difficulties, we all know that executives strive valiantly to achieve rational decisions. No amount of emphasis on the difficulties should ever be permitted to obscure this fact. Creativity, intuition, know-how, experience—all these play their role in the decision process. But the creative burst of insight precedes, it doesn't replace the rational part of the decision-making process. To convince others, to evaluate between two different creative insights, to subject the creative insight to the cold light of reason—all these require the weighing and evaluating of alternative strategies in terms of the objectives, the possible states of nature, and the competitive strategies. In other words, the rational decision-making process is called into play. . . .

Elements of Forecasting*

J. W. REDFIELD

The businessman who said, "I'd like a copy of next Thursday's newspaper," when he was asked what he'd like most in the world to have, expressed a universal wish. Who wouldn't like to know what is coming, particularly in business? Who wouldn't like to know what is going to happen in his business during the next year, or in the next five years—with the assurance of at least reasonable accuracy?

In business, a great deal of time and energy are spent in trying to figure out what is likely to happen next. It is always the first step in budgeting, scheduling, and planning; and every businessman does it at least to some extent, either consciously or subconsciously, either systematically or otherwise. There simply has to be *some* basis for setting up future financial, production, and sales requirements and objectives. However, although estimating future business by one means or another is an essential and regular practice, the way it is done often leaves much to be desired from the standpoint of the reliability and dependability of the resulting forecasts. Many executives, consequently, have only loose estimates to use as the basis for business planning—estimates that often reflect the sales manager's optimism, on the one hand, or the controller's or production manager's conservatism, on the other. In either case these estimates are likely to be highly subjective and, as a result, biased by the distinctly human tendencies toward caution, self-protection, or the desire to please.

As a matter of fact, also, many businessmen, even in large companies where forecasting is an organized staff function, tend to distrust formalized forecasting. They are inclined either to discount or reject it as a "crystal-ball" activity or, once having given it a trial, mistakenly to expect a great deal more from it

than it is intended to achieve. This is not only unfortunate, but it is also unnecessary. Business forecasting, done properly on a formalized basis, minimizes overenthusiastic as well as unduly conservative estimates, and the results can be rational, realistic, and believable.

The purpose, here, is to throw some light on systematic business forecasting in the hope that this highly useful activity will be better understood and more widely used. Rather than focusing on statistical procedures, which do play an important part in certain of its phases, the approach will be to discuss in simple but down-to-earth terms: (1) what a formal business forecasting program can contribute to management, (2) how it should be carried out, and (3) what its inherent limitations are.

ACCEPTING BUSINESS FORECASTING

Let it be noted immediately that the value of establishing a formal forecasting program is not limited to the assistance it provides in future planning. There are a number of important subsidiary advantages that should not be overlooked. Some of them are likely to have far-reaching effects on the operation of the business and can lead to a better control over and evaluation of the key functions of the company.

Such corollary benefits come automatically, as a consequence of setting up a logical basis for looking ahead. These preparations (particularly if the activities involved are not already established as regular procedures in the company), while producing information needed for the forecast, are likely also to bring to light the lack of control information on certain operations of the business or the need for improving some of the existing control reports. Not least important are the opportunities a formal forecasting program presents for encouraging teamwork among the key executives and for allocating accountability for actual results where these differ from earlier estimates.

Add these advantages to the more immediate gains in the form of sounder procurement

* Reprinted by permission of the publisher from the *Harvard Business Review*, vol. 2, no. 6, pp. 81–91, November, 1951. Mr. Redfield is associated with the management consultant firm of Cresap, McCormick, and Paget and is a well-known lecturer and instructor in management.

and production schedules, firmer budgets and appropriations for sales, advertising, and so forth, and it becomes plain common sense to approach the question of business forecasting with an open mind.

Actually, the crystal-ball tag has become attached to forecasting primarily because the process has not been fully understood. In particular, one limitation of forecasting has not been brought out into the open, recognized, and accepted: no one can foretell the future *exactly,* and all forecasting must include some elements of *guesswork.*

Once that fact is recognized, one can go on to ask himself, "Since no business can operate successfully without planning ahead, is it not sensible to make sure we obtain the best possible and most logical estimates of what will occur?" Certainly the best possible guess is infinitely better and more reliable than any substitute—including the "rule of thumb" or "feel" methods that are still used by many otherwise astute businessmen.

Guesswork being inescapable, the idea is simply to reduce the limits of error to a minimum. This can be done by following a procedure for combining mathematical analysis with the best business judgment available and then using the resulting estimates as the basis for future planning.

THE FORECASTING PROCEDURE

The forecasting process itself is approached on the premise that a general understanding of what is done and of how sound future estimates can be obtained is prerequisite to a full utilization of this activity as a practical business tool.

There are four essential elements in the process. Whether the forecast is to cover a short period (of several months to a year) or a longer period, the steps are as follows:

1. *Developing the groundwork*—that is, carrying out an orderly investigation of products, company, and industry, in order to determine generally how each of these has progressed in the past, separately and in relation to each other. In short, the aim is to build a structure on which future estimates can be based.

2. *Estimating future business*—that is, following a clear-cut plan for working out future expectancies in the form of a *mutual* undertaking with key executives and, after future business has been estimated in accordance with the predetermined step-by-step procedure, issuing an official statement of the resultant forecast. The key executives, by mutually develop-

ing the forecast, automatically assume coresponsibility and individual accountability for such later deviations of actual from estimated results as may occur.

3. *Comparing actual with estimated results*— that is, checking the attained with the anticipated status of the business periodically, and tracking down reasons for any major differences. The forecast provides bench marks for measuring unanticipated gains or losses. Once measured, the reasons for important variations can be investigated on the spot.

4. *Refining the forecast process*—that is, once familiarity with estimating the future of the business is gained through practice, sharpening the approach and refining the procedure. One must be reasonably tolerant with early forecasts, recognizing that proficiency with a new tool is not acquired overnight, and at the same time insist on constant improvement as experience with the process is gained.

Each one of these elements of the process is described below in some detail—(a) to show the part it plays in the development of the forecast and (b) to point out the subsidiary benefits which management can reasonably expect as by-products of proper forecasting procedure.

But, first, a word of warning: the accuracy and dependability of any forecast depend to a great extent on the care and analytical astuteness with which the early steps of the process are carried out. The results of the early steps become the foundation for later steps. Therefore, careful planning and a thorough job are essential. For example, the initial step, analyzing historical data, often is a lengthy operation. However, enough time must be allowed for its proper accomplishment. The common tendency of management to "hurry things along," particularly in the preparatory stages of a project involving statistical analyses, should be curbed. Putting the pressure on at this point can only lead to hastily done and poorly planned work that is likely to distort the picture later on.

DEVELOPING THE GROUNDWORK

The logical starting point is to find out everything possible about the past activities of the business and of the industry. A familiar principle is involved: that you cannot figure out where you are *going* unless you know where you *have been.*

Some of the questions about the business and industry for which answers will be wanted are presented below. Answers to such questions on the past and present situation will tell you where you have been going and will establish the basis for judging the future. In addition, unless this sort of historical analysis has already been carried out in a company, some highly interesting and pertinent information is likely to come to light that will contribute to an even better understanding of the business. This could well become subsidiary benefit No. 1.

In this initial step of the forecast process, it is wise to try to find out:

1. Did the trend of company sales return to its pre-1929 level, or did a new era at a different level set in after 1932?

2. What was the trend of the *company's* sales (by products, product lines, total, etc.) *before* and *after* World War II—through a sufficiently long period prior to the war for the trend to be significant? Has this trend been generally the same postwar as it was prewar, or has a significant change occurred?

3. What has been the trend of sales in the *industry* through the same periods?

4. Has the industry trend remained the same or has it, also, changed significantly?

5. What has been the relationship between the company trend and the industry trend? Has the company been losing or gaining ground in the industry; that is, has the company's share of the total market been increasing or decreasing?

6. Is there evidence that the market for the company's particular type of product is or may soon become saturated and, therefore, that the replacement market is likely to be the principal source of business in the future?

7. From an internal standpoint, how do the trends of the several product lines compare, one with the other? Have some shown consistent gains while others have dropped off? Have some gained more rapidly than others and consequently carried more than their share of the load?

Analyzing Company Historical Records
Now, how does one get the answer to these questions? First of all, the old company records are brought out and appropriate tabulations made showing the company's monthly and yearly sales, by products and totals, for an extended period before World War II and for the postwar years. As many prewar years as possible should be included, even going back beyond the early 1930's. Comparing the general direction of sales prior to and after 1930–1932 and before and after World War II may be revealing. In any event, the longer the period studied, the better.

It is important at this stage to plan ahead, having in mind that later comparisons based on the historical data about to be developed can be valid only if the data are set forth in comparable terms. For example, unit sales prewar and postwar are likely to be capable of direct comparison. Dollars of sales prewar, however, are less likely to be comparable because selling prices probably have been increased. In the latter case, it would be necessary to devalue the postwar dollar figures using the prewar prices as the base in order to achieve comparability.

The chances are that the best procedure will be to tabulate the monthly and yearly sales of individual products or product lines in units, and thus avoid the necessity of reducing the more recent figures to a comparable dollar base. It will be possible later to convert units to dollars for budget purposes. When it comes to over-all company sales, however, perhaps the dollar basis will be better. Part of the process is comparing company sales over the period being studied with industry sales and other figures (to be discussed) for the same period, and these are most likely to be stated in dollars. The principal idea is to look ahead, now, to the future uses for the tabulations and thus avoid the need for redoing them later on.

Tabulating sales over the selected past period by month and year for each product or line separately will be helpful. In this way each product can be studied individually. A "total" sheet for over-all company sales should also be included in order to develop a picture of the past trend of the company as a whole. (Large columnar sheets are useful for such tabulations.)

Of course, the initial going may not be so smooth as one would like. For example, the company sales records may be buried deep in the archives and have to be "dug out." Again, record-keeping methods may have changed over the years; sales may be listed only in total and not by type of product; or cancellations of orders, returned goods, and the like may not be properly accounted for. Regret that the company's record keeping has not been all it should have been and realization that more accurate records are needed will naturally result in making improvements in the record-keeping methods—and this could be subsidiary benefit No. 2.

Developing Information on the Industry
Historical data on the industry as a whole are usually fairly easy to obtain. Dollar (and/or sometimes unit) figures for an increasing number of industries are being published or are

available from the proper sources, now that managements are beginning to recognize the importance of having current figures on the industries they work in. One good source is the standard government publications of the Census Bureau, the Federal Reserve Board, the Department of Labor, or other government agencies; also, industry associations may have previous studies or may currently publish data that will be helpful. A little searching will probably turn up figures that can be tabulated on the same basis as the company figures and therefore can be used to good advantage.

Here, again, the important thing is to achieve comparability. Industry sales data which are later to be compared with company sales must be stated in the same terms—units or dollars—and they must cover all or the greater part of the same period of years selected for study.

It may happen, however, that only broad breakdowns of the industry figures are available from published sources. Though these may be used, it soon becomes obvious that finer breakdowns would be even more helpful, not only to the particular company but also to others in the same general field. Management may decide, therefore, to arouse interest among members of the industry association in having it, or some other impartial body, currently assemble and circulate more detailed industry information on a controlled basis. Setting up the mechanics for this exchange of industry information, if there is no provision for it now, certainly would lead to subsidiary benefit No. 3.

Developing Information on Competitors
Once company and industry figures have been whipped into shape for the forecast, the job of accumulating historical information on the company's chief competitors must be tackled. Of course, competitive data are not easy to obtain. Competitors are notoriously cagey about publishing their sales figures in convenient form for others' analysis. In fact, marketing analysis or field research is often needed to fill in this gap. But by digging in the right places much helpful information can be obtained.

For example, the company may be able to size up competitors fairly well through its own salesmen's knowledge of what goes on in their territories. A review of the salesmen's reports, particularly reports of business lost if they are available, and similar records will be helpful. In addition, it may be desirable to talk to the salesmen in person or send them a carefully worked-out questionnaire designed to get as many facts as possible about competitive ac-

tivities. Questions such as these will be appropriate: "Are our competitors making any greater inroads on our customers than in the past?" "How does our company stand alongside our chief competitors in the market now and as compared with past years?" "What are competitors' plans as reflected in their field activities?"

Information of this sort, obtained from all corners of the market and from the men right on the ground, and boiled down to its essentials, can be of considerable help in providing an understanding of competitive activities and of the company's status in the trade. To be most meaningful, however, such a search for information should be thought through and carefully planned. If this is done first, then all of the salesmen will understand thoroughly what they are expected to do, will answer the same questions on the competitive and company situation, and will comment on the same aspects of the market; and, of utmost importance, the questions asked will go directly to the core of the situations being explored and will cover the subject completely.

Such a tussle with past company figures sharpens the attention to other operational weaknesses that may exist. Perhaps in talking to the salesmen, reviewing sales reports, and so on, areas of information on characteristics of the market or on competitive aspects wherein some, or maybe all, of the salesmen are weak may come to notice. Perhaps it will become clear that the salesmen would sell better if they knew more about these things. If such is the case, the decision may be made to look into ways of educating them as soon as the forecast project has been completed—subsidiary benefit No. 4.

(All along, the exploratory work is likely to touch upon activities of the business which are related to, even though they may not be specifically a part of, the forecasting project— activities which perhaps could, and should, be strengthened. Once these are brought to light, corrective measures can be applied promptly and systematically, whereas these activities might otherwise have continued to limp along. Thus, there may be possibilities all the way through for additional subsidiary benefits.)

The executives should be questioned too. One or several probably have wide acquaintance with and special knowledge of competitors. This suggests making a systematic effort to find out what information these men can add about the company's competition, about competitors' progress over the years, and about their future intentions. Even though a great deal of what will be contributed may already be known, pertinent bits of added information are very likely to come to light. Perhaps Company A, for instance, has a new product in mind that could hurt the company's sales if it is marketed; or Company B may be thinking of changing its method of distribution; and so on. All of this additional information adds to the detailed background.

In addition, during this questioning the executives obviously will want to know the "why" of the interrogation. This provides the opportunity to get *them* interested in the forecast project. They are going to be brought into the proceedings later on anyway, and this is a good time to get started. Let them have a brief "run-down" on the forecast project and on the way in which any information they can supply is to be used. A little "selling" of the forecast project now will help just that much toward obtaining the cooperation of all of these interested executives during the steps to come later.

DEVELOPING TRENDS AND RELATIONSHIPS

By this time a lot of information on what the company and industry have done over the past years will have been assembled. Now the job is to find out what the various figures mean. There is nothing mysterious or difficult about this, and nothing basically complicated. What is necessary is merely knowing how to figure percentages and the like and being alert to detect relationships and trends. Native curiosity and good business judgment are two very useful aids at this stage.

The objective is to show how the sales of each product and of the company as a whole have varied throughout the period, but in such a way as to avoid the picture's being confused by individual monthly or annual variations.

Trends   For this purpose, company and industry trends are developed from the historical figures already assembled. These trends are part of the basic forecast structure, now beginning to shape up, on which the forecast itself will later be based. So long as they truly represent a broad past period, they will be highly useful as the starting point for working out the future estimates.

Once sales for each product and for the company as a whole have been tabulated by months and years for a period extending from, say, around 1920 up through the current year, it is a simple matter to plot these figures on separate cross-ruled charts. Then curves are drawn on these charts to represent the general

direction taken by the plotted points and thus show the trends of individual product and company sales over the selected period of years.

A trend curve is nothing more than a simple way to show the predominant, over-all characteristics of a series of figures. Its principal advantages lie in its ability to reconcile the wide variations in magnitude that usually occur in untreated historical figures and in its facility for showing the net effect of these variations.

These curves can be drawn by hand, or they can be developed mathematically. The latter method, of course, is preferred, but freehand curves, if drawn carefully, will serve the purpose. Whether drawn freehand or computed mathematically, the curves will not pass through all of the plotted points but will take a "middle course" leaving about as many plotted points above as below the curve, thus in essence "averaging out" the variation in magnitude of the plotted points. The purpose, remember, is to show the *general* direction of sales. Exhibit I provides a rough—and admittedly oversimplified—illustration.

At this point we must take notice of a rather common objection. It is often said that trend curves are coldly impartial and will reflect unusual as well as usual conditions with equal unconcern. How, then, can historical trend curves be used as a valid basis for future estimates? The solution is simply to make sure, in developing them, that they represent *only* the *usual* conditions: (1) The monthly or yearly historical figures are examined to discover unusual variations; (2) the cause of these variations is located; (3) the original figures are corrected as required; and then (4) the trends are developed from the *corrected* data. Almost invariably unusual past conditions are reflected unmistakably by wide variations in the historical figures, and it is not difficult to identify and find explanations for these abnormalities in corollary company and other records or in the memories of company executives.

For example, suppose the sales curve for product "X" looks something like that in Exhibit II. Only the year 1936 is shown in order to illustrate the point. It is unmistakable that all was rational until July, when for no apparent reason the bottom dropped out. Such a variation would be patently atypical.

In the actual case from which this example was taken, it was found after considerable digging that someone way back there in 1936 had "charged off" a large number of back-logged orders that had been accumulating on the books and had reduced the record of July's sales accordingly. (Perhaps it should not have been done, but it was.) It is logical, therefore,

EXHIBIT I Trend Curves for Annual Sales, in Units, over a Period of Thirteen Years, of Company A (Drawn Freehand) and Company B (Computed by the Least Squares Method)

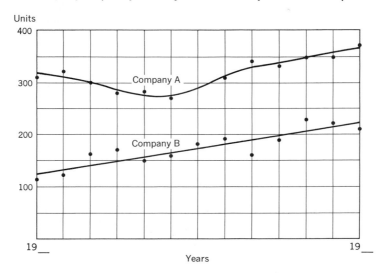

to synthesize a July figure that conforms generally with the figures for the preceding and succeeding months. This correction is indicated by the dotted line. Other such unusual variations can be adjusted in the same way once the reasons have been ascertained.

Charts showing plotted sales and trends for each product or line, for the company, and for the industry should be set up, more or less as in Exhibit III. For this example two possible company situations have been hypothecated and their sales curves shown.

Curve A is patterned after the sales curve of a large manufacturer in the midwest. Two

EXHIBIT II Trend Curve of Monthly Sales, in Units, 1936, Showing Abnormal Variation for July and Correction Made on Basis of Previous and Succeeding Month

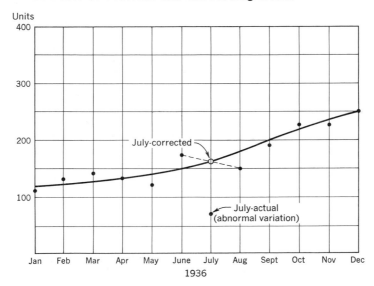

EXHIBIT III   Trend Curves of Annual Sales, in Units, 1920 to 1950,
Showing Radical Change in Company A's Level and
Recovery of Company B after 1929

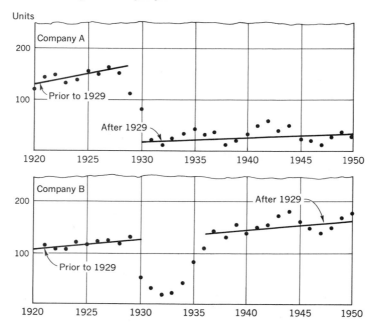

points become apparent: (1) a decided drop in business occurred *prior* to the general business decline that followed 1929; and (2) the sales curve did not return to its previous level. In the actual case from which this example was taken it was found that the market for the products involved had become saturated along about 1927, and a decline in sales had already started by the time 1929 came along. Significantly, it was apparent that during the succeeding years a new "era" had set in. Since about 1932 replacement business had accounted for most of the company's sales. The entirely new and lower level of the sales curve did not necessarily reflect successful competitive inroads.

Curve B, on the other hand, reflects a less exciting situation. This sales curve shows that ground lost after 1929 has been regained and that the trend has been generally the same throughout the whole period.

Close examination of any company's charts will reveal similar or other equally interesting information about total company sales during the period before and after 1929 and the years before and after World War II.

Relationships   In addition to charting product, company, and industry sales and developing trend curves for these, it is desirable also

to compute and tabulate percentages representing the relationship of each one to the other throughout the past period selected for study. In doing this, it is best to determine for each month and year: (1) the per cent, or share, of the industry's sales accounted for by the company; and (2) the per cent, or share, of total company sales accounted for by each of the products or lines. Then, the resulting percentage figures for each of these can be plotted on charts and trend curves developed for them.

These relationships and their trends tell their own very interesting stories. For example, examining this record of the share the company has obtained of the total market over the years will tell where the company has been heading *in relation to the industry*—that is, whether the business has increased at a greater rate than competition (which is always good to see) or whether it has been losing ground in the industry over the years. Although an increasing trend would reflect company progress compared with past years, one that has increased at a rate less than that of the industry would indicate that the competition has progressed even more rapidly. In other words, a company could have been gaining, on the one hand, and (without realizing it) losing, on the other. A little study along these lines can easily lead to subsidiary benefit No. 5.

It may appear desirable to examine the past sales of individual products or product lines the same way as total company and industry sales. Comparing the trends of the products' sales will show how successful each one has been *in relation to the others*. The fact may be uncovered that one or another of the products or lines, while showing some gains over the years, has actually lagged behind the others so far as its contribution to total company sales is concerned. To know such facts about the company's products or lines could be subsidiary benefit No. 6.

These percentage relationships and trends also will help later on in the forecast process in determining the share of industry sales that the company is likely to obtain, and the share of company sales that each product or line is likely to account for in the period ahead.

Short-term Characteristics The next step is to determine whether seasonal or other repetitive variations have been characteristic of the past sales of individual products, the company, or the industry. Preferably this is done mathematically, in order to obtain precise measures of whatever periodic swings in sales there may be. However, the same results can be obtained roughly by visually comparing the charts. If up-surges or valleys occur every year during the same season or month, the percentage of the annual total that each month of the year characteristically accounts for can be figured out.

Such a measure of past seasonal, or similar, variations will help to make the forthcoming forecast realistic. Later on future annual sales will be estimated without regard to these periodic increases or decreases, and then the annual expectancy can be distributed over the months of the year in accordance with the characteristic monthly proportions.

A National Index Finally, it is necessary to have a series of figures representing activities up to the present in some broad segment of the national economy—a series whose trend over the past period being studied closely approximates the trend of the industry.

Nationally published indexes on production or on the financial aspects of the nation's industrial activity are commonly used for this purpose, and there are often several to choose from among the many now compiled by various governmental agencies. Here the personnel of the local Federal Reserve or Department of Commerce field office should be consulted; these people are universally helpful and co-operative and are qualified to suggest still other sources.

Reflecting, as they do, activities for large segments of the nation's total economy, such indexes are not likely to be affected materially by activities within most single businesses or industries. Moreover, they will tend to maintain a relatively even course over the years, except in the event of drastic economic changes. Because this sort of index is relatively stable, the trend of the selected national series, developed for the past years and up to the present and extended out through the future period of the forecast, is particularly useful as the backbone of the forecast structure being built.

Progress to This Point Most of the preliminary work has now been done. The past activities of the individual products, of the company, and of the industry have been "boiled down"; and a related national index has been found and adapted. As a result, these things can now be seen:

1. *Trends*—that is, where the individual products, the company, the industry, and a related large segment of the national economy are heading, as of today.

2. *Relationships*—that is, how the company's progress has compared with that of the industry, and how the individual products or lines have fared in relation to each other.

3. *Inherent characteristics*—that is, whatever seasonal variations are characteristic of the company and in the industry.

In addition, certain of the control aspects of the business have had a close scrutiny. Possible improvements in these and in other control and reporting activities, particularly those that heretofore have been conducted too loosely to be relied upon as the basis for future planning, have probably been considered, if not actually initiated.

As far as the groundwork of the project is concerned, all that remains now is to extend (on the chart) the trend curve of the selected national index out through the future period to be forecast, and to extend the trend curve of the industry out through the same period in such a way as to parallel the national index curve.

ESTIMATING FUTURE BUSINESS

Actually working out the forecast from this point on should be a mutual undertaking participated in by all of the company's key executives whose knowledge and experience qualify them to contribute opinions on the future of the company and the industry.

In the first place, each of the key executives has a definite stake in the company's progress. Each one, therefore, not only should contribute to the best of his ability toward planning for its future, but also should be placed in a position of joint accountability for the accuracy of the estimates on which these plans are to be based. In the second place, a group approach avoids the mistake of placing the whole responsibility for the forecast on one head. Too often the findings of that one executive about the future of the business become the target of the remaining executives or provide them with a ready-made defensive position when future sales do not stack up with what was expected. Unless they are brought into it, these other executives, not having contributed to the forecast, can (and will) deny with impunity any responsibility and accountability for deviations of actual from forecast results.

Developing the Forecast Plans   The next step, therefore, is to bring the best brains available in the company to bear on the forecast problem. This requires planning and a spelled-out approach. These men should do some concentrated thinking about the forecast, but they are also going to be busy with other problems. The easier it is made for them to grasp and understand the forecast aims and procedures, and their individual responsibilities in connection with the project, the better chance there will be of getting their full cooperation.

Accordingly, the forecast program should be described briefly in writing, and the plan circulated among the key executives. This write-up should have the overt approval of the chief executive and should explain the purpose of the forecast project, stating what it is intended specifically to do. Above all, it should stress the cooperative part and responsibilities the key executives are to have in it. This description should also cover the mechanics of the process and should include charts and tables as required.

These points should be made and emphasized:

1. That the trend curves, the percentage relationships, and the charted historical characteristics of the business and industry, while revealing past activities, are also capable of indicating what is *likely* to happen in the future, *"all other things being equal"*;

2. That the best collective judgment and knowledge of the company's executives with re-

spect to the business and industry is now to be called into action in order to form a *composite company opinion* on (a) whether all things *will* be "equal" in the future period as compared with the past period or (b) whether things will be different; and, if different, in what ways and to what extent.

The stage is set in this way so that the forecast will be the product of: (1) precise mathematical or at least reasonably accurate measures of known facts—measures that are both objective and impersonal; and (2) a consensus of considered executive judgment—judgment that is based on a variety of experience in the business and the industry. The stage is also set so that a group executive meeting (or meetings, if necessary) may be held for working out the forecast, and so that executives included can come in fully prepared for the discussions.

Working Out the Forecast   In the executive meeting the forecast should be worked out systematically. The chief executive of the company, or another executive of adequate standing, should direct this activity. Strong leadership will be desirable because differences of opinion will need ironing out; overoptimistic and overpessimistic opinions will have to be reconciled; and a clear, hardheaded, and realistic view of the company's future must be maintained throughout. The actual working out involves two steps:

1. Determining how much business there is likely to be for the *industry* as a whole during the forecast period by (a) observing the out-and-out mechanical extensions of the past trends of the industry and of the related national index through the forecast period, and (b) adjusting this rough industry forecast upwards or downwards until it conforms with the executive group's consensus of opinion of anticipated general business conditions and the future outlook for the industry.

2. Reaching a consensus of realistic opinions concerning the trends which the company's own total business and its several products or lines are likely to take during the forecast period, based on considerations of (a) the products' and the company's past trends as shown on the charts; (b) the trends which, it is anticipated, the products, the company, and the industry will follow; and (c) the share of the industry's total business that the company has obtained in the past and is likely to obtain in the future.

These joint opinions, obviously, should take into consideration the company's own plans and what is known of competitors' plans for the future. Any unusual internal conditions of backlog, shortage of materials, and the like which threaten to affect the forecast should also be considered.

Applying the Forecast   It is a simple matter to translate this consensus of executive opinion into formal chart form showing the anticipated trends of the industry, of the company, and of the individual company products or lines throughout the forecast period. At this point the company forecasts should be adjusted according to whatever predetermined seasonal or similar variations may have been characteristic of the business in the past.

It is now time to write up a brief, final statement of the official company forecast, including a full description of the assumptions on which the forecast was based. Here is an example of the way it might go:

> In the official opinion of the company, the trend of general business, of the industry, and of the company is expected to continue to rise [or to decline, as the case may be]. The company's plans for expanding its distribution are to be implemented shortly and are expected to produce $x\%$ of additional business. On the other hand, new [or improved] competitive products, now about ready for the market, are expected to account for a loss of $y\%$ of the company's business during the forecast period. On the basis of these assumptions, such-and-such an amount of business is forecast for each product and for the company during the forecast period.

In such a forecast, developed mutually by all of the key executives of the company from a sound base of historical facts, no one executive opinion is likely to be predominant, and each participant has had free opportunity to contribute his opinions. It follows, then, that each of these executives can be expected to accept the forecast, without personal reservation, as the basis for planning his own segment of company operations. Consequently, the controller, sales manager, advertising manager, production chief, and any other of these executives can plan his respective operation with the assurance that management *as a whole* has taken into full account all major contingencies that can reasonably be anticipated.

Using an official forecast like this as the starting point for company planning is likely to produce another important subsidiary bene-

fit. Inasmuch as the group method of developing the forecast discourages individual hedging with an eye to a later accounting and particularly because it provides a mutually developed starting point for planning, certain executives begin to operate more from an aggressive and less from a defensive position with respect to their own segments of the company's operations.

COMPARING ACTUAL WITH ESTIMATED RESULTS

It would be a mistake to drop the forecast project at this point. To regard any business forecast as static and unchanging and, once having worked it out, to file it away and forget it, or, on the other hand, to accept it without a further look as the year proceeds, is the surest possible road to disappointment. Disappointments need not occur, however, if the forecast is looked on not only as the very best estimate possible at the time of its inception but also as a means of bringing to light, throughout the entire forecast period, any major variations from what has been forecast when and as such variations occur.

To avoid disappointment, and to use the forecast for all it is worth, arrangements must be made to compare actual with anticipated sales results periodically. It must be understood that minor variations from the forecast are bound to occur; so, as the months (or weeks or quarters) unfold, no one should worry about small interim swings. But major variations and also lesser deviations which begin consistently to repeat should be scrutinized closely.

These are the danger signals. As soon as a significant variation appears, and regardless of whether the actual performance is greater or less than was expected, it is important to try to determine what lies behind the difference.

Tracking Down Causes for Variations
Suppose actual sales results are appreciably less than were forecast. The immediate reaction is: "Let's get to the bottom of this." The first move is to call in the sales manager and ask him why sales, apparently, have gone sour. Things begin to happen! Developing the forecast has accustomed executives to looking at sales results from the vantage point of specific measurements; so now they want facts.

Probably one of these two situations will be revealed:

1. If the sales control and analysis function is operating properly, it is probable that the

sales manager has anticipated this action and has taken steps to find out why sales have slipped. In that case he will already have analyzed current reports and identified the sales territories, the products, or the product lines that are responsible. Perhaps he already has made a move to find out directly from the field what is happening.

2. On the other hand, perhaps what develops is that the sales control and analysis function needs strengthening; that current analysis of sales is not being carried out effectively; and that, as a result, it is proving difficult to isolate the specific reasons for the decline promptly enough to take effective remedial action.

In cases such as the former, it is usually easy to provide a logical follow-through—that is, to establish the facts and take direct and speedy action on the adverse situation. In the latter case, the need for establishing adequate sales controls or for improving the present function becomes apparent, and the required steps for improvement can be taken. Subsidiary benefits of the forecast project like this may continue to crop up.

It might be, for example, that as various problems of this nature arise, more information is needed, say, on markets or distribution methods than is regularly available in the company. A detailed study of these factors may be highly desirable. In that case, the market research department can be put to work on this specific project. Or, if no formal market research function is established in the company, expert assistance can be obtained from the outside either on a project basis or to aid in establishing a permanent market research activity within the company.

Adjusting the Forecast   Perhaps the reasons found for a major deviation from the forecast may strongly indicate that a new situation has developed that could not reasonably have been foreseen. Competitive activity may have changed radically; or there may have been some other serious alteration of the basic assumptions of the initial forecast. In that case, either the company's competitive tactics must be altered so as to counteract the change; or, if that is not possible, the forecast must be adjusted to conformity with this new situation. Significant variations of actual from forecast results, like these, can happen at any time and must be taken care of "on the spot."

It would be foolhardy, however, to limit re-examination of the forecast to the times when these danger signals appear. If it is to reflect accurately company and industry-wide influences and activities—which are always changing and are never static—the forecast, perforce, must be periodically rechecked and, if necessary, adjusted. Company plans may change, not necessarily radically but enough to have an effect on future expectancies; the trend of the industry or the national economy may shift. Of particular importance is the fact that conditions affecting the forecast in the third or fourth quarter of a year can be foreseen and evaluated with much greater accuracy at the beginnings of these quarters than at the beginning of the year, the time the initial forecast ordinarily is completed.

It should be a regular and unchanging procedure in the company at the beginning of each quarter (1) to restudy the principal measurable factors affecting the forecast and to re-evaluate the extent of their change since the last recheck, and (2) to assemble the executive group as was done for the initial forecast and mutually reaffirm or adjust the forecast as it will apply to the period then ahead. This should be done in the light of whatever changes may have occurred in the measurable factors and on the basis of the then current opinions of the executives. If a change in the forecast seems indicated, it is also advisable to repeat the procedure used initially of issuing a new official forecast statement showing and explaining the changes.

REFINING THE FORECAST PROCESS

The foregoing description of the forecasting process undoubtedly is something of an oversimplification. The primary objective, however, has been to point up the basic principles, procedures, and benefits that are involved. Some difficult problems are bound to be encountered; and, particularly at first, mistakes may be made. But it should be realized that forecasting, like anything else, gets better and more accurate with practice. One can learn only by experience how to gauge with accuracy the sensitivity of products and industry to changing company, industry, and economic conditions.

With learning will come more and more precise evaluations of the extent to which products, company, and industry are likely to react to various stimuli. Moreover, the method adopted initially for developing a forecast almost invariably is subject to some later refinements of application to the particular characteristics of the business, based on experience gained with the selected method in actual use.

For these reasons a certain latitude should be allowed the forecast when evaluating its effectiveness during its early years in the company—but not to the extent of being complacent. There is always opportunity to improve not only the mathematical but also the judgment aspects of the forecast method in use. In that way it will become more and more helpful, in fact more and more indispensable.

13

Sales Forecasting: Key to Integrated Management*

WILLIAM LAZER

Business organizations are increasingly adopting the marketing management concept. This philosophy of business operation places greater emphasis on marketing planning and forces business executives to design marketing strategies and program marketing effort to achieve realistic and predetermined objectives.

Sales forecasting can aid management greatly in implementing the marketing management approach. It is a basis for developing co-ordinated and goal-directed systems of marketing action. The sales forecast is one of the vital tools of marketing planning since adequate planning and the effective deployment of marketing resources are based on sales forecasting data.

Sales forecasting promotes and facilitates the proper functioning of the many segments of a firm's total spectrum of business and marketing activities. It influences almost every other prediction of business operations. It is used in establishing budgets and marketing controls. Sales forecasts help determine various limiting conditions for management decisions and programs and are useful tools for co-ordinating the integral aspects of business operations. They provide bases for evaluating the function-

ing and productivity of various segments of business activity. They can guide marketing and other business action toward the achievement of implicit and explicit objectives.

This article investigates three aspects of sales forecasting as a key to integrated management action: (1) sales forecasting as a component of the marketing planning process, (2) sales forecasting as a focus for integrative planning, and (3) the basic components and procedures of a comprehensive sales forecasting program.

IN MARKETING PLANNING

Figure 1 illustrates the strategic role of sales forecasting in gathering information for marketing planning. Effective planning of marketing activities can be achieved only if adequate marketing-related information is available. Marketing planning is concerned with the application of analysis and judgment to available information and the prediction of likely occurrences and trends during some future period.

Marketing-related information can refer to either the past or the future. Information about past activities is often referred to as factual information. Information about the future is anything but factual, and might be characterized as assumptive. Past information is available to every business if it has an adequate record-keeping process. It is also available

* Reprinted by permission of the publisher from *Business Horizons*, vol. 2, no. 3, pp. 61–67, Fall, 1959. Mr. Lazer is professor of business administration in the College of Business and Public Service, Michigan State University.

FIGURE 1   Sales Forecasting's Role in Marketing Planning

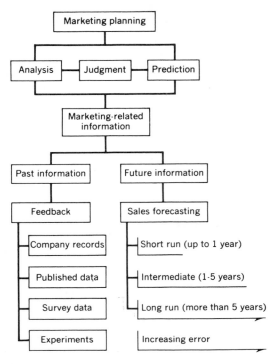

from other secondary data sources, such as information reported by governmental bureaus, university research bureaus, and trade associations. Past information may also be assembled through the use of various primary data-gathering research tools, such as surveys and experiments.

Future information requires the utilization of forecasting techniques and processes. Nevertheless, it is based on past data and is usually the result of the application of predictive tools to available past information.

Whenever a business gathers future data, varying degrees of error are bound to exist. Regardless of the forecasting techniques used and the degree of sophistication achieved, future conditions will always deviate to some degree from the predictions of the forecasters. Thus, management must expect future information to contain some error.

For effective marketing planning, both types of information must be available for executive use. From a planning and decision-making point of view, future, or nonfactual, information may be more significant than information about the past. This becomes clear if one considers that plans and decisions made today are actually based on executive expectations of what will happen during some future period.

If we consider sales forecasting from the point of view of furnishing marketing-related information, we can state that management gathers information as a result of two complementary processes: feedback and sales forecasting. Feedback consists of relating information about past events and relationships back to management. Through the use of such factual data, management can adjust existing operations and plans and thereby improve the effectiveness of all business action.

Sales forecasting furnishes management with information about what market conditions will probably be like during a future period. Management can then use this information as a basis for planning broad company goals and the strategies to achieve them. Sales forecasting data are used in establishing various types of potential volume and profit targets that become the bases for guiding and controlling operations.

Past and future information, however, are constantly blending. A sales forecast, although it furnishes future information, eventually takes the form of feedback information. Once this happens, a comparison may be made between actual and forecast sales for a specific period. Through such an audit, deviations may be noted and explanations sought for them. This information can, in turn, help refine the assumptions about future sales forecasts and increase the total effectiveness of the forecasting procedure.

The various predictions made may take the form of short-run sales forecasts of less than a year, intermediate forecasts of from one to five years, and long-run forecasts for periods of more than five years. Generally, the longer range the predictions, the greater the forecasting error.

IN INTEGRATIVE PLANNING

Another facet of sales forecasting and its role in marketing planning is its position in the integrative planning process. A sales forecast is a useful tool for integrating the external business environment with the internal forces of the company. It reduces to workable management dimensions the external business environment over which management has relatively little control. It delimits those constraints that establish the boundaries within which a company must make decisions and operate and translates them into company programs.

Figure 2 portrays sales forecasting as an aid to integrative planning. It indicates the con-

FIGURE 2   Sales Forecasting: A Focus for Integrative Planning

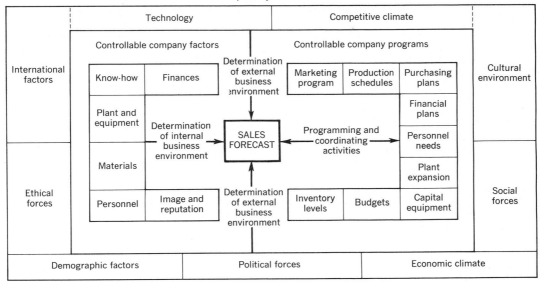

trollable, partially controllable, and noncontrollable factors that management should integrate and take into account in making effective sales forecasts.

The noncontrollable forces determine the broad environmental limits within which the company will operate. These factors include cultural forces, the economic environment, demographic forces, political factors, ethical and social forces, and various international conditions. They cannot be influenced to any degree by company action; at best, they may be recognized and appraised in an intelligent manner.

On Figure 2, broken lines separate the competitive environment and technological factors from other noncontrollable factors. This is to indicate that management action may have some influence over at least these two external forces, which are considered partially controllable factors. However, even though company action can affect competition and technology, the forces *beyond* company control generally have a more significant impact.

BUSINESS HORIZONS

As forecasts become longer run in nature, the necessity of recording the existing external climate becomes more imperative since, in the future, it will be these noncontrollable factors that set the over-all constraints and boundaries within which companies survive and grow or

fail. Through an evaluation and projection of external forces, management attempts to make realistic assumptions about the future environment. These assumptions about noncontrollable and partially controllable factors are the foundations of sales forecasts, and intelligent sales predictions can be made only by implicitly or explicitly assuming relationships about these factors.

Management should not consider this initial step of determining the external company environment as merely a theoretical exercise that is of little use in practical sales forecasting. The external variables are factors that must be dealt with practically and realistically. Their influence cannot be ignored.

As an example of the importance of external forces, consider the development of a controlled shopping center. Several years may elapse from the initiation of the original idea and the first inquiry concerning site location until the actual opening of the center. Choices must be made from among alternative sites, and considerable negotiations may follow to obtain the property and construct and finance the center. Then there are a host of operating details to attend to, including the actual leasing of stores.

The profitability of the total investment and the sales realized by retail stores in the shopping center will be affected by external forces. Existing and potential competition, for example, can have great influence on future sales.

Demographic and economic forces in the form of population shifts and income trends will shape the retail sales potential of the center. Existing and potential industrial development of the surrounding territory will influence employment and income and will be reflected in marketing opportunity.

Municipal, state, and federal regulations will have an impact on future pricing tactics, on the use of various promotional devices including trading stamps, on store hours, and even on the types of merchandise that may be sold in particular kinds of stores.

Other examples could be presented concerning such industries as wood products, chemicals, mining, petroleum, transportation, the power industry, and communications.

After determining the external business climate for a future period, the sales forecaster must estimate the impact that internal business factors will make on potential markets. This involves an evaluation of those factors over which the company has direct control. They can be adjusted over the longer run by the company itself.

For an effective forecast, the company's know-how, its financial position, the plant capacity, the material resources and personnel available, and the company's reputation, image, and position in the market place must all be evaluated. The market position that a company eventually earns and the sales that it achieves will depend on the impact made by the internal business factors as they are combined into planned management programs carried out within the external business system. A consideration of both climates, external and internal, will give management some guides by which to judge the potential sales opportunity for a company. Through the use of various analyses and by the application of sound judgment, management may map out a company's future sales position.

Thus, sales forecasting helps integrate the management-controllable factors, or the given elements of a total business system within which the company operates and the internal factors of the business itself.

The sales forecast is also a device by means of which management may integrate its objectives, its operating programs, and its targets with potential market opportunity. This can be done by translating the sales forecast into specific profit and sales-volume goals to be realized in a given future period of time. The sales forecast thus becomes a basis for marketing programs, purchasing plans, financial budgets, personnel needs, production schedules, plant and equipment requirements, expansion programs, and perhaps most other aspects of management programming.

The right half of Figure 2 presents sales forecasting as a vehicle for translating the noncontrollable, partially controllable, and internal business environments into specific controllable management programs. The figure also emphasizes the interrelationships between sales forecasts and company programs.

FORECASTING PROGRAM

Figure 3 outlines the elements of a total sales forecasting program. Four major stages of forecasting, the specific procedures to be followed, and their sequence are presented. These stages are: assembling the forecasting

---

FIGURE 3   A Total Sales Forecasting Program

STAGES OF PROCESS	TECHNIQUES	RESULTS
Assembling information		
Recognize noncontrollable and partially controllable business environment.	Observe and list significant external factors	Identification of pertinent cultural, social, economic, political, demographic, competitive, ethical, international, technological forces
Gather information about noncontrollable and partially controllable forces	Investigate outside sources of information	Selection and gathering of data from government, industry, university research, Federal Reserve Board, company records.

FIGURE 3   A Total Sales Forecasting Program (Continued)

STAGES OF PROCESS	TECHNIQUES	RESULTS
Gather information about controllable forces.	Investigate company records	Selection of relevant company forecasting information
Evaluating and projecting Data		
Analyze data	Apply analytical tools: time series analysis, least squares, simple correlation, multiple correlation, input-output tables, break-even charts	Determination of patterns and relationships: lead and lag indicators, cycles, seasonal indexes, trend lines, covariation
Forecast future sales	Employ extrapolation, constant percentage of increase, end-use analysis, executive opinion, historical analogy, panel of experts, grass-roots techniques, surveys, models, experiments, samples, hunches, judgment, and crystal ball	Prediction and definition of future dollar sales, unit sales, maximum and minimum ranges
Operationally applying forecast		
Refine sales forecast	Break sales down by volume and profit control units: product lines, territories, customers, salesmen	Establishment of specific sales targets
Translate specific targets into operational programs	Establish and co-ordinate plans: marketing program, production schedules, purchasing plans, financial requirements, personnel needs, plant expansion, capital equipment budgets, inventory levels	Identification of controllable business environment
Auditing the forecast		
Review forecast	Compare actual and forecast sales regularly and analyze discrepancies	Determination of reasons for deviations
Modify forecast and forecasting procedures	Re-evaluate projections and adjust forecasting techniques	More accurate sales forecasting

---

information; evaluating and projecting the data; applying the sales forecast operationally; and auditing the forecast. These four steps are broken down further, and some of the techniques that may be utilized at each stage and the results achieved are described. Figure 3 starts with the noncontrollable business environment and internal business climate and works down through the various predictions about controllable business plans, programs, and objectives.

The first step in a comprehensive sales forecasting program is assembling forecasting information. This involves the recognition of noncontrollable and partially controllable environments through observation and listing of significant external factors. The result is the identification of pertinent social, cultural, ethical, economic, political, demographic, international, technological, and competitive forces that will influence the projections.

Next, information can be assembled about these noncontrollable factors and an investigation made of such outside sources of information as governments, industries, and universities

The third step in assembling forecasting information is that of gathering information about the controllable company environment, which involves research into company records. This should result in the selection of relevant company forecasting information.

After forecasting information has been assembled, the data must be evaluated and projected. This activity has two components: analyzing the data and making the actual forecast. To analyze the data, such analytical tools as time series analysis, least squares methods of fitting a straight line, fitting curves, simple and multiple correlation, the use of input-output tables, and breakeven charts may be used. This leads to the determination of patterns and relationships through lead and lag indicators, cycles, seasonal indexes, trend lines, and measures of covariation.

The actual sales projections may be made through extrapolation, a straight percentage increase in sales, executive opinion polls, end-use analysis, historical analogy, a panel of experts, the grass-roots approach, samples and surveys, models, experiments, hunches, judgments, and the oft-used crystal ball. After these projections have been made, the prediction and definition of future dollar and unit sales, and maximum and minimum sales ranges is possible.

Then the forecast must be applied operationally, which involves refining the sales forecast. This is done by breaking it down on the basis of volume and profit control units by product lines, salesmen, customers, territories, and other managerial units. Specific sales targets can thus be established, and sales forecasting data become the basis for programming marketing, production, purchasing, finance, plant expansion, capital equipment acquisition, personnel, and inventory needs. Controllable business programs have now been really determined.

The last step in a comprehensive sales forecasting program is that of auditing the forecast. This involves reviewing the forecast by comparing actual and forecast sales and analyzing any deviations or discrepancies. The purpose here is to determine the reasons for the deviations. Then future forecasts and even the forecasting techniques can be modified. The end result is more accurate sales forecasts.

The total sales forecasting process is one of refinement. It starts with the more general factors—the external noncontrollable environment and the internal business environment—quantifies them, and finally establishes specific operational goals and targets.

Marketing planning often suffers because management does not develop an effective sales forecasting program. One of the great inducements to ignore or neglect sales forecasting is the difficulty of making predictions. It is a trying task for anyone to try to determine future relationships and their implications for potential sales. It is much more comfortable to turn to the consideration of current operating problems, which are more concrete, are somewhat easier to grasp, and for which some corrective action may be initiated almost immediately.

However, professional marketing management cannot afford to neglect the sales forecasting process. It must become concerned with the development of well co-ordinated, planned, and forceful systems of business action. It must plan the use of company resources so that a firm can establish itself in the market place and grow.

The future marketing climate is likely to be one of keener competition, an exhilarating pace of market change, heavier fixed costs, and an increasing emphasis on innovation. Adequate marketing planning will become the foundation for integrated marketing action. Since one of the basic components of effective marketing planning is sales forecasting, it seems obvious that in the future an increasing amount of time and resources will be spent by companies in developing more adequate sales forecasts.

The Environment of Decision*

CHESTER I. BARNARD

The acts of individuals may be distinguished in principal as those which are the result of deliberation, calculation, thought, and those which are unconscious, automatic, responsive, the results of internal or external conditions present or past. In general, whatever processes precede the first class of acts culminate in what may be termed "decision." Involved in acts which are ascribed to decision are many subsidiary acts which are themselves automatic, the processes of which are usually unknown to the actor.

When decision is involved there are consciously present two terms—the end to be accomplished and the means to be used. The end itself may be the result of logical processes in which the end is in turn a means to some broader or more remote end; or the immediate end, and generally the ultimate end, may not be a result of logical processes, but "given"—that is, unconsciously impressed—by conditions, including social conditions past or present, including orders or organizations. But whenever the end has been determined, by whatever process, the decision as to means is itself a logical process of discrimination, analysis, choice—however defective either the factual basis for choice or the reasoning related to these facts. . . .

I. THE OCCASIONS OF DECISION

The making of decisions, as everyone knows from personal experience, is a burdensome task. Offsetting the exhilaration that may result from correct and successful decision and the relief that follows the terminating of a

struggle to determine issues is the depression that comes from failure or error of decision and the frustration which ensues from uncertainty. Accordingly, it will be observed that men generally try to avoid making decisions, beyond a limited degree when they are rather uncritical responses to conditions. The capacity of most men to make decisions is quite narrow, although it is a capacity that may be considerably developed by training and especially by experience.

The executive is under the obligation of making decisions usually within approximately defined limits related to the position he has accepted; and is under the necessity of keeping within the limits of his capacity if he is continuously to discharge this obligation. He must, therefore, to be successful, distinguish between the occasions of decision in order to avoid the acceptance of more than he can undertake without neglecting the fields to which his position relates. For the natural reluctance of other men to decide, their persistent disposition to avoid responsibility, and their fear of criticism, will lead them to overwhelm the executive who does not protect himself from excessive burdens of decisions if he is not already protected by a well regulated and habitual distribution of responsibilities.

It is for this reason necessary in the making of decisions to maintain a balance between the fields from which the occasions of them arise. I suppose this is rarely a matter of conscious selection, and is probably subject to no general rules. It involves in itself important decisions. For our purposes, however, it may be helpful to note that the occasions for decision originate in three distinct fields: (a) from authoritative communications from superiors; (b) from cases referred for decision by subordinates; (c) from cases originating in the initiative of the executive concerned.

(a) Occasions for decisions are frequently furnished by instructions or by general requirements of superior authority. Such decisions

* Reprinted by permission of the publisher from Chester I. Barnard, *The Functions of the Executive,* Harvard University Press, Cambridge, Mass., 1938, pp. 185, 189–198, 201–205. Mr. Barnard was formerly president of the New Jersey Bell Telephone Company and the Rockefeller Foundation; before his death in 1961, he was also a member of the New York City Board of Education and a director of several business corporations and foundations.

relate to the interpretation, application, and distribution of instructions. These occasions cannot be avoided, though the burden may be reduced by delegation of responsibility to subordinates. They involve serious decisions when the instructions seem morally wrong, harmful to the organization, or impossible of execution.

(b) The cases referred for decision may be called appellate cases. They arise from incapacity of subordinates, uncertainty of instructions, novelty of conditions, conflict of jurisdiction or conflicts of orders, or failure of subjective authority. The control of the number of appellate cases lies in adequacy of executive organization, of personnel, of previous decision; and the development of the processes of informal organization. The test of executive action is to make these decisions when they are important, or when they cannot be delegated reasonably, and to decline the others.

(c) The occasions of decision on the initiative of the executive are the most important test of his capacity. Out of his understanding of the situation, which depends upon his ability and initiative, and on the character of the communication system of his organization, it is to be determined whether something needs to be done or corrected. To decide that question involves not merely the ordinary elements but the executive's specific justification for deciding. For when the occasions for decision arise from above or below the position of the executive, others have in advance granted him authority; but when made on his own initiative, this always may be (and generally is) questioned, at least tacitly (in the form whether decision was necessary, or related to scope of obligations, etc.). Moreover, failure to decide is usually not specifically subject to attack, except under extreme conditions. Hence there is much incentive to avoid decision. Pressure of other work is the usual self-justification. Yet it is clear that the most important obligation is to raise and decide those issues which no one else is in a position to raise effectively.

From the point of view of the *relative* importance of specific decisions, those of executives properly call for first attention. From the point of view of *aggregate* importance, it is not decisions of executives but of non-executive participants in organization which should enlist major interest. Indeed it is precisely for this reason that many executive decisions are

necessary—they relate to the facilitation of correct action involving appropriate decisions among others. In large measure this is a process of providing for the clear presentment of the issues or choices. At any event, it is easily evident merely from the inspection of the action of the non-executive participants in organization that coordination of action requires repeated organization decisions "on the spot" where the effective action of organization takes place. It is here that the final and most concrete objectives of purposes are found, with the maximum of definiteness. There is no further stage of organization action. The final selection of means takes place at this point.

It should be noted, however, that the types of decisions as well as the conditions change in character as we descend from the major executive to the non-executive positions in organization. At the upper limit decisions relating to ends to be pursued generally require the major attention, those relating to means being secondary, rather general, and especially concerned with personnel, that is, the development and protection of organization itself. At intermediate levels the breaking of broad purposes into more specific ends and the technical and technological problems, including economic problems, of action become prominent. At the low levels decisions characteristically relate to technologically correct conduct, so far as the action is organization action. But it is at these low levels, where ultimate authority resides, that the *personal* decisions determining willingness to contribute become of relatively greatest aggregate importance.

II. THE EVIDENCES OF DECISION

Not the least of the difficulties of appraising the executive functions or the relative merits of executives lies in the fact that there is little direct opportunity to observe the essential operations of decision. It is a perplexing fact that most executive decisions produce no direct evidence of themselves and that knowledge of them can only be derived from the cumulation of indirect evidence. They must largely be inferred from general results in which they are merely one factor, and from symptomatic indications of roundabout character.

Those decisions which are most directly known result in the emission of authoritative communications, that is, orders. Something is or is not to be done. Even in such cases the basic decision may not be evidence; for the decision to attempt to achieve a certain result or condition may require several communications to different persons which appear to be complete in themselves but in which the controlling general decision may not be disclosed.

Again, a firm decision may be taken that does not result in any communication whatever for the time being. A decision properly timed must be made in advance of communicating it, either because the action involved must wait anticipated developments or because it cannot be authoritative without educational or persuasive preparation.

Finally, the decision may be not to decide. This is a most frequent decision, and from some points of view probably the most important. For every alert executive continually raises in his own mind questions for determination. As a result of his consideration he may determine that the question is not pertinent. He may determine that it is not now pertinent. He may determine that it is pertinent now but that there are lacking adequate data upon which to base a final decision. He may determine that the question is pertinent, can be decided, will not be decided except by himself, and yet it would be better that it be not decided because his competence is insufficient.

The fine art of executive decision consists in not deciding questions that are not now pertinent, in not deciding prematurely, in not making decisions that cannot be made effective, and in not making decisions that others should make. Not to decide questions that are not pertinent at the time is uncommon good sense, though to raise them may be uncommon perspicacity. Not to decide questions prematurely is to refuse commitment or attitude or the development of prejudice. Not to make decisions that cannot be made effective is to refrain from destroying authority. Not to make decisions that others should make is to preserve morale, to develop competence, to fix responsibility, and to preserve authority.

From this it may be seen that decisions fall into two major classes, positive decisions—to do something, to direct action, to cease action, to prevent action; and negative decisions, which are decisions not to decide. Both are inescapable; but the negative decisions are often largely unconscious, relatively non-logical, "instinctive," "good sense." It is because of the rejections that the selection is good. The best of moves may be offset by a false move. This is why time is usually necessary to appraise the executive. There is no current evidence of the all-important negative decisions. The absence of effective moves indicates failure of initiative in decision, but error of action probably often means absence of good negative decisions. The success of action through a period of time denotes excellence of selection and of rejection of possible actions.

III. THE NATURE OF THE ENVIRONMENT

Whatever the occasions or the evidences of decision, it is clear that decisions are constantly being made. What is the nature of the environment of decisions, the materials with which they deal, the field to which they relate? It consists of two parts: (a) purpose; and (b) the physical world, the social world, the external things and forces and circumstances of the moment. All of these, including purpose, constitute the objective field of decision; but the two parts are of radically different nature and origin. The function of decision is to regulate the relations between these two parts. This regulation is accomplished either by changing the purpose or by changing the remainder of the environment.

(a) We may consider purpose first. It may seem strange perhaps that purpose should be included in the objective environment, since purpose of all things seems personal, subjective, internal, the expression of desire. This is true; but *at the moment of a new decision,* an existing purpose, the result of a previous decision under previous conditions, is an objective fact, and it is so treated at that moment in so far as it is a factor in new decision.

This is especially true because organization decisions do not relate to personal purposes, but to organization purposes. The purpose which concerns an organization decision may have been given as a fact to and accepted as such by the person who is responsible for making a new decision. But no matter how arrived at, when decision is in point, the purpose is fact already determined; its making is a matter of history; it may be as objective as another man's emotions may be to an observer.

We must next note, however, that purpose is essential to give any meaning to the rest of the environment.[1] The environment must be looked at from *some* point of view to be intelligible. A mere mass of things, atoms, movements, forces, noises, lights, could produce some response from a sensitive creature or certainly would have some

---

[1] I am under the impression that in a general way both the form of expression and the concepts stated in the next several paragraphs were derived from or influenced by A. N. Whitehead's *Process and Reality.*

effect on it, or on other things, but the reduction of this mass of everything to something significant requires a basis for discrimination, for picking out this and that as pertinent, relevant, and interesting. This basis is that in *this* situation something is or is not to be done. The situation aids, obstructs, or is neutral from *this* point of view. The basis for this discrimination is a purpose, an end, an object to be accomplished.

Purpose itself has no meaning, however, except in an environment. It can only be defined in terms of an environment.[2] Even to want to go somewhere, anywhere, supposes some kind of environment. A very general purpose supposes a very general undifferentiated environment; and if the purpose is stated or thought of it must be in terms of that general environment. But when formed, it immediately (if it is not in suspense or dormant, so to speak) serves for reducing that environment to more definite features; and the immediate result is to change purpose into a more specific purpose. Thus when I decide I want to go from A to B my idea of terrain is vague. But as soon as I have decided, the terrain becomes less vague; I immediately see paths, rocks, obstacles that are significant; and this finer discrimination results in detailed and smaller purposes. I not only want to go from A to B, but I want to go this way, that way, etc. This constant refinement of purpose is the effect of repeated decisions, in finer and finer detail, until eventually detailed purpose is contemporaneous accomplishment. But similarly with each new edition of purposes, a new discrimination of the environment is involved, until finally the last obstacle of progressive action represents a breaking up of a general purpose into many concrete purposes, each as it is made almost simultaneously associated with the action. The thing is done as soon as decided; it becomes a matter of history; it constitutes a single step in the process of experience.

Thus back and forth purpose and environment react in successive steps through successive decisions in greater and greater detail. A series of final decisions, each apparently trivial, is largely accomplished unconsciously and sums up into an effected general purpose and a route of experience.

(b) We may now consider the environment of decision exclusive of purpose. It consists of atoms and molecules, agglomerations of things in motion, alive; of men and emotions; of physical laws and social laws; social ideas; norms of actions, of forces and resistances. Their number is infinite and they are all always present. They are also always changing. They are meaningless in their variety and changes except as discriminated in the light of purpose. They are viewed as static facts, if the change is not significant from the viewpoint of the purpose, or as both static and dynamic facts.

This discrimination divides the world into two parts; the facts that are immaterial, irrelevant, mere background; and the part that contains the facts that apparently aid or prevent the accomplishment of purpose. As soon as that discrimination takes place, decision is in bud. It is in the state of selecting among alternatives. These alternatives are either to utilize favorable factors, to eliminate or circumvent unfavorable ones, or to change the purpose. Note that if the decision is to deal with the environment, this automatically introduces new but more detailed purposes, the progeny, as it were, of the parent purpose; but if the decision is to change the purpose rather than deal with the environment, the parent is sterile. It is abandoned, and a new purpose is selected, thereby creating a *new* environment in the light of *that* purpose.

This looks like metaphysical speculation if one thinks of it as individual and personal—undemonstrable assumptions, speculative reasoning. But it can be observed in an organization, at least sufficiently to corroborate it roughly. Thus if the president of a telephone company for good reasons orders[3] two poles carrying a cable removed from the north side of First Street between A and B Streets to the opposite side of First Street, it can, I think, be approximately demonstrated that carrying out

---

[2] Care should be taken to keep in mind that environment throughout does not mean merely physical aspects of the environment, but explicitly includes social aspects, although physical rather than other aspects are used for illustration as simpler. In many organizations, however, the physical aspects are constant and it is the social aspects which are pertinent. This is the case especially when the purpose is a concrete expression of social ideas or attitudes, as, for example, in ritualistic types of action whether religious or political.

[3] Partly to illustrate several statements in this essay I may say that it is necessary to imagine extreme conditions to suppose he would issue such an order. Ordinarily what he would do would be to inquire whether it would be feasible to take the action suggested, or what would be involved in doing so, or he would state the problem and ask for its solution, etc. The executive art is nine-tenths inducing those who have authority to use it in taking pertinent action.

that order involves perhaps 10,000 decisions of 100 men located at 15 points, requiring successive analyses of several environments, including social, moral, legal, economic, and physical facts of the environment, and requiring 9000 redefinitions and refinements of purpose, and 1000 changes of purpose. If inquiry be made of those responsible, probably not more than a half-a-dozen decisions will be recalled or deemed worthy of mention—those that seemed at the moment difficult or momentous, or that were subject to question or proved erroneous. The others will be "taken for granted," all a part of the business or knowing one's business. However, a large part of the decisions, purposes, and descriptions and analyses of the various environments will be a matter of record—short-cut, abbreviated, to be sure, but marking the routes of decisions with fair definiteness. Only in the case of individual workmen shall we be almost completely reduced to speculation as to the number and character of the decisions required, because many of them certainly will relate to the physiological action. . . .

[IV.] THE THEORY OF OPPORTUNISM

The opportunistic element refers to the objective field within which action must take place. The process of decision so far as it relates to this objective field is essentially one of analysis, even though in practice much of the process will be intuitive or not conscious. The analysis of present circumstances is in part the definition of purpose in immediate terms; but it is also the process of finding what present circumstances are significant with reference to that purpose. What events, what objects, what conditions aid, what prevent, the attainment of purpose?

This analysis will lead to the rejection from present interest or attention of most of the innumerable events, objects, details, circumstances of the situation, since under the conditions they are irrelevant to the purpose. This, of course, is sometimes an easy, sometimes a difficult task. It is easy if it has been done before for similar circumstances, if it yields to an established technique of analysis, if it is a solved scientific problem. It is difficult if it is novel, if there is no technique, or no science. For then the analysis is in effect partly unaided surmise, hypothesis, assumption. This fact, even when the decider is aware of it, does not permit escape from decision, though it may lead to negative decision, that is, to decision not to decide the question for the present. Hence, there is no escape from *some* decision once the

process of setting up purpose against environment has begun.

The analysis required for decision is in effect a search for the "strategic factors." The notion of the "strategic factor," a term I borrow from Professor John R. Commons,[4] is related to the term "limiting factor" which is common in scientific work. Professor Commons' use of the word is restricted to certain aspects of managerial and bargaining operations in economic systems, but the restriction to this field is unnecessary; the principle involved is the same in whatever circumstances decision is required. The theory of the strategic factor is necessary to an appreciation of the process of decision, and therefore to the understanding of organization and the executive functions as well as, perhaps, individual purposive conduct. As generally as I can state it, this theory is as follows:

If we take any system, or set of conditions, or conglomeration of circumstances existing at a given time, we recognize that it consists of elements, or parts, or factors, which together make up the whole system, set of conditions, or circumstances. Now, if we approach this system or set of circumstances, with a view to the accomplishment of a purpose (and only when we so approach it), the elements or parts become distinguished into two classes: those which if absent or changed would accomplish the desired purpose, provided the others remain unchanged; and these others. The first kind are often called limiting factors, the second, complementary factors. Moreover, when we concentrate our attention upon a *restricted* or subsidiary system or set of circumstances, we often find, on the basis of previous experience or knowledge, that the circumstances fail to satisfy the requirements of purpose because they lack an additional element or elements, that is, elements which are known to exist in the *larger* environment. These are likewise limiting factors.

The limiting (strategic) factor is the one whose control, in the right form, at the right place and time, will establish a new system or set of conditions which meets the purpose. Thus if we wish to increase the yield of grain in a certain field and on analysis it appears that the soil lacks potash, potash may be said to be the strategic (or limiting) factor. If a tank of water is to be used for cleaning purposes, and is found to contain sediment, the sediment is the strategic (limiting) factor in the use of the water for cleaning. If a machine

4 John R. Commons, *Institutional Economics*, The Macmillan Company, New York, 1934, *passim*, but especially chap. 9, pp. 627–633.

is not operable because a screw is missing, the screw is the strategic (limiting) factor.[5]

Where the crucial element or part present or absent is a thing or physical element or compound or ingredient it is convenient to call it "limiting" factor; but when personal or organizational action is the crucial element, *as it ultimately is in all purposive effort,* the word "strategic" is preferable. This preference relates to a distinction in the use of the analysis. If its purpose is knowledge for its own sake, that is, if the purpose is immediately scientific, the term "limiting factor" conveys the relatively static situation of the analyst. If the purpose is not knowledge but decision as to action, "strategic factor" conveys the relatively changing position of the analyst, in which the subjective aspects of decision interact with the objective field in which it is developed.

The fact that a strategic factor is always involved is overlooked because the personal or organization action required often seems trivial; the necessary effort is less than that required to analyze the situation or system. For example, it may require great effort to determine that the land needs potash, but little effort to get the potash. Nevertheless, when the need has been determined, a new situation has arisen because of the fact of knowledge or the assumption that potash is the limiting factor; and instead of potash, the limiting factor *obtaining* potash then becomes the strategic factor; and this will change progressively into *obtaining* the money to *buy* potash, then *finding* John to *go* after potash, then *getting* machines and men to *spread* potash, etc., etc. Thus the determination of the strategic factor is itself the decision which at once reduces purpose to a new level, compelling search for a new strategic factor in the new situation. Says Commons:

> But the limiting and complementary factors are continually changing places. What was the limiting factor becomes complementary, when once it has come under control; then another factor is the limiting one. The limiting factor, in the operation of an automobile, at one time may be the electric spark; at another the gasoline; at another the man at the wheel. This is

the meaning of efficiency—the control of the changeable limiting factors at the right time, right place, right amount, and right form in order to enlarge the total output by the expected operation of complementary factors.[6]

If we rephrase this last sentence to accord with our terminology and our broader subject, it will read: "This is the meaning of effective decision—the control of the changeable strategic factors, that is, the exercise of control at the right time, right place, right amount, and right form so that purpose is properly redefined and accomplished."

Professor Commons continues:

> But out of the complex happenings, man selects the limiting factors for his purposes. If he can control these, then the other factors work out the effects intended. The "cause" is volitional control of the limiting or strategic factors. . . . The "effects" are the operations of the complementary factors. . . .

With the distinctions in phraseology which Commons makes for his purposes we are not concerned. I think it sound to say that the strategic factor always determines the *action* that is controlling, even in the case of what he calls the limiting factor. It is not the element that is missing but the action that could procure the missing element that is the controlling factor. To determine what element should be changed or is missing is the first step in defining the *action* required. Decision relates to *action,* whether it be in the field of business transactions, political transactions, mechanical operations, chemical combinations, scientific experimentation, or whatever relates to accomplishment of intention.

The strategic factor is, then, the center of the environment of decision. It is the point at which choice applies. To *do* or not to do *this,* that is the question. Often there are tentatively several strategic factors, any one of which meets the immediate situation or satisfies the necessity of immediate purpose. This expands the horizon into the less immediate future, increases the objective field. The final strategic selection will be made on the basis of the estimate of less immediate future consequences.

---

[5] There may be more than one limiting factor, in which they may all be taken as a limiting set, or broken down to single factors for action in some order.

[6] Commons, *op. cit.,* p. 629.

15

*Basic Frameworks for Decisions**

CHARLES Z. WILSON and MARCUS ALEXIS

INTRODUCTION

Decision making has been an integral part of the management literature for more than half a century. But because of an immoderate emphasis on decision-making as an hierarchial "right," explorations of the behavioral aspects of the decision process(es) were at a minimum for much of this time. It was not until the early 50's that developments in decision theory gained a noticeable momentum. During this period we witnessed, on the one hand, the emergence of more powerful and sophisticated tools of mathematics and statistics; and, on the other hand, a revitalization of the social sciences. Together these developments forged the intellectual setting from which much of the current contributions to decision theory evolves.[1]

Unfortunately, however, the bulk of the literature on decision theory is developed along rigorous lines and spanned across several disciplines requiring more than a modest amount of mathematics, statistics, psychology, sociology, and economics. Much of these materials are incomprehensible to the non-specialist and in many cases pose a formidable challenge for the specialist. The purpose of this paper is to present a panoramic view of frameworks and related decision concepts underlying the wide range of decision models now in use. For the purposes of this paper, the discussion is anchored to two general types of frameworks. We have designated one type of framework as "closed." This is the classical decision situation where a decision maker faces a known set of alternatives and selects one or several of such courses of action by a "rational selection" process.[2] The second general type of framework is designated as "open." It parallels the "adaptive" or "learning" model.[3] This particular kind of framework is designated to facilitate a more complex view of the decision process. The act of choice spans many dimensions of behavior; rational as well as nonrational aspects.

"Open" and "closed" decision models, of course, are not mutually exclusive. One of the contentions of this paper is that both general types of decision models result from the same set of basic decision elements. Differences between the types stem mainly from the recognition and degree of emphasis accorded certain of the elements.

Decision Elements Of major interest to students of decision theory is the "complete" decision model. For a decision model to be "complete," that is, universally applicable, it must be able to prescribe behavior in the most complex as well as simplest cases. It must be capable of reflecting all dimensions of choice situations. Needless to say, the search for the "complete" model is a shifting goal and perhaps will continue to elude dynamic, aspiring

* Reprinted by permission of the publisher from the *Journal of the Academy of Management,* vol. 5, no. 2, pp. 151–164, August, 1962. Mr. Wilson is associate professor at the University of Southern California and Mr. Alexis is associate professor in the College of Business Administration at the University of Rochester. The authors . . . wish to acknowledge the assistance they have been given from the Behavioral Theory of The Firm project which is being carried on at the Graduate School of Industrial Administration, Carnegie Institute of Technology.

[1] There are several interesting summaries of developments in social science fields. See Ward Edwards, "The Theory of Decision Making," *Psychological Review,* vol. 51, pp. 380–471, September, 1954; William J. Gore and Fred S. Silander, "A Bibliographical Essay on Decision Making," *Administrative Science Quarterly,* vol. 4, pp. 97–121, June, 1959.

For a survey of quantitative developments, see Robert Schlaifer, *Probability and Statistics for Business Decisions,* McGraw-Hill Book Company, New York, 1959; Herman Chernoff and Lincoln E. Moses, *Elementary Decision Theory,* John Wiley & Sons, Inc., New York, 1959; and R. M. Thrall, C. H. Coombs, and R. L. Davis, *Decision Processes,* John Wiley & Sons, Inc., New York, 1954.

[2] Herbert A. Simon, "Some Strategic Considerations in the Construction of Social Science Models," Paul F. Lazarsfeld (ed.), *Mathematical Thinking in the Social Sciences,* The Free Press of Glencoe, New York, 1954.

[3] Kenneth J. Arrow, "Utilities, Attitudes, Choice: A Review Article," *Econometrica,* vol. 26, pp. 1–23, January, 1958.

researchers. The persistent research nevertheless has been rewarding. As a by-product of attempts to define and outline the "complete" model, we have come to recognize at least six elements common to all decisions: (1) the state of nature; (2) the decision maker; (3) the goals or ends to be served; (4) the relevant alternatives and the set of actions from which a choice will be made; (5) a relation which produces an ordering of alternatives in some arrangement; and (6) the choice itself, the selection of one or some combination of alternatives.

The state of nature refers to those aspects of the decision maker's environment which affect his choice. Included herein are the relationships between choices and outcomes. These relationships may be random, that is, probabilistic. It is also possible for the relationships not to be known by the decision maker.

The individual or group making a choice is referred to as the decision maker. The decision maker is influenced not only by facts of the choice situation; he is also a product of his environment—the total set of social, political and economic forces around him.

By goals or ends are meant those objectives which the decision maker seeks to attain. In some choice situations the goals are clearly defined and operative. In others, such as the sequential choice situation, where choices are influenced by past choice(s) and outcome(s), goals are not always identifiable, operational or stable.

Alternatives, ordering of relations, and choice will not be discussed here because of the depth of coverage given in the sections immediately following.

By specifying the nature of these elements or in some cases according them mere recognition, it is possible to define a range of frameworks.

"CLOSED" DECISION MODELS

Organizations are goal-oriented systems. That is, they are designed to improve the planning, problem-solving and decision-making abilities of individuals in pursuit of common goals. Therefore, it is not surprising that the most commonly used and accepted analytical framework for choice behavior or decision-making in organizations is the "closed" decision model.

At the center of this framework is a concept of rationality rooted in the consciousness of individual choice behavior. Usually an individual is faced in a given situation with a number of choices or several possible courses of action. Each course of action is likely to lead to a unique consequence or to one of several possible consequences. We call an individual rational if he takes into account the possible consequences of actions open to him, if he is aware of a certain preference ordering and considers it, and if, in the light of such knowledge, he chooses that course of action which, in his estimation, leads to the best or most preferred consequence. In terms of the six elements common to all decision models, the ideal rational man makes a choice(s) on the basis of:

1. A known set of relevant alternatives with corresponding outcomes.

2. An established rule or relation which produces an ordering of the alternatives.

3. Maximizing something such as money rewards, income, physical goods or some form of utility.

Many of the widely accepted decision models in management science assume a kind of administrative rationality similar to that prescribed for the ideal rational man.[4] Such models are structured in "closed" frameworks. They are "closed" because of the minimal weight given to the environment of the decision maker, and the complexity of the act of choice as such.

Linear programming problems are particularly interesting examples of rational choice or "closed" decision-making. Consider this simple production decision. Company T has two products, A and B, which can be produced in two different departments, I and II. The departments have different production capacities and unit profit per item of production. The decision is to select that combination of products A and B which best utilizes the total available capacity. Let's suppose that the following is given:

X_a, X_b—are possible quantities of product A and B

2.00, 2.50—are unit profits (dollars) for product A and B

.50, 1.0 —are percentages of capacity required to produce a unit of product A and B in department I

.80, .50—are percentages of capacity required to produce a unit of product A and B in department II

---

[4] David W. Miller and Martin K. Starr, *Executive Decisions and Operations Research*, Prentice-Hall, Inc., (Englewood Cliffs, N.J., 1960; also C. West Churchman, Russell L. Ackoff, and E. Leonard Arnoff, *Operations Research*, John Wiley & Sons, Inc., New York, 1957.

Then the model for our decision consists of an objective function

(1) profit $= 2.00X_a + 2.50X_b$

to be maximized subject to

(2) Dept. I: $.50X_a + 1.00X_b \leqslant 100\%$
 Dept. II: $.80X_a + .50X_b \leqslant 100\%$

and

(3) $X_a > 0$ and $X_b > 0$.

That is, the production of any one of the departments must not exceed its full capacity but always be positive.

The goals or ends to be served are represented by profits. In other words, profits are a substitute for the whole structure of organization goals.

The decision maker can identify all feasible alternatives. The objective function combined with the constrained set of production possibilities makes possible the generation of a complete set of feasible solutions. The growth of computer operations and effective information systems has greatly enhanced this particular aspect of "closed" models.

Finally, problem solving algorithms such as the simplex method not only generate but also order feasible solutions and hence assure the selection of an "optimal" course of action.[5] Linear programming applications, in general, use restricted but very powerful "closed" models.

Games of strategy (Game Theory) are also structured in "closed" frameworks.[6] There are (1) clearly defined goals; (2) a number of alternatives open at each phase of the situation and; (3) players or participants who can estimate the consequences of their choices. The latter implies taking into consideration that outcomes are determined not only by one's own choice but also by choices of others. Thus, we have a "rational routine": identify alternatives, order, and select "best" course of action in light of predetermined goals.

There are countless other examples of "closed" models. Organizational decision making in general is concerned with sets of problems that can be framed in the typical "closed" choice situation. Limited resources, if not other factors, will act as ultimate restraints. "Closed"

models, therefore, have enjoyed an increasing popularity. Recent developments have served to broaden the applicability of "closed" decision models by giving extensive attention to several states of nature often ignored. The remainder of this section will be devoted to a discussion of the impact of these developments on those decision elements emphasized in "closed" frameworks.

Alternatives: Action-Outcome Relations

One way that different states of nature affect decision models is through the correspondence between alternatives (choices) and the posssible outcome (consequences). There exist three knowledge states of choice-outcome relations.[7]

(a) *Certainty:* It is assumed that there is complete and accurate knowledge of the consequence of each choice.

(b) *Uncertainty:* The consequences of each choice cannot be defined by a correspondence relationship even within a probabilistic framework.

(c) *Risk:* It is assumed that accurate knowledge about the probability distribution of the consequence of each alternative exists.

Certainty implies a state of awareness on the part of decision makers that seldom exists. The emphasis on certainty or deterministic foundations in decision-making is a holdover from the early associations of social and physical sciences. Some contended that the laws of the physical sciences and the related deterministic quantitative methodology might be extended to social behavior.[8] But the contemporary revolution in both social and physical sciences has done much to minimize this view.

Genuine uncertainty is untenable in "closed" decision models. A basic premise in all "closed" decision models is that alternatives and consequences as well as goals are given. Thus, at least equal probabilistic measures can be assigned to possible outcomes of a given course of action. The current developments in subjective probability have done much to eliminate states of genuine uncertainty.

It is fair to say that models of risk dominate the kinds of foundations assumed in decision theory. The likelihood of each of the possible outcomes resulting from a particular course of action can generally be stated in either an

---

[5] There are other algorithms but the simplex approach is most widely used. See George B. Dantzig, "Maximization of a Linear Function of Variables Subject to Linear Inequalities," in T. C. Koopmans (ed.), *Activity Analysis of Production and Allocation,* John Wiley & Sons, Inc., New York, 1951.

[6] Anatol Rapoport, *Fights, Games and Debates,* University of Michigan Press, Ann Arbor, Mich., 1960, chap. 6.

[7] James G. March and Herbert A. Simon, *Organizations,* John Wiley & Sons, Inc., New York, 1959, p. 137.

[8] Rashevsky, for example, illustrates how much of the methodology of physical sciences is applicable to social behavior. See James S. Coleman, "An Expository Analysis of Rashevsky's Social Behavior Models," in Lazarsfeld, *op. cit.,* pp. 105–165.

objective or subjective probabilistic frame of reference. This is true if *all* outcomes for a given course of action cannot be specified independently. The U. S. Department of Commerce cannot, for example, list all of the consequences of a $5 billion decline in new plant expenditure. But it is nevertheless feasible for government economists to determine within a probabilistic framework the likelihood of certain major consequences.

Certainty and uncertainty may be thought of as limiting cases of risk.

Objective Probability. Objective probability is fashioned from the regularity of *en masse* behavior. Its operational meaning flows from the Law of Large Numbers which asserts: the probability of any specified departure from the expected relative frequency of an event becomes smaller and smaller as the number of events considered becomes larger and larger. Stating this differently, given a large number of events and the relative frequency with which each event takes place, a stated probability of a particular event becomes more reliable as the number of events considered are increased.

We may define the objective or *a priori* probability of an event as the relative frequency with which an event would take place, given a large but finite number of observations. More generally, the probability of an event E, denoted by $P(E)$, can be represented by the ratio:

number of possible outcomes of E

total number of possible experiment outcomes

Experiment is assumed to be any set of observed phenomena. The total number of outcomes in this case is finite and countable and the number of outcomes of E are less than or equal to the total number of outcomes. In all cases where E is not the only possible outcome, a sufficiently large number of outcome observations will show E to be less than the total and hence $P(E)$ to be less than 1.

$P(E)$ is the probability measure of a simple event, one which is not related to the occurrence of any other event. If A denotes a choice and $a_1, a_2, a_3 \ldots a_n$ denote a set of outcomes, $P(a_1|A), P(a_2|A), P(a_3|A) \ldots P(a_n|A)$ are compound events; more specifically, they are *conditional probability* measures of $a_1, a_2, a_3 \ldots a_n$ when A is chosen. The values of $P(a_1|A), P(a_2|A), P(a_3|A) \ldots P(a_n|A)$ may be determined experimentally as in coin tossing or by empirically derived frequency distributions. *Extensive* experience is a basic requirement for "good" objective probability meas-

ures. One, for example, could toss a die six times to determine the probability or likelihood of the number two occurring. Suppose one observes that two (2) occurs ⅓ of the time; i.e., $P(X=2) = ⅓$ where X is a number on the die. This is an objective measure of the relative frequency of the number two occurring in a toss of the die but it is *not* the probability of two (2). We identify the probability of an event with the relative frequency over a *large number* of tosses. If an unbiased die is tossed a sufficiently large number of times, the relative frequency and, hence, the probability of a two (2) is ⅙; $P(X=2) = ⅙$.

Also, care must be exercised to insure the selection of the "right" statistical model. Contrary to popular beliefs, the normal distribution does not always work well as a generalized theoretical framework for estimating probability measures.[9] In many cases, getting the "right" theoretical framework poses an extremely difficult problem. Selecting the statistical model may be as important an operation in obtaining objective probabilistic measures as acquiring sufficient experience.

Reasonably accurate frequency distributions are available for many types of "closed" decision models. Electric power companies, for example, have years of experience to serve as a basis for estimating the probabilities of generating outages. Likewise, commercial airlines would have little difficulty in estimating the probability of "no-show" reservations.

In recent years, there has been a growing concern about non-recurring decisions. How does one construct a probabilistic foundation when decisions are unique? To the extent that there are unique elements in United States-Cuba relations, it is impossible to assign objective probability measures to the success or failure of particular actions. To date no uniformly acceptable solution method has been devised.

Equally as important, but more hopeful of solution, is the problem of convincing decision makers to use available data. The availability of objective probability measures is no assurance that they will be used in the decision process. The decision maker and experimenter are often different persons and the decision maker may not base his action on objective probabilities developed by the experimenter. If the "staff man" informs the line manager that

---

[9] The central-limit theorem tells us that a population with finite variance and mean has the property that the distribution of sample means drawn from it approaches the normal distribution. But this is only true if the variance is finite!

an alternative T will result in outcome t_1 20% of the time or $P(t_1/T) = .20$, does the superior accept this estimate or adjust it upward (downward)?

Subjective Probability. Subjective probability has a long history, dating back to Jacob Bernoulli in the 17th Century. Renewed interest in the subject has been generated because of the probabilistic base of many decision models and the recognition that decision makers are not always completely informed. Unlike its objective relation, subjective probability is heavily behavioral in its approach.[10] The decision maker is not assumed to maximize on the basis of objective probabilities. He interprets action-outcome likelihoods in terms of personal perceptions. Unless very well informed, his estimates are likely to be different than the objective probabilities. Some experimental evidence strongly suggests a linear correspondence between subjective and objective probability but this does not necessarily mean that decision makers using subjective probability estimates behave *as if* they were acting on the basis of objective probability data. For one thing, behavior is related not only to the estimate of probability but to the subjective value of the expected outcome.

Evidence suggests that the decision maker acts on the basis of some combination of the following:

1. degrees of belief in relative frequency basis of objective probability
2. perceptions of objective probability
3. evaluation of the importance of the situation
4. revocability of the decision

Subjective probabilities may depart from objective measures because of any one of the factors.

The objective probability that an unbiased coin will fall heads on any toss is equal to the probability that it will fall tails. Thus they are both equal to one-half. An observer who is not familiar with the laws of probability might conclude that after a series of heads the coin is more likely to fall heads than tails on succeeding trials. In other words, the observer's limited experience of coin tossing leads him to "believe" that the probability of heads is greater than that of tails. The future actions of the individual may be affected by this perceptive estimate regardless how objective or reliable given probability measures may be.

Any model which seeks to predict decision behavior must recognize the likely discrepancy between personalistic (subjective) and objective probabilities.

Utility: Ordering of Alternatives

Another way of broadening the "closed" decision model to reflect a more "complete" set of elements is through the preference ordering of alternatives by the decision maker. The ordering of alternatives is an operation defined in the domain of the individual's value system. Early writers on utility discussed the ordering of alternatives as an ordinal ranking process (first, second, etc.). To this extent, a range of social or environmental forces shaping the individual's values are brought to bear indirectly in "closed" decision models.

Decision models today require that utility theory be developed beyond the ordinal stage. Each outcome must have an assigned, interval-scaled value. Structuring utility functions with such properties is not always feasible. Except where money or some easily measurable commodity can be taken as equivalent to measures of utility or at least related in an ascertainable manner, the determination of utilities, or even proof of their existence, is a most difficult matter.[11]

Contemporary utility theory starts with a set of human behavior axioms consistent with the generally prescribed concept of rationality in decision choice models. Each axiom is assumed to be testable.[12] That is, the axioms are stated such that the experimenter can assign operational meanings and relations to terms using the disciplines of logic and measure theory.

To date, several axiomatic systems for a theory of utility have been developed. Some are more "complete" than others. A "complete" axiomatic system must include what is known as the closure axiom. This axiom asserts that a person always prefers one of two outcomes or else is indifferent.

The one axiom common to all systems of rational behavior and subject to the most attention is the transitivity axiom. This axiom reads: If A is preferred to B, and B is preferred to C, then A is preferred to C. Without transivity, we could not "link" the many sub-preference systems of an individual.

Developing the Utility Index. The discussions on utility theory seem to indicate the

[10] Leonard J. Savage, *The Foundation of Statistics,* John Wiley & Sons, Inc., New York, 1954.

[11] C. West Churchman, *Prediction and Optimal Decisions,* Prentice-Hall, Inc., Englewood Cliffs, N.J., 1961, chap. 8.
[12] *Ibid.*

following are necessary for the construction of a utility index:

(a) a set of mutually exclusive independent events

(b) an axiomatic system permitting the assignment of numerical values to each outcome

(c) a probability measure of each outcome possibility

(d) the assumption that the decision maker is a maximizer

(e) a willingness to gamble on the part of the decision maker

To construct a utility index, we must be able to derive an interval scale which satisfies the requirement that none of the empirically determined relations are disturbed. This is accomplished if the ratio of two pairs of measures taken on different scales will always be the same. A linear transformation satisfies this requirement.[13] Consider the following example.

A university research team is interested in measuring the subjective value of money to each of a group of students. To measure these subjective values (utilities), the researchers construct an experiment (a choice situation) in which the student is given the alternative of a specified but uncertain (risky) cash prize and of a certain (non-risky) cash prize. To distinguish between the risky and non-risky prizes, the former is referred to as an expected prize and the other as cash reward.

The expected prize is always some probability combination of zero and $1,000. The cash reward varies. A utility value of 100 is arbitrarily assigned to $1,000 and a utility value of zero to zero dollars. The utility of any cash reward is found by multiplying the probability of $1,000 by 100.

By now it is clear that the expected prize is nothing more than a gamble with a payoff of either zero or $1,000. Each gamble is independent of all other gambles and income is stated in numerical terms. Thus we have all the necessary requirements for the construction of an interval scale.

The scale is constructed by finding gambles and cash prizes to which students are indifferent. If a student is indifferent between a gamble involving a 50–50 chance of zero or $1,000 and a cash income of $400, we say *that the utility of $400 is equal* to ½(0) + ½(100) or 50. The student may then be found to be indifferent between a cash income of $600 and a gamble in which the probability of zero is .25 and of $1,000 is .75. The interval scale

value of $600 is then equal to ½(0) + ¾(100) or 75.

This procedure is continued for a large number of cash rewards and expected prizes involving $1,000 and zero. From the data collected, it is possible to express the preference of each student as a mathematical function of money and utility. Utility functions so constructed are not interpersonally comparable. In general it is not possible to construct a function for the students as a group. An exception, of course, would be possible only if all the students had the same subjective valuation of money; that is, they had the same interval scale. This is highly unlikely.

It is easy to generalize from the gamble about the students to ones involving different sums. All that is required for an interval scale is a method by which utility can be expressed as a linear transformation.

Stochastic Choice. Ordinarily if individuals do order all alternatives, they will not be able to assign consistent utility to the same alternatives in repetitive situations without some error. This is particularly true if A is only slightly preferred to B. Instead of asserting absolutely that A is preferred to B, it would be more realistic to say, for example, that A is preferred to B "95% of the time." Or B may be preferred to A "5% of the time." In general such probabilistic preferences would give a more plausible interpretation of "indifferent" or "preferred." By weakening the "consistency requirement" in the axiomatic framework of preference orderings, extensive empirical testing would be more meaningful.[14]

With either one of the above approaches to preference ordering, there are serious obstacles to empirically deriving utility indexes.

Experiments that have been conducted to date indicate the need for an unusually high degree of sophistication in research methods.[15] This complicates the task of enlarging the collection of empirically derived utility functions. Thus it appears that for times to come, the underlying assumptions and valuations of the decision maker in choice situations will remain beyond our reach.

Optimization or Suboptimization?

The decision maker may act as if he is maximizing in "closed" decision models. But his deci-

---

[13] Rapoport, *op. cit.*, pp. 124–128.

[14] Herbert A. Simon, "Theories of Decision-making in Economics and Behavioral Science," *American Economic Review*, vol. 49, no. 3, p. 262, June 1959.

[15] See, for example, Donald Davidson, Patrick Suppes, and Sidney Siegel, *Decision Making: An Experimental Approach*, Stanford University Press, Stanford, Calif., 1957.

sions may not *in fact* be "optimal" for the organization. In organizational decision making, the decision maker may be restricted by the hierarchical arrangement of the organizations and the flows of information through channels. The "closed" decision model for most organizational decision-making postures may therefore depart from the popularized concept of "maximizing" behavior.

Suboptimization is more typical of organizational decision-making. The decision maker acts on the basis of the decision framework and information available to his particular unit or department in the hierarchy. He makes decisions from a "local" point of view.

Such decisions may be optimal for any given department, but less than optimal for the organization as a whole. The organization is affected by the total set of effects; a department may not be. Decisions beneficial to one department may create difficulties elsewhere in the organization which are much greater than the benefits received by the decision maker's department.

A company may decide to charge divisions for the use made of warehousing to assure economic utilization of facilities. The division managers have the alternative of using outside space if it is less costly. If the divisions are charged on the basis of the number of square feet occupied, it is easy for the decision maker to compare the cost of using company facilities versus independent warehouses. If company warehouses are partially empty and a division uses outside warehousing because it is less costly, the decision may well be "best" from the point of view of the division's income statement, but this is not the case for the company as a whole. The additional cost of storing in company facilities would have been zero and company profits would have been higher.

Summarizing the discussion on "closed" decision models, we find that the applicability of such models can be increased by modifying certain of the basic assumptions and relations such as action-outcome sequences and preferences orderings under different states of nature. Undoubtedly these modifications tend to broaden and add some realism to "closed" decision models, but even after such revisions, the theoretical foundations of "closed" models are inadequate to serve as points of departure for a general understanding of the human decision processes. The decision processes are far more dynamic than those depicted by the scheme of a "closed" model.

Goals are not defined in as clear-cut a manner as choice-decision models hypothesize.

Goal-striving behavior occurs within a range of structure of goals. The selection of a particular goal or goal structure is itself a decision. Moreover, information is generally inadequate to identify all alternatives, and relevant alternatives are not necessarily stable; they may change with successive decisions.

There is serious doubt as to the ability of the "closed" decision model to stimulate complex choice behavior, although it may do very well for simple choices.

"OPEN" DECISION MODELS

In "closed" models a few dimensions of the decision environment are selected and admitted into the decision process; action-outcome relations, utility and so on. The decision maker is assumed to be a logical, methodical maximizer. In contrast, the "open" decision model parallels an "open system." Like the open system, it is continually influenced by its total environment. And, of course, it also influences the environment. Decisions shape as well as mirror environment. Contrary to main elements of "closed" decision models, it does not assume that the decision maker can recognize all goals and feasible alternatives. A more realistic view of the decision maker is emphasized. He is a complex mixture of many elements—his culture, his personality, and his aspirations.

Behavioral Foundations of "Open" Decision Model The "open" decision model accents the individual's ability to control his behavior. For the most part, human behavior is learned and not controlled by biological forces shaped by "inborn" dimensions. This means that behavior is the outcome of conscious and unconscious "selective processes" and therefore must reflect the limitations of human cognition and the complexity of man's total environment.

Human Cognition. Between the stimulus or "cue" and the ultimate action which follows, lies a filtering system or image.[16] The image is a construct of relationships, experiences, values and emotions. It is characterized by an internal capacity to grow from within as well as from the retention of external experiences. This point is illustrated by man's capacity to create, from series of unrelated events, ideas that become the sources of monumental essays, names, symphonies or organizations.[17]

The image is the key element in cognitive

[16] Kenneth E. Boulding, *The Image,* University of Michigan Press, Ann Arbor, Mich., 1956.
[17] *Ibid.,* pp. 25–27.

behavior. It contains not only what is, but what might be. Man not only knows, but knows that he knows.[18] The decision maker's decision reflects his perceptions of people, roles, and organizations in addition to his own values and emotions. Even the most intelligent of us act on the basis of images including more than the objective facts of the decision situation.

But despite man's power to behave "rationally," that is to say, his ability to select and order his responses to stimuli, he is bounded by a limited perspective. He possesses limited computational skills and, therefore, does not always make the best use of available information. Often he is inclined to deal with simplified models of real situations.[19]

Thus, the assumptions of "closed" decision models loses meaning in the context of an "open" system. An individual cannot weigh *all* alternatives. And still further, if the decision maker does not possess the ability to recognize and weigh the many choices that may be available, how does he "maximize" in the sense prescribed by "closed" decision models?

Role Behavior.   If each individual's decision is the result of personalized selection process, how then does an organization, or for that matter society, channel such personal-centered behavior toward group defined ends? The answer lies in the make-up of the image. It is true that the image is a nondescript framework of experiences, values and expectations. But it is also characterized by order. Some experiences and expectations are collected and "stored" as single entities. Such programs of experiences and expectations become the basis for standardized responses to recurring stimuli. The whole collection of experiences and expectations, some developed from recurring and others from non-recurring situations are said to form premises for individual decisions.

Thus, to the extent that the organization is able to plant dominating premises it is able to control and unify the behavior of participants. Organization structures provide status systems with roles defined. These become premises for individual decisions and hence behavior. The organization likewise provides experiences and information through training and communication. These, too, are premises for decisions and can become powerful means of influencing individuals toward organizational goals.[20] The role system, however, is perhaps the most discussed method of standardizing individual behavior.

For society as a whole, we also get individual behavior that is generally structured by premises reflecting experiences and expectations associated with roles. Public approval is often dependent on the way one acts and his role. For some roles—motherhood, fatherhood, doctor, etc.—there are well-defined sets of standardized behaviors or norms that must be adhered to by the "acting" individuals. Fathers are expected to be the breadwinners in the American family; they are expected to assume financial responsibility. The laws of society frequently reflect the expectations as to how one is to act in a role. Fathers may be jailed for nonsupport. Creditors may sue husbands for debts incurred by their wives. Every person acts out at least one role for which there is an expected pattern. It may be his role as a citizen, soldier, teacher, student, corporate officer or public official.

Decisions in "Open" Models

The single-choice "open" decision model in some ways resembles a dynamic means-end or "closed" scheme. That is, the decision is made within the framework of a predetermined goal and established alternative. But the comparison ends there. Consider the model in Figure 1.

[18] *Ibid.*
[19] Herbert A. Simon, *Models of Man*, John Wiley & Sons, Inc., New York, 1957, p. 197.

[20] Herbert A. Simon, *Administrative Behavior*, 2d ed., The Macmillan Company, New York, 1957, pp. 123–125.

FIGURE 1   A Single-choice "Open" Model

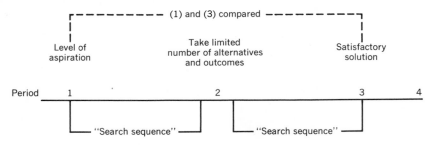

The decision maker passes through three time periods:

Period 1: The individual starts out with an idealized goal structure. He defines one or more action goals as a "first approximation" of the "ideal goal" in the structure. The action goal(s) may be considered as representative of the decision maker's *Aspiration Level*.[21]

Period 2: The individual engages in search activity and defines a limited number of outcomes and alternatives. He does not attempt to establish the relations rigorously. His analysis proceeds from loosely defined rules of approximation. The limited alternatives defined establish a starting point for further search toward a solution.

Period 3. Search among the limited alternatives is undertaken to find a "satisfactory" as contrasted with an "optimal" solution. "Satisfactory" is defined in terms of the aspiration level or action goals.

A number of differences between "closed" and "open" decision models which are not always apparent are highlighted:

1. predetermined goals are replaced by some unidentified structure which is approximated by an aspiration level.

2. all alternatives and outcomes are not predetermined; neither are the relationships between specific alternatives and outcomes always defined.

3. the ordering of all alternatives is replaced by a search routine which considers fewer than all alternatives.

4. the individual does not maximize but seeks to find a solution to "satisfy" an aspiration level.

Even in a single choice situation, the "open" model offers a "deeper" description of the choice process than "closed" decision models. If choices are defined in a stochastic context, this model can be predictive.

The Multiple-choice "Open" Model

The multiple choice "open" model is a more ambitious attempt to emphasize cognition processes in decision making. The model is a hierarchy of "single decisions"; each successive decision is an attempt to improve the outcome in light of new information gained in the previous decisions. It provides a highly realistic simulation of human problem-solving.

The key element in the multiple-choice "open" model is the attainment discrepancy or the difference between the levels of aspiration and achievement. In most cases, some attainment discrepancy is almost certain because of the decision maker's inability to equate with any degree of precision a given outcome with his aspiration level. Generally an outcome can only be identified with a region about the aspiration level. A given outcome is satisfactory (unsatisfactory) or successful (unsuccessful) according to the magnitude of the attainment discrepancy. In our model, only significant discrepancies (plus or minus) are considered.

The attainment discrepancy controls the *modus operandi* for reaching a stable solution in "open" models. The size and direction of the discrepancy induce adjustments in both the level of aspiration and search activity.[22]

In Figure 2, it is explicitly assumed that a "plus" discrepancy increases the level of aspiration and decreases the range of search for solutions. A "negative" discrepancy decreases the level of aspirations and broadens the range of search. These behavioral attributes are specifically defined to assure "bound" properties in the model. This means that the range of fluctuations is restricted. The decision and aspiration level fluctuates between positions of minimum and maximum potential. Lewin *et al.* introduce "bound" properties in a similar model by making the attainment of "highly satisfactory solution" highly improbable, and "highly unsatisfactory solutions" highly probable. The effect of this approach is to make search desirable and probable given an unsatisfactory solution. But as reasonably satisfactory solutions are reached, search becomes undesirable and improbable. There must exist a solution where search activity will cease altogether.

The model in Figure 2 is an adaptive one. The decision maker reacts to the outcome by adjusting his goals (aspiration level) and hence his definition of an acceptable outcome.

The "open" decision model promises a number of fruitful paths toward a "complete" decision model. But it, too, has limitations. The main limitation (rather serious at this point) is the difficulty of discovering and measuring attributes of complex choice situations. Beyond this such models are a source of encouragement for students of decision-making. "Open" decision models add realism to the decision-making framework. The human capacities of the decision maker are given some measure of recognition. "Open" decision models offer a richer explanation of the human decision-

[21] Kurt Lewin et al., "Level of Aspiration," in J. Mcv. Hunt (ed.), *Personality and the Behavior Disorders,* vol. 1, The Ronald Press Company, New York, 1944.

[22] Simon, *Model of Man,* p. 253.

FIGURE 2   The Multiple-choice "Open" Decision Model

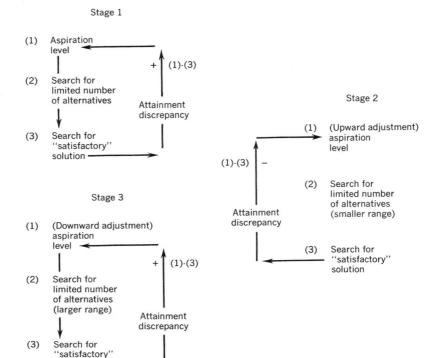

making framework; the dynamics of choice are introduced. Finally, "open" decision models bring to bear the totality of forces—external and internal to the decision maker—influencing a decision.

CONCLUSIONS

There is a growing disenchantment with "closed" decision models in economic and management science circles.[23] A serious re-

consideration of decisions that confront the organization decision maker and the required decision foundations appears to be in order. At this point there is evidence that the most vital decisions are non-recurring. "Search" is required to find feasible alternatives. And often this "search" must not be constrained by the bounds of some preferred solution. Problems solving requires a flexible and dynamic framework. Organizations grow and thus have growing aspirations; so must their problems and what constitute acceptable solutions. The future of "open" decision models, in light of these straws in the wind, seems highly promising.

[23] See, for example, Charles Hitch, "Uncertainties in Operations Research," *Journal of Operations Research*, vol. 8, no. 4, pp. 437–445, July-August, 1960; and Kenneth J. Arrow, "Decision Theory and Operations Research," *Journal of Operations Research*, vol. 5, no. 6, pp. 765–774, December, 1957.

"Operations Research" for Management*

C. C. HERRMANN and J. F. MAGEE

There is a new concept in management. It is called operations research. It has helped companies to solve such diverse business problems as directing salesmen to the right accounts at the right time, dividing the advertising budget in the most effective way, establishing equitable bonus systems, improving inventory and reordering policies, planning minimum-cost production schedules, and estimating the amount of clerical help needed for a new operation.

Operations research makes possible accomplishments like these and many others because (a) it helps to single out the critical issues which require executive appraisal and analysis, and (b) it provides factual bases to support and guide executive judgment. Thus, it eases the burden of effort and time on executives but intensifies the potential of their decision-making role. In this sense operations research contributes toward better management.

What is this thing called operations research? How does it work? How does it differ from other services to management? Where can it be used? How should management get it organized and under way? What are its limitations and potentials? These are all questions that we shall try to answer in the following pages.

ESSENTIAL FEATURES

Operations research apparently means different things to different people. To some businessmen and scientists it means only the application of statistics and common sense to business problems. Indeed, one vice president of a leading company remarked that if his division heads did not practice it every day, they would not last long. To others it is just another and perhaps more comprehensive term for ex-

isting activities like market research, quality control, or industrial engineering. Some businessmen consider it a new sales or production gimmick; some, a product of academic people interfering in the practical world. In truth, operations research is none of these things, as we shall soon see.

It should not be surprising that there has been this confusion. Operations research is not an explicit, easily identifiable concept that developed to meet the specific needs of industry. It was first applied in World War II by groups of scientists who were engaged by the government to help frame recommendations for the improvement of military activities. After the war a few soundly managed companies experimented with it and found that it worked successfully in business operations as well; and it has since gained a secure foothold in industry.

Early attempts by operations analysts to describe their activities, based on the objective of arriving at a precise and comprehensive definition of operations research, tended to be overly generalized, broad, and self-conscious, and suffered from emphasis on military applications. Some of the confusion surrounding the meaning of the term, operations research, has resulted from attempts at identification with special techniques or unnecessarily rigid distinctions between operations research and other management service activities.

Now, let us see if we can cut through some of this confusion.

The first point to grasp is that operations research *is* what its name implies, research on operations. However, it involves a *particular* view of operations and, even more important, a *particular* kind of research.

Operations are considered as an entity. The subject matter studied is not the equipment used, nor the morale of the participants, nor the physical properties of the output; it is the combination of these in total, as an economic process. And operations so conceived are subject to analysis by the mental processes and the methodologies which we have come to associ-

* Reprinted by permission of the publishers from *Harvard Business Review*, vol. 31, no. 4, pp. 100–103, 106–107, 111–112, July-August, 1953. Mr. Herrmann and Mr. Magee are both vice-presidents of Arthur D. Little, Inc.

ate with the research work of the physicist, the chemist, and the biologist—what has come to be called "the scientific method."

The Scientific Method   The basic premise underlying the scientific method is a simple and abiding faith in the rationality of nature, leading to the belief that phenomena have a cause. If phenomena do have a cause, it is the scientist's contention that by hard work the mechanism or system underlying the observed facts can be discovered. Once the mechanism is known, nature's secrets are known and can be used to the investigator's own best advantage.

The scientist knows that his analogue to nature will never be entirely perfect. But it must be *sufficiently* accurate to suit the particular purposes at hand; and, until it is, he must repeat the processes of observation, induction, and theory construction—again and again. Note that a satisfactory solution must be in quantitative terms in order that it can be predictive—the only accepted fundamental test of being physically meaningful.

The scientific method, in its ideal form, calls for a rather special mental attitude, foremost in which is a reverence for facts. Of course all modern executives are accustomed to using figures to control their operations. But they are primarily concerned with results and only secondarily with causes; they interpret their facts in the light of company objectives. This is a much different attitude from seeking out the relationships underlying the facts.

Thus, when an executive looks at sales figures, he looks at them primarily in terms of the success of his sales campaign and its effect on profits. By contrast, when the scientist looks at these same figures, he seeks in them a clue to the fundamental behavior pattern of the customers. By the process of induction he tentatively formulates a theoretical system or mechanism; then by the inverse process of deduction he determines what phenomena should take place and checks these against the observed facts. His test is simple: Does the assumed mechanism act enough like nature— or, more specifically in this case, does it produce quantitative data such as can be used for predicting how the customers will in fact behave? For example:

> In a company manufacturing specialty products, examination of account records showed that customer behavior could be accurately described as a time-dependent Poisson process —a type of phenomenon found widely in nature, from problems in biology to nuclear

physics. This concept yielded the key to establishing measures of the efficiency of the salesmen's work and of the effect of the promotion in building sales. On this basis a new method of directing promotional salesmen to appropriate accounts was constructed—and then tested by careful experiments, to see if sales increases resulted at less than proportionate increases in cost. (The results in this case were spectacular: an over-all sales rise in six figures, and a corresponding gain in net profits.)

Implementation   Through the years mathematical and experimental techniques have been developed to implement this attitude. The application of the scientific attitude and the associated techniques to the study of operations, whether business, government, or military, is what is meant by operations research.

Newton was able to explain the apparently totally unrelated phenomena of planetary motion and objects falling on the earth by the simple unifying concept of gravity. This represented a tremendous step forward in helping men to understand and control the world about them. Again, more recently, the power of the scientific method was demonstrated by the ability of the nuclear physicists to predict the tremendous energy potential lying within the atom.

Here are a few summary examples of the way this same kind of approach has been applied to down-to-earth business problems.

- A company with a number of products made at three different locations was concerned about the items to be produced at each location and the points at which the items would be warehoused. Freight costs constituted a substantial part of the delivered cost of the material. Operations research showed that what appeared to be a complex and involved problem could be broken into a series of rather simple components. Adaptations of linear programing methods were used to find the warehousing schedule which would minimize freight costs. The study is now being extended to determine the best distribution of products among manufacturing plants and warehouse locations in order to minimize net delivered cost in relation to return on investment.

- A manufacturer of chemical products, with a wide and varied line, sought more rational or logical bases than the customary percentage of sales for distributing his limited advertising budget among products, some of which were growing, some stable, and others declining. An operations research study showed that advertising effectiveness was related to three simple characteristics, each of which could be estimated from existing sales data with satisfactory reliability: (a) the total market potential; (b) the rate of growth of sales; (c) the customer loss rate. A mathematical formulation of these three characteristics provided a rational basis for distributing advertising and promotional effort.

- In a company making a line of light machines, the executive board questioned the amount of money spent for missionary salesmen calling on customers. Studies yielded explicit mathematical statements of (a) the relation between the number of accounts called on and the resulting sales volume and (b) the relation between sales costs and manufacturing and distribution costs. These were combined by the methods of differential calculus to set up simple tables for picking the level of promotion in each area which would maximize company net profits. The results showed that nearly a 50% increase in promotional activity was economically feasible and would yield substantial profits.

- An industrial products manufacturer wanted to set time standards as a basis for costs and labor efficiency controls. The operations research group studied several complex operations; expressed the effect of the physical characteristics of products and equipment and the time required to produce a given amount of output in the form of mathematical equations; and then, without further extensive time study or special data collection, set up tables of production time standards according to product characteristics, equipment used, and worker efficiency, which could be applied to any or all of the production operations.

- A company carrying an inventory of a large number of finished items had trouble maintaining sound and balanced stock levels. Despite careful attention and continued modification of reorder points in the light of experience, the stock of many individual items turned out to be either too high for sales or inadequate to meet demand. The problem was solved by a physical chemist who first collected data on the variables, such as size and frequency of order, length of production and delivery time, etc.; then set up an assumed system, which he tried out against extreme sales situations, continually changing its characteristics slightly until it met the necessary conditions—all

on paper (a technique well known to physical scientists); and thus was able to determine a workable system without cost of installation and risk of possible failure.

These examples should serve to give some idea of how the scientific method can be applied. But they represent only a few of the many scientific techniques available (as we shall see when we examine further cases in more detail). Some practitioners even take the rather broad point of view that operations research should include the rather indefinite and qualitative methods of the social fields. Most professional opinion, however, favors the view that operations research is more restricted in meaning, limited to the quantitative methods and experimentally verifiable results of the physical sciences.

BASIC CONCEPTS

There are four concepts of fundamental importance to the practice of operations research: (a) the model, (b) the measure of effectiveness, (c) the necessity for decision, and (d) the role of experimentation.

The Model The most frequently encountered concept in operations research is that of the model—the simplified representation of an operation, containing only those aspects which are of primary importance to the problem under study. It has been of great use in facilitating the investigation of operations. To illustrate with some familiar types of "models" from other fields:

1. In aeronautical engineering the model of an aeroplane is used to investigate the aerodynamic properties in a wind tunnel. While perfectly adequate for this purpose, it would hardly do for practical use. It has no seats; it may not even be hollow. It is, however, a satisfactory physical model for studying the flight characteristics of the ship.

2. Another, quite different kind of model, with which we are all familiar, is the accounting model. This is essentially a simplified representation on paper, in the form of accounts and ledgers, of the flow of goods and services through a business enterprise. It provides measures of the rate of flow, the values produced, and the performances achieved, and to that extent is useful (though it is hardly a realistic representation of *operations*).

3. Many models are used in physics. Three-dimensional models of complex molecules

are probably most familiar to laymen, but the most powerful models in this field are sets of mathematical equations.

There are several different types of operations research models. Most of them are mathematical in form, being a set of equations relating significant variables in the operation to the outcome. . . .

Another type of model frequently used is the punched-card model, where components of the operation are represented by individual punched cards; masses of these are manipulated on standard punched-card equipment. For example, in a study of a sales distribution problem, each customer, of thousands served by the company, was represented by a punched card containing significant information about his location, type of business, frequency of purchase, and average rate of business. The punched cards representing the customers could then be subjected to assumed promotional treatments, with the effects of the promotions punched into the cards. The resulting business could be calculated and an evaluation made of alternative sales-promotion campaigns.

Occasionally a model is physical like the ones often used by engineers. For example, the use of a hydrokinetic model has been proposed in the study of a mass advertising problem. The fluid flowing through the model would represent business of various types going to the company or to competitors as a result of various forms of the company's own and competitive promotional efforts (represented in the model by forces acting on the fluids).

Operations research models can also be distinguished as exact or probabilistic:

1. An *exact* model is used in operations or processes where chance plays a small role, where the effect of a given action will be reasonably closely determined. Exact models can be used, for example, in long-range production scheduling problems in the face of known or committed demand. The exact model is sufficiently accurate since it can be assumed that, barring a major catastrophe, over the long run planned and actual production will be reasonably close.

2. The *probabilistic* model, on the other hand, contains explicit recognition of uncertainty. Such models are of great use in the analysis of advertising problems, where the unpredictability of consumers plays a great role. . . . They make extensive use of the highly developed theory of probability, which has come to be of such great value in the physical science. One customarily thinks of a physicist as dealing with rather exact concepts and highly predictable experiments. Yet physicists faced a problem equivalent to the advertising problem in predicting atomic activity. Methods developed for physical problems involving mass behavior under random conditions can be applied with great facility and value to operations.

The model is a major goal of the operations research analyst. In one sense, the construction of the model, or a faithful representation of the operation, is the scientist's primary job. In doing it he develops a theory to explain the observed characteristics of the operation. . . . The remaining task is to interpret this theory through the manipulation of the model, whether mathematical or physical.

Measure of Effectiveness   Related to the concept of a model or theory of operation is the measure of effectiveness, whereby the extent to which the operation is attaining its goal can be explicitly determined. One common over-all measure of effectiveness in industrial operations is return on investment; another is net dollar profit. Measures of effectiveness down the scale might be the number of customers serviced per hour, the ratio of productive to total hours of a machine operation, etc.

A *consistent* statement of the fundamental goals of the operation is essential to the mathematical logic of the model. (It does not matter if the goals are complex.) Just as the model cannot make 2 and 2 add up to 5, so it is impossible to relate fundamentally inconsistent objectives and produce consistent and meaningful results.

Operations research has frequently brought to light inconsistencies in company goals. Take production scheduling, for instance. Very often its object has been stated as scheduling production to meet sales forecasts with minimum production costs, with minimum inventory investment, and without customer-service failure. Yet minimizing inventory investment typically requires the use of start-and-stop or at best uneven production plans, resulting in excessive production costs; and eliminating the risk of not being able to ship every customer order immediately requires huge inventories, in the face of fluctuating and at least partially unpredictable demand.

The solution is to combine and sublimate such otherwise inconsistent goals to a higher unified and consistent goal. To illustrate:

The diverse goals of customer service, production economy, and investment minimization can be expressed in terms of costs—the cost of inefficient production (hiring, training, overtime, etc.), the cost of investment in inventory (the rate of interest the treasurer wishes to charge to conserve his funds or perhaps the return on investment which can be earned through alternative uses of the available funds), and the cost of inability to meet a customer's demand (estimated loss of goodwill and future business). While the latter two costs are primarily policy costs, experience has shown that they are sufficiently determinable and realistic to afford a basis for management decision.

The three component costs can then be cast in an algebraic equation expressing their interrelationships in terms of total scheduling cost; and the minimum total scheduling cost becomes the one, consistent goal.

Note that, once set up, the algebraic equation can be worked in reverse. Thus, the sales manager might be told how much the company can *afford* to pay for an inventory large enough to avoid varying risks of failure to meet consumer demand.

This kind of clarification of goals is particularly important in relating subordinate and over-all company goals—as in the case of a department run efficiently at the expense of other departments or of a promotion budget based on a fixed percentage of sales without regard to the adverse effects on manufacturing budgets.

The statement of a complete and wholly consistent goal of company operations must be recognized as an ideal. Business goals are very complex, and to catch the full flavor of the objectives of an intricate business operation in any simple, explicit statement is difficult. Many business goals remain, and probably ever will remain, at least in part intangible—e.g., efforts to improve employee morale or contribute to the public welfare. To that extent, the objective of operations research must be more modest than the construction of a complete model and the measurement of the extent to which the operation is attaining the complete set of goals established for it. But it still can serve to clarify the interdependency of those intangibles with the company goals which in fact are measurable, thus providing a guide to executive decision.

Necessity for Decision   The third concept inherent in operations research is that of decision and decision making. An essential element in all true operations research problems is the existence of alternative courses of action, with a choice to be made among them; otherwise the study of an operation becomes academic or theoretical. This should be clear from the cases already cited.

In sum, the objective of operations research is to clarify the relation between the several courses of action, determine their outcomes, and indicate which measures up best in terms of the company goal. But note that, while this should be of assistance to the executive in making his decision intelligently, in every case the ultimate responsibility still lies with him.

Role of Experimentation   The fourth significant concept concerns the role of experimentation. Operations research is the application of experimental science to the study of operations. The theory, or model, is generally built up from observed data or experience, although in some cases the model development may depend heavily on external or a priori information. In any event, the theory describing the operation must always be verifiable experimentally. Two kinds of experiments are important in this connection:

1. The first kind is designed simply to get information. Thus, it often takes the form of an apparently rather impractical test. In one case the operations analysts directed advertising toward potential customers the company knew were not worth addressing, and refrained from addressing customers the company typically sought—and for a very simple reason. There was plenty of evidence indicating what happened when advertising was directed toward those normally addressed but not enough about its effects upon those *not* normally addressed. To evaluate the effectiveness of the advertising, therefore, it was necessary to find out what happened to those normally promoted when they were not promoted, and what happened to those normally not promoted when they were.

2. The other type of experiment is the critical type; it is designed to test the validity of conclusions. Again, what appear to be rather impractical forms of experimentation are sometimes used. Thus, in the most sensitive experiments of this type, the validity of the theory or model can often be tested most revealingly in terms of the results of extreme policies rather than in terms of the more normal policy likely to be put into practice. . . .

EVALUATION

In perspective, what is the current status of operations research? What are its contributions, its limitations, its future?

Contributions   Case histories show that operations research provides a basis for arriving at an integrated and objective analysis of operating problems. Characteristically, operations research tends to force an expansion in viewpoint and a more critical, questioning attitude. It also stimulates objective thinking, partly because it emphasizes broad purposes and partly because the mathematical nature of the model and techniques limits the influence of personal bias.

The results of operations research studies are quantitative. They provide an opportunity for sound estimates in terms of requirements, objectives, and goals, and a basis for more precise planning and decision making.

The contributions of operations research to business analysis and planning have been important and substantial. Here are two worth singling out:

1. *The application of organized thinking to data already existing within the company*—Frequently a major contribution has been the location, collection, and classification of existing data scattered through widely separated branches of the company. In one recent study, an operations research team found the same fundamental problem cropping up under various guises in a number of different parts of the company. Each division or section had its own point of view toward the problem, and each had significant information bearing on it that was unavailable to the others. This sort of thing happens despite the most sound and progressive management; operations research tends to rectify it.

2. *The introduction of new concepts and new methods of analysis*—Some of these concepts, such as information theory, control theory, and certain aspects of statistical mechanics have been carried over from other fields; the physical sciences, and in particular modern physics, have been a very fruitful source of transplanted analytical techniques. But there are also certain original contributions, such as the newborn theories of clerical organization and consumer behavior, which suggest the possibility of developing further tools for attacking important business problems. All these techniques make it possible to explore the effects of alternate courses of action before management becomes committed to one of them.

Limitations   Operations research is hardly a cure-all for every business ill; neither is it a source of automatic decisions. It is limited to the study of tangible, measurable factors. The many important factors affecting business decisions that remain intangible or qualitative must continue to be evaluated on the basis of executive judgment and intuition. Often they make it necessary to adjust or modify the conclusions drawn from the quantitative analysis of the researchers. Professional personnel in operations research strongly emphasize this distinction between the operations research responsibility for analysis and the executive responsibility for decision. They point with approval to cases like this one:

> In a recent series of conferences called to implement the results of a long and major operations research investigation, the analysts emphasized that their conclusions were based in part on the assumption that the output of a plant in question could be increased substantially at the existing level of efficiency. The executive responsible for the operation of the plant felt that this assumption was a sound one. The official responsible for the ultimate decision, however, decided to follow a more conservative course of action than the one indicated by the study, primarily because of his estimate of the psychological effect that increases in volume would have on the plant personnel.

The fact that operations research is scientific in character rather than expert means that more time is required to achieve useful conclusions than in the case of normal engineering analyses. As an applied science, the work is torn between two objectives: as "applied" it strives for practical and useful work; as "science" it seeks increasing understanding of the basic operation, even when the usefulness of this information is not immediately clear. The executive who plans to support research work of this character must be fairly warned of the need for restraint. The natural tendency to require that the studies or analyses be "practical" can, if enforced too rigidly, result in the loss of substantial benefits. Also, the results of studies of this type are necessarily somewhat speculative. When operations research is purchased, neither the specific program to be followed, the precise questions to be answered, nor the successful achievement of results can be guaranteed.

Recognition of this difference between operations research and more conventional engineering methods is essential to the satisfaction of both the controlling executive and the analyst.

Problems Ahead   Thinking ahead about the future of operations research, the principal internal problem which it faces is the development of a reserve of manpower adequately trained and motivated. There is a serious need at the present time for trained personnel to carry forward even the present limited level of activity. Lack of manpower, even now, threatens the quality of the work. The insufficient supply of adequately trained and experienced men to meet the demand can create a vacuum, drawing in poorly trained persons and making maintenance of standards difficult. The growing interest among mathematicians, physicists, and others is easing this problem somewhat, however, and colleges and universities have taken the first steps in training young men to fill the gap. The problem the academic institutions face is primarily lack of sound case material and the current amorphous state of a subject with uncertain acceptance in industry generally. Industrial support of educational efforts by providing realistic case material and opportunities for field investigations would be of tremendous help.

The most serious problem in external relationships is probably the need to develop efficient means for communicating ideas and results of research to executive users. The more experienced operations research groups have come to realize that explaining or "selling" conclusions is just as important as arriving at conclusions, if they are in fact to be useful. The communication needs are simple: in short, an ability to express clearly and concisely conclusions based on lengthy studies, to organize results in terms of interest to the reader and user, and to recognize that executives'

interests are more practical than the researchers'. . . .

New Horizons   In conclusion, the future of operations research appears reasonably bright at the present time. Successful applications in industry are fulfilling the hopes of its early supporters, and the skepticism of businessmen is tending to break down as successful case histories pile up and become available for publication.

The areas of potential application of operations research appear broad. The future holds possible extensions such as the development of strategic concepts through the applications of the much heralded (but as yet largely untested) theory of games and by the development of a fundamental understanding of the impact of advertising and merchandising methods.

How will operations research help in the future to clarify the role of the executive? Present indications are that it will live up to its expectations of helping executives to make decisions more intelligently, but the decisions will always remain to be made. The possibility of removing all subjective and qualitative factors must be deemed at the present time to be more a hope than a real possibility, and the construction of completely consistent and logical goals, while a reasonable objective in decision making, is probably unattainable. The balancing of the responsibilities to society, consumers, owners, and employees will therefore still be the fundamental task of executives.

17

Making OR Effective for Management*

ROBERT A. HAMMOND

In recent years, operations research has established itself as a remarkably potent tool

* Reprinted by permission of the publisher from *Business Horizons*, vol. 5, no. 1, pp. 73–82, Spring, 1962. Mr. Hammond is an associate in the New York office of McKinsey & Company, Inc., management consultants.

for solving business problems. Its potential increases as research produces new technical developments and as business feels the pressure to sharpen the impact of planning and decision-making procedures. Both the academic world and industry have made significant strides in improving the capability of OR by refining concepts, developing advanced mathematical techniques, and applying more effective computer hardware. At the same time, business executives have become increasingly receptive to trying out and adopting these new methods and, as a result, OR has been accepted by many companies.

Yet, despite the warm reception OR has enjoyed and despite the OR success stories in current business and technical publications, praise for OR is not unanimous. A canvass of any representative sample of companies would reveal a large number of disillusioned rather than enthusiastic managements, and discontinued rather than flourishing OR programs.

Why has OR been successful in some companies and not in others? In carrying out OR projects, what are the most common obstacles to the profitable solution of assignments? How can management deal with these obstacles to ensure adequate returns on its investment in OR? Can more managements profitably use this powerful technique?

In this article, I shall analyze these questions and explain how companies have obtained maximum benefit from OR. From this, some guidelines will be developed for use by: (1) management responsible for organizing and directing OR activities in a company; (2) operating management (the ultimate users of OR work); and (3) OR staff.

PROBLEMS IN EFFECTIVENESS

Management needs first of all a yardstick with which to measure whether or not an OR project has been a success or failure so that it can focus attention on specific problems in the effective use of OR and ways of solving them. Any one of several criteria can, of course, be used to measure OR achievement. The technical quality of the analysis and solution, for example, is one possible yardstick. Another is the improvement in management's understanding of the problem. The expected profit improvement or cost reduction is still another.

A more fundamental criterion than any of these is necessary, however, and can be found in the one element common to all three possibilities: the best solution of the business problem must be *effectively implemented*. In this lies the measure of OR success. Using effective implementation as a criterion provides a starting point for determining what obstacles most frequently delay, or totally prevent, the success of an OR project.

A review of many companies' experience in the management of OR shows that there are many impediments to the effective completion of an OR project. Of these, four seem to be particularly detrimental: (1) overemphasis on technique; (2) poor communication between the OR team and management; (3) failure to make use of the experience and judgment of operating managers; and (4) inadequate participation of management in the project.

Technique   The lack of suitable mathematical techniques is rarely a problem in OR studies. Ironically, in fact, the availability of numerous methods and computer hardware may in itself become a problem; the significance—and novelty—of these techniques misdirects OR teams and managers into enthusiasm for the mechanics rather than for the end product. As a result, OR teams have at times taken up insignificant problems, or have attempted to solve important problems incorrectly, merely because a computer is available or a technique known.

Recently, for example, a paper company studied ways of scheduling orders on a paper-making machine so that waste (called trim loss) would be minimized. The OR team developed a linear programming model to select orders in a way that minimized waste. The model proved difficult to use, however, because last-minute changes in production (not at all unusual in the paper industry) required frequent reruns on the computer. A later reappraisal of marketing needs and production scheduling showed that maintaining a finished-goods inventory of popular sizes provided the flexibility needed to schedule accurately without a computer. The decision to use linear programming not only cost the company money unnecessarily, but also left management's real problem unsolved.

In another instance, a heavy-equipment manufacturer undertook a lengthy study to improve production planning. The study was a very satisfactory scientific endeavor, which produced a complicated scheduling model. The cost reduction achieved, however, was insignificant compared with the cost of developing the model. In fact, the model produced results only slightly better than would have been achieved by using a series of simple decision rules derived from existing practice. This company lost sight of the true objective of the study: to determine better decision rules for its own needs, rather than the best decision rules theoretically possible. Unquestionably, mathematical techniques and computers are pivotal in this field, and extensive technical research is essential for continued OR progress. Too often, however, technique dominates the selection of problems to be studied, the approach to be used, and the emphasis of the study.

Communication No matter how effective the technique used to solve a problem, the technical group is always faced with the task of communicating the results of its study to operating management, in terms that can be fully understood and accepted.

A manufacturing company, interested in improving forecasts of the annual demand for its products, ran aground on a communications problem. After studying the problem, the OR team had developed a correlation method; this showed, by analysis of past data, the best relationship between product demand and a set of economic factors. To the uninitiated, these factors—gross national product, average level of population, and average family income—appeared to have little direct connection with the company.

In presenting the forecasting method to marketing management, the team dwelt at length on technical points—how the method had been developed and the mathematical relationships between the economic factors and product demand. The practical application, however, went almost unmentioned. Consequently, management assumed—incorrectly—that the OR results were an explanation of how each factor affected demand, rather than a means of determining what action to take. The method, which was perfectly sound, was never accepted because the OR team failed to interpret the results in operational terms for managers who had a marketing orientation.

It is, of course, frequently difficult for people with different technical backgrounds or functional responsibilities to come to agreement and understanding on a common problem. Yet it is in these interfunctional problems that OR can offer its greatest benefits to management. The OR team is almost certain to encounter communication problems if it presents recommendations and results in an overly technical manner or does not specify the assumptions and limitations of the work. In companies with a successful OR record, the OR team has been willing to expend considerable effort to ensure that its presentations are easily understandable and in terms that are meaningful to management.

Experience and Judgment Many studies are unsuccessful because the OR team does not stay in close touch with line managers to draw on their experience and judgment. From the outset of a project, these managers can offer guidance and know-how to the technical staff.

They can assist in defining realistic objectives and suggest solutions that may otherwise be overlooked. Their knowledge can often be incorporated in the model as inputs or, at least, be used in formulating assumptions and constraints for it.

An OR team in an airlines company neglected this valuable approach and, in consequence, worked out a solution that, while technically sound, proved to be virtually useless. During the first few months of the introduction of a new jet aircraft into its fleet, the company experienced serious spare-parts problems. Aircraft components were failing much more rapidly than expected, and a policy of low initial stocking of spares made the difficulties more severe.

The OR team tackled the problem without more than the most casual contact with purchasing and inventory management. The team worked out a complete simulation model, which determined the total requirement for spare parts and the allocation of parts to field stores. Before a computer run could be planned, this model required data on the expected failure rate of each part and the expected schedule of planes. In fact, to use the simulation model would have required a major reorganization and change of approach in the purchasing department. Unfortunately, the model did not give the company's purchasing department a means of analyzing requirements on an item-by-item basis or of using the existing procurement facilities for rapid initial ordering. Thus, the model was a complete waste of effort because the OR work was treated as a research project with no appreciation of the urgency of the situation or the practical contributions that purchasing management could have made.

Success therefore depends on the OR team's ability to use the experience of the decision makers and utilize all relevant information, both internal to the firm and—just as important—external, such as political, economic, and competitive factors. Management information on external factors is particularly significant for OR to be successful in solving: long-range problems, which require judgment on the future; problems involving profitability; and problems of marketing strategy, which, for example, could involve consideration of competition.

Management Participation There is still another reason why OR programs fail to gain acceptance and full implementation: inadequate participation by management—especially the management level that must act on the recommendations.

When OR achievements of a leading manufacturing company were recently reviewed, the record showed that, although several models of processing operations had been built, the company was lagging far behind its competitors in applying OR. In fact, few of the models had been successfully used. In tracing the causes for this failure, the review committee found that the OR group believed its responsibility ended when the mathematical model was completed. But even more important, the group was under the control of a functional head whose responsibilities were unrelated to the broad scope of OR work. Because of this organizational arrangement, the OR group did not have access to top management and was seriously handicapped in its study of interfunctional problems.

The effectiveness of an OR team depends on obtaining the cooperation and participation of the level of management responsible for all of the functions involved in the study and affected by its recommendations. Thus, in a study of inventory, in which both marketing and production are involved, the executive responsible for both marketing and production must participate. Without his acceptance of the implementation program, the interfunctional problem cannot effectively be resolved.

Furthermore, it is important to enlist the participation of operating management, as well as of management responsible for the functions involved. By contributing to an OR study, operating managers may be more profoundly persuaded of its validity and usefulness. That they be thus persuaded is essential to the full implementation of any OR solution. For among the most frequent obstacles to successful completion of a project are operating managers' prejudices against the use of quantitative solutions, their unwillingness to accept the computer as an aid to decision making, their understandable resentment of outside interference in their decision areas, and their suspicion of centralized decision-making authority, which may not provide the same degree of flexibility currently available in their decision areas.

GUIDELINES FOR SUCCESS

The OR experience of a wide range of companies of varying size and in different industries shows that the total effectiveness of OR—judged by the success of implementation—can be improved by careful planning and by close coordination between the OR problem solvers and the solution implementers. Four important guidelines will help management and the OR staff carry projects through to their practical

and profitable use: (1) solve problems rather than apply techniques; (2) organize for problem solving; (3) select projects carefully; and (4) use a planned approach to OR studies.

Solve Problems   The management point of view that is most likely to promote successful use of OR is one that views OR as an approach to problem solving and planning rather than as a collection of techniques. It is an extension of problem-solving and planning methods used by management. The results of OR studies must be practical and capable of being put into operation in decision making or planning.

The best way to prevent a study from getting too deeply involved in mere application of technique is for the OR team and operating management to define clearly from the outset the objective and scope of the study and the approach to be used. It is also necessary to consider early in the study the value and impact that achieving the objectives will have for operating management. And throughout, management and the OR team must pursue with singleness of purpose the main objective of the study: to solve the problem. To achieve this prime requisite, the method employed is secondary, whether it is linear programming, simple algebra, or merely a sound process of improving existing practical decision rules.

If, as suggested, successful application of OR depends on placing emphasis on problem solving and planning, then what are the specific benefits of the OR approach? Four of them follow:

First, some industries have problems that cannot be solved effectively or efficiently by relying solely on past experience in similar situations. This may be because there are many courses of action—with no standard solutions —or many interrelated variables. Therefore, the development of a mathematical model and analysis of alternatives, often with the aid of a computer, becomes the most profitable way of solving the problem. OR not only provides significantly better answers in these cases but occasionally makes a solution—other than judgmental—possible.

Second, when developing planning methods and decision rules involving more than one functional area, OR often provides an approach to analysis of these problems, which leads to quantitative solutions that are thus removed to some extent from the gray areas of discretion.

Third, the use of an approach to problem solving that requires a precisely defined objective and detailed resolution of significant factors and alternatives in many cases provides both a better diagnosis of the problem and a quantitative justification for a program of corrective action.

Finally, in some cases the OR approach provides a solution of more lasting value than a short-term judgmental solution. For example, a manufacturing firm experienced a rapid increase in its finished-goods inventory when production was not reduced after a cut in a competitor's price caused a sudden drop in sales. Inventories grew so rapidly that, when production finally acted, it was necessary to lay off part of the work force. The layoff caused union grievances and a strike was threatened. Inventories were slowly reduced by placing the work force on a part-time basis and, at the same time, a start was made on a long-term solution of the inventory problem by setting up an OR study on inventory and production control. This study resulted in a set of dynamic decision rules of long-term value—because they could easily be updated as conditions changed—that allowed management to plan production, work force, and inventory levels.

Although the prime use of OR study is to solve a specific business problem, there are occasions when OR can also be used to analyze an entire business system to provide information for decisions, or, in fact, to locate the real problem affecting the operation of the company. In addition, where detailed analysis is not possible, an OR approach can be used to evaluate the sensitivity of alternative decisions to a range of possible future conditions.

ORGANIZE FOR PROBLEM SOLVING

Whatever the technical means used in an OR study, its success depends in large measure on the organization and staffing of the OR activity. Management is, in fact, concerned with the organization and staffing of two kinds of OR activities: teams temporarily set up to study a specific management problem or planning process, and the permanent, specialized OR staff.

If a team is to solve specific business problems, it must consist of both OR technicians competent in developing mathematical solutions and planners familiar with existing practices in making management decisions. Furthermore, the team members must be skillful in communicating conclusions and recommendations to management. They should be able to inspire management confidence in the abilities of the team to understand and interpret the business situation and in a solution derived from the team's mathematical skills.

In organizing this kind of team, it is particularly important that provision be made for drawing on management's experience. In a study of forecasting procedures, for example, a marketing manager's knowledge of the growth and decay of demand for a new product may be a key factor. Therefore, although the OR team is using exponential smoothing (a method of forecasting using weighted averages of past sales), it should take account of management's knowledge of the growth pattern and the impact of promotional efforts, to obtain the most useful forecasting procedure.

The only way of effectively incorporating such background knowledge and experience is to have members of operating management serve on the study team. Their participation prevents the last-minute realization that some practical and significant business facts have been omitted from consideration, thus invalidating the work. At the same time, they act as a sounding board for recommendations before the results are presented to top management.

When the team is first established, the stage must be set, organizationally, for implementing the final recommendations. Thus, if the study crosses functional, departmental, or divisional lines, the results and recommendations of the study should be directed to the management responsible for all operations involved. If the study crosses all functional lines—as some studies do—the work should be designed for, and directed to, the chief executive.

Even though such temporary OR teams are important, the keystone of successful OR work is the specialized staff. To solve management problems, such an OR staff must combine technical excellence with an understanding of management's approach to decision making. They should bring to problem solving all the capabilities needed—creativity, analytical skill, an unbiased approach, and practical ideas and reasoning. In addition, companies with the most successful OR records have high-caliber OR leadership. The OR staff in such companies also takes on the important training functions of (1) developing competence in OR techniques; (2) developing interest and ability to recognize opportunities for using OR at all management levels; and (3) helping operating management to understand and use the results of OR studies.

As for the place of the OR staff in the company organization, experience shows that several locations have been successful, provided the activity is not restricted to one functional area. Further, the staff must have access to, and cooperation from, a level of management high enough in the organization to ensure implementation of results.

This does not necessarily require all of the OR staff to be completely centralized. In fact, many large companies—particularly those in the oil industry—have men with OR skills strategically distributed at divisional levels. These companies, however, maintain a small, high-caliber staff group to provide functional or technical guidance for the total OR activity. The staff group maintains close contact with top management, ensures that OR is applied wherever benefits can be derived, determines when outside technical aid is needed, and provides the technical guidance for planning programs and developing techniques.

This decentralized arrangement with central technical guidance has several advantages. The most important one is that the OR teams work in closer contact with the managers responsible for implementing results. In addition, a great deal of excellent OR work can be carried out by specialists in other areas. Economists, engineers, and EDP experts, for example, can—with technical assistance—produce the benefits of a successful OR application.

In small companies, the only people with OR skills may be two or three on the technical OR staff. They must be high-caliber men and, because they cannot be expected to possess every skill, they should be analysts and planners rather than expert mathematicians. Therefore, in small companies there may be greater need to seek consulting advice and technical assistance outside the company.

In summary, then, the essential characteristics of temporary study teams are, first, that team members be planners and problem solvers dedicated to seeking practical guides for management decision making, and, second, that quality rather than quantity be the main requirement. The exact organizational location of the permanent OR staff is not critical, but the staff must consist of people with fresh ideas, technical knowledge, ability to take an objective and systematic approach to problem solving, and, above all, ability to communicate with all levels of management.

Select Projects Carefully   With satisfactory organization and staffing, the effectiveness of OR will depend on the selection of projects and on the approach used by the teams to plan the work and meet the study objectives.

The selection of projects is a twofold responsibility. The first part is management's responsibility to identify the key decisions and problem areas and, with the OR staff, to evaluate the need for better problem solutions or planning methods. Top management, as well as operating management, should play a part in this identification process because much of the real benefit of OR comes from studies in decision areas that cross functional boundaries.

The second part of the responsibility falls on the OR staff that must assist management in identification and ranking of projects by estimating the probability of success, the expected benefits and risks, and the possible work load and timetable. All these important factors can be used later by the study team when the project is started.

The selection of OR projects is particularly important for companies just starting OR work, because the future of OR in the company will be determined by the short-term benefits derived from the first projects. Selection of projects with short-term payoff and low risk of not reaching successful implementation is the best way to establish the value of OR and gain management interest and confidence. For example, such projects may be in production or inventory control where a high degree of success has been obtained. With initial success as background, more extensive studies—usually with greater potential payoff—can be undertaken.

Because starting an OR activity presents some problems, and because the selection and ranking of profitable OR projects requires a diagnosis of management problems and a knowledge of the likely success of OR work, companies often seek outside consultant guidance in these areas. For some companies, specialized staffs trained in mathematics may not be necessary at all to obtain the fundamental benefits that OR offers.

Even in companies where OR is well established, projects that embrace total company or corporate problems should not be started without first taking significant intermediate steps. The company can benefit from analyses of parts of the larger problem that lend themselves readily to such approaches and that can be successfully completed in a reasonable span of time. Nevertheless, the long-range objective of the OR staff should be the benefits of OR that are obtained when OR contributes to improved decision making in problems that have significant profit impact, such as major marketing and financial decisions.

Use a Planned Approach   To deal with problems of conflicting goals, policies, and alternatives, the OR team should use a planned approach to the study. It is important to recognize that the prime function of OR in industry is to develop and apply a quantitative approach to specific problems, rather than carry out fundamental research. The required creativity will not be restricted by scheduling and planning the study, and the desired end result, the implementation of the selected solution, will be ensured.

Figure 1, which illustrates the total OR approach to problem solving, shows that the first step in an approach is to obtain the basic facts, opinions, and symptoms of the problem needed to define clearly management's real problem.

Next, the factors affecting the problem, the variables and constraints, must be determined. The variable factors are those on which decisions have to be made, such as level of inventory, production rate, or amount and character of promotional effort. The constraints limit the solution of the problem, such as specific out-of-stock criteria, a constant employment policy, or a minimum cash requirement. Also, the assumptions to be made when solving the problem must be identified, for example, constant product mix or price, uniform market growth, or a maximum and minimum range of future sales.

The next important step in the problem-solving approach is to develop alternative courses of action or possible solutions to the problem, and clearly stated objectives by which the alternatives can be analyzed. These alternatives are then evaluated to select the optimum solution—the course of action, plan, or rule that will best achieve the objective. The last and the most important step of all is, of course, implementation.

These steps represent a formal approach to problem solving applicable to the solution of any problem, whether the technique used is mathematical or nonmathematical. As Figure 1 illustrates, the technical elements of the OR approach are concerned with developing alternative solutions and analyzing them to determine the optimum. This is usually done by the development of a mathematical model using appropriate tools of the trade (or techniques) to allow a computer to calculate the optimum solution. The important factor to consider when using the technical elements of the OR approach is that the optimum solution of the model is not necessarily the course of action that management should take to solve their

FIGURE 1   An Operations Research Approach to Problem Solving

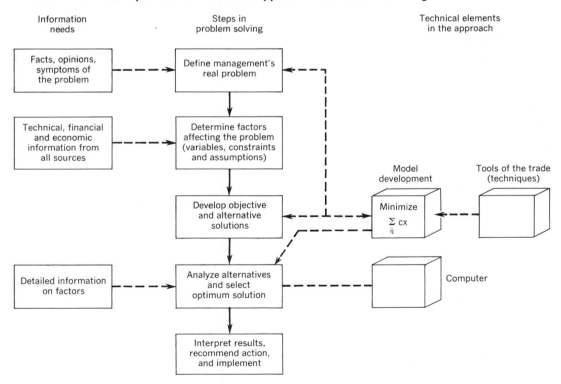

business problem. The model solution must be interpreted and evaluated in the context of the assumptions used and the total business environment, so that a detailed course of action for management is developed.

This approach, which should be used by OR teams and understood by management, formalizes the problem-solving steps so the study can be most effectively scheduled and controlled and thus achieve the two goals of solution and implementation.

CONCLUSION

The company that gets more for its OR investment is one that successfully translates OR solutions into action. The responsibility for reaching this final result is threefold, resting in part on management, in part on permanent OR staff, and in part on the temporary study teams. On top management devolves the responsibility for: (1) ensuring that the OR staff is advantageously located in the organization to facilitate communication and productive interchange of ideas; (2) initiating OR projects on key management problems; and (3) obtaining action based on accepted recommendations of OR teams. Operating management must seek advice on their problems, recognize opportunities for using OR, offer their experience, guidance, and direction to OR teams, and recognize the need for their participation in the problem-solving process.

The basis for success of OR lies with the OR staff, and in particular the head of this staff group. The group has the responsibility for: (1) promoting the beneficial use of OR; (2) communicating with all levels of management on the objectives, benefits, limitations, and approach of OR problem solving; (3) providing technical guidance and participation in studies; and (4) ensuring that the goal of seeking implementation is constantly upheld.

The temporary OR team, for its part, should concentrate on the underlying purpose of any study: to find better decision rules or better planning methods for the company, rather than the theoretically best rules. In defining the study, the team should choose the technique to fit the problem, not the problem to fit the technique. And in carrying out the study, the team should follow a planned approach in the search for practical answers to the problems on hand.

By retaining the objectivity of a consulting group, the team should cut through organizational red tape and personal prejudices. It should pull together conflicting points of view and methods, tap the company's fund of executive experience and judgment, and fuse all these with its own creativity and use of OR techniques.

By these means top management can look forward to significant profit contributions through action resulting from operations research projects.

18   F. POLICY FORMULATION

Product Planning for Future Profits*

RICHARD D. CRISP

As of March 1958, anyone's list of the half-dozen most worrisome problems of top

* Reprinted with permission of the publisher from *Dun's Review and Modern Industry*, vol. 71, no. 3, pp. 34ff, March, 1958. Mr. Crisp is director of marketing for Guild, Bascom, and Bonfigli, Inc., of Chicago, and also lecturer in marketing, Northwestern University.

management would have to include two items that quite a few of today's executives have never before encountered at first hand. One is a continuing softening of sales volume, often showing up in a shrinkage of back orders and a swelling of inventories. The other is the mounting pressure on profits, resulting from the unpleasant combination of lower-than-capacity operating levels and higher break-even points.

Serious as these two problems can be, in the long run they're far from insoluble. Many management people have learned that there is one area of constructive action that promises to contribute to the solution of both. That area, of course, is new-product development.

If management attention today is more intensely concentrated on the development of new products than ever before, the reason is simply the tremendous potential profit and volume in new products. The nature of this potential shows up in the results of a recent study by an industrial publisher. In ten different industrial classifications new products were expected to contribute from 30 per cent to 80 per cent of total volume over a period of five years—that is, from 1955 to 1960.

FIGURING THE ODDS

But while the development and marketing of new products promise important volume and profits to those who succeed, the odds against the success of a new product today are higher than most business men realize. In fact, a frequently quoted observation, that four out of five new products fail, greatly underestimates the odds. There are three reasons for this.

First, the observation was based on the experience of 200 large manufacturers of consumer products, all of whom have substantial experience and skilled, specialized personnel. If four out of five of *their* new products fail, the odds for all companies are certainly much higher. Second, the study was made in 1945. The competitive pressures against a new product in 1958 are unquestionably much heavier, and the chances of success correspondingly lower. Third, the estimate was based on the performance record of products actually placed on the market. It didn't take into consideration cases of product-mortality before launching but *after* substantial investments of time, effort, and money.

Long experience in the marketing-management field has convinced me that there are few areas of management practice today where the gap between the most effective and the least effective performance is as wide as in new-product activities.

What does this mean for companies whose experience in new-product activities has been less satisfactory? Simply this: If your company is like most others, a marked improvement in your new-product batting average can be achieved rather quickly and easily, by introducing into your operation certain approaches and principles distilled from the experience of companies outstandingly effective in new-product marketing.

HOW TO LOOK FOR TROUBLE

To help you identify the areas in your new-product program where the greatest opportunities for improvement exist, here is a rundown of the chief trouble spots.

1. *What are the objectives of your new-product activities?*

The single difference that most commonly distinguishes the successful from the unsuccessful company in the new-product area lies in the answer to this question: Do you have the specific objectives of your new-product program in writing so that they can be clearly understood by all? Failure to crystallize the objectives of a new-product program before making substantial commitments of time, money, and effort is a major source of new-product failure.

Crystallizing the objectives of a new product is essential for increasing efficiency and minimizing wasted effort. The search for a promising new product often involves considerable wasted motion. Sharply defined objectives can greatly reduce that waste by (1) narrowing the search to those products that will contribute to the attainment of the predetermined objectives and (2) insuring the early abandonment of projects inconsistent with those objectives. Dropping a product at a lower and hence less expensive point on the developmental curve results in marked savings.

An example will help to show how successful new-product marketers use objectives as a tool. The Toni Company was once actively seeking new products. The objective of the search was to find and develop products with a Winter consumption peak to offset the Summer peaks of existing products. But an important subsidiary objective was to find products that could share the cost of some of the company's expensive television commitments during the Winter months.

One product that was considered, evaluated, developed, and even carried into the test-market stage was a hand lotion. But research disclosed that hand lotion as a product class has a consumption peak in small town and rural areas. At that time, television audiences peaked sharply in larger cities. The lack of fit between the shape of the market for the product and the company's objectives counted heavily in the decision to drop the product.

A similar lack of fit was disclosed when S. C. Johnson & Sons, Inc., makers of wax products, was considering adding shoe polishes to its line. One prime objective of the company's new-product program at that time was to find products that could be sold by the consumer-product sales organization through the same distribution channels used for its other summer products. Shoe polish sells in substantial volume. Much of that volume, however, involves specialized distribution channels to reach shoe-repair and shoe-supply retailers. The company lost interest in the product when it found it would have to set up a separate sales organization or else divert a considerable amount of the present sales department's time from its regular customers. Again it was the predetermined objective that led to an early recognition that there was a serious lack of fit.

2. *How similar are the new products you are considering to those you now make?*

Getting the answer to this question can be vital to success or failure and hence should be considered as early as possible in the planning of a new product. For the experience of countless companies has led to the distillation of this principle: *The more a proposed product differs from those you are now making and know thoroughly, the greater are the odds that it will never contribute a dollar of profit.*

The explanation lies in what we might call a buried assumption. (In new-product situations, there is usually an intrinsic and implicit assumption.) That is, it is assumed that the new product can be added to the line and marketed without much more drain on the time and effort of the management team, per sales or profit dollar, than existing products require.

In the case of variations of products with which the management team is already familiar —like a new cake-mix flavor or a new industrial lubricant added to an existing line—this assumption is likely to be valid. But when management has to learn an entirely new business to produce a new product, the assumption most emphatically does not apply.

The millions of dollars that have been poured down the rathole before management faced the facts and asked, "What are we doing here?" would make a large dent in the Federal deficit.

Two factors are present in this kind of situation. The first is the high cost of the time and effort necessarily expended by a company's top management team. This added burden might be taken on without difficulty if a team began the job with time on its hands. Such a starting point is mighty unusual. The second factor is the effect that this diversion of a large share of management's time and attention will have

on a company's existing products and product lines. Such a diversion is often an important contributing factor to a decline in sales and share-of-market for existing products. When management concentrates attention on new-product activities, it's important to be sure that someone is watching the store. For it is a rare new product indeed that can contribute enough to a company's volume and profit to offset fully a significant decline in the company's established products. Such a decline is often an unanticipated and unidentified "cost" of a new product.

Incidentally, there is a big opportunity here for many companies to improve their new-product planning. An aggressive new-product program often requires the commitment of a significant share of a company's total assets, including the important if intangible one of top-management time and attention. Companies doing the best job in new products rarely lose sight of this fact. In evaluating a proposed new product, they always ask, "Would the same amount of time, effort, and money devoted to our existing products pay us a larger return on our investment?" If the answer is "yes"—and it often is—the new product is dropped.

These comments do not mean that emphasis on new-product development is being overdone. Rather, they are intended to underline this fact: A new-product program is likely to be fully effective only if it is first planned and then executed with a full awareness of its probable impact on the company's total situation.

3. *Does your new-product planning proceed from factory to consumer, or does it work in reverse?*

An accurate and objective answer to this question will do much to reveal exactly how up-to-date your company's marketing management is in its approach to the new-product area. At one time production-minded managements decided what they were going to make and proceeded to make it. The sales department was then given the task of selling the product. Often the market was restricted, or the product was unsuited to the needs of the market. Extraordinarily high sales costs were the result.

Today well-managed companies accept beyond question that it is easier and cheaper to make what customers want to buy than to sell them what you want to make. As a result, management tends to be customer-oriented. It is this shift in emphasis, more and more widely recognized, that is largely responsible for what is sometimes described as the "new marketing concept."

In new-product development and marketing,

a consumer-oriented approach prevails in those companies with the most impressive new-product record. Perhaps you think these comments are too obvious. The sad fact is that they are not. The proportion of companies devoting expensive developmental time to "getting the bugs out" of products for which there is no customer need or desire is shockingly high.

This comment isn't meant to apply to products that are too new for consumers to be aware of their need for them. I am thinking of those products with "advantages" that the customer can enjoy only by sacrificing other values more important *to the customer.*

For example, not so many years ago, Servel developed an automatic ice-cube maker that fitted inside the frozen-food storage section of the Servel refrigerator. The device, introduced with considerable fanfare, jolted other refrigerator manufacturers, one of whom quickly conducted a small-scale consumer study. When the results were laid before him, he told his design department to scrap plans for trying to top the Servel innovation. What did the research show? It disclosed that housewives being reasonable creatures, would much prefer to have the space taken up by the device given to additional frozen-food storage, which they use every day, rather than have the convenience of automatic ice cubes, which they need in quantity only on special occasions.

To determine how your company stacks up in this respect, study a list of the new products you have done major work on over the last several years. Ask yourself where the basic suggestion or idea came from that started the work on a project. What evidence was there of a real and important need for such a product among the customers you hoped to sell it to?

In the case of the industrial and consumer durable goods market, it is often difficult to secure a customer's-eye-view of a proposed product. But don't let the high costs of tooling up or the difficulties of working with a heavy or bulky product persuade you to rely on guesswork alone. Techniques for pre-evaluating proposed products, even of such kinds, are widely and inexpensively available.

4. *Have all basic assumptions underlying new-product work been exhaustively studied and tested?*

Often the initial decision to assign a high priority to a proposed new product is based on a preliminary (and sometimes superficial) appraisal of the problems involved. It is extremely important to subject such a decision to careful review, *before* committing sizable funds to the project. In particular all basic assumptions should be reviewed.

Many a new-product failure can be traced to using unsound premises as a basis for its development. Those premises may involve scale of demand, price, nature of competition, distribution channels, or almost any other element of marketing. You should be especially on guard against wishful thinking in this key area.

As an illustration of how it could happen to you, here is the experience of a well-managed company, an industry leader in a field that sells largely, although by no means exclusively, through jewelry channels. The objective of the new-product program was to expand volume by adding products similar to the company's existing line in terms both of manufacturing skills required and of distribution channels used. One product under consideration was a camera about as large as a pack of cigarettes. The analysis that led the company to embark on research and development of the camera simply stated that a product with such-and-such characteristics could be sold in volume through jewelry outlets. Hundreds of thousands of R&D dollars later, the company perfected the product. At that point they found that cameras in the same price class as theirs were sold almost exclusively through photographic outlets. The product was quietly interred.

5. *When products have been in development over a period of time, is the marketing picture periodically and routinely re-examined for new or changed factors that affect the volume outlook?*

It often takes considerable time to move a new product from the idea to the ready-for-production stage. A further lag is caused by the varying lead-times required for tooling and production. In effective new-product programs, provision is made for a periodic and routine, but far from perfunctory, re-examination of the marketing situation. Today the marketing picture changes with often breath-taking rapidity. A soundly conceived product, created to fill an unquestioned need, may fail because some other product aimed at the same need-target beat it to the market-place.

Careful attention to trends affecting basic market factors is also essential. The hazards of basic market changes are illustrated by the case of Ford's new Edsel car. When the plans to launch the Edsel were made, the middle-price automotive market was a large and expanding segment of the total. But it took three years to translate the plans for the Edsel into a product-in-being with a going dealer organization to sell it. Early Edsel sales were below expectations—partly because the middle-price share of the auto market was far smaller in 1957 when the car was introduced than it had been when plans were frozen for production.

You are unlikely to have to cope with the hazards that a three-year lead-time adds to the always risky business of developing and marketing new products. Even so, the Edsel experience is one to remember. A major competitive innovation or a sharp change in import competition may make it desirable for you to re-examine your plans. Often it is far less expensive to put the brakes on a product and "eat" the research and development costs than to market a product when the odds against its success have changed materially.

6. *Have the differences between your new products and your basic business—and especially the marketing differences—been fully recognized?*

A company's failure (especially in the planning stages of the program) to recognize the basic and striking differences between the business it is in and the business it proposes to enter spells doom for many new products even before they see the light of competition.

This problem is particularly acute in the case of companies that dominate their industry. They tend to enter new-product marketing with a rather strong "we are a leader" bias. Despite the new-product actuarial tables, they are confident of success. Often they stumble and fall, tripped by overconfidence.

Their new product goes into a market where it is often a "me, too" or "just another" product, rather than a leader. Competitors ignore (as they should) the company's acts. They fail to follow—which can be disconcerting to those who think in terms of leadership. As a result, the company finds that its appraisals of "what will happen when we do such-and-such" are grossly in error.

This is an extremely important problem area, partly because of its great and inescapable complexity. Differences between your established product and your new product may exist in almost any section of the marketing picture. They may exist in the area of product differentiation, for example. You are a leader in your basic industry because your products are clearly superior in ways that are important to the customers who use them. Your new product may be insufficiently differentiated, or differentiated in ways that are considered unimportant by the customers you're selling. What happens then? All the experience you have developed in your basic business becomes either irrelevant or obsolete. You have no basis for judging the extent to which, for example, your conversion of "triers" to users is good, fair, or poor. Besides, your estimate of the influence

of price strategy on volume is unlikely to apply to this new, strange situation.

Or consider service. Perhaps the basic products you have been selling have required very little service. Your new product takes you into an industry or product area in which prompt service is more important to your customers than what seem to you to be basic differences in the qualities of the products themselves. What do you do now? To keep the situation simple, let's assume that you anticipated this problem. But it would be far more realistic to assume that you had failed to do so and only found out about it when you tried to diagnose your disappointingly low rate of sales.

Another problem might well develop in trade practices and terms. As a newcomer in an industry, you will have to offer distributors all the attractions and advantages they have been getting from other companies. To break in, you may have to offer more. What will you do if the existing concerns equal or exceed your offers? How far are you prepared to go to "buy your way in"?

The answer to that last question can be vital. It certainly was in the case of one of the most spectacular financial flops in the new-product area. When Lever Brothers introduced Swan soap as a challenge to Procter & Gamble's Ivory, initial plans called for an advertising expenditure rate three times that of Ivory's going rate *in the planning period*. But by the time Swan was actually launched, P&G's expenditure rate for Ivory had been tripled. Published estimates of Lever Brothers' loss on Swan have run as high as $20 million.

7. *Is the scheduling of your new-product development realistically established and reasonably maintained?*

There can be no question of the difficulties implicit in establishing and maintaining an "on time" schedule in research and developmental work, particularly where that work is primarily creative. But eventually, in the development of every product, a point is reached when it is possible to predict with reasonable certainty how soon the product can be launched. It is in the scheduling of activities during this interval that the most marked differences between the practices of successful companies and average concerns appear.

Traditionally, delays in research and development are allowed to soak up a larger and larger part of the total time before introduction day. As an almost inescapable consequence, vital elements in marketing planning are telescoped or eliminated. The new product slides down the ways and sinks with only a few bubbles to mark the spot.

In contrast, those companies that make something close to a fine art of new-product activities generally enforce a carefully predetermined time schedule throughout the new product's developmental period. They have written lists of all key elements and decisions that must be made and adequate time allocated for each. That kind of detailed schedule—which might run to more than 150 different major decisions in marketing alone—is a potent planning tool, which minimizes many of the serious risks that might handicap the new product.

There are two ways to enforce such a schedule on a research-and-development team. First, successful companies often have no research and development team. Instead, they have a new-product team, on which both research-and-development and marketing management viewpoints are represented and closely integrated. Second, commercially acceptable standards of product performance are provided as a guide to research and development efforts. This eliminates the time problem, with which most executives experienced with new products are familiar. The technical research group wants "just a little more time." In return, they promise a "much better" product.

In some ways, producing a new product is like a pregnancy. A point is reached when more time in the womb contributes little to the baby, and it can be mighty hard on the mother.

8. *Is your new-product marketing routinely begun either on a test-market or on a controlled, limited area basis?*

New-product marketing is fraught with risk. It is only plain common sense to minimize that risk by reducing the scale of its introduction. Experienced companies try to do this by using a carefully pre-planned test market or a limited geographical introduction, which is also a test of sorts.

There are two important advantages in this limited-risk approach. First, when the product is a dud, the small-scale introduction demonstrates that fact, usually unmistakably, with a minimum investment of time, effort, and money. Second, almost all test-market or limited-scale introductions reveal "bugs" in the marketing plan or ways to improve its effectiveness substantially. By using a market test as the production management team uses a pilot plant, both the likelihood of success and the scale of that success if achieved can be increased.

9. *Is nonrepetitive or stock-building volume carefully considered in evaluating the limited-scale test or introduction?*

One of the most frequent mistakes is the strong (often, it seems, irresistible) tendency of management to underestimate the length of time and the volume required to build up distributors' supplies of a new product. As a result, some of this stock-building volume is incorrectly translated into actual consumer sales, thus causing estimates of the new product's market potential to be ridiculously exaggerated.

10. *Do you carefully compare the sales volume and the cost of achieving it with the pre-introduction budgets and forecasts?*

Careful and continuing attention to whether the sales achieved and the costs of securing those sales match, exceed, or run under pre-introduction budgets and forecasts is standard operating procedure in effective new-product programs. It is important to watch the vital early results so that appropriate action can be taken. The definition of "appropriate action" depends on how actual volume and expenses compare to the forecast. If the product is destined for failure, minimize losses and trip the trap on it at the earliest possible moment. If the product is running ahead of forecasts, then carefully controlled experiments to see how high volume can be pushed, perhaps with additional promotion or sales force, are indicated.

It is impossible to cover new-product development completely in a single article. But these questions and answers represent a comprehensive checklist for setting up an effective new-product program. No one can hit the ball out of the park on every new product, but if you follow these tips you'll make fewer strike-outs.

19

The Strategy of Product Policy*

CHARLES H. KLINE

The first concern of most businessmen is the content of their product lines. No other problem of management affects profits more directly. Few problems require more constant attention from management.

Active executives make decisions almost every day that affect the product line in such matters as allocations of manpower, factory space, or sales effort. Frequently they must also decide major product questions—whether to undertake a new development project, to introduce a new product, or to eliminate an old one. Mistakes in any of these are usually costly, and may even be ruinous.

To help get better and faster decisions on problems of product-line content, executives in a number of manufacturing companies have developed formal product policies. These policies summarize the business characteristics which experience has shown successful products must have. In effect, each policy is a statement of long-range strategy that defines the means for a particular company to make the greatest over-all profits.

Experience has shown that a product policy serves these three main functions:

1. A product policy helps to provide the information required for decisions on the product line. It tells lower management and professional staffs of market analysts, research workers, and industrial engineers what top management needs to know. Furthermore, it provides a convenient framework around which this information can be organized.

2. Also, a product policy gives executives a supplementary check on the usual estimates of profit and loss. Even though modern techniques of market research, sales forecasting, and cost estimating are often sur-prisingly good, the data they provide are still only approximations.

It is often impossible to make any realistic financial estimates at all—for example, at the start of a long-range research program. At other times available sales and profit data may not be significant. An unsatisfactory record for an existing product may reflect a basic mistake in product policy, but it may also be the result of poor organization, unsuitable sales and promotion, faulty design, or inadequate plant facilities.

An analysis in terms of a basic product policy shows up weak spots in the financial estimates and indicates imponderable factors that cannot easily be reduced to numbers.

3. Most important of all, a product policy guides and directs the activities of the whole organization toward a single goal. Only rarely are product decisions made solely by top executives. More often such decisions require the specialized knowledge of experts in many fields—research, development, engineering, manufacturing, marketing, law, finance, and even personnel.

The original idea for a new product may occur to an engineer at the laboratory bench, a copy writer in the advertising department, or a salesman in the field. Between the first concept and the final decision by top management to introduce the new product there comes a long series of investigations, analyses, research and development studies, pilot production runs, and marketing tests. This work is expensive and time-consuming, and it involves a great many people in the organization. To complete these indispensable steps as quickly and thoroughly as possible requires good teamwork and a clear idea of management's over-all policy.

A sound product policy, well prepared and well taught to all professional and supervisory employees, is thus an important tool for co-

* Reprinted by permission of the publisher from *Harvard Business Review*, vol. 33, no. 4, pp. 91–100, July-August, 1955. Mr. Kline is manager of the Chemical Development Division of the Climax Molybdenum Company.

ordination and direction. It applies not only to those major decisions which are the ultimate responsibility of presidents and general managers but also to the many day-to-day decisions by which lower-level employees shape the course of a business.

ANALYZING RESOURCES

The first step in developing a product policy is to make a careful inventory of a company's resources along the lines suggested in Exhibit I. Every company is unique. As a result of its history, experience, and personnel it has certain strengths and certain weaknesses that distinguish it from other business organizations. The ideal product policy makes the best use of a company's strong points and avoids its weak points.

In this sense every business enterprise is specialized, so that it is best suited to perform only certain services or to produce only certain types of product. The product lines of many large and successful corporations are so extremely varied that this point is often missed. One well-known company makes everything from light bulbs to jet engines, and another has a product line ranging from flashlight batteries to synthetic fibers. Although at first glance it may seem difficult to relate such diverse products to a single product policy, closer analysis shows that they all have in common certain strategic business characteristics which are related to company resources.

DEVELOPING THE POLICY

It is these business characteristics that make up the elements of product policy. Individually they are all well known. Every business executive deals with one or another of them daily. But in developing a product policy he must look at all these strategic points together. Let us see how they fit into an over-all policy.

Financial Strength In many respects the most important characteristic of any business is the investment required to enter it. This investment includes the land, buildings, and equipment needed for the business; the required inventories of raw material, work in process, and finished stock; and the funds necessary to carry accounts receivable and provide cash for working capital.

These components of the total investment are all related to the volume of sales. Investment in inventories, receivables, and cash varies almost directly with sales. Even the in-

---

EXHIBIT I   Inventory of Company Resources

Financial strength	Money available or obtainable for financing research and development, plant construction, inventory, receivables, working capital, and operating losses in the early stages of commercial operation.
Raw material reserves	Ownership of, or preferential access to, natural resources such as minerals, and ores, brine deposits, natural gas, forests.
Physical plant	Manufacturing plant, research and testing facilities warehouses, branch offices, trucks, tankers, etc.
Location	Situation of plant or other physical facilities with relation to markets, raw materials, or utilities.
Patents	Ownership or control of a technical monopoly through patents.
Public acceptance	Brand preference, market contracts, and other public support built up by successful performance in the past.
Specialized experience	Unique or uncommon knowledge of manufacturing, distribution, scientific fields, or managerial techniques.
Personnel	Payroll of skilled labor, salesmen, engineers, or other workers with definite specialized abilities.
Management	Professional skill, experience, ambition, and will for growth of the company's leadership.

EXHIBIT II   Size of Manufacturing Establishments for Various Products

(Source: U.S. Census of Manufactures, 1947.)

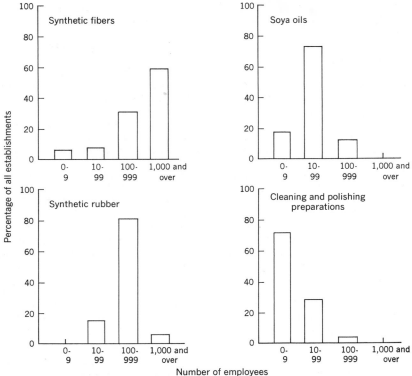

vestment in such fixed assets as land, buildings, and equipment must be scaled to the volume of product to be sold. Thus a given operation may require a high capital investment merely because the volume of sales will be large. Many merchandising ventures are of this type.

In manufacturing industries, however, capital requirements usually depend on process economics. Some products inherently require manufacture on a larger scale than others. Exhibit II compares the size of plant, as measured by the number of employees, in four types of establishment in the chemical process industries. As the exhibit shows, synthetic rubber and synthetic fiber plants are always large, soya oil mills are usually of moderate size, and plants producing cleaning and polishing compounds are generally small. The typical synthetic fiber plant has a thousand times more employees than the typical cleaning and polishing compound plant. The difference in fixed plant investment is probably much greater.

Small companies with limited financial resources are restricted to businesses that require

a relatively low investment. On the other hand, large and wealthy corporations have the choice of entering either high-investment or low-investment businesses—though experience has shown that such companies are most successful (indeed, sometimes only successful) in high-investment businesses, where large-scale operations do give them a competitive advantage.

In these connections, the observation made by Crawford H. Greenewalt, president of du Pont, is significant:

There is much misconception also about the relationship between big and little businesses. . . . No little business could compete with us in nylon for the reason that no such business could bring together the capital and technical resources required for an efficient producing unit. We, on the other hand, have no interest in competing in spheres where we can make no substantial technical contribution, and there are many activities, particularly in the fields of marketing and distribution, that small businesses can do better than we. . . .

Let me cite an example. We make nylon

yarn and sell it to whoever will buy. Your wife buys, let us say, a nylon blouse. Between the sale of that yarn and that blouse are the throwster who twists the yarn, the weaver who weaves it, the finisher who finishes and dyes it, the cutter who makes the garment, and the retail store that sells it. For the most part these are small businesses.[1]

As a general rule, the smallest economic unit that has the facilities to undertake a given operation performs it most efficiently. That is why, when large companies enter low-investment businesses they very often run into difficulties. To illustrate:

The breakeven charts shown in Exhibit III summarize the findings of a cost analysis of the manufacture and sale of a specialty product under two sets of conditions: (a) actual operating results in one of the largest corporations in the United States; and (b) the estimated results in a small independent business.

The product in question was a semifabricated material with a small but assured market potential of about $200,000 annually. The investment in plant equipment necessary for this volume of sales was about $25,000.

As the left-hand chart shows, the large corporation needed a sales volume of $216,000 per year to break even on this product. The small company, however, could make money anywhere above the breakeven point of $55,000 in annual sales shown in the right-hand chart.

[1] From a speech reported in *Chemical and Engineering News,* Oct. 10, 1949, p. 2896.

At the breakeven volume of $216,000 for the large company, the small company would net $72,000 before taxes.

Comparison of the two charts shows that the lower costs in the small company would come partly from lower fixed charges, raw material and direct-labor costs, and commercial, administrative, and engineering expenses. An operating manager primarily concerned with this one product could reasonably be expected to make small savings in these items. But the principal advantage of the small company would be its far lower variable overhead costs, estimated at less than half those of the large company.

Actually this analysis was made by the large corporation after several years of poor operating results. When this cost study became available, the product was dropped.

Sales Volume The financial strength of a company also influences the desirable level of sales for its products. A large volume of sales requires a large investment. For the reasons already mentioned, large companies are generally most successful in products with a large annual volume of sales, and small companies in low-volume specialty items. However, the acceptable range in dollars will obviously vary from one type of business to another.

Sales volume depends partly on the number of potential applications of a product, the number of potential customers, and the size of the area in which it will be distributed. These factors also determine the degree of stability in the sales volume. A product with only one

EXHIBIT III   Breakeven Charts for Manufacture of Specialty Semifabricated Product in Large and Small Companies

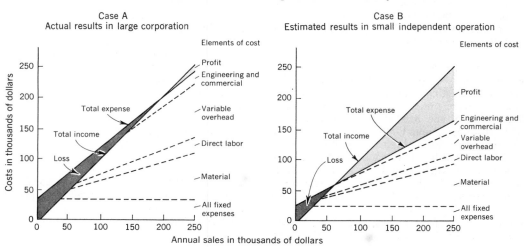

Case A
Actual results in large corporation

Case B
Estimated results in small independent operation

Annual sales in thousands of dollars

application and relatively few customers is liable to sudden obsolescence and violent fluctuations in sales. Therefore most large companies seek products with broad markets and avoid items salable only to one or two customers, the government, or the armed forces. The small company can sometimes afford to take more chances, for it has more flexibility to turn around and adjust to changing circumstances.

Distribution Channels   Channels of distribution consist largely of intangibles. There may be some investment in warehouses, trucks, and offices, but these facilities may also be rented. In any case the fixed investment is generally small. Perhaps for this reason business executives sometimes overrate the flexibility of their distribution channels.

Engineers and production men are particularly apt to assume that a salesforce can always handle "just one more" product, regardless of its market. Even sales managers sometimes say that a product will "sell itself" or "take no effort." As a result, one of the commonest problems in business today is that of the single salesforce trying to cover too many markets.

Professor Melvin T. Copeland summarizes the problem this way:

> Early in my research work in the field of marketing, I found that when a company was catering to two different markets, such as the consumer market and the industrial market, for example, better results typically were secured by segregating the salesforce into two groups, one for each type of market. It appeared that ordinarily a salesman could not be continually shifting back and forth between different types of buyers without having his effectiveness materially impaired. The buying habits and the buying motives of the two types of buyers were so different as to involve difficult mental shifts by the salesman. . . .[2]

Any new product has a great advantage when it can be sold to the same consuming groups as existing products. The new product benefits from the company's accumulated knowledge of the markets, close relationships with customers, and public acceptance which the salesforce has built up over the years.

On the other hand, a new product is at some disadvantage when it must be sold in entirely new markets. In this case the company must build entirely new distribution channels for the

product. Sales executives must develop new sales and promotional concepts, hire and train a new salesforce, perhaps select new distributors, and ultimately win new customers. These steps are costly and time-consuming, and they may prove a steady drain on executive effort that could be better spent elsewhere.

Accordingly a product intended for an entirely new market should generally have other advantages strong enough to justify the risks involved in distribution.

Effect on Present Products   A going concern cannot forget the products which are already earning assets.

Ideally every addition to the line should improve the profitability of present products. When a company such as Westinghouse develops a new electrical appliance, it increases the overall demand for electricity and thus increases the market for its turbines, generators, transformers, and other power equipment.

Unfortunately, situations of this sort are rather rare. For practical purposes a proposed new product will be satisfactory as long as it does not hurt the sale of present products. Of course, the situation is different when a new product makes an old one obsolete. It is obviously better for a company to replace its own products than to let a competitor do so.

Competition   In entering a new market a company should usually have some advantage over present and potential competitors in the field. At the least it should have no disadvantage.

The number and type of competitors a company will have to face in a new business generally depend on the capital investment required to enter the business. Where the investment is high, the number of competitors is fairly small, but they are usually strong, well entrenched, and difficult to dislodge. On the other hand, where the investment is low, there may be so many small, relatively weak companies in the field that poor pricing practices prevent any one from making a reasonable profit.

Executives in some companies with national distribution make it a policy not to enter any new market unless they believe they have enough advantages over competition to capture at least 20% of the market on a sound pricing basis.

Cyclical Stability   Steady, nonseasonal demand is nearly always desirable in a product. It is desirable also to have a product that is relatively independent of fluctuations in the business cycle.

---

[2] Melvin T. Copeland, *The Executive at Work*, Harvard University Press, Cambridge, Mass., 1951, p. 85.

Capital goods and some consumer durable goods are particularly vulnerable to periods of depression. Some companies in these fields lay special stress on new products that go into consumer nondurable markets. These products include not only items sold to the ultimate consumer, such as paints, drugs, lubricants, or antifreeze, but also industrial materials sold to fabricators or processors of consumer goods —for example, tetraethyl lead to gasoline refiners or tin cans to food packers.

Research and Patents Research brings profitable new products and leads to strong patent positions. It can also be very expensive. Products which offer the opportunity for important technical achievement are generally most attractive to financially strong companies, especially those which already have large research staffs as corporate resources. Smaller companies tend to avoid businesses requiring much development. Many small companies operate in highly technical fields, but these are usually rather specialized.

The attitude toward research and development also varies from one company to another on purely strategic grounds, regardless of size. Some companies specialize in very technical products. They carry on as much research as they can afford, continually seek out new technical fields for development, and even abandon older products that have reached a fairly stable technology and are no longer protected by patents. Joel Dean describes one such company in these terms:

> It is a fairly conscious policy of one of the large chemical companies to choose only those new products that have been developed by its product research organization and that are distinctive enough in both chemical and manufacturing requirements to be protected for some time to come. The counterpart of this policy is to abandon products when they have degenerated to the status of commonly produced commodities. The company advances to new monopoly positions as fast as economic progress wears down the walls of the old.[3]

In a company like the one just described any product that does not offer much opportunity for technical advances is not very attractive.

On the other hand, some companies concentrate on making old or relatively nontechnical products better and cheaper than any one else. Here the emphasis is usually on expert low-cost

production or aggressive merchandising. The company resources are primarily the production or sales staff, and the need for much research is an unfavorable factor.

Raw Materials In the event a company owns or controls a source of raw material, it has a resource which it should obviously use whenever possible. However, most companies must buy all or the greater part of their raw materials. These preferably should be basic commodities that are readily available in constant supply from several sources. They should also be free of any restrictive competitive control. Any raw material available from only one source is vulnerable to interruption by strikes, fires, bankruptcy, or other disasters—and even, on occasion, to the supplier's flat refusal to sell.

Distant and unreliable sources are also dangerous. For example:

> One large company is a heavy consumer of Indian mica. Because of unsettled conditions in India and throughout the world, this company always keeps a protective inventory of about one year's supply. Since the total expense of maintaining an inventory for a year (including interest, taxes, insurance, warehousing, and losses) is about 20% to 25% of its cost, this company pays a heavy penalty for its unavoidable dependence on an unreliable source.

Freedom from competitive control is especially important for raw materials used in large quantities. Thus:

> After World War II several chemical companies developed methods for polymerizing styrene to polystyrene. After spending considerable sums on technical developments, the companies all eventually abandoned these projects. Executives realized that they would have to buy styrene from the basic producers, who also made and sold polystyrene. As converters of a material under the control of competitors, they would be at the mercy of more integrated companies both as to supply and in regard to the relative price level of the two materials.

Value Added The fate of those styrene projects calls attention to the strategic value of highly integrated businesses. The best measure of integration is the value added by manufacture—that is, the spread between the cost of making the product, expressed as a percentage of total cost. Where distribution costs are high, the value added by manufacture and distribution is a more appropriate measure.

A high value added means that the product

---

[3] Joel Dean, *Managerial Economics*, Prentice-Hall, Inc., Englewood Cliffs, N.J., 1951, p. 130.

demands a high plant investment or considerable expense in engineering, labor, or supplies. These requirements give producers greater scope for improving efficiency, reducing costs, and developing a superior product. Furthermore, all these factors represent capital requirements. For this reason a high value added by manufacture is usually more desirable for the large company and less important for the small one.

Manufacturing Load   In many types of manufacturing, executives have some freedom of choice in deciding whether to produce standard products that can be sold from stock or custom products made to the individual customer's order. Standard products sold in large volume can be made most economically with equipment specially designed for mass production. The heavy capital investment and high volume of sales make such products particularly suitable for large companies.

On the other hand, the smaller company with limited capital may find it more profitable to make custom products or to supply standard products in a larger number of grades, sizes, and finishes. This type of manufacture substitutes labor for expensive and inflexible plant equipment. Operating costs are higher but can sometimes be offset by higher prices. Furthermore, since the investment is smaller, lower margins may still give a satisfactory return.

The job-shop processing of industrial goods —for example, custom molding of plastics— is an example of diversified manufacturing load where the small company has a great advantage over the large. The production of fashion goods is another. Professor Copeland describes this situation:

> From an administrative standpoint, style merchandising calls for rapid adjustment to continual and frequent changes in demand. Designing, purchasing, production, pricing, and sales have to be adjusted quickly to each change in a volatile market, and the various activities are so closely interdependent that they must all be adjusted almost simultaneously. Under these circumstances the activities of an enterprise manufacturing style merchandise are not sufficiently standardized or stable to permit the delegation of much decision-making to lieutenants. Hence, the small manufacturer who can constantly feel the pulse of the market and who can transmit his instructions directly and immediately to the operating forces is in a strategic competitive position. In such an industry the advantages of quick decision-making

and speedy transmittal of decisions to operatives more than offset the economics which might otherwise be gained from large-scale manufacture.[4]

STATING THE POLICY

Even this brief review shows that different companies may take diametrically opposite positions on each of a dozen or more points of product strategy. The contrast in over-all policy between two hypothetical companies is illustrated in Exhibit IV. Both companies are assumed to be manufacturers of synthetic organic chemicals and similar in all respects except one—size. In size they are assumed to differ by a factor of 1,000 as measured by their net worths. As the exhibit shows, this one difference is reflected in almost every aspect of their product policies.

In practice the differences between companies are never so simple and pronounced. Consequently the differences between product policies are often more elusive, though nonetheless real.

Whatever policy is adopted, it must generally be reduced to written form if executives and employees are to use it throughout a company. The statement of policy may be a series of short definitions, as in these excerpts paraphrased from the instructions of a large manufacturer of industrial goods:

> 1. *Sales volume:* Each product line should have a large potential volume of sales. It should be useful in a number of different applications and salable to a large number of customers.
>
> 4. *Patent protection:* Each line should be well protected by patents arising from the company's own discoveries or acquired by purchase or other means.
>
> 9. *Effect on present products:* Each line should improve the company's over-all sales and profit position. It should preferably help to promote the sale of the company's other products. If, however, it would hinder the sale of other company products, it should have a greater potential long-range profit than the products in conflict with it.

The statement may also be written up as a series of questions arranged as a check list. The following excerpts are paraphrased from such a statement developed by a well-known manufacturer of consumer goods, whose strat-

[4] Copeland, *op. cit.*, p. 149.

EXHIBIT IV   Examples of Product Strategy in Large and Small Companies

PRODUCT REQUIREMENTS	COMPANY A NET WORTH $500,000,000	COMPANY B NET WORTH $500,000
Capital investment	High	Low
Sales volume	Large volume Mass markets Many applications National distribution	Small volume Specialized markets Many to few applications Local or specialized distribution
Similarity to present distribution channels	High to moderate	High
Effect on going products	Good to fair	Good
Competition	Relatively few companies Sound pricing Good possibility of securing a large percentage of the market	Few to many companies Sound pricing Desirable market position variable
Cyclical stability	High	High
Technical opportunity	Great	Moderate to small
Patent protection	Great	Great to none
Raw materials	Basic materials Many suppliers	Intermediate or basic materials Many to few suppliers
Manufacturing load	Standard products Mass production Few grades and sizes	Standard or custom products Specialized production Few to many grades or sizes
Value added	High	High to moderate

egy was "to serve the market for nondurable household goods bought by large numbers of families with a fairly high frequency of purchase":

1. *Customer advantage:* Does the proposed product offer the customer an advantage?

   a. Is it superior to competition in a major property?

   b. If equal to competitive products in use properties, can it be sold profitably at a lower price?

2. *Mass market:* Is there a mass market for the product?

6. *Stability:* Will the product be free of undue breakage or deterioration from normal handling in distribution?

8. *Permissibility:* Will the product conform to applicable government regulations?

To summarize the appraisal of actual products against the product policy, one large materials processor supplements the formal statement with a simple check form. Exhibit V shows this company's summary appraisals of two proposed new businesses. In Case A, although the proposed business was quite different from the company's present lines, it did represent a favorable over-all pattern. In Case B, on the other hand, the over-all pattern was poor even though there were several favorable points, such as a general similarity to the present operations. The company in question developed Case A into a major new business but did not consider Case B further.

EXHIBIT V   Examples of Summary Product Appraisals by a Large Materials Processor

---

CASE A: A GENERALLY FAVORABLE PATTERN

	VERY GOOD	GOOD	FAIR	POOR	VERY POOR
Sales volume	x				
Type and number of competitors	x				
Technical opportunity	x				
Patent protection		x			
Raw materials		x			
Production load		x			
Value added		x			
Similarity to major business				x	
Effect on present products			x		

CASE B: A GENERALLY UNFAVORABLE PATTERN

	VERY GOOD	GOOD	FAIR	POOR	VERY POOR
Sales volume	x				
Type and number of competitors					x
Technical opportunity				x	
Patent protection					x
Raw materials		x			
Production load			x		
Value added		x			
Similarity to major business	x				
Effect on present products	x				

APPLYING THE POLICY

A product policy is especially helpful as a supplement and check on the usual estimates of profitability in three types of product activity: (a) development of new products; (b) vertical integration in manufacturing; and (c) elimination of old products.

New Products   Research and development programs usually proceed stepwise, and in a completed project executives must make at least four major decisions:

1. To undertake preliminary exploratory research, either technical or commercial.
2. To launch a full-scale development program.
3. To build a pilot plant and conduct pilot market tests.

4. To build a commercial plant and put the product on the market.

If the development does not satisfactorily meet the requirements of the company's overall product policy at each of these check points, it should be dropped or seriously changed.

Of course, at the start of an exploratory research program there will not be enough information for a complete analysis of the project. An important part of the development will be to obtain the needed information through marketing research, product research, and engineering studies. Nevertheless, early analysis of the information that is available can help prevent such wasted projects as those on the conversion of styrene already mentioned.

Executives can ensure proper consideration of product policy in development work by requiring a brief analysis of each project whenever they must authorize major operating expenditures. One company that controls research and development work by formal "development authorizations" has incorporated such an analysis in its standard authorization form. Despite some initial protests from the research department, the system has worked well for several years now.

Integration   Should a company make or buy a component part or raw material? Captive production gives certainty of supply, control of quality, and the possibility of substantial cost savings. It may also divert capital from more profitable end products and lead a company into unrelated fields in which it cannot operate efficiently. Furthermore a captive production unit lacks the spur of competition. It may produce only at high cost and lag behind in technological development.[5]

Analysis in terms of a company's product policy helps to indicate these dangers. In general, a company should produce its own parts or materials only when all three of these conditions are met:

1. The raw material considered as a product by itself meets the requirements of the company's product strategy.
2. Internal consumption is large relative to the output of a plant of economic size—say, over 50%. (Otherwise the company is adding a new product, not primarily integrating.)
3. Production will give substantial savings— or profits, if the material is to be sold externally as well.

Somewhat similar considerations apply when a company decides whether to sell an intermediate product or to process it further toward the form in which it will finally be used. Each additional step in manufacture eliminates the cost of intermediate distribution, increases the value added by manufacture, and adds to total profits. However, further processing can also lead a company into fields where it cannot function as efficiently as its customers.

Here again an analysis in terms of product policy is useful. As a general rule, further

processing is justified only when all three of these requirements are satisfied:

1. The new end product resulting from further processing meets the requirements of the company's product strategy.
2. The cost of the present product is large relative to the total cost of the new end product—say, over 50%.
3. The new processing step will improve the profitability of the over-all operation.

Old Products   The analysis of unsatisfactory products already made and sold is a less common but widely needed application of product policy. Some executives periodically review all product lines to eliminate obsolescent items and to prevent the diversion of effort on low-volume, relatively unprofitable products. For example:

After such a survey one company with annual sales of $40,000,000 eliminated sixteen different products with a total volume of $3,300,000. It also made a number of improvements in methods of handling the products retained.

Over the next three years the company's total sales increased by one-half and its profits by some twenty times. Among the many factors contributing to these spectacular increases, top executives have stated that dropping unsatisfactory products was one of the most important.

BUILDING FOR THE FUTURE

Besides helping the executive himself make better decisions on product questions such as those just discussed, a good product policy helps to build teamwork throughout the organization. If soundly conceived, clearly stated, and thoroughly understood by all supervisory and professional employees, the policy can be an important tool for control and coordination.

Finally, this approach to product strategy can also have a very dynamic effect in shaping the future development of a company. There is no need to take the present weaknesses for granted. If different resources and a different product strategy show greater promise for the future, then the analysis will indicate where the company must change and strengthen itself. On this basis management can take the constructive steps that are needed.

---

[5] See Carter C. Higgins, "Make-or-Buy Re-examined," *Harvard Business Review*, March-April, 1955, p. 109. —The editors of *Harvard Business Review*.

The Mechanics of Implementation*

GEORGE A. PECK

In launching a program of expansion, we believe that sound forward planning is absolutely essential to achieve efficiency and show a profit in such a competitive industry as ours. Intelligent planning, coupled with our present cost-reduction program, should:

1. Pave the way for a more effective sales program.
2. Improve the procurement of purchased materials.
3. Smooth out production peaks and valleys.
4. Simplify labor problems.
5. Provide a systematic basis for sound budgeting.

In our case, some definite period over which to plan had to be chosen. As stated, we think that a five-year span is the optimum period of time, since anything else is insufficient for long-range engineering, real estate, and capital assets planning, while a longer period would involve too much "crystal balling." A new year is added to the plan on December 15th, and the plan is adjusted and revised at the divisional level every June 15th. This frequency of adjustment maintains the plan as a current guide but prevents it from fluctuating to the point of confusion.

Except where specifically indicated, the following discussion will deal with those phases of the planning work carried out at the divisional or operating level.

THE SALES FORECAST

The backbone of any long-range planning, of course, is the sales forecast which is prepared by the Sales Department of each division in cooperation with the Business Research, Market Analysis, Engineering, Research, and

Production Departments of the company. This forecast is broken down into individual product lines.

Exhibit 1 is a typical flow chart outlining the group effort and individual department responsibility for furnishing various phases of information to the Sales Department for sales forecast purposes. As shown, the Production Committee is responsible for furnishing the preliminary cost estimates to the Research and Development group as well as furnishing preliminary cost details to the Sales Forecasting

EXHIBIT 1   Flow Chart

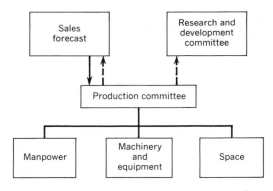

group (see dotted lines on chart). This happens in advance of the preparation of the divisional sales forecast. The information is used by Research and Development and Sales Forecasting to arrive at their final forecast. Then, once the sales forecast has become final for budget, it becomes the responsibility of the Production Committee to prepare final figures on manpower, space, and machinery needed to fulfill the forecast.

One of our recent sales forecasts (Exhibit 2) indicates a steady increase of commercial and government dollar volume for a particular division. The rate of increase was decided by our top management in the manner that has

---

* Reprinted by permission of the publisher from *Launching a Company Expansion Program,* American Management Association, Financial Management Series, no. 112, New York, 1956, pp. 23–34. Mr. Peck was formerly associated with the General Dynamics Corporation.

EXHIBIT 2   Typical Divisional Five-Year Sales Forecast

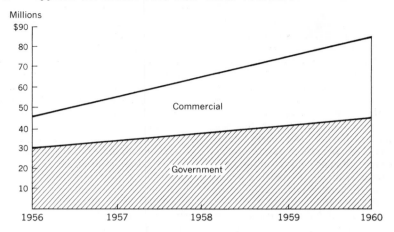

previously been described. In the case of equipment manufactured for the government, Exhibit 3 shows a sales forecast giving information upon which each prediction is based. This involves classifying the sales figures as (*a*) signed contracts, (*b*) good possibilities, and (*c*) hopeful guesses. The five-year forecast of sales is considered as relatively firm for its first two years, while the last three years are regarded as "preliminary."

While the Production Committee has done much preliminary estimating for the Research and Development Committee, it has also worked very closely with the Sales Department in preparing the sales forecast by estimating

the cost of new developments and revising costs on present production contracts. These revised cost data serve as a guide for the Sales Department to predict selling prices of the same equipment on future contract production runs.

Once a sales forecast becomes final, the Production Committee swings into a very important phase of its work. The production manager of each division heads up the Production Committees; and, with the aid of production engineers, test equipment engineers, and inspection, purchasing, and production control personnel, he prepares the requirements for manpower, space, and equipment.

EXHIBIT 3   Government Contracts: Five-Year Sales Forecast

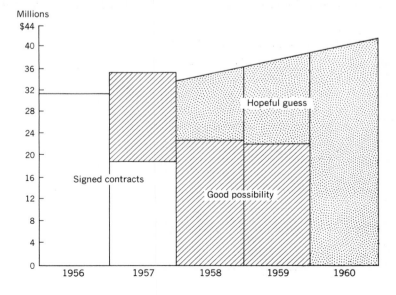

MANPOWER REQUIREMENTS

Each production manager prepares for his operational vice president manpower requirements estimated from the size and rate of production indicated by the sales forecast. These requirements are scheduled for each product line on a monthly basis for the first year and on an annual basis thereafter. The various charts are combined into two schedules: one which shows the monthly schedule for the first year and another which shows the yearly fluctuations in the divisional personnel requirements for the next five years. Because it is a well-known fact that a steady or gradually increasing workforce is the most efficient, considerable effort is expended to achieve this condition.

Exhibit 4 shows a typical manpower chart for a division. To achieve a smooth-looking chart of this nature, the production rates are juggled and rearranged for the various product lines—within reason, of course—so that an over-all manpower requirement schedule is obtained. From this schedule of direct labor personnel, needs for supervisory and indirect personnel are predicted by using ratios developed for individual departments at Stromberg-Carlson. Although these ratios vary from job to job, we have developed fairly practical estimates for the commercial and government production lines. Requirements for supervisory personnel, as well as such indirect labor as production engineers, expediters, maintenance men, janitors, and stock clerks, are estimated in this way.

Plans are made to fill these personnel needs, first, by transferring surplus personnel from other departments and, second, by hiring. The president of our local union is advised at this time of our anticipated personnel requirements and of the plans which we intend to use to meet them. This policy has met with the wholehearted approval of both the union members and the officers, and we have never experienced any difficulty in selling our plans and policies to them. The absence of job seniority in our plants allows us to transfer workers from job to job for the mutual advantage of both employee and company.

If the requirements for supervisory and indirect personnel exceed the present supply, the direct labor payroll is examined by the responsible supervisors for persons who might qualify for promotion to these better jobs. If there are sufficient numbers of such persons involved, a formal in-plant training program is initiated; and, in addition, these persons might also be enrolled in appropriate technical schools in the area. With regard to these outside courses, our company follows the practice of paying one-half of the tuition for courses successfully completed.

When the survey of personnel requirements is made, it often reveals that some of the required engineering and higher-paid supervisory personnel are not available in our plant. The Personnel Department is then provided with a personnel requisition for the needed people. This is done some months in advance of the time that we shall need these people, so that careful testing and selection of candidates can be undertaken.

Once the various manpower schedules are set up, we try to maintain a ratio of direct labor personnel to indirect labor personnel in the ratio of three direct to one indirect.

EXHIBIT 4   Typical Divisional Forecast of Manpower Requirements

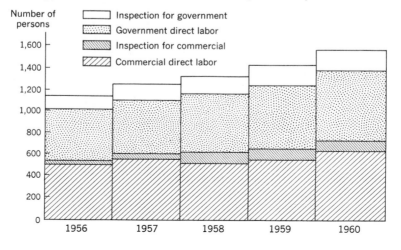

MANUFACTURING SPACE

When the manpower requirements have been set for the division and we have calculated our indirect personnel, it is possible to make an estimate of the additional space required.

The amount of space needed for the manufacturing area is calculated by multiplying the number of production and inspection workers by our standard square-foot allowance per employee. The space requirements for engineering, production engineering, and office can all be estimated in a similar manner. The requirements of all departments are then totaled and compared to the amount of space available. The difference, of course, is the amount of additional engineering office and production space required to fulfill the demands of the growth and expansion program.

Exhibit 5 shows the total manufacturing area required by one of our divisions. The three tightly crosshatched figures represent the existing space; the other figures represent the space which must be added. Space requirements cannot be fully determined without considering the type and amount of production machinery and equipment that will be required for the planned rate of production as well as the type of assembly. Past history proves a very important aid in determining some of these factors for future production.

After the exact space requirements have been determined, it is necessary to convert this information into monetary terms to determine how much the space is going to cost us; whether we are going to build or lease; and, also, the type of building that we are going to put up. Will it be single-story or double-story? Will we have available parking space? What about heating in our central plant, materials handling in the new space, and so forth?

NECESSARY EQUIPMENT

Once these questions have been answered and space requirements have been settled, we can move to the last and probably the most important of the functions—the determination of how much equipment is necessary to carry on our program.

Automation   Automatic assembly, dip soldering machines, materials handling systems, and automatic packers are only a few of the large and expensive tools which must be planned for. To determine the full impact of these and other automatic machines upon the company, Stromberg-Carlson formed an Automation group two years ago. It soon realized that automatic assembly machines would be an absolute necessity for survival in an industry as competitive as ours. Accordingly, this group was transferred to the Research Department and given the responsibility of developing an

EXHIBIT 5   Required Manufacturing Floor Space

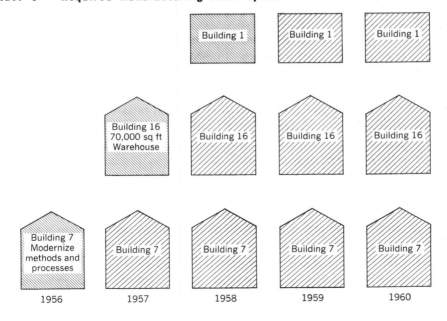

automatic assembly line for the manufacture of electronic equipment. The actual assembly equipment has recently been purchased to specifications written by this group, who will modify it to accommodate our various products.

An integral part of this automation study program was the redesign of one of our standard table-model radios to facilitate automatic assembly. It was revealed during the course of this redesign that many of the standard parts of a radio or television set must themselves be redesigned, reshaped, or packaged differently to allow their use in automatic production machinery. Now that the redesign of component parts, end product, and production equipment has been established, it is planned that this Automation group will be transferred to the vice president of manufacturing. There it will be responsible for the installation of the automatic line in the factory and for supervising the pilot run on scheduled production.

To complement the work done by the Automation group on assembly methods, our Test Equipment Engineering Department began investigation of automatic testing techniques and equipment that would further reduce manpower requirements while improving product uniformity. It is essential to our growth and expansion program that the technical manpower requirements be lessened, as there are not a sufficient number of technically trained persons available to meet even the present requirements.

The equipment developed by this department enables us to conserve technical manpower and thereby realize cost reductions in the manufacture of commercial equipment as well as government electronic gear. As to product uniformity, one of the prime virtues of automatic production equipment, to the government inspector, is the much higher degree of control that is possible. With automatic testing equipment, aligning and testing are less subject to human error, thus making statistical analysis a more potent and meaningful tool.

Standard Tools and Machinery   Funds also have to be provided for additional tools and machinery of a standard nature and for replacement of tools and machinery which are wearing out. Historically in our shop, over a period of years, insufficient funds were appropriated to maintain our machine departments properly; therefore, we have been, and are, faced with "catching up" as well as planning normal replacement and expansion. The Production Engineering Department is responsible for this program.

There are many areas where a need for replacement is apparent simply because available equipment is not capable of producing satisfactory parts within specification. It is not only a question of old and worn machinery; we are constantly faced with changes in design concept which require tolerances that were not considered feasible when the present equipment was manufactured 20 or 30 years ago. This then means that much equipment cannot be used for certain parts. For scheduling work, and for considering replacements, we have graded all machines into three classifications which indicate their condition.

It is not necessary that all equipment be of the latest design and in top condition. But a great amount of desirable efficiency and flexibility is lost if a foreman can use only a small percentage of his equipment on high-precision work. Since an increasing percentage of our requirements call for very close tolerances, he is forced to schedule more and more of his work on fewer machines. This means shorter, uneconomic runs in order to free the machines for other urgent requirements, with the resulting increases in setup time and costs.

Replacement or Redesign?   Because the older equipment is also subject to higher maintenance cost, a program has been established to provide for accumulating maintenance and repair labor and the cost of major parts by machine number. Although these are general overhead charges against the department, this statistical accumulation by machine will provide factual data which can be used to good effect in determining when a machine should be replaced. Moreover, a tabulated report of machine utilization gives us information which is increasingly useful. This shows the per cent of the normal 40 hours each week during which a machine is actually used, and also reflects certain major items, such as down time for repair. Other reasons for non-use— for example, "no requirement," or machine inadequacy—must likewise be studied.

In an increasing number of cases, we therefore have such factual data as (1) grading of the machine, (2) maintenance and repair costs, and (3) per cent of utilization, as indications that perhaps a machine should be replaced. The next step is examination of the requirements for the type of work done by the machine. Are the parts produced part of a continuing sales requirement, or is this requirement only temporary? Is Design Engineering reasonably satisfied with the product, or is a redesign under way, and would the concept of the redesign be changed if there were a possibility of using a new and different machine? Perhaps Design Engineering is partially restricted in its work by its knowledge of the equipment presently available, and its thinking might change if this restriction were removed and different equipment were available for manufacturing the part.

Choice of New Machines

Assume that as a result of these considerations a new machine is suggested. It then becomes necessary to forecast accurately production costs for the appropriate parts on the new machine. A comparison of production costs for the old and new machines provides a basis for determining the "return on investment," which is the current measuring stick being used.

It may be necessary, of course, to compare several possible new machines to determine which is the most profitable replacement. In this area, we encounter a need to anticipate future development in the field. A machine may wear out or be obsoleted by new developments in machine design. New equipment in a competitor's factory can obsolete our equipment much more rapidly than the passing years. Therefore, although it is impossible to predict many new machine developments, it is necessary for our production engineers to stay abreast of all new machines and processes. An example of this type of planning is the fact that certain equipment recommended for the 1956 program was specifically chosen because it will fit into possible automated assembly lines now in the very early planning stages.

Analysis of Results Obtained

Another very important phase of Production Engineering's responsibility is the investigation and analysis of results actually obtained by new equipment which has been purchased and installed. This continuous check is essential if we are to be certain of our approach to the problems. We must "discover if we were right" —this must not be a case of "proving we were right."

Our initial results in this type of investigation are encouraging. An example is the Stokes automatic molding machine which has recently been installed in one of our departments. The original justification contained a cost analysis indicating an annual cost saving of approximately $19,600. To date, 130,000 parts of one type have been run on this new machine with a saving of $2,600. Extended to an annual rate, our experience thus far indicates a continuing annual saving of $18,500 per year for this machine which cost $10,500.

Justifying Expenditures

Our concept of planning and itemizing a capital budget has changed considerably in recent years, and much more detailed analyses to provide proper justification of new acquisitions are now required. The limiting factor, of course, will always be the funds available, and there will be the problem of comparing the relative merits of many possible expenditures, all of which are justified, to determine which ones will produce the greatest return for the company.

The budget for capital equipment is presented in both written and graphic form. Exhibit 6 shows a typical capital expenditures budget for a division over a five-year span. It indicates the machinery necessary to maintain production at forecast levels.

EXHIBIT 6   Projected Fixed Capital Expenditures

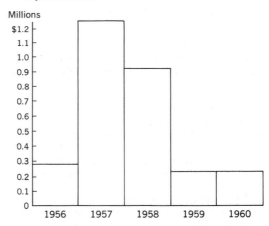

We find that capital equipment expenditures vary considerably between the divisions and that it is necessary to do juggling to provide ample protection across the years. Exhibit 6, it must be remembered, represents just one of the divisions. When all divisional requirements are added together, we show a more constant level of annual expenditures.

In these few pages, we have tried to show how our formal growth and expansion plan is handled at the operating level. The important point to keep in mind is that it takes a great deal of coordinated effort and constant attention to keep a program of this nature on the track. Needless to say, we feel that the amount of effort involved is more than justified by the results.

21

*Forecasting of Cash**

ROBERT I. PHEMISTER

Stated in simple terms, financial policy is a plan which answers two important questions: "Where will the money come from?" and "What will it be used for?" To assist management in finding the answers to these questions, we have developed a method of cash forecasting which has proved reliable under many changing conditions. . . .

HOW THE SYSTEM WORKS

The cash forecast is based on a complete budget program comprised of a series of individual forecasts covering every phase of our operations. Each forecast is carefully prepared in detail by the individual responsible for the particular operation. For example, the sales manager of a division submits a forecast of sales showing the quantity of each product he expects to sell and the price he expects to receive. In a similar manner executives in every part of our company contribute their forecasts to the budget program.

The individual forecasts thus obtained are translated in terms of cash and set down in a way which shows clearly their relationship to each other. The resulting cash forecast then becomes the framework from which definite financial policies can be developed. This forecast is prepared each month for the Board of Directors and covers a period of 24 months in advance. It shows the cash position of the company in terms of long-range planning.

The first of the two statements which comprise the cash forecast shows the estimated change in cash position for the two-year period (Figure 3). This statement is divided into two sections, the first showing the estimated sources of cash. "Estimated Earnings" as given in this

section are based on information furnished by the division general managers and include new earnings from the proposed expansion of plant facilities in addition to forecasted earnings from present facilities. Since the estimated earnings have been reduced by the estimated amount of depreciation and provision for income taxes, these items are added back to arrive at the cash earnings.

The second section of the form shows the estimated disbursements of cash. "Expenditures for Construction" are obtained from the construction budget, which lists every construction project that is seriously contemplated during the next two or more years. These budgets are submitted by each plant manager and approved by his division manager. They contain a brief description of each project, its estimated cost, and the quarterly periods in which funds will be required for construction. Here again we work from the smallest element toward the total result.

"Working Capital," as we use the term, is the money which we need to finance operations from the time raw material is purchased until the cash from the sale of finished goods is collected from customers. In addition to the funds required for regular operations, we provide for the additional working capital which will be required for the expanded facilities. This amount is determined from the estimates of construction projects which show the new working capital required in addition to the construction cost of the project.

"Investment in Associated Companies" as used on this form represents funds which these companies expect to require for construction or other purposes. "Dividends Paid" is based on the common and preference shares outstanding at that time. It is assumed that the existing quarterly rate on common shares will be maintained. Since income taxes represent a major disbursement and it is our policy to carry a balance of tax notes on hand equal to our federal income tax liability, we include in the estimated disbursements the amount of tax notes we expect to purchase.

* Reprinted by permission of the publishers from *A Program of Financial Planning and Controls: The Monsanto Chemical Company,* American Management Association, Financial Management Series, no. 103, New York, 1953, pp. 10–13. Mr. Phemister is controller, Inorganic Chemicals Division, Monsanto Chemical Company.

FIGURE 3   Monsanto Chemical Company and Consolidated Subsidiaries Estimated Change in Cash Position for the Two Years Ending September 30, 1952
(In thousands of dollars)

| | YEAR ENDING SEPTEMBER 30 | |
	1951	1952
Cash balance at beginning of period	$ 56,263	$ 27,113
Sources of cash:		
Earnings	25,622	30,461
Depreciation	13,510	15,956
Provision for income taxes	40,627	46,559
Total	$136,022	$120,089
Disbursement of cash:		
Expenditures for construction	$ 44,789	$ 79,620
Working capital, etc.:		
For new construction projects	8,920	13,200
Other	200	452
Investment in associated companies	1,000	7,000
Dividends paid	12,400	12,400
Purchase of tax notes	41,600	47,650
Total disbursements	$ 27,113	$160,322
Cash balance at end of period	$108,909	($ 40,233)

Notes:

DETERMINING FUNDS REQUIRED

On this statement the estimated disbursements of cash may well exceed the estimated cash that will be available. For example, if we have planned a large expansion program, this statement will show the need for additional funds.

The second statement (Figure 4) of the cash forecast shows the estimated balance of cash and tax notes at the end of each month during the two-year period covered by the forecast. Information for this statement is obtained by spreading each of the factors on the previous statement and computing the month-by-month change in cash. From the monthly cash balances, the Directors can determine how much and at what time additional cash will be required. Armed with the information shown in these statements, the Directors can appraise the situation and determine a course of action.

I might mention an actual forecast which we furnished our Directors in September, 1950. It was evident from this forecast that funds would be required early in 1952 and that the cash deficiency would reach a maximum of about $60,000,000 in July, 1952. As early as 1949, when our construction program began to take shape, the monthly cash forecast indicated that additional funds would be required to carry out the program. Therefore, the Directors were advised of the estimated financial picture well in advance.

In this particular instance, the Directors secured additional funds in 1951. In January, 1952, we sold $104,000,000 worth of common stock and debentures. That is one illustration of the value of our cash forecast as an aid to financial planning. Without a forecast the needs for additional funds would have become apparent eventually. It is very unlikely, however, that the requirements could have been estimated accurately either as to time or amount. Financial planning under these conditions would have been reduced to expediency, which is both risky and expensive.

The success of our cash-forecasting procedure lies in the fact that we gather together and coordinate all the individual forecasts covering each phase of our operations. Each

FIGURE 4   Monsanto Chemical Company and Consolidated
            Subsidiaries Estimated Monthly Cash Position
            for the Two Years Ending September 30, 1952
            (In thousands of dollars)

	MONTH END CASH BALANCE	TAX NOTES ON HAND
1950		
October	$54,676	$23,741
November	51,594	27,092
December	50,210	27,879
1951		
January	46,767	31,025
February	42,061	34,248
March	37,166	29,826
April	32,403	32,060
May	31,628	35,297
June	29,405	30,533
July	28,287	33,761
August	28,359	36,904
September	27,113	34,221
October	27,287	37,552
November	26,593	40,808
December	26,887	37,865
1952		
January	25,344	41,726
February	12,066	45,694
March	(2,106)	36,530
April	(17,405)	40,434
May	(34,913)	44,391
June	(49,022)	35,324
July	(60,095)	39,519
August	(52,898)	43,769
September	(40,233)	41,663

responsible executive in our company contributes a carefully prepared forecast covering those operations for which he is responsible. We believe this method yields more accurate results than one based on a few general estimates of future conditions. Because it has been reliable under many changing conditions, it has earned the confidence of management.

22

A New Way to Manage: Integrated Planning and Control*

JOHN O. TOMB

The fault is certainly not in any failure to accept the idea of planning or control. No textbook on management, no executive development program, no description of modern business practice fails to list planning and control among the central responsibilities of every manager. The fault does not lie in a lack of procedures or mechanics. There are elaborate forms, timetables, and flow charts. Nor do the difficulties stem from inadequate provision for the planning and control process in the organizational structure. Departments traditionally concerned with these two processes have grown in number and scope of responsibility. Separate groups and positions are increasingly being created to coordinate planning activities in diversified, complex enterprises. But for all the acceptance, and the mechanism, and the organization, the effort remains more often a disappointment than a triumph.

MUCH PLANNING IS UNREALISTIC

A basic difficulty is simply this—most planning and control systems are not rooted in the realities of the business. All too often they function within the straitjacket of accounting conventions. They require an estimated number for every blank space on a form, but they require little attention to the ways in which these numbers are to be achieved. As a result, they provide neither a useful guide to action nor a reliable basis for control.

So it is not really surprising that the operating manager looks upon planning as an exercise for which he must find time, rather than a useful tool to increase his own contribution to corporate goals. It is red tape that diverts his attention from the company and its objectives,

rather than an activity that identifies him more closely with them.

Clearly, what is needed is a planning process that makes things happen, a planning process that provides a secure basis for control by the man who plans and by those above him, a planning process that is an integral part of the management task.

Recently, a few pioneering companies have worked out a new approach to developing such a process. It has been called "Integrated Planning and Control" (IPC) because it integrates planning and control into a single, on-going activity, which is itself the very heart of the managerial function.

Under this approach, the planning and control process is no longer a numerical exercise so separate from day-to-day operations that it appears to be pursued as an end in itself. Nor is it a procedure restricting the actions of line managers to a pattern imposed by some other part of the organization. Instead, IPC is a job-oriented approach to planning—an approach that concentrates on planning action. For example, under IPC a sales manager is required to develop his marketing program before he sets a sales target. Thus, if poor distribution has been curtailing sales, he includes in his plan a program to obtain better outlets before indicating a sales increase. Similarly, if a plant manager wants to show reduced overhead in his plan, he must support this reduction by a program to cut back his staff by a specified number of people.

Obviously, a manager who plans this way develops a total operating program. Thus, IPC makes planning and control an integral part of his job rather than an appendage only remotely associated with the way he performs his job.

In the words of one executive, it represents, quite literally, a "new way to manage the business." The results of this new way of managing to date have been dramatic:

* Reprinted by permission of the publisher from *California Management Review*, vol. 5, no. 1, pp. 57–62, Fall, 1962. Mr. Tomb is a director in the Chicago office of McKinsey and Company, Inc., management consultants.

- A drug company had completed its conventional budget for the coming year when management decided to introduce IPC. The IPC approach resulted in a planned profit increase of 25 percent over the earlier budget figures. More important, the individuals in the company felt more confident of achieving these higher profits than the previous budgeted amount.

- A retail merchandising chain introduced IPC on a limited basis and found that expense and profit control were notably better in stores that used the IPC approach than in others that did not.

- A multidivision capital goods producer found that IPC made its managers "aware of profit improvement opportunities they never imagined existed." The result—a profit increase in one year of 47 percent.

- A large equipment producer planned for an increase in profits of more than 60 percent after it installed IPC—and then proceeded to achieve an increase of 70 percent.

HOW IPC WORKS

There are three distinctive characteristics of integrated planning and control that enable it to make unusual contributions to corporate profit. First, it multiplies the creative and constructive analysis of improvement opportunities by every manager who participates in the process. Second, it identifies him so closely with his work, his objectives, and his opportunities that he functions far more effectively in the pursuit of his goals. Third, it provides managers with a basis for positive control instead of merely giving them historical analysis or explanations. As a result, managers can deal imaginatively with change rather than defensively with their shortcomings.

Integrated planning and control requires three major steps:

- Each manager identifies the activities for which he is specifically responsible.

- Each manager selects from the entire range of his responsibilities those activities where significant improvement can be made.

- For each of these selected activities, each manager prepares a plan to achieve clearly defined improvement. Each plan is more than a statement of an expected end result; it also indicates how that end result is to be achieved and what its profit impact will be.

A manager who goes through these steps develops plans that are realistic and reliable. Because such plans incorporate his proposed actions and are not limited to accounting forecasts, he acquires a sense of personal commitment to whatever objectives his plan states. As a result, top management can have real confidence that approved plans will be carried out. The sections that follow discuss in detail each of these major steps of an IPC action plan.

RELATING PLANS TO RESPONSIBILITIES

Before any manager can effectively develop plans, he must have a clear understanding of the activities for which he is responsible. Although this statement may seem axiomatic, any experienced organization analyst knows how few managers have a full and accurate understanding of their responsibilities.

In many companies, apparently, form is mistaken for substance. An organization manual is prepared containing detailed position descriptions. Once the manual has been distributed, everyone assumes that all members of the organization understand what they are supposed to do. The fact of the matter is that this assumption is often incorrect; for the descriptions themselves are typically incomplete, highly generalized, and frequently out of date. They are full of such words and phrases as "coordinate," "collaborate with" and "keep alert to." They are often inadequate in assigning basic responsibilities for important tasks that involve several participants. And, of course, they give almost no indication of the relative importance of major elements of performance. For example:

> When describing the allocation of marketing activities in a large multidivision company, several key managers claimed responsibility for the same tasks. The product managers, marketing research manager, and sales managers each believed he had final responsibility for establishing the planned sales level. Further, the marketing research and product managers named the tasks of "determining marketing programs" and "specifying advertising media" as among their responsibilities. And there were other activities for which none of the key managers assumed responsibility. Although the company could point with pride to the manuals of position descriptions, there was an extraordinary lack of understanding of individual responsibilities among the men who filled the positions.

To ensure the understanding of individual responsibilities that is essential to developing meaningful plans, the IPC process begins by identifying all the activities that need to be performed if the business is to be successful. These activities—or "elements of performance" —are listed without attempting to assign them to a particular position.

Once these elements of performance have been defined for a functional area, responsibility for them is reviewed. This review does not embrace the larger task of an organization study. Rather, it focuses on identifying for each individual all the activities he needs to perform in order to carry out his job. The discussion of a particular element of performance with an individual manager usually helps him to think a lot more deeply about his job and to distinguish more clearly between routine, administrative tasks and those activities that can influence company profits. Because this process reveals position relationships so clearly, it identifies the critical points at which plans of individual managers have to be reconciled and consolidated to form a single, effective program for the total functional area or division.

SELECTING AREAS FOR IMPROVEMENT

The second step in effective planning is to identify opportunities for improvement. This is totally different, it should be noted, from the typical budgeting approach. There, managers are preoccupied with determining what amounts should be set for such accounting categories as salaries, overtime, supplies, telephone, and travel. These figures are often arrived at by applying percentage increases or decreases to the amounts for the previous year. Rarely does a manager free himself from this preoccupation with numbers and ask the key question: *"How* can the activities assigned to me be performed better or at a significantly lower cost?"

IPC has been designed to overcome this critical limitation. A manager does not start to plan until he thoroughly understands the performance elements making up his job. He starts his planning by using these performance elements as a check list. From this check list he selects those activities that present opportunities for significant improvement.

Thus, planning is a selective process that builds in an automatic bias for profit improvement. Of the 15 to 20 performance elements for which a manager may be responsible, he is likely to build improvement plans for only five or six. Of course, he might limit himself to one or two; or he might decide to tackle nine or ten.

For example, one marketing executive might soundly decide that his major efforts for the coming year should be aimed at increasing his field sales force in certain regions and improving his distribution structure in certain markets. But another marketing executive might add to these two goals improved packaging, a modified system of account coverage, revision in pricing structure, and a new type of sales promotion campaign. What is important in either case is that plans are developed to capitalize on what the manager considers to be his own best opportunities for significant improvement.

PREPARING PLANS

Once he has selected his improvement areas, a manager develops his detailed plan. Every such plan should indicate both the desired end result and the means for achieving it. Thus, every plan involves three key ingredients:

- **Objective**—the improvement to be achieved
- **Action program**—the specific steps required to achieve the objective
- **Profit impact**—the effect of the action on company profits and resources.

Exhibit I illustrates a typical plan for the manufacturing function which includes each of the primary ingredients outlined above. It also indicates who is responsible for each action program step and the timing of each step.

The development of the "how to do it" action program illustrated encourages a manager to explore many alternatives that may be available instead of settling for the first solution that comes to mind. More often than not, the first solution is the traditional one. The manager grows in his job and increases his worth to the company only when he begins increasingly to take fresh and imaginative looks at the way old problems are solved. IPC makes it difficult for a manager to continue in the same old rut; it prods him to break new ground.

MAKES PLANNER INVOLVE HIMSELF IN JOB

The completeness of this type of planning also gives a manager confidence in his ability to carry out his plans. Most managers who go through the IPC sequence begin to develop a much stronger proprietary interest in their jobs. The fact that they played a major role in identifying improvement opportunities and in determining how to capitalize on them tends to develop a spirit of dedication to make things happen. This sense of commitment and of self-discipline is an integral part of the IPC process and becomes a key factor in achieving desired

---

EXHIBIT I   Manufacturing Plan

OBJECTIVE   REDUCE THE FREQUENCY AND COST OF FAULTY CASTINGS RECEIVED FROM THE XYZ COMPANY.

ACTION PROGRAM

STEPS	RESPONSIBILITY	TIMING
Ensure recognition by supplier of problem with "hard spots" in castings	Purchasing manager Production manager	Completed
Negotiate price concession on all castings received during weeks when we return more than ten bad castings	Purchasing manager	Jan. 31, 1962
Set up storage area to accumulate ruined castings	Facilities manager	Jan. 31, 1962
Establish procedures to record machine downtime and cutter breakage with individual castings	Production control	Feb. 15, 1962
Submit information weekly to XYZ Company	Purchasing manager	Begin Mar. 1, 1962

PROFIT IMPACT:	1962 PROFIT INCREASE (DECREASE)
Price concessions	$ 7,000
Effect of improved quality	
Scrap	8,500
Overtime	3,500
Expense tools	9,000
Lost production	20,000
Other	12,000
Modifications in storage area	(2,000)
Recording procedures	(1,000)
Other costs	(3,000)
Total profit impact	$54,000

---

end results and controlling performance against plan.

Integrated planning and control thus creates and maintains a sense of urgency and responsibility among managers that is, in many ways, its most important aspect. It literally forces a manager to take a good hard look at the activities assigned to him, evaluate each activity and determine where improvement can be made, and decide how much improvement he can achieve and how he will achieve it.

KEEPS BOSS INFORMED

A plan like the one illustrated is also of great value to a manager's superior. Because each plan details the steps to be taken to achieve its objective, the superior knows exactly what his subordinates intend to do. He can constructively appraise the soundness of their proposed actions. The superior may be able to contribute recommendations, based on his broader experience, that lead to helpful modifications in the objectives or in the action steps. He also can integrate each subordinate's objectives with those developed by other managers. In contrast, a typical budgeting system may provide a superior with little more than accounting data, but without any indication of the action programs planned by his managers.

The section on "Profit Impact" illustrated at the bottom of Exhibit I shows how the action programs contained in each manager's plans are tied into the company's accounting and budgeting system. This section translates planned actions into monetary terms. But, by its very structure, it focuses attention on what is to be done, not on expense categories.

COPING WITH CHANGING CONDITIONS

No planning process can foresee all the contingencies that may develop—either internally or externally—during the period covered by a plan. It is important, however, that unfavorable changes do not result in watering down the objectives agreed upon when plans were developed and approved. And it is equally important that managers do not use these changed conditions as an excuse for failure to achieve planned goals.

IPC fosters a commitment to achieving planned objectives in spite of change or difficulty. When unanticipated internal or external conditions prevent the achievement of an objective through the means planned in the original action program, most managers respond by developing an alternative program rather than using changed conditions as a scapegoat.

This positive approach is illustrated by the actions of the marketing director in a company using the IPC approach:

The marketing plan for 1961—which had been developed in depth—included the introduction of a major new product during the second month of the fiscal year. It was planned that this product would account for 10 percent of the 1961 sales volume and 12 percent of the merchandising profit. At the time the marketing plan was developed, other functional areas within the company—e.g., engineering and manufacturing—also developed specific plans to ensure availability of the new product. However, when manufacturing started to produce the product in volume, it found that a critical assembly, supplied by an outside vendor, was 95 percent defective. Investigation revealed that the problem was caused by the vendor's manufacturing process and would take six months to correct. No other suppliers were available.

Rather than give up the planned additional profit, the marketing director initiated a series of revised action steps to make up for the lack of this new product. These steps involved:

- Evaluating existing products to determine those with the highest merchandising profit.

- Identifying segments of the market where sales of existing products could be increased; revamping the advertising and sales promotion program to reduce emphasis on the new product and divert funds to new promotions on existing products.

- Redeploying the sales force to maximize selling effort in markets that promised immediate response.

The net effect of these revised action steps was a gain just as large as the one the manager originally planned; the marketing division reached both its sales and its profit objective.

The marketing director could have used the unavailability of the new product as a good excuse for not achieving the sales and profit objectives. The unforeseen event was completely beyond his control or influence. But because of his deep sense of personal commitment, he was convinced that something could be done about the situation, and he did it.

This attitude is in sharp contrast with management's attitude in many companies using a conventional budgeting approach. In such companies, management tends to lower its sights whenever the going gets a bit rough. Managers look for scapegoats for failure to reach planned objectives. As the rather typical general manager of a construction materials company put it: "We are completely at the mercy of the level of housing starts. If they go down, our sales go down; if they go up, our sales go up." It simply never occurred to him that by imaginative management action he could control his company's destiny to a far greater degree than he, or many of his competitors, believed possible.

RETENTION OF SOME CONVENTIONAL STEPS

IPC by no means abandons conventional planning and control approaches in their entirety. Rather, it extends the usefulness of such conventional steps as:

- The development and communication of corporate or divisional goals and planning assumptions that provide a frame of reference for the planning efforts of individual managers.

- The review and evaluation of plans by each manager's superior.

- The consolidation of plans from individual managers into functional plans (i.e., marketing, manufacturing, personnel, etc.), and the later translation of these functional plans into accounting terms so that conventional statements of income, costs, expenses, and cash flow can be prepared.

- The consolidation of functional plans into divisional or corporate plans, and the review of these consolidated plans at successive levels of management.

SUMMARY

IPC is more than the substitution of new labels for old. It makes planning and control an integral part of the everyday thinking and acting of every manager. It lifts planning and control out of the systems and procedures category and provides the basis for a total operating program for every individual with management responsibility.

IPC does this by integrating the thoughts and actions of a manager in five ways. This new approach does these things:

- Integrates planning with each manager's responsibilities by relating his plans to the performance elements in his job.
- Integrates each manager's planning with the continuing search for ways to improve profits.
- Integrates the objectives that each manager sets with a detailed action program for achieving each one.

- Integrates into each individual's plans a measure of the overall purpose of the enterprise—effect on profits.
- Integrates into each manager's planning a commitment to "make things happen" regardless of changing conditions.

Integrated planning and control is not something that can be plugged in and then left to run itself. The installation of IPC takes time and dedicated effort. More important, its success requires the unqualified and continuing support of top management. With intelligent installation and use, however, IPC injects a dynamic element into management behavior that can produce dramatic results.

As the president of a company that has pioneered in the development of IPC reported to his stockholders: "During the past year a new planning and control process to achieve maximum effectiveness was developed and is now being established in all of the company's operations. The results from this new planning and control approach have thus far exceeded all expectations."

It is instances like this that lead enthusiastic executives to refer to IPC as "a new way to manage."

23

*Making Long-range Company Planning Pay Off**

GEORGE A. STEINER

This article is devoted to a thumb-nail sketch of two major aspects of long-range planning. First is the methodology or procedure for long-range planning. The second concerns the pay-off to a company that does long-range planning.

* Reprinted by permission of the publisher from the *California Management Review*, vol. 4, no. 2, pp. 28–41, Winter, 1962. Mr. Steiner is professor of business administration and director, Division of Research, Graduate School of Business, University of California, Los Angeles.

I have chosen to dwell on these two points for several reasons. First, while long-range planning has grown rapidly in recent years and has paid off handsomely for many companies, there still are questions raised about its value. Second, while important progress has been made in the techniques of long-range planning, there are comparatively few detailed case studies and principles which are available for those who wish to initiate the process or improve their planning.

These two factors are related. I suspect, although solid proof is not available, that the major reason for the fact that more companies do not engage in long-range planning is that they do not know precisely how to go about it. Not wishing to admit this even to themselves, other reasons are given for the lack of long-range planning.[1]

WHAT IS LONG-RANGE PLANNING?

Planning in general is the conscious determination of courses of action to achieve preconceived objectives. It is deciding in advance what is to be done, when it is to be done, by whom it is to be done, and how it is to be done. It can range from the detailed, specific and rigid to the broad, general and flexible design.

Long-range planning does this for extended periods of time. Long-range planning is a process for establishing long-range goals; working out strategies, programs, and policies to achieve these goals; and setting up the necessary machinery to insure that the company gets where it wants to go.

It is a process of choosing from among alternative courses of action and charting the use of time, resources, and effort to achieve the objective sought. The further into the future the plan stretches the less detailed are its specific parts. The subject matter of long-range plans should cover products, services, facilities, manpower, research and development, organization, marketing, financial matters, and various aspects of management itself.[2]

How Long Is Long-range?
How long a time should a long-range plan cover? The answer to this question is much like the response of Abraham Lincoln when asked how long a man's legs ought to be. "Long enough to reach the ground," said the President.

Similarly, the length of a planning period will vary considerably from company to company and subject to subject. It is not fixed or rigid. The time span of a plan should cover the period encompassing important financial commitments and their pay-off.

For example, depending upon subject matter, coverage should embrace product development time and period of major financial impact following development; resource development time (e.g., sources of supply, management talent, or labor skills); and time required to develop physical facilities plus pay-off period for major capital investments. For most businesses such factors will establish a minimum long-range planning period of from 5 to 10 years.

Formal LRP in Industry
All managers engage in long-range planning—if only to increase their own salaries. If they do not plan they are not doing their jobs. In the past, when top managers needed help in planning they often hired an assistant or created a vice-president for administration.

Large and complex organizations centuries ago had staff positions for planning. Long-range planning, therefore, is not new. What is new is charging someone with full-time responsibility for planning and giving him a staff to do the job. It is the growth of planning departments and staff specialists at the top levels of corporations and major divisions that is new.

Pressures on American companies to establish such formal organizations have been most strong during the past ten years. Among the major pressures are the following:

1. Business has become increasingly complex because of expanding enterprise size, decentralization of authority, diversification of product lines, mergers, and the growing sensitivity of internal operations to uncontrollable environmental forces.

2. Technological rates of change are increasing and placing a premium on those organizations which can foresee and adapt to them.

3. A variety of forces are squeezing profit margins.

4. End-use markets (domestic) are altering significantly and rapidly with geographic population shifts, changes in population composition, new social trends influencing market behavior of consumers, and growing competition for consumer savings.

5. End-use markets (abroad) are changing rapidly with new commercial alignments, and efforts to industrialize the underdeveloped countries of the world.

6. There has been a rapid development of tools for planning and a growing recognition of the need for skilled technical competence to apply them to long-range planning. This trend promises to accelerate. In mind are not alone the new powerful mathematical tools which have been adapted to business decision-making (e.g., linear programming, game theory, probability theory, etc.); but the application of computers, simulation and systems concepts, and new developments in economics, psychology, and other social sciences.

7. Competitors are devoting more attention to long-range planning.[3]

Under such pressures more and more companies in the past ten years have been developing long-range planning programs and extending the field of inquiry further into the future. I believe, however, that effective long-range planning in industry is not as widespread as it ought to be.

Facts about the growth of formalized long-range planning are not plentiful nor reliable. *Nation's Business* concluded that about 20 percent of businesses had long-range planning in 1953 compared to about 50 percent in 1958.[4] The National Industrial Conference Board concluded in 1956 that of 189 manufacturing companies participating in its survey only one out of four had no formalized forward planning or failed to plan ahead beyond one year. About half of those having long-range plans said they included all the major elements of the enterprise in their planning. Only half said they placed much reliance on the plans.[5]

A survey made by *Management Methods* in 1958 revealed that among its respondents, only 18 percent had formal advanced plans while another 52 percent had informal advanced plans. No advanced plans were made in 30 percent of the companies covered. When asked whether respondents felt they were doing as much advanced planning as they should, 72 percent replied in the negative. Practically all planning in companies in this survey was for five years or less.

Professors Sord and Welsch found in a study published in the same year that two-thirds of the number surveyed had long-range plans, but the subject matter varied greatly. Two-thirds had long-range sales plans, but only about one-third had long-range research or expense plans. Only about half had long-range profit or cash plans. Practically all plans were for 5 years or less.[6]

These data, while not conclusive, are helpful. My own empirical observations, together with the data cited, lead me to conclude that, while formal long-range corporate planning has grown by leaps and bounds in the past ten years, the practice is heavily concentrated in larger enterprises, and it is centered there on a few major problem areas (capital expenditures, product development, and sales) for periods less than five years. The coverage, time span, and usage is not great enough in light of potential value.

How to Make a Long-range Plan

In developing long-range plans it is helpful to think in terms of a series of steps. But, since the planner must always think in terms of retracing his thinking, allowance must also be made for some overlapping of these steps.

The sequence of steps presented in the next few paragraphs illustrates one concrete framework upon which a company may plan. It is flexible and has been used successfully. This particular sequence has the virtue of focusing attention on product which is usually, although not always, the principal theme of a business long-range plan.

The specific methodology of planning may vary much from one company to another whether or not the steps presented here are followed. This arises because the process must be flexible to accommodate an unusually complex intermeshing of variables which are subject to constant change. In mind are such factors as the technical knowledge and wisdom of the planners, the particular needs of the enterprise, the organization for planning, availability of strategic facts, subject-matter of the plans, and uses to be made of the results.[7]

First: Plan to Plan

First, is *planning to plan*. As the Cleveland Electric Illuminating Company has so well documented, company planning must be planned.[8] This may seem as redundant as Cole Porter's "Begin the Beguine." But planning does not just happen. It must be planned!

A suitable planning climate must be established, and the organization made planning conscious. Policy decisions must be made about who will do what in planning. And, step-by-step procedures must be worked out. In one major planning program of a large corporation in which I participated the first thing we did was to prepare a detailed letter covering the entire planning procedure for signature by the president. The letter was addressed to all parties involved. In this way everyone knew what was the plan to plan. The newer the plan the more important the thoroughness with which this step should be taken. But even where planning is well established the procedures should be carefully spelled out, as in, for example, the *Westinghouse Planning Guide*.[9]

On the other hand, care should be taken to avoid overdoing this step. It is easily possible to preplan too long, in too much detail and to spend too much time on clarification of procedures. There is too much feed-back in going through the sequences of planning to warrant more than just enough detail in this step to get the process moving.

Basic assumptions must be made at various stages in the planning process. At the outset, however, some of the overall assumptions upon which planning rests should be set forth. In mind, for example, are premises which provide a framework for planning, such as the course of the cold war, population movements, or competitors' activities.

Purely methodological premises may also be established, such as—plans will be based upon constant rather than actual anticipated prices. But, whatever the premises determined, the point is that standards must be developed to guide the planning program. Otherwise, lack of coordination, unnecessary emphasis and study on less important subjects, excessive planning costs, and confusion in drawing conclusions are predictive consequences of poorly devised or neglected premises.

Second: Define Objectives

Second, *objectives of planning must be clearly specified.* The purpose of the plan, the objectives to be sought in the planning process, and the relation of planning goals to other goals and objectives in the enterprise must be clarified. Setting objectives provides the key to how planning will be done, the strategic factors to be emphasized in plan development, and methods by which planning will become the basis for action.

The objective of every business, of course, is to make a profit. Otherwise the business will not survive. But saying this is far from developing a set of goals which will best serve a company and its long-range planning program.

Be Specific. Goals should be established as concretely as possible. What does this mean? Is the goal to be an aggregate absolute volume of profits? Is the goal to be expressed in terms of a percentage of sales? Is it to be in terms of percentage of investment? If it is return on investment, how is this to be calculated? Is it the E. I. du Pont de Nemours and Company or the Monsanto Chemical Company formula? Will a rising rate of return on investment be accepted even if sales do not increase?

Is sales growth in itself a goal? Is sales stability a goal? How are conflicts among goals to be resolved? Are there other objectives which need be expressed as a guide to the planning program?

Defining Corporate Goals. There has recently been a growing interest in defining corporate goals, probably in part as an outgrowth of long-range planning needs. Often-stated economic-type objectives, besides those mentioned in preceding paragraphs, are—growth, expressed in terms of sales, assets, employees, profits, or product line; stability, usually expressed in terms of sales, manpower, and profits; flexibility, expressed in numerous ways, such as, ability to innovate, speed of response to new environment, especially competition; diversity in preparedness to compete; sensitivity

to technological and market changes; and acquisition of a given status of technical skill.

Very frequently, goals express ethical or moral considerations. These are generally described in terms such as leadership of the firm in the industry, integrity and honesty in dealing with others, maintenance of amicable community relations, and assumption of social responsibilities with respect to community problems.[10]

Must Be Realistic. Long-range company goals should be given the greatest thought and formulated as realistically as possible. The validity of goals for planning should be tested upon the basis of past experience of the company and its industry, and future prospects for both. Unrealistic goals are not very helpful.

Sometimes an immediate problem will serve as the focal point for planning. If, for example, rate of return on stockholders' investment for a company has been well below the industry average for the past five years the prime goal for the company planning may be to achieve the industry average or better.

Similarly, actual or anticipated trouble with a product may provide the basis for a concrete goal, e.g., "eliminate the product and substitute others," "undertake new research on the product to improve its salability," or "cut costs of the product by X percent of sales so that it will attract a new level of demand."

Realistic projections of company operations must be placed against any goals established for the future. The difference between the two sets of numbers will reveal the magnitude of the tasks that lie ahead for the corporation. If, for example, a sales objective of 1,000,000 units is established for five years in the future, and 1,500,000 for ten years ahead, and a realistic forecast shows 750,000 units in 1967 and 1,150,000 in 1972, the magnitude of the problem for the company is revealed.

Through this process long-range company goals should be established for sales, profits, capital requirements, new and old product requirements. Then, for each of these, the gap between aspirations and projections on present plans and trends must be measured or defined.

Third: Explore Possible Strategies

The third step is to *develop strategies to fill the major gaps.* The problem here is to bring to the foreground and examine the principal alternatives open to the company in filling the gaps and then to choose from among them those most acceptable. There obviously are many ways to do this.

In this step companies must come face to

face with major questions of policy. If there is a sales gap, for example, to what extent will it be filled with old products, by further penetration of old markets, or entrance into new markets? If this is not enough, to what extent should the old product be importantly modified by research? Where can and should costs be reduced or increased? Should new products be introduced? If so, should they be developed by the present company or acquired through merger? Should all new acquisitions have an affinity with present product lines, or is this not necessary?

While the central focus of planning is naturally on products, the question of strategies is not exclusively concerned with products. Strategies may be developed, for example, for management training, management succession, organization, investments of surplus cash, dividend policy, or public relations.

The precise steps to be followed in developing strategies to answer the kinds of questions given above obviously vary from case to case. One illustrative approach is as follows.

To begin with, tentative alternative courses of action may be set forth for testing in the planning process. These may be suggested by managers at different levels. A planning group itself may, and probably will, think up alternative strategies. The planning process will apply several screenings to the suggestions, the sifting measures which will become more rigorous in successive planning stages.

It is also healthy and often indispensable to undertake an objective and honest appraisal of company strengths and weaknesses in relevant areas. For example, if a company is planning a diversification program, analysis is important in the following areas—management competence to digest proposed mergers; financial capability; marketing abilities for the new product; and, if stock is used to acquire a new company, the ability of the present management to continue control of the enterprise. Other areas of review might include basic research and engineering competence, advertising and promotion skills, labor relations, quality of management, capacity to control costs and production, and product and service acceptability.

Elemental, of course, is the build-up of information important in choosing between alternative courses of action. This is a critical stage in planning because it is frequently difficult to acquire reliable information about the most crucial strategic factors in decision-making. It is most important at this stage to concentrate on the strategic data, or those which will have the most significance in choice conclusions.

The range of phenomena about which data should be collected is very wide. For a new product possibility, for example, the analysis may cover technological matters, ranging from projection of prospective scientific advances affecting the product to costs and timing of research, development, tests, and engineering for the product. There are many economic matters of interest, including market changes, possible demand at different pricing levels, estimated fixed and variable costs, break-even volume, prospective return on investment, and probabilities of profit amounts at different price-volume-cost ranges. Where applicable, there are also, of course, social, political, military, and internal administrative matters demanding attention.

The next step is to *select strategies from among alternative possibilities.* More or less simultaneously four analytical processes merge at this point. The first is the application, where appropriate, of new mathematical techniques to get a quantitative optimization of objectives.

The second is a modification of quantitative conclusions by a broad range of qualitative factors which will have a determining impact on final choices. Included in the latter, for example, would be estimates of what competitors are likely to do under given circumstances.

Break-even Calculations.   Third, to the extent practicable, the financial impact of decisions should be measured individually and in their entirety. This should be done by the preparation of break-even calculations, cash flow analyses, and balance sheet and profit and loss statements. The detail of analysis should naturally be tailored to fit the need and importance of the data to the reliability of conclusions. Computer simulation, while not now used very extensively in this step, is a fourth process which promises to grow in importance.

The net results of this stage should be the development of strategies to fill the gaps apparent in step two. These broad plans of action should be either the best possible solutions to the problems or, at the very least, suitable ones. They should be tested for feasibility in terms of management, manpower, finances, competitor actions, technical expectations, and market acceptability. Broad magnitudes and timing should be established.

Resulting strategies can be broad or relatively narrow. One important aero-space company in the United States recently matched a frank appraisal of its strengths and weaknesses in various disciplines of knowledge used in the industry against prospective new product developments. It reasoned that it could not maintain strength in all the areas of knowledge which it now covered. The result was an increase in strength in some areas and an elimination of many other areas.

Some companies have decided to expand through merger even though the resulting product line is heterogeneous. Other companies feel it a better strategy to acquire new products through merger only when there is a close relationship with present product line. Some companies mix these two strategies. Certain companies have decided to lead their industry in research and development. Others are content to follow.

A manufacturer of ceramics ware recently decided to concentrate only on products requiring advanced scientific and engineering skills and to abandon mass production of dinnerware. One electronics producer recently decided, following an agonizing appraisal, to abandon his computer line.

A medium-sized California food processor worked out a completely new detailed strategy for timing of annual sales promotion and new product development. A large oil company recently completed a detailed strategy covering its foreign investment program. These are illustrations of results from this step.

Fourth: Subplan to Fit Strategy   The fourth step in long-range planning is to *develop derivative operational plans.* A planning process is not complete until subsidiary plans are made to put into effect the strategies developed in step three. This seems elementary but is not always followed in practice. Decisions made without methods to carry them out are ineffective. The following cover the most important functional areas where derivative plans must be made.

Research and development programs should be supported, timed, and controlled to achieve the new product or other requirements needed to reach goals. These other requirements may, for example, include improving old products, reducing production costs, hiring new scientific skills, or increasing basic research.

Production programs should reflect digestion of new equipment, scheduling, new quality controls and inspection methods, and associated activities.

Marketing and promotion plans would, of course, include new selling efforts, advertising programs, reorganization of sales territories, pricing, and perhaps packaging.

Organizational changes may be required as a result of the new program which in turn, of course, needs detailed planning before implementation. Included here might be new management training programs.

Financial plans would include preparations for new equity financing or borrowing, budgeting of capital, and detailed financial forecasts to support the feasibility of the operational plans.

Parallel Planning.   An important feature of long-range planning is parallel planning. It would be a waste of time and resources to insist that production await engineering before beginning its derivative plans, or that marketing await production, or that organization await all of them. It is true that what is decided in one functional area will have a determining impact on other areas. But planning in all areas must proceed in parallel to the fullest extent practicable to save time. This can be accomplished by good communications in planning and sharpening of abilities to guess correctly what is going on in other functional areas that will affect planning in another area.

Naturally, the nearer term plans should be sufficiently detailed to permit operations and control. For this purpose detailed budgets or other planning and control techniques should be prepared. The further away in time the less detail should be needed or justified in terms of cost.

Fifth: Integrate Plan   The fifth and final step is to *assure the integration of long-range and short-range plans and to introduce the necessary controls to be sure operations take place in conformance with plans.*

SEQUENTIAL STAGES

Short-range plans must, of course, be prepared in light of longer-range goals. Meshing the two can be accomplished by developing sequential stages to meet long-range goals, as for example, promotion plans, the near-term aspects of which would be included in specific budgetary items. Where long-range plans are not specified in concrete terms, as for example, outlines to improve the quality of management, the connection is looser.

In such instances, short-range plans should reflect the longer-range goals and policies set to achieve them. In some companies the problem of meshing short-range and long-range plans is accomplished by developing five-year plans in which the first year is the current operating budget.

The control process designed to insure that operations take place in conformance with plans extends too far beyond the planning function discussed in this paper and will not be treated here. It is perhaps unnecessary to say that plans which are not executed are only exercises. They may be important as exercises but they are not plans in the sense the term is used here. Reciprocally, efficient control of operations is rather difficult without the goals and standards of performance which plans establish.

ORGANIZATION FOR PLANNING

Too large a field of inquiry for extended treatment here is the subject of business practices and principles in organizing for long-range planning. But, since it has a direct bearing upon the way planning steps such as the above are performed, a few observations are in order.

First of all, organization for planning is not a simple matter of working out procedural or data flows. It must face the fundamental question of who is going to do what about basic decision making in an organization.

Boards of directors have superior authority but there is great variation in the extent to which they choose to use this power. At E. I. du Pont de Nemours and Company, for example, the Board has delegated great power to subcommittees of the Board, principally the Executive Committee. Long-range planning at Du Pont centers in this group. In other companies the board has delegated its planning powers to the president. In some, the president in turn has delegated his powers in varying degrees to committees, departments, or individuals.

TOP MANAGEMENT SUPPORT

Second, and closely associated with the above issue, long-range planning will be most useful and effective if the top executives of the company have confidence and faith in it. A long-range planning program is not likely to be of much value if the chief executives do not support it actively.

Third, rather widespread participation in the process should be encouraged, but not to the extent that timetables cannot be met, objectivity in analyzing facts is lost, or strategic decisions become known to too many people. Long-range plans are usually rather important to a great many people in an enterprise. Their participation in and execution of the plan will be enhanced if they can point to some contribution of theirs in it, or if they can find in it a goal worth striving for.

Effective planning requires decentralization. It is true that top management itself may define basic long-range planning strategies. But the execution of these programs requires effec-

tive coordination of many people. As Peter Drucker has pointed out, planning and doing are separate parts of the same job. They are not separate jobs. Planning proceeds best when both top management and operating people participate fully in it.

DOES PLANNING PAY OFF?

Determining pay-off is a matter of relating the value of planning results to the costs of planning. Every planning program should be examined to determine the margin between value and cost. On the whole, pay-off calculations are probably more easily determined for short-range than for long-range plans.

Long-range planning may not pay off for five, ten or more years. It is because of the difficulties in making cost-value calculations, together with the length of time needed to draw conclusions, that questions often arise about pay-off for long-range planning.

"Extinct by Instinct"   Two extreme approaches seem to be taken by companies that either ignore or improperly face the question of pay-off. One approach is to minimize costs by ignoring basic steps in planning. This method depends upon conclusions derived without encumbrances of carefully developed facts or lines of reasoning. For this approach the practitioner feels little need for a conscious and deliberate assessment of relevant considerations upon which judgments can be developed. In common parlance this is called "flying by the seat of your pants." I prefer to call it the road to becoming extinct by instinct.

"Paralysis by Analysis"   At the other extreme is overemphasis of value in relation to cost. With this approach there is recognition of the need for planning. An assignment is made to a dedicated hard-working soul with a reputation for thoroughness. Work is begun without much reference to the complexities of the task and before long a large number of people are involved at substantial cost.

Somewhere along the line, usually later than sooner, a voluminous report is prepared and promptly filed away "for future reference." Either the need for decision has long since passed or the report is too complex and bulky for busy people to read and digest. This I call the road to paralysis by analysis.[11]

Cost-Value Equation   For planning to pay off a happy balance between the two extremes must be struck. The precise pay-off for any particular planning operation is difficult to determine. No one can do this without examining the cost-value equation for that program. But planning has paid off for companies that have considered this equation and achieved the balance required.

The Stanford Research Institute studied the question "Why Companies Grow." One major conclusion of the study was that: "In the cases of both high-growth and low-growth companies, those that now support planning programs have shown a superior growth rate in recent years."[12]

The Stanford study observed that most companies with formalized planning programs were enthusiastic about their value. Well might they be if, partly as a result of planning, their growth rates have been exceptional. For these companies planning has clearly paid off.

Ford's Experience   Ernest Breech, former Chairman of the Board of the Ford Motor Company, has observed: "We believe it is our business, and that of other large companies, to make trends, not to follow them. A confident aggressive spirit, backed up by intelligent planning and hard-hitting management, can be contagious."[13] For Ford, planning has paid off handsomely as the last ten years of that company's history will testify.

On the other hand the path to bankruptcy is strewn with corpses who failed to plan or planned poorly. A study by the Bureau of Business Research at the University of Pittsburgh concluded that among the ten companies chosen for intensive study every one was guilty of poor planning and this shortcoming was the major cause of failure in the majority of cases.[14]

It is probably true that the only certainty about long-range planning is that the conclusions will prove to be in error. There is no such thing as 20/20 foresight. But, one great advantage of forward planning is that coming to grips with uncertainty by analysis and study should result in a reduction of the margin of doubt about the future. Despite the fog enshrouding the future many companies have planned ahead and hit goals surprisingly accurately.

FORWARD PLANNING

Ralph Cordiner, commenting on this point in his book *New Frontiers for Professional Managers*, has observed that one of the three principal new horizons ahead for managers lies in the area of long-range planning. As he put it, "In a time of radical world wide change, when every day introduces new elements of uncertainty, forward planning may seem to be

nearly impossible—an exercise in futility. Yet there never was a more urgent need for long-range planning on the part of every business, and indeed every other important element of our national life."[15]

The argument is often presented that for large companies the choices for investing funds are many and necessitate advance planning. But, since a range of choice in investment of funds in a small single-product company does not exist, for it, advance planning is a waste of time.

This idea is most erroneous. Small companies have just as great a need for long-range planning as large ones. They may not have the cash to support technical specialists, but there are other means to acquire the needed expertise. Many small companies, through long-range planning, have opened the door to successful expansion, new products, and new markets by multiplying ranges of desirable choices.

In considering pay-off for long-range planning, value is generally considered to lie in the areas of improved profit stability, growth, more efficient sales, capital expenditure, inventory, research and development, or cost reduction programs. Or long-range planning may prove its worth in better management replacement and improvement programs; or some other tangible and concrete activities of the enterprise.

ANCILLARY BENEFITS

It should also be pointed out that a number of important ancillary and intangible benefits have accrued to companies having formal long-range planning programs. A brief list of them is shown on page 148. The planning process constitutes an excellent channel of communication throughout the organization. It identifies problems ahead for a firm long before they become acute. It focuses attention on the principal determinants of the business. It provides an organized mechanism for testing value judgments.

It opens new horizons for profitable study. It prevents piecemeal solutions to problems. It is a good training ground for future managers, and it brings to those responsible for running the business a comprehensive, coordinated, and uniform picture of present and future business.

CONCLUSIONS

Despite the phenomenal growth of formal long-range planning, and its important pay-off to many companies there are still too many companies that do not employ the process effectively. The reasons are often anchored in their lack of knowledge about how to do it, misunderstanding of its cost-value calculation, or both.

Five operational steps for long-range planning have been set forth and examined. They are recapitulated below in graphic form.

FIVE STEPS FOR LONG-RANGE PLANNING

1. PLANNING TO PLAN

2. SPECIFYING OBJECTIVES OF ENTERPRISE
   - forecasting future prospects
   - measuring the gaps between aspirations and projections

3. DEVELOPING STRATEGIES
   - to fill in the major gaps

4. DEVELOPING DERIVATIVE OR DETAILED PLANS IN MAJOR FUNCTIONAL AREAS TO FIT THE STRATEGIES
   - research and development
   - production
   - marketing and promotion

5. INTEGRATION OF LONG-RANGE AND SHORT-RANGE PLANS
   - introducing necessary controls

For long-range planning to pay off a balance must be struck between minimizing cost by ignoring basic steps and principles of effective planning and incurring overly heavy cost by excessive analysis. While full benefits may not be derived for many years, efforts should be made to measure them and offset them against costs. This article has been devoted to the proposition that available knowledge about how to undertake long-range planning is quite sufficient, and full understanding of the cost-value equation is so pervasive, that all businesses, large and small, should have a more or less formal long-range planning program and reap rich rewards from it.

REFERENCES

(This article, translated into Italian, appeared abroad under the title "Il rendimento della Programmazione d'impresa a lungo termine" in a recent issue of the *Rivista Internazionale di Scienze Economiche e Commerciali,* a periodical published by the Università Bocconi in Milan. G.A.S.)

1. For example, other reasons given are: Our business is too cyclical. Our customers do not know their plans, so how can we know ours?

Long-range planning is too vague. Not enough time exists for short-range planning, let alone long-range planning. We cannot afford specialists needed to do the job. It costs more than it is worth.

2. For other definitions see George A. Steiner, "What Do We Know About Using Long-range Plans?", *California Management Review,* Fall, 1959; Peter F. Drucker, "Long-range Planning: Challenge to Management Science," *Management Science,* April, 1959; Bruce Payne and James H. Kennedy, "Making Long-range Planning Work," *The Management Review,* February, 1959; and William H. Newman and Charles E. Summer, Jr., *The Process of Management,* Prentice-Hall, Inc., Englewood Cliffs, N.J., 1961, pp. 430–436.

3. See Charles E. Summer, Jr., "The Future Role of the Corporate Planner," *California Management Review,* Winter, 1961.

4. "Planning Tomorrow's Profits," *Nation's Business,* August, 1958.

5. "Long-range Planning Pays Off," *Business Record,* October, 1956.

6. Burnard H. Sord and Glenn A. Welsch, *Business Budgeting,* Controllership Foundation, New York, 1958.

7. For other operational planning sequences see David W. Ewing, *Long-range Planning for Management,* Harper & Row, Publishers, Incorporated, New York, 1958; William E. Hill, "Planning for Profits: A Four-stage Method," *California Management Review,* Spring, 1959, which is a method much like that presented here; Bruce Payne and James H. Kennedy, *op. cit.; Westinghouse Planning Guide,* Westinghouse Electric Corporation, 1959; *Guide to Profit Improvement Program,* American Brake Shoe Company, 1959; and Arthur W. Lucas and William G. Livingston, "Long-range Planning and the Capital Appropriations Program," in *Financial Planning for Greater Profits,* American Management Association, Report no. 44, New York, 1960. For a detailed analytical planning sequence see Preston P. Le Breton and Dale A. Henning, *Planning Theory,* Prentice-Hall, Inc., Englewood Cliffs, N.J., 1961.

8. Ralph M. Besse, "Company Planning Must Be Planned!" *Dun's Review,* April, 1957.

9. See note 7.

10. See, for example, Stewart Thompson, *Management Creeds and Philosophies,* American Management Association, Research Study, no. 32, New York, 1958; Richard Eells, *The Meaning of Modern Business,* Columbia University Press, New York, 1960, chap. 6, "Corporate

Goals"; Peter Drucker, *The Practice of Management,* Harper & Row, Publishers, Incorporated, New York, 1954, chap.7, "The Objectives of a Business"; and George R. Terry, *Principles of Management,* Richard D. Irwin, Inc., Homewood, Ill., 1956, chap. 9, "Management Objectives and Ethics."

11. From Charles R. Schwartz, "The Return-on-investment Concept as a Tool for Decision Making" in *Improving the Caliber of Company Management,* American Management Association, General Management Series, no. 183, New York, 1956, p. 46.

12. N. R. Maines, *Why Companies Grow,* Stanford Research Institute, Palo Alto, Calif., 1957, p. 4.

13. Ernest R. Breech, "Planning the Basic Strategy of a Large Business," in Edward C. Bursk and Dan H. Fenn, Jr., (eds.), *Planning the Future Strategy of Your Business,* McGraw-Hill Book Company, New York, 1956, p. 17.

14. A. M. Woodruff and T. G. Alexander, *Success and Failure in Small Manufacturing,* University of Pittsburgh Press, Pittsburgh, Pa., 1958, pp. 48, 100.

15. Ralph J. Cordiner, *New Frontiers for Professional Managers,* McGraw-Hill Book Company, New York, 1956, p. 82.

PART THREE   ORGANIZATION   *The task of organizing is to establish a system of activity groupings and authority relationships in which people can know what their tasks are, how their tasks relate to each other, and where authority for decisions needed to accomplish these tasks rests. Organization thus establishes an environment for performance by individuals operating in a formally structured group.*

The existence of formal task groupings and authority relationships has been traced to the limitations imposed by the span of management, an important concept which is explained in L. F. Urwick's paper "The Manager's Span of Control." While many persons, including the editors, would disagree with the specific numbers he uses, Colonel Urwick's analysis is still a classic. Related to span (and to many other facets of managing) are the problem of knowing when people are really busy and the often-encountered tendency of organizations to grow. A major contribution to management literature and a stroke of genius in perception of the human being and his manipulations of the organization is the whimsical and original "Parkinson's Law," by C. Northcote Parkinson. These materials are supplemented by an article about a recent attempt to make more exact calculations of the proper span of management in practice. The program adopted by a division of the Lockheed Aircraft Corporation is reported by Harold Stieglitz in "Optimizing Span of Control."

In practice, enterprises have developed certain departmental patterns. These are described in an excerpt from one of Ernest Dale's books, under the title "The Division of Basic Company Activities." Another problem of departmentation is the allocation of activities to departments. The original research on this was done more than three decades ago by the late Prof. L. C. Sorrell, and excerpts from his study are included under the title "Business Organization and Guides for Grouping Activities." A recent study of the use of departmental forms by a number of American business concerns was made by Harold Stieglitz of the National Industrial Conference Board. "Patterns in Organizational Structuring" is an excerpt from this study, summarizing the author's findings.

One of the major developments in organization practice and philosophy in the past four decades, a development which has allowed enterprises to grow large without loss of organizational effectiveness, has been decentralization of authority. This is more than the art and science of delegation, for it involves a philosophy and an art of dispensing authority without losing control. Perhaps the most successful practitioner of decentralization in world industry has been the General Motors Company. The editors have included excerpts from a statement of Harlow H. Curtice, late president of that company, titled "General Motors Organization Philosophy and Structure." The statement of philosophy and principles of another top industrialist, Ralph J. Cordiner, recent chairman of the General Electric Company, has been taken from his writings and is presented under the title "Decentralization at General Electric." Because control so often has been lost through decentralization, the editors have included the statement of another industrialist, John G. Staiger, "What Cannot Be Decentralized."

One of the most misunderstood and misapplied concepts in management is the line and staff concept, viewed by your editors as describing a kind of authority relationship, rather than as delineating types of activities, people, or organization units. In practice, the misunderstanding of line and staff relationships has led to much friction and inefficiency. The readings selected

150

for this area include an excerpt from Notes on the Theory of Organization, *by L. F. Urwick; the summary of Louis A. Allen's findings from his extensive study for the National Industrial Conference Board; and the excellent study "Line and Staff in Industrial Relations," by Charles A. Myers and John G. Turnbull.*

Committees are special organizational forms designed for the undertaking of a task by a group, as a group, rather than by an individual. Our readings on this important subject include an article by W. H. Mylander, of the du Pont Company, which is based on his instructive experience with the operation of management committees and titled "Management by Executive Committee." Cyril O'Donnell's summary article "Ground Rules for Using Committees" analyzes how to make committees work effectively.

Organizational structures must be planned to remain effective for varying periods of time. Since they will furnish the environment for people not yet on the scene, they reflect future company plans. "Organizational Planning," by the du Pont executive, Robert L. Hershey, casts some light on this important subject. In this article, the author admirably bridges the gap between the authority-activity (structural) aspects of organizing and the aspects of organizing having to do with people, which are dealt with in Part 4.

The Manager's Span of Control*

LYNDALL F. URWICK

There is no question that in the last quarter century the work load of the executive has greatly increased. The top management man has new functions that he cannot possibly delegate completely; take, for instance, his new responsibilities in public relations and industrial relations. Businesses have grown in size, in complexity, and in geographical coverage; the duties and problems of the top executive have increased commensurately.

For this reason, one of the biggest tasks confronting the manager is that of reducing his overload of less important daily duties, thus giving himself time for reflection as well as for the personal contacts with his organization which are the mainspring of leadership—the "personal touch" which makes the executive a business *leader*.

It is in connection with this organizational problem that the "span of control" concept has received so much attention. As the first writer to apply this principle formally to business, I propose here to re-examine the concept, to analyze the main criticisms that have been levied against it, and to demonstrate why and how a restricted span of control can improve executive effectiveness, reduce pressure, inefficiency and incompetence, produce better employee cooperation, and build morale and a sense of unity within the organization.

THE PRINCIPLE

As far as I know, the first person to direct public attention to the principle of span of control was a soldier—the late General Sir Ian Hamilton. His statement (which, of course, reflects his military association) is the basis for subsequent interpretations of the concept oriented to business:

* Reprinted by permission of the publisher from *Harvard Business Review*, vol. 34, no. 3, pp. 39–47, May-June, 1956. Colonel Urwick is chairman of Urwick, Orr and Partners, Ltd., consulting specialists in organization and management. He is also an internationally known scholar, lecturer, and author on management.

The average human brain finds its effective scope in handling from three to six other brains. If a man divides the whole of his work into two branches and delegates his responsibility, freely and properly, to two experienced heads of branches he will not have enough to do. The occasions when they would refer to him would be too few to keep him fully occupied. If he delegates to three heads he will be kept fairly busy whilst six heads of branches will give most bosses a ten hours' day. Those data are the results of centuries of the experiences of soldiers, which are greater, where organization is in question, than those of politicians, business men or any other class of men. . . .

Of all the ways of waste there is none so vicious as that of your clever politician trying to run a business concern without having any notion of self-organization. One of them who took over munitions[1] for a time had so little idea of organizing his own energy that he nearly died of overwork *through holding up the work of others;* i.e., by delegating responsibility coupled with *direct access to himself* to seventeen sub-chiefs! Now it will be understood why a Battalion has four companies (and not seventeen); why a Brigade has three or four battalions (and not seventeen).

Organizations are run by rule then; a rule whereby from three to six "hands" are shepherded by one "head," each "head" in turn being member of a superior group of from three to six who are being wheeled into line one by one. . . .

As to whether the groups are three, four, five or six it is useful to bear in mind a by-law: the smaller the responsibility of the group member, the larger may be the number of the group and vice versa. That is to say, one N.C.O. in charge of three private soldiers would be too idle; one lieutenant general in charge of six divisional generals would be too busy. The nearer we approach the supreme head of the

[1] The British Ministry of Munitions in World War I.

whole organization, the more we ought to work towards groups of six.[2]

I came across General Hamilton's organizational rule in the early 1920's and called it to the attention of friends interested in management problems. The principle made its initial and rather informal appearance in management literature in 1922. H. P. Kendall of Boston, addressing a meeting of the Taylor Society, stated:

> At a dinner the other evening, I heard the President of the General Electric Company asked how many people should report directly to the President of a large industrial company. He said that eight or nine were reporting at present, but that it was too many, and he was reorganizing his functions so that only four or five would report directly to himself; and I imagine that four or five is enough. Not that a chief executive should not have contact with others; but that is about as many general functions as should regularly and directly lead up to him.[3]

Some eight years later I was walking in Paris with a friend, A. V. Graicunas,[4] and he said, "Can you come back to my flat for a good talk? You know you're always stating that the number of subordinates reporting to an executive should be limited; I think there is mathematical proof of it. I shall want your help in presenting the idea."

Group Relationships   The result of our discussion was Graicunas' article "Relationship in Organization," which appeared originally in the *Bulletin of the International Management Institute* in 1933.[5]

Graicunas' idea was basically very simple. The superior, in dealing with his subordinates, must keep in mind not only the direct relationships between himself and each subordinate as an individual but also his relationships with different groupings of the subordinates and the cross relationships between all the subordinates. These relationships vary considerably with the size of the subordinate group. While the supervisor's own direct relationships with individuals increase in proportion to the addition of subordinates, the group and cross relationships increase much more than proportionately. To illustrate:

> If A supervises two persons, B and C, he can deal with them individually or as a pair. The behavior of B in the presence of C and of C in the presence of B will differ from their behavior when each is with A alone. Furthermore, what B thinks of C and what C thinks of B constitute two cross relationships which A must keep in mind when delegating work on which B and C must collaborate in A's absence. In other words, even in this extremely simple unit of organization, with two subordinates, a superior must keep up to six relationships constantly in mind.

Then, when a third subordinate, D, is added, A's direct relationships with individuals increase by only 1 (A-D), but the various groupings he may have to deal with increase by 7 (A-B-D, A-D-B, A-C-D, A-D-C, A-B-CD, A-C-BD, and A-D-BC), and the various cross relationships he may have to reckon with increase by 4 (B-D, D-B, C-D, D-C), making a total of 18.

A fourth subordinate brings the total up to 44. The situation really gets complex when a fifth subordinate is added—even granting that many of the relationships will never need explicit attention. The superior again increases his direct relationship with individuals by 1—representing a 25% gain in his *power to delegate*. But the number of group and cross relationships he may have to deal with has gone up from 44 to 100—more than a 100% increase in the burden of *supervision and coordination*.

If a sixth man is added, the group and cross relationships jump to about 200. A seventh subordinate puts the figure at between 450 and 500. And so on.

Graicunas, had he expanded on his principle, would probably have agreed that no executive should have to deal directly with more than a half-dozen men. Actually, because of the psychological concept known as "the span of attention," which limits the number of items that the human brain can keep within its grasp simultaneously, it seems doubtful if any individual can keep track of and understand the large number of group relationships involved with more than five subordinates. Graicunas did qualify his observations to some degree. He noted that since it is the cross relationships between subordinates which render the task of supervision more complex, this

---

[2] Sir Ian Hamilton, *The Soul & Body of an Army,* Edward Arnold (Publishers) Ltd., London, 1921, p. 229.

[3] H. P. Kendall, "The Problem of the Chief Executive," *Bulletin of the Taylor Society,* vol. 7, no. 2, April, 1922.

[4] Believed dead. He was in Lithuania, his native country, when it was occupied by the Russians.

[5] Reprinted in Luther Gulick and Lyndall E. Urwick (eds.), *Papers on the Science of Administration,* Institute of Public Administration, New York, 1937, p. 183.

difficulty will not occur to the same degree where the work is of such a nature as to require few working contacts between the subordinates concerned. This is the same premise which General Hamilton had stated earlier in his bylaw: "The smaller the responsibility of the group member, the larger may be the group. . . ."

In reducing Graicunas' work to a definite statement of principle a few years later, I was careful to include his exception to the rule, and the wording of the concept now stands as:

> No superior can supervise directly the work of more than five or, at the most, six subordinates *whose work interlocks.*[6] [Italics added.]

CRITICISM OF CONCEPT

The "span of control" is not a rigid rule to be applied woodenly in all situations. But is is a very useful general principle and a valuable diagnostic instrument in cases where organizational weakness exists. However, the concept has met with substantial opposition, encountering objections both on theoretical and on practical grounds.

Theoretical Attack   Herbert A. Simon has questioned the validity of the span of control in terms of theoretical soundness. He writes:

> . . . A contradictory proverb of administration can be stated which, though it is not so familiar as the principle of the span of control, can be supported by arguments of equal plausibility. The proverb in question is the following:
> "Administrative efficiency is enhanced by keeping at a minimum the number of organizational levels through which a matter must pass before it is acted on."
> In many situations the results to which this principle leads are in direct contradiction to the requirements of the span of control.[7]

Mr. Simon finds further fault with the span of control, which inevitably produces, he thinks, excessive red tape. As he sees it, each contact between organization members must be carried upward until a common superior is found, thus involving needless waste of time and energy.

In general, industry is now tending to pay more attention to the inefficiencies of extended levels of organization than it is to those of the span of control. The International Business Machines Corporation, for example, recently cut one entire level of middle management from its organization and increased the span of control of the remaining executives. One organization expert, commenting on this type of action, has said, "You have a place in which good people can grow rather than stagnate when you discard this traditional idea of the span of authority."[8]

The drive to shorten the chain of command, which in effect denies the importance of careful limitations on the span of control, is an attempt to improve communications, as well as to force some authority and responsibility down into the organization structure. Both these objectives are commendable; nevertheless, the limits of the span of control are real and important restrictions. It is clear that a careful balancing of the inefficiencies of levels against those of spans is necessary—and this is entirely possible, as I shall try to point out later.

Concern for Democracy   Other people object to the idea of a limited span of authority on the ground that it prohibits democratic participation within the organization. According to Burleigh B. Gardner of Social Research, Inc.:

> There is good reason to believe that the gain in productivity achieved by overspecialization and its twin brother, overcentralization of authority, has been lost in the debilitating and enervating effects they have had on employee morale and willingness to cooperate.[9]

In current organization practice and experience, there seems to be a general concern with the relative merits of the highly centralized, pyramidal system with a tight span of control and the flat, more decentralized system. At present, there are many in favor of the flat setup. Proponents of this form of organization argue that it makes for a minimum of social and administrative "distance," and that although the great number of subordinates creates a certain looseness of supervision, this same looseness promotes initiative in a way that no bonus system can match.

[6] Lyndall F. Urwick, *Scientific Principles and Organization,* American Management Association, Institute of Management Series, no. 19, New York, 1938, p. 8.
[7] Herbert A. Simon, *Administrative Behavior,* The Macmillan Company, New York, 1947, pp. 26–28.

[8] Harold Koontz and Cyril O'Donnell, *Principles of Management,* McGraw-Hill Book Company, New York, 1955, p. 98.
[9] William H. Whyte, Jr., and the Editors of Fortune, *Is Anybody Listening?* Simon and Schuster, Inc., New York, 1952, p. 129.

In fact, there appears to be a practical dilemma overshadowing management organization—a dilemma between morale and efficiency. In this connection, psychologist Alex Bavelas and a group at M.I.T. have staged some interesting experiments with different types of communication networks in order to measure effects on performance:

> Bavelas arranged one group of five people so that they communicated with each other in a circular pattern—this would be representative of the flat, democratic organizational structure. He set up another group of five in a hierarchical pattern—this representing the stricter, chain-of-command organization. Both groups were given the same problem and were instructed to solve it by exchanging messages.
>
> Bavelas found that the group in the circular pattern was very happy—but not very efficient; and that the hierarchical group got much more efficient results—but was not very content or satisfied with the manner in which its decisions had been reached. This experiment did seem to prove that morale is very closely tied in with the degree of participation; it is understandable that many managements feel "there is a potential choice to be made. Which is to be emphasized—morale or efficiency?"[10]

Actually, I do not think that efficiency is incompatible with organizational morale. In fact, I feel that one of the strongest arguments for the span of control is that it can, if used intelligently, combine these two vital elements.

Denial of Concept   In addition to the criticisms based on size of organization and lack of democracy, there is the type of criticism which merely states that a given organization is efficient despite apparent infraction of the span of control and that, therefore, the principle is incorrect. For instance, here is a statement describing a wartime administrative situation:

> With three squadrons on the station the C.O. had as many as eleven officers under his immediate control (the total strength being about 2500 men and women). Senior R.A.F. officers handle such concerns efficiently, thus denying the oft-repeated statements of leading businessmen that the span of control of one man should be a maximum of six. The Captain of a large battleship has the same wide span of control and can fight his ship just as well. Either

the theory of the limited span of control [Graicunas'] is false, or the businessmen who make such statements would do well to learn from the Navy and the R.A.F.[11]

I have found, after 20 years' experience as a management consultant, that the span of control is a principle which is very frequently broken in practice at all levels of business. The fact is, however, that neglect of the concept often underlies the severest management difficulties. When the principle is recognized as valid, it can point the way to simple changes in structure in organizations that are suffering from malmanagement. Such changes have, it is true, added to the number of administrative levels in the instances I have observed. But they have also proved most valuable in improving effectiveness and in rescuing individuals from misdirected charges of personal incompetence.

In some such situations, the manager or foreman concerned had simply been overstraining his capacity by trying to deal with too many subordinates directly. Once this was realized, and the stress was reduced by grouping a certain number of subordinates under an appropriate intermediate control, the effect was marked and almost instantaneous. In many such instances the individual who had previously been under criticism proved more than equal to his responsibilities after the change.

Human Failings   There are, of course, some very strong human temptations to ignore this principle of span of control in business:

1. Business has so far failed to distinguish rank or status from function, and today we attach an exaggerated importance to unofficial symbols of status. To report directly to the chief rather than to some intermediate authority is such a symbol; subordinates feel they can enhance their status by doing this. Here is one reason why the span of control is not widely accepted in business circles.

2. Businessmen have always been and always will be cost-conscious. There is sometimes pressure on management to avoid making new appointments, however necessary from the standpoint of better organization, because additional personnel will increase the company's overhead cost.

3. Sometimes there is the higher level manager who cherishes a misleading stereotype

[10] *Ibid.*, p. 134.

[11] T. F. Paterson, *Morale in War and Work*, Max Parrish, London, 1955, p. 23, note.

of the "efficient executive." He sees his value as a businessman measured by his busyness; he feels that the number of individuals reporting to him directly is an index of his value to the organization. He likes the sense of power and self-importance generated by a queue on his doormat. Personal ambition sometimes finds an outlet in acquiring additional responsibilities, without too nice a regard for organizational refinements. This tendency, usually described as "empire-building," is universal in all forms of human organization.

Of course, the top executive cannot always take all the blame for the confusion. It is hard for him, as a human being, to resist pressure from his subordinates who want to be directly accountable to him, especially when these men are individuals of weight and value to the company. They may be creative men, whose new ideas and fresh departures need the personal attention of the boss if they are to be introduced successfully.

If, in addition to these pressures, the practical validity of the span of control is itself called into question and those who are tempted to ignore it can defend themselves as being more "democratic" and avoiding administrative and social "distance," the moral courage to enforce the principle sufficiently—and this often requires real moral courage—will be lacking. Business organization will suffer accordingly.

UTILIZING THE CONCEPT

At this point, I should like to examine the criticisms of the principle more closely and show how it may and should be applied in organizational situations.

Taking first the apparent dilemma between managerial efficiency and democratic participation, this "practical" objection to the span of control is not really valid. There is no greater stimulant of morale than a collective consciousness of efficiency. There is nothing which rots morale more quickly and more completely than poor communication and indecisiveness—the feeling that those in authority do not know their own minds. And there is no condition which more quickly produces a sense of indecision among subordinates or more effectively hampers communication than being responsible to a superior who has too wide a span of control.

Needed: A Leader   The choice in managerial practice should not be between the executive who wants to overcentralize—i.e., the

man who cannot delegate properly and therefore demands a tight span of control so that he can pass on every subordinate decision, important or not—and the executive who is prepared to trust his subordinates and therefore wishes to see little of them. The first type of manager is simply one who does not know how to *lead* and hence tries to *dominate*. The latter type is one who does not realize that leadership calls for as much constant personal contact as circumstances permit.

However much responsibility may be delegated, subordinates like to have fairly frequent opportunities of ensuring that their chief's mind is in step with their own and vice versa. They need a chance to cement confidence between themselves and the boss, even though at such interviews they may not discuss actual administrative detail at all.

The chief with too wide a span of control tends to frustrate this very proper wish to cultivate mutuality; here is where the argument for "democratic participation" falls flat. In a loosely organized business with no strict limits on the executive's span of authority, subordinates will line up in his secretary's office and will be constantly frustrated when they want a word with him. They will feel that he is too absorbed in business to take time to get to know his men and try to understand and appreciate their problems.

Both the man who cannot delegate and the man who neglects to make a point of meeting frequently with his subordinates have failed in exercising their leadership duties, and consequently confusion and inefficiency are rife. This situation occurs often in organization structures which, in principle, are quite satisfactory and should work well. The trouble can usually be traced to an insufficient appreciation on the part of the chief that leadership has other functions besides administration— functions of representation, initiation, and interpretation.

Above all, the difficulty is due to an inability to see the business enterprise as a social group —rather than only an organization with an economic purpose. This in turn is the reason for neglect of one of the major responsibilities of leadership, as expressed by an official regulation of the British Army in World War II: "The first duty of an officer is to care for, that is to know, his men."

Actually, the problem of morale is largely one of giving the business executive time to be a business *leader*, and this can only be accomplished through cutting down some of the other demands on him.

Misconceptions Moreover, it is not true that a correct span of control necessarily results in "administrative distance"; that assumption is based on two unfortunately widespread misconceptions:

1. "That a superior should never have direct contact with individuals at lower levels except through or in the presence of their immediate superior." This is nonsense, and is a clear indication of poor morale within the organization. It shows that the lower-level manager concerned is doubtful of the good sense and loyalty of both his subordinates and the higher executive. The intermediate manager may feel that his own authority is being bypassed by the superior; he has visions of his subordinates using this opportunity to criticize him and advance their own interests with the boss. All this indicates that the lower-level manager is sadly out of touch with his chief—that there has been no chance for confidence and trust to be established—and this condition is particularly apt to occur where the top manager's span of control is too wide.

2. "That 'the official channels' should be the only avenues of communication." Official channels should, of course, be the only avenue of *official* communication which goes "on the record." But the individual who thinks they are the *only* means of communication has little notion of business as a social activity. He is probably preoccupied with the economic purpose of the undertaking and its formal structure; he doesn't recognize the importance of the unofficial and informal relationships which occur at all levels of any organized activity and which are usually far more important to morale and effectiveness than the official relationships. In any organization where morale is high, most of the important work is done by verbal contacts between men who trust each other, talk the same language, and share the same doctrine. The "record" comes later.

There must, of course, be official records, but the recording procedure is a secondary one. It is the tendency to regard it as all-important which makes so many of our large businesses excessively bureaucratic, and it is because some chiefs elevate paper work to a position of significance which it should not occupy that they are overworked. Many managers spend too large a proportion of their time mulling over documents and too small a proportion cultivating good individual relations with their subordinates. The resulting lack of confidence between people forces them into an elaborate machinery of committees which further restricts their time for personal contacts.

Problem of Levels Once businessmen have overcome their misconceptions about the span of control, the need for limiting the number of levels in an organization can be appraised in a clearer light.

Herbert Simon has said that the principle of minimizing organizational levels directly contradicts the requirements of the span of control. But the cure for "administrative distance" is not to extend the executive's span of authority beyond what he can reasonably handle in order to reduce the number of levels. Rather, the method is to ensure (a) that at each level the executive has a pattern of organization which enables him to devote ample time to getting to know and understand his immediate subordinates, and (b) that he regards maintaining such personal contacts as one of his principal duties—in other words, that he is a leader before he is an administrator.

Subject to these two limitations it is, of course, desirable to restrict the number of levels as much as possible. Any level which is not vital is an organizational complication which should be eliminated. But in determining the number of levels which are necessary, prime regard should be paid to the span of control, not vice versa. Forcing managers to exceed their feasible span of control merely in order to reduce the number of levels will *increase* administrative and social distance. In effect, the executives will no longer have time to meet with their subordinates and find out what is going on in the organization.

One good way of reducing the difficulties connected with structural divisions is to encourage lower-level personnel in developing cross relationships and communication to the maximum. There are many matters which never need come to the attention of a top executive, many problems which could be solved quickly and satisfactorily at the subordinate level if the habit of communication and cooperation is accepted and promoted. For example:

An employee at the third level of responsibility in Department A (let us call him A3) who has business with an employee at the same level of responsibility in Department B (B3) should not have to climb wearily up the hierarchy to the head of Department A, across to the head of Department B, and down that chain of command until he finally arrives at his destination—his opposite number in Department B's third level. He should go to him direct.

"Excessive red tape" is easily avoided if cross communication is fostered within an organization. Of course if either A3 or B3 thinks the matter is sufficiently important to interest an immediate superior—A2 or B2—the superior should be informed and/or consulted. But action should not have to wait on an extended communication process justified only by the fact that the two department heads distrust each other or have no confidence in their subordinates.

Apparent Exception At this point I might emphasize again the qualification to Graicunas' span of control principle—that a superior's authority should extend over no more than six subordinates *whose work interlocks.*

In cases where there does not happen to be any interlocking of the work of subordinate units, there is most certainly less need for extensive subdivisions or levels of control. This can be demonstrated by a look at the organizational setup of Sears, Roebuck and Co.—ostensibly a "flat" arrangement.

The chart of the organization of Sears' buying department (the company keeps such charts for the information of visitors) shows close to 100 buyers reporting directly to one manager. However, when the organization is examined more closely, we find that:

- Each of these buyers purchases a clearly defined range of articles; there is no reason why the men should encroach on each other's bailiwick.

- Where the buyers have common problems or use common services (transport facilities, for example), the manager of the buying department has the aid of four assistants, each of whom specializes in one of these problems or services.

Thus, since there are five people dividing between them the work of supervising the buyers, the real span of control is nearer 20 than 100. And, since the buyers are each responsible for a clearly defined unit of goods, their areas of responsibility only touch occasionally and then just at the circumference. Provided that the buyers have been properly selected and trained, there is not too much for the supervisor to do except to make sure that predetermined standards are being maintained and to deal with casualties.

Similar situations characterize most stores and departments within one store. There is no reason why 20 stores situated in different towns and operating on a more or less standardized pattern should not be controlled effectively by a single chief. These are isolated units with few working contacts with each other. Their departments sell different kinds of goods. Once appropriate personnel have been found and trained, there is little occasion for the type of interdepartmental or interbranch connections and conflicts which would occur in a manufacturing business set up along functional lines. This latter type of organization does demand authoritative supervision if failures in coordination are to be avoided.

I know of a case in Great Britain where the director of a parent company was controlling quite successfully some 30 or more subsidiary companies. Considerable autonomy was allowed to the boards of the subsidiary companies—which were all in different countries. The top manager in this case had only to satisfy himself that each subsidiary was developing "according to plan"; he had none of the daily stresses found in the unified manufacturing concern organized on a functional basis.

THE GENERAL STAFF

The one criticism of the span of control which I have not yet touched on concerns the military experiences which seem to deny the need for any limitations on the top officer's scope of command. T. F. Paterson stated that an officer commanding an air force station in World War II had eleven immediate subordinates and that the captain commanding a battleship had just as many.

I could not agree more with Mr. Paterson that "businessmen . . . would do well to learn from the Navy and the R.A.F." But what businessmen should learn from the military services is how to organize so that the chief executive of a functionally arranged business can handle directly a larger number of specialized subordinates, all of whom have the right of direct access to him, without overstraining his span of control. The answer to this problem lies in the correct use of *general,* as opposed to *special,* staff officers—a form of organization which business has, as yet, rarely understood or applied successfully. This form of relationship, though not necessarily with the title "general staff," is found in an air force station such as T. F. Paterson has described and also in the British Navy.

"Commanding Machine" During 1917–1918 I had the opportunity to observe at firsthand the organization of a British infantry division. There were 18 persons directly responsible to our Divisional Commander—a dozen more than we have said the ordinary business executive can effectively handle. And yet the Commander seldom spent more than a couple of hours a day in his office, and he maintained very close contact with all his subordinates. How had this apparently successful neglect of the principle of span of control been made to work?

First of all, a clear distinction was drawn between the *nominal* right of direct access to the Commander and the *frequent* use of that right. Normally heads of specialized branches, and indeed all subordinates, were expected to take up all *routine* business through the appropriate general staff officer in the first instance. Only if they regarded the matter as one of outstanding importance which justified them in approaching the Commander—and this only *after* they had failed to secure a satisfactory settlement with one of his general staff officers—would the Commander accept a direct discussion. However, the subordinates' *right* to require direct access to the top officer was clearly recognized, and this safeguarded their independent responsibility in the exercise of their functions as well as their professional or organizational "status."

The Commander had thus only six immediate subordinates who usually approached him directly—the three Brigadiers General in charge of infantry brigades, the Brigadier General of Artillery, and his two principal general staff officers. The latter were able to relieve the Commander of all the routine work of coordinating line and specialist activities. They did virtually all the paper work, drafting operational and routine orders, conducting correspondence, etc. However, the responsibility for every word they wrote was the Commander's; they had no personal authority.

The Commander utilized much of the time saved him from office routine in visiting personally all 18 of his subordinates. The object of his visits was to give them the feeling that he was interested in their problems, that he was concerned with their progress. He did not encourage them to discuss routine business at these meetings. Indeed, if a subordinate did raise a routine question, the Commander almost invariably replied: "Well, you know, I keep out of administrative detail. I'll have to look into it, but I'll see you tomorrow."

Then he would put the paper into his pocket and, when he got back to headquarters, would ask the general staff officer concerned for an explanation of the situation. The Commander would see the subordinate the next day and do

his best to satisfy him that the matter had been dealt with correctly, and he would keep tabs on the situation to make sure that everything turned out well.

Thus, at one and the same time the Commander protected his general staff officers from resentment and unjust accusations and satisfied all his subordinates that they had constant access to him and that anything which went wrong would be taken care of promptly. The effect of this system was that while the Commander's nominal span of control was 18 persons, his actual span of control—the number of people with whom he had constant personal contact on *business* matters—was only 6.

Also, the problem of the multiplication of levels was avoided. The general staff officers did not constitute a separate level between the chief and the chief's immediate subordinates. The whole general staff setup was regarded as an extension of the Commander's personality, a "commanding machine" rather than an individual. Communications took place directly between the subordinate units and the Commander; the fact that a letter might be opened and answered by some general staff officer and that the Commander might never see it had no bearing on this principle or on the way in which the communications channel was regarded by subordinate units. All acts of Headquarters were the Commander's acts and no one else's.

Implications for Business

The principle that a chief may delegate a great deal of the daily business of commanding and of coordinating to subordinate officers whose formal communications carry his authority is clearly understood in the combat services. Unfortunately, it is not so commonly appreciated in business circles.

What appears to have happened in business, particularly in the United States, is that, with the growth of industrial specialization, second-line positions in an organization have become increasingly functional or specialist positions. Different functions do have different orientations and interests which sometimes conflict— take manufacturing and marketing, for example—and these conflicts of interest have thrown a very much increased burden of coordination on chief executives. This fact is responsible for much of the pressure on the chief and on higher executives to enlarge their spans of control.

Also, the number of specializations which business must use is always growing, and this means that more and more line units want to have direct access to the top manager. If specialized ideas and methods, particularly when they are new and untried, do not have the chief's interest and support, they cannot gain the recognition they need for successful entry into the field, and the criticisms of the limited span of control cited in this article are probably, in part, a reflection of this "pressure of specialization."

It seems to me that there is only one possible answer to the dilemma. Business should not weaken on the principle of the span of control in a vain attempt to induce already strained executives to stretch a little farther. Rather, it should re-examine its assumptions about organization, and it should give special attention

to the use of general staff officers. As I have pointed out, military experience suggests a solution which, while not denying to the specialist his status and final right of access to the chief, allows the top executive to reduce his effective span of control.

The chief will then have time to consider important problems and proposed improvements. He will have the opportunity to see personally and talk with those subordinates who need his help and his approval. The result should be more "democratic participation," greater efficiency, and substantially improved organizational morale.

25

*Parkinson's Law**

It is a commonplace observation that work expands so as to fill the time available for its completion. Thus, an elderly lady of leisure can spend an entire day in writing and despatching a postcard to her niece at Bognor Regis. An hour will be spent in finding the postcard, another in hunting for spectacles, half-an-hour in a search for the address, an hour and a quarter in composition, and twenty minutes in deciding whether or not to take an umbrella when going to the pillar-box in the next street. The total effort which would occupy a busy man for three minutes all told may in this fashion leave another person prostrate after a day of doubt, anxiety and toil.

Granted that work (and especially paper work) is thus elastic in its demands on time, it is manifest that there need be little or no relationship between the work to be done and the size of the staff to which it may be as-

signed. Before the discovery of a new scientific law—herewith presented to the public for the first time, and to be called Parkinson's Law[1] —there has, however, been insufficient recognition of the implication of this fact in the field of public administration. Politicians and taxpayers have assumed (with occasional phases of doubt) that a rising total in the number of civil servants must reflect a growing volume of work to be done. Cynics, in questioning this belief, have imagined that the multiplication of officials must have left some of them idle or all of them able to work for shorter hours. But this is a matter in which faith and doubt seem equally misplaced. The fact is that the number of the officials and the quantity of the work to be done are not related to each other at all. The rise in the total of those employed is governed by Parkinson's Law, and would be much the same whether the volume of the work were to increase, diminish or even disappear. The importance of Parkinson's Law lies in the fact that it is a law of growth based upon an analysis of the factors by which the growth is controlled.

The validity of this recently discovered law must rely mainly on statistical proofs, which

* Reprinted by special permission of the *Economist*, vol. 188, pp. 635–637, Nov. 19, 1955, in which this unsigned article (later ascribed to Professor C. Northcote Parkinson, prominent lecturer and writer, and formerly Raffles professor of history at the University of Singapore in Malaya) first appeared; and by Houghton Mifflin Company, Boston, publishers of *Parkinson's Law* in which this article was reprinted in 1957.

[1] Why? Why not?—Editor.

will follow. Of more interest to the general reader is the explanation of the factors that underlie the general tendency to which this law gives definition. Omitting technicalities (which are numerous) we may distinguish, at the outset, two motive forces. They can be represented for the present purpose by two almost axiomatic statements, thus:

Factor I. An official wants to multiply subordinates, not rivals; and

Factor II. Officials make work for each other. We must now examine these motive forces in turn.

THE LAW OF MULTIPLICATION OF SUBORDINATES

To comprehend Factor I, we must picture a civil servant called A who finds himself overworked. Whether this overwork is real or imaginary is immaterial; but we should observe, in passing, that A's sensation (or illusion) might easily result from his own decreasing energy—a normal symptom of middle-age. For this real or imagined overwork there are, broadly speaking, three possible remedies:

1. He may resign.
2. He may ask to halve the work with a colleague called B.
3. He may demand the assistance of two subordinates to be called C and D.

There is probably no instance in civil service history of A choosing any but the third alternative. By resignation he would lose his pension rights. By having B appointed, on his own level in the hierarchy, he would merely bring in a rival for promotion to W's vacancy when W (at long last) retires. So A would rather have C and D, junior men, below him. They will add to his consequence; and, by dividing the work into two categories, as between C and D, he will have the merit of being the only man who comprehends them both.

It is essential to realize, at this point, that C and D are, as it were, inseparable. To appoint C alone would have been impossible. Why? Because C, if by himself, would divide the work with A and so assume almost the equal status which has been refused in the first instance to B; a status the more emphasized if C is A's only possible successor. Subordinates must thus number two or more, each being kept in order by fear of the other's promotion. When C complains in turn of being overworked (as he certainly will) A will, with the concurrence of C, advise the appointment of two assistants to help C. But he can then avert internal friction only by advising the appointment of two more assistants to help D, whose position is much the same. With this recruitment of E, F, G and H, the promotion of A is now practically certain.

THE LAW OF MULTIPLICATION OF WORK

Seven officials are now doing what one did before. This is where Factor II comes into operation. For these seven make so much work for each other that all are fully occupied and A is actually working harder than ever. An incoming document may well come before each of them in turn. Official E decides that it falls within the province of F, who places a draft reply before C, who amends it drastically before consulting D, who asks G to deal with it. But G goes on leave at this point, handing the file over to H, who drafts a minute, which is signed by D and returned to C, who revises his draft accordingly and lays the new version before A.

What does A do? He would have every excuse for signing the thing unread, for he has many other matters on his mind. Knowing now that he is to succeed W next year, he has to decide whether C or D should succeed to his own office. He had to agree to G going on leave, although not yet strictly entitled to it. He is worried whether H should not have gone instead, for reasons of health. He has looked pale recently—partly but not solely because of his domestic troubles. Then there is the business of F's special increment of salary for the period of the conference, and E's application for transfer to the Ministry of Pensions. A has heard that D is in love with a married typist and that G and F are no longer on speaking terms—no one seems to know why. So A might be tempted to sign C's draft and have done with it.

But A is a conscientious man. Beset as he is with problems created by his colleagues for themselves and for him—created by the mere fact of these officials' existence—he is not the man to shirk his duty. He reads through the draft with care, deletes the fussy paragraphs added by C and H and restores the thing back to the form preferred in the first instance by the able (if quarrelsome) F. He corrects the English—none of these young men can write grammatically—and finally produces the same reply he would have written if officials C to H had never been born. Far more people have taken far longer to produce the same result. No one has been idle. All have done their best. And it is late in the evening before A finally quits his office and begins the return journey to Ealing. The last of the office lights are being turned off in the gathering dusk which marks the end of another day's administrative toil. Among the last to leave, A reflects, with bowed shoulders and a wry smile, that late hours, like grey hairs, are among the penalties of success.

THE SCIENTIFIC PROOFS

From this description of the factors at work the student of political science will recognize that administrators are more or less bound to multiply. Nothing has yet been said, however, about the period of time likely to elapse between the date of A's appointment and the date from which we can calculate the pensionable service of H. Vast masses of statistical evidence have been collected and it is from a study of this data that Parkinson's Law has been deduced. Space will not allow of detailed analysis, but research began in the British Navy Estimates. These were chosen because the Admiralty's responsibilities are more easily measurable than those of (say) the Board of Trade.

The accompanying table is derived from Admiralty statistics for 1914 and 1928. The criticism voiced at the time centred on the comparison between the sharp fall in numbers of those available for fighting and the sharp rise in those available only for administration, the creation, it was said, of "a magnificent Navy on land." But that comparison is not to the present purpose. What we have to note is that the 2,000 Admiralty officials of 1914 had become the 3,569 of 1928; and that this growth was unrelated to any possible increase in their work. The Navy during that period had diminished, in point of fact, by a third in men and two-thirds in ships. Nor, from 1922 onwards, was its strength even expected to increase, for its total of ships (unlike its total of officials) was limited by the Washington Naval Agreement of that year. Yet in these circum-stances we had a 78.45 per cent increase in Admiralty officials over a period of fourteen years; an average increase of 5.6 per cent a year on the earlier total. In fact, as we shall see, the rate of increase was not as regular as that. All we have to consider, at this stage, is the percentage rise over a given period.

Can this rise in the total number of civil servants be accounted for except on the assumption that such a total must always rise by a law governing its growth? It might be urged, at this point, that the period under discussion was one of rapid development in naval technique. The use of the flying machine was no longer confined to the eccentric. Submarines were tolerated if not approved. Engineer officers were beginning to be regarded as almost human. In so revolutionary an age we might expect the storekeepers would have more elaborate inventories to compile. We might not wonder to see more draughtsmen on the payroll, more designers, more technicians and scientists. But these, the dockyard officials, increased only by 40 per cent in number, while the men of Whitehall increased by nearly 80 per cent. For every new foreman or electrical engineer at Portsmouth there had to be two or more clerks at Charing Cross. From this we might be tempted to conclude, provisionally, that the rate of increase in administrative staff is likely to be double that of the technical staff at a time when the actually useful strength (in this case, of seamen) is being reduced by 31.5 per cent. It has been proved, however, statistically, that this last percentage is irrelevant. *The Officials would have multiplied at the same rate had there been no actual seamen at all.*

It would be interesting to follow the further progress by which the 8,118 Admiralty staff of 1935 came to number 33,788 by 1954. But the staff of the Colonial Office affords a better field of study during a period of Imperial decline. The relevant statistics are set down be-

Admiralty Statistics

	1914	1928	PERCENTAGE INCREASE OR DECREASE
Capital ships in commission	62	20	−67.74
Officers and men in Royal Navy	146,000	100,000	−31.50
Dockyard workers	57,000	62,439	+ 9.54
Dockyard officials and clerks	3,249	4,558	+40.28
Admiralty officials	2,000	3,569	+78.45

low. Before showing what the rate of increase is, we must observe that the extent of this department's responsibilities was far from constant during these twenty years. The colonial territories were not much altered in area or population between 1935 and 1939. They were considerably diminished by 1943, certain areas being in enemy hands. They were increased again in 1947, but have since then shrunk steadily from year to year as successive colonies achieve self-government.

Colonial Office Officials

1935	1939	1943	1947	1954
372	450	817	1,139	1,661

It would be rational, prior to the discovery of Parkinson's Law, to suppose that these changes in the scope of Empire would be reflected in the size of its central administration. But a glance at the figures shows that the staff totals represent automatic stages in an inevitable increase. And this increase, while related to that observed in other departments, has nothing to do with the size—or even the existence—of the Empire. What are the percentages of increase? We must ignore, for this purpose, the rapid increase in staff which accompanied the diminution of responsibility during World War II. We should note rather the peacetime rates of increase over 5.24 per cent between 1935 and 1939, and 6.55 per cent between 1947 and 1954. This gives an average increase of 5.89 per cent each year, a percentage markedly similar to that already found in the Admiralty staff increase between 1914 and 1928.

Further and detailed statistical analysis of departmental staffs would be inappropriate in such an article as this. It is hoped, however, to reach a tentative conclusion regarding the time likely to elapse between a given official's first appointment and the later appointment of his two or more assistants. Dealing with the problem of pure staff accumulation, all the researches so far completed point to average increase of about 5¾ per cent per year. This fact established, it now becomes possible to state Parkinson's Law in mathematical form, thus:

In any public administrative department not actually at war the staff increase may be expected to follow this formula:

$$x = \frac{2k^m + p}{n}$$

where k is the number of staff seeking promotion through the appointment of subordinates; p represents the difference between the ages of appointment and retirement; m is the number of man-hours devoted to answering minutes within the department; and n is the number of effective units being administered. Then x will be the number of new staff required each year.

Mathematicians will, of course, realize that to find the percentage increase they must multiply x by 100 and divide by the total of the previous year, thus:

$$\frac{100\ (2k^m + p)}{yn}\ \%$$

where y represents the total original staff. And this figure will invariably prove to be between 5.17 per cent and 6.56 per cent, irrespective of any variation in the amount of work (if any) to be done.

The discovery of this formula and of the general principles upon which it is based has, of course, no emotive value. No attempt has been made to inquire whether departments ought to grow in size. Those who hold that this growth is essential to gain full employment are fully entitled to their opinion. Those who doubt the stability of an economy based upon reading each other's minutes are equally entitled to theirs. Parkinson's Law is a purely scientific discovery, inapplicable except in theory to the politics of the day. It is not the business of the botanist to eradicate the weeds. Enough for him if he can tell us just how fast they grow.

26

Optimizing Span of Control*

HAROLD STIEGLITZ

There is no really neat, packaged formula that anyone can use to determine the proper span of control for a particular supervisor. Nor is there anything close to a foolproof device for determining the proper number of levels that should exist in an organization. If management could come up with a formula for one, the other would be solved. For obviously, in any organization, the span of control determines the number of levels, or vice versa. This is just a matter of building pyramids—for any given number of people, the broader the base of the pyramid, the fewer the layers of pyramids required.

Pragmatically speaking, a really proper span of control is one that is not improper. And there are tell-tale signals indicating when spans are too broad or too narrow. Harassed supervisors and frustrated subordinates often mean that the supervisor has too broad a span. Conversely, harassed subordinates and frustrated supervisors often indicate too narrow a span. Likewise, the proper number of levels, pragmatically speaking, is the number that is neither too few nor too many. Delayed decisions and distorted communications are the chief signals that there are too many levels of supervision. Too few levels is seldom, if ever, a complaint.

Many pressures are behind companies' constant search for optimum spans of control and

levels of management. One of the more compelling of these is money—or saving money. Where this pressure operates, "optimum" in terms of spans or levels is spelled out to mean fewer levels and broader spans than now exist.

Mathematically speaking, it can be shown that an increase in the span of control brings about a proportional decrease in the number of supervisors. Assume, for example, 3,200 rank-and-file employees. If the first level supervisors have a span of sixteen and middle managers (those that supervise the supervisors) have an average span of four, the result is 266 supervisors and five levels of supervision. But increase the span of supervision by 25%. Give the foremen a span of twenty, let the middle managers' span average five rather than four, and the result is 199 supervisors and four levels rather than five.[1] In this case, increasing the span by 25% has cut the number of supervisors by roughly 25%.

The nagging feeling that such savings—to say nothing of the increased efficiency they bring—may be attainable leads companies to continue to experiment with span of control.

There are at least two ways that have been used to reduce the number of supervisors and supervisory levels. One is by fiat—a wholesale cut in the ranks of supervisors is ordered and the work is redistributed to a lesser number. The other is through periodic organizational analyses aimed at reevaluating the nature of the work and the degree of authority vested with various managerial levels. One company found, for example, that it could increase the

* Reprinted by permission of the publisher from *Management Record*, vol. 24, no. 9, pp. 121–129, September, 1962. Mr. Stieglitz is assistant director, Division of Personnel Administration, National Industrial Conference Board.

[1] The following table shows this comparison:

	FOREMAN'S SPAN —16 MIDDLE MANAGER'S SPAN —4	FOREMAN'S SPAN —20 MIDDLE MANAGER'S SPAN —5
Employees	3200	3200
Foremen	200	160
Managers	50	32
	12	6
	3	1
	1	

span of its first-line supervisors by eliminating most of the nonmanagerial work they were performing. Another was able to eliminate a full level of supervision by delegating more authority to lower-level supervisors.

The Lockheed Missiles & Space Company (a group division of Lockheed Aircraft Corporation) has been experimenting with still another—and somewhat novel—method. It has developed a device somewhat similar to job evaluation to assist it in determining proper spans of control. And this device—plus a lot of judgment in its application—so far has helped to broaden spans, to reduce levels and to effect a substantial reduction in the supervisory payroll.

LOCKHEED'S APPROACH

Like some other companies, Lockheed shies away from the term span of control because of the restrictions connoted by the word "control." Instead, it speaks of span of management. And while span of control most often refers to the number of people that report to a supervisor, Lockheed's span of management excludes assistants, assistants-to and other personal staff assigned to the supervisor. Instead, for purposes of its analyses, the supervisor and his assistants are viewed as one.

In attempting to arrive at an optimum span of management, the organization analysts at Lockheed asked themselves a few critical questions—and proceeded to supply answers to them. The questions were of this type:

- What are some of the critical factors that affect span of management?

- Among these factors, are there some that are more critical than others?

- Would it be possible to weight these factors with point values to reflect their relative importance?

- Could a scale of point values be established as a standard to set spans of management?

- Would the result provide a practical tool for determining proper spans of management?

The questions themselves and the procedures implied by the questions resemble those used in job evaluation. And, in Lockheed's case, the organization analysts were able to work out satisfactory answers to each of the questions.

The Factors Lockheed's analysts selected seven factors as being most significant to the span of management:

1. Similarity of function: the degree to which

functions performed by the various components are alike or different.

2. Geographic contiguity: the physical location of the components and personnel reporting to a principal.

3. Complexity of functions: the nature of the duties being performed by the organization components or personnel. Takes into account the skills necessary to perform satisfactorily.

4. Direction and control: the nature of the personnel reporting directly to a principal. Includes the degree of the principal's attention which they require for proper supervision of their actions.

5. Coordination: the extent to which the principal must exert time and effort in keeping actions properly correlated and in keeping his activity keyed in with other activities of the company.

6. Planning: the importance, complexity, and time required to review and establish future programs and objectives.

7. Organizational assistance: the help received by the principal from direct-line assistants, staff activities, and assistants-to. (In the case of first-line supervision, lead men would be included.)

Weighting the Factors Having isolated these seven factors, Lockheed next tried to determine which factors are more critical than others—which factors have a greater impact or are more burdensome to the supervisor and thus place a greater limitation on the number of people that can be supervised. Is geographic dispersion a greater limitation than dissimilar functions? Does planning pose more of a burden than coordination? The answers to these questions—in the form of point values reflecting the degrees of supervisory burden—were based on common sense, experience and experimentation. Differing degrees of each factor with different point values for each degree were tested against actual cases. Finally, a combination of point values was found that showed the most consistent correlation with existing spans of management that were broad. The point values assigned six of the factors are shown on the chart and the accompanying text on pages 167 to 169.

The seventh factor, organizational assistance, was treated differently. Inasmuch as organizational assistance is designed to lighten rather than increase the supervisory burden, it was felt that a supervisor with a line assistant should be able to handle a broader management span than one without. So instead of giving this factor a straight point value, Lockheed assigned percentage values to various types of assistants. A direct line assistant, for example, is given a percentage value of 70%; an assistant-to, 95%; three leadmen reporting to a first-line supervisor are given 55% (see box on page 169 for multiplier factors). These percentages are then used as multiplier factors to reduce the total point value applicable to a given position.

As explained by Lockheed:

> A unit's functions would be analyzed against the six basic span factors, and a numerical value would be determined. This number would be called the supervisory index. If there were a full direct line assistant, this number would then be multiplied by .70. If the index were 38, the new index would be $38 \times .70 = 26.6$ or 27.

Setting Standards for Spans   The point values arrived at were then set up as a supervisory index to "suggested spans." The higher the point value the greater the supervisory burden and the lower the suggested span. Relating the actual span, in terms of numbers of people, to the point values was done by analyzing a number of different supervisory situations and fitting a trend line to the result. From the analysis, it became apparent that two scales would be required—one for middle managers; another for first-line supervisors.

For middle managers the scale is as follows:

SUPERVISORY INDEX	SUGGESTED STANDARD SPAN
40–42	4–5
37–39	4–6
34–36	4–7
31–33	5–8
28–30	6–9
25–27	7–10
22–24	8–11

Four is the minimum span because no situations were found in which fewer than four people were actually supervised.

For first-line supervisors, the same index numbers provide for approximately twice the span.

How Useful A Tool?   So far, Lockheed has used this program in only a few units of the company. One extended the average span from 3.8 people to 4.2 and reduced supervisory levels from five to four; another broadened the average span of middle managers from 3.0 to 4.2 and cut levels from six to five; and in a third case, the average span went from 4.2 to 4.8 persons and levels dropped from seven to five. The reductions in managerial personnel and supervisory payroll were "substantial."

It can be taken for granted that the mere application of this program did not bring about these results. Lockheed's organization analysts who worked out this plan quickly emphasized that it is a guide, and only a guide. Judgments must still be made in any organizational problem, and under no circumstance does this device become a substitute for judgments.

Judgment, for example, is called for in evaluating the extent to which the six factors are present in a particular job situation. And even greater judgment is needed in deciding whether the "suggested span" is truly appropriate in a given situation.

Obviously, if only three or four subordinates are required, the span would not be widened merely because the supervisor could handle more. But more significantly, it might well be that a given factor—such as coordination—may weigh so very heavily in one supervisory situation that it would be specious to apply the point values called for in the plan.

For another thing, there are factors other than the seven selected that affect span—whether it be called span of control or span of management. The degree of competence possessed by both the manager and those he manages is one such factor.[1] These are just some of the considerations that come under the heading of "judgment" in applying this plan.

To what extent, if any, is such a plan applicable to companies other than Lockheed? Are the factors and their point values unique to Lockheed? An answer to the second question is supplied by Lockheed's organization analyst:

> It is possible that different companies would find different combinations and different weightings of the factors, but I believe that managerial conditions are sufficiently similar in all companies that these values would apply. The units which we sampled were taken from a cross section of our company, including engineering, scientific, marketing, manufacturing, procurement, quality assurance, etc. While the technology of our business is probably distinctive, the basic managerial conditions are remarkably similar to businesses everywhere.

[1] For other factors affecting span of control, see "Analyzing the Span of Control," *Management Record,* July-August, 1960, pp. 7–10.

As for the first question—how widely could such a plan be used—the answer is also implicit in Lockheed's emphasis upon the use of judgment in applying the plan. In this respect, too, the device for determining optimum span is like job evaluation. For wage and salary administrators constantly emphasize that any job evaluation plan is simply a tool that managers may use to sharpen their judgments about the price to be paid for a particular kind of work.

Its usefulness as a tool for any company depends upon its design and the understanding of its limitations.

In a sense, Lockheed has applied similar reasoning to span of management. The plan it has come up with represents an attempt to bring a little bit more objectivity, a little bit more organized thinking, to the determination of span and levels of management.

SPAN FACTOR	DEGREE OF SUPERVISORY BURDEN				
Similarity of functions	Identical 1	Essentially alike 2	Similar 3	Inherently different 4	Fundamentally distinct 5
Geographic contiguity	All together 1	All in one bldg 2	Separate bldg's one plant location 3	Separate locations one geographic area 4	Dispersed geographic areas 5
Complexity of functions	Simple repetitive 2	Routine 4	Some complexity 6	Complex, varied 8	Highly complex, varied 10
Direction & control	Minimum supervision & training 3	Limited supervision 6	Moderate periodic supervision 9	Frequent continuing supervision 12	Constant close supervision 15
Coordination	Minimum relationships with others 2	Relationships limited to defined courses 4	Moderate Relationships easily controlled 6	Considerable close relationship 8	Extensive mutual non-recurring relationships 10
Planning	Minimum scope & complexity 2	Limited scope & complexity 4	Moderate scope & complexity 6	Considerable effort required guided only by broad policies 8	Extensive effort required, areas & policies not charted 10

POINT VALUES ASSIGNED TO FACTORS

Similarity of Functions

One point—identical. Employees would be of the same occupation doing the same type of work. In a typical situation, a particular function (such as assembly) would be organized by teams or groups working on identical units or giving identical service.

Two points—essentially alike but having distin-

guishing characteristics in the nature of the functions. This rating would be applied to those components which perform similar work or work of the same nature at different geographic locations.

Three points—similar but with distinct differences in approach or skills required. Typically, each employee or component would be doing work in a general classification (e.g., general accounting, physics, manufacturing engineering) but in different segments of that field (nuclear physics vs. ionic physics, or payroll accounting vs. property accounting, etc.

Four points—inherently different but with common purpose. This rating would apply, for example, to those components (such as development manufacturing) which are closely tied to a single end product or result but where each component performs different phases of the total process (such as development assembly, electronic assembly, final assembly and production control within a development manufacturing activity).

Five points—fundamentally distinct, with different areas of responsibility and requiring entirely different types of personnel skills. The scope of responsibility is fairly broad and the components are organized on a functional basis, each function requiring specialized skills and knowledge.

Geographic Contiguity

Location of personnel or subsidiary components are: one point in one contiguous area in one building; two points—in separate locations within one building; three points—in separate buildings within a plant location; four points—in separate buildings in a geographic area (in different cities of one country); five points—in widely dispersed geographic areas (in several separate parts of the state or country).

Complexity of Functions

Two points—simple, repetitive duties which require little training (less than six months) and which follow simple and well-defined rules and procedures. Examples would include typing, stock handling, mail handling, simple assembly.

Four points—routine duties of little complexity requiring individuals to exercise some but not a great amount of skill and/or judgment in following rules and procedures. Examples would include production machine operations, reproduction operations, receiving and shipping.

Six points—duties of some complexity requiring two or three years' experience and training and which require the application of reasonable judgment and/or skills. Examples would include production planning and scheduling, equipment maintenance, accounts payable, etc.

Eight points—complex duties involving a variety of differing tasks, requiring four-six years experience and training and which require the application of considerable creativity, judgment and skills. Examples would include personnel administration, management planning, industrial engineering, buying, financial planning, test mechanics, special tool builders.

Ten points—extremely complex duties which might involve a wide variety of tasks and which require long training and experience (eight–ten years). Abstract or creative thinking and/or the necessity for consideration of many factors in driving at courses of action. Examples: research scientists, engineering development.

Direction and Control

One to three points—minimum supervision, direction, and control. Subordinate positions would be filled by highly qualified, trained, and experienced individuals who perform within general assignments and with limited direction by the supervisor. Subordinates would not be expected to secure detailed approvals from their supervisors. Subordinates would be top-level directors or are high-level professional, technical, and scientific personnel.

Four to six points—limited supervision, direction and control. Subordinate positions need only occasional contact with the supervisor. Such contact would be necessary, for example, to obtain over-all counseling on a project, to assure that actions are in keeping with company directives and the objectives of the supervisor. Relations with other activities in most cases would be resolved by the subordinates. Internal problems would generally be worked out by the subordinate. Typical subordinate positions would include senior engineers or supervisory personnel in technical and professional areas.

Seven to nine points—moderate periodic supervision, direction and control. Subordinates would be working to a set of fairly well-defined rules of conduct either by professional practices or by company policy and procedure. Exceptions requiring supervisor action and unusual circumstances could be expected to occur with moderate frequency.

Ten to twelve points—frequent supervision, training, and control. Subordinates require continuous regular checking and instruction. The supervisor would be expected to check frequently to assure that subordinates do not make errors in their work.

Thirteen to fifteen points—constant and close supervision, instruction and control. The closeness of supervision could result from the type of work (very important and costly experiments); or from the type of employees (knowledge and skills are such that continual, careful instruction and direction are required). Unusual occurrences would be referred to the principal for decision. Regular rules, guides, or procedures would be very difficult or impossible to prepare.

Coordination

Two points—a minimum amount of coordination. The functions of the components are such that their work is not dependent on the output of others and their work or output does not have a significant effect on other activities. This situation might occur in a pure research activity whose output is not required to meet any precise objectives.

Four points—a limited amount of coordination. The principal would meet occasionally with his subordinates and/or other components to make sure that their functions and/or output are properly conforming to quantity, timing, or procedure requirements. The resolution of problems would be readily determined from well-defined courses of conduct. Coordination might be substantially performed by other departments, such as a scheduling department.

Six points—a moderate amount of coordination. Supervisors would be required to integrate output, timing, and procedures. Functions of subordinates might be so closely related as to require the principal to keep them coordinated.

Eight points—a considerable amount of coordination. A significant amount of the principal's efforts would be required in discussing and resolving mutual problems of timing and quality of output and matters of procedure. The functions of his component would be rather closely tied in with other activities so that mutual and complementary action would be desirable. Some of these relationships could be defined, but others could not.

Ten points—extensive coordination. A great amount of the principal's time would be spent with subordinates and with others in keeping activities in balance. This would apply to certain staff positions that work closely with others

in developing programs or resolving mutual problems of a nonrecurring nature. This might also occur with a responsibility cutting across several organizational lines. In applying the point values to the supervisory job, a distinction must be made between those situations which require the principal to perform these duties and those where subordinates can accomplish the desired coordination without the principal's assistance.

Planning

Two points—of minor importance and complexity, requiring a minimum of time and effort. Functions which are routine in nature where the plans are simple and easily determined, based on very precise criteria, or where plans are prepared by some external organization.

Four points—of limited importance and complexity requiring some measurable time and effort. Activities which do not require a great amount of planning. The criteria for plans and the boundaries within which plans are to be prepared are broadly defined.

Six points—of moderate importance and complexity requiring a moderate amount of time. Planning would be necessary to accomplish objectives and programs, and there would be some criteria to follow.

Eight points—of considerable importance and complexity requiring a large amount of time. Some guidance on planning is available but there would be a number of variables without clear guideposts.

Ten points—of great importance and complexity requiring a considerable amount of time and effort. Planning is largely uncharted and deals with many variables, requiring abstract thinking.

Organization

Direct line assistants and staff activities or personnel which have administrative, planning and control responsibilities: multiplier factor—.60

Direct line assistant: multiplier factor—.70

Staff activities or personnel which have administrative, planning and control responsibilities: multiplier factor—.75

Staff activities or personnel which have administrative, or planning or control responsibilities: multiplier factor—.85

An assistant-to, performing limited planning and control functions: multiplier factor—.95

Leadmen (applicable to first-line supervisors only). The number of leadmen (and the accompanying multiplier factors) in the organization are: one leadman—.85; two leadmen—.70; three leadmen—.55; four leadmen—.40; five leadmen—.25. (This assumes that a leadman will give guidance to eight–twelve employees and spend some 20%–30% of his time in duties of guidance, job assignment and training.)

The Division of Basic Company Activities*

ERNEST DALE

The alternative methods for dividing the work of a company toward the accomplishment of its objectives are numerous. They include, traditionally, function, product, location, customers, process, equipment, and time. It should be noted that in many companies these various bases of division are combined, and coordinated by checks and balances. But there is usually one predominant type of subdivision of the major company activities, made by the chief executive officer himself, called "basic subdivision," "basic delegation," or "departmentation."

The first step in the division of work is the determination of the primary responsibilities of the enterprise—that is, the purpose of the enterprise, and the major functions necessary to accomplish it. Thus, in a manufacturing enterprise, production is one basic responsibility; in merchandising, it may be advertising; in public utilities, the mantenance of equipment; in the liquor business, the determination of credit risk; in flour milling, the purchase of flour.

The principal or primary subdivision of the activities of an enterprise may then be divided on the following bases:

1. *Function.* Major subdivision by function, subject-matter or principal activities is found in many enterprises where actual control throughout all hierarchies and over all locations is exercised by the heads of managerial functions—such as finance; production (including plant design, construction and maintenance, purchasing); manufacture; engineering (product design or research, possibly quality control); law (claims, tax laws, corporate affairs); human relations (relations to stockholders, employees, community, government); sales (mar-

keting, advertising). Many companies are so subdivided at the top. This arrangement has the advantages of specialization. More importantly, it should make possible adequate time for basic long-run planning and major decision-making and consultation for those in charge of the major management functions. But it may result in inter-departmental jealousies and conflicts over the limits of authority. It is also subject to considerable conflict among the local plant managers in multi-plant organizations. An example of a functional type of organization setup is shown in the organization chart of the Dictaphone Corporation (Figure 1).

There appears to be a certain degree of uniformity in basic managerial functions of the top organization structure, at least in very large companies, as is shown in the accompanying illustrations of abbreviated organization charts (Figures 2–4). Of particular interest is the abbreviated organization chart of Standard Oil Company of California (Figure 2), which employs the use of the conventional line and staff organization plan and, in addition, identifies in vertical arrangement the following basic functional groups: Policy Making, Administration and Coordination, Staff and Service, and Operations.

2. *Product.* Management activities may be grouped on the basis of the major types of products or services marketed, and sold separately. This kind of grouping is used by some large companies manufacturing a diverse product line.

At General Foods Corporation and International Harvester Company, the major subdivisions of work are on a product basis. Other examples are found in merchandising, automobile, chemicals and meat packing. Grouping by product has the advantage of bringing together and coordinating in one place major activities required to make a particular product (purchasing, engineering, production, distribution, etc.). Such an arrangement provides a particularly sound basis for decentralization.

* Reprinted by permission of the publisher from *Planning and Developing the Company Organization Structure,* American Management Association, Research Report, no. 20, New York, 1952, pp. 25–38. Mr. Dale is professor of management at Cornell University and senior partner of Ernest Dale and Associates, management consultants.

FIGURE 1   A Functional Organization: The Dictaphone Corporation

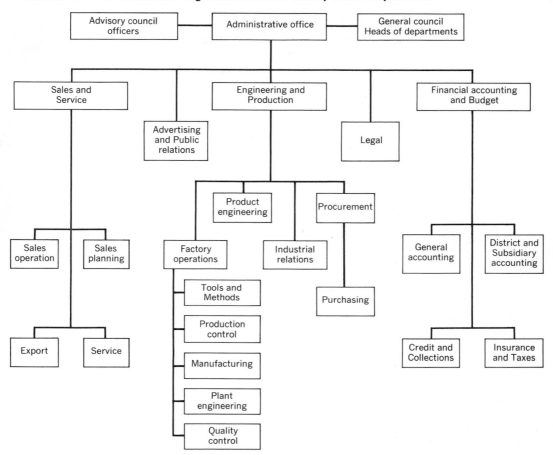

It may also make possible close control and accounting comparability through central staff agencies.

Even in the "mono-product plants" (as General R. Johnson, President of Johnson & Johnson, describes them) it may be wise to make "little ones out of big ones." For example, at the General Electric Company the refrigerator cabinet is made separately from refrigerator compressor units. Or in the production of locomotives, the cabs and running gear are made in separate sections, erected and assembled in another section; the rotating units are made in another shop; and control gadgets in still another. In making control gadgets of infinite variety, the necessity for a multi-product plant really arises.

Figure 5 shows the product organization at The Kendall Company, a medium-sized company which is famous for its work in scientific management. It shows a basic organization built about three major products. It also shows in an interesting way the provision of staff services to these line divisions, the operation of which is decentralized, while coordination and control are centralized.

3. *Location* (also called territorial or geographical division or departmentation). Under this type of arrangement, all activities performed in a particular area are brought together. It is found in companies serving customers on a national or international scale— e.g., the liquor business, railroads, chain stores, life insurance companies, the overseas branches of motor car and oil companies. The product and locational principles may be combined, with different factories in different locations devoted to the production of different types of products (e.g., General Motors).

The major subdivisions of oil companies are often on a regional basis, since the natural unit of work centers around the major oil-producing

FIGURE 2   Abbreviated Organization Chart: Standard Oil Company of California

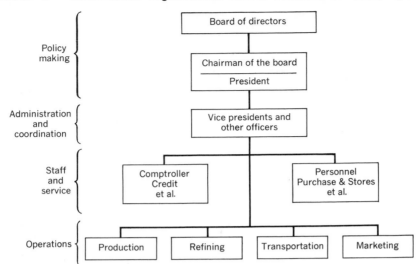

fields. Production and selling or the selling function alone may often be subdivided on a regional basis. The advantage of such a division is that the power of decision-making is concentrated near the source of origin and is all-inclusive, with functional central control. It prevents the losses of efficiency that arise when a company spreads out too thinly. It ensures that careful account is taken of local conditions—an important factor, since the problems of selling may be different in different parts of the country. It makes it possible to take advantage immediately of favorable opportunities arising on the spot. It permits co-ordination on a manageable scale. It facilitates operation in times of emergency or war. Finally, it provides opportunity for training of lower executives in a wide range of activities so that qualified men will be available to fill vacancies in higher jobs.

Figure 6 illustrates territorial or geographical division of company activities.

4. *Customers*. Major subdivision on a customer basis occurs in certain fields—radio and television, for example. Here emphasis is principally on selling programs to individual clients, such as a cigarette company, a soap manufacturer, etc. Lower level subdivisions on a customer basis are found, for example, on railroads (Pullman and Coach travellers), and insurance companies (type of policy-holders, sometimes divided by groups of serial numbers).

In a broader sense, not only customers, but other parties connected with the enterprise may be represented on the organization chart. Figure 7 shows such a division of functions in terms of management communications to its own people at all levels—stockholders, suppliers, financiers, the consumer audience and the general audience. While the usual organization chart shows the structure of the management hierarchy, this chart shows the inter-relationships (and their absence) between the

FIGURE 3   Abbreviated Organization Chart: General Motors Corporation

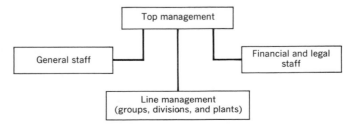

FIGURE 4   Abbreviated Organization Chart: Du Pont

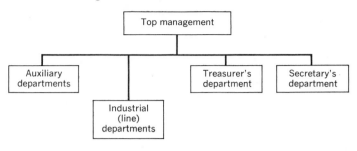

various "publics" connected with the enterprise. It shows the functions which fall into natural groupings and the combinations of functions which are possible in various managerial activities. For instance, in preparing the company annual report, its uses and the varying interests of the different groups may be indicated by such a chart [Figure 7]. (This chart was prepared by A. F. Arnold, designer and management consultant to industry.)

FIGURE 5   Product Organization: Kendall Company

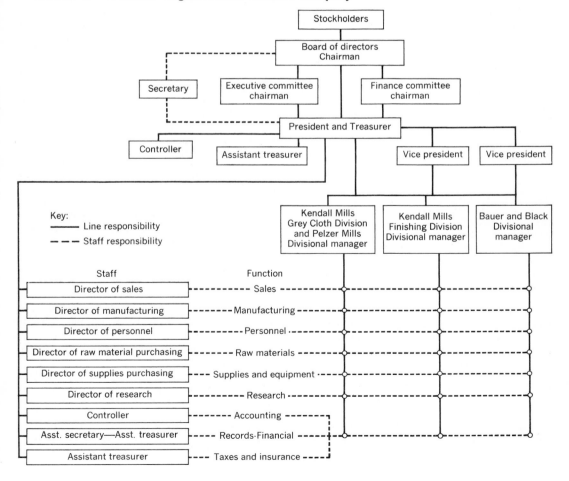

FIGURE 6   Territorial Division of Activities: American Felt Company

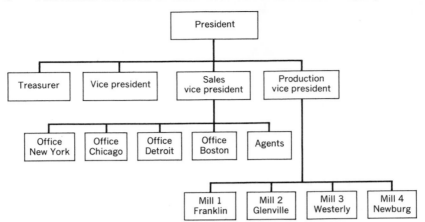

5. *Process*. In integrated textile concerns, major divisions may be made on the basis of operational sequence—e.g., spinning, weaving, bleaching, dyeing, inspection, boxing, shipping. In steel and men's and women's clothing subdividing is often based on the process.

6. *Equipment*. In certain fields, equipment determines major subdivisions. In a secretarial school, for example, the subdivisions may be determined by the chief instruments whose operation is taught, such as the typewriter, the stenotyping machine, the comptometer, etc. (often identical with process).

7. *Time*. Division of work may be based on time sequences, with the work broken down under the categories of planning, execution and control. Thus the first major business division would be devoted to the formulation of objectives, methods of accomplishing them, forecasts and budgets. The second major division would be devoted to the execution of the plans, and would correspond roughly to the major operating group in a business. The third major division is devoted to the control of the results of execution in the light of the objectives and plans of the business.

To present an illustration, at one prominent company the general manager has three principal assistants, each of whom is responsible to him for one of the three main aspects of management, i.e., planning, execution, and control. There are three aspects of planning. In order to do a job one must analyze it carefully and study the available resources. Next, one must balance resources against the job, and design the job to fit the resources. The program must be scheduled on a time basis, and must meet certain set standards of quality and quantity.

All these activities are found under the First Vice President. In another corporation this might be a continuing function of the secretariat of a general policy or planning committee. Although the committee may be made up of certain heads of subordinate departments, the permanent secretariat is in fact the Office of the Vice President. Second, general management is supplied with a Vice President for Operations, charged with the execution of the company's program. He is responsible for the day-to-day coordination, direction and supervision of the company's affairs. To his desk come the thousand and one issues which demand prompt decisions to expedite the efficient execution of any large and complex program. And, finally, in the jurisdiction of the Third Vice President is the function of controllership. His is the job of keeping the progress of the company under scrutiny, comparing it constantly with its program. One might say that this Third Vice President serves the other two. He serves the planner by making prognosticative analyses, and by analysis of past performance which can serve as the basis for future program activities. Obviously, he is a most valuable aid to the General Manager, because he is able to make decisions on the basis of *all* the facts—not merely those which happen to come to him in connection with specific problems.

8. *The "harmonious overlap."* Another method of work division may be useful, particularly in research work which must be speedily completed to meet competition or fulfill an urgent customer requirement. It can sometimes be applied to a variety of rush jobs.

This method of work division may be best

FIGURE 7   Division of Functions Shown in Terms of Management Communication

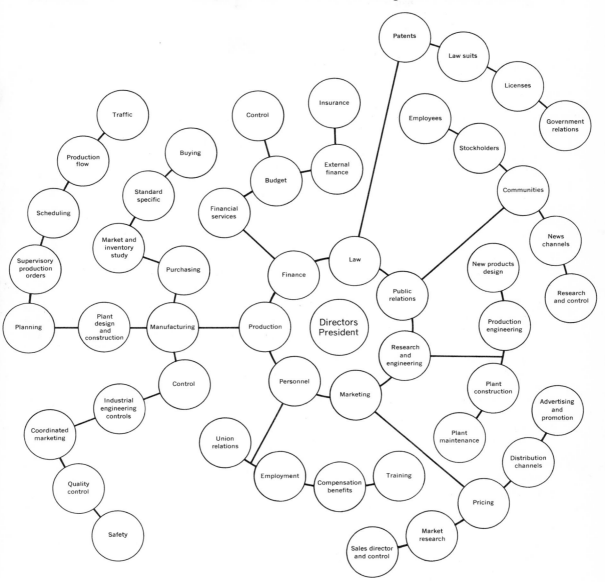

explained by recounting Dr. Alexander Sachs' conference with the late President F. D. Roosevelt in 1939 on dividing the work on the atomic bomb construction:

F.D.R. was worried whether an atomic weapon could be ready in time to decide the outcome of the war. Dr. Sachs had estimated the project might cost two billions, and honestly told the President that, ordinarily, it would take 25 years to do the job. He explained to F.D.R.

that he had searched the history of human thought for an example of how time could be telescoped.

He found the example in music, he says. The composer of music had ways of making time three-layered. Remember the old round you used to sing: "Are you sleeping, etc.?" Three tunes going at once, harmoniously overlapping each other. This, he advised, was what must be done with the atomic project.

"When you start one part of the project,

assume you have finished it successfully, and start the next as if you had." That is exactly what was done, probably for the first time with such a huge undertaking. It worked.[1]

9. *Coordination and balance.* An attempt has been made to bring together the various factors of organizational planning in such a way that each acts as a check or balance on the others. In his *Design for Industrial Co-ordination,*[2] Robert W. Porter set out a technique for coordinating the basic functions in the field of industrial organization. He set up seven major categories for classifying industrial activities, with three subsidiary classifications for each:

1. The problems of policy, performance and compensation, identified as technical problems.

2. The problems of planning, production and inspection, identified as functional problems.

3. The problems of administration, management and operation, identified as jurisdictional problems.

4. The problems of communication, cooperation and control, identified as organizational problems.

5. The problems of executive capacity dealing with intellect, volition and ethics, identified as leadership problems.

6. The problems of employee stimulation, application and discipline, identified as institutional problems.

7. The problems of expectancy, efficiency and economy, identified as measurement problems.

The author attempts, on the basis of wide practical experience, to bring out the inter-operation and relationships of the 21 elements of performance, so that staff needs can be reduced, while the coordination process is improved. It is claimed that this plan of division has the advantages of economizing staff services, improving communication, cutting down jurisdictional problems, and providing better balance in general.

The foregoing are some general guides for determining how the work of the organization may be subdivided, and what consequences may follow. Their specific application will depend upon the special needs of the enterprise.

---

[1] From "How F.D.R. Planned to Use the A-Bomb," by Nat S. Finney, *Look Magazine,* Mar. 14, 1950, p. 25. Copyright 1950 by Cowles Magazine, Inc.

[2] Robert W. Porter, *Design for Industrial Co-ordination,* Harper & Row, Publishers, Incorporated, New York, 1941.

There is no indication from this list that any one way of grouping activities is better than another. If one basis is adopted, then other bases will have to be intermixed. Even when a proper primary basis of dividing work has been decided on, its specific limits must be determined. For example, suppose it has been decided that it will be best to divide sales activities on a territorial basis. This still leaves open the question as to how the territories are to be split up. It is not always practical to determine sales territories by geographical boundaries. The problem must be solved in terms of selling a particular article in a particular situation.

For these reasons it is necessary to develop criteria which are helpful in deciding which method of grouping to use. That method should then be chosen which satisfies best the criteria under consideration, and is best adapted to individual needs.

CRITERIA FOR DETERMINING THE DIVISION OF BASIC ACTIVITIES

In general, the various functions which must be performed to accomplish the objectives of the enterprise should be so assigned as to obtain the greatest possible advantage from the division of labor:

1. Work should be so divided that the incumbent of a position should be able to become a specialist and increase his knowledge on the particular job assigned to him.

2. Special abilities should be used to the full.

3. Groups of people (divisions, departments) should comprise a workable, homogeneous and separate field of activity. The nature of their work should be similar or complementary (the former is probably more important in the lower executive ranks, the latter more important in the upper ranks).

Three major criteria may be distinguished for dividing work—economic and non-economic criteria and the size of the company.

Economic Efficiency　　Economic criteria relate to business efficiency. These in turn may be evaluated in terms of saving money, contributing more to the company's revenue, in the speed or accuracy of transacting business.

That particular grouping of activities should be chosen which will make the greatest contribution to the profitability of the enterprise. This may take many different forms, some of which are discussed below:

1. *Major Contributions to Survival and Profitability.* In the early stages of a company's

growth the fundamental problem is that of economic survival. This may require improvement of the production process so that goods will be turned out on time and within the proper cost limits. It may require successful acquisition of sources of raw materials, as in the timber industry and mining. Or, most commonly, it may require acquisition of cash through sales to meet current expenses and to build up a reserve of working capital. These basic objectives tend to become the major function in the business, with the executive in charge becoming in fact the most important official in the business.

Once production or sales have reached satisfactory levels and have become more or less stabilized, they may well lapse into secondary activities, while research and control become dominant. The primary aim at this point may be technical superiority. If this is under pressure by competitors, or the company itself is forging ahead, this very instability will greatly increase the importance of the technical function—especially if the firm's competitive superiority rests on it. The development by the research or style department of innovations which will accelerate the growth of the company are likely to be primary functions. Or the primary activity, from the standpoint of profits, may be that of integration, consolidation and establishment of central control. Once the firm has reached its final stage of growth and is at the point of defending its share of the market, sales may again become predominant.

2. The company may wish to take full advantage of *specialization* and therefore may group together similar functions or specialties. Thus the selling function is often divided into groups of closely related products—in a food company, confectionery products, for example, may be grouped together so that salesmen can devote themselves to selling one product group well rather than dissipate their efforts over many products. Similarly, activities which serve the same purpose may be most efficiently grouped together—e.g., recruitment, interviewing, testing, hiring and induction may be handled by the employment department, while the employee benefit activities are handled separately by a welfare department.

3. *Lines of communication* may be shortened by a particular type of grouping. Thus specific functions in subsidiary plants may communicate directly with the corresponding headquarters function without going through the local plant manager—e.g., control and auditing.

4. *Duplication* may be reduced or abolished by consolidating a particular function which was previously widely scattered, e.g., the consolidation of the personnel function into a headquarters department.

5. *Balance* may be improved and better operating results attained by combining different parts of a job under several men into one complete job under one man. Joseph B. Hall, President of The Kroger Company, describes such a change in operations as follows:

> Until the past few years, we operated on a functional basis with one man responsible for buying and another man responsible for selling. Sometimes there was friction between these men. If, for instance, merchandise failed to sell, the sales promotion man claimed that the merchandise was inferior; whereupon the buyer would intimate that the sales promotion man had missed his true vocation and should be farming or cleaning the streets. The situation was somewhat like that between the meat managers and the grocery managers; in both cases it was difficult to hold men responsible when each man handled only a part of the complete job.

Railroads have experienced similar cleavages between different parts of the system.

6. The extent of delegated authority may be widened so that lower executives have a greater *power of decision-making*. This has the advantage that people on the spot who are most familiar with the problems can make better and speedier decisions.

7. *Uniformity and consistency* of policy may be brought about. For example, if a personnel department is set up, there is likely to result greater uniformity in pay for similar jobs, more consistent policies with regard to merit rating and promotion, hiring and training.

8. *Control* may be improved. Work may be so divided that similar units are created so that there is better comparability of selling and production efforts. On the other hand, control may be improved by separating inspection activities from the group—e.g., separation of the financial or auditing function from a subsidiary plant, separating credit from sales for fear salesmen will be too easy on the creditors.

9. Activities may be grouped in the department ment which makes the *most effective* use of them. For example, a company might consider having the production department take over the training function from the personnel department if this is the best way to gain acceptance from foremen and hourly-rated employees.

10. *Competition* may be the criterion for dividing activities. Accordingly, the work may be split up into different departments or factories so that the results are fairly comparable. For example, in cement companies the work is distributed to different plants which are usually highly comparable. Sometimes it may be necessary to proceed on the opposite line of reasoning and join two types of work in order to suppress competition which hurts the total effort of the company.

11. *Job interest* may be severely impaired by over-specialization of individual jobs as well as of whole departments. Where work is divided too finely, with little variation or change, the monotony may obscure the meaning of the job and its relation to the end product, and give rise to job dissatisfaction and quits. Over-specialization is likely to require extra supervision (to deal with the resulting discontent) and an elaborate system of formal controls.

Non-economic Factors   There may be important *non-economic* factors to consider in the division of work. These frequently make for *autonomy* in a particular activity. Thus a special division may be set up to look after special interests connected with the enterprise, e.g., a division on stockholder relations or local community relations. Or the division is created to arouse *attention* to the particular activity— defense work, governmental relationships, safety (Central Maine Power Company), executive health, or salary evaluation. At the National Biscuit Company, for example, the head of the Sanitation Department reports directly to the president because the company attaches primary importance to the maintenance of sanitary conditions. Or a special division may be created for a *particular man*—to feather his ego, to "kick him upstairs," to take account of reduced abilities, or to retain some of his services on retirement (e.g., the position of Honorary Chairman of the Board). Division of work may have to be fitted to traditional arrangements within the company. For example, both the production and sales manager may have equal standing in a subsidiary and be given equal powers, but there may be no plant manager. Or the office manager may take over personnel work because there may not be enough of it to justify a full-time division. Or a particular division may continue to occupy an important position within the company simply because it has existed for a long time— e.g., in one company the engineer in charge of bridge-building (the oldest activity in the company) headed up a major division and reported to the president long after bridge-build-

ing had become a minor activity. *Preconceived ideas* and principles, and excessive reliance on formality may also be powerful factors in structuring a business enterprise.

Finally, the *personal interests* or hobbies of the chief executive may play a role. For example, Mac Fisheries were originally added to the Lever soap business in order to facilitate sale of the catch of fishermen of some islands on the West Coast of Scotland in whose development the first Lord Leverhulme took a private interest.

Obviously, not all the factors mentioned above are either rational or desirable determinants of the division of work within an enterprise. However, their existence should be taken into account and the reasons for their existence understood before any attempt is made to change the status quo.

Size of Company   The final major criterion for dividing the work of the organization is the size of the company. The importance of the chief problems faced by the top management varies as the company grows. Hence the major functions exercised and supervised by the chief executive are likely to change also. This may be illustrated by the Work Table which the great French industrialist, Henri Fayol, drew up.[3]

From this table the following conclusions may be drawn:

1. The most important ability of the head of the small industrial company is technical ability.
2. As one goes up the chain of command, the relative importance of managerial ability increases and that of technical ability declines. Equilibrium between these two obtains in medium-sized companies.
3. The most important ability on the part of the heads of large companies is managerial ability or skills, and the more important the company the greater the place occupied by this ability.
4. Commercial and financial ability play a relatively more important part in the case of heads of small and middle-sized companies than they do in the case of larger companies.
5. As one goes up the scale of industrial concerns the managerial coefficient increases at the expense of the rest, which tend to even out, approximating up to one-tenth of the total evaluation.

---

[3] From Henri Fayol, *General and Industrial Management,* trans. Constance Storrs, Sir Isaac Pitman & Sons, Ltd., London, 1949, pp. 10–11.

Relative Importance of Requisite Abilities of Personnel in Industrial Concerns

	REQUISITE ABILITIES						
	MAN-AGERIAL, %	TECH-NICAL, %	COM-MERCIAL, %	FINAN-CIAL, %	SECU-RITY,* %	ACCOUNT-ING, %	TOTAL EVALUA-TION, %
One-man business	15	40	20	10	5	10	100
Small firm	25	30	15	10	10	10	100
Medium-sized firm	30	25	15	10	10	10	100
Large firm	40	15	15	10	10	10	100
Very large firm	50	10	10	10	10	10	100
State enterprise	60	8	8	8	8	8	100

* Safeguarding property, avoiding social disturbances in the broad sense and any influence endangering the life of the business.

It is clear that the larger the size of the business the greater the emphasis on broad managerial functions, such as planning, forecasting, organizing, commanding, coordinating and controlling.

CONCLUSION

The most important criterion for the division of work is that of economic efficiency. This should lead to specialization, full utilization of abilities and homogeneity between groups.

Where this criterion is paramount, the basic functions (i.e., those supervised by the chief executive) are those which make the greatest contribution toward profitability. However, the economic criterion, it should be remembered, must usually be modified in the light of non-economic needs. Both need to be fitted to the particular stage of the growth and the special requirements of the company.

28

Business Organization and Guides for Grouping Activities*

L. C. SORRELL

BUSINESS ORGANIZATION FOR MANAGEMENT

Like many other business expressions, the term, "organization," is loosely used. Often it simply means the business entity or company. Accompanied by the adjective, "legal," it means the corporate versus the partnership or single proprietorship methods of adjusting the legal rights and duties of owners and creditors. Preceded by the word, "financial," it refers to the capital or capital stock structure of the business —for example, the amounts of bonded indebtedness as compared with descriptions of assets and liabilities. Its derivative, "reorganization," has even wider usage. Thus, a business is said to undergo reorganization when its policies are revised, its operating methods and practices are changed, as well as when its financial structure is altered, the personnel replaced, and the allocation of authority and responsibility among the executive personnel is under investigation. In a stricter sense it means the authority relationships between the personnel employed in the enterprise, and it is this last meaning that will be employed in this discussion.

To organize involves doing—precisely what? Say that any given task is one of some complexity and requires the cooperation of several human beings, the process of organizing requires, first, that it shall be analyzed, or split up into more elementary ones; next that these shall be so grouped that they may be assigned to an individual for performance; then that particular individuals shall be obtained who will perform them. The requirement must not

be forgotten that these individuals must all work together. Analysis, specialization, delegation of authority, and coordination of specialists are associated phases of this organizing process. Stated differently, organizing is the process of determining the kind and extent of the specialization to be employed in performing tasks. The same is true even though a single individual only is involved; he must allocate his energy at different times to different parts of the task. He may likewise be said to be planning his work.

But our present concern does not lie with the planning of all kinds of business tasks. It is commonly recognized that two general classes of personnel are encountered in any large business—those who perform various tasks and those who manage those who perform. A distinction exists between managers and those who are managed. This simply means that a specialized kind of work—managerial—is assigned to specialists, called managers, or executives, and the organization of this type of work, termed management, is an important phase of business organization. Indeed, it is this phase that especially concerns us in this series of articles.

Another view of the management organization is often helpful. As already stated, a group of activities may be assigned to a single individual for performance. Similarly, a group of individuals may be assigned to a subordinate executive to manage, the same constituting a section or bureau. Then several bureaus may be combined to form a department and the several departments form the business as a whole. This combination of sections, bureaus, divisions, districts, and departments forms what may be termed the mechanical framework of the organization. In order to visualize the scheme better, many firms draw up an organization chart that shows someone's idea of the organization at a given time. If correctly

* Reprinted by permission of the publisher from "Organization of Traffic and Transportation Activities," *Traffic World*, vol. 46, pp. 1505–1507, 1569–1571, December, 1930. Mr. Sorrell was professor of transportation in the Graduate School of Business at the University of Chicago.

drawn, it should show the result of the process of organizing and reorganizing the business activities.

BUSINESS DEPARTMENTATION

This process of sub-division and grouping of activities under specialized managers results in departmentation. It is a familiar fact that business enterprises of any considerable size are divided into departments and sub-departments, each supposedly in the charge of a single executive. As soon as the business passes beyond the capacity of a single controlling head to supervise each individual worker, the need for departmentation is realized. For departmentation essentially is a grouping of workers for the purpose of direction and control. An alternative method of organizing the work of management does, indeed, exist. For example, without grouping the workers themselves, it is possible to assign specialist managers to different phases of the work performed by each worker. Thus, one manager might supervise the training of each worker, another the condition of his machines and tools, still another the inspection of his output, and so on—a scheme of organization associated with the late Frederick W. Taylor and oftentimes called "functional control." Difficulties inherent in this method have prevented any widespread use of it. Most business organization thought contemplates a grouping of workers under a single executive who is responsible for their efforts. This grouping of workers is departmentation.

Now, different methods or bases for departmentation exist.[1] It is possible, for example, to assign all the workers located in a given place to a single executive; this may be regarded as a territorial grouping of workers for the purpose of management. It is commonly encountered in railroads, chain retail stores, and the field organizations of sales forces. Thus, under prevalent practices of American railroads, the operating and maintenance forces employed on a certain section of the road are placed under the authority of a division superintendent; and, if the property is of great extent, division superintendents are grouped under district superintendents and the latter under regional man-

agers. Or a number of chain stores located within a specified district of a salesman supervisor whose jurisdiction is confined to that territory.

Again, it is possible to assign to a given executive all or a defined part of the workers engaged in the production and selling of a given commodity or group of commodities. This basis of grouping is commonly encountered in department stores, wholesale companies, and also in manufacturing enterprises. Thus, the merchandising function of department stores, which is a combination of buying and selling activities, is commonly so organized; buyers are specialized in terms of commodities; groups of buyers are placed under assistant merchandise managers who, in turn, respond to a general merchandise manager. In such cases only the merchandise function is so organized. Other activities, such as store operation, are differently grouped.

A third basis of grouping is commonly called functional. This word is variously used but, fundamentally, it means an activity or group of activities. Thus, when we speak of the sales department, we are speaking of a functional group of activities: It includes those who engaged in the activity of selling. Likewise, the terms production, purchasing, accounting, finance, and traffic more or less accurately indicate a functional classification of activities.

Now, territorial departments group together activities performed within a prescribed area; commodity departments bring together those affecting certain commodities; but what is the basis of functional departmentation? Since this method of analysis must be employed in further discussion of traffic organization, a more careful examination is warranted.

FUNCTIONAL DEPARTMENTATION

Functionalization may be defined as that fundamental of organization which requires that all the proper functions of a business be recognized, granted existence, combined where similar or complementary, and placed under the direction, supervision, and control of properly qualified executives who have only one, or at the most but a few, similar functions to perform.[2]

We have, therefore, to determine the functions of management in such a way that, firstly, each function forms a compact group of intimately

---

[1] Production Executives Series, no. 83, American Management Association, New York, p. 9. Mr. Thomas R. Jones, of the Cincinnati Milling Machine Company, enumerates as possible bases for grouping, the following: product, process, equipment, geography, function, and combinations of the foregoing. In my opinion equipment and process merge into product and function.

[2] Webster Robinson, *Fundamentals of Business Organization,* McGraw-Hill Book Company, New York, 1925, p. 36.

associated activities; secondly, each function is clearly distinguishable from other functions; thirdly, each function is suitable for single control.[3]

In spite of the awkwardness of these formulations, two ideas seem to emerge. One is that a functional departmentation requires the grouping of activities that are similar to each other, and the other is that it may also require the grouping of activities that are intimately associated with each other.

What constitutes likeness or similarity of activities to warrant grouping as a function? Presumably, not identical or repetitive activities, such as are encountered in a machine drilling operation. Presumably, the concept means likeness from the point of view of interest, aptitude, attitude, training and education, personality, and physique required for performing given tasks. Approaching it negatively, sales activities are commonly regarded as unlike production ones. Clearly, a salesman requires personality, attitude (like to meet people), knowledge, capacity for expression, tenacity (not easily discouraged); an operator of a machine drill requires some skill, strength, quickness, and a capacity for enduring monotonous repeat operations. In these cases the contrast is quite clear, the activities are quite unlike, and it would be difficult for the same individual to perform both effectively. And it is assumed that it would also be difficult for the same individual to manage such unlike activities.

Take another problem. Advertising, too, is quite unlike selling by personal effort. It deals with humanity in the mass, whereas the latter deals with it as individuals. Advertising employs the written or pictured idea, salesmanship the spoken word. The techniques and attitudes required appear strikingly different. And yet, unlike as these activities are, save in purpose, they are often placed in the same major department and under the control of the same departmental executive. Here the second idea of functional grouping comes into play; they are so disposed of because they are very intimately associated in purpose. That purpose is selling goods. Advertising is one method and personal salesmanship is another. They must both operate closely. Advertising is but the initial part of the selling process, completed by personal effort.

Observe another illustration. In department stores, the buying and selling functions are commonly committed to merchandise managers who are responsible for both types of activity —an organization arrangement that generally does not prevail in manufacturing establishments. One reason that may be assigned for this practice is that responsibility could not readily be obtained if these two activities were placed under separate and coordinate authorities, for then selling would be prone to explain its failure to make sales on the ground that the goods were not properly bought, and buying would rejoin that the goods were all right, but that poor salesmanship was the cause. This situation suggests that the two activities are so closely associated that they may properly be treated as a single function for organization purposes. The presence of style goods naturally renders this problem more acute than where staples are purchased or where purchasing buys for factory consumption rather than for sale.

Hence, the functional grouping seems to require, in some cases, similarity of the activities and in others, inquiry concerning the intimacy of their association. The justification of functional departmentation rests on the assumption that an executive can better manage activities so grouped than when some other principle is chosen. In part, it is a protest against illogical methods of allocation, such as the accidental interest of an executive in some subject, or an assignment to a certain executive in order that he may have a more imposing array of activities under his control, or because no one else cares to adopt the orphan, or because of the incapacity of an executive to surrender any subject that has ever been under his authority. In part, its justification depends on an assumption that, in many situations, functional grouping is superior to commodity or territorial departmentation. All three are types of managerial specialization. If functional departmentation may properly be regarded as more economical in the employment of high-grade managerial ability, railroad experience, at least, suggests that territorial specialization may produce better all-around managers.

Where complexity results from the presence of very diverse products or extensive territories, usually some combination of these methods is necessary. The combinations may be simultaneous or successive and may actually overlap. They are simultaneous if they occur at the same organization level. For example, the United States Bureau of Foreign and Domestic Commerce has an assistant director in charge of foreign offices, another in charge of domestic offices, and another in charge of the commodity divisions. In the latter the gathering of

[3] Oliver Sheldon, *The Philosophy of Management*, Pitman Publishing Corporation, New York, 1923, pp. 51–52.

information is organized along commodity lines. Here territorial and commodity organizations parallel each other. Or an organization may be functionally departmented at the top and territorially organized farther down. A sales department is a functional grouping; the next order of grouping may be territorial; and then a branch house, as a territorial unit, may itself be organized functionally. Here a successive application of these methods is observed. Once more, suppose a business, like meat packing, is functionally departmented, but, at the same time, one executive has general supervisory power over all pork operations, another over all cattle operations, and so on. In this case an overlapping of the methods of grouping is evident. . . .

SOME INSTANCES OF VARIATION IN ASSOCIATION OF ACTIVITIES

The organization of manufacturing and mercantile companies, as well as railroads, reveals a large amount of variation in the association of specific groups of activities.

We shall mention a few examples only. Purchasing may be treated as part of the production function, or it may be linked to selling as in department stores, or it may be considered a major function, coordinate with both production and sales. Similarly, engineering is commonly found within the production field. Sometimes it is associated with selling and occasionally it is a major department. Railroad freight claims may be domiciled in the operating, traffic, legal, or accounting department. Sometimes overcharge claims are assigned to accounting and loss and damage claims go to the legal division. Commercial research wavers between an independent status and that of a subordinate division of sales. Accounting is often allied with finance, but probably more frequently these two activities are segregated. Commercial invoicing may belong to sales or to accounting. Office management may be construed to include accounting or may be separated therefrom. Industrial traffic departments often include shipping, receiving, and trucking activities; often the latter are assigned to the production department. Freight claim activities of industries sometimes are concentrated in the accounting division, and, on the other hand, some phases of freight accounting may be found within the traffic department itself. A similar question exists concerning the wisdom of assigning the store's function to the control of the purchasing department. Industrial traffic departments themselves are assigned to sales, purchasing, production, office

management, or may have coordinate rank. Production and general accounting dispute control over cost accounting activities. What is true concerning these larger groups of activities also applies to the narrower ones—much diversity exists.

Most business concerns are organized for the purposes of buying or producing goods and services and selling them. Production and sales, thus, appear as distinct groups of services. Finance, accounting, and personnel are involved in each of them. Establishing these activities as coordinate departments necessarily removes some activities that otherwise would be embraced within sales and production. It is not surprising that conflict arises. Furthermore, it appears that some activities may be quite closely associated with several other groups and this fact occasions variation in practice. It is desirable to inquire briefly concerning the bases on which allocation is predicted.

BASES FOR THE ASSOCIATION OF ACTIVITIES

Generalizing from a number of cases of variation and the arguments advanced to support some particular association or dissociation of activities, certain theories appear to be accepted.

First may be mentioned the theory that a given activity may properly be associated with the group of activities (i.e., department) that can make most of it. Call this the principle of use. It is well stated by Donaldson Brown, Vice-President of General Motors Corporation,[4] in discussing the organization of that company:

> Where any given plant produces a component entering into the finished product of just one of our divisions, it is deemed proper, unless the manufacture is of a highly specialized character, that the investment in that plant and its operation be placed under the jurisdiction of the consuming division. Generally speaking, where the product of a given plant enters into the product of two or more of our divisions, it is deemed desirable to place the investment in such plant and the full responsibility for its operation under the jurisdiction of a separately organized division.

The same reasoning may apply to a service as well as to a product. Thus, if industrial

---

[4] *Decentralized Operations and Responsibilities with Coordinated Control,* American Management Association, Annual Convention Series, no. 57, New York.

traffic activities are performed chiefly in connection with outbound shipments, this theory might, in the absence of other considerations, warrant assignment of traffic to sales. If commercial research or engineering is mainly employed in selling, a similar allocation might be made. On the other hand, should these activities be extensively utilized by several departments, segregation might be the solution.

A second theory holds that an activity may properly be assigned to that department whose executive is interested and capable of giving intelligent direction to the same. Thus, one encounters the argument that the training and conduct of the sales people in a department store should be assigned to the personnel division of the store operating department, rather than to the merchandise (buying) department, because the buyers, although responsible for sales, generally speaking, are not interested in or capable of administering this activity. It is also argued that commercial research should not be assigned to the selling department, especially if the latter is managed by a salesman manager type, rather than a real director of sales, and that production managers, by reason of training and bias, are often incapable of inadequately supervising the purchasing function. This theory may merge into the first, because the executive who uses the services of a given bureau may be more interested in its administration than anyone else. This theory, however, does not justify assignment simply on the basis of accidental interest.

THE COMPETITIVE THEORY

A third theory of association or dissociation may be termed the competitive one; that is, certain groups of activities may be segregated rather than associated, in order to permit the fullest possible development of each and to prevent domination of one by the other. This basis has been used, sometimes, to justify a foreign sales department completely divorced from the domestic sales department and involving coordination only at the level of the chief executive. With a sales manager more interested in domestic than foreign sales, the latter probably would languish, and the opposite result might accrue if the sales manager were more interested in foreign sales. Give each an independent status and let them develop competitively. It has also been used to justify the maintenance of parallel organizations of salesmen, selling different products, or competing brands of the same product. In the field of transportation it has seemed to warrant

the exercise of governmental authority to prevent railways from absorbing waterway and highway transportation agencies. While conceding that some loss may follow the duplication of services that accompanies competition, some believe that it serves as a spur to each of the agencies to improve service and reduce cost. The sailing vessel reached the highest pitch of success under the stress of competition with steam; railways have reached their greatest efficiency in the period of growing highway competition. This theory seems to be more vital to the newer instrumentalities because, if they are grouped in operation with the older, men trained in the older and, therefore, possessing the viewpoint of the dominant methods, are likely to give less vigor to the development of the new. In this aspect it resembles somewhat the second theory—that of interest and capacity.

A variant of this idea is encountered in the practice of attempting to place certain activities on their own feet and practically conduct them as though they were independent business units. Thus, the foreign department of a bank may be considered simply as a service bureau for domestic operations and little consideration may be given to the profit aspect of foreign exchange. Or, that department may have a capital and personnel of its own and be required to show profits as well as the rest of the banking operations. The trust functions of a commercial bank may be treated in a similar fashion and so might the trucking activities of a mercantile firm. The discussion of General Motors, cited above, affords another example of a conscious application of this theory:

> If the advantages of such a type of organization are to be enjoyed fully, it is absolutely essential that each unit be constituted so that it represents a self-contained business enterprise. The capital placed under its jurisdiction must be identified definitely with its own business and no other; and prices at which its products are sold must be based upon actual competitive values. Otherwise there is no tangible basis upon which the general effectiveness of the direct management can be gauged reliably.

COORDINATION OF ACTIVITIES

A fourth theory is the opposite of the third. Activities may be associated so that competitive development may be diminished or prevented and so that coordination may be obtained, in the sense that each facility may be used to perform the tasks for which it is best fitted. This may be effected simply by means of joint ownership, affecting policy, but not the management organization; or it may go the length of changing the latter. Thus, a transportation company may own railways, waterways, and trucks, but may leave each to a separate department. Or, it might give its division superintendents authority over all transport instrumentalities. The latter, of course, would be a closer form of coordination. Unified ownership and/or operation would not eliminate all competition between them, but it is likely that it would be held within narrower bounds. Say that an industrial concern has intra-plant transport facilities consisting of standard gauge electric, narrow gauge electric, highway trucks, and small industrial tractors and trailers. These may be organized competitively or they may be welded into a unified operating organization.

Fifth, a bureau may be assigned to a given department because of a supposed necessity of controlling the policy of the former in the interest of the latter, or, conversely, it may be withheld from a certain department because of the fear that the latter would contribute too much bias to the administration of the bureau.

Railroad claims seem to be a good illustration of this line of reasoning. This activity might be assigned to operation on the ground that operation causes loss and damage claims, at least, and should be charged with that responsibility so that it will have an incentive to prevent them. Traffic might allege that it is much interested in the maintenance of the shipper's good-will—that claims constitute a prolific source of ill-will and can be administered so as to maintain good-will, if correct policies prevail. Law, of course, can point to the fact that claims of all kinds involve questions of law, and accounting, too, can point to the accounting aspects of claims, particularly over-charge claims. The association with operation is predicated on responsibility and prevention; with traffic, on good-will; with accounting and law, on the basis of technical matters. The policy in the settlement of claims may be strict or lenient; it may range all the way from a tendency to evade all responsibility to a tendency to regard the customer as being always right. Operation possibly might tend toward strictness, because claims are a reflection on their own performance. Traffic might be too lenient, because of a disposition to pacify the customer. Law or accounting might be more balanced between these two viewpoints

—more neutralized. Moreover, with railroads, the anti-rebating provisions must not be overlooked. A non-public utility, per contra, might readily reason that commercial claims should be assigned to sales, in order that the latter might control the policy of the former.

SOME ACTIVITIES NOT EASILY SEGREGATED

Sixth, the fact is encountered that some activities are not easily separated from others; the break is not "clean"; they must be kept together, if responsibility is to be obtained. This seems to be the theory that underlies the association of buying and selling goods in department stores. That goods well bought are more than half-sold is a maxim that seems to incorporate the idea. It is probably less omnipresent where staples are being sold and where manufacturing is involved. Again, it may happen that one bureau or division cannot effectively perform its function unless some other bureau will faithfully carry out instructions. To some extent this pervades all business organizations, but it does seem that the functioning of certain departments is more inter-related than is that between others. Charge traffic with the responsibility of effecting the most economical purchase of transportation; this cannot be achieved unless shipping and receiving will faithfully carry out instructions. Traffic might thus argue that these activities are so interdependent that they should be associated in management. Cooperation may be gained otherwise, but association under the same manager, at least, removes one possible barrier. Some activities are so integrated physically that separation for organization purposes seems impossible—for instance, conveyor systems that feed machine or assembly operations. And if a personnel department can force an employee on an unwilling foreman, the latter's authority and capacity to maintain discipline will probably be diminished.

Seventh, a negative principle is often encountered—that an activity may not properly be associated in organization with activities that it should check. Thus, some accountants argue that that function may not properly be combined with treasury, first, because it should operate as a check on financial activities as well as on other departmental functions and, second, because it is likely to reflect too much of the financial point of view. In discussing the authority of the controller over cost accounting and accounts receivable ledgers, as compared with the authority of manufacturing and credit departments, respectively, J. P. Jordan[5] presents a similar argument:

> As a blanket argument, however, the guiding thought in respect to the controller's department is that of its being a check upon all operations of the business in order that such a check will be entirely separated from either the line or staff departments which may be too vitally concerned whether with covering up or overlooking laxity in some form or other.

This principle may establish what associations should not exist; it does not say what should be done.

GROUPING DEPENDS ON NECESSITIES OF COORDINATION

Finally, it should be observed that the grouping of activities into departments depends on the necessities of effecting some type of coordination. For example, take a branch house organization. Within a branch house are several functions—selling, storing, shipping, receiving, accounting, collections and credits, trucking. In a large branch house a considerable personnel may be found in each activity. The manager will probably be someone with sales experience, because that is the main function of a non-manufacturing branch. Definitely, he belongs to the sales organization. But not all the branch house activities may be so classified. It may, nevertheless, be desirable to give the branch house manager authority over all of the branch house activities and employees, because he is so situated that he can supervise them, whereas the specialists in each of these functions can exercise only absentee supervision. The necessities of coordination at that selling point and the maintenance of discipline

[5] J. P. Jordan, in *Yearbook,* National Association of Cost Accountants, 1929, p. 18.

seem to require this grouping of associated activities.

Railroad transportation in the United States offers another illustration of the same point in the long standing argument concerning the merits of the divisional and departmental methods of organization. As traffic men know, this relates wholly to the operating and maintenance activities. Under the departmental system, if completely carried out, engineering, mechanical, and operating appear as major sub-departments within the operating and maintenance department. The chief engineer has direct authority over the division engineer, the chief mechanical officer over the master mechanics on the division, and the superintendent of transportation over the division superintendents. But the division superintendents have no authority over division engineers and master mechanics. But, under the divisional system, though these same departments exist, the division superintendent does have direct authority over division engineers and master mechanics. So far as the organization plan itself goes, the pure departmental system makes no provision for coordination among these three activities short of the general manager, whereas the divisional system ties them together at the level of the division superintendent. The question, of course, is at which point in the organization scheme it is most necessary to obtain that coordination. Exponents of the departmental system emphasize the economy of man power and uniformity of standards secured. Adherents of the divisional system point to the necessity of obtaining cooperation quickly for dealing with emergencies, such as floods and wrecks, and affirm that this method develops better all-around managers. It hardly needs to be emphasized that neither method exists in pure form and that personalities and devices quite outside the organization plan may modify the actual working of both schemes.

29

*Patterns in Organization Structuring**

HAROLD STIEGLITZ

Change is the only constant in company organization structuring. The truth of this cliché, which is both a refuge and a vested interest of the organization planner, becomes evident when one attempts to examine the structure of a large number of companies. In gathering material for this particular report, the Conference Board was frequently told: "Our latest organization chart is no longer current," or "We are just in the process of reorganizing," or "A new chart reflecting recent changes will be sent as soon as possible."

Many of the organization changes these companies refer to are minor in that they reflect a shift in one or two functions, or a change in several reporting relationships, or merely a change in the personnel occupying given positions. On the other hand, a sizable portion of the changes are major in that they reflect large-scale regroupings of activities or basic changes in the authority structure of the company.

Even some seemingly minor changes may be major. For example, the insertion of an executive vice-president in an organization where none has existed before, may be represented by a relatively small change in the chart, but it may well be a major redistribution of authority. And in some companies, a series of small, seemingly unrelated organization changes takes on a pattern after a while and begins to add up to a major change.

At such a point even a detached observer, not privy to the inside working of the company, begins to realize that a company's chart, at any one time, represents merely one stage in an ever-evolving organization plan. Similarly, the charts of a variety of organizations, taken at any one time, may depict an evolving pattern of business in general adapting its organization structure to change. For conceiva-bly, instead of looking at the separate charts of three or four different companies, one might be looking at the chart of one company at four different stages of its development.

Among the sixty-one different companies whose charts make up the bulk of this report, such a pattern is discernible. The pattern reflects the attempts of companies to build organization structures consonant with the requirements of larger and—more importantly—far more complex business. The increase in size and complexity which has confronted many companies has come about through the new markets they are serving, the new products they are producing, and the resulting changed legal and economic climate they are operating in. In some companies the increased complexity has resulted from self-generated expansion; in others it has come about through mergers and acquisitions.

How to manage a large, highly complex business is a problem a relatively few giant companies faced many years ago.[1] The solutions that they reached at the time were viewed as pioneering. But it is becoming more evident that as more companies reach a certain size and complexity, they reach for organizational solutions that are somewhat similar. For some companies this similarity results from emulation of what seems to have been successful for another company with similar problems. But more often today it seems to result from the application of the principles of organization to a given set of circumstances.

The observable pattern among the sixty-one companies has four major elements to it, some more evident than others:

1. A more concerted move to divisionalized organization structures accompanied by greater decentralization.

2. The elaboration and changed role of corporate staff.

* Reprinted by permission of the publisher from *Corporate Organization Structures*, National Industrial Conference Board, Studies in Personnel Policy, no. 183, New York, 1961, pp. 12–15. Mr. Stieglitz is assistant director, Division of Personnel Administration, National Industrial Conference Board.

[1] For one recent investigation of this point, see Ernest Dale, *The Great Organizers: Theory and Practice of Organization,* McGraw-Hill Book Company, New York, 1960.

3. The emergence of another level of general executives, most often labeled "group executives."

4. The elaboration of the chief executive's office.

The elements of this pattern are by no means unrelated. All stem from the same root problem. All might be viewed as part of the answer to the same question: "How can one man—the chief executive—manage to manage a larger and more complex enterprise?"

GREATER DIVISIONALIZATION ACCOMPANIED BY DECENTRALIZATION

As companies move into new fields of operations occasioned by expanded product lines or wider sales regions, they are confronted by new problems of competition, new technological problems, and new marketing problems. For example, a company historically identified with the production and sale of glass containers meets a whole new field of competitors when it expands its product line to include metal and paper containers. A service company operating in one region meets a new field of competitors when it expands its services to new regions.

The functional-type organization so well fitted to the single-product company or the company operating in one socio-economic region has difficulties in adequately coping with the new problems. For example, it is difficult for a single head of manufacturing to deal with all the different manufacturing problems associated with a variety of different products; or for a single head of sales to give adequate attention to the sale of different products to different customers in different regions. More importantly, it is hazardous to leave the overall coordination of the production, engineering and sale of a variety of products serving a variety of regions and customers to one man. But that is the case in a strictly functional type of organization: one man, the chief executive or his deputy, coordinates all line elements.

For several reasons—adequate emphasis on different product lines, easier identification of profitability, greater flexibility of operations, and increased ability to compete in a variety of markets—more companies have grouped functions on a product basis and delegated responsibility for their coordination to the head of a product division. This divisionalization, almost by definition, has brought with it a greater degree of decentralization. For, in a divisionalized organization, the authority to make decisions involving the coordination of the activities relating to one product and accountability for profits occurs at a level lower in the organization than the president or the executive vice-president.

Of course, divisionalization may proceed from two different directions. Most often it occurs in a company previously organized along functional lines. But it may also proceed from a totally different direction: for example, where wholly-owned subsidiaries are more closely integrated into the operations of the parent company; or where merged or acquired companies operate as divisions of the over-all company. In the process of becoming a division, the subsidiary, merged, or acquired unit loses some of its autonomy.

It has been argued that this loss of autonomy amounts to recentralization rather than decentralization. But from the point of view of the parent or over-all company, it is still decentralization. (Because there are other aspects to this point, it will be touched on later.)

Among the companies participating in this report, the tendency to divisionalize operations is noticeable. For some, the move began after World War II and has continued; for many others, it is more recent. It is most noticeable, naturally, among those diversified manufacturing companies whose operations lend themselves readily to grouping of activities on the basis of product. But even companies engaged in businesses whose production processes historically have lent themselves to a functional organization (steel, for example), or those who have a common market for a variety of products (foods, for example), have adopted divisionalized organizational structures.

The move to divisionalize has not been without its problems. One is that as more specialized product groupings are attempted, it becomes increasingly difficult to meet the three basic criteria for optimum divisionalization along product lines: differing production technology, differing markets, and sufficient demands for the product. As a result, some companies have regrouped production (but more often sales) of previously established product units. Instead of having ten different product units, for example, they may regroup to eight, with one unit handling sales of the products that have the same customers.

A second problem arises, in establishing product or regional divisions, over the allocation of staff or service units to the product divisions. Need a division have a full staff complement in accounting, personnel, public relations, and research? Judging from the charts and manuals of the participating companies, economics, tempered by considerations of decentralization, seems to provide the answer. If the requirements of the division are such as to require a full-time staff component in any of the mentioned fields of specialization, the unit is set up. But if the services can be more economically provided by a central unit or a unit serving several divisions or a group of divisions, the staff service is not placed within the division.

However, as mentioned above, this purely economic consideration is tempered by the nature of delegated authority. If the division head or other unit head is held accountable for results, he may require or feel that he requires certain staff units at his elbow.

The companies participating in this report show a variety of staff arrangements so far as their divisions are concerned. In companies whose divisions are virtually major operations, or whose divisions are geographically dispersed, a full staff complement often exists within the division and/or units of the division. More often, when the company is smaller or not so widely dispersed, the product divisions may have less staff or none at all. The head of the product division in such a situation can avail himself of central staff services or, depending upon the degree of decentralization, hire outside consultants to furnish his requirements.

ELABORATION AND CHANGING ROLE OF CORPORATE STAFF

As a company grows, staff also grows. Part of this growth in staff is a natural consequence of the need for more services of the same type: it takes a larger accounting department to service a company with $1 million in sales and 1,000 employees than to service one with $500,000 in sales and 400 employees. Part results from companies setting up units to carry on activities previously bought on a contract basis: the company may have grown to the point where it needs a full-time staff department to provide services that were formerly provided by an outside public relations firm or legal counsel on a part-time basis.

Another reason for the growth of corporate staff is evident in the charts of participating companies: many of them are finding a need for types of service that had not been of concern previously. Thus, in some companies certain staff components are now appearing at the corporate level for the first time. Some examples of the "newer" staff functions are: community relations, government relations, stockholder relations, computer technology or electronic data processing, research, product development, marketing and market research,

manufacturing, executive development, organization planning, long-range planning, organization development, management services, and control.

Some of these functions arise from the changed competitive environment the business operates in; research, product development, and market research are prime examples, and government and community relations might also come under this heading. Some are more directly attributable to the move to divisionalized operations; for example, organization planning, executive development, and the emergence of marketing and manufacturing as corporate staff activities. And some are consequences of both; for example, electronic data processing, long-range planning, organization development, and management services.

Although the types of staff activity at the corporate level have been increasing, it is not accurate to say that the number of personnel engaged in corporate staff work has also increased. For much of the service-type work with which staff is identified is carried on by staff personnel within the divisions, leaving a smaller but more specialized, versatile, and highly skilled staff at corporate headquarters.

This fact points up another aspect of the elaboration of corporate staff: the general shift of emphasis from its role as a primarily service agency to its role as an agency assisting in planning and control. This change in emphasis is partly apparent in the titles of the merging corporate manuals and position guides that detail the responsibilities of corporate staff. The shift is especially common in companies that have moved to divisionalized organization. For in a divisionalized company that practices decentralization, corporate staff takes on the major job of assisting in the formulation of overall corporate objectives and policies. And it acts as the agent of the chief executive in measuring and appraising performance within functional specialties relative to the established objectives and policies.

Possibly the change in the role of corporate staff in a divisionalized and decentralized company might be more easily viewed from the perspective of the chief executive. In a functional type of organization he (or his deputy, the executive vice-president) has responsibility for coordinating the line elements—production and sales.

But, in a divisionalized organization, the chief executive delegates responsibility for coordination of what amounts to separate businesses to two, five, or more division heads. However, if his aim is decentralization rather than fragmentation, he attempts to set up objectives and policies that act as a cohesive and unifying force. Thus, the chief executive concentrates on those responsibilities that affect the organization and its future as a total entity: determination of objectives and long-range plans, policy formulation, surveillance, and control. As the business becomes more complex, the exercise of these reserved responsibilities calls for more and better information. Corporate staff has been characterized as the lobes of the brain that make it possible for the chief executive to carry out these essential responsibilities.

The emergence of corporate staff as a major force in the planning and control of corporate objectives and policies has been characterized as "recentralization"—as a reaction to too much decentralization.[1] Upon analysis, it can be seen that this claim contains some truth. But it can also be seen that other factors may contribute to what has been loosely termed recentralization.

First, some companies attempted to set up "divisionalized, decentralized" operations without first establishing over-all corporate objectives, objectives for each of their divisions, and corporate policies. After the effects of such disorganization became evident, the companies sought to establish those unifying elements that had been lacking. In such situations, organization analysts argue, the company was not decentralized in the first instance; it was atomized.

Second, some companies that have decentralized find that over a period of time there are changes in the three factors affecting the degree of decentralization.

1. *Competence.* The demonstrated competence of a position incumbent may fall short of the requirements of the job or a new replacement may lack the competence required. In either case, the position may be redefined with less authority.

2. *Information.* The information required at a given level of decision making may not be available at that level. Authority is moved up to the level at which it is available.

3. *Scope of impact.* Because of a change in circumstances, certain decisions made by lower level heads may be found to have a widening scope of impact. Authority to make such decisions is moved up to the level at which all affected units are coordinated. Or where the company decides that a uniform

course of action is necessary, the authority to make separate decisions is withdrawn.

In all three of the situations above, there is less decentralization than before; "recentralization" has occurred.

The use of these terms serves to emphasize a basic point: decentralization is a matter of degree. It varies from one company to another; it varies within a given company when, for example, certain organizational units may exercise a higher degree of delegated authority than others.

Other problems confront companies as a result of the elaboration and changing role of corporate staff. One is determining the types of controls the company can use and still maintain a decentralized organization. It is possible for central staff, in the name of control, to set up detailed audits and reporting procedures that amount to a constant check on division heads. The alternative stressed by organization planners is control or appraisal of performance on the basis of established objectives and accountability for results.

Another problem arises from the fact that, in a divisionalized organization, corporate staff heads tend to be less involved in servicing operations than under a functional type of organization. Also, former heads of such traditionally line functions as manufacturing and sales may now find themselves heading a corporate staff manufacturing or marketing unit. In both cases, changes in relationships and methods of operation are called for. Reports from companies indicate that not all executives find it easy to make this adjustment.

EMERGENCE OF GROUP EXECUTIVES

As divisionalized companies increase the number of product divisions, effective coordination of the separate divisions becomes a greater problem. A fairly common organizational device many companies have used, and still use, is the setting up of an executive vice-president to ease the load of the president. In some companies, the executive vice-president coordinates staff activities. Far more often he coordinates the operating units or divisions and the president retains direct supervision of the corporate staff units vital to his over-all planning and control responsibilities.

However, with the proliferation of product divisions and corporate staff units, some companies are finding that even an executive vice-president cannot adequately provide the required direction. So they have added general executives accountable for the performance of two or more product divisions that are some-

---

[1] See, for example, "Top Management Tightens Control," *Dun's Review and Modern Industry,* July, 1959.

what related in terms of production technology or markets served. Most often, these executives carry the title of group vice-president or group executive. In some companies, they constitute an additional level between an executive vice-president and product divisions; in others, they are apparently in lieu of the executive vice-president.

The emergence of group executives is not confined to the giants among the companies in this report.

In a few companies, a position somewhat similar to that of group executives also appears at the corporate staff level. Two, three, or more corporate staff units may be grouped together under a senior vice-president or a position titled vice-president, administration.

Cutting down on the chief executive's span of control is the reason most often given for the increased number of group executives. The factors that seem most relevant to the determination to set up a group executive are:

1. Increased demand on the chief executive's time: when the extent of the chief executive's external relations and over-all responsibilities rises so that the time remaining for him to furnish personal contact with major unit heads is inadequate, the new level is created to act in lieu of the chief executive.

2. Increased interaction between divisions: when the objectives or plans of several divisions begin to have greater effect on each other, possibly by virtue of overlapping markets, closer coordination is provided by means of a group executive.

For many practical purposes the group executive, like the executive vice-president, may be likened to an assistant president (rather than assistant to the president) as far as the divisions reporting to him are concerned. And as is often the case with assistants, the responsibilities and authority of the group executive, and their impact on the degree of responsibility and authority of those reporting to him, are not always clearly defined. It certainly cannot be found in the charts of companies where this position exists. But judging from position guides and organization analyses, some companies attempt to have it clearly understood that the division head's accountability for profitable performance, and his attendant authority, are in no way diminished by the insertion of a group executive; the group executive in these companies exercises some of the authority formerly reserved to the president relative to divisional operations. However, it is recognized that in such cases, although there

is no lessening of the formal authority of the division head, he may feel he has less "authority" (in a prestige sense) because he is one level removed, or one level further removed, from the president.

ELABORATION OF THE CHIEF EXECUTIVE'S OFFICE

The elements so far discussed can be viewed as means used by the chief executive to manage a growing and far more complex business; all three allow him to devote more of his time to those responsibilities uniquely reserved to him.

Some of the unique responsibilities of the chief executive have already been mentioned, or at least implied, in the preceding discussion. Analyses of organization indicate that the following are the hard core of the chief executive's reserved responsibilities:[1]

• *External relations*—The chief executive is the company as far as external relations with the public, stockholders, government, and business associates are concerned.

• *Objectives and long-range planning*—The chief executive determines the appropriate long-range and short-range objectives and plans for their accomplishment.

• *Over-all policy formulation*—The chief executive sets the code of ethical conduct that the company will adhere to in pursuit of its objectives.

• *Surveillance and control*—The chief executive sees to it that all components of the organization are moving in the direction of established objectives and are conforming with corporate policies.

• *Development of a successor*—The chief executive assures the continued survival and perpetuation of a company by developing the next chief executive.

There seems to be little question that the nature of these reserved responsibilities is the same for a chief executive of a small company, a medium-sized company, or a large or very large company. But as the company grows in size and complexity, the scope of these reserved responsibilities grows to such an extent that they are beyond the capabilities of one man. External relations alone may so preoccupy the chief executive of a giant enterprise

---

[1] For a fuller discussion of these reserved responsibilities and some of the organizational device structures used by the chief executive, see "Organization of the Chief Executive's Job," *Management Record,* February, 1961.

as to leave inadequate time for proper attention to the other responsibilities. Or at different stages of development, the other responsibilities may demand the full attention of the chief executive.

Not only does the scope of the reserved responsibilities grow beyond the capabilities of one man; but also, the abilities required for their performance become so increasingly varied that one individual cannot supply them.

It is evident from the organization structures in this study that companies—or more particularly, chief executives—are using several methods to cope with the expansion of the reserved responsibilities of the chief executive. All the methods elaborate the office of the chief executive so that these reserved responsibilities —the "chief executive function"—are being performed by more than one man. Accountability still rests with the chief executive office alone, but the function, it might be said, is "decentralized."

One fairly widespread method, by no means new, is the use of personal staff assistants. In some companies, their responsibilities are rather general. They carry out whatever jobs of a temporary or a continuing nature the chief executive may assign to them. In others, the assistants specialize in fields of interest that the chief executive has chosen to reserve to himself; possibly, organization planning, technical development, and market development.

The distinction between these more specialized staff assistants and corporate staff units is not always sharp. Often they provide functional assistance to other units of the organization. Their major emphasis, however, appears to be on studies or plans, sometimes of a confidential nature, that fall within the reserved responsibilities of the chief executive.

Another method that appears quite frequently among the participating companies amounts to an upgrading of the president-executive vice-president relationship. An increasing number of companies are allocating the chief executive function to a chairman of the board designated "chief executive officer." The president in these companies is sometimes designated "chief operating officer," or sometimes "chief administrative officer." In some companies there is a definite split in responsibility of the two men, but quite often they "share the same box" and share responsibilities.

In a very few of the participating companies, not just two but three (a chairman, president, and an executive vice-president) and even four men (a chairman, president, and two executive vice-presidents) share this top box and the duties of the chief executive.

Still another method of coping with the increased complexity of the chief executive function calls for the creation of a council of top executives to carry out this chief executive function. The concept involved here cannot be adequately depicted on any chart. But a few companies use a special charting device to emphasize the idea. One box labeled "executive office" or "executive management" or "office of the president" appears at the top of the chart. It includes not only the chief executive and the executive vice-president(s) but also those group executives and general staff executives accountable for coordinating the operating and corporate staff components of the business.

In effect, the group executives and general staff executives making up this top council wear two hats. As group or general staff executives they are accountable for the performance of the units reporting to them. But, as members of the executive office, they lose their identities as line or staff men and become, to quote one company:

> A group of executives free of detailed administrative and operating matters to assist the president in policy development and the over-all leadership and coordination of the company's business and management.

Having men with specified areas of functional and business responsibilities and with complementary abilities in this "office of the president" is viewed as assuring more adequate consideration of all factors that bear on any over-all decision. And, the chief executive function, instead of being the sole responsibility of the chief executive officer, becomes the resibility of a composite personality, the chief executive office. The chief executive officer under this concept has the job of coordinating the component parts of his office and gives direction and purpose to their work so the company can reach the objectives for which he is accountable.

General Motors Organization Philosophy and Structure*

HARLOW H. CURTICE

I. FOUR BASIC REASONS UNDERLYING OUR GROWTH

May I first make the point that the growth of General Motors has taken place principally over the past 35 years. This period coincides with that in which the policies and business of the corporation have functioned under the existing management organization.

In my opinion there are four principal reasons for our success. These are, first, the dynamic growth of our country; second, the even more rapid growth of the automobile industry; third, our management structure; and, fourth, our approach to problems.

It is obvious that our country has grown tremendously since the early 1920's. To cite just one measure of growth, our gross national product has increased three-fold on a constant dollar basis. Actually, in terms of current dollars the increase has been from about 80 billion to a current rate of 395 billion. The country has grown and businesses of all kinds have grown.

General Motors would have grown substantially over the past 35 years had it done no more than keep pace with the growth of the country.

However, the automobile industry, and with it General Motors, has grown faster than has the country. Over the years our industry has become an increasingly important factor in the economy, supplying the vital needs of transportation of goods and people. Its contributions to the nation's expanding output of useful goods and services have become increasingly significant.

General Motors has grown faster than has

the automobile industry as a whole. Quite obviously, we have made things that people wanted, and people in increasing numbers have bought them. We have built up customer satisfaction in our products and, equally important, the constant improvement in our cars has created customer desire for the new model by making him dissatisfied with the old. As one newspaper expressed it, to find the reason for General Motors' success it is necessary to "get out of the hearing room and into the show room. The reason GM is big is because people want to buy its products. The reason people want to buy its products is that they are good and they are priced right."

General Motors has been able to offer greater dollar values in its products, and at the same time it has been able to operate efficiently to provide dividends for its shareholders and substantial sums for reinvestment in the business.

But, one may well ask why and how; and this brings me to what to my mind are the two fundamental reasons for the success of General Motors.

Both fall under the heading of what might be termed management philosophy. When this General Motors philosophy was formulated in the early 1920's—and I might add that the credit for its formulation largely goes to one man, Alfred P. Sloan, Jr.—it was unique as applied to industry. That it is no longer unique is in itself evidence of its soundness.

The first element of this philosophy has to do with organizational structure, the second with our approach to problems. Both, of course, concern people—in fact, can only be put into practice by people.

It is in this sense that in General Motors we often speak of the importance of people, and stress the fact that it is people that make the difference between one organization and another. In a more fundamental sense, however, the people of one organization are more

---

* Reprinted from "The Development and Growth of General Motors," a Statement before the Subcommittee on Anti-Trust and Monopoly of the United States Senate Committee on the Judiciary, Dec. 2, 1955, pp. 5–12. Mr. Curtice was President of the General Motors Corporation.

effective than those of another because the organizational structure enables them to work as a more effective team and because the organization's philosophy gives them a better approach to problems. . . .

II. UNIQUE ORGANIZATIONAL STRUCTURE

To fully appreciate the revolutionary nature of the organizational structure developed by Mr. Sloan in the early 1920's, it is necessary to appraise it in the light of conditions as they existed at that time. The business enterprise which the present management took charge of in 1921 had been put together, beginning in 1908, by W. C. Durant, and it largely bore the stamp of his personality. Durant had genius as a creator and super-salesman. He was not an administrator and did not develop an effective organization. Twice under his administration the Corporation was in serious financial difficulties—first in 1910 and again in 1920.

Prior to 1921 there existed no real concept of sound management in General Motors. Operations were neither integrated nor coordinated. There was no consistent policy with respect to product programs. Frequently poor judgment was exercised in making capital expenditures and establishing production schedules. The Corporation did not have a properly developed research and engineering staff nor any sound concept of budgetary control.

The central administration did not exercise adequate control over the operations of the individual divisions. There were wide variations in the competence of divisional managements. In short, the Corporation was unorganized and the individual units largely out of control.

It is not surprising, therefore, that this (see Chart I) was the competitive picture in 1921 when the management changed and Mr. Sloan began to put into effect the policies with respect to organizational structure which I will now outline.

Even before the crisis of 1920 materialized, Mr. Sloan was very conscious of the need in General Motors for a new and clearly defined concept of management philosophy. He had observed that much time was being consumed in solving detailed administrative problems and in meeting the critical situations which were constantly arising. He recognized that too great a concentration of problems upon a small number of executives limited initiative, caused delay, increased expense, reduced efficiency and retarded development.

He realized that centralization, properly established, makes possible directional control, coordination, specialization, and resulting economies. He also realized that decentralization, properly established, develops initiative and responsibility; it makes possible a proper distribution of decisions at all levels of management, including the foreman—with resulting flexi-

CHART I   General Motors Per Cent of Industry Vehicle Sales for the Year 1921
(Source: F.T.C. "Report on Motor Vehicle Industry," page 27.)

General Motors:
1.	Buick	4.77%
2.	Cadillac	0.66%
3.	Chevrolet	4.04%
4.	Oldsmobile	1.13%
5.	Oakland	0.70%
6.	GMC Truck and misc.	0.49%
	Total	11.79%

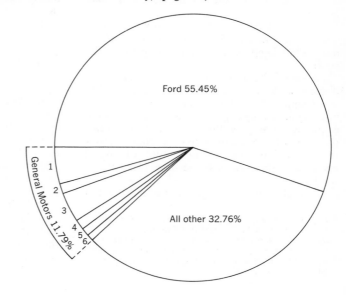

bility and cooperative effort, so necessary to a large-scale enterprise. His objective was to obtain the proper balance between these two apparently conflicting principles of centralization and decentralization in order to obtain the best elements of each in the combination. He concluded that, to achieve this balance so necessary for flexibility of operation, General Motors management should be established on a foundation of centralized policy and decentralized administration.

Mr. Sloan's concept of the management of a great industrial organization, expressed in his own words as he finally evolved it, is "to divide it into as many parts as consistently as can be done, place in charge of each part the most capable executive that can be found, develop a system of coordination so that each part may strengthen and support each other part; thus not only welding all parts together in the common interests of a joint enterprise, but importantly developing ability and initiative through the instrumentalities of responsibility and ambition—developing men and giving them an opportunity to exercise their talents, both in their own interests as well as in that of the business."

In pursuance of that plan (Chart II) each of the various operations was established as an integral unit under a General Manager. Then, those operations which had a common relationship were grouped under a Group Executive for coordinating purposes. These Group Executives reported to the President who was the Chief Executive Officer.

To perform those functional activities that could be accomplished more effectively by one activity in the interest of the whole and to coordinate similar functional activities of the different operating units and promote their effectiveness, a General Staff, and in addition, Financial and Legal Staffs, were established to operate on a functional basis.

Over a period of years, the functions of the General Staff have varied and have been expanded with business experience and changed conditions but within the framework of the general concept. Today, the General Staff concerns itself with the following functions: distribution, engineering, manufacturing, personnel, public relations, research and styling.

Since the adoption of the foregoing plan of organization, each staff Vice President has been a coordinating executive and has no direct authority over the operating units or their departments. With his staff he contributes to the development of better and more advanced policies and programs within his functional area through research and study. Certain of these staffs cooperate directly with those departments of the operating units whose activities are in the same functional areas. This provides coordination for the divisional operations, which are subject to local leadership and have local responsibility for functioning.

These decentralized operations function under the overall jurisdiction of the Board of Directors and committees of the Board of Directors which operate within the authority granted to them by the Board of Directors in the establishment of financial and operating policies. In addition, there were during the early period and subsequently, certain advisory committees or groups, the membership and functions of which have varied from time to time.

Today, General Motors has two principal committees of the Board of Directors—the Financial Policy Committee, which is concerned with the financial and legal affairs of the Corporation, and the Operations Policy Committee, which deals primarily wih the operating affairs of the business.

There are two additional committees of the Board of Directors, namely, an Audit Committee and a Bonus and Salary Committee, consisting of directors who are not members of management.

The membership of the Financial Policy Committee includes, in addition to three members of the management, representatives of large stockholder interests, and men with broad experience in business and finance. This representation provides a diversification of viewpoint and opinion. The Operations Policy Committee is made up entirely of members of the management of General Motors Corporation. Three of its members are also members of the Financial Policy Committee.

In addition, for several years past the Corporation has had an Administration Committee that functioned under the jurisdiction of the Operations Policy Committee. Its membership includes all of the members of the Operations Policy Committee and the General Managers of representative divisions of the Corporation. The Administration Committee reports on the manufacturing and selling activities of the Corporation and makes recommendations with respect to such operations. Assisting the Administration Committee are certain policy groups headed up by staff Vice Presidents and Group Executives which consider and recommend policies within their respective areas.

In the structure and function of a decentralized organization such as General Motors, no part can properly be understood and appraised separately from the whole, if that part is to

CHART II   Organization Chart: General Motors Corporation

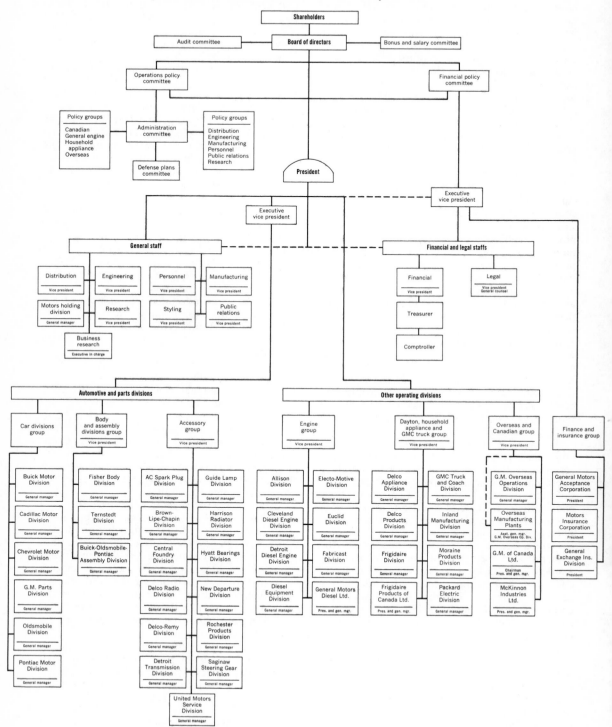

be properly evaluated in relation to performance and efficiency. The major parts of the General Motors operations are its Central Office Staff coordination and its decentralized divisional operations. Necessarily, there must be continuing cooperation and exchange of ideas between these two groups and among the divisions. In the final analysis, it is this cooperative effort, properly stimulated and developed, which makes for maximum efficiency.

The balance between decentralized operations, on the one hand, and coordinated control, on the other, varies according to areas. It also varies according to the temperaments and talents of executives, and the way in which they work. While the relationships of physical things are inherent in the business, it is men who establish and govern these relationships. The relationship between the Central Office Staff and the Divisional line operations may vary according to conditions and circumstances.

In summary, the organization of General Motors Corporation under the Board of Directors consists of the Financial Policy Committee and the operations Policy Committee, supported by other committees and policy-groups; staff operations; component product divisions; end product divisions; and service operations; all headed up by staff executives or general line officers who report to the Chief Executive Officer, except for the executives in charge of the financial and legal activities who report to the Chairman of the Financial Policy Committee.

The two principal committees of the Board pass on all major issues in the field of policy and administration. As already stated, the other committees or groups make reports and recommendations, serving as a channel for the flow of information and advice through the central management, to and from the committees and the operations in the field.

The Group Executive, through discussion, counsel and advice, directs and coordinates the activities of his divisions. However, within the established policies of the Corporation and under the Chief Executive Officer, the Group Executive has complete administrative authority over these divisions. Under the Group Executive, and within the framework of uniform policies and procedures, the General Manager has full administrative authority over the operations of his divisions.

The Central Staffs operate in more or less specialized areas. The Distribution Staff concerns itself with policies and problems in the sales and distribution area and cooperates with the divisions in the development of effective merchandising and service procedures. It collects, evaluates and distributes information, makes reports and recommendations and generally guides the operations within its policy area. It concerns itself with broad problems which I will deal with more specifically later.

The Engineering Staff works on forward engineering policies and coordinates the product programs of divisions. It also concerns itself with long-range engineering projects and developments. The day-to-day engineering work and the short-term engineering problems are handled by the engineering staffs of the manufacturing divisions, although they also undertake special long-range projects both in their own interests and in the interests of the Corporation as a whole. The Engineering Staff is also available to any division for advice and assistance.

The Development Groups of the Engineering Staff carry out engineering studies of new products and of new engineering developments of existing products which are beyond the basic research stage, but are not sufficiently close to production to warrant test or final development by divisional engineering staffs.

The Engineering Staff also operates the General Motors Proving Ground. Here comparative tests are made of products of General Motors and competitors to keep management informed about our engineering progress and to assist the divisions in the fulfillment of their responsibility for the development and quality of General Motors products.

The Manufacturing Staff undertakes technical studies and experimental projects for the improvement of manufacturing methods and facilities; the development of new processes for greater efficiency of operations; and the continuing quality improvement of General Motors products. In addition it has the vital function of planning ahead for the coordination and balanced in-flow of basic materials so necessary to the efficient operation of the Corporation's facilities. In this connection, during the postwar period, this staff has searched for and located materials in short supply for the divisions.

The Personnel Staff assists in the development of policy in the area of employee relationship for all employees. It develops and recommends employee benefit plans, including safety, health and insurance programs of all types. This Staff negotiates and is responsible for the administration of national collective bargaining agreements with international labor unions. It also assists in the negotiation of local labor agreements. At present, the Corporation has several national agreements and a large number of local agreements.

The Public Relations Staff assists in the development of policies and activities insofar as public relations aspects are concerned. It keeps Management informed of public attitudes and interprets General Motors policies and actions to the public. It helps build good relations in the various communities in which General Motors operates. Divisions frequently consult with this staff operation and utilize its services in connection with their own public relations activities.

Two of the Central Office staffs operate in an area in which there is no staff or departmental activity, as such, in the divisions. They are the Research and the Styling staffs.

The Research Staff directs its efforts primarily to the more fundamental studies which are the basis for long-range programs beyond the immediate scope of divisional operations. Fundamental research in this activity has developed new methods and new products. The Staff also provides advice and assistance to the divisions on current problems.

The Styling Staff has the responsibility of creating and developing advanced styling for all products. It works with the divisions in presenting to management the product styling to be considered, not only for the next model year, but for many model years ahead. All of our consumer products are re-styled annually. The leadership which General Motors enjoys in the market is due in a very large degree to the contributions made by the Styling Staff.

The Financial and Legal Staffs report to the Financial Policy Committee. There is no departmental area, as such, in the divisional operations in connection with legal activities. Similarly, the Financial Staff is responsible for taxes, insurance, and banking relationships for the Corporation as a whole. The Financial Staff also assists the divisional operations and coordinates their activities in the financial area, and it furnishes, supervises and audits a gen-

eral accounting system which is the guide and control for all operations in reflecting and reporting their costs, expenses, reserves and profits.

Such a management concept provides a continuous flow of ideas and information upward and downward through the management organization, by means of reports, meetings and conferences of both staff executives and line executives at all appropriate levels. This results in mutual education and understanding with respect to the authority, responsibility, objectives and purposes of management at all levels from the foreman to the Chief Executive Officer. It provides interpretation and understanding of policy and procedure as it is or may be established or changed. It produces an upward flow of information with respect to situations arising in operations, full knowledge of which is necessary if appropriate changes in policy or procedure are to be accomplished intelligently and promptly. It provides maximum initiative at every managerial level and at every point requiring administrative judgment, by the men closest to all the facts of the situation having full responsibility for their decisions. Finally, it makes possible accurate and prompt appraisal and evaluation of the contribution of the individual executive at every level of management, and of the contribution as well of every divisional organization and staff operation.

Although for many years this form of decentralized industrial management was identified primarily with General Motors, in more recent years decentralized management has been adopted by other large industrial companies.

The success of General Motors is the proof of the soundness of this management philosophy and its effectiveness in its application to a large industrial organization. Testifying to this has been a growing consumer preference expressed in the purchase of General Motors products.

31

Decentralization at General Electric*

RALPH J. CORDINER

Every company should be managed in accordance with some workable, ethically responsible philosophy of management. That is, the managers of the company should be in general agreement on a set of underlying principles that will guide their work in providing leadership for the company.

For some companies, the set of principles that guide the managers may be tacitly understood, without ever being presented systematically. They may be part of the company's tradition or may even reflect the personal philosophy of the chief executive.

While General Electric's present philosophy of management has had a long evolution in Company tradition and reflects the personalities of its great leaders in years gone by, considerable effort has been devoted in the past ten years to "thinking through" and presenting this managerial philosophy in a systematic way.

In this lecture, I should like to discuss the results of these studies: the philosophy of decentralization, and how it has been applied by General Electric in building an organization structure to meet the challenges of an expanding economy.

At the very outset, let me make clear that I am not selling our particular approach to organizing and managing as a solution for the problems of other companies. If I have any thesis, it is that each company should study, for itself, the particular conditions that will determine its future, and out of such detailed study should evolve a philosophy and structure that is fully appropriate for an individual company. The patterns of organization with which I shall deal are General Electric's solutions to General Electric's problems, and may or may not be applicable elsewhere.

* Reprinted with permission of the publisher from Ralph J. Cordiner, *New Frontiers for Professional Managers*, McGraw-Hill Book Company, New York, 1956, pp. 40–79. Mr. Cordiner is chairman of the board and chief executive officer of the General Electric Company.

REVIEWING THE CHARACTERISTICS OF GENERAL ELECTRIC

The General Electric Company faces certain opportunities and challenges that are natural results of its own particular characteristics. At the risk of being repetitious, let me summarize these characteristics here:

1. General Electric is the leading manufacturer in the electrical industry, which is probably the most sustained and dynamic growth industry of the twentieth century.

2. General Electric is owned by 358,000 share owners, one of the most widely owned companies in the world. Approximately one half of the Company's quarter million employees are now or are becoming share owners in the Company.

3. General Electric is managed by professional managers, who are not the owners of the business but employees hired by the share owners through their elected directors and the Company Officers, to manage their business in the balanced best interests of all concerned. Seventeen of the nineteen directors are non-officers, or "outside" directors.

4. The Company has a long tradition of public responsibility and integrity, as demonstrated by its participation in national, community, and educational affairs, and its services in the national defense.

5. General Electric is a customer-focused Company. Through this emphasis on serving the customer, it has also provided great benefits for share owners, employees, suppliers, retailers, and others who share in the work of serving these customers.

6. This is a Company with outstanding technical skills and facilities, where one out of every thirteen employees is a scientist or engineer.

7. General Electric has the capacity—and the inclination—to take large, long-term risks

in introducing new products, new businesses, and ultimately new industries.

8. General Electric grows from within. It is expanding not by merger or purchase of other companies, but by developing new products and markets—and hence new businesses.

9. General Electric is one of the most diversified companies in the world, with some 350 distinct product lines and about 3 million catalog items. These products have an original basis in the technologies involved in producing equipment to generate, transmit, distribute, and utilize electric power.

10. General Electric is a large company that has grown in service to the nation and the world. Its sales volume in 1955 was more than $3 billion, and its net earnings were $201 million. It provides rewarding opportunities for 252,000 employees in the United States and 29,000 employees in foreign lands, for 40,000 suppliers, and for 400,000 distributive-type businesses which derive all or part of their income from selling and servicing General Electric products.

11. General Electric needs to be managed with a long-range point of view, which is natural for a company in the business of innovation.

Out of these eleven characteristics of the General Electric Company arise its particular challenges and opportunities, and the particular forms of management and organization that are practiced in the Company.

EXPLOSIVE GROWTH RAISES ORGANIZATIONAL QUESTIONS

Up until 1939, the Company was able to operate efficiently under a highly centralized form of management. During World War II, however, General Electric began a period of almost explosive growth which caused its managers to question whether it might not be necessary to evolve new techniques to be used in organizing and managing the Company.

From 1920 to 1939, the Company's sales volume had risen slowly from $200 million to $342 million a year. By 1943, under the pressure of war production, it rose suddenly to $1,370,000,000 a year—over a four-fold increase in four years. Postwar experience and forecasts indicated that this was only the beginning of an opportunity for continuing, rapid growth in serving the nation's demands for electrical and related products. The Company produced over $3 billion worth of goods and services last year; and if we do the job we should do of satisfying customers, this figure may well rise—as the Company has publicly stated many times—to $6 billion early in the 1960's.

It is obvious that a Company with such growth characteristics, and operating on such a scale, requires a different managerial approach than the Company of the 1920's and '30's. This was, of course, recognized by Gerard Swope, who served as president during those decades when the foundations for future growth were carefully laid, and by Charles Wilson, the Company's president during the hectic, war-torn '40's. Under their leadership, I was asked to study the new problems of organizing and managing such a rapidly growing enterprise.

From the beginning of the study, it was apparent that the Company was going to require increasingly better planning, greater flexibility, and faster, more informed decisions than was possible under the highly centralized organization structure, which was suited for earlier and different conditions. Unless we could put the responsibility and authority for decision making closer in each case to the scene of the problem, where complete understanding and prompt action are possible, the Company would not be able to compete with the hundreds of nimble competitors who were, as they say, able to turn on a dime.

In addition, General Electric faced the need to develop capable leaders for the future; the need for more friendly and cooperative relationships between managers and other employees; the need to stay ahead of competition in serving the customers; and the very human need to make the work of a manager at all echelons of the organization more manageable. The work had to be made more manageable so that it could be understood and carried out by people of normally available energy and intelligence, thus leaving no requirement for the so-called indispensable man.

THE SOLUTION: DECENTRALIZATION

To these and many other challenges which were described in my previous lecture, the philosophy of decentralization seemed to provide useful solutions.

Now, decentralization has different meanings for different people. The decision to decentralize General Electric did not mean that it was decided to "break up the Company" into smaller pieces. This would be self-defeating, because it would lose to the public and to the Company those advantages that are the distinctive contribution of large enterprises: the ability to serve as a source of major innovations in the nation's economic life, creating new products, new industries, new employment, and new outlets for smaller businesses; the ability to energize the flow of mass production and mass distribution; and the ability to provide a broad range of advanced technical capacity in order to produce the more complex products and systems of our times.

In General Electric, decentralization is a way of preserving and enhancing these contributions of the large enterprise, and at the same time achieving the flexibility and the "human touch" that are popularly associated with—though not always attained by—small organizations.

Under this concept, we have undertaken decentralization not only according to products, geography, and functional types of work. The most important aspect of the Company's philosophy is thorough decentralization of the responsibility and authority for making business decisions.

Here is the underlying logic. The share owners, through their Board of Directors, delegate to the President responsibility for the conduct of the whole business. The responsibility carries with it all the authority required to get the work done, except such authorities as are specifically withheld by the Board and the share owners. The total responsibility also carries with it full accountability for results. General Electric may be unique in that the Board of Directors has issued a position guide for the President, stating in detail his responsibility, authority, and accountability.

Now, the President is of course unable to do all the work himself, and so he delegates the responsibility for portions of the total work through organization channels to individuals who have the talents and knowledge required to do it. This is done by planning and building the work of the Company into an organization structure which consists of all the necessary positions and components required to do all the work in the most effective and efficient manner.

Each employee thus takes on responsibility for some part of the overall Company work. Along with this responsibility, each position naturally carries with it full accountability for measured results, and all the necessary authority required for the position except those authorities that are specifically stated as withheld. Therefore each employee of the Company has, in his position, full responsibility, authority, and accountability for a certain defined body of work and teamwork. Through teamwork he recognizes his relationships to the other employees who perform a share of the total work of the Company.

With this philosophy, General Electric achieves a community of purpose between leaders and their associates, and is able to attain that voluntary integration which is the hallmark of a free and decentralized enterprise.

In such compressed statement, this management philosophy may sound somewhat obscure, but its practical result is to put the responsibility for making business decisions not with a few top executives, but with the individual managerial and functional employees who have the most immediately applicable information required to make sound decisions and take prompt action. When such responsibility—along with commensurate authority and accountability—has been delegated according to a carefully planned organization of work, then each individual in the Company has a challenging and dignified position which will bring out his full resources and enthusiastic cooperation.

TEN GUIDING PRINCIPLES

Since philosophy is, by definition, a system of first principles, I should like to list for you ten principles which express General Electric's philosophy of decentralization.

1. Decentralization places authority to make decisions at points as near as possible to where actions take place.

2. Decentralization is likely to get best overall results by getting greatest and most directly applicable knowledge and most timely understanding actually into play on the greatest number of decisions.

3. Decentralization will work if real authority is delegated; and not if details then have to be reported, or, worse yet, if they have to be "checked" first.

4. Decentralization requires confidence that associates in decentralized positions will have the capacity to make sound decisions in the majority of cases; and such confidence starts at the executive level. Unless the President and all the other Officers have a deep personal conviction and an active desire to decentralize full decision-making responsibility and authority, actual decentralization will never take place.

The Officers must set an example in the art of full delegation.

5. Decentralization requires understanding that the main role of staff or services is the rendering of assistance and advice to line operators through a relatively few experienced people, so that those making decisions can themselves make them correctly.

6. Decentralization requires realization that the natural aggregate of many individually sound decisions will be better for the business and for the public than centrally planned and controlled decisions.

7. Decentralization rests on the need to have general business objectives, organization structure, relationships, policies, and measurements known, understood, and followed; but realizing that definition of policies does not necessarily mean uniformity of methods of executing such policies in decentralized operations.

8. Decentralization can be achieved only when higher executives realize that authority genuinely delegated to lower echelons cannot, in fact, also be retained by them. We have, today, Officers and Managers who still believe in decentralization down to themselves and no further. By paying lip-service to decentralization, but actually reviewing detailed work and decisions and continually "second-guessing" their associates, such Officers keep their organization in confusion and prevent the growth of self-reliant men.

9. Decentralization will work only if responsibility commensurate with decision-making authority is truly accepted and exercised at all levels.

10. Decentralization requires personnel policies based on measured performance, enforced standards, rewards for good performance, and removal for incapacity or poor performance.

DESIGNING ORGANIZATIONAL STRUCTURE

Now, given this philosophy, how can it be expressed in an organization structure suitable to the General Electric Company? In our experience, the following work must be done to attain a sound, flexible, and dynamic organization structure:

1. Determine the objectives, and the policies, programs, plans, and schedules that will best achieve those objectives; for the Company as a whole and in turn, for each component of the business.

2. Determine the work to be done to achieve these objectives, under such guiding policies.

3. Divide and classify or group related work into a simple, logical, understandable, and comprehensive organization structure.

4. Assign essential work clearly and definitely to the various components and positions in the organization structure.

5. Determine the requirements and qualifications of personnel to occupy such positions.

6. Staff the organization with persons who meet these qualifications.

7. Establish methods and procedures which will help to achieve the objectives of the organization.

This is the procedure which has been followed in carrying out General Electric's current decentralization program, which had its beginnings in studies started in 1943, and went into the actual application phase in February, 1951. As you can imagine, the entire process involves a tremendous amount of self-analysis and education throughout the organization. Not only new ideas, but new attitudes need to be developed and accepted. Many former positions and organizations need to be discontinued, and many new and responsible positions and components are created. Persons may feel, under such changing circumstances, that their careers and livelihoods are threatened, so that they may be inclined to be suspicious, or at least over-cautious, until the new philosophy has been thoroughly assimilated, refined, and established. Timing is of the utmost importance, and I personally felt in 1951 that five years would be required to evolve the new structure and have it implemented with understanding and enthusiasm. The program appears to be just about on schedule.

Through all these difficult conditions, the General Electric men and women have performed with admirable wisdom and maturity, maintaining the momentum of progress in serving their customers while absorbing this latest phase in the Company's evolution. The work of organization is never done and the structure has to be continuously adapted to new and anticipated conditions. Nevertheless, it is safe to say that the new type of decentralized organization structure has been substantially established and manned, with outstanding personnel, products, and facilities to make it effective. The results, in terms of better values for customers and better earnings for share owners and employees, are reflected in the Company's statement for the first quarter of 1956, which shows an increase of 14% in sales and 30% in orders, over the first quarter of 1955.

GENERAL ELECTRIC'S OBJECTIVES

I indicated that the first step in organization is to sharpen up the objectives of the Company as a whole, to provide a framework for the objectives of each organization component and each position in the Company.

These Company objectives have been subjected to deep study, and are still undergoing review by managers throughout the organization. At present, they are ten in number and broad in character, and they are reflected in the Company's organization structure. Briefly summarized, General Electric's objectives are as follows:

1. To carry on a diversified, growing, and profitable worldwide manufacturing business in electrical apparatus, appliances, and supplies, and in related materials, products, systems, and services for industry, commerce, agriculture, government, the community, and the home.

2. To lead in research in all fields of science and all areas of work relating to the business in order to assure a constant flow of new knowledge that will make real the Company theme, "Progress Is Our Most Important Product."

3. To operate each decentralized business venture to achieve its own customer acceptance and profitable results, by taking the appropriate business risks.

4. To design, make, and market all Company products and services with good quality and with inherent customer value, at fair, competitive prices.

5. To build public confidence and friendly feeling for products and services bearing the Company's name and brands.

6. To provide good jobs, wages, working conditions, work satisfactions, stability of employment, and opportunities for advancement for employees, in return for their loyalty, initiative, skill, care, effort, attendance, and teamwork.

7. To manage the human and material resources of the enterprise for continuity and flow of progress, growth, profit, and public service in accordance with the principles of decentralization, sound or-

ganization structure, and professional management.

8. To attract and retain investor capital through attractive returns as a continuing incentive for wide investor participation and support.

9. To cooperate with suppliers, distributors, retailers, contractors, and others who facilitate the production, distribution, installation, and servicing of Company products and systems.

10. To meet the Company's social, civic, and economic responsibilities with imagination and with voluntary action which will merit the understanding and support of all concerned among the public.

To the casual reader or listener, these broad objectives may sound vague and obvious, but thoughtful study will reveal that each of them represents a number of deliberate and important managerial decisions. They provide a direct expression of the Company's ethical standards, its managerial philosophy, and its continuing purposes—in a form which makes them understandable and acceptable, after study, to every member of the organization.

GENERAL ELECTRIC'S ORGANIZATION STRUCTURE

In order to achieve these objectives on a continuing and profitable basis, an improved organization structure was devised in accordance with the principles of decentralization. This structure and the reasons for it are outlined in considerable detail in a paper I presented before the American Management Association in June, 1952, but here we shall sketch only the main outline of the structure.

The organization of General Electric is essentially a three-part structure which carefully distinguishes between Operating work, Services work, and Executive work.

The Operating Components First let us consider the Operating work. Today, General Electric's products are engineered, manufactured, and marketed by nearly a hundred decentralized Operating Departments, each of them bearing full operating responsibility and authority for the Company's success and profitability in a particular product or service field. The special skills and knowledge required for each operating business are thus brought to bear by a local business managerial team which can concentrate on the opportunities of a specific product or marketing area. Through these integrated managerial teams, each with a specific profit-and-loss responsibility for the operation of a defined business, we achieve the flexibility, drive, and the "human touch" that comes from direct participation in the daily problems of a business.

To demonstrate that the responsibility, authority, and accountability of these Operating Departments is real, not window dressing, consider their pricing authority. The price of a product can be raised or lowered by the managers of the Department producing it, with only voluntary responsibility on their part to give sensible consideration to the impact of such price changes on other Company products. In one area of General Electric products, the major appliances such as refrigerators, ranges, and home laundry equipment, there are two Divisions competing directly with each other. The Hotpoint Division in Chicago and the Major Appliance and Television Receiver Division in Louisville have different facilities, different product designs, different distribution, and different prices. They compete at the market place very aggressively, and incidentally, very profitably. Other Departments compete with each other by presenting different types of products that perform essentially the same function. For example there is the competition between electronic tubes and transistors, or between room air conditioners and central air conditioning.

As further evidence of the freedom provided by decentralization to the Operating Departments, consider the fact that the operating budget of the General Electric Company is not a document prepared by the Executive Offices in New York. It is an addition of the budgets prepared by the Operating Department General Managers, with the concurrence of the Division General Managers and Group Executives. These budgets include planned sales volume, product development plans, expenditures for plant and equipment, market targets, turnover of investment, net earnings, projected organization structure, and other related items.

In the days when the Company had a centralized organization, it was the custom for Operating components to submit budgets which were promptly blue-penciled, modified, expanded or contracted, and "second-guessed" by the headquarters Executives. As a result, Operating people did not usually take their budgeting too seriously.

Now they are taking it seriously because they know they will be measured on their ability to achieve the budgeted results which they, themselves, have established as proper goals for their organizations.

We are frequently asked how these Operating Departments can do accurate forecasting and budgeting, and how the Executives can delegate this difficult function to persons less broadly experienced than themselves. The Operating Departments can do better forecasting and budgeting because they are intimately informed as to the conditions which prevail and will prevail in their line of business.

Since they are better informed, they are authorized to make whatever prudent commitments they should on materials, and we have recently increased the approval authority of the Operating Department General Managers over capital expenditures so that they can, by their own decision, make commitments up to $500,000.[1]

In such a diversified company as General Electric, it is impossible for the Executives in New York to have detailed knowledge of such a variety of businesses and markets. Executives can help by supplying some general aiming areas for the Company as a whole, and information as to the probable general trends of business. But this information is to be factored in, and not to dominate the budgeting of the Operating Departments, nor does it do so.

The fact is that the Operating Departments are now doing better budgeting than was done by headquarters in years gone by. Last year the Company as a whole was within 1% of its budgeted sales results, although some individual Departments were off by substantially greater percentages one way or another.

The Operating Departments are now making plans and budgets which are firm commitments for five years and estimates for ten years. This is not on the Soviet model of the so-called "Five Year Plan" which regards each plan as a separate batch of work, to be succeeded by the next plan. Instead, a General Electric operating plan is a continuous and dynamic structure based on a rolling forecast, always ten years ahead of current operations. Frequent reviews and annual adjustments keep the plans realistically attuned to new conditions and competitive developments. Thus each is a dynamic business plan, not a rigid strait jacket of the "planned economy" type.

It is important to emphasize the voluntary nature of a position in General Electric. For

---

[1] I believe that too much of a fetish has been made in the past of capital expenditures. A manager can lose a lot more money on inventory, foolish pricing policy, careless personnel staffing, or poor production scheduling. Let me illustrate. In General Electric, capital expenditures in 1955 amounted to $153 millions, but we bought $1.400 millions of materials and had a payroll of $1,200 millions.

every position in the Company, including these Operating General Managers, a man has the personal right to accept or refuse the position —along with accountability for the results expected, and the risks involved in accepting such responsibilities. If for personal or other reasons he decides not to accept a particular position, there is no prejudice against him. He will receive other offers for which he is qualified as such positions become available. Voluntary and whole-hearted acceptance is of course a necessary condition if a man is to be held accountable for results in risk-taking ventures.

At the present time the Company has nearly 100 manufacturing Operating Departments, plus a number of sales and service business departments. For purposes of management, these departments are grouped into 21 Operating Divisions. Each division must be described as a family of businesses; for example, the Turbine Division consists of the Gas Turbine Department, the Large Steam Turbine–Generator Department, the Medium Steam Turbine, Generator, and Gear Department, the Small Turbine Department, and the Foundry Department.

After he has proven his capacity to be an Officer, the General Manager of a Division is usually elected a Vice President of the Company. Most of the Division General Manager's time is devoted to long-range planning for the Division as a part of the over-all Company, while operating responsibilities for the specific businesses are clearly delegated to the Department General Managers.

To assure that the Operating Departments and their customers will receive the full benefit of the Company's broad resources in knowledge and risk-taking capacity, two other types of work are provided for in the Company's over-all organization structure: Services work and Executive work.

The Services   The functional services are components at the corporate level, staffed with the Company's most experienced personnel in the major business functions: accounting, engineering, legal and corporate, management consultation, manufacturing, marketing, public and employee relations, treasury, and research. It is important to note that, in contrast with the powerful Operating authority wielded by headquarters functional Executives under the earlier centralized structure, these Services people have no authority whatsoever over the Operating Departments and Divisions, except the authority of knowledge. They have, instead, two Company-wide responsibilities: to do research, teaching, and long-range guidance in personnel development in their functional field; and to do such functional operating work for the Company as a whole as can best be done at the corporate level.

First, let us consider the research and teaching—what we call "Services functional work." In each busines function, such as accounting or marketing, General Electric is trying to apply the same principles of fundamental research and creative study that have long kept it ahead in the area of science and technology. The Services have been deliberately freed of Operating responsibility so that they can think ahead, developing through research the most advanced knowledge, principles, and techniques in their functional field, as well as keeping abreast of current knowledge developed elsewhere.

Services also have the responsibility to convert this new knowledge into usable forms and patterns, and to make it available through advice and teaching, to the Operating Departments and Divisions. Services also help to formulate Company policies appropriate to their function, and maintain a "clearinghouse" of current practices and standards within the Company to help facilitate a free flow of functional knowledge across the entire organization.

Of course, communications should never bog down in channels. If a Section Manager in steam turbine engineering at Schenectady, for example, wants some information pertaining to the engineering of aircraft gas turbines in another section, in Evandale, he does not have to go all the way up through channels to a Group Executive and down the other channel. He is expected to get the information straight across the Company just by picking up the telephone and talking to the fellow in Evandale who has the information.

The duties of Services also include long-range personnel development planning, to assure a continuing supply of outstanding people with the required changing functional skills.

Thus the emphasis in Service functional work is on the future: anticipating future opportunities and future problems, so that when they arrive General Electric will have the personnel and knowledge ready to meet them unsurprised.

The other important duty of the Services is to perform such operating work as can best be done at the corporate level, for the Company as a whole.

This includes, for example, the work of Treasury Services in handling corporate financing and investment activities on an efficient basis. There would be great confusion if the 21 Operating Divisions or 100 Operating Departments were to deal with the banks entirely separately. It should be remembered, however, that the authority to deny the use of capital from the Company's treasury to Operating General Managers who wish prudently to invest is not part of the Treasurer's responsibilities.

Another example of Operating work in the Services is the conduct of public relations programs such as institutional advertising and television, preparation of the annual report, and similar informational activities that deal with the Company as a whole. It is important that Services perform such corporate operating work with great distinction, to serve as a high standard for functional work throughout the Company.

The Executives   Leadership and long-range planning for the Company as a whole constitute the Executive classification of work in the Company structure. To understand this Executive aspect of the General Electric organization, it is important to understand two unusual organizational devices: The President's Office and the Executive Office.

The President's Office is a group of Executives who share the work of the President. In addition to the President, it includes the Chairman of the Board, and five Executive Vice Presidents. The Chairman of the Board, in addition to the duties assigned him directly by the Board, represents the President in such areas as financial affairs, public and governmental liaison, and international matters, and each of the Executive Vice Presidents represents the President in relationships with a specific group of Operating Divisions. This unique organizational device was created in recognition of the fact that no one man would have the time and knowledge required to provide effective Executive leadership for the variety of businesses in a Company as large and as diversified as General Electric. Thus each Executive Vice President serves as the President in a defined Operating area, without in any sense relieving the President of the ultimate responsibility placed upon him by the Board of Directors for the success of the enterprise as a whole.

The Executive Vice Presidents, in General Electric, are true Executives. That is, they have been freed of Operating responsibility and administrative details so that they can devote their time to long-range planning, appraisal of current performance, bringing divisional objectives and plans into a working pattern with over-all Company needs, and making sure of the needed continuity of competent managerial

and other personnel in the decentralized businesses.

These seven members of the President's Office, together with the nine Company Officers in charge of the Services, form what is known as the Executive Office. These Senior Officers deliberately set aside about 20% of their time to serve, not as Executives for their particular area of Operations or Services, but as a well-balanced group of general Executives who advise the President on matters that concern all functions and all operations—in other words, the Company as a whole. In this way, the Executive Office provides a melding of extensive business judgment and advanced functional knowledge to help the President plan the Company's management, growth, and course ten or more years ahead.

There you have the organizational structure of the General Electric Company: a three-part structure consisting of the Executives, who provide leadership and long-range planning for the Company as a whole; the Services, which provide leadership and advanced research in each functional field; and the Operating components, which have decentralized responsibility for the success, growth, and competitive profitability of the Company's diverse Operating businesses.

A significant feature of this organization is that it has no place for assistants, "assistants-to," or "administrative assistants." It is our firm belief that such titles or positions create confusion as to responsibility, authority, and accountability, and tend to retard the growth of men and the Company. If a position is too big for one person and appears to require assistants, then the work should be divided up and reorganized into as many positions as are required to do the work efficiently. Each position in the Company should be able to "stand on its own," with a specifically defined area of responsibility, of authority, and of accountability.

Likewise, General Electric structure has no place for committees as decision-making bodies. It is my feeling that a committee moves at the speed of its least informed member, and too often is used as a way of sharing irresponsibility. Before decentralization, an official tried to get on a great number of committees. He would lead a very calm, safe, orderly life. Not much would happen, but nothing would ever happen to him.

Today, a committee may be helpful as an advisory group, and indeed the Executive Office of the General Electric Company meets twice monthly as an Advisory Council for the

President. In any such arrangement, however, it must be made abundantly clear that the authority for any particular decision lies with the responsible individual, even if he makes it while sitting with the other Council members.

Such a deliberate avoidance of assistants and decision-making committees is directly in keeping with the decentralization philosophy, which requires full delegation of responsibility, authority, and accountability to the person who is best qualified to make the decisions for a certain area of work.

Challenges of Decentralization Bringing this decentralized organization structure to full effectiveness poses a number of immediate challenges to every member of the organization, and particularly to the managers. These include:

The development of men.

Leadership by persuasion rather than command.

The achievement of teamwork, integration, and balance.

The measurement of results.

Proper use of all types of compensation.

Criteria for determining the scope of a business at Department and Division levels, and for the Company as a whole.

We can touch on only a few of these challenging topics, but in the next lecture I will take up in greater detail these and other frontier areas for professional managers.

Development of Men First, consider the development of men. Our studies indicate that this challenge will be met by applying four concepts:

The first concept is self-development. The Company has a policy of equal opportunity for every employee to develop and advance just as far and as rapidly as he can. It is part of each manager's work to challenge and guide those who report to him, in their self-development planning. But the initiative, the spark, must be provided by the man himself.

The second concept is "climate for growth." The Company's research into the processes of manpower development indicates that the growth—or lack of growth—of strong leaders and self-reliant individuals depends a great deal on what we call "managerial climate." This "tone" or "atmosphere" in an organization can be subjected to analysis and a certain degree of measurement. Furthermore, the manager and the individuals in the component can do specific things to improve the climate, so

that men will develop faster and work will be done more effectively and enthusiastically.

The third concept is manpower planning. This is the manager's work. He needs to plan ahead specifically for his future requirements and then begin to develop people who will be qualified for future openings in his own component and throughout the Company.

The fourth concept for manpower development is increased education. The complexities of modern business demand ever higher levels of education among employees. Industry is therefore obliged to step up its own adult educational activities, and to utilize more fully the resources of the nation's educational institutions. In General Electric, one out of eight General Electric employees at all levels of the organization takes advantage of Company-conducted courses, in an average year. The cost of this educational and training activity in General Electric is on the order of $35 to $40 million a year.

Such activities range all the way from factory courses to retrain employees for changes in assignments, to advanced educational courses for professional employees in every function, including the function of management. By the end of the year 1956, about 4,000 General Electric men will be taking the Professional Business Management Course in decentralized components across the country.

Within three years it is expected that 25,000 employees will have completed this course of study.

Just this year, General Electric completed construction and began operation of a Management Research and Development Institute at Crotonville, New York. In addition to training leaders for the Professional Business Management Course, the Institute conducts an Advanced Management Course for classes of 80 carefully selected employees who spend 13 weeks at the Institute, away from their regular duties. The Institute is thus serving as a focal point for a major Company-wide effort in manager education.

Leading by Persuasion Another major challenge posed by the decentralization philosophy is the challenge to lead by persuasion rather than command. This is inherent in the very idea of decentralization. I do not think that I exaggerate when I say that about 20% of the time of the Officers is spent talking to employees at all levels, exploring and answering questions to arrive at a common understanding of what the Company is and what it is trying to do.

A centralized organization implies control from a central point, with close supervision and issuance of orders and mandatory courses of action, so that the centralized control can be effective. Decentralization, on the other hand, implies freedom for individuals everywhere in the organization to act on the basis of their own knowledge of the particular conditions that apply to the particular problem at hand. This does not mean that a decentralized organization should be loose-jointed or uncoordinated. On the contrary, even more effective and flexible integration can be achieved through the formulation and communication of common objectives and policies, and common means for measurement, so that the man in the decentralized components of the organization will voluntarily and responsibly make sound decisions beneficial to the entire enterprise.

In this situation, the manager's work is to lead others by drawing out their ideas, their special knowledge, and their efforts. Since self-discipline rather than boss-discipline is the hallmark of a decentralized organization, the manager resorts to command only in emergencies where he must admit temporary failure to make the situation and the necessary course of action self-evident. To the degree that the contributions of every individual are made voluntary and are self-disciplined, the manager is leading by persuasion rather than command.

Integration, Teamwork, and Balance   A third challenge of decentralization is the challenge of integration, teamwork, and balance. There is no question but that decentralization can set up powerful centrifugal forces that could pull a company apart. We have had to discourage managers from pre-empting, through squatters' rights everything they could see. They had been suppressed by strong hands, and the power and authority given to them under decentralization was raw meat. Maybe they were "overtrained" because they sometimes became so independent that they wanted neither advice nor restrictions in the interests of the whole Company. I am greatly concerned when a man talks about "my organization," "my Division," or "my men," for all of us are just passing by.

There is a need for some practical instruments to assure that local decisions will recognize and advance the interests of the Company as a whole, rather than work at cross-purposes with the rest of the organization.

One basic instrument is the formulation and communication of clear objectives for the Company as a whole. Then each component can establish its own objectives to help attain, rather than contradict, the objectives of the whole enterprise. This is why it is important that a company's objectives be studied and understood by everyone in the organization.

Another need is for policies which clearly express the common interests and the common purposes of all members of the enterprise. It is important that the number of policies be kept to a minimum, and my opinion is that about 50 policies should suffice to spell out the policy considerations of the General Electric Company. In most situations, the policy merely requires that conscious and orderly thought be given to the over-all business enterprise before important local decisions are made. Only in a very few fields is use made of directive policies which prescribe a mandatory course of action based on a corporate rather than a local decision.

Yet another instrument of integration is a system of common nomenclature, a common language in describing the work classifications, and positions, and the organizational components of the Company.

However, beyond such formal means as common objectives, policies, and nomenclature, the integration of a decentralized company requires an active understanding and acceptance of the concept of deliberate and voluntary teamwork. The concepts of teamwork, integration, and balanced effort need to prevail or the company can drift inevitably toward recentralization. Hence the Company's managers, in order to preserve their freedom of decision-making, need deeply to learn the habits of voluntary teamwork in the interests of the enterprise as a whole.

A PHILOSOPHY OF FREEDOM

What I have said of decentralization as a philosophy applies with equal force to any large organization of free human beings, whether it be a government, a university, a union, or a business. Decentralization is a creative response to the challenges of our time, a way of preserving and enhancing the competitive enterprise system as it evolves into the new forms that have been so aptly named the "people's capitalism."

The economy of the United States, and its position as a world power, make large enterprises both an irreversible fact and an actual necessity for economic and national security reasons. Any attendant perils lie not in bigness itself, but in the way the energies of large organizations are organized and managed. Centralized administration of large institutions of any kind can lead to irresponsibility, shortsightedness, inefficiency, and the abuse of power—but this need not happen under wise and self-disciplined guidance. Responsible decentralization—as a philosophy—makes it possible to provide at once the big results that come from big enterprises, with the human freedom that comes from respecting the competence and dignity of every individual in the enterprise.

General Electric's particular form of decentralization may or may not be applicable elsewhere, but it is built firmly on the chosen philosophy that recognizes the dignity and capacity of the individual human being, and recognizes his responsibility and authority for making the decisions that count. This philosophy, I deeply urge, must prevail if freedom is to survive in the world.

32

What Cannot Be Decentralized*

JOHN G. STAIGER

Before a decision can be made as to what can or should be decentralized and what should remain centralized, certain questions must be answered. These can best be determined by first examining certain considerations.

When a company's organization plan is oriented to a single product or geographical marketing region, divisionalization often takes place, usually with some delegation of authority and decision-making responsibility. When, however, local management attention applies fairly equally to each of several products or geographical segments of the business, then decentralization rather than merely divisionalization has taken place.

The principle upon which decentralization is carried out is most often stated thus: "Authority to take or initiate action should be delegated as close to the scene of action as possible."

But decentralization is not merely a matter of delegation on paper. In our own organization manual we state:

> Delegation of authority must be real. It includes not only what a superior says to his subordinate, but also the way in which he acts. An important ingredient in delegation is the willingness to permit the subordinate to make a reasonable number of mistakes.

* Reprinted by permission of the publisher from *Management Record*, vol. 25, no. 1, pp. 19–21, January, 1963. Mr. Staiger is vice-president-administration, North American operations, Massey-Ferguson, Limited.

The question in delegation is: "When does delegation and permission to make mistakes become softness?" Within the broader context of company management, decentralization poses the question: "When does top management give up effective control of business?"

There are three practical considerations that determine the extent to which decentralization of decision making is possible and desirable: (1) The competence to make decisions on the part of the person to whom authority is delegated. A derivative of this must be his superior's confidence in the subordinate's competence. (2) Adequate and reliable information pertinent to the decision is required by the person making the decision. Decision-making authority, therefore, cannot be pushed below the point at which all information bearing on the decision is available. (3) The scope of the impact of the decision: if a decision affects more than one unit of the enterprise, the authority to make the decision must rest with the manager accountable for the several units affected by the decision.

Companies have not always paid attention to these limitations on effective decentralization. In particular, top managements often inadequately consider the scope of impact of the authority they are delegating, allowing operating executives to make decisions that have major effects on company profits.

In the July–August 1962 issue of *Harvard Business Review*, for example, there appears an article, "The Second Squeeze on Profits."

This article comments, in part, on the excess capacity in many industries traceable to over-decentralization of decision making in regard to plant location, plant size, plant equipment and the products to be made in the plant. Therefore, I think it is fair to ask such questions as these: How often have unprofitable products, even entire product divisions, been carried because excessive decentralization had eroded profit-focused control? How often have profitability waned and staff costs multiplied while top management did only the long-range planning jobs?

MASSEY–FERGUSON'S EXPERIENCE

How do these general considerations apply to an individual company? On the assumption that one actual case study is worth a half-dozen hypothetical examples, I want to talk to you briefly about the company I know best—Massey-Ferguson, Limited. Massey-Ferguson is a Canadian company actively carrying on business in ten different countries. These are Australia, Brazil, Canada, France, Germany, India, Italy, South Africa, the United States and the United Kingdom. We market farm equipment products in over 160 different world markets.

Structurally, the Massey-Ferguson organization plan for operating this worldwide business does not present noticeable differences from standard, textbook organizational plans. The organization chart shows a president with the usual, functionally identified, corporate staff to advise and assist him. At the operating level, there appear the following operating units: Australian, French, German, North American, Perkins and United Kingdom.

In addition, there are the Brazilian, Italian, South African and Indian operations which have recently been organized. While they develop organization strength and maturity, they will be the responsibility of the special operations function located within the corporate staff.

In the 160 regional markets our company sells in around the world, our business is handled by an export agency, which reports directly to the corporate staff marketing function.

A WORLDWIDE STRUCTURE

What is unique about our company is the concept by which these greatly dispersed operating entities are structured, managed and controlled. There is no foreign or international-operations division at Massey-Ferguson. We do not make a distinction between foreign and domestic operations. We sell in the world market and we give equal emphasis to each operating unit. Massey-Ferguson has a truly worldwide organization plan and structure.

In the Massey-Ferguson organization plan, the objectives of the company, the nature of the enterprise, and the geographic-political areas in which we operate have been the factors which determine the extent of decentralization. Three objectives, in particular, establish the limits of control. These are (1) to be worldwide in scope; (2) to have a full product line; (3) to be an integrated producer.

The world farm equipment industry is today a picture of vivid contrasts. It ranges from the highly competitive mature markets of North America to agriculturally undeveloped areas whose potential remains largely untapped.

There are marked differences from one market area to another with respect to type of agriculture, farming practices, equipment needs and distribution patterns. The rising tide of nationalism, the emergence of new countries and the formation of new trading blocs have all played a role in the shaping of this world-wide market.

From one region to another within this market, Massey-Ferguson's position fluctuates widely, ranging from a subordinate place in some areas to preeminence in others. To achieve the objective of becoming worldwide in scope means drastic upgrading in some areas while holding position in others. Success in this effort depends upon our ability to react appropriately and quickly to local marketing conditions. Marketing decisions must be made at local levels, and these are, therefore, always decentralized to local-operations-unit levels.

Manufacturing costs are substantially influenced by volume, mix and inventory "pipeline" considerations. To the extent feasible within the limits of broader worldwide requirements, control of manufacturing is decentralized to local-operations-unit levels.

To present a full line of agricultural machinery, it is necessary to coordinate the product needs of regional markets with available product-development funds and manpower. The goal is to develop a common unit that probably satisfies somewhat less than the total potential in each market, but achieves optimum worldwide market penetration and profitability.

Product decisions—product development decisions—are highly centralized in Massey-Ferguson because they involve a number of markets and a number of operational units.

As an example of what this control upon product development and product design can achieve, it might be noted that the North American tractor manufacturing operation in

Detroit may use diesel engines from Perkins and transmissions from our tractor plants in the United Kingdom, rear axles from France, castings and machined components from Canada and, of course, the major complement of components from the United States. This can also be done in reverse: components can be sent from the Detroit factory to any location in the world and be mated with components from these other factories in such a way that we always get the same high quality and the same properly performing units.

AREAS OF CENTRAL CONTROL

Some other decisions that are made centrally are those determining what products will be manufactured, where and for whom. Since demand for certain products in many market areas is too small to support local manufacture, these decisions are centralized to ensure maximum use of facilities, cash and other such assets.

To achieve our objective to become an integrated producer, we require continual exploration for opportunities for acquisition and expansion. Since every additional integrated source of agricultural equipment can affect each Massey-Ferguson worldwide operation, facility-addition decisions that increase total integration are centralized. Of course, centralized planning and control of the product line, of product development and engineering, and of manufacture implies centralized controls upon capital expenditures and investments as well. They are complementary.

The international business environment, including such things as tariffs, exchange rates, import quotas and taxes, not to mention political situations that alter relationships between sources and markets, are obviously important to us. We are quite convinced that our success as an international enterprise depends in large part on our ability to react with maximum flexibility and speed to such changes. For this reason a central group constantly analyzes developments that influence the flow of trade within our world to ensure that all company operations create the most desirable cash flow and profits.

From the foregoing discussion of Massey-Ferguson's objectives and the nature of the worldwide farm equipment business, you can see that the organization plan that best serves our total requirements is a blend of centralized and decentralized elements. Marketing and manufacturing responsibilities, together with supporting service functions, are located as close as possible to local markets. Activities that determine the long-range character of the company, such as the planning and control of the product line, the planning and control of facilities and money, and the planning of the strategy to react to changes in the patterns of international trade, are highly centralized.

The board of directors of the company establishes basic policies and objectives. These are executed by the president and the corporate staff, who also play an important role in all major decisions that affect worldwide strategy in transactions between operations units.

The president is an active, participating executive, maintaining constant personal contact with heads of all operating units.

From all of these considerations we can draw up a list of those responsibilities that cannot be decentralized at Massey-Ferguson:

1. The responsibility for determining the over-all objectives of the enterprise
2. The responsibility for formulating the policies that guide the enterprise
3. The final responsibility for the control of the business within the total range of the objectives and policies, including control over any changes in the nature of the business
4. The responsibility for product design, where a product decision affects more than one area of accountability
5. The responsibility for planning for the achievement of over-all objectives and for measuring actual performance against those plans
6. The final approval of corporate plans or budgets
7. The decisions pertaining to the availability, and the application, of general company funds
8. The responsibility for capital-investment plans.

Truly, any such list must be custom tailored to the needs of each individual enterprise. It might include all, a few, or none of the kinds of items which I have listed.

The Nature of Line and Staff*

LYNDALL F. URWICK

The number of informal and personal relationships found in any undertaking are, of course, very numerous. The number of formal organization relationships usually found are, in fact, only three. The fact that there are three is, however, very seldom realized. It has been obscured by a general misunderstanding that there are only *two* such relations as implied in the widespread use of the phrase "staff and line." This error is due to a curious verbal confusion. In the Army of the United States the word *staff* has tended to be used in two different meanings—of specialists who assist the "line" in its duties by the contribution of special skills and services and also of officers who assist the commander in carrying out his functions of command.

General staff officers assist the commander by performing such duties pertaining to the functions of command as may be delegated to them by regulations or given them by the commander. Technical and administrative staff officers assist the commander and his general staff in an advisory capacity in matters pertaining to their special branches. The staff does not form a link in the Chain of Command, or in any other way take from or add to the authority and responsibility of commanders.[1]

But, by whatever name they may be called, there is a difference between the activities of assisting a commander or executive in carrying out *his* functions of command and providing advice and assistance to such a commander or executive and his subordinates *on some special-*ized subject*. In modern American military and naval organization this distinction is recognized.

The staff is provided to assist the commander in the performance of his four functional duties, which are as follows: (1) Personnel (2) Military Intelligence (3) Operations and Training and (4) Logistics. . . . In addition to the general staff or unit staff, all units have a special staff . . . which may include all or some of the following: chaplain, surgeon, munitions officer, reconnaissance officer, communications officer, etc., etc.[2]

Most Naval Staffs . . . are composed of a Personal Staff, a Coordinating Staff and a Special Staff. . . . The Personal Staff consists of those officers ordered as aides to the admiral (Chief of Staff, Flag Secretary, Flag Lieutenant). . . . The Coordinating Staff is divided into four or five standard military staff sections [Administration Section, Intelligence Section, Operations Section, Logistics Section Communications Section. A footnote reads "Communications Officer in some staffs is a member of special staff."] . . .
The Special Staff consists of those officers with special training whose duties do not fall logically within the sphere of responsibility of the Personal Staff or of any Section of the Coordinating Staff.[3] [Air Officer, Gunnery Officer, Legal Officer, Medical Officer, Chaplain.]

But in transferring the term *staff* to business, writers on management have failed to distinguish between the duties and relationships of the general staff (Army) or personal and coordinating staffs (Navy) on the one hand, and of the special staffs on the other. And this failure is of importance, because the two groups of duties are in one respect incom-

---

* Reprinted with permission of the publisher from *Notes on the Theory of Organization,* American Management Association, New York, 1952, pp. 67–74. Colonel Urwick is chairman of Urwick, Orr and Partners, Ltd., consulting specialists in organization and management. He is also an internationally known scholar, lecturer, and author on management.
[1] "Command, Staff and Tactics," prepared by the General Service Schools, Fort Leavenworth, Kans. Quoted by H. S. Dennison, *Organization Engineering,* McGraw-Hill Book Company, New York, 1931, p. 146.

[2] *The Officer's Guide,* Military Service Publishing Company, September, 1951, p. 373.
[3] Arthur A. Ageton, *The Naval Officer's Guide,* McGraw-Hill Book Company, New York, 1951, pp. 402–410.

patible. One of the main duties of an officer who is assisting his chief in "carrying out his functions of command" is to relieve him of the growing burden of coordination already emphasized. If he is a specialist he is, by definition, unable to do this. Indeed he must add to his chief's burden of coordination, since necessarily he brings to bear a further specialist point of view in addition to those which his chief has to coordinate already. Secondly the relations of the specialist (a supply or medical officer for instance) to his chief and to his chief's "line" subordinates are necessarily somewhat different from those of a general or coordinating staff officer. The former carries the authority of his special knowledge and training; he renders a specialized service, the need for which is generally accepted. The latter merely represents his chief's authority, relieving him of much of the detail of actual command. This representative function is a very delicate one. And owing to the confusion between the two uses of the term *staff* in civil life the complex series of regulations and conventions which the fighting services have built up to govern this "difficult" relationship have never been correctly worked out in business.

In consequence, many executives, and particularly chief executives, are grossly overworked. In many cases their lives are abbreviated drastically and unnecessarily. Specialization is the way of more exact knowledge and more exact knowledge spells efficiency. Its evolution and extension are inevitable. But specialization unaccompanied by the organization devices necessary to relieve leaders at all levels of the increased burden of coordination which it imposes, must mean jurisdictional disputes and other frictions which dissipate much of its advantage in personal disunity. Chiefs who should expend the major proportion of their time in leading their units or undertakings become incurably desk-bound. The magnificent training opportunities offered by true "staff" positions (general or coordinating staff posts) do not exist. Not only is the present generation of leadership frustrated and exhausted before its time; its successors perpetuate its errors because they come to overall responsibilities without the irreplaceable experience of looking at the undertaking intellectually from an overall angle while their minds are still fresh and comparatively flexible.

THE THREE RELATIONSHIPS

It is therefore of great importance that business men should learn to understand that there are not *two* relationships in formal organiza-

tion, but *three*. There are not only *line* relationships and *staff* relationships: there are *line* relationships, *specialist* relationships and *general staff* relationships.

The differences between the three can be defined very simply by indicating the kinds of authority and responsibility involved in each of them.

Line Relations everyone understands. They are the normal relations between superior and direct subordinate. What is not so generally appreciated is that they persist whatever the function of the superior or of the subordinate. A subordinate may be a general staff officer ("Assistant to" an executive) or he may be a specialist of some kind. The superior may be a "line" superior or a specialist or a senior general staff officer. The relations between the two are always "line" relations. Broadly, the superior is responsible to the undertaking for the subordinate: his authority is direct. And the subordinate has to do whatever his superior directs him to do: his responsibility is general.

A second difficulty is encountered because men are doubtful which activities in any undertaking should be regarded as "line." The working rule here is "without which not." "Line" activities are those in the absence of which it is impossible to imagine the undertaking continuing even for a brief period. In a manufacturing business they are usually making and selling. All other activities are ancillary to these: they are not the basic things which the undertaking exists to do. Generally the Principle of Authority should always be expressed through the "line" activities of an undertaking: the Chain of Command, the central skeleton of authority and responsibility should be built up round the delegation of responsibility for the "line" activities of that particular enterprise. But, as already emphasized, the relations between superior and direct subordinate remain "line" relations whatever the function either is discharging.

Specialized or "Functional" Relations arise wherever an individual is charged with authority for a particular subject and in relation to an equal discharging another function or to a subordinate directly responsible to somebody else. Here the "functional" officer can have no direct authority. An equal in another function or the subordinate in a "line" relation to somebody else already have a chief and "no man can serve two masters." Hence the authority of the specialist is necessarily indirect. Theoretically it is always exercised *through* the other individual's "line" superior. In practice in any healthy situation, once the "line" authority of the direct superior is fully acknowledged by the specialist and he is not afraid that it will be infringed, the specialist can do 95% of his work direct. "Official channels" are not the way to do business. They are there "for the record" in case good personal relations break down or there is a sudden change of personalities. But the real work of the world is always done by individuals who trust each other and whose good relations are informal. The formal procedure is necessary— as necessary as are drains in a house. In fact it performs exactly the same function as drains in a house: it carries off the waste matter of bad human relations. But to imagine that effective collaboration can be secured by the formal procedure alone is lunatic, as eccentric as if a householder decided to live in his drains.

The responsibility of the subordinate towards the specialist is strictly limited to the specialist's subject. That is obvious, since by definition the subordinate is in a "line" relation to someone else. The specialist who goes outside the strict limits of his subject is "asking for trouble."

General or Coordinating Staff Relations
It is this relationship which is most usually misunderstood. The true "staff" officer, the "Assistant to" an executive, should never have or be allowed to imagine that he has any authority of his own. He is merely an extension of his chief's personality, expressing his chief's authority. This does not mean that he may not do a great deal of work for his chief. He may draft and issue over his own signature almost every instruction which emanates from his chief's headquarters. But he does so as the representative of his chief's authority. The instructions are his chief's instructions, not his. And since they have been issued in writing his chief's direct subordinates are "covered": they can point to the written order as the justification to the chief for any action they

have taken in accordance with it. One of the conventions developed to safeguard this position in the British Army is that no "staff" officer should ever give a verbal order to any of his chief's direct subordinates or to their subordinates.

Another is that he should not offer them advice unless it is requested. And vis-a-vis the chief no direct subordinate can quote verbal advice offered by a "staff" officer: the responsibility remains wholly his. This follows logically from the fact that the "staff" officer has no authority of his own: applying the Principle of Correspondence, since he has no authority he cannot relieve his chief's direct subordinates of any of their responsibility. His responsibility is purely advisory.

A second convention by which true "staff" relations overcome the limitations imposed by The Span of Control is that chiefs of specialist branches, while retaining their nominal right of direct access to the commander, normally always approach the appropriate "staff" officer in the first instance. He is thus enabled to relieve his chief of a very large proportion of the detailed work of coordination, to forestall friction between specialists and "the line," and generally to see that the day by day housekeeping of the undertaking proceeds without constant reference of minor disputes to higher authority. A British divisional commander in 1917 had nominally some 16 or 18 direct subordinates. Actually the vast majority of his work of command was confined to two principal staff officers, an artillery commander and three commanders of infantry brigades. Since the last three did not interlock, this was in practice a span of control of four. Because he was relieved of an enormous mass of office work and daily details he was able to keep in constant personal contact with his specialist chiefs. Because they understood the convention they did not take up administrative detail with him and he was thus able to exercise his true function of leadership.

34

Developing Sound Line and Staff Relationships*

LOUIS A. ALLEN

In many companies, there is no clear recognition of the proper role of line and staff. In addition to misunderstanding, there is frequently rivalry and even animosity. Where these exist, the unfavorable repercussions are clearly evident.

EVIDENCES OF STAFF–LINE FRICTION

One evidence of the inability of staff and line to get along is delay and disagreement in decision-making. For example, in one case, a multiplant company in New Jersey built a new plant in the South. This plant required phenol as a raw material in one of its basic processes. The phenol was produced in another company plant located in the Midwest. The new Southern plant was geared to start operations on the first of April. However, a disagreement developed between the division manager, who was responsible for the new plant and the central staff traffic manager, who handled interplant shipments. Should the phenol go by rail or by water? The argument was carried back and forth for several days. Finally it reached the president for arbitration. The net result was late shipment. The start-up date for the new plant had to be delayed for three days with attendant losses in time, money, and patience.

This loss of money brought the whole issue into the open and led to a careful examination of the proper role of line and staff and the relationships necessary for effective teamwork.

In another case, a manufacturer of electrical products developed a new type of unit heater. The company spent large sums on development and tried to get the model into production as quickly as possible. However, many delays

intervened. A competitor finally captured the market by coming out first with a similar product. This led to a personal investigation by the company president. At first, material and design delays pointed to technical inefficiency. After continued probing, however, the president found that there had been a good deal of disagreement behind the scenes between the director of engineering and the vice-president of the manufacturing division. This, in turn, was reflected by pulling and hauling between individual engineering and manufacturing people further down the line, who were directly involved in the design and development of the new product.

In a midwestern company, both the staff personnel department and the line sales division placed "blind" advertisements in local newspapers for field salesmen, without one knowing what the other had done. In a multiplant metal fabricating company, the staff production department in central headquarters completed part of a detailed analysis of the cost of installing an intricate conveyor system in one of the plants, before it found out that the division manager had already placed a consultant on retainer to do the same job.

There is often running warfare between line managers and their staff counterparts. This is sometimes apparent even to casual observation. In other instances, it is camouflaged, but none the less menacing to company productivity. This antagonism may exist in the lower echelons of the organization as well as at the top. Foremen frequently resent the services of specialists from staff departments. For example, in one company the production superintendent complained to the plant manager, "That training director keeps my department in an uproar. He pulls my foremen off the floor to attend his conferences and gives them ideas I don't agree with." In another company, the manager of an operating division sent a letter to the president telling him that he had ordered the

* Reprinted by the permission of the publisher from *Improving Staff and Line Relationships*, National Industrial Conference Board, Inc., Studies in Personnel Policy, no. 153, New York, 1956, pp. 70–80. Mr. Allen is president of Louis A. Allen Associates, management consultants.

public relations director off the lot and that he didn't want to see him back. The reason: "He talks big about the company to local people and says things I can't live up to."

Both line and staff managers sometimes come to regard their opposite numbers as natural opponents and often present a common front in their attempts to justify their own actions and discredit or outwit the "opposition." In a large Eastern chain store operation, for example, the inventory control unit in the central headquarters was responsible for maintaining the company policy of bringing inventories to a specified level by January 1 of each year. Store managers developed their own methods for protection from this "staff" policy. Immediately after Christmas each year, a procession of trucks paraded from one store to another within each city in which stores of the chain were situated. The store managers were making sure that their inventories were at requisite levels before the staff people came "snooping around."

There is another side to the picture, however. In some companies line and staff mesh smoothly together. They work as a coordinated team, attacking problems with great effectiveness. In these cases, staff finds it hard to keep up with demands for its services by the line. For example, the training manager of an Eastern manufacturing company saw his department grow from one to seven persons and from a budget of $10,000 to $145,000 within three years. The reasons for this growth is obvious in the training director's concept of his relationship with the line organization. As he expressed it: "The only reason we're here is to help the line. We count our success in terms of the number of calls for help we get. I feel that if we can't offer something that the operating people need, we don't belong in the plant at all."

The experience of companies that have arrived at satisfactory solutions to this problem indicates that there is no simple, and certainly no standard, answer. The part played by staff and line differs among companies as widely as do methods of doing business, objectives, and personalities.

CAUSES OF CONFLICT

What is at the root of the difficulty? In most cases, the causes of staff-line conflict can readily be identified. Questioning of a large number of both line and staff managers brings out two viewpoints with considerable consistency.

The Line Viewpoint   Line managers most often have these complaints about the staff organization:

Staff tends to assume line authority.

Staff does not give sound advice.

Staff steals credit.

Staff fails to keep the line informed.

Staff fails to see the whole picture.

Staff Tends to Assume Line Authority. Many line managers feel that a basic cause of friction is the failure of staff to recognize its place. Line managers are generally keenly aware that they are accountable for results, including profits. While they may recognize that the staff specialist is a necessary and valuable part of the business scenery, they frequently resent what he does, or what they think he is trying to do, because they feel it encroaches upon their duties and prerogatives. Where there is friction, line managers often feel that the ready solution is to "put staff in its place."

As one production manager said, "After all, we have the headaches of getting the stuff out the back door. We worry about scheduling and costs and customer returns. Staff people want authority, but they are not held for results the way we are. They should realize that their job is to help us, not to be telling us what to do."

According to some line managers, this usurpation of authority may extend to actual encroachment on the work being done. A number of instances were cited in which personnel people assigned new employees to production departments without first consulting with or getting the agreement of the foreman concerned. In a candy company, the sales manager pointed to a small sticker advertising a statewide charitable appeal. "These go on every box of candy we sell in this state during the next two weeks," he said. "The public relations manager talked the president into it without consulting me. It might be a good idea from a public relations viewpoint, but I think I should make this kind of decision, not a staff man."

Staff Does Not Give Sound Advice.   Many managers complain that while staff is supposed to give counsel and advice, the ideas they come up with are not always fully considered, well-balanced, and soundly tested. In some companies, staff is considered "academic," "ivory tower," "unrealistic," and "too theoretical."

The reasons for this attitude on the part of line are clear. For one thing, since staff is not held to account for ultimate results, some staff managers show a tendency to propose new ideas without thinking through or testing them. One common reason for this is the tendency to take over a program bodily because some other company has used it successfully. The fact that the idea is not adapted to the particular conditions which exist locally does not become evident until after a good deal of time and effort have been devoted to trying to make it work.

Another reason for this attitude of line is that the staff specialist often neglects to explain to and consult with the line man. And even if he does both of these, he frequently neglects to give the line man time to absorb and "catch up" with the specialist's thinking and knowledge. As one plant manager said, "Central Staff came down here and put up some racks and started to give away comic books and manuals by the truckload on how to grow a garden and how to wave your own hair. I figure we have to sell a couple hundred units of our product a day just to pay for this. Personnel says it will make people appreciate free enterprise, but I think that's wishful thinking."

The tendency of staff to use technical or "professional" jargon also contributes to this line attitude. "That psychologist we have for a personnel manager is always talking about 'motivation' and 'correlation' and 'personality traits,'" said one supervisor. "I wish he would talk plain English so I would know what he was getting at."

Staff Steals Credit. Another common complaint centers about the tendency of staff to assume credit for programs when they are successful and to lay the blame on the line when they are not. In one company, a new program of statistical quality control was developed and installed under staff auspices. The first year the program was in operation several flaws showed up, resulting in an unusually high percentage of customer returns. The staff quality control department wrote a lengthy memo which tended to prove that the fault was the foremen's because they allowed drilling and reaming operations to get out of specification limits. An intensive training program was instituted, with the result that both rework and returns went down to record lows. Both the quality control and training departments then prepared reports showing that their efforts were responsible for the considerable savings in factory costs that resulted.

The Conference Board found that members of line management are particularly vocal about this. "We take the rap until we get the bugs ironed out," one superintendent said, "then every staff man in the shop rushes in to grab the credit."

Staff Fails to Keep the Line Informed. Many line managers complain bitterly about cases in which the staff works with the line manager's subordinates but does not let the boss himself know about it. In a chemical company, for example, the training department installed a job training program in three production departments before letting the production superintendent know what they were doing. In the superintendent's eyes, the fact that they had gained his consent to introduce a general training program did not warrant their starting this new activity without informing him. "I first knew that I was doing job training when the plant manager complimented me on it," said the production superintendent. "I realize the training people are doing a good job for me, but I'd like them to let *me* know about it too."

Staff Fails to See the Whole Picture. Line executives frequently point out that staff people tend to operate in terms only of the limited objectives of their own specialty, rather than in the interests of the business as a whole. The difficulty here seems to be that the staff man becomes so involved in his own area that he fails to relate it fully to the task of the line and to the over-all objectives of the company.

The personnel administration manager may be more concerned with building up a large central personnel group and increasing the technical proficiency of his own unit rather than with the development of effective personnel people in the operating divisions of the company. The industrial engineer may carry the investment in a methods improvement program past the point of profitability because he is over-concerned with perfecting the system.

A manufacturing vice-president in a large, multi-unit company cites what he feels is a classic example. "The personnel department has spent a great deal of money developing psychological tests for the selection of executives," he said. "It has reached the point now that you have to pass a whole battery of tests before you are favorably considered for promotion. Some of the men who have built up fine records of performance on the job have done poorly in the tests. Several have left us. Many are frustrated and discouraged because they feel they are up against something that is arbitrary and inaccurate. The personnel people simply do not realize that it takes all kinds of people to make a good team. If we have too many star performers, we won't have teamwork. What we need is balance. The personnel people don't know enough about running the business as a whole to see that. If they'd put more time and effort on helping us develop the people we now have, instead of figuring out reasons why they're no good, we'd all be better off."

The Staff Viewpoint   Complaints in the staff-line relationship are not entirely one-sided. Many staff men have strong opinions as to their treatment at the hands of the line. Their views usually center about these specific points:

Line Does Not Make Proper Use of Staff. "I feel about as useful as an appendix around here," said one personnel manager. "The production vice-president I report to figures he is an expert on human relations and personnel administration. Instead of my advising and counseling him, he calls me in once a week and lays out detailed instructions that I'm supposed to follow to the letter."

Some line managers have strong and dominant personalities and are intelligent and well-enough informed to feel that they do not need advice. When this is true, the line manager probably needs only a personnel staff assistant and not a full staff complement.

In other instances, however, the line manager requires the help of staff specialists, but either because of personal inability to accept advice, or distrust of his advisors, he rejects the suggestions he receives.

Staff specialists point out that when this situation exists, they cannot possibly do a good staff job. "I can't come up with a good proposal if the old man just tells me he wants 'a program for forecasting the economic picture,' " said the sales manager of a metal goods manufacturer. "He and the board of directors talked all afternoon about that one, but he is very reluctant about giving me the details I need to do a job. He says the information is confidential, but if he doesn't trust me, he should get a new man."

In still other cases, staff people say that some line executives who most need their specialized help rarely invite the specialist into the picture. The staff people say the line man either is "afraid" of interference or he fails to appreciate the help that is available for the asking. (In rebuttal, some line people say that the staff people whom they "overlook" inviting into the picture are too weak and ineffectual to be of real assistance.)

Line Resists New Ideas.   Many staff men feel that line management tends to be short-sighted and resistant to new ideas. In one company, the personnel manager pulled out copies of memoranda which he had forwarded to the president. They dated back to 1946. All reiterated the need for a program of management development to provide a continuing supply of management replacements. The company had recently expanded its basic product line, and several key management positions were open.

The personnel manager was bitter. "We had to go outside and hire people at fancy prices. It knocked our whole salary structure out of line," he said. "Yet I recommended a program nine years ago that would have prevented this."

Line Does Not Give Staff Enough Authority.   A common theme in the staff manager's complaints is lack of authority. "We're paid to be experts. Most of us know a lot more about our specialty than the line people. But we haven't got the authority to make it stick," said one purchasing agent.

When questioned, many staff managers express themselves strongly that, if they have what they feel is the best solution to a problem they should be able to enforce action on the line man involved. In one instance, a personnel manager mentioned that a general foreman had turned down four people consecutively who had been referred to him for an opening in his department. "He wants us to agree to his hiring a fellow-member of the military society to which he belongs," the personnel manager explained. "But we tested the man and he simply doesn't have the intelligence or aptitudes that are needed on this job. We should be able to ring the curtain down ourselves without making all these false passes."

SOLUTIONS

What is the answer to the problem of staff and line? How can better teamwork be developed? The answer seems to lie first in better understanding of the basic relationship between line and staff. Many companies which have investigated the problem find that neither line nor staff is very clear as to what the other is supposed to do. Improved cooperation usually follows clear definition of the role of each, and thorough indoctrination and education of both line and staff people.

The Basic Line-Staff Relationship   The basic relationship which exists between line and staff in many companies may be summarized as follows:

1. The units that are designated as line have ultimate responsibility for successful operation of the company. Therefore, the line must also be responsible for operating decisions.

2. Staff elements contribute by providing advice and service to the line in accomplishing the objectives of the enterprise.

3. Staff is responsible for providing advice and service to appropriate line elements when requested to do so. However, staff also has the responsibility of proffering advice and service where it is not requested, but where it believes it is needed.

4. The solicitation of advice and the acceptance of suggestions and counsel is usually at the option of the line organization. However, in some cases, it must be recognized that only the top level of the line organization has this option and that its decision on the use of staff advice or service is binding throughout lower levels. In these cases, subordinate levels in the line may have no option in the use of specialized staff services, but may be required to use them.

For example, the engineering department may analyze the use of machines, tools, jigs, and fixtures and present recommendations to the line. The operating line organization does not ask for this advisory service. Higher management provides it as a means of improving operations by bringing to the problem the most highly skilled and best informed specialists.

In this case, it is the line manager's responsibility to make most effective use of this advice. If he disagrees with it, he should have the opportunity to appeal to higher authority.

The same holds true with certain services. Because the line manager cannot possibly equip himself to perform highly specialized parts of his job, staff units may perform this service for him. For example, the services of the cost accountant are provided to help the line manager determine his costs. If the line manager disagrees with the methods of collecting this data or with the figures themselves, he may appeal to higher authority. But since he is not equipped to gather and analyze this data himself, and since cost standards are necessary to effective operation, he must use the services of the accountant.

5. Line should give serious consideration to offers of advice and service made by staff units and should follow it if it is to the company's best interest to do so. However, except in those cases where the use of staff advice and service is compulsory and subject only to appeal to higher authority, it is not mandatory that the advice of staff should be followed unfailingly. Except as

noted above, line managers have the authority to modify, reject, or accept such advice.

6. Both line and staff should have the right of appeal to higher authority in case of disagreement as to whether staff recommendation should be followed. However, this right to appeal should not be permitted to supersede the line's responsibility for making immediate decisions when required by the operating situation.

How Staff Can Do a Better Job   In spite of the widespread difficulties arising from poor staff-line relationships there is abundant evidence that staff specialists can improve their relationships with line. Many companies find that if staff observes the following points, it can increase both the acceptance and the overall value of the work it does.

Operate in Terms of the Objectives of the Company as a Whole.   Staff exists to help the line organization accomplish the objectives of the company. It follows that to operate effectively, staff should know what the company is trying to accomplish in terms of operations, costs, and sales. The purchasing agent who does not know how the end products of the company are made, sold, and used is operating as blindly as the personnel manager who does not know the trend of total labor costs to sales or to what extent indirect labor costs are increasing over direct labor.

Operating people are generally concerned with day-to-day operating goals. Many operating managers rely upon staff specialists to think ahead for them. As the president of a large processing company in Philadelphia said: "If the personnel department does not think ahead and anticipate personnel needs ten years from now, who is going to do it? I expect the personnel staff to tell me what our objectives related to people should be, but I expect them to find out what the rest of the company is doing and plans to do before they come up with their own recommendations."

Encourage and Educate Line Components to Use Staff Effectively.   This requires education of line personnel to the point where they know what the staff specialty is concerned with and what it can do for them. In some companies, this is accomplished through meetings, talks and discussions, in which staff people describe their specialties to line managers. In other cases, position descriptions of staff jobs are prepared and distributed to line managers. Brochures and booklets of various kinds may also be used to outline staff duties. In some instances, where the company has no prepared program for acquainting line with staff duties, the individual staff managers make it a point to talk informally with line managers about their operation, using this opportunity to outline their own activities and how they can be useful to the line man. (Yet, the staff activities that seem to be overburdened with requests from line executives for help, service and advice also appear to be manned with unusually competent and alert people. This may indicate that a good job by the staff department is an effective method of encouraging and educating line components to use staff.)

Prerequisite to this approach, of course, is the need for the staff man to brief himself thoroughly on the line man's operation. In fact, the more he knows about the operating picture, the quicker his own ideas will be accepted and the more effective he will be.

Many successful staff specialists point out that certain personal qualities are necessary if the staff man is to secure acceptance. Because of his specialized knowledge, the staff manager frequently is tempted to "expert." This usually arouses antagonism and resistance. Most staff managers find that a humble attitude, the use of many questions, and a *sincere* desire to be of help are likely to be more productive.

The staff manager also must be able to satisfy his need for personal recognition from satisfaction with a job well done and the favorable remarks of his own superior, rather than with public identification with the success of the program which he may have personally sponsored and developed. Staff managers usually find that it is best to give full credit to the line organization for the results that are accomplished.

Recognize and Overcome Resistance to Change. One of the important reasons for line opposition to ideas presented by staff is the psychological factor of resistance to change. People automatically tend to resist ideas that threaten to change the way they have been doing things. The fact that a change is suggested is in itself an implied criticism that the old way was not good enough.

People resist changes in the way they do their work or in the work itself. But it is not commonly recognized that they are even more set against changes that threaten disturbance or alteration in personal relationships. For example, a maintenance supervisor may be offered a change in his job responsibilities. Perhaps he has always been responsible for the installation of new equipment and he does not want to give it up, even though he is being given responsibility for the lubrication program in its place. It is to be expected that he would

be opposed to this change unless he saw some immediate personal gain in it for himself. His opposition would be intensified if he saw any threat to himself in the change. Under the same conditions the supervisor's resistance would be still greater if the change meant that he would also have to move to another part of the plant and work with another group of people. Here the gains to himself would also have to be even greater to offset this threatened disruption of his social pattern of group relationships.

Resistance is to be expected any time a change is proposed. This fact is of particular importance to specialized staff people, who continually deal in change and proposals for change.

Staff specialists can anticipate and overcome this natural resistance to change. Many companies have found these points helpful:

A. Determine to what extent the change proposed will affect the personal relationships of the people involved. Is the staff man advocating a major, sweeping change which will affect the social patterns established in the group he is working with? Can the change be broken down into smaller, more numerous moves which will have less negative impact?

B. When major changes are involved, which will modify the relationships between a line manager and the people who work for him, opposition from the manager will be minimized if he participates from the early planning stages. When announcement of the change is to be made the line manager can make it as a working partner, and not as an unwilling associate. In effect, the line manager has an opportunity to make the idea his own.

C. The people who will be affected by the change will accept it better if:

  • They realize it will benefit them personally—that it will make their work easier, faster or safer. The change should be tied in as closely as possible with the individual's personal goals and interests—his job, family, future.

  • They have an opportunity to offer suggestions, ideas, and comments concerning the change as it affects them—provided these suggestions are sincerely wanted and are given serious consideration.

  • They are kept informed of the results of the change.

  • They are able to check up on how well they are doing in terms of the change.

Acquire Technical Proficiency. A primary reason for the existence of staff is that it is highly informed and expert in a specialized field. It follows that the staff specialist needs to have a detailed and extensive knowledge of his field. To be most effective, the staff man also needs a breadth of knowledge concerning the whole company and its operations. The more familiar he is with the problems and operations of line and of other staff specialities, the better he can develop effective recommendations in his own area. The director of personnel administration, for example, is not entitled to a hearing for his ideas unless he is able to orient and evaluate them in terms of the other problems of his company's management. He must, in other words, appreciate the problems of finance, production, procurement, sales, profits, costs, product research, planning, and so forth. Line managers tend to distrust the staff manager who operates in a vacuum, even if he is well informed about his own specialty. Glib recital of "text book" solutions, failure to recognize practical operating conditions, and adherence to a strictly theoretical point of view, quickly alienate line executives.

Technical proficiency, for a staff man, means more than subject knowledge. Since his value lies in how well he can apply and communicate this knowledge, he requires training and education in the techniques of creative and logical thinking. More than this, the staff man also needs to develop the basic skills of writing and speaking so that he can convey his ideas clearly and succinctly.

How Line Can Make Better Use of Staff

It is important for line to learn how to use specialized staff assistance effectively because the value of the line manager to the organization depends to a large extent upon the use he makes of staff services. This, in turn, depends to a large extent on his ability to secure the interested help of the individuals supplying and performing these services.

In spite of this, staff advice and services are relegated to a secondary position by many line managers, even when the staff people are highly competent executives. These line managers call upon staff only as a last resort— and then only after they have exhausted every other available resource. One widespread reason is that there is a carefully camouflaged rivalry between the line and staff manager. The line manager wants to demonstrate that he can do it "on his own." The staff man wants an ample share of credit if the results are good, and he is constantly striving to maneuver himself into a protected position

where he can also say, "I-told-you-so," if the project goes to pieces.

This credit-grabbing, "I-told-you-so," attitude often stems from the staff man's sense of insecurity. But, regardless of the reason, the more he displays this attitude, the more the line manager displays resentment and lack of confidence in the staff man. The vicious circle is completed as the staff man thus grows increasingly insecure from the fear that the line manager will eventually try to dispense with his services and eliminate his job.

Make Maximum Use of Staff. Specialized skills are made available in the staff departments so that the line manager can use them to help him perform his job more effectively. The more the line man calls upon and makes use of staff, the better the specialist will become with the line manager's problems and his way of working. Highly successful line executives find that it is only common sense to make habitual use of staff. They have learned that this enables them to bring to bear on their problems special abilities and a fresh viewpoint. Where competent staff is available, the line manager has, in effect, a consultant or retainer who can help him to do his job better.

As one large company points out, when advice or service is volunteered by a specialized staff department, the line man should accord it the same recognition and careful consideration that he would if he had requested it. Otherwise, he is spurning the specialized advice and assistance made available to him by the corporation.

Make Proper Use of Staff. It is to be expected that qualified staff specialists want to put their abilities and experience to work on problems of real importance. They become annoyed and frustrated, however, when a line manager asks them to help and they later find out that their time was wasted because he had incorrectly identified his problem. In one case, a plant manager asked the purchasing agent to secure some data on the costs of a pusher-bar conveyor installation as compared with those of the existing crane and magnet operation. After the purchasing agent had completed his study at considerable time and effort, the plant manager told him, "We haven't got the money for new equipment. I guess what I really wanted to know was how to operate that crane with two men instead of three." He then called in the industrial engineer to make the new study for him.

In another case, the production superintendent in a processing plant was having difficulty getting acceptance of the methods improvement program he had recently installed. He felt that the training director, who had been teaching management courses in the plant, would be able to help him. The production superintendent outlined the program, but left the impression that the program was lagging because the foremen did not understand it. The training director came up with a suggested communications program for helping employees to understand the details of methods improvement. He was greatly confused when the production superintendent declared that this was not what was needed. It was only after prolonged discussion that the staff man found that the production manager's introduction of the program had been arbitrary and had antagonized the foremen. What he needed was a retake of the whole program to secure maximum participation and a sound basis for motivating people to make suggestions for improving of operations.

The line manager saves his own time and that of his specialized staff associates if he thinks through his problem until he can identify the key factor that is causing his difficulty. It is not until he has defined the real problem that the staff man can proceed with assurance.[1]

---

[1] Many executives have also found it desirable (where the cause of a problem is not clearcut) to call in the staff specialist and ask him not only to suggest a solution but also to start out by identifying the real problem.

There is another important way in which staff is improperly used by line. Some line managers frequently encourage staff to give orders by asking them to make final decisions that are line prerogatives. For example, a line manager who gives the personnel manager authority to hire employees and to place them without consent of the foreman or supervisor involved needs to recognize in advance that he is giving away his line prerogative. The president who asks the labor relations manager to travel to a distant plant, negotiate the union contract for the plant manager, and to sign it himself, needs to recognize the hazards of asking the staff man to exceed his proper scope.

Keep Staff Informed.   Line managers at the corporate level frequently fail to keep their staff managers fully informed of decisions which affect them. For example, an executive vice-president and a division manager decided to install a fully automatic assembly line in one plant of the company. This necessitated the use of many more maintenance and technical people over a period of years, together with several additional engineers. The personnel manager found this out only when a request for additional personnel came through when the work was completed. Instead of having an opportunity to train and upgrade people from within the company over a period of months, he was forced to hire people from the outside.

35

Line and Staff in Industrial Relations*

CHARLES A. MYERS and JOHN G. TURNBULL

* Reprinted by permission of the publisher from *Harvard Business Review*, vol. 34, no. 4, pp. 113–124, July–August, 1956. Mr. Myers is professor of Industrial relations and director of the Industrial Relations Section at the Massachusetts Institute of Technology. Mr. Turnbull is professor of economics and industrial relations at the University of Minnesota.
Authors' note: We wish to acknowledge the help of Maynard N. Touissoint, Graduate Assistant in the Industrial Relations Section, Massachusetts Institute of Technology, who helped with some of the interviews on which the findings presented in this article are based.

The industrial relations function in American management has developed rapidly over the past 20 years as unionization, labor shortages, and growing management recognition of the importance of the human factor in industry have combined to raise its stature and position in the company organization.

The "proper" organizational role of the industrial relations director or personnel officer has been the subject of much discussion. Probably the most widely held view is that it is a staff function. This means giving advice, assistance, and counsel to the line organization in the formulation of industrial relations policies and in the handling of industrial relations problems, but not taking from the line the responsibilty for making decisions affecting people. This responsibility is held to be one which the line officers, as *managers,* cannot effectively delegate if they are to do their jobs.

How close is this "ideal" concept of the industrial relations function to actual practice in American industry?

EXAMINATION CALLED FOR

We start with the fact that the industrial relations officer performs a variety of functions which are not uniform among companies or even within the same company.[1] But we do not know whether this is simply the result of haphazard organization or whether it indicates that no basic organizational principles can be applied to the industrial relations function. We do not even know how much the decision-making process varies with the type of problem under consideration, or what difference there is, if any, between the location of *formal* authority to make a decision (usually the line) and the place where the decision is *effectively* made.

Obviously there is real need for a more systematic examination of what the industrial relations director or personnel officer actually does in a number of problem and policy areas. With more knowledge and understanding, individual companies can better organize their own industrial relations activities. The aim of this article is to provide such an approach, with particular emphasis on these questions:

- How does the industrial relations director view his own role in the organization?
- How are personnel policies formulated, and who initiates and approves changes?
- How are the personnel administration functions—hiring, promotion, layoff, discipline, training, safety, and so on—handled?
- Who negotiates with the union, interprets the contract, and handles grievances?
- What problems does the industrial relations director see as a consequence of his organizational role and activities in the company?

Survey of Experience   To get the answers we conducted a small but intensive research project:

[1] See John T. Dunlop and Charles A. Myers, "The Industrial Relations Function in Management," *Personnel,* March, 1955, p. 3.

Interviews were held with industrial relations officers in 34 firms with which the Industrial Relations Section at the Massachusetts Institute of Technology had previous contacts. These officers were interested in re-examining with us the organizational role of industrial relations in their firms.

The 34 companies in the sample consisted of 24 manufacturing firms in 10 different industries, 2 food distribution chains, 2 department stores, 5 banks and insurance companies, and 1 engineering and construction firm. They ranged in size from 500 employees to nearly 30,000; 25 had collective bargaining agreements with unions; and 29 had multiplant operations.

Since most of these firms were in the Boston area, 8 companies in the middle Atlantic states and in the Midwest were checked to guard against the chance of geographical bias. Common patterns of experience began to emerge early in the interviews, and our belief is that a much larger sample with wider geographical distribution would not have materially affected our conclusions.

In each case, personal interviews averaging two hours in length were held with the principal industrial relations officer or officers (who were associated, in several cases, with different branches of the company). A schedule of questions was used, but free and detailed responses were encouraged.

Apparent Contradiction   One of the most striking results of the interviews was the contradiction between belief and practice. Not one industrial relations director, when asked to define his organizational role, answered, "I operate primarily in a line capacity" (except of course, with respect to his own department). Rather, the typical response was that he operated in a staff capacity or, at most, in some combination of staff and line capacity. But when he went on to describe how he handled particular personnel or labor relations functions, it was clear that in a number of situations *he made the effective decisions.* He may not have had the formal authority to do so, but he "called the shots." To illustrate:

In one rather extreme instance, the industrial relations director, who called himself a staff man, also said he made decisions on most promotions, could overrule the foreman on disciplinary action without getting higher approval for his action, disciplined foremen for failing to follow established personnel policies, had rather complete discretion in negotiating the terms of a new contract with the union, was sole interpreter of the union agreement for management, and handled all grievances after the first step!

How can such contradictions be explained? We suspect that the answer is that the term "staff" has become so customarily associated with the "proper" functioning of an industrial relations department that most practitioners simply give what they consider the expected or acceptable response to the question of their status. In any event, it is clear that we must go far beyond any generalized examination of the industrial relations function in management.

5 TYPES OF ADMINISTRATION

In order to understand the variations that are found in practice, it is helpful to visualize a spectrum or a theoretically possible range of methods of administering the industrial relations function:

Type 1. The line handles a personnel function completely, as for example when a foreman recruits, selects, places, and inducts workers for his own department, in the absence of a formal industrial relations department. Or the plant manager negotiates the collective bargaining agreement, and various levels of the line organization administer it.

Type 2. The line delegates to an industrial relations unit the responsibility for providing advice only. For example, the industrial relations department may counsel a foreman on the best methods of recruiting and selecting his work force, or on request it may give advice on negotiating a collective bargaining agreement or settling a grievance.

Type 3. The line formally delegates to an industrial relations department the responsibility for providing advice *and* service, with the line retaining and utilizing *continuing* decision-making and review authority. Thus, the industrial relations officer recruits and screens candidates for employment, but the final decision to accept or reject any candidate always rests with the foreman in whose department he would work. In the labor relations sphere, the staff specialist may assist the line in preparing for and in negotiating the collective agreement, and he may recommend to the line methods for settling grievances at the second or third step.

Type 4. The line formally delegates to an industrial relations department the responsibility for making final decisions in particular functional areas, subject only to *periodic* review of the effectiveness of the delegation or subject to the right of the affected line official to appeal to higher authority. Thus, the personnel officer may recruit and actually select all employees, with the foreman or supervisor having no authority to accept or reject any individual candidates, except possibly having the right of appeal. Or the labor relations specialist may be given broad, effective decision-making power to negotiate agreements with unions and in settling grievances. (This method can also be used when an industrial relations consultant or attorney from outside the company is hired to negotiate the union agreement or settle the grievance.)

Type 5. The industrial relations department gets by default (or may even usurp) the decision-making authority in a given functional area.

Type 5 and even Type 4 go beyond what commonly has been considered good organizational practice. The type corresponding to the staff role recommended in much of the literature on industrial relations is Type 3.[2]

Companies Classified   In our studies we did not encounter any Type 1 cases, because the firms interviewed were large enough to have personnel or labor relations departments. We also found no Type 2 cases; these are probably rare because most industrial relations departments provide important services for the line organization and go beyond the "advice only" stage. Type 5 cases were difficult to detect in the interviews, but we suspect that a strong personality in the industrial relations position often succeeds in getting control of decision-making authority without formal or explicit delegation, or that authority may "gravitate" to him because of his special skill—in the settlement of grievances, for example.

All except one of the nonunionized companies were of Type 3. That is, the majority of their industrial relations functions (primarily personnel administration, since they were not unionized) were handled by the line. However, in each case there may have been some specific exceptions. Thus, in discipline and discharge, safety, management development programs, and wage and salary administration, the effective decision-making power often rested in the personnel officer. The one other nonunion company could be classified as Type 4 in the majority of its personnel functions.

[2] Type 3 has been spelled out in detail by Robert Saltonstall, "Who's Who in Personnel Administration," *Harvard Business Review*, July–August, 1955, p. 75.

Most of the unionized companies also fell into the Type 3 category in both their personnel administration and labor relations activities. But again there were exceptions in the personnel functions, as noted above, and in specific labor relations practices. For instance, it was not uncommon for the labor relations personnel to make effective decisions on contract interpretation and on grievance settlements. Routine problems in particular were handled in this manner, while decisions on critical issues more frequently required line approval.

A few of the unionized companies were basically Type 4 in their labor relations activities. In at least five cases, this department had extensive authority in the negotiation of the collective bargaining agreement, in its interpretation, and in the settlement of grievances. There may even have been a trace of the Type 5 pattern in some of these instances.

12 SPECIFIC FUNCTIONS

With these general conclusions in mind, let us turn now to a more detailed examination of the specific tasks or functions that confront the industrial relations department. How are they handled in the companies interviewed? What do industrial relations and personnel managers have to say about them?

Industrial Relations Policy   Except where the collective bargaining agreement is involved and the union initiates changes, suggestions for introducing or altering industrial relations policies most commonly originate in the industrial relations department. According to one man:

> We're paid to be experts in this field. Our main task is to keep ahead of current developments; we'd be in a mess if we didn't. The last thing in the world I want is for one of our line people to come back from a convention and ask, "How come we don't have this or that policy?"

Regardless of the source from which policy suggestions arise, in all the companies we looked at the industrial relations unit is charged with the responsibility of investigating the suggestion, working up a concrete proposal if the idea has merit, and otherwise processing the proposal. However, consultation with people in the line organization is frequent, and in some firms policy committees consider proposed changes.

If the proposal is minor in nature, the industrial relations unit frequently will be given specific authority to approve. Any major pro-

posal customarily requires final approval by a vice president, president, executive committee, or board of directors. But, except for the critical cases, this final approval is of the rubber-stamp variety in a number of companies; the staff executive makes the effective decision. Thus, one industrial relations director noted:

> Over the years I've built up a fair amount of experience in this business; moreover, over the years top management has learned to trust my judgment. So I guess in most cases top management does rubber stamp most of my proposals. They've come to accept my advice. This doesn't mean I've never made any mistakes. Far from it. But it illustrates the case.

Hiring & Promotion   In the majority of cases we studied, line officers effectively decide who is to be hired, promoted, transferred, laid off, and retired. The staff provides advice and service—service in the way of recruiting, interviewing, testing, and keeping records.

Here again, however, the staff may exert considerable influence if not formal decision-making authority. For instance, it may be consulted on a promotion case, where its competence in psychological testing may be utilized. (This is frequently true for all promotions to and at managerial levels.) Indeed, in many companies the staff executive's expertise is so respected that the line will hesitate to recommend a promotion unless the personnel people concur. Hence the staff has an effective influence which may be tantamount to making the decision. As one personnel manager noted:

> In a really critical case, if I disagreed with the line on a promotion, I'd take the battle up higher. Otherwise I'd make my feelings known, and if they were disregarded, I'd let the line have its way. But I have been right in enough critical cases so that the line hesitates if I do not concur.

One or two other variations can be noted. In tight labor markets the personnel people effectively do the actual hiring; the foreman customarily has the right to discharge a man before the end of his probationary period, but he more or less accepts all candidates sent to him. In the hiring of salaried and managerial employees, by contrast, there is a tendency to give the department head (or equivalent line officer) much more discretion; he has the privilege of looking over eligible candidates before any decision is made.

In the hiring of college graduate trainees,

the personnel department often has full authority. The reason for this is interesting. As
one personnel spokesman noted:

> We know the needs from our replacement
> tables. But if we let the line department heads
> look over and interview prospective candi-
> dates, we would have a big battle as to who
> was going to get whom. This way we hire the
> college boys and ration them out.

Discipline & Discharge

Here again, basic
authority is usually held by the line, with the
staff providing a policy framework and con-
sultative assistance. But the personnel staff has
much more actual decision-making authority
here than in hiring, promotion, and transfer.
In a majority of cases the actual *approval* of
the personnel department has to be secured
before a discharge can be effected; in some
cases the personnel staff may even be able to
overrule lower line decisions. There are several reasons for this:

1. Management feels that discharge is a severe
   penalty and should not be exacted unless a
   clear case can be shown. The personnel staff
   can provide the means for investigating the
   validity of the discharge.
2. There is a need for uniformity in the application of discipline and of discharge
   penalties. Supervisors and middle management men could be trained to do this, but
   in many firms it appears more easily accomplished by a specialized staff unit.

Conflicts may still be resolved by appeal to
higher line authority, but many cases are really
decided by the industrial relations officer. In a
majority of companies, however, the line *ad-
ministers* the penalty; the personnel people are
not the "axe men." As one director put it:

> We are not the whipping boys. This is some-
> thing best done by the supervisor. In the old
> days our office had a bad name; we were sup-
> posed to have a closet full of whips; and if you
> ever got called up here, you would quake in
> your boots. But all that is changed now.

An interesting sidelight to the discipline
problem existed in two companies where authority to discipline and discharge had recently
been restored to the line. One personnel manager commented:

> You hear that the supervisor feels he ought to
> have disciplinary authority in order to control
> his department. In our company this right was
> recently returned to them. And you should

have heard the howls. They felt we weren't
earning our money. Discipline is a dirty business. And they were only too happy to let us
do it, as had been done for the past 30 years.

Employee Training

The common practice
is for the line to make the final decision as to
whether an employee training program would
or would not be used, with the personnel staff
customarily "training the trainers" and helping
to decide course content and teaching procedures when programs were introduced. Although the line had the final authority to accept or reject a training course, most personnel
men indicated they gave a lot of time and
effort to "selling" the line men on training. In
a small number of multiplant companies with
sizable central training staffs, there was a
greater tendency for the staff group to make
effective decisions, particularly with respect to
training programs at the branch level.

Management Development

As for train-
ing at higher levels, the interviews revealed
that the industrial relations director frequently
makes decisions as to whether or not to establish a supervisory training or management development program. When a program is set
up, he often decides on its content, presentation, and general administration. These decisions occasionally lead to a broadening of the
staff's implicit authority.

We found a number of cases where lower
and middle management officers (and new
college trainees) were aware that the industrial
relations officer had an important voice in
management development and therefore in
promotion. Hence "advice" given by the staff
man to the line manager became an "order,"
since it would not be wise for the latter to
cross a person with some degree of control
over his future. One personnel director indicated that this had become a serious problem
with respect to college trainees who came to
him for job training assignments:

> It's a standing custom among the trainees who
> see me to ask each other, "Did you get the
> $100 look this morning? Or only the $10
> look?" And it's more than a joking matter.

Safety Programs

While the day-to-day en-
forcement of safety is the responsibility of the
first-line supervisor, the staff has considerable
authority over line supervisors in matters of
plant safety policies, procedures, and equipment (in contrast to accident prevention programs of an educational nature, where they
remain in a staff capacity). This practice ap-

pears to rest in part on a practical legal consideration: safety requirements and workmen's compensation demand close adherence to a set of legal regulations. Hence rigorous control is necessary. While it is preferable to work through the line wherever possible, there may be cases in which time or other circumstances do not permit it.

Wages & Salaries

In compensation matters personnel staffs operate in two basically different ways. After a formal wage and salary program has been introduced (a line decision in the companies that we examined), personnel tends to have rather complete authority in its administration. This includes the power to decide, for example, on the job evaluation system to be used, the specific rate structure, and procedures for moving within and between grades. In some instances, even where there were job evaluation and salary administration committees which included representatives of the line organization, the personnel director, or his deputy, frequently dominated these committees through his special knowledge and skill.

All this is a perfect illustration of how "expert knowledge" breeds decision-making authority. As one personnel man explained:

Our policy is to keep the rate structure in line. So we make wage surveys periodically. We are the ones who get and interpret the information. And our suggestions are in effect decisions. Why? Because we have the knowledge. Line management could go out and make its own survey. But this is unthinkable, unless we should go off the deep end.

By contrast, in the assignment of individual pay rates the line tends to maintain a higher degree of control. Where discretion is involved in initially assigning a rate to a man and in changing his rate (as in increases within rate ranges), the immediate supervisor plays the key decision-making role. In a minority of companies the personnel department has to be advised of any changes, and in a still smaller number of cases its approval has to be secured. The purpose of requiring approval is precautionary; it is not held wise to permit a rate increase if all the individual's personnel records, located centrally, indicate otherwise.

The Control Function

In a majority of cases, the personnel department is responsible for "policing" personnel policies—especially when trouble occurs, as when a complaint or grievance is brought to the attention of the personnel staff. Our respondents stressed that *how* the staff executive talks to the line is as important as *what* he says. An informal approach is generally preferred. For example, the staff man might go to the foreman charged with violating company policy and say:

Joe, I'm sure you know company policy on this matter. But we've had some complaints, and I thought I'd kick it around with you.

Personnel men feel that it is better to work directly with the "violator" at the first step rather than to go to his superior. But if the violations continue, "we go to his superior and lower the boom," one personnel director added.

In a small number of cases the personnel officer initially takes a stronger attitude toward the erring line supervisor:

I bring the fellow in and say, "These are the rules. Get on the ball or there is no place in the organization for you!"

If I find the line not making adequate checks, I raise hell with them.

Does this "control" function create difficulties for the personnel staff in its relation with the line organization? The majority view is that it does, but that this is inherent in the situation and that it can be minimized appreciably by "not trying to appear as if we were running the show, but speaking softly and cooperatively." It is clear, however, that this entire area is one in which personnel people do not feel comfortable. Enforcement of personnel policies is not likely to win anyone first prize in a popularity contest.

Labor Negotiations

The majority of industrial or labor relations directors in our study are involved in the contract negotiation process either as principal or alternate spokesmen.

Where they are principals, their ultimate authority tends to be limited, since basic questions, such as union security or the amount of a wage increase, are almost without exception decided by top line management. But within these specified limits, the labor relations specialist may be given considerable discretion in negotiating the details of the collective bargaining agreement.

In addition, the specialist may have a good deal of authority by virtue of his power to advise top management, prior to negotiations, regarding "what it will take to settle." Because of his expert knowledge, he may, in effect, make the decision on the probable settlement;

the line executives may hesitate to overrule his judgment—especially if he has been proved right in the past.

In a small number of cases examined, the labor relations specialist exercised what approximated "unlimited authority" in negotiating the agreement. In one company, the labor relations director excluded all line personnel, except the president, from the negotiations and, moreover, did not report to them at any stage of the negotiation on what was transpiring or on how matters were developing. It was his belief that such reporting would "foul up the situation."

Why do some companies use this approach? Apparently some line managers, especially those with backgrounds in merchandising, engineering, and research, feel that labor relations is a distasteful, strange, and tough business which is best shifted to specialists. More frequently, however, line managers in manufacturing firms accept labor relations as part of their operating responsibilities.

Interpreting the Agreement The common practice is for the industrial or labor relations department to interpret the agreement on a decision-making rather than a purely advisory basis. Even when the line management takes the lead in negotiating the agreement, the responsibility for interpretation is frequently placed on the staff man who has participated in the bargaining process and whose expertise has assisted the line in the details of contract phraseology and meaning. More than this, managements feel the need for uniform interpretation of the agreement throughout the company, and uniformity is best achieved by delegating the responsibility to a specialist.

This is especially true in the routine cases where the supervisors and middle managers seek guidance on the application of a particular clause in the agreement. The specialist's view becomes decisive. None of the executives interviewed reported any difficulties with the line organization in centralizing the responsibility for contract interpretation in the hands of the specialist. Apparently the line accepts this as a perfectly logical delegation in a specialized area affecting the whole organization.

Processing Grievances In a majority of cases the line processes grievances through the first and second steps. Customarily, the advice of the labor relations unit is sought, and in a number of instances the advice becomes an order. "Sell, then tell" was the way several industrial relations directors characterized their approach.

Why should the labor relations specialist have any authority to "tell"? The chain of reasoning appears to be as follows:

In most unionized companies, enough grievance cases have arisen so that there is a body of precedent on almost every issue that arises. The labor relations department, as interpreter of the agreement, has a record of these precedents. It can indicate, therefore, what equity and consistency would call for in any case. It can also indicate whether a case, if processed to arbitration, would be likely to be won or lost. Therefore, expert knowledge permits it to make effective decisions.

In a majority of companies, the labor relations director is listed at the third stage in the grievance procedure. Can he negotiate a settlement? Yes. Can he do it on his own authority? Commonly, no. In the majority of cases, clearance with higher line authority is required. But such clearance is frequently only nominal. According to one staff man:

I called the president and told him if I settled this way, we'd probably avoid a strike, which I knew from our competitive position he was anxious to do. He told me, "Is that your view? Go ahead and settle. That's what we hired you for."

In a minority of cases the labor relations director feels free to settle even without recourse to higher authority.

Contract Enforcement While the collective bargaining agreement tends to be enforced by its very institutional setting (the union pressing grievances if it is not), there are still some problems analogous to those involved in enforcing personnel policies. And they tend to be resolved in the same way: informal discussion with the "violator" followed, where necessary, by discussions with his superior. A tougher attitude is likely to be taken, however, probably because of pressure from the union. When labor relations personnel were asked, "What would you do about a supervisor who persistently violated the spirit of the agreement?" a frequent response was, "We'd get rid of him." And while the line would do the actual "ridding," the labor relations officer would have an important voice in the process.

5 SETS OF INFLUENCES

What accounts for the many variations in the authority and responsibility of the industrial relations director? Our study indicates that five sets of influences are at work.

Unionism　　This is probably the most important single factor shaping the role of the industrial relations function in management. Where a strong labor organization exists, and where its decision-making processes are also centralized, a similar pattern develops in the management organization. A central, specialized labor relations unit is needed. The specialization becomes so technical that it appears more difficult to "teach" the line than it does for the specialists to handle the problems themselves. Hence, there is a natural drift, if not always a specific delegation of authority, toward decision-making responsibility in the labor relations functions.

The following section from one of the interviews illustrates the importance of union pressure on the location of the responsibility for labor relations.

> *Interviewer:* "Are you listed in any stage of the grievance procedure?"
>
> *Respondent:* "Yes, at the third stage."
>
> *Interviewer:* "Can you settle the grievance yourself, or do you have to secure approval up the line for your decision?"
>
> *Respondent:* "I have complete power to settle. I call the shots. I do not consult higher authority unless it is a higher authority issue. Then I would solicit their thinking."
>
> *Interviewer:* "Suppose you had a foreman who was in the wrong on a grievance, and the case came to you. Would you let it go to arbitration, let the arbitrator lose face to save the foreman's face?"
>
> *Respondent:* "No, we'd let the foreman hang."
>
> *Interviewer:* "Why?"
>
> *Respondent:* "We've got a hell of a militant union breathing down our necks. We can't afford to get the organization into trouble merely to save an individual."

Size & Organization　　We found some tendency for the industrial relations department to exercise line responsibility in more of its functions when the size of the company increased and as multiplant operation became more common. The need for company-wide uniformity of policy and practice is the main factor here, and apparently it is best achieved through centralized responsibility. But the larger firm is also likely to be confronted with the more centralized union, and it is difficult to evaluate the relative importance of these two influences. In fact, in several of the smaller firms in our sample the industrial relations director was

most conspicuously operating in a decision-making rather than advisory or service capacity toward the line organization.

Expert Knowledge　　When the industrial relations officer makes effective decisions in the functional areas outlined above, he does so frequently because the line executives have become increasingly dependent on his expert knowledge and informed judgment. It would seem that the longer the industrial relations man has served the organization and the more often his advice or suggestions to line managers have proved to be right, the stronger has become his position in their eyes, and the less they are inclined to "go their own way." What happens is that when a few individualists get "burned" by ignoring the industrial relations director's advice, the die is cast. His advice thereafter becomes the effective decision. Frequently, also, formal delegation of authority to him will be increased.

Strong Personalities　　The drift of decision-making authority, in fact if not in precise organizational delegation, to the industrial relations department has been accelerated by the presence of strong personalities. Some of the men interviewed turned out to be close to the staff type idealized in the literature; they operate through patient advice and persuasion, and consider themselves successful if they can increase the skill and responsibility of the line officers in handling problems in personnel and labor relations. But other industrial relations men obviously enjoy more authority, and the force of their personality is such that authority "gravitates" to them.

The collective personality of top line management also is important, as noted earlier. In collective bargaining, negotiating agreements, and settling grievances, the staff executives tend to have more authority in merchandising, engineering, and research-oriented firms than in the average manufacturing firms.

Effective Ideas　　Professional journals, books, and education are influential in shaping the role of the industrial relations director in some companies. For example, the personnel department in one company was moving from a line to a staff role because the new director had been a student in the advanced management course of an authority who convincingly expounded the staff principle in personnel administration. In another case, a personnel textbook with the same point of view had been instrumental in shaping the manner in which the industrial relations department functioned.

In contrast with the foregoing factors, geographic and economic differences do not appear to account for many differences in the industrial relations director's authority (although perhaps our sample was too small to support a generalization on this point). Type of industry and product also do not seem to be important influences in the firms we studied (this would not necessarily be true of industries in which multi-employer bargaining has emerged).

THE HIDDEN DANGER

Most discussions of organizational theory take the position that the staff should operate in an advisory service capacity in relation to the line, and that it should not issue orders to the line. A recent crystallization of this view spells out meticulously the nature of and reasons for this concept of the staff function.[3] But some writers who stress organizational practice more than theory, particularly industrial relations practice, have given support to the view that staff activities may, on occasion, properly include "direct command" vis-à-vis the line, in addition to advice and services. For example:

- Ernest Dale suggests that the staff official may issue orders either in his own name or for the line superior in exceptional cases, when it is necessary to insure uniformity of company practice.[4]

- Peter Drucker notes that, while the line organization still has the primary responsibility for managing people, delegation of certain activities to specialists may be necessary—for instance, the negotiation of union contracts.[5]

- L. Urwick, while in general supporting the view that the "personnel manager is a staff officer," believes that he should be in direct ("line") control of all those units in the enterprise that specialize in such aspects of

personnel work as employment and medical and welfare programs (but *not* those aspects which are of such a character that they can only be handled effectively in the last resort by the chief executive—e.g., trade union negotiation and the development and promotion of higher executives).[6]

Thus, the discussions of organization practice tend to support the view which has emerged from our study that a variety of patterns may exist in different companies and may work well. This is essentially a pragmatic rather than a doctrinaire view. Logically the staff concept of the industrial relations function makes sense; yet the experience of some companies indicates that the personnel officer can make decisions affecting the line without any *apparent* ill effects on the line. This can be explained on two grounds:

1. It appears that people can work under a variety of organizational arrangements. "People get used to it" was the typical explanation offered when we tried to probe about the "exceptions" to the staff role which we found in certain companies.

2. There may be a "unity of purpose" between the staff and line—they may "think alike"—which makes it possible for staff executives to share in certain line responsibilities without staff-line friction. (If there are strong differences in viewpoint between staff and line, such joint responsibility would not, of course, be practical.)

In our study we did not attempt systematically to evaluate in each company the impact of the particular pattern of industrial relations functions that we found. This could only have been done by extensive interviewing at different management levels to discover whether line supervisors and department heads (a) found their ability to manage their work force curtailed and limited by what the industrial relations director did, or (b) were using the staff groups as a "crutch." Some of the staff officers we interviewed were aware of resentment toward their role, as we have seen; but the effects of this resentment on the functioning of the entire organization could not be evaluated.

[3] Robert C. Sampson, *The Staff Role in Management, Its Creative Uses,* Harper & Row, Publishers, Incorporated, New York, 1955; see also Paul E. Holden, Lounsbury S. Fish, and Hubert L. Smith, *Top Management Organization and Control,* McGraw-Hill Book Company, New York, 1951, pp. 36–58, particularly p. 40.

[4] Ernest Dale, *Planning and Developing the Company Organization Structure,* American Management Association, Research Report, no. 20, New York, 1952, pp. 71–73. For a similar view, see Louis Allen, "The Line-Staff Relationship," *Management Record,* September, 1955, p. 346.

[5] Peter Drucker, *The Practice of Management,* Harper & Row, Publishers, Incorporated, New York, 1954, p. 244.

[6] See L. Urwick, *Personnel Management in Relation to Factory Organization,* London Institute of Labour Management, 1943, particularly pp. 16–20, 23–27. For a useful overall view of line and staff problems, see, by the same author, "Organization as a Technical Problem," in Luther Gulick and L. Urwick (eds.), *Papers on the Science of Administration,* Columbia University, Institute of Public Administration, New York, 1937, pp. 49–88.

Here is a "hidden danger" area deserving further empirical research, since there is at least some earlier evidence that centralization of the industrial relations function has damaging effects on the morale of the lower line organization.[7] Furthermore, there are reasons for believing that, when a staff man is given the responsibility for decision making, particularly with respect to rewarding and punishing employees, the line supervisor's role is considerably weakened as a manager; he is no longer in such a good position to influence behavior.[8]

4 PROPOSED DISTINCTIONS

Recognizing that there may be some uncertainty about the probable effects on the line organization of placing decision-making power in the hands of the industrial relations officer, we can still ask how much authority the line managers should delegate to the staff.

In this connection our study indicates that it is important to distinguish between the different functions which an industrial relations department performs. In a sense any attempt to break them down represents an oversimplification, but for convenience of presentation we have developed a four-fold classification in terms of (a) supervision; (b) policy making and negotiation, (c) interpretation, and (d) service.

Supervisory Decisions   One group of industrial relations functions directly involves the relationships between the line supervisor at any organizational level and his subordinates. Since he is responsible for the results which his work group produces, the supervisor must have the authority to make the initial effective decision when problems arise involving members of his work group. The industrial relations staff, however, should have the right to appeal to the superior of the line supervisor if it believes that a mistake is being made or a company policy violated. The staff can offer advice and service

to the line, but the effective decision, made at the level at which the problem arises, is a responsibility of the line. Likewise, a final or critical decision, made in cases if an appeal arises, rests at some point in the line organization.

Hiring affords an excellent example of this group of industrial relations functions. The industrial relations staff may offer general advice on the hiring process; it may provide recruitment and screening services. But the effective decision to accept or reject an applicant should rest (even if only at the end of the probationary period) with the supervisor in whose department the individual will work. Staff appeal might arise in a case where, for example, the supervisor brings in his own candidate and the personnel department believes this candidate is clearly unfit. The staff should have the right to protest his being hired, but the final resolution of the conflict—the critical decision—needs to be made by higher line authority.

Other personnel functions in which this approach seems logical include all those where the employee is directly involved: promotion, demotion, transfer, layoff, discharge, discipline, determination of the individual wage rate within a rate range, initial disposition of grievances at the first step in the grievance procedure, and so on. Lack of authority to make initial decisions on these matters robs the line supervisor of the means by which he can do an effective job of developing and motivating the people whose efforts he is expected to supervise.

Policy Making & Negotiation   There are some industrial relations functions vital to the organization as a whole, where it is clear that effective decision-making authority cannot be delegated to an individual line manager below the top-management level. These are in the policy-making area.

For example, in unionized firms, many functions must be handled within the framework of a collective agreement. Even in nonunion companies, consistent personnel policies are clearly needed to operate as guides to the individual supervisor's decisions.

One workable arrangement is for the staff to give both advice and service in policy making and negotiation and for top line management to make both the initial and critical final decisions in negotiating an agreement or in formulating personnel policy. A staff possessing the expertness and the knowledge to perform these functions may have broader powers delegated to it by the chief line executive—especially if

[7] See, for example, F. L. W. Richardson, Jr., and Charles R. Walker, *Human Relations in an Expanding Company*, Labor and Management Center, Yale University, New Haven, Conn., 1948; and, by the same authors, "Work Flow and Human Relations," *Harvard Business Review*, January, 1949, p. 107; see also Glenn Gardiner, "The Operating Executive and the Personnel Department," *Personnel Functions and the Line Organization*, American Management Association, Personnel Series, no. 121, New York, 1948, p. 3.

[8] See Douglas McGregor, "Line Management's Responsibility for Human Relations," *Building Up the Supervisor's Job*, American Management Association, Manufacturing Series, no. 213, New York, 1954, particularly p. 29.

there is a strong sense of common purpose between the line and staff personnel. While this practice is defensible, it should be emphasized that there are two responsibilities of which the line can*not* divest itself: (1) the making of key decisions which materially affect the substance and direction of policy, such as the amount of a wage increase or the granting of a union-shop clause; and (2) the critical decision to accept or reject the total collective bargaining agreement (as negotiated) or the policy framework.

Problems of Interpretation   A third group of industrial relations functions includes the interpretation and application of the collective agreement or of personnel policies. Like policy making and negotiation, this work applies to the organization as a whole, and it affects the relationship between the individual supervisor and his subordinates. But because its impact is not so decisive as policy making, it is possible to justify delegating more authority to the staff. Here management could properly authorize the staff official to make the effective decision subject to the right of the line officer affected to appeal to his superior.

Such decisions are most likely to be needed in the labor relations area, especially when the firm is confronted with a strong union ready to raise grievances over alleged violations of or inconsistencies in the application of the collective agreement. For the same reasons, the staff may be made responsible, in the grievance procedure, for making settlements at the second or, more often, the third stage, when these settlements usually affect more than the individual and his supervisor.

A line supervisor who does not agree with a particular interpretation or grievance settlement by the staff should have the right to appeal to higher line authority to resolve the difference. It should not be surprising, however, if this right of appeal is rarely used in practice. Line officials may be afraid to or prefer not to appeal to higher authority because of the weight which the staff man carries in the organization; the staff man's special knowledge and expertise may seem too compelling to contest.[9] These are the realities which compel line management to recognize and accept the role of the specialist in labor relations—even when that role makes inroads on the line official's authority.

Service Activities   Finally, there are industrial relations functions which neither involve directly the relationships between the supervisor and his subordinates nor relate to policy formulation or application, but which so clearly apply to the organization as a whole that effective decision-making authority on most matters can be delegated to the staff. These functions include employee and other service activities usually handled by industrial relations departments. Once a determination has been made by the appropriate level of line management to undertake a service activity, and a budget has been set up, authority can be delegated to the staff to make decisions on content, methods, and administration.

Activities linked to relations within the firm, such as in-plant feeding, health and welfare programs, sports and recreation, and information programs (including company house organs), would, of course, be handled exclusively by personnel or industrial relations managers. But in the case of activities which are extra-company in nature, such as legal phases of collective bargaining legislation, wage and hour laws, Social Security, workmen's compensation, and so on, formal delegation of authority to handle problems may be made to the legal staff within or outside the industrial relations department. Management may also give slices of decision-making authority to such other external specialists as actuaries and pension consultants.

Conclusion   In summary, our study confirms the concept that the industrial relations department should be limited to its traditional role of advice, service, consultation, and control *in connection with functions which directly involve the line supervisor and his work group*. But in (a) policy making, particularly where a strong centralized union is involved, and in (b) policy or contract interpretation, our evidence indicates that more authority for making initial decisions is frequently delegated to the staff specialist. We cannot say with positive assurance that the delegation of such authority has no ill effects on the line organization. Further research is needed to clarify this point. We can only say that if there are dangers, they have not made much impression on most of the staff executives interviewed.

Clearly, every company that does give the staff man added authority in policy making and interpretation, or is contemplating doing so, ought to consider carefully the possibility of harm to the morale of the line organization and to its ability to do an effective manage-

---

[9] This point has been made effectively by Herbert A. Simon, *Administrative Behavior*, The Macmillan Company, New York, 1947, p. 135.

ment job through the efforts of other people.

With this caution in mind, the appropriate combination in a particular company should emerge from a review of the existing organizational structure, the pressures (such as strong unions) facing the organization, and the personalities and skills of those involved in the line and staff responsibilities for handling industrial relations. The larger the company, the stronger the union pressures, the more skilled the staff, and the greater the common purpose of line and staff executives, the more logical it is to delegate to the staff the authority to make decisions in policy interpretation and to take a more active role in policy formulation.

36   E. COMMITTEES

Management by Executive Committee*

W. H. MYLANDER

- What are the advantages, and the disadvantages, of committee management for the modern American business corporation?
- At what point in a company's growth, or product diversification, should consideration be given to committee management?
- How does committee management work, and what kind of people are required to make it work successfully?

Questions of this kind were put to 12 of the top executives of E. I. du Pont de Nemours & Company, which has pioneered in using the executive committee form of organization, and this article represents a composite of their replies—their expressions of judgment based on the test of experience.

FORM OF ORGANIZATION

Du Pont, now in its 153rd year, began as a manufacturer of powder on the banks of the Brandywine Creek near Wilmington, Delaware. Its 72 plants in 26 states produce some 1,200 chemical product lines with a sales volume of close to $1.7 billion in 1954.

Until 1921, du Pont was operated with the customary line organization headed by a president assisted by vice presidents in charge of

specialized functions such as finance, production, and sales. Then, under the farsighted presidency of Irénée du Pont, now honorary chairman of the board, the company adopted a committee-line system regarded as unique in American industry.

At the top is an executive committee of the board of directors consisting of President Crawford H. Greenewalt and nine vice presidents. These men devote full time to the company's affairs, although relieved of day-by-day functional responsibilities. As a committee, they meet each Wednesday, and oftener if necessary. The bylaws provide that between the monthly meetings of the board the executive committee:

> . . . shall possess and may exercise all the powers of the Board of Directors in the management and direction of all the business and affairs of the company . . . in such a manner as the Executive Committee shall deem best for the interest of the company in all cases in which specific directions shall not have been given by the Board of Directors.

The only other limitation on the executive committee's powers involves certain financial decisions which are reserved for the board's committees on finance, audit, and bonus and salary. The executive committee constitutes about one-third of the board's membership, and is, in effect, a daily "working board."

Strangers in Wilmington sometimes are told

* Reprinted by permission of the publisher from *Harvard Business Review*, vol. 33, no. 3, pp. 51–58, May, 1955. Mr. Mylander is an administrative assistant of E. I. du Pont de Nemours & Company.

that "the executive committee runs the company and the general managers run the business." This is because du Pont operations are decentralized below the committee level into ten manufacturing departments headed by general managers with full authority to run their businesses as they please—so long, as they observe over-all company policies and earn a satisfactory return on the investment of plant and working capital entrusted to them. At present these departments are electrochemicals, explosives, fabrics and finishes, film, Grasselli chemicals, organic chemicals, photo products, pigments, polychemicals, and textile fibers.

Du Pont also has fourteen staff or auxiliary departments. Twelve of these—advertising, chemical, development, employee relations, engineering, foreign relations, general services, legal, public relations, purchasing, traffic, and economist—are headed by directors who are appointed by and report to the executive committee. The other two are the departments of the secretary and the treasurer, who are elected by the board and report to the president and the finance committee.

The company principle that "authority must be commensurate with responsibility" extends to the staff groups. The directors organize and run their own departments. In serving the manufacturing departments, their relations by and large are similar to those of outside agencies selling specialized services. There is no rule that requires a manufacturing department to utilize du Pont's staff facilities, but it is rare when a general manager prefers outside counsel. The staff departments also provide institutional services for the company as a whole.

The general managers and directors hire their own personnel. Each selects an assistant who must be approved by the executive committee since he should be capable of taking over in event of illness or disability of the general manager or director. "It makes you a little more careful in your choice," said one general manager.

While careful to preserve the independence of the departments in personnel matters, the committee keeps a watchful eye on the training of managerial talent. Potential executives are noted usually when they are in the early thirties and have been with du Pont from five to ten years. Those who show ability are given the opportunity to round out their experience by taking a hand in all aspects of the business. They are moved across functional fields, such as from research to production or sales, and are even transferred from one manufacturing department to another, in order that their development may be furthered.

The general managers have their own technical, production, and sales divisions, and such others as they deem advisable. They, along with the directors of staff departments, report regularly to the executive committee on their operations. "Our general managers," said one vice president, "have substantially as much power as the average company president."

ORIGIN OF THE SYSTEM

When Irénée du Pont and his associates conceived the executive committee-line system of management under which the company has grown and prospered for 34 years, they were seeking a better way to deal with the problems presented by product diversification. The old line organization had been adequate when the company was just making and selling explosives, but by 1921 a deliberate program of expansion into the broad field of chemical products was well under way.

Product Diversification As early as the turn of the century came the modest beginning of du Pont's now famed program of research. Pending the time when its own laboratories would create the present steady flow of new and improved products, the company had bought chemical concerns with know-how and experience in various lines here in this country and had purchased patents and scientific knowledge abroad. Consequently du Pont, with a sales volume in 1921 of $55 million, was suffering growing pains with the new products.

It was one thing to make and sell explosives and quite another to make and sell paint, as du Pont's centralized sales and product divisions soon discovered. The salesmen who knew explosives and how to sell them knew little about paint. Unfamiliar sales and production problems also stemmed from other new products, such as plastic-coated fabrics, dyes, pigments, and the "fibersilk" now known as rayon.

Most chemicals are sold to other industries rather than directly to the consumer (consumer purchases today account for less than 9% of du Pont's production). The successful chemical salesman, therefore, not only must know his own wares, but must be familiar with the needs and problems of the industries to which he sells. He must be able to demonstrate how a chemical can be used to improve the end product manufactured by his customer. Obviously it was demanding too much to expect the sales expert in explosives to be equally expert in dyestuffs.

The centralized manufacturing department encountered the same troubles as the centralized sales department. But unfamiliarity with new products was not the only headache. A veteran of those days recalls an instance when the manager of a paint plant insisted on turning out all the white paint he could make because he knew how to make it at a good profit. The salesmen, however, discovered that the public wanted colored paint. They reported the demand for colors to their manager, who passed the word up the line to the vice president in charge of sales. This vice president in turn took the matter up with the vice president in charge of manufacturing, who sent the word back down the line to the plant manager. But by the time it reached the plant manager and production had been geared to sales, the inventory tanks contained an appalling amount of white paint.

"Our principal difficulty," recalls Walter S. Carpenter, Jr., now chairman of the board, "was that when trouble occurred anywhere in the organization, it had to filter all the way up to the top and all the way back down again before it was corrected."

Company Growth   All the executives interviewed felt that the need for the new organization stemmed primarily from diversification and complexity of products, although company growth in itself was a factor.

- There would be far less need for an executive committee," said one, "if a company had only one product line regardless of its size. But even then, the committee might be valuable in considering broad trends and developments without having to be tied down with live issues."

- "It would be impossible," said another, "for any one person to administer such diversified operations as we are engaged in. It is necessary always to think in terms of what is best for the company as a whole, rather than for any one of the various components."

- "When a company is big enough," said a third, "complex enough or diverse enough to need more than one man to see the sum of the whole, the committee system should be given consideration."

- A fourth simply observed, "Ten heads are better than one."

HOW THE COMMITTEE OPERATES

The vice presidents sometimes tell the general managers: "You are the bosses, and we are the philosophers." No one in du Pont, however, and least of all a general manager,

would make the mistake of attributing top company authority anywhere but to the executive committee.

Responsibilities   Fundamentally, the committee exercises three important responsibilities:

1. It determines the broad, basic policies for the operations of the company.

2. It selects the men to carry out these operations.

3. It maintains a continuous review, and seeks to make an honest and objective appraisal of the conduct of the business to make sure that the men selected are doing a good job.

The opinions of the committee members command the respect of general managers and other executives down the line. Each member is recognized as an expert in specific fields, which gives to the committee as a whole a prestige seldom possible for a single individual to attain. If a weakness appears in a department, the committee is quick to assist the general manager in determining whether the trouble is in sales, research, or production. When the weak spot is located, committee experts in that field help the general manager to find a solution.

The Wednesday Meetings.   Each manufacturing department presents a monthly operating report, which the committee usually considers on the first and last Wednesdays of each month. In addition, the committee averages one meeting a month in a chart room, where the performance and forecasts of sales and earnings for each department are reviewed with the general manager. (A series of departments is considered each time, with every department averaging about four reviews a year.) If there is a slump in either performance or forecast, the general manager is expected to provide a satisfactory explanation and to discuss with the committee the steps which should be taken to bring operations up to standard.

Capital expenditures or long-range commitments of the departments which are above certain amounts must go to the committee for approval, and those above higher limits must be approved by the finance committee as well. This insures committee scrutiny of projects such as new plant construction, plant expansion, or new commercial ventures. The projects, however, are initiated by the general managers.

The committee passes on agreements and contracts proposed by the departments. The staff departments present annual budgets for approval. The operating departments and the chemical and engineering departments present their own research budgets. Construction forecasts are presented four times a year by the engineering department.

Decisions on operating schedules, prices, individual salary raises, and other day-by-day operating problems are left to the general managers, but are subject to the policy framework established over the years by the executive committee. However, if a department gets out of line in these respects with the rest of the company, the committee quickly calls in the general manager for a talk. It should be noted that such talks are rarely necessary.

"The heart of our operation is the Wednesday meeting," said President Greenewalt. "We spend the rest of the week directly or indirectly preparing for it."

Each Friday afternoon, committee members find on their desks a stack of reports two inches high which they are expected to read and digest prior to the next Wednesday. "We are supposed to have time to think," said one vice president indicating the stack. The members, however, do find it helpful to study a proposal in writing before taking it up in oral discussion with the officials concerned.

In the Wednesday meetings, each member of the committee has one vote, including the president, who usually votes only to make or break a tie. Split decisions are uncommon. Five members constitute a quorum, and four affirmative votes are required for the adoption of any resolution. Occasionally the members of the minority ask to have their opposition recorded. Otherwise the action is simply noted as taken, or as taken unanimously.

The practice in some companies of requiring unanimity for committee action finds no support at du Pont. Each member pays careful attention to the views of the others when a question is debated, and minds have been changed by debate. The members feel, however, that it would be stultifying to have to go along with a decision if they sincerely believe it to be wrong, and they pride themselves on being "rugged individualists." A showdown on important questions usually is postponed until all members are present, although, as stated above, five constitute a quorum for ordinary business.

As chairman of the meetings, President Greenewalt has the usual presiding officer's responsibility to see that there is opportunity for full debate, to narrow the issues to their essence, and to call for a decision after adequate discussion. Other members praise his objectivity as chairman, although they know he does not hesitate to speak his mind and express his own views when they differ from others. When fuller explanation of a decision than the customary "advice of action" is warranted, he calls the general managers together and does the explaining.

The agenda for an executive committee meeting averages at least 12 items. The regular required reports from the manufacturing departments provide the framework, and either the departments or members of the committee can initiate additions. "In a live organization, the agenda will take care of itself," was one comment. (See Exhibit 1 for a sample agenda —typical in breadth and variety though not necessarily in specific subject matter.)

"Court of Appeals."   Since the manufacturing departments compete with each other as well as with outside rivals, and the staff departments have their own differences of opinion, the executive committee is available as a court of last resort to settle intracompany disputes. The committee does not like to be placed in this role, however, and this fact is emphatically made known to the disputants. When all consultation and mediation fails, the committee if called upon will step in and resolve the issue—and the disputants will resolve never again to let it go as far as the committee.

Review of Department Projects.   Members of the committee believe that the system functions at its best when they are able to stimulate and encourage the initiation of ideas and projects from down the line. They do not hesitate, however, to inject their own proposals when they believe them to be for the best interests of the company:

- "It is rare when a general manager is turned down on a project," said a vice president. "He knows his proposal will be reviewed by experts; and since our general managers are able men, they don't bring anything to us unless they are pretty sure."

- "Sometimes we don't agree with a general manager," said another, "but it is better to let a mistake be made than to order a general manager to act against his judgment—unless too many people would be hurt."

- "We err on the side of letting the general managers run their businesses according to their own lights," said a third. "When I was a general manager, they let me spend half a million dollars playing around with superpressures without getting any results."

There is a readiness among the vice presidents to concede that du Pont has made mistakes—"some of them beauts"—but they do point out that the initiation of projects by the departments, followed by executive committee review, provides a built-in weeding-out process

EXHIBIT 1   Agenda for a Wednesday Meeting

Chart room

1. Fabrics and Finishes Department regular report for January.
2. Grasselli Chemicals Department regular report for January.
3. Photo Products Department regular report for January.
4. Pigments Department regular report for January.
5. Foreign Relations Department—annual report and operating budget.

Committee room

Unfinished business

6. Engineering Department—operating budget.
7. Motion picture program based on the Company's programs re "How Our Business System Operates." Joint report from Advertising, Employee Relations, and Public Relations Departments.

New Business

8. Organic Chemicals Department regular report for January.
9. Appropriation project covering partial design, procurement of long delivery equipment, and preparation of construction cost estimate New River Pump House, ash and waste retention facilities, Old Hickory Rayon and Cellophane Plants.
10. Appropriation project—replacement of worn-out pirns, Waynesboro Plant.
11. Credit appropriation—additional power facilities, Spruance Rayon Plant.
12. Appropriation—project for synthesis gas via coal partial combustion—Step #1, Belle Works.
13. Adjustment of permanent investment—QY catalyst facilities, Arlington Works.
14. Supplemental report on accomplishment—second year's operation—continuous polyvinyl alcohol and monomer process, Niagara Falls Plant.
15. History, present status, and future prospects of the "Elvanol" polyvinyl alcohol business. Report from Electrochemicals Department.
16. Miscellaneous items.

which disposes of most ill-considered proposals before they ever reach the action stage.

Long-range Considerations. The committee feels strongly its obligation to look into the future for national trends, and in 1939, for example, it anticipated a country-wide pattern of wage increases. The general managers were called in and encouraged to grant increases promptly in the interest of sound employee relations. It took some convincing in certain departments where general managers were reluctant to curtail department earnings, but the result was regarded as worthwhile.

Operating officials in their planning, too, are encouraged by the committee to take into account long-range considerations of the public interest. For example, du Pont is the sole supplier of neoprene rubber for the free world. When expanded production of this product seemed advisable, the general manager proposed and the committee approved the construction of a scond plant rather than enlargement of existing facilities. Among other reasons given in support of this proposal was that a second plant would guarantee an alternate source of neoprene for defense and commercial use in case one plant should be shut down by fire or disaster. As far as the company itself was concerned, the enlargement of the single plant, obviously, would have meant a greater return on investment over the near term.

One of the ways in which the committee seeks answers to its own questions, and stimulates thinking in the departments, is by requesting "whither" reports. These are so named because they ask "whither nylon?" or "whither titanium?" The studies involved in preparation of these documents dealing with the future of specified products are enlightening to the general managers as well as to the committee.

Study and consultation constitute a continuous process at du Pont. In fact, most decisions of the committee are reached only after careful examination of all available facts and opinions and consultation with everyone in a position to make some contribution.

Advisory Duties In a secondary role, members of the committee serve as individual advisers in areas where they are best qualified by skill, training, and experience. But in contrast to formal committee decisions in which they have a vote, as advisers their influence is indirect, and they are quick to say that they can't give orders as individuals "to anybody but my secretary."

Although committee members advise, rather than dictate, it takes a strong-willed general manager or staff department director, who is sure of his ground, to take counteraction after soliciting counsel. This is not because the committee members seek to impose their will upon management down the line, but because everyone in the company looks up to them as experts in specialized areas. Thus:

Vice President Walter J. Beadle, a former treasurer, advises on foreign relations and legal matters. Another former treasurer, Vice President T. C. Davis, is adviser to the treasurer's department. Vice President Charles A. Cary, up from assistant general manager of the old rayon department, advises on traffic, purchasing, and general services. Vice President J. Warren Kinsman, up from general manager of fabrics and finishes, the company's largest direct sales area, is adviser on advertising and sales. Vice President Henry B. du Pont, who came up from engineering research, advises on engineering. Vice President William H. Ward, a former general manager of explosives, advises on personnel, salaries, and employee relations.

Vice President Walter Dannenbaum, up from general manager of the old ammonia department, advises on manufacturing. Vice President Roger Williams, who was chemical director of the ammonia department and later was in charge of the Hanford atomic energy project as assistant manager of explosives, advises on chemical research and development. President Greenewalt is the adviser on public relations, and is also consulted along with Mr. Williams on technical and scientific problems. Vice President Robert L. Richards, promoted last fall from general manager of textile fibers, awaits his advisership assignment.

Executive committee members also serve on other committees. Messrs. Beadle, Ward, and Williams are members of the company's subcommittee on "B" bonus, while Mr. Dannenbaum is chairman of the "A" bonus committee. Messrs. du Pont, Kinsman, and Dannenbaum are members of a subcommittee on purchases and sales, while Messrs. Beadle, Cary, and du Pont are members of a subcommittee on construction forecasts. In addition, some members of the executive committee are directors of certain subsidiary corporations.

- "We give advice, solicited or volunteered," explained one. "There is no compulsion to follow it, although we sometimes resort to tactful persuasion."
- "It is cooperation, contact, the development of a common understanding, and talking out problems," said another. "The key to the company's success is how the general

managers run the business. Our task is to create an environment which will help them do a better job."

- "We should never attempt to exercise too much power for that would destroy the autonomy of the departments," said a third.
- "It is always desirable to avoid sending down pronouncements from on high," observed a fourth. "We try to get the viewpoints of others involved and work out a mutually satisfactory answer."

While individual members of the committee are frequently consulted in advance for their views on special aspects of a project—for example, Mr. Williams on the technical end, Mr. Kinsman on sales, or Mr. Dannenbaum on manufacturing—they are not expected to commit themselves on the project as a whole. The project, as a *project*, is considered on its merits when the general manager formally presents it to the committee, even though the financial, legal, technical, sales, and manufacturing problems connected with it may have already been discussed individually with the special advisers in these fields.

QUALIFICATIONS FOR MEMBERSHIP

In selecting the executive committee, the board of directors, in the words of one director, "tries to create a superman by combining the great breadth of experience represented by the various members, so each can contribute his own viewpoint for the benefit of the others and the group as a whole." Specifically, the following qualifications are looked for:

Basic experience and expertness in one or more fields, especially research, production, sales, finance, or engineering, constitute a primary qualification.

A well-rounded background is desirable beclause, as another put it, "when a man goes on the committee, he is not supposed to look at an issue from the standpoint of his old department or activity, but in the interest of the company as a whole."

Sound judgment, objectivity, breadth of vision, and a willingness to cooperate are essential qualities.

The prospective committee member should be well read, versed in industrial problems, and aware of what's going on in the nation and the world.

He should enjoy good health, and be of an age which will permit him to serve at least 10 years before compulsory retirement at 65.

Other specifications as they were expressed by the board members interviewed include:

His head should be screwed on right.

He should be an individualist—we don't want go-alongers.

He should balance independence of opinion with the grace to submit to the will of the majority.

He should have ideas but be willing to see them turned down without waiting for an opportunity later to say "I told you so."

He should have a specialty and as much else as he can bring with him.

He should be a self-starter willing to be an adviser—with all that the term implies and all that it doesn't imply.

We want men who won't be earth-bound by logic but have the instinct or intuition to do the right thing whether logical or not.

He should have forbearance, and recognize that the other fellow has strong convictions, too.

He should have profound tolerance, and avoid getting provoked.

He needs personality, a fine mind, and a quick wit.

Two members of the committee separately mentioned "dedication" as a qualification. One defined this quality as "a will to devote all your time and interest to the company's affairs," while the other remarked, "I told a general manager the other day that coming on the committee is like joining a monastery—you work 16 hours a day and get your fun out of the job. You must be dedicated."

It is acknowledged that fate has a hand in the selections. A man with all of the qualifications may miss promotion to the committee because there are no suitable vacancies while he is in the proper age bracket. One of the vice presidents also suggested that "an individual might be an excellent general manager and a poor vice president, or vice versa."

The size of the committee has varied from time to time. Asked why it numbers ten, instead of five or fifteen, a member explained that it was essential to have technical, financial, manufacturing, sales, and engineering experience represented. Then, he continued, it is better to have two from each field, both to insure a quorum for the weekly meetings, despite illnesses, vacations, or business trips, and to make available the judgment of two experts, rather than one, on specialized issues. Also, he felt that ten could function as a committee

without the loss of individualism, but twice that number might lead to "herd thinking" or the development of cliques.

"We need a good, wide spectrum," said another, "but not so many as to become unmanageable."

All present members of the committee have come up through the ranks of du Pont, which practices a policy of promotion from within. They absorbed the spirit and became familiar with the theory and practice of the company before assuming their present posts. Committee members believe that outsiders could be brought in if necessary and would soon become accustomed to the system, but they concede it might take time and result in some dissatisfaction.

ADVANTAGES OF THE SYSTEM

When questioned concerning the advantages of the committee-line system, the executives interviewed stressed the following:

1. *The strength and security of group decisions—*

We are less likely to go to extremes, since the committee assures a balanced viewpoint on every issue.

If one individual could always come up with the right answer, we would not need a committee.

When seven men out of ten—all intellectually honest—can reach agreement, the chances are that it is sound.

It may take longer to get action, but this pays off handsomely in better decisions and ability to follow through on long-range policies.

We reap the benefit of diversified experience. One of the ten will think of some important angle that may be a blank to everyone else.

2. *Objectivity in decision making—*

The system permits discussion and consideration of policy by men relieved of day-to-day decisions. This means more than "time to think." It means that nobody on the committee will be influenced consciously or unconsciously by the effect of the decision on an operation for which he is responsible, because we aren't responsible for operations.

We all have more to do than we can get done, but we do have time to concern ourselves with things we couldn't do if we had line responsibilities.

The discipline of having to work out an agreement with nine others promotes objectivity and thorough analysis of the problems.

There is some duplication of effort, but we get a combined judgment based on all considerations and weighed without bias.

3. *Continuity of administration—*

The committee changes so gradually that our management is always on an even keel, whereas, when a dictator dies, there is no successor.

The committee assures the company of an averaging-out of temperament and ability in top management.

4. *Development of personnel—*

The system accommodates a greater diversity of executive talent. There is a place for the man who sings solo, and also for the man who sings best in the chorus.

General guidance by suggestion through the adviserships encourages initiative throughout the organization.

Our advice always is so worded that a general manager is free to disregard it if he wishes.

Where there is decentralization at the top, there is initiative down the line.

Other advantages briefly mentioned included: increasing the stature of departmental manager, relieving part of the burden which usually falls upon the president or chief executive officer, encouraging the resolution of problems at lower management levels, and flexibility.

DISADVANTAGES OF THE SYSTEM

The executives were at a loss for a ready answer when asked to list the disadvantages of the system. After some thought the following were brought out:

1. A few who had come up through departmental management mentioned a certain sense of frustration.

On the committee you feel inhibited. You move up to it from an active to an ethereal field, and have to get things done by advice and suggestion.

Men who have been on the firing line, making day-to-day decisions, suddenly find when they move up to the committee that they can't give

orders as individuals to anybody but their secretaries.

There is difficulty in making the transition from line management to the committee, with the danger that departmental allegiances will stay in the picture.

Compromise isn't always easy, and expediency must be paid for.

2. Some of the others cited as a minor disadvantage the fact that outsiders frequently are unaware of the division of responsibilities at du Pont, and expect the president and the vice presidents to make decisions on sales or other matters which lie within the province of the general managers.

3. One of the more individualistic members pointed out that ten people had to read every report, but added that there is compensation in the fact that one of the ten occasionally spots something the other nine miss.

4. It was also suggested that in a small company an executive committee might not have enough to do, that autonomy of the departments would be weakened if the committee set up too many rules, and that there might be room even at du Pont for "something to fall between the slats of responsibility."

On the whole, however, the members of the committee were unable to cite serious disadvantages, and two of them suggested that the question be put to one of the general managers.

After some thought the general manager consulted answered that with his title he did find it a little difficult to compete for customers' attention against the head of a competing company, who had the title of president, even though his own department's total output is five times larger than that of the competitor.

"But I just can't think of any other disadvantages of our system," he said. "I would much rather go to ten men with a project than take my chances on one."

In conclusion, the 12 top executives stressed that (1) they are not urging other companies to adopt their committee-line system, (2) they believe unanimously it has been successful for du Pont, and (3) they feel it should work for any other large producer of diversified lines.

Ground Rules for Using Committees*

CYRIL O'DONNELL

A camel, someone has said, is a horse designed by a committee—and this is fairly typical of the current attitude toward this form of group activity. The use of committees has been criticized as a way of avoiding individual executive action, as a means of covering up managerial inadequacies, as a form of inefficient corporate "togetherness," and as a device for legitimizing procrastination and indecisiveness. What's more, every one of these accusations is justified, at least in many cases.

What is frequently overlooked, however, is that these are not valid criticisms of committees, but rather of the *misuse* of committees. For a committee that can be charged with any of these faults is not being employed as a committe should be used. Committees do have legitimate functions and, properly used, they constitute an invaluable management tool. The question is, how should they be properly used?

One common error is the confusion of committees with other kinds of joint action. Many people apply the term "committee" to any meeting of two or more people, but this definition is obviously too flexible and imprecise. It would necessarily include such diverse activities as business conferences, staff meetings, meetings of department heads, executive committee meetings, and even luncheon engagements, all of which are designed to serve quite different purposes. Conferences and typical staff meetings are primarily communication devices, utilized for economic purposes; a meeting of department heads may be called to clear up snags or overcome delays in some area that concerns all of them; meetings of an executive committee on which the president

sits are held primarily for communication purposes. In none of these instances does a true committee exist.

THE TRUE COMMITTEE

What, then, is a committee? We might define it as *two or more persons appointed by their immediate superior for the purpose of acting or advising their superior about a subject that is not clearly within the competence of any of them.*

This implies that the superior does not sit in on the committee meetings; that the membership is confined to two or more of his immediate subordinates; and that the subject matter to be considered is not within the assigned duties of any individual member. Such a committee is properly considered an organizational device because it is performing an activity that, for various reasons, is not otherwise assigned. It may or may not have authority to take action, and it may be either an *ad hoc* group or a permanent committee.

BASIC REQUIREMENTS

The proper use of committees is based on two fundamental assumptions. In the first place, it assumes that the structure of the enterprise and the association of activities in this structure conform to the principles of good organization. Experienced business managers recognize that it is not possible, even in a well-organized company, to cover all types of activities or to assign all duties to specific individuals. Even when it is possible to make such assignments, they sometimes prefer not to do so. The important point is that the committee device is not a crutch for poor organization structure—it supplements good structure.

The second basic assumption is that the enterprise has effective managers. Too often the committee device is used to supplement

* Reprinted by permission of the publisher from the *Management Review*, vol. 50, no. 10, pp. 63–67, October, 1961. Mr. O'Donnell is professor of business organization and policy and vice-chairman for management theory in the Graduate School of Business Administration, University of California, Los Angeles.

and buttress inefficient men. The use of a committee to support mediocrity in management is an extremely poor and even dangerous device. True, it may sometimes be necessary in the short run. But this situation should be clearly recognized, and vigorous effort should be made to achieve good organization and employ effective managers as quickly as possible.

The one time when a committee can be legitimately used—and the only circumstance in which its use can be justified—is when it can do a job better than a single manager. This means that the net effect must be superior in the light of such factors as cost, time, decisiveness, justice, and sound judgment.

Pooled Experience   There are three situations in which a committee may meet this criterion. To begin with, a committee is a sound organizational device when it is used to obtain the considered views of subordinates about a subject beyond the experience of their superior. If the superior has the breadth and depth of experience represented by the members of a committee, it is obvious that he has no need of group action. Lacking this experience, the superior might conceivably ask for the advice of individual subordinates without organizing a committee. This is quite often done—as, for example, when an executive calls on a department or division manager for his views on a particular subject. Quite often, however, such an informal approach will result in the subordinate's giving views that are narrow in conception and not fully considered. As a member of a committee, the same subordinate would frame his views with an eye to potential questions or criticism of his fellow members, and he would thus be likely to be less extreme and insular in his viewpoint.

A good example of this kind of committee is the typical policy committee, whose purpose is to formulate policy to best fit the needs of the enterprise. For example, the question in the mind of the president may be, "Do we need a policy on pricing, and, if so, how should it be framed?" If he has come up through engineering or production, the president may lack the technical knowledge and experience required to decide a matter of this type. Consequently, he would find it advisable to refer the matter to his policy committee. The members of the committee would develop their views, not only with respect to special interests of the division or function they represent, but also from the viewpoint of the welfare of the company as a whole. Their considered views would result in a consensus which they would report to the president. In this instance, the committee would be acting in a staff capacity, and it would probably be a standing committee.

Too Much Power   A second appropriate use of a committee as an organizational device is to exercise authority that is too great for any one man. The authority may be considered too great because it requires broader knowledge than any one man can be expected to have, because there is too much risk of bias or prejudice, or because it is difficult to find a person willing to exercise the authority. Good examples of such committees are investment committees, wage–and–salary committees, and boards of directors. It would be unusual to find a treasurer or a chairman of a board of directors who would be willing to take it on himself to decide how the surplus funds of a firm should be invested—and, indeed, it is likely to be too risky for the firm to rely on the judgment of any one man. Similar considerations are involved with respect to the wage–and–salary committee and the board of directors, which is a committee representing the stockholders. Committees of these types are standing committees that are delegated line authority. They make decisions on a majority basis and are true "plural executives."

Spreading Responsibility   A third appropriate reason to use a committee as an organizational device is to diffuse responsibility among several executives. Very often it is undesirable to pinpoint responsibility for action on one person. A good example of this type of committee is the bonus committee, which determines the exact distribution of a fund among the qualified members or recipients. Although the total amount of a bonus fund may be expressed, in terms of a percentage of profits before taxes, the method of distributing the bonus is not always directly related to the salaries of the potential recipients; distribution is frequently made on the basis of an evaluation of their contributions to the company in the past year. One manager might well find the assignment of making this evaluation very uncomfortable, and he would be the target of complaints and accusations form those who felt that they were unfairly treated. When a committee is used for this purpose, responsibility is spread among the members, and disappointed recipients are less disposed to complain; they are more likely to be satisfied that no bias or prejudice was involved in the decision of a group.

A committee of this type is likely to be an *ad hoc* group, and it normally has a staff position with respect to the chief executive officer.

However, at the option of their superior, the committee may be delegated line authority to act in the situation.

COMMITTEE OPERATION

Three important elements are necessary to make committees truly and effectively operational. First, the purpose for which the committee is being established must be distinctly defined. A written statement will help to achieve clarity, and it will eliminate the need for committee members to spend time deciding exactly what they are supposed to be doing.

Second, the authority of the committee must be clearly specified. This is an easy matter, but it should be given careful attention. The committee may perform a staff function, having authority only to investigate and recommend to their superior, or it may be given authority to make decisions. Which is the case must be clearly determined and communicated.

Finally, the chairman of a committee should at all times be appointed on the basis of his ability to conduct an efficient meeting. Efficiency requires that the chairman prepare an agenda in advance so the members will have time to study the subject and consider their views. It means that the chairman must insure that all members are heard from, encouraging the reticent and keeping the loquacious in check. When all the contributions of the members are in, he should state the consensus of the meeting to be sure that he has properly understood it, and he should see that minutes of the meeting are distributed in rough form for correction and review prior to their final distribution.

If these points are given adequate consideration, management can be sure that its committees will operate effectively.

AN ANNUAL CHECKUP

It is an efficient practice for a company to make an annual audit of its committees, evaluating each one to determine whether it can be justified as an organizational device. If any existing group fails to meet one of the three basic purposes of committees, there is a serious question of its legitimacy.

As this audit is conducted from year to year, managers will gain a thorough understanding of the appropriate use of committees. They will shy away from using committees as crutches for inadequacies, as excuses for delay, or as devices to shift decision-making responsibility, and they will learn to use them to do the jobs for which they are uniquely suited.

When this has been accomplished, the committee will have attained its proper and respected place in the organization structure of the enterprise.

38 F. ORGANIZATION PLANNING

Organizational Planning*

ROBERT L. HERSHEY

All human organizations have three essential features. First, they have an objective—a result to be achieved. Second, there are people, the implements by which the organization gets its work done and produces the results which

* Reprinted by permission of the publisher from *Business Topics,* vol. 10, no. 1, pp. 29–40, Winter, 1962. Mr. Hershey is vice-president of E. I. du Pont de Nemours and Company.

are the reason for its existence. Third, there is structure, the way the people are placed in working relationship with each other. For greatest effectiveness, both the people and the structure of an organization must be well tuned to its objectives. The people will need to have whatever special skills are required, and the structure must bring the people together in a way which stimulates maximum use of those skills on the essentials of the job to be done. Proper structure provides for doing those things necessary to attain the objective, and at the same time firmly excludes the doing of those things which are unnecessary.

Organizations are temporary or permanent. The expedition which some years ago finally put two men on the top of Mt. Everest was a relatively uncomplicated example of a temporary organization. As the results clearly show, it had all the essential characteristics of an efficient organization: clearly recognized objective, competent people with the proper skills, a simple but appropriate structure for using those skills.

Businessmen are concerned with the far more complicated problems of essentially permanent organizations. The problem under examination is how to maintain permanent organizations, and indeed a specific kind of permanent organization—that is, business organizations—at top levels of effectiveness as the months and years roll by. The three features of an organization, its objectives, its people, and its structure will all need attention if it is to achieve this goal. In the nature of things there is no reason why an organization's objectives or structure need change with time. There are indeed some organizations, not business ones I may say, of considerable antiquity, whose structure seems not to have changed essentially for centuries. Time will, however, inexorably guarantee a change in the people. No organization, however stable otherwise, can afford to neglect the problem posed by this simple fact.

MOTIVES AND CONCERNS

While some kinds of organizations may find it unnecessary to adjust their structural arrangements from time to time, and may for years have unaltered objectives, business organizations will neglect the matters of reexamining objectives and altering structures only at great peril. The reasons for this are quite simple. However a business organization may view its objectives, the organization must be oriented to its market or markets. Its structure must be consonant with the demands and peculiarities of the market it has set itself to serve. Markets, however, are almost as fickle and mortal as humans. At any rate they do change, and indeed one of the goals of most dynamic business enterprises is precisely to change them by some kind of profitable innovation. Thus new products, new services, and sometimes wholly new markets come into being, or more accurately are created by the actions of businessmen. Markets grow and change in character. Sometimes they slowly fade away. While structural adjustment in the organization may not always be necessary to accommodate to these market changes, wise management will be prepared to make such adjustments promptly when needed. One of the great difficulties, of course, is recognition of the need.

Apart from the influences of changing markets there are other reasons for structural changes. One of the most important of them is changing technology of every kind. Changes in methods of manufacture, of communication, of transportation, even of computation can all require structural adjustment if the organization is to use them to best advantage.

Thus if organizational planning is an activity having as its purpose the preparation for those changes which will be necessary to keep the organization at top efficiency, it will be seen that it must certainly concern itself always with the problem of people, perhaps much of the time with organizational structure, and probably even now and then with a reexamination of broad objectives.

Organizational planning, in its relationship to effective management control, warrants consideration from both the viewpoint of personnel and that of structure. In the final analysis, of course, it is people who are all-important. If a situation is improved by a structural change, it is because some thoroughly competent people have analyzed a problem, devised a solution, and acted. So the ultimate problem is one of recruiting, training, and selecting for promotion the best people available. However, before discussing this management development phase and how we attempt to deal with it in the Du Pont Company, I should like to turn to the matter of structure and in doing so recount some company history.

STRUCTURAL PLANNING

The present general structure of the Du Pont Company has been in existence just over forty years; this September marked the fortieth anniversary of its formal adoption. At the time it was a major change in structure for the whole company, and it came after a considerable period of most intensive organizational planning, though it is not likely that anyone in those days used any such term to describe the process.

Because the organization concept underlying the change was then something rare in business practice and because it has served the company well over the intervening years, it may be useful to take a brief look at what the change was and how it came about.

Company History   Until about the second decade of the century Du Pont was essentially a one-business company. It was organized internally along functional lines; there was a manufacturing department, a sales department, and so forth. This internal structure, and with it a fully developed set of operating procedures, had proved excellently well suited to the company's older business. During the second decade the company began to diversify, mainly by acquisitions, into other phases of the chemical business, until by the end of the decade, in addition to the old explosives and powder business, it was engaging in the manufacture and sale of such diverse products as paints, coated fabrics, dyestuffs and nitrocellulose plastic, and articles made therefrom, such as toilet sets. It seemed a perfectly natural and reasonable thing to merge these newly acquired activities into the existing organizational structure, which had adequately proven its virtues in the years past. Thus the manufacture of all products became the responsibility of the manufacturing department and the single sales department bore the responsibility for selling such different things as dynamite and paint, as well as many other products.

Decentralization   I wish I could give a succinct but detailed view, as it might have appeared to a participant in those days, of the difficulties that arose from this arrangement. Unfortunately, I cannot. Perhaps at this distance and with a greater ' .iowledge of organizational theory we can adequately imagine some of them. I can, however, report that sometime in 1920 members of the top management of the company became concerned that something less than the desired effectiveness was being achieved. The question of organization structure was raised in the top councils of the company and a developing discussion followed. A fact-finding survey by an *ad hoc* committee of upper, but not top, level management was undertaken.

As fact-finding and discussion proceeded, the idea that the purposes of the company would be better served if all the activities relating to each of the company's "businesses" could be segregated into a single unit and placed under a single responsible manager became clarified and accepted. The germ of this idea had appeared in the very early phases of the discussion, as had the analysis that "diversifica-

tion of industries and products" and not size was at the root of the company's difficulties. One of the symptoms of the difficulties which was much complained about in those days was the inordinate number of large and indecisive meetings. It is clear in retrospect that there was lacking a focus of responsibility, except at the very top of the company, for those decisions which required coordinated judgment on the manufacturing and sales aspects of a particular product, or related group of products.

The practical application to the company as it then stood of this idea of decentralized responsibility for a business required the study and solution of many problems of detail. How was the company to be divided into the new departments? How completely was a department to be staffed with its own specialists? How was corporate coordination to be provided? How was the new structure to be supplied with personnel?

Functional to Industrial   The division of the company into the new departments was to be according to the "industries" the company was then in; hence they were called "industrial departments" in distinction from the former functional departments, and this is still the company term for them. The businessman's vocabulary has changed over the years; perhaps today it would be more meaningful to say the division was made generally according to marketing areas. Five industrial departments were finally established. Their heads were designated General Managers.

Although the manufacturing and selling functions in each department were always clearly to be the responsibility of the General Manager, there was not in the beginning clear-cut agreement about some other functions. Research in those days was not what it is today; indeed the old functional department doing research was called the Chemical Department. Each of the new industrial departments was given a research responsibility at least in its own industry, since otherwise the General Managers could, to quote from a document of the time, "escape responsibility for unsatisfactory performance." The Chemical Department did not disappear, but research of a more fundamental nature and on products not related to the existing businesses was assigned to it.

Departmental Reorganization   A somewhat different conclusion was reached with respect to the purchasing function; it was concluded that the advantages of a central and specialized purchasing group outweighed the prospective advantages of industrial department purchasing. The existing Purchasing Department was retained, but the authority and responsibility of the General Manager was safeguarded by requiring his approval of purchase contracts and leaving him the opportunity to appeal to the top company management to handle specific purchasing situations. Traffic was a Purchasing Department function.

The other corporate departments were: Treasurer's, Legal, Engineering, Development, Advertising, and Service (which encompassed a great miscellany of services which are today spread among several departments). All these had been in existence before the change. With a few name changes, splits and additions, we have the same departments today: the Chemical Department is now Central Research; Traffic is a separate entity; the functions of the old Service Department are now distributed among the Employee Relations Department, the General Services Department which manages the company's central office buildings and supplies a number of services to them, the Secretary's Department, and the Public Relations Department.

Corporate Level Coordination Coordination of this structure at the corporate level was provided by utilizing two subcommittees of the Board of Directors which had been in existence for some years, the Finance Committee and the Executive Committee. There was essentially no change in the responsibilities of the Finance Committee. Both before and after the change, and today, the Treasurer is responsible to the Finance Committee, which sets financial policy, oversees financial operations and authorizes capital expenditures over a specified amount. There were, however, rather drastic changes in the composition and functions of the Executive Committee, which became the principal managing and coordinating agency at the corporate level.

The members of the old committee had in general been heads of the old functional departments; the President was not a member. There is evidence that the scrutiny in the committee of the performance of a department had been somewhat less penetrating than it might have been had the department head not been a committee member. However that may have been, no head of the new industrial departments was a member of the new Executive Committee and the members of the committee had no direct operating responsibilities. They were instead given functional advisory responsibilities in areas for which their skills and experience fitted them. The President became

a member of the committee and its chairman. All departments, including the new industrial departments, except the Treasurer's, as already noted, reported to the Executive Committee.

The company found the required personnel to staff this radically changed organization within its own ranks; in at least one instance a senior executive and board member who had given up direct operating duties returned to become one of the new General Managers.

President's Letter The new organization was formally adopted by the Board of Directors in September of 1921, and was made effective with remarkable rapidity thereafter. A letter of the President (then Mr. Irénée du Pont) to the employees announced the change. Sections of the letter read as follows:

> We have come to the conclusion that in order to obtain the best results each line of business should be put in charge of a General Manager who will be given full authority and responsibility for the success of his Department. There will accordingly be formed five industrial departments. . . . There will also be auxiliary departments which will act in a consulting capacity and perform also staff and service functions for the Company as a whole and for the other departments. . . . The Executive Committee will have charge of all the operations of the Company under this plan. . . . This type of organization fixes responsibility. When a man is made responsible for results, his interest is stimulated; hard and effective work follows, which brings successful results. The Directors believe this plan will have a strong appeal to our employees because it will give to their efforts a more direct and definite influence upon the profitable operation of this business.

As the event showed, the Directors' belief was wholly correct.

Significance This is old history; as business history goes it is almost ancient. I have dwelt upon it, not only because the present company, of which I will have more to say, still has the same basic structure but also because I believe there are in it significant points for organizational planning in situations of any type.

There was first of all an appraisal of performance, which was found to be unsatisfactory. There was a period of fact-finding to identify the causes of the difficulty. There was the formulation of a basic organizational plan —which in this instance more sharply defined areas of responsibility and authority, and provided better concentration and coordination of effort on each of a number of differing business problems. There followed a considerable period during which the basic plan was worked out in detail, and indeed given a trial run in at least one limited area, before it was finally put into operation. I do not mean to imply that all this was done without much discussion and debate. Ideas, however good, are not refined and developed by mild acquiescence with their original proponents. Vigorous, thoughtful, and penetrating discussion between intelligent, honest, and dedicated people is the only way to that result. The men who participated in this piece of business history were just such people, and this emphasizes once more the importance of first-rate people to the whole organizational problem.

Present Structure   In the forty years since, there have been many changes in detail in the Du Pont Company but the basic organizational structure remains. There are today eleven industrial departments of the kind created in 1921; the International Department has had, since 1958, the status of an industrial department but the overseas character of its operations rather than the homogeneity of its business provides the definition of its scope. Only one of the present industrial departments has the same name it had forty years ago. Some of the products made in those days have long since disappeared from the market place; Others have been involved in many changes, in methods of manufacture, for example, or in modification of product characteristics. Of course many, many new products and a considerable number of new "industries," in the 1921 sense, have appeared. The relentless working of time has brought about, with a single exception, a complete change in the people in active managerial positions of the company. That single exception is Mr. Walter S. Carpenter, Jr. In 1921 he was a member of the Executive Committee, today he is the Chairman of the Board. The sales of the company have grown from less than $100 million to more than $2 billion.

Throughout this period of growth and change certain principles have provided the beacon lights by which the company's course was charted. First there was and is the concept that the company's business operations should be divided among several independent departments, each of which should operate in as homogeneous a business area as possible. Each of the departments was to have in it and under the control of its management all the functions necessary to profitable operation in its business area. All of our domestic industrial departments do marketing, manufacturing, research and accounting, and are responsible as well for the development and training of their personnel, as I will discuss more fully later. This decentralized management was a rare thing in 1921, perhaps partly because there were then not many widely diversified companies. Today it is commonplace.

Re-alignments   In the application of this concept the Executive Committee has not thought it wise to establish as a new department in the earliest days of its development every new venture which might appear to have in it the germ of a new industry. Thus, in its infancy, neoprene (Du Pont's and indeed the country's first synthetic rubber) was originally developed in the Organic Chemicals Department, which was then most skilled in the techniques required in its manufacture. Some years later when neoprene had acquired an established position, a new department, the Elastomer Chemicals Department, was created to exploit neoprene and certain related products in the synthetic rubber field.

Over the years there have also been departmental re-alignments of other kinds brought about by changing technology and changing markets. For example, in 1949 two departments were merged primarily because (to give an oversimplified explanation of all the factors involved) the manufacturing skills of one were needed to support the marketing effort in a brand new market area which was just opening up for the other. These are only two examples of a process which is going on more or less continuously and which has as its purpose the maintenance of departmental homogeneity in the interest of economy and efficiency.

Authority and Responsibility   This concept of departmental decentralization would not have been workable without the companion principle of delegation of authority and responsibility to the departmental manager. Mr. Irénée du Pont said in 1921 in commenting on the relationship between the new Executive Committee and the newly established General Managers, "The Executive Committee has to keep its hands off the General Manager or it cannot hold him responsible." This is of course the great secret of successful delegation. When responsibility for achieving a result is handed over there must go with it fully commensurate authority to do those things necessary for the desired accomplishment, and he who delegates cannot properly interfere with the exercise of that authority so long as the responsibility remains delegated. This principle does not deny, on the contrary it positively affirms, that the recipient of the delegated authority must be held accountable for results, but it is the results and not the details of every tactic employed in their production for which he must be held to an accounting. Such success as the Du Pont Company has achieved over the years has been to a large extent due to the positive response of the Executive Committee to Mr. du Pont's admonition of 1921.

I have sometimes had the impression that people not fully familiar with the operation of the Du Pont Company, but aware of the prominence of its Executive Committee in its organizational structure, conclude that it is run by "committee management" with all that implies for lack of speed in the decision process. If this belief is held, it is a misunderstanding. Indeed, it is precisely those decisions which require speed in their making which the organizational structure intends to place in the province of the industrial departments. The Executive Committee concerns itself with the establishment of broad policy, the selection of departmental management, the periodic review of departmental performance, the approval and authorization of capital expenditures beyond the limit of departmental authority, and the general coordination of the several departments. These are all matters which we believe can be decided with benefit and with ample speed in a properly constituted and self-disciplined committee.

Technique of Overhauling   How is the planning of organizational structural adjustments carried out in the company today? As will be realized from what I have already stated, the internal structure of each industrial department and adjustment of it to new conditions is a part of the responsibility of the department and adjustment of it to new conditions structures of the departments would show many broad similarities but also many differences in detail, occasioned of course by the differing necessities of the departments. Some structural adjustments, often minor but occasionally of major size, are in process somewhere in the company's departments almost all the time. Some years ago, as an Assistant General Manager, I participated intimately in a pretty complete overhauling of the marketing arm of one of our departments. In this instance we had the help of a well known management consulting firm, primarily to ensure objectivity in our work, there being some rather strongly-held differing opinions in the

department as to the proper course to be followed. It took us a good many months to complete the necessary fact finding, appraisal and analysis of the facts, development of proposals for organizational changes, selection of a specific plan, and choice of the key personnel in the new structure. We were very careful when we reached the point of putting the plan into operation to explain to each individual involved—and this was the whole marketing organization—the reasons for the new structure, and his place in it before general and public announcement of the change. Although of course not everyone was satisfied, everyone knew what his new job was from his own supervision, and I feel confident we avoided the feeling of frustration, dismay, and wonderment which can and usually does follow the unexpected announcement of a new organization by means of a bulletin from the front office. This procedure was time-consuming and involved a lot of work, but the acceptance of the new plan was immediate and enthusiastic; more important, improved results were apparent in a very few months. In the years since, other changes have been made in that marketing organization, primarily to adjust to new complexities in the market, and I am confident still others will appear in the future.

Although in this instance and some others, use was made of outside consultants, and they were really very helpful, most of such structural changes are carried through without such outside assistance. Of course the advice and experience of other departments and of the Executive Committee members are always available in attacking these problems.

In doing such organizational planning as comes within its specific area of responsibility, for example the readjustment of departmental lines, and the creation of new departments, the Executive Committee has at its disposal any and all resources of the company relevant to the problem at hand, but in particular it has in the Development Department a management staff to study and advise on such matters. A lot of hard thinking, however, is done in this area by the individual Executive Committee members. To give them time to do just such thinking was one of the reasons they were freed from direct operating responsibility in the 1921 reorganization.

We in the Du Pont Company know very well that the company's organizational structure can and always could be improved, and that the effort must constantly be made to improve it. We think it is good but certainly not perfect. It has served us well, but it is shaped to the necessities of our situation and should not be considered as anything other than just that: an organizational suit custom-tailored to a particular corporate body. We think the du Pont history is more significant for what it shows about building an organizational structure than for what it shows as to structural details.

PERSONNEL PLANNING

I have already commented on the critical importance of the people in an organization. It is, perhaps, significant that the only group in the Du Pont Company bearing the title "Organization Planning Division," or any similar title, is a part of the Employee Relations Department and concerns itself entirely with matters related to the personnel, rather than to the structural aspects or organization planning.

I should like to mention briefly something about how the Du Pont Company tries to get the right people in the right places in the organization as time and circumstance generate movement of people through the structure. The effort concerns primarily, of course, the problem of tomorrow's managers. There are four separate but closely related aspects of this matter:

- the recruitment of new employees into the organization;

- the training and development of individuals both to improve their present performance and, especially, to prepare them for greater future responsibility;

- the coordination of the program of training of individuals with the future requirements of the organization, or organizational planning in the personnel sense;

- the selection of individuals for promotion.

Promotion Policy   Historically the Du Pont Company has followed a policy of promotion from within. Many of the present top management personnel, indeed nearly all of them, have spent their entire working careers in the company's service. There have occasionally been older men of established competence brought into the company in key positions, but this has been done to obtain the benefit of highly specialized skills not previously available in the company. Such a policy obviously requires a constant flow into the lower ranks of able young people with potential for development. Accordingly we mount a vigorous and continuing recruiting effort aimed primarily at young people just completing their college or university training. Although much of this re-

cruiting is done with the active assistance of a professional recruiting staff which serves the whole company, the specifications as to number and qualifications of the people to be employed are set by the individual departments and the offers of employment are made directly by, or on the specific behalf of, a particular department. As an obvious consequence, the new employee begins his service in a specific department, at a particular location and in an activity at least broadly limited, e.g., research or manufacturing.

Training and Development   As to training and development, I have already mentioned that each department is responsible for this activity with respect to its own personnel. Indeed the development of future managers is regarded as one of the major responsibilities of departmental management. The methods used by the departments differ somewhat in detail, but there are significant generalizations which can be made.

Fundamentally we attempt to deal with each individual as an individual. In the first days of his employment there are, of course, certain more or less standardized orientation procedures used to assist him in feeling at home in his new environment. However, early in his career we begin appraising his performance and his potentialities, and try to assist in his development in ways tailored as much as possible to his needs. Thereafter this procedure becomes a continuing process. Our objective is to utilize the skills of each individual to the maximum capacity he is able to fulfill, and willing to undertake. Our view is that the continued growth of a man is a highly personal matter which is greatly influenced by his own inner drive to develop himself—his ambition or his motivation, if you will—but which we can assist in various ways.

Some of the ways we think are helpful to the developing manager and which we try to use are these: coaching on the job by supervision; adequate and objective appraisal of his potentiality and discussion of his performance; assignment to jobs of different types for variety of experience; off-the-job education, both inside and outside the company. About all of these, and particularly about the matter of appraisal and performance review, volumes could be and indeed have been written. I do not propose to elaborate on them here.

The Duty of Appraisal   If the development of people is to be well done it must be recognized throughout the organization as an important objective, and every member of supervision must look upon the development of his subordinates as an essential part of his daily supervisory task. Supervisors will have unequal skills in this area and the job will never be perfectly done. It will assuredly be less well done if positive performance in training and developing subordinates is not expected and demanded as an integral part of the supervisory job.

Though I do not wish to discuss in detail the complicated and controversial subject of personnel appraisals, it should be emphasized that though appraisal forms and methods of many kinds have been used in various parts of the company over the years, this is still an area of trial and experiment. We strive always for more objectivity, and for means of judging by actual performance rather than by subjective appraisal of characteristics. Much reliance is placed in many of the departments upon discussion of a man's performance and potentialities by several of his superiors who have had significant opportunities of observing him. In this way it is hoped a reliable and responsible consensus can be reached, particularly on a man's ability to take on greater responsibility.

However such appraisals are made, they are an essential factor in planning for the inevitable future movements of people in the organization. A device much used in Du Pont Company departments in doing such planning is the so-called replacement chart. This is in effect a hypothetical future organization chart which shows, based on the latest appraisals of each individual, the possibilities in the replacement moves which would be necessitated by the removal of any of the current, and especially the key, incumbents. Study of such a chart will show whether adequate replacements are immediately available, or may be expected to be in the near future, and will often aid in suggesting additional kinds of training or experience which should be planned for specific individuals, and of course such study is of tremendous value if the unexpected necessity arises for an actual replacement. I hardly need say that periodic revisions and restudy of such charts are a necessity; an annual review is probably adequate in normal circumstances.

As an assistance in corporate and cross-department planning, the Organization Planning Division (referred to previously) receives annually from each company department a statement of its appraisal of the promotability status of certain of its people. From this statement the division prepares a Personnel Inventory Chart which points up the present and future problems the department may face in replacing personnel. From these statements the division also has always available company-wide lists of men believed currently qualified for positions at certain organizational levels and above. These lists are used in our attempts to be sure that sound cross-departmental moves are made when necessary or desirable.

This whole process of development, appraisal, and planning culminates in the succession of selections of individuals for promotion. If the various preliminary phases have been well done, the final selection will usually not be too difficult or controversial; whether it be the very best selection or not, it at least will not have been capriciously or irresponsibly made. It is, I am sure, too much to hope that in every instance the selection can be the uniquely right one. In my opinion, it is not too much to hope that the really bad selections, which sooner or later need to be painfully corrected, can be avoided.

CONCLUSION

In summary, I want to point out that important as planning is in the Du Pont Company both as to the structural and the personnel aspects of the organization, we do not deal with either aspect in a highly centralized way. We believe both phases of the job will on the whole be better done when they are approached as an integral part of each department's responsibilities. Nor do we have rigidly standardized procedures in either area. While we fully recognize the necessity for such procedures in many operating areas, the decision made in any phase of organizational planning always requires the use of judgment. We prefer to avoid the narcotic effect which overelaboration of rules and procedures so often produces when judgment is essential.

The art of building and maintaining an effective organization requires a clear identification of the organization's objective, an organizational structure suitable to the attainment of that objective, and—here finally is the very heart of the matter—good people, to set the objective, to shape the structure and to make the whole organization go.

PART FOUR

STAFFING *Staffing is the management function which has to do with putting people into the framework of organization. It is thus the selection, inventory, appraisal, and training of people for enterprise activities.*

The staffing function necessarily starts with the specification of jobs to be done to accomplish plans, as these jobs are grouped and allocated to positions within the organizational structure. Of particular importance to students of management is the staffing of managerial positions. Nicely bridging the gap between the organization and the staffing function is Wilfred Brown's excellent article "What is Work?" in which he points out that there can be no freedom without restriction and no work without definition of tasks.

Closely related to Wilfred Brown's definition of work is Eli Ginzberg's article "Man and His Work," in which the role of work and the importance of the proper training and selection of people to the economic and social development of a nation is emphasized. The role of the top manager in assuring the proper selection, motivation, and training of people is discussed in the article by Ralph E. Gillen and Herbert Hubben, "Motivating the Boss: The Key to Managerial Development."

In the special area of managerial selection, our readings include the practical and highly important contribution of J. Watson Wilson, "Toward Better Use of Psychological Testing." In this article the author points out the misuse of psychological tests in personnel selection and sets forth some "ground rules" for using such tests properly. Another important contribution to an understanding of the problem of selecting managers is the excellent essay, "Predictors of Managerial Effectiveness," by Thomas A. Mahoney. This article is one of the most terse, but at the same time thorough, treatises on what we should look for when selecting effective future managers.

In the area of managerial training, the editors have included a summary of the well-developed Sperry Gyroscope management program, Earl R. Zack's "An Integrated Approach to Management Development." This article shows how one prominent company integrates its management development program into the entire process of company operation and management. And, to show some of the pitfalls in management training programs and to summarize some new approaches, the editors have included Bernard J. Bienvenu's provocative article "What Kind of Training for Tomorrow?"

As a major supplement to standard training devices and programs, a large number of companies have used the "management game"—a simulated exercise, under controlled conditions, of the management process itself. Because of the widespread interest in games for this purpose, the editors believe that the reader will find William R. Dill's article "What Management Games Do Best" of special interest.

The key to management training, and perhaps even to management itself, is effective management appraisal. If management does not know the strengths and weaknesses of individual managers, it is very difficult to develop the most effective training program. Moreover, nearly any enterprise would like to have a group of effective managers, and this requires that management appraisals be as accurate as possible. Despite the importance of management appraisal, the editors were not impressed with the appraisal practices of most companies until they began to develop evaluations based upon predetermined objectives. When this is done, management appraisal becomes much less subjective; the manager is evaluated on the basis of what he does rather than what people think of him. Thus, the establishment of objectives becomes an integrate part of the management process.

To cast some light on the newest methods of appraisal as well as some of the newest thinking about it, the editors have included an excerpt from Edward G. Schleh's book Management by Results, *under the title of "The Basic Management Design: Management Objectives." A special study made by the management consulting firm of Booz, Allen & Hamilton, "Management Appraisal: Key to Building Executives," and the very useful and perceptive article by Arch Patton, "How to Appraise Executive Performance" are also included. The article by Mr. Patton, particularly, sets forth the latest approach—measuring management performance by assessing ability to set and meet verifiable objectives.*

What Is Work?*

WILFRED BROWN

Consider the following "want ad" from a leading Sunday newspaper:

> Shop Superintendent. Competent and experienced man required to take complete charge of sheet metal and machine shop engaged on commercial work. The aim is expansion particularly in the stainless steel field and applicants must be up to date in methods. . . .

Hundreds of such advertisements appear each Sunday, but only about 20% make any attempt whatsoever to describe the work required to be done. And in those 20% the description leaves much to be desired, as does the quotation above. A closer look makes it clear that:

1. *The ad is incorrect.* For example, the term "complete charge of" implies that nobody else in the company has *any* responsibility for the "sheet metal and machine shop."

2. *Nobody reading the description obtains any real knowledge of the work involved except through inference.* If the reader already has considerable knowledge of the sort of work done by superintendents of machine shops, he can make some reasonable guesses, but these may prove erroneous if the hiring company uses the word "superintendent" in an unusual way.

TOO GENERAL A TERM

The fact that particular "want ads" are vaguely worded is not important. The point is that advertisements of this kind are symptomatic of a more serious problem. Businessmen, in general, simply do not understand the exact meaning of the term *work*. People in industry have not yet reached the stage where they talk about work in objective terms. (My idea of a realistic job description is shown in Exhibit 1.) Many of our attempts to describe *work* are nothing more than descriptions of the *people* who do the work. For example, we refer in airy terms to managerial work, accounting work, skilled or unskilled work, and engineering work, and sometimes to boring work or interesting work, and so on. Obviously these are terms which are more descriptive of the type of person who does the work or his state of mind while working than of anything else.

Nor are we any better off if we move just one step closer to a specific definition. Suppose we say, as many companies do, that Mr. X is responsible for production or for sales. Are we not still misstating the facts? It is the board of directors who actually is responsible for seeing that these functions are adequately performed. The president in turn has to set up organizations to get these functions adequately performed at the many levels of the corporation. Separate individuals, subordinate to the president, work exclusively in the area of production or sales.

But as one descends the hierarchy of organization, it is clear that every person in the enterprise is responsible for some sort of work that is connected with these basic functions. Therefore, to say that Mr. X is responsible for sales or Mr. Y for production tells one nothing about the work either does. The real question is: What distinctive part of production work does Mr. Y do and in what terms is it to be described so as to distinguish it from the work done on production by other people in the company?

Better Breakdown   One answer has been suggested by the findings of the Glacier Project, so-called because it was conducted in my company, The Glacier Metal Company Limited,[1] which indicate that the work of any

* Reprinted by permission of the publisher from *Harvard Business Review*, vol. 40, no. 5, pp. 121–129, September–October, 1962. Mr. Brown is chairman and managing director of the Glacier Metal Company, Ltd., England.

[1] In 1948 Glacier Metal Company Limited, in collaboration with the Tavistock Institute of Human Relations, London, initiated a joint sociological project for the study of organization, supported by gov-

---

EXHIBIT I   Realistic Job Description

How might the actual work of a "shop superintendent" be described? Essentially, in specific terms which spell out the rules and regulations that he must observe, as well as the type of decisions which he, personally, is authorized and expected to make. Naturally, any job description cannot be truly complete, for work changes dynamically in line with the demands of customers, the availability of new methods, new plant, capital resources, and the skills and experiences of people. Nevertheless, a relatively unchanging hard core of duties and responsibilities remains, and this can and should be defined in specific terms.

SHOP SUPERINTENDENT

1. The shop superintendent is immediately responsible to the plant general manager and has an immediate command over nine subordinates (six foremen managers, three specialists—one for production control and one each for personnel and organization) plus an extended command over 170 machine operators.

2. With this team, he will be responsible for the management of a department consisting of _____ sq. ft. of factory space, with machinery and tools for the manufacture of up to _____ units of _____ per week.

3. He is allotted work programs by the general manager to be achieved at weekly intervals, with the requirement that products be delivered to stores on dates named, that all products meet specified quality standards, and that all are produced at the lowest possible expenditure of resources, which, in any event, should not exceed a stated total budget without prior reference to the general manager.

4. He must work within the range of company policies covering such matters as pay rates, holidays, relations with trade unions, manufacturing techniques to be used, quality standards, and records to be kept. In addition, he must adhere to the policy boundaries established by the general manager relating to overtime, nightshifts, pay, provision of services, maintenance of plant, purchases, analysis of expense, and so on. Since all these company and plant

---

role can be objectively and distinguishably described in terms of its prescribed and discretionary content.

By prescribed content we mean the things that the occupant of the role must do if he is to avoid a charge of negligence or insubordination. One of the characteristics of prescribed work is that one knows when he has completed it. For example, a manager may pre-

scribe that his subordinate produce for him each month a written report in four parts, detailing:

- Results of operations for the month.
- Developments in hand.
- Recommendations for changes.
- Problems on which assistance is required.

Although the content of the report is largely at the dictate of the subordinate's judgment (i.e., discretionary), there is no discretion given as to whether or not he renders such a report, and he certainly will know whether or not he has complied with the instruction. The manager may, after receiving the report, criticize its content as a display of substandard use of discretion, but he cannot accuse its writer of insubordination if it is on his desk at the due date.

On the other hand, discretionary work is composed of all those decisions that we not only are authorized to make but also are held

---

ernment research funds. This continued for three years and, at the end of that period, Dr. Elliott Jaques, who led the original project, assumed the position of Independent Sociological Consultant to the company; and the research continued, having a life so far of 14 years. For other findings stemming from this study, see the article by Dr. Jaques, "Objective Measures for Pay Differentials," *Harvard Business Review*, January–February, 1962, p. 139. Also see Wilfred Brown, *Exploration in Management*, 1960; and Elliott Jaques, *Equitable Payment*, 1961. Both books published by John Wiley & Sons, Inc., New York, and William Heinemann, Ltd., London.

EXHIBIT I   Realistic Job Description (Continued)

---

policies have been set down in writing, the superintendent must know them and either conform to them or immediately report any inability to do so.

5. Within these policies, the superintendent will carry the duty of making a wide range of decisions. For example, he must determine:

   a. How to allot work among his subordinates and judge the effectiveness with which it is carried out. If he is not satisfied, he must decide how to correct the situation: by criticism, training, advice, reallocation of work, or even by removal of the subordinate from the post.

   b. In the light of the program of work that he is given, what jigs and tools to order, what supplies to requisition, what level of overtime to allow, how best to use the service of his production engineers, and what priorities to set on the work to be done.

   c. What recommendations to make to the plant general manager of his resources that are, in his opinion, insufficient for the program of work he is given to do.

   d. Whether the rate of expense in his department is the lowest possible and, if not, how it can be reduced.

   e. Whether the expense created by his subordinates is appropriate and, if not, how it can be reduced.

   f. Whether the various analyses of expense provided to him are sufficient for his purpose and what changes to recommend if they are not.

   g. What changes (within policies set by the general manager) in manufacturing methods should be explored in order to improve output, quality, shorten throughput time, reduce expense, save material, and, so on.

   h. What changes in the policies set by the company and the general manager he should recommend, if any of these are inconsistent, in his opinion, with optimum efficiency of his department.

Note how different this is from the vagueness of the want ad mentioned at the beginning of the article!

---

responsible for making. As soon as a man grows familiar with this way of thinking about work, it becomes clear that although the mere carrying out of the prescribed content of work is the *sine qua non* of retaining the job, he earns no medals simply for obeying instructions. If he doesn't, he gets fired! Ideally in business, we are judged to be good, indifferent, or poor, on the basis of the quality of our decision making.

Discretion in Decisions   Many people in industry feel that the "top brass" makes all the decisions and that factory and office workers only do routine work which does not involve the use of discretion. Any objective analysis of a specific job, however, soon explodes this assumption. Take, for example, a filing clerk's job. Surely, we might think that there are no decisions to be made in this situation. But this is not so. For example, a filing clerk might spend considerable time deciding:

- How to rate concurrent demands for filing service coming from several sources at the same time; that is, which should be met first?

- Whether to go to his supervisor and ask for assistance to meet a temporary flood of work, or to allow himself to get temporarily into arrears.

- When to open new files for correspondence which was previously filed under a bulging "miscellaneous" category.

- Whether particular documents are or are not intended for filing in his center.

- How to develop original work methods in order to get through more quickly.

Immediate availability of back correspondence is very important to managers, but even the most thoroughly prescribed routine will not ensure this, because much depends on the wise use of discretion by filing clerks.

Differences in Responsibility There are decisions being made at all levels in a company. Further proof of this is shown by the fact that a manager will allocate work of varying difficulty to subordinates (all of whom, superficially, are doing the same type of work) on the basis of his personal confidence in their individual capacities to make what he assesses as being wise decisions. Actually, then, since each employee is given different levels of assignment, everyone does not have the same job, despite the fact that an individual may be labeled a tool designer, or an assistant director of marketing, or what have you. Therefore, if the employee who bears the most responsibility is not paid more than ones with less responsibility, a sense of injustice may properly arise. The best man should be rewarded fairly while the manager should assist the other subordinates in developing their own competence.

Thus, a manager's decisions set the bounds of his subordinates' work. A manager's use of discretion sets the prescribed content of the roles of his subordinates. If one examines the nature of the work of an entire corporation, it soon becomes clear that the work of a single operator in a production department is bounded by an ascending array of policies set by managers at ever higher levels above him. This situation can be most simply described diagrammatically, as in Exhibit II.

WORK AS IT EXISTS

Recently I lectured to various groups of students in the United States on the subject of work. I found, as I nearly always do, a strong tendency to assume that I was really recommending something new. But this was not my intention at all. Nor is it now. My whole purpose is to describe what, in fact, exists.

I claim that it is a fact that work has these two discrete components—prescribed content and discretionary content—and that, at the intuitive level, managers already know this. May I, therefore, emphasize that I am describing what I believe to be reality. I am not trying to tell people what they ought to do; I merely wish to describe what I and others have observed. There are too many "oughts" in the teaching of management, and not enough attempts to observe, generalize, and describe.

Gains through Explicitness I am trying to behave like a scientist, for the main task of science is to describe the world in which we live in ever more precise generalities. There is, however, some advocacy in my remarks, for I

EXHIBIT II   How Superiors' Decisions and Policies Set Bounds on Subordinates' Work

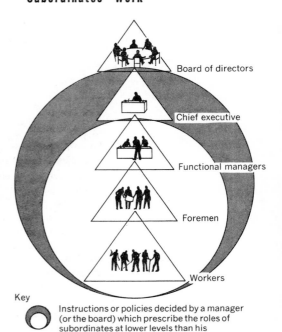

Board of directors

Chief executive

Functional managers

Foremen

Workers

Key

⬤ Instructions or policies decided by a manager (or the board) which prescribe the roles of subordinates at lower levels than his immediate command

△ Instructions or policies set by one manager which prescribe the role of an immediate subordinate or of the whole of his immediate command

believe it to be important that, as far as possible, we cease relying on intuitive knowledge and attempt to make this knowledge explicit in our minds, at least. Thus, it would seem to me to be a substantial contribution toward the effectiveness of the way in which we operate industry, if —

- Every manager could be more formally aware of the prescribed bounds within which he is working and the decisions which he alone is responsible for making.

- Managers became explicitly aware of the policies they set which bound the area of discretion allocated to *their* subordinates.

In our company, we have found it helpful, when a job falls vacant, to draft a specification of the *prescribed* and *discretionary* content of the optimum level of work which the manager in charge of that role will want the appointee to be able to perform. Those who become alarmed at this procedure often assume that the specifications remain static and are unchangeable by the manager. They assume, further, that such specification necessarily would *curtail* opportunity for a display of initiative and insight by the person in the role, which would introduce a degree of rigidity into the organization and inhibit growth in the amount of responsibility taken on by its members.

One of these questioners went so far as to say:

> The manager in charge of that part of our organization responsible for development of new products feels free to use his and his staff's inventive genius to think up new products and to spend resources in developing them that would keep our company ahead of competition, without going to his boss every time to ask if he can go ahead. If his role were tightly prescribed, he could not do this.

My reply to him was this:

> A wise chief executive prescribes the role of the manager responsible for the development of new products by stating that he has a budget within which he must work. If he feels that the interests of the company are best served by spending beyond this, he has the *duty* of raising the matter with the chief executive. He has an establishment of personnel, plant, factory, office space, and so on, which are available to him. And he works within a wide range of coordinating policies, which are set by the chief executive. Within such prescribed limits, he is charged with the responsibility of making decisions to optimize the probability of our products keeping ahead of competition. He also knows that if the company does fall behind, he is liable to be assessed as having shown poor judgment and, in the last analysis, will lose his job.

Under these circumstances I think that there is less danger of the product-development man in our company falling down on his job than there is that his counterpart in the company of my questioner will be unsuccessful.

BOUNDARIES ON DECISIONS

In a large company employing thousands of people, work has to be integrated toward the development, production, and sale of a broad range of products or services. Unless prescribed boundaries are set on the decisions that each individual can make, it is impossible to get each one of those thousands working toward a common end.

For example, if the company is developing an airplane, then the president must lay down the general specifications for construction:

- Is it to be a small executive aircraft or a 150-passenger airliner?
- What is its flight range to be?
- What is to be its weight and general performance, and the like?

If the president does not do this, his immediate subordinate who is responsible only for design may well go astray and produce something that does not fit the company's manufacturing capacity or is unsuitable for sale in the particular sector of the market in which the company is operating. Within the general specifications as to the type of plane, performance requirements, ultimate market, and so forth laid down by the president, the manager who is responsible for design must split up the job between his subordinates. He has to set prescribed limits on each of the subassemblies which he delegates to each of a number of subordinates so that those subassemblies will fit together in the total aircraft. If one man is responsible for the landing gear, he must see its relationship to the main fuselage, while the man in charge of tail design must envisage its relationship to the wing areas. Thus, all parts of the main task must be prescribed in such a way as to make them fit together.

Now, this can be clearly seen with regard to the task of designing a complex product. But the same prescribed boundaries on decisions are not so easily approved when applied to the framework of policies regarding the use of resources, pay, hours of work, status, and services within which every person in an organization must work. It should, however, be clear to those who have management experience that unless top management sets coordinating policies which prescribe the discretion of managers throughout the company, individual managers would be entitled to make decisions that could create chaos. For instance:

- If one departmental manager is allowed to approve excessive overtime while another has to lay off a number of people, serious trouble will arise.
- If a superintendent decides to reward a particular type of work at a level of pay which differs substantially from that paid for similar work in other departments, then pressures are set up for every other department to follow suit.

• If one office manager provides all staff
working at a particular level with private
offices and other office managers do not,
then considerable emotional pressures arise
in the company.

Clearly, therefore, some generalized control
with regard to many aspects of business has
to be brought into existence to prevent these
things from happening.

Indeed, whether or not companies are consciously aware of it, they, in fact, do have
policies which prescribe the manner in which
work is to be done and which bring about the
necessary degree of uniformity and coordination. And it is not a question of choice: they
exist. The only thing we can choose is whether
or not to recognize the existence of these policies verbally. Surely there is only one answer.
Without explicit awareness we cannot describe
what work we want of the individual; we cannot teach him his job; we cannot maintain
consistency of effort; and, above all, we are
unable to increase the level of work which we,
as managers, demand of our subordinates as
their level of personal capacity rises with experience and age.

Depth of Penetration   It is important for
managers to think explicitly about the nature
of work; for, until they do, the importance
which should be attached to depth of penetration of an instruction does not seem to occur
to them. Whenever a manager makes a decision and issues an instruction within the prescribed bounds set by his immediate manager
and by the organization as a whole, he should
consider whether this instruction is directed
only to those under his immediate command
(that is, those subordinates who report directly
to him) or whether it is also binding on other
layers of his extended command (all those who
are under his command and who report to
his subordinates). This, as I shall show, is an
important issue.

Let us take a simple example. A plant manager is worried about an increase in the
number of products which fail to pass final
inspection from his part of the plant. He
wishes to issue instructions which will start
the process of reducing the scrap percentage.
Now, he can do this in two different ways.

He can call together the superintendents
who are his immediate subordinates and instruct each one to carry out a critical analysis
of the cause of reject work in his own department. Within four weeks, each superintendent
is to present a full report to the manager stat-

ing the results of the analysis, the steps taken
to improve performance, and to list any recommendations, outside the bounds of his own
discretion, which would assist him in reducing
waste. The plant manager might further instruct each superintendent that until further
notice from him a progress report on operation
"reduce scrap" is to be in his office by eight
o'clock every Monday morning.

By phrasing his instructions in this way, the
manager has left the superintendents a great
deal of discretion for the action required to
correct the situation, but he has prescribed the
carrying out of an analysis and the sending of
reports to him.

Alternatively, the plant manager can himself
issue additional instructions, because he is exceedingly anxious about the situation and not
confident that his superintendents will achieve
the results he requires. He might, for example,
specify that, in carrying out the faulty work
analysis, each foreman must list every operation in his section which, during the last three
months, has averaged over 5% rejects. The
employees who perform these operations, the
tools, the machines, and the incoming material,
all are to be analyzed in order to locate the
cause and sources of the scrap work. Any foreman unable to cope with the analysis will seek
assistance, through his superintendent, from
the engineering department.

In this second case the plant manager has
greatly reduced the discretion of his superintendents by prescribing the work of the foreman also. Thus, the level of penetration of the
plant manager's instructions is down to his
foremen.

Influence on Subordinates   It is possible
for a manager to give an instruction which
prescribes the work of everybody in his extended command. In the Glacier Metal Company we use the word contraction to refer to
that element of a manager's instruction which
prescribes the work not only of his immediate
subordinates but also of all the lower levels in
his extended command. It refers to the idea of
a manager giving an instruction which reaches
down beyond his immediate subordinates into
his extended command, and, therefore, contracts or reduces the command of the subordinates. Some instructions given by managers
have this characteristic of contraction, some
do not. If any reader is in doubt about this
concept, I urge him to read or listen to some
of his own, or his manager's instructions.

Again, I am not advocating, but merely describing, what actually is. The important point,
however, lies in the fact that many managers

have no real awareness of the contraction element in their own instructions. Now, the contraction instruction always introduces a greater degree of uniformity than one which is addressed only to a manager's immediate command. Thus, it comes about sometimes that managers, who are emotionally very opposed to placing limitations on the use of initiative by their immediate subordinates or to the introduction of uniformity of practice, are, through lack of insight into their own acts, doing precisely what they wish to avoid!

Insight on Authority The terms centralization and decentralization are much used in industry nowadays but without an exact meaning. Using the notions of prescribed and discretionary work and contraction we can now, if we wish, give them precise content. For example, the giving of an instruction with the characteristic of contraction is a move toward centralization, but the giving of an instruction without the characteristic of contraction is a move toward decentralization.

In recent years, I have noticed that corporations have been breaking up big conglomerations of manufacturing capacity by building subplants hundreds of miles away from headquarters and reducing the size of the central organization. This could appropriately be called "geographical decentralization," but I think that such a plan is often carried out also in the hope of obtaining a higher degree of decentralization of authority.

Note, however, what often happens. The anxiety raised by geographical separation leads to the issue of far more contraction instructions than were previously felt to be necessary when the whole of the company's resources were situated at one site. Thus, geographical separation, which is often assumed to lead to decentralization of authority, has frequently limited the degree of discretion of the distant plant managers. Authority, therefore, has actually become further centralized.

FREEDOM WITHIN THE LAW

There is a widely accepted (though seldom stated) policy in industry about organization, which runs something like this:

Do not formalize the work of specific jobs closely, for, in appointing people to these roles, one has no means of prediscovering the differential ability of people, and therefore it is best to leave each individual to assume the maximum responsibility which he himself feels capable of discharging. By creating this situation, the innate intelligence and personality of each employed person will determine the work which he does, and this will ensure that the fullest use will be made of the capacity of the people employed.

Although I recognize the controversial nature of my belief, I strongly feel that this doctrine is quite unrealistic. I contend that the work of all jobs is bounded by prescribed policies. The only question is one of an explicit recognition of the bounds.

Many management theorists and sociologists use the categories formal and informal when talking about organization. Most of them approve of informal organization because "it provides freedom of action for the individual." But I suggest that there is a fundamental error in their thinking, based on their failure to perceive that all human work involves the use of judgment, choice, or discretion. As soon as human judgment is not required to get work done, then that work is mechanized. You can think up hypothetical jobs which involve no discretion, but you will not find them in reality. If this fact is not recognized, then it is easy to assume that a completely formalized or explicit organization deprives everybody of freedom to act.

Anxiety without Bounds If nothing is formalized in an organization (if there are no written or explicitly recognized prescribed bounds to the work roles), then clearly no one really knows what decisions he or anybody else is authorized to make. Every time an individual in the company faces a problem, his first thought would have to be, "Is it my responsibility to deal with this or is it not?" In the absence of prescribed bounds to his role, he does not and cannot know. Therefore, he will have to decide first whether or not to act. Then, if he decides to do so, he will have to make a decision on what action to take. But once he has made his decision, others may question his right to do so. His manager may "bawl him out" or may praise him for "showing initiative"; the individual does not know in advance which response he will get.

Making decisions is always difficult because there is always a lapse of time before we know whether or not we have acted wisely. But if we are to be judged, on every occasion, not only on the wisdom of our decisions themselves, but also on whether or not we were correct in assuming that the responsibility was or was not within our authority, then our work lives will be intolerable. We will live in a state of constant uncertainty about our own duties, which would unfortunately affect our work.

Thus, I personally believe that the more formalization that exists, the more clearly we will know the bounds of the discretion which we are authorized to use, and will be held responsible for using. Formalization of organization delineates authority or roles, and prescribed policies make clear to people the area in which they have freedom to act. Without a clearly defined area of freedom there is no freedom. This, in fact, is a very old story reaching down through the history of mankind: there is no real freedom without laws.

Some readers may tend to reject these ideas because the corporation that is their employer has no explicit policies—a circumstance enabling them to assume (through sheer courage) an ever greater responsibility. But these readers may remember that if one of their colleagues wants to usurp some of their responsibility through equal courage and initiative, then, according to their own set of rules, that colleague is entitled to do so! Presumably, an interesting battle will result! Likewise, if some of their subordinates decide to stop doing the job the superior expects of them, then what, according to their set of rules, should they do? It seems to me that they must either let the situation ride (which would be disastrous from a work point of view), or else move in and prescribe the work content of their subordinates' roles.

In short, there are always prescribed bounds to roles in organizations, but often they are not explicit. When they are not, there is an endless possibility of political maneuvers by company employees.

MANAGING CHANGE

Nowadays in business there is much talk about resistance to change. But change always involves alterations to existing policy. If a policy is not explicit in the first place, then changes are difficult, if not impossible, to articulate. Suppose that a plant manager faces a steady and dangerous rise in the level of expense in consumable supplies. He wants to halt this advance and eventually bring the expense back to a level which he considers to be reasonable. However, he has formulated no policy on the subject before, so that he does not know how many employees at various levels throughout the company are responsible for all the thousands of decisions which cause the expense. Thus, the first thing he must do is to determine which roles are authorized to use discretion to expend these supplies. In other words, the prelude to effective change is to make existing policy explicit.

The plant manager who does not cause this to be done many, instead, make assumptions about who is responsible for such expenditure; but if his assumptions are inaccurate, then his change of policy will be ineffective as well. Unless there is a reasonably accurate and well-defined appreciation of the current situation in the mind of the manager who wishes to introduce change, the decisions he makes about what is to be changed are likely to be inconsistent with reality. Consequently, his subordinates will act puzzled and anxious, and they will probably begin to resist change. If the manager adopts the conventional outlook, he will probably think his subordinates are obstinate, anxious, lacking enough imagination to see the benefits arising out of his ideas. This would be quite unfair.

I am not suggesting that there is no such thing as genuine resistance to change, but it is clear to me that much of the seemingly uncooperative behavior of people is due to their genuine concern about the operational folly of the proposed changes stemming from the lack of insight into the reality of the situation. Thus, some resistance to change is a result of organization and not of the character of people.

Forestalling Difficulty   Many years ago in our company we drafted, in conjunction with representatives of our employees at all levels, a series of standing orders covering such issues as personal expenses, travel arrangements, working overtime, shift working, holidays, sick pay, absence from work, appeals procedures, responsibility of representatives, and so on. Each order may have involved 20 to 30 people in many hours of work, but over the years these standing orders have saved us tens of thousands of hours, eliminated countless disputes, and delineated the discretion of hundreds of managers. They have enabled the managers to make decisions which are backed by clear authority agreed to by all parties. When circumstances changed, these orders were revised relatively easily because everyone could appreciate the fact that they had become outmoded.

This is just one of the many benefits which arise out of facing the reality of work and substituting explicit objectivity for the inconsistencies and haziness of intuitive thinking. My contention is that a similarly scientific approach to all phases of organization (such matters as role, role structure, sources of managerial authority, specialist work, appeal mechanisms, representative systems, legislation, and so on) would prove that many problems in industry and commerce believed today to be a result of the behavior of individuals, actually reflect sociological factors.

CONCLUSION

The study of management is not merely a study of man, involving an understanding of his character, his motivation, his aims, and his behavior in different circumstances. Such a study involves the structure of roles which make up an organization, the work content of those roles, the relationship among roles, and the manner in which this structure of roles and their work content should be adapted to the environment in which a company operates.

Thus, it is not sufficient that managers recognize only the psychological aspects of work. They must understand (and be able to describe) how work is bounded by organizational policies. By pretending that such limitations to our work do not exist—on the basis that by so doing we give initiative free rein—we often end up with employees who, undecided about whose job it is to catch the ball, allow it to fall between them.

By contrast, managers who define jobs objectively in terms of their prescribed and discretionary content and who are aware of how the policies they themselves set impinge on and bound the area of discretion of their subordinates will find that they have far fewer organizational and human relations problems to contend with.

Managerial Training   This more realistic view of the nature of work has a further, and vitally important, implication for the many institutions whose efforts are devoted to the training of managers. I am convinced that such training tends to emphasize the supposed irreconcilability of the organizational and the psychological aspects of management, and I am equally strongly convinced that a thorough study of management would in fact show that these two views are not irreconcilable after all.

When, in this article, I have argued that the behavior of an individual at work is partially a function of his structural position in the organization and the work content of his role, this does not mean that I deny the influence of psychological factors. As a matter of fact, I am quite willing to admit that:

- Different people put into the same role will behave in different fashions.

- Increasing the efficiency and bettering the relationships among people in various roles are also a function of the character and personality of the individuals concerned.

- The actual work established in any particular role must be varied (within authorized brackets) according to the capacity for work of the individual in that role.

What I would like to see, on the part of those involved in management training, is an equal willingness to admit the influence of organizational factors.

The training of managers should be concerned with both the psychological aspects of management and the sociological aspects of organization. To treat these as mutually exclusive alternatives is to try to construct a bicycle with one wheel. That many institutions concerned with the training of managers ignore the organizational aspects of the subject to an alarming extent is evidenced by the fact that they are without definitions of such social entities as manager, specialist, work, representative, policy, instruction, and so on—without, in effect, the kind of vocabulary of clearly bounded terms which has proved so essential to the teaching of the physical sciences. Without such a necessary means of communication about organization, how can a body of knowledge emerge? And in the absence of knowledge, how can teaching proceed very far?

40

Man and His Work*

ELI GINZBERG

The modern world faces many problems arising from man's industrial and technological development; unemployment; the obsolescence of skills; lack of work opportunities for the aged, young people, and minority groups; individuals' difficulties in adjusting to rapid change; the necessity of improving personnel practices; and the uncertain future of underdeveloped areas, to name but a few. All of these relate to the efficient use of resources in modern society, particularly human resources.

Except for the war years between 1942 and 1946, my associates at Columbia and I have been engaged in research investigations in the conservation and utilization of human resources since 1939. We have worked from the start as an interdisciplinary team. Our studies could never have been planned, and certainly not executed, by any one person. Though we have neither sole nor even primary claims to the findings that follow, they represent the highlights of what we have learned.

Our point of departure and the focus of our interest have been the centrality of work in human life. We believe that the best way to understand the behavior of human beings—the behavior of groups—is to start from a consideration of how work regulates the life of the individual, the operating units in the economy, and the total society. I have grouped our findings under these three rubrics: work from the point of view of society at large; work from the point of view of the employer; and work from the point of view of the individual. These are somewhat arbitrary distinctions but they do provide a framework for discussion.

The first proposition is a simple one: human resources are the key to economic development. This is a very old proposition which stems from Adam Smith's *The Wealth of Nations*. Our group has long believed that Smith had a deeper understanding of the inner workings of a dynamic economy than any of his followers. Our own adaptation of his premise is this: how people think about work, and what they consider to be important goals in life, will determine whether their country will develop or not. The notion that material resources are the key to development is fallacious. Brazil has tremendous material resources. Israel has very poor resources. The difference in the level of these two economies is largely a reflection of the differences in quality of the human resources of the two countries.

The kind of an economy a country develops depends in considerable measure on the kind of economy it wants. For example, people can decide to sit and fish. For a very long time, the French did just that. But more recently they decided that they wanted refrigerators and automobiles, and their economy has undergone a major transformation. Incidentally, this is largely due in my opinion to the export of American values. We are Americanizing the world. The key element in this proposition is that the values, attitudes, and general orientation of the people of a country determine its economic development.

The next point in my catena is the scourge of unemployment. Our work at Columbia began in the late 1930's with studies of people who had been unemployed for a long time. One study dealt with unemployment in South Wales, a region where people had been out of work for so long that they had forgotten the meaning of time; no day of the week was distinguished from any other.[1] Unemployment is a scourge because it destroys not one generation but two. It destroys the adults, and prevents their children from growing up properly. A country must have a national policy aimed at preventing and alleviating unemployment.

* Reprinted by permission of the publisher from *California Management Review*, vol. 5, no. 2, pp. 21–28, Winter, 1962. Mr. Ginzberg is professor of economics, Graduate School of Business, Columbia University.

THIRD FINDING

The third finding in this category of work as it relates to the society concerns the major transformation of the role of work in contemporary life. This is the first time in the history of the world that the masses have options, somewhat similar to those previously known only by the wealthy, about the kind of life they want to lead. They can decide whether they want to throw the major part of their efforts and energies into the job or into activities unconnected with the job. For the first time the mass of the population has enough free time and enough money to make such options meaningful. When I first went to California years ago, billboards urged us to "Work and Play." Now they suggest that we "Stay and Play"; soon they may simply command us to "Play!" This suggests the nature of the transformation.

The fourth finding can be subsumed under a heading called the reach of democracy. The notion that democracy relates solely to the political arena is an incorrect one. The values that people hold, the objectives that they seek, the motives to which they respond, penetrate all aspects of their lives. My children are constantly telling me that my decisions "aren't fair." Such complaints seem to have particular attraction for children brought up in a democracy. Children in an autocratic society are unlikely to challenge their parents on points of fairness. Likewise, the major thrust of trade unionism must be seen not from the viewpoint of wages and hours but in terms of control of work in the shop. This reflects the determination of workers in a democracy to control their own lives as much as possible and to reduce to a minimum the authority of others over them. This is the nub of the issue; it helps to explain the reach of democracy into the industrial arena.

DYNAMIC AMERICAN ECONOMY

The fifth point has to do with the moving escalator. The dynamic American economy makes it possible even for people who are standing still to get ahead. All one has to do is to step on the escalator. Many people who do not want to work very hard can still enjoy a substantial gain in real income. Time alone will push them ahead.

The next point relates to the family, which, having long been the consumption unit, is now becoming the employment unit. With 30 million women working for wages at some time during the course of a year, the question of whether a man will change his job depends increasingly on whether his wife must also change her job. The issue is no longer the optimization of a man's income and career opportunities but of the family's. This first showed up in the armed services. Married women officers would remain in the service only if their assignments could be dovetailed with their husbands'.

This proposition can be broadened to include considerations affecting the education of one's children. Several years ago I discovered that one of the big advantages that California had over the East in procuring technical personnel was its superior public education system. Many scientists and engineers, who generally are greatly interested in the education of their youngsters, have moved to the West not only because of the weather but because of the schools.

Next, I believe that work as a mechanism of social adjustment has not been properly appreciated. Much pathology in our society reflects interferences with people's opportunities to work. If you lock people in mental institutions . . . or men and women in prison . . . or young adults in schools, you almost insure their deterioration. Human beings require an opportunity for expression through work, which is the best tie between themselves and reality. We have failed to use work properly as an instrument of therapy and rehabilitation.

Now I want to look at work from the viewpoint of the employer. The first proposition is that performance must be considered as multifaceted. How people perform depends on (1) their capacities and limitations, (2) management policy, and (3) the pressures and opportunities in the larger society. The performance of an individual cannot be measured without reference to the kinds of policies governing his work and to the pressures in the society that are exerted upon him. Meaningful understanding of performance requires a multifaceted approach.

Our second theory concerns the adjustment potential. This represents a more sophisticated approach to performance than those which lay stress on emotional adjustment alone. The adjustment potential was developed because human beings are usually able to meet the demands that are made of them. This is particularly true if they are part of an organization and if their future depends on their meeting certain demands. A second element implicit in the concept of the adjustment potential is the availability of a wide range of jobs, so that an individual is able to choose one within his limits. One of the advantages of an

intricate economy is the wide difference between the demands made on a doorman and
those made on a president.

ADJUSTMENT POTENTIAL

Such elasticity helps the individual to adjust,
for he can determine his own level of aspiration and performance. Moreover, most human
beings have strengths that compensate for their
weaknesses. We tend to focus on people's
weaknesses and forget their strengths. The
adjustment potential takes into account the individual's compulsion to perform, the variations in the levels of aspirations, and the existence of compensatory mechanisms.

The third theorem is the vulnerability of
selection. Most personnel divisions would like
to solve their personnel problems through
selection, because they believe that then they
would have no further problems. But it does
not work out that simply. Selection always has
logistical implications. One can never select
better people than exist in the pool from which
they are drawn. Industry, for example, wants
creative scientists but the pool contains Ph.D.'s.
The two are by no means synonymous. Moreover, there are serious limitations to assessment. All one knows about a Ph.D. is that he
has gone through school and was able to give
his professors the answers they wanted. There
are no diagnostic tools for discerning the drive,
self-confidence, and special qualities that will
make one man creative and not the other.

SIMPLIFY PROCEDURES

The question of costs must also be weighed.
We contend that large corporations should
simplify their selection procedures. They should
ignore the upper 5 per cent of a graduating
class because most of these men will probably
not be happy in a large corporation, and they
should ignore the lower 15 per cent of the class
because they may not have the capacity to
work effectively. The personnel officers should
concentrate on those in the middle, paying
special attention to those who say that they
would like to work for a particular company.

The next principle is called deviation tolerance. In recent years in this country we have
misapplied psychiatric concepts in personnel
work. We have used clinical categories such
as misfit, unfit, unbalanced, unstable, without
really understanding the terms. There is no
direct link possible between the categories of
mental illness and work adjustment.

Moreover, people's emotional states vary.
Our study, *The Ineffective Soldier*, revealed

that many severely disturbed Army people
stabilized very quickly once they got out of the
service. The only importance of emotional deviations derives from the extremes, and there
one does not need subtle theories. There are,
of course, seriously disturbed people who cannot fit into any normal work group. But most
people are only a little disturbed and only
at times, and they can fit into most work
groups.

COMPULSIVITY OF POWER

The fifth point has to do with the compul-
sivity of power. In a society organized around
power some people spend a great deal of
energy playing the game of power. Large
organizations, profit and non-profit alike, are
characterized by constant struggles of people
to gain more power. The major skill of the
successful contestants often is not technical or
intellectual; it is political, and their advancement depends primarily on how well they
manipulate people. Some years ago, the Chairman of the board of one of America's great
public utilities commented that he could see
very little difference between his company and
Tammany Hall. Part of the continuing shortage
of good scientific and technical personnel is an
outgrowth of the way in which power and
rewards are distributed. If in addition to being
a good chemist or physicist an individual is
interested in power, he moves very quickly
away from the laboratory into the administrative hierarchy. He is not pulled away; he wants
to move into the arena where the payoff is.
In the United States we do not like to face the
reality of power and its influence on behavior.
But it is essential that we do, if we ever expect
to understand our society.

The sixth proposition is called the evaluation
trap. Most work is performed by groups, not
by individuals; hence it is very hard to assess
individuals. Moreover, supervisors assess the
supervised, and this results in serious contami-
nation of the evaluation procedures, for those
who do the ratings are the potential or actual
competitors of thse whom they rate. The more
able the subordinate, the more likely that the
evaluation will be faulty.

The seventh point deals with the accelerated
obsolescence of skill. Promotions in large organizations depend primarily on years of service. A man becomes a vice president or president of a large organization in his late forties
or early fifties. In a rapidly advancing scientific
and technological society men get close to the
top when they are already obsolete. At least it
is likely that their knowledge of the science and

technology on which the company's future depends will be out of date. Recently, at least one large American corporation has perceived this danger, and has taken steps to retrain its senior technical personnel who hold important managerial positions.

The eighth proposition is the creativity dilemma. The genius of American industry was the development of the mass production of standardized goods, based for the most part on simple line organization. However, we are now entering a period in which the production of ideas is essential for our further progress. The success of many companies will depend less on the operation of the plant and more on the efficiency of its research and development laboratory. The problem here is that we have an antiquated system of management. New, flexible rules and procedures must be introduced for the management of professional people. Professionals cannot be treated in the same manner as hourly employees.

CAREER DEVELOPMENT

We come now to work from the viewpoint of the individual. This includes a consideration of the individual's preparation for work. Our first contention is that occupational choice is a process resolvable only by compromise and in its later stages is more or less irreversible.[3] We have found that the process of occupational decision-making starts in the preschool period and remains largely subconscious until around the age of eleven. At this point it intrudes on the individual's consciousness, where it remains for many years while he explores his interests, capacities, values, and reality. Toward the end of adolescence—about eighteen to twenty—the decisions that are made become increasingly irreversible. It is too late for a senior in medical school to decide that he really wanted to be a lawyer.

In our current research on talent and performance we have discerned important differences in career patterns. There are those whose career development appears to progress without handicap, while others encounter serious impediments. Some of the differences may lie in different values held by people: some are willing to work for seven days a week, while others prefer to go fishing on their days off. Some of the differences may reflect external circumstances: one young man may have been deferred during the Korean War, while another is set back two years. It will be some time before we have classified and evaluated the complexities that we have uncovered in the process of career development.

ILLITERACY

The third proposition is one of fact; it relates to the pervasiveness of illiteracy in American society. Earlier studies disclosed that one out of every nine young men screened for military service in World War II was either totally illiterate or borderline literate, which meant that he could be trained only as a duty soldier. This is not "ancient history," however; the Commissioner of Motor Vehicles of North Carolina recently discovered that about 20 per cent of the applicants for drivers' licenses were illiterate. They were unable to fill out simple blanks. And this situation is not peculiar to North Carolina. Inadequate education is a particular characteristic of older workers, whose employability frequently is hindered more by lack of education than by considerations of age.

A fourth proposition is the infantilization of youth. We have elongated the school system to a ridiculous extreme. While I have a positive view toward education in general, I believe that many youngsters are forced to remain in school beyond the point of diminishing returns. I submit that by the age of fifteen, or the latest sixteen, many boys, possibly one out of every three or four, have learned all that they are able to learn from books, at least at this point of their lives. They may be able to learn more at a later stage. But at this age these youngsters need the opportunity to work; they need close relations with adults; they need to learn by doing and to earn some money.

These remarks also have pertinence for girls. One-fourth of all the girls in the United States are married by the age of eighteen; half of them are married before they are twenty-one. Since many stay in school until they are twenty or twenty-two, many marry before they have acquired much adult experience. I submit that this lack of experience may be related to the lack of permanence of many first marriages.

The next proposition is the inequality of equality. This doctrine relates to disadvantaged groups. If these groups are presented with the same opportunities as the more advantaged, they will continue to lag behind them in accomplishment. What they need are extra services, special help, so that hey can truly achieve an approximate equality with the more favored sectors of society.

Next is the desirability of a second chance. Adolescence is a period fraught with disturbance. It is impossible to communicate effectively with adolescents. It is not possible to influence them directly. Many young people will inevitably make decisions which they will later find to have been wrong. In a rich society like ours, it is important that they have a second chance. It is important to keep avenues open to them.

THE SEQUENCE OF CAREERS

The seventh proposition relates to sequential careers. To cite an unusual example: in Iran by the time a young person reaches fifteen he must be ready to start on a second career. The very young children who weave rugs lose their nimbleness by the time they are adolescents and must look for a second career. In the United States we have always had some experience with sequential careers, especially for those in professional sports. An athlete slows down by thirty, thirty-five, or forty at the latest. The necessity to shift from one major area of activity to another will probably become much more prevalent. Consider the instance of married women. By their middle thirties, they have finished having children and their youngest child is in school. They have many years stretching ahead of them—one-quarter of all the women in the United States will live to be at least eighty-five.

More and more groups will have sequential careers. Recently the Air Force has recognized that its requirements for pilots will drop over time. Hence it is writing contracts for pilots to cover a ten-year tour of duty. The lesson here for large corporations is to restudy their personnel policies to see whether they might not be able to encourage some people to leave earlier than they otherwise would—while they still have time to get in somewhere else.

The eighth point stipulates that only a small minority is work-oriented. Only a small proportion of any work group is really interested in working very hard. I submit that the world's work is always carried by a small minority. Management should seek to discover the work-oriented individuals. It is very difficult to force people to work, and this enhances the importance of locating those who like to. One way to do this is to allow more scope for self-determination.

My final point is that success is different from satisfaction. Success relates to the objective world, satisfaction, to the way in which a man feels about his work. An interesting characteristic of affluent societies which presents a problem is the large number of options open to people. The more successful a man is, the more chance he has to become dissatisfied, because of the many options that he sees but cannot exercise. Possibly it was arranged that there be some balance between poor and rich. The

poor are frustrated by lack of options; the rich, by an excess of opportunities.

Let me point out very briefly some of the more important implications of these propositions for public and private policy. In the arena of public policy the importance of a continuing high level of employment is the major implication. With a high level of employment, many problems can be solved; without it most problems become intractible. The most important single domestic challenge is to increase the number of jobs available. Even the number of mental patients is sensitive to the employment index: in good times, marginal people find it possible to keep jobs. The problems set out above relating to youth, minority groups, older people, cannot be solved unless employment is at a high level.

ESSENTIAL INVESTMENT

Next, in a world characterized by rapid advances in science and technology substantial and sustained investment in human resources is essential. There is much waste of the nation's scientific and technical personnel, stemming directly from the fact that the skills of many trained people have been permitted to obsolesce because employers would not invest in their future development.

Third, we need to experiment with work as an instrument for social adjustment. We need work-study programs for the nonintellectual youth, for mental hospital patients, for inmates of prisons, for older persons. We need new patterns of employment for workers too old to obtain jobs through regular competitive channels but too young to retire. We have demonstrated very little social imagination to date and it has been an expensive lack; we put people on the relief rolls but we are unwilling to secure them jobs.

Next, we need new designs for the more effective guidance, education, and employment of the "mature woman." This is the woman in her early or middle thirties whose family responsibilities are beginning to lighten and who sooner or later may be interested in entering or re-entering the labor force. Again, we are doing very little that is imaginative.

The fifth point is the tremendous need for improved articulation between the school system and the education and training provided by the armed services, industry, and other adult education units.

The above are five areas for consideration from the point of view of public policy. Now let me suggest five in the domain of business management. The first stresses the need to shift

MAN AND HIS WORK

attention from selection to assignment. I indicated earlier my conviction that selection is a weak reed on which to lean. Much more attention should be devoted to improving assignment and evaluation techniques. Moreover, indoctrination programs have become overelaborate. Some companies force a young man to spend a year or even more before he is permitted to get to work. My recommendation is to let him learn by working.

RE-EXAMINE THE SYSTEM

The second suggestion stresses the need to reexamine the career system. Thirty years ago the petroleum companies and some other large companies established career systems. At that time this was a progressive move. They said to the young man, "You come with us and attend to business, and your future will be secure." They established elaborate systems of deferred benefits, including liberal pension schemes. But this is the wrong tack for companies operating in the economy of the 1960's and 1970's. It should be made easier, not more difficult, to separate people who no longer are productive. A company will always, without even trying, accumulate people who have begun to lose energy and initiative. The problem is to separate people who have become liabilities because they block others from efficient performance. Recently, a junior college in California had the imagination to find good jobs for youngsters who were doing badly in their studies. Industry can learn from this example. It too should make special efforts to move people on just as fast as it discovers that it cannot use them effectively.

SPECIAL PROBLEMS

The third recommendation centers on the need to alter policies and procedures developed for hourly employees to meet the special problems presented by scientific and technical personnel. Many problems must be reconsidered: freedom to work, hours of work, freedom to publish, freedom to study. People who work with their minds cannot be controlled. They must control themselves. At best they can be encouraged. The incentive system must be reappraised and reordered, if necessary.

Even the ponderous Army recognized this in 1946 when it provided that a senior medical officer who remained in his specialty could go to the top of the Medical Corps and become a major general without having to assume administrative duties. I know of no industrial corporation where the top scientist is recompensed

at a rate that even approaches that of the chief executive officer. There is great need for basing remuneration on contribution, not on title.

The fourth point has to do with the urgent necessity for more experimentation with the restructuring of research and development. I do not think that every large American company can hope to build up and maintain a first rate research and development effort. They can maintain development laboratories, but there just is not enough talent available for twenty or thirty, not to mention fifty or one hundred, concerns in an industry to attract, on a full-time basis, the order of talent required to solve the more difficult scientific and technological problems that they face. We need radical new departures in the employment of scientists. Here we may be able to pick up a clue or two from the Germans, the Dutch, even the Italians, who have long been forced to economize in the use of scarce resources.

The fifth suggestion relates to the adjustments implicit in the transformation of work and the need for corresponding changes in personnel policies and procedures. For example, further studies are needed in such areas as assessing plant location in relation to the places where well-trained people prefer to live; better identification of the work-oriented person; introducing more self-selection for the work-oriented; deeper understanding of the reasons why workers seek greater control over their work.

In conclusion, let me say that our group at Columbia fully appreciates that we do not have mastery over all the propositions that have emerged from our research. Nor do we claim that all these findings are unique to our work. But we believe that they are important, and we appreciate that we were able to contribute to their formulation only because of a constructive environment that facilitated cooperation between the university, business, and government. The extent to which we as a people succeed in advancing knowledge of human resources and applying it will depend on the strengthening of such co-operative efforts. Basic and applied research must progress hand in hand.

REFERENCES

1. Eli Ginzberg, *Grass on the Slag Heaps: The Story of the Welsh Miners,* Harper & Brothers, New York, 1942.
2. Eli Ginzberg, James K. Anderson, and others, *The Ineffective Soldier: Lessons for Management and the Nation,* Columbia University Press, New York, 1959. (3 volumes: *The Lost*

Divisions, Breakdown and Recovery, and *Patterns of Performance.*)

3. Eli Ginzberg, Sol W. Ginsburg, Sidney Axelrad, and John L. Herma, *Occupational Choice: An Approach to a General Theory,* Columbia University Press, New York, 1951.

   Collateral reading for those interested in further study might include: *What Makes an Executive: Report of a Round Table on Executive Potential and Performance,* Eli Ginzberg, Chairman, Columbia University Press, New York, 1955. Eli Ginzberg and Ewing W. Reilley, *Effecting Change in Large Organizations,* Columbia University Press, New York, 1957; Robert W. Smuts, *Women and Work in America,* 1959; and Eli Ginzberg, *Human Resources: The Wealth of a Nation,* Simon and Shuster, Inc., New York, 1958.

41

*Motivating the Boss: The Key to Executive Development**

RALPH L. GILLEN and HERBERT HUBBEN

"Within the next five years, one third of my department heads will retire, and I don't know where to get the replacements," the president of a medium-sized utility company said recently. "We have had a full-scale executive development program that the personnel people have been riding herd on for several years, but I can't see any results."

Further discussion with this executive, however, disclosed that his efforts at planning replacements had so far been limited to approving the program and making a speech to his executives about self-development. Investigation showed that present department heads did not believe in the program that had been established, considered it too time-consuming, thought that it took them away from their operating responsibilities, and, hence, were not relating it to the company's operations.

The president who made these comments understood one vital principle, that a big difference between successful and unsuccessful executive-building may be the involvement and drive of the executive or near-executive himself. He did not understand that enthusiasm of this sort does not start by itself; it needs the encouragement of someone whose influence is important.

The top management of this company believed (and rightly so) that the primary function of any business enterprise is to conduct operations profitably, not to develop executives. But they failed to realize that finding and training managers is a key (if not *the* key) to the maintenance and expansion of profitable operations.

Developing executives is a slow process. There are many techniques that can be used, but all of them are designed to accomplish one major objective: to build an executive into a better executive by widening his experience, sharpening his decision-making skill, and strengthening his ability to understand and put together the pieces that make up a business. A good executive will do so in a way that will lead to profitable operations.

PROGRESS IN TECHNIQUE

Much has been written about executive development. Management literature has reflected grave concern over the short supply of potential business leaders. Considerable public and private effort has gone into the formulation and application of philosophies, programs,

* Reprinted by permission of the publisher from *Business Horizons,* vol. 3, no. 3, pp. 49–54, Fall, 1960. Mr. Gillen and Mr. Hubben are management consultants for the firm of McKinsey & Company, Inc., Washington, D. C.

courses, and tests to find and develop executives. Psychologists have developed executive recruiting programs; professional societies have often become swapping-grounds for exchanging résumés and job openings; professional magazines have studied and analyzed executive backgrounds, behavior, interests, and hobbies.

All this has been to the good. Attention has been focused on the need; useful techniques have been discovered and communicated; and as a result, some top executives have developed who might otherwise have remained buried in positions requiring less than their full capacities. Many chief executives in this country have come up the same way; presidents who started out shoveling coke in the foundry and managers of field offices or branch plants who started as clerks or as claims adjusters are not uncommon. But for every one of these who became an executive, there are hundreds, with perhaps the same intelligence, the same personalities, and the same potentials, who have not.

THE BASIC PROBLEM

What then is the problem? Why are executives still in short supply? Why are the available techniques not used effectively enough to ensure an adequate and continuing source of business managers? If the potential is there, why can't it be utilized? The answer suggested by the chief executive of a trucking company was that any man with potential and the drive to bring himself to top management's attention could succeed—as long as top management's attention was focused inside and down. So it may be true that lack of concern—continuing, tireless concern—may inhibit the opportunities of people down the line.

Others have suggested that business is becoming increasingly complex and that not all human beings can develop fast enough to keep up; that the courage, risk-taking, and enterprise necessary in an executive are being replaced by an obsession with security, stability, and conformity; and that a sharply increased standard of living has provided so much material well-being that dissatisfaction, the prime motivation for progress and ambition, is rapidly disappearing.

These conclusions are difficult to accept. Man seems able to grasp ever-expanding horizons of complexity. To the cave man the wheel and fire were objects of greatest perplexity; to King Richard the Lion-Hearted the written word was more than he could comprehend; and many of today's managers view electronic computers with fear and uneasiness. There is

also some evidence that new business starts are falling off, not because of less adventurousness, but because it takes increasingly more money and more paper work to start an enterprise. And the infinitely expansive nature of human wants overcomes the satiation of demand and the alleged loss of ambition resulting from a high standard of living.

We are not persuaded that lack of motivation or ambition to become capable managers is the key problem; but lack of opportunity and top management interest may be. The complexity of industry, the general desire for economic security, and the contented state of the economy make it difficult for the man with potential to get his head above the crowd, especially if his superior puts no premium on this. Top management encouragement has to be an active thing; it cannot be merely the statement of a policy of encouraging employees to qualify themselves for better positions.

In brief, the real problem is getting those in a position to do the job of developing executives to work at it; the techniques for building business leaders can have no real value unless the boss is motivated to use them. By boss we mean not just the chief executive, but every independent manager down the line who has responsibility for people's work and whose subordinates are not regularly exposed to headquarters or the front office. This includes managers of branch plants and sales offices, regardless of how little operating authority they may have.

THE ROOTS OF THE PROBLEM

In our competitive society, material achievement has long been the main standard of success. Recognition of personality, genius, scholarship, artistic ability, and idealism is usually subordinated to respect for practical results. In the business world, it is axiomatic that the successful corporate executive is most often one who builds profits, not one who builds people. It is true that building people can be one means of expanding profits, but it is not the usual standard by which performance is measured, not the one that the stockholders will strongly support.

In the face of the prevailing standard, it is hard to criticize the man who devotes more attention to increasing profits than to developing executives. At the root of a manager's failure to use the techniques available for building people is his consuming concern with current profits. His performance at a given instant will be measured largely by the current profit and loss statement; he is likely to test his immediate personal success by the size of his compensation, not by his contribution to the growth of his subordinates.

Is this wrong? If an enterprise is established to make money, or to provide a service, or to serve the community, why shouldn't the top man make these his own principal objectives? Why should he devote more time and effort to developing executives, when the scope and pace of current economic and political activity give him more than enough to do? Could he delegate this executive development function to someone else? These questions can best be answered by considering what an executive stands to gain if he does concentrate on developing people and what he is likely to lose if he avoids this job.

SUPPORT FOR PARTICIPATION

The thesis that the key to executive development is motivating the boss to active participation is supported by three propositions:

1. The growth and profitability of an enterprise depend heavily on the long-range planning capacity of its management.
2. The ultimate measure of an executive's success is the usefulness and long-term value of what he leaves behind.
3. Subordinates will not undertake active change or self-improvement without support from their superiors.

PLANNING FOR LONG-TERM GROWTH

It has been said that, in the field of government, the principal obstacle to effective public administration is the four-year term of the president. This is an obstacle the corporate executive typically does not face. He can plan many aspects of company, division, or plant operations for years ahead, confident that continuity, or inertia, will permit them to be carried out.

Excessive emphasis on current short-term profits, however, limits the extent to which long-range growth can be considered. If the success of a modern corporation is largely dependent upon practical and effective planning, the responsibility for planning falls logically on the top executives. Their function is to provide not only for adequate day-to-day results, but for continuing and expanding profits.

The long-range planning function must necessarily include careful attention to the development of executives capable of directing a business that is larger and more complex than the present one. The current man at the top, if he is to provide properly for long-range growth, must ensure that he builds even more competent executives than are presently needed.

The significance of this requirement is seen in the degeneration and ultimate disposal of many family businesses in which the founder has not ensured that his heirs are capable of handling a larger enterprise than he himself began. In one small machine-tools company, the founder dies suddenly. Only the heroic and unexpected efforts of an in-law, who was assumed to have no talent at all, forestalled complete chaos and permitted orderly and profitable sale of the company. The founder's concern with building a profitable business had left no room for the development of a sound executive structure, and his death forced disposal of the company, even though it turned out to be an orderly one.

Concern with building sales and profits now and postponement of attention to building people until later is natural. Long-range consideration of company well-being requires a reversal of this position, however, and this can be instigated only by the manager who is willing to devote the necessary effort to providing for the perpetuation and expansion of his business.

THE MEASURE OF SUCCESS

It is not difficult to accept the concept that a business will benefit if its top executive provides for its future managerial needs, even at the expense of attention to current profits. It is much harder to accept the idea that an executive himself will be better off, in the long run, by concerning himself with building people.

The fact that a manager's performance is measured by current results is not the only factor that is likely to cause him to oppose, at least subconsciously, the building of executives. Rather than ensure that his subordinates will grow, the executive may actually restrict their growth for a variety of reasons. The executive may be jealous of or uneasy about capabilities greater than his own; he may resent a rate of progress that exceeds his, or a youthful flair for handling responsibility evident earlier than was his own; he may be reluctant to relinquish authority, particularly if he anticipates a number of years of active work for himself or has any doubts about subordinates; he may fear the diminishing of his reputation as a result of the growth of the reputation of his subordinates.

These are natural reactions. Analysis of any individual will reveal one or another of the human weaknesses—pride, jealousy, insecurity

—that result in an unwillingness to accept the responsibility for providing for his own replacement and the replacement of those on whom he depends for current success.

For many executives, preoccupation with these considerations, as well as with the more legitimate and socially accepted ones such as increasing profits and sales, obscures the lasting advantage of building people. Few executives are so successful at building profits and amassing wealth as to ensure that such achievements will be remembered for long; Morgans, Rockefellers, and Fords are rare. An executive who is recalled as outstandingly successful is probably placed in this category because he has developed the organization through people who rely on his training and leadership to manage their affairs and those of the company successfully.

As a measure of success, the building of people to stand as conspicuous and productive symbols of an individual's achievements is much more easily attained by top men at all levels than are some of the more commonly recognized success symbols, such as profit-building and personal wealth. This observation becomes even more meaningful as the professional manager (who may have little or no share in the ownership of a business) replaces the owner "captain of industry" in making the day-to-day decisions that spell the difference between success and near-success. The economic facts of life—income taxes in particular—have made empire builders infrequent exceptions to the rule.

As a result, top men in business today have limited opportunity to achieve the success that is measured by the size of the businesses they build or the size of their estates. Despite this fact, few appear to recognize that failure to provide a "living legacy" in the form of trained people limits the extent to which their achievements, ideas, and philosophies will be carried on after their own active participation ceases. Current operations may also suffer, since lack of attention to executive development may put a damper on subordinates' incentive, or cause them to leave before their real contributions are made.

SUPPORT FROM THE TOP

People are inclined, on the whole, to be modest and to underrate themselves, even in their own minds. It requires faith in their potential and a measure of inspiration to bring them to recognize what they could achieve, and stimulate them to strive for it.

The executive who recognizes the basic importance of executive development to his business and to himself will actively encourage the progress of his promising employees. He will keep abreast of new techniques, such as appraisal ratings, replacement tables, and coaching, and will utilize them constructively. But he will also recognize that the tools and techniques for building a business through people are really not as important as the underlying philosophy. The significance of this management cliché becomes apparent when top men at all levels begin to recognize that executive development is not a job that can be delegated to the personnel director or the vice-president for administration; it is a job that every manager must do for himself. The bank president who knows each of his employees by name has no right to be proud of this fact unless he also knows a good deal more: What are the individual employee's capabilities? Where is he going? What will it take to get him there? And most important, does he know it?

Interestingly enough, this inventory of employees' abilities and potential will make possible a more thorough planning job. It will stimulate constructive thinking about such questions as where an organization will be in two months, or two years; what kind of people are necessary in order to get there and to stay there; whether these people are in the organization now; or where they may be found. Hiring experienced men from the open market is a legitimate business technique, but the prudent manager does not rely on it. The two-man hot-dog stand owner assumes that he can get better talent than he has by paying a little more. The 200-man electronics company, however, would be better off in assuming that executive development, not higher salaries, is the key to progress.

The president with the problem described at the beginning of the article—that of replacing his retiring department heads—should have been doing far more than approving a program and making speeches. He should not have limited himself to appraisal of his key subordinate's sales results or success in cost control. He should have considered the degree to which they were building for the future of their organizations and their people, setting tough goals for promising subordinates, analyzing their strengths and weaknesses, and providing for corrective and developmental training. It was clear, however, that the company's executives would adopt this policy only if the president convinced his department heads (and, in effect, himself) that the business would be better off in the long run if attention were given to these factors.

THE SOLUTION

The boss sets the pace and the organization reflects his attitude. If he sincerely believes that one of his principal responsibilities is building people—and works at it—the job will be done, to his own benefit and that of the enterprise. Despite elaborate executive development programs and verbal manifestations of top-management interest, little of lasting value will be accomplished without this belief. Conversely, even with rudimentary techniques, effective development of people is possible and probable if the top man believes in it and gives to it at least as much time and attention as he devotes to other activities. How does he go about it? Or, if he is failing to realize the need, how can a younger executive motivate him to consider the development of people as an important, if not critical, job? This question can be approached from two viewpoints.

THE TOP EXECUTIVE'S VIEWPOINT

What can the top executive do to demonstrate and carry out his belief in the importance of developing people? He may use any of several approaches:

Devoting time to direct and personal training by keeping up with what younger executives are doing, coaching them on promising projects and ideas, and periodically reviewing their progress.

Finding ways to observe directly how people perform through assigning them to special projects or to short tours of duty in the executive or division office, or by making them personal assistants to key executives for limited periods.

Insisting that people be promoted as rapidly as their abilities will permit, rather than following conventional seniority patterns. The occasional promotion of an able young executive over the heads of others can have a dramatic impact on motivation.

Taking aggressive steps to keep people with limitations from becoming obstacles to the promotion of others by encouraging lateral movements or by limiting the duration of assignments of promising men as subordinates to managers who have reached their capability ceilings.

Reviewing compensation arrangements and forms continually to be sure they are producing the expected results; recognizing that people respond to different stimuli and that selective use of a variety of forms of compensation and status symbols can harness individual drives and personal motives.

Bringing in from the outside people whose new ideas and ambitions show the younger executive that ability, interest, and initiative will be recognized, no matter where they are found.

On the other hand, what can the younger executive do to stimulate his superior to greater concern over developing people for the future? Tactfully used, the following approaches provide a range of opportunities:

Writing articles on executive development to demonstrate concern about personal growth and ways to achieve it, and making sure they are seen by the boss.

Initiating demands for coaching, rotation, and periodic evaluation to assure that there is no confusion about personal interests, aims, and progress.

Insisting on room for growth by identifying and expressing interest in functions, positions, or locations that offer opportunities for development.

Finding out what motivates the higher executive and demonstrating to him that by encouraging his employees to assume more responsibility, he will have more time for those things he needs and likes to do.

Volunteering for special projects or studies that promise to broaden him through his learning new skills, meeting new problems, or contacting new people.

Bringing in new ideas constantly, even at the risk of having many of them rejected. This will demonstrate that originality and initiative still exist in the organization and that the executive will not need to look elsewhere for his future managers.

Viewed separately or undertaken sporadically, none of these approaches is earth-shaking. The motivation of present executives and the development of new ones is a long process. Immediately discernible results from any one or even several actions are unlikely. Persistent effort, tact, and perception are necessary for executives who seek to stimulate the development of people in their organization, and for those who want to motivate their superiors to increase their emphasis on this activity. Although there is no easy way to achieve the objective, no other program is likely to pay off as well.

Toward Better Use of Psychological Testing*

J. WATSON WILSON

As many a high school student can gleefully point out, none of our "laws" of aerodynamics is capable of explaining just how it is that the bumble bee flies. The fact of the matter is, according to some of these laws the bumble bee cannot possibly fly at all. Luckily, the bumble bee, as he blithely wings his way, knows nothing about aerodynamics and assuredly cares even less.

Psychologists occasionally find themselves in the same embarrassing position as the aerodynamicists, for there are some people who succeed brilliantly at jobs that psychological tests will "prove" they are unfitted for. This does not mean that the laws of psychometrics should be ignored any more than the case of the bumble bee means that there is something fundamentally wrong with the design of our airplanes. Rather, it indicates that we do not yet understand the laws of testing as well as we might. Unfortunately, the inadequacy of our present knowledge often leads to rashness, rather than caution, in the use of tests. Thus the flames of controversy over the value of testing, which have burned ever since tests were introduced into industry shortly after World War I, are stoked ever higher.

As in many controversies, atypical instances are frequently cited.

There is the example of the tense, shy young man who got the bright idea of becoming an insurance salesman in order to overcome his timidity and self-consciousness. His test scores, taking no account of his determination, predicted failure. Within three years, he joined the elite group of million-dollar producers.

Or take the case of a company that selected its salesmen by means of a very expensive mail-order testing program. The tests were accompanied by great claims to objectivity on the grounds that the people who interpreted them never saw the company or its candidates. They had objectivity to be sure, but some very elementary research proved that this particular company would have done better to hire men turned down by the tests than to hire those that the tests recommended, for the test scores showed a negative correlation with on-the-job performance.

Some years ago—to take just one more example—the agency vice president of a large insurance company offered a psychologist $100,000 to study one of its salesmen, who had sold more than a million dollars' worth of life insurance in his first ten months of employment. All the psychologist had to do for his tidy fee was to find out what made this man a million-dollar producer and devise a test that would uncover others just like him. The psychologist was flattered, but had to refuse the offer. Similar performance on the part of different individuals, he explained, may stem from very different personality characteristics—especially as one moves up the occupational scale from the more specific jobs to the more abstract, or creative, ones.

These anecdotes illustrate some of the more basic things that need to be said about tests and testing.

THE IMPORTANCE OF INDIVIDUAL DIFFERENCES

The most important point is that it is people who are being tested, and people differ. They differ in such general abilities as intelligence. They differ in aptitudes and talents, both general and specific. They differ in interest and temperament and motivation. Moreover, what accounts for one man's success or failure may be very different from what accounts for another's, and the ways in which a

* Reprinted by permission of the publisher from *Personnel*, vol. 39, no. 3, pp. 55–62, May–June, 1962. Mr. Wilson is managing partner of Nordli, Wilson Associates, of Westport, Connecticut.

certain individual differs from other people may be an asset or a liability to his employer, depending on the job he is in, the nature of the difference, and the degree of the difference.

Psychological tests, as part of a selection or appraisal program, may be a very important tool for managers, a means of helping them identify and understand individual differences and thereby perform their functions better. Tests cannot, however, be substituted for managerial judgment, or action, and they have limited value except insofar as they help the manager to judge well. Any manager who treats them as ends in themselves is guilty of abdicating his responsibilities.

In passing, it should be noted that the old concept of putting "square pegs" into "square holes" is quite obsolete. There are, of course, some people in this world who just cannot find a place for themselves. Generally speaking, however, people aren't square and neither are jobs. There are many things that any one individual can do and do well; hence, there are many people who can competently perform more than one kind of job. For this reason, tests ought never to be used for pigeonholing people, and their results ought never to be considered a final verdict on anybody.

GROUND RULES OF TESTING

If you are using tests or contemplating their use—and every company of any size should at least consider them—there are certain ground rules you should observe:

1. *The test data should be weighed in the context of the subject's history.* There are many tests whose results cannot be validly interpreted without consideration of other information about the person being tested. Trying to interpret these results in a vacuum is like trying to diagnose a man's physical condition on the basis of his height, weight, pulse rate, and blood pressure without knowing anything about his medical history.

Take, for example, personality tests, which are very popular and can be highly useful in many situations. A so-called adverse score on an emotional scale may mean any number of things. One person with such a score may find it hard to hold a job because his emotional problems lead to difficulty in getting along with other people; this will be reflected in a history of frequent job changes. Another person with an adverse emotional pattern may take his feelings out on himself rather than others and may have a history of ulcers or some other physical disorder. Still another with such a

score may manage his emotions in a way that does not affect either his health or his job history and may even make him a more diligent worker. Thus the personal history makes the bare test score meaningful.

The same holds true of interest tests, which are commonly used for uncovering vocational preferences. To interpret these tests properly, one must know whether the picture the individual has presented in his responses describes him as he really is or as he would like to be. The extroverted young man who sold magazines as a child and was a leader all through school will probably score high, naturally enough, in persuasiveness—but so may the introverted young man who wishes he were more outgoing. Only by interpreting the test data in light of the individual's history can you know what such a score really means.

2. *Know the job in question. Have valid and adequate job descriptions and analyses.* How specific or detailed your testing program is should be determined to a very large degree by job analysis. After all, tests are tools, and should therefore be chosen for their suitability to the particular selection job to be done. Whether you should use a typing aptitude test or a typing achievement test depends on whether you want to train your personnel within the company or to hire them fully trained. Whether you should use a test of clerical aptitude or one of general intelligence depends on whether the tests involved in the particular job at issue are highly standardized or not.

Unless your company is a very unusual one, it will not be able to find one test, or even one battery of tests, that can yield adequate information about all its jobs and all its applicants. This may sound too obvious to be worth mentioning. Yet I know one New England company where all prospective employees are given a test originally intended to select butter wrappers. As it happens, this company doesn't make butter, and its product is rarely wrapped.

3. *Know your tests—what they will do and what they won't do.* It is constantly amazing how little some people know about the tests they use daily. Yet every test worth using comes with a carefully prepared manual that describes its use, gives its reliability rating and probably its validity rating as well, and tells how the scores on the test usually run. Never —and I can't be too emphatic about this— never use a test that is not accompanied by information of this kind. Furthermore, don't use any test until you have mastered the material given in its manual.

A brief explanation of the terms "reliability" and "validity" is probably in order. A test is reliable if the person taking it today scores the same (or almost the same) as he would have scored last week or as he would score next week. Reliability is measured on a scale running from zero to 1. Perfect reliability is very hard to achieve, but ratings of .86 to .92 are fairly common in good tests. A rating of .24, for example, would be an indication of poor reliability.

The importance of reliability is obvious, and reliability ratings are easy to come by, for every good test is accompanied by such data. Yet one test that is now among the most widely used instruments for selecting salesmen has a reliability of only .14. Apparently, companies that will spend hundreds, and even thousands, of dollars evaluating the reliability of a machine they are thinking of buying will hardly give a second thought to the tools with which they propose to choose people to run the machine or sell its products—though on the basis of tests like the one just mentioned they make decisions that may cost thousands of dollars in salaries, advances, and the like.

Along with their reliability ratings, many good tests are accompanied by validity data. Broadly speaking, validity is an index of the degree to which a test measures what is it supposed to measure. A validity rating answers the question how well test scores correlate with job performance. To the degree that a sales test, say, is valid, the best salesmen will get the highest scores, the worst salesmen will get the lowest scores, and so on. Incidentally, all sales talks and rationalizations to the contrary, it is unlikely that a test with low reliability will have significant validity either.

Generally speaking, reputable test builders and publishers determine the validity of their tests by analyzing the scores of people whose productiveness or effectiveness is known. They publish the results of these analyses either in the test manuals or in separate research studies. *Don't use tests about which such data are not available unless you are prepared to do your own validity research.* Remember, in these test-happy days there are many patent medicines. Some are good, some are indifferent, and some are downright harmful.

Not too long ago, for example, the research department of a trade association conducted a validity study on a test used by many of its member companies. The test scores, it found, showed a negative correlation with on-the-job performance. Here too, the companies would have been better off in hiring the people who "failed" the test than they were in hiring those who did well on it. And yet, despite the published research of their own association, many of these companies are still using this test, which is, incidentally, a fairly expensive one. This sort of thing, which happens over and over again, is not only poor management; it is also a grave injustice to the people who must take the tests.

4. *Insofar as possible, use tests that have both general and specific norms.* Test builders who approach their work scientifically often provide data on the scores of different population groups. This enables the test user to compare his candidates not only with people in general but also with people performing the same job in companies like his own. Since we live in a competitive society, both comparisons may be important. The first one tells you how your candidates compare with the man in the street, and the second tells you how they compare with the people selected by other companies— perhaps your competitors.

One eastern manufacturing company has a policy of selecting only those candidates whose test scores are 50 per cent higher than the selection norms of other companies in the same business. The result is that its costs are lower, and its profits higher, than those prevailing in the industry, and the company itself is more stable than its competitors.

On the other hand, I know of another company that only recently installed a testing program. Management was appalled to discover that the employees scored much lower than people performing the same jobs in other companies. No wonder this company's unit cost was higher than that of its competitors.

5. *Don't confuse recruiting and selection.* The chances are, your testing program will be of little avail if you too readily move your hiring standards up and down to suit the market— particularly if you ignore test data when people are hard to come by. In times of a tight labor market, it is much better to intensify your recruiting efforts than to adapt your standards to the pressures of the situation. Once you have established sound and realistic test norms, stick by them; you'll find that the people you select will stick by you when the going is really rough.

A couple of examples will serve to illustrate the point.

One company, dissatisfied with the performance of the people it was hiring, installed a new testing program with norms that were correlated with what it considered satisfactory performance and were as high as those of other companies in the industry. When it began to give the tests to applicants, it found that only one out of twelve met the new standards—a far smaller ratio than it had been accustomed to. The tests quickly became "impractical," "unrealistic," and a lot of other things. The fact of the matter was, of course, that the tests had begun to highlight glaring inadequacies in the company's recruiting program. Management had not counted on this turn of events and, unable to face up to it, used the tests as a scapegoat.

Another company takes quite a different attitude toward the problem of selection standards. Its standards are high, and it refuses to lower them. When things get tougher, it recruits harder. Not long ago, the company went through a slate of 25 applicants to find one acceptable candidate. "We can afford to spend money on recruiting," one of its executives has remarked, "but we cannot afford to hire incompetent or marginal people."

6. *Have as high a "selection ratio" as you possibly can.* The "selection ratio" is the number of candidates available for each job to be filled. With or without tests, you don't really *select* when you decide whether or not to accept the only candidate you have. Genuine selection takes place when you have several candidates to choose among—and it is then that testing is most useful. It can be shown statistically that even a test of only moderate validity can be very helpful if you administer it to a large number of candidates—in other words, if you have a high selection ratio. Conversely, the most valid and reliable test in the world will be of limited value if your selection ratio is very low.

One company, recognizing the importance of the selection ratio, has a rule that at least three candidates must be considered for every position, be it the job of machine operator or that of vice president. In the latter case, the number of candidates considered may run as high as 50. The money this company invests in its recruiting program is returned many times over, as one can see from its balance sheet.

7. *Before adopting any test, try it out on your own employees.* Though this is often expensive and time consuming, it is an essential part of the testing program. There are two reasons for this:

First, trying out each test on a known quantity—your own personnel—will help you to choose the tests you need. You should never assume that because a test is applicable in some situations it is necessarily applicable in yours. Its usefulness may be affected by any number of subtle, easily overlooked differences in the job or the environment. There are, for example, dozens of clerical aptitude tests; some situations call for one test, others for a different test. In prescribing various tests, the trained psychometrician makes educated guesses that are usually right. Their rightness, however, should always be carefully and accurately tested in the situation in question.

Second, try-outs of all tests under consideration may yield valuable information about your present employees and even about your recruiting and selection processes. If the companies using the invalid sales test mentioned earlier had done some elementary research before adopting it, they probably would not have become so emotionally involved that they continued to use it despite its poor reliability and its complete lack of validity.

8. *Have your testing program installed by experts.* Approach the installation of a testing program with the same enlightened skepticism that the head of an accounting department would use in selecting bookkeeping equipment. Remember that knowing how to administer tests is one thing, knowing how to interpret them is another, and knowing how to install a testing program is yet a third. Unless you are training in psychometrics, or are willing to spend years learning psychological principles and statistics, don't make this a do-it-yourself project.

In one southern company, do-it-yourself installation has led to increases in the turnover and accident rates. The personnel man was eager to save money by cutting the amount of time new employees spent in learning their jobs. Reasoning that the smarter men are, the quicker they learn, he set high standards of intelligence for *all* the company's jobs. What he did not realize is that in many jobs too much intelligence is as bad as too little. Employees whose intellectual capacities are greatly above those needed for their work will soon become bored and will either begin looking for more stimulating jobs or become so inattentive that they are likely to have accidents.

9. *Avoid the role of counselor.* The minute some people see test data, they are unable to resist the urge to manage other people's lives.

Our world seems to be filled with people who mistakenly think that tests furnish the answer to every human problem. If your testing program is well designed, it may help you decide how well a certain person can do a particular job in your own company. Don't ask it to do more. The testing done for purposes of selection is very different from testing done for purposes of guidance—educational, emotional, or vocational.

> Not long ago, a young man who had taken a battery of tests in applying for a factory job consulted a psychologist to check the advice given him by the factory's employment manager. Among other things, the employment manager had suggested that, in the light of his ability, he should take advantage of the G.I. Bill and go to college rather than take a training position in a factory. The employment man had also told him that when he finished college he should study medicine. What the tests didn't show was that the young man was color-blind and had a history of fainting at the sight of blood.

All this adds up to the simple conclusion that psychological tests, like any other tool, can be effective only when they are handled well. Unfortunately, testing is so often misused that it is scarcely any wonder that its value is a matter of constant controversy.

Many companies, having begun by expecting too much of tests in the first place and ended by getting less from their programs than they might have done, may well be tempted to write off the entire testing movement as a bad mistake. Experience shows, however, that companies that choose their tests as carefully as they choose their equipment and do not delegate to tests the management function of making basic decisions will find them a valuable aid in the complicated task of making the best use of industry's most valuable asset—its human ones.

43

Predictors of Managerial Effectiveness*

THOMAS A. MAHONEY

The search for predictors of managerial effectiveness usually begins with an attempt to define and measure management potential. It is assumed that many factors influence and determine the future effectiveness of individual managers, and that management staffing decisions concern only potential for development and effective performance. Development of this potential and motivation for performance must be accomplished through means other than selection for assignments.

Two different approaches to the definition of effectiveness and the potential for achieving this effectiveness can be observed. Many stu-

* Reprinted by permission of the publishers from *Building the Executive Team*, Prentice-Hall, Inc., Englewood Cliffs, New Jersey, 1961, pp. 186–197. Mr. Mahoney is an associate professor in the School of Business Administration, University of Minnesota.

dents of management view managing as a general process common to all positions of leadership and management, implying that there are general measures of managerial effectiveness and that management potential can be viewed as a single phenomenon. This approach seeks the identification of predictors of effectiveness which can be employed in all managerial staffing situations. The second approach views managerial effectiveness as specific to the situation. It is argued that different situations require different management performance to be considered effective performance, and that each situation must be considered unique. Thus, a number of varying potentials must be considered in the prediction of effectiveness. Stogdill, for example, concluded from an examination of leadership studies that the characteristics of successful leadership in non-business situations vary considerably from one situation to another, implying that potential for managerial effectiveness is highly specific.[1] There is no need, however, to choose between these two approaches to the definition of managerial effectiveness and management potential; both are relevant. Certainly management and leadership situations do vary, and the most efficient predictors would be those related to the exact situation. The studies of management jobs and predictors of managerial effectiveness suggest that there are characteristics or elements of effective performance and measures of potential which are common to a number of staffing situations. We probably should expect certain common predictors of managerial effectiveness which can be used for gross predictions in a number of situations, and other more specific predictors which improve the efficiency of prediction for any single situation. The apparent conflict between these two approaches is not likely to be solved through discussion and speculation; further research and study of management potential are necessary.

Definitions of management potential and predictors of managerial effectiveness are found in company practices in the selection and appraisal of managers as well as in suggested programs for the identification of management potential. Some of these predictors are based upon hunches and others have been discovered and validated in specific studies. Practically every suggested predictor is used in the prediction of effectiveness in one or another situation, regardless of the demonstrated validity of the predictor. Certain of the differences among suggested predictors stem from the vague and inadequate definitions of effectiveness applied both in logical deduction and in validation studies. Other differences stem from the generality and vagueness of the concepts of predictors which are suggested. Consequently, there is a great deal of overlap, duplication, and conflict among the numerous lists of suggested predictors of managerial effectiveness. A review of the thinking and research concerning predictors can be useful in developing a firmer concept of management potential and in suggesting leads for further study and research. Certain rather general recommendations also can be drawn from this review.

No generally satisfactory system for the classification of personal characteristics and traits exists at present. The lack of precision in

many of the concepts and definitions of characteristics makes it possible to classify each characteristic under any of a number of different groupings. The classification employed here includes four general classifications: physical characteristics, abilities and skills, interests, and personality characteristics. However, certain characteristics are difficult to classify even with this broad, general system, and characteristics are rather arbitrarily grouped in some instances.

PHYSICAL CHARACTERISTICS

Various physical characteristics have been suggested repeatedly as qualifications for effective managerial performance and as indicators of management potential. Poor health usually is recognized as a deterrent to managerial performance, but few of the suggested physical characteristics have been found positively related to effectiveness. Build and physique sometimes are suggested as indicators of management potential, although studies indicate little if any relationship between them and effectiveness.[2] One study in 1918 revealed that executives in industry and government tended to be slightly taller and heavier than nonexecutives, and studies of leadership characteristics in non-business situations report a consistently low positive relationship between leadership and height and weight.[3] More recent studies comparing managers of varying degrees of effectiveness report no consistent relationship between managerial effectiveness and these physical characteristics, however.[4]

The most frequently mentioned physical characteristics of leaders in business and government concern vitality, energy, and physical endurance. Vitality and energy of the leader are suggested as aids to leadership because they inspire confidence and motivate subordinates. The energetic leader sets an example of work and performance that stimulates subordinates to like efforts. Physical endurance is suggested as necessary to permit the work and effort required in acquiring the knowledge and experience necessary for management, as well as the extraordinary physical demands of prolonged periods of work and effort. There are certain critical periods when the presence of the leader is required, and absence at this time can de-

---

[1] Ralph M. Stogdill, "Personal Factors Associated with Leadership: A Survey of the Literature," *Journal of Psychology*, vol. 25, pp. 35–71, 1948.

[2] See Glen U. Cleeton and Charles W. Mason, *Executive Ability*, The Antioch Press, Yellow Springs, Ohio, 1946; and Stogdill, *op. cit.*, p. 37.

[3] Stogdill, *op. cit.*, p. 37.

[4] Thomas A. Mahoney, Thomas H. Jerdee, and Allan N. Nash, "Predicting Managerial Effectiveness." *Personnel Psychology*, Summer, 1960.

stroy the manager's ability to lead. Health characteristics of effective management have received increased attention in recent years with the recognition of the physical demands of the job of the manager and with several studies indicating obesity, nervous tension, and heart trouble prevalent among executives.[5] However, more recent studies suggest that fears of special health hazards associated with management jobs probably are exaggerated. In summary, health and physical factors probably are important in so far as they may restrict the extraordinary attention and efforts required in management. Reasonably good health is demanded, but this probably is more a result of preventive medicine than of unusual qualifications.

ABILITIES AND SKILLS

Various abilities and skills have been suggested as predictors of managerial effectiveness, and measures of a number of abilities and skills are included in management selection and placement programs. Probably the abilities most frequently mentioned as comprising management potential are intellectual and mental abilities. Numerous studies have indicated a positive relationship between measures of intellectual factors and managerial effectiveness, and it is generally accepted that managerial candidates should possess above-average intelligence. While above-average intelligence appears important to managerial effectiveness, there is some doubt about the relationship of highly superior intelligence to effectiveness. Stogdill reports from his review of research that the intelligence of a leader should be above that of his subordinates or followers, but that a marked difference of intelligence appears just as destructive of managerial effectiveness as does lowered intelligence.[6] The exact nature of the relationship is not known, however, and further study is required to determine the relationship between markedly superior intelligence and managerial effectiveness.

Intelligence is a rather complex characteristic with many different facets which may be related in varying degrees to managerial effectiveness. Abstract reasoning ability is one facet

of intelligence usually included in discussions of managerial potential; the manager is expected to be able to summarize information, to generalize with abstract concepts, and to view relationships within the organization as abstract concepts. At least one measure of abstract reasoning ability has been found predictive of managerial effectiveness, suggesting the usefulness of this concept as a predictor in managerial staffing.[7] Mental flexibility is another such facet of intelligence, the effective manager being expected to accept new ideas and concepts readily and fit them into his total body of knowledge. Judgment also is an intellectual factor frequently cited as an element of management potential. Although the concept of judgment is difficult to define precisely, it appears to be the ability to consider alternative courses of action, draw the proper implications from each, and assign the proper weight to each consideration in making a choice. Several measures of judgment have been employed in studies of predictors of managerial effectiveness with positive results. General ability to learn and problem-solving abilities are additional facets of intelligence considered as predictors of managerial effectiveness. Various measures of general intelligence, which supposedly measure these facets, have been developed and tested in studies of management potential. Results of these studies indicate that above-average intelligence is a directly contributing factor in managerial effectiveness. Intelligence is a factor in other measures found related to managerial effectiveness, measures which also reflect influences other than intelligence. For example, level of education, grades earned in school, and age of graduation have all been found related to managerial effectiveness. In summary, intelligence appears to be a general predictor of managerial effectiveness, although the implications of markedly superior intelligence are not yet known. The measure of intelligence most useful in predicting effectiveness probably will vary with the situation, but some measure of intelligence should be included in most attempts to predict managerial effectiveness.

Empathic ability—the ability to predict and understand the reactions of others to various ideas and situations—is mentioned frequently in theories of management potential. It is argued that the successful leader must know and understand the feelings and attitudes of his followers, and must use this knowledge in

---

[5] See Jack Kirk, "R. I. P.: The Overworked Executive," *Journal of Commerce*, Dec. 30, 1953, p. 1; "Executive Health Problems: Fact or Fancy?" *Advertising Age*, Oct. 4, 1954; *Industrial Relations News*, vol. 6, no. 14, Apr. 7, 1956; and Life Extension Foundation, "Job Stress and the Executive: 6,000 Managers Report Their Experience," *The Management Review*, vol. 47, pp. 13–22, May, 1958.

[6] Stogdill, *op. cit.*, pp. 44–45.

[7] See Milton M. Mandell, "Research Findings in the Field of Supervision and Executive Selection," *Personnel*, vol. 27, no. 3, pp. 215–216, November, 1950.

shaping programs and directives to enlist the support of followers. In short, this ability enables the leader or manager to better secure the willing cooperation of subordinates and to motivate them to improved performance. Various attempts have been made to measure empathy and to measure the relationship between these measures and managerial effectiveness. Thus far, these attempts have had little success, either because the measures developed are not truly measuring empathic ability, or because empathy is not important in the prediction of managerial effectiveness.

Verbal ability is another ability mentioned frequently in theories of management and leadership. Verbal ability is considered involved in the ability to speak persuasively, the ability to write clearly and convincingly, and the ability to read—all specific abilities mentioned as important for managerial effectiveness. The manager accomplishes the objectives of his position through the direction and coordination of the efforts of others, a task which calls for communication. Thus, verbal ability, as seen in both receiving and transmitting information and communications, is listed as an element of management potential. Relatively little research has been reported concerning the relationship between verbal ability and managerial effectiveness. Various vocabulary measures—measures of one aspect of verbal ability—have been investigated and found related to effectiveness in specific situations.

Certain other abilities and skills are included in the concept of management potential for specific situations. For example, mechanical aptitude has been found related to managerial effectiveness in a number of situations requiring this aptitude. Specific knowledges also are related to effectiveness, again in situations where these knowledges are specific requirements of the position(s) being staffed. The majority of these additional abilities and skills appear to be useful in the prediction of managerial effectiveness only in those specific situations, however, and are not generally predictive of effectiveness.

INTERESTS

Measures of aptitudes, abilities and skills are indications of what an individual "can do," while measures of interests are designed to indicate what the individual "will do." Interests and values are considered important in the motivation of an individual and, thus, important in the prediction of effectiveness. Both ability and motivation or interests are thought

to be related to performance in a somewhat compensatory manner—strong interests may compensate for certain lacks in aptitude if the individual is motivated to exert more effort. The motivation required for effectiveness is expected where the individual's interests coincide with job requirements. Thus, we might expect to identify general interest patterns related to over-all managerial effectiveness and rather more specific interest patterns associated with effectiveness in specific job situations.

Interests and values might be considered part of the concept of personality, since they probably are related to various personality aspects, such as motivation, social adjustment, and initiative. We shall treat them as separate from personality in this discussion, since they are somewhat easier to define and measure than are other aspects of personality.

Various patterns of interests and values have been found related to managerial effectiveness in studies of management potential. In general, the effective manager appears to possess broad interests with particular interest in practical matters and in literary and persuasive activities and a lack of interest in mechanical, technical, and social service activities. The University of Minnesota studies of management potential indicate that interests of effective managers in general are similar to the interests of managers of sales, purchasing agents, and manufacturing company presidents; they are dissimilar to the interests of men engaged in the biological sciences and in technical crafts.[8] Another study, this one within a large retail organization, indicates that effective managers tend to have high economic and political interests and relatively low aesthetic interests.[9] Important differences in interests of effective managers in different types of work also were indicated in this study. By comparison, effective managers within government appear to have high theoretical and social values and relatively low economic values. Several studies have indicated that effective managers in various job situations tend to have relatively broad interests, reflected either in hobbies or in extracurricular activities during high school and college.[10] In summary, interests and values of the individual appear to be an important element in the prediction of managerial effectiveness in general or in specific job situations. Interests found specifically related to the performance desired should be investigated and

[8] Thomas A. Mahoney, Thomas H. Jerdee, and Allan N. Nash, *op. cit.*
[9] Cited in Mandell, "The Selection of Executives," p. 267.
[10] *Ibid.*, pp. 270–272.

employed wherever possible, although the Minnesota study suggests that interest measures can be used with value in the prediction of general managerial effectiveness.

PERSONALITY

Personality is a complicated, vague, and ill-defined concept of certain personal characteristics. It commonly is viewed as the complex of attitudes, values, and traits which underlie individual behavior. There is no single integrated concept of personality, and most discussions of personality focus upon various characteristics considered as elements of personality. Certain of these characteristics refer to observable behavior while others refer to rather fixed traits assumed to be influences of behavior. Almost every conceivable aspect of behavior has been classed as an element of personality by one or another author; some 3,000 to 5,000 characteristics have been counted in various discussions of personality. Discussions of personality lack precision, as do attempts to measure personality characteristics. Part of this difficulty stems from conceptual and semantic problems. Many of the characteristics mentioned in various discussions undoubtedly refer to the same general characteristics, the disagreement stemming from the interpretation of terminology or from the fact that these listed characteristics refer to different dimensions of the same general characteristic or trait. For example, what one observer calls "aggressiveness" another observer might call "perseverance." A somewhat more basic problem in the examination of personality stems from the apparent inconsistency of personality characteristics; people do not display the same behavioral tendencies in all situations. Thus, a person described as generous and kind in one situation might appear stingy and mean in another situation. In short, we are not sure what personality is or exactly how to describe it. Nevertheless, there is a widespread conviction that personality characteristics play an important role in determining the effectiveness of a manager; certain characteristics are required for effective performance while others hinder it. Thus, personality usually is considered in assessing management potential and in predicting managerial effectiveness. We shall consider a number of personality characteristics commonly suggested as predictors of managerial effectiveness, recognizing that few of them have been tested and proven useful in this prediction. This lack of demonstrated relationship probably stems from our present lack of reliable and valid measures of person-

ality, although it may result from a lack of anything stable which we can class as personality and which is related to managerial effectiveness in fact. The personality concepts discussed here are generalizations based upon the many discussions of personality and managerial effectiveness. These generalizations are intended to provide a framework for our discussion and are not intended as a definitive classification of personality characteristics.

One grouping of personality characteristics, suggested as predictors of managerial effectiveness, includes the concepts of ambition, motivation, and drive-to-achieve. The potentially effective manager is described as possessing a high level of aspiration and a real desire for achievement; it is this which furnishes the motivation to undergo the necessary development and to withstand the pressures encountered by the manager. Several studies report the relationship between effectiveness and some measure of ambition or drive, although no generally satisfactory measure has been discovered. Indications of this drive may be sought in experiences, such as work during the individual's education and other early work experiences. It is difficult to suggest any single best motivation for managers, whether it be social prestige, money, family security, authority, power, or merely the thrill of achievement. In fact, the studies of values reported earlier suggest that the motivations will vary for managers in different fields of endeavor. It seems reasonable, however, that there should be some motivating factor which provides a real desire to succeed and which goads the manager to seek successful performance.

Another set of closely related concepts refer to the energy, drive, and activity of the manager. The effective manager has been described as an individual who works long and hard and who drives himself. These concepts also are closely related to the concept of vitality discussed earlier as a physical characteristic. Again, there is no commonly accepted measure of this group of characteristics, and little research which does more than suggest the predictive value of possible measures.

A third set of concepts may be described as including the concepts of self-confidence and social poise, freedom from inferiority, emotional or personal adjustment, and maturity. In general, these concepts point up the need for a realistic understanding of one's abilities and shortcomings and an acceptance of them. Several studies employing measures purporting to measure self-confidence and emotional maturity have found a positive relationship between these measures and managerial effectiveness, suggesting that measures of these concepts may be predictive of effectiveness, although, again, there is no general acceptable measure of these concepts, and any measure employed should be validated carefully.

Closely correlated with the characteristics of confidence and adjustment are the concepts of courage and decisiveness. In fact, these characteristics might be included with the previous group. It is argued that the effective manager must be a leader and must inspire confidence in others, and that courage and decisiveness are necessary for this. The effective manager is expected to make decisions, even unpopular decisions, and then to stick by his convictions. Despite the appeal of this argument, there are no conclusive studies indicating a positive relationship between courage and effectiveness. These concepts certainly would be difficult to measure and may already have been measured in the measures of self-confidence.

The successful manager also is expected to possess a sense of dominance. This is interpreted to mean that the effective manager must desire to lead and to direct, and that he takes the initiative in his relationships with others. He is not expected to dictate, but to dominate through leadership. Several studies have employed measures of dominance and report a positive relationship with effectiveness. Further study is necessary to determine the extent of relationship, however. It is entirely possible that extreme dominance, like extreme intelligence, may be detrimental to effectiveness as a manager.

The concepts of agreeableness, cooperativeness, and sociability comprise another set of characteristics suggested as predictive of managerial effectiveness. In short, the effective manager is described as a "likable" person. Perhaps it is this set of characteristics which tempers the characteristic of dominance. Measures of these characteristics are far from re-liable, and studies of their relationship with effectiveness are only suggestive of relationships.

A final group of characteristics refers to characteristics usually mentioned as most important in the determination of managerial effectiveness. These concern the integrity, character, and ethical standards of the individual. The effective manager is described as possessing a real respect for individuals and as conducting himself in accordance with this respect. He is expected to possess relatively high ethical standards in his dealings with others and in his relationships to gain and hold the respect of subordinates and colleagues. Although difficult to measure with any precision, this group of characteristics is accepted generally as a prerequisite for effective management. Probably the best measures of them are obtained through observations of behavior and experience, deviations from the required standards being easier to note than the exact degree of the standards possessed.

In summary, personality characteristics generally are included in any attempt to assess management potential. Few of these characteristics are defined with any precision, and they are quite difficult to estimate or measure. Research results to date are far from conclusive in the discovery of relationships between presently available measures of personality and effectiveness. This is not to imply that further research will not result in improved measures of personality or reliable predictors of managerial effectiveness. Rather, it should suggest that all assessments of personality characteristics be viewed with skepticism, and that little reliance be placed on predictions of effectiveness based upon these assessments. All use of personality measures in the prediction of managerial effectiveness should be carefully validated in the specific situation where they will be used.

An Integrated Approach to Management Development*

EARL R. ZACK

One reason, perhaps, why many formal management development programs fall short of the high hopes set upon them is that they lose sight of the fact that, so far as the organization is concerned, individual growth is not an end in itself but a means to an end—improved company performance, both now and in the future.

At Sperry Gyroscope, where we have been slowly and carefully developing our program over the past five years, we have always borne in mind that the ultimate goal of our management development activities is to give the customer a better product, faster, at lower cost, and at the highest attainable profit. In short, we are not in the business of developing people. We endeavor to help them achieve their fullest potential because we recognize that if we do not we shall one day find ourselves out of business.

Materialistic though this may sound, it is well in line with current thinking on the vexing problem of how to motivate people to top performance. Thus, in his recent book, *The Human Side of Enterprise,* Douglas McGregor has pointed out how essential it is for employees at all levels to feel that their personal goals are tied to organizational goals. One of the manager's most important functions, he stresses, is to create a climate in which the individual can best attain his own goals by directing his efforts toward attaining the goals of the enterprise.

And in *Landmarks of Tomorrow,* Peter Drucker said pretty much the same thing:

> An organization belongs on the sick list when "good human relations" become more important than performance and achievement.

* Reprinted by permission of the publisher from *Personnel,* vol. 38, no. 5, pp. 51–60, August, 1961. Mr. Zack is management consultant and professor of management in the graduate division of Pace College, New York City.

Our own concept of "management development" derives from this basic philosophy. As the company stated at the inauguration of its management development program in 1956:

> The growth of the individual is inseparable from the company's achievement of its business and operating objectives. Employees can best attain their personal goals in a company that operates at a profit and continually enhances its growth potential and competitive stature.

There is a tendency in industry to look upon "management development" as a "department" or as a guest-expert "program" complete with pat formulas, pushbuttons, and magic wands. Our own feeling is that if a company is to achieve its development goals management development must be a dynamic way of life for the entire organization, a continuous concentration by managers at all levels on the development of individual and organizational performance. Within this frame of reference, we have assigned the responsibility for devising and providing specialized tools and services to a company unit labeled the Personnel Development Department. The actual development of people, however, remains essentially a line function.

The stated objectives of our program are much the same as those of many other companies:

1. To bring the current performance of each supervisor up to the highest attainable level and to develop whatever potential he may have for growing into positions of higher responsibility.
2. To insure the availability of qualified managerial manpower as required to meet the organization's current and future needs.
3. To insure consistently high utilization of individual managerial capabilities.

The approaches we are taking to achieve these objectives differ, however, from those in general use. Before discussing these approaches in detail, it might be advisable to take a closer look at what the attainment of each one of the objectives entails.

Developing individual performance, whether in terms of the manager's current assignment or in terms of some growth spot for which he may be considered a short-term or long-term prospect, requires clear and specific identification of each man's strengths and potential, as well as of his development needs. In other words, it requires a system of performance appraisal aimed at pin-pointing the developmental activities that can help him to realize his potential, satisfy his needs, or both. In addition, it requires a high level of motivation on the part of both the man who is to be developed and the people who are, along with him, accountable for his development.

Insuring the availability of qualified managerial manpower requires the building and maintenance of an adequate managerial reserve. The appraisal and developmental activity just mentioned constitutes one of the crucial requisites for this. Also required is a continuous program of organization analysis that can provide a valid basis for assessing the company's manpower needs in both short-range and long-range terms.

Insuring consistently high utilization of the company's resources of managerial abilities requires that consideration be given to all appropriate people whenever a position becomes vacant. Thus it also requires the provision of some mechanism whereby across-the-board consideration can in fact be made.

Two–step Performance Appraisal So much, then, for what each of our objectives requires. Now let's take a closer look at the first one—improving current performance and developing individual potential. In the very first stage of this process, performance appraisal, Sperry uses a two-step approach: we begin by evaluating the manager's performance in terms of what he and his subordinate organization achieved during the period covered by the appraisal; only then do we look at the "how" and "why" of this achievement.

This is, of course, an "objectives-oriented" approach. Its underlying idea derives from the pyramidal nature of managerial organization. The chief executive is charged with the responsibility for achieving a fairly specific set of objectives that are in essence a summation of the business and operating objectives of all the units in the company. These objectives are usually expressed in terms of sales volume, profit margins, expansion and diversification of product lines, company growth, public and employee relations, and the like.

Simply because they do represent the objectives of the entire company, the responsibility for achieving parts of the set resides in managers at all levels, from the president down through the assistant foreman. This comes about as the end result of the process of delegation. (Accountability, of course, always rests with the manager who did the delegating.)

Since the company's over-all performance is evaluated in terms of how well certain specific objectives have been met, there is little or no point in evaluating individual managers in terms of stereotyped definitions of "what every good manager should be." It is for this reason that the first part of every appraisal at Sperry consists, as I have said, of an evaluation of the extent to which the manager and his subordinate organization are achieving their business and operating objectives.

In preparation for this, a statement of position objectives, including suggestions for the appraisal coverage, is drawn up by the Personnel Development Department in consultation with the manager to be appraised, his superiors, and managers whose relation to him is functional rather than direct. Copies of these documents are turned over to the manager and his immediate superior as far in advance of the actual appraisal as possible. The statement of position objectives becomes the basis for a series of discussions in which they draw up plans, set specific goals, and augment the suggestions for appraisal coverage by the inclusion of concrete standards of measurement that, in their opinion, constitute realistic indices of the manager's performance.

An excerpt from a typical statement of position objectives and suggested coverage, as prepared by the Personnel Development Department, is given in Exhibit 1. This is for the position of Manager of the Surface Armament Division, a 4,500-man operation.

The second part of each man's appraisal, dealing with the "how" and "why" of his performance, focuses on his understanding, skill, and ability in the areas of performance common to all managerial positions: planning, decision making, creating, staffing, directing and controlling, human relations, and personal efficiency.

As part of this half of the appraisal, the manager's present and potential capacity for growth is evaluated. This evaluation, repeated in every annual appraisal, is conducted by an appraisal committee consisting of managers

---

EXHIBIT 1   Excerpt from Statement of Objectives

STATEMENT OF OBJECTIVES FOR APPRAISAL PURPOSES

POSITION: Manager, Surface Armament Division
ORIENTING SUMMARY OF MAJOR OBJECTIVES:

1. To attain an optimum profit, currently and in the long run, through the development, design, manufacture, and sale of:

    A. Naval surveillance and weapons systems

    B. Land surveillance and weapons systems.

2. To manufacture and provide at minimum cost, consistent with quality and delivery requirements, such foundry products as may be requisitioned by the various units of the Company.

3. To provide engineering computing services to other Divisions and to assist them in the development of digital systems.

4. To see that factors related to the operations and profitability of the Surface Armament Division receive proper consideration in all management decisions.

POSITION OBJECTIVE	PERFORMANCE (SUGGESTED COVERAGE)
Naval Surveillance and Weapons Systems	Has an optimum profit been attained from the development, design, manufacture, and sale of these products and services? Are the current picture and future outlook favorable?
(Objective 1A.)	Are any of the products, services, or contracts in this line in need of special attention to improve their profitability?
	Has the Company's competitive share of the total market for these products and services increased under his leadership?
	Are new products, services, relationships, and capabilities being developed in a manner calculated to secure, on a long-term basis, an optimum share of the market?
	Does he (and does his organization) keep abreast of new principles and techniques and pursue the development of those most applicable to the requirements of potential customers? Does he use the results of these preliminary investigations effectively in procuring contracts?
	Are customer quality and product performance requirements fully met and, when feasible, exceeded?
	Are customer delivery requirements and all commitments fully met?
	Are costs and prices competitive (to the extent that these are and have been under his and his subordinates' control)?
	Are any improvements desired in the development, design, manufacture, or sale of these products and services?

from at least the two levels of supervision above the man in question and a representative of the Personnel Development Department.

The function of this representative is not to appraise but to guide the discussion, keeping it factual and making sure that all important points are covered. At the end, he condenses the appraisers' comments into specific descriptive statements in what we call an "Appraisal Summary," which must then be approved by the appraising managers. This summary also includes information about the manager's age, physical condition, interests and ambitions, education, experience, and so on, supplied in advance by the manager himself, his superiors, and others.

The end result of an appraisal of this kind is a concise, documented description of the man, his performance, and his potential.

Counseling: An Exercise in Cooperation

In most management development programs, formal appraisal is followed by a counseling session between the manager and his boss. As numerous reports have abundantly testified, the superior is often reluctant to do this counseling, and the subordinate responds to it with either defensiveness or anxiety. Sperry's program does include performance-improvement counseling, but our approach differs in two major ways from most of the others with which I am familiar.

First, the discussions between superior and subordinate nearly always begin far in advance of the formal appraisal. As I have pointed out, our appraisal system requires that the two men meet before the appraisal session to set objectives and draw up performance indices. Post-appraisal counseling, therefore, is simply a periodic summary of the discussions they have been holding ever since they first began to consider and discuss the statement of position objectives for the man's job. It is also a formal supplement to the planning and problem solving that these discussions have involved.

Second, the chain of accountability running through the objectives-oriented framework of our program gives every superior a high personal stake in his subordinate's effectiveness. When he appraises the subordinate's performance, he is appraising part of his own performance. When he counsels the subordinate, his goal is to improve his own total performance. As a result, we have found that more and more of our managers are coming to see these counseling sessions as opportunities for joint planning and goal setting rather than for blaming their subordinates for poor performance.

This development counseling is supplemented by a variety of other methods, including guided on-the-job experience, job rotation, outside course work, seminars, visits to other companies, and in-company training programs. Individualizing the development program makes it possible to take a pragmatic point of view and selectively use whatever development media seem most likely to meet the individual's needs.

Group Training for Individual Development

This does not mean, however, that we reject the group training approach. Indeed, we are actively engaged in group development work, though we have tried to be as aware as possible of the dangerous traps into which group training efforts can easily fall.

I think it is generally agreed that there are two kinds of operational problems to which group training can be a partial or total answer. At one end of the total spectrum of problems are those caused by clearly identifiable lacks in knowledge or specific skills. These problems are relatively easy to overcome. In fact, their identification is almost synonymous with their solution.

At the other end are the operational problems whose outward symptoms are easy to perceive but whose causes are complex because they involve basic attitudes, sensitivities, and understandings. In dealing with these, we use participative training approaches, which, we feel, offer the best hope of curing the underlying diseases.

Our group training activities involve all levels of personnel, from hourly through managerial.

The guiding philosophy of our training program is a pragmatic one. It holds that training must be problem-oriented and that it is justified, therefore, only to the extent that, by improving work performance, it clearly contributes to the attainment of the company's basic operating and business objectives.

The Personnel Development Department conceives its role in training mainly as one of providing specialized tools, assistance, and guidance to training activities that can be adequately handled by line and staff people in the various divisions. There are, of course, a few kinds of training that require specialized knowledge or skills not to be found among the divisional people. These may be handled directly by the Personnel Development staff or by qualified outsiders—or the company may seek them from outside institutions and programs.

Information on training needs is obtained from several sources:

1. The Personnel Development Department's continuing studies of development needs as revealed in management development appraisals.
2. Supervisors and managers.
3. Division management.
4. Higher levels of management.

These higher managerial levels, consisting of officers, division managers, and people of similar rank, offer an invaluable contribution to the program—their deep understanding of current operating problems, of the company's over-all objectives and plans, and of short-range and long-range trends in technology, markets, and manufacturing processes. They are therefore assigned a dual function—providing information about certain kinds of current and projected training needs and, in addition, acting in an advisory and policy-formulating capacity.

Each manager's progress under individualized or group development programming is closely followed by the Personnel Development Department and is formally evaluated at the time of his annual appraisal.

Determining Who's on First   When appraisals for all the managerial people within a major unit of the company have been completed, the results are summarized in an "Organization Analysis and Manpower Planning Chart." As can be seen from Exhibit 2, this chart takes the form of a conventional organization chart but includes significant information from the appraisal of each man whose name appears on it.

Such charts give an overview of the company's various departments from a number of perspectives, including the strengths and weaknesses of the organization structure, the supervisory manpower resources available for meeting current and longer-range needs, the back-up situation for all key spots, and the blocked positions—that is, those that cannot serve as avenues of growth and advancement for people at lower levels because their incumbents are not themselves promotable.

All this affords us a basis for planning the development of individual employees and of the company as a whole. In other words, all the programs so far described—appraisal, counseling, training, and organization analysis—are integrated into a method of working toward the second objective of management

development—to insure the availability of qualified managerial manpower.

As I suggested before, achievement of the third and last objective—to insure maximum utilization of the abilities of all the company's managers—requires that all qualified people be considered for whatever vacancies may arise. To make sure that this happens, Sperry has issued a Standard Practice Instruction stating that every opening in a position covered by the management development program must be reported to the Director of Personnel Development, who then supplies the line manager (or managers) responsible for the final staffing decision with detailed information on everyone who ought to be considered for the post.

This regulation, I hasten to point out, does not involve Personnel Development's guest-experting managerial placements all over the lot. Nothing could have been further from our intention, and the practice is one that I would resist were it ever to be proposed.

Needless to say, in any but the smallest of companies a procedure like ours is feasible only if it is accompanied by some mechanism for processing personnel data. For this reason, personnel selection at Sperry is a three-step process that begins with the use of our "Personnel Register." This is an automated system for storing and recalling information on all Class I personnel—that is, all managerial people, all key nonmanagerial specialists, and all sub-supervisory scientific personnel. The Register contains an average of 150 items of factual background information on each of roughly 5,000 people. This information is organized in a manner that permits the automatic selection of everyone who meets certain sets of requirements.

Thus the Register constitutes a practical method of insuring that no qualified and interested person is overlooked when new projects must be staffed, open positions filled, or the company's capacity for taking on new business assessed. It operates as follows:

1. Each employee supplies data on his background, job interests, ambition, and the like on a multi-page "Individual Qualifications Form" distributed by the Personnel Development Department. These data are updated annually or more often, if necessary, on supplement sheets.
2. The information thus obtained is coded and punched on cards.
3. To obtain a tentative list of candidates for an open position, the requirements of the

EXHIBIT 2 **Excerpt from Dummy Organization Analysis and Planning Chart**

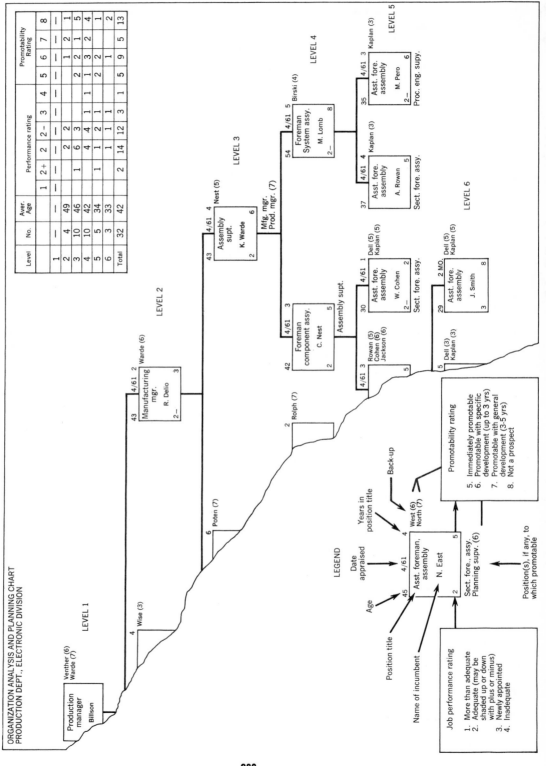

position are recorded on an appropriate form. They are described in the same terms as those used by the employees in supplying the original Register data.

4. The Personnel Development Department then uses these qualifications to control a search of all the cards in the Register. The end result is a list of the names of those employees who meet the specified requirements. This completes the first step in the search—the part based on specific background data.

In the second step, the Personnel Development staff examines its personnel files, which contain the Individual Qualifications Forms and data from performance appraisals. (Appraisal data on supervisory personnel are, of course, generated through the management development appraisal procedure. Appraisal data on non-supervisory personnel are generated through the Sperry Performance Development Plan, which was inaugurated in 1958.)

The third step in the selection process consists of personal interviews of all the people who survived the first two steps. Most often, the interview is conducted by the candidate's prospective superior plus anyone else who may be appropriate.

It is perhaps worth noting here that the selection process is related not only to the particular evaluations that emerge from our appraisal program but to the very first step in appraisal—the development of specific business and operating goals. Once the objectives of all our supervisory positions, actual or proposed, have been clearly delineated, each set of objectives is used to suggest the criteria that should be applied in searching through the Personnel Register and the appraisal records to find suitable candidates for the position.

In the few years of its existence, our program has made great strides toward creating a climate in which superior and subordinate recognize the commonality of their performance goals and the need for continuous joint planning to achieve them. In addition, it has proved a useful tool for organization analysis and short-range and long-range organization planning. Needless to say, no program so extensive as this can be said to have proved its worth in the short span of five years. Our experience to date, however, suggests that the approaches we are using can go far toward overcoming some of the major problems encountered in management development in recent years.

45

What Kind of Training for Tomorrow?*

BERNARD J. BIENVENU

"I have often reflected," Niccolo Machiavelli once wrote, "that the causes of the successes or failures of men depend upon their manner of suiting their conduct to the times."

Though the particular kinds of conduct

* Reprinted by permission of the publisher from *Personnel*, vol. 38, no. 6, pp. 8–17, December, 1961. Mr. Bienvenu is professor of management and head of the Department of Management at the University of Southwestern Louisiana.

Machiavelli advocated as being suitable to his times are hardly to be recommended here, the point he was making is just as applicable to the individual man today as it was in the sixteenth century. It is equally applicable to the successes and failures of organizations, both public and private.

To put the matter more simply, if an organization is to survive, it can do so only by orienting itself to changing circumstances. The significance of this statement need scarcely be pointed out, for it is generally agreed that the main objective of any organization should be to insure its own continuity and to insure it in an increasingly effective manner.

To survive over a long period of time, an organization must return more to society, in the form of material accomplishment and human betterment, than society pays in human and material costs to perpetuate it. It must, therefore, adjust itself to changes in society's needs and wants. A business organization, for example, cannot endure unless it constantly orients itself to the demands of society so as to furnish the type of product or service that society needs, at the price society is willing to pay, and in the quantity and quality society desires. Moreover, society insists upon receiving more from the product or service than the organization spends in human and material costs to produce it.

This basic principle applies not only to organizations of all kinds but to the various groups or activities within them and thus to the particular activity that is the subject of this article—training and development. To insure its own continuity, the training function must see to it that the returns it provides to the organization are greater than the costs incurred in its operation. The people in charge of training must be able to suit their own conduct to the times if they are to go on teaching others to do so.

What, then, are "the times"? The last 20 years have seen more changes than any comparable period in history. Scientific breakthroughs stimulated by World War II and the continuing fight for survival have brought forth more new products, new methods, and new ideas than had ever been thought possible.

Products manufactured five or ten years ago have either been replaced by new and different products or been so radically changed that the current versions scarcely bear any similarity to the originals. Principles recently held to be beyond dispute have given way to new principles, which will undoubtedly be discarded in their turn. The procedures and methods that were the last word in efficiency only a year ago are already outmoded. Tried-and-tested policies once thought everlasting have become part of history. Organizational growth, the development of rapid ways to process information, and advances in our understanding of human behavior have wrought drastic changes in managerial methods and organizational concepts. The introduction of new industrial processes has radically altered long-standing skill requirements, making the physical realm subordinate to the intellectual.

In view of the scope and rapidity of all these changes, it seems clear that a critical reexamination of the training function is badly needed. Have the assumptions and methods of industrial training kept pace with industry itself? Are they, in other words, suitable to the times?

SOME OUTWORN ASSUMPTIONS

Among the prevailing training assumptions one of the most basic—an assumption that is in fact basic to education in general—is that all people profit equally from training. This may have been true once, but there is much to indicate that in industry, at all events, it is true no longer. Because of the rapidity of change itself and the increased importance of mental skill at the expense of manual strength and dexterity, most industries are finding that they now need, and are likely to go on needing, a much higher caliber of work and supervision than in the past. For this reason, there can be but little profit in training employees of low caliber. It may be true that every employee can derive some benefit from training, but the effort and costs involved in training an entire workforce will undoubtedly exceed the results obtained—a violation of the basic principle of survival.

Moreover, a program of universal training can prove downright harmful, for it is likely to create dissatisfaction and cause serious problems if the impression is conveyed, intentionally or not, that training will result in promotion. In organizations where training really is synonymous with promotion, the training must be performed on a very selective basis or the organization structure will be seriously impaired.

Another basic assumption in need of reexamination is that all training is good, that training can *ipso facto* cure all the problems of the organization. This assumption is of course related to one of the prevailing dogmas of Western society—that education can solve all problems and cure all ills. Both assumption and dogma derive from the premise that all problems are the result of the lack of adequate formal education.

But this is fallacy, for there are many situations that training cannot remedy. It cannot counteract unwise promotions or ineffective methods, nor can it replace intelligent supervision, favorable environmental conditions, individual willingness to accept responsibility, and the like. Furthermore, when training is seen as a panacea, executives and supervisory personnel can easily cover up their own inadequacies by ascribing all their problems to deficiencies in their subordinates' training.

Blind faith in training often results, too, in the establishment of training divisions vested with the authority for developing people at the lower levels of the organization. This in turn often leads supervisors to conclude that training is no longer part of their responsibility. Such abdication, frequent though it is, is really very much like trying to delegate the authority for handling all human problems to the personnel department—something that would be regarded as preposterous by line managers and personnel men alike. Training and development, like human problems, cannot be completely delegated to a particular department, for they are by their very nature the responsibility of all supervisory personnel.

Even when this principle is recognized by top management, there is a good chance that the mere establishment of a training department will prove self-defeating, for line people often seize upon it as a chance to evade their own responsibility. The training director, besieged by requests to handle line problems and make and implement line decisions, had best tread very carefully lest he find that instead of developing supervisors and employees he is being developed by them.

THE BANDWAGON ASSUMPTION

The final assumption in need of critical review displays its fallaciousness as soon as it is made explicit, though it is probably responsible for most of the training programs now in existence. This is the assumption that since nearly everybody is running such programs they must be worthwhile. It should go without saying that the value of training ought to be judged not by its popularity but by its results and by the needs of the individual company.

In fact, a training program can be successful only if it is based on careful examination of the company's situation and its problems. In the final analysis, the program's success does not depend on feeling or fad; it depends, rather, on knowledge of what should be taught, why it should be taught, and to whom and in what way it should be taught.

The answers to these questions are determined by the internal conditions of the organization and, to an even greater extent, by the external conditions that affect its continuity. Clearly, then, the objectives of the program must derive from the total organizational picture and must be in tune with the most general objectives of the organization. In addition, they must take account of the temper of the times and the organization's environment, for only in this way can training and development be truly productive, solving the problems of the future along with those of the present.

TRAINING IN WHAT?

Training programs themselves, as has already been noted, are as badly in need of re-examination as are the assumptions that underlie them. In terms of subject matter, they fall into four major categories—training in company policies and programs, training in particular skills, training in economics, and training in human relations—each of which should be considered on its own.

Training in company policies or programs, the first kind, is really indoctrination or orientation rather than training and thus has very little to do with development and nothing to do with training for the future. Though programs of this kind fill an important need, they should not be thought of as giving any substantial aid to the development of the individual or enhancing his ability to contribute to the organization. In fact, they can be harmful to both parties if they try to "brainwash" the employees into conforming to the mode of existence that the organization thinks desirable.

When they are successful at this, the organization becomes a church or a religion, an object of blind love and absolute faith. Needless to say, the atmosphere thus created makes it very difficult for people to recognize the organization's faults or to perceive the need for change. Even if inadequacies are recognized, they are unlikely to be pointed out, for in the eyes of the "church" to be vocal about such things is to indicate a lack of love and a failure to apprehend the greatness of the organization; it is to be disloyal and therefore undeserving of consideration or advancement.

Thus when such "brainwashing" is carried on intensively, the maintenance of the *status quo* becomes more important than flexibility, and smugness and complacency replace humility and dynamism. The training does nothing to help the organization adjust to changing times; indeed, it is training for self-abolition.

The second major type of training—training in particular skills to be used on the job—is, like the first, indoctrination for a specific purpose rather than development. In essence, it is training for today rather than for tomorrow. This is not to say that such training is not advisable; actually, it is probably essential in most situations. But its aim is narrow: to guarantee a certain minimal contribution to the organization; and it does very little to help the worker contribute any more than the minimum. Moreover, if it lays too much stress on particular ways of performing the tasks in question, it will act to block the imagination and develop a resistance to change.

Training in economics, another popular type of formal program, cannot be considered necessary activity like technical training and is unlikely to yield returns greater than the efforts and expenses it entails. As commonly practiced, it is nothing but a propaganda tool, for most programs explain our economic system solely from the standpoint of the employer. This kind of presentation is generally regarded as deceitful by the employees, and thus, far from creating understanding and cooperation, serves only to create distrust. Indeed, it is rather naïve in the first place to think that a program in economic education can shift the loyalty of employees from their own group to the employer, for it is well known that pressures to remain loyal to one's own group usually prevail even over the individual's better judgment.

THE BOOM IN HUMAN RELATIONS TRAINING

The fourth type of training mentioned earlier, training in human relations, has been the great fad in American business and, in fact, in all organizations, since the end of World War II. Though it is commonly regarded as the solution to all organizational problems, writings and pronouncements on the subject exhibit nothing even approaching a consensus about its purposes or objectives.

For some, its objective is to foster individual and group happiness. For others, it is to enable the individual to adjust to his environment. And for still others, it is to win acceptance for the great doctrine of "bringing everybody along." Rarely does one find the purpose of this training expressed in terms of productivity and individual contributions to the organization.

Even when top management does recognize these as the major objectives of human relations training, the training programs actually carried out at the lower levels may work toward entirely different goals, for the conduct of these programs is very often given over to people whose natural inclination or educational background makes it hard for them to recognize the realities of organizational survival. As a result, a good many human relations training programs revolve around the assumption that the organization exists to serve the purposes of its workforce rather than vice versa. Given certain other conditions, management may well find itself being managed by its employees.

This is by no means the only hazard presented by human relations training programs. By making the employees conscious of frustrations that they never thought about before, the training may lead them to engage in constant bickering. It may encourage individuals to manipulate for their own purposes rather than for those of the organization. It may bring the workforce around to the belief, often advocated by human relations practitioners, that everybody ought to be given uniform treatment regardless of ability.

This is perhaps the greatest danger of all. If this principle takes hold, the organization's future will undoubtedly be bleak and may be brief as well, for uniform treatment breeds conformity and uniform mediocrity, both of which are inimical to the flexibility and adaptability upon which survival depends.

In sum, then, the four most common kinds of training do little to insure organizational survival in an age of constant and pervasive change. At their best, they are useful for the here and now. At their worst, they develop attitudes and habits that preclude internal change and growth.

THE NEW TRAINING

If this is so, then what *should* training consist of? It is obviously not enough merely to say that training should be concerned with developing flexibility and adaptability rather than with explaining the company's absence policy or extolling the importance of good communications. A brief examination of the broader educational context in which industrial training now operates should, however, provide some further guidelines.

This context is nothing less than American society as a whole. Today, more than half the people in our nation's labor force, including those engaged in agriculture, hold high-school diplomas, and the technical workforce is growing three times as fast as the total population. Because we have become an "educated society" and are constantly becoming still better educated, the kind of training that sufficed in the past is no longer adequate to our needs; for the same reason, the adoption of new training methods should present less difficulty than it has ever done before. As Peter Drucker has pointed out:

> . . . tomorrow, if not today, more and more of the people in the normal traditional organization, in the day-to-day operations of a business,

are going to be people with very high education . . . people who do everyday "line" work
and yet who are different in their background,
their expectations, and the way they work from
the people who did these line jobs yesterday.
. . . Their work is not physical; it is work of
the mind. The only way to increase their productivity is to increase the output and the
effectiveness of the mind. This can be accomplished only if we succeed both in making each
of these men more productive in his own right
and then in making this contribution more
effective throughout the entire company.[1]

The change of which Mr. Drucker speaks
imposes a significant new responsibility upon
the training function, for increasing the output
and effectiveness of the mind is, of course,
largely a matter of training. More important
still, it is a matter of a special kind of training
—the development of conceptual skill, imagination, and judgment. These three qualities
must take their place alongside the two already
mentioned, flexibility and adaptability, as the
chief concerns of training for tomorrow.

Admittedly, it is hard to say at this point
just how these aims can be realized. The principles of training outlined here are still in their
infancy, so that detailed suggestions for implementing them cannot yet be advanced. Some
general guidance may, however, prove useful.

To begin with, industry could learn a great
deal from the way in which educators are responding to the changes taking place in society
and in their own fields. Dean Stanley F. Teele,
of the Harvard Business School, reports that
at a conference in which he participated along
with educators from schools of medicine, law,
engineering, and other professions the following consensus was reached:

> There is now so much to know about medicine
> or law or engineering, that we cannot possibly
> teach a man to be a doctor, lawyer, or engineer
> in the years that we have to work with him.
> From now on what we must do instead is to
> teach him to think like a doctor, a lawyer, or
> an engineer and rely on him to learn as he goes
> along.[2]

In line with this thinking, MIT is now beginning to teach engineering as a concept rather

than as a skill. It hopes thus to enable its engineering graduates to move along with the
times.

If business organizations are to preserve
their continuity, they too must institute this
new kind of training. It must be used at the
lowest levels as well as at the highest, for the
organization as a whole cannot move forward
unless all levels are oriented to the future. The
foreman must be taught to think as a foreman
and to view his job in the widest possible perspective. The worker must be made to think of
his job in relation to the larger task of which
it is a part.

Instead of being taught a skill that will soon
become outmoded, the worker should be given
an intensive theoretical grounding (by lecture
and demonstration, for example) in the basis
and purposes of the larger task and should also
be acquainted with its various phases. Through
a rotation system he might even be given a
chance to work at each of these phases and
thus broaden his understanding of his work
and of its relation to the total production
process.

This training will enable the worker to think
about his job in terms of general concepts and
will increase his mental flexibility. By freeing
him from the narrow traditional view of his
work, it will also enable him to see the need
for change, to grasp new processes quickly, to
retrain himself when necessary, and to develop
creativity, judgment, and imagination. What is
being recommended here is a liberal training,
which should yield all the benefits traditionally
associated with a liberal education.

TRAINING IN WHAT'S YET TO COME

In an age of continuous change, training
inevitably becomes, as education has always
been, a continuous and organized process. In
essence, training has now become education.
There is no reason, therefore, why part of the
worker's time should not be devoted to directed
reading and study. Lectures and demonstrations
acquainting him with changes in his work and
in the industry should be conducted on a continuous basis. This training should deal with
changes anticipated for the future as well as
those currently taking place, for it is of utmost
importance that the worker's thinking be oriented toward long-term future developments.
Such an orientation will counteract the natural
tendency toward complacency and narrowness
and will also help to foster mental flexibility
and creativity, traits that depend in part on the
ability to foresee the future.

All this emphasis upon enhancing creativity

---

[1] P. F. Drucker, "The New Challenge—Managing the
Educated," in Dan H. Fenn, Jr., (ed.), *Manage-
ment's Mission in a New Society*, McGraw-Hill
Book Company, New York, 1959, pp. 165, 169–170.

[2] S. F. Teele, "Your Job and Mine: What Change Is
Doing to Them," *Harvard Business School Bulletin*,
August, 1960, p. 13.

at the bottom level may perhaps need some defense or, at the least, explanation, for it is often assumed that these qualities are necessary only at the higher echelons. What must be remembered is that the great bulk of any organization is at the bottom level, so that in the final analysis it is this level that is most immediately involved in the production of goods and services. Thus it is this level that is best acquainted with the production process and is consequently in the best position to recognize ways in which productivity might be increased. When, by training or environment, this group's thinking is limited to the immediate task, then the organization and, in fact, the entire nation are deprived of their most fertile source of new ideas.

Neither the upward trend in the educational level of the workforce nor the kinds of training advocated in this article will produce significant results if the worker is so closely supervised and his work made so inflexible that he has no opportunity to exercise imagination and flexibility. Indeed, the best way of developing these qualities is to force their use and to create an environment that encourages this and accepts the consequences. Workers should therefore be given as much responsibility as possible, and a policy of self-supervision should be followed.

SELF-SUPERVISION FOR FLEXIBILITY

This will of course necessitate some additional training at the supervisory level, which will find that the new policy demands major adjustments in its traditional operating methods. Whereas, for example, the supervisor has traditionally encouraged his workers to bring their problems to him, he must now encourage them to work out the solutions themselves;

instead of forcing them to follow a specific plan of work, he must allow them to develop their own.

The intellectual vacuum in which many workers are placed has tended to dull their ability to contribute to the organization. Self-supervision should help to replace this vacuum with a rich and stimulating atmosphere and should thus help the workers to make their maximum contribution.

The importance of developing an environment that accepts, and in fact demands, change should not be underestimated. It is well known that the educational productiveness of higher educational institutions is in large part the result of their receptive environment and their reliance on self-supervision. With industrial work becoming increasingly mental in character, industrial organizations will need a type of environment and supervision much like those of educational institutions.

Finally, it should be noted that, as John W. Gardner has said,

> More and more we are coming to see that high performance . . . takes place in a framework of expectation. If it is expected it will often occur. If there are no expectations, there will be very little high performance.[3]

All phases of training should therefore include efforts to develop an attitude of expectation. Creativity, mental flexibility, judgment, and imagination are more likely to be part of the worker's standard operating equipment if they are expected to be than if they are viewed as something above and beyond the call of duty.

[3] J. W. Gardner, *Excellence,* Harper & Row, Publishers, Incorporated, New York, 1961, p. 101.

46

What Management Games Do Best*

WILLIAM R. DILL

Today there are more than a hundred management games being used in executive development; they range from simple games that can be played at home as a substitute for bridge and poker to games that can keep teams of twenty men busy night and day for a week or more. Hundreds of executives have taken part in games at the American Management Association seminar, in university executive programs, or within their own companies. The self-styled "experts" on games have built up a large bibliography of articles and speeches in the last five years.

With games, experts, and opinions aplenty, there has been surprisingly little systematic talk and even less reliable evidence about what games teach or how they should be chosen or designed to need specific training goals. "Gaming" has been promoted and accepted, but sometimes with more enthusiasm than sense. Yet beneath the promotions and promises, there is general agreement that management games rank as one of the most promising educational innovations of the last few years and perhaps the most significant one in management training since the case method was introduced four decades ago.

Games can be used in programs of executive development in three ways:

1. To discredit old ways of thinking and to build up interest in learning
2. To give men experience with the problems that managers face
3. To help evaluate a manager's performance.

In brief, games can be used to stimulate, to simulate, and to test.

GAMES TO STIMULATE

When the American Management Association introduced its first game a few years ago,

it was undeniably fun to play. Their formula was a good one, and it has been imitated by many others: devise a game that is easy to learn but not so easy to master. Set it up so that the people who play it will have top management titles and will make top management "decisions." Play it in a situation where spirited competition among teams is encouraged, but where no team or individual is clearly a winner or loser. Play the game intensively on a full-time basis, for a day or a week when the players have nothing else to do.

Something that is fun to do is not to be scorned. It is obviously a fine innovation if your idea of executive development is simply to assemble people in an attractive place for a vacation at company expense. But it is also good for starting a more substantial program on the right foot—to get participants acquainted and working together, to remind them of the learning they still have to do, to stir them up and start them thinking. A game can set the stage for the work to follow. Likewise, the right game, administered with efficiency and showmanship, can later restore interest in a program where, for various reasons, enthusiasm drops off. In one of the most imaginative and successful executive development programs in Europe, a variant of the first AMA game is being used to help hold the attention of participants during the final weeks when other approaches to learning have lost their novelty.

If your aim is to stimulate the men in a training program, then the following considerations are probably most important in selecting, developing, and conducting a game:

First, the game should fit the men who will play it. It must be complex enough to be interesting, but not so difficult that it takes hours of advanced study to learn to play. It ought to seem like a reasonable test of their skills and experience. If it has to be built around a kind of industry different from the one they are working in, it is probably better that the industry be completely fanciful, rather

* Reprinted by permission of the publisher from *Business Horizons,* vol. 4, no. 3, pp. 55–64, Fall, 1961. Mr. Dill is associate professor of industrial administration and assistant dean of the Graduate School of Industrial Administration, Carnegie Institute of Technology.

than an approximation of an industry that they recognize and care little about.

Second, the game should be easy to administer with the given facilities (staff, space, computer, and so on). Teams may get a perverse satisfaction from an occasional machine breakdown or umpire's error, but it is hard to maintain interest and competitive spirit if teams have to wait long periods of time for results or if they discover that they have been the unfortunate victims of a "bug" in the computer program or an error in interpretation of the rules by a statistical clerk.

Third, the lessons that the game teaches should be fairly obvious and pertinent to the contents of the rest of the program. If, for example, a goal of the game is to break up players' traditional patterns of thought, you want a game that tempts players to follow their own prejudices but rewards them for taking a fresh and original point of view.

Fourth, the player should "respect" the game. Although this item has lower priority than the others, it is probably most exciting for players to look forward to taking part in a well-publicized game (such as the AMA, IBM, or McKinsey exercises) or in a game developed within their company. If the game is a widely used one, you may have the advantage of being able to compare the performance of your players with the records compiled by teams elsewhere. If the game has local origins, players may be more willing to accept the game's rules and challenge.

The games that are best as stimulators are not necessarily good simulations of what executives are called upon to do. Running a company involves more than working as a three- or four-man committee to make a dozen decisions every fifteen minutes about gross levels of production, gross investment in research and development, and the like. A manager has a more substantial job. At least one large company has dropped simpler games from its training programs because it could not get a reading on anything but their entertainment value. A developer of one of the best-known games admits that about the most his game does is to bring about what he calls "spiritual purification"—it loosens up men for other kinds of training.

GAMES TO SIMULATE

If the purpose of the games is to simulate the job of an executive and the problems he faces, specifications other than simplicity and fast pacing become desirable. Not all managers get ulcers, but being a manager is not at the same level of entertainment as a cold hand of poker or a game of touch football. Management involves hard work. It requires analysis and attention to detail as well as a willingness to make judgments under the pressure of time. It means an ability to plan as well as to act, to innovate as well as to operate in a stable environment, to explore and evaluate alternatives, and to carry out decisions.

Developing Skills   A game that aims to give a man the experience of being a manager is one that is designed to develop the following:

- The ability to recognize new situations for what they are—to question, to probe and to analyze before making assumptions or starting to carry out programs developed in another situation.

- The ability to set goals, to use these goals to distinguish important from trivial information, and to plan and control the execution of his own job and the job activities of others

- An unwillingness to sit back and work with only the information available to him, a skepticism about the quality and completeness of what he is getting, and a willingness to define what he really needs and to go out and find it

- An understanding of the relationships among specialized activities within a firm, along with a willingness to go after new concepts and to broaden his horizon of awareness and interest.

- A willingness to assume effective responsibility—whether as "chief" or as "Indian"—for the success of efforts that involve efficient and cooperative interaction among a large group of people with different kinds of experience and status

- An ability to assess and classify experience, to delegate work to subordinates, or pass it on to a successor in ways that will keep the organization headed towards its goals.

Such specifications call for a relatively complex game—one that provides players with a great deal of information about their environment; one that gives them the task of evaluating, interpreting, and perhaps regrouping this information; one that requires decisions at several levels, from long-range policy and investment decisions to those about specific problems within production, marketing, and finance departments. Such a game would also provide enough work to keep a large team busy and to encourage specialization of function and differentiation of authority levels within the organization; it would test a team's ability both to manage a going concern and to adapt to change.

An effective training game should provide its players with ample information, but not all of it in the form of direct accounting statements from a computer. Great amounts of information make the important problems hard to dig out and, in addition, make it difficult for one man to run the organization. Both effects can be accentuated further if the inputs to the team are divided, so that no one member of the team has direct access to all the material that he needs.

Most simple games present teams with accurate information at no cost. In a real training game, less information should be provided automatically than most games provide. More of it should be available on an optional basis, but at a price. Reasonable degrees of error and bias should be built into the information itself (and even perhaps into the functions that tell the team how much the information costs).

Players need not always know exactly what kinds of information are and are not available to them. Some experimentation is in order in giving players more freedom to pose questions to the umpires or to the computer about information they have decided they need.

Decision-making   A second important dimension of a training game is the decision structure that it provides. The measure of a good game is not the number of decisions but the number of kinds of decisions that a team must make. It is important, for example, to build into a game the opportunity to make long-range capital investments in machinery, buildings, and the like; but if you have built in such decision opportunities for rolling mills, you are adding little to the game by adding a decision opportunity for hydraulic presses.

The game should provide not only for making decisions but also for determining which decisions need to be made and for developing and implementing rules to simplify decision-making. In one of the AMA games, for example, the computer is perfectly capable of running the company and keeping it going on a routine basis. Executives do not have to tend to all decisions every "quarter" of play. Their job is to decide where their attention and participation is most needed and to set up new policies in these areas. In our game, players first have to learn what duties must be tended to "monthly" to keep their company going. Once a routine is established, we simply ask them to turn in decisions or decision rules for three months at a time. These must be policies or rules that "subordinates" can follow, though, depending on what the intermediate results are after the first and second months. They are judged not on the elegance of their policies but on the end results. They must explain their rules and policies to subordinates in advance of plays, but they have no further control on how the subordinates interpret the rules. Since they have no further contact with their subordinates for three moves, poorly defined or poorly explained rules will get them into trouble.

Environment   A third dimension is the environment of the "world" against which the teams are pitted, that is, the computer model or the rules that the umpire uses to determine results. This is important, for it is reflected in the kinds of information that the teams receive and the kinds of decisions they must make but it is important in other ways, too.

The world should be complex so that results will not depend inordinately on one or two kinds of decisions that the team may make. On the other hand, it should not be so complex that it cannot be analyzed and does not respond to action. An unresponsive environment may be a realistic imitation of some businesses, but it is damaging to team motivation. The world should include surprises for the teams, but these should not be totally unreasonable in their eyes. A random model—such as the McKinsey game uses—can produce demoralizing results for players whose experience tells them that the environment is relatively stable.

The environment against which players compete also ought to put a premium on action that is well planned and intelligently coordinated over a period of time. Procter and Gamble accomplishes this in some of their scheduling games by charging teams high costs for each change in the level of production; we have similar penalties built into ours. We also lag the effects of expenditures on such things as advertising, maintenance, and research, and the effects of hiring and firing on productivity so that actions have to be planned well in advance of anticipated results.

For some products, four playing periods are necessary from the time materials are bought until finished goods are sent to consumers. Other planning sequences cover up to a year or more of simulated play. Players on one team for which I was director projected forecasts of sales, income, and balance sheet position two to three "years" (24 to 36 moves) ahead in order to get their board's approval for a long-run dividend policy.

To meet the kinds of requirements we have been specifying, the environment almost has to be simulated by computer. Human umpires and clerks are too slow, too expensive, and too inaccurate. Some of the simpler computer games can be calculated by hand, but the time for doing so increases from a few minutes by machine to 45 minutes or more per move. The Carnegie game requires about 45 minutes of time on an IBM 650 to generate one period's results for three teams in competition with one another. It would be impossible to run except by machine.

Yet, although the computer is necessary for a complex game, our experience has convinced us that the kinds of things that a computer can generate provide only part of the environment with which a trainee should be confronted. One major shortcoming of most game experiments today, one that can be easily corrected within the framework of existing games, is that there is not enough attention to the live interactions that managers have with other persons even within the playing teams. Attempts have been made to provide more of this kind of experience.

I have already mentioned the attempt in our game to force players to develop instructions, policies, and decision rules that men who are not members of management can use; to teach these rules to those who will apply them; and then to live with the results of actions taken by subordinates in the absence of the players who manage the team. (So far, poor rules or poor training has led to passed dividends, unauthorized liquidation of investments, unwanted changes in production schedules, and disastrous pricing decisions for some teams.)

Members of the Program for Executives at Carnegie last spring did not apply to the computer for a bank loan; instead they applied in person to a team made up of faculty members and Pittsburgh bankers, presented their case, and negotiated the terms of the loan. The terms then became computer inputs and part of the team's record.

After several moves with the Carnegie game, Tulane University has confronted players with demands from a union representing hourly production workers for higher wages and other fringe benefits. A faculty member with long experience as a mediator and arbitrator in labor disputes represented the union and, under the threat of a strike deadline, negotiated new contracts with the game teams. The teams had to live from then on with the additional labor costs that the negotiations incurred.

Last year, in our graduate program, we asked groups of first-year graduate students who were not playing the game to audit the books of the second-year men who were. They combined a traditional audit with a general management survey and analysis. Several benefits of this are already apparent. In the view of a partner in one of the city's leading C.P.A. firms, the students who did the audit learned more about the philosophy, the tactics, and the standards of a good management audit than they could have learned in several semesters of accounting. Not the least that they learned were some of the problems involved in getting the management group to accept a report that was highly (and rightfully) critical of management. They came to appreciate the distinction between responsible and irresponsible criticism. The teams learned how their performance looked to outsiders, and they learned some of the standards to which they might expect to be held in the real world.

A game for use with federal government executives was developed by Norman Martin and John Howard Sims at the University of Chicago. It placed a great deal of emphasis on testing men's reactions to a day of crisis. A number of outsiders were on hand to harass the top echelons of management with news that one of their best employees was about to accept a job in private industry; with word that the Philadelphia warehouse had burned down; with unannounced visits from congressmen and the FBI; with a slowdown among the secretarial staff; and with assorted other problems. When the players were inept, the net result of a day's work was chaos.

In using the Carnegie Tech game with graduate students at Carnegie, Indiana, and Tulane, a board of directors was established for each team. The job of these boards was not to teach men how to play the game, but to question them on how they are playing it, and, as they learn to do a better job, to keep raising the standards by which their performance is judged.

Boards have been important for three reasons. First, there is a principle in learning theory that the points made explicit stick longer with trainees than the ones not brought to the surface by discussion, experience, reflection, or argument.

Second, the boards of directors can emphasize that analysis is as important as action for success in top management. If a man has to explain to an outside board why he thinks 50 per cent is a good dividend payout ratio, he is less likely to give an arbitrary figure than if he only has to justify it to himself.

Third, a key element to executive success is the ability to present and justify ideas to others.

Suppose we could trust our finance officer to do a careful job of analysis in arriving at 50 per cent as a payout ratio. In real life, his analysis may be to no avail unless he can get his superiors to accept it. The directors can stimulate a well-planned and substantial presentation of facts, opinions, and recommendations.

Considerations   The possibilities for other games exercises are many. For a program aimed at men who have had no supervisory experience, for example, why not give them the opportunity to hire, train, and control some clerical people to do routine accounting and analysis? Or if the game is rich enough and complex enough for players to employ men with knowledge of modern operations research or management science techniques, why not let them commission special staff studies, both as a means of training the staff men and of educating future managers as to the potential of these new techniques?

Another intriguing possibility is to permit teams to negotiate with one another over the long run on the licensing of products, the sale of equipment and buildings to one another, or the terms of mergers. If it can be done without creating lasting personal frictions among the players, it might also be instructive to let teams hire men from one firm to another, setting up an open market for managerial talent.

Personnel men and training directors have a major stake in the success or failure of management games; yet as a group they have contributed relatively little to the design of games. I know of only two games that involve indices of employee morale and that provide basic structure to generate employee grievances and strikes. I know of no game that really poses questions of organizational efficiency, except within the small team of players who make up the top management group. There are specialized games to teach concepts and strategies in marketing, production, and finance, but I know of none in personnel, labor relations, or organizational planning.

To get the most from a game in an executive development program, two further conditions are perhaps obvious but worth mentioning since they are often overlooked. First, there should be adequate time and leadership for discussing the results of the game and the experiences that players are having. The men who most need training are the men who do not learn easily and automatically from their own experience. Sessions may be held with individual teams at intervals during play of the game to review their progress in organizing and in working toward their goals. Sessions may be held with several teams present to discuss what are appropriate standards of team performance and, after the game, to compare the teams' objectives and strategies with their results.

Second, efforts should be made to integrate the game with what the men do on the job. Our experience at Carnegie shows that three kinds of integration work well: (1) asking players in discussion sessions to draw on their experience in the game as data for exploring the meaning of new ideas and concepts; (2) providing opportunities and incentives for men to use ideas and methods gained from lectures, discussions, and readings in their play of the game; and (3) examining the computer model in the game as a way of teaching players how companies and industries function in an economy and how to construct games and simulations of their own.

These, then, are the major specifications for games that are meant to simulate what the manager does. They are offered, tentatively, as plans that have worked well for us and for others. I want now to re-emphasize one theme that underlies them all.

My concept of what an executive development program should do and of what a game in such a program should do emphasizes hard work, a fair degree of stress for the participants, and an open (and, if necessary, a critical) evaluation of how they are doing. For various reasons at Carnegie, we have pushed our students harder in playing the management game than we have our executives. The executives have more freedom to pace themselves and to set their own standards of performance. It is not particularly surprising, as a result, that a few executive teams have only half-played the game and that the best teams in a comparative match have been made up of students, not executives.

These are harsh words to implement where senior executives as students may outrank the trainer and where they are looking for a respite from the stress and strain of their regular jobs. On the other hand, it seems as clear for mature and experienced men as it does for college students that real learning involves hard work and that one does not learn to cope with the stresses and strains of a management job except by experiencing them and conquering them.

A well-designed, well-run game does not offer an easy path to learning; but it offers a way to present some of the problems, challenges, and stresses of managerial work to men who must learn them under conditions where the costs of failure, to the man and the individual, are real but much smaller than in real life.

GAMES TO TEST

The third possible contribution of games to executive development is as a tool for assessment. One company, Procter and Gamble, has tried this year to evaluate college students employed for the summer by their performance in a game exercise. Other companies are also using games to judge the potential of employees. The motivation is much the same, I think, as that which leads us to try "stress interviews" or that which led the Office of Strategic Services in World War II to test men by putting them through mock-ups of situations they might have to face behind enemy lines.

The promise and the problems are roughly the same. It is reasonable to use games to assess men if—but only if—three conditions are met:

1. We must have a criterion so that we know what kind of men we are looking for. (This gets increasingly difficult as we move into the more individualized upper echelons of management.)
2. We must have a theory, a system of measuring behavior, and some experience that will let us interpret the meaning of the behavior that our candidates display.
3. We must have adequate control over the way the game develops so that we understand the stimuli that the man is responding to and the reasons why he chose to behave as he did.

But until we get more experience, it is probably best simply to observe what happens in games, to try to infer the reasons for various people's behavior and for their success or lack of success, and then to pool our observations with the impressions we have from other sources. The best measures to try to derive from observing the players in a game are probably not the "traits" for which we search with objective personality tests and about which we talk so vaguely in management. Instead, we can often see the players duplicating the specific behaviors we would expect of a good or a poor manager. At Carnegie, we think that the game has helped us to distinguish men who have an aversion to routine work from those who seem greatly attracted by it. We think it has helped us to identify men who take their tasks seriously and who work hard and men who show very great or very little insight into how to manage critical relationships with their peers. The presentations to the boards have

helped to identify men who have the ability to express ideas clearly, to get jobs done on schedule, and to argue their positions forcefully.

The danger is that we may assume that behavior displayed in the artificial environment of a game will also be displayed in the real world of management. We need to keep in mind that this was the basic problem in the O.S.S. testing program, which, perhaps more than any other to date, has explored the issues that we would face in using games to predict executive success. Even in a carefully planned and varied set of "test" situations, the O.S.S. found that it was not able to anticipate many of the conditions that the men would face behind enemy lines. Similarly none of the business games now in existence lets us anticipate with any degree of adequacy the world that the men we select for management will perform in five to twenty years from now.

At Carnegie we have examined the personality characteristics of individuals who turn out to be most influential on their teams and of members of the teams that have done best in the game. Raw intelligence, which counts highly in academic course work, is happily not a good predictor of success in the game. I say "happily" because we have ample evidence that among college graduates intelligence alone is not a good predictor of managerial potential. None of the other personality variables that we have looked at is related either to individual or to team performance. The qualities of a good game player may be as elusive as the qualities of a manager.

THE COST OF GAMING

Relatively little has been published about the costs of gaming. Clearly, it is expensive to start from scratch—to design and program a management game, to prepare and revise manuals of instructions for players and administrators, and to experiment with ways of exploiting the game's educational potential. The company that wants its own game, even a relatively simple one, must be prepared to make a substantial investment of time, money, and talent. The company that wants a complex game modeled after its own problems will have to make a very large investment.

To develop the Carnegie Tech management games, six faculty members worked part time for two months to map out the basic design. At least three man-years have gone into the initial programming for the computer, into debugging efforts, and into modifying the program so that the game could be used more widely. The manuals for players have been through several revisions, and it will take many more months to write up a complete manual of instructions and advice for others who use the game.

On the other hand, in the process of developing a game, companies obtain many important side benefits. By bringing line executives, staff specialists, and computer technicians together to plan what the game should be like, it is possible to:

- Provoke a thorough review of the purposes and methods of training programs within the organization

- Create closer working relationships between men who know the company and its problems and the newer, younger employees who have the special skills needed to construct the game model and to program it for the computer

- Explore in detail many important questions about the effects of managerial decisions and about the interdependence between the company and its environment.

The out-of-pocket costs (and the indirect gains) are much less if a company decides to use one of the many games already available. Some of the simpler games—both with and without a computer—can be run for small groups by one man who has taken the time to learn how to manage them and to anticipate and prepare for some of the emergencies that may arise. A noncomputer game, though, it not necessarily easy or inexpensive to run. It probably takes more advance planning, more preparation of playing materials, and more man power to referee the game and check players' calculations in a concentrated run of the McKinsey game, a noncomputer game, than it does in a similar run of the IBM game, which requires a computer. The real costs for man power and for computer time on any of the games are hard to estimate, because they depend in each situation on the degree to which the men and computers would otherwise be involved in gainful work for the company. The costs of even a complex game for a company that has training department personnel and a large computer standing idle some of the time may be very low.

The right game for stimulation is one that is relatively simple to learn, easy to administer, not very subtle in what it teaches, and basically interesting to the men who are to play it.

Games can also be used to educate—to simulate the opportunities, the challenges, and the pressures that an executive is confronted with and to provide a setting in which men can develop managerial skills. These skills include an ability to adapt to new situations; an ability to set goals and to work from these goals in defining problems and planning action; a skepticism that causes men to ask questions and to go out looking for information; an understanding of relationships among specialized jobs in the firm; a willingness to work responsibly and effectively with others; and an ability to learn from experience and to learn how to organize and transmit experience to others.

This article might have been entitled "Management Games—Recreation or Education?" It was meant to convey the excitement and the promise, along with the problems and the confusion, that surround the discussion of what games can contribute to executive development.

We have progressed farthest in using management games as a recreational tool. When used to start an executive program or to bolster it toward the end when interest in other activities lags, a management game that is administered with efficiency and showmanship has great powers to stimulate and to entertain. It can help to shake men loose from old habits and stir their enthusiasm for new learning.

The game that will best develop these skills is a complex one that provides players with lots of information, asks them to make a variety of decisions, and calculates the results of their actions in an elaborate and realistic way. Such a game puts a premium on planning and on intelligently coordinated action over a period of time. Players are pitted against a "model" of the world, simulated with the help of a computer; but in addition, they must deal face to face with other groups; subordinates, bankers, boards of directors, labor representatives, and the like. The greatest need in the games we now have is for more flexibility in their design and for more stress on decision problems in the areas of organizational design and personnel management.

Where games are used to develop managerial skills, players should have time and incentives to discuss their experience. What they do in the game should be integrated with other parts of the training program. Learning is most likely to be effective if the men are challenged to work hard and are not protected in an extreme degree against stress and possible failure.

The wisdom of using games to evaluate managers is not yet clear. It is hard to predict who will do well in a complex management game just as it is hard to predict who will do well on a real management job. Nevertheless, observations of how well men do in a game may be a valuable supplement to other information that is available to assess their potential.

The Basic Management Design: Management Objectives*

EDWARD C. SCHLEH

Individuals may easily get out of touch with the central purpose of the enterprise, a process encouraged by the natural inclination to specify the activities that are required of a man instead of the results. But even though there has been a general statement of the results that should normally be expected of a position, the definition process has not gone far enough unless specific objectives have been well set for all management people in the enterprise. Objectives should be set for personnel all the way down to each foreman and salesman and, in addition, to staff people such as accountants, industrial engineers, chemists, etc. It is only then that the individual becomes personally and positively involved in the success of the enterprise. He has his definite part to play.

What are objectives? Objectives are really a means for carrying delegation down to a specific period, probably one year. Management objectives state the specific accomplishment expected of each individual in a specific period of time so that the work of the whole management group is soundly blended at a particular moment of time. Each one has a known accomplishment to make leading to the over-all accomplishment expected of the enterprise in that period. To the extent that this is well done, each man knows exactly what is expected of him. To the extent that it is poorly done, delegation is weak, leading inevitably to weak operation, to weak accomplishment, and to a division of interest between the enterprise and the men, no matter what the level.

Because of the interweaving and necessary blending of the work of a number of people to get a final corporate accomplishment, it often seems difficult to set specific objectives for certain positions. It may seem especially difficult to define objectives that are measurable because of the record system in the firm. There is then a natural tendency to define activities rather than results with the rationalization that the activities, if properly carried out, will lead to the hoped-for result. This is very often wishful thinking. In almost every activity there is quite a broad range for interpretation of the direction it could take if end results have not been defined. Under these conditions the individual on the job will often make interpretations counter to those made by his superior. The accomplishment is then less than was expected and perhaps in a different direction. In addition, difference in interpretation may give the man the impression that the rules have been changed on him during the period. He will lose some of his enthusiasm.

To the extent that you can *state the objectives in terms of final measurable results,* such as dollars, percentages, amounts, etc., you tend to get better understanding and better direction. The man is encouraged to accept the philosophy that he does have to contribute to the actual accomplishment of the enterprise in this particular period. Without measurable objectives, this point is very frequently missed at various levels in the operation. The man may become divorced from the central drive of the enterprise.

One of the stumbling blocks in the way of setting measurable objectives is that the record system does not appear to be good enough to measure progress toward objectives with accuracy. We should point out that extreme accuracy is not critical. In many cases, *crude measurements are serviceable* to start out with. They are often adequate permanently. One of the common errors in going into an objective program is the assumption that there must be completely measurable results and that the measurement must be perfectly accurate. In

---

* Reprinted by permission of the publishers from Edward C. Schleh, *Management by Results: The Dynamics of Profitable Management,* McGraw-Hill Book Company, New York, 1961, chap. 3, pp. 18–30. Mr. Schleh is president of Schleh Associates, Inc., management consultants, Minneapolis.

many cases, this is almost an impossibility. Even if the measurement is somewhat inaccurate, men are better stimulated with measurable objectives than without them. They better understand the direction of the enterprise and their own responsibility in it.

UNDERLYING PRINCIPLES OF MANAGEMENT OBJECTIVES

In an effort to cover all parts of a position, managers will frequently try to define everything that they wish a position to accomplish. Because job descriptions often attempt to describe all the duties of a job, each duty is used as a basis for an objective. This inevitably leads to objectives on many subparts of a job, frequently minor subparts. Very often these objectives are simply phases of projects and cannot be measured in terms of final result. The manager feels quite satisfied, however, with having completely outlined "all the parts" of the position. He may wind up with anywhere from 10 to 30 specific items. He has "completely" described the requirements of the job (see Figure 2).

The difficulty is that the individual on the job may actually be steered away from final results by this catalogue list. He often fails to see the final accomplishment to which some of the minor results should be contributing. In addition, he is not given as much leeway to pick and choose and blend these minor items to get the best overall total accomplishment. He is restricted in the judgment he may exercise. In a sense, the specific items tend to reduce his authority and leeway to take action. There is also a tendency for a man to feel secure in the accomplishment of, say, 90 per cent of these minor items even though 10 per cent were not accomplished. The 10 per cent not accomplished may be more difficult and more important, however, so that the net accomplishment is considerably less than 90 per cent. The catalogue list approach generally does not give proper emphasis to the most important items. It can therefore easily lead a man away from maximum valuable accomplishment.

Too many objectives tend to take the drive out of an objective program. As a working rule, *no position should have more than two to five objectives.* If there are more, they should ordinarily be combined in some way. A program with too many objectives tends to highlight the minor ones to the detriment of the major ones. Any objective that is less than 10 or 15 per cent of the job should probably be combined with another one.

FIGURE 2   Typical "Duties" Type of Description, Often Used Instead of "Results" Statements

To approve purchase requisitions in his office

To plan budget requests for his operations

To develop plant production policies

To supervise production scheduling methods; to make sure that Sales is notified of promise dates

To make sure that new construction is adequately supervised

To recommend appropriate incentive systems for his production employees

To supervise activities of repair, quality, material handling, plant engineering and get maximum efficiency from them

To determine methods of handling obsolete equipment

To aid in development of by-product uses

To establish a policy for technical services in his departments

To determine standards for processes and equipment

To provide staff services for planning new construction

To get all his employees to be on the alert for patentable items

To recommend equipment needed

To determine industrial engineering policy

To supervise production office

To maintain control over plant inventories

Even though a small number of objectives has been set, the man on the job may weigh them differently from the way his superior does. For example, he may feel that all objectives are of equal value. This is rarely the case. Or he may feel that one objective overrides all others. A typical example of this is in purchasing, where price of goods purchased is often held to be the important item. (Such an emphasis usually comes from past experience of commendation or reprimand.) In many cases, this may not be true. Timing of deliveries, quality of materials, packaging, and inventory investment may be as important, and in some cases even more important.

When you *assign a percentage value to objectives,* they become much more effective. For example, if there are three objectives, the executive should be able to say that one objective is 40 per cent, another 40 per cent, and the third 20 per cent of the job. He will encourage a better-balanced effort from the man on the job. The delegating executive will be forced to do a much more realistic job of planning the results that he has to get. He will frequently find that objectives he believed to be important are so small in value compared with others that they should not be given special emphasis. They should, perhaps, be combined with other objectives. To the man on the job it becomes clear that he cannot get recognition for a job well done unless good accomplishment can be shown on each objective. The percentage weight of each one is too large to ignore.

With the growth of accounting records, particularly since the advent of high-speed data-processing equipment, there is a greater and greater tendency to centralize record control. These records usually tend to highlight costs and may lead to what can be an undermining characteristic in any operation, that of over-emphasizing costs to the detriment of the creative goals of a position. Ordinarily, any position is set up to accomplish something, not necessarily to control costs. This point is frequently lost sight of when objectives are set directly from a P & L statement or a cost statement, as they are likely to be. (It is true, of course, that the accomplishment should be made as efficiently as possible so that costs can be held under control.)

It is usually advantageous for an executive to *first set the creative goals of a position.* What is the accomplishment to be made that will forward the enterprise? Is it to get sales, produce a product, make loans, or give a service? Secondarily, *then, cost objectives* should enter the picture. Ask yourself first in regard to the job, "What is the reason for its existence? What is it supposed to contribute?" Then, and only then, should you ask yourself, "What is the estimated cost that we can permit in order to get this result?" In other words, you should look at cost in light of accomplishment. One of the most expensive violations of this principle can occur in sales. While sales cost is important, sales accomplishment, whether represented in terms of more volume, more outlets, better price, or better tie-in to plant operation, is probably the first essential. Then, secondarily, the cost of realizing the creative goals must be kept within reason. Salesmen who are badgered by cost considerations may do less creative selling.

The same philosophy can apply to other positions, however. For example, in plants or offices emphasis on costs (very frequently through budgets) may easily develop a philosophy that one should not take chances and spend money on new methods. New methods may be a gamble and throw off the budget. The discouragement of improvement is one of the most enervating effects of overemphasis on cost. Management people at all levels may be subtly discouraged from creatively experimenting with new or improved methods.

Some executives feel that it is good practice to set objectives that are far out in "the wild blue yonder." In other words, they feel that it is sound to set objectives that are almost impossible to attain. "Give them something to shoot for." This philosophy is ordinarily based on an unrealistic approach to human beings and their motivation. *Objectives should be reasonable.* It takes a great deal of fortitude and drive for a man to consistently react well to an objective set beyond his reach. In most cases such an objective will take the heart out of a good man rather than be a stimulus to him to work harder. People are usually more stimulated by success than they are by failure. In addition, if goals are too stiff, a man may begin to accept nonaccomplishment as normal and lose his sense of personal accountability— the real driving force that spurs men on in any operation. The bad effect of stiff goals was demonstrated by an executive who was perfectly willing to specify a 10-million-dollar sales volume goal for a branch where 6 million had been the highest ever achieved in the past. There was comparatively little drive toward high goals in that firm. Instead, there was a constant flow of alibis, cover-ups, and reasons for lack of accomplishment.

Many executives feel that any one responsibility can be delegated to only one individual. This feeling appears to grow stronger when specific objectives are discussed. Such an attitude, however, can lead to an unrealistic approach to management operation. It is not only perfectly proper, but almost essential, that *objectives should be set for a man in any area where he has a strong influence on the result even though he does not have full control.* This will mean that the same objective may be set for more than one person. In actual practice it is a rare objective that does not require the work of more than one person for accomplishment. Setting the same objective for two people forces sound cooperation between men—in time schedules, quality of work, etc. It makes the accomplishment of the objective of value to both men. Cooperation becomes increasingly a part of normal operation. It is advantageous to each of the two men to cooperate in order to achieve the result. Lack of accomplishment will react to the disadvantage of each. The accomplishment of the objective will redound to their mutual advantage, generally a more effective spur to effort that exhortations to "cooperate" or to be good company men. Contrary to the belief of many executives, one of the major values of a sound objective program is that it makes cooperation advantageous to the individuals in the firm. It encourages rather than discourages cooperation.

In our competitive economy, firms must constantly improve or they are left by the wayside. Improvement must become a way of life for every person in the enterprise. Unfortunately, a counterphilosophy often develops that improvement is a responsibility of a certain small number of individuals, very frequently staff men or higher management men. As a consequence, management people down the line do not embrace improvement as part of their individual responsibility. Improvement will not come automatically. It must be built in as part of the basic organization setup. (It is extraordinary how much creative ability often lies dormant in individuals. Management objectives provide one of the soundest ways we know of for tapping this ability.) *Objectives should require some improvement in operation from each man every period.* They provide a basis for recognition of improvement for each man.

Without objectives it is common for management to demand improvement in some areas but not in others. As a consequence many management people feel that last year's methods are good enough. Such a feeling should be discouraged. Objectives should force some improvement in every position every year. After all, good performance last year is easier for the man to attain this year. He ordinarily has last year's gains to help him. A word of caution! Improvement means improvement in method, not necessarily in results. For example, a 10 per cent decline in sales volume may reflect substantial improvement if the industry has declined 20 per cent.

This improvement philosophy appears to be at odds with the normal industrial engineering approach in time-study incentive plans, where there is usually a guarantee that the standard will hold indefinitely unless the procedure changes. This approach is not sound when applied to management people. In effect, the standard changes every year. A little better job is required. However, there is more consistency with the industrial engineering approach than at first appears. The achievement of last year will probably be easier this year. An average job done by a man applying himself reasonably well should be better this year than it was the year before. He has the new ideas that were developed the year before to work on. His job is easier.

If you do not write into the job requirement a specific accountability for some improvement every year, you have taken the first step toward a relaxation of individual drive. The very setup will eventually develop a lagging, desultory, and nonaggressive team. As the firm grows it will frequently find itself faced with key openings and no one to fill them. Its men will not grow to realize the full potential of their own abilities. Management has not been developed to man new positions and to meet new challenges. A firm is well on the way to this stagnation if it allows a new idea to be killed with the comment, "We're doing all right. We are better off than the industry"; or, "We don't want to stir up any trouble now. Things are going all right."

Closely allied to the question of improvement is the question of changing objectives. As we stated earlier, objectives reflect the requirement for accomplishment for a particular year. It is part of any changing enterprise that requirements, and therefore *objectives, should change from year to year.* What was most important one year may be of lesser importance the following year. Operating conditions change, companies change, and outside conditions change. One of the great advantages of objectives is that they force flexibility. They should be carefully reviewed at the beginning of every period so that they will reflect those changes in conditions that must be met. The firm will be more virile and up to date. It is unrealistic to assume that objectives or requirements will not change from period to period in any dynamic company. In fact, one of the reasons for the gradual relaxation of employees in many firms is the almost unconscious acceptance of the fact that, once set up, requirements should hold for years to come. This change in philosophy must, of course, be sold to all management people as being part of normal operation.

Generally, *objectives are most effective if they are set in advance of the period they are to cover.* There is a tendency on the part of a number of executives to want to have all the facts available before they set any objectives. They suffer from the fear than an objective may be set that is either too tight or too loose, generally the latter. As a consequence, when they set objectives they frequently set them later in the period. You can readily see the effect of this on the employee. He probably believes that the executive has made sure of his performance and then set the objective so that he will get a certain amount of recognition but no more. In addition, the man does not have the full period in which to work toward the accomplishment of the objec-

tives. Much of the stimulating effect of objectives may be lost. A flagrant example of this
error was made by a large mill supply manufacturer where sales managers' objectives—and
incidentally, bonus plans—were issued on the
first of September for the current calendar
year. You can well imagine the effect on the
employees concerned.

Objectives should ordinarily be in writing,
with a copy for the man and a copy for his
boss. We should point out, however, that the
fact that they are in writing is not significant

except as a matter of reference. Objectives
should always be discussed face to face between the supervisor and the man until they
are mutually understood and accepted. The
copy in writing is merely a reflection of an
understanding that has been arrived at personally. In every case, of course, it is *the supervisor* who *should make sure that his men have
a clear understanding of these objectives*. The
subordinate is always at a disadvantage if he
must take the initiative in this.

48

Management Appraisal: Key to Building Executives*

BOOZ, ALLEN & HAMILTON

Business leaders know that building a successful enterprise depends upon people—their
proper selection, development and use. The
discovery of executive talent and its development emerges constantly in discussions with
business leaders as an abiding and central concern. The search for management talent is un-
ceasing, not only to get today's job done better
but also to provide for expansion and to build
for the future.

The president of a corporation, therefore,
spends a large part of his time trying to find
able people and to use their talents to best advantage. To do this, he must identify and appraise ability. Appraisal is the key. Many techniques for measuring management ability have
been devised to help a president with his vital
task, but the shortcomings of any individual
measure have often left him uncertain as to
the reliability of the result.

The search for greater reliability in executive evaluation has led us to review appraisal
practices in prominent companies and our own
experience, for the purpose of developing a

program that is valid and practical for management to use. The results of our research convince us, more than ever, that reliability can be
substantially improved by the use of several
differing methods of appraisal, all integrated
into a single, final evaluation on a carefully
planned basis. Such a multiple method looks
at a man from all sides and pulls together results that can be cross-checked and confirmed.
It is this integration, this accumulation of evidence behind every conclusion, that provides
reliability.

As a first step in our research to make
evaluation more dependable, current practices
of prominent companies were reviewed. These
findings are given below. Following this and
drawing on our own long experience in executive appraisal, the report (1) shows by case
history how a practical evaluation can be
carried out, (2) lists the standards for a reliable program, and (3) demonstrates the use of
appraisal results.

PRESENT APPRAISAL PRACTICES

As a survey of management appraisal programs in 50 prominent companies was undertaken as background research for this report.

* A brochure published in 1955 by Booz, Allen &
Hamilton, management consultants, and reprinted
with their permission.

One half of these companies relied solely on a single supervisor's opinion for appraisal, and results appeared inadequate. Another 15 companies, or 30%, had persons in addition to the supervisor make appraisals, usually the supervisor's supervisor or a rating committee. Improved appraisals and better records for manpower planning resulted. Ten companies, or only 20%, had gone beyond the usual evaluation practices. Even here the appraisal records kept for manpower planning were far less complete than plans for manufacturing, sales or distribution in the same companies.

These are the research findings for the most prominent companies having organized programs. If all companies are considered, appraisal appears to be largely unplanned and sometimes amounts to little more than impressions of key supervisors. Human resources are then not inventoried or well known. The range of ability and the total value of a man may be overlooked. This creates a tendency for management to judge men by the things they do wrong, rather than by their entire ability. Under these conditions, a company's primary asset—management talent—is not used as well as it could be.

Despite shortcomings in present practice, the benefits from adequate appraisal are clear to most executives. People will be better placed, more capable backer-ups will be chosen, and development of talent will be more effective. The general quality of management will improve.

A CASE HISTORY OF A PRACTICAL APPRAISAL PROGRAM

To realize these benefits, management needs a practical, as well as a reliable, appraisal program. In our experience four appraisal methods can be successfully woven into such an evaluation. Less than this number enlarges the margin of error; and more than four makes the program costly and difficult to carry out. Each of the four methods serves as an independent measure, and they are later integrated to confirm appraisal findings.

The four elements in the appraisal program are:

1. Analysis of experience
2. Appraisal by associates
3. Personnel tests
4. Planned interviews

Perhaps the best way to demonstrate how an appraisal program is carried out, and how the integration is made, is to follow through the appraisal of one individual. The case history will have to be shortened greatly because the actual forms and appraisal facts are too lengthy to discuss in detail here. However, the essentials of the appraisal program and integration may be shown in the case of James Smith, age 34, an assistant controller in a medium-sized company.

Analysis of Experience

An analysis of Mr. Smith's background was undertaken to determine his past pattern of accomplishment, or its lack. Successful work performance and rapid advancement in the past are important indications of promotional potential. The assumption of responsibility, both on the job and in civic and social life, reflects leadership ability. A comparison of such background with that of fellow workers, on a planned basis, is the first step to find men who can develop into leadership positions.

In the case of Mr. Smith, an analysis of his background showed that his work experience had been narrow and confined to accounting. Salary increases had been rapid, and internal company ratings had been high. His promotions in position level had been faster than usual. Mr. Smith was a member of two professional associations. The experience analysis showed that he had not taken part in other professional organizations or in civic activity. He had held no leadership positions outside his company.

Appraisal by Associates

Five business associates were used to appraise Mr. Smith in order to achieve objectivity and accuracy. Each business associate made an independent and confidential evaluation. These appraisers were chosen for their knowledge of Mr. Smith from positions above and beside him in the controller's department and from positions in other departments with which he worked. The objective was to look at Mr. Smith from every angle and eliminate "blind spots." The appraisers were forced to make a choice on Smith's strong points and weaknesses. Mr. Smith was rated by his associates on position, performance, mental qualities and human relations. Mental qualities and human relations were included because these qualities are increasingly important at higher management levels.

The five business associates who appraised Mr. Smith were in substantial agreement that the strong points of his position performance were his job knowledge and his drive. Turning to his weak points, they questioned the work accomplishment in his section and his ability to delegate and control the activity under him.

As to mental ability, his business associates felt that he was exceptionally alert and flexible, but there was doubt about his creativeness.

On human relations, his associates felt that his attitude was good, but they agreed that he was weak on supervision, the training of subordinates and self-control.

Overall, his business associates thought that he probably had a promotion potential to the departmental or vice presidential level in the accounting field. They felt his main training needs were in the handling of people and a broader outlook on the company's activity.

Personnel Tests

Tests were used in four areas—basic mental ability, interests, personal characteristics and knowledge of supervisory principles. The tests were chosen to integrate with other parts of the program. Test results were compared with company norms, or the scores made by other individuals within the organization. The tests were used to confirm and explain other appraisal findings. In short, tests were used only in a supporting role and not as a sole evaluation technique.

The test profile confirmed Mr. Smith's high mental ability. It showed that he had a strong accounting interest and maintained a rapid work pace. The tests indicated that he tended to assume responsibility readily. Test results confirmed the appraisal of his business associates on his weakness in handling people. He had poor knowledge of proper supervisory principles. He lacked the basic desire to help others, was deficient in self-control and tended to work things out alone. It is interesting to note that Mr. Smith's tendency to work individually rather than in a team effort is confirmed by the tests, by associates' appraisal and by his experience record.

Planned Interviews

A planned appraisal interview was arranged with Mr. Smith to pick up the loose ends and balance out the total appraisal. The interview was intended to provide facts not obtained elsewhere, such as personal appearance, poise, personality, mental organization and fluency, as well as to clear up queries raised by other findings. It played an important part in the integration process, by probing, resolving and confirming results.

The interview with Mr. Smith indicated that he had a very pleasing personal appearance, a high verbal facility and demonstrated good mental organization. His job knowledge was outstanding. The weak points indicated by the interview were a narrowness of interests, irrita-

bility and poor self-control, and lack of interest in or knowledge on how to deal with people.

Appraisal Summary

The most important thing to note about this appraisal case history is that the four parts—experience analysis, associate appraisal, personnel tests and planned interview—are consciously designed and applied to yield related results. It thus becomes possible to accumulate appraisal findings. Confirmed facts are assembled; isolated findings are dropped from consideration. Each accepted appraisal fact is backed by accumulated evidence.

In combining the appraisal findings on Mr. Smith, it was concluded that he was strong in mental qualities, job knowledge and performance but that he possessed deficits in administration, supervision and training. Each of these points could be substantiated in the accumulated evidence from each section of the program. The evaluation of Mr. Smith further indicated that he probably could advance ultimately to the vice presidential level. This would be his ceiling, unless he broadened very considerably under a development program.

At the time of the appraisal, Mr. Smith did not seem to possess the background, training, interest, administrative facility or human relations skill needed to become president. Still he could be very valuable to the company, ultimately, as vice president in charge of accounting and finance. However, for this position he needed additional training and development. He needed a better knowledge of treasurer functions, training in administration and personnel management, personal counsel on his deficits and a better understanding of company operating problems.

The appraisal results on Mr. Smith, therefore, gave management a list of his strengths and weaknesses, his advancement potential, the position that he seemed most eligible to fill, and the training and development necessary to qualify for that position. The appraisal provided the basic material needed for Mr. Smith's placement, promotion and development. Taken together with similar appraisal findings on all management personnel within the organization, appraisal thus proves to be an effective tool for manpower planning, utilization and development.

STANDARDS FOR RELIABLE APPRAISAL

Although the case history of Mr. Smith has been given as a narrative of appraisal results, the evaluation actually took place on a carefully planned basis. The appraisal was planned to meet ten specifications that have been derived from our consulting experience with a wide range of companies. These specifications may be regarded as the bylaws of good appraisal, for they are the means by which reliability can be obtained. They have been tested in use and their practicality has been proved. A soundly constructive program should include the following elements.

1. The appraisal factors and methods should be selected to key in with a company's needs. The program must, therefore, have individuality and conform to the practical requirements of a company's operation.

2. Several appraisal methods should be used, and these methods should differ. Diverse methods provide a balance appraisal that eliminates "blind spots."

3. An appraisal system should be integrated in such a way that findings from one part of the program can be cross-checked with those from others. Real appraisal accuracy is the outgrowth of confirmed findings and accumulated evidence.

4. A direct evaluation of an individual's performance on the job, and a comparative measure of the man against other jobs and other people, should be made. This provides a practical test of whether a man can meet new job requirements and whether he is the best man for the job.

5. An appraisal program must be operated on a periodic basis to discover individuals who may have been missed on the first appraisal and to measure the development of those who are striving to get ahead.

6. A careful written appraisal is essential to permit the step-by-step course of evaluation to be followed and the accumulation of evidence to be observed.

7. An appraisal program should be flexible enough to be applied to all management levels because there is a constant transition in management staff as promotions, replacements and transfers are made.

8. Management appraisal should be applied to all executive personnel because everyone in a management position is part of the reservoir of future talent.

9. The appraisal program must be easy to understand to gain management confidence and to provide ease of administration.

10. Appraisal records must be kept confidential to prevent lowering of morale and to insure honest evaluation.

The planning and carrying out of an appraisal program that meets these standards requires experience and objectivity as well as full company participation. This combination of qualities can be obtained by using experienced consultants who help plan an appraisal program and who then take company personnel through the appraisal skills. This enables the company staff to carry on the program and to assume their responsibility to develop better management personnel.

USING APPRAISAL RESULTS

The case history of Mr. Smith also suggests how appraisal findings help in the development and use of executive talent. Given appraisal results of demonstrated reliability, management can use these conclusions for counseling, planning of replacements, improved executive selection and setting up of training schedules to meet individual needs.

Using Appraisal Results to Build Men

The first use of appraisal results is to counsel with each employee about his future development. This can be accomplished when the supervisor reports on the evaluation and tells each individual how he is doing and how he can improve.

> Admittedly, this counseling and coaching procedure is difficult. It is hard to talk to a man about his weaknesses and to do it in such a way that he is motivated to try to improve himself. This is certainly one of the primary responsibilities of the executive today and promises to be even more so in the future. By the manner in which the executive carries out this vital function, he sets up a gauge of his own effectiveness.[1]

Counseling is a difficult art not born of textbooks and manuals. For the supervisor, as for the subordinate, it is a point of self-improvement and growth.

> When the evaluation is thoroughly discussed in a friendly, private conference, the immediate superior has an opportunity to:
>
> Recognize the individual's outstanding accomplishments.
>
> Tell him exactly where he stands.
>
> Show him in what areas it is felt he can improve.

[1] Louis A. Allen, "Building Executives for the Future," *Advanced Management*, November, 1952, p. 20.

Explain why it is to his advantage to undertake this improvement.[2]

This counseling step should help the management person improve his present job performance, point the way for qualification to higher jobs and help him develop those broad characteristics important in a top management position.

Planning Replacements   Management is not a permanent thing—replacement needs are always impending. ". . . we find that American business needs enough men to do the work of today, to replace losses through illness, old age, and death, and to meet the requirements of expansion."[3] To this must be added replacements for those whose performance is unsatisfactory.

One way that future executive needs can be soundly planned is through the use of a replacement table. This is a top management report giving a view of the road ahead. It lists each key position and indicates the approximate time when the position may be vacated. It also lists the most likely candidates for each position and shows when they will be ready for promotion. In addition, positions are indicated

[2] William F. Wrightnour, "Management Development: A Practical Application," *Personnel*, January, 1952, p. 288.
[3] Earl G. Planty and Carlos A. Efferson, "Developing Leadership for Tomorrow's Tasks," *Dun's Review*, February, 1952, p. 32.

for which a qualified replacement cannot be found or developed in the present organization.

The replacement table may also be translated into a replacement *chart*. The organizational chart is coded to show present position incumbents and the most qualified backer-ups, together with each person's present and ultimate promotion potential. One form of replacement chart, frequently employed, is shown in the figure below. The coding of this chart has been simplified in this illustration to show only the broad gradations of a man's ultimate potential. Red [the hatched space] indicates that the man has the potential ability to be president, white that he has potential for vice president, gray that he can be promoted one position level, and black that the man is at his ceiling. The timing of advancement appears alongside the man's name and age. It shows whether he can be promoted now, soon or later.

This excerpt from a replacement chart indicates its advantages as an administrative tool. Three positions are shown in the sales organization. The top position is that of a vice president of sales. The present incumbent is Thomas A. Jones, 61 years of age, who is satisfactory in the position but possesses no promotional possibilities beyond it, indicated by the black color. Mr. Jones will retire in four years; hence plans should be made shortly to fill the position.

There are two candidates, Peter Smith and William Brown, both of whom are ready to be vice president of sales now and both of whom

Forward Planning and Replacement Chart

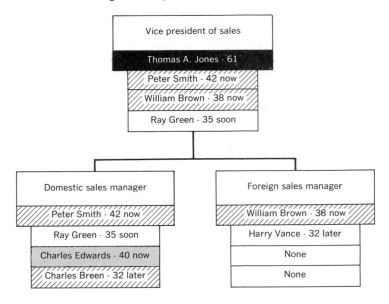

have the ability, as shown by the red, ultimately to become president of the company. Mr. Smith has a good replacement in Ray Green, who could be readied for the domestic sales manager's position soon. Charles Edwards is also an adequate replacement and is ready for promotion now but has less long-range potential than Mr. Green. The chart suggests that the decision rests on whether immediate replacement is more important than ultimate potential.

Now look at the foreign sales manager's position. The good candidate is Harry Vance, who is rather young (32) and could be readied for the position only after a considerable time. Moreover, no further candidates seem available for the foreign sales manager's job. William Brown has a job left to do, to develop backer-ups for the foreign sales manager's position.

Under these circumstances, if something were to happen to Vice President Jones today, Peter Smith is the logical choice because replacements are available. If the position is not to be filled until Mr. Jones retires, then William Brown is aware that he must develop proper backer-ups if he wants to be a strong vice presidential candidate. This example shows how useful appraisal is for manpower planning and replacement.

Improving Management Selection   A third major use of appraisal results is to improve management selection. This process goes on continually in employment, placement, transfer and special assignment.

Placement and Transfer.   Appraisal results will disclose management persons who might serve more capably in other positions. The findings will identify weaknesses and misfits. They will also disclose management strengths that might be better capitalized on if the persons were transferred.

Employment.   Appraisal results identify the qualities of successful executives in relation to their positions. The abilities of these top-flight management personnel can then be used to derive employment standards for each key position, thus improving recruitment and employment.

Special Assignment.   To cover special assignments, management in the past has had to select men solely on the basis of job performance and availability. The selection of individuals for special assignments can be more intelligently done when it is based upon a complete catalog of individual abilities.

Wherever management personnel are to be selected, the appraisal process yields an inventory of management strengths, weaknesses, abilities and personal characteristics that provides an excellent base for intelligent decisions.

Providing a Base for Management Development   The fourth major use of appraisal results is to provide a base for management development. This can be approached by the construction of a development guide for each management person. This guide includes an identification of the individual, the positions for which he seems best qualified, the limitations or training needs derived from a comparison of appraisal results with position requirements, and recommendations for training to fill out the person's competence. A schedule showing the timing of the development program should also be provided. This schedule will disclose when the candidate can be promoted to the next higher position with promise of successfully carrying out its duties.

Hence the entire training program for each management employee can be developed from appraisal results. Group development programs can be devised to meet the "clusters" of needs appearing in the various individual records. The appraisal results therefore provide a basis for tailoring a sound development program to company needs.

CONCLUSION

Business has grown rapidly in recent years, and the number of management employees has multiplied. This has compounded executive personnel problems. Business has had some difficulty improving its techniques for handling management people in keeping with business expansion. Objective inventorying of executive talent has become more urgent as size and complexity have increased. Yet some companies still rely on supervisory opinion for personnel decisions, and this type of evaluation is falling short of the present task.

The pressure of events is likely to bring an improvement in present company practices, for evaluation deals with the most important asset of a business—its manpower talent. The need for more executives in growing organizations, for one thing, is focusing attention upon effective means to develop management talent from within. As long ago as 1936, a prominent personage put his finger on this need when he stated

> To me the crux of the situation (finding business leaders) is not so much the need for men, nor the scarcity of proven leaders, as it is the failure of American business management gen-

erally to introduce an orderly and methodical system for the discovery, development and assignment of executive personnel.[4]

A second reason for expecting more attention to be devoted to executive appraisal and manpower planning is that orderly evaluation is now practical. The principles and methods presented here embody a form of appraisal developed from programs installed in a wide

[4] Edward R. Stettinius, Jr., Address before the 1936 graduating class of Harvard University.

range of companies. The principles are tested and their reliability proved.

Third, the return of rigorous competition is forcing the improved use of executives. In many instances the margin of competitive success or failure is locked up in the quality of management talent. Experience indicates that the right personnel organized into an effective management team is essential to the continuing success of an enterprise. This is the reason that we foresee growing emphasis on organized appraisal—the key to building better management.

49

*How to Appraise Executive Performance**

ARCH PATTON

What makes an executive successful? Why does one man forge his way to the top, while another, equally trained, fails to live up to company expectations? How can we better understand the process by which executives develop?

In hopes of finding answers to these important questions, one of the country's largest corporations made a survey, a few years ago, of the educational, economic, and social backgrounds of more than 100 top-echelon executives. The objective of the study was to discover if the early life experiences of this demonstrably successful group of men had common elements that could be used to improve the corporation's executive selection and development process.

AS DIVERSE AS AMERICA

The research team carefully studied the early family life of each top-management executive, including his family's financial and social status, the extent of his formal educa-

* Reprinted by permission of the publisher from *Harvard Business Review*, vol. 38, no. 1, pp. 63–70, January-February, 1960. Mr. Patton is a director of McKinsey and Company, Inc., management consultants.

tion, subjects studied, marks received, and his early work experience. When the results of the survey were reviewed, it was found that the environment of the company's key executives during their formative years tended to be as diverse as America itself. These highly successful executives came from poor as well as wealthy families, some had Master's degrees while others failed to finish high school, and outstanding and average students were found in equal numbers.

Only one common historic relationship was discovered: *within two years after joining the company, the compensation of each executive topped the average for his age group, and this pay differential above the average widened at an accelerating rate throughout his career.*

The results of this study underscore the dangers inherent in a recruiting process that slavishly follows preconceived ideas of what it takes to make an outstanding executive. The results indicate, furthermore, that intelligence, courage, aggressiveness, and other qualities making for business success are incubated in virtually every conceivable early environment.

The most significant contribution of the survey may turn out to be a better understanding of the executive development process. For if we cannot prejudge the *capacity* of the individual with any certainty, it follows that we must assign critical importance to the ability to judge on-the-job *performance*. This performance appraisal is a never-ending process, for individuals reach the peak of their ability, or willingness, to accept responsibility at different stages in their careers. As every top executive knows, many apparently well-endowed individuals reach "plateaus" of arrested development early in their careers, while others seem able to draw indefinitely on hidden reserves of strength to take on ever larger responsibilities.

In effect, this means that the soundest basis for judging an individual's ability to handle a higher level job is how well he is dealing with similar problems in his present job. Or, to put it another way, an executive's past and present performance is the most reliable key to his future performance. This being the case, the ability of management to judge an individual's performance is basic to the continuing success of the enterprise.

EARLY APPRAISAL EFFORTS

The need for sound appraisals of executive performance has been recognized in industry for many years. The first efforts in this direction tended to have psychological overtones and usually consisted of appraisals of traits that were deemed important to a successful executive. Thus, these early approaches did not appraise performance in terms of the results stemming from decisions made or influenced by an individual, but rather in terms of preconceived characteristics that management personnel were presumed to have. Particularly in the years following World War II, performance appraisal was often looked on as an integral part of an executive development program.

Subjective Approach   Unfortunately, the executive characteristics appraised in development programs—leadership, initiative, dependability, judgment, getting along with people, ambition, and so on—do not necessarily measure a man's *effectiveness* on the job. Indeed, all too often judgments of performance under such plans reflect what is *thought* of the man rather than what he *does*.

The great weakness in this approach has proved to be the lack of performance criteria that are related to job responsibilities. Such concentration on personality traits ignores the more objective measures of on-the-job performance that are developed from budgets and accounting reports. This highly subjective approach, in turn, has made it difficult for management to communicate its judgment of an executive's performance to the man who has been evaluated. It is the rare individual who will concede that he does not display executive characteristics, and an even rarer boss who can comfortably explain shortcomings of so personal a nature to his subordinate. By contrast, the more objective criteria—rising or falling sales, profit margins, scrap losses, employee turnover, absenteeism, machine down time, and the like—are more readily understood by the subordinate and easier to explain because they are in quantitative terms that are part of the operating language of the business.

Another factor that tends to obsolete trait-oriented appraisals in recent years has been the increasing use of executive incentive plans in industry. More and more companies have found their bonus plans "in trouble" because eligible executives do not believe that incentive payments based on subjective appraisals reflect their individual efforts. This belief apparently results from an instinctive revulsion among executives to having their compensation largely dependent on what senior executives *think* of them. First, they suspect favoritism, and second, they exhibit a subconscious desire to have their performance measured by yardsticks that are based on more tangible, quantitative targets they have learned to understand and trust.

Mathematical Approach   Some companies have taken steps to overcome the "popularity contest" aspects of subjective appraisals and to meet the growing need for judging performance in terms of individual targets. Often, however, such procedures have swung to the other extreme in bonus plan administration: setting individual goals for the year in quantitative terms (e.g., increase sales 10% or cut scrap losses 7%) and paying off on "performance" directly keyed to those goals. This approach has the great advantage of eliminating subjective judgment as the determinant of an individual's bonus. Furthermore, it does measure performance, and in terms that are understandable to the individual.

But the experience of many companies that have adopted this mathematical approach indicates that it, too, has serious shortcomings. The most important weakness revolves around the fact that once the individual targets have been established, mathematics takes over the basic responsibility of management to manage. If the individual goals set at the beginning of the year are not consistent between divisions, or between functions within divisions, the mathematically derived payoff at the year's end, undoubtedly, will be unfair. Some executives will be over-paid and others underpaid as a result of forces beyond the control of the individual. An un-expected price war, for instance, may seriously reduce profit margins in one division, while margins in another division benefit from the liquidation of a competitor. With mathematics deciding who gets what bonus, such basic eco-nomic shifts go unrecognized.

Then, too, the mathematically derived payoff that results from preset goals permits no ad-justment in rewards for the *difficulty* of accom-plishment. A manufacturing department, for example, may have surmounted major prob-lems in fulfilling commitments that were easily attained by the sales department, or vice versa. But unless the program permits the *judgment* of management to reflect the difficulty of accomplishment, great incentive values are lost to the inflexibility of mathematics.

Because unfavorable results frequently stem from these relatively extreme approaches to performance appraisal—the wholly subjective and the mathematically determined evaluations —a number of leading companies have blended the best of the two into what appears destined to become a formidable management tool. The remainder of this article will examine in some detail the philosophy underlying the new con-cept, the administrative problems encountered, and the benefits derived from its use.

PLANNED PERFORMANCE

Essentially, this composite approach to appraisal is aimed at providing a sound basis for judging the relative performance of ex-ecutives, expressed in terms of their individual responsibilities. It establishes annual targets for the individual that are implicit in the job he holds. And it provides for *judging* performance in terms of these targets rather than a purely mathematical measurement. In addition, it re-lates these individual targets to the short- and long-term goals of the enterprise. This means that each member of the management team is working toward the same agreed-on objectives of the company or division and will be judged by how well he performs these tasks.

Company Goals   This approach is called by a variety of names: programed management, management by objective, or planned perform-ance programing. But whatever the title, its users have a common objective: that indi-vidual performance be judged in terms of agreed-on tasks reflecting the goals of the busi-ness. The first step, therefore, involves the de-velopment of long- and short-range company goals. The longer-term objectives are useful in "stretching" executive thinking—in making managers think "bigger"—but are also valuable as a guide to the practicability of the forecast targets:

Let as assume, for instance, that a single-product manufacturer, after considerable study, sets a five-year goal of doubling his unit vol-ume. As a result, he has decided how much must be added to current sales in the first, second, and later years to attain this goal. The practicability of these estimates, of course, needs to be checked against the ability of the company to manufacture, sell, and finance such increases in volume. It makes no sense, for example, to set goals beyond the company's ability to provide funds at reasonable cost, or to agree to sell more of a product than facilities can be expected to turn out.

Once it is decided that a 15% increase in company volume is a realistic target for the first year, the next step is to determine what must be accomplished by each functional group in order to attain such a goal. To do so neces-sitates a careful assessment of interfunctional relationships. For instance, perhaps it is possible for the sales department to develop 15% more business by a greater utilization of salesmen's time; but if this is accomplished, new facilities might be needed by manufacturing in order to meet this goal. (These new facilities, in turn, would obviously have to be considered in rela-tion to the forecast needs of future years as well.)

On the other hand, production facilities might be adequate to attain the necessary vol-ume, but the sales department might have to introduce a new line of products in order to reach this figure. If this occurs, of course, other functional areas are likely to be involved. In addition to changes that a new line might neces-sitate in the sales department, i.e., the introduc-tion of a specialized sales force, the engineering department would be expected to design the new line, credit standards might have to be tightened or loosened, transportation costs or lead times might need alteration, and so on.

Functional Tasks   Experience has shown that translating short-term company objectives into 12-month goals for individual functional executives is best done by setting up both quan-titative and qualitative tasks to be accom-plished during the period. In other words, ex-ecutive responsibilities include (a) those that can be *measured,* such as sales, behind-schedule production, or credit losses, and (b) those that must be *judged,* made up of the intangibles that arise when an executive develops a new process, establishes a training program, improves the quality of engineering candidates, and the like.

The advantage of separating qualitative and quantitative tasks lies in the very human tendency among executives to "let the numbers decide." It appears to be much easier for a superior to point out shortcomings to a subordinate when he can blame such an unpleasant conclusion on the results of a quantitative evaluation. Explaining weaknesses that must be *judged* impressionistically, while frequently more important to the training process, causes greater discomfort to the superior. The separation of the two induces a deeper awareness of the importance of both elements.

Further, these tasks need to be set up for both line and staff positions—a process that has proved to be a serious stumbling block to performance appraisal programs. Trouble results largely from line-oriented senior executives finding it difficult to visualize the possibility of setting realistic targets for staff jobs. There appears to be an unfortunate tendency among some senior executives to write off the entire approach because of this blind spot where staff is concerned. Thus:

> Dislike of this approach frequently occurs when the responsibilities of staff functions are vague, and their contribution to the management process has not been adequately developed. The senior executive subconsciously questions the value of the staff function, yet has come to believe that "staff is a hallmark of modern management." He remembers the time, a few years ago, when his company had two vice presidents—sales and manufacturing. Today, there may be vice presidents for finance, engineering, personnel, administration, and so on, but the senior executive does not have the same "feel" for these jobs that he has for the line sales or manufacturing jobs with which he grew up.

This problem has been reduced, however, as top management more and more recognizes the need for spending as much *time* in establishing company and functional goals at the outset as it spends in appraising performance at the end of the year. This more thoughtful approach to task setting results in a better understanding of staff activities, as well as a more practical evaluation of the contributions that can be made in this area.

A number of techniques have been found helpful in cutting the problem down to size. If the tasks of the line organization are worked out first, for example, the process of thinking through the supporting goals of the staff functions is simplified. Similarly, there appears to be an advantage in setting up quantitative goals first and, subsequently, building the qualitative tasks on this foundation. One company has developed a master list of general goals for each functional area, some quantitative and some qualitative. While individual tasks will vary, of course, from year to year, these general goals have been found to be worth keeping in mind.

Examples of annual tasks developed as a basis for appraising the performance of a division head, a personnel executive, and a manufacturing executive are shown in Exhibits I, II, and III. The tasks in these examples are obviously fewer than would be the case in real life, but they are adequate to show the kind of tasks that can be used as a basis for appraising the performance of top line and staff executives.

EXHIBIT I   Planned Performance Targets for Division Manager

Annual target plans

List of major accomplishments needed this year to meet corporation, division, or department goals.

Quantitative targets

Objectives for the year ahead that can be appraised in terms of *how much;* for example, "increase return on investment from 12% to 15%."

1. Increase billings by 17%, maintaining a 50%-30%-20% product mix in Departments A, B, and C.

2. Increase over-all profits (BT) by 35%.

3. Increase asset turnover from 1.3 times a year to 1.5 times.

4. Increase return on total assets from 18% to 21%.

5. Increase inventory turnover from 6.1 to 5.8 months.

6. Expand market share from 21% to 24%.

Qualitative targets

Objectives that can best be appraised in terms of *how well;* for example, "improve technical appraisal program," or "make more effective use of budgetary control."

1. Develop a new line of motors for introduction in 1961. Complete engineering phase, start production engineering.

2. Develop a more effective basis for testing

EXHIBIT I   Planned Performance Targets for Division Manager (Continued)

candidates for supervisory positions, with particular reference to individual aptitudes for specific positions.

3. Increase the number of promotable executives by better training methods, including the introduction of job rotation and the establishment of a special assignment program designed to broaden the skills of outstanding men.

4. Start weekly department head meetings as a training and information medium.

EXHIBIT II   Planned Performance Targets for Director of Personnel

Annual target plans

List of major accomplishments needed this year to meet corporation, division, or department goals.

Quantitative targets

Objectives for the year ahead that can be appraised in terms of *how much;* for example, "increase return on investment from 12% to 15%."

1. Reduce clerical costs of operating the employment function (recruiting and screening applicants) 60%.

2. Reduce cafeteria operating loss 3%.

3. Increase the typing pool from 25 to 30 employees.

4. Reduce the number of secretaries in headquarters staff by 15.

Qualitative targets

Objectives that can best be appraised in terms of *how well;* for example, "improve technical appraisal program," or "make more effective use of budgetary control."

1. Develop a safety training program for the operating divisions.

2. Simplify and reduce the number of clerical salary classifications.

3. Complete the management inventory.

4. Develop an approach to executive performance appraisal that will improve bonus plan administration.

5. Speed up new-employee indoctrination procedure (estimated target—one hour).

6. Develop a program to provide the negotiating

EXHIBIT II   Planned Performance Targets for Director of Personnel (Continued)

group with information that anticipates union demands more accurately.

7. Work with the manufacturing function to eliminate "assistants to" general foremen and plant superintendents within five years.

EXHIBIT III   Planned Performance Targets for Director of Manufacturing

Annual target plans

List of major accomplishments needed this year to meet corporation, division, or department goals.

Quantitative targets.

Objectives for the year ahead that can be appraised in terms of *how much;* for example, "increase return on investment from 12% to 15%."

1. Cut lead time on component purchases from 120 to 100 days.

2. Reduce WDC to 70% in terms of present prices.

3. Manufacturing's phase of the cost reduction program for the division is one third of the $1,500,000 excess saving over last year.

4. Improve delivery schedule performance by 5 percentage points (to 83%).

5. Reduce spoilage ratio by 2% net from 1959 figure.

6. Improve net allowed hours ratio by 3%.

Qualitative targets

Objectives that can best be appraised in terms of *how well;* for example, "improve technical appraisal program," or "make more effective use of budgetary control."

1. Speed up the recognition and utilization of suggestions developed in the suggestion system.

2. Improve production planning on the assembly floor to reduce the need for stand-by stocks of sub-assemblies.

3. Restudy the manufacturing process now used for product "X" to reduce the direct labor needs.

Lower Level Tempo   The annual tasks established for the key functions naturally set the tempo for executives below the top functional level. The goals of subordinates are necessarily tied in with the targets set up for the boss. However, some confusion has crept into the picture at this point. There are those who regard goal setting as the job of the subordinate, with the supervisor merely helping the subordinate relate his own tasks "to the realities of the organization," as one commentator put it. The great advantage of this method, in the eyes of its supporters, is psychological. The executive sets his own tasks, hence paces his own development.

My experience indicates that it is unrealistic to expect middle-management executives to be broad-gauged enough to set their own tasks. They do not fully comprehend the goals that have been established for their boss by top management in order to maintain integration between functions. Further, there is little evidence that lower echelon executives (those without full functional responsibility) are likely to set personal targets that fully "stretch" their capabilities. The political environment in most companies is such that it is very important for executives to "hit the target" they have agreed on. Since "stretched" goals are more difficult to attain, the incentive to play it safe is frequently overwhelming.

This does not mean that lower level executives should not have an important voice in their job targets. The record indicates they should. But since their tasks are keyed directly to the goals of the functional executive, the latter must determine the targets of a subordinate, virtually in self-protection. Indeed, many of the tasks of the top functional executive are delegated directly to the subordinate:

- For example, when a chief engineer has responsibility for reducing the number of motor frames in the product line, he almost certainly delegates this particular chore to someone on his staff.

- When the top manufacturing executive is charged with cutting 20% off the lead time in component purchases, this too will be passed along if he is a good executive.

Thus, the tasks of this lower level group are much like those of their superiors. The main difference is in the number of special, short-term assignments that do not appear in any job description because they change so rapidly.

Judging Performance   With job targets set up for top and middle-management executives, the next step involves determining where each executive's performance of agreed-on tasks falls in the spectrum from outstanding to poor.

Companies doing the best job of appraising the performance of their executives appear to have a number of points in common. For one thing, most of them have incentive bonus plans. The existence of this constant prod to developing better appraisal techniques seems to pay off in good results. Perhaps this reflects top management's willingness to spend more time on something involving a lot of money.

Another common attribute of such companies is top management's recognition that in the most important aspect of the entire appraisal process lies in the identification of outstanding and poor performers. Many appraisal programs bog down because of the time spent trying to identify minuscule differences in performance among the middle 60% to 70% of the executive group whose performance approximates the average! As a result of the effort spent in this direction, the 30% to 40% of the executives who are either outstanding or poor performers receive inadequate attention. Naturally, this becomes a critically important roadblock to success if the appraisal program includes an unwieldy number of executives.

In this connection, a technique so simple that it hardly seems worth mentioning has proved of considerable value. The outstanding performer and the poorest performer are first identified; then, in pairs, the second most outstanding and the second poorest are determined; and so on in pairs until it becomes difficult to distinguish between the performance of individual executives. Thus, a sense of proportion and reality is built into what otherwise tends to be a swampy morass.

One of the most difficult problems in judging performance lies in the values to be assigned line verus staff contributions. A few companies have developed an approach that appears helpful and sounds practical. While its use seems to be limited to those with incentive plans, there is no apparent need for such a limitation. This approach involves appraising the performance of fully profit-responsible executives (such as division managers) first, line executives (sales and manufacturing) second, and staff executives only after tentative values have been set for the profit-responsible and line executives. In other words, the performance of staff executive is "slotted" around already established relationships among the line executives.

This technique makes sense. The performance of the fully profit-responsible executive can be measured with a good deal of accuracy, by means of share-of-market, return-on-investment comparisons, and the like. Yardsticks for appraising sales and manufacturing executives are also good. However, measures of the staff executive's performance still leave much to be desired, and the evaluation of his performance should benefit from being tied in to the more tangible landmarks used for line executives.

The risk, of course, is that staff executives will be "slotted" on a position-in-the-hierarchy basis, or, in other words, judged by their position on the organization chart rather than by their performance. But a hardheaded judgment of the relative value of the tasks agreed on, as well as a careful assessment of performance will go a long way toward protecting against this risk.

Action Needed   Having determined where individual performance falls in the continuum from outstanding to poor, it is necessary to do something about these findings. One of the recurring problems in appraisal programs is that lower echelon executives come to believe "nothing happens" as a result of the admittedly time-consuming appraisal effort.

An obvious first step is to see that the individual knows what is thought of his performance, and why. Since management's judgment of his performance is based on results racked up in the attainment of specific tasks, the individual's weaknesses and strengths are clearly delineated, and the supervising executive can discuss reasonably concrete "hits and misses" with the subordinate. This overcomes the natural reluctance among executives to criticize purely personal traits in their subordinates. Further, it focuses attention on specific opportunities for improvement. The planned performance approach, therefore, provides a basis for self-development on the part of the individual, as well as an assessment of "how he is doing."

For performance appraisal to be firmly rooted in a company's way of life it should play a key role in promotions, merit increases, and bonus payments. The outsider reviewing corporate administration practices all too frequently finds top performers, as measured by the appraisal program, doing no better than the average performer where bonuses, merit increases, and promotions are concerned. It may not make sense, but the rationalizations are plentiful. For instance, a top performer will be passed over for a merit increase "because his bonus was boosted this year"; or his bonus will be held unchanged despite outstanding performance "because he recently received a merit increase."

The point is this: if performance appraisal is worthwhile, it should provide the backbone for executive personnel administration.

Early Problems   To date at least, only a handful of companies have seriously attempted to set up such a programmed approach to performance appraisal. Because most of these pioneering efforts were started in the past few years, it is too early to look for success stories. However, the top executives of companies that have tackled task planning are almost uniformly enthusiastic with results achieved so far. The principal accomplishment, in their view, is the establishment of a task-oriented way of life. Job objectives are morely clearly defined and, therefore, better coordinated. Individual executives know what is expected of them and can target their activities more effectively. Last but certainly not least, the annual review of "hits and misses" between superior and subordinate becomes more realistic and more productive of improved future performance.

Needless to say, there have been problems. It is significant, however, that the major problem areas follow a reasonably consistent pattern from company to company. For example:

1. The detailed probing of individual job responsibilities essential to this approach takes a great deal of time and necessitates some highly creative thinking. Since executives are human, many of them tend to resist both the effort and the thought processes that are involved. For this reason, it is essential that that the chief executive be solidly behind the project. If, for instance, executives come to suspect that their own bonuses may suffer from any neglect of the necessary time and thought requirements, so much the better.

2. Another common problem of successful performance programing is the need for a competent and creative "control function." Executives who are to be rewarded or penalized, in part at least, on results developed by the budgeting and accounting function should have great confidence in the control techniques used, as well as the skill and honesty of this group. It is relatively simple to devise yardsticks, but the objectivity and courage of the top control executives must be respected at all levels if these measures are to be effective. Executives need to have faith that tasks set for the various functions are equally difficult, and that figures are not going to be juggled to protect someone's favorite.

The judgment of individual performance in terms of agreed-on tasks (such as those in Exhibits I, II, and III) requires maturity of a high order at the top level. One of the great advantages of the approach is the coordination of effort that results from its thoughtful, orderly task-setting process. If top management is overly arbitrary in its judgments, understandable problems develop. The chief executive who looks only to the results, without a careful weighing of the difficulties encountered in the accomplishments, is storing up future trouble.

3. The planned performance approach also calls for a personnel staff of unusual competence. This group necessarily plays a key role in advising top management when an imbalance occurs between functions. Several appraisal programs have suffered because the top personnel executives were unwilling or unable to convince top management of developing problem areas. In one instance, the personnel executive knew that the annual tasks set for one functional group were consistently more difficult to attain than were those of other groups. As a result this group had lost about 25% in bonus income over a four-year period. Top management became aware of the problem only after several promising young executives quit, and a subsequent study disclosed the source of the trouble.

Since this approach to performance appraisal is most effective when confined to executives who importantly influence company profits, many personnel executives find themselves dealing with new and complex problems when an executive appraisal program is adopted. As one personnel vice president put it, "I used to spend 95% of my time on problems dealing directly or indirectly with moves having union overtones. Now, more than half my time is spent on the recruitment, development, organization, and motivation of executives!"

Many personnel executives have found it difficult to effect a changeover. Thus, top management faces a serious handicap, since a strong, capable personnel group is a major ingredient in a successful appraisal program.

4. The "cutoff point" of executives to be included in the appraisal program has proved to be another problem area. If too many are included, the programing task becomes monumental. The most effective course appears to involve starting off with a relatively limited group of key executives whose profit impact is unmistakable, and adding levels of executives to the program as its usefulness "proves out." The temptation to include too many, however, is almost overwhelming and needs to be consciously restrained.

Results to date indicate that the programed approach to performance appraisal is not for the laissez-faire management. It is a new way of life—and as difficult as it is rewarding.

CONCLUSION

The planned performance approach provides several important advantages over earlier attempts at executive appraisal:

- The long- and short-term objectives of the enterprise become an integral part of the performance appraisal process

- The job responsibilities of executives provide the basis for setting individual targets. As a result of the necessity for thinking through the interrelationships between job activities, there is a more effective targeting of individual effort

- The outstanding and poor performers receive primary attention, spotlighting those eligible for promotion or merit increases and those requiring training or elimination

- Personality plays a less important part in the final evaluation of performance, for the focus is on what a man does rather than what is thought of him. Thus, subjective criteria are replaced by objective ones

- Mathematics is put in its proper role, providing guidelines rather than final decisions.

Companies using this appraisal approach believe its greatest contribution stems from the disciplines it imposes on the management process. Planned performance forces a company:

- To think hard about its objectives and review them constantly.

- To study the responsibilities involved in individual positions and determine their relative importance to the business

- To set practical work tasks for individuals and hold them accountable for their attainment

- To take whatever action is called for by the information presented to it, in order to build a more effective management team.

In a sense, therefore, such a program involves a down-to-earth executive development program. Since people learn by doing, on-the-job training has great advantages over the more formal executive development programs that bloomed in profusion after the war.

The planned performance approach requires an enormous investment of top management's time in its early years. Since it usually involves a more disciplined way of life in the management process, it needs strong support from the chief executive and those directly under him. Because of the great time demands involved, companies have found it advantageous to limit the number of positions included in the program to those having a clearly recognizable impact on profits.

The approach also requires unusually skilled and resourceful control, market, and economic research functions. Because quantitative yardsticks play a major role in establishing targets and judging performance, they must be demonstrably good or executive belief in the fairness of the process will be undermined. It should be recorded, however, that the performance of executives is subject to constant scrutiny, for decisions bearing on promotions, merit increases, and bonuses are being made by top management almost daily. The question is whether the planned performance approach is worth the time and the effort that are needed to make it effective.

Companies that have worked hardest to develop their skill in this area believe it to be a major improvement over earlier efforts. And the fact that these concerns are pacesetters in industry implies that the competitive pressure exerted by their success with this new management tool will force an ever-widening circle of companies to think in similar terms about executive performance appraisal.

PART FIVE

DIRECTION *Direction is the managerial function of guiding, overseeing, and leading people. It is preeminently, therefore, that portion of the management process which involves personal relationships, even though the reader will recognize that all aspects of managing must be designed to make it possible for people to work together effectively. But direction, as a function, goes peculiarly outside of the formal organization and the enterprise for its roots, since people are necessarily a product and a part of a culture far wider than any undertaking or its immediate industrial environment. The editors have, therefore, chosen to group reading dealing with this function of managing into "The Direction Process," "Motivation," "Leadership," and "Communication."*

Because the handling of people is central to direction, the study of human relations has been of major interest to management, particularly since the famous Western Electric Hawthorne experiments more than three decades ago. This widespread interest in and study of human relations has resulted in illuminating research on the one hand, and many excessive claims, on the other. In the summary, "Changing Concepts of Human Relations," a chapter from one of Carl Heyel's books, the author skillfully and accurately traces the development of human relations concepts in management, emphasizing the major research and objectively dealing with various concepts as they have changed over the years.

The editors have also selected an excerpt on "informal organization" from Keith Davis's book Human Relations in Business. *He shows that systems of informal relationships, related to but quite apart from formal organizational relationships, exist in any enterprise and describes the factors which influence personal interaction. Of particular value—especially since many managers, in the period since World War II, have perhaps become overly enthusiastic about "practicing human relations"—is the incisive paper by Prof. Malcolm P. McNair, "What Price Human Relations?" In the view of the editors, Professor McNair's paper has been of tremendous influence in removing from management teaching and practice some excessive and impractical notions.*

In the area of motivation, which is so important to effective direction and management, the editors have selected four outstanding articles. One is "Motivation: The Core of Management," in which Prof. Rensis Likert emphasizes the importance of recognizing people as members of a group, rather than as individuals, and of using participation and employee-centered supervision to produce effective motivation. The problem of differences in the consideration which motivate people is well presented in the article by Robert N. McMurry, "Conflicts in Human Values." A concern about the overemphasis of "complete involvement" of the individual and about the tendency of many psychologists to believe that management should be interested in an individual's total *needs is expressed by Fremont E. Kast in his article "Motivating the Organization Man." Albert F. Watters, also, argues for the better use of means now at our disposal—including mutual involvement, better communication, and systems of compensation—for achieving more effective motivation of the human beings in an enterprise. His point of view is presented in "Management and Motivation: Releasing Human Potential."*

Because it is hoped that managers may be effective leaders and because it is recognized that leadership lies at the center of direction, a considerable amount of writing about and research into leadership has been generated.

The editors have included three articles on this important subject. In "The Anatomy of Leadership" Eugene E. Jennings attempts to develop some concepts about leadership and some approaches to the question of what leadership is. In the second article, "Requisites of Effective Leadership," Robert G. Wall and Hugh Hawkins emphasize the relationship of leadership to what the individual needs from the environment and from the group. In the third article, "Three Styles of Leadership and Their Uses," Robert T. Golembiewski attempts to analyze the conditions under which various styles of leadership are most useful. His discussion is organized around the generally accepted major styles of leadership: participative or democratic, autocratic, and free-reign leadership.

The ability to communicate is obviously essential to direction since, to deal with people, managers must communicate. This important topic is dealt with in three interesting articles. One is Frank E. Fischer's "A New Look at Management Communication," in which he analyzes some of the difficulties in communication and discusses ways of improving communication. Another selection is "Ten Commandments of Good Communication," issued some years ago by the American Management Association. This terse and effective statement presents guidelines by which a manager may improve his communication with superiors, subordinates, and associates. The excellent article by Carl R. Rogers and F. J. Roethlisberger, "Barriers and Gateways to Communication," analyzes the failure of communications and suggests how communication between superiors and subordinates can be made more effective.

Changing Concepts of Human Relations*

CARL HEYEL

A man who was trying to read his newspaper was continually interrupted by his small daughter as she played on the floor beside him. In desperation, he persuaded her to try her older sister's jigsaw puzzle. He was quite certain that the puzzle, picturing a map of the world, was difficult enough to keep her occupied indefinitely. To his surprise, after but a few minutes she tugged at his arm and showed him the completed map.

"How on earth did you do it so fast?" he exclaimed.

"Well, you see," she replied, "there was a picture of a man on the other side. I put the man together in the box lid and flipped it over. When the man was right, the whole world came out right too!"

The moral, of course, is obvious in our threatened age. But it applies with special aptness to the individual plant and departmental situation—when the man is right, the department and the company are right too.

Ever since the late 1920's, and intensified by the social problems of the Great Depression, advanced management has increasingly been preoccupied with the human side of its operations. Prior to that time, industrial engineers had been seeking most of the answers to efficient operation in improved production processes and more refined budgeting for cost controls and the like. Even in the stress and strain of World War II production, the question of employee morale and motivation was always of high-priority concern. "Put the worker at his ease" was a prime injunction of JIT, the Job Instructor Training program of the War Manpower Commission's Training Within Industry Division; and human relations was further stressed in its JRT, or Job Relations Training, program.

Human relations has been much belabored in supervisory training courses. "How to Get Along with People," "How to Motivate," "How

to Handle Grievances" are stock titles in all such training programs—to say nothing of the shelves of books and stacks of magazine articles on the same subjects. What more should be said about "new concepts in human relations" here?

The fact is that there have been some wide pendulum swings in management attitudes on the subject ever since the famous "Hawthorne experiments" of the Western Electric Company in 1923–26 and 1927–32 triggered the so-called "human relations movement." Some pages of review and perspective are therefore in order. . . . Our purpose here, . . . will be to see if we can attain a balanced view. . . .

SOME BACKGROUND

The Hawthorne experiments had such a profound effect in ushering in the new preoccupation with worker motivation, participation, satisfaction, and the like that it may be well to tell the story again briefly, despite the risk of familiarity. These experiments represent the most ambitious single investigation ever attempted up to and since that date to determine what factors significantly influence the efficiency and productivity of working groups.

The investigators began what they at first thought would be a more or less routine study of the effect of illumination on production. A test group of employees was chosen, and a suitable assembly operation was set up. Conditions were standardized, and it was found that production did indeed increase as illumination increased. But when the analysts *decreased* the illumination within very broad limits, they found to their surprise that production still continued to go up! Obviously, some variable or variables were at work that were more important than illumination.

As a result of the unexpected findings a second, more ambitious research study was undertaken. This experiment consisted of an exhaustive investigation of the production of five girls who were continuously engaged in the

* Reprinted by permission of the publisher from *Management for Modern Supervisors,* American Management Association, New York, 1962, pp. 44–67.

repetitive assembly of small electrical relays. The girls were subjected to all sorts of changes in their working conditions. They took six rest pauses a day, worked without rest pauses, worked short hours and long hours. They were switched around in their chairs, and given different kinds of relays to assemble. Detailed records were kept on such factors as the weather outside and whether the girls came to work tired after parties or fresh after a good night's sleep. There were changes in the form of incentive payments and in the quality of supervision.

The results of all these observations were again unexpected. No matter what the changes were, total output continued to rise throughout the period of the experiments, reaching a total increase of 30 per cent. The conclusion reached was that the increases in output were due, not to any of the changes in tangible working conditions, but rather to the *social relationships* of the girls and *their attitude toward supervision.*[1]

The girls were interviewed in depth and were asked to reply to detailed questionnaires. The investigators, in their final explanation of the results, placed great emphasis on the apparent influence of the *sense of participation and belonging.* The girls knew that they were taking part in an interesting experiment, and they were consulted on details that affected them. They realized that they were part of something that management considered important, and this affected the pride they took in their work. The investigators also concluded that the informal organization and social relationships which the girls developed by working together were as important as the formal organization.

The final report stated that "the operators have no clear idea as to why they are able to produce more in the test room; but as shown in the replies to the questionnaires, there is the feeling that better output is in some way related to the distinctly pleasanter, freer, and happier working conditions." Professor Elton Mayo stated that "comment after comment from the girls indicates that they have been relieved of the nervous tension under which they previously worked. They have ceased to regard the man in charge as a 'boss.'" The social influences were rated as being of more significance than physical factors and changes in pay.

The study of the relay-assembly girls was followed by a study of 14 male operators in a bank wiring room with a view to obtaining more exact information about social groups within the company. This second study reinforced the findings from the relay test room.

Following the Hawthorne experiments there was a tremendous swing by management to a deep preoccupation with the human and social aspects of work. In industrial relations literature and from the platforms of management gatherings the Hawthorne findings were quoted extensively ("interminably," as one commentator has since put it). This is not, of course, to say that the swing was due solely to this work—but the findings did provide an apparent scientific basis for the arguments that were increasingly being advanced by socially conscious spokesmen for government, business, and academic circles. These arguments held that human relations had been a neglected factor in productivity; that too much attention had been given to money incentives and to impersonally engineered standards of performance; that management in general and supervisors in particular had to be much more concerned with "what made people tick," with problems of informal organizations in any working group, and with problems of *communication, participation,* and *understanding.*

This new trend in management thinking had a marked influence on the type and content of supervisory training programs—and in many cases the preoccupation with the human reactions on the job led to rather extreme emphasis on psychological and even near-psychiatric approaches. While there has been a justified reaction against giving analysis and advice to subordinates on alleged personality defects and a concomitant swing back to stressing performance on the job, the net result has been a salutary concern in getting supervisors to think about what constitutes constructive leadership on the job; about effective techniques of communication and teaching, overcoming resistance to change, instilling pride in work, and achieving identification with company objectives.

Another direct result of the Hawthorne experiments was the impetus they gave to "undirected" employee counseling. This was carried to great lengths by the Hawthorne management, which made a skilled interviewer available to each shop department. As soon as he felt that he had a fairly good knowledge of the special human problems in question, this interviewer began meeting with individual employees in a special room. Complete confi-

---

[1] The experimental room was devised and maintained by the Western Electric Company. Much of the analysis was done by Prof. T. N. Whitehead and his associates at the Harvard Graduate School of Business Administration, under the direction of Prof. Elton Mayo. The story is told by F. J. Roethlisberger and W. J. Dickson, *Management and the Worker,* Harvard University Press, Cambridge, Mass., 1939.

dence was absolutely guaranteed. Nothing the employee could say could shock the interviewer—and the interviewer never argued and never gave advice. Management felt that the interviews were eminently worthwhile, even though the interviewer actually did nothing!

Under this philosophy, whatever corrective action takes place comes about through increased understanding, through thinking and self-help stimulated by the questions. Not many companies, of course, could afford the luxury of such an elaborate setup, but the techniques of this form of counseling—that is, largely listening—are now widely applied as part of formal employee and executive appraisal plans.[2]

NEW INSIGHTS INTO MOTIVATION

In the years under our review, a great deal of attention has been given to the question of human motivation. Social scientists have sought to develop theories about the motivation of people at work on the basis of their own observations in industrial situations, the results of studies by clinical psychologists, the reactions under controlled experiments of non-industry groups such as school children and military units, and the "living examples" furnished by the practitioners of work simplification and by programs such as that of the Lincoln Electric Company.

We shall come back to all of these later. At this point, however, we should mention some ideas about motivation advanced by A. H. Maslow.[3] These ideas have since won general acceptance by psychologists and provide valuable insights to anyone concerned with getting the best out of people in our industrial society today.

Dr. Maslow postulates five basic needs which, he says, are organized into successive levels. For example, hunger is a basic physiological need. But when there is plenty of food, higher needs emerge. When the higher needs are satisfied, newer and still higher needs come to the fore, and so on. Thus gratification becomes as important a concept in motivation as deprivation. A want that is satisfied is no longer a want.

Below we give, necessarily simplified, these levels of basic needs, starting with the lowest. (It should not be assumed that a need must be entirely satisfied before the next one emerges. Most normal people are partially satisfied in all of their basic needs at the same time.)

1. *The physiological needs.* These are hunger for food, sexual gratification, and shelter.

2. *The safety needs.* If the physiological needs are relatively satisfied, a set of needs emerges for protection against danger and threats. In an ordered society a person usually feels safe from extremes of climate, tyranny, violence, and so on. Expressions of safety needs are thus seen in preferences for job security, insurance, and the like. Other manifestations are preferences for the familiar rather than the unfamiliar, the known rather than the unknown. These are normal reactions. Arbitrary management actions giving rise to uncertainty can have an adverse effect at any level in the organization. The tendency toward resistance to change is human and universal.

3. *The love needs.* (Some writers term these "social" needs.) If the physiological and safety needs are fairly well taken care of, the needs for love and affection and "belongingness" will emerge, and the cycle will repeat itself with this new center. The person now seeks affectionate relations with people in general, a place in his group. If he is deprived of these goals, he will want to attain them more than anything else in the world, and, in Dr. Maslow's words, "he may even forget that once, when he was hungry, he sneered at love." In our society, the thwarting of these needs is the most common cause of severe psychological maladjustment.

4. *The esteem needs.* Practically everyone has a need for self-respect and for the esteem of others. This results in the desire for strength, adequacy, confidence, independence, reputation or prestige, recognition, attention, and appreciation. These "egoistic" needs are rarely completely satisfied. They are of special importance in our discussion because the typical industrial and commercial organization does not offer much opportunity for their satisfaction to employees at the lower levels. It is the recognition of these needs that has focused so much attention upon ways to provide employees with a sense of participation. Extreme advocates call for very broad participation indeed, covering even allocation of work and setting of the work pace, and criticize "scientific management" as deliberately thwarting these esteem needs.

5. *The need for "self-actualization," for self-fulfillment.* Even if all the needs thus far men-

---

[2] That this was no short-lived enthusiasm at Hawthorne is indicated by the fact that the counseling procedure was in force for 20 years, 1936 to 1956. Since then the program has been curtailed, and the counseling techniques have been incorporated into Western Electric's general supervisory development programs.

[3] A. H. Maslow, "A Theory of Human Motivation," *Psychological Review*, vol. 50, 1943.

tioned are satisfied, we can still expect that a new discontent and restlessness will develop unless the individual is doing what he is fitted for. Dr. Maslow writes: "A musician must make music, an artist must paint, a poet must write, if he is to be ultimately happy. What a man can be he must be. This need we may call self-actualization." The clear emergence of these needs rests upon prior satisfaction of the physiological, safety, love, and esteem needs. People who are satisfied in these needs are basically satisfied people, and it is from these that we can expect the fullest and healthiest creativeness.

An important point about these basic needs is that in the average person they are more often unconscious than conscious. A supervisor who is aware of them will often obtain a clarifying insight into seemingly contradictory behavior. ("We agreed to their wage demands—now why can't we get productivity?")

"DEMOCRATIC" VERSUS "AUTHORITARIAN" SUPERVISION

All the foregoing ties in with the continuing emphasis that has in recent years been given by many industrial psychologists and others interested in the industrial application of the social sciences to the advantages of so-called "democratic" versus "authoritarian" supervision and to more "participative" management in general. A supervisor who is "democratically oriented" is one who thinks of himself as a coordinator of his group rather than "boss." He believes subordinates should have more voice in running the department and listens to ideas and suggestions from them. He passes adequate explanations on to his subordinates when changes are made and is prepared on occasion to give in to a subordinate if there is disagreement on how something should be done.

The advocates of democratic supervision contend that with all that is now known about the reactions of people in groups, about individual motivations, and about worker satisfaction, an entirely new theory of management is called for, one that permits more self-fulfillment or self-actualization by the worker.

Under this concept, the supervisor is seen not so much as the directive head of his group but rather as its representative in the next higher group in the organization. The supervisor and the members of his work group are interdependent, whereas under the authoritarian system the supervisor's authority and the subordinate's dependency are emphasized. The latter view is considered unrealistic by the proponents of democratic supervision, since, they point out, in many situations the superior must depend on his subordinate. The principle is illustrated by what Rensis Likert has called the "linking pin" concept of supervision, illustrated in Exhibit 3.[4] In (a), loops are drawn around each individual and his boss, indicating that the pairs represent the primary working and communication relationship. In (b), illustrating the "linking pins," loops are drawn around each supervisor and all of his subordinates.

INCENTIVE PLANS AND THE NEW CONCEPTS OF MOTIVATION

It is understandable that developments such as those discussed thus far would cause many people to question individual incentives or piecework plans. By the beginning of the "human relations movement" such plans had been brought to a point of wide application in industry, and they are still very widely used. (We include under the term any system of wage payment under which the earnings of an employee or a small group of employees are directly related to output by means of a formula linking their measured performance to a predetermined standard.)

These plans, of course, rely practically altogether on a single motivation—additional monetary reward for additional effort—and if recognized industrial engineering procedures are followed, the production standards against which individual performance is measured are set by a professional methods department. In management literature there has been increasing advocacy of replacing such plans with group bonus plans and companywide profit-sharing plans, relating the bonus either to company profits or company savings as a whole or to departmental savings effected by voluntary group effort. These, it is claimed, are much more conducive to harmonious relationships, continuing productivity, and dedication to the objectives of the enterprise as a whole.

In an attempt to support this view industrial psychologists and others have cited numerous

---

[4] Rensis Likert, "Developing Patterns in Management," in *Strengthening Management for the New Technology,* American Management Association, General Management Series, no. 178, New York, 1955; and *Changing Patterns and Concepts in Management,* American Management Association, General Management Series, no. 182, New York, 1956, part 2.

EXHIBIT 3   "Man to Man" (*a*) and "Linking Pin" (*b*) Concepts of
Supervisory Relationships

(*a*)

(*b*)

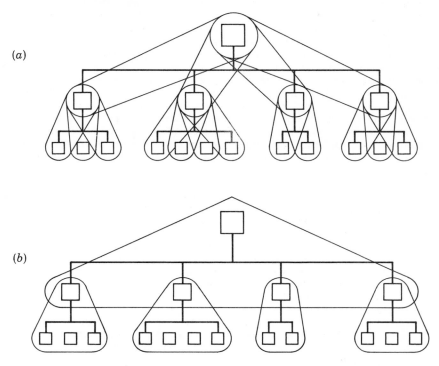

case study examples of worker opinions polled in specific plants, showing shortcomings of engineered performance standards and incentive systems or citing beneficial results when the newer philosophies of participation, group cohesiveness, and the like were applied. We cannot take the space to review the literature extensively; but, to give the flavor of the general nature of these reports, we offer two examples as typical. Presently we shall comment on the validity of such criticisms if an incentive plan is soundly engineered and installed in such a way as to achieve employee cooperation. . . .

Our first example, as related by William Foote Whyte,[5] concerns a paint room, where women spray-painted wooden toys and hung them on hooks which carried them into a drying oven. The girls were expected to reach engineered performance standards in six months.

But there was a serious problem of absenteeism and turnover. The girls claimed that the standards were impossible, and many hooks went into the oven empty. They complained of the oven heat, fumes, and general messiness.

[5] William Foote Whyte, *Money and Motivation,* Harper & Row, Publishers Incorporated, New York, 1955.

The foreman decided to meet with the girls and discuss their problems. They claimed that the room was poorly ventilated and too hot and asked for some large fans. The foreman got management approval to install three fans.

The girls' attitude was so improved that the foreman arranged for another meeting. The girls then complained that the time study men had set the conveyor too fast. They asked to be allowed to control the conveyor speed themselves—to be able to vary it during the day.

After meetings between the foreman and the standards men, it was decided to try the girls' idea, and a control was installed, containing a dial for "low," "medium," and "fast." Medium speed was just a little above standard. The girls experimented with this and established the following pattern: For the first half-hour each day the control was set at slightly above medium. The next two and a half hours were at high speed. For a half-hour before and after lunch the speed was set at low. Thereafter the control was again changed to high and left there until the last 45 minutes, when it was changed to medium.

The girls now reported that the pace was comfortable. Scarcely a hook went by empty, and rejects leveled off. Two months before the end of the six months' learning period, production was 30 to 50 per cent above standard, and the girls were collecting base pay, learner's bonus, and regular bonus.

This story typifies case studies purporting to show the possibilities, even in fairly mechanized operations, of applying the new concepts of participation—although in this instance there was a sad ending. The girls were earning more money than many skilled workers, and the latter knew it. Whyte reports that without consultation the superintendent revoked the learning bonus and returned the painting operation to its original status: The hooks again moved at a constant speed, production dropped, and within a month all but two of the girls had quit. The foreman stayed for several months but then left for another job.

Our second example is from Douglas McGregor:[6]

> The practical logic of incentives is that people want money, and that they will work harder to get more of it. . . . Incentive plans do not, however, take account of several other well demonstrated characteristics of behavior in the organizational setting: (1) that most people also want the approval of their fellow workers and that, if necessary, they will forego increased pay to obtain this approval; (2) that no managerial assurances can persuade workers that incentive rates will remain inviolate regardless of how much they produce; (3) that the ingenuity of the average worker is sufficient to outwit *any* system of controls devised by management.
>
> A "good" individual incentive plan may bring about a moderate increase in productivity (perhaps 15 per cent), but is also may bring a considerable variety of protective behaviors—deliberate restriction of output, hidden jigs and fixtures, hidden production, fudged records, grievances over rates and standards, etc. It generally creates attitudes which are the opposite of those desired.

THE REACTION

The cumulative effect, in some companies, of all the emphasis on human relations was to swing the pendulum pretty far—to a "do-gooder's" philosophy of personnel administration. Inevitably, there were second thoughts. Was all this talk about the human factor in industry taking on the aspects of a fad? Was "democratic" supervision simply "soft" supervision? (As one executive put it, "Are we running a pink-tea party, or operating a business?") Were all the interesting case studies nothing more than anecdotes—isolated casebook material without any general significance?

Participative management is all well and good, but should girls really be allowed to set conveyor speeds? Are we overly concerned with patting workers on the head, giving them expressions of approval to bolster their self-esteem? Do engineered performance standards really rob a worker of human dignity? Where should management draw the line in giving up its prerogatives?

These implied doubts were accentuated by the recession of the late 1950's. Cost-conscious managers felt that there were many frills that could be cut from industrial relations practices, and many felt that they were in a position to adopt somewhat more of a "get tough" policy with organized labor. Typical of the questioning attitude are the following observations by Malcolm P. McNair in the *Harvard Business Review*.[7]

> My quarrel is not with the solid substance of much that is comprehended by the phrase "human relations," but rather with the "cult" or "fad" aspects . . . which are assuming so much prominence.
>
> . . . The world's work has to be done, and people have to take responsibility for their own work and their own lives. Too much emphasis on human relations encourages people to feel sorry for themselves, makes it easier for them to slough off responsibility, to find excuses for failure, to act like children. When somebody falls down on a job or does not behave in accordance with accepted codes, we look into his psychological background for factors that may be used as excuses. In these respects the cult of human relations is but part and parcel of the sloppy sentimentalism characterizing the world today. . . .
>
> It has become the fashion to decry friction, but friction has its uses; without friction there are no sparks, without friction it is possible to go too far in the direction of sweetness and light, harmony, and the avoidance of all irritation. . . .
>
> The overemphasis on human relations, with all its apparatus of courses, special vocabulary, and so on, tends to create the very problems

---

[6] Douglas McGregor, *The Human Side of Enterprise*, McGraw-Hill Publishing Company, New York, 1960.

[7] Malcolm P. McNair, "Thinking Ahead: What Price Human Relations?" *Harvard Business Review*, March–April, 1957.

that human relations deals with. It is a vicious circle. You encourage people to pick at the scabs of their psychic wounds.

THE SEARCH FOR PROOF

To seek answers to questions such as those raised above, there have been numerous attempts by social scientists to put a somewhat firmer scientific base under all the admonitions to encourage participation, to provide scope for individual goal setting, to consider social relationship, and the like. To see whether such human relations practices could actually be tied in to increased production, a number of controlled experiments were undertaken, incorporating as much as possible of the rigor employed in experiments in the physical sciences.

But, before discussing such experiments, let us note that in this search for hard-boiled evidence, the sacrosanct Hawthorne experiments themselves came under some critical review. In 1953, 20 years after the original Hawthorne reports, a British social scientist, Michael Argyle, published a paper entitled "The Relay Assembly Test Room in Retrospect."[8] He carefully re-examined all the reported results, subjecting them to tests for statistical significance, evaluated the types of controls that had been set up, and reconsidered all the possible influences on the final measurements. He flatly stated:

> The conclusion drawn was that the reported increase of output was not due to the experimental periods, to the wage change, or to certain other physical factors, but to social changes, and in particular to the new attitude of the girls toward supervision. . . . It is clear that the three groups of physical factors considered [rest periods, shorter hours, changes in pay] could easily have been responsible for the whole of the observed increase of output, although there is insufficient evidence to show whether they were or not. . . . It was concluded that only about half of the 30 per cent increase was due to the method of payment. This figure was arrived at by comparison with two control groups, but no conclusions can be based on comparisons of single case studies where there is no control of other important conditions. . . . It is thus not possible to say how much increase was due to the wage change. . . . There is no quantitative evidence for the conclusions for

which this agreement is famous—that the increase in output was due to a changed relationship to supervision.

It is interesting to note that this British paper has as yet apparently made no impression upon American management literature.

THE HARWOOD MANUFACTURING CORPORATION STUDY

Getting back to the laudable efforts to assemble quantitative data under controlled conditions, we can remark that carefully controlled statistical studies are still relatively few in number. One of the most widely quoted is that of the Harwood Manufacturing Corporation.[9] The company manufactures clothing, chiefly pajamas, and at the time of the study employed 500 women and 100 men.

When girls were transferred to new work because of, say, a change of style, their output dropped below the 60 units per hour standard for fully trained workers and tended to stay down, even after a reasonable readjustment period and even when the changes were quite small. Those who succeeded in regaining standard did so slowly, taking longer than a "green" worker. There was also a good deal of conflict with supervisors, time study men, and management generally.

To test the effect of allowing the girls to participate more in a needed change, the company developed a series of experiments when four groups of girls had to be transferred to new work. The work was all about equally difficult, and the changes were of about the same magnitude. One of the groups was used as a control, and for it the customary transfer procedure was used.

For the other groups, meetings were set up at which a manager discussed the need to cut costs. He showed two seemingly identical pairs of pajamas. The one had been made the year before, and the other was made by the new method at half the cost. Animated discussion ensued. The workers agreed that cost reductions were possible and necessary and came forward with suggestions. Management then presented its plan for making a job study and training operators for the new job and explained how the new rate would apply.

The control group showed all the typical symptoms found in previous transfers. Its output after transfer averaged only about 50, with

[8] Michael Argyle, "The Relay Assembly Test Room in Retrospect," *Occupational Psychology*, vol. 27, 1953.

[9] L. Coch and J. P. French, Jr., "Overcoming Resistance to Change," *Human Relations*, August, 1948.

close standardization of output around the average. In the first 40 days of the experiment about 17 per cent of the group left the company. The rest caused trouble with supervisors and time study men and brought in the union to dispute the new rate.

Results with the participating groups showed a remarkable contrast. Output not merely recovered, but climbed quickly to about 70. Interest and cooperation shown in the initial discussions carried over to the jobs. Workers referred to "our job" and "our rate." There were no difficulties with supervisors and no major grievances, and none of the workers left the firm. The investigators reported that intergroup competition quickly developed and sped the process of achieving higher output.

A further experiment was then made: When the first group had adequately proved the deficiencies of the old procedure, it was broken up, and its members were scattered to other departments. Several left the firm. Later, the 13 surviving members were reassembled and once more launched on a new job under the "total participation" procedure. This time there was no question of their output sticking at around 50: Like the others, it quickly rose to and stayed at 70.

THE NORWEGIAN SHOE FACTORY

A group of Norwegian investigators[10] was impressed with the Harwood findings but felt they should be confirmed by a more detailed study which would be more closely controlled and would employ more refined methods of statistical analysis to be sure that the results could be attributed to the variables under study and not to random or unknown causes. They chose for their study a shoe factory in southern Norway, with 1600 employees. The department studied employed 400 men and women organized in almost identical work groups. Nine four-employee groups took part in the experiment, because they were going to be assigned to work on a new product.

Four areas of decision making were used: (1) allocation of articles to be produced, (2) length of training, (3) division of labor, and (4) assignment of jobs. Two of the experimental groups were allowed "moderate participation," and the other three were allowed only "weak" participation—that is, they participated only in allocating the articles. The control group was permitted *no* participation. Detailed production records for all groups were

[10] John P. French, Jr., Joachim Israel, and Dagfinn Ås, "An Experiment in Participation in a Norwegian Factory," *Human Relations,* no. 1, 1960.

supplied by management. Each of the five experimental groups met with its foreman and representatives of the planning department to decide which of the five new products should be assigned to it. The two groups with greater participation held additional meetings in which they helped decide about the division of labor into four jobs, the assignment of these jobs to group members, and the training for the new jobs.

Ten weeks after the training, extensive post-experimental questionnaires were answered by the group members. The variations in the production of the groups, and in the answers to the questionnaire, were subjected to extensive statistical-significance analysis to determine the statistical probability that the results could have been due to other factors than the ones under review.

As far as tangible results—actual production—were concerned, the experimental groups did *not* differ significantly from the control groups. All kept fairly close to standard. However, the two groups that had been permitted the greater amount of participation took a relatively shorter time to reach the standard level of production. One of these groups increased beyond the level but took 15 weeks to do so.

This experiment must be disappointing to anyone who wants to make an open-and-shut case for participation in terms of increased productivity. With respect to attitudes toward management and job satisfaction in general, the authors concluded from the questionnaire analysis that they had adduced statistical support for their hypothesis (which might appear obvious) that the effects of participation hold only for subjects who experience only as much participation "as they consider right and proper" and that the effects of participation increase with decreasing resistance to the methods adopted by management to assure participation.

We have, of course, given only the bare bones of these Norwegian results, limiting ourselves to the tangible effects on production. The authors speculate on participation in general and on employee attitudes revealed by the questionnaires. They find moderate support for relating participation to feelings of satisfaction, and to labor/management relations. Despite the apparent inconclusiveness of this much more statistically refined version of the Harwood experiment, the authors surprisingly conclude that it seemed to yield consistent results, but that "the American experimental manipulation was more relevant to production and hence produced stronger forces affecting production."

UNIVERSITY OF MICHIGAN STUDIES

Another widely quoted source of quantitative analytical data on human relations in industry is the University of Michigan Research Center. In recent years this group has conducted extensive research into the effect on productivity of various organizational variables, with emphasis on the type of supervision. Included are studies of 72 foremen in charge of maintenance gangs for the Baltimore and Ohio Railroad; 224 Prudential Insurance Company office supervisors; over 300 supervisors in the Caterpillar Tractor Company; and employees of The Detroit Edison Company. The general conclusion of the investigators is that "democratic" supervision, as against close or "autocratic" supervision, is related to higher output. Job satisfaction on the part of employees is also reported as generally greater under democratic leadership. In the Prudential study, an average difference of 10 per cent in production was found between matched departments under different supervisors. The studies seemed to indicate that pressure for production on the part of the supervisors was completely unrelated to productivity, even to be inversely related to it. Surprisingly, when other data of the studies were analyzed, the evidence indicated that the foremen who spent more time on supervision had more productive sections, even though the same studies showed that close supervision was related to low output. It was concluded that to obtain high output a foreman had to tread a narrow path, spending a lot of time on supervision and yet not supervising too closely!

THE INDUSTRIAL CONTROLS CORPORATION

Industrial Controls is the disguised name of a medium-sized company (1,000 employees) in which a group of investigators from the Harvard Business School made an exhaustive six months' study, in 1955, of a department with 45 industrial workers. The stages of this research, including selection of the company, collection of preliminary data, and processing and reporting upon the data, extended over more than two years.[11] The study was designed to test a large number of hypotheses about factors which were thought to determine the behavior of any work group and the individuals in it. Findings were subjected to elaborate statistical tests for significance.

Eighteen basic hypotheses and resultant predictions are discussed in detail in the published report. The researchers had established these on the basis of prior studies and speculations by themselves and other social scientists. The hypotheses ranged over a wide field, covering the effects on productivity and worker satisfaction of such factors as acceptance by the group, differences in social and educational background, degree of interaction required by the job, rewards by management, and differences in social and educational background of an individual as compared with the norms of the group. They also covered observations about informal leadership, factors determining acceptance by the group, tensions arising from confusion as to "status" with the group, and the like.

Statistically speaking, the results of this detailed study were decidedly mixed. In the words of the authors:

> A document of some 200 pages was prepared which recorded our hits, our near-misses, our gross errors, etc. It compared the actual results with the results we had predicted from each hypothesis as well as from the combination of hypotheses we had used. . . . In some few cases we were right "on the nose"; in some more cases we were not "on the nose" but in "the right direction"; and then there were a substantial number of cases in which we were "way off." In some cases the actual behavior in terms of productivity and satisfaction was at a variance of 180 degrees from the behavior we had expected and predicted.

But the published study is valuable, nevertheless, in terms of the insights into motivation and behavior which are provided by the speculations and extended discussions of the authors in which they glean illuminating perspective out of varying and sometimes contradictory results. . . .

ARGYRIS'S "PLANTS NO. 5 AND 6"

Professor Chris Argyris of Yale has long been attempting to find laws of organizational behavior. In recent publications[12] he has documented in detail his interpretations of observations and depth interviews in "Plants No. 5 and 6" of a worldwide corporation. Both plants

[11] A. Zaleznik, C. R. Christensen, and F. J. Roethlisberger, *The Motivation, Productivity, and Satisfaction of Workers: A Prediction Study*, Harvard University, Division of Research, Graduate School of Business Administration, Boston, 1958.

[12] Chris Argyris, "Organizational Effectiveness Under Stress," *Harvard Business Review*, May–June, 1960; and *Understanding Organizational Behavior*, Dorsey Press, Inc., Homewood, Ill., 1960.

were approximately similar in size (500 employees), type of employees, products manufactured, and type of corporate controls and management leadership.

The management of Plant No. 5 had always paid the highest wages in the community. It had instituted liberal employee benefits long before the unions championed them. Indexes such as turnover, absenteeism, and grievances were very low. Excessive scrap and waste did not exist; stealing, gambling, rule breaking, late arrival, and refusal to work overtime on short notice hardly ever occurred. Surprisingly, after his detailed probings, Professor Argyris arrived at the following conclusion, despite the observed results which any factory manager would yearn to achieve:[13]

> The traditional indexes of low absenteeism, low turnover, low grievance occurrences, and high productivity are questioned. Given such indexes, management should not assume that it also will have employees who desire to be identified with the company . . . to worry about making the company more effective, to feel some responsibility for the over-all health of the company. . . . Such a climate will develop few employees who want to promote themselves into positions of responsibility. . . . The employees . . . will slowly become "simplified" human beings.

Two years later, Professor Argyris had the opportunity to round out his study by going into the "Siamese twin," Plant No. 6. Here management had just begun a drive to cut costs. Pressure was applied to cut production waste, errors, and down time and to increase quality. New control procedures were introduced. One of the "tightening up" actions of management was the elimination of what appears to have been an unusually loose feature of the incentive pay system—a so-called "kitty" —and much of Professor Argyris's discussion of worker attitudes and resentments has to do with the kitty's demise. Briefly, an employee could restrict his reported production by holding back work tickets, "banking" them in his kitty until a day when he was assigned a tough job, when he was not feeling well, or when his machine broke down. (There is no report as to the effect of this informal system on production scheduling and inventory control!)

Professor Argyris does not present any results of Plant No. 6's "pressure" in terms of output or costs, but he does give some adverse

results in terms of absenteeism, turnover, and quality. The high-skill departments had a considerably poorer record on quality than the low-skill groups, although no control figures are given for the period preceding the study.

Like the Norwegian experiment, this exhaustive study under almost ideal experimental conditions (two like plants, one subject to stress, the other available as a control) must be considered disappointing to anyone seeking positive proof supporting theories on human relations. It produced few quantitative results that one can sink his teeth into.

WHAT IT ALL ADDS UP TO

What we have been saying in this chapter may be summed up as follows:

1. Studies at the Western Electric Company some 30 years ago got everyone to thinking much more than before about the human relations factor in industry. There was a great swing toward human relations skills in supervisory training and in executive development programs. Great stress has been laid on the findings that social relationships within a working group and the attitudes of employees toward their supervisors were actually more important than physical aspects of the job and often more important than pay. "Democratic foremanship" rather than "authoritarian direction" has been advocated. There has been emphasis on the need of employees to participate in decisions affecting their work, to give them a sense of belonging.

   In their concern about allowing people in industry to work as mutually helpful members of groups rather than as highly competitive individuals, some loud voices have been raised against piecework and other individual-incentive plans. Many case examples have purported to show that better results are obtained when groups of employees are allowed to set their own pace.

2. In more recent years, there have been a number of attempts at scientifically controlled experiments to get a quantitative basis for the assumptions made about the beneficial effects (in terms of tangible increases in productivity or production-related reductions in worker dissatisfaction or reductions in problems of quality, turnover, absenteeism, and so on) of a management policy of permitting a high degree of participation, providing a sense of belonging, and exercising democratic supervision.

   As a whole, the results are not statisti-

[13] Chris Argyris, "The Organization: What Makes It Healthy?" *Harvard Business Review*, November–December, 1958.

cally impressive, and some of the interpretations have been challenged. But, even where the results seem quite inconclusive, many conductors of experiments apparently are uninfluenced by their own findings and remain stanch advocates of the "human relations thesis," on the basis of side speculation flowing from their work rather than on quantitative proof.

3. In recent years there have been some strong criticisms of the emphasis on human relations and even some critical review of the original Hawthorne studies. There has been a tendency in many executive appraisal programs and supervisory development courses in industry to return to an emphasis on tangible performance results. This has implied a more "hard-boiled" approach to achieving engineered performance standards by employees with less concern for subtle motivations and formally "structured" human relations.

SIGNIFICANCE FOR THE SUPERVISOR

What should the balanced appraisal be? The following remarks are offered as a guide to the supervisor who is confronted with practical problems of output and quality but who also has an awareness of the importance of the individual human being in every production group.

1. There is as yet no exact science of human relations. It is not possible to predict the specific results in terms of *worker output* to be obtained by extending the degree of participation by employees, improving their "job satisfaction," clarifying their attitudes toward management, and so on.

2. The supervisor will be well advised to take heed of the swing toward greater stress on cost and immediate output as measures of his supervisory effectiveness and insist upon results from his people without too many qualms about friction and harmony and the workers' liking for him as a person. But this does not mean that he should dismiss as "bunk" all the preoccupation with human relations that has become increasingly prevalent over the past few decades. Without trying to develop a host of formalized techniques, he should take the common-sense view that "treating people like people" results in a more responsive working force.

3. Putting real thought into overcoming resistance to change, into effective communication, into putting workers at their ease when instructing them or checking on them, into getting them to work as a team for the objectives of the company—all of these are definitely part of good supervision. At the same time, it will be well to beware of going overboard on some of the notions advanced about seeking employee views on every change, about allowing employees to allocate work or set their own pace, and the like.

4. The concept of "democratic supervision" is sound—within limits. Yes, if it means careful indoctrination of the worker by the supervisor on what is expected of him, careful teaching of methods, solicitation of suggestions, voice for the employee *to the extent feasible* in work allocation, and then a minimum of "breathing down the employee's neck." Yes, *if by his experience in his own department* he knows that his people are ready for it. No, if he has "green" help, or if methods in his department have undergone a significant change, or if the quality record is poor, or if there has been a past record of poor management/employee relationships. Of course, the application of the principle depends upon the type of operation. Supervisors of highly creative departments (such as research and development) are the best candidates for the "linking pin" concept and are most effective when they consider themselves largely as representative of the employees to higher management rather than as strict directors of their efforts. The same could be true in almost any highly skilled, low-turnover department.

5. Contrary to much of the human relations literature, individual-incentive systems, *properly engineered* and installed in a way to achieve full employee understanding and cooperation, are still a powerful motivator. As recently as October 1960, Arthur A. Rath, a pioneer in the field, had this to say:[14]

> Based on observation in hundreds of plants, large and small, in every type of industry, it is my conviction that nothing will stimulate an employee to perform at his top capacity as will individual incentives—a system of compensation which links his reward as directly as possible with his *own efforts*. This position is based not only on 40 years of personal contact with problems of worker productivity, but also on parallel profes-

[14] Arthur A. Rath, "The Case for Individual Incentives: Management's Most Potent Motivational Tool," *Personnel Journal*, October, 1960.

sional experience of others, the testimony of operating executives, and by confirming evidence of published surveys.

It goes without saying that the supervisor must be thoroughly acquainted with the workings of the plan in force (and the plan must be one that adheres to modern industrial relations principles). The attitude cannot be that an individual-incentive system is "automatic" and requires less skilled supervision. (The "kitty" with which Professor Argyris is so preoccupied would not be tolerated in advanced practice.)

6. Employee participation should be encouraged *in matters which are within the employees' province.* They should be given ample explanation about changes, and their opinions and suggestions should be welcomed. Key employees will often have good ideas on how work can be done better, and, as is advocated by the practitioners of work simplification, the supervisor can use these ideas in supplementing the work of the professional methods and systems people in plant or office. Management should have a policy of paying well for any usable ideas. However, management should not step away from its right and duty to manage. The supervisor should be wary of those who advocate that workers set the pace of their work. This is something for engineers to determine. Even James F. Lincoln, famous for the "incentive management" system he instituted at the Lincoln Electric Company,[15] centers all his motivational philosophy around instilling a sense of belonging and participation in employees and flatly attests, "It is the responsibility of management to find the most efficient way of doing any job. This is not the responsibility of the operator."

With engineered performance standards in use, the opportunities for democratic supervision are, if anything, enhanced. Since methods and expected output are established, the supervisor can leave conscientious employees to be their own taskmasters and concentrate on planning for and servicing the department.

7. There is no conflict between the concept of *participation,* as exemplified in successful group incentive plans, and the drive of *individual competition,* as shown in the success of individual-incentive plans—as long as there is ingrained acceptance of the idea of individual responsibility for performance. To be successful, group plans require that employees be ready for them. Engineered group incentives can, with proper management philosophy, develop a feeling of solidarity, of individuals helping one another. Perhaps the Lincoln Electric plan is the best example of combining the drives of *both* individual competition and teamwork: Every encouragement is given, by dividing a fair share of profits among employees, to constructive efforts by them as members of a group, and to fostering pride in belonging to the group. But *within* each group each man is judged individually and given individual recognition so that he can benefit both ways. As Mr. Lincoln puts it, "All men want to be part of a group—but they still want to be outstanding in that group. . . . Competition and pride are fundamental urges."

8. Even though there is no solid statistical evidence correlating job satisfaction with tangible output, the supervisor should not forget about satisfaction and concentrate solely on output. The conclusion to be drawn from research is that we should revise a fundamental notion about job satisfaction: It is not the *cause* of something (for example, increased production) but rather the *result* of something (the conditions under which the work is done). Hence, job satisfaction is an *output,* not an *input.* But it should always be a desired output, and for long-run operating efficiency it is intelligent to take the position that a balance may well be struck which sacrifices some productivity for job satisfaction.

[15] James F. Lincoln, *Incentive Management,* Lincoln Electric Company, Cleveland, 1951.

51

*What Price Human Relations?**

MALCOLM P. McNAIR

In 1956 the Inland Steel Company appointed a vice president of human relations. The Inland Steel Company, of course, is big business; but little business is not being neglected, for I note that the McGraw-Hill Book Company, Inc., is publishing a book on *Human Relations in Small Industry*. The Harvard Business School has had a chair of Human Relations since 1950; by now the number of courses in Human Relations in schools and colleges throughout the country has multiplied substantially. Even more marked is the rapid growth of executive development programs, some in schools, some in industry, but almost all of them placing emphasis on human relations.

Doctoral theses increasingly carry such titles as "A Case Study of the Human Aspects of Introducing a New Product into Production," "An Intensive Study of Supervisory Training in Human Relations and Foreman Behavior at Work," "A Case Study of the Administration of Change in the Large Modern Office," and "Emergence of Leadership in Manufacturing Work Groups." And recently the *Harvard Business Review* has reprinted a dozen articles on human relations, under the title "How Successful Executives Handle People, 12 Studies on Communications and Management Skills," which include such intriguing subjects as "Making Human Relations Work," "Barriers and Gateways to Communication," and "The Fateful Process of Mr. A Talking to Mr. B."

It is obvious that human relations is very much the fashion in business thinking today. And fashions in business thinking are not a novelty; there have been many others. I can well recall that when I first joined the Harvard Business School faculty, the reigning vogue in

business thinking was scientific management. Only a few years later, however, the grandiose claims of scientific management were sharply debunked. What was of solid worth remained —but a considerable amount of froth had been blown off the top.

Must we go through the same process—with all its waste and possible damage along the way—to get to what is worthwhile in human relations?

My quarrel is not with the solid substance of much that is comprehended by the phrase "human relations," but rather with the "cult" or "fad" aspects of human relations, which are assuming so much prominence.

There can be no doubt that people are of absorbing interest to other people. To verify this fact you have only to look at what makes headlines in the newspapers. There is a fascination for most of us in speculating about people and their behavior. So it is not surprising that human relations has assumed so much prominence as a fashionable mode of thinking. But, as with any kind of fashion, it can be carried to the point where people accept it without questioning—and certainly this can be dangerous when we are dealing with such an important segment of man's activity.

Therefore, just because the tide has gone so far, I must make my points in the most emphatic manner possible. Though I feel I have not distorted the picture, I do not care whether businessmen accept my interpretation in full, or even in large part, *so long as they get stirred up to do some critical thinking of their own.*

Before going any further let me try to indicate the things in this area of human relations which are really basic and with which there is no conceivable quarrel. In the first place, there can be no dispute with research in the social sciences, including the behavioral sciences. Obviously such research is highly important to business management and to business education. Business management and education must seek to understand the behavior of people as

* Reprinted by permission of the publisher from *Harvard Business Review*, vol. 35, no. 2, pp. 15–23, March-April, 1957. Mr. McNair is Lincoln Filene Professor of Retailing at the Harvard Business School and a director of Indian Head Mills, Inc., Allied Stores Corporation, the National Retail Dry Goods Association, and several large department stores.

workers, the behavior of people as members of organizations, and, of course, the behavior of people as consumers. In all these areas we need more and better understanding of human behavior.

Neither is there any dispute in regard to the things that are important for a man's conduct in relation to his fellow men. The foundation is good Christian ethics, respect for the dignity of the individual human being, and integrity of character. On these we should stand fast. Personally I have always liked this paraphrase of what Theodore Roosevelt once said in a commencement address: "On the Ten Commandments and the Sermon on the Mount, uncompromising rigidity; on all else, the widest tolerance."[1] But between acceptance of high moral principles and the exigencies of day-to-day conduct of affairs there can be, with the best intentions, a very wide gap. This is the gap which by better understanding of human motivation we should try to fill.

Also there can be little dispute about the observations on the behavior of people at work which Professor Fritz J. Roethlisberger, the leader of the human relations group at Harvard, summed up half a dozen years ago:

> People at work are not so different from people in other aspects of life. They are not entirely creatures of logic. They have feelings. They like to feel important and to have their work recognized as important. Although they are interested in the size of their pay envelopes, this is not a matter of their first concern. Sometimes they are more interested in having their pay reflect accurately the relative social importance to them of the different jobs they do. Sometimes even still more important to them than maintenance of socially accepted wage differentials is the way their superiors treat them.
>
> They like to work in an atmosphere of approval. They like to be praised rather than blamed. They do not like to have to admit their mistakes—at least, not publicly. They like to know what is expected of them and where they stand in relation to their boss's expectations. They like to have some warning of the changes that may affect them.
>
> They like to feel independent in their relations to their supervisors. They like to be able to express their feelings to them without being misunderstood. They like to be listened to and have their feelings and points of view taken into account. They like to be consulted about and

participate in the actions that will personally affect them. In short, employees, like most people, want to be treated as belonging to and being an integral part of some group.[2]

In other words, "People behave like people." They have feelings. They don't always behave logically. The concept of the economic man can be a dangerous abstraction. Every individual wants to feel important, to have self-esteem, to have "face." Everybody likes to feel that he is "wanted." He likes to have a "sense of belonging." Group influences and group loyalties are important. The desire for psychological "security" is strong. People don't always reveal their feelings in words.

That all these human attitudes have important consequences for management is likewise not open to dispute. It is well accepted in management thinking today that leadership has to be earned, it cannot be conferred; that authority comes from below, not from above; that in any business unit there will be "social" groups which will cut across organization lines; that good communication involves both the willingness to listen and the ability to "get through" but not by shouting.

Dean Stanley F. Teele of the Harvard Business School recently made the statement,

> As we have learned more and more about a business organization as a social unit, we have become increasingly certain that the executive's skill with people—or the lack of it—is the determining element in his long-range success or failure.[3]

Here we are down to the nub of the matter. What is this skill? Can it be taught? Are there dangers in the teaching of it? Is skill an appropriate concept?

Perhaps I can give a clue to the line of thought which I am developing when I say that I am essentially disturbed at the combination of *skill* with *human relations*. For me, "human relations skill" has a cold-blooded connotation of proficiency, technical expertness, calculated effect.

There is no gainsaying the fact that a need long existed in many businesses for a much

---

[1] From Farida Wiley (ed.), *Theodore Roosevelt's America*, The Devin-Adair Company, Inc., New York, 1955, Introduction, p. xxi.

[2] Fritz J. Roethlisberger, "The Human Equation in Employee Productivity," Speech before the Personnel Group of the National Retail Dry Goods Association, 1950.

[3] Stanley F. Teele, "The Harvard Business School and the Search for Ultimate Values," Speech at the presentation to the *Harvard Business Review* of a citation from The Laymen's Movement for a Christian World, New York, Oct. 25, 1955.

greater awareness of human relations and that, in some, perhaps in a considerable number, the need still exists. The very avidity with which people prone to fashionable thinking in business have seized on the fad of human relations itself suggests the presence of a considerable guilt complex in the minds of businessmen in regard to their dealings with people. So it is not my intent to argue that there is no need for spreading greater awareness of the human relations point of view among many businessmen. Nevertheless it is my opinion that some very real dangers threaten.

The world's work has to be done, and people have to take responsibility for their own work and their own lives. Too much emphasis on human relations encourages people to feel sorry for themselves, makes it easier for them to slough off responsibility, to find excuses for failure, to act like children. When somebody falls down on a job, or does not behave in accordance with accepted codes, we look into his psychological background for factors that may be used as excuses. In these respects the cult of human relations is but part and parcel of the sloppy sentimentalism characterizing the world today.

Undue preoccupation with human relations saps individual responsibility, leads us not to think about the job any more and about getting it done but only about people and their relations. I contend that discipline has its uses in any organization for accomplishing tasks. And this is especially true of self-discipline. Will power, self-control, and personal responsibility are more than ever important in a world that is in danger of wallowing in self-pity and infantilism.

Most great advances are made by individuals. Devoting too much effort in business to trying to keep everybody happy results in conformity, in failure to build individuals. It has become the fashion to decry friction, but friction has its uses; without friction there are no sparks, without friction it is possible to go too far in the direction of sweetness and light, harmony, and the avoidance of all irritation. The present-day emphasis on "bringing everybody along" can easily lead to a deadly level of mediocrity.

We can accept the first part of a statement by Peter Drucker:

> The success and ultimately the survival of every business, large or small, depends in the last analysis on its ability to develop people. . . . This ability . . . is not measured by any of our conventional yardsticks of economic success; yet it is the final measurement.

Drucker, however, goes on to add a further thought, which opens more opportunity for debate. He says,

> Increasingly from here on this ability to develop people will have to be systematized by management as a major conscious activity and responsibility.

In this concept there is the familiar danger of turning over to a program or a course or an educational director a responsibility that is a peculiarly personal one.

The responsibility for developing people belongs to every executive as an individual. No man is a good executive who is not a good teacher; and if Drucker's recommendation that executive development be "systematized by management as a major conscious activity" is interpreted as meaning that someone trained in the new mode of thinking should be appointed as director of executive development, then the probable outcome will be simply another company program in human relations. While this may be good for some of the executives, no long-run contribution to the development of good people will be made unless the good individuals personally take the responsibility for developing other individuals.

Please do not misunderstand me. I am not talking about old-fashioned rugged individualism or the law of the jungle, and I am not holding up as ideals the robber barons of the nineteenth century, or even some of the vigorous industrialists of the early twentieth century. But I ask you to consider whether some of today's business leaders, well known to all of us—Clarence Randall, Gardiner Symonds, Neil McElroy, Tex Colbert, Earl Puckett, Fred Lazarus, and so on—are not primarily products of a school of friction and competitive striving. We need more men like them, not fewer. It may be appropriate here to cite the recent observations of Dean Teele on "inner serenity" and "divine discontent":

> Any realistic approach to the nature of top business management, and therefore to the problems of selection and development for top business management, makes abundantly clear that the balance between these two [attributes] is perhaps the most important determinant of success in top business management. Let me elaborate.
>
> Psychiatrists, psychologists, and religious advisers join with ordinary lay observers in noting how often human efficiency is greatly reduced by sharp inner conflicts—conflicts which usually center around value judgments. That is to say,

conflicts as to basic personal purposes and objectives, as to the values to be sought in life, are far more often the barriers to effective performance than intellectual incapacity or lack of necessary knowledge. The goal then from this point of view is the development of that inner serenity which comes from having struggled with and then resolved the basic questions of purpose and values.

On the other hand, in business as in the world generally, discontent is an element of the greatest importance. Dissatisfaction with oneself, with one's performance, is an essential for improvement. So important to the progress of the world is discontent on the part of the relatively few who feel it, that we have come to characterize it as divine discontent. Here . . . the need is for both inner serenity and divine discontent—a need for both in a balance between the two appropriate for the particular individuals.[4]

To keep that important balance of inner serenity and divine discontent in our future business leaders, we need to focus educational and training programs more sharply on the development of individuals than is the fashion today. What is important for the development of the individual? Obviously, many things; but one prime essential is the ability to think, and the nurturing of this ability must be a principal objective of all our educational effort.

In the field of business education this ability to think, to deal with situations, to go to the heart of things, to formulate problems and issues, is not an innate quality. It has to be cultivated, and it requires long and rigorous and often tedious practice in digging out significant facts in weighing evidence, foreseeing contingencies, developing alternatives, finding the right questions to ask. In all business education, whether at the college or graduate level or at the stage of so-called executive development, we must not omit the insistence on close analysis, on careful reasoning and deduction, on cultivation of the power to differentiate and discriminate.

There is a very real danger that undue preoccupation with human relations can easily give a wrong slant to the whole process of education for business leadership. For one thing, it tends to give a false concept of the executive job. Dealing with people is eminently important in the day's work of the business executive, but so are the processes of analysis, judg-

---

[4] Stanley F. Teele, "The Fourth Dimension in Management," Address to the American Management Association, New York, May 25, 1956.

ment, and decision making. It takes skill and persistence to dig out facts; it takes judgment and understanding to get at the real issues; it takes perspective and imagination to see the feasible alternatives; it takes logic and intuition to arrive at conclusions; it takes the habit of decision and a sense of timing to develop a plan of action.

On the letterhead of the general policy letters that are sent periodically to the managing directors of all 80-odd stores in the Allied Stores Corporation there is this slogan:

> To LOOK is one thing.
> To SEE what you look at is another.
> To UNDERSTAND what you see is a third.
> To LEARN from what you understand is still something else.
> But to ACT on what you learn is all that really matters, isn't it?

An executive's ability to see, to understand, to learn, and to act comprises much more than skill in human relations.

Awareness of human relations as one aspect of the executive's job is of course essential. But, in my view, *awareness of human relations* and the *conscious effort to practice human relations on other people* are two different things, and I think this is crucial.

As soon as a man consciously undertakes to practice human relations, one of several bad consequences is almost inevitable. Consciously trying to practice human relations is like consciously trying to be a gentleman. If you have to think about it, insincerity creeps in and personal integrity moves out. With some this leads by a short step to the somewhat cynical point of view which students in Administrative Practices courses have described by coining the verb "ad prac," meaning to "manipulate people for one's own ends."

A less deliberate but perhaps even more dangerous consequence may be the development of a yen for managing other people's lives, always, of course, with the most excellent intentions. In the same direction the conscious practice of human relations leads to amateur psychiatry and to the unwarranted invasions of the privacy of individuals.

Hence I am disturbed about the consequences to business management of human relations blown up into pseudoscience—with a special vocabulary and with special practitioners and experts. In fact, to my mind there is something almost sinister about the very term "human relations practitioner," though I am sure that all sincere devotees of human relations would vigorously disclaim any such imputation.

For me much of the freshness and the insight which characterized a great deal of the earlier work in this field—exemplified by the quotation from Professor Roethlisberger which I cited in my introductory statement—has been lost as the effort has progressed to blow human relations up into a science—something to be explored and practiced for its own sake.

I realize that many people in the human relations field—Professor Roethlisberger in particular—are also disturbed about this trend, and about its unintended repercussions. But it was almost inevitable that other people would run away with such a fruitful concept, and set it up as an idol with appropriate rituals of worship (usually called "techniques"). Once you throw yourself into trying to "listen," to "gain intuitive familiarity," to "think in terms of mutually independent relationship," and so on, you can easily forget that there is more to business—and life—than running around plying human relations "skill" to plumb the hidden thoughts of everybody with whom you come in contact, including yourself.

This is the same mistake that some consumer motivation researchers make, as Alfred Politz has pointed out—trying to find out the attitudes, opinions, and preferences in the consumer's mind *without regard* to whether these factors are what determine how he will act in a given buying situation.[5] In his words, the "truth" that such researchers seek—and he always puts the word in quotes—is not only of a lower order than the scientifically established facts of how consumers react in real life, but it is also of less use to managers in making marketing decisions.

The whole things gets a little ridiculous when . . . foremen are assumed to have progressed when they have gained in "consideration" at the expense of something called "initiating structure"—yet such was the apparent objective of one company's training program.[6]

From the standpoint of developing really good human relations in a business context, to say nothing of the job of getting the world's work done, the kind of training just described seems to me in grave danger of bogging down in semantics and trivialities and dubious introspection. I am totally unable to associate the

conscious practice of human relations skill (in the sense of making people happy in spite of themselves or getting them to do something they don't think they want to do) with the *dignity of an individual person created in God's image.*

Apparently this "skill" of the "human relations practitioner" consists to a considerable degree of what is called "listening." The basic importance of the ability to listen is not to be gainsaid; neither is it to be denied that people do not always reveal their inward feelings in words. But in the effort to blow human relations up into a science and develop a technique of communication, some of the enthusiasts have worked up such standard conversational gambits as "This is what I think I hear you saying," or "As I listen, this is what I think you mean."

No doubt there are times when a silent reaction of this kind is appropriate, but if the human relations practitioner makes such phrases part of his conversational repertoire, there are times when these cute remarks may gain him a punch in the nose. Sometimes people damn well mean what they are saying and will rightly regard anything less than a man-to-man recognition of that fact as derogatory to their dignity.

That a group of foremen who were given a course emphasizing human relations and thereafter turned out to be distinctly poorer practitioners than they had been before taking the course, as in the above case, would not, to my mind, be simply an accident. I think it a result that might well be expected nine times out of ten. In other words, the overemphasis on human relations, with all its apparatus of courses, special vocabulary, and so on, tends to create the very problems that human relations deals with. It is a vicious circle. You encourage people to pick at the scabs of their psychic wounds.

In evaluating the place of human relations in business, a recent incident is in point:

At a luncheon gathering Miss Else Herzberg, the highly successful educational director of a large chain of stores in Great Britain, Marks and Spencer, Ltd., described at some length the personnel management policies of that concern and the high state of employee morale that existed. Throughout her description I was listening for some reference to human relations. I did not hear it, and when she had finished I said, "But, Miss Herzberg, you haven't said anything about human relations." Immediately she flashed back, "We live it; we don't have to talk about it."

[5] Alfred Politz, "Science and Truth in Marketing Research," *Harvard Business Review*, January–February, 1957, p. 117.
[6] Kenneth R. Andrews, "Is Management Training Effective? II. Measurement, Objectives, and Policy," *Harvard Business Review*, March–April, 1957, p. 63.

In point also is a recent remark of Earl Puckett, chairman of the board of Allied Stores Corporation, when in discussing a particular management problem he said, "Of course you treat people like people."

And so, although I concede that there is still too little awareness of human relations problems in many business organizations, I think that the present vogue for human relations and for executive development programs which strongly emphasize human relations holds some real dangers because it weakens the sense of responsibility, because it promotes conformity, because it too greatly subordinates the development of individuals, and because it conveys a one-sided concept of the executive job.

I turn now more specifically to the dangers to business education at the college level which seem to me inherent in the present overemphasis upon human relations. Business executives should have as much concern with this part of the subject as teachers—perhaps more, because they must use the young men we turn out; furthermore, they represent the demand of the market and so can have a real influence on what the educators do.

The dangers to the education of young men, in my opinion, are even more serious than the dangers to business executive development programs for mature men. After all, we are well aware that businessmen follow fads, and so fairly soon the human relations cult in business will begin to wane and operations research or something else will become the fashion. Also, as remarked earlier, there is still a substantial need in business for greater awareness of human relations, and more businessmen are sufficiently adult to separate the wheat from the chaff. Thus in advanced management training programs for experienced executives there is no doubt greater justification for courses in Human Relations than there is in collegiate and immediate graduate programs.

From the general educational standpoint perhaps the first question is whether human relations can be taught at all. I do not deny that something can be learned about human relations, but I do maintain that direct emphasis on human relations as subject matter defeats the purpose. When things must come from the heart, the Emily Post approach won't do; and if behavior does not come from the heart, it is phony. Clarence Budington Kelland, that popular writer of light fiction, in a recent *Saturday Evening Post* serial entitled "Counterfeit Cavalier," makes one of his characters say:

A very nice person has to start by being nice inside and have an aptitude for it. . . . They don't have to learn. It comes natural. No trimmings, but spontaneous. . . . If you have to think about it, it is no good.[7]

Good human relations do not lend themselves to anatomical dissection with a scalpel. How do people normally acquire good human relations? Some of course never do. In the case of those who do enjoy success in human relations and at the same time retain their sincerity, the result, I am convinced, is a composite product of breeding, home, church, education, and experience generally, not of formal Human Relations courses.

Hence in my view it is a mistake in formal education to seek to do more than develop an awareness of human relations, preferably as an integral part of other problems. This does not mean, of course, that the results of research in human behavior should not be utilized in the teaching of business administration. Certainly such results should be utilized (with due circumspection to avoid going overboard on theories that are still mostly in the realm of speculation). To take account of human relations in marketing problems and in personnel management problems and in labor relations problems and industrial management problems, and so on, of course makes sense. What I am decrying is the effort to teach human relations as such. Thus, I applaud the training of personnel managers, but I am exceedingly skeptical of training human relations practitioners.

I should like also to venture the personal opinion that human relations in its fairly heavy dependence on Freudian psychology is headed the wrong way. In the long history of mankind, the few centuries, dating perhaps from the Sumerian civilization, during which we have sought to apply an intellectual and moral veneer to man the animal are a very short period indeed as compared with the time that has elapsed since our ancestors first began to walk erect; and it seems to me that a large part of the job of education still must be to toughen and thicken this veneer, not to encourage people to crack it and peel it off, as seems to have been the fashion for much of the last half century. I suspect that modern psychiatry is in a vicious circle, that some of the principal causes of increased mental disease lie in morbid introspection, lack of strong moral convictions, and leisure that we have not yet learned how to use.

I believe that one of these days a newer

7 Clarence Buddington Kelland, *Counterfeit Cavalier, Saturday Evening Post*, May 26, 1956, p. 24.

school of thought in these matters will re-emphasize the importance of will power, self-control, and personal responsibility. I can well recall hearing Charles William Eliot, on the occasion of his ninetieth birthday, repeat his famous prescription for a happy life: "Look up, and not down, look forward and not backward, look out and not in."

Our present preoccupation with the emotional and nonlogical aspects of life seems to me in many ways responsible for the prevalent wishful thinking of the American people. As a higher and higher proportion of American youth goes to college, it might be supposed that intelligently realistic ways of looking at things would be on the increase, but the contrary seems to be true. As people we are more prone than ever to let our desires color our thinking. More and more the few people who have the courage to present realistic viewpoints on national and world affairs find that the public will not listen to what it does not wish to hear. Why isn't education bringing us a more intelligent outlook on life?

Can it be that one of the reasons is that education itself has surrendered so far to the ideas that are concerned primarily with the current fashionable interest in the emotional and nonlogical aspects of living? In reviewing Joan Dunn's book, *Why Teachers Can't Teach —A Case History,* E. Victor Milione remarks, "Our educational system has substituted training in life adjustment for education."[8] Obviously there are many analogies between the doctrines of the progressives in education and the over-emphasis on human relations. Personally I prefer a more rigorous educational philosophy. I can well recall a remark of A. Lawrence Lowell that "the business of education is making people uncomfortable."

In any event, I think it is the job of education to push for more and not less emphasis on logics and morals in dealing with social problems. The following quotation from C. C. Furnas, chancellor of the University of Buffalo, makes much sense to me:

> We must recognize, of course, that it takes much more than pure intellect to answer social questions. Great problems involving many people are usually handled in an atmosphere of high emotion and the participants often show but little evidence of being rational human beings. But, even though it acts slowly, it is certainly true that intelligence can and does have some influence in shaping mass emotions. It is in this slow modification of mass emotional

patterns that the average intelligent person can and should play a continuing role within his own sphere of influence.[9]

How can we do this if we encourage immature minds to regard the nonlogical aspects as the most important? Not that teachers necessarily intend it this way—though I am sure some have been carried so far—but simply that putting so much explicit emphasis on the emotional and irrational makes the student feel it is all-important. No protestation to the contrary can undo that impression—that perhaps *nonlogical* impression—which is exactly what an understanding of human behavior ought to lead us to expect in the first place.

But perhaps my principal quarrel with the teaching of human relations has to do with timing. Discussion of such problems as what men should learn, and how they should learn it, is probably as old as education itself, but much less attention has been given to the question, "When should men learn?"

The whole modern development of adult education has brought into disrepute the old adage that you can't teach an old dog new tricks. In fact, in the area of business administration it is quite plausible that teaching of certain managerial skills is best accomplished in later years, after men have gained considerable experience in business activities. William H. Whyte, Jr., the author of *Is Anybody Listening?* and *The Organization Man,* in discussing the Alfred P. Sloan Fellowship Program at the Massachusetts Institute of Technology, has this to say:

> But on one point there is considerable agreement: to be valuable, such a course should be taken only when a man has had at least five years' business experience. The broad view can be a very illusory thing. Until a man has known the necessity—the zest—of mastering a specific skill, he may fall prey to the idea that the manager is a sort of neutralist expediter who concerns himself only with abstractions such as human relations and motivation. Those who study these subjects after ten years or so of job experience have already learned the basic importance of doing a piece of work; in the undergraduate business schools, however, the abstractions are instilled in impressionable minds before they are ready to read between the lines and to spot the vast amount of hot air and wishful thinking that is contained in the average business curriculum.[10]

[8] E. Victor Milione, *The Freeman,* March, 1956, p. 59.

[9] *Ibid.,* p. 24.
[10] William H. Whyte, Jr., *Fortune,* June, 1956, p. 248.

Among those managerial skills the specific teaching of which had better be left to later years is the handling of human relations. Thus I should not only rewrite the old adage in the form, "There are some tricks you can teach only to an old dog," but I should go on to the important corollary, "There are some tricks that you had better not try to teach to young dogs." The dangers in trying to teach human relations as such at the collegiate or immediate graduate level are substantial. Indeed, by developing courses in human relations for college graduates in their early twenties without previous business experience we are essentially opening Pandora's box.

Such courses lead to a false concept of the executive's job. There is a de-emphasis of analysis, judgment, and decision making. Someone has said that the job of the modern executive is to be intelligently superficial. This statement is true in the sense that when a man reaches an important executive post, he does not have time to go to the bottom of every problem that is presented to him, and he certainly should not undertake himself to do the work of his subordinates. If he does these things, he is a poor executive. But if an executive has not learned at some stage to go to the bottom of problems in one or more particular areas, he will not in the long run be a successful manager.

Human relations expertise is not a substitute for administrative leadership, and there is danger in getting young men to think that business administration consists primarily of a battery of experts in operations research, mathematics, theory of games, and so on, equipped with a Univac and presided over by a smart human relations man. Undoubtedly many of the new techniques are substantial aids to *judgment,* but they do not fully replace that vital quality. One of the great dangers in teaching human relations as such at the collegiate or immediate graduate level is that the student is led to think that he can short-cut the process of becoming an executive.

The study of human relations as such also opens up a wonderful "escape" for the student in many of his other courses. Let's admit it: none of us is too much enamored of hard thinking, and when a student in class is asked to present an analysis of some such problem as buying a piece of equipment, or making a needed part instead of buying it, he frequently is prone to dodge hard thinking about facts in favor of speculation on the probable attitudes of workers toward the introduction of a new machine or new process.

For some students, as for some businessmen, the discussion of human relations aspects of business management problems can even lead to the development of the cynical "ad prac" point of view, which assumes that the chief end of studying human relations is to develop skill in manipulating people; this perhaps is the present-day version of high-pressure selling.

A different but equally dangerous result occurs in the case of the student who becomes so much interested in human relations that he turns himself into an amateur psychiatrist, appraises every problem he encounters in terms of human relations, and either reaches an unhealthy state of introspection or else develops a zeal for making converts to human relations and winds up with a passion for running other people's lives.

The sum of the matter is this. It is not that the human relations concept is wrong; it is simply that we have blown it up too big and have placed too much emphasis on teaching human relations as such at the collegiate and early graduate level. A sound program in business education, in my opinion, will of course envisage research in human behavior; it may, with some possible good results, venture on offering specific courses in Human Relations for mature executives; but for students in their twenties who have not yet become seasoned in practical business activities we should keep away from specific courses in Administrative Practices and Human Relations, while at the same time inculcating an awareness of human relations problems wherever they appropriately appear in other management courses. In other words, let us look closely enough at what we are doing so we can be sure that the gains we make in this area turn out to be *net* gains.

Finally, to express a personal conviction on a somewhat deeper note, I should like to refer again to Dean Teele's comments, cited earlier, on "inner serenity." The attainment of that all-important goal, in my opinion, is not to be sought through the present vogue of interest in human relations. Inner serenity is an individual matter, not a group product. As Cameron Hawley puts it, "A man finds happiness only by walking his own path across the earth."[11]

Let's treat people like people, but let's not make a big production of it.

[11] Cameron Hawley, "Walk Your Own Path!" *This Week Magazine,* Dec. 11, 1955.

52

Informal Organization[*]

KEITH DAVIS

Beneath the cloak of formal relationships in a business there exists a more complex, complicated system of informal relationships. The informal organization is significant to management because it is a powerful influence upon productivity and job satisfaction. . . .

THE NATURE OF INFORMAL ORGANIZATION

Informal organization is that network of personal and social relations which is not established or required by formal organization. It arises from the social interaction of people, which means that it develops spontaneously as people associate with each other. The emphasis within informal organization is on people and their relationships, whereas formal organization emphasizes positions in terms of authority and functions. Informal authority, therefore, attaches to a *person,* while formal authority attaches to a *position* and a person wields it only by virtue of his position.

Characteristics of Informal Organization

Managers sometimes wish they could order the informal organization abolished with the stroke of a pen. Most of them would prefer to work with only the formal organization, because this would make their job simpler and involve less worry. From their point of view the informal organization is a "thorn in the side" which regularly offers resistance to their formal orders, or amends them, or accomplishes them by a procedure different from the intended one. Regardless of how helpful or harmful it is, managers soon learn its first characteristic—it cannot be absolutely abolished. A manager can rescind any formal organization which he has established, but he did not create the informal organization and he cannot rescind it. As long

* Reprinted by permission of the publisher from Keith Davis, *Human Relations in Business,* McGraw-Hill Book Company, New York, 1957, pp. 98–118. Mr. Davis is professor of management, School of Business, Arizona State University.

as there are people in business there will be informal groups.

Authority in informal organization is earned or given permissively, rather than delegated. Informal authority comes from those who are the object of its control; but formal authority comes from "outsiders" who are "higher up the line," rather than from the people who are controlled by it. In contrast to the downward flow of formal authority, informal authority more often flows upward or horizontally. It is more of a privilege than a right. It is usually more unstable than formal authority, since it is subject to the sentiments of people. Because of its subjective nature, informal organization is not subject to management control in the way that formal organization is.

As a result of the differences between the two sources of authority, formal organization may grow to immense size, but informal organizations (at least the closely knit ones) tend to remain smaller in order to keep within the limits of personal relationships. There are, therefore, many different informal organizations within a large business. They exist at all levels. Some of them are wholly within the business; others are partially external to it.

Informal Leaders

The leaders of informal groups arise from various causes. Some of these causes are age, seniority, technical competence, work location, freedom to move around the work area, and a pleasant, responsive personality. The causes are actually as multitudinous as there are situations because each leader arises under slightly different circumstances. Informal groups overlap to the extent that one person may be a member of several different groups, which means that there is not just one leader but several of varying importance. The group may look to one employee on matters pertaining to wages and to another to lead recreational plans. In this way each person in a department may be some type of informal leader. Perhaps there is an "oldtimer" who is looked upon as the expert on job problems, a "listener" who serves as counselor, and a "spokesman" who is depended upon to convey key problems to the manager. In return for his services, each leader usually enjoys certain rewards and privileges. Perhaps the "oldtimer" is permitted to punch the clock first, and so on. One significant reward is the esteem in which the leader is held.

Although each person in a work group may be leader of some small informal organization, there is usually one primary leader who stands out above the rest. His influence is predominant. Each manager needs to learn who the informal leader of his subordinates is and to work with that person to assure that his leadership is furthering the company's objectives, rather than hindering them. When the informal leader is working against the company, his effect is far greater than his numerical proportion in the group. He is in a biological sense the "dominant gene" in his interaction with others. His influence is illustrated statistically in the following example.

Assume that A is the informal leader in group $ABCDE$. In this group there are 26 interpersonal combinations as follows:[1]

AB	DE	BDE
AC	ABC	CDE
AD	ABD	ABCD
AE	ABE	ABDE
BC	ACD	ACDE
BD	ACE	ABCE
BE	ADE	BCDE
CD	BCD	ABCDE
CE	BCE	

Assuming that A is the leader and that each of the 26 combinations occurs as often as any other, it is seen that A (who is one-fifth of the group) is involved in approximately three-fifths (58 per cent) of the interactions. The result would be identical selecting B, C, D, or E as the informal leader. Since an anticompany informal leader "poisons" a majority of the interpersonal contacts, it is easy to see how one such person can quickly undermine a manager and ruin morale in a whole department. The informal leader in this instance is the one bad apple who ruins the barrel.

[1] The number of combinations for any group may be computed by the combinatorial formula $C \dfrac{N}{r} = \dfrac{N!}{r!(N-r)!}$ which indicates the number of ways in which n things can be combined r at a time. See Acheson J. Duncan, *Quality Control and Industrial Statistics*, Richard D. Irwin, Inc., Homewood, Ill., 1952, pp. 81–82.

The informal organization is a good place for potential formal leaders to develop, but it should be remembered that an informal leader does not always make the best formal manager. Business history is replete with incidents of good informal leaders who became arrogant bosses once they received formal authority. Informal authority, since it comes from those acted upon, holds arrogance in check, but there is no such check on formal authority.

Some informal leaders fail as formal ones because they fear formal responsibility, something they do not have as informal leaders. They often criticize management for lacking initiative, not daring to be different, or being overcautious; but when they take a management job, they become even more conservative because they are afraid to make a mistake. Other informal leaders fail because the area of formal management responsibility is much broader than the tiny functional area in which they had informal authority. The fact that Joe is the leader in departmental social activities does not mean that he will be equally good as the departmental manager.

Functions of Informal Groups   Informal groups arise and persist because they satisfy wants of their members. These wants are determined by the group members themselves. A want which seems to be felt by all groups is the necessity to perpetuate its culture, and this is an important function of any informal organization. A second informal group function is communication. In order to meet wants and to keep its members informed of what is taking place that may affect want satisfaction, the group develops systems and channels of communication.

A third function is social control by which the behavior of others is influenced and regulated. Social control is both internal and external. Internal control is directed toward making members of the group conform to its culture. In an accounting office an employee wore a bow tie to work. Comments and "razzing" from other workers soon convinced him that a bow tie was not an "accepted" style in the group, so thereafter he did not wear it. External control is directed toward those outside the group such as management, union leadership, or other informal groups. Pressures of external control can be quite strong, as when a walkout strike occurs.

Benefits of Informal Organization   Informal organization is sometimes looked upon as a negative force in the work group, but this is not necessarily so. If its interests and goals are integrated with the company's, it will then work for company objectives rather than against them. The manager's big responsibility is to do all he can to effect this integration so that the two groups will mesh instead of clash. This is effective management, and its over-all result is that the informal organization helps get the work done. Dubin, Shartle, and others recognize that this blending of the formal and informal is the most effective way to accomplish work. Formal plans and policies cannot meet *every* problem in a dynamic situation, because they are preestablished and partly inflexible. Some requirements can be met better by informal relations, which can be flexible and spontaneous. Dubin states, "Informal relations in the organization serve to preserve the organization from the self-destruction that would result from literal obedience to the formal policies, rules, regulations, and procedures."[2] Shartle, in reporting his field research on leadership, comments "The informal structure is one index of the dynamics of getting work done, and it appears that for efficiency it will necessarily deviate from the formal structure."[3] This idea can be stated as the *principle of informal organization* as follows: an integration of the interests, goals, methods, and evaluation systems of formal and informal organizations tends to increase productivity and job satisfaction.

The over-all result of "helping get the work done" can be subdivided to show the different types of specific benefits which informal organization brings. First, it may act to lighten the work load of the formal manager. If employees know that their manager has the support of the existing informal organization, they are more likely to respond to his ideas, to be motivated to work efficiently, and to proceed with their assigned tasks without bothering their manager "just to be sure." The manager in this situation feels more free to delegate and decentralize because he is confident that his group will cooperate. This confidence in his people will also act to lighten the mental burden of his responsibility, but not the responsibility itself.

Informal organization acts to fill in gaps in formal orders or in the manager's abilities. If a manager is weak in planning ability, one of his employees may informally help with planning, either through suggestions or open action, so that the over-all result is the same as if the manager did good planning. Shartle reports

that executives tend to choose principal assistants who complement their own abilities.[4] This may be because the situation has been ripe for that type of informal leader to arise within the group. As mentioned earlier, informal organization is a good place to develop leaders, although informal leaders are not always the best formal leaders.

A significant benefit of informal organization is that it gives satisfaction and stability to work groups. It is the means by which workers achieve a sense of belonging and security. It is a device to protect themselves from outside influences and to preserve their culture. The new employee joins a work group as an outsider, and he collides with this protective attitude of the group. Although his formal induction is achieved in a day, his social (informal) induction may take weeks or may never be achieved. He may remain an isolate or outsider. He does not *join* the group in the true sense of the word; he has to be accepted into it.

A well-known benefit of informal organization is that it can be a useful channel of employee communication. Management, in fact, often depends on the informal system to convey certain types of information. Another benefit is that it is a safety valve for the frustrations and other emotional problems of group work. If a man is unhappy and feels he cannot talk to his supervisor, perhaps he will talk to a friend. If a worker has leadership abilities, but the formal organization cannot use them, perhaps he will use his abilities by becoming an informal leader.

A benefit of informal organization which is seldom recognized is that its presence encourages a manager to plan and act more carefully than he would otherwise. Any manager who recognizes its power knows that it is a check and balance on his unlimited use of authority. He will introduce changes into his group only after careful planning because he knows that the informal group could provide the impetus to undermine an ill-conceived and shaky project. He wants his projects to succeed because he will have to answer to *formal* authority if they fail.

Each of the benefits of informal organization can be reversed to become disadvantages under different circumstances. The informal group can lighten the load of the manager, but it can also cause him extra burdens when it works against him. Its communication system can carry useful information, or it may carry useless rumor and gossip. One of the worst effects

[2] Robert Dubin, *Human Relations in Administration,* Prentice-Hall, Inc., Englewood Cliffs, N.J., 1951, p. 68.

[3] Carroll L. Shartle, "Leadership and Executive Performance," *Personnel,* March, 1949, p. 378.

[4] *Ibid.*

of informal organization is its support of restriction-of-work practices in order, supposedly, to protect its members.

Types of Informal Groups   Sociologists have classified three types of informal groups: friendship-kinship groups, cliques, and subcliques.[5] In addition there is a fourth category "isolates," who are not a group but a number of individuals with negligible informal work-group ties. Their differences are illustrated in Figure 6-1. Friendship-kinship groups denote close personal ties as friends or relatives. They most frequently exist in pairs. This type of group in business is especially significant to the *spread* of influence or information. Two close friends or relatives may be members of two separate cliques and thereby carry from one clique to the other an idea or bit of news.

Cliques are composed of persons who commonly associate with each other and maintain certain social practices and standards. Acceptance of a person into the clique requires acceptance by the group, rather than by an individual in it. Subcliques are attached to a clique through having one or more members in it. Subclique members not in the main clique are given only partial acceptance by it.

Charting the Informal Organization   The diagram of group attraction in Figure 6-1 may be called a *sociogram*. This study and meas-

urement of feelings of group members toward each other was pioneered by J. L. Moreno in the 1930s and is called *sociometry*. Moreno classed feelings as attraction, repulsion, and indifference. To learn these feelings in a work group he asked members to rank their choices of people with whom they would like to work or not to work. The person receiving the most votes is the star or sociometric leader. This person is the one liked the most, but is not necessarily the true informal leader who motivates the group to take action. The star can make or break a social fad, but he may be secondary to someone else in leading the group toward a work goal. When the patterns of feelings are charted, the result is a sociogram. Sociometric rankings have been used to build work teams to achieve better teamwork and efficiency. In one instance carpenters and bricklayers were organized into sociometrically selected teams, which reduced their labor cost index from 36.66 to 32.22 and the materials cost index from 33.00 to 31.00 during the eleven-month period after the teams were organized. The over-all result was a saving of five per cent in total production costs, plus more satisfied workers.[6]

Another charting approach is to diagram the actual informal interactions of people, such as with whom one spends the most time and with

[5] Delbert C. Miller and William H. Form, *Industrial Sociology*, Harper & Row, Publishers, Incorporated, New York, 1951, pp. 282–283.

[6] Raymond H. Van Zelst, "Sociometrically Selected Work Teams Increase Production," *Personnel Psychology*, Autumn, 1952, pp. 175–185. See also "Foremen by Popular Acclaim," *Business Week*, Mar. 26, 1955, pp. 171–172.

FIGURE 6-1   Types of Informal Groups

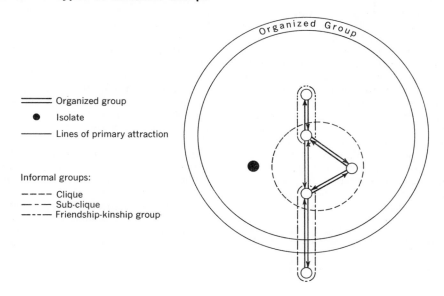

Organized group

● Isolate

Lines of primary attraction

Informal groups:

– – – – Clique
– · – · Sub-clique
– · · – · · Friendship-kinship group

whom one checks when he does not check with his supervisor. Charts of these relationships are usually called interpersonal charts, interaction charts, or informal organization charts. These interaction patterns can be superimposed on the formal organization chart in order to show variation between the two. This is illustrated in Figure 6-2, from a study made by the author. Superimposed on the formal chart are lines showing the patterns of contact which developed from an event known to the managers in positions 27 and 234. Most of these contacts were neither with a direct supervisor nor direct subordinates. Contacts were largely *outside* the direct chains of command. Some of these contacts were required by procedure and were consequently formal, but a large portion of them were informal.

Surveys of employees to determine their interpersonal contacts are called *contactual surveys*. These surveys show informal and procedural relationships and aid management in the following ways:[7]

1. Checking and charting the informal organization
2. Making plans to change organization or procedures
3. Setting up management controls
4. Solving communication problems
5. Locating people who are active communicators and/or facilitate action
6. Locating persons with leadership potential

[7] William B. Seiniger, "Charting the Informal Organization," *Advanced Management,* November, 1951, pp. 24–27.

STATUS

Status refers to the social rank of a person in comparison with others. There are two kinds of status, formal and informal. Formal status refers to the relation of supervisor and subordinate as designated by the chain of command in any organization. Informal status refers to the social rank which others accord to a person because of their feelings toward him. It is the position which one has in a social system. Since this chapter concerns informal organization, the term "status" used hereafter will refer to informal status unless the context implies otherwise.

Status relationships require ranking and comparison. It always takes two or more persons to make a status relationship. One must be higher and the other lower. Status also has certain external markings, such as fancy desks. These are the symbols of status. Since status implies rank, people in business are concerned about it. The desire for status is one of the strongest motivating factors among business people. They sometimes will make unreasonable effort and sacrifice in order to achieve slightly more status. The term "lose face" is often used as a synonym for loss of status in personal interaction, and its seriousness is widely recognized in business. When a person becomes seriously upset over his status and his inability to change it, he is said to have *status anxiety.* Individuals are bound together in *status systems* or *status hierarchies,* which define their relative rank to others in the system.

In addition to its function of distinguishing

FIGURE 6-2   Patterns of Contact about an Event Known to Managers in Positions 27 and 234

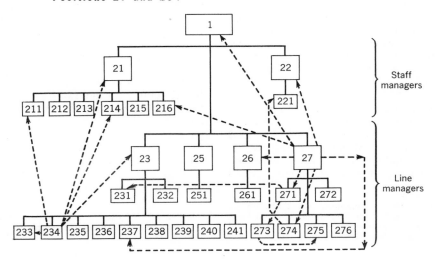

and ranking people, a status system serves three other functions in the business organization. First, it provides a framework for communication and cooperation. Second, it is a basic means of giving people a sense of responsibility. Loss of status is more than loss of prestige. It seriously affects personality. People, therefore, become quite responsible in order to protect and develop their status. Barnard comments, "The desire for improvement of status and especially the desire to protect status appears to be the basis of a sense of general responsibility."[8] Third, and related to responsibility, is the incentive function of status. Since status is important to people, they will work hard to achieve it. Many will seek it for its own sake, even if it provides no additional pay, improved working conditions, or other tangible benefits. When status is attached to actions which further the company's goals, strong incentives are released toward their accomplishment.

> By way of illustration, a laundry manager used to devote negative attention and reprimand (low status) to workers whom he found idle, even when they had finished their work and were waiting for more from another operator. He wanted them to help other operators, but he found that his approach simply caused them to work slower. Upon reexamination of his approach, he decided to try to build the status of his "idle" employees who finished their work ahead of others. He visited with them in a friendly way as he walked through his shop. He permitted them to go to any other work station to talk and visit, or to get soft drinks for themselves or others. The slow workers began to work faster to achieve this status, and the fast workers improved in order to preserve their relative position. As the fast workers visited other work stations they developed friendships and did considerable informal training and helping of the slow workers. The manager later commented, "I am amazed by the changed attitudes of the workers and their increased productivity."

The importance of status requires management to give attention to how it arises and whether managment actions affect it. The total causes of status probably stretch to infinity, because each situation is different. There are, however, several status causes generally found in most business situations, such as age, working conditions, and type of work done. A factor such as age cannot be changed by management, but its influence on status can be modified. Other factors such as working conditions can be somewhat changed.

In-company Causes of Status   Following are some of the status influences which occur within a company.

Organizational Level.   A basic cause of informal status is the rank which a person has in the formal organization. Higher formal rank places him in a position to make decisions about others and to initiate action affecting them. It places one "closer to the top." If people with lamps on their desks originate action on people without desk lamps, then desk lamps eventually become symbols of status. A person who acquires a desk lamp augments his status at the same time, even though he does not initiate action on others. Consequently company desk lamps become sought after, and some persons may even offer to buy their own lamps if the company cannot supply them. Status of a particular level attaches also to those who closely assist that level. The secretary to a vice-president usually has more status than the secretary to a department head.

Type and Level of Skill.   Society generally attaches more status to mental skills than to physical skills, but this relationship is further affected by the skill level which is applied. An unskilled machine operator tends to have less status than an unskilled clerk, but a skilled toolmaker will have more status than the unskilled clerk. The toolmaker acquires his status by virtue of his high skill, even though his work is considered to be largely physical by those who accord him status. Status is also affected by the amount of formal education and effort which was required to prepare for the job.

Sometimes an "insignificant" detail such as the material used affects status. W. F. Whyte in his study of the restaurant industry discovered that cooks who prepare chicken have higher status than those who prepare meat, and that within the zone of chicken preparation the informal scale of jobs falls from white meat to dark meat![9] These relationships tend to exist even when the pay and working conditions are almost identical.

Working Conditions.   Better working conditions generally accord higher status to the

---

[8] Chester I. Barnard, "Functions and Pathology of Status Systems in Formal Organizations," in William F. Whyte (ed.), *Industry and Society,* McGraw-Hill Book Company, New York, 1946, p. 69.

[9] William F. Whyte, *Human Relations in the Restaurant Industry,* McGraw-Hill Book Company, New York, 1948, pp. 33–46.

person having them. This is one of the reasons white-collar jobs throughout the world usually carry more status than blue-collar jobs of equal skill. Most people seem to prefer such white-collar surroundings as soft chairs, air conditioning, and clean hands. Because these things are sought after and there is limited supply relative to demand for them, they eventually achieve higher status. In this respect the status *value* given to different conditions has a supply-and-demand relationship similar to that in economics. When supply is small relative to demand, high status value is attached. When the supply is adequate relative to demand, status value will be less. To illustrate, in an office where a few people are accorded desk pads they may become important status symbols, but when everyone gets desk pads, they assume less status value and the group starts looking for some other way to distinguish their members. As one status symbol becomes generally available to everyone and therefore no longer a mark of distinction, another status symbol will arise to take its place, because the group exhibits a basic need to distinguish its members. The result is that status symbols vary somewhat from department to department, company to company, and time to time.

Pay.   Skill level, working conditions, and other factors determine pay, which in itself becomes a symbol of status. In any work group, status hierarchies are built around differences in pay, and any disturbance of this hierarchy by job evaluation or incentives may produce major disruptions in the social system. When management revises wage scales, it does not simply change a job rate, but it also changes the informal rank of people.

Even the way that pay is computed has its status implications. It is a real mark of distinction to graduate from time-clock punching to merely signing a weekly time sheet. Even more status is achieved when a person makes no time report at all. In a similar way, great prestige is attached in some companies to a listing on the semimonthly payroll instead of the weekly payroll, even though the pay check received is identical.

Seniority.   Being an oldtimer in a company usually merits higher status than do the newcomers. Having been there longer, the oldtimer "knows the ropes" and is in position to assume informal leadership of the newcomers. His group has also secured certain seniority privileges, either through formal agreement with management or as a matter of custom. Some of these privileges seek to protect his job security, because he recognizes that older workers tend to have more difficulty finding employment. Other privileges are purely for personal convenience and status. Vacation dates, overtime, day-shift work, and other privileges are awarded by seniority. Management sometimes permits these practices to exist even when they are detrimental to the company.

Shift preferences were determined by seniority in one firm with the result that nearly all experienced personnel were on the first shift. The night shift suffered greatly from lack of technically qualified men, but management chose not to upset this long-established situation. Night-shift productivity was only 80 per cent of the day shift's. Even foremen and superintendents were assigned shifts by seniority, which gave the night shift young, inexperienced leadership.

External Status Causes   A worker's status is not wholly determined in the company. There are external cultural factors which affect the rank of people in the company social system.

Age.   Though related to seniority, age has an influence all its own. Age is a physiological measurement, but it has its social significance. Younger workers often "look up" to older workers, partly as a carryover of the father-son relationship. Older workers tend to have mutual interests and associate closely.

Sex.   Custom in each plant has decreed certain jobs for men and others for women. Especially in factory work, a woman sometimes is thought to be an intruder who is taking a job away from a man, and is consequently rejected and given secondary status. There is a secular trend toward equal work status for women, but differences still exist.

Racial and Cultural Status.   Social status of a particular racial or cultural group outside the plant affects the status of that entire group in the informal organization. Many business units are located in a *plural community,* which is defined as one in which distinctly different racial or cultural groups coexist within one over-all political and economic unit without mingling in the other aspects of their daily lives.[10] One example is a community having native-born workers and immigrants who cling strongly to customs of the "old country." The group with lesser status in the community will tend to have lesser status in the plant.

In a plural community management must learn to interpret some of its in-plant problems

[10] Cyril Sofer, "Working Groups in a Plural Society," *Industrial and Labor Relations Review,* 1954, p. 68.

in the light of existing social distinctions in the community. Each worker brings to the work situation a set of viewpoints and feelings conditioned by the place his group occupies in the whole society. He reacts to his supervisors, subordinates, and co-workers partly as an individual and partly as representative of the different groups to which he belongs. They, in turn, react to him the same way. A business which enters a community with distinctly different racial or cultural groups will find that its human relations problems are made tougher by preexisting conditions. Though the firm did not cause these conditions, it may be blamed for permitting them to continue at work, because they are fundamentally not related to jobs. The firm is sometimes unrealistically blamed because, although it can ignore racial or cultural differences on the job, they still exist in the minds of men and will continue to influence the informal organization. Management's practical responsibility, therefore, is to make a precise compromise between recognizing differences and not recognizing them.

> In one company, a certain culture of immigrants and their descendants had always held all of the foundry jobs. Other members of the community were just as capable of learning foundry work. At no time did management prohibit outsiders from taking foundry work because it felt that would open it to a charge of discrimination, but it did discourage others from taking foundry work to the extent that foundry work largely remained the special vocation of a certain cultural group.

Occupational Status. A job's status within a plant is partly affected by the general prestige rating of that occupation among the public. This general prestige rating is the one which a company should expect for its jobs, except where there are significant in-plant factors to cause variation. A study of 90 occupations based on 2,920 interviews with a representative sample of people, showed that the highest rankings were U.S. Supreme Court Justice, physician, and state governor, in that order. Lowest ranked jobs were garbage collector, street sweeper, and shoe shiner. The occupational status of selected business jobs, indicated by rank from the top, follows: member of the board of directors of a large corporation, 18; accountant for a large business, 29; official of an international labor union, 40.5; electrician or trained machinist, 45; carpenter, 58; local official of a labor union, 62; machine operator in a factory, 64.5; and janitor, 85.5. People were generally consistent in the ratings,

except that they rated their own and related occupations higher than others did.[11]

Occupational status is significant to human relations in several ways. It often helps a counselor diagnose status problems and conflicts. It definitely influences the employee's reaction to promotion, transfer, and wage administration. In general, employees expect pay to be positively related to status, especially within each promotion hierarchy. A machine operator, for example, expects each job on his promotional route to give him higher status as well as pay. If management's job-evaluation scheme gives higher pay to a lower-status job, he may not want to promote to it even though it pays more. Occupational status also helps determine who will be informal leader of a group composed of different occupations. It definitely serves as a motivation to those seeking to advance in the organization. Some persons are status seekers, wanting a job of high status regardless of its other conditions. These persons can be encouraged to qualify themselves for high-status jobs so that they can become better adjusted—or their level of aspiration must be lowered.

Status of an Industry. Just as occupations have status, so does any industry. People attach more status to one industry than to another, which tends to affect recruiting for that industry. It probably also affects job satisfaction because a worker tends to be sensitive about what his friends and neighbors think about the industry that employs him. A study by Brayfield shows that men and women college students generally agreed on the rank of an industry, which indicates that industry status is not materially influenced by sex. Each industry's status attached to all jobs of its employees, because it was largely unaffected by whether a respondent considered himself a manager or a laborer in the industry. This means, for example, that a vice-president in an industry ranked 4th would tend to have higher community social status than one in an industry ranked 7th or 13th. The same would be true for a laborer. The five industries with highest status were, in order of rank: medical services, banks, education, Federal government, and farming.[12]

Symbols of Status The status system of business reaches the ultimate of observable

[11] Carroll L. Shartle, *Occupational Information,* 2d ed., Prentice-Hall, Inc., Englewood Cliffs, N.J., 1952, pp. 114–117.

[12] Arthur H. Brayfield, Carroll E. Kennedy, Jr., and William E. Kendall, "Social Status of Industries," *Journal of Applied Psychology,* pp. 213–215, August, 1954.

evidence with its *status symbols*. These are the visible, external trappings which attach to a man's person or workplace and serve as evidence of his social rank. They exist in the office, shop, warehouse, refinery, or wherever works groups congregate. They are most in evidence among different levels of executives because each successive level usually has the authority to provide itself with surroundings just a little different from those lower in the structure.

In one office the size and type of wastebasket is a mark of distinction. In another, significant symbols are type of desk, stapling machines, and telephones. In the executive offices, such paraphernalia of rank as rugs, bookcases, curtains, and pictures on the wall are important.

All of this concern for symbols of status seems amusing, and at times it is, as illustrated by Figures 6-3 and 6-4. Managers enjoy poking fun at themselves, but at other times status symbols are a deadly serious problem. They endanger morale because an executive who does not have a certain symbol and thinks he should, can become a gloomy, nervous man. They lead to conflict, because executives vie with each other to get particular symbols. And finally, symbols can affect the company budget if executives try to acquire too many of them. One writer comments: "If one vice-president hangs a few abstract oil paintings on his walls, and bills the company, what's to keep the other seven V.-P.'s from doing the same and turning the shop into an annex of the Museum of Modern Art?"[13]

Since symbols of status exist in every company, a manager needs to be alert to them. They will serve as a disruptive force or as positive motivation, depending on the skill with which management handles the problem. When, for example, an employee gives unreasonable attention to status symbols, this is evidence of status anxiety which requires management attention. Status symbols seem to be growing in importance in modern business. They are becoming a larger part of the over-all "compensation" which an executive receives. Income-tax structure prevents a company from giving an executive large increases in spendable income, but the trappings of status which it can provide are almost unlimited. Evidence already exists that executives, as well as workers, do respond to status motivation.

What should be management's policy toward status symbols? Some managers go so far as

to deny the existence of status symbols in their firms, but this is hardly realistic. Others allow symbols to develop as a part of tradition. It is understood that when a corner office becomes vacant the next man in line gets it, and so on, but nothing is put in writing. This policy works under conditions of stability, but a move to a new office building may so upset relationships that there has to be some codifying of the rules. Codification reduces friction, is the most efficient way to allocate space, and gives positive budget control over symbol purchases, but it also smacks of regimentation. Regardless of which approach is used, the rule usually is that executives of equal rank in the same department receive approximately equal status symbols. There may be some variation between broad departments, such as production and sales, because work is distinctly different and rank is not so easily comparable. In any case, managers face the fact that status exists and must be dealt with. They do have the power to influence and control status relationships somewhat.

SOCIAL GROUPS IN INDUSTRY

Of all the influences on status, type and skill of work and level of work are probably the most important. They are the primary determinants of the five broad social groups typically found in any business large enough for these distinctions to be made. The groups are:[14]

Top managers
Middle managers and supervisors
Technical and professional workers
Office and clerical workers
Shop workers

Members of each group have common interests, possess similar status, tend to associate together, and so on. Their problems and relationships are discussed throughout this text.

The Wives of Management   In addition to the five company social groups, there is a sixth semi-company group—the wives of employees, especially of management. Although they are not employees, they are sometimes interviewed and screened when their husbands are employed or promoted.[15] They are increasingly

[13] "The Big Puzzle: Who Gets How Much of What," *Business Week*, Oct. 16, 1954, p. 66.

[14] F. J. Roethlisberger, *Management and Morale*, Harvard University Press, Cambridge, Mass., 1941, pp. 35–36.
[15] "Roughly half the companies on which *Fortune* has data have made wife-screening a regular practice and many others seem ready to do so." William H. Whyte, Jr., "The Corporation and the Wife," *Fortune*, November, 1951, p. 109.

FIGURE 6-3 A Ready Guide for Evaluating Executives, or R-H-I-P, In Use by Chemists, Engineers, Trainees, and Students Throughout the General Office—Hundreds of Satisfied Users*

VISIBLE APPURTENANCES	TOP DOGS	V.I.P.s	BRASS	NO. 2s	EAGER BEAVERS	HOI POLLOI
Brief cases	None—they ask the questions	Use backs of envelopes	Someone goes along to carry theirs	Carry their own—empty	Daily—carry their own—filled with work	Too poor to own one
Desks, office	Custom made (to order)	Executive style (to order)	Type A "director"	Type B "manager"	Cast offs from no. 2s	Yellow oak—or cast-offs from eager beavers
Tables, office	Coffee tables	End tables or decorative wall tables	Matching tables type A	Matching tables type B	Plain work table	None—lucky to have own desk
Carpeting	Nylon—1 inch pile	Nylon—1 inch pile	Wool-twist (with pad)	Wool-twist (without pad)	Used wool pieces—sewed	Asphalt tile
Plant stands	Several—Kept filled with strange exotic plants		Two—repotted whenever they take a trip	One medium-sized—repotted annually during vacation	Small—repotted when plant dies	May have one in the department or bring their own from home
Vacuum water bottles	Silver	Silver	Chromium	Plain painted	Coke machine	Water fountains
Library	Private collection	Autographed or complimentary books and reports	Selected references	Impressive titles on covers	Books everywhere	Dictionary
Shoe shine service	Every morning at 10:00	Every morning at 10:15	Every day at 9:00 or 11:00	Every other day	Once a week	Shine their own
Parking space	Private, in front of office	In plant garage	In company garage—if enough seniority	In company properties—somewhere	On the parking lot	Anywhere they can find a space—if they can afford a car
Luncheon menu	Cream cheese on whole wheat Buttermilk and Indigestion tablets	Cream of celery soup Chicken sandwich (white meat) Milk	Fruit cup - Spinach Lamb chop - Peas Ice cream - Tea	Orange juice Minute steak French fries - Salad Fruit cup Coffee	Tomato juice Chicken croquettes Mashed potatoes Peas - Bread Chocolate cream pie Coffee	Clam chowder Frankfurter and beans Rolls and butter Raisin pie à la mode Two cups of coffee

* Used with permission of the author, K. B. Bernhardt.

352

FIGURE 6-4   A Humorous Description of Office Status Problems (Source: By I. H. E. Otto, Reproduced with permission of the American Management Association, *Management Review*, April, 1953, p. 186.)

Totemism and Protocol in the American Enterprise System

This is the way it is in offices:

First you start at desks that are
huddled together back to back with
barely squeeze room between them

      Then you work

        at desks that

        all face the

        same way and

        are neatly spaced.

And if yours occupies a space by

        ITSELF

all know that you must be a
Senior whatever-it-is
till the rare day when you ascend
to the Supervisory or Middle Management level
and get a desk that is *catty-cornered.*

(If you never get another promotion, of course, in due time

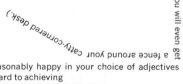

But if you are reasonably happy in your choice of adjectives
you may look forward to achieving
    AN OFFICE OF YOUR OWN
with your name on the frosted panes that extend to eye level,
all above being clear glass; for you will never get a solidly
walled-in office until you are in like Flynn and have become a

        w

    !   h

    l   e

        e

---

being invited to orientation programs, and company parties are definitely swinging toward including wives. This is concrete evidence that companies consider them a significant part of the company informal organization. Their influence is felt in several ways:

1. They are a chain of communication to other managers through their wives.

2. They are a part of many company social functions for employees, executives, and customers.

3. Their attitudes will significantly affect the job performance of their husbands.

The wife's role is assumed to be that of helping her husband progress upward in the corporation. She is expected to be a gracious hostess and social agent. She should be gregarious and eager to make "constructive friendships" appropriate to her husband's place in the social structure at that time. As he moves upward in the corporation, she too should be easily mobile to new friends, new neighborhoods, and new modes of social life. She needs to be understanding of the stringent requirements, such as night work and travel, which the firm makes of her spouse.

Since the wife is not an employee, the corporate demands on her which have just been described can be easily overdone. It is evident that she should be motivated toward these requirements, rather than coerced. To do otherwise might result in an informal revolt and do more harm than good. Further, there are ethical questions concerning just how much the corporation should expect of one only informally related to it. Neither is the husband a twenty-four-hour servant of the firm, and his family life for the most part is beyond the scope of his employer's control. It is clear that too much control produces uniformity and regimentation, and tends to destroy the individualism and freedom which corporate leadership professes to support. It is quite true that management needs to be concerned about the wife because she affects the firm; but management cannot expect to control everything which affects its operations!

CONTROL OF INFORMAL ORGANIZATION

It has been noted that management did not put informal organization in business, and neither can management take it away. Nor would it want to do so. But management can exercise a measure of control. Since the informal organization operates during work as well as away, management exercises partial control over it by such means as what management communicates, what people are permitted to work close together, and how management recognizes informal leaders. Management's job is:

1. To let employees know that management accepts and understands informal organization

2. To influence it (exercise a measure of control over it)

3. To control it so that its interests and objectives are integrated with those of the formal organization
4. To keep formal activities from unnecessarily threatening or disrupting it

The formal organization has one set of values and system of evaluating people. The informal has another. If these two evaluation systems are far apart there will be conflict. Pace of work serves as an example. If the informal management standards give high status the low producer who restricts work and if formal management standards give high status and wages to high producers in accordance with an incentive plan, then the two evaluation systems are far apart and conflict is certain. If the two evaluation systems can be brought into closer agreement, there tends to be less conflict and better morale and productivity in accordance with the principle of informal organization. This is management's control objective with informal organization.

Management in order to maintain control is cautious to keep informal organization secondary to the formal organization. Arguments have been advanced that when formal management is incompetent an *overriding* informal organization is necessary and desirable in order to keep the group working effectively. The statement, "We get along here in spite of the boss, rather than because of him," is descriptive of actual situations. But is this desirable? Normally it is better to discover incompetent leadership early, because informal leadership will not forever keep the group on a course toward the formal objective. Sooner or later formal and informal interests will conflict and then formal authority is needed to resolve the conflict. This concept, which is widely accepted in management, may be stated as follows: *Considering all an organization's activities, formal organization should be the primary control, although certain single activities may be primarily controlled informally.*

THE PERSONALITY OF A BUSINESS

Formal and informal organization, as they are adapted to meet the changing environment, give to each business a personality, just like a person has. This personality is sometimes called *organizational charter.*[16] Each company has its own culture, traditions, and characteristic methods of action. Some companies are bustling and efficient, others are easy-going. Some are quite human, others are hard and cold. They change slowly, being influenced by their leaders and their environment. Like people, some are more susceptible to change than others. A company tends to attract and keep people who fit its personality so that its patterns are to some extent perpetuated. A certain manufacturing company serves as an illustration. Its management stresses seniority, centralized control, and cautious decisions. It has difficulty attracting and retaining young, educated men with promotion potential. What else could be expected? Men of this personality do not fit the company's pattern of living, *its personality.* In order to achieve maximum results, managers as they deal with human problems in a business need to know that firm's particular personality pattern, just as they need also to know an individual worker's personality.

SUMMARY

Informal organization exists permanently with business because it arises from the interaction of people. Along with formal controls, it influences human behavior at work and is consequently of concern to management. It is indirectly subject to some management control. The basic control objective in this instance is to integrate closely the long-run interests of the formal and informal systems so that they will operate to evaluate and reward people in about the same way.

Rank of people in informal organization is determined by their status. There are innumerable causes of status both within and without a business. Various physical surroundings become associated with a certain status and therefore become symbols of that status. Like magical herbs these symbols are much sought after because they distinguish one person from another and are supposed to accord status to their possessor. Groups with similar status constitute the broad social groups in industry: managers, supervisors, shop workers, office workers, and professional people. A semi-company group is the wives of employees.

Formal and informal organization together give a company its personality as it interacts with other influences. In many companies the major additional human relations influence is a second formal and informal organization—the union.

[16] E. W. Bakke, *The Fusion Process,* Labor and Management Center, Yale University, New Haven, 1955, p. 9.

53

Motivation: The Core of Management*

RENSIS LIKERT

It is widely recognized that there are large differences in the productive efficiency of different companies. Even within a company there are usually substantial differences in productivity among the different plants or departments. These differences in productivity are often due to differences in managerial policy and practice.

There is too little information on what a good management does that makes the difference between high and low productivity, between high and low employee morale. American business is spending millions of dollars every year applying the scientific method to product development and the improvement of production methods, but it is not similarly applying its resources to discover how the most effective managers and supervisors function and how their principles and practices can be applied more generally.

The Institute for Social Research of the University of Michigan is one of the few organizations conducting systematic research on this problem.[1] It is trying to find what makes an organization tick; trying to discover the principles of organizational structure and the principles and practices of leadership that are responsible for high productivity and high job satisfaction.

The Institute program is designed to provide a mirror for business so that it can see in its own operations and experience what works best and why. Studies have been conducted or are under way in a wide variety of organizations. These include public utilities, an insurance company, an automotive company, a heavy machinery factory, a railroad, an electric appliance factory, and some government agencies. The work of the organizations studied has varied from highly routine clerical and assembly operations to complex scientific research.

One of the basic concepts underlying this research is that no matter how varied the task—whether in government, industry, or any part of the military organization—there are common fundamental principles applicable to the effective organization of human activity. In addition to these general principles, there may be specific principles that apply to particular types of work—such as selling, as opposed to office management. But the philosophy behind this whole program of research is that scientifically valid data can be obtained which will enable us to state general principles. Once we know the general principles, we must learn how to transfer them from one situation to another. We are doing this research at all levels of organization—not only at the employee level and the small-unit level but at the plant level and the company level. We expect that some principles will carry right on through; others will be specific, perhaps, for the different levels or parts of an organization.

In carrying forward this program of research, two major criteria have been used to evaluate administrative effectiveness:

1. Productivity per man-hour or some similar measure of the organization's success in achieving its productivity goals.

2. The job satisfaction and other satisfactions derived by employees or members of the group.

The results being obtained show that a consistent pattern of motivational principles and their application is associated with high productivity and high job satisfaction, irrespective of the particular company or industry in which the study is conducted. I shall present some of these results and briefly summarize some of the generalizations that are emerging from this research.

* Reprinted by permission of the publisher from Rensis Likert, *Motivation: The Core of Management,* American Management Association, Personnel Series, no. 155, New York, 1953, pp. 3–21. Mr. Likert is director of the Institute for Social Research and professor in both the Psychology and Sociology Departments at the University of Michigan.

[1] This program was started by a contract with the Office of Naval Research. Since its initiation, business organization and governmental agencies, as well as ONR, have contributed to its support.

FACTORS IN HIGH AND LOW PRODUCTIVITY

There are some factors which are commonly assumed to increase productivity but which, when actual results are examined, are found not to be related to productivity or else to have a negligible relationship. Thus we are finding very little relationship, *within a company*, between employees' attitudes toward the company and their productivity. The more productive employees or sections do not have appreciably more favorable attitudes than do the less productive employees. Chart 1 illustrates the pattern of relationship that we are finding. The common assumption that developing a favorable attitude among employees toward the company will result in increased productivity does not seem to be warranted.

A favorable over-all attitude toward one's company and job does result in less absence from the job. I suspect also that it may result in less turnover and may attract a better labor force in a tight labor market, but we do not yet have any data on these points.

Illustrative, again, of the kind of variables that show no relationship to productivity or even a negative relationship is the material in Chart 2. We are finding, in some situations at least, that there is a negative relationship between the extent to which employees participate in a recreational program and their productivity. The less productive sections participate in recreational activities more often than do those sections that are more productive.

THE SUPERVISOR: EMPLOYEE-CENTERED OR PRODUCTION-CENTERED

In contrast to these patterns involving factors of a nonpersonal nature, we are consistently finding that there is a marked relationship between the kind of supervision an employee receives and both his productivity and the satisfactions which he derives from his work. When the worker (or a person at any level in a hierarchy) feels that his boss sees him only. as an instrument of production, as merely a cog in a machine, he is likely to be a poor producer. However, when he feels that his boss is genuinely interested in him, his problems, his future, and his well-being, he is more likely to be a high producer. Some typical results are shown in Chart 3.

The employee-centered supervisor not only trains people to do their present job well but tends to train them for the next higher job. He is interested in helping them with their problems on the job and off the job.

The following illustrations represent typical viewpoints of supervisors whom we have classified as employee-centered or production-centered:

Employee-centered supervisors are those who describe their work as did this one:
I've tried to help my girls in getting better jobs and to get advanced, but there're so few positions for them to go to. That's why I teach them how to supervise. A lot of my girls are assistant section heads today.

In spite of the fact that this supervisor has promoted many of her ablest girls to better positions, she still has a high-production section. By giving her girls supervisory experience or letting one of them supervise two or three others in small groups, she builds effective teamwork and a friendly, cooperative atmosphere.

Another supervisor, also employee-centered, commented as follows:
I study the girls' work, find out who works together and put them together. The main thing is to keep the girls happy. I talk with them and learn what their peculiarities are so that if a girl gets excited, I know whether it is important or not. Your girls have to feel that you are one of them, not the boss. Some girls get sort of cranky, and you can't just say, "Do it." It is much better to ask them to do the work in other ways; that's only human nature.

Another employee-centered section head commented as follows:
I try to understand each girl. I remember I was

CHART 1   Relation of Attitude toward Company and Productivity

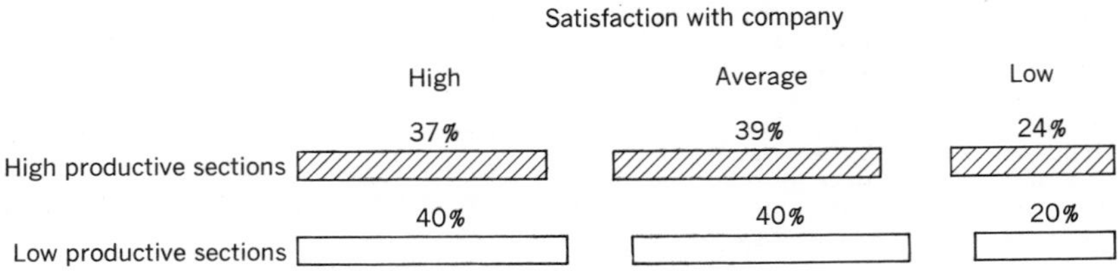

Satisfaction with company

	High	Average	Low
High productive sections	37%	39%	24%
Low productive sections	40%	40%	20%

CHART 2   Participation in Company Recreational Activities

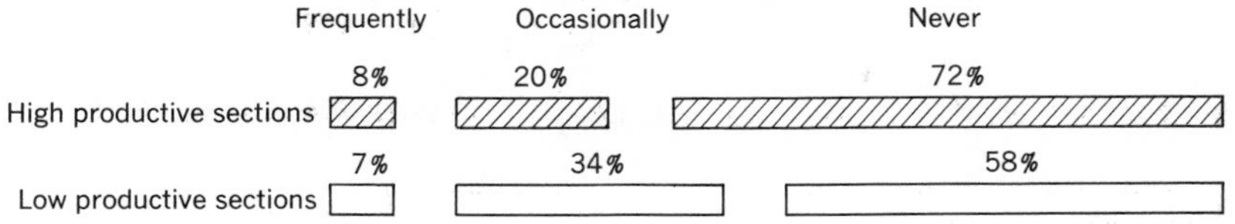

	Frequently	Occasionally	Never
High productive sections	8%	20%	72%
Low productive sections	7%	34%	58%

one once and that I liked to be the kind that was known by my supervisor. Knowing the girls helps with handling the work here. You also have to know what happens outside to help them inside here at their work.

In contrast, this comment is illustrative of the attitude of a production-centered supervisor in charge of a low-production section:

I know we're doing what is supposed to be done in our section. Hit the work in and out—and hit it right—not slipshod.

Another production-oriented, low-producing section head commented as follows:

It is my job to get the employee to stay on the job and produce. I have to work up efficiency charts. My efficiency chart is my argument if I have to make any complaint. My biggest headache is to get the employees to do their best.

Still another production-centered supervisor commented as follows:

The girls sometimes stop work before the bell rings; I have been after them and I keep them overtime to do the work. You have to do something drastic and make examples of them.

PRODUCTIVITY AND CLOSENESS OF SUPERVISION

Related to pressing for production is the *closeness* of supervision that a person experiences. Close supervision tends to be associated with lower productivity and more general supervision with higher productivity. This relationship is shown in Chart 4.

Low productivity may at times lead to closer supervision, but it is clear that it may also cause low productivity. In one of the companies involved in this research program it has been found that switching managers of high- and low-production division results in the high-production managers raising the productivity of the low-production divisions faster than the former high-production divisions slip under the low-production managers. Supervisors, as they are shifted from job to job, tend to carry with them and to maintain their habitual attitudes toward the supervisory process and toward their subordinates. This suggests that supervisory attitudes and habits tend to be the causal influence. For example, an assistant manager of a low-production department, in discussing his situation, said, "This interest-in-people approach is all right, but it is a luxury. I've got to keep pressure on for production, and when I get production up then I can afford to take time to show an interest in my employees and their problems." Being under pressure for increased production, and being primarily concerned with it, seem to cause supervisors to neglect important human dimensions of the supervisory process which in the long run determine the production of their groups.

Heads of low-producing sections seem to recognize that close supervision adversely affects their work. They show more dissatisfaction with the way their job is organized than do high-producing section heads and give as the reason for this dissatisfaction "too little delegation of authority."

CHART 3   "Employee-centered" Supervisors Are Higher Producers Than "Production-centered" Supervisors

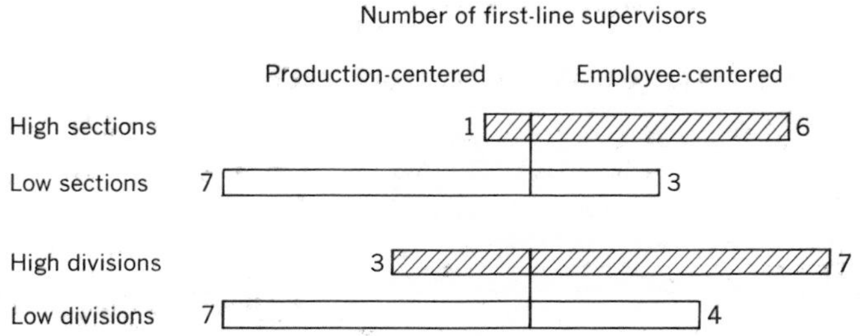

Number of first-line supervisors

	Production-centered	Employee-centered
High sections	1	6
Low sections	7	3
High divisions	3	7
Low divisions	7	4

CHART 4   Low-production Section Heads Are More Closely Supervised Than Are High-production Heads

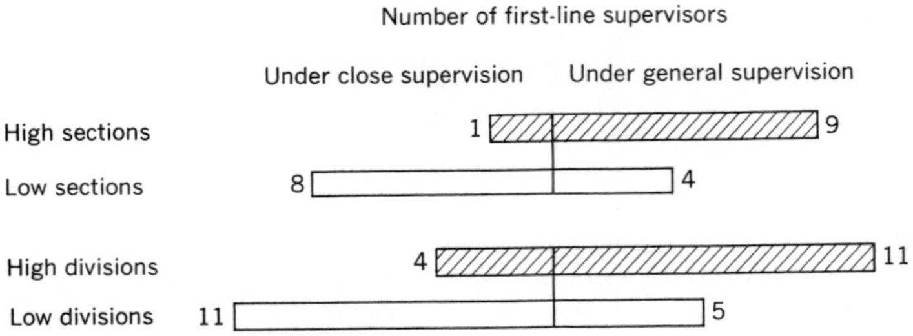

Number of first-line supervisors

Under close supervision   Under general supervision

High sections   1   9

Low sections   8   4

High divisions   4   11

Low divisions   11   5

In studying the results one gets the impression that persons who use general supervision tend more often to specify the goal or tasks to be accomplished and give subordinates some leeway in how it is accomplished. Persons using close supervision, however, are more likely to specify the precise activities of subordinates. Those using general supervision may, of course, make available to subordinates the resources of work simplification, etc., but do not specify in every detail precisely how they will be used.

When people are given general supervision, it is necessary to keep them well-informed. As shown in Chart 5, supervisors in charge of high-production groups report more often that they are kept informed about developments than do supervisors in charge of low-production groups.

We are finding conflicting patterns of relationship between morale and productivity. In some situations there is high morale and high productivity; in others we find high morale and low productivity or the converse. There are good reasons for these variations, and they are related to the kind of supervision that exists. But the significant finding for this discussion is that the kind of supervision which results in the highest productivity also results in the highest morale. Thus, for example, employee-centered supervision produces high levels of job satisfaction as well as high productivity.

Chart 6 illustrates the kind of findings being obtained. Where work groups with the highest

and lowest morale were asked to describe what their supervisors did, the results were as shown in Chart 6. The workers in low-morale groups mentioned just as often as workers in high-morale groups that their supervisors performed such production-centered tasks as "enforces the rules," "arranges work and makes work assignments," and "supplies men with materials and tools." But the high-morale groups mentioned much more frequently than the low such employee-centered functions as "recommends promotions and pay increases," "informs men on what is happening in the company," "keeps men posted on how well they are doing," and "hears complaints and grievances."[2]

IMPORTANCE OF THE GROUP RELATIONSHIP

Books on management and administration tend to deal with the relationship between superior and subordinates, between supervisors and employees, as *individuals*. Research on management similarly has tended to focus on the relationship between the superior and the subordinates as individuals. We are encountering increasing evidence, however, that the superior's skill in supervising his subordinates *as a group* is an important variable affecting his success: the greater his skill in using group

[2] In this discussion the term "morale" is used as meaning the total satisfactions the individual derives from his work situation. It is not being used as synonymous with the degree to which the individual is motivated to do his work.

CHART 5   Supervisory Communications and Productivity

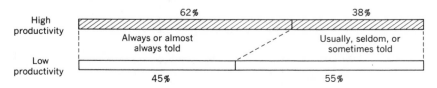

High productivity   62%   38%

Always or almost always told   Usually, seldom, or sometimes told

Low productivity   45%   55%

CHART 6 Percentages of High and Low Morale Groups Describing What Their Supervisors Do

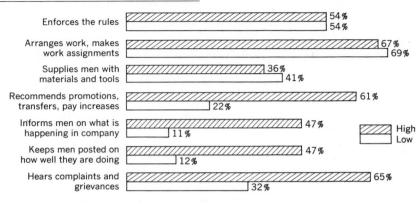

Enforces the rules — 54% / 54%

Arranges work, makes work assignments — 67% / 69%

Supplies men with materials and tools — 36% / 41%

Recommends promotions, transfers, pay increases — 61% / 22%

Informs men on what is happening in company — 47% / 11%

Keeps men posted on how well they are doing — 47% / 12%

Hears complaints and grievances — 65% / 32%

High / Low

methods of supervision, the greater are the productivity and job satisfaction of the work group.

Chart 7 shows the relationship between the feeling that the "company is interested in employees' ideas and suggestions" and the level of employee morale. For both blue-collar and white-collar workers, there is a marked relationship between worker morale and how much employees feel that their boss is interested in discussing work problems with the work group.

Another important and striking relationship is shown in Chart 8. Foremen of high-production work groups report much more frequently than the foremen of low-production groups that their work groups perform well when they, the foremen, are absent. High-production supervisors, through group methods of supervision, apparently develop within the work group the expectation and capacity to function effectively whether the foreman is present or not. This ability to function well in the absence of the supervisor is, no doubt, one of the reasons for the greater productivity of the high-production groups.

Chart 9 shows the relationship between group pride (or loyalty) and group productivity. The high-production groups show greater

CHART 7 Relations of Employee Morale to Feeling That Company Is Interested in Employees' Ideas and Suggestions

Percentage who feel that discussions with supervisor help

Level of morale	White collar	Blue collar
High	93%	87%
Medium	72%	57%
Low	42%	24%

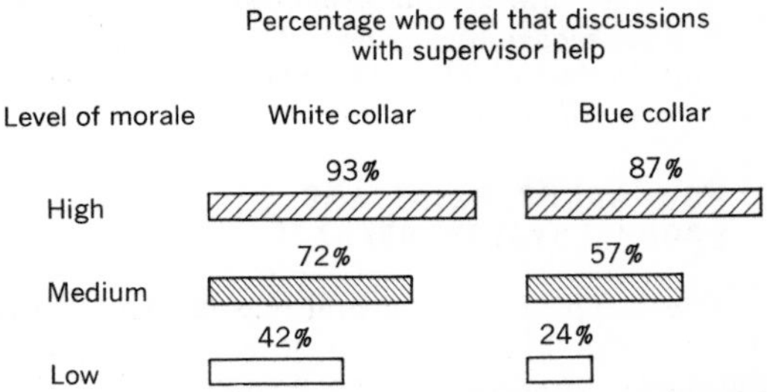

R 53-7

group loyalty and greater group pride than do the low-production groups. We are finding that this relationship holds for many kinds of

CHART 8 High-productivity Work Groups Perform Well When Foreman Is Absent

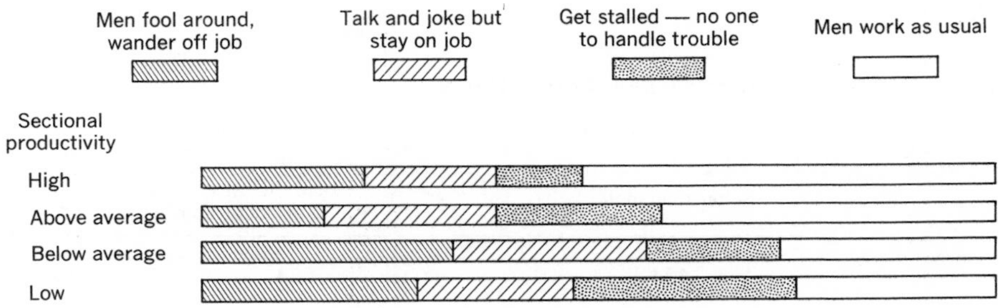

Men fool around, wander off job | Talk and joke but stay on job | Get stalled — no one to handle trouble | Men work as usual

Sectional productivity

High

Above average

Below average

Low

CHART 9   Relation of Pride in Work Group to Productivity

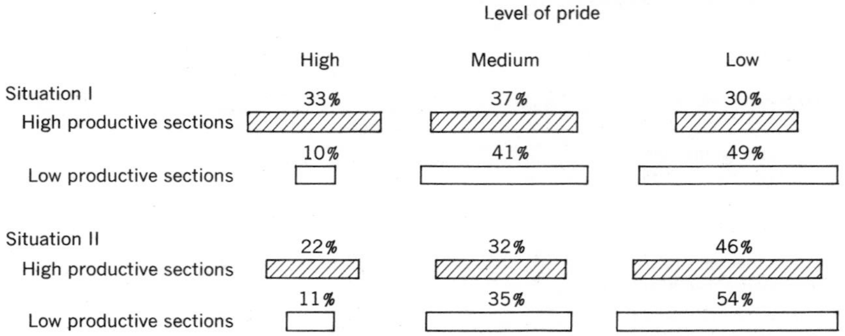

Level of pride

	High	Medium	Low
Situation I			
High productive sections	33%	37%	30%
Low productive sections	10%	41%	49%
Situation II			
High productive sections	22%	32%	46%
Low productive sections	11%	35%	54%

groups and many kinds of work. In Chart 9, for example, "Situation I" deals with clerical workers and "Situation II" deals with maintenance-of-way crews on a railroad.

In the study of the clerical operations, the workers and supervisors who displayed pride in their work group would make such comments as: "We have a good group," "We work together well," or "We help out each other." One supervisor said about her group:

They all have definite assignments, and they're a nice cooperative crowd. They just jump in and do things and never bother me. They have a responsibility toward the group.

HOW GROUP PRIDE AND GROUP LOYALTY OPERATE

There appear to be several reasons why work groups with high group pride and loyalty are the more productive. One reason is that the workers cooperate more and help one another in getting the work done. Work groups with high group loyalty show more teamwork and more willingness to help each other than do those with low group loyalty. In the high-loyalty groups there tends to be a flow of work back and forth between the workers depending upon the load. In groups with low group loyalty there tends to be more of a feeling

that each worker is on his own and that how he gets along with his work is his own responsibility.

The effect upon productivity of workers helping one another is shown in Chart 10. When foremen were asked, "How does your section compare with other sections in the way the men help each other on the job?" the answers showed a marked relationship to group productivity. The foremen of high-production groups reported much more often than the foremen of low-production groups that their men helped one another in getting the work done.

The workers in the high-production work groups not only have greater group loyalty and help one another more but give this help on their own initiative. Workers in groups with low group loyalty at times help one another, but then it is more often upon the request of the foreman. The willingness to help one another displayed by the groups with high group loyalty seems to come from a better team spirit and better interpersonal relationships that the foreman has developed in the group. This atmosphere seems to come from group methods of supervision and assigning work tasks as a whole to the group. Low group loyalty seems to occur where the foreman deals with workers individually and makes individual work assignments. One supervisor of a low

CHART 10   Group Solidarity and Productivity

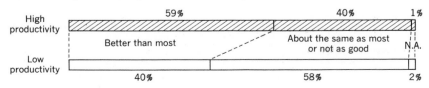

High productivity	59%	40%	1%
	Better than most	About the same as most or not as good	N.A.
Low productivity	40%	58%	2%

productive clerical group described his pattern of supervision as follows:

I apportion out the work to the people in my section and generally supervise the work handled. If a clerk is out, I have to make arrangements to have her work done. The work must go on even though there are absences. This involves getting work redistributed to those who are there.

Another factor contributing to the higher productivity of groups with high group loyalty is their lower rate of absence from the job.

CHART 11   Group Solidarity: White-collar Men

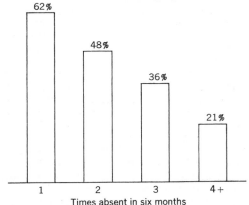

Per cent saying—"Our crew better than others at sticking together"

62%
48%
36%
21%

1   2   3   4+
Times absent in six months

As Chart 11 shows, persons in groups with high group loyalty are much less likely to be absent from work than persons in groups with lower group loyalty. This chart is based on data from white-collar workers. Similar results were obtained for blue-collar workers. Liking the work group clearly results, for all kinds of workers, in less absence from the job.

As might be expected, work groups with high group loyalty have more favorable attitudes toward production than do groups with low group loyalty. Thus we find that high-loyalty groups differ from groups of low group loyalty in having higher production goals. Their opinion as to what is reasonable production is higher and is more nearly the same as that of their foreman. Moreover, the high-loyalty groups have a more favorable attitude toward the high producer. This is shown in Chart 12.

We are finding that the high-loyalty groups differ from the low in ways that form a consistent pattern. In addition to the differences already mentioned, the following characteristics have been found. The groups with greater group loyalty are more likely to

- Have greater identification with their group and a greater feeling of belonging to it.
- Have more friends in the group and in the company—rather than outside the company.
- Have better interpersonal relations among the members of the work group.
- Have a more favorable attitude toward their job and their company.
- Not only have higher production goals but produce more with less sense of strain or pressure.

There is evidence that whenever a supervisor (or manager) abdicates his leadership role and does not develop a good team spirit, other persons within the group will take over and develop some kind of group loyalty. Often the informal leadership which emerges establishes groups with goals counter to the goals of the over-all organization. Human nature is such that there seems to be no question as to whether or not groups will be formed. If constituted leadership lacks group skills and fails to establish group leadership, other leadership will emerge and take over.

CHART 12   The Relationship of the Employee's Attitude toward the Highly Productive Worker and Sectional Pride in Work Group

Feeling toward highly productive worker	Employees in high pride sections	Employees in medium pride sections	Employees in low pride sections
Admire	44%	24%	32%
Neutral	28%	37%	35%
Resent	23%	45%	32%

CHART 13   The Relationship of the Supervisor's Attitude toward His Employees and the Employees' Degree of Pride in Work Group

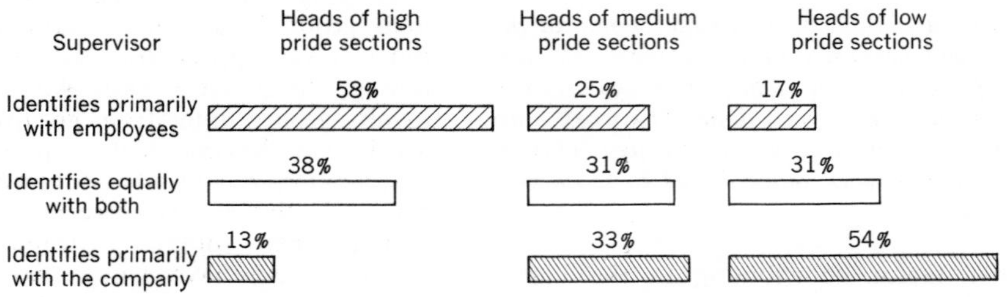

Supervisor	Heads of high pride sections	Heads of medium pride sections	Heads of low pride sections
Identifies primarily with employees	58%	25%	17%
Identifies equally with both	38%	31%	31%
Identifies primarily with the company	13%	33%	54%

DEVELOPING GROUP LOYALTY AND TEAM SPIRIT

Since high group loyalty and a good team spirit seem to result in greater production, greater job satisfaction, less absence, and, I suspect, less turnover, it is important to ask, "How can group loyalty be developed?" One factor which exercises an influence is shown in Chart 13. When a superior treats subordinates as human beings, it results in greater group loyalty and pride. Moreover, as Chart 14 shows, when supervisors stay sufficiently close psychologically to their workers to be able to see the problems of the workers through the eyes of the workers, the supervisors are better able to develop good group loyalty.

The good supervisor is able to identify with his employees and keep psychologically close to them. This seems to foster a good team spirit with open communication. It permits the supervisor to understand problems as employees see them and to interpret for top and middle management the employees' points of view. The supervisor who fails to identify with employees becomes psychologically far from them. This makes him incapable of seeing and dealing with problems as employees see them and hence unable to arrive at mutually satisfactory decisions. This supervisor is also unable to help middle and top management to see problems as employees see them and thereby to help

management to arrive at policy decisions which will be mutually satisfactory.

Our research results indicate that it is important for supervisors to accept the goals of the over-all organization and to have a clear understanding of the role and function of their work group in achieving the over-all goals. When supervisors recognize and accept responsibility for performing the functions required of their work group and at the same time have the capacity to identify with their employees, effective results are obtained.

There are, of course, many other factors which are important in developing group loyalty and team spirit. Scattered research in industry and elsewhere indicates that commonly recognized methods of group leadership will yield good group loyalty when used. These methods and skills include those developed and taught by the National Training Laboratory in Group Development. Among the most important of these methods are those involving group participation in decisions affecting the group. There is evidence that group participation and involvement are beneficial at all levels in an organization. One of the best ways, for example, to have supervisors become aware of the job that needs to be done by their work group and to have them accept responsibility for it is to involve them in decisions where the functions and responsibilities of their work group are examined and reviewed.

CHART 14   The Relationship of the Supervisor's Attitude toward His Employees and the Employees' Degree of Pride in Work Group

Supervisor	Heads of high pride sections	Heads of medium pride sections	Heads of low pride sections
Considers employees as human beings	47%	20%	33%
Considers employees primarily as people to get the work out	26%	35%	39%

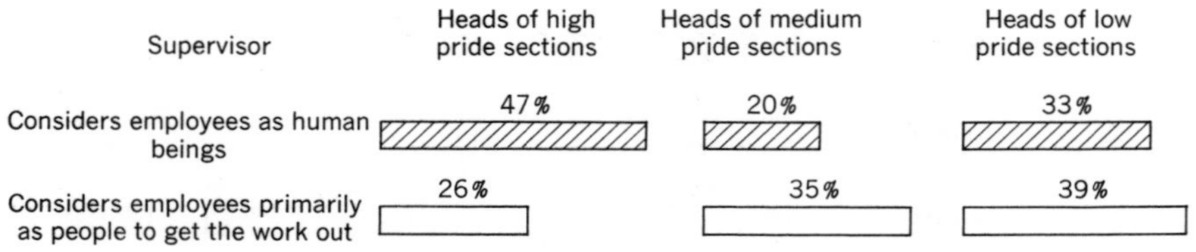

CONCLUSION: NATURE OF HUMAN MOTIVATION

Some general conclusions have been stated here as the different results were presented. Additional conclusions emerge, however, as the results are looked at in an over-all manner. Thus these results suggest an important conclusion as to the nature of human motivation. An examination of the results presented here and of results from other research shows that every human being earnestly seeks a secure, friendly, and supportive relationship and one that gives him a sense of personal worth in the face-to-face groups most important to him. The most important face-to-face groups are almost always his immediate family group and his work group. If his formal face-to-face work group is hostile, he develops new friendly informal groups. Human nature seems to motivate each of us to establish and maintain these friendly supportive relationships in those face-to-face groups in which we spend most of our lives. Either we successfully establish these friendly and supportive relationships or we crack up.

It is not surprising, therefore, that we see people generally striving for a sense of dignity and personal worth. We all seem to seek recognition and a sense of importance in terms of the values and goals which we cherish and which our most important face-to-face groups also cherish.

To say that people seek friendly and supportive relationships does not mean that they seek to be coddled. Quite the contrary. People seek to achieve a sense of importance from doing difficult but important tasks which help to implement goals which they and their friends seek.

THE FINDINGS APPLIED

If there is anything of value in the results presented and the conclusions drawn, then when these findings are applied there should be an increase in productivity and in job satisfaction. We have been running several tests applying these results. These tests involve hundreds of employees in widely different kinds of industries. I shall report briefly the results obtained in one of these tests.

Chart 15 indicates the effect of participation upon productivity. This chart is based on the experiment by Coch and French[3] designed to employ three variations in participation procedure.

The first variation involved participation through representation of the workers in designing the changes to be made in the jobs. The second variation consisted of total participation

[3] Lester Coch, and John R. P. French, Jr., "Overcoming Resistance to Change," *Human Relations*, vol. I, no. 4, 1948.

CHART 15   The Effect of Participation on Production

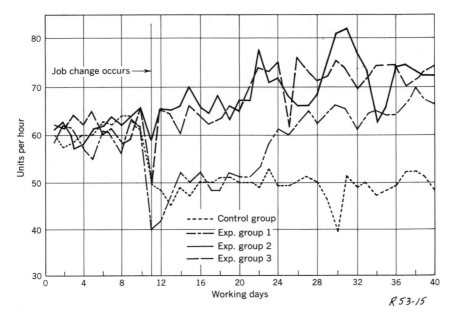

Working days

R 53-15

by all members of the group in designing the changes. A third (control) group was also used. Two experimental groups received the total participation treatment. The (control) group went through the usual factory routine when they were changed. The production department modified the job, and a new piece rate was set. A group meeting was then held in which the control group was told that the change was necessary because of competitive conditions, and that a new piece rate had been set. The new piece rate was thoroughly explained by the time study man, questions were answered, and the meeting dismissed. Experimental group 1 was changed in a different manner. Before any changes took place, a group meeting was held with all the operators to be changed.

The need for the change was presented as dramatically as possible, showing two identical garments produced in the factory; one was produced in 1946 and had sold for 100 per cent more than its fellow in 1947. The group was asked to identify the cheaper one and could not do it. This demonstration effectively shared with the group the entire problem of the necessity of cost reduction. A general agreement was reached that a savings could be effected by removing the "frills" and "fancy" work from the garment without affecting the folders' opportunity to achieve a high efficiency rating. Management then presented a plan to set the new job and piece rate:

1. Make a check study of the job as it was being done.

2. Eliminate all unnecessary work.

3. Train several operators in the correct methods.

4. Set the piece rate by time studies on these specially trained operators.

5. Explain the new job and rate to all the operators.

6. Train all operators in the new method so they can reach a high rate of production within a short time.

The group approved this plan (though no formal group decision was reached) and chose the operators to be specially trained. A submeeting with the "special" operators was held immediately following the meeting with the entire group. They displayed a cooperative and interested attitude and immediately presented many good suggestions. This attitude carried over into the working out of the details of the new job; and when the new job and piece rates were set, the "special" operators referred to the resultants as "our job," "our rate," etc. The new job and piece rates were presented at a second group meeting to all the operators involved. The "special" operators served to train the other operators on the new job. Experimental groups 2 and 3 went through much the same kind of change meetings. The groups were smaller than experimental group 1, and a more intimate atmosphere was established. The need for a change was once again made dramatically clear; the same general plan was presented by management. However, since the groups were small, all operators were chosen as "special"

CHART 16   A Comparison of the Effect of the Control Procedure with the Total Participation Procedure on the same Group

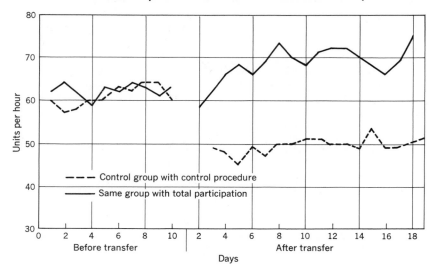

Units per hour

– – – Control group with control procedure
——— Same group with total participation

Before transfer   After transfer

Days

operators; that is, all operators were to participate directly in the designing of the new jobs, and all operators would be studied by the time study man. It is interesting to note that in the meetings with these two groups, suggestions were immediately made in such quantity that the stenographer had great difficulty in recording them. The group approved of the plans, but again no formal group decision was reached.

The results shown in Chart 15 clearly demonstrate the effectiveness of participation upon production. It is significant that the control group, when treated like experimental groups 2 and 3 in another change that occurred some months later, showed a productivity record identical to that shown by experimental groups 2 and 3. Chart 16 shows these curves.

The following, also taken from Coch and French, presents evidence on the power of group standards:

> Probably the most important force affecting the recovery under the control procedure was a group standard, set by the group, restricting the level of production to 50 units per hour. Evidently this explicit agreement to restrict production is related to the group's rejection of the change and of the new job as arbitrary and unreasonable. Perhaps they had faint hopes of demonstrating that standard production could not be attained and thereby obtain a more favorable piece rate. In any case there was a definite group phenomenon which affected all the members of the group. . . . An analysis was made for all groups of the individual differences within the group in levels of production. In Experiment I the 40 days before change were compared with the 30 days after change; in Experiment II the 10 days before change were

compared to the 17 days after change. As a measure of variability, the standard deviation was calculated each day for each group. The average daily standard deviations before and after change are shown in the left-hand column. There is indeed a marked decrease in individual differences with the control group after their first transfer. In fact the restriction of production resulted in a lower variability than in any other group. Thus we may conclude that the group standard at 50 units per hour set up strong group-induced forces. . . . The table of variability also shows that the experimental treatments markedly reduced variability in the other four groups after transfer.

This experiment by Coch and French shows that the results from research can be applied in the shop and can yield substantial improvements in production. This experiment also yields improvement in attitudes toward the job.

Personnel departments have a very large and important task to perform in helping the line organization to apply the results of human relations research. This includes helping the line organization to appreciate that employee-centered supervision yields better production and better job satisfaction than production-centered supervision. Chart 17, which shows what the foremen in a very well-managed company say are the most important things they have to do, gives an indication of the magnitude of the job that personnel people face

CHART 17   What Foremen Say Are the Most Important Things They Have to Do

Production	78%
Human relations	7%
Both	15%

GROUP	VARIABILITY	
	BEFORE CHANGE	AFTER CHANGE
Experiment I:		
Control group	9.8	1.9
Experimental 1	9.7	3.8
Experimental 2	10.3	2.7
Experimental 3	9.9	2.4
Experiment II:		
Control group	12.7	2.9

in helping the line organization to become employee-centered in its supervision. Over three-quarters of the foremen in that company state that pushing for production is the most important part of their job. The line organization, moreover, needs help in learning the skills required for using employee-centered supervision effectively. Research results pointing to effective ways to develop these skills are available, but that is a topic for other discussions.

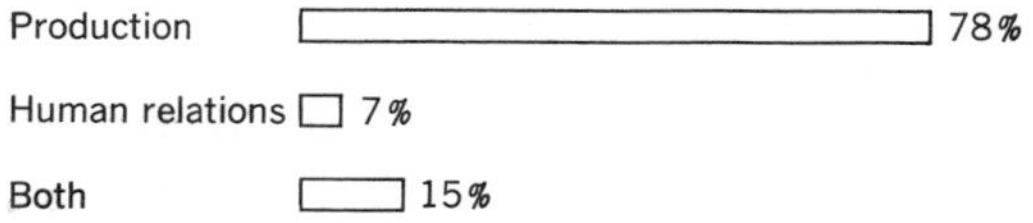

54

Conflicts in Human Values*

ROBERT N. McMURRY

One of man's most prized possessions is his intellect. Of all his attributes, it is probably his *reason* in which he takes the greatest pride. He even describes himself as "Homo sapiens," the thinking man. Yet much of his behavior, if observed impartially by a visitor from Mars, might better be characterized as "unreasoned," rather than "reasoned."

In the realm of business and industry alone, he provides ample evidence that logic and reason are far from the sole determinants of his actions. For example:

- Management—like the Bourbon kings— often fails to learn from its errors and perpetuates practices which successfully alienate it from the workers.

- The workers, in turn, not infrequently limit their output, even though this diminishes their earnings, and engage in other practices that endanger the security of the jobs on which they depend for a livelihood.

- Superiors and subordinates as well as principal divisions and departments within a business are often unable to work in harmony with each other even though it is clearly in their interest to do so.

- Nor are management and the workers always able to communicate effectively with each other even though their messages may be exquisitely logical and beautifully reasoned.

- Intellectuals and politicians are constantly launching attacks on the businessman designed to denigrate and disparage him. Yet the businessman, through his gifts and taxes, is a principal supporter of both.

Since this behavior is costly and sometimes self-destructive, the question may be asked: Why is there so much "unreason" in inter-

personal relations in industry? The tendency these days seems to be to blame the failure on poor communications, conflicts of interest, lack of knowledge, or inadequate management control. I readily agree that such matters are frequently factors in the picture—but not always the most important ones. In case after case with which I am familiar the real cause of breakdown is conflicting *values*. This diagnosis throws many key management problems in an entirely different light and suggests radically different prescriptions for action.

Before proceeding with the discussion, let me comment briefly on the terms to be used:

A value, according to Webster, has, among other meanings, "the quality or fact of being excellent, useful or desirable; worth in a thing." As a verb it means "to place in a scale of values; as to value honor above riches." An ideology, according to Webster, is the "manner or content of thinking characteristic of an individual or class; as, bourgeois ideology." A belief, by contrast, is "a conviction or persuasion of truth." Typical management values are the sanctity of property and the desirability of the free enterprise system. Values more commonly held by all Americans include the worthwhileness of the idea that virtue tends inevitably to be rewarded in the end and that motherhood is sacred.

"PEOPLE PROBLEMS"

Everyone has opinions and attitudes, many of which, being highly toned emotionally, are coeval in influence with the intelligence that people use in determining what they think and how they act.

Because of these emotional influences, despite mankind's pretensions to the contrary few persons are wholly reasonable in a strict sense of the word; they do not go from fact to fact to form conclusions or revise opinions in the light of new observations.

Many of industry's most costly, frustrating, and chronic dilemmas arise from aberrant

* Reprinted by permission of the publisher from *Harvard Business Review*, vol. 41, no. 3, pp. 130–145, May–June, 1963. Mr. McMurry is head of the McMurry Company, consultants in personnel, industrial relations and market research, Chicago.

opinions and attitudes on the part of management, supervisors, and workers. These, in turn, often lead to behavior which is eccentric, unrealistic, and self-defeating, when not inescapably irrational and deviant. This is why many of management's greatest difficulties have their roots in "people problems."

Significantly, these peculiarities of thinking, acting, and behaving are in no sense the products of mental deficit. They are not limited to the mentally handicapped and ignorant. Nor are they limited to the emotionally disturbed. They appear with equal frequency among experienced, highly trained, happy, and intelligent executives; among intellectuals, scientists, and engineers; among labor leaders and union officials at all levels; and among faithful plant and office employees of long service. The aberrant thinking of these people, too, contributes to management problems. Witness, for instance:

- The usually "rational" owner who will liquidate his business rather than be forced to negotiate with a union.

- The scientist who, perhaps because he happens to be a misguided idealist, becomes a poor security risk.

- The labor leader who foments a long and costly strike simply to demonstrate his "muscle."

- The hourly rated worker who welds pop bottles inside the body of the automobile he is assembling simply for "kicks."

- The intellectuals and politicians who advocate confiscatory taxes on the grounds that profits are unwarranted.

The fact that the motives of an individual or group are indisputably exalted does not mean that the people are realistic. This was dramatically demonstrated by the "noble experiment" of national prohibition of alcoholic beverages.

How Values Alter Behavior   The common denominator of nearly all of these people problems is to be found in the area of *values*. While it is commonly recognized that values differ widely from person to person and from culture to culture, their influence on people's thinking, acting, and behavior tends to be seriously underestimated. Their influence on the individual is powerful because:

1. They principally determine what he regards as right, good, worthy, beautiful, ethical, and so forth (thus establishing his vocation and life goals and many of his motivations,

for it may be assumed that he will seek that which he deems desirable).

2. They also provide the standards and norms by which he guides his day-to-day behavior. (In this sense they constitute an integral part of his conscience.)

3. They chiefly determine his attitudes toward the causes and issues (political, economic, social, and industrial) with which he comes into contact daily.

4. They exert a powerful influence on the kinds and types of persons with whom he can be personally compatible and the kinds of social activities in which he can engage.

5. They largely determine which ideas, principles, and concepts he can accept, assimilate, remember, and transmit without distortion.

6. They provide him with an almost unlimited number and variety of moral principles which can be employed to rationalize and justify any action he has taken or is contemplating. (If his stand is totally unrealistic, ludicrous, or even harmful, he can still defend it "on principle.")

Conflicts and Inconsistencies   Human values would be of only minor concern to industry were it not for the fact that they are often extremely unreliable guides to thinking and acting. They tend to create internal and external conflict, to show internal inconsistency, and to deny reality. Few, if any, of a person's values are the products of ratiocination. Instead, they reflect faithfully the mores and ideologies of the cultures in which the individual has lived. The principal sources of his values are:

- The heroes he has worshiped in the course of his development (the parental, school, athletic, theatrical, political, and other authority figures with whom he has identified himself) and whose values, beliefs, and standards he has introjected—usually quite uncritically.

- His associates and peers whose acceptance and esteem are vital to him. (Many people feel they must conform absolutely and blindly to the beliefs, standards, and values of their groups on penalty of ostracism. This is why the behavior of young people is frequently so bizarre and unrealistic.)

Everyone's values have had a wide variety of sources and have been acquired over a long period of time; hence, in the aggregate a person's value system may be riddled with inconsistencies. He may have spent his childhood in

a religiously orthodox environment and acquired a corresponding system of values. Later
in life, he may have attended a very liberal
university, come under the influence of in-
structors and associates who were atheists, and
acquired values that are the polar opposites of
his earlier ones.

These internalized value conflicts are often
both painful and anxiety-provoking. Not knowing which set of values to use as a guide, the
individual resolves the problem as he does
others by repressing (putting out of consciousness, i.e., locking away in logic-tight compartments of his mind) those values which are in
conflict.[1] In consequence, he is no longer
aware of the conflict between and among his
values. Thus, he can be opposed to integration
with the Negro but employ him (or her) for
the most intimate personal services: cooking,
laundry, as a wet nurse, even as a mistress.
Normally he is conscious of only one set of
values at a time—those that are appropriate
to the circumstances which happen fortuitously
to prevail. At the same time, he also has a
wide variety of values from which to draw in
rationalizing and defending his beliefs and
actions. Hence, in terms of values he is comparable to the churchgoer who can justify an
act or opinion by an apt quotation from the
Bible, paying little attention to the apparent
inconsistencies in his interpretation.

EFFECT ON BEHAVIOR

Some values help us build productive human
relationships; some do not. But in any case
there is one outstanding characteristic of the
effect of values on behavior. The more important a value to us, the more likely we are to
believe that it is indisputably the *right* one.
Commonly, in my observation, people are
neither open-minded nor tolerant in the field
of values. More often than not the manager,
worker, union official, or public official whom
I see believes that all values which are inconsistent or in conflict with his are *wrong*. Their
possessors are misinformed, ignorant, stupid,
or wilfully benighted and evil, in his judgment. He tends thus to be wholly unreceptive
to others' values. Many things are seen by him
as either black or white; there are no grays.
(Attitudes favoring or against Communism are
typical.) Moreover, attempts by others to convince him that his values are faulty are rarely

---

[1] For a fuller explanation of the theory behind various
aspects of psychology, see Harry Levinson, "What
Killed Bob Lyons?" *Harvard Business Review*,
January–February, 1963, p. 127.

effective and often provoke violent outbursts
of hostility. This is because to question *his*
values is to undermine the foundations of his
way of life. He must be sure that his values
are the right ones, or he will be at sea with
neither chart nor compass.

In extreme cases, the person believes that
anyone who possesses values other than his
must be set right, using persuasion or logic;
failing in this, through imposition by force. In
both the radical right and radical left, this
missionary zeal easily becomes fanaticism.

No Testing   How often do we wish to subject our values to careful, controlled reality
testing? *We are afraid that they might be
proved false.* It is safer to assume that the
"authorities" or other sources of the values are
infallible. In consequence, many superficially
plausible but clinically questionable assumptions relative to human nature are regularly
made in industry without ever being tested.
To illustrate:

• Many people who value hard work, self-
  improvement, the Horatio Alger tradition,
  group participation, and democratic progress
  believe that the typical employee sincerely
  desires a high degree of job autonomy and
  is eager to accept responsibility for guiding
  his own and his group's activities. On this
  premise, it has been argued that decision
  making should be pushed to the lowest possible rank in the organization, ideally to the
  machine-tender level. (This is the philosophy
  of so-called "bottom-up management.") It
  is believed that this exercise will not only
  strengthen and develop the employees, but
  will improve their morale as well.

• On the other hand, there are people with
  more authoritarian (and perhaps more
  cynical) values who are led to feel that
  most employees, because of their acute need
  for certainty, security, and structure, wish
  to participate in an absolute minimum of
  decision-making activities. They point to
  evidence that employees want a high degree
  of relatively authoritarian supervision. Decisions entail risks which may threaten their
  security, they argue. Hence, there is a constant tendency for problems and questions
  to be "bucked upward" to the top levels of
  the enterprise for adjudication. (This is why
  President Truman characterized his office as
  "the level at which the buck stopped.")

Are there not possibilities for objectively
testing such values and beliefs? To be sure, the
intangible, evanescent, and idealistic nature of

many values does render them difficult to subject to controlled experiment, but this is not true of all values all the time. For example, part of the value of democratic progress and group participation is the idea that people are perfectible and that everyone sincerely desires to learn of his limitations in order to take constructive action to overcome them. The validity of these assumptions is not difficult to test empirically. For instance:

All that is necessary is to study two groups of "problem" employees in an identical industrial setting. One group, perhaps 50 in number, is intensively counseled; its members' shortcomings are clearly defined for them, and opportunities are provided for them to correct the conditions causing them to be unsatisfactory as employees. The second matched group of like size, serving as a control, receives only conventional supervisory guidance. At the end of one year, the status of the members of the two groups is compared. If the hypothetical assumption is valid, the first group will show a marked degree of improvement, the second none.

Such a test might be conducted at various levels of responsibility under different conditions. It might be found that both democratic and authoritarian values are vulnerable; i.e., that the assumptions about people on which they are based hold up only part of the time or under limited circumstances.

Cult of Masculinity

Certain traits, such as masculinity, boldness, aggressiveness, self-reliance, and decisiveness—the concept of the "winner," the person who invariably triumphs—have come to be widely overvalued in the prevailing business and industrial culture. While these traits are certainly helpful, if not always essential, to success in management, sales and related occupations, there are many vocations in which they are neither required nor particularly advantageous. Such vocations are often unfairly patronized and depreciated; and those who tend to be rather passive, submissive, and dependent are characterized by many as "weak," a term of disparagement in the prevailing value system of business.

In consequence, many persons are driven to attempt to exhibit masculinity, aggressiveness, and decisiveness, and to seek positions which call for these qualities when they do not have them. As a result, such people often find themselves in jobs for which they are totally unsuited. In their efforts to exhibit the esteemed qualities or to fill positions which demand such qualities, they often subject themselves to pressures and tensions which, because they are in

excess of their ability to tolerate them, often induce such psychogenic symptoms as ulcers and allergies, and such flight manifestations as obesity, excessive smoking, alcoholism, frantic random activity, or overpreoccupation with detail. These effects figure prominently in some of the company problems we shall look at later on.

Identifying Situations

If management is to cope successfully with its people problems, it must take into greater account than it usually does the roles played by values, with all of their inconsistencies, conflicts, and unrealities. And it should attack the problems discriminately, without attaching value labels to whole groups.

In view of the number and variety of values involved in most "people problem" situations, and because of the complexity of their interrelationships, each must be considered on its own merits. In the following pages I shall focus on six situations that top executives find particularly troublesome:

1. Labor-management strife.
2. Poor employee morale, especially if resulting from ultra-authoritarian management.
3. Declines in performance standards.
4. Failures in superior-subordinate relations.
5. Communication problems.
6. Attacks on business by intellectuals and politicians.

LABOR–MANAGEMENT STRIFE

Conflicts of values between labor and management cause strife more often than is usually recognized. Economic factors are often of lesser importance than are value conflicts. Each party naturally regards its goals, standards, and shibboleths—especially insofar as these can be identified with values—as indisputably the right ones; each side is intolerant of the values of the other. Each contestant suports his position by appeals to logic, by moral arguments, and by reference to the principles on which he stands; but the basic problem lies in conflicts of values. Typical was the Studebaker–United Auto Workers strike of 1962:

Its cause was management's desire to become more competitive with Detroit by reducing its men's wash-up time from 39 to 24 minutes per day. This, it was estimated, would save $600,000 per year in production costs with no corresponding reduction in wages.

The union, in response, charged that to reduce the wash-up allowance by 15 minutes per day was an evidence of management's desire to exploit the workers. It stated emphatically that it "would not bow the head and bend the knee to management greed and exploitation," and went on a six-week strike marked by some violence.

The strike cost the workers $750,000 in lost pay and the company $21,000,000 in lost production. (It was ultimately settled by a compromise—a reduction in wash-up time by 5 minutes, effective at model-change time in 1963.)

Steps to Improvement   There is no simple, inexpensive, sovereign remedy for conflicts of this nature. Improved communication, for instance, is no answer. The roots of conflict are too deep and complex, and the values of both parties are too bitterly opposed. The important thing to face is the fact that when the causes of strife are primarily value-oriented, the arguments are more emotional than rational. They are not only manifestations of unreason, frequently by both parties, but, by the same token, largely proof against logic. In fact, the application of logic often succeeds in *exacerbating* the difficulty.

However, it is realistic to try to lessen the bitterness of the strife. To that end, the following principles and steps are valuable:

Initiative. Management must realize that it must take the initiative in seeking remedial action. It usually has greater freedom and latitude in which to act than the union has, and is less compelled to follow a rigid course shaped primarily by the ideologies of its members.

Recognition of Union's Role. Management must also recognize the fact that the typical union member's value system is so constituted that he *must* prove to his employer, to the world, and to himself that he fears no one; and that he is a wholly autonomous, independent individual who should have as influential a voice in what he does on the job as does the company. This he must do to deny his passive, dependent needs and to compensate for his deeply rooted feelings of helplessness, of inadequacy. Since the union is both the instrument by which he can express his defiance with impunity and his only protection against mistreatment by the company, he is doubly dependent on it. (This is a condition which the union exploits for its own ends.) This emotional need to prove his "manhood" frequently leads to the eruption of violence.

Self-review. Management should openly, honestly, and candidly review its own values, par-

ticularly as they impinge on the lives, duties, and responsibilities of its employees. It must define its own goals vis-à-vis its people, establish what it wants from them, and, at the same time, decide what it proposes to contribute to their welfare.

Evaluation of Situation. Executives should ascertain by means of a joint analysis of (a) union policies and demands and (b) the results of employee information and opinion polls, the content and goals of prevailing worker ideologies. In conducting the polls, particular effort must be made to ascertain the precise conditions which not only give the workers legitimate grounds for complaint but also justify existing antimanagement sentiments —conditions such as poor working facilities, low pay, and weak or incompetent supervision. It is also essential to discover the "facts" about the enterprise which are believed by the employees but do not happen to be true. For example, it may be believed that the company nets 25% profit after taxes.

Executives who have not been close to the blue-collar scene may be surprised at the results of a probing survey. Such convictions as the following are likely to emerge:

- A worker acquires a property right to his job which grows greater the longer he holds it.

- He has a right to a share of the profits he helps to produce.

- He should have a voice in determining the conditions under which he works; work rules are a fit subject for negotiations.

- In some instances he may even feel that it is all right for him to keep his production at the level of the least competent to protect the latter's job security.

- Likewise, he may even go so far as to believe that any profit made by the employer is at his expense; accordingly, it is all right for him to steal from the employer or at least to soldier on the job.

Value Comparison. Management must compare, as objectively as possible, *its* values with those of its employees, within the broad frame of reference of conditions which prevail within the company, its industry, and the economy. The aim of this study is to find *common goals and values,* i.e., to seek to integrate conflicting desires. For instance, it may be possible to find a solution, such as profit sharing or the Scanlon Plan, which will offer a common goal and minimize conflicts of interest.

Where great psychological and cultural distances separate top management and members of the bargaining unit, it will never be possible to integrate their ideologies completely. The key to the minimization of conflict lies, therefore, in a willingness by management to take an impartial, objective, and tolerant view of opposed values and ideologies. Management must accept the fact that since most worker values cannot be significantly modified, the only thing left for it to do is to accept them as unchangeable facts of life and plan its communications and labor relations programs accordingly.

A direct, frontal attack on an opposed ideology accomplishes nothing other than the stimulation of greater intolerance and, often, of violence. Bitter as this pill may be to some intransigent members of management, a desire for understanding and a search for a common ground with labor may be much more productive of labor peace and cooperation than will a more direct and aggressive anti-union campaign.

POOR MORALE

Poor employee morale with consequent excessive labor turnover, substandard productivity, and "poor attitudes" often arises from the arbitrary implementation of authoritarian, sometimes ultrarightist management values. The values in these cases often tend not only to be unnecessarily rigid and restrictive but to constitute an affront to the employee's image of himself as an intelligent, autonomous human being. Thus the time clock is commonly regarded as a symbol of worker bondage.

Moreover, many managements are not content simply to promulgate their values; actively, sometimes brutally, they seek to *impose* their values on their employees. Their thinking is solely in "blacks and whites," and in their minds their values are always the right ones. Some of them attempt to build good morale by force, by disciplining or discharging all nonconformists and damning them as "troublemakers" or "communists." Other managements reportedly have even attempted to dominate the private lives of their personnel and to exercise thought control over those who were tenants in company housing projects (e.g., those developed by Henry Ford, the elder, and by the Kohler Company).

Problems of Remedial Action The outlook for remedial action in such cases is poor, in my opinion. Most executives I have seen in authoritarian organizations have the "John Birch society mentality," i.e., they have a compulsive, obsessive drive to impose their values on everyone else, particularly their subordinates. With this mentality, they are completely impervious to reason and are aggressively hostile to all values which conflict even in the slightest with theirs; to question their values is, of course, to exacerbate their underlying insecurities.

Furthermore, they cannot tolerate strong subordinates. Hence it is to be expected that the law of diminishing competence will come into play, resulting in considerable weakness at the first, second, and third levels of supervision. And since such executives tend to select subordinates in their own image, it is to be expected that these managers, superintendents, and foremen will not only be weak but also autocratic, and will subscribe to the same rigid values as their superiors. Thus, they too become petty tyrants.

Only the replacement, retirement, or death of the more autocratic members of such a management offers any lasting solution to the problem. For then there is the possibility that the successors will be more secure. Hence, they would be capable of assessing their own values with reasonable objectivity and of ascertaining the appropriateness, validity, and acceptability of these to employees. This would mean they could adopt a tolerant, understanding, and open-minded attitude toward their employees' ideologies. Only under these circumstances can management initiate the necessary remedial steps to ensure that company values, policies, and practices are reasonably consistent with worker needs and ideologies.

Probably the executives' greatest difficulty will lie in assessing objectively the qualifications of supervisors. Since these men and women will be technically competent, of long service, and loyal, their superiors may see no reason why any of them should be replaced. After all, "They think right." Authoritarian executives tend to be quite insensitive to evidences of weaknesses such as their own in subordinates. Because many of these subordinates will be loud, dictatorial "bulls of the woods," they will be regarded by their superiors as strong and decisive.

In the meantime, if not already organized, companies with such managements will be exceptionally vulnerable to unionization. When the employees join a labor organization to provide themselves with some defense against management and supervision, and to find a group sympathetic to their ideologies, company executives will fail to understand why the workers are "disloyal" to them after they have "done everything possible for their welfare."

Unable to comprehend the role that they themselves have played in creating disaffection among their people, they will seek scapegoats elsewhere. They may even charge union organizers and sympathizers with being "communists" and "traitors to the American (their) way of life." The chances are good that they will succeed not only in winning sympathy for the union but in "proving" to employees that management is indeed the villain it is often pictured to be.

DECLINE OF WORK STANDARDS

Charles H. Brower, president of Batten, Barton, Durstine & Osborne, Inc., a leading advertising agency, stated some time ago in a widely publicized talk before the Sales Executives Club of America:

Here in America we have reached the high tide of mediocrity, the era of the great goof-off, the age of the half-done job. The land from coast to coast has been enjoying a stampede away from responsibility. It is populated with laundry men who won't iron shirts, with waiters who won't serve, with carpenters who will come around someday maybe, with executives whose mind is on the golf course, with teachers who demand a single salary schedule so that achievement cannot be rewarded, nor poor work punished, with students who take cinch courses because the hard ones make them think, with spiritual delinquents of all kinds who have been triumphantly determined to enjoy what was known until the present crises as "the new leisure."[2]

These persons' consciences do not trouble them because in the mores of the prevailing welfare state, as they see it, craftsmanship and excellence of performance in general have ceased to be as widely accepted values as they may have been in the past. How many employees, short of those in the topmost echelons (and not even some of these), can be characterized today as "dedicated"? The motto of many is "I only work here." In large corporations, it is not unusual for a number of the employees to regard the company as many people think of the government: as having unlimited resources. Hence they feel no obligation to consider the economic welfare of their employer.

[2] Charles H. Brower, Address before the National Sales Executives Convention, May 20, 1958, *Speeches and Articles by BBDOers*, Gen. 1202.

As a result of this and other influences, the prevailing worker ideology in a company may contain such sentiments as:

- The employee has little obligation to his employer; after all, the latter is making an excessive profit on each worker's efforts.
- No employer has any right to deny a spirited boy the privilege of engaging in some good clean fun, e.g., welding pop bottles in a gasoline tank, even though this may necessitate the subsequent disassembly of the entire car in order to locate the source of the noise.

Perhaps the greatest paradox is the fact that the same employee who soldiers on the job may be extremely industrious off it, building an addition to his home or making a hi-fi set.

Steps to Improvement   Attempts to change the attitudes and consequent productivity of such employees by reason or admonition are rarely fruitful, because:

- Their ideologies and value systems are very resistant to change, especially where there is little identity with or respect for the author of the proposed change.
- They have little or no incentive to change their individual values or way of life; they are quite content with themselves as they are.
- Most of their associates and personal heroes subscribe to the same values as their own; an employee would be a nonconformist in his group were he to change, possibly an outcast.
- The motives of management are distrusted; the employer is seen as grasping and greedy, seeking only to make a profit at the workers' expense.

Since, with many employees, little or no improvement can be expected to occur spontaneously, it must be understood that improvement has to be induced *from without and above* by the provision of comprehensive job structuring and the application of fair but firm discipline. This entails:

- A clear definition of company rules and policies as they relate to the employee.
- A clear definition of each employee's job duties, responsibilities, and authority.
- A clear definition of the expectations of each employee's supervisor as to his job performance.

- An understanding by all personnel that management does not believe in appeasement; that offenders will be disciplined at once, union or no union.
- The provision of first-, second-, and third-line supervision of sufficient competence and strength to win and hold employee respect, to implement company policies, and to ensure that reasonable discipline is maintained.

Management must recognize that no business organization which intends to remain solvent can afford to function continually as a rehabilitation center for the delinquent and a home for the indigent. It cannot afford the luxury of being "democratic" or practicing "human relations" at the cost of order and discipline. Over the long pull, management must —

- assess its own values objectively and try to ensure that its policies are sound;
- make clear its expectations to its marginal "problem" cases, with the understanding that they are being warned to improve the quality of their performance;
- act decisively if, after due warning, the employee does not show improvement (all new hourly rated employees should, ideally, be on probation for at least 90 days);
- establish comprehensive selection techniques to ensure the exclusion of potential "problem employees" (those whose previous records, test results, and interview findings indicate that they are chronic troublemakers, irresponsible, emotionally immature, psychopathic personalities, or borderline psychotics)·
- recognize those, even among the well-adjusted, whose values do not preclude their joining in antimanagement activities (these may include some brilliant technicians, but they must always be regarded as questionable security risks).

INDIVIDUAL RELATIONSHIPS

Values also play an important (although not all-inclusive) role in personal relationships. Both incompatibility and excessive compatibility are troublesome.

Four factors are critical if the character of any superior-subordinate relationship, particularly when those involved work close to each other, is to be a good one:

1. The superior's technical expectations and standards must be met by the subordinate.

2. The superior's personal values must be relatively similar to those of his subordinate.

3. The subordinate's competence must not be so great as to make him a threat to his superior's job security.

4. As far as possible, the superior must meet his subordinate's expectations technically and personally, so that he is respected by him.

In cases of either overcompatibility or undercompatibility, the true causes are rarely enunciated because often the parties themselves are unaware of their nature. For example, the anxious (and correspondingly incompatible) superior is rarely able to face the fact that it is his subordinate's competence which frightens him. All he knows consciously is that he somehow does not like his subordinate, as in the old bit of doggerel about Dr. Fell:

> I do not love thee, Dr. Fell
> The reason why I cannot tell
> But this alone I know full well
> I do not love thee, Dr. Fell.

Under such circumstances, the superior often finds a value-oriented rationalization for his attitude, such as that his subordinate has execrable taste in clothes.

Realistic Approach   In coping with cases of incompatibility, little is to be gained by any attempt to influence the relationship by a straightforward, logical approach. This is because the primary determinant of any such relationship is the congruence or dissonance of the parties' values (with overtones of anxiety where the superior fears his subordinate). Where incompatibility exists, corrective or preventive action must include the determination of the kind of person who *is* compatible with the superior, particularly by observing those of the superior's present subordinates who are clearly compatible with him. What kinds of persons (technically, value-wise, and in terms of competence) can he tolerate comfortably? And to what values must the subordinates subscribe in order for them to be acceptable to him?

Where overcompatibility exists, a study must made to determine what needs (for support, reassurance, or flattery) current favorites satisfy in the superior. On the basis of these findings, standards can be established for use in evaluating candidates for the position of subordinate to a particular executive. An intensive appraisal of the candidate can then be made, using very thorough interviewing techniques to ascertain the extent to which his technical qualities will meet his superior's expectations, the extent to which the pattern of his values is consonant with those of his prospective boss, and the extent to which he is or is not a potential threat to his superior.

Since neither supervisory values nor the capacity in the superior to tolerate a strong subordinate is susceptible to significant change in a few months or years, where actual overcompatibility or undercompatibility are encountered corrective actions usually consist of:

- Separating *over*compatible superiors and subordinates. (In many such instances, the subordinate is so weak and pliable that he is little more than a clerk regardless of his title. To keep him there will simply be to perpetuate a bad situation. The superior will rarely part with him voluntarily. Hence the initiative for change must come from management.)

- Studying each case of incompatibility to ascertain whether the roots of the difficulty lie principally in a conflict of basic values or in a threat to the superior from the junior, or because both these elements are involved in the situation.

- Recognizing that where the difficulty lies in a conflict of basic values, the two men had best be separated and teamed up with more compatible associates.

- Recognizing that where the cause of the problem lies in the fact that the superior fears his junior, *they should be left together.* (Otherwise the law of diminishing competence will almost certainly come into play, and a weaker man will be selected by the superior to take his junior's place. The weak senior will resent a strong, competent subordinate and constantly emphasize his faults, but if management is aware of the situation, it can be on guard against being misled by the superior to the subordinate's disadvantage.)

- Using care in initial employment, transfers, or promotions to match prospective superiors and subordinates. (This attention should ensure that their technical and personal values are reasonably in agreement and that a condition of overcompatibility will not develop in which the junior is too little of a threat to his superior.)

No business can expect to have a completely harmonious staff; a reasonable degree of dissonance and conflict is, in most instances, healthy. Successful management faces the fact that some discord is inevitable, and it attempts only to maintain a balance between harmony and conflict. Its goal, in view of this, is to discourage open internecine warfare, and at the same time to ensure that no subordinates are discriminated against unfairly by incompatible or frightened superiors.

BARRIERS TO COMMUNICATION

Many companies are constantly plagued with failure of their internal communication systems, both horizontally (between departments and divisions) and vertically (between top management and the hourly rated employees). In such cases messages often fail to get through to their intended recipients or become distorted and garbled in transmission. Most critical, the effects of intensive educational, morale-building, and attitude-changing campaigns are often negligible.

One of the primary reasons for these failures of communication is a conflict of values. The breakdown can occur where (as in the Studebaker case) the standards of management are not only unacceptable to the workers but may create violent hostilities; intermediate supervision is unable to transmit the message effectively because many of its members are, say, ex-machine tenders and hence have retained the values of their men; the recipients are unable to accept, assimilate, and remember the message without distortion (as was the case with the members of the Studebaker bargaining unit). In office groups, interdepartmental rivalries may exist (i.e., each unit—sales, production, engineering, and so on—may have its own unique constellation of values) so that what is acceptable to one division will not necessarily be so to another.

Building Rapport Management or interdepartmental communications must, of course, be clear, concise, and unambiguous. But this is only the first step. *It is still essential that the content of communications be oriented to take into account existing union, worker, or departmental ideologies.* These can be ascertained by an analysis of union demands, by information and opinion polls, and by studying employee complaints, grievances, or other expressions of departmental attitudes.

Communications must express only those values of management or the department which are reasonably consonant with the recipients' ideologies. They must not reinforce convictions prevalent in worker ideologies. Thus, direct pleas for greater productivity reinforce the belief that the company is greedy and seeks to exploit its employees. Nor should a communication conflict with prevailing divisional ideologies. It is also imperative that the message contain no sentiments derogatory to worker self-images. For example, it should not imply that they, the employees are unimportant (faceless automatons or clock numbers), that their attitudes are wrong, or that their leaders have betrayed them. Likewise, there must be no implication that the contributions of one group in the business are more important than those of another.

The more egregiously erroneous beliefs revealed by information polls, e.g., that company profits are 25% after taxes, should be corrected where unassailable factual information can be offered in refutation. Opportunities can also be provided for personal contacts with top executives, permitting personal discussions with a direct "feedback" from the workers. These can be of great help in dispelling misunderstandings. Finally, wherever possible, all intracompany communications should be limited to matters of fact. Care must be employed to exclude value-oriented statements such as those often expressed in monthly letters from the president which stress the merits of the free enterprise system, and so on. *All communications should be designed to emphasize common values*—for instance, the merits of the company profit-sharing plan, if there is one. This is suitable because it represents an integration of the values of both management and the workers.

To ensure clear channels of *upward* communication, management must make clear, by its responses to employee opinions, that it will tolerate expressions of values which conflict with its own. This means that it will not be necessary for employees to tell management only "what it wants to hear." Management must demonstrate that it is open-minded toward values which conflict with its own and will do its best to integrate them with its own.

In the final analysis, however, company executives must face the fact that there will be failures of communications whenever a message must be filtered through the minds of one or more persons. What *is* possible is to keep the number and gravity of failures down so that operations are not needlessly disrupted.

ATTACKS ON BUSINESS

Business often is subjected to scathing attacks by intellectuals and politicians. It is charged with degrading the public taste, seducing people by promotional campaigns into making purchases which they neither need nor can afford, setting prices that are too high, and foisting shoddy and even deleterious merchandise upon the public. For example:

- Bertrand de Jouvenal, the French economist and political theorist, says that the hostility of the intellectuals toward the businessman is the result of a clash between their value systems. The businessman's philosophy is: give the public what it wants. The intellectual's is: give the public what it ought to have.[3]

- According to Joseph Schumpeter, noted Harvard economist, intellectuals do not have direct responsibility for practical affairs; they stand outside the circle, as it were, and can only gain recognition by making a nuisance of themselves.[4]

Thus, the intellectuals' attacks often consist of plausible, value-oriented rationalizations designed to gratify a profound underlying envy and hostility. This is why their attacks are sometimes violent and vitriolic to the point of unreason.

Similarly, many politicians who are opportunists of the first order are not above the cynical use of such an issue as the high price of certain ethical pharmaceutical products to dramatize themselves colorfully. To publicize themselves as defenders of the public weal, they will charge that businessmen are greedy and make excessive profits.

Indirect Steps Needed   To attempt to meet charges of this character head-on (whether leveled by intellectuals or by politicians) and to try to demolish them by force of logic is usually futile, because most of these accusations lie in the realm of values. They are, therefore, often evanescent, elusive, and extremely difficult to pin down and counter factually and categorically. Furthermore, there is a constant danger that in attempting to disprove charges of this nature, the businessman may find himself taking a position or making allegations which will conflict with prevailing ideologies in business, social, and political circles. Antagonisms can be created which will be as damaging to the businessman as the original charges against which he is attempting to defend himself. Where the issues are vague, nebulous, and cloudy, or the charges difficult

---

[3] Quoted in LeBaron R. Foster, "The Businessman: Through the Eyes of the Intellectual," *Encore,* Spring, 1962, p. 13.
[4] *Ibid.,* p. 12.

to refute, it is easy for the businessman to become involved in endless, specious argument.

In view of this, the most expeditious course for the businessman is as follows:

1. He should disdain to answer the irresponsible charges directly, implying that they are not worthy of his serious attention. (This is the same tactic commonly used by both intellectuals and politicians when faced with rebuttals and counter-charges.) The businessman should learn to simply shrug them off.

2. Immediately upon learning of any grave charges—regardless of their source—management should attempt to ascertain by market research studies in depth, employing the techniques of motivational research, the exact character of the public's prevailing ideologies relating to business in the area in question.

3. Using these research findings as a basis, management can then conduct a positive, value-oriented campaign to stress the *positive* contributions of business to the public welfare. These statements must, of course, be designed to confirm, never to conflict with, prevailing public ideologies. Under no circumstances should the statements directly refute existing beliefs, even blatantly erroneous beliefs such as that anything left in a tin can will spoil and become poisonous. Instead, the campaign should emphasize what the business or industry has already done in the public interest (e.g., the misery and suffering that the new antibiotics have prevented) and what it will offer in the future. If this story is properly dramatized and is consistent with the values of the audience to whom it is directed, it will tend to erase the memory of the original charges and substitute a more favorable public image.

It is well to remember that, in the final analysis, the net effect of the intellectuals' and politicians' attacks, even when they are not answered, is usually negligible. They are rarely a cause for great concern, no matter how flamboyant. This is because many of the issues are only of incidental concern to the public. Also, neither the intellectual nor the average politician is usually a heroic figure to the man in the street. Therefore, he has little incentive to identify himself with them, and their pronouncements ordinarily have little impact or influence on his thinking. His interest in the charges is only a passing one and rarely leads him to take action of any sort, at the polls or elsewhere. In short, most of these harangues

where the businessman and his works are viewed with alarm by intellectuals and politicians are actually of little significance.

LIVING WITH VALUES

Despite the fact that many human values are inconsistent, conflicting, and unrealistic, and so are dubious guides to beliefs, attitudes, and actions, they are a fact of life. They are here to stay. Everyone must have his quota of values; without them, he is a ship without a rudder. If management is to build and maintain an effective, well-integrated work force, it must constantly test its own values and the policies which result from them to make certain that they are:

- Reasonably consistent internally.

- Not too acutely in conflict with the values of other members of the management group, with those of company employees, and with those of the public.

- Reasonably consistent with reality.

- Not arbitrarily imposed on the company personnel.

- Recognized not to be infallibly correct but at least subject to debate.

Values are not only ubiquitous but indispensable in every culture. However, if their limitations and proneness to error are not recognized by management, they may do great harm. Heretofore, their role has not been adequately understood and evaluated, particularly in the fields of employee, labor, and public relations. In consequence, much unnecessary friction, strife, and even violence have occurred. Production has often been held to unnecessarily low levels. Superior and subordinate relations have not been as compatible and productive as they should be. Individuals and businesses have pursued courses of action which were less than fully productive, sometimes even deleterious to the enterprise. Intracompany communications have often been ineffective, and businessmen have sometimes been unnecessarily terrified by the attacks of intellectuals and politicians.

The best approach to the problem of dealing with inconsistent, conflicting, or unrealistic values is a relatively simple one. It is based on the recognition that, as already stated, *nearly everyone has more than one set of values which relate to a given topic.* Often these values are of a totally opposed character. Instead of questioning expressed values, the individual or the group must either be researched thoroughly, using sophisticated interviewing techniques, or encouraged to "talk the problem out" at length. By this means, alternative and, hopefully, more appropriate values which are already a part of their ideological systems (though not always clearly appreciated) may often be discovered. These can then be seized on by management and strongly advocated. Since they already were held by the persons or groups whom it is desired to influence, their advocacy by management will constitute no affront to the employees' self-respect and create few resentments.

Obviously, most such solutions are in the nature of compromises; hence few are perfect. Nevertheless, their consequences are often far superior to the results obtained by direct, frontal attacks on aberrant values.

Of all problems in the entire field of value judgments in industry, the greatest one probably is to convince top management of some simple truths. Its members are often accustomed to believing that their standards are infallible and should prevail. Great progress can be made if they can be led to see that:

1. Their points of view are not the only ones.
2. Most issues are not absolutely black or white but do have some gray areas.
3. They personally do not enjoy a monopoly of the truth.
4. Because someone espouses a system of values which differs from theirs, he is not necessarily ignorant, stupid, or disloyal.

55

*Motivating the Organization Man**

FREMONT E. KAST

Management frequently expresses a frustrating inability to motivate workers toward meeting organizational goals and objectives. Complaints are often heard that run something like this: "What does it take to get these fellows in the plant to stop complaining? We increased their direct pay by over 50 per cent in the past ten years and gave them a retirement program, a sickness and accident plan, and other benefits. Yet their complaints are increasing, and the only way we can maintain output is through more mechanization. Looks like a recession is the only thing that will straighten them out."

Moreover, the problem is not limited to rank-and-file employees; motivating and satisfying engineering and technical personnel is equally troublesome. Even though orbiting space vehicles and rising scientism throughout the nation have increased the status, monetary rewards, and prestige of scientific and technical personnel, their effective integration into the corporate family has been difficult. The prime asset of scientific personnel is creativity and independence of mind, which must be relatively unrestricted by formal organizational requirements. Yet they must be motivated to work as part of the corporate team and have to be willing to subordinate individual and even professional requirements in favor of corporate objectives.[1]

At a recent management conference, a high-level line executive said, "How can I get these independent characters to see that they have to operate within the organization and that corporate needs are sometimes more important than requirements of the scientific method? Why, they don't really understand what we are in business for, and every time I try to pin them down to do something for the company,

* Reprinted by permission of the publisher from *Business Horizons*, vol. 4, no. 1, pp. 55–60, Spring, 1961. Mr. Kast is associate professor of policy, personnel relations and production in the College of Business Administration at the University of Washington.

[1] William L. Swager, in "Improving the Management of Research," *Business Horizons*, vol. 2, pp. 42–49, Winter, 1959, points up the problems facing management of research and development and suggests several sound programs for their solution.

they run off to another meeting where they can read high-brow papers and get their egos inflated."

Nor has the question of effective motivation escaped the inner circles of higher management. The president of one of our larger corporations, in discussing the problems of motivation, stated that it was increasingly difficult to find means of inducing his top executives to higher levels of performance. He put the blame directly on the progressive income tax because it has limited the effectiveness of monetary incentives in high-income brackets. He seemed to feel that when monetary incentives are taken away, few alternatives remain for stimulating executives to greater effectiveness.

These statements indicate a major dilemma facing modern management. Every organizational activity, from the small informal group to the large-scale business, governmental, or religious organization, requires that the individual subordinate his independence and discretion in favor of organizational requirements. What can the business organization offer as a reward for this sacrifice? Or is there an insoluble conflict between the needs of the individual and the objectives of the organization?

Perhaps some light can be shed upon these problems if we attempt to define the characteristics of an organization and to determine what motivates its participants. Possible conflicts between organizational requirements and individual needs will then be revealed.

THE ORGANIZATION

An understanding of the basic characteristics of all organizations is fundamental to the discussion of alternative means of motivating people for effective participation. Any organization involves the integration of human and physical resources for accomplishing objectives, and by its very nature is a social structure. E. Wright Bakke defines the social organization as:

. . . a continuing system of differentiated and coordinated human activities utilizing, transforming, and welding together a specific set of human, material, capital, ideational, and natural resources into a unique problem-solving whole whose function is to satisfy particular human needs in interaction with other systems of human activities and resources in a particular environment.[2]

---

[2] E. Wright Bakke in Mason Haire (ed.), *Modern Organization Theory,* John Wiley & Sons, Inc., New York, 1959, p. 50.

This definition, although complex, is appropriate for all of man's organizations and emphasizes the following characteristics: (1) a system of differentiation of human activities; (2) a system for integration of human activities; (3) objective orientation for satisfaction of human needs; and (4) interaction with environment.

Although each of these characteristics has received a great deal of attention, most of the current "organization theories" deal with one rather than with all of them. In this article, I will concentrate on the third, the orientation of the organization toward the satisfaction of human needs, for herein lies the problem of motivation.

In simpler organizations, such as family or kinship groups, the objective of need satisfaction of the various participants is obvious. The needs are easily determined, and the relationships between organization members, determined primarily by physical characteristics or sociocultural forces, are clear-cut. However, in the more complex organization, such as the business corporation, the objective of need satisfaction is not so simple. Questions such as "Which needs will be satisfied for whom?" must be answered. Obviously, in any social organization there are likely to be conflicts among the various participants; thus, the complex organization must develop elaborate means for allocating need satisfaction among its participants.

The question remains of why individuals participate in the organization. Theoretically, each employee will continue working effectively in an organization when the inducements are greater than the contributions that he is asked to make. In this Barnard-Simon theory of organizational equilibrium, the central postulates are:

1. An organization is a system of interrelated social behaviors of a number of people whom we shall call the participants.
2. Each participant and each group of participants receive from the organization inducements; in return, they make contributions to the organization.
3. Each participant will continue in an organization only so long as inducements offered to him are as great as or greater (measured in terms of his values and in terms of the alternatives open to him) than the contributions he is asked to make.
4. The contributions provided by the various groups of participants are the source from which the organization manufactures the inducements offered to participants.

5. Hence, an organization is solvent and will continue in existence only so long as the contributions provide enough inducements to draw forth these contributions.[3]

The inducements that the organization provides and the willingness of the individuals to contribute to organizational goals are dependent upon many variables, including the aspiration level of participants, the alternatives available, the formal reward and punishment system, and the state of the external environment. However, the types of satisfaction that the organization can bestow depend mainly upon the nature of individual motives.

Motives and Needs In any social organization, the extent of the individual's effective participation depends, basically, upon the degree to which the organization satisfies his needs. What are the needs that motivate man's behavior? There are many ways of classifying man's motives but perhaps the most basic is in terms of their origin. Sherif and Sherif distinguish motives as:

1. *Biogenic motives.* These originate in the physiological requirements and self-regulation process of the organism that maintain equilibrium in the "internal environment," within certain limits. The self-regulating processes are referred to as homeostasis.

2. *Sociogenic motives.* These motives are acquired in the course of the individual's development in a social setting. They are formed in connection with interpersonal relationships, group relations, or established social values or norms in institutions.[4]

This distinction of human motives emphasizes that behavior is a joint result of interrelated factors both from within the individual and from sociocultural influences. Although this breakdown of motives is useful in a general way to indicate the origin of human motivation, it is not sufficiently detailed to provide adequate guidelines for management. A. H. Maslow has set forth a theory of motivation that provides insight into the kinds of organizational forces that may influence behavior.[5] He distinguishes man's basic needs as:

1. The physiological needs such as hunger, thirst, the activity-sleep cycle, sex, and evacuation.

2. The safety needs for protection against danger, threat, and deprivation.

3. The love needs for satisfactory associations with others, for belonging to groups, and for giving and receiving friendship and affection.

4. The esteem needs for self-respect, for self-esteem, and for the esteem of others, often referred to as the ego or status needs.

5. The self-actualization or self-fulfillment needs to achieve the potential within himself, for maximum self-development and for creativity and self-expression.

Of what value is the theoretical discussion of human motivation to the executive who has to direct human and physical resources toward corporate objectives? These objectives can be accomplished only by inducing the cooperation and enthusiasm of all organizational participants (including management itself) through the satisfaction of their needs. Certainly it is not difficult to understand the necessity for satisfaction of physiological needs, but, as we move up the scale to the higher needs, we run into considerable confusion. Sociological and cultural forces have a great impact upon the means for satisfaction of sociability, status, and self-fulfillment.

The satisfaction or thwarting of needs has a pronounced influence on man's behavior. But not all are of the same intensity, nor do they influence behavior similarly at all times. There is substantial experimental and experiential evidence that man has a hierarchy of needs with the physiological needs having a higher level of prepotency. When a man is deprived of a basic need such as food, frustration influences his entire behavior. Under conditions of semistarvation for an extended period (a period like that encountered in a concentration camp or through a self-imposed diet), hunger comes to dominate more and more of the individual's thoughts and activities. With deprivation of biogenic needs, the sociogenic or higher-level needs become less important.[6]

Motivation in an Affluent Society In an advanced society where basic physiological needs have been substantially satisfied, the whole concept of motivation for organizational effectiveness must be re-evaluated. Once a

[3] James G. March and Herbert A. Simon, *Organizations,* John Wiley & Sons, Inc., New York, 1958, p. 84.
[4] Muzafer Sherif and Carolyn W. Sherif, *An Outline of Social Psychology,* Harper & Row, Publishers, Incorporated, New York, 1956, pp. 365–387.
[5] A. H. Maslow, "A Theory of Human Motivation," *The Psychological Review,* pp. 370–396, July, 1943.
[6] For a full discussion of the impact of a deprivation of biogenic needs upon sociogenic motives see Sherif and Sherif, *op. cit.,* p. 443.

lower-level need is satisfied, it no longer serves as a prime motivator. Thus, the physiological needs, when chronically gratified, cease to be active determinants of behavior. Furthermore, the more unlikely the possibility of an unsatisfied need (in the thinking of the individual), the less his behavior will be influenced by this need.

The American economic system has had phenomenal success in meeting the subsistence and safety needs of its citizens. With greatly increased productivity and higher levels of employment, our gross national product (measured in constant dollars) has increased by 150 per cent since 1929 and by nearly 60 per cent in the period since 1947.[7] Per capita personal income increased from $1,268 in 1946 to $2,148 in 1959. Even though there are instances of people living at the subsistence level, our economy has provided rewards substantially above this level for the majority of citizens. Our safety and security needs have also been basically satisfied by the growth of business, union, and governmental social security plans over the past thirty years. The future promises an even greater ability of our economic system to meet the primary subsistence and security requirements of our population.

What, then, is the problem? If we have been so successful in meeting these fundamental needs for human happiness, why don't we have a higher level of satisfaction and more cooperation in our corporate enterprises?

The means of satisfaction of human needs are not necessarily interchangeable. An increase in pay or fringe benefits will not generally satisfy employees' needs for sociability, status, or self-fulfillment. Any attempt by management to supply greater satisfaction of one need will not sublimate the behavioral influence of others. It appears that, while we have been successful in meeting the physiological and safety needs of employees, we tend to undervalue the higher-level social, status, and self-fulfillment needs. These have assumed a much more important position in our motivation structure than they would in a society of scarcity. Zaleznik, Christenson, and Roethlisberger, in reporting their research on motivation and productivity, summarize this concept as follows:

Thus management finds itself in a tough situation. By satisfying its workers' subsistence needs it has lost its conventional controls for motivating them. It has released new wants which

its old motivational tools cannot satisfy. Morever, it has unwittingly organized its work in ways which do not provide the conditions which will allow these new needs to be satisfied. As a result, many of the workers' new needs for membership, status, and growth become thwarted and so-called human relations experts are hired to deal with these thwarted needs which management has unwittingly produced in the first place.[8]

Their conclusions, strongly influenced by their ideological and ethical framework, suggest that management must direct its efforts toward satisfying higher needs in order to increase satisfaction and productivity.

THE CONFLICT

The preceding conclusion, while offering promise, fails to appreciate many hurdles and also assumes a position of responsibility (and authority) for the business corporation, which may be in conflict with our democratic concepts of a pluralistic society.

While the organization is a means for the fulfillment of the individual's needs, it also requires him to subordinate certain wants. Every organization, even the most voluntary social activity, demands that the individual direct his behavior toward the accomplishment of group objectives. The assumption that the business organization should be able to satisfy *all* of the needs of its participants and still accomplish its goals is in direct conflict with the requirements of organized behavior.

The business organization is most effective in providing for the fulfillment of the primary needs of participants. The basis for the satisfaction of these needs is a direct result of the productive effort of enterprise. However, the higher-level social, status, and self-fulfillment needs are more abstract and often outside the control of the formal business organization. Fulfillment of these cannot be provided directly by management, but are the result of influences such as the informal work group, the employee's outside professional relationship, his home life, his social activities—in fact, his entire sociocultural environment.

Many researchers have investigated this conflict between the requirements of the formal organization and the personality development of an individual. Chris Argyris states that the

[7] *Economic Report of the President,* Government Printing Office, Washington, D.C., 1960, pp. 156–157.

[8] A. Zaleznik, C. R. Christensen, and F. J. Roethlisberger, *The Motivation, Productivity, and Satisfaction of Workers,* Harvard Graduate School of Business, Boston, 1958, p. 403.

emphasis of the formal organization on the rationality of task specialization, a chain of command, a unity of direction, and span of control runs directly counter to the development of the human being in our Western culture. As a result of this basic incongruency, the individual is frustrated and does not work effectively to accomplish organizational goals.[9]

Inherent in this conflict between the individual and the organization is the question of balance between the centralized, bureaucratic organization and participative, democratic processes.[10] Specifically, to what extent are the democratic, individual self-determination processes practical or possible in the business organization?

Bureaucracy and Democracy Questioning of business responsibility and the concern over the subordination of the individual to the organization has been expressed by William H. Whyte, Jr. in *Organization Man,* C. Wright Mills in *The Power Elite,* and Alan Harrington in *Life in the Crystal Palace.*[11] Certainly any large organization, to be effective, must have an internal environment for decision-making and control that provides for a uniformity of action and an accepted pattern of individual behavior. The corporation must have disciplined behavior—actions must be anticipated and predictable. How can these requirements of rationality and uniformity be made compatible with democratic processes? Peter Blau in *Bureaucracy and Modern Society* clearly sets forth the conflict and explains the distinction between a bureaucracy and a democracy in terms of the goals to be accomplished.[12] He suggests that, if an organization is established for the purpose of realizing a specific objective, it is expected to be governed by criteria of efficiency. He defines such an

organization as a bureaucracy. Bureaucratization implies that considerations of efficiency outweigh all others in the formation and development of the organization.[13] However, in the democratic organization, considerations of efficiency are expected to be subordinated to the central aims of stimulating free expression of conflicting opinions. Bureaucratic and democratic structures can be distinguished, then, on the basis of the dominant organizing principles: efficiency or freedom of dissent.

The bureaucratic organization is geared to efficiency. For the business organization, the measurement of efficiency is, typically, long-run profitability and growth; these are essential in our competitive society. One of the major concerns of management is to direct and motivate organizational participants so that they will cooperate in meeting these objectives. The business organization has rewarded participants through the satisfaction of their needs —traditionally the subsistence and safety needs. But in the very satisfaction of these needs, the higher-level social, status, and self-fulfillment needs have often been sacrificed. Some authors take the viewpoint that our entire basis of organization is at fault and suggest a major change in administrative concepts. It is, apparently, their view that management should be oriented toward the satisfaction of *all needs.* While I certainly agree that management should seek new motivational methods, we may be asking the impossible to suggest that any organization primarily geared to economic objectives can or should be the vehicle for total need satisfaction. In fact, a society where the individual has a wide latitude of freedom in the selection of his organizational relationships —in his work, religious, political, and social life—is the essence of our democracy. To ask a business organization to fulfill all of these needs might seriously interfere with our broad opportunities for democratic participation in many organizational relationships.

Management must use effective motivation to secure cooperation from organizational participants and should give greater recognition to the higher-level needs. Total reliance upon monetary rewards, fringe benefits, and employment security as the only vehicles for motivation drastically limits the reward that the

[9] Chris Argyris, *Personality and Organization,* Harper & Row, Publishers, Incorporated, New York, 1956.

[10] The term "bureaucratic" is not utilized herein in an adverse sense. Rather it is used to define the rational organization with the characteristics of specialization of labor, a hierarchy of authority, a consistent system of rules and regulations, employment based upon technical qualifications, and rationality of decision-making.

[11] William H. Whyte, Jr., *The Organization Man,* Simon and Schuster, Inc., New York, 1956; C. Wright Mills, *The Power Elite,* Oxford University Press, Fair Lawn, N.J., 1956; Alan Harrington, *Life in the Crystal Palace,* Alfred A. Knopf, Inc., New York, 1959; and the German philosopher Karl Jasper, *Man in the Modern Age,* Humanities Press, New York, 1957 provide a profound analysis of the problems man faces in adapting to an "organized" society.

[12] Peter N. Blau, *Democracy in Modern Society,* Random House, Inc., New York, 1956, pp. 101–118.

[13] As Blau points out, this efficiency is in terms of organizational objectives rather than the objectives of the client. Quite frequently we, as clients, accuse the bureaucratic organization of red tape and inefficiency when in fact these contribute to the standardization, impersonality, and efficiency of the organization but fail to meet our own requirements.

organization may bestow. Yet it does not follow automatically that management can and should take on the responsibility for total fulfillment of all needs. The objectives of uniformity and efficiency in the business organization mitigate against the operation of a truly democratic administration. Without democratic processes, the corporation attempting to satisfy all human needs could easily become a paternalistic, monolithic structure. When the business organization, with its requirements for a bureaucratic autocracy, seeks to meet the total requirements of the individual, it runs the grave risk of completely subordinating the individual's freedom—not only in his work life but in his total life. I am increasingly concerned over the current trend to demand "complete involvement" of all participants by the corporate organization. Perhaps we would do better to recognize that man has many needs, some fulfilled by his participation in the business organization, some by other organizations such as educational institutions, churches, social groups, and families; some will not be fulfilled but will be powerful motivators to higher levels of achievement.

56

Management and Motivation: Releasing Human Potential*

ALBERT F. WATTERS

The ferment now sweeping the world is rooted in man's deepest instincts—instincts that have been amply documented in his long struggle up from the cave. The efforts to achieve economic security, equality of opportunity, tolerance of diverse races and creeds, and cultural and scientific progress are but a reflection of man's intense concern about his individuality—his inherent need to develop his potential to the full.

Because individual man is the means through which society achieves its objectives, it seems logical that management should develop a deeper understanding of his nature and of the influence of our changing times on the way in which he lives and works. Indeed it can be said that lack of this understanding underlies the failure of many companies to secure full support from their employees for the goals of the enterprise.

The knowledge about human nature that has accumulated over the centuries contains much that is of direct relevance to the management of people at work. At the risk of some oversimplification, we can say that all men possess the same inherent characteristics; or, to put it another way, that man is an organism whose behavior is conditioned by natural laws. These laws tell us that man is:

1. A *unit of energy* that seeks to spend itself and, in the process, both possesses and exercises the choice of how to expend this energy; that is to say, whether to conserve it, waste it, or use it productively.

2. *An organism possessing the dynamic ability to grow and adjust and select qualitatively.* In other words, man has the power to extract from his environment the nourishment he needs to build more of himself, both physically and mentally. Because the environment within which he moves can be conditioned, growth may be accelerated or slowed down as long as life lasts.

3. *Purposeful.* This characteristic manifests itself in man's instinctive search for food, security, achievement and recognition. It is the

* Reprinted by permission of the publisher from *Personnel,* vol. 39, no. 2, pp. 8–16, March–April, 1962. Mr. Watters is vice-president–personnel services for the General Foods Corporation.

force that induces him to expend his energy to become more perfectly what he wants to become. This drive may be conscious or unconscious—conscious in the struggle to attain ever-higher objectives, less conscious in the search for the things that are essential to simple self-preservation.

4. *Unique.* Each human being has his own personality, and each has the capacity to direct his energies. This capacity for self-direction increases man's uniqueness and magnifies the effect of experience upon his ultimate development. No two people react in precisely the same way to the same experience. Each does, however, react in his own way, and is therefore always in the process of becoming more and more different from his fellows.

Thus man can be viewed as a unit of energy wanting to produce; having the dynamic ability to grow and adjust; being purposeful; and possessing unique capabilities to respond to experience. It is also apparent that side by side with these characteristics must be placed the fact that man cannot be separated from his environment and that his knowledge, attitudes, and values largely derive from it.

The most vital and dynamic force in our environment today is the universal and continuously accelerating phenomenon of change. We live in a milieu of movement, and what we are, what we do, and what we can become in the future all stem from our ability to relate ourselves to this movement. Because we cannot halt change or always control its pace, we are forced to adapt both to the idea of change and to its effect on the human situation.

In our lifetime, we have all seen sweeping changes influencing our environment:

- International change—the growth of formerly underdeveloped countries to new power and independence.
- The population explosion at home and the rapid expansion of the middle class overseas.
- Domestic economic and political developments.
- Growth in the availability of higher education.
- Changing markets and methods of distribution.
- The changing role of labor.
- Accelerated research and technological progress.
- Shifts in the composition of the population and of the workforce.

Man is responding to these changes both negatively and positively. The increase in juvenile delinquency, mental illness, divorce, restlessness, and conflict reflect his negative responses to the rapid shifts in his environment. On the positive side, we see people developing new needs and expectations, achieving greater intellectual independence, acquiring deeper insights, experiencing new freedoms, cultivating broader interests, and gaining wider perspectives on life and on human relationships.

Few will deny that the work environment is largely created by the managerial processes employed by the business organization. Does not the art of effective management lie, then, in the development of managerial skills and processes that recognize, and are consistent with, the unique capacity of man to respond, positively or negatively, to the influences of this environment? But we may well go on to ask whether our managerial processes have changed as fast as man has. How often in the past have we reluctantly accepted change that we could have initiated?

Do present managerial processes, rooted deeply in the past, rely on outmoded concepts of authority and control? To what degree are we using and experimenting with new processes that can excite energy, induce growth, build on purpose, and stimulate the release of each man's unique potential?

We might examine, in this light, some managerial processes that can capitalize on this potential, particularly among our key people—the group whose contributions account for an ever-larger share of corporate growth and profitability. Among such key people are the researcher, the engineer, the marketing specialist, the manager, and the salesman—the individual contributors whose influence on profitability far outweighs their proportionate share of the pay-roll.

Among the processes that may deserve greater exploration in our effort to establish a more "motivating" work environment, I would particularly single out (1) mutual involvement; (2) communication; and (3) compensation.

THE PROCESS OF MUTUAL INVOLVEMENT

Throughout history, cooperative effort has been the key to human progress. It is the joint effort of creative and industrious families, groups, and nations, united in a common cause, that has moved mankind forward. Today, with his sense of intellectual independence and his consciousness of the significance of his own competence, initiative, and freedom, the individual man rebels at being denied full opportunity to participate in decisions on matters ultimately affecting his own destiny—such as, for example, the job at which he spends the greater part of his waking hours.

Social scientists, in fact, now take the view that poor performance on the job is due more to *lack of involvement* than to laziness or incompetence. Thus Douglas McGregor, of MIT, suggests that the question we have to consider is not whether people are lazy, but rather what they are going to direct their energies toward. Passiveness, he believes, is misdirected energy and a direct result of the work situation—for human nature is not in itself perverse. If people have a hand in setting targets for themselves, they'll set good targets, and they'll see that what's good for the company can also be good for them.

Rensis Likert, of the University of Michigan, also maintains that employees would not be indifferent and apathetic if they had more influence on the decisions that affect them and a sense of identification with both the problems and the solutions.

These conclusions suggest that in organizing our work groups we should move away from the rigid, formal patterns of the past toward greater consideration for the dynamic relations among people as one way to unlock the potential of the workforce. Key employees especially must be given freedom to work at the highest levels of which they are capable, and ways must be found to provide this freedom within the disciplines of the business organization.

This may mean greater decentralization of authority and responsibility for end results—the establishment of teams having profit-making or creative responsibility, yet operating within the formal framework of multi-purpose organizations. It suggests form and structure of organization but flexibility and movement within the form. It also suggests that job relationships and responsibilities should be organized in terms of agreed-upon end results, with full latitude being provided within the framework for the accomplishment of individual goals.

There are many opportunities for the manager to provide for employee participation in the day-to-day work situation:

- Setting work goals.
- Planning for work accomplishment.
- Planning for work or performance improvement.
- Reviewing progress.
- Providing exposure to developmental activities.

When key people help decide what should be done and how it can be accomplished, with their superior acting as a resource person—suggesting, guiding, and stimulating—they usually:

- Have a better understanding of what the job is and what results are expected.
- Establish more imaginative and challenging job goals in keeping with their purposes and within the framework of the job.
- Work more productively, using the methods most effective for them.
- Assume responsibility and a sense of commitment for accomplishment.
- Actively search for, and develop, their own solutions to problems.
- Become more aware of how their achievements measure up to agreed-upon objectives.

In short, mutual involvement follows logically from our recognition of individual abilities. It capitalizes on *differences* rather than *similarities*—and these differences may be of extra value in the accomplishment of work by high-talent people.

INTEGRATING THE COMMUNICATIONS FLOW

The process of mutual involvement, in and by itself, does not necessarily insure mutual understanding of purpose, problem, plan or action. Its natural bridge is communication—the tool for understanding. Through the use of this tool individuals acquire the information they need to solve problems, make decisions, reach agreement. When communication is lacking, there is little communal cohesion.

It cannot be said that management has failed to recognize the need to convey and exchange information. It may, however, have lacked skill and sophistication in the use of this tool and dedication to the improvement of business communication.

In using the human communications network, we might well take a lesson from automatic data processing, which stores, integrates, and sorts information and, to the extent that the right questions or problems are fed into it, feeds back usable information and results. The machine will always work, but it works more effectively at some times than at others—depending on the information we give it.

In the same way, man will always expend his energy; but he will use it productively, with minimum waste and confusion, only to the extent that he is given the right information. Among other things, he needs to have full understanding of his responsibilities, authority, objectives, and expected results. But the lack of this kind of understanding remains one of the most frequent complaints of high-talent people in business organizations today.

Admittedly, mutual involvement and adequate communication are not new ideas to management. Can it be that our reluctance to make more effective use of these interdependent and interrelated tools lies in the fear that in so doing we may grant too much freedom to the individual? Yet knowledge and understanding of what is going on are essential to the growth of both the individual and the enterprise. Out of experience come analysis, evaluation, and learning—the basis for more effective planning and action in the future. And knowledge of both "satisfactory" and "unsatisfactory" results gives the individual the opportunity to gear his energy, purpose, and unique attributes to producing even more effectively henceforth.

Recognizing the individual's tendency to seek the whole and to see his relationship to the whole, we should stimulate the integration of all information—from all employees—that might have a bearing on common problems or projects. We should also take greater advantage of the opportunity to discuss problems and accomplishments as they happen, so that communication on the job becomes a work-oriented, ongoing, mutual exchange of views between superior and subordinate, rather than a judgment handed down once a year by higher authority.

Management can further capitalize on the individual's unique qualities by raising questions, encouraging the free exchange of opinion, opening the channels of upward communication, and listening to ideas and problems—in short, taking every step to encourage the creative response that is too often inhibited in companies that are run by rigid adherence to form.

COMPENSATION AS AN INCENTIVE

We turn now to the third tool available to management for establishing a more motivating work environment—compensation. It is, of course, well known that money seldom heads the list of environmental factors that spur men to more productive use of their energies. Yet it seems equally clear that the compensation program has a major and specific role to play in creating the positive climate within which people work. Among the purposes the compensation program serves are:

- To attract and retain key people of superior caliber.

- To stimulate key people to improve their performance and to improve the results of operations for which they are responsible.
- To encourage individuals to strive for advancement.
- To reward significant achievement.
- To give individual recognition of status and achievement.
- To foster a sense of loyalty to, and identification with, the company.

Before the various elements of an effective compensation program are discussed, perhaps it should be stressed that to be successful the program must be an integrated whole. In my opinion, it is a frequent failure of compensation programs that they are built piece by piece without sufficient consideration of the effect of each element on the over-all program.

The three central elements of the compensation program are: (1) the base salary plan; (2) the incentive plan; and (3) the deferred compensation plan. Of these, the first is, of course, fundamental to the success of the entire program. Base salary must be equitable in relation to other salaries both inside and outside the organization. If the base salary plan is not "right," then the rest of the program cannot be "right" either.

There is more to base salary than equitable measurement, however. In addition to being, in most cases, the largest single element of compensation, in terms of both outlay by the employer and income to the employee, base salary can be a powerful incentive force. Fair determination of salary levels is admittedly important. But the way salaries are administered within these levels—how a raise, for example, is conceived and handled—is also a significant incentive in itself and may reinforce the impact of the other elements of the compensation program.

Equitable Measurement   So far as equitable measurement is concerned, it probably is safe to say that few management techniques have been so amply documented as have those of job description and evaluation. Yet I think we still need to pay more attention to job evaluation techniques with particular relevance to the needs and aspirations of key people. Especially needed here, for example, are:

- A means of giving measured recognition to the large and growing importance of *innovation* and *creativity,* not only in research jobs where it is so apparent, but in management, marketing, and staff positions generally.

- Methods of developing realistic and meaningful relationships between the important but intangible differing *responsibility* of different staff positions, as against the more easily measurable *accountability* of line functions.

Still on the matter of techniques, I might add that not only can the individual employee gain incentive from job descriptions that are stated clearly, consistently, and fully, *in terms of the end results expected,* but management benefits from them too. Developed in this way, the job description becomes a tool of managing, not just a device for measuring human effort.

If jobs are described in terms of end results expected and are evaluated accordingly, the task of performance appraisal is immeasurably simplified. Here, however, it is important to remember that we are talking about appraisal as a tool for stimulating and rewarding individual achievement. If instead the program is aimed at fostering growth and development, then, obviously, different appraisal techniques are required.

Unfortunately, it should be added that there is no known cure for the presence within a large organization of "hard" and "easy" performance raters. Nevertheless, this problem needs to be worked at constantly to insure equity and consistency in the end results. Careful, explicit definitions of performance standard, and continuing training and retaining of managers in appraisal concepts, probably are the most important steps in this direction.

The Bonus Plan   Incentive, or bonus, plans for key employees are the second ingredient in the compensation program—and an extremely important one. These plans afford perhaps the most direct and measurable means of stimulating individual performance. Needless to say, they must be geared to the actual contribution made by the individual to the profitability of the business.

Though it may be difficult to measure staff executives' contributions, they are so substantial and so real that bonus arrangements have a valid place in the compensation program for staff as well as for line people. This requirement reinforces the need for sophisticated appraisal techniques and meaningful performance standards.

To be truly effective, an incentive plan should represent a "plus" for extra effort; it should not be merely a device for making up for deficiencies in the base salary program. The extra award then need be made only when

and to the extent that performance is above standard and has produced results that are better than the merely acceptable.

Here, as in the area of salary administration, management must take certain steps to get the most for its dollars. It must insure that the plan provides for:

- Common understanding of the role of bonus payments and their relation to the total compensation program.
- An appraisal technique that insures that awards represent recognition of "plus achievement." Implicit in this requirement is a clear and commonly understood definition of "standard" versus "plus."
- Adequate communication on the role of objectives in planning, appraising, and measuring performance.
- Significant differences in bonus awards, to reflect differences in performance and contribution. Without this provision, the impact of the cause-and-effect relation between "plus performance" and the bonus payment, or between a downturn in performance and a decrease in bonus payment, is lost.

Deferred Compensation   Now for the third major ingredient of a compensation program— the deferred compensation plan. Here again, the plan should form an integral part of the company's total compensation picture. If, for example, it takes the form of stock options, these should be granted in amounts that bear a consistent relation to the recipients' base salaries, as well as to their performance.

Too often, the incentive value of stock options is diluted because in trying to keep individual details confidential, as must be done, we neglect to explain clearly to the participants just what the stock option plan means and what it is intended to accomplish. More often than not, participants have only a very general idea of the purpose of the stock option and its meaning to them. Management can gain significantly from a stock option plan if it clearly establishes its relation to the total compensation program and if it also makes clear to participants that a stock option poses the requirement for continuing and important contributions to the company's growth and success.

In short, the total compensation program when effectively communicated and administered, offer management the opportunity to recognize the individual contributions made by its key people and to stimulate them to still greater achievement. It thus serves to reinforce and support the other positive factors in the work environment.

What I have tried to show here is that a more penetrating analysis of man and his needs can lead to better use of the means now at our disposal to provide more effective motivation for human effort in the business community. As we have seen, modern man is increasingly aware of his uniqueness and impatient with environments that tend to force him into preconceived patterns. At the same time, the infinite variety of human skills and ambitions can reinforce and strengthen the entire business organization when it is wisely channeled toward constructive team objectives. It is the task of management—as well as its opportunity—to provide the work environment that will release the creative potential of its employees for the gain and satisfaction of all concerned.

57   C. LEADERSHIP

The Anatomy of Leadership*

EUGENE E. JENNINGS

We often hear that ours is an age without heroes and that business is without leaders. The towering personalities of the past seem, to some, to have considerably more specific gravity than their successors of today.

This indictment, while containing some truth—more, in fact, than should leave us feeling comfortable—overlooks the rugged individualists still on the business stage; more than a handful of flamboyant entrepreneurs and, throughout the ranks of business, aggressive, assertive individuals who openly or secretly hunger for leadership roles.

Nonetheless, the charge that we have allowed leadership to lapse as a necessary executive art deserves close examination. In too many companies the careful man has replaced the tycoon who was willing, in an earlier time, to take uncommon risks by boldly seizing initiative. Decision-making has become diffused, decentralized and impersonal in many organizations.

Why this has happened is, to some extent, an inevitable result of social and economic change. The unrestrained, owner-managed enterprises of the late 19th and 20th centuries are no more. Ownership of our largest and even many of our smallest organizations is today dispersed, and direction flows not from an ownership caste but from cadres of professional managers who are responsible to boards of directors, to government regulators, to organized workers and to a fickle consuming public.

But more important than why the climate of leadership has changed is that today's business organization, and tomorrow's, will require a new breed of restless men with imagination—men perhaps not cut from the same cloth as the old titans but nonetheless ready and able to break free of conventional procedure and move into untried fields. The problem, therefore, is: How can business encourage its managers and managerial aspirants to assume a more vigorous leadership role?

TODAY'S APPROACH TO LEADERSHIP

The term "leadership" is indiscriminately applied to such varied activities as playground supervisor, committee chairman, club president, business executive, and politician. Furthermore, research has produced such a variegated list of traits presumably to describe leadership that, for all practical purposes, it

* Reprinted by permission of the publisher from *Management of Personnel Quarterly*, Autumn, 1961. Mr. Jennings is associate professor of business administration at Michigan State University.

describes nothing. Fifty years of study have failed to produce one personality trait or set of qualities that can be used to discriminate between leaders and non-leaders.

This failure to identify leadership traits in individuals has led us to look elsewhere for the keys to leadership. If a person does not become a leader because he possesses a particular pattern of personality characteristics, maybe he becomes a leader because of something outside of him; that is, the situation determines which men will rise and be chosen to leadership.

The transfer from the personality to the situation has altered our whole approach to leadership. The situational approach appealed to our ideal of democracy, our belief in the impact of the environment on the individual and our need to do something quickly about our shortage of leaders. Because it denied that leaders are born and affirmed that leaders are made, this approach stimulated a deluge of executive training and leadership development programs.

No doubt leaders often need propitious moments to rise. Without such occasions they might remain unknown. In this sense, the situation is indeed influential, but need not be determining. *First,* aggressive action can sometimes overcome a difficult situation. *Second,* initiative often helps determine what the situation actually is. The individual manager can never know the exact situation unless he pits himself vigorously against it. It is in striving to overcome adversity that he finds his full capacity for leadership. This is a fact too often forgotten today.

Admittedly, great events in history are always a marriage between the man and the circumstances, but what is crucial is which predominates. The fact is that the situation holds within it the distinct possibility of several different leaders rising to power. The "right man for the right situation" is a subtle but lethal kind of fatalistic thinking that must not be cultivated if business is to maintain its necessarily dynamic and creative nature.

What Leaders Do   Where modern measurement fails to define leadership, history offers some suggestions. Plato, for example, conceived his ideal society as having three occupational classes—workers and slaves, guardians, and philosophers. In this society the king would draw up the plans and the philosophers would carry them out with the aid of the civil service and military officers comprising the guardian class. Here we have a specific distinction between leadership and execution. Leadership determines the overall plan and infuses the system with a character and direction that could not come by keeping close to the day-to-day stream of problems.

Hence the leader is a beginner of plans carried out by an executive. Machiavelli, Carlyle, Nietzsche, William James, Woodrow Wilson, John Dewey, Lenin, Franklin D. Roosevelt and Churchill all made similar distinctions. Few who have given thought to this distinction have failed to find merit in it. The leader's role is initiating, beginning. It is born of imagination and a sense of mission. It involves great personal risk.

The executive may bring about changes too, but they are of the type warranted by the situation and appropriate to the organization. He operates more in terms of active needs than can be handled by immediate supervision. Consequently, he does not substantially change the character or direction of his organization.

Although both types are needed, few leaders make good executives and few executives make good leaders. It is the rare man who excels at both.

Who Are Today's Leaders?   If, in today's society, we are replacing dynamic men with efficient men, the next question is: What causes this imbalance? The answer may be provided by a closer look at the qualities of leaders. They are found in the sense of purpose, power and self-confidence. In numerous studies of both contemporary and historical figures, these three qualities stand out as essential to fulfilling the role of leadership. When any one of these qualities is lacking, leadership suffers.

BUREAUCRACY LIMITS LEADERSHIP

Men who lead must have vision of real possibilities of the future and must articulate them to the people. This ability to raise one's sights, to get above the struggle, to see beyond triviality, is becoming increasingly rare. We may disparage the men who today see only dimly what tomorrow will clearly need to be done, but there is a condition which subsumes all of us. This condition is one of bureaucratic stagnation. In a society such as ours, there is the strong tendency to develop a civil-service mentality. Our whole society is developing this bureaucratic mind in business, unions, church, school and government.

The individual's role is largely identified by the position he occupies, and these positions, in turn, are systematically integrated to provide the highest degree of coordination and efficiency possible. Public distrust of the bureaucracy is not a reaction against inefficiency, however. The bureaucracy is quite efficient in most cases, due to its emphasis on coordination and efficiency to the exclusion of all other goals. It is a common characteristic of the bureaucratic individual that, while his singlemindedness brings specific events into sharper focus, he is blind to the periphery beyond which lies a different world.

Bureaucratic society assigns each individual his functions, the area of his authority and the standards of proficiency. The worker is harnessed in to ensure the exact performance essential to keep the huge system under control. If any sort of decision is assigned to him or demanded of him, it is duly taken within the limited province of his function without his having to delve to the bottom of things. Duties and regulations laid down to guide him are applied meticulously in such a manner that risk is avoided. There is no semblance of a genuinely creative community of action, let alone sensitive insight into things above and beyond. Initiative is not possible to any great degree or the whole system would fall apart. Risk is eliminated by the sacred adoption of the system's rational rules and regulations, even though they appear irrational to the individual.

Greatness or Efficiency?

In a society becoming heavily bureaucratic, as we are, great men are subordinated to efficient men. The executive type has dethroned the leader. Plato's "achievement" is without its antecedent "beginner." No one person really "begins." Man is enmeshed at all times in an intricate set of relationships that prohibits his seizing the helm and steering a course of his own choosing. Our community "leaders" of today rarely want to shoulder responsibility. They seldom want to decide anything without endorsement. Some committee, group or precedent must be represented in everything they do and upon which they can shift the onus if things go wrong. In the bureaucratic society, the ultimate court of appeals is a previous set of actions that have become a method or system held consecrate because at one time, when things were less complex, it more visibly promoted the general interest. The ends were more within assessment. Upon this method or system, in one of its multifarious forms, accrues the individual's final responsibility. Each individual is a tiny wheel with a fractional share in the decision, but no one effectively decides.

But all of this is consciously realized by many people; many rebel, some silently and some openly. They feel so intimately interlocked in social processes that they do not know how much they rely upon others and their system. Leadership is not a conscious problem to people today because they are not conscious of themselves as leaders. They wonder curiously about what people mean who refer to them as leaders.

The bureaucratic mode of human existence destroys heroic vision. We are today a relatively unpurposeful society. So much is this the concern today that Eisenhower ordered a commission to look into national goals. Luce of Time-Life, Inc., ordered a series of articles on "What Is Our National Purpose?" It is interesting that neither endeavor created much of a national reaction. No great movements for change and reform have emerged. But yet, to speak intelligently today of our national purpose is beyond our ability, so long have we become accustomed to seeing the parts, not the whole, immediate aims rather than long-range goals.

Bureaucracy and the civil-service mentality have contributed in the past to the destruction of the Roman and British empires. They are presently engulfing the individual in America, his ability to see and feel beyond his role or commitment.

Organizations Demand Conservatism

This lack of heroic vision makes individuals "all too executive." Today all too many executives merely add their dots to a series of dots reflecting the evolving histories of their organizations. Under the ethic of finishing the unfinished task started by his great predecessors, this type of executive receives the advantages and benefits of power-seeking without incurring the risk of the leader's attempt at major innovation. In short, he seeks success and personal advantage but does not have a sense of purpose or historical opportunity.

The illusive and masquerading feature of all of this is that the organization typically continues to get bigger. Someone usually gets credit for the growth partly because giving credit is a strong habit carried over from our heroic past. The mania for bigness is, however, a perfect example of how many executives today fit into the on-going direction and character of their organizations in such a manner that they merely mid-wife the enterprises through what are actually predetermined courses. There is no change from the normal or expected pattern of growth as a consequence of his personal efforts, but rather only a continued increase in size and complexity under the illusion of heroic leadership. It simply is not fair for the executive under these circumstances to be given the title of a leader since change is really not change after all.

THE POWER STRUGGLE

In other words, power is a disruptive and reformative—a creative—tool in the care of a leader. The power of one who acts as an executive is a sustaining and maintaining—a conservative—tool. Many executives today do not have a strong creative opportunity or sense of purpose but have the same drive for power as their predecessors. An individual who has a strong drive for power, but who does not have a strong purpose to which he can attach that drive, would, necessarily appear more power-seeking than he might actually be. There is, of course, a lot to be said for the argument that his power drive may tend to increase in the absence of an objective goal that will give it form and sanction. But in either case, the very "nakedness" of his power-seeking would seem to prompt him to inhibit it, which in turn brings on a psychological condition whereby it becomes even more difficult to develop heroic thrust. If we keep in mind, then, that the problem of many executives today is that they must appear to be thrusting and aggressive while at the same time not appear to be too power-seeking, we have in capsule the essence of what they are trying to do. In other words, how to extricate themselves from these paradoxical demands is indeed the key to their success today.

One reason why all too few executives wish to have power to accomplish great and noble things is that the power struggle involves considerable personal risk. To remove the risk one must, of course, make his power permanent. But in making his power permanent the executive cannot make it apparent, for in doing so he necessarily makes enemies of both those who are equally driven by the same urge and those who abhor the evil effects that power brings to both the organization and the personality of the individual. Implementing the power drive subtly and silently is a delicate skill that separates the power élite from the more common contenders. It is extremely difficult to learn the rules of acquiring through subtle means the necessary power with which to control others. It is for this reason that many executives fail to achieve the power necessary to effect major changes.

We might note that the price of failure is, often more than not, forfeiture of the gains won by the attempt at leadership. This penalty often includes the loss of executive position. So the accepted pattern of many executives has become to gain power and make it permanent by not personally causing or sponsoring major innovations. For them it is safer to use power as a conservative force than as a creative force. Consequently, this kind of executive is not only as interested in gaining power as was his predecessor, but he is today incomparably more skilled in gaining and maintaining his power than in knowing and using his power for creative purposes.

The executive who makes the mistake of emerging into the fierce light of daring leadership is apt to become caught in dilemmas his talents are inadequate for resolving. Furthermore, a major innovation is something that requires time to work itself out. Even if the program goes on to achieve success in heroic proportions, the executive could be knocked off because of an errant move in the interim. Anyone who takes long chances will find that the averages are against him. This we found to be an axiom of political experience. Major changes set loose unknown forces that gather a momentum of their own and smash through to results unwanted by anyone, including the executive. Consequently, it is far wiser to sponsor many minor changes that only appear to be tests of ability although they must, of course, be beneficial to the organization, and many executives are becoming aware of this fact.

Using Group Responsibility   One favorite technique of many executives today is to place the responsibility for major changes in the hands of groups and thus shield themselves from the responsibility of complete failure. The idea here is to delegate to the "responsible group" those problems that are of major significance. By this means, the executive assumes more "individual responsibility" for the more numerous minor innovations with the thought that many minor innovations will give heroic stature more easily than one major change, especially one that hazards failure or is cushioned by group responsibility. In effect, the strategy is to become cumulatively heroic through acts that are so integrated as to compound themselves.

It may be argued that this new conservatism is made possible partly by large bureaucratic organizations wherein decisions must be increasingly made by the group method. Since the group is generally more conservative than the individual, the executive naturally becomes less radical and creative. Then too, the increasing use of group meetings, both formal and informal, has forced out into the open the good intentions of the executive. As long as the executive could personally and privately deal with his superiors, subordinates and peers, he did not have to reveal or fear to reveal his intentions toward power. He received ethical justification under the code of enlightened self-interest.

But the convening of a group makes it imperative for the ambitious executive to manifest the most noble intentions simply because a group has a moral quality that is not found in the members taken separately. All good princes today know that in such quasipublic gatherings as conferences, committees and even informal meetings, one must never be anything less than noble and moral and, above all, never appear too eager or overtly ambitious. The revealed ambition of an executive is grossly magnified by the ratio of the number of group members who witness the accidental dropping of his disguise. This means that in group meetings the executive today must hide his apparent need and drive for power by not being radically different, or at least not standing pat on a radical program. He knows that sponsoring a terribly different idea automatically forces him to draw upon the total power resources available to him. This is never done today.

Taking the Limited Offensive   The third characteristic of a leader is his strong inner will to resist forces that might move him away from his mission or purpose. He must be strong in character and use the full force of his personality. There is a growing tendency today in our society to assume a limited offensive. For many, the mark of the successful individual is that he never uses the full potential of his personality. Of course, no one ever uses the full potential of his personality, but we are concerned here that many an executive uses increasingly less. This lack of self-directedness shows up in his interpersonal relations. He is calm but engaging, argumentative at times but not disagreeable, alert but not too trusting. He approaches people easily but also he is able to move out when he gets involved. The word is "heavy" when he talks about the conversations he seeks to avoid. When caught unavoidably in a "heavy," he has the skill to work problems through to a convenient and acceptable solution, but in those cases his personality is invariably engaged on behalf of calming the disturbances, restoring the equilibrium and thwarting accusations of being "difficult."

In all cases, blows of lethal and total effec-

tiveness must never be swung, even in the form of words. It is far better to succeed a little bit than to destroy the opposition completely, which always brings trouble later because of bitterness and recrimination. Pleasantries can never remove the pain of a grievous offense. This kind of individual believes strictly in a limited offensive with maximum opportunity for numerous engage-disengage sequences that will persuade but not offend. Above all, he must not make apparent his resources as an individual apart from his position, because of the tendency to impute ambition to the individual who shows personal talents that are not directly identified with the accepted norms and practices of his function and position. In other words, there is a tendency to confuse the individual with his formal rank and function in the hierarchy.

NO SENSE OF MISSION

Many individuals generally have no grand design, no mission, no great plan calling for change and progress. It is the true leader who has a grand design, which is reflected by a chain-like sequence of relevant and integrated events that serve as stepping stones. Of course, the grand design may not be easily deciphered until it is completed. Contrariwise, the individual lets each situation dictate to him his special set of techniques and plans of action. He sees no overall strategy except that which reflects the on-going and established interests of the various claimant groups involved in his organization. This allows him maximum flexibility without the personal risk of long-range programs.

It is difficult for the typical individual to have a deep and disturbing sense of mission when he is so specialized and boxed in by bureaucratic formulas that he cannot rise above the trivia to see what is ahead, above and behind. But if he suffers from "administrivia," he more importantly suffers from annihilation of all privacy.

Escape from Thinking   Heroic leadership requires not so much a determination to outmaneuver the other fellow, but an ability to anticipate the effects of action now in progress and to devise plans that will be essentially preventive rather than remedial. But who is doing the thinking? Telephone any executive during business hours and you will probably be told he is "at a meeting," for he spends most of his time "in conference." The executive has a genius for cluttering up his day, and many have somehow managed to persuade themselves that they are too busy to think, to read, to look back and to see into the future. Being busy is more than a national passion, as some believe, and it is more than an excuse— it is a means of escape. The real question concerning the opportunity for leadership is not the time or lack of it that is provided for thought, but the value that is placed on thought. Our society has always been action oriented, but lately what little thought has existed has been largely sacrificed to meetings where thinking is done in haste and geared to specific problems at hand, to say nothing of the power tactics that consume vast amounts of intellectual and emotional energy.

The individual today has a passion for discussion. He may use grave and decisive words, may even adopt divergent attitudes at strategic moments, but never stands his ground, especially for a radical idea or program. The stance that he takes is commonly referred to as "a convenient point of reference," but this reference is subject to shifting. By this means he is able to transfer the discussion to a new plane, insisting upon complete objectivity when it is necessary to ensure avoiding any subjective or emotional involvement. The individual's true home is a kind of superficial intellectualism in which his thoughts appear to have a logical coherence, his word choices are for maximum effect. He oozes with intuitions and hunches, or he reports on the latest research findings from scientific studies of elaborate detail, rigorous methodology and unimpeachable authorship. The use of anonymous authorities is itself an indication of how he has become abstracted from the reality about him.

Executives Fight a Phantom Battle   Now what all of this amounts to is that the power struggle going on within these vast human systems found in business, government, education and union organization is without a fighting front. It is a phantom battle. The clever use of the "littles" of sophistry, the impersonalization of arguments, the resorting to anonymous authorities, and the appeal to the "powers that be" (which somehow always remain nameless), make the development of a purposive life futile. The executive fights among the shadows and the noble myths are subject to momentary change. What appears at first to be a united front becomes later divided against itself, where adversaries join forces and the man on the right or left of the large oval conference table stands ready to pose as a friendly "devil's advocate" or "his majesty's loyal supporter," depending upon what the situation warrants. The attempt to discover the true fighting front and

unveil the nameless powers for even a brief moment is to destroy ambiguity and oddly enough to promote general resistance and unrest. Apparently a modern truth today is that to be safe one must never feel secure.

Executives Lack Creativity   In summary, and in preparation for the challenge and conclusion, the individual is rapidly becoming a kind of power-seeker who appears to be a leader because he is skillful in getting support, popularity and rapport with a minimum of "heavy" involvement. He is trying hard to become skillful at working with people and using resources of committees and decision-making groups. He appears to be a good human relations practitioner or social engineer, but actually considers these human relations principles as means by which he may intelligently and subtly play the power game. But in playing this game he does not cause major innovation.

This is the new rule which makes the power game drastically different from that of his predecessors such as Carnegie and Rockefeller, Senior. Seeking only to fulfill the expectations of others and to live within the established imperatives of his organization, the executive finds it unnecessary to the pursuit of self-interest to champion radically new and great programs and to risk willingly the greater inner resources available to him as a unique individual. What at first glance appears to be a lack of self-direction due to a kind of cunning or strategy turns out, after a second look, to be a result of inner weakness. The executive today is not to be seen as a malicious power-seeker; he is not to be morally castigated. His problem is not completely his fault. He is to be understood as one who lives in a high pressure system in which there are few opportunities available to him whereby he can attach his ambition and desire to succeed to the top to a great and noble purpose. In short, it is not out of choice that the executive wears the face that he does. Unfortunately this feature makes his problem incomparably more difficult.

Although we do not know how many have taken to the anonymity of large-scale organization as their avenue of escape from the responsibilities of leadership, it seems plausible that this picture represents many of the top executives in our major large institutions, including business and government. We might further believe that as the scale and complexity of these institutions increase, and the pressures they necessarily generate become more imperative and inhibiting, even the strongest-willed executive will find it necessary to operate without greatly engaging his unique and effective personality. The increasing pattern of half-hearted attempts at leadership is tending toward drastic consequences of which the annihilation of the individual's productive or creative resources is one of the more imminent possibilities.

WHAT IS THE IDEAL LEADER?

With these possibilities besetting the aspiring leader today, what are the conditions of ideal? What is an ideal type of leader? Our superior man is necessarily a "free man," but not free in the sense that he exists outside of an organizational system. Our ideal is not a hermit because a hermit is still a prey to the world. While fighting against his world, a hermit only escapes it in order to continue to exist as a human being. He thus takes on a kind of sincere falseness which negates his virtuous intentions. It is simply foolhardy, in a society as heavily populated and as massively organized as ours is today, to believe that one can escape physically. And it is unheroic.

The fact that the individual cannot escape places limitations on Clark Kerr's recommendation for coping with organizational society. Mr. Kerr rebelled at the current practice of human relations and recommended that the individual should give himself to many organizations rather than to one and reserve for himself the aspiration of limitlessness rather than project this quality into the character of organization. This is precisely what the contemporary person is doing to-day, but he does not get in return this feeling of limitlessness.

Only becoming half-involved in any one organization prevents the individual from realizing his true and full powers within. He cannot come into meaningful grips with his huge organization unless he firmly resolves that he is going to play an active aggressive role in it. It is only through active participation in molding events with a sense of direct responsibility for their consequences that one can achieve the personal strength necessary to live in harmony with the pressures of the organization without being absorbed by them. And this is what the executive needs today. Rather than a social ethic with which to justify and give sanction to the enormous power of the organization over him, the individual needs a stronger will with which to put his total productive resources to work for him and his organization.

The concept of our ideal shows us that only through struggle, through meeting directly the harshness and tyranny of the real world, can a man come to his own self. Until then he feels extremely abstracted from the stream of life, and he consumes vast amounts of physical and psychological energy trying to overcome his feelings of powerlessness.

But more importantly, he can never really get the feel of the true character and direction of the organization if he does not become totally involved in it. Without this feeling and grasping kind of intellect, it is difficult to become intimately involved in a creative plan to make over the character or re-chart the direction of the enterprise or some part thereof. One can only fall back on the drive for power —the common denominator among the alienated—when he does not have the inspiration to lead and accomplish a great and noble life purpose. But this purpose must of necessity be intimately tied to the character and direction of the organization in which the individual seeks his principal source of livelihood. No amount of leading and accomplishing great and noble purposes in extra-organizational endeavors, as seen in the current rage for charity, community and recreational activities, will overcome the psychological vacuity brought on by the lack of purposeful involvement in an individual's major activity throughout the day. This fad of finding purpose in life outside of the business or government or union organization is a prime example of the modern individual's tendency to distribute himself among too many organizations. While the organization balloons to gigantic proportions and the executive comes to find less and less personal involvement in it, he is, so to speak, busily passing the charity hat around in his community to help the needy and the suffering. It is not fanciful to suggest that this extra-organizational effort is the executive's way of escaping from his primary leadership responsibilities. Nor is it disrespectful to suggest that this escape mechanism is a desperate attempt to recapture his lost sense of personal worth.

For some executives, however, the extra-organizational activity is done merely because this is what a successful and well-adjusted executive should do today. In this case he cannot be classed as a leader for he is not really sincere. But we must reaffirm that in many cases the executive becomes an extraorganizational man not because of choice but rather because of a compulsive need to escape from an environment that offers less and less opportunity for personal thrust. The extraorganizational pattern is an important means whereby the executive who has a strong drive for power can more fully satisfy this need. It is not possible to relate this type of activity to virtue because it results from compulsiveness, from inner weakness, rather than from inner strength. That is to say, the executive becomes an extraorganizational man not because he is a superior person whose vast reserve of energy cannot be adequately used by any one organization, but rather because he has a low reserve of energy owing to a lack of both power and opportunity to use whatever productive resources he has within his principal organization.

We now arrive at the heart of the matter. The leader of the future will be that individual with the great mission to overcome the mass feeling of alienation and self-inadequacy. He will recognize that this struggle starts not with his community, not even with his principal organization, but rather it starts with *himself*. He puts his own house in order; he gradually and diligently develops the necessary values, courage, and self-control whereby he can successfully become identified with, but not absorbed by, his organization. He disciplines himself to wholeness, and from this newly acquired inner strength he dominates the pressures of his organization and leads the people about him. In this way power over others comes to him because he is inwardly a superior person. The emergence of this hero, who is admittedly a rare gift to any organization or society, will by the changes he helps bring about prepare the way for other executives to become better leaders.

There are many executives today who are on "crusades" to restore the uncommon man, bring back the independent spirit, destroy the organization man and revive the Titan's inner-directed conscience. They write books, give speeches, appear in only the most proper public gatherings and social circles, associate with the elites of their choice, buy and in some cases read the best literature, and identify with the most sophisticated authors. If it were not for the fact that they are so noisy and public about this build-up we would actually think of them as somewhat sincere. Contrarily, we cannot help but believe that this eagerness to appear to be something akin to our superior person is really the attempt to assure themselves that they are what they are not. It follows that only a few will be able to recapture the will to lead. Of course, it never has been absolutely extinct, but the point is that these few promising executives need to be encouraged or they will find that their way back to conspicuous leadership will be too strenuous for them. Some may believe that everything must be done, every available resource must be used to help develop the promising executive into a superior type of person. The danger of this advice is that the appearance of a leader with

the hero's sense of historical purpose cannot be well planned and predicted. This, however, makes it all the more imperative that we should do certain things that are within our power to create a conducive atmosphere for the reappearance of the man of exceptional talent.

How Today's Organizations Kill Leadership

To this end there are certain specific practices within our society that warrant special criticism at this time. To begin with, the organization today has achieved a life of its own. It goes rambling on seemingly immune to the personal advances of any one executive. It has created a kind of social or impersonal system of leadership which is the product of many individuals acting expertly at their chosen tasks. Then, too, the reduction of competition allows the oligopolistic or monopolistic firm to ramble on without apparent need for the great and personal mastery of the heroic monarch of the past. As Crawford Greenewalt has said, the "responsible group" has replaced the "responsible individual" and the corporation's health and future is that much more assured. This, however, is questionable.

But with the replacement of the responsible individual by the responsible group, the executive is merely given a more concrete and convenient unit whereby he can advance his own individual interests without any more opportunity for heroic thrust when the responsible group has replaced the responsible individual. The last thing that the executive needs today is to have this additional obstacle placed before him which he must hurdle in his attempt to be aggressive and creative. One does not place another obstacle before an individual who already feels alienated and powerless. Nothing has caused as much arrestment of his leadership opportunity as the responsible-group concept. We have previously suggested that it will make all the more the power artist and that much less the purposeful leader.

There are few features of our society that show less faith in personal, conspicuous leadership than in this growing concept of the responsible group. It may be suggested at this time that the growth in acceptance and use of the responsible group portrays, in dramatic form, our growing loss of faith in conspicuous leadership and our feelings of inadequacy. The group might very well be used to keep the individual informed of what is going on, but he should not be allowed to use it as a chief tool for power-seeking. Executives should be encouraged to seek power that comes from a superior inner awareness and sensitivity to what the future character and direction of the firm should be, not power that comes from an ability to manipulate people and to use social techniques.

The need for inner strength may indicate that the executive should be protected from groups by having conferences formally scheduled. At present many committees are called on an informal basis which often amounts to calling a conference whenever someone pushes the panic button. Since the panic button is pushed often in an alienated society, the executive is always in conference. By having conferences as infrequently as possible, the executive will not be at the mercy of the panic-button pusher. At least this might be tried until the promising executive has developed sufficient inner reserve to restrain from pushing the panic button or jumping mechanically to the alarm whenever he or some other executive gets into a little difficulty. He will then have to look within for the resources with which to work himself out of difficulty—an almost unheard of practice today in many organizations. This too may be too much of a struggle for him today so that care must be taken that he is not given too much freedom from the group without an adequate recovery of his individual resources.

Who Will Be Our Leaders?

It is impossible to determine who the future leaders will be. Any attempt at scientific selection will produce a contemptible arrogance resulting from a lack of awareness of the limitations of technical kinds of identification and selection. Attempts to determine exactly the traits of a leader have resulted in complete failure. In spite of this we all have a crude but amazingly efficient sensitivity to the essence of leadership and to the existence of great leaders. We can recognize them even though their characteristics cannot be scientifically measured. The tendency today is to deny these rare men any psychological room, let alone social status and organizational prestige. We have tried to present some of the characteristics by which we can identify leaders, but these traits were only roughly described because words can only approximate the emotional quality with which we identify our heroes. To be sure the actual worship of heroes today has acquired a grotesque posture as seen in current biographical literature. But the essential spark is still there in the minds and hearts of many people and needs only to be rekindled.

In other words, it is not that we cannot recognize our leaders, but rather that we no longer value them as highly as we once did. Therefore, scientific tests should definitely be discouraged so that our eminently more superior powers of observation and intuition can once again help us to find and to raise to our highest positions men of rare and exceptional leadership potential. In this way talent and ability will be brought into line with position, all of which will help, but of course not guarantee, a return to heroic leadership.

Recommendations as to how to structure and reorganize for the rebirth of leadership could become so demanding and pervasive that the tendency to rely too heavily upon organization to eliminate the organization man could move us one notch back rather than one notch forward. All suggestions to help bring about a superior man in our organization should be tempered by judicious concern for the extreme fallacy of organizing to return to independence. We must be careful to place our reliance upon the individual to find his way to psychological recovery and not upon the forces inherent in the group and organization.

Time Out to Think

With this due caution, there is still another recommendation reflected in our concept of the superman. This recommendation concerns the value we place upon thought that is private deliberation resulting from a well-disciplined use of one's intellectual reserves. Each executive who shows promise of heroic leadership should be allowed ample opportunity to think. Perhaps once every five or seven years he should be given a year off with pay so that he can read and study and perhaps even write. When it is possible to organize his time and responsibilities, he should be given time off to think—to get away from his office, and become aware of the broader possibilities found in studying literature, philosophy, art and the social sciences. Under proper and well-conceived circumstances this effort will not be an escape from leadership responsibilities, although this is a distinct danger. However, this program can be effective only with men who are willing and able to make major innovations and assume great responsibility and risks and who will profit from getting out and seeing a broader or higher purpose to which their organizations and they may become devoted. A vigorous emphasis on the value of the thoughtful man will allow a leadership to come forth that will be devoted to great and noble missions not out of compulsive needs but out of choice that comes from inner wisdom.

Of course, finding ways to give the promising executive this opportunity to develop his intellectual resources will require a change in present-day values. The direction and character of the typical business organization will have to be changed since the man of action has theretofore been its standard breed. While we wait for some great innovator to show us the way toward the major innovation, there are some small things we can do ourselves. Most important among these is to reverse our tendency to walk into offices and homes, and backyards for that matter, because of an overpowering need to have friends and acquaintances. We can afford to be hard on ourselves and others who want not privacy but companionship. A good brother's keeper is one who helps the other person to suffer a little by leaving him alone and unengaged because this will in the long run help him to struggle and perhaps find himself.

THE CHALLENGE

Human progress occurs to a great extent through the intellectual efforts of its great men. Leadership might well be viewed as thought in command, while action and implementation might be the limitations imposed upon the individual who does not have or cannot use superior intellectual resources. Displacing or eliminating this great resource will assuredly reduce our opportunity and potentiality for change and progress.

In conclusion ours is a society whose chief characteristic is a lost sense of self-direction as seen in the tendency to escape from leadership responsibility. The challenge is to revive the individual's unique powers of purposive striving and his courage to assume and sustain great risks. To be sure, there are many recommendations that could be made to this end, but because the purpose of this article is to diagnose our problem today, we have highlighted only a few. They include denial of the value of extraorganizational effort, resistance to the responsible-group trend, respect for a man's privacy, faith in men of rare ability and giving highest value to that talent reflected in thought deliberation.

58

Requisites of Effective Leadership

ROBERT G. WALL and HUGH HAWKINS

Like any other skill, the ability to lead has a number of requisites for its development. It requires an understanding of human behavior; it requires certain personal qualities; it requires practice. And—probably more important than any of these—it requires knowledge about leadership itself.

It is unfortunate that, despite an abundance of literature on the subject of leadership, much remains to be discovered, and there is still a good deal of disagreement about many aspects of leadership. Nevertheless, research has already yielded a fair amount of knowledge about the

* Reprinted by permission of the publisher from *Personnel*, vol. 39, no. 3, pp. 21–28, May–June, 1962. Mr. Wall and Mr. Hawkins are members of the personnel department of the International Milling Company, Minneapolis.

subject, and there *are* some areas of general agreement. Whether these advances are cause for rejoicing on the part of practicing managers, however, is still another question, for to find out what is now known about leadership one must read the works of 20 or 30 authorities in the field. Needless to say, few managers have the time for such an undertaking.

This article is an attempt to provide practicing managers with the fruits of just such a survey. The six principles that will serve as a framework for the summary that follows are not to be taken as unequivocal statements of cause and effect, nor are they so many easy steps to better leadership. The relationships they describe are, however, fairly well substantiated and accepted, and the principles themselves should provide a basis for the application of particular insights and research findings, as well as a useful background for further reading on the subject.

1. *The effective use of leadership contributes to the achievement of the goals of the group.* As obvious as this principle seems, it is worthy of a few words, for it is a prerequisite of the principles that follow. Indeed, unless the principle is a true one, there is little practical reason for studying leadership at all.

To accept this principle, one need only believe that leadership has some effect on group action and that every group must necessarily engage in some form of action, if only the action involved in maintaining itself as a group. Actually, however, most definitions of leadership take the matter quite a bit further. Leadership, they hold, is a process whereby a group is directed toward a goal, and its chief function is to make the achievement of group goals more efficient. In the business situation, group goals are not necessarily the goals of the individuals who make up the groups, but are rather the group's reasons for being—production, service, innovation, and the like. A secondary function of leadership, but one that, in the long run, is closely tied to the efficient achievement of group goals, is to control interactions within the group in such a way as to increase the group's cohesiveness and morale and to accelerate the personal development of its members.

The importance of leadership, then, is undeniable. In fact, most authorities agree that some form of leadership will inevitably arise in nearly every group activity. Since most of the work of the business world is accomplished, in one way or another, through group activity, it is obviously to the advantage of the business enterprise to provide itself with the most effective leadership possible. Here, of course, the leadership is formal rather than informal, for every work group is given an appointed leader. The benefits that can be derived from effective formal leadership are widely recognized throughout industry as well as by the researchers in the field.

2. *Effective leadership is a function of the characteristics of the leader, the group, the situation, and the interrelations among these factors.* Most investigations of leadership have employed one or another of three approaches, focusing on the individual, the group, or the situation.

The individual approach, also called the "great man" theory or the trait approach, was the first way of thinking about leadership, and probably is still the most common. Its basic premise is that leadership is a quality, or set of qualities, possessed by an individual; or, in

other words, that one who has the ability to lead will most likely be a successful leader in any situation.

Researchers employing this approach have long tried to uncover a cluster of traits common to all effective leaders in the hope that these could then be measured and used to predict success in leadership in almost any situation. Their efforts have borne little fruit. A review of over a hundred studies aimed at discovering such traits has revealed that of all the physical, intellectual, and personal determinants of effective leadership supposedly uncovered by these studies only 5 per cent showed up in four or more of the studies.[1]

Nevertheless, there are indications that the trait theory contains an element of truth. Helen Jennings, though not a whole-hearted supporter of the theory, has reported finding some characteristics that seem to be common to effective leaders;[2] and Cecil Gibb, who is equally dubious about it, has said,

> There do seem to be, however, certain general characteristics of personality, the possession of which does not necessarily cause a man to have leadership status conferred upon him, but which does place him higher than he would otherwise be on the scale of choice in any group.[3]

The failure of the individual approach to uncover the clear-cut set of traits it seeks has led investigators to try other approaches. One of these is the group approach, which holds that the success of the leader is determined principally by the characteristics of the particular group he is leading. Unlike the trait approach, which assumes that the leader is free to mold the group's activities as he will, this approach sees him as bound by the needs and norms of the group.

THE GROUP APPROACH

Effective leadership, the group approach maintains, consists of structuring the group's interactions in a way that satisfies the group's needs. Moreover, this structuring must take place within the framework of the group's norms. As George Homans, analyzing leadership in several different situations, has ex-

[1] R. Stogdill, "Personal Factors Associated with Leadership: A Survey of the Literature," *Journal of Psychology*, January, 1948, pp. 35–71.

[2] A. Gouldner, *Studies in Leadership*, Harper & Row, Publishers, Incorporated, New York, 1950.

[3] C. Gibb, "The Principles and Traits of Leadership," *Journal of Abnormal and Social Psychology*, pp. 267–284, July, 1947.

plained, the maintenance of the leader's authority depends on how well he conforms with
certain of the group's norms.[4]

The importance of consideration for the
group has also been pointed out by Ferenc
Merei, who found that groups tend to develop
their own unique patterns of interaction and
that an individual can become an effective
leader only if he accepts the tradition of the
group and operates within it.[5]

The third approach, the situation, is similar
to the group approach except that it places
even more emphasis on the characteristics of
the specific situation or environment in which
the leader is operating—the particular job to
be done, for example. Proponents of this
approach believe that the qualities necessary
for effective leadership vary with the situation
and that, in fact, almost any trait or skill can
become a "quality of leadership" in the right
situation. The fact that someone has been successful as a leader in one situation, they hold,
does not necessarily indicate that he will be
successful in another. This approach has, like
the others, generated a good number of research studies, and there is now considerable
evidence indicating the importance of situational characteristics.

The fact that each of the three approaches
seems to be able to make some contribution
to our understanding of leadership attests to
the importance of all the factors involved.
Coupled with the inability of any one approach
to yield completely adequate explanations, it
strongly suggests that the answer lies in a combination of the three approaches. Leadership,
in other words, seems to be neither a quality
possessed by an individual nor a product of
the group or the situation alone, but, rather,
a function of the interaction between the individual and the total social situation.

3. *The effectiveness of a leader depends largely
on how well he and his organization define his
role and how completely they accept it.* This
principle is concerned primarily with the environment in which the leader is placed. It
involves two problems: organization and communication.

In informal group settings, solving these
problems is the job of the leader. In industrial
situations, however, the two problems, and
especially that of organization, must be solved
mainly by top management. The individual

manager's position within the organization is
seldom of his own creation. Instead, he is generally assigned a place in an already established, and usually rigid, organization structure,
and there is little he can do to change the
status or influence of his position except in the
direction established by top management. Basically, then, this principle involves the question
of how to set up the leader's environment so
that he can function effectively.

THE PROBLEM OF THE FOREMAN

That there is a problem of role definition
and acceptance is particularly evident in the
case of the first-line supervisor. A number of
studies at this level have shown that the foreman's superiors and subordinates evaluate him
in terms of different criteria. He is expected to
accept the values of his superiors, but he must
at the same time behave in such a way as to
win the willing cooperation of his subordinates.

How can this dilemma be resolved? Most
authorities now think that the solution lies in
promoting the foreman's identification with
higher management. Management's thinking
should be more extensively communicated
down to first-line supervisors, they urge, and
foremen should be brought in on the discussion and solution of problems traditionally reserved for the higher levels.

This does not mean that it is unimportant
for foremen to be oriented to the workers' interests and to recognize their problems. Indeed, this need is commonly recognized in the
various forms of supervisory training in human
relations. It does, however, involve a subordination of worker orientation to management
identification. Though some people may object
to this, it is generally felt that this is the only
way to provide the supervisor with   well-
defined and secure position and to achieve
aggressive leadership in the pursuit of company
goals.

Not only must the foreman be encouraged
to identify with management, but he must be
given enough authority to make this identification realistic. In a survey reported by Sufrin
and Gaynes, foremen in 20 large firms in the
Syracuse area were found to have very little
authority to handle grievances, even in instances where they could rely on precedent
or a clear-cut policy.[6] Most of them were little
more than messengers between workers and
management. Naturally enough, the foremen
felt insecure in their work, for they were un-

---

[4] G. Homans, *The Human Group*, Harcourt, Brace &
World, Inc., New York, 1950.

[5] F. Merei, "Group Leadership and Institutionaliza-
tion," in Swanson, Newcomb, and Hartley (eds.),
Readings in Social Psychology, Holt, Rinehart and
Winston, Inc., New York, 1952, pp. 318–328.

[6] S. Sufrin and G. Gaynes, "Foremen and Their Labor
Relations Authority," *Personnel*, November, 1948,
pp. 199–203.

sure of what they could do and of what support they would get from management.

Similarly, Donald Wray, who observed foremen's activities on a day-to-day basis, has reported that the foremen he studied were primarily transmitters of decisions made by their superiors.[7] Again, the difference between the actual authority of the foremen and the norms of their position led to feelings of insecurity and conflict. Many other studies have confirmed the importance of defining the supervisor's position in such a way that everyone concerned is aware of its authority and responsibility.

THE LEADER'S BEHAVIOR

Proper organization must be supplemented by proper behavior on the part of the leader. To be effective, he must accept his role as it has been defined by the organization and must behave according to the norms of the role. It is important in this regard that he maintain the position of leadership given him by the organization and that he help to establish himself as a source of authority. The subordinates' recognition of the leader's effectiveness and their trust in his ability will result in the establishment of a "zone of indifference"—an area in which his orders are followed without question.

To gain this recognition, the leader must preserve a delicate balance betwen subordinate-centered behavior and aloofness. Obviously, he will never win the loyalty of his men if he does not show concern with their needs and their welfare. On the other hand, continued interaction between the leader and his followers in social situations can only result in one of two things: Either the effective rank of the leaders will be lowered, or he will be put in a position of leadership in the informal social situation.

Both these results are detrimental, as Homans has clearly pointed out.[8] The first weakens the leader's position, and the second, by introducing elements of formal leadership into a situation that would otherwise be marked by a free interaction among equals, forces the subordinates to be dependent upon the leader and, therefore, resentful of him.

THREE ENVIRONMENTAL NEEDS

In sum, then, the third principle indicates three environmental requirements for effective leadership:

(1) a proper organizational setup,
(2) careful definition of the leader's place within the organization, and
(3) acceptance of this position by both the leader and those above and below him. Though the individual leader can do much to promote his own effectiveness by accepting his role and performing within its limits, the basic responsibility here belongs to top management, and forms part of its responsibility for organization planning and effective communication.

4. *To be effective, a leader must be able to analyze his group and determine what courses of action will best help to achieve the group's goals and promote its morale.* The third principle stressed the importance of the organizational environment and considered the leader as an individual only in pointing out how his behavior should be related to his organizational position. This fourth principle gives further consideration to the leader as an individual. What it says, in essence, is that in order to perform as effectively as possible he must understand both the work of his group and the group itself and must know how these will be affected by his actions.

The need for this understanding and knowledge arises from the prime importance of the leader's ability to make decisions that will promote efficiency and productivity in his group. Studies have shown that the adequacy of a leader's decisions is closely related to the adequacy of his perceptions and his analyses of group problems. Unless he has a good idea of what the roots of these problems are and what alternatives are possible, he cannot consistently make the best decisions. In their discussion of things a leader must do, Ross and Hendry suggest some reasons why understanding of the group seems to be essential for the leader's success:

> What may be involved here is that the leader, sensitive to feelings and attitudes in the group, is more understanding, is better able to communicate with group members, is able to become a communication center, is able to help the group formulate its goals, and is able to take the steps necessary to help the group move toward its goal.[9]

At this point in the discussion one may well revive the question of the individual approach to leadership, for it seems clear that the leader's sensitivity to feelings and attitudes in the

[7] D. Wray, "Marginal Man of Industry: The Foreman," *American Journal of Sociology*, January, 1949, pp. 298–301.
[8] Homans, *op. cit.*
[9] M. Ross and C. Hendry, *New Understandings of Leadership*, Association Press, New York, 1957.

group has a good deal to do with his individual personality. It should be recalled, therefore, that though investigations taking this approach generally failed to isolate any characteristics closely related to success in all situations, their results did not by any means indicate that individual traits are unimportant. In fact, many people believe that the failure of these studies was due to weaknesses in the research techniques they used, rather than to the lack of general characteristics of leadership.

It is also possible, however, that the studies failed because they paid too much attention to the effect of purely personal traits or characteristics and too little to that of interactional abilities. It is in the latter category that one finds the requirements specified in this principle—analytical and decision-making ability.

Individual skill in analysis and decision making may very well be a common characteristic of effective leaders, but this is precisely because leadership is a matter not just of individual traits but of many group and situational factors as well. All these factors and the varying interrelationships among them require accurate analysis if the leader is to initiate the proper action and eliminate as far as possible any unforeseen results of that action.

5. *It is important to the leader's success that his followers perceive him as effectively responding to group needs.* This principle covers another facet of the leadership problem—relations between the leader and his men. Needless to say, the leader's effectiveness depends largely on whether or not he has the willing support of his subordinates, which in turn depends on how they perceive his ability and actions. If they see him as someone who can satisfy their needs in terms of promoting group survival, goal achievement, and a desirable working environment, they will give him the necessary support, thus making it easier for him to attain the goal of effective leadership.

What is it, then, that the leader must do in order to be perceived in this way? Studies have shown that effective foremen spend considerably more time in supervisory duties than do relatively ineffective foremen. They spend more time planning, are regarded by their men as better planners, and are more likely to feel that supervision is the best way for them to get their job done. Less effective foremen spend

more time participating in the work of their group and apparently regard supervisory duties as routine tasks. The better foremen are also more interested in workers as individuals. They do a good job of representing their men, and the men are well aware of it.

The close identification with management emphasized under the third principle does not mean that the leader must not thoroughly understand his followers and be recognized by them as a strong supporter of their interests. Ross and Hendry lay great stress on this point, maintaining that the leader must be associated with the group and must be able to help group members in practical ways.[10]

6. *The effectiveness of the leader must ultimately be judged in terms of the group's survival and its progress toward its goals.* This final principle turns to the subject of evaluating leaders or styles of leadership. Evaluation is obviously necessary for the study of leadership, as a basis for further research. But it is no less important for business organizations, which must determine their leadership needs in order to make sound decisions about selection, training, and promotion and must assess the various styles or techniques of leadership in planning programs to raise the general caliber of their leadership.

Though there is more than one way to measure the effectiveness of a leader, the group-centered approach is the most basic. Here the assessor tries to evaluate the leader's success by looking at the activities of his group and trying to measure its progress toward the goals for whose achievement it exists. This is clearly the most logical criterion of success, for if leadership is basically a tool for the efficient achievement of group goals, then it must ultimately be evaluated in terms of this achievement.

In sum, then, if the organization sees to it that the roles of its managers and supervisors are properly defined and are accepted by everyone concerned and that the people in positions of leadership are able to analyze the needs of their groups, prescribe practical courses of action, and demonstrate responsiveness to their groups' interests, it will have done much to insure that its various activities will be performed as efficiently as possible.

[10] *Ibid.*

59

Three Styles of Leadership and Their Uses*

ROBERT T. GOLEMBIEWSKI

Managers who have tried to keep track of research and thinking on the subject of leadership may well sympathize with the centipede that was asked how it managed its legs, for this innocent question, the limerick tells us, reduced the unfortunate creature to lying "distracted in a ditch considering how to run."

The question asked in the leadership literature—"How does one lead men?"—is every bit as disconcerting as the one put to the centipede. Nevertheless, the parallel between them is not quite exact. The centipede, until he had to think about it, was only doing what came naturally and doing it well. Leadership in the work situation, however, does not belong to the order of instinctive behavior. Doing what comes naturally in striving for leadership often leaves much to be desired.

Though management has tended to be all too receptive to endorsements for this, that, or the other leadership approach, its interest has sound foundations. In the first place, a considerable body of evidence shows that the productivity of a work unit is affected by the kind of leadership the unit receives. In the second, decisions about what style of leadership to adopt must to some extent be made for the company as a whole rather than being left to the intuitions of individual managers. Still, management's interest has not been satisfied, for the evidence supporting any one leadership style can always be countered, and frequently is, by evidence supporting its precise opposite. The bewildered organization that has tried and abandoned one style after another may well be pardoned for asking, "Where do we go from here?"

Fortunately, it is beginning to look as if a theory based on empirical findings is at last in the making. No one yet knows exactly what its ultimate content will be, but its outlines can now be perceived and—even more important—can be put to use to improve managerial practice.

At this point, it may be useful, therefore, to review the research findings that form the skeleton of this theory and to examine their practical implications. But before doing so, it is necessary to define the term "leadership"— though this in itself is a question that has stirred up endless controversy. For the purposes of this article, however, "leadership" will be taken to mean the consistent ability to influence people in desired ways.

On the classification of leadership styles, fortunately, there is more agreement. Most authorities recognize three basic types: "leader-centered," or "autocratic"; "group-centered," or "democratic"; and "individual-centered," or "free-rein."[1] The supposedly modern view, of course, is that the group-centered style is the most conducive to productivity. By contrast, the traditional view admits only the leader-centered style, regards the group-centered style as a plaything of psychologists, and dismisses the free-rein style as constituting not leadership, but rather its surrender.

EACH IN ITS PLACE

Supporters of any all-or-nothing view have one thing in common: they will often be surprised to find that the research literature does not consistently support any one leadership style. The reason for this lies not in any failing of the research itself but in the simple fact that there is no "best" style. Indeed, the question "Which kind of leadership should we use?"

* Reprinted by permission of the publisher from *Personnel*, vol. 38, no. 4, pp. 34–45, July–August, 1961. Mr. Golembiewski is an assistant professor in the College of Commerce and Business Administration at the University of Illinois.

[1] For a typical treatment, see A. Uris, *How to Be a Successful Leader*, McGraw-Hill Book Company, New York, 1953, pp. 32–39.

prevents any useful answer. The question should be, rather, "Which kind of leadership *when?*"

This "when," it is worth pointing out, constitutes an integral part of the question, for every scientific formulation must at some point specify the conditions it covers. Even the well-tested law explaining what happens when objects are dropped holds true only for objects that are heavier than air. If the objects are dropped at certain points in space, moreover, they will "fall up," or float.

This approach provides a partial explanation of the apparent chaos of the research literature. Many studies that seem to contradict each other are simply accounts of leadership phenomena under different conditions. Studies based upon observation of similar conditions, on the other hand, have yielded a pattern of consistent results.

Fortunately, leadership study has now taken on a "situational" approach. The main point of this approach has been well expressed in popular terms by Auren Uris, who advises the would-be leader as follows: "The skill with which you apply the three basic tools of leadership—autocratic, democratic, and free-rein techniques—determines your personal success as a leader."[2]

What, then, are the conditions that should be taken into account in the choice of a leadership style? There are many. Four among them, however—personality, task characteristics, task roles, and group characteristics—are particularly important and have been explored in a number of research studies. A separate examination of each of these conditions should provide some guidelines for translating such advice as Uris' into action.

Personality   As the advocates of group-centered leadership often fail to realize, not all people can function well under the same kind of leadership. There are, for example, many people whose personalities make them unfitted for a group- or individual-centered style.[3] Such a person was Administrator H, described in Harold Lasswell's *Psychopathology and Politics.*[4] A childhood marked by unfortunate sexual experiences and domination by an over-

bearing, prudish father had left him sharply, though unconsciously, ambivalent toward authority. Consequently, he worked well under supervision but invariably became careless when he was given substantial freedom on the job.

Needless to say, giving free rein to a subordinate like H would bring nothing but trouble, though over the long run his personality might possibly change enough to permit a looser kind of supervision. Studies of "authoritarianism" confirm these common-sense conclusions about how to deal with men like Administrator H. Authoritarians behave in ways that reveal compulsive conformity based upon a view of the world as menacing and unfriendly. Though they are not necessarily people of low intelligence, they think in relatively few channels, from which they cannot be moved. In addition, they seek security through the exercise of authority or, better still, through surrender to some powerful authority figure.

Studying authoritarianism in military groups, Medalia formulated and tested the following two hypotheses:[5]

1. People with strong authoritarian tendencies will be more likely to accept formal military leaders with the conventional traits of the "good officer" than will people with weak authoritarian tendencies.

2. People with strong authoritarian tendencies will be more likely to re-enlist than will people with weak authoritarian tendencies.

The data that emerged from his study are shown in Table 1. Not only do these findings support both hypotheses but, when one takes into account certain technical factors in the study that tended to obscure any relations, they suggest a very strong relation between personality and leadership style.

The practical advantages of adapting leadership style to personality characteristics seem clear from this study. In the groups analyzed, it could mean a 23 per cent increase in the acceptance of the formal leader by his subordinates and a 14 per cent increase in the intent to reenlist. These figures indicate the need for developing a valid diagnostic indicator of the leadership style to which an individual will respond best. Comparable changes in a business organization would certainly prove well worth the cost of meshing leadership style and personality factors.

---

[2] *Ibid.,* p. 31.
[3] Many personnel men are aware of these personality effects and therefore recruit only from those groups of people whose general social training seems likely to produce the personality characteristics appropriate to the organization's leadership style. Thus some companies seek out rural workers because of their alleged amenability to formal discipline.
[4] *The Political Writings of Harold D. Lasswell,* The Free Press of Glencoe, New York, 1951, pp. 127–135.

[5] N. Z. Medalia, "Authoritarianism, Leader Acceptance, and Group Cohesion," *Journal of Abnormal and Social Psychology,* vol. 51, no. 2, pp. 207–213, 1955.

TABLE 1   Relation of Authoritarianism in Members of a
Military Group to Acceptance of Formal Heads
and Intent to Re-enlist

	AUTHORITARIANISM			DIFFERENCE BETWEEN
	HIGH	MEDIUM	LOW	HIGH AND LOW
Leader acceptance				
Above median	59%	52%	36%	+23
Below median	41	48	64	−23
Total	100%	100%	100%	
Intent to re-enlist				
Yes or undecided	38%	34%	24%	+14
No	62	66	76	−14
Total	100%	100%	100%	

A word of qualification must, however, be inserted here. Most people have wide "response repertoires." That is, they are able to perform the wide range of behaviors required by the various styles of leadership despite their personal preference for a particular style.

This adaptability was demonstrated by Berkowitz in an experiment with a communication network that channeled a great deal of information to some positions and very little to others.[6] Half the subjects were assigned to communication positions in which they would have to act in ways that were not congruent with their personalities: submissive people were placed in central positions, dominant people in peripheral positions. The other half were assigned to the positions appropriate to their personalities. Though the two kinds of subjects at first performed quite differently, Berkowitz found, the "misplaced" subjects generally managed to adjust to the demands of their positions by the last of the three trials in the experiment.

Berkowitz' experiment, however, was brief. The findings of other research projects indicate that if it had continued, the subjects in the first group would ultimately have displayed reactions ranging from dissatisfaction to attempts at sabotaging the work process. Just when it is that such reactions begin to appear will be determined by circumstances and personalities. But when they do hit, they hit hard.

A manager, then, may vary his style of leadership, but he cannot force people to act forever in ways that are uncongenial to their personalities. This imposes a difficult task upon the manager and the organization—ascertaining the behavior preferences of the individual subordinates and then arranging the work so as to allow them to carry out their tasks in the manner they prefer. Unless this is done, the formal head will remain just that, rather than being accepted by his men as their leader.

Task Characteristics   The second major condition affecting the usefulness of any given leadership style is the nature of the task to be performed. Though little work has so far been done in classifying tasks, it should be adequate here to note that tasks may be distinguished in terms of (1) the obviousness of the solution to the problem or of the work itself and (2) the amount of cooperation the task requires.

Unfortunately, research to date has for the most part assumed that all tasks are quite complex and require a great deal of interpersonal cooperation. Because socio-emotional factors affect performance most strongly when the task is of this kind, the leader-centered style, which tends to generate emotional flare-ups, usually shows up poorly under these circumstances, while the group-centered style shows up well.

Many tasks, however, do not have these assumed characteristics. One of Deutsch's experiments illustrates the value of distinguishing between kinds of tasks.[7] The prediction to be tested was that internally cooperative groups would be more effective than internally competitive groups. When groups of both kinds attempted to solve human relations and puzzle

---

[6] L. Berkowitz, "Personality and Group Position," *Sociometry*, vol. 19, no. 4, pp. 210–222, 1956.

[7] M. Deutsch, "The Effects of Cooperation and Competition upon Group Process," in D. Cartwright and A. Zander (eds.), *Group Dynamics: Research and Theory*, Harper & Row Publishers, Incorporated, New York, 1953, pp. 319–353. See especially tables 23.5, 23.7, 23.9, and 23.11.

problems, it was found, the "cooperative" groups did indeed perform better on a number of measures of effectiveness, including quantitative and qualitative output, member satisfaction with group functioning and output, and amount of aggressive behavior. But on several measures the differences between the two kinds of groups were more marked for the human relations problem than for the puzzle problem. It seems as if the objectively demonstrable nature of the puzzle solution made it difficult for members of the "competitive" groups to block each other in subtle ways. (Certainly, the nature of the task would have made direct blocking seem ridiculous.) The open-endedness of the human relations problem, on the other hand, gave them ample opportunity to run each other ragged.

In terms of leadership style, these data suggest that the leader-centered style is particularly inappropriate to tasks that have more than one possible solution and that require a considerable amount of interpersonal cooperation. More important still, the data seem to leave little room for the leader-centered style even on tasks with just the opposite characteristics, for, as has already been noted, the group-centered style generally proved the more effective not only for the human relations problem but for the puzzle problem as well. In actual business and industrial situations, it should also be pointed out, emotional tensions can affect performance adversely at any number of points in the operation—at far more points than in Deutsch's experimental situation. Moreover, the marked preference most people show for the group-centered style furthers its claim to being the more useful of the two.

This does not mean, however, that the leader-centered style should be rejected out of hand. A situation in which most of the operators are strongly authoritarian and the task is a simple one requiring little cooperation is obviously tailor-made for authoritarian leadership.

The Role of Intelligence. Calling a task "simple" of course implies some relation between the task itself and the intelligence of the people who are to perform it. The importance of taking this relation into account in deciding upon a leadership style has been demonstrated by a simple experiment with a game based on "Twenty Questions."[8] As Table 2 indicates, though all the subjects worked on essentially the same task, the "Brights" did their best under a group-centered style, and the "Dulls" under a leader-centered style. The relation was especially marked for the "Dulls," whose problem-solving efficiency was only half as high under group-centered leadership as under authoritarian leadership.

Regulating work assignments by task and personality characteristics may seem like a great deal of bother, but the 100 per cent performance difference for the "Dulls" suggests that the extra bother will more than pay its own way. Indeed, business would most likely find it profitable to subsidize the research necessary for the development of even more precise ways of differentiating people than those now available. The "Brights" in this experiment—to give just one illustration of the value of this greater precision—probably included some authoritarian subjects. (Though low intelligence is frequently accompanied by

[8] A. D. Calvin *et al.,* "The Effect of Intelligence and Social Atmosphere on Group Problem-solving Behavior," *Journal of Social Psychology,* vol. 45, 1957, First Half, pp. 61–74.

TABLE 2   Effects of Leadership Style and Members' Intelligence upon Group Performance in "Twenty Questions" Game

MEMBERS' INTELLIGENCE AND LEADERSHIP STYLE	MEASURES OF PERFORMANCE	
	MEDIAN NO. OF QUESTIONS ASKED PER PROBLEM	PER CENT OF PROBLEMS SOLVED
Bright		
Group-centered	15.5	100.0
Leader-centered	18.5	87.5
Dull		
Group-centered	31.0	37.5
Leader-centered	24.5	75.0

high authoritarianism, high intelligence is not so frequently accompanied by low authoritarianism.) Excluding the authoritarians from the "Bright" sample would probably have had two effects: the performance of the remaining "Brights" under group-centered conditions would have improved, and that of the "Brights" under leader-centered conditions would have deteriorated. In the industrial situation, both the individual and management could profit from a more comfortable "fit" of employees to their tasks.

Task Roles   Still another question to be considered in choosing a leadership style is "Who does what?"—that is, "What are the roles of the leaders and followers?" Though the very notion of leadership implies a set of roles different from those of followership just what functions are covered by each set cannot be rigidly prescribed. Indeed, the distribution of functions is often the product of social consensus, and may vary even among work teams performing the same operation in the same organization.

Roles do, however, fall into three broad categories: roles peculiar to the superior, roles peculiar to the subordinate, and "mixed" roles, whose functions are performed by either or both. The general argument here, by way of preview, is that each of these three classes implies a different leadership style.

Evidence indicates that supervisors who are successful in influencing their subordinates' behavior in the desired directions—that is, supervisors who are leaders—work at sharpening these differences in roles. In a study by Kahn and Katz, supervisors of section gangs on a railroad and supervisors of clerical sections in an insurance company were asked how much of their time was usually spent in supervisory matters, and how much in other matters.[9] Their answers, shown in Table 3, revealed that the supervisors with low-producing sections were two or three times more likely to perform the same duties as their men, or to perform the paperwork aspects of their jobs, than the supervisors with high-producing sections.

These findings can be explained by a little common-sense reasoning: The behavior of the low-producing supervisors reflects either a lack of consensus about roles in their work groups or their own failure to respect an existing consensus. Whatever the case, conflict is likely, and must inevitably result in productivity losses.

Not only should the superior differentiate his functions from those of his subordinates, but he should, of course, perform certain *specific* functions. The amount of planning he does, for example, is directly related to the productivity of his section. Some interesting data on this score were obtained by asking foremen in a tractor factory whether they were able to plan their work ahead as much as they liked.[10] Though their answers, given in Table 4, suggest that the high-producing foremen actually did more planning than the low-producing foremen, it should be noted that the foremen were talking about the fulfillment of their planning expectations, not about how much planning they actually did or how much they thought necessary. It seems reasonable to assume that high-producing foremen were

[9] R. L. Kahn and D. Katz, "Leadership Practices in Relation to Productivity and Morale," in Cartwright and Zander, *op. cit.*, p. 615.
[10] *Ibid.*, p. 619.

TABLE 3   Time Spent in Supervising in Relation to Section Productivity

SECTION PRODUCTIVITY	50% OR MORE OF TIME SPENT IN SUPERVISING %	LESS THAN 50% OF TIME SPENT IN SUPERVISING %	NOT ASCERTAINED %	TOTAL %
Insurance company				
High	75	17	8	100
Low	33	59	8	100
Railroad				
High	55	31	14	100
Low	25	61	14	100

**TABLE 4   Foremen's Perception of Opportunity for Planning
in Relation to Section Productivity**

| | FOREMEN'S RESPONSES | | | |
SECTION PRODUCTIVITY* %	CAN PLAN AHEAD AS MUCH AS NEEDED %	SOMETIMES HAVE TROUBLE PLANNING FAR ENOUGH AHEAD %	CAN SELDOM OR NEVER PLAN AHEAD %	TOTAL %
97–101	37	42	21	100
91–96	51	32	17	100
86–90	29	41	30	100
80–85	29	46	25	100
50–79	14	40	46	100

* Productivity is expressed as per cent of standard.

more aware of the importance of planning than the others. Thus their less-than-complete satisfaction may reflect high hopes rather than low accomplishment. If this is so, then they must have been even more active in planning their work than the table suggests.

Tables 3 and 4 deal with but two of the three categories of roles outlined above: roles peculiar to the subordinate and roles peculiar to the superior. There is, however, substantial evidence of the harm that superiors do in failing to respect the third category of roles: those whose performance is "mixed." The conflict generated by supervisory insensitivity to this third category is, of course, the subject of much of the human relations literature.

But what leadership styles do these three categories demand? As the provisional model in Table 5 shows, it seems likely that the superior's roles are best handled with a leader-centered style, "mixed" roles with a group-centered style, and the subordinate's roles with a free-rein style. This does not, however, mean that the superior should surrender all his power over certain functions. On the contrary, every role assumes a set of guidelines for behavior, and the three leadership styles are merely different techniques for developing and enforcing them. When the guidelines are violated—whatever the leadership style under which they were developed—the supervisor is put into a decisive position.

If, for example, a worker insisted on tightening bolts with his teeth, his fellow workers and his supervisor would undoubtedly be scandalized and would agree that the worker's freedom in deciding how to perform this operation did not extend quite so far as all that. Group pressure—especially in a work unit operating under group-centered leadership—might en-

**TABLE 5   A Provisional Model of Roles
and Appropriate Leadership Styles**

CATEGORY OF ROLES	TYPICAL FUNCTION	GENERALLY APPROPRIATE LEADERSHIP STYLE
1. Roles peculiar to the superior	Setting general goals	Leader-centered
2. "Mixed" roles	Relocating machines on which individuals have worked for many years	Group-centered
3. Roles peculiar to the subordinate	Deciding how to use a tool	Free-rein

courage him to change his ways. But the supervisor would still be on the spot, formally and socially. He would have to supplement this pressure and perhaps take formal action. When violations of the behavioral guidelines are winked at, the supervisor invariably comes off a loser.

The supervisor who would be a leader, then, must have a deft touch. A useful criterion for determining when to step in can be found in the concept of "relevance," that is, in how the issue ranks in terms of its importance to, say, the employees, the organization as a whole, or the boss.

The more relevant an issue is to the group, experimental evidence shows, the more willing the group is to accept a relatively authoritarian way of dealing with it. Thus a leader who is strongly supported by his group may depend primarily on free-rein and group-centered styles, which encourage member involvement. When a relevant issue arises, however, he will exercise substantial influence, and, in fact, the group will expect him to do so. (The leader-centered superior with a work unit of authoritarians will, of course, hold a tight rein on most matters and therefore need not have such a delicate touch. But such situations are rare.)

An issue may, of course, be relevant to the formal organization but not to the group. If, for example, the work unit neglects its responsibilities to the company on the question of the level of production, the superior may have to use a leader-centered style despite the group's reluctance to have him do so. On less relevant matters, however, he would do well to balance it with a group-centered or free-rein style, which would reduce any tension generated by the leader-centered style. The "relevance" concept, in other words, supplements the model in Table 5, for an unanticipated relevant item may appear in any one of the three categories. The handling of such items will in the long run determine whether the formal head continues to function as a leader or loses his control over the group.

Group Characteristics   Discussing the relevance of an issue for a work group implies that the group has developed certain common standards *of* its own and *on* its own. This characteristic of groups—the tendency to develop group norms and group goals—may be accompanied by fairly powerful mechanisms for imposing the group's will upon its members and upon the outside world. The group therefore plays a large part in determining the success of the various leadership styles. Group properties have, of course, been examined at

length in the social science literature, and this author has sketched their broad implications for organization performance elsewhere.[11]

One aspect worth considering here is the degree to which the group *as a group* accepts its formal head. If the group feels that its supervisor is not fulfilling its needs, it may find itself a more satisfactory leader from within its own ranks. This should not be a matter of indifference to industrial managers, for the emergence of an informal leader who acts as spokesman for a work unit is often associated with low productivity. In the Kahn and Katz study, workers in railroad section gangs were asked, "Is there some one man in the section who speaks up for the men when they want something?" Fewer than one in six respondents in the high-producing sections answered *yes,* while over half the respondents in the low-producing sections did so.[12]

Must the Leader Be Liked?   Such data as these, however, should not be taken as an endorsement of group-centered leadership. All three styles are equal to the task of winning informal acceptance for the formal head, though under different conditions. Moreover, the supervisor is not always well advised to try to raise his informal status to the level of his formal status. He must consider, among other things, the nature of his group's norms, which he will have to respect if he is to gain informal acceptance. If, as is by no means uncommon, the norms favor low output, his attempt to gain high informal status may force him to compromise his formal position.

The dangers of such an attempt are illustrated in a study of aerial bombardment crews by Adams.[13] Each member of each crew was ranked on several measures of status within the crew—formal rank, popularity, reputed flying ability, and so on. When the formal ranks of the members of any crew were quite similar to their ranks on the other measures, Adams found, the crew as a whole did well on "social performance" (harmony, intimacy, and the like). The crews that showed up best in these two respects, however, were not the best in "technical performance" (e.g., bombing accuracy). These findings seem reasonable. The popularity of the formal leaders of these crews was probably based in part upon their respect of a norm opposed to outstanding technical

[11] R. T. Golembiewski, "The Small Group and Public Administration," *Public Administration Review*, vol. 19, no. 3, pp. 149–156, 1959.
[12] Kahn and Katz, *op. cit.*, p. 616.
[13] S. Adams, "Status Congruency as a Variable in Small Group Performance," *Social Forces*, vol. 32, no. 1, pp. 16–22, 1953.

performance. Obviously, it did not make them particularly effective in their formal position. On the contrary, their closeness with their men helped the crews resist the demands of the "outside" organization.

A supervisor inheriting a work unit with a low-output norm faces a difficult task in choosing a style of leadership. If he employs a free-rein style, he will most likely succeed only in supporting the group norm. At the other extreme, the use of a leader-centered style may well harden the group's resistance to the formal organization. Even if the supervisor succeeds in breaking the group norm, he will most likely arouse antagonisms bound to affect the work process sooner or later.[14] (One major exception must be noted here: Groups of authoritarians, as has already been pointed out, will generally respond well to a leader-centered style. But this offers little practical consolation, given the apparent rarity of such groups.) Finally, it is the group-centered style, paradoxical though it may seem, that offers the best chance of success in changing a low-output norm, and group-centered leadership has actually proved useful in a number of instances. The reason for this seems to be that low output is a means by which the members of a work unit protect themselves against some perceived threat. A group-centered style often acts to make the group members feel less threatened and thus reduces their need for the low-output norm. But this is not inevitable.

In sum, every leadership style stands liable to failure in the attempt to develop and enforce a more acceptable output norm. If none of them works, the supervisor has no choice but to stop being a practicing psychologist and recommend that the unit be broken up.

---

[14] Such a situation is analyzed in R. T. Golembiewski, "O & M and the Small Group," *Public Administration Review*, vol. 20, no. 4, pp. 205–212, 1960.

CONCLUDING NOTES

The difficulties of choosing a leadership style, then, are great even if only a single condition is considered. From the two preceding paragraphs alone it should be clear that the question of how to lead any given work group is far more complex than is recognized by any existing generalizations, all of which call for a single leadership style. To compound this complexity, however, the four sets of conditions discussed in this article always appear in combination, so that some elements in a situation may favor one style while some elements favor another.

In fact, our increasing knowledge of the complexity of the question has outmoded the traditional designations of leadership styles. These designations, which suggest exclusive categories, ought to be modified so as to express the ways in which leadership styles continuously change in response to changing situations. The suggestions presented above outline the nature of the necessary changes. Needless to say, though these suggestions are consistent with the available research findings, they will need further verification before they can be considered rules for action.

Finally, it must be noted that the foregoing discussion has centered on the question "What are the conditions under which various leadership styles are most useful?" and has, in effect, neglected the question "What *should be* the dominant leadership style?" This neglect should not be taken as indicating that the question of value is unimportant. Rather, it recognizes that in practice the choice of a leadership style implies, and is preceded by, a value choice. In the field of leadership, as in every other, the use of empirical regularities must always be guided by considerations of what ought to be.

A New Look at Management Communication*

FRANK E. FISCHER

Over a decade ago Alvin Dodd, then President of the American Management Association, said, "The No. 1 management problem today is communication." Offhand, we seem to have come a long way since those benighted times. A number of colleges are now offering seminars and courses for executives in some phase of communication. Management books and periodicals are full of information about new communication devices and techniques. Lecturers by the score have spread the gospel of communication throughout the business world. Many companies have installed specialists in newly created "Communications" Departments. Consultants in communication have sprouted all over the land. The International Council of Industrial Editors estimates that management spends over $112,000,000 a year in publications designed to influence the thinking of employees, stockholders, and customers.

And yet . . . the editors of *Fortune* and Peter Drucker have charged that all this communicating is not worth a damn. All the talk, the activity, the gimmicks, and the prescriptions have failed to build a bridge between labor and management, between superior and subordinate. "We have been inept," says A. S. Igleheart, formerly Chairman of the Board and President of General Foods, "in communicating the ideas and information which create understanding among people who work together in an enterprise."

Why Communication Fails   Is this true? Has management lost its way? Not really, but many are foundering for one or more of the following reasons: First, many executives have mistaken the form of communication for its substance. They have paid too much attention

to media and devices, too little to purpose and content. It is this phenomenon that led *Fortune's* W. H. Whyte, Jr. to conclude that "the great enemy of communication is the illusion of it."

Second, executives have gone astray because they have considered communication a simple, isolated problem instead of a complex and dynamic process. They have overemphasized one form of communication—the employee magazine, personnel counseling, good reading racks, economic indoctrination—at the expense of other equally important elements.

Third, they have talked too much and listened too little. They have sought to extinguish the fire of discontent by dousing employees with information on every subject from taxes to taxidermy. But, as an industrial psychologist, Charles Flory, has warned,

> We can't assume that all communication is done through words . . . that people behave in uniform ways, and that any failure to understand an executive pronouncement lies with the receiver and not with the initiator.

The real problem is more often lack of understanding than lack of information.

The fact of the matter is that many executives still do not understand what communication is and what it can do. They underestimate its complexity, its power, and its importance. Too few appreciate that communication is at the heart of all business operations, that it encompasses all those activities by which we influence others. Actually, communication is the most important tool we have for getting things done. It is the basis for understanding, for cooperation, and for action.

The Cost of Miscommunication   Many of management's problems are traceable to failures in communication: Someone neglects to

* Reprinted by permission of the publisher from *Personnel*, vol. 31, no. 6, pp. 487–495, May, 1955. Mr. Fischer is director of seminars and courses, American Management Association.

tell the production manager that a critical material will be in short supply for the next few weeks; someone forgets to notify the advertising agency that the new product will not reach the market as scheduled; a promising junior executive accepts an attractive offer from a competitor because his boss gave him no indication how his work was appreciated; a grievance is filed because the foreman paid no attention to a worker's grumbling about the need for a safety guard on his machine; a department head's 50-page report goes unread because his superior wanted only a brief summary of the problem.

The cost of miscommunication of this sort is beyond calculation—not only in terms of time and money but in misunderstanding, inefficiency, and hostility. John Kusik, Vice-President of Chesapeake and Ohio Railroad, states that his company handles at least a billion written messages a year and many times that number of oral communications. Two-thirds of the payroll, he estimates, is spent for the sending, transmitting, and receiving of messages. Beyond question, a great deal could be saved by eliminating, combining, and condensing the simple routine messages that pulsate through a modern business. The first step in this direction is to improve the executive's *personal* skill as a sender and receiver of communications. This would require greater sensitivity to language and attention to the emotional content of messages. It demands awareness of communication barriers and how to overcome them, and the ability to tap the ideas and experiences of others.

THE COMMUNICATION PROCESS

As Lawrence Appley has pointed out, skill in communicating depends upon mastery of the basic communication process and involves the following steps:

1. Clarifying the idea or problem.
2. Getting participation in developing a solution to the problem.
3. Transmitting ideas or decisions.
4. Motivating others to take action agreed upon.
5. Measuring the effectiveness of communications.

1. Clarification Communications often misfire because one or more of these steps are omitted or mishandled. Customarily, the busy executive limits his attention to the third phase of the process: transmitting ideas. Of course, messages must get through if communication is to be complete. But, as Clarence Randall has said, "The beginning of all communication is an idea." Unless the idea is first clearly formulated in the mind of the transmitter, the message is likely to be misunderstood by the receiver. You can't make a clear print from a blurred negative. The study of communication, therefore, must begin with a careful and precise identification of the problem that requires action. It helps to try to reduce the problem to a simple statement for, as John Dewey has observed, "A problem well stated is half solved."

The executive's next task is to gather from all available sources data that bear upon the problem. After collecting this information he must evaluate it. He selects what is important and relevant to the problem, then proceeds to develop alternate solutions. He examines assumptions, weighs precedents, and anticipates consequences. He chooses finally what appears to him to be the best alternative and outlines this solution to test its logic and completeness.

2. Participation At this point he draws others into the problem. He does this primarily for three purposes:

(a) To clarify and test his *own* thinking by sharing his ideas with others.

(b) To gather the ideas and suggestions of others in a position to contribute to the solution of the problem.

(c) By inviting their participation, to motivate those responsible for carrying out the decision.

There are few problems so simple, few answers so obvious, that an executive's thinking cannot be sharpened by consulting with others. Some executives who can create or plan most brilliantly are inept in stirring the interest or gaining the cooperation of other people. Productive participation demands careful preparation, a permissive climate, sensitive listening, and the willingness to credit others for their contributions. In addition it requires skill in leading conferences, meetings, and committees where people can speak freely and responsibly. And most important, it requires confidence in the ability of people to make effective decisions. If you don't *expect* people to act responsibly, the chances are they will justify your expectations. Sensibly handled, participation is *not* a device for evading responsibility or syndicating the risk of making decisions.

3. Transmission   Having arrived at a solution or a decision, the executive's next step is to communicate it to those who will carry it out or who will be affected by it. Here he must plan carefully what to communicate, to whom to communicate, and how best to do it. Whether the communication is written or oral, the same care must be taken that he says what he has to say simply and clearly. He has to consider the nature of the person or group with whom he is communicating, the organizational and psychological barriers that may get in his way. He must remember that language that is clear to him may be obscure to others. Words that seem neutral to him may create feelings of suspicion or hostility in those who read or hear them.

4. Motivation   Clarity alone, then, is not enough. Most communications require not only that they be understood, but that they be accepted and acted upon. This leads directly into the fourth phase of the communication process, namely, motivation. If the communication not only states clearly what is to be done but inspires the recipient to want to do it, then we have truly communicated. This is basic in every situation requiring coordination and teamwork. It is particularly important when the communication threatens the established ways of doing things or thinking about things.

Evidence is accumulating that the morale of an organization and in large degree its productivity are related directly to the communication process. Employees who know what is expected of them, who know how their work ties in with the objectives of the company, who learn about changes before they take place, will obviously work with heightened interest and enthusiasm. Likewise, their motivation is better if they feel free to discuss problems with their supervisor and contribute to decisions that affect their work.

This factor was demonstrated long ago in the famous Hawthorne experiments of the Western Electric Company. It is confirmed by more recent surveys conducted by the University of Michigan in industries like steel, railroading, and insurance. Evidence from many sources points to the fact that free communication between the parts of a business generally results in improved morale and productivity. In each of these studies one major point keeps coming to the fore: Improvement in communication depends not so much on lavish investment in mass media, but on the daily work relations between superior and subordinate.

The National Industrial Conference Board surveyed the production employees of two plants operated by the same company.[1] The two groups were matched except that Plant "B" had participated in an active communication program for a number of years. Plant "A" had not been influenced by any such program. The following highlights from the survey's findings underline the intimate relation that seemingly exists everywhere between morale and the freedom to communicate:

1. Q. *Does your company do a good job of telling you what's going on and what's being planned?*

ANSWER	PLANT A	PLANT B
Very good job	18%	55%
Doesn't do much	22%	14%

2. Q. *Does your foreman ask your advice before deciding things that affect you?*

ANSWER	PLANT A	PLANT B
Hardly ever	65%	40%
Almost always	11%	26%

3. Q. *Can you talk things over with your foreman when you want to?*

ANSWER	PLANT A	PLANT B
Yes, I always can	34%	56%
Hardly ever	5%	0%

4. Q. *Do you feel a part of your company?*

ANSWER	PLANT A	PLANT B
I feel I really belong	29%	62%
I feel I just work here	42%	14%

5. Q. *How does your company compare as a company to work for with other companies?*

ANSWER	PLANT A	PLANT B
Worse than average	4%	3%
Just average	35%	19%
One of the very best	20%	45%

5. Evaluation   Just as communications often suffer from lack of planning, so they suffer from failure to evaluate their effectiveness. Much has been learned about why some conferences succeed and others don't, why some memos are clearer than others, why some talks get results and others produce indifference,

[1] See "Communicating with Employees," National Industrial Conference Board, Inc., *Studies in Personnel Policy, no. 129,* New York, pp. 36–40.

why counseling in one instance results in improved performance and in another produces only resistance. It is possible also to trace the impact of communications from attitude surveys, from records of productiveness, absenteeism, turnover, and the like.

HOW TO ACHIEVE EFFECTIVE COMMUNICATION

There is little need today for special pleading in the cause of communication. Progressive managers everywhere recognize it as the basic skill of management. They know that it is not an independent activity but an essential part of everything the manager does. Executives have become painfully aware how often carefully laid plans and programs have foundered on the rocks of faulty communication. That's why so many executives are asking, "What can be done throughout the company to establish and maintain a sound system of communication? What can I personally do to help my managers become better communicators?"

The Essentials   A volume could be written in answer to such questions. However, two fundamental recommendations can be outlined. First of all the executive must set an example that will announce to all of management his belief in the importance of communication. "Every organization," says Douglas Lynch, Executive Vice-President of Brush Electronics, "is colored by the man at the top to a degree that very few of us would like to admit." By his precepts, his policies, his actions—in short, by the leadership he exercises—he can nourish or stifle the communication in his organization. In defining the responsibility of his executives, in setting standards for their performance, and in rewarding them for their efforts, he must consider skill in communication as one of the main attributes of leadership. If this seems obvious, glance through the descriptions and standards for executive positions in your company. Is there any mention of the communication responsibilities of the executive? Think also of the basis on which you last promoted an executive. Without question, you considered his record as a planner and producer. But did you review his ability to coordinate others into a well-informed, highly motivated team?

Secondly, most executives, regardless of natural endowment, can improve their abilities to communicate—if they are properly guided and encouraged. How much is being done in your company to help the executive clarify his thinking, secure the participation of others, transmit ideas clearly and persuasively, moti-

vate others to act affirmatively, or to evaluate the effectiveness of their communications? Recently, AMA made a survey of companies with formal management development programs. Only 10 to 20 per cent offered training in communication.

Other Requirements of an Effective Program   In addition to these broad fundamentals, a survey of industrial practices, both good and bad, indicates that, to be effective, a communication program must meet the following requirements:

1. *Express the needs and character of the organization.* It makes a difference whether the company is small or large, old or new, manufacturing or retail, centralized or decentralized, union or non-union. It makes a very great difference whether the company has a tradition of secrecy or freedom of information, of authoritarianism or democracy. Every communication is judged in the context of a company's traditions and practices. That is why it is so risky to copy someone else's communication program—no matter how successful it was. You may remember how the March Hare in *Alice in Wonderland* tried to fix the Mad Hatter's watch with butter. When it failed, he could only say, in pained surprise: "And it was the *best* butter, the *best* butter."

2. *Communication grows best in a climate of trust and confidence.* Managements that have a record of keeping faith with their employees, reporting the facts honestly, and listening sincerely don't have to depend upon high-pressure indoctrination or slick handouts. An employee's knowledge that he has free access to information is more important than any specific information we can give him. Paul Arnold, President of Arnold Bakeries, recently said in this connection: "If your employee relations program is a sound one, if your intent is true, if your people believe in that intent, and in that truth, then and only then are you successfully communicating."

3. *Communication should form an integral part of each executive's job.* Though personnel specialists can advise the line and administer a program of formal communication, each executive is responsible for maintaining clear and consistent communication with his associates. This is one responsibility that he cannot delegate.

4. *Communication must be a continuing program, not a brief campaign.* It is not a panacea for sudden ills, but a day-in, day-out way of managing people. We must not, like the famous blind men who reconstructed the whole of an

elephant from a single part, identify the whole of communication with one of its devices. Exploitation of one particular medium will often create more problems than it will solve. This is a lesson some companies have learned when, after a long history of indifference to employees' interests, they have begun an all-out drive to indoctrinate them on some particular subject. The fanciest annual report, the fattest pay insert, the busiest reading rack, or the loudest public address system in and of themselves win few friends and influence few people.

5. *Communication must be stimulated.* Management must show what Alexander Heron, Vice President of Crown Zellerbach Company, has called "an *aggressive* willingness to share information with its employees." Stonewall Jackson is said to have been so secretive that he often misled his own staff more than he did the enemy. In their fear of competitors too many executives do likewise. It is not enough to correct misinformation or even to tell employees only what they *have* to know or what *management* thinks they should know. The proper starting point is to find out *what employees are interested in hearing.*

6. *Communication must be directed to a purpose and a person.* It is not, as Lawrence Appley has warned, an end in itself. Its true end is "effective management." Perhaps executives think too much about *how* to communicate and too little about *why* they are communicating. "I don't advise you," says Clarence Randall, "to start talking until you have begun thinking. It's no good opening the tap if there is nothing in the tank." It is equally risky to communicate without taking into account the individual or group you are deailng with. Every individual brings to the communication process certain personal equipment—experiences, attitudes, feelings, expectations—that must be considered if we are to achieve understanding with him. Alexander Heron has expressed this idea very forcibly:

> The foundation for any program for understanding between us and our employees is a complete respect on our part for the personality and individuality of the employee. While there may be a hundred or a hundred thousand employees on our payroll, and while we may bargain collectively with them through their chosen representatives, our relations are not with a mass of men; our relations are with each one of a hundred or a hundred thousand individual persons. We cannot share information with an abstract, imaginary entity such as "the public," "labor" or "the union," or "the rank and file." We can share information with Al Adams and Bill Brown and Carl Casey and Dan Davis, who work with us and receive their income in wages which we deliver to them.

7. *Communication must move freely in both directions.* It is commonplace today to emphasize that communication is a two-way street. In actual practice, however, management devotes far more attention to telling, informing, and commanding than it does to listening, asking, and interpreting. Only 4 per cent of the 160 executives polled by the Bureau of National Affairs disagreed with *Fortune's* recent article on management's failure to listen to its people. One way to learn what people want to know about is to encourage them to communicate upward in the organization. To find out whether its story is understood and accepted by employees, management must stimulate them to express their ideas and questions—and then management must *do* something about the problems that are raised.

8. *Communication must consider the supervisor's role.* In building a bridge between top management and employees, we must never forget that the prime communicator is the supervisor. He is in the most critical position to interpret—or misinterpret—top management thinking for the employees. H. J. Ruttenberg, the well-known labor leader, has said that in his experience the unionization of almost every plant has been preceded by the distortion of top management's attitudes and policies by minor functionaries. Useful as they are, such devices as president's letters, suggestion boxes, employee counselors, attitude surveys, and company magazines all represent detours. They route the employee's thinking and his problems around the supervisor. "First-line supervisors and foremen," said L. W. Tate, Vice President of Dallas Railway and Terminal Company, "are in the best position to feel the pulse of the workers in their day-to-day contacts on the job." Management must do everything in its power to keep the supervisor continually informed and to tap his knowledge of what employees are doing and thinking.

9. *The lines of communication should be as clear and direct as possible.* Many communications become diluted or distorted as they pass through levels of management. Others lose their usefulness because of delays in their journey down the management hierarchy. In establishing policy in communication, top management is haunted by the dilemma of maintaining the formal organizational channels and the necessity for speed and timeliness. One com-

pany prescribed exactly the channels through which communications must flow. When executive "A" wished to make a contact with executive "B" not prescribed in the standard procedure, he had to submit a request to his own boss, "A¹," that started the labyrinthine process shown in Figure 1.

FIGURE 1   Lines of Communication

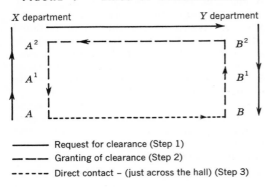

——————— Request for clearance (Step 1)
— —— — Granting of clearance (Step 2)
- - - - - - Direct contact – (just across the hall) (Step 3)

Contrast this with the sensible policy on communication developed by Jones and Laughlin: "The plan of organization should permit and require the exercise of common sense and good judgment at all levels in determining the best channels of contact to expedite the work." In other words, management is told to communicate in the most direct way consistent with good sense.

10. *Communication must reflect the everyday policies and practices of management.* The important word here is "practices." In the long run, employees are influenced not by what management says but by what it does. It is the context of behavior that gives words their meaning. Employees are not fooled when the boss says good morning or asks about an ailing wife because the manual tells him that this is good human relations. The boss who levels with his people, who listens to their problems, who is genuinely interested in them, can exercise effective leadership even though he may forget sometimes to say good morning. It is useless for an executive to announce an "open-door" policy if employees do not feel comfortable once they go through the door. The manager who tells a foreman that he is interested in his problems but ignores his requests for help or information is, in effect, really telling the foreman that he is *not* interested in him.

We must never forget that the most powerful communication isn't what you *say*, it's what you *do*. What counts, in the final analysis, is not what people are *told* but what they *accept*. It is this concept of the role of communication in industry that characterizes effective leadership. This is the key that will unlock the gates to higher morale and productivity. To use this key we must have the faith that induced Charles McCormick to launch his plan of multiple management. We must act on the belief, as he did, that people can do anything if (1) they want to do it, (2) they are trained to do it, and (3) they understand the reason for doing it.

61

*Ten Commandments of Good Communication**

As a manager, your prime responsibility is to get things done through people. However sound your ideas or well-reasoned your deci-

* Reprinted by permission of the *American Management Association.* Copyright, 1955.

sions, they become effective only as they are transmitted to others and achieve the desired action—or reaction. Communication, therefore, is your most vital management tool. On the job you communicate not only with words but through your apparent attitudes and your actions. For communication encompasses all human behavior that results in an exchange of meaning. How well you manage depends upon how well you communicate in this broad sense. These ten commandments are designed to help you improve your skills as a manager by improving your skills of communication—with superiors, subordinates, and associates.

1. *Seek to clarify your ideas before communicating.* The more systematically we analyze the problem or idea to be communicated, the clearer it becomes. This is the first step toward effective communication. Many communications fail because of inadequate planning. Good planning must consider the goals and attitudes of those who will receive the communication and those who will be affected by it.

2. *Examine the true purpose of each communication.* Before you communicate, ask yourself what you *really* want to accomplish with your message—obtain information, initiate action, change another person's attitude? Identify your most important goal and then adapt your language, tone, and total approach to serve that specific objective. Don't try to accomplish too much with each communication. The sharper the focus of your message the greater its chances of success.

3. *Consider the total physical and human setting whenever you communicate.* Meaning and intent are conveyed by more than words alone. Many other factors influence the over-all impact of a communication, and the manager must be sensitive to the total setting in which he communicates. Consider, for example, your sense of timing—i.e., the circumstances under which you make an announcement or render a decision; the *physical setting*—whether you communicate in private, for example, or otherwise; the *social climate* that pervades work relationships within the company or a department and sets the tone of its communications; *custom and past practice*—the degree to which your communication conforms to, or departs from, the expectations of your audience. Be constantly aware of the total setting in which you communicate. Like all living things, communication must be capable of adapting to its environment.

4. *Consult with others, where appropriate, in planning communications.* Frequently it is desirable or necessary to seek the participation of others in planning a communication or developing the facts on which to base it. Such consultation often helps to lend additional insight and objectivity to your message. Moreover, those who have helped you plan your communication will give it their active support.

5. *Be mindful, while you communicate, of the overtones as well as the basic content of your message.* Your tone of voice, your expression, your apparent receptiveness to the responses of others—all have tremendous impact on those you wish to reach. Frequently overlooked, these subtleties of communication often affect a listener's reaction to a message even more than its basic content. Similarly, your choice of language—particularly your awareness of the fine shades of meaning and emotion in the words you use—predetermines in large part the reactions of your listeners.

6. *Take the opportunity, when it arises, to convey something of help or value to the receiver.* Consideration of the other person's interests and needs—the habit of trying to look at things from his point of view—will frequently point up opportunities to convey something of immediate benefit or long-range value to him. People on the job are most responsive to the manager whose messages take their own interests into account.

7. *Follow up your communication.* Our best efforts at communication may be wasted, and we may never know whether we have succeeded in expressing our true meaning and intent, if we do not follow up to see how well we have put our message across. This you can do by asking questions, by encouraging the receiver to express his reactions, by follow-up contacts, by subsequent review of performance. Make certain that every important communication has a "feed-back" so that complete understanding and appropriate action result.

8. *Communicate for tomorrow as well as today.* While communications may be aimed primarily at meeting the demands of an immediate situation, they must be planned with the past in mind if they are to maintain consistency in the receiver's view; but, most important of all, they must be consistent with long-range interests and goals. For example, it is not easy to communicate frankly on such matters as poor performance or the shortcomings of a loyal subordinate—but postponing disagreeable communications makes them more difficult in the long run and is actually unfair to your subordinates and your company.

9. *Be sure your actions support your communications.* In the final analysis, the most persuasive kind of communication is not what you say but what you *do*. When a man's actions or attitudes contradict his words, we tend to discount what he has said. For every manager this means that good supervisory practices—such as clear assignment of responsibility and authority, fair rewards for effort,

and sound policy enforcement—serve to communicate more than all the gifts of oratory.

10. *Last, but by no means least: Seek not only to be understood but to understand—be a good listener.* When we start talking we often cease to listen—in that larger sense of being attuned to the other person's unspoken reactions and attitudes. Even more serious is the fact that we are *all* guilty, at times, of inattentiveness when others are attempting to communicate to us.

Listening is one of the most important, most difficult—and most neglected—skills in communication. It demands that we concentrate not only on the explicit meanings another person is expressing, but on the implicit meanings, unspoken words, and undertones that may be far more significant. Thus we must learn to listen with the inner ear if we are to know the inner man.

62

Barriers and Gateways to Communication*

CARL R. ROGERS and F. J. ROETHLISBERGER

PART I

It may seem curious that a person like myself, whose whole professional effort is devoted to psychotherapy, should be interested in problems of communication. What relationship is there between obstacles to communication and providing therapeutic help to individuals with emotional maladjustments?

Actually the relationship is very close indeed. The whole task of psychotherapy is the task of dealing with a failure in communication. The emotionally maladjusted person, the "neurotic," is in difficulty, first, because communication within himself has broken down

* Reprinted by permission of the publisher from *Harvard Business Review*, vol. 30, no. 4, pp. 46–52, July–August, 1952. Mr. Rogers is Knapp Professor at the University of Wisconsin. Mr. Roethlisberger is Wallace Brett Donham Professor of Human Relations at Harvard University.

Editors' [of the *Harvard Business Review*] note: Mr. Rogers' and Mr. Roethlisberger's observations are based on their contributions to a panel discussion at the Centennial Conference on Communications, Northwestern University, October, 1951. A complete report of this conference may be secured by writing to the Publications Office, Northwestern University, Evanston, Ill.

and, secondly, because as a result of this his communication with others has been damaged. To put it another way, in the "neurotic" individual parts of himself which have been termed unconscious, or repressed, or denied to awareness, become blocked off so that they no longer communicate themselves to the conscious or managing part of himself; as long as this is true, there are distortions in the way he communicates himself to others, and so he suffers both within himself and in his interpersonal relations.

The task of psychotherapy is to help the person achieve, through a special relationship with a therapist, good communication within himself. Once this is achieved, he can communicate more freely and more effectively with others. We may say then that psychotherapy is good communication, within and between men. We may also turn that statement around and it will still be true. Good communication, free communication, within or between men, is always therapeutic.

It is, then, from a background of experience with communication in counseling and psychotherapy that I want to present two ideas: (1) I wish to state what I believe is one of the major factors in blocking or impeding communication, and then (2) I wish to present what in our experience has proved to be a very important way of improving or facilitating communication.

Barrier: The Tendency to Evaluate

I should like to propose, as a hypothesis for consideration, that the major barrier to mutual interpersonal communication is our very natural tendency to judge, to evaluate, to approve (or disapprove) the statement of the other person or the other group. Let me illustrate my meaning with some very simple examples.

Suppose someone, commenting on this discussion, makes the statement, "I didn't like what that man said." What will you respond? Almost invariably your reply will be either approval or disapproval of the attitude expressed. Either you respond, "I didn't either; I thought it was terrible," or else you tend to reply, "Oh, I thought it was really good." In other words, your primary reaction is to evaluate it from *your* point of view, your own frame of reference.

Or take another example. Suppose I say with some feeling, "I think the Republicans are behaving in ways that show a lot of good sound sense these days." What is the response that arises in your mind? The overwhelming likelihood is that it will be evaluative. In other words, you will find yourself agreeing, or disagreeing, or making some judgment about me such as "He must be a conservative," or "He seems solid in his thinking." Or let us take an illustration from the international scene. Russia says vehemently, "The treaty with Japan is a war plot on the part of the United States." We rise as one person to say, "That's a lie!"

This last illustration brings in another element connected with my hypothesis. Although the tendency to make evaluations is common in almost all interchange of language, it is very much heightened in those situations where feelings and emotions are deeply involved. So the stronger our feelings, the more likely it is that there will be no mutual element in the communication. There will be just two ideas, two feelings, two judgments, missing each other in psychological space.

I am sure you recognize this from your own experience. When you have not been emotionally involved yourself and have listened to a heated discussion, you often go away thinking, "Well, they actually weren't talking about the same thing." And they were not. Each was making a judgment, an evaluation, from his own frame of reference. There was really nothing which could be called communication in any genuine sense. This tendency to react to any emotionally meaningful statement by forming an evaluation of it from our own point of view is, I repeat, the major barrier to interpersonal communication.

Gateway: Listening with Understanding

Is there any way of solving this problem, of avoiding this barrier? I feel that we are making exciting progress toward this goal, and I should like to present it as simply as I can. Real communication occurs, and this evaluative tendency is avoided, when we listen with understanding. What does that mean? It means to see the expressed idea and attitude from the other person's point of view, to sense how it feels to him, to achieve his frame of reference in regard to the thing he is talking about.

Stated so briefly, this may sound absurdly simple, but it is not. It is an approach which we have found extremely potent in the field of psychotherapy. It is the most effective agent we know for altering the basic personality structure of an individual and for improving his relationships and his communications with others. If I can listen to what he can tell me, if I can understand how it seems to him, if I can see its personal meaning for him, if I can sense the emotional flavor which it has for him, then I will be releasing potent forces of change in him.

Again, if I can really understand how he hates his father, or hates the company, or hates Communists—if I can catch the flavor of his fear of insanity, or his fear of atom bombs, or of Russia—it will be of the greatest help to him in altering those hatreds and fears and in establishing realistic and harmonious relationships with the very people and situations toward which he has felt hatred and fear. We know from our research that such empathic understanding—understanding *with* a person, not *about* him—is such an effective approach that it can bring about major changes in personality.

Some of you may be feeling that you listen well to people and yet you have never seen such results. The chances are great indeed that your listening has not been of the type I have described. Fortunately, I can suggest a little laboratory experiment which you can try to test the quality of your understanding. The next time you get into an argument with your wife, or your friend, or with a small group of friends, just stop the discussion for a moment and, for an experiment, institute this rule: "Each person can speak up for himself only *after* he has first restated the ideas and feelings of the previous speaker accurately and to that speaker's satisfaction."

You see what this would mean. It would simply mean that before presenting your own point of view, it would be necessary for you to achieve the other speaker's frame of reference —to understand his thoughts and feelings so well that you could summarize them for him. Sounds simple, doesn't it? But if you try it, you will discover that it is one of the most difficult things you have ever tried to do. However, once you have been able to see the other's point of view, your own comments will have to be drastically revised. You will also find the emotion going out of the discussion, the differences being reduced, and those differences which remain being of a rational and understandable sort.

Can you imagine what this kind of an approach would mean if it were projected into larger areas? What would happen to a labor-management dispute if it were conducted in such a way that labor, without necessarily agreeing, could accurately state management's point of view in a way that management could accept; and management, without approving labor's stand, could state labor's case in a way that labor agreed was accurate? It would mean that real communication was established, and one could practically guarantee that some reasonable solution would be reached.

If, then, this way of approach is an effective avenue to good communication and good relationships, as I am quite sure you will agree if you try the experiment I have mentioned, why is it not more widely tried and used? I will try to list the difficulties which keep it from being utilized.

Need for Courage.   In the first place it takes courage, a quality which is not too widespread. I am indebted to Dr. S. I. Hayakawa, the semanticist, for pointing out that to carry on psychotherapy in this fashion is to take a very real risk, and that courage is required. If you really understand another person in this way, if you are willing to enter his private world and see the way life appears to him, without any attempt to make evaluative judgments, you run the risk of being changed yourself. You might see it his way; you might find yourself influenced in your attitudes or your personality.

This risk of being changed is one of the most frightening prospects many of us can face. If I enter, as fully as I am able, into the private world of a neurotic or psychotic individual, isn't there a risk that I might become lost in that world? Most of us are afraid to take that risk. Or if we were listening to a Russian Communist, or Senator Joe McCarthy, how many of us would dare to try to see the world from each of their points of view? The great majority of us could not *listen;* we would find ourselves compelled to *evaluate,* because listening would seem too dangerous. So the first requirement is courage, and we do not always have it.

Heightened Emotions.   But there is a second obstacle. It is just when emotions are strongest that it is most difficult to achieve the frame of reference of the other person or group. Yet it is then that the attitude is most needed if communication is to be established. We have not found this to be an insuperable obstacle in our experience in psychotherapy. A third party, who is able to lay aside his own feelings and evaluations, can assist greatly by listening with understanding to each person or group and clarifying the views and attitudes each holds.

We have found this effective in small groups in which contradictory or antagonistic attitudes exist. When the parties to a dispute realize that they are being understood, that someone sees how the situation seems to them, the statements grow less exaggerated and less defensive, and it is no longer necessary to maintain the attitude, "I am 100% right and you are 100% wrong." The influence of such an understanding catalyst in the group permits the members to come closer and closer to the objective truth involved in the relationship. In this way mutual communication is established, and some type of agreement becomes much more possible.

So we may say that though heightened emotions make it much more difficult to understand *with* an opponent, our experience makes it clear that a neutral, understanding, catalyst type of leader or therapist can overcome this obstacle in a small group.

Size of Group.   That last phrase, however, suggests another obstacle to utilizing the approach I have described. Thus far all our experience has been with small face-to-face groups—groups exhibiting industrial tensions, religious tensions, racial tensions, and therapy groups in which many personal tensions are present. In these small groups our experience, confirmed by a limited amount of research, shows that this basic approach leads to improved communication, to greater acceptance of others and by others, and to attitudes which are more positive and more problem-solving in nature. There is a decrease in defensiveness, in exaggerated statements, in evaluative and critical behavior.

But these findings are from small groups.

What about trying to achieve understanding between larger groups that are geographically remote, or between face-to-face groups that are not speaking for themselves but simply as representatives of others, like the delegates at Kaesong? Frankly we do not know the answers to these questions. I believe the situation might be put this way: As social scientists we have a tentative test-tube solution of the problem of breakdown in communication. But to confirm the validity of this test-tube solution and to adapt it to the enormous problems of communication breakdown between classes, groups, and nations would involve additional funds, much more research, and creative thinking of a high order.

Yet with our present limited knowledge we can see some steps which might be taken even in large groups to increase the amount of listening *with* and decrease the amount of evaluation *about*. To be imaginative for a moment, let us suppose that a therapeutically oriented international group went to the Russian leaders and said, "We want to achieve a genuine understanding of your views and, even more important, of your attitudes and feelings toward the United States. We will summarize and resummarize these views and feelings if necessary, until you agree that our description represents the situation as it seems to you."

Then suppose they did the same thing with the leaders in our own country. If they then gave the widest possible distribution to these two views, with the feelings clearly described but not expressed in name-calling, might not the effect be very great? It would not guarantee the type of understanding I have been describing, but it would make it much more possible. We can understand the feelings of a person who hates us much more readily when his attitudes are accurately described to us by a neutral third party than we can when he is shaking his fist at us.

Faith in Social Sciences. But even to describe such a first step is to suggest another obstacle to this approach of understanding. Our civilization does not yet have enough faith in the social sciences to utilize their findings. The opposite is true of the physical sciences. During the war when a test-tube solution was found to the problem of synthetic rubber, millions of dollars and an army of talent were turned loose on the problem of using that finding. If synthetic rubber could be made in milligrams, it could and would be made in the thousands of tons. And it was. But in the social science realm, if a way is found of facilitating communication and mutual understanding in small groups, there is no guarantee that the finding will be utilized. It may be a generation or more before the money and the brains will be turned loose to exploit that finding.

Summary In closing, I should like to summarize this small-scale solution to the problem of barriers in communication, and to point out certain of its characteristics.

I have said that our research and experience to date would make it appear that breakdowns in communication, and the evaluative tendency which is the major barrier to communication, can be avoided. The solution is provided by creating a situation in which each of the different parties comes to understand the other from the *other's* point of view. This has been achieved, in practice, even when feelings run high, by the influence of a person who is willing to understand each point of view empathically, and who thus acts as a catalyst to precipitate further understanding.

This procedure has important characteristics. It can be initiated by one party, without waiting for the other to be ready. It can even be initiated by a neutral third person, provided he can gain a minimum of cooperation from one of the parties.

This procedure can deal with the insincerities, the defensive exaggerations, the lies, the "false fronts" which characterize almost every failure in communication. These defensive distortions drop away with astonishing speed as people find that the only intent is to understand, not to judge.

This approach leads steadily and rapidly toward the discovery of the truth, toward a realistic appraisal of the objective barriers to communication. The dropping of some defensiveness by one party leads to further dropping of defensiveness by the other party, and truth is thus approached.

This procedure gradually achieves mutual communication. Mutual communication tends to be pointed toward solving a problem rather than toward attacking a person or group. It leads to a situation in which I see how the problem appears to you as well as to me, and you see how it appears to me as well as to you. Thus accurately and realistically defined, the problem is almost certain to yield to intelligent attack; or if it is in part insoluble, it will be comfortably accepted as such.

This then appears to be a test-tube solution to the breakdown of communication as it occurs in small groups. Can we take this small-scale answer, investigate it further, refine it, develop it, and apply it to the tragic and well-nigh fatal failures of communication which threaten the very existence of our modern world? It seems to me that this is a possibility and a challenge which we should explore.

PART II*

In thinking about the many barriers to personal communication, particularly those that are due to differences of background, experience, and motivation, it seems to me extraordinary that any two persons can ever understand each other. Such reflections provoke the question of how communication is possible when people do not see and assume the same things and share the same values.

On this question there are two schools of thought. One school assumes that communication between A and B, for example, has failed when B does not accept what A has to say as being fact, true, or valid; and that the goal of communication is to get B to agree with A's opinions, ideas, facts, or information.

The position of the other school of thought is quite different. It assumes that communication has failed when B does not feel free to express his feelings to A because B fears they will not be accepted by A. Communication is facilitated when on the part of A or B or both there is a willingness to express and accept differences.

As these are quite divergent conceptions, let us explore them further with an example.

> Bill, an employee, is talking with his boss in the boss's office. The boss says, "I think, Bill, that this is the best way to do your job." Bill says, "Oh yeah!" According to the first school of thought, this reply would be a sign of poor communication. Bill does not understand the best way of doing his work. To improve communication, therefore, it is up to the boss to explain to Bill why his way is the best.
>
> From the point of view of the second school of thought, Bill's reply is a sign neither of good nor of bad communication. Bill's response is indeterminate. But the boss has an opportunity to find out what Bill means if he so desires. Let us assume that this is what he chooses to do, i.e., find out what Bill means. So this boss tries to get Bill to talk more about his job while he (the boss) listens.

For purposes of simplification, I shall call the boss representing the first school of thought "Smith" and the boss representing the second

* Author's note: For the concepts I use to present my material I am greatly indebted to some very interesting conversations I have had with my friend, Irving Lee.—*F. J. R.*

school of thought "Jones." In the presence of the so-called same stimulus each behaves differently. Smith chooses to *explain;* Jones chooses to *listen.* In my experience Jones's response works better than Smith's. It works better because Jones is making a more proper evaluation of what is taking place between him and Bill than Smith is. Let us test this hypothesis by continuing with our example.

What Smith Assumes, Sees, and Feels
Smith assumes that he understands what Bill means when Bill says, "Oh yeah!" so there is no need to find out. Smith is sure that Bill does not understand why this is the best way to do his job, so Smith has to tell him. In this process let us assume Smith is logical, lucid, and clear. He presents his facts and evidence well. But, alas, Bill remains unconvinced. What does Smith do? Operating under the assumption that what is taking place between him and Bill is something essentially logical, Smith can draw only one of two conclusions: either (1) he has not been clear enough, or (2) Bill is too damned stupid to understand. So he either has to "spell out" his case in words of fewer and fewer syllables or give up. Smith is reluctant to do the latter, so he continues to explain. What happens?

If Bill still does not accept Smith's explanation of why this is the best way for him to do his job, a pattern of interacting feelings is produced of which Smith is often unaware. The more Smith cannot get Bill to understand him, the more frustrated Smith becomes and the more Bill becomes a threat to his logical capacity. Since Smith sees himself as a fairly reasonable and logical chap, this is a difficult feeling to accept. It is much easier for him to perceive Bill as uncooperative or stupid. This perception, however, will affect what Smith says and does. Under these pressures Bill comes to be evaluated more and more in terms of Smith's values. By this process Smith tends to treat Bill's values as unimportant. He tends to deny Bill's uniqueness and difference. He treats Bill as if he had little capacity for self-direction.

Let us be clear. Smith does not see that he is doing these things. When he is feverishly scratching hieroglyphics on the back of an envelope, trying to explain to Bill why this is the best way to do his job, Smith is trying to be helpful. He is a man of goodwill, and he wants to set Bill straight. This is the way Smith sees himself and his behavior. But it is for this very reason that Bill's "Oh yeah!" is getting under Smith's skin.

"How dumb can a guy be?" is Smith's attitude, and unfortunately Bill will hear that more than Smith's good intentions. Bill will feel misunderstood. He will not see Smith as a man of goodwill trying to be helpful. Rather he will perceive him as a threat to his self-esteem and personal integrity. Against this threat Bill will feel the need to defend himself at all cost. Not being so logically articulate as Smith, Bill expresses this need, again, by saying, "Oh yeah!"

What Jones Assumes, Sees, and Feels

Let us leave this sad scene between Smith and Bill, which I fear is going to terminate by Bill's either leaving in a huff or being kicked out of Smith's office. Let us turn for a moment to Jones and see what he is assuming, seeing, hearing, feeling, doing, and saying when he interacts with Bill.

Jones, it will be remembered, does not assume that he knows what Bill means when he says, "Oh yeah!" so he has to find out. Moreover, he assumes that when Bill said this, he had not exhausted his vocabulary or his feelings. Bill may not necessarily mean one thing; he may mean several different things. So Jones decides to listen.

In this process Jones is not under any illusion that what will take place will be eventually logical. Rather he is assuming that what will take place will be primarily an interaction of feelings. Therefore, he cannot ignore the feelings of Bill, the effect of Bill's feelings on him, or the effect of his feelings on Bill. In other words, he cannot ignore his relationship to Bill; he cannot assume that it will make no difference to what Bill will hear or accept.

Therefore, Jones will be paying strict attention to all of the things Smith has ignored. He will be addressing himself to Bill's feelings, his own, and the interactions between them.

Jones will therefore realize that he has ruffled Bill's feelings with his comment, "I think, Bill, this is the best way to do your job." So instead of trying to get Bill to understand him, he decides to try to understand Bill. He does this by encouraging Bill to speak. Instead of telling Bill how he should feel or think, he asks Bill such questions as, "Is this what you feel?" "Is this what you see?" "Is this what you assume?" Instead of ignoring Bill's evaluations as irrelevant, not valid, inconsequential, or false, he tries to understand Bill's reality as he feels it, perceives it, and assumes it to be. As Bill begins to open up, Jones's curiosity is piqued by this process.

"Bill isn't so dumb; he's quite an interesting guy" becomes Jones's attitude. And that is what Bill hears. Therefore Bill feels understood and accepted as a person. He becomes less

defensive. He is in a better frame of mind to explore and re-examine his own perceptions, feelings, and assumptions. In this process he perceives Jones as a source of help. Bill feels free to express his differences. He feels that Jones has some respect for his capacity for self-direction. These positive feelings toward Jones make Bill more inclined to say, "Well, Jones, I don't quite agree with you that this is the best way to do my job, but I'll tell you what I'll do. I'll try to do it that way for a few days, and then I'll tell you what I think."

Conclusion

I grant that my two orientations do not work themselves out in practice in quite so simple or neat a fashion as I have been able to work them out on paper. There are many other ways in which Bill could have responded to Smith in the first place. He might even have said, "O.K., boss, I agree that your way of doing my job is better." But Smith still would not have known how Bill felt when he made this statement or whether Bill was actually going to do his job differently. Likewise, Bill could have responded to Jones in a way different from my example. In spite of Jones's attitude, Bill might still be reluctant to express himself freely to his boss.

The purpose of my examples has not been to demonstrate the right or wrong way of communicating. My purpose has been simply to provide something concrete to point to when I make the following generalizations:

1. Smith represents to me a very common pattern of misunderstanding. The misunderstanding does not arise because Smith is not clear enough in expressing himself. It arises because of Smith's misevaluation of what is taking place when two people are talking together.

2. Smith's misevaluation of the process of personal communication consists of certain very common assumptions, e.g., (a) that what is taking place is something essentially logical; (b) that words in themselves apart from the people involved mean something; and (c) that the purpose of the interaction is to get Bill to see things from Smith's point of view.

3. Because of these assumptions, a chain reaction of perceptions and negative feelings is engendered which blocks communication. By ignoring Bill's feelings and by rationalizing his own, Smith ignores his relationship to Bill as one of the most important determinants of the communication. As a result, Bill hears Smith's attitude more clearly than the logical content of Smith's words. Bill

feels that his individual uniqueness is being denied. His personal integrity being at stake, he becomes defensive and belligerent. As a result, Smith feels frustrated. He perceives Bill as stupid. So he says and does things which only provoke more defensiveness on the part of Bill.

4. In the case of Jones, I have tried to show what might possibly happen if we made a different evaluation of what is taking place when two people are talking together. Jones makes a different set of assumptions. He assumes (a) that what is taking place between him and Bill is an interaction of sentiments; (b) that Bill—not his words in themselves—means something; (c) that the object of the interaction is to give Bill an opportunity to express freely his differences.

5. Because of these assumptions, a psychological chain reaction of reinforcing feelings and perceptions is set up which facilitates communication between Bill and him. When Jones addresses himself to Bill's feelings and perceptions from Bill's point of view, Bill feels understood and accepted as a person; he feels free to express his differences. Bill sees Jones as a source of help; Jones sees Bill as an interesting person. Bill in turn becomes more cooperative.

6. If I have identified correctly these very common patterns of personal communication, then some interesting hypotheses can be stated:

   (a) Jones's method works better than Smith's, not because of any magic, but because Jones has a better map than Smith of the process of personal communication.

   (b) The practice of Jones's method, however, is not merely an intellectual exercise. It depends on Jones's capacity and willingness to see and accept points of view different from his own, and to practice this orientation in a face-to-face relationship. This practice involves an emotional as well as an intellectual achievement. It depends in part on Jones's awareness of himself, in part on the practice of a skill.

   (c) Although our colleges and universities try to get students to appreciate intellectually points of view different from their own, very little is done to help them to implement this general intellectual appreciation in a simple face-to-face relationship—at the level of a skill. Most educational institutions train their students to be logical, lucid, and clear. Very little is done to help them to listen more skillfully. As a result, our educated world contains too many Smiths and too few Joneses.

   (d) The biggest block to personal communication is man's inability to listen intelligently, understandingly, and skillfully to another person. This deficiency in the modern world is widespread and appalling. In our universities as well as elsewhere, too little is being done about it.

7. In conclusion, let me apologize for acting toward you the way Smith did. But who am I to violate a long-standing academic tradition!

PART SIX

CONTROL

Control is the management function of making sure that plans succeed. In other words, it is the measuring and correcting of activities of subordinates to ensure that these activities are contributing to the achievement of planned goals. The reader can see, of course, that planning and control are very closely interrelated. He will note also that effective control implies more than measuring. In many instances it requires revised planning, additional organizing, improved staffing, and better methods of directing. It is thus a means of "closing the loop" in the entire management process.

The control process is regarded by the editors as one of establishing standards against which performance can be measured, the measuring of performance, and the correcting of deviations from the standards or plans. In "The Meaning of Control," Douglas S. Sherwin points out that control is an important responsibility of every manager and emphasizes significance of information, particularly forecasting, to effective control. The second article is Arnold F. Emch's "Control Means Action." Mr. Emch points out the dangers of burdensome control systems, as well as the risks involved in insufficient control. He also makes clear that planning is the basis for control, that information must be used to guide control, and that action by people with appropriate delegated authority is the essence of control.

Because of the importance of information to both planning and control— and because electronic data processing has made information available in unprecedented amounts—the editors have selected three articles on information. One of these is the concise but insightful paper of Philip Gustafson, "Business Reports: How to Get Facts You Need." Mr. Gustafson outlines eight requirements for effective management reporting and uses the report systems of the Du Pont Company and United Airlines to illustrate them. A second article is D. Ronald Daniel's "Management Information Crisis." Mr. Daniel alerts managers to the crisis which is being created by the tremendous flood of undigested information and suggests ways of establishing an integrated information system. The stimulating paper by Marion Harper, Jr., "A New Profession to Aid Management," also deals with the problem of information and the dangers of unprocessed information. Taking the position that a manager manages through information and that information, in order to be useful, must be processed like any raw material, Mr. Harper suggests that the modern manager needs a specialist who can digest and translate a wide variety of information into a form more easily comprehended and therefore more useful to the manager who must use it to take action.

One of the most interesting developments in management has been the rapid growth of new techniques for achieving more effective planning and control. The reader should not overlook, however, the existence of several rather old and well-tested means of obtaining effective planning and control. The authors have therefore included the excellent article on budgets by James L. Peirce, "The Budget Comes of Age"; "The Breakeven Concept," by the acknowledged specialist in this area, Fred V. Gardner; and an excerpt entitled "Internal Auditing Control," from Internal Auditing for Management, *by F. A. Lamperti and J. B. Thurston, who are the generally recognized pioneers in the development of this technique.*

Among the newer techniques for planning and control which have grown out of the recognition that systems theory, long used in the physical sciences, can be applied with great profit in management, are physical distribution management ("rhochrematics"), program evaluation review technique

(PERT), and other devices of a mathematical nature. The editors have included, on the subject of physical distribution management, the instructive article by Stanley H. Brewer and James Rosenszweig, "Rhochrematics and Organizational Adjustments." R. W. Miller's "How to Plan and Control with PERT" describes the nature of PERT, and, to cast further light on this interesting device for planning and control and to give a clearer picture of how management can use it, the editors have included Ivars Avots's paper "The Management Side of PERT."

Because there has been so much discussion concerning the use of computers for achieving more effective management planning and control, the editors have included the article by D. G. Malcolm and A. J. Rowe, "An Approach to Computer-based Management Control Systems." Drawing from experience in their companies and applications in military systems, the authors of this article discuss the importance of designing management control systems and of recognizing the interdependence of control and planning in the development of the most effective control systems.

The possible future impact of the computer and the application of the methodology of the physical sciences to management have been the subjects of considerable discussion and speculation. The tremendous computing power of the electronic data processing machine is being combined with the mathematical tools of the physical sciences and applied to management. What does this mean in terms of the development of a mathematically based science of management? The editors have selected two articles on this subject. One, "Potentials of Management Science," by Peter F. Drucker, is a sober reflection on the potentialities and the limitations of management science and contains a strong warning to the specialists in this field that they must use these scientific instruments and methods for better business management, not as an unrealistic "management gadget bag." The second article, by Prof. Herbert A. Simon, is an optimistic view of the future of scientific management, entitled "The Automation of Management." Professor Simon is among those few scholars who believe that it is entirely possible for future machine programs to simulate much, if not all, of the thinking which goes into the management process itself, although he admits that there may be many places where this would be prohibitively expensive. Thus Professor Simon takes one of the more extreme positions, it appears to the editors, by forecasting a greater degree of automation of the management function through the use of the new mathematical techniques and the computer.

One of the major aspects of control is the measurement of overall performance of a company or of an integrated division of it. Perhaps the most widely used device for measuring overall performance of a company or an integrated division has been the rate-of-return-on-investment method, developed by the Du Pont Company in 1919 and used by it since that time as a major means of divisional control. Included, therefore, is an exposition by a Du Pont executive, T. C. Davis, titled "How the Du Pont Organization Appraises Its Performance." Related to this presentation is the explanation, by T. G. Mackensen, of how the H. J. Heinz Company has used the rate-of-return-on-investment approach to judge the profitability of product lines in a company which cannot easily be divisionalized, included under the title, "Return on Invested Capital."

Since it is often overlooked in measuring the total performance of an enterprise, Prof. Rensis Likert has aptly called attention to the importance of measuring the human franchise in an enterprise. This point of view by Professor Likert, supported by his observations that means are available for measuring the attitudes of people in an enterprise, is included under the title, "Measuring Organizational Performance."

In the opinion of the editors, the most direct of all controls is control over the total quality of management. All other controls are indirect in the sense that they are designed largely to detect failures on the part of those who undertake managerial tasks. Despite the considerable interest of management scholars and practitioners in developing means for auditing the total quality of management, the literature is quite limited.

Pioneering efforts in this area have been the work of the American Institute of Management, under the leadership of Jackson Martindell. Mr. Martindell, long a successful investment counselor, years ago came to the conclusion that the quality of management in a company was the most important single factor, from the standpoint of investment. He therefore founded the American Institute of Management for the purpose of making management audits of companies. While the thoroughness of this pioneering effort may be subject to criticism, it nonetheless is an original and valuable technique which, in the editors' judgment, will become increasingly important. A summary of how the institute undertakes its management audits and the factors which they have included is presented under the title, "Management Audits Simplified."

One of the early approaches to the management audit was the "Outline for a Management Audit," developed by the Metropolitan Life Insurance Company. Although this audit approach attempted to encompass functional fields of company operation as well as management practice, it is an interesting and novel outline of the kinds of things to look at when assessing the managerial functions of organizing and control. Our last selection is Robert B. Buchele's informative article "How to Evaluate a Firm," which gives heavy emphasis to the importance of management but includes other factors as well.

The Meaning of Control*

DOUGLAS S. SHERWIN

"What exactly do you mean by management control?" When this question was asked of a number of managers, in both Government and industry, the answers showed a surprising lack of agreement—surprising, since in a field for which theory has been developed to the extent it has in business management, terms should be precise, specific, and unambiguous. The literature, as one might expect, reflects about the same variety of views as entertained by management men themselves, and so does little to clarify the situation.

Is it important that managers have a clear understanding of this concept? The question almost answers itself. A manager who does not understand management control cannot be expected to exercise it in the most efficient and effective manner. Nor can staff men whose duty it is to design systems and procedures for their organizations design efficient systems unless they possess a clear understanding of management control. And certainly (though the truth of this is seldom sufficiently appreciated) anyone who is subject to control by others has to understand clearly what that means if he is to be contented in that relationship.

Indeed, when management control is *not* understood, good management is a very improbable result. This is especially true when—as frequently it is—control is identified with management, or is confused with certain devices of management, such as objectives, plans, organization charts, policy statements, delegations of authority, procedures, and the like. The manager who believes managing and controlling are the same thing has wasted one word and needs a second to be invented. And one who believes he has provided for control when he has established objectives, plans, policies, organization charts, and so forth, has made himself vulnerable to really serious consequences. A clear understanding of control is

therefore indispensable in an effective manager.

Understanding control really means understanding three principal things about it: What is control? What is controlled? And who controls? By proposing answers to these questions, I will try to frame a concept of control that will be useful to practitioners of the managerial art.

The conception of control which I advocate can be simply and briefly stated as follows:

The essence of control is action which adjusts operations to predetermined standards, and its basis is information in the hands of managers.

We have a ready-made model for this concept of control in the automatic systems which are widely used for process control in the chemical and petroleum industries. A process control system works this way. Suppose, for example, it is desired to maintain a constant rate of flow of oil through a pipe at a predetermined, or set-point value. A signal, whose strength represents the rate of flow, can be produced in a measuring device and transmitted to a control mechanism. The control mechanism, when it detects any deviation of the actual from the set-point signal, will reposition the valve regulating flow rate.

BASIS FOR CONTROL

A process control mechanism thus acts to adjust operations to predetermined standards and does so on the basis of information it receives. In a parallel way, information reaching a manager gives him the opportunity for corrective action and is his basis for control. He cannot exercise control without such information. And he cannot do a complete job of managing without controlling.

As mentioned earlier, some students of management have defined control as what results from having objectives, plans, policies, organization charts, procedures, and so forth; and they refer to these elements of the management system, consequently, as controls or means of control. It is not difficult to understand why

* Reprinted by permission of the publishers from *Dun's Review and Modern Industry*, pp. 45ff., January, 1956. Mr. Sherwin is assistant coordinator, Rubber Chemicals Division, Phillips Chemical Company.

these devices of managing are so described by proponents of this point of view. Without objectives, for example, we all know results are likely to be other than desired, so it is assumed they function to control the results. And so it is with the other elements of the system.

Nevertheless, these elements are neither controls nor means of control. They do have, however, as we shall see later, an important role to play in a control *system,* and we can therefore examine them now in a little detail.

Certainly, to accomplish a task except through accident, people must know what they are trying to do. Objectives fulfill this need. Without them, people may work quite industriously yet, working aimlessly, accomplish little. Plans and programs complement objectives, since they propose how and according to what time schedule the objectives are to be reached.

But though objectives, and plans and programs are indispensable to the efficient management of a business (or, for that matter, to the management of almost any human endeavor) they are not means of control. Control is checking to determine whether plans are being observed and suitable progress toward the objectives is being made, and acting, if necessary, to correct any deviations.

Policy is simply a statement of an organization's intention to act in certain ways when specified types of circumstances arise. It represents a general decision, predetermined and expressed as a principle or rule, establishing a normal pattern of conduct for dealing with given types of business events—usually recurrent. A statement of policy is therefore useful in economizing the time of managers and in assisting them to discharge their responsibilities equitably and consistently.

POLICY VERIFICATION

Nothing in these advantages, however, makes policy a means of control. Indeed, by their very nature, policies generate the need for control; they do not fulfill that need. Adherence to policies is not guaranteed, nor can it be taken on faith. It has to be verified. Without verification, there is no basis for control, no control, and incomplete managing.

Organization is often cited as a means of control. This detracts both from its own significance and from the concept of control.

Organization is part of the giving of an assignment. The organization chart, for example, is a first crude step in the defining of assignments. It gives to each individual, in his title, a first approximation to the nature of his assignment, and it orients him as accountable to a certain individual. But it is not in a fruitful sense a means of control. Control is checking to ascertain whether the assignment is being executed as intended—and acting on the basis of that information.

The relation between 'internal check' and 'internal control' is likewise not well understood. The two terms refer to quite different aspects of the managerial system. 'Internal check' provides in practise for the principle that the same person should not have responsibility for all phases of a transaction. This makes it clearly an aspect of organization, rather than of control. For how do we provide for internal check? We provide for it through segregating the duties of recording and those of custodianship and assigning them to different employees or groups of employees.

Assigning duties is, of course, the very essence of organizing, and thus internal check is simply organizing in a special way in order to realize special objectives. Internal control, on the other hand, observes the actual performance of duties as against the assigned duties and acts, where necessary, to correct deviations of the actual from the assigned.

Internal check and internal control are obviously both very necessary in an enterprise. But they operate differently. The objective of internal check is to reduce the opportunity for fraud or error to occur. The objective of internal control is to restore operations to predetermined standards. Internal check is thus static or built-in; it is provided before-the-fact; and its operation is preventive in its effect. Internal control, in contrast, is active and continual; it is exercised after-the-fact; and its operation is corrective in its effect.

Assignments are far from defined, however, by the preparation of an organization chart. Among the ways we have for supplementing the titles and lines of authority of an organization chart are delegations of authority. Delegations of authority clarify the extent of authority of individuals and in that way serve to define assignments. That they are not means of control is apparent from the very fact that wherever there has been a delegation of authority the need for control increases, and this could hardly be expected to happen if delegations of authority were themselves means of control.

MANAGER'S RESPONSIBILITY

Control becomes necessary whenever a manager delegates authority to a subordinate, because he cannot delegate, then simply sit back and forget all about it. A manager's accountability to his own superior has not diminished one whit as a result of delegating part of his authority to a subordinate. It is therefore incumbent upon managers who delegate authority to exercise control over actions taken under the authority so delegated. That means checking results as a basis for possible corrective action.

The question whether budgets are a means of control does not yield a straightforward answer because budgets perform more than one function. They perform three: they present the objectives, plans and programs of the organization and express them in financial terms; they report the progress of actual performance against these predetermined objectives, plans, and programs; and, like organization charts, delegations of authority, procedures, and job descriptions, they define the assignments which have flowed down from the chief executive.

In expressing the objectives and plans of the organization, budgets are of course not means of control, for reasons examined earlier when objectives and plans were considered. Nor do budgets qualify as means of control in their function of defining assignments. Though this service of budgets is frequently overlooked, defining an assignment, as I have suggested previously, is neither a means of control nor the exercise of control.

Budgets are a means of control only in the respect that they report progress of actual performance against the program,—information which enables managers to take action directed toward bringing actual results into conformity with the program.

In the previous paragraphs I have tried to show that objectives, plans and programs, organization charts, and other elements of the managerial system are not fruitfully regarded as either 'controls' or 'means of control.' They nevertheless do bear a very important relationship to the control function. They are the pre-established standards to which operations are adjusted by the exercise of management control.

It may seem unfamiliar to some to view these devices of management in that light. Perhaps 'standards' is not the very best word. Yet these elements of the system are standards in a very real sense, for they have been laid down by competent authority as models or standards of desired performance.

These standards are, of course, dynamic in character, for they are constantly altered, modified, or revised. But for a moment let us give our attention to their static quality.

An objective is static until revised; a plan or program is static until it is abandoned. They possess a kind of temporary durability or limited permanence. They are in force until

superseded. This same static quality inheres also in the other elements of the managerial system we spoke of. Policies, organizational set-up, procedures, delegations, job descriptions, and so forth, are, of course, constantly altered and added to. But, like objectives and plans, they retain their force until they are either abandoned or revised.

Suppose, for convenience, we use the phrase 'framework of management' to mean all the elements of the managerial system taken together—objectives, plans and programs, policies, organization, and the like. Doubtless, a more descriptive phrase could be invented, but this one at least suggests the notion that there is something of a semi-permanent nature in the managerial system. Now we can in a new way identify what is controlled. Managers control adherence to the objectives, plans, policies, organizational structure, procedures, and so forth, which have been laid down. In brief, managers control adherence to a predetermined 'framework of management.'

Now we can turn to the very important question that must be answered: "Who should act?"

It has become almost axiomatic as a management principle (which is unfortunately not always given effect in practise) that that person should act who is responsible for the results. 'Results' has to be interpreted here in a broad sense. For results include not only profits and costs—obvious items—but the conformity of all operations with all standards. Hence, whoever had responsibility for specifying and establishing a particular standard has to be ultimately responsible for controlling adherence to it and responsible, therefore, for such corrective action as is necessary. Of course, those below him in the chain of command may help him, but they cannot relieve him of final responsibility for control. Therefore, authority for managers to establish standards should be delegated as far down in the organization as practical wisdom permits. It then becomes their responsibility to control adherence of operations to the system they establish.

It is not only a responsibility, but a right; and it is asking for trouble to place in anyone else's hands the responsibility for controlling results in the operating manager's sphere of responsibility.

If the basis of control is information in the hands of managers, 'reporting' is elevated to a level of very considerable importance. Used here in a broad sense, 'reporting' includes special reports and routine reports; written, oral, and graphic reports; staff meetings, conferences, television screens, and any other means whereby information is transmitted to a manager as a basis for control action. Even the non-receipt of information, as where management is by exception, can be informational and imply the existence of control.

We are often told that reports should be timely and designed to meet the needs of managers. We are in a better position to appreciate this when we realize the important role that reporting plays in the control function. Certainly if it is to be the basis for control, information should be assembled with that objective in view. It should exclude material extraneous to the problem of control and must be placed at the disposal of managers quickly so that operations do not deviate any further from the desired norm—or for a longer period—than can be avoided.

That control occurs after the fact is a point that sometimes troubles managers. It should not —since this is simply part of the nature of the concept. The situation is entirely comparable in the process control system described earlier. In that system the detecting device continuously evaluates results and transmits them back to the control mechanism, which, sensing the difference between the actual and the desired results, acts to restore results to the desired value. The results, just as in management control, precede the exercise of control. Control systems, human or mechanical, deal with transfers of energy and a transfer of energy takes time. We learn from this—and it underscores the importance of speed in reporting—that all we can do for the management problem is to minimize the time lag between results and action.

CONTROL SPECTRUM

There is another sometimes troublesome aspect of control, namely, that control over some things must be relinquished as successively higher echelons of management are reached. This again we must simply face. Managers in the first echelon require certain information as their basis for controlling. But in the next higher echelon, the character of required information changes; some information is dropped, some is added. There is thus a kind of 'control spectrum.' For the process of fading out and shading in of information is continued as you move up the pyramid until, just as in the visible spectrum the colors at one end are wholly unlike those at the other, the information reported to the top is wholly different from the information reported to first line managers.

This would hardly be worth pointing out except that some managers are burdened with a persistent sense of insecurity which undermines their self-confidence and ability to do the job, because they are unable to keep track of all the details under their management. Of course, they should not be able to keep track of all the results, or more accurately, should not allow themselves to do so. Relinquishing control over some operations is a calculated risk, taken so that managers can assume more important tasks.

It will bear mentioning that information serves other purposes than as the basis for control. The notion of a 'framework of management,' which we suggested earlier, is helpful in describing one of these purposes. This 'framework,' we said, is constantly undergoing change in one or another of its aspects. Such change takes place, not accidentally, but following conscious decisions for change by those responsible for such decisions. And decisions for changes in the framework are based on information that is conceptually different from information used for controlling adherence to the framework.

WHERE FORECASTS FIT

Forecasts and projections, for example, have no place in the problem of control (since control is after-the-fact while forecasts are before) but they are very important for setting objectives and formulating plans. Of course, information for aiming and for planning does not have to be before-the-fact. It may be an after-the-fact analysis proving that a certain policy has been impolitic in its effect on the relations of the company with customer, employee, or stockholder; or that a certain plan is no longer practical; or that a certain procedure is unworkable. The prescription here certainly would not be 'control' (since in these cases control would simply bring operations into conformity with obsolete standards), but the establishment of new standards—a new policy, a new plan, and a new procedure—to be controlled to.

Besides furnishing evidence of a need for reconstructing the managerial framework, information is, of course, the basis of all communication. But since that subject is one of the most discussed in the management field to-day, there is no need to discuss it further here.

Control, we have seen, means something quite specific in the managerial art. This is certainly as it should be in an area of thought as well developed as business management. For in any field for which theory has been developed to an appreciable extent, terms should be precise and unambiguous. Control, when used in a management context, should mean one thing and one thing only. I have suggested that it means action directed toward bringing operations into conformity with pre-determined standards and goals; that it is exercised by managers; and that its basis is information in their hands after-the-fact.

In addition to being a specific part of managing, control is also, quite evidently, an extremely important part of managing. In organizations, therefore, where the responsibility for control is not placed in the hands of managers, or not accepted by them, difficulties are certain to arise. Managers must control. Staff members of the organization may, by furnishing information, help a manager discharge this responsibility, but may not share in it. Where this philosophy is adopted by top management as the policy of the organization, the probability is enhanced that the energies of the organization will be channeled in fruitful directions.

TERMINOLOGY

Control is admittedly a term with emotional connotations. The denotation of the term, however, suffers from no such objection. Control is not supervision. Experienced managers perceive that as their authority is broadened, their superiors must place increased reliance on control as a means of safeguarding their own accountability. But at the same time, supervision of their activities by superiors becomes less close. There seems every reason to believe, therefore, that as the real nature of control becomes better understood, managers will come to recognize that their being subject to it in increasing measure is as sure a sign as any of their progress in the organization and in the fulfillment of their position.

Managerial Control

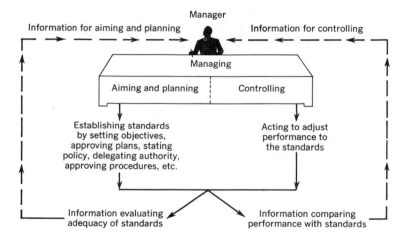

64

*Control Means Action**

ARNOLD F. EMCH

In today's competitive economy there is a tremendous premium on initiative in management. Although intelligent policy making and planning are, as always, of decisive importance, top-level planners feel more dependent than ever on those "centers of initiative" down the line. Many companies have greatly increased in size; more important, new techniques, processes, and products are changing industry patterns. Unless the management organization is alert and alive to these changing conditions, the most intelligent efforts of top planners may be futile in the face of shrewd competitors exploiting new ideas and approaches.

How does the concept of "control" fit into this picture, particularly with respect to the problem of initiative on the part of executives who are charged with the responsibility of getting things done? Is control a boon or a barrier to initiative? This question is widening a four-way split of executive opinion in industry as well as in governmental and nonprofit enterprise. One group is unqualifiedly for something or other they call "control"; a second group looks on the whole business with a jaundiced eye; a third group finds itself uncomfortably in the middle with the feeling that there is something wrong with each of the extreme points of view; and a fourth group subscribes to the functional concept that will be presented in the following pages.

In this article I shall examine the practical consequences of these different approaches, highlighting some of the abuses and the misconceptions of control as well as suggesting ways of establishing effective control in management. The following points, among others, will be discussed:

- The "Captain Queeg" approach to management—with its excessive, detailed, and of-

* Reprinted by permission of the publisher from *Harvard Business Review*, vol. 32, no. 4, pp. 92–98, July–August, 1954. Mr. Emch is a partner in the management consulting firm of Booz, Allen & Hamilton.

ten useless control measures—is ineffectual as well as highly repugnant to red-blooded executives.

- The "Will Rogers" top executive—the antithesis of Captain Queeg—usually finds himself engaged in a weird performance of subterfuge as he tries to run his business with some semblance of order and direction without recognizing or acknowledging that it is a "controlled" situation.

- A common mistake is to treat control systems and plans of organization independently of each other. Control must not only provide measures for adequate planning and for performance evaluation, but also stimulate initiative on the part of executives and employees.

- The controller should not try to control in the sense of encroaching on the authority of those who have been charged with the responsibility of getting something done.

- Planning and budgeting are only devices to assure correlated and consistent actions in the future.

- Control techniques can be better understood and applied if control is equated with action. And action should be taken only by those having authority and responsibility for the activities which are affected.

- Information can be tailored effectively to executive needs for taking imaginative action by following certain definite criteria (which will be spelled out). Neither a famine nor a surplus of data is necessary.

INEFFECTIVENESS AT THE TOP

The bewildering difference of opinion and practice in this area makes no sense at all until we remember that control—perhaps more than any other major management function—reflects the personalities and attitudes of those at the top. Let us see what some of these executives look like.

Captain Queeg: Excessive Control   At one extreme is the Captain Queeg type of *Caine Mutiny* fame, who insists on the letter of the law to such an extent that war can rage all around him while he is trying to find out who ate the quart of strawberries. From this standpoint of management, what was the matter with Captain Queeg? Two things—one psychological, the other methodological.

As Herman Wouk, the author of the book, painted him, Captain Queeg was fundamentally so insecure and suspicious that he had to know every last detail of what every last tar aboard the U.S.S. *Caine* was doing in order to protect himself and to assure himself that all policies, rules, and regulations of the Navy were observed down to the last minutia. What he forgot in this preoccupation with detail was (a) that he and his kind might lose the war, and (b) that he was stifling all initiative, interest, and enthusiasm on the part of his men. In short, he was, through his interpretation of control, forgetting the strategic objectives of the war and, at the same time, creating a serious morale problem in his crew.

The situation on Captain Queeg's ship was a typical example of the stultifying effect of rigidly confining strait-jacket "control procedures" on the imagination and intellect of men. In the words of Keefer, one of the principals of the story, it was a situation in which "the work has been fragmentized by a few excellent brains at the top, on the assumption that near-morons will be responsible for each fragment."

In business this type of control does not of course bring about mutiny in the usual sense. What it does instead is to create (a) an undertone of frustration and a sense of futility; (b) a pattern of alibis, truth-slantings, and downright dishonesty; (c) outright conflicts among executives, due to exercise of control by some who have no corresponding responsibility for action; (d) a gradual diminution of the use of initiative and judgment to the point where executives are absorbed in clerical detail and meticulous line-by-line paper-pushing practices; and (e) an increase in executive turnover as a result of the more intelligent and courageous personnel looking elsewhere for a more favorable condition for the exercise of their real talents.

I have cited a fictitious character as an example; but actually, in business, government, and nonprofit enterprises, there are literally hundreds of Captain Queeg's counterparts. These men build up a system of control that in the end defeats the purposes for which it was originally intended. The paper, the personnel, the money, and the time expended on forms, reports, manuals, bulletins, and statistics in support of these misbegotten control systems are enough to stagger the most eager imagination. As pointed out in the *ACME Reporter* (bulletin of the Association of Consulting Management Engineers):

> It often develops to the point where mere following of procedures becomes more important than carrying out policies and striving toward objectives. The result is a creeping, self-propagating bureaucracy.

Do these burdensome control systems ever accomplish their original purpose? Do they not have some merit? All I can say is that in my experience as a management consultant to different kinds of businesses over the past 20 years, I have never seen such a setup or such an operation pay off.

Quite the contrary! I have found all the shortcomings of the usual dictatorial and all-embracing regime, including the inevitably weak, insecure, or overambitious executive at the top; mountains of forms, reports, manuals, directives, and interpretative bulletins which nobody reads or which, if they are read, require special staffs to pore over them to keep executives abreast; bad morale in the second and third layers of management; and, believe it or not, usually poor planning and lack of significant management information when and where it is needed—the very things you would think *could* be accomplished by these immense, involved, and demanding systems of control.

Will Rogers: Insufficient Control   Now let us look at Captain Queeg's opposite, the executive who is pretty sure of himself and who inclines to be a "good egg" with democratic impulses. He does not like control and he does not want any part of it. It is repugnant to him. His philosophy of management is to shove his men off the dock and make them swim. That is the way they can learn best. "Sure, they'll make mistakes," he says with a confident, genial grin; "that's good for them; that's the way they'll learn the facts of life." His is the freedom-of-enterprise point of view in the extreme.

But despite his rodeo-bronco-swim-for-your-life approach to management, this Will Rogers sooner or later will want to know where his business is going and how well it is doing on its way. Instead of having a "controller" in any usual sense—this of course he would not tolerate—he sets out to find himself a bright, young, likable, willing fellow, and without much ado appoints him "assistant to the president."

There are all kinds of things that Mr. Rogers will want to know—usually pronto—and no ready information will be available to supply this need. So he will call in his assistant, throw him the ball without concern or premeditation, and let it go at that.

It takes no genius to figure out what this apparently simple practice will lead to. The assistant is eager, able, and willing; and he goes about these repeated assignments with energy and dispatch. It does not take long for him to realize that he does not have certain formation at hand. He begins to build up a little system all his own. His desk drawers and filing cases fill up with special data. He takes an increasing interest in the budget and begins to question department heads as to the justification of certain items. He even has misgivings on just how he ought to go about getting some of the information that he knows he will eventually need.

But the rest of the staff soon comes to realize that, although the newcomer is only the assistant to the president whereas they are vice presidents or managers, this young fellow has the ear of the boss and is beginning to analyze things and increasingly make judgments for the president. Perhaps they had better play ball with the young man, they think, if they are to stay in the good graces of Mr. Rogers. And so it goes. A roundabout way of control is devised —never direct, never through channels, never through organization objectives, or policies, or clear-cut statements of basic procedure. Nobody quite knows any more what he should or should not do, but everyone is quite certain that "cooperation" with the assistant is the order of the day.

FUNCTIONAL CONTROL

Now what is the matter with all this? What is the matter with Captain Queeg's or Mr. Rogers' approach to control? It boils down to this: Each approach shows a complete lack of understanding or appreciation of what control is trying to accomplish in an enterprise, and of how to get executives to assume and carry out effectively their proper responsibilities. Put very simply, there can be too much control and there can be too little control; in both cases there is a misunderstanding or a corruption of control in the necessary and sound sense.

Let us look at it in another way. What is the problem we are dealing with when we talk of "control"? Actually it is simple: We have a job to do—a line of services or products to make and sell at a profit. There are a number of persons involved in the doing of that job. Hence we organize ourselves in some fashion so that each one of us has specific, assigned tasks, all more or less related to one another. And we try to see that each key individual has a clear understanding of his functions, of his lines of authority downward, and of his line of responsibility upward.

But if we should go only this far, we would not go far enough. We must also determine what each of these individuals needs in the way of facts and figures in order to perform his job effectively. This, then, is the problem of control: to match the responsibilities of every key position with the management information necessary for the effective and efficient execution of those responsibilities. Control itself can be defined as the making of decisions and taking of actions required by the responsibilities of each position, i.e., the proper performance of each executive according to the requirements of his position.

Now, some readers may object to this concept on the ground that it does not even mention the familiar rudiments of control, traditionally conceived. You may be prompted to say: "Control means making sure that actual results conform to desired results, and this involves three basic functions: (a) setting standards of satisfactory performance; (b) checking results to see how they compare with the standards; and (c) taking corrective action where actual results do not meet the standards."

I have no quarrel with this concept, except that these functions ought to be, and in fact must be, built *into* the organization structure as part and parcel of the responsibilities and authorities of every key position. They should not be segregated and put on a list of functions under the heading "control."

This brings us to the basic flaw of most control systems as well as of most plans of organization. Control and organization have generally been treated independently of each other, thus missing the point of how the organization is to work in practice, or of what the executives are trying to control in the operations. Actually organization and control are inseparable when there is effective management; they cannot function properly without each other.

How many times have you pored over an organization plan only to find yourself saying: "In general I think it is good, but how do I do this particular job; how can I carry out the responsibilities entrusted to me?" The answer here to a very large extent is in the informational and control system that is established. What are the "management dials" necessary for you to do your job? What are the significant management factors you should have before you in order to make executive judgment, and what is it you do when certain things take place? Do you know what you should do, and why, and what are the probable consequences of your decisions?

This is the problem of control in every executive position in the enterprise, up and down the various levels in the organization. In short, the answer to the effective operation of the plan of organization is primarily through a system of control which is part and parcel of it.

An effective system of control, in turn, depends on the plan of organization. If you tried to look at your control problem without considering the plan of organization, you would soon find yourself asking, "Who gives me this information? Why do I get it? What do I do with it?" Obviously you could not answer until you knew who was responsible for what in the scheme of things—in other words, the organization again.

Relating control to the specific responsibilities and authorities of each executive position is what I have chosen to call "functional control." In this sense control is an integral element of every function in the organization, and every function will then be truly under control.

RULES AND GUIDES

If management accepts the concept of control just described, it will find that a number of challenging corollaries follow in consequence. I should like to discuss them now, with particular attention to their implications for the everyday realities of company operations.

Controllers Don't Control   First, the new concept of control will require some reorientation in the traditional or prevailing practices and tendencies of controllers or control offices. It will require recognition of the fact that a controller does not actually control, and that any effort on his part to take over the function of control from the operating personnel will lead inevitably to the abuses and misunderstandings I have already mentioned.

The word "control" itself has no doubt led to the misconception that the control function of an enterprise is a highly centralized activity in the office of a controller; that management reports, statistics, and information generally are not only collected by the controller but are also specifically for his use; and, finally, that he has the authority to bring about executive actions throughout the organization without assuming corresponding responsibility for those actions.

Nothing of course could be farther from the application of effective control in a well-managed enterprise. Although the controller is or should be a major executive at the same level as the other divisional executives of an enterprise, and hence is or should be a part of the top-management team, it should be noted that, apart from his usual departmental activities such as keeping records, paying bills, receiving cash, preparing invoices, maintaining the office and routine accounting, he has no direct operating responsibilities.

In fact, the more important and delicate tasks the controller must perform have to do with advising the president and other executives on the broad, over-all picture of the enterprise; coordinating basic plans and budgets; preparing and issuing special control reports; and standardizing methods of accounting and other procedures. Note the predominantly *informational* character of each of these responsibilities.

Let me illustrate what can happen when this is forgotten and the controller is allowed to get out of hand.

I recall the case of a large city administration which had the usual bureau of the budget with a controller in charge. The extent to which the powers of this office had been stretched to make decisions or to stop decisions in the actual operations of the various city departments was beyond belief. No powers of a foreign monarchy were ever exercised with greater authoritarian finality.

Yet the end result scarcely justified the appellation "control." Instead there were phony figures, tampered statistics, and endless ingenious manipulations on the part of department and division heads in order to accomplish some degree of operating effectiveness within the restrictive patterns and requirements of the controller—and in order to conceal the true facts from the authorities above. The result was more nearly the *opposite* of control!

Here, for example, is what happened when the controller decreed that new personnel for a newly constructed establishment would have to be employed at the lowest end of the salary ranges. (Staffing patterns had been worked out for various types of city establishments, with the usual minimum-maximum salary ranges for each kind of position.) The operating heads soon found that they could not employ this lower and inexperienced level of talent and expect any degree of competence in running the new plant. Appeals to the controller were of no avail.

So they embarked on a weird set of thimble-rigging operations, whereby they hired employees for the new plant at the lowest level decreed by the controller and forthwith began to distribute these to various other installations, and in turn quietly "loaned" some of the more experienced and competent personnel from these other installations to the new plant to get it under way.

Of course the records and the statistics and the payrolls never reflected what went on, and the subsequent budgets and staffing patterns were continued year after year without ever revealing the true state of affairs. The budget actually turned out to be a device for the concealment of the facts.

The operating personnel chuckled with cynical satisfaction; the controller's pride and vanity were assuaged through "compliance" with his rules and regulations; the files of the bureau of the budget were replete with dubious reports, figures, and statistics. But there was no real, honest, or effective control in the best sense of modern management.

If, instead of these attitudes and practices, the controller had been motivated by a deep sense of service and had realized that most of what he did had value only insofar as it was *helpful* to someone else in doing his job, there would have been a much more effective and efficient operation.

Lest executives in business react to this example from government by thinking, "It can't happen here," let me add that, in my observation at least, it *does* happen in industry—and oftener than we think! In fact, many of those unexciting profit statements that are being written today are a direct result.

Planning Is the Basis   The misuse of the control function has far-reaching consequences in the planning and budgeting process. The budget is a primary means of assuring that actions conform to basic plans. It is a device for measuring the actions taken and for determining the actions required. But it does not, *of itself,* control.

Almost as important as the budget itself is the planning of the operation that is finally translated into the budget. In the planning phase, as we all know, actions are proposed, opposing points of view are resolved, and a consistent course of action is set. Conditions expected are appraised, and proposed actions to meet these conditions are devised. To the extent that planning determines the actions that need to be taken and stimulates thinking ahead about those actions, it is a most effective basis for control—but, again, it is not control itself.

Thus, plans and budgets together provide a picture, in common related terms, of what is intended and expected and the means by which

the goals are to be achieved. They provide a means for reporting back the progress made against the goals, and a general framework for new decisions and actions in an integrated pattern of development. A good example of a planning and budgeting basis for control is provided by the postwar experience of a company that was producing large, expensive precision equipment.

The management of this company decided to prepare a report called a "production forecast." It was based on an estimate of sales and was adjusted for both engineering and manufacturing loads. When finally approved by the executive committee, it became an 18-month plan which was to be adjusted periodically in accordance with manufacturing lead times and in terms of what the company expected to make (the rate and volume of production).

The plan was eminently successful and, even to this day, is eagerly awaited each quarter by all operating executives, since it has become the basis for many decisions throughout the company. From it can be calculated such figures as number of direct workers required, number of workers needed in service areas (payroll and accounting), adjustments in the level of inventory, and adjustments in purchasing loads and selling programs.

Prior to adoption of this plan the company was continually faced with unexplained increases in inventories, with serious imbalances between number of production workers and actual requirements, and with the sales department and the manufacturing department working at cross purposes. For instance, it was found that the sales department was selling custom designs for delivery at times when the manufacturing department was unable to produce even its normal load of standard lines.

Properly conceived and used, such plans and budgets can become important elements in implementing effective control. Rather than impeding judgment, they should contribute to initiative in avoiding undesirable conditions and in meeting such conditions when they do arise.

Action Is the Essence   Control is being exercised when the operations of the enterprise are guided within the plans adopted, are held in line in the face of varying conditions, or are returned to an in-line state after deviations are located. Note that action is implied in each case. This is important. In a very real sense, control means action—action to correct a condition found to be in error, or action to prevent such a condition from arising—and is never achieved without having action as an essential step.

Thus, in the case of the precision equipment company whose planning procedure was just described, control was actually achieved through a series of specific steps taken by the various department heads acting in response to the production forecast:

1. Idle workers, approximating 10% of the total number, were reassigned to other areas.

2. Personnel requirements in all service and staff areas were recalculated.

3. Personnel were added in the sales area in order to step up sales effort.

4. Order points and ordering quantities on two major product lines were reset.

5. Deliveries on open orders with vendors were extended.

6. For the near future, purchasing requirements were frozen at minimum levels.

7. Sufficient cause was found to re-examine the company's entire inventory, which resulted in scrapping $500,000 in materials and using materials on hand in lieu of ordering new materials.

Note that management had first made a cooperative planning and budgeting effort; then came control in the form of action.

Delegation Is the Key   But control action can be taken only by the individual executives who hold delegated responsibility and authority for the operations affected. Certainly it makes little sense to assign someone the "responsibility" for a specific operation; set the achievement of certain results as a goal; and then, through a series of denials, restrictions, limitations, specifications, and decisions, allow him no initiative.

In such instances, the wise, loyal, and experienced executive will try to conform and to achieve the desired results. If he succeeds, it will probably be because of his own ingenuity, patience, flexibility, and doggedness, rather than because of any superimposed decisions coming from above. If he fails, however, there is a real question of accountability, since many of the decisions and actions will have been precipitated by others not directly responsible for the operation. This of course is a perfect setting for alibis and for passing the buck when the going gets rough; someone has to be the scapegoat for miscalculations or poor performance.

To sum up, merely discovering out-of-line conditions, or having detailed information

about a situation, does not achieve control. Control is exercised by taking action, and action must be taken within the authority delegated. And just as no person can be said to control directly the activities assigned to another's jurisdiction, so the only person who can directly control activities is the one directly responsible for them. This is fundamental to the healthy and successful operation of any enterprise; at the same time it is probably one of the least observed principles of management. There are a great many more instances of its violation than there are of its wholehearted acceptance and practice.

Information Is the Guide   Now we can see more clearly where information, such as provided by the controller, fits into the picture. Many enterprises have grown beyond the size where they can be managed by decisions arrived at through direct observation alone. So there must be control; and control requires a system of information tailored to the specific management needs of every key executive— information that is *timely* and *adequate*.

Let us take the timeliness factor first. While information *as such* does not control, it is needed by executives as a guide to actions which do control. Because they overlook this, controllers frequently miss the mark in being of real service to operating personnel. In general, they submit too many historical reports which merely relate what has taken place. Management would rather have approximate information that is prompt than highly accurate information after it is too late to be of value in decision making.

Turning now to the second factor, what is the criterion of "adequate" information? What *kind* of information is adequate, and how *much*? Frequently controllers solve this problem by giving the line executives everything there is to know—by virtually swamping them in facts and figures. But the effect of too much is likely to be almost as bad as too little or too late.

A system of control should require no more than is absolutely necessary in the way of reports, data, and statistics. The determination of what is "necessary" should conform to this simple dictum: In accord with your responsibilities and authority, can you or should you do anything about the information that is presented to you and, if so, what? This is the final criterion of management or control information. If you can do nothing about the material that is presented, then it is purely informative and not strictly necessary for you for management purposes.

For example, I recall the instance of a very successful insurance company whose president was far ahead of most chief executives in wanting to renovate the company operations and to introduce modern management practices. He was completely sold on the idea of decentralization, with a small central headquarters and a top policy and planning level.

But in his attempt to supply the necessary information to all key executives throughout the country, he embarked on a colossal and expensive statistical program that included computations on all manner of items. He distributed this information routinely and at frequent, regular intervals to all concerned. There was a thick, 18-inch by 30-inch book of these tabulations, statistics, and data on the desk of every executive throughout the land. It was so voluminous that each executive had to have an assistant or "analyst" who devoted himself almost exclusively to the problem of keeping up with the most recent data supplied. It became a byword in the company that "wherever there is an executive, you will also find an analyst."

The data were there in generous quantity, and the figures were accurately reported and fairly up to date. But it was standard information for all alike. What was missing was the specific bit of significant management information that each key executive needed in order to watch and control his own particular operation or department. What each of these executives could use to advantage might have been put on one page, but what they got instead was 200 large pages of involved, mechanically tabulated statistics which were largely academic and irrelevant from the point of view of any given executive.

Every key position in an enterprise is or should be related to some objective or set of objectives. These, in turn, should be translated into specific goals for specific calendar periods. The executive in charge of any operation or department, in order to achieve these specific goals within certain time limits, should have before him specific performance data—"management dials"—so he can know how well his operation is progressing and, if significantly out of line, what he individually must do to correct the situation.

CONCLUSION

What is needed is an understanding that the functions of planning and performance evaluation are part and parcel of the entire organization, and must therefore be distributed to each and every appropriate level of responsibility—instead of being concentrated in a highly centralized office that usually carries the name of "the controller." Every key executive, in fulfilling his responsibilities, is or should be his own "controller." In this sense, control can be as much an energizing as a steering function. So conceived it should no longer be a barrier but a tremendous boon to initiative.

If controllers, in turn, will recognize that real control is achieved only through actions taken by executives other than themselves, they will be well on the way to realizing that theirs is basically a service to render and that, however difficult this role, its sole value is to assist the key executives in the proper performance of their functions. A very wise man once said: "Control is primarily a state of mind." Let us make certain that it is a *healthy* state of mind.

Business Reports:
How to Get Facts You Need*

PHILIP GUSTAFSON

New and dynamic forms of management control are being worked out and applied today throughout the business world.

As business becomes increasingly decentralized and complex, more and more does today's executive need a sensitive instrument panel to keep from flying blind, to see what's going on and whether people are doing what they're supposed to be doing.

Today's instrument panel is management control, and this is a highlight report on what some of the leaders are doing in the field.

Control is bound up with planning and, taken together, the process consists essentially of three basic steps:

1. Deciding in advance what should be accomplished and what will constitute good performance. These decisions frequently take the form of budgets, cost standards, operating programs and the like.

2. Finding out actual performance, then measuring and evaluating it.

3. Taking corrective action.

There are many ways to check actual performance. A few of the commonest include direct observation by a line supervisor, consultation through informal contacts with subordinates, regular operations or financial audits, special investigations or analyses and the formal management control report, which is the most commonly used type of control in medium to large-scale business organizations.

All of these forms of control are used in the average business today. However, as business has grown in size and complexity, informal and intermittent methods of keeping in touch with

what's going on, such as personal contact, have diminished in value. The method of growing importance in large-scale business is the written or graphic management report. This is today's instrument panel.

A growing number of managements, however, are finding that the instrument panel in the front office hasn't kept pace with the complex instrumentation they have built into the factories. Thus, many companies are overhauling their formal reports—statistical, accounting, narrative and graphic. A survey of what some of these companies are doing has produced the following guides.

1. GIVE STANDARDS FOR COMPARISON

Since the object of control is to see that everything is carried out according to decisions already made, every control report should facilitate the evaluation of actual results by comparing them with what they should have been.

"Your report must have built-in standards as a basis of comparison," says Paul Hamman, partner in Touche, Niven, Bailey and Smart, Certified Public Accountants, of Detroit, Mich.

"One manufacturing company used to get out a report on scrap losses that was a horrible example of what not to do. In the first place it had no basis of comparison.

"The vice president wanted to know 'Is one per cent of the material going through, or 10 per cent?' He wanted an area of tolerance, let's say below three per cent. If they got out of this area, he wanted to raise Cain. As it was, he was left without a bogey."

Since control can be exercised only by people, management control reports must follow the structure of the organization and be set up by individual responsibilities.

* Reprinted by permission of the publisher and author from *Nation's Business*, vol. 44, no. 8, pp. 78–82, August, 1956. Mr. Gustafson is now a professional journalist and was a public relations consultant in New York.

"Operating reports rest on a cornerstone of well-defined responsibility," says Mr. Hamman. "You must give a man a goal and then measure his progress against this goal."

2. POINT OUT DANGER AREAS

A good report focuses attention on matters requiring action by accenting the significant trends or out-of-line performance. This is known as reporting by exception. Such reports highlight the exceptions which require management attention. You want your reports to tell you:

What is good?

What is bad?

Who is responsible?

The man making the report should report on the pertinent areas of his own responsibility. The recipient should be able to tell where he should go for more information if he wants it.

3. BE TIMELY

Reports should be issued promptly and at appropriate intervals. Operating information is perishable and must be made available in sufficient time for necessary action. Besides, the report must reflect current operating conditions.

4. COVER CRITICAL AREAS

"There are two major areas of need that are not covered by the structure of management reports that exist in most companies today," says Richard Neuschel of McKinsey and Company, management consultants. "The first of these includes those elements of performance that can be expressed quantitatively but which are not covered by the accounting system nor by budgets or standard costs. These might include such factors as facilities utilization, customer turnover, market penetration, delivery performance and the like.

"Second, there is a need for some kind of reporting on elements of performance that cannot be expressed either quantitatively or in terms of contribution to short-term profits. This category includes practically all important performance factors comprising such functions as engineering, research and development, industrial relations, controllership, etc."

"The structure of formal management reports in many companies today is a pretty sorry thing," Mr. Neuschel adds. "The typical approach to improving the reports has three basic weaknesses:

"It is self-limiting because it ties the mind to the make-up of existing reports.

"It provides no reasoned basis for determining what information is needed. The principal criteria for cutting or keeping existing reports are personal preference and preconceptions.

"It is not dynamic. It does not go deeply enough in trying to rebuild the structure of management information into a real profit-making tool. It is a negative approach aimed primarily at cutting office expense through the elimination of unnecessary or duplicate information.

"Furthermore, no system of management control or of management reports is anywhere near complete if it is limited to the elements of performance covered by the accounting system —that is, income, cost and expense . . . those elements which have a direct and measurable effect on short-term profits."

5. AIM FOR SIMPLICITY

"A lot of companies don't realize how old fashioned their top management reports have become," says Mr. Hamman. "The reports of most companies have the atmosphere of the middle '20's. One company used a page full of close-packed figures that looked like a bookkeeper's summary of the year's work. It was a transcription of a bookkeeper talking to himself.

"The company directors couldn't have been helped less if a bushel basket full of figures had been poured out on the table in front of them."

"One of the big problems is that posed by electronics equipment," says another consultant. "We've gone through an era of office mechanization and automation to such an extent that the capacity to produce management information has outstripped the capacity to assimilate it and use it intelligently in running the business."

6. CLARITY IS ESSENTIAL

Make sure your reports are easy for a non-figure-minded executive to understand and use. Few top management executives today come up through the accounting department, though most reports are prepared as if they did.

The real object of reports is to get them used. If they are not in a form in which they can be used, they're no good. They simply lie around. The report should not only be expressed in the language of the report user but it should report only the essential facts so the reader can learn the whole story without becoming confused.

A good report should have eye appeal. Eye appeal requires that the report should be readable, with information organized to lead the eye through a well-aligned format rather than through a labyrinth of words and figures.

Graphs, charts and other visual presentation techniques are becoming increasingly popular in business.

"We design a report not to be read," says one consultant. "We don't want the reader wasting time reading reports. We want him just to look at the paper and say, 'Here's what I wanted to know'—then not have to read any farther. The real test is whether a stranger to the business can read a report effectively."

7. FOCUS ON THE FUTURE

"Management reports should include a liberal number of predictions and predictors rather than aim solely at a meticulous reporting of historical data," says Mr. Hamman. "Indicated trends are far more useful to management than determination of so-called exact profits for a short-time period."

8. INTEGRATE YOUR REPORT SYSTEM

Instead of being a coherent, understandable whole, a report structure often tends to be a hodgepodge of unrelated bits and pieces—some overlapping, or conflicting, some clear, some confusing. It is not difficult to see why this condition develops. In most companies, the structure of management information is neither the product of one mind nor one time. Its parts are seldom developed according to any conceptual scheme. Each came into being without any thought as to how that part related to the whole.

The report structure as a whole should represent an integrated plan of control under which the information given to all levels of management is tied together and simply becomes more condensed as higher levels of management are reached.

This means that the reporting system must have unity. One should be able to follow logically step by step from one report to another and from summary to supplementary or subsidiary reports.

A well-designed structure of reports should:

1. Provide each executive with the planning information necessary to make the decisions for which he is responsible.

2. Provide each executive with the control information necessary to relate performance with the planned goals covering the activities for which he is responsible.

A number of progressive corporations, usually those with facilities spread throughout the country, have worked out highly successful systems of management reporting.

Two of these are taken up here in detail.

The Du Pont System   The whole structure of top management information at E. I. du Pont de Nemours & Company, Inc., is based on graphic presentation. It is centered around the chart room, an amphitheater on the ninth floor of the company's offices at Wilmington, Del. The charts are mounted on 30 by 40 inch metal frames suspended by wheels from an overhead network of trolleys, specially designed and constructed so that, in a matter of seconds, any series can be brought to a central display room for review. There are more than 400 of these charts and they carry a running account of the operations of Du Pont's 10 manufacturing departments and of the company as a whole. This is the nerve center of the business.

When an executive at Wilmington wants to review any division, he comes to the chartroom and says,

"I want the facts of life about X Department."

A member of a special reports and charting staff from the treasurer's department, constantly at work on these reports, brings him the information he wants.

The Du Pont company believes that effective reporting of internal data is fully as important to the company as good public reporting. Its chart system was conceived as a means of enabling the company financial staff to report to executive management the financial results of an operation in a manner at once simple and yet complete. The basic concept emphasizes return on investment and the factors contributing to it.

Return on investment is shown on the charts as the financial end result of operations; it is the product of two percentages—turnover multiplied by earnings as per cent of sales. Turnover is obtained by dividing sales by total investment; it reflects the rapidity with which plant and working capital is being employed. The separate effects of these two percentages on return on investment may be determined through an analysis of charts showing sales, elements of cost of sales, earnings and the details of plant inventories, accounts receivable and cash.

The principal advantage of the chart system is to point up immediately the places where further analysis, review and attention may be desirable or necessary. The charts are intended to show what happened in terms of profit return on investment, and to put the finger on the broad underlying factors which caused the results to be what they were. They do not displace the customary financial statements such as forecasts, budgets or historical reports.

On the fourth Wednesday of each month, the executive committee reviews the operations of a group of departments, so that each department averages about four reviews a year.

A member of Du Pont's treasurer's department presides at the session, moving each chart or series of charts in place before the executive committee. He is prepared to give background reasons for normal variations in current data against past performance or against forecasts.

If an unusual variation shows up, however, the general manager of the department under review is on hand to explain, and the reason is traced back to its source through the chart system.

The charts used for review by the executive committee in general show the results of departmental operations for the current year against a background of exactly the same data for the ten preceding years and a forecast for the next 12 months.

Similar chart series are employed to some extent by all levels of departmental management. The company has a thoroughly developed method for following up on one-shot decisions. It has, for example, a hard-headed system for following up on capital expenditure results.

Each one of the major departments, when seeking to expand, must submit to the executive committee an appropriation request spelling out the facility it wants to build, then give a complete long-term evaluation on:

Anticipated sales volume

Price projections

Competitive outlook

Profit prospects

Prospects for return on investment

After the authorized facility has been in operation one year, the general manager submits a "Report of Accomplishment," which is a statement of actual sales volume and earnings contrasted with expectations at the time the appropriation request was initiated.

If the over-all picture is not entirely favorable, the executive committee may request another accomplishment report at the end of the second year.

Sometimes the series of reports for a particular project is continued for three or four years. Meanwhile, the departmental management gets interim reports more frequently.

Such reporting has become so much a part of the procedure that it's part of the thinking and working habits of the people who do it.

Plans for the Du Pont people are something to be carried out, not predictions of probability. For them, good planning plus good follow-up equals a programmed decision.

This process of follow-up, company executives say, has forced people to be a lot more hard-headed and realistic in the estimates on which they base their decisions. They know they are going to be followed up. Also, it forces them to be more realistic in programming their efforts to make sure the results are going to be achieved.

Decision-making and planning complement each other. The better the plan, the more effective the control—the more realistic the goals.

The United Airlines System One of the fastest and most dynamic reporting systems in business is operated by United Airlines with the aid of electronic machines. It produces a profit and loss statement which is laid on the desk of President W. A. Patterson in Chicago every 24 hours.

The statement has its birth every day in the statistical production room at United's Denver operating base. Passenger and cargo volumes, collected from each flight, are combined at the end of the day. The results are wired to United's Chicago offices ready for processing at 8:30 A.M. Economic research employees apply revenue rates predetermined by experience and expense rates based on current operating budget requirements to the previous day's volume appearing on the wire. Within an hour, an operating profit or loss is estimated and passed on to top management.

The daily report shows the day's operating profit or loss along with a month and year to date accumulation. Also, daily revenue passenger miles and the passenger load factor are given. Data are broken down in such a way as to give the passenger department information on which to decide whether to put more planes on the Chicago to San Francisco run or advertise to get additional passengers.

An intrinsic part of United's reporting system is what company executives like to call "the room with the 14,000-mile view." This is an information and planning center at Denver which is the business world's equivalent of the military briefing room. Facts funneled daily into this center present a clear picture of operations throughout United's 80-city system.

In keeping with the idea of expansive vision,

the room has glass walls on one side. Modern white plastic chairs are grouped before a map of the United States, eight feet high and 20 feet wide, on which United's routes are outlined. Colored lights (red for weather, green for maintenance and white for passengers) at major terminals show current operating conditions. If the red light glows steadily, for example, it means adverse weather; if it is flashing, the weather is marginal. Electric clocks above the map show the time in each zone through which United operates.

The room is designed to provide management with operational facts in the most convenient form. Data, such as mileage flown, delays at terminals by type of plane and total number of departures, are posted on lucite panels, flanking the map. Dozens of supplementary charts deal with payload volumes and load factors, weather, actual performance as compared with schedule and related information.

Daily at 8:30 A.M., MST, United's operations executives meet in the room for a 14,000-mile view. Four briefing specialists review operations of the past 24 hours and outline what the next 24 are expected to bring. The opening summary is presented by a meteorologist who analyzes the decisive factors in yesterday's weather conditions from the Atlantic seaboard to the Hawaiian Islands. He then gives his forecast for the next 24 hours, accenting developments which may affect operations.

A mechanical specialist follows with information on the status of the company's fleet. He reports the number and types of aircraft withdrawn from service for overhaul and comments on the progress of various engineering projects at the San Francisco base.

A traffic specialist then gives a résumé of the previous day's performance in terms of any customer service problems which arose. Approximately 750 plane departures are scheduled daily. Those which deviate from schedule are spotlighted for management study to prevent possible recurrence.

The remaining gaps in the 14,000-mile view are filled in by a flight operations specialist who discusses the availability of equipment, and weather outlook on the line. The session then adjourns. Immediately afterwards, some department chiefs may call their staffs together to act on particular facets of the day's operating plan.

No matter how highly-developed a management report system may be, it's only as good as the action management takes. So once a good reporting system is set up and all the information is in, what does management do to improve the situation?

Here are ten possibilities, depending on conditions:

1. It supplies additional skills.
2. It provides more guidance or training to improve the ability to meet the goal.
3. It sets up a new program.
4. It obtains new finances.
5. It procures more facilities.
6. It finds a better product.
7. It supplies better incentives.
8. It replaces people not functioning properly.
9. It changes the program by which the objective is to be achieved (perhaps by adding more facilities, money, etc.).
10. Or, it might change the goal itself.

No business can be run by formula nor can any system of control replace the need for perception, vision, imagination, inventiveness, leadership or executive qualities.

66

*Management Information Crisis**

D. RONALD DANIEL

- In late 1960 a large defense contractor became concerned over a major project that was slipping badly. After 15 months costs were running far above the estimate and the job was behind schedule. A top-level executive, assigned as program manager to salvage the project, found he had no way of pinpointing what parts of the system were causing the trouble, why costs were so high, and which subcontractors were not performing.

- Recently an American electronics company revamped its organization structure. To compete more aggressively in international markets, management appointed "area managers" with operating responsibility— e.g., in Latin America, Western Europe, and the Far East. After nine months it was apparent that the new plan was not coming up to expectations. On checking with three newly created area managers, the company president heard each say, in effect:

   > In half of the countries in my area the political situation is in flux, and I can't anticipate what's going to happen next.

   > I'm still trying to find out whether our operating costs in Austria are reasonable.

   > I don't know where in South America we're making a profit.

- A small but highly successful consumer products company recently followed the lead of its larger competitors by establishing product-manager positions. Although outstanding men were placed in the new jobs, an air of general confusion soon developed, and the product managers began to show signs of frustration. After much study it became apparent that an important

cause of the trouble was that no one had determined what kind of information the product managers would need in order to perform their new functions.

In retrospect it is obvious that these three companies were plagued by a common problem: inadequate management information. The data were inadequate, not in the sense of there not being enough, but in terms of relevancy for setting objectives, for shaping alternative strategies, for making decisions, and for measuring results against planned goals.

ASSESSING THE GAP

In each company the origin of the problem lay in the gap between a static information system and a changing organization structure. This difficulty is not new or uncommon. There is hardly a major company in the United States whose plan of organization has not been changed and rechanged since World War II. And with revised structures have come new jobs, new responsibilities, new decision-making authorities, and reshaped reporting relationships. All of these factors combine to create new demands for information—information that is usually missing in existing systems. As a result, many leading companies are suffering a major information crisis—often without fully realizing it.

Far-reaching Trends   Some idea of the scope of this problem can be gained by reviewing the intensity of the three major causes of recent organization changes in American business:

Growth.   Since 1945 the Gross National Product has risen 135%. In specific industries the growth rate has been even greater. Plastic production, for example, tripled between 1948 and 1958; electronics sales nearly quadrupled in the decade from 1950 to 1960. Many individual companies have shown even more startling growth. This growth, in turn, has fostered organizational change:

* Reprinted by permission of the publisher from *Harvard Business Review*, vol. 39, no. 5, pp. 111–121, September–October, 1961. Mr. Daniel is associated with the management consulting firm of McKinsey & Co., Inc.

- Divisions have been created and decentralization has been encouraged.
- Greater precision in defining line-staff relationships has been necessitated.
- Organization structures that were once adequate for $50-million businesses have proved unworkable for $500-million enterprises.

Diversification. Merger and acquisition have accounted for the growth of many large organizations. For these companies, the task of finding, evaluating, and consummating diversification deals—and assimilating newly acquired products and businesses—has required continuous organizational adjustment. Some corporations have diversified by developing new product lines to satisfy shifting market requirements; some have used other means. But always the effect has been the same: different organization structures for parts of or perhaps for the entire enterprise.

International Operations. There has been a threefold increase in the value of United States investments abroad since World War II. Major companies that once regarded foreign markets as minor sources of incremental profits, or as markets for surplus production, now look overseas for the bulk of their future profits and growth. They are setting up manufacturing and research as well as marketing organizations in foreign countries. Consequently, we are growing used to seeing a company's "export department" evolve into the "international division," and national companies grow into world-wide enterprises.[1] All this calls for extensive modifications of organization structure.

The impact of any one of the above factors alone would be sufficient to create great change in an enterprise, but consider that in many cases at least two, and sometimes all three, have been at work. It is easy to see why so many company organization structures do become unstable and how this creates a management information problem large enough to hamper some firms and nearly paralyze others.

Linking Systems and Needs   Organization structure and information requirements are inextricably linked. In order to translate a statement of his duties into action, an executive must receive and use information. Information in this case is not just the accounting

---

[1] See Gilbert H. Clee and Alfred di Scipio, "Creating a *World* Enterprise," *Harvard Business Review,* November–December, 1959, p. 77.

system and the forms and reports it produces. It includes *all* the data and intelligence—financial and nonfinancial—that are really needed to plan, operate, and control a particular enterprise. This embraces external information such as economic and political factors and data on competitive activity.

When viewed in this light, the impact of organization structure on needs for management information becomes apparent. The trouble is that in most companies it is virtually taken for granted that the information necessary for performance of a manager's duties flows naturally to the job. To a certain extent this is so. For example, internally generated information—especially accounting information—does tend to flow easily to the job or can be made to do so. Also, in companies doing business in only one industry and having a small, closely knit management group much vital interdepartmental and general information is conveyed by frequent face-to-face contact and coordination among executives. Economic and competitive information from outside is similarly transmitted, the bulk of it coming into the concern informally. Further, through trade contacts, general reading, and occasional special studies, executives toss bits of information into the common pool and draw from it as well.

The point is, however, that while such an informal system can work well for small and medium-size companies in simple and relatively static industries, it becomes inadequate when companies grow larger and especially when they spread over several industries, areas, and countries. At this point, most large companies have found that information has to be conveyed in a formal manner and less and less through direct observation.

Unfortunately, management often loses sight of the seemingly obvious and simple relationship between organization structure and information needs. Companies very seldom follow up on reorganizations with penetrating reappraisals of their information systems, and managers given new responsibilities and decision-making authority often do not receive all the information they require.

Causes of Confusion   The cornerstone for building a compact, useful management information system is the determination of each executive's information needs. This requires a clear grasp of the individual's role in the organization—his responsibilities, his authorities, and his relationships with other executives. The task is then to—

- Design a network of procedures that will process raw data in such a way as to generate the information required for management use.
- Implement such procedures in actual practice.

Such action steps, while demanding and time-consuming, have proved to be far less difficult than the creative and conceptual first step of defining information requirements. Seldom is the open approach of asking an executive what information he requires successful. For one thing, he may find it difficult to be articulate because the organization structure of his company is not clearly defined.

Further, and more important, there is a widespread tendency among operating executives to think of information exclusively in terms of their companies' accounting systems and the reports thus generated. This way of thinking can be a serious deterrent because:

1. Many conventional accounting reports cause confusion in the minds of nonfinancially trained executives. Take, for example, the profit-and-loss statement, with its arbitrary treatment of inventories, depreciation, allocated overhead expenses, and the like, or the statistical sales report, which is often a 40-page, untitled, machine-prepared tabulation of sales to individual customers. Such reports have made an indelible impression on managers' thinking, coloring their understanding and expectations of reports in general.

2. By its very nature traditional accounting fails to highlight many important aspects of business operations. Accounting systems often are designed primarily to meet SEC, Internal Revenue, and other statutory requirements—requirements that, more often than not, fail to correspond to management's information needs. Accounting describes the past in dollars, usually without discriminating between the critical and noncritical elements of a business—the elements that control competitive success in a particular industry and the elements that do not.

3. Accounting reports generally describe what has happened inside a company. Just consider what this approach omits:

   - Information about the future.
   - Data expressed in nonfinancial terms— e.g., share of market, productivity, quality levels, adequacy of customer service, and so on.

- Information dealing with external conditions as they might bear on a particular company's operations.

Yet all of these items are essential to the intelligent managing of a business.

PLANNING NEEDS DEFINED

The key to the development of a dynamic and usable system of management information is to move beyond the limits of classical accounting reports and to conceive of information as it relates to two vital elements of the management process—planning and control. In the pages to follow I shall focus largely on the planning aspect.

We hear more and more these days about new techniques for inventory, cost, and other types of control, but information systems for business planning still represent a relatively unexplored horizon.

Planning, as used in this article, means: setting objectives, formulating strategy, and deciding among alternative investments or courses of action. This definition can be applied to an entire company, an integrated division, or a single operating department.

As Exhibit I shows, the information required to do planning of this kind is of three basic types:

1. *Environmental information*—Describes the social, political, and economic aspects of the climate in which a business operates or may operate in the future.

2. *Competitive information*—Explains the past performance, programs, and plans of competing companies.

3. *Internal information*—Indicates a company's own strengths and weaknesses.

Now let us consider each of these categories in some detail.

Environmental Information   The environmental data category is one of the least formalized and hence least used parts of a management information system in most companies. Specific examples of the data included in this category are:

- Population—current levels, growth trends, age distribution, geographical distribution, effect on unemployment.
- Price levels—retail, wholesale, commodities, government regulation.
- Transportation—availability, costs, competition, regulation.

EXHIBIT I   Anatomy of Management Information

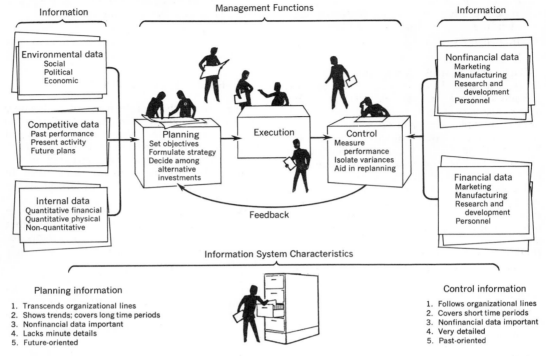

Information System Characteristics

Planning information
1. Transcends organizational lines
2. Shows trends; covers long time periods
3. Nonfinancial data important
4. Lacks minute details
5. Future-oriented

Control information
1. Follows organizational lines
2. Covers short time periods
3. Nonfinancial data important
4. Very detailed
5. Past-oriented

• Foreign trade—balance of payments, exchange rates, convertibility.

• Labor force—skills, availability, wages, turnover, unions.

To this list a company operating internationally would add another item—systematic collection and interpretation, on a country-by-country basis, of information on political and economic conditions in the foreign areas where business is being done. Here is an example of what can be accomplished:

A well-established international corporation with a highly sophisticated management makes a three-pronged effort to get data on local political and economic conditions. (a) There is a small but highly competent and well-paid four-man staff at corporate headquarters which travels extensively and publishes, using its own observations plus a variety of other sources, a weekly commentary on world events as they relate to the company. (b) This corporation has trained all its country managers to be keen observers of their local scene and to report their interpretive comments to headquarters regularly. (c) There is a little-talked-about group of "intelligence agents" who are not on the company's official payroll but are nevertheless paid for the information they pass along.

Certainly, not every organization has to go to these ends to keep itself informed of the situation in which it operates. However, those organizations that ignore environmental data or that leaves its collection to the informal devices of individual executives are inviting trouble. Those companies that are knowledgeable concerning their environment are almost always in tune with the times and ahead of their competition. To illustrate:

1. Good intelligence on the sociological changes taking place in the United States led several heavy manufacturing companies to enter the "leisure time" field with a great deal of success.

2. Insight into the possible impact of foreign labor costs on parts of the electronics industry caused some U.S. corporations to acquire their own manufacturing facilities abroad. As a result, the firms were able not only to protect their domestic markets but also to open up profitable operations overseas.

3. Knowledge of trends in age distribution in the United States added to an awareness of the rate of change of scientific learning provides ample proof for some firms of the desirability of being in the educational publishing field for the next decade.

To be of real use, environmental data must indicate trends; population figures, balance-of-payment data, or political shifts are of little significance when shown for one period because they don't help management make *analytical* interpretations.

The collection and transmission of good environmental data are often problematical. Even in the United States some kinds of information are not readily available and must be pieced together from several sources or acquired *sub rosa* from officially inaccessible sources. Transmitting environmental data, particularly political information, is so awkward that sometimes the data collector must sit down personally with those who need to know the information.

In sum, environmental data are an aspect of planning information that requires more attention and warrants formalization, especially in large geographically dispersed companies. The emergence of the corporate economics department[2] is one development that could lead to better results in this area, but it is my impression that so far the progress of these units has been uneven.

Competitive Information   Data on competition comprise the second category of planning information. There are three important types to consider:

1. *Past performance*—This includes information on the profitability, return on investment, share of market, and so forth of competing companies. Such information is primarily useful in identifying one's competitors. It also is one benchmark when setting company objectives.

2. *Present activity*—This category covers new product introductions, management changes, price strategy, and so on—all current developments. Good intelligence on such matters can materially influence a company's planning; for example, it may lead to accelerating research programs, modifying advertising strategy, or switching distribution channels. The implication here is not that a company's plans should always be defensive and prompted by a competitor's moves but simply that anything important a competitor does should be recognized and factored into the planning process.

3. *Future plans*—This includes information on acquisition intentions, facility plans, and research and development efforts.

2 Clark S. Teitsworth, "Growing Role of the Company Economist," *Harvard Business Review*, January–February, 1959, p. 97; and the article by Henry B. Arthur (*Harvard Business Review*, January–February, 1959).

Competitive information, like environmental data, is an infrequently formalized part of a company's total information system. And so there seldom is a concerted effort to collect this kind of material, to process it, and to report it to management regularly. But some interesting exceptions to this general lack of concern exist:

- Oil companies have long employed "scouts" in their land departments. These men report on acreage purchases, drilling results, and other competitive activity that may be pertinent to the future actions of their own company.
- Business machine companies have "competitive equipment evaluation personnel" who continually assess the technical features of competitors' hardware.
- Retail organizations employ "comparison shoppers" who appraise the prices and quality of merchandise in competitive stores.

Commercial intelligence departments are appearing more and more on corporate organization charts. An excerpt from the charter of one such group states its basic responsibility thus:

To seek out, collect, evaluate, and report information covering the past performance and future plans of competitors in such a manner that the information will have potential utility in strategic and operational planning of the corporation. This means that in addition to reporting factual information, emphasis should be on determining the implications of such information for the corporation.

Internal Information   The third and final basic category of planning information is made up of internal data. As it relates to the total planning process, internal data are aimed at identifying a company's strengths and weaknesses—the characteristics that, when viewed in the perspective of the general business environment and in the light of competitive activity, should help management to shape its future plans. It is useful to think of internal data as being of three types:

1. *Quantitative-financial*—e.g., sales, costs, and cost behavior relative to volume changes.

2. *Quantitative-physical*—e.g., share of market, productivity, delivery performance, and manpower resources.

3. *Nonquantitative*—e.g., community standing and labor relations.

In reporting internal data, a company's information system must be discriminating and selective. It should focus on "success factors." In most industries there are usually three to six factors that determine success; these key jobs must be done exceedingly well for a company to be successful. Here are some examples from several major industries:

- In the automobile industry, styling, an efficient dealer organization, and tight control of manufacturing costs are paramount.

- In food processing, new product development, good distribution, and effective advertising are the major success factors.

- In life insurance, the development of agency management personnel, effective control of clerical personnel, and innovation in creating new types of policies spell the difference.

The companies which have achieved the greatest advances in information analysis have consistently been those which have developed systems that have (a) been selective and (b) focused on the company's strengths and weaknesses with respect to its acknowledged success factors. By doing this, the managements have generated the kind of information that is most useful in capitalizing on strengths and correcting weaknesses. To illustrate:

An oil company devised a system of regularly reporting its "finding" costs—those costs incurred in exploring for new reserves of oil divided by the number of barrels of oil found. When this ratio trended upward beyond an established point, it was a signal to the company's management to consider the acquisition of other oil companies (together with their proved reserves) as a less expensive alternative to finding oil through its own exploratory efforts.

In the minds of most executives the accounting system exists primarily to meet the company's internal data needs; yet this is often an unreasonable and unfulfilled expectation. Accounting reports rarely focus on success factors that are nonfinancial in nature. Moreover, accounting practices with respect to allocation of expenses, transfer prices, and the like, often tend to obscure rather than clarify the underlying strengths and weaknesses of a company. This inadequacy should not be surprising since the *raison d'être* of many accounting systems is not to facilitate planning but rather to ensure the fulfillment of management's responsibility to the stockholders, the government, and other groups.

TAILORING THE REQUIREMENTS

If a company is to have a comprehensive, integrated system of information to support its planning process, it will need a set of management reports that regularly covers the three basic categories of planning data—i.e., environmental, competitive, and internal. The amount of data required in each area will naturally vary from company to company and will depend on such factors as the nature of the industry, the size and operating territory of the company, and the acceptance by management of planning as an essential function. However, it is important in every case for management to *formalize* and *regularize* the collection, transmission, processing, and presentation of planning information; the data are too vital to be ignored or taken care of by occasional "special studies." It is no accident that many of the most successful companies in this country are characterized by well-developed planning information systems.

What is gained if such an approach is taken? What difference does it make in operations? We do not need to conjecture to answer these questions; we can turn to concrete company experience. For instance, Exhibit II illustrates how the information used by the marketing department of an oil company changed as a result of a thorough study of the information needed to formulate effective plans. In this instance, the study indicated an increase in the data required by the vice president and his staff. (However, this result is not inevitable; it holds only for this particular situation. In other circumstances reviews of this kind have led to significant *cutbacks* in information.)

Several points should be noted in examining Exhibit II:

1. The information shown is not all for the *personal* use of the vice president, although much of it is generated and used in his field.

2. For simplicity, most of the information listed in the exhibit was presented to company executives in graphic form.

3. The exhibit highlights only the reports used for retail gasoline marketing; omitted are fuel oil marketing, commercial and industrial marketing, and other topics which the new reporting system also covered.

Many companies have found that the most effective approach to determining requirements for planning information, whether it be for one executive or an entire company, is to relate the three types of planning data described earlier

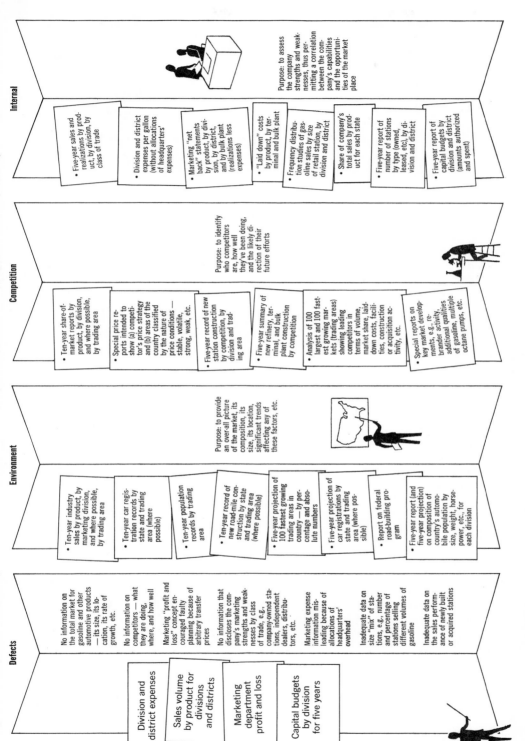

Defects

Division and district expenses

Sales volume by product for divisions and districts

Marketing department profit and loss

Capital budgets by division for five years

- No information on the total market for gasoline and other automotive products — its size, its location, its rate of growth, etc.
- No information on competitors — what they are doing, where, and how well
- Marketing "profit and loss" concept encouraged faulty planning because of arbitrary transfer prices
- No information that discloses the company's marketing strengths and weaknesses by class of trade, e.g., company-owned stations, independent dealers, distributors, etc.
- Marketing expense information misleading because of allocations of headquarters' overhead
- Inadequate data on size "mix" of stations, e.g., number and percentage of stations selling different volumes of gasoline
- Inadequate data on the sales performance of newly built or acquired stations

Environment

- Ten-year industry sales by product, by marketing division, and where possible, by trading area
- Ten-year car registration records by state and trading area (where possible)
- Ten-year population records by trading area
- Ten-year record of new road-mile construction by state and trading area (where possible)
- Five-year projection of 100 fastest growing trading areas in country — by percentage and absolute numbers
- Five-year projection of car registrations by state and trading area (where possible)
- Report on federal road-building program
- Five-year report (and five-year projection) on composition of country's automobile population by size, weight, horse-power, etc., for each division

Purpose: to provide an over-all picture of the market, its composition, its size, its location, significant trends affecting any of these factors, etc.

Competition

- Ten-year share-of-market reports by product, by division, and where possible, by trading area
- Special price reports intended to show (a) competitor's price strategy and (b) areas of the country classified by the nature of price conditions — stable, volatile, strong, weak, etc.
- Five-year record of new station construction by competition, by division and trading area
- Five-year summary of new refinery, terminal, and bulk plant construction by competition
- Analysis of 100 largest and 100 fastest growing markets (trading areas) showing leading competitors in terms of volume, market share, laid-down costs, facilities, construction or acquisition activity, etc.
- Special reports on key market developments, e.g., re-brander activity, additional qualities of gasoline, multiple octane pumps, etc.

Purpose: to identify who competitors are, how well they've been doing, and the likely direction of their future efforts

Internal

- Five-year sales and realizations by product, by division, by class of trade
- Division and district expenses per gallon (without allocations of headquarters' expenses)
- Marketing "net back" statements by product, by division, by district, and by bulk plant (realizations less expenses)
- "Laid down" costs by product, by terminal and bulk plant
- Frequency distribution studies of gasoline sales by size of retail station, by division and district
- Share of company's total sales by product for each state
- Five-year report of number of stations by type (owned, leased, etc), by division and district
- Five-year report of capital budgets by division and district (amounts authorized and spent)

Purpose: to assess the company strengths and weaknesses, thus permitting a correlation between the company's capabilities and the opportunities of the market place

EXHIBIT II   Comparative Analysis of Marketing Planning Information

to the steps in the planning process—i.e., setting objectives, developing strategy, and deciding among alternative investments. Thus, one asks himself questions like these:

- What political data are needed to set reasonable objectives for this company?
- What sociological and economic data about the areas in which this company operates are needed to formulate new product strategy?
- What competitive intelligence is necessary to develop share-of-market objectives?
- What internal cost information is needed to choose between alternative facility locations?

Contrast with Control In Exhibit I, I have listed the five principal characteristics of planning data compared with the characteristics of control data. Note that in all but one case (nonfinancial information) they are different. It is most important to keep these differences in mind, lest the "fuel" for the planning system be confused with the "fuel" for the control system, and vice versa. Hence, I should like to emphasize the contrasts here:

1. *Coverage*—Good planning information is not compartmentalized by functions. Indeed, it seeks to transcend the divisions that exist in a company and to provide the basis on which *integrated* plans can be made. In contrast, control information hews closely to organizational lines so that it can be used to measure performance and help in holding specific managers more accountable.

2. *Length of time*—Planning information covers fairly long periods of time—months and years rather than days and weeks—and deals with trends. Thus, although it should be regularly prepared, it is not developed as frequently as control information.

3. *Degree of detail*—Excessive detail is the quicksand of intelligent planning. Unlike control, where precision and minute care do have a place, planning (and particularly long-range planning) focuses on the major outlines of the situation ahead. In the words of two authorities, L. Eugene Root and George A. Steiner, "The further out in time the planning, the less certain one can be about the precision of numbers. As a basic principle in planning it is understood that, in the longer range, details merge into trends and patterns."[3]

4. *Orientation*—Planning information should provide insights into the future. Control information shows past results and the reasons for them.

FUTURE DEVELOPMENTS

The heightened interest of management in its information crisis is already unmistakable. Dean Stanley F. Teele of the Harvard Business School, writing on the process of change in the years ahead, states:

> I think the capacity to manage knowledge will be still more important to the manager. . . . The manager will need to increase his skill in deciding what knowledge he needs.[4]

Ralph Cordiner of General Electric Company in his book, *New Frontiers for Professional Managers*, writes:

> It is an immense problem to organize and communicate the information required to operate a large, decentralized organization. . . .
> What is required . . . is a . . . penetrating and orderly study of the business in its entirety to discover what specific information is needed at each particular position in view of the decisions to be made there. . . .[5]

Invariably, increasing attention of leaders in education and industry precedes and prepares the way for frontal attacks on business problems. In many organizations the initial reaction to the management information problem is first evidenced by a concern over "the flood of paper work." Eventually, the problem itself is recognized—i.e., the need to define concisely the information required for intelligent planning and control of a business.

Following this awakening interest in business information problems, we are likely to see the acceleration of two developments already in view: (a) improved techniques relating to the creation and operation of total information systems, and (b) new organizational approaches to resolving information problems.

Improved Techniques While the crisis in management information has been growing, tools that may be useful in its solution have been under development. For example, the evolution of electronic data-processing systems,

---

[3] L. Eugene Root and George A. Steiner, "The Lockheed Aircraft Corporation Master Plan," in David W. Ewing (ed.), *Long-range Planning for Management*, Harper & Row, Publishers, Incorporated, New York, 1958, p. 151.

[4] Stanley F. Teele, "Your Job and Mine," *The Harvard Business School Bulletin*, August, 1960, p. 8.

[5] Ralph J. Cordiner, *New Frontiers for Professional Managers*, McGraw-Hill Book Company, New York, 1956, p. 102.

the development of supporting communications networks, and the formulation of rigorous mathematical solutions to business problems have provided potentially valuable tools to help management attack its information problems. Specifically, progress on three fronts is an encouraging indication that this kind of approach will prove increasingly fruitful:

1. Managements of most companies are far more conversant with both the capabilities and the limitations of computer systems than they were five years ago. This growing understanding has done much to separate fact from fancy. One key result should be the increasing application of electronic data-processing concepts to the more critical, less routine problems of business.

2. Computer manufacturers and communications companies are learning the worth of their products. They show signs of recognizing that it is not hardware but an information system which is extremely valuable in helping to solve management's problems.

3. Significant improvements have been made in the techniques of harnessing computers. Advances in automatic programing and developments in creating a common business language are gratifying evidence that the gap is being narrowed between the technical potential of the hardware and management's ability to exploit it.

Organizational Moves   The development of new organizational approaches is less obvious. Earlier in this article I noted that: (a) progress in the systematic collection and reporting of information dealing with a company's environment or with its competitive situation has been slow, and (b) traditional accounting reports are often inadequate in providing the data needed for business planning. These conditions may result from a very basic cause; namely, that most organization structures do not pin down the responsibility for management information systems and tie it to specific executive positions. Controllers and other financial officers usually have been assigned responsibility for *accounting* information—but this, of course, does not meet the total need.

Nowhere has the absence of one person having specific and *total* responsibility for management information systems had a more telling effect than in defense contractor companies. In such organizations the usual information problems have been compounded by the rapid rate of technological advance and its attendant effect upon product obsolescence, and also by the requirement for "concurrency,"

which means that a single product or product complex is developed, tested, produced, and installed simultaneously. Under these conditions, some companies have been nearly paralyzed by too much of the wrong information.

Having recognized this problem, several corporations have attacked it by creating full-time management information departments. These groups are responsible for:

1. Identifying the information needs for all levels of management for both planning and control purposes. As prerequisites to this responsibility it is necessary to (a) define the authority and duties of each manager and (b) determine the factors that really contribute to competitive success in the particular business in question.

2. Developing the necessary systems to fulfill these information needs.

3. Operating the data-processing equipment necessary to generate the information which is required.

To some extent these departments, reporting high in the corporate structure, have impinged on responsibilities traditionally assigned to the accounting organization since they are concerned with financial as well as nonfinancial information. But to me this overlapping is inevitable, particularly in companies where the financial function operates under a narrow perspective and a preoccupation with accountancy. The age of the information specialist is nearing, and its arrival is inextricably tied in with the emergence of some of the newer tools of our management sciences. This notion is not far removed from the concept of Harold J. Leavitt and Thomas L. Whisler, who foresee the evolution of information technology and the creation of a "programing elite."[6]

CONCLUSION

The day when management information departments are as common as controller's departments is still years away. But this should not rule out concerted efforts to improve a company's information system. In fact, I would expect many broad-gauged controller's organizations to assume the initiative in their companies for such programs.

To this end, the nine questions listed in Exhibit III are for the executive to ask himself as a guide to assessing the improvement potential in his organization's planning information.

[6] Harold J. Leavitt and Thomas L. Whisler, "Management in the 1980's," *Harvard Business Review*, November–December, 1958, p. 41.

EXHIBIT III   How Good Is Your Planning Information?

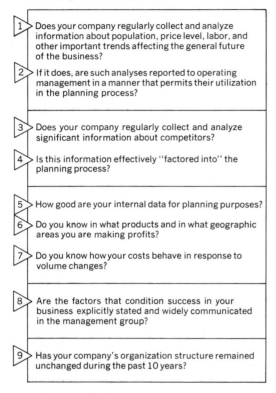

1 > Does your company regularly collect and analyze information about population, price level, labor, and other important trends affecting the general future of the business?

2 > If it does, are such analyses reported to operating management in a manner that permits their utilization in the planning process?

3 > Does your company regularly collect and analyze significant information about competitors?

4 > Is this information effectively "factored into" the planning process?

5 > How good are your internal data for planning purposes?

6 > Do you know in what products and in what geographic areas you are making profits?

7 > Do you know how your costs behave in response to volume changes?

8 > Are the factors that condition success in your business explicitly stated and widely communicated in the management group?

9 > Has your company's organization structure remained unchanged during the past 10 years?

If the answers to these questions tend to be negative, the chances are strong that changes are in order.

The impact of the information crisis on the executive will be significant. To an increasing extent, a manager's effectiveness will hinge on the quality and completeness of the facts that flow to him and on his skill in using them. With technology changing at a rapid rate, with the time dimension becoming increasingly critical, and with organizations becoming larger, more diversified in product lines, and more dispersed geographically, it is inevitable that executives will rely more and more on formally presented information in managing their businesses.

What is more, some organizations are concluding that the easiest and most effective way to influence executive action is to control the flow of information into managerial positions. This notion holds that the discipline of information can be a potent factor in determining just what an executive can and cannot do— what decisions he can make, what plans he can draw up, what corrective steps he can take.

To the extent that this is true, information systems may be increasingly used to mold and shape executive behavior. Better data handling might well become a substitute for much of the laborious shuffling and reshuffling of positions and lines of authority that now goes on. Most reorganizations seek to alter the way certain managers or groups of managers operate. But simply drawing new organization charts and rewriting job descriptions seldom ensure the implementation of new concepts and relationships. The timing, content, and format of the information provided to management, however, *can* be a strong influence in bringing about such purposeful change.

Thus, developments in management information systems will affect the executive in two ways. Not only will the new concepts influence what he is able to do, but they will to a great extent control how well he is able to do it.

67

A New Profession
to Aid Management*

MARION HARPER, JR.

Research has progressed from a secondary level of fact-finding activity to participation in the development of policy. However, we are confronted today with a glaring shortage of research professionals.

This rise in the importance of research has not been equaled by an increase in the number of research people who are qualified for policy participation. Research here does not refer to a narrow sub-species, such as advertising research or even marketing research. Rather, it is social science research in general.

One means to alleviate this shortage would be through the development of a new profession, with qualified professionals being designated as "Director of Intelligence Services." To understand how research can make a greater contribution in the future, it is worthwhile to consider several premises.

MANAGEMENT AND THE FUTURE

The first is: *To manage a business well is to manage its future; and to manage the future is to manage information.*

A good manager today can afford little time with the present and still less with the past. His concern must be for the future growth and success of the business or institution in his charge. He must make decisions every day, every hour, every minute—decisions affecting the future, and to some degree involving forecasts. Persons having responsibility for decision —whether in business, government, or wherever—hope that they are right decisions. But they seldom know. One trouble, or maybe it is a blessing, is that the consequences of most decisions remain obscure—and, short of going

* Reprinted by permission of the publisher from the *Journal of Marketing*, vol. 25, no. 3, pp. 1–6, January, 1961. Mr. Harper is chairman of the board, McCann-Erickson Co., New York.

into bankruptcy, executives hardly ever find out how bad their decisions sometimes are.

Management can never have all the facts to cover all contingencies in a forecast. A decision to act or not to act must always be partly rational and partly visceral. There will always be a last step involving personal courage, personal commitment, and personal responsibility.

Sometimes business leaders attempt to buttress this last step by consulting a committee. It is sometimes thought that, if enough facts are assembled and varied consideration given, a conclusion will evolve almost by itself. But a decision is more than a procedure or a set of facts or a certain amount of consideration. It is an election requiring individual will.

Over the years kings, generals, officials, and managers have not been wanting in courage, but nevertheless they have always felt the need to fortify themselves with as much certainty about the future as possible. Ancient chiefs had medicine men whose survival, like many since, depended more on their ability to sense the chief's wishes than on their vision of things to come.

With the Age of Reason and the rise of rational philosophy, institutions such as Royal Commissions in England developed; they supplied facts for the deliberations of Parliament. Current counterparts are government commissions and committees of investigation.

In modern business, reliance on facts has reached proportions of a virtual explosion of research—in technology, operations, and marketing. Research-and-development investment is now at the level of $9 billion and may rise to $18 billion over the next ten years. This expenditure can be considered as investment in management decision-making—to help determine the future environment for a particular course of action, or to indicate the superiority of one course of action over another.

TYPES OF DECISIONS

A related premise is this: *The term "informed decision" is a relative one.*

The expression is used almost as if there were two kinds of decisions—informed and uninformed—but obviously there are many different kinds of decisions, involving different proportions of information.

No decision is wholly informed or wholly intuitive. By definition, any decision that involves unknowns is a speculation. Management earns its authority as it takes steps to reduce speculation and deals with unknowns decisively and in good time. Business competition will always involve some of the strategy of poker. However, thanks to research, a manager can sometimes assess other hands at the table and predict the next play.

COMPLEXITIES OF DECISION-MAKING

Another premise: *Management decision-making is becoming an increasingly complex process, with a multiplication of both knowns and unknowns.*

The point of greater complexity need not be belabored. But to take one example: Not many years ago, the problem of locating a plant was a matter of checking on shipping facilities, raw materials, and available labor supply. Now it is the subject of a whole catalog of factors and special studies. You can follow a set procedure to arrive at a solution.

On the other hand, there are many problems for which procedures or research data are not available. For these, management makes—or fails to make—judgments in virgin territory.

To mention a recent example: A congressional committee was asked to appropriate funds for an atomic accelerator. The decision turned on whether to build a proton or an electron accelerator. It was said that, if you had asked ten atomic scientists, five would have favored one kind and five another. In this instance, the Democratic committee members favored the electron, and the Republicans the proton. The issue was resolved—as issues sometimes are—by postponement. Neither electron nor proton could muster enough political strength to win the day.

The problems of management are less esoteric and usually can be illuminated with some help from research. But, in general, it is true that good solutions depend on a large number of factors and on information-gathering from many different fields. They are, of course, complicated by new patterns of national and international competition, new forms of communications, the proliferation of new products, and by the emergence of new market segments involving not only age, sex, national background, and geography, but taste and individual psychology.

All these factors strain our present resources for research. They also point to some inherent limitations in our information sources.

Sometimes managers try to apply researching areas where it cannot help or can help only very little. There is an illusion abroad that almost any social or organizational problem can be solved if it is only "researched" and investigated. Unfortunately, this is not so. On the contrary, the bigger the problem, the less useful is the social science research employed to solve it. For instance, the social sciences can probably contribute very little toward the lessening of world tensions or juvenile delinquency—although immense sums are now spent on their study. The social sciences throw light on such problems only through small insights here and there, with ultimate solutions still remote. But, if our ambitions are kept within realistic limits and magic answers are not expected, research can serve as a most effective tool.

GROWING INFORMATION REVOLUTION

The next premise is this: *We are entering upon an Information Revolution in which the supply of data increases by geometric progression.*

In this era, the most successful decision-makers will be those who can best process, interpret, and put facts to use. One of today's data-processing machines can read or write at the rate of four full-length novels a second; its 640 cartridges hold 220 miles of magnetic tape. Machines such as this will be fed by a growing corps of government, business, and scientific researchers, stimulated by today's greater appetite for knowledge.

Production of the sheer mass of information will increase at a far higher rate than our Gross National Product or any other production growth. It is not unthinkable that some day the storage bins of the farm surplus program may be needed to accommodate the outpouring of data we will have at hand.

The key question, then, is—how well will we use this mass of raw information?

If a little learning is a dangerous thing, then too much—that is, knowledge not put to good use—can be a costly waste. Too many undigested facts can turn a man of action into a

Hamlet, paralyzed by indecision. Like the raw materials of industry, information must be *converted* into something. What is required is a discriminating selection which can deliver relevant data in a form usable at the echelon of decision. The research study that collects dust on shelves may very well have merit; the fault is a failure to relate its data to the problem it was designed to help solve.

Information may involve anything from the most minute and finite to the universal. Processing information today calls not only for distinguishing the forest from the trees, but distinguishing between leaves and chlorophyll —while still not losing sight of the forest.

SPECIALIST VERSUS GENERALIST

Another premise: *As information multiplies, management needs "protection" from the specialist.*

By the nature of his work, a manager is a generalist. He must, of course, have access to the knowledge and ideas of specialists to arrive at solutions that best serve his company's goals.

Specialists are necessary, even indispensable, but they have their shortcomings. Their view is often limited and their inclinations one-sided. Sometimes a specialist in a given field, through his traditional status, or the glamor of a new body of knowledge, or through personal influence, can exert undue influence on a company's destiny. Just as a surgeon is not always the best judge as to whether or not to operate so the research specialist can be trusted in his judgment only part of the way.

One answer would be that the specialist in the social sciences contributes best when his proposals are reviewed by a generalist. In the social sciences, hardly anything is absolutely certain *except the things we know anyway without the benefit of research.*

It is in this valuable buffer role that a Dr. James R. Killian, Jr., or a Dr. George B. Kistiakowsky served as scientific adviser to President Eisenhower, reviewing the proposals of different specialists.

In the marketing field, too, it is essential for specialists to report to a senior arbiter or interpreter. In the past, management has usually assumed this task and will always hold final responsibility; but it would be more appropriate for this function to be assigned to a research generalist who would be an adviser to management.

To fulfill such a co-ordinating role, a man must know what the various specialties are about. It is not necessary that he achieve the same competence as the specialist, but he should have a thorough understanding of each field. An analogy is the function of a good orchestra leader. The best conductors play a number of instruments very well and must have familiarity with all of them.

MEN AND METHODS

Another premise is: *Too many people take part in decisions—and too many decision-makers use the wrong tools.*

One reason for calling meetings is probably an impulse to assemble anyone who knows anything about the problem—so that people are brought in for their basic information, not necessarily for their abilities to deliberate.

Very often their information might be quite as well gathered and summarized by an able reporter, and in this way fewer people would be required to pass upon the problem. Thus, everyday reporting, in some instances, is a better research tool than holding a meeting.

Another poor device for decision-making is the office-routing system. Too many problems are forced *upward* through an organization— with the result that there is a misplacement of decision-making. Common examples are the evaluation of personnel, the selection of equipment, or the purchase of technical services. In such cases, pertinent information may fail to rise to the level where the question is to be decided. Data may be too voluminous, or too technical, or too time-consuming for management to consider. A certain "packaging" of information is appropriate to a given level. When confronted with too much detail, management may react like the boy who was asked to review a book on penguins. He wrote simply, "This book tells more about penguins than I want to know."

The failure to direct usable data where the decision should be made also aggravates a fault of all levels of management—a reluctance to make decisions. It is unlikely that we can change human nature overnight to develop a more courageous breed of executive; but we can support whatever courage there is with risk-reducing facts.

There is also too great a reliance on obsolete information that often goes under the venerable name of Experience. The world today changes at such an accelerated speed that, if you make a decision for 1963 or 1967 on the basis of your experience in 1953 or 1957, or even 1961, it may prove embarrassing and costly.

Today's research must not only be up-to-date, but must develop techniques for forecasting facts for the future. In the field of marketing, this means the forecasting of consumer tastes and preferences—as formidable a task as that may be.

Still another fault is that too much decision-making is on an instant or *ad hoc* basis. This is sometimes unavoidable, but the result is decision-making that seldom has the benefit of current information. Nevertheless, even a trainee knows that if we have some fore-knowledge of the kinds of decisions we will have to make—if we have time to think about them and to document alternative solutions, if we have time to discuss them with people who have some tools and some perception of the problems—then we gain a clearer perspective of the consequences. And so better results can be obtained.

Management decision-making is a continuous process. It is desirable that it be supported by a continuous program of research. Such a program will particularly benefit key decisions.

If you ask a manager how many of the decisions he made in the last year affected the development of his company, he may say not more than five, or at the most, ten. If the manager tries to anticipate the five or ten really critical decisions which he will be called upon to make during any succeeding year, he can then initiate a series of research projects which will facilitate and improve these decisions.

Today much research is conducted on a "crisis" basis, usually to reverse a declining curve or to correct a negative development. It is feasible, however, to conduct studies, especially in marketing, on much the same basis as research in a laboratory or development center. Such programs of research yield information to help solve problems that can be foreseen, and also those that arise unexpectedly.

In marketing research today, managed programs may include studies of retail outlets, pricing, product features, media, and copy effectiveness—among other subjects.

NEEDED NEW PROFESSION

Therefore, *we should encourage the development of a new profession to provide an intelligence service for the shaping of strategy and policy.* Such a profession would rise out of the fine record of all the technical achievements of research up to the present, and it would strive for a still higher stature. A member, through special training comparable with that of other professions and through proved capability, would occupy a post of "Director of Intelligence Services." Reporting to him would be such specialists as the director of marketing research, or economic research, or product research.

Management would look to the Director of Intelligence Services as someone who would develop information for different possible recommendations and who would outline the probable consequences of moving in any direction. His contribution would be measured by his ability to relate technical specifics to broad courses of action. With this ability he would commit himself to a scale of probabilities. He would not invent policy—although he might—but he would measure and help to shape it. His chief executive officer would still be charged with final formulation of policy.

The function suggested is sometimes carried on by forward planning departments; but usually their executives do not have the broad technical background which can link the all-important fact to the all-important policy. It is also, of course, a function of government intelligence services.

Thus, a Director of Intelligence Services in business might analyze and present a problem in much the same way as an intelligence adviser to the government.

Assume, for example, the cloak-and-dagger hypothesis that an intelligence officer would have appraised the consequences of dropping an agent down near Sverdlovsk, Russia. The officer might have outlined the assets and liabilities of such a venture in relation to a Summit Conference. He might have argued, conceivably, that to dramatize Russia's vulnerability would exert pressure to win acceptance for the "open-skies" proposal. And he might have weighed this possible advantage against the propaganda potential of the incident and the exposure of our intelligence methods. He would, of course, have marshaled all available information on the weather, the feasibility of the flight, the likely alertness and location of Russian ground forces, and many other details. He might also have committed himself to the probabilities involved in different alternatives—with his conviction flowing plausibly out of his documentation.

Many problems in business are not quite so spectacular, but the consideration of them could benefit from the same kind of *informed* balancing of possibilities.

Against the desirability of having such a Director of Intelligence Services, we are confronted today with a shortage of research professionals—at least, of well-rounded professionals trained to relate the various social sciences to the problems of business; men who know the relevance of research, who know its function in the decision-making process, who have a working knowledge of the many new intricate techniques at our disposal.

Here we have arrived at the crux of our difficulties: How many research people are there who measure up to this standard? Relatively few. But demand for trained men and women who can help to improve our decisions is increasing by the day; and, despite the attraction of salaries raised by competitive bidding, the supply is far below the demand.

Proposed Academic Center

One reason is that there is no academic center for the training and development of such people. There is no advanced school today which offers a specific curriculum for the development of an intelligence executive.

What is needed is a professional school—very much like a law school, medical school, or engineering school. It could launch young men and women on a highly rewarding career which could place them at the exciting nerve centers of business and bring them into the highest counsels of management.

The object of such schooling would be to give students at least a working familiarity with business operations, and the basic knowledge required for planning and executing a broad-gauge research program. It would indoctrinate young men and women in the business of problem solving through the management of information. The chief executive would still practice the *art* of problem solving; but the intelligence director would learn what can be learned about the *science* of problem-solving.

The need for a professional intelligence school can be understood by looking into the diverse background of today's best research directors.

We find academic degrees in mathematics, sociology, law, anthropology, psychology, and the humanities. The majority have a background in one of the social sciences.

One must recall that the research carried on today by business, government, and institutions may involve definitions of markets; analysis of community, trade, and labor relations; auditing of promotion; appraisal of opportunities for expansion. Most of these problems cut across more than one social science—economics, sociology, business administration, and so on—and can be solved more perceptively under direction of the research generalist.

The fact is that progress in the social sciences that are involved in broad decision-making has outstripped not only the technical competence of the administrator, but the general technical background of the specialist.

Proposed Curriculum

Today we know fairly well the technical skills required for a good intelligence director. Actually they are already being taught in a number of universities, and some are taught very well. But usually you find them not only in different departments but in different schools. Even if they are all available under the roof of one university, there is no provision for a student to train in a single curriculum.

What might such a curriculum include? It would offer: Survey Techniques, currently taught well in only a few places; Statistics, indispensable to the modern researcher, and given usually in a statistics, mathematics, or psychology department; Econometrics, in economics departments; Projective Psychological Research, which goes under the name of motivational research, taught in psychology departments. The Theory and Practice of Experimentation, found in the department of industrial engineering or, sometimes, in the statistics department; and Operations Research, also in the department of industrial engineering.

Other courses for a research generalist might include Computing-Machine Techniques; Analysis of Administrative Data, such as information compiled by the Census or by industrial trade association; and related study in Library Technique. And finally, to complete such an intelligence curriculum, there would be training in The Design and Management of Research, that is, the managerial supervision of research.

Such a curriculum can be projected from everyday observation; but its formulation into a program leading to an academic degree is obviously the prerogative of a university. It is hoped that a university faculty will design such a curriculum, to be offered in the earliest possible academic year, so that the needs of government and business for research generalists will be at least partly satisfied over the coming years.

The Budget Comes of Age*

JAMES L. PEIRCE

Any technique of management reaches maturity when, after its earlier mistakes have antagonized human beings sufficiently, it emerges with a new outlook and practice that is in harmony with the basic motivations of people. Budgeting now seems to be undergoing this metamorphosis. Out of the disturbance it has created is appearing a calmer, more orderly, more positive approach.

It is my purpose in this article to add weight to the spreading view that budgeting rests on principles which have more in common with concepts of human relationship than with rules of accounting; and that, if these principles are applied, successful practice is inevitable.

DEFENSIVENESS: THE TROUBLE

There is no doubt that thousands of management people are well grounded in constructive budget practice and derive from it a sense of balance and direction in their business affairs. No businessman who has had extensive experience with an ably managed budget system appears to doubt its value. But there are many more thousands who are so confused on the subject that it might indeed be better for them to discard their budgets entirely than to continue as they are. Surveys have shown that in some quarters budgeting is about as popular among foremen as a layoff, and analyses stress the damage that results from the misuse of budgeting procedures.

Some executives freely admit the shortcomings of their budget practices and acknowledge that they could be remedied by the application of more intelligent human relations. If it is as simple as that, then why cannot budgets be made a welcome and productive feature of all business operation without delay? The answer, I think, is that the problem is not such a simple one—just as human beings are not simple, just as the science of human relation-

ships is not simple, as witness the many failures to apply it effectively.

How shall we go about the task of instilling revitalized ideas in place of negative or shortsighted attitudes?

We can accomplish nothing until we face up to the fact that many of us have acquired a defensive approach to the subject through painful experience. Here we must dig deep into the recesses of thought—not omitting the realm of emotional misconception that colors our word associations. Why do the two words "budgets" and "people" repel each other? Why should they, when taken together, suggest the image of a problem? Why, in fact, should it even be necessary to discuss a positive approach to the matter of budgets and people?

This unhappy reaction comes from the fact that people generally do not like budgets. We must remember that foremen are people first and supervisors second; so are department managers and top executives. Budgets represent restriction. They are in the same category as school bells and Monday mornings. Each of us has entered business life with a primitive aversion to restraint, only thinly veneered by academic training.

Someone should have presented the budget ideas to us very constructively in order for us to accept it, much less to enjoy it. If from the very beginning of our careers we have been told, with accompanying evidence, that budgets were a help to us, affording us guidance, stability, and strength, as well as keeping us out of innumerable troubles, our responses would by now be quite different.

But what was our actual experience? Have not many of us been introduced to budgets in business when the budget was blamed, rightly or wrongly, for our failure to get a raise in pay? Have not many of us become acquainted with the budget only as a barrier to spending what we felt were necessary amounts of money for better equipment or performance? Is it surprising, then, that budgets are associated in many people's minds with paucity and niggardliness rather than with planning and direction?

---

* Reprinted by permission of the publisher from *Harvard Business Review*, vol. 32, no. 3, pp. 58–66, May–June, 1954. Mr. Peirce is vice president and controller of the A. B. Dick Company.

Fortunately, it is not too late to effect a correction in the thinking of the current generation of managers.

ATTITUDES: THE KEY

In probing further, it quickly becomes evident that good attitudes are the key to successful budgeting. When the attitudes of people toward each other are generous, understanding, and based on mutual respect, any technique adopted by management to further effective performance is apt to be successful. When human attitudes are dominated by distrust, criticism, and recrimination, any technique designed to improve performance is likely to fail miserably. In such cases, by a strange twist of human nature, the budgets and those who defend them bear the brunt of the blame for more fundamental errors which are entirely unconnected with budgets.

Budgeting is a trained, disciplined approach to all problems, which recognizes the need for standards of performance in order to achieve a result. Hence it must be built on a base of good organization; otherwise, favorable attitudes have no chance to operate. But at the same time it lives in an atmosphere of perpetual adjustment to the needs and capacities of people. It thrives on such fundamentals as recognition of accomplishment, consideration for the rights of individuals, fair play—in other words, enlightened relationships among people.

Motivation for Budgeting   In exploring budgeting principles as they relate to people, the first consideration should be the motivation for the budget system. Why have one at all? Is the budget a part of a system of over-all planning, in order that all concerned may have a measure of the amounts to be spent, and in order that action may be by design rather than by expediency? Or is the budget a pressure device designed to goad people into greater efforts? It takes a little soul-searching to determine honestly which of these concepts represents the position of a particular management.

Both concepts are prevalent. They may be symbolized by two wooden sticks—one neatly divided into thirty-six one-inch spaces, and the other sharply pointed at one end. The yardstick, symbolizing the planning concept of budgets, may be used, for example, by a foreman to establish standards of performance and cost and to measure actual results in relation thereto; in this sense, it is a tool used by the foreman and his boss in partnership. The pointed stick, a symbol of the pressure type of budget, is always found in the hand of the superior, turned menacingly toward his foremen or workers. The yardstick concept elicits the voluntary effort of men to do their best work. The pointed stick forces a reluctant and minimal performance.

There is plenty of evidence that the choice of the yardstick concept will not diminish the yield from the budget tool in terms of cost reduction. It has been shown again and again that high costs which stubbornly resist all efforts of the pressure type will melt away under the warmth of an approach which is attuned to the basic responses of humanity. The attitude to be adopted here is an enlistment of all concerned in a common effort, with a complete explanation of objectives and methods.

PLANNING: THE FOUNDATION

Next in the line of exploration of principles is the dependence of budgets on general company planning. Although budgeting can be separately applied to any unit of the business, it is far more effective when it rests on a foundation of integrated planning for the entire operation. In the proper sense, it is only one phase of planning. When the planning concept has been adopted, budgets emerge of necessity —budgets with a purpose as deep as the stream of ideas giving direction and drive to the business itself.

The presence or absence of intelligent planning is reflected to a surprising degree in the effectiveness of the people who are asked to operate with a budget system. And this means all the people—from top executives to production-line workers. Individuals are usually more intuitive than we realize. When a budget is built on sound business planning, they respond to that fact without always knowing why.

Meaning of Planning   As used in this discussion, *planning* refers to the predetermination of a course of action in such detail that every responsible unit of the company may be guided thereby. It includes sales forecasting, production scheduling, expense budgeting, and estimating of manufacturing costs and inventory levels. It involves making advance decisions concerning new product development and introduction, merchandising methods, material procurement, and labor rates. In short, planning implies anticipating all the knotty problems to be met by a business during the planning period—usually a year so far as operations are concerned, longer for financial and developmental activities—in other words, facing the problems and making decisions about them *ahead of time* (subject to later revision if necessary).

These decisions are frequently so hard to make in advance that they border on the impossible. Yet they insure a reasonable net profit as no other method can. And on this planned net profit figure—the apex of the planning structure—depends our ability to attract new capital as needed and to compensate management and shareholders.

I need not elaborate the importance of profit planning. I am only concerned here that it be recognized that when budgeting has a hard core of deliberate planning, adhered to by the company's top, middle, and all other management, the budget idea takes on real meaning for all concerned. Without this basis, it can never be completely palatable to those who do not understand how it can benefit them.

Effect on People Let us examine the effect of the planning process on the people involved in it. In particular, we might first consider the impact on administrative people, for their outlook in the long run determines the attitudes of the larger non-administrative group. What is the planning technique doing to foremen, department managers, division heads? Is it building up or tearing down their confidence in their company's future? Is it affecting favorably or adversely their independence of thought, their self-assurance, their capacity to understand and rely on those around them?

It seems self-evident that planning alone does not afford the entire answer. If a company's administrative personnel are exhibiting what is called "good morale" before the installation of a planning system, the chances are that turning their eyes to the future and asking them to construct together a plan for better achievement can do them no harm, but can do them untold good. With proper explanations, the management can hold forth the legitimate promise of better accomplishment, greater satisfaction, more confident operating, and, ultimately, opportunity for increased compensation.

If, on the other hand, the management is struggling with a discordant staff, perhaps suffering from the blight of fuzzy organization lines or any of the other impediments to good work resulting from a mediocre job of personnel administration, it might be better off to defer trying the planning and control idea until it has put its house in order. Too frequently a well-designed budget system has collapsed after being superimposed on a faulty base of administrative personnel policy. Then the budget is discarded and all concerned return to their familiar bad habits.

CONTROL: THE COMPLEMENT

But there is another phase of budgeting which tests the fiber of men even more than planning. I am referring to control, which is the eternal complement of planning. Neither one is useful without the other, and to budget even the smallest unit of a business implies the presence of control also.

Budget Abuses It is in the control area that the colossal mistakes of budgeting are made. It is here that the amateurs have censured their subordinates for exceeding budgets, without realizing that they themselves were to blame for inadequate training. It is here that men have become so frustrated under maladministered budgets that they have resorted to all sorts of tricks to conceal the actual results and have padded their budgets to give themselves breathing room. It is here that staff men have usurped authority, merited pay increases have been denied because of budget limitations, and tales have been carried around supervision and up to the top under the guise of budget reporting.

The list of abuses could be prolonged indefinitely. There are many wrong ways to exercise budget control. There is only one right way. Let us then discard the negative approach, since the assertion of an affirmative truth will dissolve all counterfeits.

Control might be quickly and simply defined as a disciplined effort to follow a plan or explain deviations from it. The effort referred to takes the form of self-discipline—voluntary, unified, and cooperative. The deviations from plan are deliberate, foreknown, and authorized. If they are apparently beyond anyone's ability to prevent—as for instance a failure to reach budgeted sales volume—at least they are spotlighted as early as possible, and management has the chance to take whatever action is indicated. Control is simply the modern form of the old formula, "management by exception."

It is, of course, at the point of deviation from the budget that most of the human problems are born. This is, by design, the central point in the entire system—the moment which demands explanation, instruction, decision, argument, or even discipline, as the case warrants—the flash point for management in action.

Common-sense Departures It should be evident that the effect of control on people is commensurate with their training and conditioning for it. If they understand thoroughly the meaning and uses of control, they will view it in the light of common sense. They will neither resent it nor be awed by it. They will turn it to the constructive use for which it is intended, and it will become an aid rather than an obstacle.

Perhaps the best way to clarify this common-sense approach is to examine a typical situation in which a manager wishes to make what he believes to be a desirable expenditure not covered in his budget. This problem is encountered daily and solved without friction by management people equipped with knowledge of budget principles and skill in their application— in other words, by the trained minority which shows the same attitudes-in-action of a manager grounded in good budget practice as illustrated in the following case.

The case of a sales promotion manager who is also responsible for advertising—Having been instructed to prepare a budget, he has first carefully completed his sales promotion and advertising plans for the coming period, basing them on discussions with the sales vice president and others responsible for policy and sales objectives. After constructing an acceptable plan, he has converted it into dollars in the form of a budget, which has been approved.

Because he has prepared this budget himself, he is thoroughly familiar with it. It is supported with adequate detail, including schedules of space insertions, estimates of costs of mailings, salary lists, and so on. He has reached an understanding with his "boss" concerning all of these items as a preliminary to approval of the budget. He feels confident that the plan and budget are as nearly right as he can make them.

Furthermore, he knows the implications of accepting this budget as his guide to operations. It is not to be exceeded without approval. It is a commitment that must be honored, and he well understands its importance to the company, his associates, and himself.

Nevertheless, he senses in the attitudes surrounding his budget an element of flexibility. If conditions change, the budget will have to be altered, either upward or downward. The sales promotion manager is not uneasy about this prospect. He is simply alert to recognize such a situation if it should develop.

Now let us suppose that an opportunity is presented to exert extra pressure on a certain market, and it appears that a special direct-mail campaign, supplemented by some local newspaper advertising, will yield good sales results. He knows enough not to throw the whole idea aside simply because it is not provided for in his budget. He has already had a clear understanding with the top sales executive about what

to do in such cases. So he goes about preparing a report, including proposed action, cost, and anticipated results; and he presents this report, knowing that it will be given proper consideration, even though it represents an expenditure in excess of budget limits.

The important point here is that this man, as manager of sales promotion, will not be subjected to injustice, censure, or negative treatment of any sort in advancing his ideas. He is fully aware of having a plan and a commitment to abide by it; yet he has assurance that if the interests of the company will be best served by breaking the budget, permission to do so will be forthcoming. All concerned will have an opportunity to evaluate the proposal and to weigh the desirability of deviating from the adopted plan.

How simple this miniature study in budget attitudes! How mature the responses governed by common sense! And yet how often common sense is violated! Is there any reason not to extend this frank approach to the foreman who sees a need for maintenance expenses or a merit increase not embraced in his budget? The frictions, frustrations, and other evils supposed to be inherent in budgets must all be susceptible to eradication in the same sensible manner.

Essential Prerequisites   All this presupposes, of course, that the supervisor in question —regardless of which division of the business he may be in—enjoys a satisfactory working relationship with his immediate superior. It also rests on clear-cut organization lines and the disposition to delegate authority along with responsibility.

Further, the accounting principles used must be well tested, and the accounting administration of high caliber. Strict honesty must govern the determination of the content of budget accounts and of the charges made thereto. Nothing confuses budget operation more quickly than the charging of costs over which the supervisor has no control, unless such items are set out separately and so labeled.

A last important requisite is understanding of the make-up of the budget. Flexible factory budgets especially can be complicated and subject to dispute. The factors used must be clearly explained, with full recognition of their weaknesses. If an item—such as machine repairs, for example—is neither wholly fixed nor wholly variable, but must be treated one way or the other for budget purposes, the shortcomings of the resulting budget figure should be conceded frankly. If scrap and rework costs are subject to dispute between foremen, the situation must be talked out in an air of give-and-take. No plant management should encourage or permit embittered arguments between foremen on such a matter. If all concerned have a clear understanding of the function of the budget and a reasonable attitude toward each other in the framework of modern industrial organization, such disputes will not occur.

COST REDUCTION: THE GOAL

The attitudes we have been discussing should add to, rather than detract from, the effectiveness of budgets in the field of cost control. Most companies operate continuously, in good times and bad, under the pressure of relentless competition, which forces them in turn to devote ceaseless effort to cost reduction. It is perhaps this circumstance more than any other that has given impetus to the spread of budgeting. And it has doubtless given rise to the abuses falling under the general heading of "pressure."

The usual tone of the complaints in this category is to the effect that budgets are used only as a hammer on costs (and at the same time on people), and particularly that the budgets are constantly being tightened and compliance with them enforced indiscriminately. The impression received by a supervisor in this situation is one of constant insistence on better and better performance, continuous blame for failure to meet the budget, and complete absence of credit for his good work. The budget becomes purely a pressure device, against which he must defend himself or lose his job.

The only really effective cure for such a distorted outlook is to substitute, as rapidly as possible, a "let's do it together" attitude for the shortsighted "you do it or else" attitude. The latter may have gained more ground in a plant or office than the management realizes. To correct this attitude may take time and patience, but it is never impossible to blank out negatives and substitute positives in human thinking.

Cost reduction drive is a feature of the American competitive system and is admittedly responsible in large measure for our high living standard. Budgets can be used for such stimulation without enslaving people. They furnish the standard from which to explore cost-savings possibilities. They provide the measure of yield from improved methods. But the attitude surrounding the practice must be right.

Incentives, True and False   This line of thought runs directly into the question of incentive. What incentive does a production super-visor have to reduce costs? Certainly the incentive supplied by threat is negative and, in the long run, ineffective. Direct money incentives, correlated to budget factors, claim some merit but, as we shall see, are fraught with problems. The true incentives, becoming clear after generations of management experiment, are those usually referred to as "intangible," supplemented by wages carefully determined and sympathetically explained.

But as an alternative let us examine for a moment the possibilities of direct money incentives. Some companies use and defend them—and we can have no quarrel with success. The line of reasoning on which they are based runs something like this: "If simple piecework can be an effective incentive for the workman, then the same principle can be applied to the foreman. We will provide a supervisory bonus and include in its computation a factor measuring success in complying with the budget. Savings against the budget will benefit the company and, at the same time, will provide funds for rewarding the foreman."

The fallacies in this reasoning begin to appear early in the process. They arise from two sources: (a) from the almost insurmountable difficulty of setting a completely fair and acceptable budget for this purpose, especially in the light of unforeseeable changes in operating conditions, and (b) from the tendency for the foreman to emphasize budget performance to the detriment of necessary action. It is a distinct temptation to defer maintenance when the need is not urgent and the expenditure would reduce one's own pay check.

As the foreman grows to the stature of a responsible manager, as he becomes more and more able to carry added responsibilities independently (and this is the goal of enlightened management today), the problems of basing incentive pay on budget factors become progressively tougher to handle. The experienced foreman is conscious of the importance of cost reduction, both by training and by virtue of the understanding of the job which his company has given him. He is also conscious of the need to spend money. He is likely to resent being rewarded for unwise penny-pinching as much as being penalized for exceeding his budget when the need for it is evident to everyone.

To a supervisor properly informed and aware of his role as a part of the management team, the real incentive is the satisfaction that comes from knowing that he has given his best effort, evidenced by suitable recognition both financial and in the manner and words of the superior. There is no substitute for the positive kind of understanding that can be developed between a supervisor and the rest of management if all concerned resolve to cultivate it.

By the same token, there is nothing better to assure the success of a cost-reduction program than a foreman with an inspired attitude and a real comprehension of the company's objectives, needs, and policies. To such a man, the budget will be a tool used to measure common achievements, rather than an irritant to the men and women entrusted to his leadership.

MANAGEMENT SUPPORT: THE NEED

One of the rocks on which many systems founder is the lack of top-management support. This is a strange commentary on a management group which, in this country, is generally supposed to have reached the acme of sophistication in the motivation of people. Nevertheless, examine any limping, halfhearted budget system, and note how the "chickens come home to roost" in the president's office.

Even more surprising, it frequently turns out that the top man does not really understand the planning and control concept and the simple interplay of attitudes that make it work. Consequently his allegiance to it is tentative and lukewarm. He constantly questions the methods used and is instinctively distrustful of results. This frame of mind permeates the organization. It bolsters opposition to the budget idea and weakens its proponents.

No budget system can realize its potential value without the unqualified support and understanding of top management. The solution, of course, lies in a process usually known as "education." Actually, it is even deeper than that. The budget idea is an expanding, growing concept—usually pioneered by one man with vision in a company. Little by little, this man— be he president or controller—patiently inculcates the advancing idea on his associates, until it is tested and accepted by all.

Controllers' Mistakes   There is another enemy of successful budget practice which may well be the cause of more of the friction between budgets and people than all the other errors put together. I refer to the misconception on the part of controllers, budget managers, accountants, and other staff people concerning their part in the process.

When a controller takes operating personnel to task for exceeding the budget, he is inviting trouble of the worst kind. His correct course is to report the situation to responsible operating management and, if necessary, to the president, using the same figures and terms in each case.

The problem then rests with the president and his operating subordinate, which is exactly where it belongs. It should be discussed and action determined in the direct line organization. No controller should permit himself to be placed in the position of representing the president in such matters—of giving approval to budgets or disapproval to results.

The same principle applies to all staff people concerned with coordinating the budget system, whether they report to a controller, treasurer, or factory accountant. There is impressive evidence that overzealous budget people have caused a great deal of mischief in this field, practically all of it unnecessary. They cannot be blamed individually, of course, for the failure of management to provide the principles needed for good budget practice. The remedy is in the eradication of a vicious set of faulty notions concerning the relationships of staff and line.

One of the first steps is to insist that each manager or foreman establish his own budget. He knows best his potential performance and the extent to which he can commit himself. He may enlist expert help, of course, from the budget man, but under no circumstances should the budget man or controller establish the budget, nor should the foreman be permitted to feel that this is happening. The penalty for violating this rule is the sacrifice of the sense of responsibility that locks a man securely to his budget when he knows it is his own.

Another misconception sometimes indulged by budget men is that they are almost solely responsible for cost reduction; that they alone are expected to seek and find opportunities for cost savings, such as excessive waste, dispensable overtime, carelessness in handling tools, and so on. In some cases, they have apparently been instructed to report such instances to a factory superintendent or even to top management rather than to the responsible first-line supervisor. It is difficult to conceive of a practice that violates more completely the basic principles of good human relations.

Line Organization   This medieval mess will clear itself up once management has established the fact that the line organization is responsible for cost control—fully and absolutely. Using a familiar type of organization, let it be clear that the vice president of manufacturing is charged with the duty of conducting the manufacturing cost reduction campaign; he delegates this work as he sees fit to plant managers, and they in turn to factory superintendents, who then look to the front-line men, the foremen, for control of costs.

The controller and budget men still fit into this picture importantly:

1. They are equipped to establish and coordinate the budget system, with all of the tools of accounting and cost analysis.

2. They should be able to teach the operating people how to use it.

3. They should provide timely and intelligible reporting on performance against budget. (This reporting should of course be tailored to the organization level to which it is addressed. For instance, at the top, the controller is obligated to report that which is pertinent to the president of the company.)

The attitude which should govern the staff people in this field, as in all other staff assignments, is one of maximum helpfulness to the line personnel. Only in this way can the budget man gain the foreman's confidence. If he finds cost-saving ideas, they should be volunteered promptly to the foreman for what use the latter can make of them. Personal credit is not the primary consideration. The budget man's own superior should be adept enough in detecting a skillful job to accord it the recognition it deserves—and one primary evidence of such performance will be a satisfactory relationship with the operating personnel. It is a preposterous notion that a budget man vaults to success on the failures and errors of the line.

CONCLUSION

The specific steps to be taken to improve budgeting practice depend, of course, on the mistakes an organization has been making. A searching self-examination in the light of the known principles of budgeting would seem to be the first move. Having identified the practices in an organization which most clearly abuse these principles, management will find that the corrective steps will present themselves. Courage and patience are needed to follow them.

Summary of Principles   Here, for your convenience, is a summary of points to be considered by any management wishing to establish its budget practice on a sound foundation:

1. Establish your budget system on the highest possible level of motivation. To be specific, this means using it as a means for setting standards of performance, for measuring actual results, and for guiding management to satisfactory achievement. It means rejecting the use of budgets primarily as a pressure device to goad people into greater efforts. Accept this as a part of the philosophy of your company. Think about it, talk about it, make it a reality. And give more than lip service, even if it is difficult at first to separate the two conflicting motives. A budget program cannot be advanced to the stage of maximum fruition without this step.

2. Anchor your budgeting firmly in a foundation of company planning. Do not permit it to float unattached—a technique without a clearly thought-out reason for being. The budget is not the plan; it is merely the statement of the plan in the language of figures. First turn the thinking of your organization to basic planning; then ask your people to prepare budgets to effectuate their plans. Plan sales by markets and products, plan development, plan methods of manufacturing, purchasing, and merchandising. Determine the performance required of each department of the business; then budgets become simply the standard of dollars needed to do the job. This is the approach that makes managers out of men.

3. Establish the meaning of control, and then put it into practice. In particular this requires the manager of each department to establish his own budget, based on his understanding of the job to be done. Top management may not be able to approve as high a figure as he asks for, but it can reach agreement with him as to what he is expected to accomplish and what it will cost. Having done this, he is responsible for planned performance. If he finds it necessary to exceed the budget, he should discuss this action with his superior and ask for advance approval. A budget is neither to be considered sacred nor to be taken lightly. Managers will respond with better attitudes when they understand that the use of the budget is to permit them to control their own operations.

4. Insist on a clear-cut organization structure. A budget system cannot thrive without it. Each department should have a responsible manager, vested with authority commensurate with his responsibilities. He should have a clear understanding both as to the individual to whom he reports and as to the people who report to him. These are well-known precepts. A searching organization audit may be needed to determine whether they are being followed. The limitations on budget success are precisely marked by the degree of organization soundness.

5. Arrange for good, common-sense accounting and complete, simple, and prompt explanations of the content of the items. This re-

quires an accounting staff that is more concerned with the operating facts than with the techniques of balancing the books. Extreme care should be devoted to seeing that no supervisor has in his budget any item over which he does not have control. This area is fraught with debatable items and unending technical complications. If your house is not in order in this respect, almost any amount of effort is justified to put it in shape. And unless you are the exception to the rule, it will cost more money initially than you expect to pay, in terms of staff salaries and, perhaps, outside consulting services. The cost is usually well justified, however, in the end result.

6. In the field of cost control, use your budget as a tool to be placed in your foremen's hands—not as a club to be held over their heads. To implement this rule, it may be a good idea to design an educational program. Meetings attended by line and staff supervisors may prove an effective vehicle. Cost reduction must be placed on the basis of mutual effort toward a common aim. The creation of this atmosphere is an essential, definitive step in budget practice.

7. Insure the active participation of top management. The budget program cannot succeed otherwise. The way of going about this step depends on your organizational status. If you are the president and question how well you measure up to this requirement, examine your thinking critically and ascertain which of the points in this article, if any, arouse resistance in your thought. Discussion with a controller other than your own may afford a fresh view. In any case, set aside the time to explore and understand the subject fully and to practice budgetary control in your daily affairs. If, however, you are a controller, your course in enlisting top-management support is one of patient, untiring teaching, until your case is won and the planning and control idea is in the warp and woof of your company's thinking.

8. See that the controller and his staff express the correct attitude for the responsibility they undertake with respect to budgets. It is the controller's job to establish, maintain, and coordinate a budgetary system—in fact, a complete system of planning and control. But this work must be accomplished through authorized management. He must not enforce his instructions nor issue orders. He and his staff must be devoted to producing, reporting, and interpreting information—to making the planning and control machinery

run. He is wholly a staff executive, and his only honors stem from the confidence of his associates. This he earns by honestly providing the control service and refraining from making operating decisions. Perhaps the cultivation of this attitude is the most productive single step of all, because from it the impetus to take the other steps may flow.

I have refrained from specifying the manner in which these ideas might be made known, or "sold," to the administrative groups. The task is essentially one for controllership. It is the most challenging project the controller is privileged to conduct, and it gains momentum as he enlists the support of top management and of supervision at all levels.

The actual method of carrying on this unremitting campaign varies from company to company, but there is a predominant tendency to rely largely on daily contacts. The controller and his staff—all the budget men and cost accountants—spread the idea in their working conversations. Meanwhile, special attention is continuously given the top echelon by the controller himself. Relatively few companies appear to hold regular educational or discussion meetings for this purpose.

It is interesting that all of the eight steps listed have their roots deep in personnel administration—that each one is, in the final analysis, the reflection of a problem involving people.

Deeper Significance   The present era demands a new appraisal of our daily work. The symptoms of budget irritations may point to deeper meanings in the spiritual emancipation of mankind. We are beginning to learn that no tool can be used effectively unless the hand that guides it is rightly motivated. Like all other techniques of business, the budget should be a door open to more satisfying and profitable work—not an instrument of torture.

Then it will be known that what you can do without a budget you can do better with one. It will be seen that the entire planning and control procedure, under whatever name, is a device for freeing men to do their best work—not a machine of restriction and condemnation. This better view is within our grasp today.

Planning is but another word for the vision that sees a creative achievement before it is manifest. Control is but a name for direction. The genius of management cannot fail to turn the budget idea finally into positive channels, so that people individually, as well as business leadership generally, will reap the harvest that it promises.

69

The Breakeven Concept*

FRED V. GARDNER

INTRODUCTION

An inquiring reporter with the knack of getting to the heart of a subject would find that those who manage business affairs and who are responsible either for guiding profit performance or for measuring it know very little about what breakevens are, why they are what they are, or what to do about them when they show eccentric characteristics.

Do You Know Your Breakeven Point?   It is true that when the question is first put to management men they are prone to say, "Of course I know what breakevens are. They are the place where profits turn to losses or losses to profits, depending upon whether you are going up or down." It is surprising how many first-class, high-ranking executives shrug off the whole problem with this type of comment.

A *Business Week* magazine article made three important points:

Most management men talk about breakeven points, but they often mean a lot of different things.

A few companies really figure the points closely —and swear by the results.

Most companies know—or guess—that their breakeven points have risen little in terms of capacity.[1]

These statements agree with our findings. The 19th hole on the breakeven point is played in about the same vein as on the golf course. The poorer the performance, the louder the excuses.

Breakevens and Capacity   It is true that the breakeven point is that point of capacity at

which operations pass from profits to losses or vice versa. The only trouble with this concept is that this point in terms of either capacity or income is not rigid or static. It changes with every decision of management. It changes when selling prices change and when operating efficiency rises or falls. It changes as the relationship between product lines varies even for short periods of time. These and many other reasons cause a breakeven point to move in a definable orbit. Unless the path of this orbit can be measured, conclusions reached about breakevens may be as dangerous as a bottle marked "Poison" if not used correctly.

RESISTANCE TO BREAKEVEN CONTROL

Because the postwar years were so lucrative that management energy was concentrated on the problem of keeping up production, many executives have built up "straw men" of resistance in their minds against the breakeven concepts without thinking of the consequences.

Most management men have adopted the term "breakeven" as a part of their vernacular and the word bobs up everywhere. Yet most of those in authority who toss the word around in conversation have little concrete knowledge about the structure of a breakeven point, its habits, or its characteristics, and know even less how to harness the breakeven concept in guiding their operations. To offset these shortcomings in advanced management thinking, alibis and excuses have developed.

The major excuses run about as follows: "Why worry about the breakeven point today? We will get it down when we have to." Or, "It will work all right for others perhaps, but it just won't work in our company," or, "It's all theory and not very practical."

These are but a few of the hundreds of defensive comments used daily in explaining all types of performance to all kinds of people who are interested in these problems. Were we

* Reprinted by permission of the publisher from Fred V. Gardner, *Profit Management and Control*, McGraw-Hill Book Company, Inc., New York, 1955, pp. 19–26. Mr. Gardner is senior partner of Fred V. Gardner and Associates, management consultants.
[1] *Business Week*, Dec. 13, 1952, p. 158.

to attempt cataloguing the variations and ramifications of the statements above, they would
range from the ridiculous to the sublime.
Many of them, if put together in proper sequence, would be as interesting and entertain-
ing as the proverbial three-ring circus.

Today's Breakeven Too Easy to Attain

To
answer broadly . . . the foregoing comments,
. . . the following observations are appropriate.
Why worry about the breakeven point today if
we can get it down when we have to? We did
not bring it down from 1929 to 1932, when it
was a fight for survival. To be sure, that was
over 20 years ago, and we have learned much
in management techniques since then. Nor did
many industries demonstrate ability to hold on
to their breakeven-point positions in the 1937–
1938 recession. And breakeven-point control
was widely lacking in 1949–1950. The truth is
that each faltering and falling-off business, however slight the hiatus, again demonstrates the
need for better control mechanisms to protect
against the "close-haul" years.

The average company today will find it difficult even to maintain its existing breakeven
point when volume falls off, let alone attempt
to reduce or improve its breakeven picture. Inflexible labor contracts, sheer size and diversity,
multiplicity of operating locations, and un-
streamlined methods of selling are just a few of
the present conditions leading to less cost flexibility and greater difficulty of control.

Companies that have run contra to the pattern of constant growth which has been so
typical of industry in recent years are living
monuments to attest to the fact that breakeven
reduction is not a "sleight-of-hand" process. It
requires hard work to build techniques based
on dynamic and forceful controls, controls
which tell why profits vary as well as what
profits are.

"Breakeven Concepts Won't Work for Our Company"

Holding that breakevens may
work all right in other companies but not in
your own runs counter to experience in retailing, service, and manufacturing, from capital
goods to soft goods, from technical to highly
competitive lines. Whether it be the airline
industry with its peculiarities (including people
who think you can be good only if you are a
flyer) or a chain of lumber yards or a chemical
plant, breakeven concepts will work, provided
the idea has executive support, the controls are
honestly built, and the findings honestly followed. Of course they will not work for you if
you do not want them to.

Are Breakevens Theory?

Some say break-
evens are all theory. If you think breakevens
are simply theoretical, it is because you are
theoretical. The breakeven point does not
harness you. It records what you harness. If it
appears to be unrealistic, if it presents conditions which you do not believe, that is not the
fault of the breakeven point. Like the thermometer which measures the temperature in
your office or home, it measures facts. If the
thermometer tells you it is cold, that is not the
fault of the thermometer but of the temperature being measured.

Breakevens are the mirror of your business,
nothing less, nothing more. Their application
and use will tell you how your business looks
and will help you decide whether it is "time for
a change."

Delving deeply into the objections to
breakeven-point analysis and control, one finds
but few real bases for opposing application of
this scientific and sensitive aid to business operation. Plain lack of understanding can be cured,
but more disturbing are the resistances rooted
in downright indifference and in personal ego.

Indifference arises in prosperous periods during which profits are easy to come by. Simple
evolution will jar lethargy of this kind because
it is inevitable that the going will be more
difficult in some years than in others. In the
meantime both employees and owners suffer.
Personal ego objections are more difficult to
meet. In such cases the chief executive is proud
of his ability, likes to run by the seat of his
pants, and despite protestations to the contrary,
enjoys the role of local god and crystal-ball
gazer extraordinary. He does not want science
in management if he will lose the zest of his
mysterious maneuvering. Even such a manager
will find breakeven control useful in lightening
his load. Apart from the better performance his
executives will register, his own life will be
more free of ulcers, hardening of the arteries,
and frightening heart disturbances.

The *Business Week* article cited earlier gives
a clue which is worthy of note:

> Relatively few companies make explicit opera-
> tional use of breakeven points, or even figure
> them very closely. The companies that do use
> breakeven points frequently build intricate sys-
> tems out of them, and swear by their usefulness.

To refresh our thinking of what a breakeven
point is, how it is determined, and how it gives
dynamics to static information, an illustration
from a section of the history of Caterpillar
Tractor will be helpful.

CATERPILLAR TRACTOR COMPANY BREAKEVEN CHART

For illustration, a simple breakeven chart of the Caterpillar Tractor Company is shown for the most recent years (Chart 2).

The base scale of the chart is the reason for incurring cost—therefore we have plotted the annual net sales in millions of dollars horizontally. The vertical scale is assigned to the value to be compared with the reason for incurring cost. Since we are concerned with the behavior of costs in relation to sales income, the vertical scale is assigned to annual costs (before income taxes) in millions of dollars.

It is axiomatic that "breakeven" means balance of sales income with cost outgo. Therefore we draw a "sales" line (really a line of 100 per cent correlation between costs and sales income) from the zero point at the left to Point B on the chart. At that point the line indicates, according to our scales, that there is a "breakeven" condition if sales and costs are both 500 million dollars; and the breakeven condition will be shown if costs fall on any point of the broken "sales" line down to zero.

Then we take the adjusted costs from Table II and plot the costs for each year, measuring up on the cost scale, and recording its point directly over the sales value plotted for that year along the base line. It is apparent that in the years 1946, 1947, 1948, and 1950 cost and sales relationships were such that a straight line could be drawn through them. But we are dealing with the record through 1953. A straight line drawn through the 1949 and 1953 points falls through an approximate average of the 1950 and 1951 points. Furthermore such a line closely imitates the slope of the 1946–1948

TABLE II Caterpillar Tractor Company Sales and Costs 1946–1953

YEAR	NET SALES	ADJUSTED COSTS*
1946	$128,437	$126,069
1947	189,120	172,816
1948	218,037	193,686
1949	254,872	228,482
1950	337,285	276,727
1951	393,756	356,903
1952	477,600	406,106
1953	433,800	371,465

* Depreciation for all years restated to that used in 1951 to eliminate effect of changed plant capacity and accelerated amortization. Income share not included in costs.

points. Therefore, for illustrative purposes it is a fair assumption that this higher line, marked "costs of output" on the chart, is fairly representative of the more recent cost-value-income relationships realized by the Caterpillar management.

It is evident that the slopes of the sales line and of the cost line are substantially different. Running the cost line down to the zero net-sales axis (extreme left) we find that this "cost pattern" indicates a substantial remainder of cost even though sales income were zero. This remainder is the standby or constant relationship common to certain kinds of costs in every business. There would be no such thing as a breakeven point (point of crossover between the cost and sales lines) unless this were true. Accounting statements do not suggest the pres-

CHART 2   Breakeven Chart: Caterpillar Tractor Company

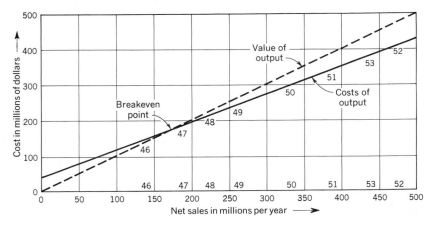

ence of this kind of costs nor afford any means of estimating the relative importance of the variable and standby costs.

We are not concerned here with the specific value of Caterpillar's breakeven point. Rather, using data which can be checked with public sources, we seek only to demonstrate that the slopes of the cost and sales lines for Caterpillars, and, indeed, for every company no matter what the nature of its business, will disclose two kinds of costs.

As we have drawn the line, the cost line rises from the standby constant at a rate of approximately $79 for each $100 of sales. This was the rate at which Caterpillar added costs (as sales volume rose from some 228 million dollars in 1949 to 406 million dollars in 1952), a little more or a little less, year by year. Over the term of years as the adjusted years are plotted, this could be said to represent Caterpillar's quality of control on the upside. But should sales volume decline, we could not attribute the same quality of control *unless Caterpillar also removes $79 of cost for each $100 of sales decline*. That kind of cost control is necessary to hold the breakeven point at the indicated 150 million dollars of sales.

To control costs and their resultant profits, the problem of management is one of understanding how the two elements—standby and variable time factors—are affected by specific decisions. So long as there is no means of separating them, as in the conventional accounting statement, management cannot but confuse its people and confuse itself in its efforts to "do something about the breakeven point."

Why Fly Blind?   Fly blind if you are happy, but if you prefer instruments to control your course, they must be used correctly and with sufficient knowledge to bring you out of the overcast and land you safely at some selected objective. The breakeven chart is an excellent instrument panel for your guidance in controlling your business. The ten salient points of the breakeven-point chart are so many gauges for checking out your management decisions. Study Chart 3 carefully. Let your imagination take hold. With good understanding of these points you can appraise your own breakeven point and can interpret the signals for important management action. The ten points of significance in a breakeven chart are:

1. The breakeven point itself
2. The profit path above the breakeven point as an indication of inherent profitability
3. The standby cost relationship to other costs and sales values at the breakeven point and at other capacity levels
4. The breakeven point as a percentage of normal output capacity—the margin-of-safety index
5. Point of maximum output as measured by existing plant or organization capacity, or point at which diminishing returns appear as a higher rate of variable costs because of major productive inefficiencies
6. Variable cost rate, an approximation of true "direct" or out-of-pocket costs
7. Selling price per unit
8. Relationship of variable and standby costs at any level of activity

CHART 3   The Important Points of Breakeven Analysis

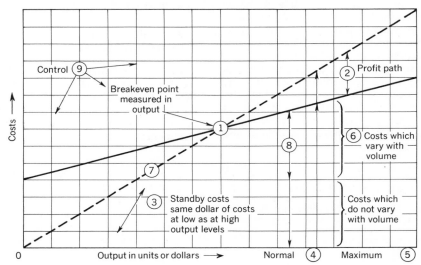

9. Tie-in with profit and loss statement as a test of validity

10. Competitive comparison with other companies . . .

CONCLUSION

As with any control-instrument panel, much is needed behind the breakeven chart to make it work and to make it the reliable, ever-ready management aid that it can and should be. Take warning: we have but started on the road to dynamic business control and costing; there is much hard work ahead.

There must, however, be a basic understanding and acceptance of the breakeven concept. Remember that you are trying to bring order out of the chaos of the conflicting *time* effects of different kinds of business cost. Unproved promises and "guesstimates" will be more harmful than helpful. Your breakeven chart must be thoroughly supported with detailed cost planning and structuring, carrying the concept down into each phase, department, and account within your business.

70

*Internal Auditing Control**

F. A. LAMPERTI and J. B. THURSTON

INTERNAL AUDITING CONTROL

Modern internal auditing is one of the essential means for establishing and maintaining management control of a business. It rounds out all of the basic elements of management control and is in itself the main element of the appraisal, measurement, and evaluation control.

The rapid growth and widespread acceptance of modern internal auditing results primarily from the fact that it has provided executives with an important control which was lacking before its development and use. The acceptance of this function as a medium of control was accelerated by World War II, not only through specifications in governmental regulations and the requirements of war contracts, but also through the sheer necessity on the part of owners and managers to maintain close supervision over rapidly expanding companies and large industrial organizations.

* Reprinted by permission of the publisher from F. A. Lamperti and J. B. Thurston, *Internal Auditing for Management*, Prentice-Hall, Inc., Englewood Cliffs, N.J., 1953, pp. 83–84, 86, 89–92. Mr. Lamperti is an internal auditor and organization consultant, and Mr. Thurston, now deceased, was the first president of the Institute of Internal Auditors and a consulting management engineer.

Since the war, a variety of factors have contributed to its continuing growth, among them being the further development and perfection of internal auditing itself; the postwar growth of many relatively new as well as older companies to a size where internal auditing is required to establish adequate coordination; and, finally, management's increasing familiarity with, and recognition of, the importance of this new control technique.

RESPONSIBILITIES OF THE INTERNAL AUDITOR

In 1947, the Institute [of Internal Auditors] published a statement outlining the responsibilities of the internal auditor. . . . The following paragraph, captioned "Nature of Internal Auditing," summarizes the highlights of the statement:

Internal auditing is the independent appraisal activity within an organization for the review of the accounting, financial, and other operations as a basis for protective and constructive service to management. It is a type of control which functions by measuring and evaluating the effectiveness of other types of control. It deals primarily with accounting and financial matters but it may also properly deal with matters of an operating nature.

RELATIONSHIP BETWEEN CORPORATE ACCOUNTING AND INTERNAL AUDITING

It is important to recognize at the outset that internal auditing is not just another accounting function. In fact, it is not an accounting function at all but a management-control function.

A great many executives, however, still consider internal auditing as a branch of accounting, with its activities limited to the verification of accounting and financial transactions. This is no doubt a result of the close historical association that has existed between the two functions. Internal auditing was born of accounting. It came into being as soon as the need for establishing accountability developed. The need for someone besides the owner to handle revenues and transactions brought with it the need for someone to verify these revenues and transactions objectively. The association has been close for centuries and is still close.

New interests have come into the life of internal auditing until it has reached a point where it is time to leave the parental shelter and branch out into an independent life. It is associated closely but objectively with every activity and every transaction which contributes to its company's profit dollar. It issues no orders, originates no transactions, but is everywhere as a searching, appraising, and open evaluating function, with the object of helping those who do issue orders or originate transactions.

In many instances accounting data are limited in scope. Consequently, management decisions based on them alone may be faulty if the actual conditions behind the statements are not known. Because the limitations of accounting have been recognized, increasing attention is being paid by management to internal auditing and other control techniques.

Aside from the statement of responsibilities, the internal auditing function is difficult to define in precise terms. It varies materially with the size and type of each organization and with other contributing circumstances. Many smaller companies do not have an internal auditor; the public accountant's services include the responsibilities usually given him. On the other hand, larger companies and corporate entities which have expanded materially have found a definite need for a management representative who could replace the personal contact which formerly existed between management and person-

nel. This need is being filled today by the internal auditor.

Larger companies have found it necessary also to develop a system of administration which may be called *management by exception.* Under this system, top management determines and provides the policies and procedures best suited to meet the objectives of the company. It assumes then that these policies are being carried out effectively and that the only items which come to its attention thereafter represent exceptions from established policy and procedures or suggestions for improvement.

This form of management technique calls for extensive reliance on reports covering all phases of operations. If properly designed and compiled, these reports should reflect the effectiveness of management's policies and the thoroughness with which they are observed. It is the internal auditor's responsibility, and one he is particularly fitted to carry out, to see that the operations are in accordance with the policies and that the reports reflect these operations properly. In so doing, he is in a position to keep management informed of how effectively it discharges its responsibilities. The very nature of the auditor's examination discloses also the propriety and effectiveness of the procedures and the results obtained through them.

This brings us to another contribution of the internal auditing function, namely the determination of the adequacy of the procedures in force, as well as the recommendation of improved procedures wherever necessary. As a result of the examination of records and procedures throughout all organizations of the company, the internal auditor is in a good position to (a) recommend improvements in existing procedures, (b) suggest new ones which will serve management objectives better, and (c) make available to other divisions of any particularly effective practice developed in a specific unit of the company. Conversely, where an undesirable change has been made in established procedures in a particular unit, the auditor can point out its disadvantages from an over-all point of view and bring about necessary corrections.

There is a marked difference between the establishment of well-defined controls and their day-to-day use. Variances are bound to creep in as a result of any number of reasons. Someone may believe that he has found a shortcut, another person misinterprets a directive, others may willfully desire to see certain steps circumvented. Only periodical objective examination and appraisal can maintain the efficiency of these controls. The internal auditor provides these examinations. Internal auditing is the inspection unit of the system, constantly on the alert for any weakness or breakdown of controls. It challenges every feature examined from a multiplicity of angles, determining particularly whether:

1. It conforms with company policies.
2. Controls are adequate, effective, and efficient as a transaction flows through company processes.
3. Accounting and operating procedures are proper.
4. External regulations are complied with.
5. All records are prepared and stored with adequate care.
6. Controls provide necessary safeguards against fraud, removing all sources of temptation as much as possible.

What are the means available to the internal auditor for determining compliance with management directives? The fundamental source of information is to be found in instruction manuals. Most companies have manuals covering each of the major functions. For example, the accounting manual will delineate the accounting procedures for the home office, or a branch sales office, or a factory, or any other unit of the company. The manual contains an expression of accounting management's policies as well as applicable procedures. This is essential in fostering uniformity of practice and coordination of operations. It is the internal auditor's duty to see that performance is in accordance with the manual. Consequently, his first job is to be thoroughly versed in its contents. The same is true of any other function to be audited.

In addition to the question of compliance and effectiveness of procedures, the auditor must be able to assure management of the accuracy of records and reports. This can result only from thorough checking. He must always determine the facts, note all exceptions, and follow every avenue of investigation before he can be satisfied as to the accuracy of the work and the effectiveness or desirability of existing practices.

What is true of accounting is true also of other service departments such as purchasing, traffic, advertising, personnel and others. Management establishes policies in respect to each one. Large sums of money are expended by each of these groups and the internal auditor must determine whether these funds are spent in accordance with management policies.

Again, the auditor's examination and appraisal of results should indicate whether these monies are being expended to the best interests of the company. Frequently such departments, most of which are directly under management supervision, are audited only indirectly, if at all. There have been instances of serious misapplication of company funds in some of these areas which might have been avoided or lessened through proper coverage by internal auditing.

Obviously it is difficult to define the functions of the internal auditor except in general terms, since his duties are prescribed by specific companies and vary substantially from firm to firm. However, there is a basic pattern which runs through most established auditing units, namely, the function of continuously measuring and evaluating all other controls. It is the inspection department of management controls, necessitated by the ever-increasing complexity of business administrative problems associated with the increasing decentralization of authority, with corresponding realignment of responsibilities. Other general areas of responsibility would include the following:

1. Examination of the financial transactions of the business, such as cash balance, customers' accounts, and adherence to credit terms; investigation into suppliers' accounts, into expense accounts, and so on.
2. Examination of the administrative procedures of the company to insure that the policies laid down by the management are adhered to, particularly in connection with the exercise of authority and the adherence to limits of expenditures.
3. Examination of methods with a view to the elimination of unnecessary and repetitive work, reduction of paper work, and the clearing of channels of communication.
4. An examination of procedures, both mechanical and otherwise, throughout the business with a view to suggesting improvements.
5. Checks upon the investment policy of the company with particular regard to the building up of stocks and their relation to the scale of the business; maintenance of a proper relation between the size of each department and the scale of its activities.
6. Investigation into the management functions of branches and subsidiaries, and comparison between such sections of the company with a view to improving administrative and other techniques in general.

71

Rhochrematics and Organizational Adjustments*

STANLEY H. BREWER and JAMES ROSENZWEIG

Rhochrematics, which is the new science of material and information flow, has many implications for top management. Developed to foster a systematic, integrated approach to managing the flow of raw materials, parts, components, and finished goods, its chief concept is that of maintaining the flow of the product from raw materials to the ultimate consumer.

In maintaining this flow it cuts across the traditional organization chart, and undermines some time-honored management practices, but companies practising Rhochrematics have discovered that it also cuts costs and compresses lead time.

In the case of the Boeing Airplane Company, whose Transport Division adopted this new approach following a survey in June, 1960, savings to date in reduced inventories and lead times are conservatively estimated to exceed $300,000 per year.

Boeing's experience with Rhochrematics and that of the Purex Corporation, another recent convert to the new science, will be discussed in detail later in this article, as cases in point, but the essential thesis here is that managements wishing to profit from this new science must also be willing to accept its chief concept which is continuous concentration on the flow of the manufacturing process and may involve a complete restructuring of management's accepted channels of authority and ways of doing things.

The term Rhochrematics is a coined word and stands for the flow of things. It comes from two Greek roots, "rhoe" which means a flow as of a river or a stream and "chrema"

which stands for products, materials, or things, including information. The abstract ending "ics" has been added here as for any of the sciences, such as mathematics, physics, etc.[1] From the time requirements are established and production planning is accomplished until an end product is delivered to the final consumer, many decisions are made which should be coordinated in order to optimize the entire material flow process.

Aspects of this process are being analyzed continually by almost every producer, wholesaler, or retailer. More and more attention is being devoted to physical distribution, materials management, inventory control, and other aspects of the material flow process. In most cases, however, analyses are carried out in each of these areas with little regard for the effects of changes on other areas. Hence, optimal solutions are often proposed for a segment of the flow process without due consideration for the resultant changes in the total flow pattern. Separate functions are optimized while the total operation proceeds in a suboptimal fashion.

This article attempts to ascertain the benefits that might accrue from a systematic, integrated approach to the over-all problem of material flow. Since material and information flows cut horizontally across typical vertical organizations, it will be vital to assess the impact on the organization structure of a change in approach. We will point out the benefits that might accrue, set forth some ideas on how organizations might be adjusted, and assess the likelihood of such changes in the future.

"PRODUCT MISSION"

A total concept, the flow of material and information from the raw material stage through production and distribution to the ultimate consumer, is difficult to conceive and, as such, has not been the target of concerted efforts toward optimization. The total flow is

* Reprinted by permission of the publisher from the *California Management Review*, vol. 3, no. 3, pp. 52–71, Spring, 1961. Mr. Brewer is professor of transportation in the College of Business Administration at the University of Washington. Mr. Rosenzweig is professor of policy and administration in the College of Business Administration at the University of Washington.

often so complex, involving many separate organizations and agencies, that no one agency has assumed total responsibility for the entire process.

However, when the entire "product mission" is visualized, it is easier to fit the separate parts together and make a systematic, integrated analysis of the entire system of material and information flow. While the time is not far off when such complex systems can be analyzed, via simulation or similar techniques, most attention has been devoted to one or the other of the two major sub-parts of the total flow process, production or distribution.

The flow of material from the raw material stage through the production process to the finished goods stage has been the subject of analysis for management scientists, efficiency experts, and industrial engineers for many years. A great deal of attention has been focused on isolated segments of this internal flow; e.g., costs of acquisition vs. costs of storage, inventory control, production control, expediting, and materials handling. However, little attention has been given to an integrated approach which focuses on the flow process itself rather than on individual functional areas.

Flow Concept   The flow of materials from the finished goods stage to the final consumer also has been the subject of many cost reduction efforts. There has been much furor over the fact that in many cases distribution costs actually exceed costs of production. Accordingly, much attention has been devoted to developing more efficient systems.

However, improvements in the distribution system are often made without reference to possible effects on the production function. More attention must be devoted to analysis of the over-all flow of material and information to optimize the entire process. Continued attention to individual departments, sub-areas, or functions will, of course, develop increased efficiency in isolated segments. However, such increased efficiency may be detrimental to the overall operation.

In this article we will discuss both of the major subdivisions of the material flow process, production and distribution. Attention will also be given to an integrated approach to the over-all flow process, including both internal and external flows.

Organizing for Performance   In all cases, an attempt will be made to show how improvement in isolated functional department areas may not lead too over-all efficiency. Since this problem of optimizing material and informa-

tion flow is inexorably tied to organization, it will be desirable to set the stage for later analysis by discussing some of the basic concepts of organization, and pointing out their effect upon the problem of material and information flow.

While it is obvious that contemporary organizations must be concerned with multiple goals, the business organization's primary task is that of translating raw materials into goods or services for producers or consumers through efficient utilization of capital and human resources. Business organizations have been growing continuously in size and complexity and undoubtedly will continue in this direction as long as the economy increases in complexity and society becomes more sophisticated.

In their chapter on "Molding of Organization in Modern Society," Pfiffner and Sherwood sum up the factors leading toward greater complexity as follows:

> The many factors that have operated to make modern organizations complex are just those which have served to complicate the entire fabric of society. They include: 1) the liberation of the individual in our social philosophy and policies; 2) the development of new understandings of the nature of human cooperation; 3) the broadening range of organization goals; and 4) the movement toward task specialization.[2]

Specializing Invites Fragmentation.   This latter point is of particular importance for our purposes here. As organizations grow, the many functions that must be performed tend to be split off into various divisions, departments, groups, or units. As this fragmentation occurs, the need for specialists within the organization increases.

Each specialist tends to assume his role and to become more proficient in carrying out his particular duties. The larger the company and the greater the degree of specialization, the more the tendency to lose track of over-all objectives of the firm and to concentrate on strengthening the individual function.

The specialist is motivated by a desire to perform efficiently and move up in the organization; but, for the most part, he is limited by departmental boundary lines. Normally, he can assume more duties within his particular department, but he does not take over functions that are being performed by other departments or divisions unless there is a reorganization. Often, therefore, specialization becomes identified with functionalization. While separating duties and responsibilities on the basis of functions is only one of a number of possible alternatives, it turns out to be an over-riding consideration in many cases.

Work might be divided on the basis of time sequences; for example, planning, execution, and control. However, formal organization structure does not ordinarily follow such a pattern. Equipment is not often the basis for departmentation. Processes such as milling, grinding, or heat treating often serve as a basis for organizing work groups. However, process and function are often hard to distinguish and processes might be considered as sub-functions to production.

If two or more classes of customers are entirely different, a company might well organize separate work groups to produce for different customers. Companies producing for both the military and consumer sectors of the economy might be well advised to separate completely their operations in order that entirely different requirements can be met efficiently. Geographic location of divisions or branches is a typical approach to dividing the work.

Dividing the Work. However, within each of the decentralized units there is also an organization structure which is likely to stem from some more basic factor. Multi-product companies may divide the work according to individual products or product groups in order to focus attention on the objectives of subunits of the organization. In such cases, conflicts may arise between product or product group managers and functional managers who have traditionally been responsible for carrying out the basic functions of the enterprise.

Is Vertical Organization Best? Traditionally, organization has been predominantly vertical and hierarchical with authority and responsibility resting in individual functions. Typically, superior-subordinate relationships have been established on a functional basis, with orders and instructions going down the line and reports and requests going up the line. Recently, this traditional approach has been questioned as the most suitable for over-all efficiency of the operation.

For example, the flow of material and information in the typical manufacturing operation tends to flow horizontally, cutting across the vertical structuring of functional authority. In discussing new technology and its impact upon organization, Jasinski states:

> But technology, including both integrated data, processing and integrated machine production, has developed on what might be called a horizontal plane. That is, the machine cuts across superior-subordinate relationships, affecting the

jobs of people in different areas, departments, and work groups. Superimposing a strictly vertical organization structure on a technology which emphasizes horizontal and diagonal relationships can and does cause obvious difficulties . . . Certainly it is management's job not only to recognize these new relationships, but also to take steps to enable them to function definitely and smoothly. A few managers have recognized the discrepancy between organization and technology, and have taken steps to integrate the two. They have achieved such integration in a variety of ways, which essentially may be classified as: 1. Changing the technology to conform with the existing organizational structure. 2. Changing the organization so as to define and formalize the relationships required by the technology. 3. Maintaining both the existing organization and the existing technology, but introducing mechanisms to reduce or minimize the discrepancies between the two.[3]

Focusing attention on the *flow* of material and information as stressed in Rhochrematics, allows the rethinking called for by Jasinski. The problem, in short then, is that most companies organized in the traditional functional fashion are not set up to take advantage of conceptualizing the total flow process.

The remainder of this analysis will approach this problem by discussing: (1) how differences in orientation result in different emphasis in organization structure; (2) how traditional functional specialization may suboptimize the over-all operations; (3) alternative approaches to controls over material movement; (4) some case studies; (5) some generalizations; (6) developments facilitating a Rhochrematics approach; (7) possible approaches to implementing such thinking in existing organizations.

DIFFERENCES IN ORIENTATION

Regardless of the formal organization structure, the strengths and weaknesses of a company may well depend upon its orientation. Some functions may be stressed with little attention devoted to others, according to the importance of the particular functions to the company's success.

A study of organization charts for companies producing identical products shows that there are often differences in emphasis but that there is a tendency toward similarity, at least formally. A marked similarity can be seen in the way companies producing the same product are organized at the top management or department level, but differences are found within the sub-departments, groups and units.

Intra-departmental differences indicate that similar functions are performed in vastly different ways among companies producing the same or similar products. The performance of functions often revolves around personalities, interests, and abilities. The background and capability of the departmental manager influence performance, but many times the differences result from physical location with respect to markets, raw material, labor supply, or other factors of importance to the enterprise.

Products Shape Organization Chart   The organization charts of companies producing different products are more likely to be dissimilar than those of companies producing the same product. Yet the pressure of precedent and the similarity of basic functions to be performed tend to set patterns for the organization of all companies. Top management's interest in, or orientation to, any one or combinations of these functions is the greatest stimulus for setting patterns of organization.

The two most basic (or organic) functions of any organization are normally conceded to be production and distribution. As a consequence, they receive the greatest amount of attention, interest, and analysis. Accordingly, greater proficiency tends to develop in the performance of these functions. There also seems to be some interest in integrating the effort that goes into the performance of these basic functions. Other sub-functions tend to be performed (without much integration) by specialists whose role or mission is considered to be support of and service to marketing and production departments.

Should Production Lead Flow?   This is characteristically true of the various phases of the material flow process. Companies that distribute products to almost every community in the United States tend to be sales oriented. Normally, their products are marketed in a highly competitive atmosphere. Without large budgets for advertising and promotion, plus constant pressure to sell stemming from top management, a share of the many markets each company is trying to serve may be lost. Once a competitor captures a disproportionate share of the available customers in any one market, he tends to hold them. This does not mean that production can be slighted, because, of course, availability of good quality products is one of the keynotes to success for the salesman.

Sales are important to all companies, but engineering and production get more attention in companies producing capital equipment and some types of durable goods. Established companies producing airplanes, heavy equipment, and machinery, for example, know that if they develop a superior product their salesmen will be able to capture their considered share of the total market.

Physical distribution of products is often a relatively simple task, maybe little more than delivering orders. The internal flow of material during the production process is of concern to such companies, however. Regardless of orientation, all companies are faced with some aspects of the total material flow process and can benefit from rethinking along the lines of Rhochrematics.

SUBOPTIMIZATION BY SPECIALIZATION

Although many companies tend to be oriented to the finance function, the legal function, the purchasing function and others, sales and production remain as the basic subdivisions in most organizations. Within each of these organic functions, many subfunctions are set up as separate departments or units.

The resulting fractionalization makes visualizing the total flow process difficult. Each department, in an effort to protect itself against possible delays and to make a good showing for economy, tends to pad the time schedule in its favor with the result that the entire time schedule, or flow process, is slowed down and paper "economies" prove very costly.

In the average firm, material flows originate with the tool and production planning phase. Although planning may build considerable flexibility into the schedule of production runs, this fact is seldom apparent in the paperwork issued to purchasing.

Padding the Time Schedule   With the schedule in hand, purchasing sets up a program for acquisition of needed materials and builds in safeguards to protect itself against delays in delivery and all other possible contingencies. Next, traffic takes over and builds in a second time "hedge" against unscheduled contingencies regardless of what this may do to slow down the flow of the total operation.

Since both purchasing and traffic are service departments, they are extremely cost conscious. Holding down or reducing costs is a concern to top management, and cost reduction is a way for service units to bring attention to themselves; usually by trying to optimize the particular functions delegated to them. For purchasing this normally means buying at the lowest unit cost consistent with company policies and programs.

Also, the traffic manager is motivated to purchase transportation services at the lowest unit cost, normally meaning large quantity movements, either truck load or carload lots.

Optimization of these two functions normally results in the creation of inventories, establishing requirements for warehousing or storage. This, in turn, enforces requirements for inventory management or control.

Coordinating Material Flow   Within the plant or factory there may be several stops for material—receiving, receiving inspection, storage, processing, quality control, and the production line. From the production line the material—in a different form or as finished goods—is again moved to storage or the shipping dock.

The flow of the outbound material is also influenced by several functional departments or units. Prompt delivery service may be the primary consideration insofar as the sales manager is concerned.

Shipping is normally concerned with getting the order ready and loading it aboard the carrier, after which time it becomes the responsibility of traffic. Other complexities enter the picture when regional company owned or public warehouses are used in the distribution process.

In extremely large companies many of these functions are performed in widely separated departments with a tendency toward optimization of individual functions and little consideration of the total material flow process. This is the concern of Rhochrematics. The further companies go in their growth patterns, the greater the tendency toward functional specialization within each of the units involved in the material flow process, making coordination, integration, and managerial controls extremely important.

THE QUESTION OF CONTROLS

Managerial controls are normally exercised over departments or functions, by establishing criteria, standards, or expectations. Deviations are analyzed with reference to predetermined tolerances. The greater the degree of specialization and orientation toward a particular function, the more precise the standards for controlling the activity. For small units within major departments, all deviations must be carefully explained.

Extraneous factors or influences are often the only acceptable explanation in the face of pressures from the department manager to increase the output of activities or services rendered by a small unit. And, the efficiency of the unit is judged by its ability to hold costs at the lowest possible level. Such pressures increase the tendency toward optimization of specialized functions. In the absence of good managerial controls, the specialist normally attains his position through loyalty and conscientiousness; traits which might lead to efficient performance of the specialized function.

Rethinking   The larger the company, the greater the degree of organization, resulting in the establishment of standards and procedures for the disposition of discipline. A high degree of discipline normally results in greater efficiency insofar as specialized functions are concerned. It also tends to destroy initiative and this in turn results in more and more suboptimization of the total flow process.

This is sometimes carried on to the extent that individuals within a particular group or unit end up virtually working for themselves and do not coordinate their activities with other employees in their own unit or group. They almost completely lose sight of the over-all objectives of the business organization.

The desirability of managerial controls for the total flow cannot be over-emphasized, but the limitations on these controls, cannot be overstated. Controls can only be exercised when standards have been established and information is available to measure deviations from these standards. When functions are so fragmented that information is never brought together at a central source, standards cannot be established and managerial controls can, therefore, not be exercised. Rhochrematics fosters rethinking which may facilitate a fresh, integrated approach to controls.

Managerial Orientation   One approach to better control of material flows is flexible management orientation. Since top management is ordinarily concerned with major functions such as sales, production, and finance, minor subfunctions such as traffic, inventory control, receiving, inspection, materials management, warehousing, shipping, order processing, and purchasing are left to specialists. Specialists tend to establish their own standards, and managerial controls are exercised around these self-imposed standards. There is very little germination of ideas for the integration of interrelated minor functions.

Major pressures that arise in the sales oriented organization seldom develop in terms of a minor function. Problems of the sub-departments often seem insignificant in light of the major objectives of the organization. While material flows are regarded as necessary and extremely important to the conduct of the sales function, the units responsible for this activity are normally regarded as service groups, and the quality of that service is often the only concern of the sales department.

There are constant pressures to give better service regardless of cost, and the most important consideration is probably lost sales or out of stock situations that result from inefficiency on the part of those responsible for material flow. In extreme cases, these service groups begin to incur costs greater than the profits made from individual sales. Since physical distribution is considered a "necessary evil," material flow costs become a disproportionately high percentage of the sales dollar.

Pressures that develop in a production oriented organization will often act as deterrents to good management practices for the control of material flows. Planning in such organizations revolves around the production schedule. An important aspect of the production schedule is the need to meet predetermined load dates; a requirement that is continually impressed upon the minds of the managers of service or support groups that have the job of getting the materials to the load point on the production line.

Distorted Production Schedules   The importance of meeting the production schedule cannot be taken lightly, but side effects should be given some consideration. In order to make absolutely sure that no load date is missed, the many groups that are responsible for managing isolated phases of material flows are likely to build successive high margins of safety which can become extremely costly to the company.

Estimaters are likely to be generous on the theory that some of the material may not meet specifications. Purchasers will often have vendors ship early on the theory that vendors may not be able to meet their own production schedules. Traffic is likely to have buyers plan for maximum transit time rather than median or minimum transit time. Receiving inspection will want more than ample time to perform their function.

Rework and quality control are motivated to plan for the maximum amount of time that might be required to accomplish their task. Inventory control and warehousing will normally add a protective cushion of time to allow for unknown contingencies. All these protective cushions of time add substantially to the capital costs of carrying pipeline inventories of the various materials destined for the production line.

In spite of all the effort to the contrary, shortages do occur. The larger and more complex the production activity, the greater is the concern over shortages. This is understandable because a shortage of one small part can conceivably tie up the entire production line. Hence, much effort is devoted to the shortage problem, including the use of premium forms of transportation to expedite needed materials. While some companies consider such extraordinary measures for solving a shortage problem to be a cardinal sin, little thought is given to the fact that hundreds of thousands of dollars worth of material may have arrived weeks or months prior to the time that they were required.

The cost of carrying such inventories and the overages that result from service units protecting themselves against all possible contingencies may receive little attention in the production oriented company. There is often a substantial amount of frenzied activity and many thousands of dollars spent on the shortage problem, but inconspicuous overages may be more costly than shortages that are spotlighted for attention.

Often Takes Drastic Action   Each department manager who has responsibility over some element of the material flow process seems to feel that his special function is more important than that of other department heads. The independence with which people in one department are able to operate is a deterrent to implementation of the Rhochrematics concept. The need for coordination and cooperation between departments in the organization is usually stressed, but as long as pressures come vertically down the hierarchical chain and the security and protection of broad departmental boundary lines remains, there is little likelihood that something as complicated as the material flow process can be properly integrated.

Communications Breakdown   Even when there is an extreme desire to work together, there is often a breakdown in communication and flows of information. The many activities related to material flows tend to be extremely complex and require much documentation and record keeping. The many forms and memoranda that are developed in connection with a particular transaction involving the movement of any one of many thousands of items are seldom if ever brought together in one file in a large organization.

Each individual functionally specialized unit has its own records to provide primary information for the activity of the department. Secondary information that is of value to some other unit or combination of units normally is extracted only when something goes wrong. There is seldom any attempt to extract at each stage secondary information that is related to the material flow process.

It is obvious that fairly drastic steps must be taken by companies if controls are to be established around the flow process rather than around the traditional functional departments. These steps include management rethinking and reorientation plus some obvious organizational adjustments which may include authority and responsibility channels cutting horizontally across (flowing) the traditional vertical arrangements. The following section presents several cases where innovations have been made or are being considered to allow the organization to focus on its primary responsibility, the flow of material and information.

HOW TWO FIRMS DID IT

Two examples will be used to illustrate the kinds of innovation that can produce results. In one case, emphasis is placed on the external flow of material and information, primarily the physical distribution of finished goods. In the other case, emphasis is placed on the internal flow of material and information because the company involved is production oriented.

The Purex Story

The Purex Corporation has changed from an organization that could be considered traditional, with many of the materials flow functions fragmented and responsibility divided between several of the major departments, to an organization stressing integrated management of material flow functions. The old organization, as shown in Figure 1, had a traffic manager responsible for arranging transportation of outbound products from major production plants to warehouses and other distribution points.

The production planning function was not formalized at that time and was handled by informal committees with members from sales, manufacturing, and finance. The warehousing function was handled by the sales department for the most part, as was inventory control. Managers of a number of the smaller plants reported to finance.

These plants produced liquid bleach throughout the country and handled some warehousing of finished products produced at other major production facilities. Outbound movements from these plants were the responsibility of the plant manager and, as a result, the lines of authority for these functions emanated from the vice president of finance. Some functional authority was exercised by the traffic manager because it was his duty to furnish routing guides and common carrier rates. Inasmuch as the sales department was responsible for inventory control and maintenance of stocks at regional public warehouses, it also exercised control over outbound movements from these facilities.

Realignment of Duties. Purchasing in this

FIGURE 1   Organization of Purex Corporation Prior to Adoption of Distribution Management Concept

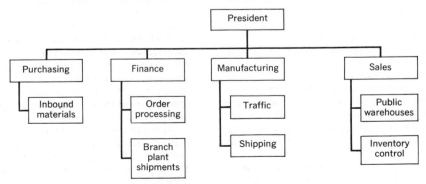

FIGURE 2   Organization of Purex Corporation for Control of Material Flows after Adoption of Distribution Management Concept

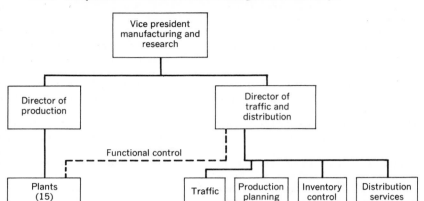

organization was responsible for control of all inbound movements of raw materials and supplies. Order processing was a function of finance, and shipping reported to manufacturing. There was no attempt to exercise over-all control of the material flow process and, as a result, many inefficiencies developed leading to substantially higher costs than warranted.

Flow System Streamlines Planning. The current organization of the Purex Corporation's material flow function is shown in Figure 2. Production planning has been formalized and put directly under the jurisdiction of the director of traffic and distribution. In addition to the planning function, he has direct line authority over inventory control, distribution services, and traffic.

Regional traffic managers report directly to him and, in addition, he has functional control over the distribution function at the various branch plants. Since these branch plants now report directly to the director of production, who in turn reports to the vice president of manufacturing and research, this functional authority almost achieves line status because the traffic director can exercise a great deal of control over all activities affecting materials movement at the branch plant level.

Direct line authority over inventory control now gives him the power he needs to control movement both into and out of public warehouses located throughout the country. Although the chart does not depict it, the director of traffic and distribution also works closely with the director of purchasing in controlling inbound shipments of raw materials and supplies.

Savings Effected. The new organizational arrangement has resulted in many benefits to

the company. Although cost reductions are difficult to determine, especially when a corporation is growing as rapidly as is the Purex Corporation, most officials of the company agree that total savings are in the high six figures. Public warehouses have been cut by nearly one-half, from 65 to 35. More efficient management controls are now exercised over inventories and production planning.

Integrated management of many of the functions related to the material flow process is being exercised. Information on all these related functions is converted to punched cards, and the data are analyzed in various ways by means of an electronic computer to obtain day-to-day operating data that are used to plan efficient production, hold inventories at minimum levels, and reduce transportation costs. Continuing attention to and sophistication of the management of material flows is planned by the Purex Corporation.

The Boeing Experience

Investigation of possibilities for better integration of the management of material flows resulted in a case study of the Transport Division of the Boeing Airplane Company in the summer of 1960 conducted by University of Washington faculty members. The initial study resulted in plans to reduce inventories and cut lead times, moves that are conservatively estimated to save the company more than $300,000 per year.

Although reorganization of the functions related to material flows has not as yet resulted, company officials are most enthusiastic about the opportunities and are giving serious consideration to inaugurating a program of re-

FIGURE 3   Present Organization of Transport Division, Boeing Airplane Company Control of Material Flows

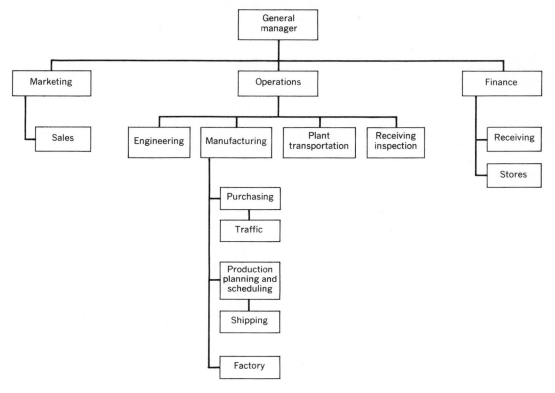

organization. Figure 3 shows the manner in which different activities concerned with material flows are now organized in the Transport Division of the Boeing Airplane Company. Serious thought is being given to a plan for realigning these functions into one department.

Here we see two differently oriented companies. The Purex Corporation, with its more than 200 finished products that must be distributed from many plants and warehouses to wholesalers and retailers through the United States, is primarily concerned with outbound movements of finished goods. The heavy moving inbound materials are few in number and consist primarily of bulk shipments of chemicals, oils, and tallow. Packaging materials are also heavy moving inbound items.

The primary concern of the Boeing Company, on the other hand, is inbound and internal movement of the more than 100,000 different parts, pieces, and raw materials that go into the production of each airplane. The parts, together with the machinery and supplies that are used in the factory, must be assembled from nearly every state in the country. For the

most part, each individual shipment is very small. The end product is the airplane, which is flown away by the customer. Distribution activities are concerned primarily with spares that must be moved to a limited number of airline companies plus the military organizations that purchase airplanes. Boeing is very much production oriented but, of course, sales is an important activity.

System Works in Both Plants

Purex, on the other hand, might be considered sales oriented; yet, production plays a vital role. These companies are the antithesis of one another insofar as their orientation and interest in the material flow function are concerned. Transportation costs alone in the Purex Company amount to more than $8 million a year or approximately 10 per cent of the sales dollar. Boeing, on the other hand, pays out a fraction of one per cent of its sales dollar in transportation costs.

Traffic and distribution play a major role in management of the Purex Corporation, whereas traffic is a minor function in the Boeing Company. However, if the many activities related to the material flow function could be organized under one head at Boeing, and sophisticated approaches developed for managing the material flow process, substantial cost reductions would result.

Other Applications. Many industries should be able to benefit from a Rhochrematics approach to management of their material flows. Service industries such as transportation companies tend to be operations and sales oriented. Since they are not concerned with selling a product, little thought may be given to material flows. The operations oriented company is in many respects like the production oriented organization. An important function is that of keeping the equipment in good condition so that schedules can be met.

These companies often accumulate hundreds of thousands of dollars worth of supplies and spare parts. Since purchasing of supplies and parts plus the various aspects of moving, storing, and issuing them, may be minor functions relative to the primary concern of the corporation, they may get little attention from top management. The fact that a train or truck or airplane or ship cannot move for lack of spare parts would be spotlighted for top management. In order to prevent this, all possible contingencies are planned for, resulting in multiple cushions and an oversupply of many items. Better control and integration of activities could result in substantial cost reductions.

Lumber. Bound industries also tend to be production oriented, with little attention given to company-wide integration of the material and information flows. For example, in the lumber industry when a log is moved to the sawmill it is turned over to a sawyer whose decision is all-important to the operation. Production orientation can influence his decision so that he cuts the best lumber, holds waste to a minimum. Little consideration may be given to the problems of inventory or lack of markets for the end product. Markets might be glutted with the items being produced with shortages developing for other products. Integrated management of raw materials procurement, production, inventory control, sales, and distribution has received little attention in this industry.

Agriculture. The agricultural industry could benefit substantially from an integrated approach to managing of the flows of their products, but since there is very little control exercised by any one individual over the many functions involved in the movement of material from original sources to final consumer, this would be most difficult to organize.

Other industries could be cited whose conceptualizing the total flow could prove extremely beneficial. However, the above examples are representative of the opportunities that can be tapped by rethinking along the lines of Rhochrematics.

GENERALISTS, NOT SPECIALISTS

The growing need for more scientific approaches to the management of material flows arises out of the increasing complexity of the productive effort of most large corporations. Business philosophy is gradually shifting from concern and need for trained specialists to concern and need for managers with broad perspective and knowledge of a number of related functions. The realization that substantial benefits can be derived from integrating many related functions should result in organization around material and information flows.

The complexity of these functions cannot be overemphasized. The existence of extreme specialists in management capacities in the many fragmented functions and the longstanding efforts that these people have made to professionalize such activities means that innovators will be faced with much inertia and outright resistance to change.

Many traffic managers, warehouse managers, purchasing managers, and others now hold key positions on the management team of most large organizations. Their organizations have been built over a period of years on the theory of functional specialization within the corporation.

There are very few senior people on the American business scene today who have the experience, background, or inclination to take over and manage an integrated approach to material flows. Many feel that the activities are so complex that it will take a long time to develop executives with the proper perspective. However, the tools and developments of the last few years make it possible to reorganize some of these activities in the interest of the over-all corporate objectives.

FACILITATING DEVELOPMENTS

While innovations stemming from the application of Rhochrematics are likely to come slowly because of the inherent resistance to change, there are a number of facilitating developments which should enhance the likelihood of progress. Separating, for the moment, the two basic elements of the flow process, material and information, we can trace some of these developments.

The technology surrounding the mass production process has been accelerating since the industrial revolution and a typical production line cuts across traditional vertical organizations. Attention in industries utilizing highly integrated production lines is focused on the material flow rather than upon individual functionally specialized units. As more sophisticated mechanization is introduced, the flow of material becomes more and more critical.

Automation Forces Flow Approach   Automation, with its self-adjusting controls over the manufacturing operation, also puts increasing emphasis on the flow process. Typically, the most highly automated operations are those such as processing industries, for example, milling or refining. However, automation is gradually spreading to other operations where concentration on the material flow process has not been as evident. As inroads are made via increased mechanization, integrated machine processing, and automation, management will be forced to think in terms of the flow of material through the plant. Hence, managerial control should be established along these lines.

The external movement or physical distribution of material is also undergoing a number of changes which will facilitate new approaches to the over-all problem of material flow. The elimination of handling through the use of containerization and integration of various modes of transportation is revolutionizing the movement of general merchandise as well as some bulk products.

Air freight is likely to be a new dimension in transportation within the next few years. The cost of moving freight through the air will be cut in half this year as new turbo-prop aircraft are delivered to some of the freight carriers. Several national companies are already using this means to reach national markets from one central production facility. They indicate that elimination of regional warehouses and multiple handling more than repays the added transportation cost.

As airfreight rates are brought down closer to the levels of truck and rail, many more companies will be able to benefit from a revised approach to material flows. Such changes in the external flow of material will often allow rethinking with regard to the internal flow of materials; for example, high-speed movement of finished goods through the normally lengthy distribution pipeline will allow companies to refine production schedules and to control inventories with much less reserve.

Information Flow   While changes in the physical flow of material, both internal and external, have been progressing, some of the most startling advances have been made in the area of information flow. Systems of information flow are critical to the control of the material flow process. The advent of high speed electronic computers has allowed companies to deal with much larger quantities of information.

Fantastic speeds allow computer processing of tremendous amounts of data which heretofore were unusable. More than that, however, the computer has stimulated rethinking on the part of innovative managements with the result being sophisticated new systems of information flow. Real progress has been made where the computer has been used to process information in new and different ways rather than to process the same old data in the same old way, only faster.

High speed data transmission over leased wires or other means has facilitated the use of the computer as a processing device. The most critical problem for systems of information flow as control mechanisms has been the collection and transmission of data rather than processing. Currently, much effort is being devoted to source recording; and once this problem is solved, the goal of integrated data processing will be within reach.

The technology necessary to achieve integrated processing of material and integrated processing of data necessary for controlling the system is either on hand or forthcoming very soon. However, management's ability to utilize these technological advances lags. The organizational adaptations necessary to take full advantage of available technology are slow in coming. Such lethargy is particularly deplorable since many of the advantages or benefits could be achieved through organizational adjustments even without the technological innovations. According to Jasinski:

> The impact of recent technological innovations has forced many managers to take a second look at their organization, particularly with the advent of modern data processing equipment. This equipment requires information in a certain form. Where managers have used it as more than simply a change in 'hardware,' equipment has triggered sweeping revisions of data processing departments. To prepare information efficiently for the processing equipment, managers have completely reorganized traditional departments. In this connection there are the telling, perhaps exaggerated, stories of companies that revised their organizations in

anticipation of delivery of data processing equipment only to realize such great savings through the reorganization process itself that they canceled their orders for the equipment.[3]

How can such benefits be achieved? How can the ideas embodied in the Rhochrematics concept be applied throughout industry?

IMPLEMENTING RHOCHREMATICS

The first and most important step in implementing a systematic, integrated approach to managing material flows is awareness on the part of top management that substantial benefit could be derived from changes in orientation. Moreover, if the Rhochrematics concept is to be applied, there must be genuine interest on the part of top management. As is the case with nearly all innovations, there will be considerable initial resistance.

Without support from the upper echelons, proposed changes are usually doomed to failure. For example, if the chief executive merely refers the subject to a committee for further investigation the odds are overwhelmingly against further action unless he maintains an active interest in the project. Committee members, particularly those with vested interests, can ordinarily marshal considerably more "why nots" than "whys."

Since Rhochrematics, the science of material and information flow, stresses the flow process, considerable attention must be given to reorganization in order that controls can be centered around this process. The interrelatedness of and interaction between the various specialized functions must be highlighted. Management attention must be focused on this problem. According to Jay Forrester, "industrial dynamics" must be recognized as an important consideration. He says:

Our industrial systems are becoming so large and sophisticated that a knowledge of the parts taken separately is not sufficient. In management, as in engineering, we can expect that the interconnections and interactions between the components of the system will often be more important than the separate components themselves.

Managing is the task of *designing* and *controlling* the industrial system. Management science, if it is to be useful, must evolve effective methods to analyze the principle interactions amongst *all* the important components of a company and its external environment. In the same sense that we can analyze complex physical systems, so will it become possible to understand better the interactions within industrial and economic systems.[4]

Management must be willing to step back and re-evaluate its traditional organizational arrangement; it must be willing to restructure traditional arrangements in order to capitalize on the advantages that can accrue by concentrating on the material flow process. The exact nature of new organization structures cannot be pinpointed. For companies emphasizing physical distribution, the distribution manager with authority over both production and distribution might be the answer. For other companies, where the internal flow of material is a more critical problem, a different approach might be appropriate. There will normally be a temptation to impose an additional agency to coordinate or expedite material flows. While this may improve the situation somewhat, it still does not get at the basic problems of empire building in the various functionally specialized departments. Until the concept of primary control based on material flows is accepted, little real benefit will be achieved.

Because of this problem of changing the atmosphere in the company and the attitude of traditionally oriented department heads, it seems that some fairly major innovations are called for in order to instigate a process of rethinking. While the initial stages of such an approach might create considerable turmoil, the long run payoff should be substantial. Management must take some giant strides in the near future if its organizational adjustments are to keep up with technological advancements.

SUMMARY AND CONCLUSIONS

Rhochrematics literally translated means the science of product or material flows. The term is connoted to mean scientific or systematic approaches to the management of material flows.

Any system is made up of a number of sub-units or operations all of which perform functions of major or minor proportions. Any of these functions might be performed independently in optimal fashion, but not necessarily in the best interests of the system as a whole. Focusing attention on the material flow process enhances the probability of optimizing the whole system rather than its separate parts.

Over the years, various aspects of the management of material flows have been receiving increased attention. Some companies have recently taken an integrated approach to the basic subfunctions of the total material flow process, production or distribution. More and more attention is being given to "distribution management," "materials management," "industrial logistics," "landed costs," or other segments of what might be called a total systems or Rhochrematics approach.

Organization theorists and practitioners have paid little attention to proposals for bringing all of the activities related to material flows under one head. Traffic, inventory management, in-plan transportation, production planning, receiving, storing, and shipping are functions that are often analyzed separately in relatively isolated departments of any one company.

In the past there was little reason to consider a systems approach to the performance of these functions because there were few alternatives and standard straightforward approaches sufficed. In recent years these activities have been complicated many times over by production of many new products, models, sizes, colors, and other variations. There are many new alternatives in transportation that did not exist even 20 years ago; for example, the long haul private, contract, or common carrier truck; "piggy back" and many other innovations in containerization on land, sea, and in the air; and the rapidly developing air freight industry with its promise of much lower rates and improved service.

The revolution that is now going on in information gathering, transmission and processing provides new dimensions for managing material flows. Growing sophistication in the field of management sciences holds excellent promise for developing even better tools for handling and combining the data that must now be used in Rhochrematics. Analyzing the data with simple machine techniques is useful;

the application of operations research techniques can prove helpful; and simulation of the material flow process seems to offer additional promise.

Top management must become interested in the Rhochrematics approach before any progress can be made. A thorough study of company goals, plans, programs, and organization will reveal the possibilities for integrating activities related to the material flow function. When such activities are fragmented in different organizational units, there is no way to even approach maximum results.

In the final analysis, serious consideration must be given to adjusting the organization of the company so that many of the interrelated functions become the responsibility of one executive. This executive must be well trained, imaginative, and broad enough in his orientation to make a complex total system function optimally.

REFERENCES

1. See Stanley H. Brewer, *Rhochrematics,* Bureau of Business Research, University of Washington, Seattle, June, 1960, 30 pp.

2. John M. Pfiffner and Frank P. Sherwood, *Administrative Organization,* Prentice-Hall, Inc., Englewood Cliffs, N.J., 1960, pp. 14–15.

3. Frank J. Jasinski, "Adapting Organization to New Technology," *Harvard Business Review,* January–February, 1959, p. 80.

4. Jay Forrester, "Management and Management Science," unpublished paper, copyrighted by Dr. Forrester, School of Industrial Management, Massachusetts Institute of Technology, p. 7.

72

How to Plan and Control
with PERT*

R. W. MILLER

The last three years have seen the explosive growth of a new family of planning and control techniques adapted to the Space Age. Much of the development work has been done in the defense industry but the construction, chemical, and other industries have played an important part in the story, too.

In this article we shall consider what is perhaps the best known of all of the new techniques, Program Evaluation Review Technique. In particular, we shall look at:

- PERT's basic requirements, such as the presentation of tasks, events, and activities on a network in sequential form with time estimates.

- Its advantages, including greatly improved control over complex development and production programs, and the capacity to distill large amounts of data in brief, orderly fashion.

- Its limitations, as in situations where there is little interconnection between the different activities pursued.

- Solutions for certain difficulties, e.g., the problem of relating time needed and job costs in the planning stage of a project.

- Policies that top management might do well to adopt, such as taking steps to train, experiment with, and put into effect the new controls.

LEADING FEATURES

The new techniques have several distinguishing characteristics:

1. They give management the ability to plan the best possible use of resources to achieve a given goal, within over-all time and cost limitations.

2. They enable executives to manage "one-of-a-kind" programs, as opposed to repetitive production situations. The importance of this kind of program in the national and world economy has become increasingly clear. Many observers have noted that the techniques of Frederick W. Taylor and Henry L. Gantt, introduced during the early part of the century for large-scale production operations, are inapplicable for a major share of the industrial effort of the 1960's—an era aptly characterized by Paul O. Gaddis as the "Age of Massive Engineering."[1]

3. They help management to handle the uncertainties involved in programs where no standard cost and time data of the Taylor-Gantt variety are available.

4. They utilize what is called "time network analysis" as a basic method of approach and as a foundation for determining manpower, material, and capital requirements.

CURRENT EFFORTS AND PROGRESS

A few examples may serve to indicate for top management the current status of the new techniques:

- The Special Projects Office of the U.S. Navy, concerned with performance trends in the execution of large military development programs, introduced PERT on its Polaris Weapon Systems in 1958. Since that time, PERT has spread rapidly throughout the U.S. defense and space industry. Currently, almost every major government and military

* Reprinted by permission of the publisher from *Harvard Business Review*, vol. 40, no. 2, pp. 93–104, March–April, 1962. Mr. Miller is manager of administration for the equipment division of the Raytheon Company.

[1] See "Thinking Ahead: The Age of Massive Engineering," *Harvard Business Review*, January–February, 1961, p. 138.

agency concerned with Space Age programs is utilizing the technique, as are large industrial contractors in the field. Small businesses wishing to participate in national defense programs will find it increasingly necessary to develop a PERT capability if they wish to be competitive in this field.

- At about the same time the Navy was developing PERT, the DuPont company, concerned with the increasing costs and time required to bring new products from research to production, initiated a study which resulted in a similar technique known as CPM (Critical Path Method). The use of the Critical Path Method has spread quite widely, and is particularly concentrated in the construction industry.

- A very considerable amount of research now is taking place on the "extensions" of PERT and CPM time-network analysis, into the areas of manpower, cost, and capital requirements. As an ultimate objective, "trade-off" relationships between time, cost, and product or equipment performance objectives are being sought. This research is being sponsored in two ways—directly by the military and privately by large companies. Anyone familiar with the current scene will be impressed by the amount of activity taking place in this field. For example, at least 40 different code names or acronyms representing variations of the new management controls have come to my attention.

- Applications of the new techniques, beyond the original engineering-oriented programs for which they were developed, are increasing every day. The PERT approach is usefully introduced in such diverse situations as planning the economy of an underdeveloped nation or establishing the sequence and timing of actions to effect a complex merger.

WHAT IS PERT?

Now let us turn to PERT in particular. What are its special characteristics and requirements?

The term is presently restricted to the area of time and, as promulgated by the Navy, has the following basic requirements:

1. All of the individual tasks to complete a given program must be visualized in a clear enough manner to be put down in a *network,* which is comprised of *events* and *activities.* An event represents a specified pro-

gram accomplishment at a particular instant in time. An activity represents the time and resources which are necessary to progress from one event to the next. Emphasis is placed on defining events and activities with sufficient precision so that there is no difficulty in monitoring actual accomplishment as the program proceeds. Exhibit I shows a typical operating-level PERT network from the electronics industry.

2. Events and activities must be sequenced on the network under a highly logical set of ground rules which allow the determination of important critical and subcritical paths. These ground rules include the fact that no successor event can be considered completed until all of its predecessor events have been completed, and no "looping" is allowed, i.e., no successor event can have an activity dependency which leads back to a predecessor event.

3. Time estimates are made for each activity of the network on a three-way basis, i.e., optimistic, most likely, and pessimistic elapsed-time figures are estimated by the person or persons most familiar with the activity involved. The three time estimates are required as a gauge of the "measure of uncertainty" of the activity, and represent full recognition of the probabilistic nature of many of the tasks in development-oriented and nonstandard programs. It is important to note, however, that, for the purposes of computation and reporting, the three time estimates are reduced to a single expected time (t_e) and a statistical variance (σ^2).

4. Depending on the size and complexity of the network, computer routines are available to calculate the critical path through it. Computers can also calculate the amount of slack (viz., extra time available) for all events and activities not on the critical path. A negative slack condition can prevail when a calculated end date does not achieve a program date objective which has been established on a prior—and often arbitrary—basis.

Time Estimates   Interpretation of the concepts of optimistic, most likely, and pessimistic elapsed times has varied over the past few years. The definitions which, in my opinion, represent a useful consensus are as follows:

- *Optimistic*—An estimate of the *minimum* time an activity will take, a result which can be obtained only if unusual good luck is experienced and everything "goes right the first time."

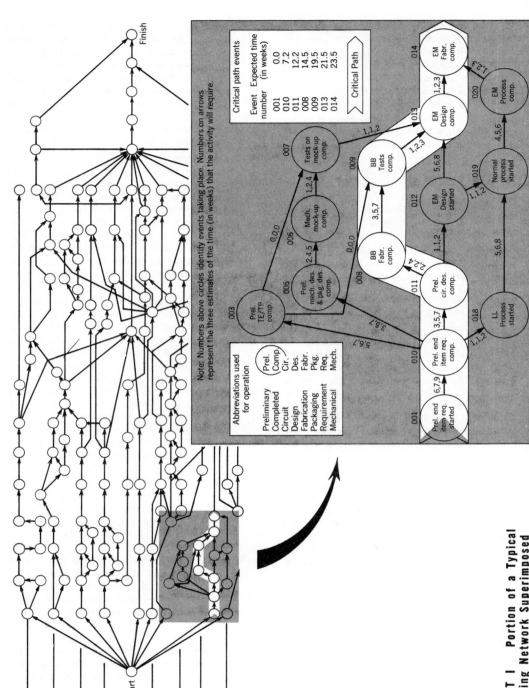

Note: Numbers above circles identify events taking place. Numbers on arrows represent the three estimates of the time (in weeks) that the activity will require.

Abbreviations used for operation

Preliminary	Prel.
Completed	Comp.
Circuit	Cir.
Design	Des.
Fabrication	Fabr.
Packaging	Pkg.
Requirement	Req.
Mechanical	Mech.

Critical path events

Event number	Expected time (in weeks)
001	0.0
010	7.2
011	12.2
008	14.5
009	19.5
013	21.5
014	23.5

Critical Path

EXHIBIT I Portion of a Typical Operating Network Superimposed on Total Network

488

• *Most likely*—An estimate of the *normal* time an activity will take, a result which would occur most often if the activity could be repeated a number of times under similar circumstances.

• *Pessimistic*—An estimate of the *maximum* time an activity will take, a result which can occur only if unusually bad luck is experienced. It should reflect the possibility of initial failure and fresh start, but should not be influenced by such factors as "catastrophic events"—strikes, fires, power failures, and so on—unless these hazards are inherent risks in the activity.

The averaging formulas by which the three time estimates are reduced to a single expected time (t_e), variance (σ^2) and standard deviation (σ) are shown in Appendix A. The approximations involved in these formulas are subject to some question, but they have been widely used and seem appropriate enough in view of the inherent lack of precision of estimating data. The variance data for an entire network make possible the determination of the *probability of meeting an established schedule date,* as shown in Appendix B.

Critical Path   In actual practice, the most important results of the calculations involved in PERT are the determination of the critical path and slack times for the network. Exhibit II contains data on the critical path and slack times for the sample network shown in Exhibit I (they are based on the method of calculation given in Appendix C). The data are shown in the form of a *slack order report* (lowest to highest slack), which is perhaps one of the most important output reports of PERT.

Other output reports, such as event order and calendar time order reports, are also available in the PERT system.

The actual utilization of PERT involves review and action by responsible managers, generally on a biweekly basis. Because time prediction and performance data are available from PERT in a "highly ordered" fashion (such as the slack order report), managers are given the opportunity to concentrate on the important critical path activities. The manager must determine valid means of shortening lead times along the critical path by applying new resources or additional funds, which are obtained from those activities that can "afford" it

EXHIBIT II   Slack Order Report

PERT SYSTEM   AIRBORNE COMPUTER — SLACK ORDER REPORT

DATE 7/12/61   WEEK 0.0   TIME IN WEEKS   PAGE 1

EVENT	T_E	T_L	T_L-T_E	T_S	P_r	
001	0.0	0.0	0			T_E = Expected event
010	7.2	7.2	0			date
011	12.2	12.2	0			
008	14.5	14.5	0			T_L = Latest allowable
009	19.5	19.5	0			event date
013	21.5	21.5	0			
014	23.5	23.5	0	23.5	.50	T_L-T_E = Event slack
020	20.6	21.5	+ .9			T_S = Scheduled event
019	15.6	16.5	+ .9			date
012	14.4	15.3	+ .9			
018	9.4	10.3	+ .9			P_r = Probability of
						achieving T_S date
007	18.2	20.3	+2.1			
006	16.0	18.1	+2.1			
005	13.2	14.3	+2.1			
003	14.2	19.5	+5.3			

because of their slack condition. Alternatively, he can re-evaluate the sequencing of activities along the critical path. If necessary, those activities which were formerly connected in a series can be organized on a parallel or concurrent basis, with the associated tradeoff risks involved. As a final, if rarely used, alternative, the manager may choose to change the scope of work of critical path activities in order to achieve a given schedule objective.

It should be pointed out that the PERT system requires constant updating and reanalysis; that is, the manager must recognize that the outlook for the completion of activities in a complex program is in a constant state of flux, and he must be continually concerned with problems of re-evaluation and reprograming. A highly systematized method of handling this aspect of PERT has been developed. An example of the input transaction document involved is given in Exhibit III.

BENEFITS GAINED

Perhaps the major advantage of PERT is that the kind of planning required to create a valid network represents a major contribution to the definition and ultimate successful control of a complex program. It may surprise some that network development and critical path analysis do, in fact, reveal interdependencies and problem areas which are either not obvious or not well defined by conventional planning methods. The creation of the network is a fairly demanding task, and is a sure-fire indicator of an organization's ability to visualize the number, kind, and sequence of activities needed to execute a complex program.

Another advantage of PERT, especially where there is a significant amount of uncertainty, is the three-way estimate. While introducing a complicating feature, this characteristic does give recognition to those realities of life which cause difficulties in most efforts at planning the future. The three-way estimate should result in a greater degree of honesty and accuracy in time forecasting; and, as a minimum, it allows the decision maker a better opportunity to evaluate the degree of uncertainty involved in a schedule—particularly along the critical path. If he is statistically sophisticated, he may even wish to examine the standard deviation and probability of accomplishment data, which were mentioned previously as features of PERT. (If there is a minimum of uncertainty in the minds of personnel estimating individual activity times, the single-time approach may, of course, be used, while

retaining all the advantages of network analysis.)

And, finally, the common language feature of PERT allows a large amount of data to be presented in a highly ordered fashion. It can be said that PERT represents the advent of the management-by-exception principle in an area of planning and control where this principle had not existed with any real degree of validity. An additional benefit of the common language feature of PERT is the fact that many individuals in different locations or organizations can easily determine the specific relationship of their efforts to the total task requirements of a large program.

This particular benefit of PERT can represent a significant gain in the modern world of large-scale undertakings and complex organizational relationships.

COPING WITH PROBLEMS

A new and important development like PERT naturally is attended by a certain amount of confusion and doubt. PERT does indeed have its problems. However, they are not always what businessmen think they are, and often there is an effective way of coping with the restrictions. In any event, it is time to compare the situations in which PERT works best with situations in which real (or imagined) troubles occur.

Uncertain Estimates   One key question concerns the unknowns of time and resources that management frequently must contend with.

In PERT methodology an available set of resources including manpower and facilities is either known or must be assumed when making the time estimates. For example, it is good practice to make special notations directly on the network when some special condition (e.g., a 48-hour rather than a 40-hour week) is assumed. Experience has shown that when a well-thought-through network is developed in sufficient detail, the first activity time estimates made are as accurate as any, and these should not be changed unless a new application of resources or a trade-off in goals is specifically determined. A further caution is that the first time estimates should not be biased by some arbitrarily established schedule objective, or by the assumption that a particular activity does not appear to be on a critical path. Schedule biasing of this kind, while it obviously cannot be prevented, clearly atrophies some of the main benefits of the technique—although it is

EXHIBIT III   Input Transaction Document

PERT
REPORT OF TIME INTERVAL
ESTIMATES & PROGRESS

REVISION NO. 2
13 FEBRUARY 1959

CLASSIFICATION:

REPORT PERIOD

FLOW CHART NO.

CONTRACT NO.

FROM:
TO:

FROM: (NAME & LOCATION OF CONTRACTOR)

TO:

FOR OFFICE USE ONLY			ACTIVITY IDENTIFICATION		TIME INTERVAL ESTIMATES			COMPLETION DATE	REMARKS
			BEGINNING EVENT NO.	ENDING EVENT NO.	OPTI-MISTIC (WEEKS) *	MOST LIKELY (WEEKS) *	PESSI-MISTIC (WEEKS) *		
(A)			(B)	(C)	(D)	(E)	(F)	(G)	(H)
(1)	(2) (3)	(4)						60 — 65 MO. DAY YR.	
12	13 — 16	17	18 — 26	34 — 42	44 — 47	48 — 51	52 — 55		
1			010	003	5.0	6.0	7.0	—	—	—	New Activity
1			003	007	0	0	0	—	—	—	New Activity
1									
2			010	018	2.0	1.0	1.0	—	—	—	Re-estimated Activity (Change)
2			018	019	5.0	6.0	8.0	—	—	—	Re-estimated Activity (Change)

SIGNATURE OF RESPONSIBLE OFFICIAL:

DATE SIGNED:

CLASSIFICATION:

* Columns D, E, and F. These estimates should be given for the full activity even though the activity has already started.

491

more quickly "discovered" with PERT than with any other method.

Because of the necessity for assumptions on manpower and resources, it is easiest to apply PERT in *project-structured* organizations, where the level of resources and available facilities are known to the estimator. PERT does not itself *explicitly* resolve the problem of multiprogram planning and control. But there is general recognition of this problem, and considerable effort is being devoted to a more complete approach to it. Meanwhile, in the case of common resource centers, it is generally necessary to undertake a loading analysis, making priority assumptions and using the resulting data on either a three-time or single-time basis for those portions of the network which are affected. It should be pointed out, however, that in terms of actual experience with PERT, the process of network development forces more problems of resource constraint or loading analysis into the open for resolution than do other planning methods.

Although PERT has been characterized as a new management control approach for R & D effort, it has perhaps been most usefully applied in those situations where there is a great deal of interconnection betweeen the activities of a network, or where there are interface connections between different networks. Certainly, network development and critical path analysis are *not* too appropriate for the pure research project, where the capabilities of small numbers of individuals with highly specialized talents are being utilized at a "constant rate" and where their activities have no significant dependence on other elements of the organization.

Justifying the Cost   One of the most frequently raised objections to PERT is the cost of its implementation. A fundamental point to examine here is whether or not a currently established planning system is giving value commensurate with its cost—or perhaps more basic still, whether the system is used at all effectively to pinpoint and control problem areas. It is quite true that, by the very nature of its logical requirements for networking, the PERT approach calls for a higher degree of planning skill and a greater amount of detail than is the case with conventional methods. In addition, the degree of detail—or the "level of indenture," as it is called—is a function of:

1. What is meaningful to the person or persons who will actually execute the work.

2. The depth of analysis that is required to determine the valid critical path or paths.

It is perhaps more appropriate to view the implementation of PERT as costing *initially* something in the order of twice that of a conventional planning system. This figure will vary significantly with such factors as:

- The degree of planning capability already available.

- The present effectiveness and homogeneity of the organization.

- The amount and quality of PERT indoctrination given.

The advocates of PERT are quick to point out that the savings achieved through better utilization of resources far outweigh the system's initial implementation costs. This better utilization of resources is achieved through concentration on critical path activities—for example, limiting overtime effort to these key activities as opposed to across-the-board use of overtime. Even more important are the "downstream" savings which are achieved by earlier and more positive action on the part of management to resolve critical problems.

Use of Standard Networks   Because of the considerable impact of PERT on many organizations where detailed planning has not had major emphasis, a trend has recently developed which can be characterized as "model or standard networking." This has to do with efforts to use the typical or established pattern of carrying out a new program in a particular industry. Model networking has many advantages (particularly in handling the large amounts of data involved in PERT), but it may also compromise one of the real objectives of PERT—i.e., *obtaining a valid network which is meaningful to the person or persons who will actually execute the work*. In the area in which PERT is used most effectively no two programs are ever exactly the same, and no two individuals will have exactly the same approach to the development of a network. Therefore, model networks should be introduced with this caution: management should always allow for the possibility of modifications which will match the realities of the program.

In addition, the introduction of so-called "master plan networks" and the top-down structuring of networks for large programs involving many different firms, while very necessary from the point of view of long-range planning and the ultimate management of such programs, should be handled with a philosophy of flexibility. The cardinal principle is that a management control structure is no better than the adequacy and accuracy of the data at its base. In the future, the top-down structuring approach—which is already evident on some major defense and space programs—will probably increase; but internal objectives, at least, will be subject to reconfirmation or realignment at the level of industry, depending upon the development of actual operating networks. The top-down structuring approach is necessary, however, in order to preserve the mechanics of *network integration;* it is important that the data from lower level networks be properly and meaningfully summarized into higher level management data.

Application to Production   A final problem, and one that is often viewed as a disadvantage of the PERT technique, is the system's lack of applicability to all of the manufacturing effort. As has been stated, PERT deals in the time domain only and does not contain the quantity information required by most manufacturing operations. Nevertheless, PERT can be, and has been, used very effectively through the preliminary manufacturing phases of production prototype or pilot model construction, and in the assembly and test of final production equipments which are still "high on the learning curve." After these phases, established production control techniques which bring in the quantity factor are generally more applicable.

Note, however, that many programs of the Space Age never leave the preliminary manufacturing stage, or at least never enter into mass production. Therefore, a considerable effort is going forward at this time to integrate the techniques of PERT within some of the established methods of production control, such as line-of-balance or similar techniques that bring in the quantity factor.

Computer or No Computer   As a result of the Navy's successful application of PERT on the Polaris program, and other similar applications, there is a common impression that the technique is only applicable when large-scale data-processing equipment is available. This is certainly true for large networks, or aggregations of networks, where critical path and slack computations are involved for several hundred or more events. It is as desirable to have a computer handle a PERT problem when a large volume of data is involved as it is to use a computer in any extensive data-processing assignment.

Probably equally significant is the fact that several ingenious manual methods have been developed in industry by those organizations which have become convinced of PERT's usefulness. These manual methods range from simple inspection on small networks to more organized but clerically oriented routines for determination of critical path, subcritical path, and slack times on networks ranging from fifty to several hundred events.

This is sufficient proof that PERT can be applied successfully to smaller programs wherever the degree of interconnection and problems of uncertainty warrant it. For those organizations practiced in the technique, both the creation of small networks and the formation of time estimates and their reduction to critical path and slack analyses can be done in a matter of hours. Exhibit I shows the network for a relatively small electronics program. Developed in less than a day, the whole network required only two hours for manual computation.

It seems clear that the small business organization which wishes to participate in national defense and space programs, or to improve its own internal schedule planning and control, should not hesitate to adopt PERT merely because it does not possess large-scale data-processing equipment.

PERT Extensions   Variations of PERT to accommodate multi-project and manufacturing situations have already been mentioned, and these are merely representative of a basic movement to *extend* the approach into the areas of manpower, cost, and the equipment performance variable. The ultimate objective of these efforts is to quantify the trade-off relationships which constantly come up in development programs but are rarely acted on with explicit data in hand.

Though none of these extensions have as yet attained as much maturity and acceptance as PERT, anyone familiar with the current scene will be impressed by the amount of effort being given to them throughout the country in both the military and industry. One healthy offset to this particular trend is the fact that the U.S. Air Force has withdrawn its code name PEP (Program Evaluation Procedure), which was an equivalent for PERT. There remains, however, a great need for government agencies to standardize input and output requirements of basic PERT time before uniformly effective extensions can be made into the area of PERT cost.

COST OF PERT

Much of the research effort on the new management controls which has taken place throughout the country is concentrated on the problem of manpower and cost. This is probably a reflection of certain facts well known to most managers of complex development programs:

- The job-costing structures generally found in industry on such programs need a great deal of interpretation to relate *actual costs* to *actual progress*. They are rarely, if ever, related in any explicit manner to the details of the scheduling plan.

- Cost constraints, either in the form of manpower shortages or funding restrictions, have a great deal to do with the success with which a program of this type can be managed.

It seems clear that both of these problems must be solved in any valid PERT cost approach.

Solutions Required The first problem means that an explicit relationship must be established between the time network and the job-cost structure, either on a one-to-one basis for each network activity, or for a designated chain of activities. As a minimum, it seems clear that more detailed job-cost structures are required than are currently in general use, although this requirement should present no serious limitation for organizations which possess modern data-processing methods and equipment.

With regard to the development of actual cost figures *from the time network,* an estimate of manpower requirements, segregated by classification, is usually considered the easiest place to start, since these requirements were presumably known at the time the network was established. In fact, however, the actual summation of such data often reveals a manpower or funding restriction problem, and forces a replanning cycle if no alternatives are available. (The summation may also reveal inefficiencies in personnel loading which can be removed by proper use of slack activities.)

Two other problems that should be mentioned are:

- *Handling of nonlabor items*—The costs for these items are often aggregated in a manner quite different from that which would result from analysis of a time network. For example, there is a tendency to buy common materials on one purchase order for a number of different prototypes, each one of which represents a distinct phase of progress in the program. A refined allocation procedure may be needed to handle this problem.

- *Coordination and control efforts* (e.g., those carried out by project or systems engi-

neering[2])—These are often not indicated on time networks unless they result in specific outputs. For PERT costing, the network in all cases must be complete, i.e., it must include all effort which is charged to the program. This is one of the areas of deficiency in many present-day networks, and one which must be overcome before an effective PERT cost application can be made.

Each of the foregoing problems can be handled if the underlying network analysis is sound and subject to a minimum of change. As a result, a number of different approaches are being attempted in the development of costed networks which have as their objective, the association of at least one cost estimate with a known activity or chain of activities on the network.

The ultimate objective of all this is not only improvement in planning and control, but also the opportunity to assess possibilities for "trading off" time and cost, i.e., adding or subtracting from one at the expense of the other. It is generally assumed that the fundamental relationships between time and cost are as portrayed in Exhibit IV. Curve A represents *total direct costs* versus time, and the "U" shape of the curve results from the assumption that there is an "optimum" time-cost point for any activity or job. It is assumed that total costs will increase with any effort to accelerate or delay the job away from this point.

Some companies in the construction industry are already using such a time-cost relationship, although in a rather specialized manner:

In one application, an assumption is made that there is a *normal* job time (which might or might not coincide with the theoretical optimum), and that from this normal time, costs increase linearly to a *crash* time, as indicated in Exhibit IV. This crash time represents the maximum acceleration the job can stand. On the basis of these assumptions, a complete mathematical approach and computer program have been developed which show how to accelerate progress on a job as much as possible for the lowest possible cost. The process involves shortening the critical path or paths by operating on those activities which have the lowest time-cost slopes.

Challenge of Cost Data Making time-cost data available for each activity in usable form is one of the fundamental problems in using

[2] See Clinton J. Chamberlain, "Coming Era in Engineering Management," *Harvard Business Review,* September–October, 1961, p. 87.

EXHIBIT IV   Assumed Time-Cost Relationships for a Job

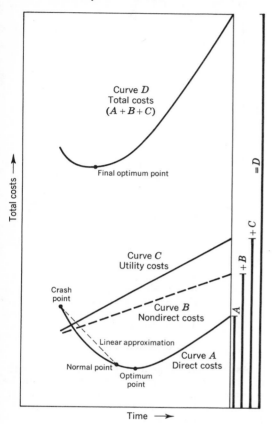

Curve C is a representation of a *utility cost curve,* which is needed to complete the picture for *total time-cost* optimization (indicated as the final optimum point on Curve D). The utility cost curve represents a quantification of the penalty for *not accomplishing the job at the earliest possible time,* and is also shown as a linear function increasing with time.

The difficulties of determining such a curve for many programs, either in terms of its shape or dollar value, should be obvious. But it is significant to note that in certain industrial applications such utility cost data have already been developed, typically in the form of "outage" costs or loss-of-profit opportunities, and used as the basis for improved decision making. Further, in the military area, utility cost is the converse of the *benefit* concept in the *benefit-cost* ratio of a weapon system; this factor varies with the time of availability of a weapon system, even though judgments of benefit are made difficult by rapidly changing circumstances in the external world.

CONCLUSION

It is clear that there are difficulties yet to be overcome in advancing the new management controls—particularly in the new areas into which PERT is being extended. Yet it is equally clear that significant progress has been made during the last few years. Assuming that developments continue at the rate at which they have taken place up to this time, what position should top management adopt *today* with regard to its own internal policies on the new management controls? Here are the most important steps:

1. Management should review its present planning and scheduling methods and compare their effectiveness with that of the PERT system. (I refer here to time networks only—not time-and-cost networks.) If the company has no direct experience with PERT, it will certainly want to consider training and experimentation programs to acquaint the organization with the technique. Management may even decide to install PERT on all of its development programs (as some companies have done), even though it has no contractual requirement to do so.

2. Management may wish to enter directly into research efforts on the new management controls or, if such efforts are already underway in the organization, place them on a higher priority basis. As a minimum, it will probably want to assign someone in the

PERT in development programs. At the planning stage, in particular, it is often difficult to determine time-cost relationships in an explicit manner, either for individual activities or for aggregates of activities. (There are often good arguments for characterizing time-cost relationships at this stage as nonlinear, flat, decreasing, or, more likely, as a range of cost possibilities.) If alternative equipment or program objectives are added as a variable, the problem is further compounded. While posing the problem, it should be pointed out that solutions for the technical handling of such data, in whatever form they are obtained, have recently been developed.

Curve B of Exhibit IV indicates *total nondirect costs,* which are assumed to increase linearly with time. Clearly, accounting practices will have to be reviewed to provide careful (and probably new) segregations of direct from non-direct costs for use in making valid time-cost trade-off evaluations.

organization to follow the numerous developments that are taking place in the field.

3. Executives should consider carefully the problem of organization to make the most effective use of the new management controls. They should consider the responsibilities of the level of management that actually uses PERT data in its working form, and the responsibilities of the levels of management that review PERT in its various summary forms. Clearly, the usefulness of the new management controls is no greater than the ability of management actually to act on the information revealed. It should be realized that problems of "recentralization" will probably accompany the advent of the new tools, particularly when applied to the planning and control of large projects throughout an entire organization.

4. Finally, management may wish to assess the longer range implications of the new management controls, both for itself and for the entire industrial community, since the forces calling for centralization of planning and control within the firm can apply equally well outside it. In the Age of Massive Engineering, the new controls will be utilized to an increasing extent in the nation's defense and space programs, which are in turn increasing in size and complexity. It seems clear that the inevitably closer relationships between government and industry will require the establishment of new guidelines for procurement and incentive contracting where these management control techniques are used.

APPENDIXES

Readers interested in applying PERT may find it helpful to have a more precise formulation of certain calculations mentioned earlier in this article. The mathematics involved is basically simple, as the following material demonstrates.

Appendix A. Expected Time Estimate   In analyzing the three time estimates, it is clear that the optimistic and the pessimistic time should occur least often, and that the most likely time should occur most often. Thus, it is assumed that the most likely time represents the peak or modal value of a probability distribution; however, it can move between the two extremes. These characteristics are best described by the Beta distribution, which is shown in two different conditions in the figures that follow.

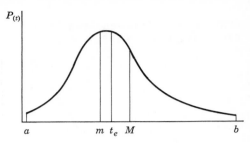

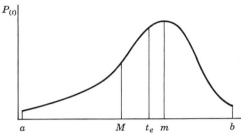

where:

$$a = \text{optimistic time}$$
$$m = \text{most likely time}$$
$$b = \text{pessimistic time}$$
$$M = \text{mid-range}\left(\frac{a + b}{2}\right)$$
$$t_e = \text{expected time}$$

As a result of analyzing the characteristics of the Beta* distribution, the final approximations to expected time (t_e), variance (σ^2), and standard deviation (σ) were written as follows for a given activity:

1. $\quad t_e = \dfrac{1}{3}(2m + M)$

$\qquad = \dfrac{1}{3}\left(2m + \dfrac{a + b}{2}\right)$

$\qquad = \dfrac{a + 4m + b}{6}$

2. $\quad \sigma^2 = \left(\dfrac{b - a}{6}\right)^2$

3. $\quad \sigma = \dfrac{b - a}{6}$

The first equation indicates that t_e should be interpreted as the weighted mean of m (most likely) and M (mid-range) estimates, with weights of 2 and 1, respectively. In other words, t_e is located one third of the way from the modal to the mid-range values, and repre-

* Note: The Beta distribution is analyzed in the PERT Summary Report, Special Projects Office, Department of the Navy, Washington, D.C., Phase I, July, 1958.

sents the 50% probability point of the distribution, i.e., it divides the area under the curve into two equal portions.

Appendix B. Probability of Meeting Schedule Times

On the basis of the Central Limit Theorem, one can conclude that the probability distribution of times for accomplishing a job consisting of a number of activities may be approximated by the normal distribution, and that this approximation approaches exactness as the number of activities becomes great (for example, more than 10 activities along a given path). Thus, we may define a curve which represents the probability of a meeting on established schedule-end date, T_S:

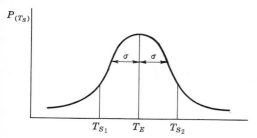

where:

$$T_E = \Sigma t_{e1} + t_{e2} + \cdots t_{en}$$
$$\sigma^2(T_E) = \Sigma \sigma^2(t_{e1}) + \sigma^2(t_{e2}) + \cdots \sigma^2(t_{en})$$
$$T_{S_1} = \text{Scheduled Time (earlier than } T_E)$$
$$T_{S_2} = \text{Scheduled Time (later than } T_E)$$

The probability of meeting the T_S date when given T_E and σ^2 for a chain of activities is defined as the ratio of (1) the area under the curve to the left of T_S to (2) the area under the entire curve. The difference between T_S and T_E, expressed in units of σ, is:

$$\frac{T_S - T_E}{\sigma}$$

This will yield a value for the probability of accomplishing T_S by use of the normal probability distribution table. Thus:

$$\frac{T_{S_1} - T_E}{\sigma} = -1.2\sigma, \ P_r \text{ (accomplishment of}$$
$$T_{S_1}) = .12$$

$$\frac{T_{S_2} - T_E}{\sigma} = +1.2\sigma, \ P_r \text{ (accomplishment of}$$
$$T_{S_2}) = .88$$

Appendix C. Determining Critical Path and Slack Times

The computation steps required to determine the critical path and slack times for the network shown in Exhibit I are as follows:

Step 1. Determine t_e for every activity on the network in accordance with the equation:

$$t_e = \frac{a + 4m + b}{6}$$

Step 2. Starting with Event No. 001, determine T_E (or cumulative T_E) for all succeeding events by summing small t_e's for each activity leading up to the event, *but choosing the largest value for the final T_E figure in those cases where there is more than one activity leading into an event.* For example, Exhibit I indicates three activities leading into Event No. 013 (EM design complete). The three preceding events are No. 007 (test on mock-up complete), No. 009 (breadboard tests complete), and No. 012 (EM design started). The cumulative T_E figures for these three preceding events, as can be seen from Exhibit II, are 18.2 weeks for Event No. 007, 19.5 weeks for Event No. 009, and 14.4 weeks for Event No. 012. Now, add the respective activity times between these three events and Event No. 013 and examine the results:

EVENT NO.	T_E	ACTIVITY TIME T_E TO EVENT NO. 013	TOTAL WEEKS
007	18.2	1.2	19.4
009	19.5	2.0	21.5
012	14.4	6.2	20.6

The largest figure, which represents the longest path or earliest time at which Event No. 013 can be completed, is 21.5 weeks, and this path leads through Event No. 009. As will be noted from Exhibit I, Event Nos. 009 and 013 are on the critical path, since the T_E values of all other paths leading into final Event No. 014 are smaller.

Step 3. Having determined the critical path through the network of Exhibit I to be 23.5 weeks, we can now set the final date of Event No. 014 at 23.5 weeks, or we can use some arbitrary scheduled time. The process covered in Step 2 is now reversed. Starting with the final event, we determine the *latest allowable time*, T_L, for each event so as not to affect critical path event times. For example, Event No. 007, with a T_E of 18.2 weeks, can be delayed up to a T_L of 20.3 weeks, before it will affect critical path Event No. 013.

Step 4. The difference between T_L and T_E, known as slack, is next computed for each event. These computations are shown in Exhibit II in the form of a slack order report, i.e., in order of lowest to highest values of *positive* slack. Note that along the critical path there is zero slack at every event, since by definition there is no possibility of slippage along the critical path without affecting the final event date. In this example, if the end schedule date of Event No. 014 were set at 23.0 weeks rather than at 23.5 weeks, there would be 0.5 weeks of negative *slack* indicated for every event along the critical path.

Step 5. The computation of variance and of standard deviation for this network is optional and involves adding the variances for each activity along the critical path, which are obtained from the formula:

$$\sigma^2 = \left(\frac{b - a}{6}\right)^2$$

The interested reader may verify that the variance for final Event No. 014, with a T_E of 23.5 weeks, is 1.46 weeks.

73

The Management Side of PERT*

IVARS AVOTS

No management technique has ever caused so much enthusiasm, controversy, and disappointment as PERT. Within the past two years PERT or, to use its full name, Program Evaluation and Review Technique, developed originally for the United States Navy as part of the Polaris program as a mathematical method for defining the minimum time for completion of a complex project, has moved from the realm of production theory to the solid status of becoming a contract requirement in the nation's major defense programs.

It has also entered the business world where it is referred to not only as PERT but sometimes as "network analysis" and "critical path planning," depending upon the industry in which it is employed. Specific aspects of the PERT theory have become items of controversy and concern in management circles. In addition, hundreds of thousands of dollars have been spent only to find in some cases that a given approach to PERT was not feasible within the context in which its use was planned.

What are the reasons which have caused PERT to make an impact unlike that of any

other management technique? What has management learned about the application and limitations of this technique? What can be expected of PERT in the future? These are some of the questions managers need answered if they are to avoid the cost of experimentation. This article attempts to provide these answers with particular attention to problems of implementation on large programs.

PERT burst upon the management horizon in 1958 when it became part of the Polaris program. It was developed by the firm of management consultants, Booz, Allen & Hamilton for the Navy in order to coordinate the thousands of activities and individual processes required to bring to completion the complex project of creating a missile which could be fired under water.

The Air Force also adopted this technique. Its initial name for its program was PEP (Program Evaluation Procedure). Now it uses the same terminology as the Navy for its program evaluation technique. In the construction industry this method of networking time and procedures is called the Critical Path Method.

Despite the dissimilarity in nomenclature, all perform essentially the same logistical function of getting each of the components of a complex procedure completed at the precise

* Reprinted by permission of the publisher of the *California Management Review*, vol. 4, no. 24, pp. 16–27, Winter, 1962. Mr. Avots is a member of the operations planning staff of the Boeing Company.

time and delivered to the exact proper place to be smoothly integrated into the final fabrication and launching of the product. The obvious advantages of such a technique, its streamlining of production, its essential tidiness and economy, its promise of optimum use at all times of men and material have made it a "natural" for business use wherever and whenever practicable. It is these very factors which have contributed to management's enthusiasm for PERT and also provided background for some of its controversies.

Foremost among them is the change in basic management philosophy which characterizes PERT against other management techniques. While it is true that considerable attention has been given in their day to bar charts, improvement curves, and other techniques, all of these were deterministic in nature. Planning resulted in a static system against which status was measured.

Introduction of PERT suddenly brought a change in traditional management thinking. The new technique did not look forward to meeting a schedule, but accepted uncertainty as part of the system. The effects of this change can be identified both in the enthusiasm for the technique as well as in resistance to it. Both conditions are often observed side by side even within the same organization.

THE SELLING POINTS OF PERT

Writers in technical publications have cited a complete line of selling points for the PERT technique. High on the list is the system's ability to predict the impact of schedule status. While other systems record status at a given time and require separate analysis to determine its effect on program objectives, PERT readily provides this information.

Moreover, PERT is primarily an analytical planning rather than a control method, and therefore does not suffer from the stigma associated with some management control techniques. In fact, as much as sixty percent of the benefits of PERT have been ascribed to its planning function rather than to its use as a control media.

This is because PERT forces integration of planning and thereby shows significant benefits even before it is used as a control tool. In the control area, PERT format cuts across organizational lines, eliminating the effect of defensive interpretation of reports along the lines of responsibility. At the same time, however, activities selected for the network usually recognize changes in responsibility and form the basis for positive control.

Predictive Quality   As a background for our discussion of PERT limitations, let us take a closer look at each of these selling points. Four features of the PERT technique give it the unique predictive quality which is not shared by other management control techniques. They are

• Critical path analysis
• Program status evaluation
• Slack determination
• Simulation

A typical PERT network is shown in Exhibit 1. The critical path is the longest series of activities which must be performed from the beginning to the end of the network. Obviously, there can be more than one critical path for a program, and, depending on the completion status of individual activities, the critical path may change.

The Critical Path.   The advantage of the critical path is not only the fact that it permits determination of the effects of any schedule delays on program completion, but it also brings into use the exception principle focusing management attention to those areas where schedule maintenance is critical. When problems arise, critical path analysis highlights the areas where action must be taken to maintain over-all program schedule.

As work progresses and status information is obtained, the PERT technique shows the time required to reach any event in the network. Together with the critical path analysis, this feature permits rapid evaluation of program status. Considering the fact that the status information can be integrated from a large number of sources and cover various levels of program effort, benefits to management can be quite significant.

Time Trade-off.   Time estimates are assigned to the activities in a PERT network on the basis of normal manpower assignment and resource allocation. When compared to the concurrent critical path, some activities require less time and therefore possess a certain amount of slack. Listing of activities having slack identifies the area of effort where trade-off in time, resources, or technical performance may improve the schedule along the critical path.

At any time during the program, the effect proposed schedule changes can be easily simulated by the computer. This feature permits management to examine detail activities, especially those critical to the program, for possible adjustments resulting in schedule or cost improvement.

EXHIBIT I   Typical PERT Network*

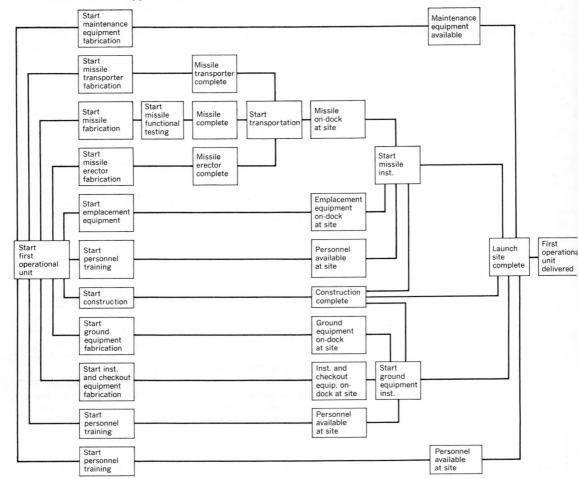

* The PERT network consists of a series of interrelated symbols representing principal events and activities in a program. An event is shown by a box and an activity is indicated by a line or arrow connecting events. When time estimates are assigned to activities, it is possible to compute the critical path of the program, as well as identify activities which have slack time. These may be extended without affecting program schedules.

Analytical Planning Method.   Observers have rightfully noted that for maximum benefits PERT application must start during or before the planning phase of a new program. The major reason for this is the fact that networking forces integration of planning and helps to discover innumerable conditions which, in a complex program, may easily be overlooked.

Traditional program planners are usually skeptical about any benefits the PERT technique may give them, and quite often there is open antagonism on their part to use of the technique. They maintain that phasing charts and master schedules have been refined to a point where they can sufficiently cover the programming of complex efforts.

However, in some cases where PERT has been applied to a going program, the planning incompatibilities which have been detected have staggered even the proponents of the technique. As a result of networking, one defense manufacturer found that the existing plan called for placing of two missiles on the same launcher on the same day.

PERT has pointed out beyond any doubt the serious weaknesses of traditional scheduling methods when applied to a program such as major missile development, manufacture, and test. In a PERT network, where each event must be preceded and followed by another event, complex relationships and interdependencies can be identified. It is the discipline of planning logic required to develop a network which forces a planner to take a new look at his task, and in the process, opens to him significant new horizons.

Positive Control.   In its entirety, a PERT network normally covers a program from its inception to at least the completion of the first article. Unlike schedules which tend to be related to organizational responsibilities, the network cuts across organizational lines. One week, the design group may be in the line of critical path, another week the line may have shifted, and the test group may be pacing the schedule. Whatever the case, management can readily identify the problem areas and initiate corrective action.

Although the network approach puts emphasis on the total program rather than particular elements, it should be remembered that if the network is sufficiently detailed, each of these elements, described by events and activities, can often be related to a functional organization or even a budget number.

Networking.   To permit this, events selected for a network must include those events which represent a change in responsibility for activities within the network. In other words, each activity needs to be identified with a particular organization. By comparison of actuals with activity estimates, the performance of each group can be evaluated, and causes for schedule difficulties can be pinpointed to responsible organizations.

Another contribution and selling point which cannot be overlooked results from the fact that networking requires adoption of positive and unambiguous definitions of all events and activities. Getting everybody in a large organization to talk the same language can be a difficult task, and if this can be accomplished as a side effect of PERT networking, it certainly deserves consideration.

Early in the development of PERT, statisticians recognized that although the technique was superior to existing flow and bar charting techniques for program planning and control, it had basic mathematical weaknesses. They also recognized that because of these weaknesses, careful decisions would have to be made as to the scope and method of application of the technique.

This recognition is well illustrated by the present PERT applications in the Boeing Company. Dictated by specific program characteristics and customer requirements, the applica-

tions on Minuteman, Dyna-Soar, and Bomarc programs are basically different in their approach and coverage, highlight different problems of application, and also show different degrees of success.

LIMITATIONS OF PERT TECHNIQUE

Some of the limitations of PERT application are very rudimentary. For example, because of its "time to completion" variable, PERT cannot be used when it is not possible to estimate the occurrence of events. This is true of any project in which there is a reasonable expectancy that a break-through in the state-of-the-art may change the sequence of events at any given stage of development. Alternate routes or paths are therefore required, both of which need to be followed to a point of no return.

Similarly, PERT cannot be used on activities which are under a recurring cycle, such as in manufacturing. PERT networks usually stop with the completion of the first production article at which point the traditional scheduling techniques or the line-of-balance method takes effect. This range of applicability is very real, and should be kept in mind throughout development of a PERT program.

Military Project Experience   From the standpoint of limitations, it is of particular interest that PERT has never been implemented on a total weapon system. For example, on the Polaris program, certain portions were networked and reported on, but the Navy concedes that at no time did a total Fleet Ballistic Missile System network exist. The reasons for this are several:

1. *Accuracy of the Model*—The network model does not yield itself to the incorporation of computer checks, and there is no known method for verification of the logic of a network. For this reason, accuracy of the network depends on the process of preparing it. In practice, network development involves cycling through computer runs, progressive evaluation, and detection of possible inaccuracies, followed by revisions.

2. *Data Handling*—When network size exceeds approximately 5,000 events, it becomes difficult to maintain the purity of computer input and quick system response. A large number of events means that a large number of people are involved in the processing of network data. Consequently, the exposure to error becomes greater. Time required for the PERT cycle also increases.

3. *Computing Large Networks*—Experience shows that it is almost impossible to manually calculate networks larger than 700 events. Therefore, larger networks, such as those for a major weapon system, require a computer. The number of events which can be economically handled by the computer depends on the amount of data which the computer can process in high-speed memory without extensive use of magnetic tapes. For example, the IBM 7090 computer has a storage capacity of 32,000 words. This capacity provides for approximately 10,000 activities or events. When networks exceed this size, it is necessary to utilize magnetic tape storage. Use of magnetic tape considerably increases the required number of computer passes and the associated cost.

4. *Summarization and Integration*—Large networks are awkward to handle. There is no known method for summarization or reducing the size of a network to a smaller equivalent net. Also, it is difficult to automatically assemble separate networks into a master network and compute it. This can be accomplished only through a special computer program and extensive cross-referencing.

5. *Reporting*—As the size of networks increases, the technique of translating computer outputs into management information becomes more difficult. Theoretically, network outputs identify problem areas as well as indicate where trade-offs in resources may be desired. While this information can be visualized when networks are small, reporting techniques have not been developed to the extent that similar use can be made of large networks. This factor limits PERT as a management tool on major programs.

PERT as a Management Problem

The nature and the far-reaching effects of the limitations of the PERT technique are such that the total problem cannot be left to the program planner or to an operations research man. Any large scale implementation of the technique has to follow careful analysis and soul searching and demands careful attention from top management.

Even when a company is required to adopt PERT by the military customer, it is necessary to keep an objective viewpoint. For example, a degree of enthusiasm would help to accelerate the application of network analysis to routine projects, such as installation of a piece of machinery, design of a generator, or construction of a building. However, it would be foolish to use the same approach to a major weapon system. When exercised apart from experience and existing knowledge of limitations, enthusiasm may cause unsound PERT applications which result in unnecessary cost, adverse psychological effect, and possible delay in the implementation of a workable PERT system.

Must Ride Herd on It. The limitations also make it obvious that active adaptation of PERT in any company will cause a considerable amount of developmental research in the technique and may result in the support of particular approaches by various parts of the organization. For this reason, especially if the company is large, PERT is not a technique which, like most management techniques, can be turned over to the departments for implementation. It requires continuous top management attention and guidance during the implementation period.

If this is not done, time and effort are lost when several departments attempt to solve similar problems, and the situation is even more serious when, upon implementation, it is discovered that the system will not work in total or includes portions which are incongruous with the over-all system. Top management attention is also important if the use of PERT techniques is required by a military customer or a major military prime contractor. In this case, definitive policy is required regarding the level of detail which will be effectively reported under the system.

Top management involvement in PERT is not restricted to over-all guidance and policy formulation. Whenever more than one PERT application takes place in a company, certain technical problems immediately become apparent which need over-all coordination. For example, the events in a PERT network can be numbered serially, sequentially, or at random. Computer programs are in existence to handle a network of each type. However, once a particular computer program is adapted by a company, it becomes impractical to introduce variations for each internal application. It should be easy to issue a company policy prescribing the use of a particular numbering system; however, such action would not solve the technical problem.

Major PERT networks may be tied into similar networks at other companies and selected data submitted in card form to military services which have their own PERT staffs. Unless the numbering systems are compatible, application of the technique will result in large workload and undue increase in cost. Unless top management is ready to assist subordinates and outside organizations to come to mutually acceptable terms, there will be disagreement, wasted effort, and an unfavorable impression on involved parties outside the company. Typical of the PERT technical problems, on which management attention will continue to be centered, are matters of system networking, scheduling, and reporting to management. Here are some of the facts concerning each of these problems.

System Networking

The usual approach to PERT on a major program starts with an overall master network. However, some people feel that this network may never be computed, and would serve primarily as a map for the selection of critical functional or subsystem areas in which detail networks would be developed. The critical path would be computed from the detail networks after practically all elements of the program have been covered. The master network would be adjusted as more definitive information becomes available in the detail networking process.

Another approach, sponsored mainly by the Boeing Company, takes the viewpoint that critical program areas cannot always be determined from a broad master network without actually computing a critical path. If functional areas are selected and networked in detail, interfaces between such functional networks are not readily apparent and integration of such networks may be extremely difficult. Even if integration is accomplished, such networks may not yield correct results and yet, because of the inability to check the network's logic, the computations have to be taken at face value.

An alternative approach recommended by the proponents of this viewpoint is to expand the master network in subsystem areas only and to use the master network for all computations. While such network would not have detail coverage in specific critical areas, it is believed to give a more dependable picture of the overall program.

Although PERT was developed basically as a planning and control tool, attempts have also been made to use it as a scheduling technique. Theoretically, PERT networks are a convenient base for preparation of bar charts and detail schedules. Networking should precede any bar charting of the program from the top down and may, in fact, eliminate the need for most bar charts and master schedules. When networks are established at proper detail, they can be used for end-to-end scheduling.

PERT as Scheduling Technique

While this theoretical approach is feasible on relatively simple programs, it breaks down when the complexity of the program is large, as in the case of major missile efforts. To utilize PERT as a scheduling tool on a complex program would require networking of hundreds of thousands of activities. Even at our advanced stage in computer technology, it is not practical to handle such vast networks. As the pressures arise to include more and more detail into the networking effort, management must recognize the limitations of the technique and draw a line.

A definition as to what PERT application should accomplish must be made and the level of detail to which the technique should be extended must be outlined. The Boeing Company, which unsuccessfully tried the scheduling approach on its Dyna-Soar program, has come to the conclusion that in the present state of development, PERT techniques cannot be used for detailed scheduling of large programs, and their application to such programs should be limited to planning and control purposes.

Reporting to Management

The principal objective of PERT reports is to call management attention to situations requiring decisions and action. In small, manually computed networks, status information can be reflected on a bar chart or some other easily visualized form. When larger programs are covered, the reporting output necessarily is in machine print-out form which does not have the visibility required for analysis.

The situation is almost paradoxical since large programs which demand quick action by top managers, necessarily generate a greater amount of reporting paper. Since there is no method to summarize networks automatically, the process of extracting data, analyzing, and then displaying these data requires progressive evaluation and permits some defensive interpretation along the way.

THE BIG PICTURE

In approaching any of these problems, management must avoid focusing on a small number of exceptions and give all its attention to the workability of the total program. It should always be kept in mind that one of those features which makes PERT excel over other techniques is the fact that it cuts across organization lines and looks at the total program. Detail logic and accuracy may have to be overlooked in order to arrive at a workable PERT program. The network should not be expected to be perfect in every detail to make it complete. As a mathematical model, the network should be sufficiently true to reality to yield practical solutions through exercise of its predictive quality.

COST OF PERT

Extensive application of PERT techniques obviously is expensive. Skilled technical personnel are required to plan networks, and engineering and operating men must take time to explain activities to planners and to make time estimates. Data processing and computer costs are impressive, to say the least.

The Special Projects Office of the Navy estimated it cost them $200,000 a year in computer time to conduct biweekly analyses of the Polaris program. While one contractor has priced its contractual PERT requirements at $300,000, other firms feel that PERT can replace a portion of the traditional planning tasks and that very little additional cost is involved.

This, of course, depends on the complexity of the program and the level of detail which may be handled within the limitations discussed earlier. The Air Force has estimated that PERT costs average 0.5 per cent of total cost on research and development programs and 0.1 per cent of major programs generally.

Less Costly Than Coffee Breaks In one instance, the Air Force found that engineering time consumed in contractor's PERT activity was less than a fourth of the time authorized for coffee breaks. This does not sound like much, however, just ten minutes per engineer per day amounts to over $300,000 a year when applied to one of the major missile programs.

To date, insufficient consideration has been given to the costs of large scale PERT applications. There is no doubt that only small applications can claim to offset these costs with savings in planning and scheduling. It is also true that on some programs, especially in construction, critical path planning can yield immediate tangible savings. For example, the Catalytic Construction Company credits network planning with a 25 percent reduction in cost on an $800,000 project. In most applications of PERT, however, the dollar savings are not quite so tangible. Costs, nevertheless, are real and should be considered in determining an optimum level of application for PERT.

OUTLOOK FOR PERT

During the first two years of PERT, discussions on the subject were limited to technical journals and companies where the technique was being applied. Early in 1961, the technique suddenly emerged as a major selling point of several management consultants. Courses on the subject were announced. American Management Association organized a briefing seminar, and the Aerospace Industries Association formed a PERT task group.

The Department of Defense initiated efforts to achieve some standardization in PERT requirements of the military services. All these activities affected the growth of the technique, shaking out some of the marginal features, such as three time estimates and computation of variance, and advancing the extension of PERT to resource factors.

Resource Incorporation Incorporation of resource factors, especially cost and manpower is currently the immediate problem in PERT development. From a theoretical standpoint, resource incorporation is not a serious problem. However, the issue becomes clouded when the methods of data collection and assignment to activities come under consideration.

To begin with, introduction of resource factors will further limit computer capacity and the number of events which can be economically processed. Resource application, therefore, will be more easily accomplished on some programs than on others. For example, programs differ in the desired level of detail in cost estimating and collection. If the networks were to be maintained at a gross level, the major problem in cost incorporation may well be that of identifying existing accounts with activities in the network, rather than assigning new account numbers to activities.

Until the problems of planning and control nature are successfully solved in PERT applications to large programs, the incorporation of costs, manpower, reliability, etc., cannot take place. These factors should be incorporated only on smaller networks where PERT technology has been sufficiently developed.

General Systems Theory Needed From a long-range standpoint, the potential of PERT extends even beyond resource incorporation. In the past few years, both industry and government have recognized a growing need for a general systems theory which would consolidate the existing scientific management methods and thereby extend the field of management sciences. Russell D. Archibald of Hughes

Aircraft Co. has pointed out that PERT may be an important step toward the development of such a theory, at least in the area of project-type programs. When all business is viewed as a system of interrelated and integrated systems and subsystems, PERT networking technique can serve as one of the necessary catalytic agents.

PERT's Weaknesses   The PERT technique is a logical refinement of planning and control techniques. Its theory is deceivingly simple, and the potential appears unlimited. Experience, however, has shown definite limitations of the technique, particularly in regard to application on large programs. Because of the initial success on military contract applications and the enthusiasm over the technique by the military services, PERT has permeated industry at an accelerated rate. As a result, application of the technique has in some cases resulted in disappointment. This has been a reflection of overenthusiasm, lack of sufficient experience, and the basic weaknesses in the technique when applied to large programs.

PERT's Strengths   Generally, PERT is a superior system for (a) integration of planning, (b) rapid evaluation of program status, (c) identification of potential trouble spots, and (d) reallocation of resources. In its application to large programs, it is one of the first computer techniques in the management field which not only processes data, but actually helps to make decisions. On small programs, it becomes a highly flexible management tool which does not require computer support.

Its Future in Management   Until such time when PERT becomes as common as the bar chart, top management attention is required to coordinate those aspects of PERT which have management and broad technical implications. Experience gained in other companies must be translated in relation to the requirements of each new application, keeping in mind the limitations of applicability, size and accuracy of networks, technical approaches, and cost.

As the technique matures and further experimentation takes place, PERT can be expected to include elements of manpower distribution and cost. The resulting tie-in with operating budgets may bring management a decade closer to the overall control system which it has been seeking.

74

An Approach to Computer-based Management Control Systems*

D. G. MALCOLM and A. J. ROWE

In an era of automated information technology, the ability to formulate decision criteria precisely and process information electronically should prove valuable in the design of management control systems. One can look forward to organizational structures which more nearly conform to the communication and informational requirements.

In an attempt to explore the problems facing management of large organizations and persons responsible for the design of management controls, the authors have embarked on an intensive research program in this area. Started in April of 1959, the research has been primarily concerned with studying computer-based management control systems.[1] By examining the

* Reprinted by permission of the publisher from the *California Management Review*, vol. 3, no. 3, pp. 5–15, Spring, 1961. Mr. Malcolm is vice-president of the western division of Operations Research, Inc. Mr. Rowe is manager of industrial dynamic research for the Hughes Aircraft Company.

flow of information and decision processes using computer simulation, insights into the behavior of these complex systems appear possible.

NATURE OF THE PROBLEM

Examining the problems confronting designers of management control systems, one is readily aware of the magnitude of the task. Although management and organizational specialists have been concerned with these same problems for many years, there still remain a large number of questions to be answered. For example:

- To what extent should top management go in developing a philosophy of "management by system?"
- How can top management determine the depth in the organization to which it should extend day-to-day personal influence?
- How can management evaluate proposed computer-based, information-processing, decision-making systems?
- How should management plan the development of an organization to achieve control?

These in turn raise a number of questions for the researcher as follows:

- What is a suitable method for determining the cost and effectiveness of management information or control systems?
- How can appropriate systems be designed prior to their actual installation?
- By what method can various types of information be expressed in terms of a company's over-all objectives?
- What is the best configuration of an integrated management control system?

Specialists have applied a wide variety of answers and approaches to these problems. Examples of traditional methods include: organizational planning, scheduling of operations, inventory control, quality control, and cost control.

It is significant to note that each of these is a component or single aspect of a business and the concept of an integrated total-system control remains practically unexploited. However, it is possible that concise, quantitative, and unequivocal answers to these questions may not be found for a long time.

DEFINING MANAGEMENT CONTROLS

For the purpose of this paper, a management control system is described as a set of policies, procedures, and associated information processing designed to give direction to corporate activities in the following ways:

- By clearly establishing goals;
- By measuring progress in achieving these goals;
- By indicating the need for corrective action.

To achieve an optimal set of management controls, however, it is necessary to "design" a management system in much the same way that equipment itself is designed. As part of this design process, it is a basic requirement that the system designer clearly understand the objectives of the business.

In this regard the traditional statements of maximizing profit or return on investment are not sufficient guides. Modern business is conducted to serve many diverse objectives, making the problem of control more sophisticated than attempting to have each and every action directed toward such goals. Management, therefore, can be considered as the custodians of the resources of an organization with the mission to organize the effort to achieve purposeful objectives and to assure survival of the business.

As part of the control process, a communication network is used to link management with the resources of the business and to provide the information needed for feedback control. The information available to the manager, is therefore used as the basis for control and operating decisions. The core of the design problem, therefore, is in determining which operating decision rules can be reduced to a routine, computerized approach.

The characteristics of information flow and decision rules provide the basic inputs for a study of management controls. It is obvious that the interlinkage between decision points, as well as the density of information flow, has a direct effect on the nature of the organizational structure required for successful operation. Thus, the constraints of the existing organization must be ignored, and the specifications for an effective organization to make required decisions should be based on the system design activity.

CURRENT APPLICATIONS OF COMPUTERS

Although there is an ever-increasing use of electronic data-processing equipment in the automating of existing information systems, the need to integrate the over-all informational requirements and to redesign a given system is often overlooked.

More generally, applications are made in one area of the business, such as finance or manufacturing, and little more than checks for compatibility are made with respect to the total system problem.

This piecemeal approach is most frequently justified on the grounds that one must build gradually in developing a total system. However, there is a growing recognition that this approach leads to suboptimal results.

In current applications, the use of electronic computers does not tap one-tenth of their ultimate potential. Although this condition is particularly true of industrial, as contrasted with military, applications, it is a situation that will become a matter of increasing concern to those who use computers, especially as they realize the nature of this potential. The situation, conceivably, could become worse before effective long-range programs are designed and in use.

Applications in Military Systems   If one examines the Air Defense Command, it is readily apparent that the prototypes of highly automated information systems are currently being established for management use. Examples of such systems which operate with extremely short feedback time, often referred to as operating in real-time, can be seen in SAGE[2] (Semi-Automatic Ground Environment) and SACCS (Strategic Air Command Control System). Both of these systems are computer-based, command-control systems.

In the course of the design and implementation of these Systems, a number of changes were made in the Air Defense Command structure. The computer control system itself was used as the basis for organizational changes which led to the centralization of many activities.

A further development which was necessitated by the requirement for design and implementation was the concept of a system manager. The ESSPO (Electronic Support Systems Project Office), was given the mission of properly managing the joint efforts of system analysis, system design, computer manufacturing, computer programming and system training.

Real-Time Control   In military applications, the computer has been used as an integral, on-line controlling device. In this context, the terms, "real-time control," "communication," and "information system," emerge as system design concepts.

"Real-time" is used to mean that the desired information is transmitted into a centralized computer instantaneously and without conversion. The significance of "real-time" control lies in the fact that information is used as it is developed and that elements in the system are controlled by the processed information immediately, not after the fact, or by making periodic forecasts of the expected future state of the system.

To achieve "real-time" control, the computer processes information, compares it with predetermined decision criteria and issues instructions to men or machines, or both, for corrective or purposeful action. Further, the computer, by means of direct outputs, informs affected parties of this information as it is developed. This is "real-time management information."

By examining the best known examples of systems of this type currently found in the military, one may find some guidance in design approaches that may be useful in evolving better on-line management control systems for industry.

MILITARY SYSTEMS

The experience gained in the development of military command control systems can be summarized under the following topics:

- Use of the Systems Analysis Approach,
- Problem Formulation for Computer Programming,
- Use of New Computer Applications, and
- Use of Formalized System Training.

While the following are broad generalizations, it would appear that the quickest route to effective development of a truly integrated management control system involves a proper point of view on the part of management in regard to the possible effects of information flow on the organization structure. That is, the possibility of recentralizing and the eliminating of certain functions must be within the system designer's scope.

Further, to perform a system analysis there must be proper organizational status for the design function and top management must plan for the necessary lead time to perform its activities. Finally, while it should be evident, it is worth emphasizing that top management participation and support is vital to obtain desired results.

Systems Analysis Approach   In reviewing the development of a system such as SAGE, one is impressed with the magnitude of the design process. The design of this system necessitated spelling out precise system requirements. This, in turn, provided the basis for more effectively meeting the needs of the air defense system.

In contrast to the systems approach, the

question that is often asked is "What can be done to improve or automate existing practices?" In looking over the process of creating new management control systems, it becomes obvious that this latter approach is often the easiest to justify and, thus, has been the route traditionally followed.

In essence, the design process is based on answering the question "What is the best system?" and is generally called the systems analysis, or systems engineering, approach. Thus, one principle in creating a new system involves a careful look at the requirements of the system via the systems engineering approach. A brief description of the steps generally involved is as follows:

1. *Establish criteria for management information needs:* (a) Establish the objectives or mission of the system. (b) Determine current information, decision, display, and report practices, by use of graphical flow analyses.

2. *Develop the preliminary design:* (a) A preliminary statement of system requirements; i.e., specific reporting frequencies, types, and routings of reports, type of equipments, displays, etc., should be established. (b) Determine what can be automated using computer programming and what to leave as currently performed. We must remember here that technology is changing rapidly. Simon[3] predicts that by 1984 it will be technically possible to automate any and all functions in an organization. (c) Balance current requirements with growth considerations.

3. *Evaluate the preliminary design:* (a) Determine the cost of hardware and applicable costs. (b) Assess training implications and requirements. (c) Establish the nature of the improvements to be gained.

4. *Develop a revised model of the proposed system:* (a) Use of systems analysis or an experimental approach involving simulation or gaming, to test the design. (b) Obtain the participation of the ultimate users.

5. *Determine system specifications:* (a) Evaluate alternative means of achieving the proposed design. (b) Consider the relationship to other system requirements.

6. *Install, de-bug, modify, extend the system:* (a) Provide for maintenance and updating. (b) Allow for flexibility in operating and modifying the system.

Computer Problem Formulation   In the application of computer-based systems, it has become evident that there is a need for precise formulation of the computer program. Descriptive statements are not sufficient, rather quantitative or analytic formulation of problems is required.

Furthermore, factors such as kind and size of memory, speed of computation, manner of indexing, and rounding must all be taken into account in computer programming. Methods of filing information, data accumulation, and reporting requirements are also significant aspects of program design.

It is often necessary to reformulate a problem to conform to the computer requirements; although this consideration is becoming less important with the availability of large-scale digital computers.

At the outset of a given computer program, a decision must be made whether to have a flexible, general purpose program or one designed for the immediate specific use. Modular programming which treats each section of a program separately provides considerable flexibility at only a small cost in computation time and storage.

Computer "Language."   Probably the most difficult aspect of the problem is the actual coding or programming language. Not only is the coding a time-consuming and difficult process, but the system designer must convey the intent of his work to programmers, thus compounding the problem.

Considerable effort is currently being expended in the development of computer languages which can be used more readily by system designers. This, in part, recognizes the fact that as much time is often spent in coding a problem as in the formulation. In this regard, then, considerable work remains to be done to develop computer languages which will simplify the operational instructions for the computer programming task.

Use of New Computer Applications   The capability of the computer to process information rapidly, store information conveniently and provide accuracy has made significant inroads on long-standing problems. Some of these computer applications are:

1. *On-line control:* As has been mentioned previously, on-line, direct read-in and read-out, integrated computer operation has been used in military systems. The importance of this technical achievement should not be underestimated. However, the feasibility of utilizing this on-line control feature for industrial application requires research and analysis to determine the cost and effectiveness of a given application.

2. *Management-by-exception:*[4] The data processing capability of high-speed computers, as used in the military, has made possible central-

ized operations using large masses of data which have been carefully sorted by built-in criteria. Only exceptions requiring attention are presented to decision makers by the computer. This feature could be extended to provide centralized control in management systems. PERT (Navy Polaris program) is an example.

3. *Interrogation, or fast-simulation possibilities:* Using a computer-based system, the human monitor can, in a sense, ask "What would happen if I issued this command?" This interrogation feature, often called "fast-simulation" requires the building of analytic models which incorporate desired predictive capabilities. Appropriate computer models for business situations may eventually provide the potentiality of on-line management control systems.

Use of Formalized System Training   In the course of developing major new military systems, it has been found that provision for training people in the on-going operations of the new systems is needed. The training in a system such as SAGE involves elaborate simulations of a predicted attack environment. This represents a new concept to the management world. The justification for this elaborate training stems from the fact that there is no other way to adequately train the people to perform under an attack situation.

However, a significant additional value in this approach should be pointed out. The proficiency of a system is determined by its operation as a whole, involving the communications and interrelations of many people and machines. Therefore, the proficiency of individual acts must be judged by measures appropriate to the system context.

It would hardly be desirable to emphasize performance at one part of the system that would be detrimental to the total system performance. In short, each person should be trained to act in an optimal way from the total system point of view.

Therefore, to adequately provide for proper performance in such broad systems, a comprehensive means of training using simulated exercises is required. Furthermore, the need for this training is not dependent on whether the environment is real or hypothetical.

SIMULATION MODELS ESSENTIAL

It appears that when radically new concepts in management control are installed, quite likely simulation models will be required. The installation time, the acceptance, and therefore even the ultimate efficiency attainable by the control systems will be considerably enhanced by appropriately designed simulation exercises along with proper criteria for measuring performance in relation to the total system.

Using a systematic design approach, as shown in the preceding discussion, it is possible to develop improved, total, computer-based management control systems. In view of the requirements of current air defense systems, the need for computer-based systems was readily justified. However, industrial systems have not reached the point where objectives can be set forth in clear and unequivocal terms and thus it is difficult to evaluate a given system design.

In short, the only feasible means for meeting the military requirements for rapid, high volume, and accurate data handling was the use of computer systems. Given these requirements, one could systematically design a feasible system. On the other hand, the capability of rigorous evaluation of a number of alternative designs has generally been considered too costly. However, the acceptability of the military approach for the business world will undoubtedly be predicated on the ability to evaluate control concepts prior to actually installing new systems.

If the advantages of information recentralization are to be achieved in practice, they must first be proved beneficial to the organization; and secondly, they must be both desired by and acceptable to management.

In practice, however, these two requirements are often in conflict. Although it is difficult to assess the value of a new system, it appears desirable to develop a design approach that is both evaluative and instructive. Such an approach can be instrumental in the realization of promised benefits of an integrated management information system. An approach which appears to be the most suitable, and perhaps the most effective in the long range, is the use of computer simulation.

Computer Simulation   As a problem-solving tool, computer simulation has been used for a number of years. It has enabled management to experiment with and test certain types of policies, procedures and organizational changes in much the same way an engineer tests new designs. With the use of computers and the development of probability methods, computer simulation can also be applied to complex operating plans or management controlling systems in addition to day-to-day operating problems. The method is similar to war gaming techniques used by the military and the paper and pencil techniques used by systems and procedure specialists.

In a sense, simulation is a synthetic means used to imitate the behavior of a system for the purpose of studying the response to specific changes. Where the problem is entirely physical in nature, such as in testing aircraft, a physical model can be used. However, in studying management control systems, which deal with the flow of information and decision networks, an exact analogue of the problem may not be possible.

An approximation, usually in the form of a mathematical or symbolic model, is used which describes the elements and properties of the system under study. Thus, a model for a management control system is a means for providing a formalized statement of system behavior, rather than a physical analogue of the system.

A Design Tool.   Simulation has only recently been considered as a useful tool for the design of management control systems.[5] A similar approach has been taken in the research program conducted by the authors,[6] where computer simulation is used as a laboratory for examining system behavior. To conduct such experimentation, an analytic model of a total business system has been developed which explicitly characterizes the information flow, decision rules and physical processes of a business system.

To the extent that this model describes the behavior of the elements of the system in a realistic manner, the conclusions drawn should prove useful in the design of management controls as applied to large-scale, complex organizations and their associated information processing.

However, in view of the intricately complex nature of a total business system, intuition alone cannot be considered sufficient to evaluate new concepts or designs. While on the other hand, extensive experimentation directly in an actual plant to evaluate alternate designs poses almost insurmountable problems.

Aside from the inevitable disruptions and possibly unrealistic results, valuable time would be lost in gathering performance data. In addition, costly mistakes might result if the consequences of actually carrying out a given experiment cannot be predicted in advance, and there is no control. These considerations, therefore, strongly support the use of computer simulation both as a research and design vehicle.

Experiments with Models   Research in Management Controls implies experimentation; however, the manner of experimenting is dependent upon the results desired. An exploratory type of experimentation is possible by simply changing parameters of the simulation model and observing the resultant system behavior.

Thus, insights into the response characteristics of the system are obtained by examining the results shown in the computer output. Another manner of experimentation is to specify given system designs and subject these to many conditions and observe the effects. This latter method is principally used to test the significant differences among alternative designs.

"Policy Laboratory."   Since the computer output provides a summarization of information reflecting system behavior generated during simulation, it is possible to obtain a continuous time trace of the changes in system performance and the interdependencies among the elements of the system. It is this capability of being able to examine, in considerable detail, the changes which result from alternate system designs that has led to the term "policy laboratory" being applied to computer simulation.

The Model and Its Role   To simulate management controls, then, it is necessary to have a model which provides a formal statement of the business system's behavior. Computer simulation, however, is seldom an exact analogue of the operation of an actual system. Rather, simulation performed on a digital computer can only approximate continuous, simultaneous activity. If the elements and properties of the system have been properly defined, then the parameters and variables can be readily controlled and measured.

The model may be symbolic, mathematical, or descriptive; however, it should be constructed so as to include properties which are sufficient to define the behavior of the system.

Forcing Function.   The variables describe behavior for a given set of parameters. The forcing functions provide the external stimuli which cause the system to react—for example, orders which enter a system cause men to work, machines to run, and so on. In this way, orders become a forcing function for the system. Whatever particular form is used, a model provides the frame of reference within which the problem is considered.

A model often indicates relationships which are not otherwise obvious. However, it should be noted that a model need not duplicate actual conditions to be useful. A model should be designed to predict actual behavior resulting from changes in the system design or application of new decision rules. Such prediction implies an understanding of the manner in which the system reacts; that is, being able to specify the outputs for a given set of inputs. This approach differs from the conventional concept of treating the system as a "black box."

Since a simulation model is merely a means for testing new ideas, the simpler the model, the more effective for research or design purposes. It is not necessary to incorporate all possible aspects of system behavior in the model; rather, only those variables which contribute substantially to system response characteristics need be incorporated.

To this end, a model can be considered as an initial experiment to determine what factors are most significant in a business system. The model can be refined or expanded as experimental data describing the system performance and sensitivity to various factors become available.

Developing a Business Model   For the purpose of studying management controls, modeling should be centered about the information, decision-making and control aspects of the business. The majority of simulations to date, however, have been concerned with the physical activities within a business, such as scheduling of products,[7] control of inventory, movement of vehicles, and maintenance of aircraft, to name a few.[8]

On the other hand, since management control is concerned with the more intangible aspects of the business, modeling is a far more difficult problem.[9] Reviewing some of these modeling considerations in detail indicates the task involved:

Decision-making Process.   If the decisions in an organization are associated with the physical points where they occur, then the decision-making process can be characterized by the decision rules and associated information. Interlinkages among the decision points represent the communication channels.

To simulate an organization with an appropriate degree of reality, it is necessary to establish a suitable communication network. In addition, the many decision criteria and decision rules have to be stated analytically to be amenable to computer programming.

Queuing Effects.   If a decision maker is viewed as a processor of information, the rate of arrival of information and the time taken to process decisions will result in an average delay or queuing effect. Analysis of such delays will provide one important measure of system effectiveness.

The speed of information transmission, as well as the number of decision points, however, must be closely coupled with the capability of the system to respond to varying inputs. By assigning costs to alternate means of informa-

tion transmittal, the cost of on-line controls can be assessed.

Organizational Considerations.   Since delays in decisions are a function of information flow and queuing, they have a direct effect on the organization structure. For example, introducing alternate decision channels to permit more effective information flow might lead to radical changes in an organization. A simulation model could thus examine different forms of organization structure and evaluate the effect of changes on the system performance.

Decentralization in an organization leads to the possibility of distortion in information due to the number of levels through which the information must pass; whereas this effect may be avoided in a more centralized organization. Therefore, the modeling must treat with this consideration in order to provide a suitable basis for studying management control systems.

Uses of the Computer Model   Up to this point, the discussion has been primarily concerned with the modeling process itself. Let us now turn to some of the specific problems which can be studied using such a simulation model.

Principles of System Design.   An important consideration in management control is the relationship of the total business system to the control methodology employed. In a sense, management controls are embedded in the broader consideration of total system design.

In view of the sparsity of knowledge in this area, computer simulation provides a means for examining a multitude of alternate designs with the possibility of developing basic design principles.

Testing System Objectives.   As has already been discussed, the formalizing of business objectives is probably one of the most difficult aspects in establishing useful management controls. This aspect of the problem is particularly important since there are a number of competing objectives in any system which must be taken into account to avoid suboptimization.

Using a computer model, the possible consequences of different combinations of objectives can be examined. It is evident that there may not be a set of universal objectives which apply to all businesses; rather, actual objectives are generally dependent upon the willingness of managers to take action in the face of uncertainty and with inadequate information.

Measuring System Performance.   During the course of running a computer model, a means for explicit measurement of system performance must be provided. In actual practice, methods of measurement have involved long delays from occurrence to reporting of events due to the lack of high-speed data-processing equipment. However, with the increased use of computers, processing and summarizing data will prove a less formidable task, and measures of system performance can be based on actual operations.

Using fast simulation as discussed for the SAGE system, managers will have the option of periodically introducing real-time control. In addition, using a simulation model new measures of performance can be developed and tested.

Design of Management Controls. A number of design concepts that should be explored in the development of new management control systems are:

- The use of information feedback loops, providing on-line control;
- The use of variable control limits in place of arbitrary standards as the basis for corrective action;
- Inclusion of formalized decision rules in the control system to (a) provide for optimization of the business system, (b) provide for improved response characteristics of the system;
- Use of a sampled data approach for providing information on system performance. This is similar to the "exception principle."

Although these four items do not constitute an exhaustive list of all considerations, they do provide some idea of the complexity of designing management control systems.

All too often, management controls are treated as ends in themselves rather than as the means of improving total system performance. In the case of corporate budgeting, for example, funds may be spent unnecessarily to forestall budget cuts at a later date.

Another illustration of the misuse of the control concept is traditional costing practices that force the business to conform to arbitrary standards. As stated by Warren Alberts of United Airlines,[10] controls should be considered as guides for obtaining improved performance and not as a means of restricting performance.

If the design process, as discussed here, is at the system level, there is greater assurance that management controls will truly be integrated. The process of modeling and formalizing the structure of the business system should itself bring clarity to the interdependency of management control with planning, policies, objectives, and decision rules. As our understanding of the behavior of business systems improves, we should be in a position to develop effective design principles for management control systems.

REFERENCES

1. A. J. Rowe, "A Research Approach in Management Controls," *Journal of Industrial Engineering,* vol. 11, pp. 251–258, May–June, 1960.

2. A computerized air defense system using data automatically correlated with known flight plans to detect presence of unknown aircraft. Also provides automatic guidance of interceptors.

3. H. Simon, "The Corporation: Will It Be Managed by Machines?" *Management Review,* November, 1960.

4. D. G. Malcolm, J. H. Roseboom, C. E. Clark, and W. Fazar, "Application of a Technique for Research and Development Program Evaluation," *Operations Research,* vol. 7, pp. 646–669, September–October, 1959.

5. D. G. Malcolm, "A Bibliography on the Use of Simulation in Management Analysis," *Operations Research,* vol. 8, pp. 169–177, March–April, 1960.

6. *System Simulation Symposium Proceedings,* American Institute of Industrial Engineers, New York, May 16–17, 1957.

7. D. G. Malcolm and A. J. Rowe, *Management Control Systems,* John Wiley & Sons, Inc., New York, 1960. (The proceedings of a symposium held at System Development Corporation.)

8. A. J. Rowe, "Toward a Theory of Scheduling," *Journal of Industrial Engineering,* vol. 2, pp. 125–136, March–April, 1960.

9. C. W. Cragin et al., "Simulation: Management's Laboratory," Simulation Associates, Bradford, Mass., April, 1959.

10. W. E. Alberts, "The Concepts of Management Control," in Malcolm and Rowe, *op. cit.,* p. 14.

75

*Potentials of Management Science**

PETER F. DRUCKER

Some time ago I was asked by one of the management associations to make a speech on "Management Science in Business Planning." I used this invitation to do something I had long intended to do, which was to scan the last four or five years of literature in the areas of management science: operations research; statistical theory and statistical decision making; systems theory, cybernetics, data processing, and information theory; econometrics, management accounting, and accounting theory; and so on. I also looked fairly closely at the management science work done in a number of businesses, either by their own staffs or by outside consultants.

No one, I am convinced, can read this literature or can survey the work done without being impressed by the potential and promise of management science. To be sure, managing will always remain somewhat of an "art"; the talent, experience, vision, courage, and character of the managers will always be major factors in their performance and in that of their enterprises. But this is true of medicine and doctors, too. And, as with medicine, management and managers—especially the most highly endowed and most highly accomplished managers—will become the more effective as their foundation of organized systematic knowledge and organized systematic search grows stronger, and as their roots in a real discipline of management and entrepreneurship grow deeper. That such a discipline is possible, the work already done in management science proves.

But no one, I am also convinced, can survey the work to date without being worried at the same time. The potential is there—but it is in danger of being frittered away. Instead of a management science which supplies knowledge, concepts, and discipline to manager and entre-preneur, we may be developing a "management gadget bag" of techniques for the efficiency expert.

The bulk of the work today concerns itself with the sharpening of already existing tools for specific technical functions—such as quality control or inventory control, warehouse location or freight-car allocation, machine loading, maintenance scheduling, or order handling. And, in fact, a good deal of the work is little more than a refinement of industrial engineering, cost accounting, or procedures analysis. Some, though not very much, attention is given to the analysis and improvement of functional efforts—primarily those of the manufacturing function but also, to some extent, of marketing and of money management.

But there is almost no work, no organized thought, no emphasis on managing an enterprise—on the risk-making, risk-taking, decision-making job. In fact, I could find only two examples of such work: the industrial dynamics program at Massachusetts Institute of Technology[1] and the operations research and synthesis work done in some parts of the General Electric Company. Throughout management science—in the literature as well as in the work in progress—the emphasis is on techniques rather than on principles, on mechanics rather than on decisions, on tools rather than on results, and, above all, on efficiency of the part rather than on performance of the whole.

However, if there is one fundamental insight underlying all management science, it is that the business enterprise is a *system* of the highest order: a system the "parts" of which are human beings contributing voluntarily of their knowledge, skill, and dedication to a joint venture.[2] And one thing characterizes all genuine systems, whether they be mechanical like

---

* Reprinted by permission of the publisher from *Harvard Business Review*, vol. 37, no. 1, pp. 25ff., January–February, 1959. Mr. Drucker is professor of management at New York University and is also a well-known management consultant, lecturer, and author.

[1] See Jay W. Forrester, "Industrial Dynamics: A Major Breakthrough for Decision Makers," *Harvard Business Review*, July–August, 1958, p. 37.
[2] See Kenneth E. Boulding, "General Systems Theory," *Management Science*, April, 1956, p. 197.

the control of a missile, biological like a tree, or social like the business enterprise: it is interdependence. The whole of a system is not necessarily improved if one particular function or part is improved or made more efficient. In fact, the system may well be damaged thereby, or even destroyed. In some cases the best way to strengthen the system may be to *weaken* a part—to make it *less* precise or *less* efficient. For what matters in any system is the performance of the whole; this is the result of growth and of dynamic balance, adjustment, and integration rather than of mere technical efficiency.

Primary emphasis on the efficiency of parts in management science is therefore bound to do damage. It is bound to optimize precision of the tool at the expense of the health and performance of the whole. (That the enterprise is a social rather than a mechanical system makes the danger all the greater, for the other "parts" do not stand still. They either respond so as to spread the maladjustment throughout the system or organize for sabotage.)

This is hardly a hypothetical danger. The literature abounds in actual examples—inventory controls that improve production runs and cut down working capital but fail to consider the delivery expectations of the customer and the market risks of the business; machine-loading schedules that overlook the impact of the operations of one department on the rest of the plant; forecasts that assume the company's competitors will just stand still; and so on.

Technically this is all excellent work. But therein lies its danger. The new tools are so much more powerful than the old tools of technical and functional work—the tools of trial and error and of cut and fit—that their wrong or careless use must do damage.

For management science to become a gadget bag, therefore, not only means a missed opportunity; it may also mean loss of its potential to contribute altogether, if not its degeneration into a mischief maker.

Hence the questions arise: Is it inevitable that management science become a gadget bag? Or would this be the result of something management science does today or fails to do? And what would be the requirements for a real management science that supplies the knowledge and the methodology we need?

The first clue lies, perhaps, in the origin of this new "management science" approach—and the origin is an unusual one indeed.

Every other discipline of man began with a crude attempt to define what its subject was. Then people set to work fashioning concepts and tools for its study. But management science began with the application of concepts and tools developed within a host of other disciplines for their own particular purposes. It may have started with the heady discovery that certain mathematical techniques, hitherto applied to the study of the physical universe, could also be applied to the study of business operations.

As a result, the focus of much of the work in management science has *not* been on such questions as: What is the business enterprise? What is managing? What do the two do, and what do the two need? Rather, the focus has been on: Where can I apply my beautiful gimmick? The emphasis has been on the hammer rather than on driving in the nail, let alone on building the house. In the literature of operations research, for instance, there are several dissertations along the lines of "155 applications of linear programing," but I have not seen any published study on "typical business opportunities and their characteristics."

What this indicates is a serious misunderstanding on the part of the management scientist of what "scientific" means. "Scientific" is not—as many management scientists naively seem to think—synonymous with quantification. If this were true, astrology would be the queen of the sciences. It is not even the application of the "scientific method." After all, astrologers observe phenomena, derive the generalization of a hypothesis therefrom, and then test the hypothesis by further organized observation. Yet astrology is superstition rather than science because of its childish assumption that there is a real zodiac, that the signs in it really exist, and that their fancied resemblance to some such earthly creature as a fish or a lion defines their character and properties (whereas all of them are nothing but the mnemonic devices of the navigators of antiquity).

In other words "scientific" presupposes a rational definition of the universe of the science (that is, of the phenomena which it considers to be real and meaningful) as well as the formulation of basic assumptions or postulates which are appropriate, consistent, and comprehensive. This job of defining the universe of a science and of setting its basic postulates has to be done, however crudely, *before* the scientific method can be applied. If it is not done, or done wrongly, the scientific method cannot be applied. If it is done, and done right, the scientific method becomes applicable and indeed powerful.

This idea is, of course, nothing new. It goes back to the distinction between the premises that are generally valid and those that pertain to a specific discipline, made in Aristotle's

Analytica Posteriora. On the rediscovery of this principle during the last century rests the power of modern science and of its methods.[3]

Management science still has to do this job of defining its "universe." If it does this, then all the work done so far will become fruitful—at least as preparation and training ground for real achievement. The first task for management science, if it is to be able to contribute rather than distort and mislead, is therefore to define the specific nature of its subject matter. This might include as a basic definition the insight that the business enterprise is a system made up of human beings. The assumptions, opinions, objectives, and even the errors of people (and especially of managers) are thus primary *facts* for the management scientist. Any effective work in management science really has to begin with analysis and study of them.

Starting, then, with this recognition of what there is to be studied, management science must next establish its basic assumptions and postulates—without which no science can develop proper methods. It might first include the vital fact that every business enterprise exists in economy and society; that even the mightiest is the servant of its environment by which it can be dismissed without ceremony, but that even the lowliest affects and molds the economy and society instead of just adapting to them; in other words, that the business enterprise exists only in an economic and social ecology of great complexity.

The basic postulates might include the following ideas:

1. The business enterprise produces neither things nor ideas but humanly determined values. The most beautifully designed machine is still only so much scrap metal until it has utility for a customer.

2. Measurements in the business enterprise are such complex, not to say metaphysical, symbols as "money"—at the same time both highly abstract and amazingly concrete.

3. Economic activity, of necessity, is the commitment of present resources to an unknowable and uncertain future—a commitment, in other words, to expectations rather than to facts. Therefore risk is of the essence, and risk making and risk taking constitute the basic function of enterprise. And risks are not only taken by the "general manager," but right through the whole organization by everybody who contributes knowledge—that is, by every manager and professional specialist. This risk is something quite different from risk in the statistician's probability; it is the risk of the unique event, the irreversible qualitative breaking of the pattern.

4. Inside and outside the business enterprise there is constant irreversible change; indeed, the business enterprise exists as the agent of change in an industrial society, and it must be capable both of purposeful evolution to adapt to new conditions and of purposeful innovation to change the conditions.

Some of this is often said in the preface of books in management science. It generally stays in the preface, however. Yet for management science to contribute to business understanding, let alone become a science, postulates like the foregoing ought to be the fabric of its work. Of course we need quantification—though it tends to come fairly late in the development of a discipline (only now, for instance, can scientists really quantify in biology). We need the scientific method. And we need work on specific areas and operations—careful, meticulous detail work. But, above all, we need to recognize the particular character of business enterprise and the unique postulates necessary for its study. It is on this vision that we must build.

The first need of a management science is, then, that it respect itself sufficiently as a distinct and genuine discipline.

The second clue to what is lacking in management science as applied today is the emphasis throughout its literature and throughout its work on "minimizing risk" or even on "eliminating risk" as the goal and ultimate purpose of its work.

To try to eliminate risk in business enterprise is futile. Risk is inherent in the commitment of present resources to future expectations. Indeed, economic progress can be defined as the ability to take greater risks. The attempt to eliminate risks, even the attempt to minimize them, can only make them irrational and unbearable. It can only result in that greatest risk of all: rigidity.

The main goal of a management science must be to enable business to take the right risk. Indeed, it must be to enable business to take *greater* risks—by providing knowledge and understanding of alternative risks and alternative expectations; by identifying the resources and efforts needed for desired results and by mobilizing energies for the greatest contribution; and by measuring results against expectations, thereby providing means for early correction of wrong or inadequate decisions.

[3] For a statement of the modern position, see Howard Eves and Carroll V. Newsom, *Foundations and Fundamental Concepts of Mathematics,* Rinehart & Company, Inc., New York, 1958, pp. 29–30.

All this may sound like mere quibbling over terms. Yet the terminology of "risk minimization" does induce a decided animus against risk taking and risk making—that is, against business enterprise—in the literature of management science. Much of it echoes the tone of the "technocrats" of a generation ago. For it wants to subordinate business to technique, and it seems to see economic activity as a sphere of physical determination rather than as an affirmation and exercise of responsible freedom and decision.

This is worse than being wrong. This is lack of respect for one's subject matter—the one thing no science can afford and no scientist can survive. Even the best and most serious work of good and serious people—and there is no lack of them in management science—is bound to be vitiated by it.

The second requirement for a management science is, then, that it take its subject matter seriously.

There would be little reason for concern about the trend of management science if we did not need so badly a genuine discipline of entrepreneurship and business management. This point has been made very often in many different contexts. Here are two good examples, expressing the same need but from different viewpoints:

- Speaking of the kind of manager required if we are to move toward a real profession of business management, Stanley F. Teele, dean of the Harvard Business School, says: "The utilization of mathematical-statistical methods, the rapid refinement of equipment for high-speed processing of information, the adaptation of a variety of research methods in the physical sciences to problems in business management are all important parts of the process to which I refer [managerial decision making]. Nevertheless, the steady increase in the habit of seeking facts and ways to relate facts to each other and to the whole situation will be far more important."[4]
- Referring to new industrial procedures and

outmoded decision-making processes, Melvin L. Hurni, operations research consultant to the General Electric Company, concludes: "In general, what is still needed is the organization of the new rational methods into a single discipline that makes them specifically applicable to the broad problems of management as a whole."[5]

I do not have to belabor the point. We know what we need: a systematic supply of organized knowledge for the risk-making and risk-taking decisions of business enterprise in our complex and rapidly changing technology, economy, and society; tools for the measurement of expectations and results; effective means for common vision and communication among the many functional and professional specialists—each with his own knowledge, his own logic, and his own language—whose combined efforts are needed to make the right business decisions, to make them effective, and to produce results. We need something teachable and learnable if only because we need far too many people with managerial vision and competence to depend on the intuition of a few "natural-born" geniuses; and only the generalizations and concepts of a discipline can really be learned or taught.

We know that these are urgent needs. In fact, the future of the free enterprise system may depend on our ability to make major managerial and entrepreneurial decisions more rationally, and to make more people capable of making and of understanding such decisions.

There would be little reason for concern here if management science had not demonstrated its great potential to fill our need. Of course, it is only in its infancy; real knowledge and understanding in vitally important areas may be decades away—may indeed never be obtained. But the work already done is exciting and powerful, and the talent at work is of a high order of competence, ability, and dedication.

All this, however, may come to naught if management science permits itself to become a management gadget bag. The opportunity will be lost, the need will go unfulfilled, and the promise will be blighted unless management science learns to respect both itself and its subject.

---

[4] Stanley F. Teele, "The Businessman of the Future," Address delivered at the Fiftieth Anniversary Conference of the Harvard Business School, September, 1958. Reprinted in Dan H. Fenn, Jr. (ed.), *Management's Mission in a New Society*, McGraw-Hill Book Company, New York, 1959.

[5] Melvin L. Hurni, "Decision Making in the Age of Automation," *Harvard Business Review*, September-October, 1955, p. 57.

76

The Automation of Management*

HERBERT A. SIMON

I have several times sidestepped the question of how far and how fast we could expect management activities to be automated. I have said something about supervision, but little about the large miscellany of management activities involving decision making, problem solving, and just plain "thinking."

In what follows I shall use the terms *decision making* and *problem solving* in a broad sense to refer interchangeably to this whole range of activities. Decision making in this sense involves much more than the final choice among possible courses of action. It involves, first of all, detecting the occasions for decision—the problems that have to be dealt with—and directing the organization's attention to them. It involves, secondly, developing possible problem solutions—courses of action—among which the final choice can be made. Discovering and defining problems, elaborating courses of action, and making final choices are all stages in the decision-making process. When the term *decision making* is used, we generally think of the third stage, but the first two account for many more man-hours of effort in organizations than the third. Much more management effort is allocated to attention-directing functions and to the investigation, fact gathering, design, and problem solving involved in developing courses of action than to the process of selection. Decision making, defined in this broad way, constitutes the bulk of managerial activity.

The problems that managers at various levels in organizations face can be classified according to how well structured, how routine, how cut and dried they are when they arise. On the one end of the continuum are highly programed decisions: routine procurement of office supplies or pricing standard products; on the other end of the continuum are unprogramed decisions: basic, once-for-all decisions to make a new product line, or strategies for labor negotiations on a new contract, or major styling decisions. Between these two extremes lie decisions with every possible mixture of programed and nonprogramed, well-structured and ill-structured, routine and nonroutine elements.

There is undoubtedly a rough, but far from perfect, correlation between a manager's organizational level and the extent to which his decisions are programed. We would expect the decisions that the president and vice-president face to be less programed, on the average, than those faced by the factory department head or the factory manager.

We are now in the early stages of a technological revolution of the decision-making process. That revolution has two aspects, one considerably further advanced than the other. The first aspect, concerned largely with decisions close to the programed end of the continuum, is the province of the new field called *operations research* or *management science*. The second aspect, concerned with unprogramed as well as programed decisions, is the province of a set of techniques that are coming to be known as *heuristic programing*.

OPERATIONS RESEARCH

I will not recount the history of operations research. It is largely the product of efforts that began on a large scale during World War II. Nor will I essay a careful definition, for operations research is as much a social movement—a migration of natural scientists, econometricians, and mathematicians into the area of business decision making—as it is a definable body of knowledge.

Operations research attempts to apply mathematics and the capabilities of modern electronic computers to business decision making. By now it is clear that the attempt is going to be highly successful. Important areas of business and engineering decision making have yielded

* Reprinted by permission of the publishers from Melvin Anshen and George Leland Bach, *Management and Corporations 1985*, McGraw-Hill Book Company, New York, 1960, pp. 39–52 (originally published as "The Corporation: Will It Be Managed by Machines?"). Mr. Simon is professor of business administration and psychology at the Carnegie Institute of Technology.

to these techniques, and the area of possible and actual application continues to grow.

Let me be more concrete and show how operations research is affecting management and how it will affect it. I shall ignore business data processing—the automation of clerical activities—and look exclusively at management activities. I can describe the situation by examples, for we are interested in the technical and economic potential of these techniques, not the present extent of their use.

1. Managers make a whole series of decisions to control inventory and production: purchasing decisions, setting the production rate and product mix, ordering stock for warehouses, shipping decisions, and the like. Several alternative mathematical techniques are now available for making such decisions; these techniques have been more or less extensively tested in practical situations, and they are being used in day-to-day decision making in a number of companies. The evidence seems to me convincing that decisions of these kinds can now be made, in most situations, with the aid of operations research techniques and with the virtual elimination of managerial "judgment," far better than such decisions have been made in the past. Moreover, in most tests that have been made, even at this early stage in the development and application of such techniques, they have shown that they can justify themselves economically. There is little or no excuse for purchasing agents, production control managers, factory managers, or warehouse managers intervening in such decisions any more. (I hasten to add that, as with any new technique, a company that wishes to make use of it must be willing to incur some development and training expense.)

2. The injection of the mathematical techniques just mentioned into the clerical processes involved in procurement, factory production control, and filling customers' orders can permit virtually complete automation of this flow in many situations, with the removal of both clerical and low-level management participation from the day-to-day activity. Customers' orders can be received and filled, the customer invoiced, orders placed on the factory, and raw-material stocks replenished —all untouched by human hands and unthought of by human decision makers.

3. Mathematical techniques for detailed scheduling of factory production, while less far advanced than the techniques just described, will almost certainly have reached within five or ten years the point where scheduling can also be completely automated, both in its clerical and in its decision-making aspects.

4. In the early years of the computer, one of its main applications was to relieve engineering organizations of the bulk of routine calculations in design. The computer initially was a clerical aid to analysis. Within the past three or four years, we have discovered how the computer can also take over the design-synthesis job in many relatively simple situations. (Though these situations are "simple," they were complex enough to require the services of college-trained engineers.) To put it simply, computers can now take customers' orders for many types of electronic motors, generators, and transformers, synthesize devices that meet the design specifications, and send the manufacturing specifications to the factory floor— again untouched by human hands. Where these techniques are now used, it is reported that they yield improved designs at about the same cost as the human design process they replace.

5. Computers, programed to carry out linear programing calculations, are now widely used to determine product mix for oil refineries and to determine formulas for commercial feed mixes. The Iowa farmer who tunes in to the morning radio reports of hog prices now learns from the commercial that XYZ feed gives him the best nutrition at the lowest cost because it is blended by electronic computers using modern mathematical techniques.

6. A large commercial airline has used computers to simulate major parts of its flight and terminal operation and has used the simulation to decide how many reserve aircraft it needed—an investment decision of great magnitude.

The plain fact is that a great many middle-management decisions that have always been supposed to call for the experienced human judgment of managers and professional engineers can now be made at least as well by computers as by managers. Moreover, a large part of the total middle-management job consists of decisions of the same general character as those that have already yielded to automation. The decisions are repetitive and require little of the kinds of flexibility that constitute man's principal comparative advantage over machines. We can predict with some confidence, I think, that persons making such decisions will constitute a much smaller fraction of the total occupied group within a few years than they do now.

HEURISTIC PROGRAMING

The mathematical and computing techniques for making programed decisions replace man but they do not generally simulate him. That is to say, a computer scheduling a refinery does not make the same calculations as would be made by an experienced refinery scheduler—even if it comes out with a very similar solution.

This fact has led to some misconceptions about the nature of computers and about their potentialities. "Computers are just very speedy morons for carrying out arithmetic calculations," it is often said. "They only do what you program them to do." These statements belong to that class of half-truths that are important just because their implications are so misleading. I shall have to pause long enough to make some categorical statements about computers. I do not have space here to develop them at length.

1. Computers are very general devices capable of manipulating all kinds of symbols—words as readily as numbers. The fact that computers generally do arithmetic is an historical accident. If a particular decision-making situation is not quantitative we cannot handle it with traditional mathematical techniques. This constitutes no essential barrier to computerization. Much successful research has been carried out in the past five years on the use of computers for processing nonnumerical information.

2. Computers behave like morons only because we are just beginning to learn how to communicate with them in something better than moronic language. There now exist so-called compiling techniques (e.g., FORTRAN) that instruct computers in general language very similar to the ordinary language of mathematics. With these compilers, we now can program a computer to evaluate a formula itself and the instruction: Do. Compiling techniques of almost comparable power have been developed for nonnumerical computing. They have not reached the point where they permit the programer to communicate with the computer in idiomatic English, but only in a kind of simple pidgin English.

3. Computers do only what you program them to do, but (a) you can program them to behave adaptively and (b) you can program them to improve their own programs on the basis of their experiences—that is, to learn. Hence, the more accurate statement is: Computers do only what you program them to do in exactly the same sense that humans do only what their genes and their cumulative experiences program them to do. This assertion leaves little room for free will in either computer or human, but it leaves a great deal of room in both for flexible, adaptive, complex, intelligent behavior.

4. It has now been demonstrated, by doing it, that computers can be programed to solve relatively ill-structured problems by using methods very similar to those used by humans in the same problem-solving situations: that is, by highly selective trial-and-error search using all sorts of rules of thumb to guide the selection; by abstracting from the given problem and solving first the abstracted problem; by using analogy; by reasoning in terms of means and ends, goals and subgoals; by adjusting aspirations to the attainable. There is no longer reason to regard phenomena like "judgment" and "insight" as either unanalyzable or unanalyzed, for, in some forms at least, these phenomena have been simulated—computers have exercised judgment and exhibited insight. The range of capabilities of computer programs of this sort is still extremely narrow, but the significant point is that some such programs have been written, tested, and even compared in their behavior with the behavior of human laboratory subjects performing the same tasks.

Computer programs that handle nonnumerical tasks, use humanoid problem-solving techniques (instead of the systematic algorithmic techniques of classical mathematics), and sometimes include learning processes, are called *heuristic programs.* They incorporate, in their processes, one or more aspects of what has been called "the art of plausible reasoning," an art that guides us through the numerous, diverse, ill-structured decisions of everyday life.

The engineering design programs I mentioned earlier are really heuristic programs, for they involve inductive reasoning. Heuristic programs have now been written for such tasks as playing checkers, playing chess, finding proofs for geometry theorems and for theorems in elementary symbolic logic, solving trigonometric and algebraic identities, balancing a factory assembly line, composing music (the ILLIAC Suite), and memorizing nonsense syllables. One program, the General Problem Solver, while not as general as its name may suggest, is entirely free from reference to any particular subject matter and is, in fact, a quite flexible scheme for reasoning in terms of goals and subgoals about any subject.

Let me make my point perfectly clear. Heuristic programs do not merely substitute machine brute force for human cunning. Increasingly, they imitate—and in some cases improve upon human cunning. I can illustrate this by describing briefly the three existing computer programs for playing chess.

One of these, the Los Alamos program, depends heavily on machine speed. The program examines, at each move, almost one million alternative possibilities, evaluating them on the basis of simple, crude criteria and selecting the one that appears best. Clearly it is doing something quite different from the human chess player—the human neither could nor would select moves in this way. The second program, Bernstein's program, is much more selective. It examines about 2,500 alternatives, chosen on the basis of rules of thumb a chess player would use and evaluates them in a slightly more complicated way than does the Los Alamos program. The third program, the RAND-Carnegie program, is still more selective. It seldom examines as many as. fifty alternatives but selects those to be examined and evaluates them in a rather involved way. All three programs, at present, play about the same level of chess—a very low level, it should be said. But they achieve this result in quite different ways. The Los Alamos program, though it embodies certain heuristic ideas, calls for machine speed rather than machine intelligence. The RAND-Carnegie program begins to approach, in the rules of thumb it embodies, the processes a human uses in choosing a chess move. Bernstein's program lies midway between the other two. Thus, in talking about our increasing capacity to write heuristic programs that simulate human problem solving, I am speaking of programs that lie toward the RAND-Carnegie end of this continuum rather than the Los Alamos end. I am speaking of programs that reason, think, and learn.

The microcosm of chess may still appear to you far more structured and programed than the macrocosm of the everyday world. Perhaps it is, although the point could be argued. However that may be, the microcosm of chess is sufficiently complex, sufficiently rich in alternatives, sufficiently irregular in structure that it poses to the problem-solving organism or mechanism the same *kinds* of difficulties and requirements that are posed—perhaps in higher degree—by ill-structured problems in general. Hence, the fact that chess programs, theorem-proving programs, music-composing programs, and a factory-scheduling program now exist indicates that the conceptual mountains have been crossed that barred us from understanding how the human mind grapples with everyday affairs. It is my conviction that no major new ideas will have to be discovered to enable us to extend these early results to the whole of human thinking, problem solving, decision-making activity. We have every reason to believe that within a very short time—I am even willing to say ten years or less—we will be able technically to produce computers that can grapple with and solve at least the range of problems that humans are able to grapple with and solve—those that are ill-structured as well as those that are well-structured.

If the technical prediction is correct, what about the economics of the matter? Again, we must apply the doctrine of comparative advantage. To what extent, in 1985, will managers and other humans be occupied in thinking about and solving ill-structured problems, as distinct from doing other things? On this point the image in my crystal ball is very dim. I will nevertheless hazard some guesses. My first guess is that man will retain a greater comparative advantage in handling ill-structured problems than in handling well-structured problems. My second guess is that he will retain a greater advantage in tasks involving sensory-manipulative coordination—"physical flexibility"—than in ill-structured problem-solving tasks—"mental flexibility." If this is true, a larger part of the working population will be mahouts and wheelbarrow pushers and a smaller part will be scientists and executives—particularly of the staff variety. The amount of shift in this direction will be somewhat diminished by the fact that as income and general productivity rise, the demand for work involving ill-structured problem solving will probably increase more than the demand for work involving flexible manipulation of the physical environment. The demand for psychiatric work will increase more rapidly than the demand for surgical work—but the rate of automation of the former will be much greater than the rate of automation of the latter.

A SUMMARY:
THE AUTOMATION OF MANAGEMENT

Our analysis rests on the assumption that managers are largely concerned with supervising, with solving well-structured problems, and with solving ill-structured problems. We have predicted that the automation of the second of these activities—solving well-structured problems—will proceed extremely rapidly; the automation of the third—solving ill-stuctured problems, moderately rapidly; and the automation of supervision more slowly. However, we have also concluded that, as less and less work becomes man paced and more and more of it machine paced, the nature of supervision will undergo change. There is no obvious way to assess quantitatively all these cross currents and conflicting trends. We might even conclude that management and other professional activities, taken collectively, may constitute about the same part of the total spectrum of occupations a generation hence as they do now. But there is reason to believe that the kinds of activities that now characterize middle management will be more completely automated than the others and hence will come to have a smaller part in the whole management picture.

SOME OTHER DIMENSIONS OF CHANGE IN MANAGEMENT

There are other dimensions for differentiating management and professional tasks, of course, besides the one we have been using. It is possible that if we described the situation in terms of these other dimensions, the change would appear larger. Let me explore this possibility just a little bit further.

First, I think we can predict that in future years the manager's time perspective will be lengthened. As automated sub-systems take over the minute-by-minute and day-to-day operation of the factory and office, the humans in the system will become increasingly occupied with preventive maintenance, with system breakdowns and malfunctions, and—perhaps most important of all—with the design and modification of systems. The automatic factory will pretty much—and subject to all of the qualifications I have introduced—run itself; the company executives will be much more concerned with tomorrow's automatic factory. Executives will have less excuse than they now have to let the emergencies of today steal the time that was allocated to planning for the future. I don't think planning is going to be a machineless function—it also will be carried out by man-machine systems, but with perhaps a larger man component and a smaller machine component than day-to-day operations.

Does this mean that executives will need a high level of technical competence in the engineering of automated factories or data-processing systems? Probably not. Most automation calls for increased technical skills for maintenance in the early stages; but the farther automation proceeds, the less those who govern the automated system need to know about the details of its mechanism. The driver of a 1960 automobile needs to know less about what is under the hood than the driver of a 1910 automobile. The user of a 1960 computer needs to know less about computer design and operation than the user of a 1950 computer. The manager of a highly automated 1985 factory will need to know less about how things are actually produced, physically, in that factory than the manager of a 1960 factory.

Similarly, we can dismiss the notion that computer programers will become a powerful elite in the automated corporation. It is far more likely that the programing occupation will become extinct (through the further development of self-programing techniques) than that it will become all-powerful. More and more, computers will program themselves; and direction will be given to computers through the mediation of compiling systems that will be completely neutral as far as content of the decision rules is concerned. Moreover, the task of communicating with computers will become less and less technical as computers come—by means of compiling techniques—closer and closer to handling the irregularities of natural language.

I suppose that managers will be called on, as automation proceeds, for more of what might be described as "systems thinking." They will need, to work effectively, to understand their organizations as large and complex dynamic systems in involving various sorts of man-machine and machine-machine interactions. For this reason, persons trained in fields like servo-mechanism engineering or mathematical economics, accustomed to dynamic systems of these kinds, and possessing conceptual tools for understanding them, may have some advantage, at least initially, in operating in the new world. Since no coherent science of complex systems exists today, universities and engineering schools are understandably perplexed as to what kinds of training will prepare their present students for this world.

How the Du Pont Organization Appraises Its Performance*

T. C. DAVIS

Once again our attention has been directed to the function of the profit incentive in holding an industrial enterprise to a successful course and one which will best serve the whole economy. Because the profit system is misunderstood by a considerable segment of our population and is actually under attack from some quarters, no effort should be spared to present at every opportunity a clear picture of the function of profits. Certain principles cannot be ignored if capital and manpower are to be successfully utilized in the production of goods, stimulated on the one hand by the incentive reward of profits and on the other hand by the prospect of a rising standard of living.

As far back as I can remember, both the measuring and reporting of profits have been controversial subjects. Although they have been debated at great length by business men, economists, bankers, accountants, lawyers, labor leaders, legislators, educators, and even statesmen, nothing definitive seems to have emerged. We appear to have made very small progress in this particular field during the past two decades. While this is discouraging, certainly we cannot abandon effort to bring about public understanding that the profit incentive is both the carrot and the stick which prods an industrial enterprise to its best performance, and that from this relationship the entire population benefits.

The stock market crash of 1929 seems in retrospect to have been the flare that set off an economic depression of great magnitude. Business management was quickly made the whipping boy. One of the charges hurled with great frequency and vigor was that the public had been misled by the information made available

to it concerning corporate business operations. Some said these data were incomplete; some said they were presented in a manner which was misleading; and some even made charges that trickery in accounting had been employed which resulted in false reports. Out of this great clamor emerged the Securities and Exchange acts, with an ever-growing body of law and regulation concerning the disclosures to be made upon the public sale of securities, and the manner of reporting to stockholders by companies with listed securities.

Under the impetus of these requirements, and because of the natural desire of business men and accountants to present to stockholders all the data they want which is at once meaningful and yet not unduly helpful to competitors, much study has been given the so-called public reporting by corporate business. And I think we may say that some improvement has been made in public reporting, although there still exists a widespread belief that all financial reporting is double talk. We haven't yet solved the problem of making a public statement of the financial results of an operation which is so simple yet so complete that it can withstand attack from every quarter. Perhaps this is a great deal to hope for, but, as I said before, we simply cannot relax in our effort to achieve this goal.

These remarks with respect to external reporting have only an indirect bearing upon my subject, but they serve as background for an important observation: Unfortunately, financial management probably has had no greater degree of success in solving the problem of reporting financial data to executive management (i.e., internal reporting) that can be claimed for financial reporting to stockholders and other public interests. My assignment has to do with internal reporting as distinguished from external reporting—in fact, it is to say something about one important part of the system of internal reporting actually in use in the duPont Company.

---

* Reprinted by permission of the publisher from *How the Du Pont Organization Appraises Its Performance*, American Management Association, Financial Management Series, no. 94, New York, 1950, pp. 3–4, 6–7, 20–22. Mr. Davis is a director of E. I. du Pont de Nemours & Company.

FUNCTION OF THE CHART SYSTEM

Any system of financial control, to be of maximum usefulness, should include a forecast of sales and profits, a forecast of working capital requirements and cash resources, and capital-expenditure budgets and working-capital standards, together with statements which show the actual operating performance and balance-sheet condition promptly after the close of an accounting period. It is the duty and responsibility of the financial staff to make these data available to executive management when required, and in a form which will reveal the operating results of each particular product line. The complexity of operations and/or the diversity of product lines complicate the financial accounting problems, and clarity in the presentation of operating results should be the objective through which solutions to specific financial and accounting problems are worked out.

At duPont one of my predecessors saw one phase of this problem of internal reporting in clear perspective. Slightly more than 30 years ago he conceived and guided the design of what we have come to call *the chart system.* This system utilizes charts and tabulations for presenting to the Executive Committee data pertinent to the performance of each operating investment. We maintain approximately 350 individual charts, a number of which are presented to the Executive Committee each month, so that in a year's time, all charts have been reviewed several times. . . .

The Executive Committee Charts   The charts [discussed] here are of the kind utilized by the Executive Committee in its direction of the business. While these or similar chart series are employed to some extent by all levels of departmental management, our considerations will here be directed toward the charts which the Treasurer's department maintains for the Executive Committee. These charts and tabulations do not displace the customary financial statements—whether forecasts, budgets or historical reports. They are used by the Executive Committee in reviewing with a general manager the operations of his department.

Once each month the Executive Committee reviews charts, the schedule being so arranged that the charts for each department are reviewed no less frequently than once every three months. At least one set or series of charts and tabulations is set up for each department. In some cases the operations of a particular department are sufficiently diverse that it has been found necessary to set up several sets of charts and tabulations, each set bracketing a portion of the department's activities which it is desired to treat as a separate unit. Thus, for our nine industrial departments we have 20 separate operating investment chart series, representing approximately 350 charts.

For each of these series the results of operations for the current year are shown against a background of exactly the same data for the 10 preceding years and a forecast for the ensuing 12 months.

We place primary emphasis upon *return on investment,* and the central theme around which the chart series is built is to focus attention upon this end result, without neglecting the factors that produce return on investment —*gross profit on sales* and *turnover.* It might be helpful if at this point we examine an outline of the formula (Figure B) which is controlling in the chart concept. . . . From this formula you will see that we wish to present *return on investment* through the factors of *earnings as a per cent of sales* (which is the gross profit margin) and *turnover.*

The return on investment responds to movement in these two factors. If there has been no change in selling price, an improvement in turnover indicates that capital is being worked harder, i.e., *the business is getting increased sales out of the same plant and working capital.* Again, if there is no change in selling prices an improvement in gross profit margin indicates that the cost in proportion to sales dollar is being reduced.

The figures used in these charts are hypothetical; they do not depict the operating results of any one of duPont's investments. However, the chart series is complete and we have borrowed from actual experiences in deciding upon what trends to present through the medium of these hypothetical figures. We have used our own experience merely as a starting point, and where it was felt that a point could be more forcefully illustrated, have exaggerated the figures in order to accomplish this. . . .

Special Advantages of the Chart System
If you have concluded that there is nothing new in these charts, you are right. Our chart series and tabulations present nothing which cannot be portrayed in a score of ways, and perhaps with even greater clarity. Not by way of defense, but rather by way of explanation, then, I want to call your attention to several points which in our opinion give this particular method of presenting the financial results of operations special merit and appeal.

First, you will note the complete absence of narrative. There is no opportunity for one re-

FIGURE B   Relationship of Factors Affecting Return on Investment

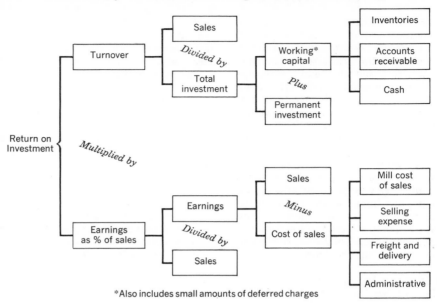

*Also includes small amounts of deferred charges

viewing the figures to bog down under the weight of particular words or phrases which may be chosen by an individual to explain a given variation in operating results. In the course of presenting the charts to our Executive Committee, the chart supervisor is always prepared to answer questions, or even to propose an answer without question, giving the background reasons for sharp variations in current data against the past or against forecasts. However, the primary purpose of reviewing data presented on the charts is to point up the places where further analysis, review and attention may be desirable or necessary. The charts are intended to show what happened in terms of *profit return on investment,* and to put the finger on the broad underlying factors which caused the results to be what they were. This identification of broad factors leading to a particular result enables the Executive Committee to raise questions with a general manager regarding possible trouble spots and, of course, may lead to further analysis and presentation.

Second, note the comparative ease with which the attention of an entire group can be held to one item at the same time. I imagine most of us have had some experience in analyzing schedules, tabulations, charts and the like with a group of men, each of whom has the data in hand, on a table or elsewhere, and have had to deal with the perplexing problem presented by the proneness of each individual comprising

the group to pursue his own analysis in his own way. The manner in which we use these charts minimizes this problem. You can be pretty well assured that each member of the group is giving attention to the same item at the same time.

Third, more or less rigid rules govern the assembly of data for the presentation. To the maximum extent possible the data for all periods shown on the charts are on a uniform basis and afford common measurement of performance for all investment lines. If we find that changing conditions require a new approach to presenting any one or more of the chart series, then all the data for the current year and the 10 preceding years are re-set on the new basis. We all know the loss of confidence in financial presentations that can be experienced when those using the data are able to allege, and perhaps to show, that a lack of uniformity or comparability has destroyed their value. To a very large extent we avoid that pitfall by keeping our charts comparable throughout.

Fourth, strict adherence to format is observed until such time as it becomes clear that a change would substantially improve the presentation. Then a new format is brought into use, complete at one time, including a re-set for the entire 10-year period. Admittedly, this means slow progress at times in improvement of format, because a helpful minor change brought to light by experience must be held on the shelf until an important change or an aggregate of minor changes makes it worthwhile to modify the whole format.

This chart series was inaugurated more than 30 years ago—in 1919, to be exact. We consider it a tribute to the foresight of those who designed and installed it that whereas the format has been changed and perhaps improved several times, *the basic concept which emphasizes return on investment, supported by the factors contributing to it, has not given way to any other.*

Fifth, the Executive Committee, for whose use these charts are primarily maintained, makes the rules governing the division of lines of business into chart series; and the classification of financial data into the several items which are set forth in the presentation. To be sure, the Executive Committee requests and receives the recommendations of the Treasurer, but in the final analysis it is the Committee's decision, after full consideration of all the pros and cons presented by the Treasurer, which is final.

This approach to data presentation, i.e., as a rule by decision of the executive management group—the group by which the data are to be used—serves to remove a potentially wide area for possible disagreement on the classification of the basic data to be presented. Disagreement in these matters dissipates energies and dilutes the value-in-use of internal financial reporting. We are disposed to think our approach to this phase of the problem goes a long way toward getting the maximum value out of presentation of the financial results of our operations.

Calculation of Return on Investment

You will note that on this chart series we calculate the return on investment on the gross value of plant and working capital rather than on stockholder-invested capital. Calculations based on stockholder-invested capital would require the deduction of reserves and liabilities from the cost of plant and working capital. The general managers of the Company are responsible for the production and sale of the products assigned to them, and for the necessary investment in plant facilities and working capital. The charts are uniform and are designed to afford a comparison of past and current performance for the same operating investment, as well as a comparison with the performance of other operating investments made in corresponding periods.

In this chart series we are seeking a clear portrayal of the profitableness of the employment of plant property and working capital. Funds provided by reserves and liabilities are invested for varying periods of time in operating properties upon which a profit must be earned if a business is to be successful, but these funds are not reflected in stockholder-invested capital. You will readily appreciate, therefore, that a deduction for liabilities and reserves from the amount invested in operating properties would show a fluctuation in operating investment due to growth of reserves and change in amount of liabilities, which, in turn, would produce such a distortion in the return on investment as to render meaningless the very figures intended to disclose the profitableness of employment of plant property and working capital.

It is entirely proper, in some instances and under some conditions, to measure corporate-entity profit performance against stockholder-invested capital, and we do it ourselves for many purposes. But it would not serve our purpose in the chart series. I am sure you will agree, upon brief reflection, that for all purposes of securing an indication of the profitableness of dollars devoted to plant and working capital—which dollars must at some time be returned intact to the corporate entity—the dollar profits made during each and every period of the use of the property must be related to the total dollars dedicated to the particular operation.

Construction of the Charts

The charts and tabulations which we show to our Executive Committee in Wilmington are hand-drawn on cardboard measuring 30 by 40 inches. The letters, numerals, and arrows are purchased from a supplier of such items. They come coated with an adhesive and are pasted on the boards by our chart clerks. Each chart or tabulation is mounted in a metal frame suspended on wheels so that it can be moved from one place to another in the chart room on specially designed and constructed overhead track. The network of track is so arranged that in a matter of seconds any series of charts can be brought to the central display point for review.

We are aware that presentation of this type of data is more and more being made by means of projection on a screen. The projection method enjoys some flexibility over our method but we have not yet found that a clear visual presentation of our charts can be obtained by projection in the physical setup presently at our disposal. In addition, we find that the preparation of material for screen projection requires time, skills and processing equipment which we are not yet prepared to devote to it. There has been some improvement in projection equipment and methods since the end of the war, and no doubt still further improvements are in the offing. We do not intend to lag behind where progress is being made, and it is entirely possible that we shall at some future date abandon the hand-drawn charts conveyed on overhead track in favor of some projection method.

CONCLUSION

In closing, permit me to say that we who are charged with varying degrees of responsi-bility for the financial and accounting matters of our respective companies must remain alert, must continue in our determination to find and employ the most effective means of presenting financial data to executive management. Our success in doing this is so closely linked with the effective application of executive manage-ment talent that it is not out of order to say that effective internal reporting is quite as im-portant to a business organization as good external reporting.

78

*Return on Invested Capital**

T. G. MACKENSEN

As men advance to positions of responsi-bility in management, it is only natural that their judgments remain heavily weighted with their specialty training and background.

Yet, across the collective judgments of man-agement, runs a certain age-old fundamental principle around which all business enterprise revolves, and which was the original and pri-mary reason for forming the business—to earn a profit on the capital employed.

I shall first endeavor to show how in our company we attempt to rally the diverse talents and capacities of management around this principle, and then discuss some of the tech-niques we employ in applying it.

THE SUCCESSFUL COMPANY

Among the characteristics of a successful business enterprise are expanding sales, in-creased employment and production, respected name, dollars of profit, acceptable products and services, and many others. All of these are unquestionably desirable, yet separately or to-gether they are not enough to guarantee con-tinued existence or growth. One other impor-tant characteristic is needed—the ability to earn a satisfactory return on the capital employed.

Increased sales volume is at best a short-term indication of successful growth and, with-out additional information, must be viewed as such. In the long run, it may prove to be a misleading guidepost if there is not a proper return on the capital necessary to support those sales. True growth comes from the ability of management to employ successfully additional capital at a satisfactory rate of return. This is the final criterion of the soundness and strength of a company's growth, for in a free competi-tive economy capital gravitates toward the more profitable enterprises. The company that is merely expanding at declining rates of return on investment will eventually be brought to a stop for lack of expansion capital.

Thus any appraisal of a company's effective-ness must be based on the successful employ-ment of capital. Proposed projects and activ-ities should be evaluated in the final analysis in the light of their demands on company assets and their probability of earning a satisfactory return on those assets. Projects that fail to meet this standard have an exhausting effect that tends to neutralize the value of other projects and may seriously limit the company's ability to press advantages in more promising

* Reprinted by permission of the publisher from *How H. J. Heinz Manages Its Financial Planning and Controls,* American Management Association, Finan-cial Management Series, no. 106, New York, 1953, pp. 37–45. Mr. Mackensen is coordinator, special accounting studies, of the H. J. Heinz Company.

areas. The over-all ability of a company to employ its present assets profitably and to develop opportunities for the successful employment of additional capital is dependent upon the individual contributions of its various activities and products and their opportunities for true growth.

THREE CATEGORIES OF PROFIT POTENTIAL

The 57 Varieties, over the many years, have undergone extensive changes in so far as the composition of the line is concerned. This continuing evolution is, of course, characteristic of any long-established business. In view of the ever-changing nature of things, we find it very helpful in keeping our long-range sights in focus to have an awareness that, as of any given time, our entire line is divisible into three categories of profit potential. These are:

1. *The Strong and Established Items of the Line.* These are the products on which the company depends for adequate dollar profits to meet dividend requirements and to provide capital for expansion. They are capable of further growth and produce a satisfactory return on their investment. Normally, these are the products that should constitute the major portion of sales volume and command the major portion of capital investment. They are entitled to priority in day-to-day managerial attention to assure that they remain strong and flourish in accordance with their possibilities for as many years into the future as possible.

2. *Products That Are New and As Yet Unproved.* These are the products that management believes to have extraordinary growth possibilities and is willing to subsidize during their development period. Since their justification lies in the expectation of future profits, they require specialized attention and frequent review and re-appraisal as experience and knowledge are acquired. To assure an adequate flow of such promising new products, there should be an effective research and development program.

3. *Products That Have Passed Their Peak in Growth and Profitability.* These products can justify little consideration for increased capital investment, since they offer no reasonable prospect for future growth and improved profit contribution. Many are logical items for pruning so that their capital requirements and managerial demands can be diverted to more profitable products.

We endeavor to maintain a sound financial balance among these three groups of products.

The company's strength today is dependent upon Group 1, the predominant items of the line producing a satisfactory return on the capital they employ. The future depends on Group 2, the flow of new products that is needed to perpetuate the vitality of the line. Group 3, the products that have passed their peak in growth and profitability, can seriously sap the company's strength, both present and future, unless eliminations are made from time to time.

Records for Each Product Line Experience has shown us, also, that no class of expense or investment remains fixed in amount over a period of continuing expansion in volume, even though it may be called fixed during a specific limited interval within the growth period. Accordingly, since we cannot expect profits to improve automatically with volume increases, we have adopted the view that management must have an effective program for the employment of capital if it is to realize an adequate rate of return on the assets it employs.

In order that our management will have the necessary facts and figures to aid in making its decisions, we augment the usual operating income statements, wherein profits are measured against sales, with records of capital employed and rates of return on investment for each of our product lines. These records are kept on a consistent basis, and comparative figures for a long term of years, including the current year's budget, are in handy form for ready reference. We group *The 57 Varieties* into a lesser number of related product lines, and we strive to make our allocations accurate and realistic, so that the resulting figures will represent as nearly as possible the results for each product line as if it were a separate business.

I shall try by means of four simplified exhibits to show the methods employed by our company in allocating capital to product lines and in making the rate of return on investment determinations. All the figures used are purely hypothetical, but they have been set up in such a way as to show the unfavorable results that can easily accrue over a period of time if the rate of return on investment is not carefully controlled and steps are not taken to correct adverse trends.

These exhibits will illustrate four product lines—A, B, C, and D—and will show comparative figures for two years, designated as "base year" and "current year." These are not successive years, but embrace a longer interval for purposes of this presentation in order better to emphasize the changes that can take place over several years.

Operating Income Compared. Chart 19 is a comparative income statement showing sales, costs, and operating income for the four products mentioned earlier for the base year and the current year.

Operating income is defined as the profit from operations before deduction of interest on borrowed capital employed and before federal income taxes. Sales dollars are analyzed by product lines, and changes in product mix are disclosed by showing the percentage that each line bears to total company sales. Cost of product, transportation from factory to sales warehouses, and product advertising are charged directly to each product line on an actual basis. Sales branch operating expense is prorated on the basis of sales, since *The 57 Varieties* are sold in mixtures. Institutional advertising and general administrative expenses are also prorated on the sales basis. The objective is to charge as many of the posts as practical on an actual basis, in order that a minimum need be prorated. Operating income is shown in dollar amount and as a per cent of sales.

The example reflects a considerable increase in dollar sales for the current year over the base year. Similarly, a handsome increase in dollars of operating income is shown. While a slight decline in rate of return on sales is indicated (10.4 per cent to 9.6 per cent), it is

nevertheless understandable that the performance shown could appear quite acceptable in the absence of any statement showing the return in terms of assets employed.

THE BALANCE SHEET AS A BASIS

Chart 20 is a comparative statement of total assets employed. It represents the asset side of the balance sheet averaged for the four quarters of each year shown.

In order to determine the assets by product lines, it is first necessary to exclude certain items appearing on the balance sheet, because they were not used in the production of operating income. Investments that represent outside financial holdings are thus excluded, as is the income from such investments. Similarly, construction in progress is excluded until such time as the facility under construction comes into use. Funds obtained to finance such construction programs would also be excluded from the cash allocated to current operations.

The treatment accorded depreciation might well be mentioned. We have elected to show fixed assets at net depreciated values. We take the position that the depreciation reserve represents that portion of the initial investment which has been recovered through charge-offs against operations and is re-invested in other

CHART 19 Multi-product Company
Comparative Operating Income Statement
(In thousands)

| | TOTAL SALES | | COSTS | | | OPERATING INCOME* | |
| | | | DIRECT | | PRORATED | | |
	AMOUNT	% OF TOTAL	AMOUNT	% OF SALES	16.1% OF SALES	AMOUNT	% OF SALES
Base year:							
Product A	$ 39,300	40	$ 28,200	71.7	$ 6,300	$ 4,800	12.2
Product B	29,500	30	21,900	74.5	4,800	2,800	9.4
Product C	19,600	20	14,400	73.1	3,100	2,100	10.8
Product D	9,800	10	7,700	78.3	1,600	500	5.1
Total	$ 98,200	100	$ 72,220	73.5	$15,800	$10,200	10.4
					17% OF SALES		
Current year:							
Product A	48,100	25	34,300	71.4	8,200	5,600	11.6
Product B	96,200	50	71,400	74.2	16,300	8,500	8.8
Product C	38,500	20	28,000	72.8	6,600	3,900	10.2
Product D	9,600	5	7,500	78.0	1,600	500	5.2
Total	$192,400	100	$141,200	73.4	$32,700	$18,500	9.6

* Before interest on borrowed money and federal income taxes.

CHART 20 Multi-product Company Comparative Statement of Assets Employed
(Four-quarter average, in thousands)

	BASE YEAR			CURRENT YEAR		
	TOTAL	PRORATED TO ALL SALES	ANALYZED BY PRODUCT	TOTAL	PRORATED TO ALL SALES	ANALYZED BY PRODUCT
Cash	$ 6,100	$ 6,100	$	$ 12,100	$12,100	$
Accounts receivable	4,800	4,800		10,000	10,000	
Inventories	20,100		20,100	55,700		55,700
Other current assets	600	600		1,700	1,700	
Total current assets	$31,600	$11,500	$20,100	$ 79,500	$23,800	$55,700
Investments	excluded			excluded		
Plant and equipment net	17,200	2,100	15,100	45,000	4,600	40,800
Construction in progress	excluded			excluded		
Other fixed assets	400	400		1,200	1,200	
Total fixed assets	$17,600	$ 2,500	$15,100	$ 46,600	$ 5,800	$40,800
Total assets employed	$49,200	$14,000	$35,200	$126,100	$29,600	$96,500

fixed assets, or is being used as working capital. To the extent that recovery and re-investment have been made, we relieve the old asset of the obligation of earning a return. Instead, we look to the new asset in which the value is now lodged for such earnings. Eliminating depreciation from the base gives a realistic investment figure which our operating people can accept without raising the question of duplication of asset values. At the same time, this treatment places a relatively greater demand for earnings on the new, modern installations than on the old, worn, and partially obsolete ones.

Management is charged with the responsibility of earning a rate of return on all the capital it employs, whether it be equity capital or borrowed money. The risks to financial security from the use of borrowed capital justify the requirement that such funds be placed at least on a par with equity capital in so far as earnings requirements are concerned. Accordingly, we do not deduct liabilities; and, in compensation, rate of return is computed before deduction of interest paid for the use of outside capital.

DETERMINATION OF INVESTMENT BY PRODUCT LINES

The next step is to determine asset usage by product lines.

Cash. We prorate cash to product lines on the basis of sales. Total cash requirements of each product line for costs, equipment replacements, interest, income taxes, and dividends approximate sales income from each product line. Therefore, sales is an appropriate basis for allocation of cash.

Accounts Receivable. We prorate accounts receivable on a sales basis. In our company, credit terms on all our varieties are identical; and, therefore, every dollar of sales is regarded to be outstanding for the same average length of time.

Inventories. We analyze inventories by product lines. Finished goods are readily identifiable, while work in process and raw materials require somewhat more detailed analysis to trace them to the end products.

Other Current Assets. This is a small item with us, and we prorate it on the basis of sales.

Factory Plant and Equipment. We analyze this important item by product. Where an entire factory is devoted to one product, the allocation is, of course, simple. Where more than one product is produced at a factory, departmental breakdowns are made, and from these we arrive at allocations by product lines.

Administrative and Sales Facilities. This item includes general offices, sales warehouses, etc., and is prorated on the basis of sales.

Other Fixed Assets. This is another small item with us, and we prorate it on the basis of sales.

The resulting analysis is Chart 21, where the applicable balance sheet values appear by the product lines. Inventory, factory plant and equipment, the prorated assets (cash, receivables, etc.), and the total assets are shown for each product line both in total amount and in usage per dollar of sales. Such a statement is indispensable in measuring the efficiency with which capital is employed. This is particularly true with respect to inventories. When all other methods of controlling inventories fail, it discloses when a need for tightening of purse strings is indicated.

This record is valuable, also, for projecting capital requirements when changes in volume levels or in product mix are contemplated.

COMPARATIVE RATES OF RETURN

Thus we arrive at the all-important exhibit (Chart 22) which shows—for each product line—sales, assets employed, and operating income expressed as an amount and as a per cent return on sales and on assets employed.

It is to this statement that we look for the results earlier discussed. It will be recalled from Chart 19 that, while the amount of operating income practically doubled, the rate of return on sales showed an apparently minor

decline from 10.4 per cent to 9.6 per cent. When the same dollars of operating income are measured against the assets employed, it will be seen that the rate of return on investment decreased from 20.8 per cent to 14.6 per cent, a substantial reduction in profitability. Thus the conventional profit and loss statement measuring profit in terms of sales dollars gives way to the more relevant comparison wherein profit is measured in terms of assets employed.

This statement makes possible investigation into at least four major areas, and in each of them there are questions to which satisfactory answers must be found.

1. *Increases in Investment.* What has happened to the promised rates of return on the appropriations approved during the period? Were they overstated? Mythical? Unattainable? Were costs understated? Why was so much approved for Product B when its profits were subnormal? Is Product A suffering from lack of capital expenditure? Are we employing existing assets at capacity and most profitably? Are we deploying available capital to its most useful purpose?

2. *Product Mix.* The threefold increase in sales for Product B is accompanied by a fivefold increase in assets for that line, and its profits were below normal, measured both as per cent

CHART 21   Multi-product Company Allocation of Investment by Product Line
(In thousands)

| | NET SALES | ANALYZED BY PRODUCT | | | | PRORATED | TOTAL ASSETS EMPLOYED | |
| | | INVENTORIES | | FACTORY PLANT AND EQUIPMENT | | CASH ACCTS. REC., ETC. | | |
	AMOUNT	AMOUNT	PER $ SALES	AMOUNT	PER $ SALES	14.3¢ PER $ SALES	AMOUNT	PER $ SALES
Base year:								
Product A	$ 39,300	$ 8,000	20.4¢	$ 7,100	18.2¢	$ 5,600	$ 20,700	52.9¢
Product B	29,500	7,500	25.3	5,200	17.7	4,200	16,900	57.3
Product C	19,600	3,300	16.7	2,800	14.1	2,800	8,900	45.1
Product D	9,800	1,300	13.2	....	...	1,400	2,700	27.5
Total	$ 98,200	$20,100	20.4	$15,100	15.4	$14,000	$ 49,200	50.1
Current year:						15.4¢ PER $ SALES		
Product A	48,100	11,800	24.5	9,200	19.1	7,400	28,400	59.0
Product B	96,200	35,400	36.8	25,100	26.1	14,800	75,300	78.3
Product C	38,500	7,100	18.4	6,500	16.9	5,900	19,500	50.7
Product D	9,600	1,400	14.5	....	...	1,500	2,900	29.9
Total	$192,400	$55,700	28.9	$40,800	21.2	$29,600	$126,100	65.5

CHART 22   Multi-product Company Comparative Rates of Return
(In thousands)

| | TOTAL SALES | | ASSETS EMPLOYED | | OPERATING INCOME* | | |
	AMOUNT	% OF TOTAL	AMOUNT	PER $ SALES	AMOUNT	PER CENT RETURN ON SALES	ON ASSETS
Base year:							
Product A	$ 39,300	40	$ 20,700	52.9	$ 4,800	12.2%	23.1%
Product B	29,500	30	16,900	57.3	2,800	9.4	16.4
Product C	19,600	20	8,900	45.1	2,100	10.8	23.9
Product D	9,800	10	2,700	27.5	500	5.1	18.5
Total	$ 98,200	100	$ 49,200	50.1	$10,200	10.4	20.8
Current year:							
Product A	48,100	25	28,400	59.0	5,600	11.6	19.7
Product B	96,200	50	75,300	78.3	8,500	8.8	11.2
Product C	38,500	20	19,500	50.7	3,900	10.2	20.1
Product D	9,600	5	2,900	29.9	500	5.2	17.2
Total	$192,400	100	$126,100	65.5	$18,500	9.6	14.6

* Before interest on borrowed money and federal income taxes.

of sales and per cent of assets employed. Increases in profitability did not come automatically with volume. What must be done to bring this important product into a better earnings position? Are we penetrating a market that is saturated?

While Product A has had a modest increase in sales, are we developing a sufficient market share? Are we keeping pace with industry growth? Is sufficient management attention being given to this important product?

Are we alerted to possible deterioration of some varieties? What provisions are we making to replace them? Are we holding on to unprofitable varieties too long?

Is the unsatisfactory showing of a product line due to problems involving particular items within the line?

3. *Volume of Sales.* While a large increase is apparent, we must ask ourselves what per cent of total market we have. Have we lost ground in any of our lines, particularly Product A? Have we gained ground in any of our lines, particularly Product B? How have we fared in relation to our competitors in regard to share of the market?

4. *Operating Costs.* We notice a consistent drop in profit per dollar of sales. In what areas of expense has this occurred? Is our pricing policy achieving our purposes? Is our budget holding in check both our manufacturing costs and commercial expenses?

These and many other areas of investigation are opened. Through the answers we seek for them, we attempt to outline a balanced program for management, alerting the members to the most profitable employment of capital and helping them understand the meaning of even minor shifts which might be compounded into major situations which would hamper future earning power.

LEASING VERSUS OWNING

The subject of leasing versus owning is no more than a specialized application of capital management. In determining the most productive means of putting capital to work, we are faced with such questions as whether to make or buy, to lease or own, etc. In seeking the basis for decision, many considerations will appear, such as the availability of funds, the stability of demand, the reliability of outside sources, and the seasonality of requirements, to name a few.

In those cases where the decision is not forced by some obvious consideration, and where alternative choices are open to management, the ultimate criterion for decision is the adequacy of the rate of return on the capital involved.

In our manufacturing operations, we own practically all the land, buildings, and equipment we require. We do, however, supplement our outright ownership in this area with short-term leases for facilities such as temporary warehouse space for peak-load, seasonal requirements. At the same time, in our selling and distribution areas, we acquire most of our branch warehouses on long-term leases. We find that outside investors have funds for such

purpose on which they are willing to accept lower rates of return than we must demand from our working capital.

In all cases, however, the final test applied is the best use of capital measured by the rate of return it provides.

79

Measuring Organizational Performance*

RENSIS LIKERT

- Does top management's emphasis on immediate earnings, production, cost reduction, and similar measures of end results encourage division managers to dissipate the organization's human assets?

- What measurable changes occur in the productivity, loyalty, attitudes, and satisfactions of an organization where decision levels are pushed down and group methods of leadership are employed? What measurable changes occur in an organization where decision levels are pushed upward and close control is exercised at the top? How do the results of each type of management compare in the short and long run?

- What qualities of an organization can and should be measured for the purposes of appraising the leadership of division managers and others to whom authority is delegated?

Decentralization and delegation are powerful concepts based on sound theory. But there is evidence that, as now utilized, they have a serious vulnerability which can be costly. This vulnerability arises from the measurements being used to evaluate and reward the performance of those given authority over decentralized operations.

This situation is becoming worse. While companies have during the past decade made greater use of work measurements and measurements of end results in evaluating managers, and also greater use of incentive pay in rewarding them, only a few managements have regularly used measurements that deal directly with the human assets of the organization—for example, measurements of loyalty, motivation, confidence, and trust. As a consequence, many companies today are encouraging managers of departments and divisions to dissipate valuable human assets of the organization. In fact, they are rewarding these managers well for doing so!

NEW MEASURES NEEDED

The advocates of decentralization recognize that measurements play a particularly important function. Ralph J. Cordiner, one of the most articulate spokesmen, has stated his views on the question as follows:

> Like many other companies, General Electric has long felt a need for more exact measurements and standards of performance, not only to evaluate past results, but to provide a more accurate means for planning future activities and calculating business risks. The traditional measures of profits such as return on investment, turnover, and percentage of net earnings

* Reprinted by permission of the publisher of *Harvard Business Review*, vol. 36, no. 2, pp. 41–52, March–April, 1958. Mr. Likert is the director of the Institute for Social Research at the University of Michigan and professor in both the Psychology and Sociology Departments.

to sales provide useful information. But they are hopelessly inadequate as measures to guide the manager's effectiveness in planning for the future of the business—the area where his decisions have the most important effects.

When General Electric undertook the thorough decentralization . . . , the need for more realistic and balanced measurements became visibly more acute. For with the decentralization of operating responsibility and authority to more than a hundred local managerial teams, there was a need for common means of measuring these diverse business operations as to their short-range and long-range effectiveness....

It was felt that, if a system of simple, common measurements could be devised, they would would have these important values . . . .

1. Common measurements would provide all the managers of each component, and the individual contributors in the component, with means to measure and plan their own performance, so that their individual decisions could be made on the basis of knowledge and infomed judgment.

2. Common measurements would provide each manager with a way of detecting deviations from established standards in time to do something about it—the feedback idea, in which current operations themselves provide a means of continuous adjustment of the operation.

3. Common measurements would provide a means of appraisal, selection, and compensation of men on the basis of objective performance rather than personality judgments, which is better for both the individual and the Company.

4. Common measurements would provide an important motivation for better performance, since they make clear on what basis the individual is to be measured and give him a way of measuring his own effectiveness.

5. Common measurements would simplify communications by providing common concepts and common language with which to think and talk about the business, especially in its quantitative aspects.

You will notice that all these points are directed at helping each decentralized manager and individual contributor measure and guide his own work, through self-discipline; they are not designed as a way for others to 'second-guess' the manager of a component or the workers in his component. When measurements are designed primarily for the 'boss' rather than for the man himself, they tend to lose their objectivity and frequently become instruments of deception.

An adequate system of common measurements, moreover, would have the additional advantage of providing the company's executives with a way of evaluating performance in some hundred different businesses without becoming involved in the operational details of each of them.[1]

TRADITIONAL THEORY

These specifications point to serious inadequacies in the measurements now being obtained. Virtually all companies regularly secure measurements which deal with such end results as production, sales, profits, and percentage of net earnings to sales. The accounting procedures of most companies also reflect fairly well the level of inventories, the investment in plant and equipment, and the condition of plant and equipment.

But much less attention is given to what might be called "intervening factors," which significantly influence the end results just mentioned. These factors include such qualities of the human organization that staffs the plant as its loyalty, skills, motivations, and capacity for effective interaction, communication, and decision making. At present there is not one company, to my knowledge, that regularly obtains measurements which adequately and accurately reflect the quality and capacity of its human organization. (But in two companies experimental programs are underway to develop measurements of this kind.)

There are two principal reasons for this situation: (1) The traditional theory of management, which dominates current concepts as to what should be measured, largely ignores motivational and other human behavior variables. (2) Until recently the social sciences were not developed enough to provide methods for measuring the quality of the human organization.

The traditional theory of management is based on scientific management, cost accounting and related developments, and general administrative concepts taken from military organizational theory. As a consequence, it calls for measurements that are concerned with such end result variables as profits and costs, or with such process variables as productivity.

Substantial research findings show, however,

[1] Ralph J. Cordiner, *New Frontiers for Professional Managers*, McGraw-Hill Book Company, New York, 1956, pp. 95–98. This volume comprises the McKinsey Lectures, which Mr. Cordiner delivered in 1956 at the Graduate School of Business, Columbia University.

that the managers in business and government who are getting the best results are systematically deviating from this traditional theory in the operating procedures which they use.[2] The general pattern of these deviations is to give much more attention to motivation than the traditional theory calls for. High-producing managers are not neglecting such tools and resources provided by scientific management as cost accounting; quite to the contrary, they use them fully. But they use these quantitative tools in special ways—ways that achieve significantly higher motivation than is obtained by those managers who adhere strictly to the methods specified by the traditional theory of management.

MODIFIED THEORY

The exact principles and practices of high-producing managers have been integrated into a modified theory of management, which has been discussed elsewhere.[3] What I am interested in discussing here are the implications of this modified theory for control. Management needs to make extensive changes in the measurements now being obtained. It should take into account such factors as the levels of confidence and trust, motivation, and loyalty, and the capacity of the organization to communicate fully, to interact effectively, and to achieve sound decisions.

It is important for all companies to obtain these new kinds of measurements to guide their operations, but it is especially important for companies making extensive use of decentralization to do so. The logic of decentralization and the underlying theory on which it is based point to the need for this. In the absence of the new measurements, as we shall see presently, many managers are enabled and may even be encouraged to behave in ways which violate the logic of decentralization and which run contrary to the best interests of their companies.

It is easy to see why. Managers, like all human beings, guide their behavior by the infor-

mation available to them. The measurements which a company provides them as a basis for decision making are particularly important. They are used by top management not only to judge the performance of departmental and division heads but also, through promotions, bonus compensation, and similar devices, to reward them. If the measurements which companies use for these purposes ignore the quality of the human organization and deal primarily with earnings, production, costs, and similar end results, managers will be encouraged to make a favorable showing on those factors alone.

Management and Productivity   Let us examine the evidence for these statements. A central concept of the modified theory is (1) that the pattern of interaction between the manager and those with whom he deals should always be such that the individuals involved will feel that the manager is dealing with them in a supportive rather than a threatening manner. A related concept is (2) that management will make full use of the potential capacities of its human resources only when each person in an organization is a member of a well-knit and effectively functioning work group with high interaction skills and performance goals.

A test of these concepts, and thereby of the modified theory, was made recently using attitudinal and motivational data collected in 1955 in a study done by the Institute for Social Research, University of Michigan:

> Data are from a company that operates nationally. The company comprises 32 geographically separated units, varying in size from about 15 to over 50 employees, which perform essentially the same operations, and for which extensive productivity and cost figures are available continuously.
>
> A single score was computed for the manager in charge of each of the 32 units. These scores, based on seven questions in the managers' questionnaire, measure the manager's attitude on the two concepts which represent the modified theory. These two concepts were found to be highly related, and consequently have been handled in the analysis as a single combined score—labeled, for convenient reference, *attitude toward men*. The results obtained are shown in Exhibit I.

This study demonstrates clearly that those managers who, as revealed in their questionnaires, have a favorable *attitude toward men* score achieve significantly higher performance than those managers who have an unfavorable

---

[2] See, for example, R. Likert, "Motivational Dimensions of Administration," *America's Manpower Crisis*, Public Administration Service, Chicago, 1952, p. 89; "Developing Patterns of Management," American Management Association, *General Management Series, no. 178*, New York, 1955, pp. 32–51; and D. Katz and R. Kahn, "Human Organization and Worker Motivation," *Industrial Productivity*, in (ed.), L. Reed Tripp, Industrial Relations Research Association, Madison, Wis., 1952, p. 146.

[3] R. Likert, "Developing Patterns of Management: II," American Management Association, *General Management Series, no. 182*, New York, 1956, pp. 3–29.

EXHIBIT I   Relationship of Attitude toward Men Score of Manager to Unit's Productivity

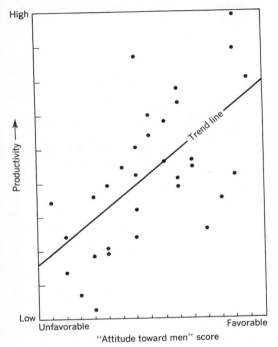

"Attitude toward men" score

score. Managers who have a supportive attitude toward their men and endeavor to build them into well-knit teams obtain appreciably higher productivity than managers who have a threatening attitude and rely more on man-to-man patterns of supervision. (The correlation coefficient is 0.64.)

Information obtained from the nonsupervisory employees under these managers confirms the supervisory pattern reported by the managers. The material from the employees also confirms the character of the important intervening human variables contributing to the better productivity of the high-performance units. The men in those units in which the manager has an above-average *attitude toward men* score differ in their descriptions of their supervision and experience from the men in units whose managers are below average in their *attitude toward men* score. More specifically, the men in units whose managers had a favorable *attitude toward men* score are more likely than the men in the other units to indicate that:

1. The supervision of their unit is of a supportive character. This involves such supervisory behavior as being more interested in the men, friendlier, more willing to go to

bat for them, and being less threatening, less punitive, less critical, and less strict (but still having high performance expectations).

2. There is more team spirit, group loyalty, and teamwork among the men and between the men and management.

3. The men have more confidence and trust in management and have higher motivation. Moreover, there is better communication between the men and management.

4. The men work under less sense of pressure, feel much freer to set their own work pace, and yet produce more.

The findings from this study are consistent with the results obtained in a number of other studies in widely different industries.[4] These other studies have also yielded evidence showing important differences in the way the managers of high- and low-producing units conceive of their job and deal with their subordinates:

- The units achieving the best performance are much more likely than the poor performance units to have managers who deal with their subordinates in a supportive manner and build high group loyalty and teamwork.

- The poor performance units are much more likely than the best units to have managers who press for production and treat their subordinates as "cogs in a machine."

- The supportive managers tend to supervise by establishing goals and objectives for their subordinates; in contrast, the pressure-oriented managers tend to focus on the processes they want their employees to carry out in order to achieve the objectives of the manager.

Dangers of Pressure   These research findings, therefore, provide a pattern of results which confirms central concepts of the modified theory of management. These results demonstrate that, on the average, *pressure-oriented, threatening, punitive management yields lower*

4 R. Kahn, "The Prediction of Productivity," *Journal of Social Issues*, vol. 12, no. 2, p. 41, 1956; D. Katz, N. Maccoby, G. Gurin, and L. G. Floor, "Productivity, Supervision and Morale among Railroad Workers," Institute for Social Research, *SRC Monograph Series*, no. 5, Ann Arbor, Mich., 1951; D. Katz, N. Maccoby, and N. Morse, "Productivity, Supervision and Morale in an Office Situation," Institute for Social Research, *SRC Monograph Series no. 2*, Ann Arbor, Mich., 1950; and R. Likert, "Motivation: The Core of Management," American Management Association, *Personnel Series, A155*, New York, 1953, pp. 3–21.

productivity, higher costs, increased absence, and less employee satisfaction than supportive, employee-centered management which uses group methods of supervision coupled with high-performance expectations.

Since the supportive pattern of supervision tends to yield the best results, clearly this is the pattern which boards of directors and top company officials should foster in all situations including those that involve decentralization and delegation. Company officers believe, no doubt, that they are achieving this pattern of management in their operations. But, unfortunately, the performance measurements now being used by most top managements put pressures on lower levels of management to behave otherwise.

What often confuses the situation is that pressure-oriented, threatening supervision can achieve impressive *short-run* results, particularly when coupled with high technical competence. There is clear-cut evidence that for a period of at least one year supervision which increases the direct pressure for productivity can achieve significant increases in production. However, such increases are obtained only at a substantial and serious cost to the organization.

TESTING PERFORMANCE

To what extent can a manager make an impressive earnings record over a short-run period of one to three years by exploiting the company's investment in the human organization in his plant or department? To what extent will the quality of his organization suffer if he does so?

Contrasting Programs   On this further question, we also have some concrete evidence from an important study conducted by the Institute for Social Research in a large multi-division corporation:

The study covered 500 clerical employees in four parallel divisions. Each division was organized in the same way, used the same technology, did exactly the same kind of work, and had employees of comparable aptitudes.

Productivity in all four of the divisions depended on the number of clerks involved. The work was something like a billing operation; there was just so much of it, but it had to be processed as it came along. Consequently, the only way in which productivity could be increased under the existing organization was to change the size of the work group.

The four divisions were assigned to two experimental programs on a random basis. Each program was assigned at random a division that

had been historically high in productivity and a division that had been below average in productivity. No attempt was made to place a division in that program which would best fit its habitual methods of supervision used by the manager, assistant managers, supervisors, and assistant supervisors.

The experiment at the clerical level lasted for one year. Beforehand, several months were devoted to planning, and there was also a training period of approximately six months. Productivity was measured continuously and computed weekly throughout the year. Employee and supervisory attitudes and related variables were measured just before and after the period.

Turning now to the heart of the study, in two divisions an attempt was made to change the supervision so that the decision levels were pushed *down*. More *general* supervision of the clerks and their supervisors was introduced. In addition, the managers, assistant managers, supervisors, and assistant supervisors of these two divisions were trained in group methods of leadership, which they endeavored to use as much as their skill would permit during the experimental year. (To this end we made liberal use of methods developed by the National Training Laboratory in Group Development.) For easy reference, the experimental changes in these two divisions will be labeled the "participative program."

In the other two divisions, by contrast, the program called for modifying the supervision so as to increase the closeness of supervision and move the decision levels *upward*. This will be labeled the "hierarchically controlled program." These changes were accomplished by a further extension of the scientific management approach. For example, one of the major changes made was to have the jobs timed by the methods department and to have standard times computed. This showed that these divisions were overstaffed by about 30%. The general manager then ordered the managers of these two divisions to cut staff by 25%. This was to be done by transfers without replacing the persons who left; no one was to be dismissed.

As a check on how effectively these policies were carried out, measurements were obtained for each division as to where decisions were made. One set of these measurements was obtained before the experimental year started, and the second set was obtained after the completion of the year. The attempts to change the level at which decisions were made were successful enough to develop measurable differences. In the hierarchically controlled program a significant shift upward occurred; by contrast, a significant shift downward occurred in the levels at which decisions were made in the participative program. Also, in the participative program there was an increase in the use of participation and in the extent to which employees were involved in decisions affecting them.

Changes in Productivity   Exhibit II shows the changes in salary costs per unit of work, which reflect the changes in productivity that occurred in the divisions. As will be observed, the hierarchically controlled program increased productivity by about 25%. This was a result of the direct orders from the general manager to reduce staff by that amount. Direct pressure produced a substantial increase in production.

EXHIBIT II   Changes in Productivity

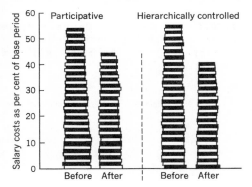

A significant increase in productivity of 20% was also achieved in the participative program, but this was not so great an increase as in the hierarchically controlled program. To bring about this improvement, the clerks themselves participated in the decision to reduce the size of the work group. (They were aware, of course, that productivity increases were sought by management in making these experiments.) Obviously, deciding to reduce the size of a work group by eliminating some of its members is probably one of the most difficult decisions for a work group to make. Yet the clerks made it. In fact, one division in the participative program increased its productivity by about the same amount as each of the two divisions in the hierarchically controlled program. The other participative division, which historically had been the poorest of all of the divisions, did not do so well and increased productivity by only about 15%.

Changes in Attitudes   Although both programs had similar effects on productivity, they had significantly different results in other respects. The productivity increases in the hierarchically controlled program were accompanied by shifts in an *adverse* direction in such factors as loyalty, attitudes, interest, and involvement in the work. But just the opposite was true in the participative program.

For example, Exhibit III shows that when more general supervision and increased participation were provided, the employees' feeling of responsibility to see that the work got done increased. Again, when the supervisor was away, they kept on working. In the hierarchically controlled program, however, the feeling of responsibility decreased, and when the supervisor was absent, the work tended to stop.

Another measurement of the extent to which an employee feels involved in his work is his attitude toward workers who are high producers. The changes in attitudes toward the high producer by the employees in the two programs are shown in Exhibit IV. Here again there was a statistically significant shift in opposite directions. In the participative program the attitudes became more favorable, and there was less pressure to restrict production. In the hierarchically controlled program the opposite effect occurred.

EXHIBIT III   Employees' Feeling of Responsibility to See That Work Gets Done

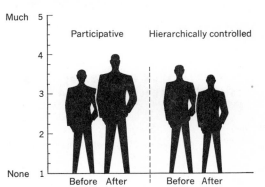

In industrial organizations that are effective in achieving their objectives, extensive research in a variety of organizations shows that superiors and subordinates are linked by loyalty, a mutual feeling of understanding and closeness, and a feeling that influence and communica-

EXHIBIT IV   Employee Attitudes toward High Producer

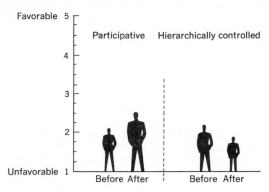

tion (both upward and downward) function well.[5] How are these attitudes and feelings achieved? Our study of the four divisions throws some light on the answer.

As Exhibit V shows, the employees in the participative program at the end of the year felt that their manager and assistant manager were "closer to them" than at the beginning of the year. The opposite was true in the hierarchically controlled program. Moreover, as Exhibit VI shows, employees in the participative program felt that their superiors were more likely to "pull" for them, or for the company *and* them, and not be solely interested in

[5] R. Kahn, F. Mann, and S. Seashore (eds.), "Human Relations Research in Large Organizations, II," *Journal of Social Issues,* vol. 12, no. 2, p. 1, 1956; and D. Katz and R. Kahn, "Some Recent Findings in Human Relations Research in Industry," E. Swanson, T. Newcomb, and E. Hartley (eds.), *Readings in Social Psychology,* Holt, Rinehart and Winston, Inc., New York, 1952, p. 650.

EXHIBIT V   How Close Manager and Assistant Manager Were Felt to Be to Employees

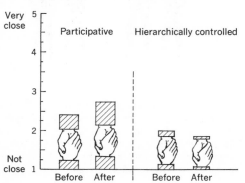

the company; while in the hierarchically controlled program, the opposite trend occurred.

As might be expected from these trends, a marked shift in opposite directions showed up during the year in the employees' feeling of satisfaction with their superiors. Exhibit VII shows the shifts in employees' feelings as to how well their superiors communicated upward and influenced management on matters which concerned them. Once again the participative program showed up better than the hierarchically controlled program. One significant aspect of the changes in attitude in the hierarchically controlled program was that the employees felt that their superiors were relying more at the end of the year on rank and authority to get the work done than was the case at the beginning of the year. "Pulling rank" tends to become self-defeating in the long run because of the hostilities and counterpressures it evokes.

EXHIBIT VI   Employee Opinions as to Extent to Which Superiors "Pulled" for Company Only or for Employees and Company

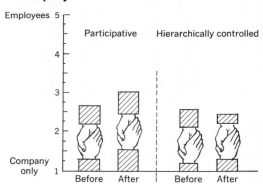

The deterioration under the hierarchically controlled program showed up in several other ways. For instance, turnover increased. Employees began to quit because of what they felt to be excessive pressure for production. As a consequence, the company felt it desirable to lessen the pressure. This happened toward the end of the experimental year.

Unfortunately, it was not possible to conduct the participative and hierarchically controlled programs for more than one year because of changes in the over-all operations of the company. However, the significant trends in opposite directions which occurred in these two programs are the trends which would be expected in the light of the studies cited earlier

EXHIBIT VII   Employees Satisfaction with Superiors as Representatives

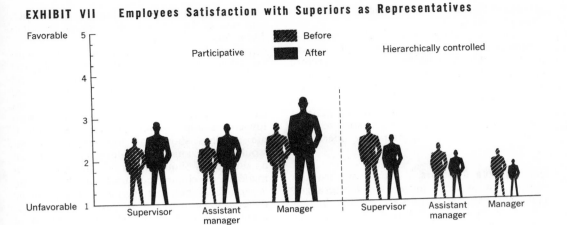

in the article. The attitudes which improved the most in the participative program and deteriorated the most in the hierarchically controlled program are those which these studies have consistently shown to be most closely related *in the long run* to employee motivation and productivity. This gives us every reason to believe that had the clerical experiment been continued for another year or two, productivity and quality of work would have continued to increase in the participative program, while in the hierarchically controlled program productivity and quality of work would have declined.

IMPLICATIONS FOR POLICY

What are the implications of all this for management policy—particularly in the company that is decentralizing its operations or otherwise delegating a good deal of authority to various managers?

Treatment of Human Assets   To begin with, most executives will readily agree that it costs money to hire and train personnel. And, after personnel have been hired and trained, it takes additional time and money to build them into a loyal, well-knit, effectively functioning organization with well-established goals. Most businessmen will also agree with the research findings which show that the more supportive the supervision and the better the organization (in terms of loyalty, level of performance goals, communication, motivation, and so forth), the greater is its capacity for high-quality performance at low cost.

If we make these assumptions, we can come, I believe, to only one conclusion. As was demonstrated in the hierarchically controlled

program of the experiment, putting pressure on a well-established organization to produce can yield substantial and immediate increases in productivity. *This increase is obtained, however, at a cost to the human assets of the organization.* In the company we studied, for example, the cost was clear: hostilities increased, there was greater reliance upon authority, loyalties declined, and motivations to produce decreased while motivations to restrict production increased. In other words, the quality of the human organization deteriorated as a functioning social system.

If the company had had an accounting procedure which showed the investment in the human organization, it would have shown that in the two divisions in the hierarchically controlled program the value of the human organization was less at the end of the experimental year than at the beginning. In other words, some of the increased productivity was achieved actually by liquidating part of the investment which the company had in the human organization in these divisions. The increase in productivity should have been charged with this cost.

On the other hand, had the company's accounting records reflected the value of the company's investment in the human organization in the two divisions in the participative program, they would have shown an opposite picture. During the year, the value of this investment increased. The management of the two divisions had been of such a character as to increase the productive capacity of the organization as a functioning social system: loyalties had increased, hostilities had decreased, communication was improved, decisions were better since they were based on more accurate and adequate information, and production goals and motivations to produce were increasing.

While a company's investment in its human organization is less tangible than the investment in plant and equipment, and therefore has not yet been given the kind of evaluation an accountant would give it, *it can be measured approximately with the methods now available*. These methods can enable management to size up present trends, analyze their relationships, and guide company operations accordingly.

Quantitative Controls   Companies are very careful not to let managers of decentralized plants show spurious profits and earnings by juggling inventory or by failing to maintain plant and equipment. Their accounting procedures measure and report regularly on inventory and condition of plant and equipment. "Earnings" achieved by liquidating the assets represented in the human organization are just as spurious as though achieved by liquidating the investment in plant. Yet they are encouraged by compensation formulas that urge managers to press unduly for immediate production, cost reduction, and similar goals; by the present-day emphasis on measuring only the end results of the activities of the lower echelons or of decentralized operations; and by job evaluations focused on the immediate contribution to earnings and profits.

In the long run, of course, such measurements are valid. The executive who "milks the human franchise" today will not be in a position to show good profit-and-loss figures tomorrow. The catch is that, by the time the symptoms of trouble are clear, the human organization has deteriorated to a point where steps to correct it are difficult and costly. As a practical matter, moreover, there is often so much rotation in executive responsibilities, and so much change in the conditions of business, that short-run tests which will provide adequate measures of current performance, including trends in the human organization, are worth much more than long-run evaluations.

There is only one solution to this problem, and it does not yet lie in more precise accounting data. The solution is to obtain adequate periodic measurements of the character and the quality of the human organization. Judgment alone is notoriously inaccurate and tends to be most inaccurate in those situations which are unsatisfactory or deteriorating. Measurements and compensation formulas are needed which will penalize managers financially and otherwise when they permit the quality of the

human organization under them to deteriorate, and reward them when they improve the quality of this organization.

Identically the same point can be made with regard to consumer attitudes, good will, and confidence in the company, in its products, and in its service. A manager of a decentralized operation can substantially increase current earnings by reducing the product quality with low-cost, shoddy output. However, the immediate earnings shown on the company books would be spurious and would actually represent a substantial liquidation of the investment made in developing consumer confidence and acceptance. Therefore, periodic measurements of consumer perceptions, attitudes, and acceptance should be made not only for the usual purposes, such as to provide direction in product development and to guide advertising and marketing, but also to protect the company's investment in consumer good will.

Adequate Appraisals   It is not sufficient merely to measure morale and the attitudes of employees toward the organization, their supervision, and their work. Favorable attitudes and excellent morale do not necessarily assure high motivation, high performance, and an effective human organization. A good deal of research indicates that this relationship is much too simple. Favorable attitudes may be found, for example, in situations where there is complacency and general contentment but where production goals are low and there is little motivation to achieve high performance.

Similarly, measurements of behavior which reflect the past condition of the human organization, while useful, are also inadequate for current appraisals. Such measurements as absence, turnover, and scrap loss tend not only to be insensitive measurements but also to reflect changes in the human organization *after* they have become substantial. More sensitive and more current measurements than those are needed.

Progress in the social sciences in recent years enables any company which so desires to obtain measurements needed for adequate appraisals of the quality and performance capacity of its human organization. Instruments to measure many of the important variables are now available; for those variables for which measuring instruments are not now available, the basic methodology now exists to develop the necessary tools. The organization for which these measurements are obtained can be an entire corporation or any of its divisions.

The following illustrate the kinds of variables which are now being measured in some companies or for which satisfactory measuring instruments can be developed:

1. Extent of loyalty to and identification with the institution and its objectives.

2. Extent to which members of the organization at all hierarchical levels feel that the organization's goals are consistent with their own needs and goals, and that the achievement of the company's goals will help them achieve their own.

3. Extent to which the goals of units and of individuals are of a character to enable the organization to achieve its objectives.

4. Level of motivation among members of the organization with regard to such variables as:

   a. Performance, including both quality and quantity of work done;

   b. Concern for elimination of waste and reduction of costs;

   c. Concern for improving product;

   d. Concern for improving processes.

5. Degree of confidence and trust among members of the organization in each other and in the different hierarchical levels.

6. Amount and quality of teamwork in each unit of the organization and between units.

7. Extent to which people feel delegation is being effectively achieved.

8. Extent to which members feel that their ideas, information, knowledge of processes, and experience are being used in the decision-making processes of the organization.

9. Level of competence and skill of different groups in the organization to interact effectively in solving problems and other tasks.

10. Efficiency and adequacy of the communication process upward, downward, sidewise.

11. Level of the leadership skills and abilities of supervisors and managers, including their basic philosophy of management and orientation toward the processes of leadership.

12. Aptitude scores of the members of the organization. If aptitude scores are obtained as people join the organization, then trends in these scores will show whether the current management is improving the basic quality of the personnel through its hiring practices or is letting quality deteriorate through unfavorable turnover.

Job for Experts   The measurement of these variables is a complex process and requires a high level of scientific competence. It cannot be done by an untrained person, no matter how intelligent he is. Nor can it be done simply by asking people questions that have not been pretested or by handing them a ready-made questionnaire. Few companies trust cost figures obtained by inexperienced personnel. It is equally dangerous to trust the untrained to obtain measurements of the state of a human organization.

CONCLUSION

Industry needs more adequate measures of organizational performance than it is now getting. Progress in the social sciences now makes these measurements possible. As a consequence, new resources are available to assist company presidents in their responsibility for the successful management of their companies.

The president's responsibility requires that he build an organization whose structure, goals, levels of loyalty, motivation, interaction skills, and competence are such that the organization achieves its objectives effectively. As tools to assist him and the other members of management, a president needs a constant flow of measurements reporting on the state of the organization and the performance being achieved. The measurements proposed here would provide a president with data which he needs to fill the current serious gap in the information coming to him and to his organization.

Management Audits Simplified*

JACKSON MARTINDELL

Intimate knowledge of the corporate history of an organization and of the attainments, personalities and capacities of a company's officers must be assembled before any sense of the degree of team spirit imbuing an organization can be grasped. This is the first indispensable step to management appraisal.

There is no way whereby this part of an audit can be simplified. A comprehensive study of the personalities involved is required because the activities and modes of conduct of the individual corporation are determined by the character of the men who lead it and the relationship between them.

Intimate knowledge, in this sense, does not require personal intimacy. The career of the average corporate officer is well documented. The viewpoints of his associates, colleagues, customers, suppliers and rivals regarding his abilities and characteristics are readily enough obtainable for sound appraisal of each man to be possible by any trained inquirer. In fact, the Institute's attempt at simplification of corporate analysis demonstrates that the best judgments regarding the personalities involved are usually obtainable from outside sources.

Requisite information concerning the management personnel of a corporation is obtainable in many quarters. Retired executives and employees are among the valuable sources of such information. The opinions of these men are usually unbiased, or, if biased, are usually swayed only by concern for the welfare of the organization in which they spent their business lives. Their philosophy of management may be outmoded, their grasp of production or marketing may be that of a past generation, but their sense of the devotion to duty of individual corporate officers is uncannily accurate.

Other, and equally important informative sources as to the qualities of men in management are labor unions, credit agencies, banks,

investment brokers, officials of insurance companies, auditors, executives of advertising agencies, and the company's own competitors and main suppliers. The latter are particularly important. The company's customers are an obvious source of sound judgment.

In simplifying the process of evolution, the Institute has found that a cooperative management willing to undertake evaluation of itself, upon the basis of the Institute's 10 Functional Categories of the Rating System, is of great value. This does not mean that if the management rates itself, the Institute need not thereafter rate it. On the contrary, the weighting given by the management to the various functional subdivisions of its own organization is evidence of the relative importance placed by the executive group upon the separate phases of its activities. It indicates the quality which men in management ascribe to the functions which they are called upon to carry out.

Under the Institute's simplified procedure, companies are now asked to appraise themselves under each of the ten categorial subdivisions, to give the reasons for the weightings they award themselves, and to supply supplementary information in substantiation of their findings.

The attempt at justification of a self-rating compels the officers to re-examine the findings it has arrayed, and assists toward better understanding of the varying degrees of importance and excellence of its several operations.

It is the Institute's experience that only after such self-appraisal has been supplied by the company, individual officers and directors need be approached directly. This is because management evaluation must not at first be concerned with broad generalities as to what a company's officers claim to have achieved in the past or hope to achieve in the future, but in discovering whatever special traits may exist within the management group.

Simultaneously, the 10 largest stockholders are consulted as to what influence they believe themselves to have upon the board of directors

* Reprinted by permission of the publisher from *The Corporate Director*, Special Issue, no. 15, pp. 1–6, December, 1951. Mr. Martindell is president of the American Institute of Management.

and as to their opinion of the directorate as a whole. It does not matter whether these 10 largest stockholders are themselves members of the board. It is not in their capacity as board members that we consult them, but as representative stockholders.

Finally, a list of prepared questions is submitted to the officers and directors. The answers to these questions are intended to supplement information already gathered, or to provide information otherwise unobtainable.

SUBDIVIDING THE MANAGEMENT ANALYSIS

The American Institute of Management has subjected over 3000 corporate managements to comparative examination. In doing so, it has discovered that the basic categories of the managerial function resolve themselves to ten, no matter what the industry. These ten categories are functional subdivisions of the management process. They do not coincide with the formal structure or organization of any single corporation. They represent the functions performed by the corporation as a whole and not the form of organization adopted to carry out that function. As such, they cut across the nominal business structure. By so doing, they bring into visible relief the separate activities carried on by the several divisions of the corporation and its officers.

Economic Function   Corporations, like individuals, develop distinctive characteristics over the years. These characteristics derive from the purposes which the corporation—like the individual—attempts to accomplish, and by its habitual way of doing so. Over the span of time, each company develops its own tradition. These traditions are truly important. They express the moral quality of the whole organization; a quality which in turn depends upon the relative importance of the company's purposes.

In evaluating this, it is important to discover:

1. When, why, where and by whom the present company was founded?

2. What changes have occurred in the fundamental nature of the business? When, why and how did these occur?

3. Has the competitive standing of the company in its industry risen since the company was founded?

4. What important changes have occurred in management since the company's inception and why did these occur?

5. Has the company always enjoyed a reputation for fair dealing with all who come in contact with it?

6. What important changes have occurred in the ownership of the corporation during its life span?

7. What contribution do the company's operations make to the national economy, regardless of the size of the company?

Among leading companies which meet the Institute's rigid tests to qualify as excellent under "Economic Function" are the following: American Telephone and Telegraph Corporation; Great Atlantic and Pacific Tea Company of America; Merck and Company; National Steel Corporation; B. F. Goodrich Company; and Procter & Gamble Company. A number of smaller companies also qualify for top rating. We mention the foregoing companies mainly because their names are familiar to almost every person in the United States—perhaps because their devotion to worthy purposes has become synonymous with their names themselves.

Corporate Structure   In any continuing organization, an established way of doing things must ultimately result in a formal organizational structure. In terms of the corporation, this amounts to saying that, with the passing of time, distinct lines of communication develop within the enterprise. The way these lines of communication intersect determines how decisions are arrived at, how they are put into effect, and how and by whom their results are appraised. In certain corporations, the making of fundamental decisions is often untimely. On occasion, fundamental decisions are not even arrived at. Instead, problems are allowed to "sort themselves out." In other corporations, basic policy decisions are made but are not followed through or, too frequently, are carried out half-heartedly. In still other companies, no attempt is ever made to evaluate the results of policy decisions and the way that they have been carried out. It is astonishing that perhaps in the majority of corporations, job evaluation and merit rating has not been extended systematically up to the top executive levels.

The essential questions in corporate structure are:

1. Who exercises the principal authority?

2. How many individuals report directly to this principal authority?

3. Is the president also the general manager?

4. Is the business decentralized geographically, or is control exercised over all functions from a central point?

5. To what extent does the company operate on product-division lines?

6. Is the structure such that profitableness or unprofitableness of each product is at all times apparent to the men responsible for its supervision, and to the principal executive officers?

7. Is there a system of job evaluation and merit rating reaching up to the president himself?

In terms of corporate structure, the Institute is particularly impressed by the soundness of internal procedures and lines of communication in General Motors Corporation, General Foods Corporation, National Dairy Products Corporation, Bethlehem Steel Corporation, E. I. Du Pont de Nemours & Company, and Sears, Roebuck & Company.

Health of Earnings Growth   Because corporate taxes bear unequally upon corporations during periods of excess profits tax levies, the essential measure of the growth of earnings must be the net profit after prior charges but before taxes. Nevertheless, such earnings must be translated into dollars available to the outstanding common stock. This is particularly true in terms of growth. The Institute's studies have uncovered many examples of corporations with large apparent growth in net earnings but with virtually no growth of earnings expressed in terms of earnings available for the payment of dividends to the common stockholder.

Size of earnings is not in itself a criterion of health of earnings growth. The earnings record during years of general prosperity or of unusual temporary demand for a company's main products is no criterion whatever. Most emphatically, earnings which derive from a natural or artificial monopoly cannot be regarded as basically healthy, no matter what their size. Therefore, it is not the size of earnings alone which determines the health of earnings growth, but the conditions under which that growth has come about, its continuousness, and its ability to be sustained, at least moderately, even during depression years.

The best corporate managements pursue policies intended to prepare the company for unforeseen contingencies. As a result, the most efficiently managed corporations show satisfactory profits even during times of bad trade. How these profits are earned, whether they result largely from the sale of new products continuously generated by development and research work, or whether they merely bear a statistical relationship to the growth of population and national income, cannot be left out of account. Merck & Company, for example, now gains more than three-quarters of its profit from products—and from methods of producing them—unknown a decade ago. In numerous other companies, Procter and Gamble and the Du Pont Company being prime examples, substantially the same is true.

To arrive at a decision as to whether the growth in a corporation's earnings has been healthy, the Institute seeks to know:

1. What growth in earnings does a study of a 10, 20, and 30 year record reveal?

2. How has the company fared in all the significant trade cycles of the past 10, 20, and 30 years?

3. How have its operating ratios compared with those of its leading competitors?

4. What percentage of the company has been owned by the common stock at the close of each year since its inception?

5. Over an extended period, what has been net before taxes in % of sales?

6. Over an extended period, what has been net before taxes in % of gross fixed assets?

7. Over an extended period, what has been net before taxes in % of net investment?

Among outstanding examples of corporations whose growth of earnings has been pronouncedly healthy, the Institute regards the following companies as exemplary: U.S. Plywood Corporation; Merck & Company; E. I. Du Pont de Nemours & Company; B. F. Goodrich Company; Grand Union Company; Minnesota Mining and Manufacturing Company; Minneapolis Honeywell Regulator Company; Standard Oil Company (New Jersey); International Paper Company; Union Carbide and Carbon Corporation; Cities Service Company; Formica Company; and Marathon Corporation.

Fairness to Stockholders   So far, we have concerned ourselves with the basic factors of the company's economic function, the reputation for probity which it has earned over the years, its form of executive organization which determines whether the business will be conducted smoothly and efficiently, and the health of its earnings growth. These three points are closely interrelated and lead to the next point to be examined: What benefits the proprietors of the company have received from their investment in it, directly in the form of dividends, and indirectly in the form of growth in their equity value.

The individual investor gains no benefit from a corporation whose own advance has been at the expense of exposing the stockholder to undue risks or of failing to pay him an adequate return for the risks he has voluntarily assumed. In the course of its researches, the Institute has uncovered numerous instances of companies well-run in other respects, but whose officers have disregarded both the private interest of the shareholders and the general interest of the public. Such companies are not well conducted; their operations are out of harmony with the needs and trends of our time.

Fairness to stockholders is perhaps the most difficult category of evaluation to define. There can be few, if any, hard and fast rules whereby quality under this heading may be measured. However, comparative study within an industry gives strong evidence of managerial quality in this respect.

The questions most carefully examined by the Institute are the following:

1. What percentage of earnings available for dividends has been paid out of dividends in each of the past thirty years?
2. Is there an established dividend policy and how long has it been established?
3. Have the dividends paid out by the individual company borne the same percental relationship to earnings as in the industry as a whole?
4. Have dividends consistently been so large as to prevent an adequate rate of growth in earned surplus?
5. Has the company shown a consistent effort to deal fairly with stockholders in all respects?

The stockholder attitudes of the following corporations appear particularly impressive to the Institute: Pennsylvania Salt Manufacturing Company; Container Corporation of America; Grand Union Company; National Cash Register Corporation; CIT Financial Corporation; General Electric Company; and American Telephone and Telegraph Company.

Research and Development   It is by now an axiom of management quality that increasing attention must be paid to research and development work as the years go by. Top management which fails to give adequate attention to ground-breaking experiments is simply failing its managerial purpose.

Unfortunately, the term "experiment" is misunderstood in the average corporation. Perhaps because the chemical and petroleum industries have done an outstanding job of research, most businessmen seem to feel that unless this specific type of work is undertaken,

no research worthy of the name is being done. With this attitude is coupled the apparent belief that research can stop at this point and yet prove wholly adequate. The fact is, however, that the areas in which profitable research can be undertaken are co-extensive with every activity of the corporation, no matter what the nature of its products or the scope of its operation.

The neglected areas of research, even in companies aggressive in the development of new products, are usually the following: market research is neglected or underemphasized; few companies have properly developed research as to the most fruitful forms of advertising; inquiries into economical handling, packaging, shipping, and many other individual phases of manufacturing and distribution are given insufficient attention.

Opportunities for profitable research exist even in commercial banking, although the bank's main functions are the safekeeping and employment of money. Almost every department of the average bank would benefit from the installation of new and more efficient methods. The markets available to some banks have been extended by the development and employment of new forms of the banking business. The National City Bank of New York is a case in point. As a result of investigating the potential profitableness of the small loan business, it now has more than 800,000 clients in this category and does more than 80 per cent of this type of business in the territory it serves.

Under the category "research and development" the broadest questions the Institute attempts to have answered are:

1. What research activities are conducted and how long have they been established?
2. Who is the executive head of research and what roles does he play in the top management?
3. Are research budgets established by projects, or is there an over-all research allotment?
4. What has been the history of research expenditures and what results were achieved?
5. Have research activities been concentrated in one direction or do they embrace the whole scope of the company's activity?
6. What annual procedure is followed in determining the results achieved by individual research projects and by the over-all research activity?

Self-evident examples of companies whose research and development activities have proved particularly fruitful are: Merck & Company; E. I. Du Pont de Nemours & Company; B. F. Goodrich Company; General Electric Corporation; Grand Union Company; Procter & Gamble Company; Standard Oil Company (New Jersey); Phillips Petroleum Company; Union Carbide & Carbon Corporation; and Minnesota Mining and Manufacturing Company.

Directorate Analysis   The Institute, after studying thousands of corporations, is convinced the greatest single weakness in American business organization lies in the composition of the average board of directors. Less effort is devoted towards improving this phase of the organization than to any other. Until two years ago, this was true beyond question. Since then, however, increasingly critical expressions by stockholders have led to some improvement. In fact, more than one-half of the correspondence of the American Institute of Management, in answer to inquiries from the outside, is now concerned with matters regarding directors.

In evaluating the board of directors, the crucial questions are:

1. Is the board an inside board or an outside board?

2. Who are the members of the board, and when and why was each added to the board?

3. What civic activities is each board member engaged in and what is his military record?

4. To what extent does the chief executive dominate the board of directors?

5. What percentage of the directors consists of lawyers, bankers, customers, suppliers, or competititors?

6. Which directors exercise the greatest influence over the board, and what form does that influence take?

Companies characterized by first-rate boards of directors are none too common. Certain paramount examples of excellence in this respect include the following companies: Procter & Gamble Company; General Foods Corporation; National Gypsum Company; Travelers Insurance Company; National City Bank of New York; National Cash Register Company; Pittsburgh Consolidation Coal Company; and Owens-Illinois Glass Company.

Fiscal Policies   The studies pursued by the Institute indicated that most of the financial difficulties experienced by corporations during the past thirty years have originated less in the development of an adverse economic environment than in defective fiscal policies pursued by managements. There is remarkable variance in the fiscal policies of companies, even within the same industry. During periods of general refinancing, one company may be selling preferred stock in order to retire bonds, while its competitor may be selling bonds to retire preferred stock. The former is sacrificing an immediate tax advantage in the search for long-term safety; the latter, sacrificing long-term safety in return for the temporary tax advantage.

It is astonishing that dividends being paid at the present time by many corporations are not proportioned to current additions to earned surplus, but actually constitute a liquidation of capital, without top management being aware of the fact. This is caused by the inflation from which we are suffering and by the fact that more than one management seems unaware that the cash it will ultimately require in order to replace its plant facilities at increasing costs may prove higher than the whole current depreciation charge and earnings combined. Management with a sound concept of fiscal conduct should be aware of this fact. It should be especially aware—and no difficulties prevent such awareness—that, perhaps within a decade, significant fluctuations in earnings and in the replacement cost of plant assets may occur. Proper fiscal procedures would deter management from dissipating liquid assets which may be needed to make up for the deficiency between annual depreciation charges and the replacement cost of annual wear and tear.

Sound fiscal policy must at all times be consistent, must be coordinated with the over-all needs of the enterprise, and must have the main purpose in view of preserving the corporation from perhaps unforeseeable stresses whose effects could be disastrous if the unforeseen were unprepared for.

The following questions are particularly weighty in this regard:

1. What has been the history of operating and financial ratios over an extended number of years?

2. Are daily financial reports made to the top executives?

3. What form of budgetary control is exercised?

4. Are reserves being established to cover the increased replacement cost of plant facilities over and above the depreciation charge against earnings?

5. How has expansion been financed in the

past and what changes have occurred in the company's capital structure in recent years?

Financial administration is particularly laudable in the following corporations: E. I. Du Pont de Nemours and Company; Procter and Gamble Company; General Electric Company; Minneapolis-Moline Company; Electric Auto-Lite Company; National Dairy Products Corporation; American Telephone and Telegraph Company; Hooker Electrochemical Company; Archer-Daniels-Midland Company; National Steel Corporation; St. Regis Paper Company; and International Paper Company.

Production Efficiency Production efficiency is the outstanding contribution made to world progress by American business. The larger markets of America, and the resulting possibility of long-line productions, are in part the cause of our increasing superiority over European production methods. In turn, the vast potentialities of the American market have spurred us to surprising competitive efforts. Our competitive standing is paramount throughout the world in all mass production items.

Nevertheless, there is discernible need on the part of management to re-appraise its plant locations, the relative advantages of horizontal or vertical integration, the efficiency which might be achieved by discarding multiple product operations within one plant or vice versa; and the advantages to be gained by permitting greater autonomy at separate production centers. Labor management relations are the primary management concern today. This is certainly true of the larger corporation. Friction is less apt to develop in smaller companies between workmen and top management but the distressing effects of the employment of untrained department heads, due to a smaller area of selection, and of incompetent direction by unsatisfactory foremen are more likely to be felt.

In general, a corporation becomes successful because of the competitive superiority resulting from its lower cost methods of production. No matter what the product, this is a basic axiom of corporate progress. Therefore, production efficiency must be gauged otherwise than by mere volume of output.

The Institute, in examining a company's past record, seeks to determine:

1. What has been the growth in productivity per capita of production employees?
2. Are the company's production costs competitive with, similar to, or higher than those of the rest of the industry?
3. Do the production executives operate mainly on the floor or from behind their office desks?
4. What machinery exists for the handling of employee grievances?
5. What labor disputes have occurred in the company in recent years?
6. What percentage of the plants now in use were built for the specific operations now performed?
7. Is production [segregated so] that the profitability of each product is at all times apparent?
8. How important is the engineering division to the over-all operation?
9. What procedures are followed in job evaluation and merit rating?

Companies with outstanding production records include: Bethlehem Steel Corporation; Standard Oil Company (New Jersey); Interchemical Corporation; Fruehauf Trailer Company; A. O. Smith; Procter & Gamble Company; Olin Industries, Incorporated; E. I. Du Pont de Nemours and Company; Chrysler Corporation; Humble Oil and Refining Company; Standard Oil Company of California; Johnson and Johnson (N.J.); Borg-Warner Corporation; Signode Steel Strapping Company; Marathon Corporation; Scott Paper Company; and Dow Chemical Company.

Sales Analysis More expressions of concern are presently being made by managements over the inadequacy of their sales division than over any other single aspect of business administration. For more than a decade, the problem of competitive selling has affected but few companies for more than a few months at a time. Some companies, because production is on an allocation basis, are now channelling their sales activity into the building of good will, a unique variant of institutional advertising. This is especially true of the General Electric Company.

In the past, the contrary has been the case. The greatest single achievement of American business has been sales promotion, exceeding even our production efficiency to the need for which it has contributed markedly. The aggressive search for markets is an American characteristic, compared with the European attitude of waiting for the purchaser to materialize. In most European companies, sales executives are not regarded as top level officers. In a number of languages, indeed, there is no phrase meaning sales manager.

The Institute gives greater weight to the

sales effort than to any other single departmental activity of the corporation. The ultimate purpose of every corporation working for profit is to transform a stated sum of cash into a larger sum of cash. The incidental cost of labor, materials, and overhead are necessary expenses in this expanding transformation. They would be of no value whatever were the final product not translated into money through sales. Consequently, selling is the main single activity of any business organization. The vigor with which markets are exploited and the wisdom with which items are priced are therefore paramount evidences of managerial excellence.

In the modern world, sales are more closely related to advertising in all its forms than to direct salesman-customer contact. The supermarket has become the leading medium for distribution to the consumer. Major sales of appliances are now made through dealers who display the items in salesrooms and stores instead of by door-to-door selling as in the past. Because of this, the Institute pays increasing attention to the effectiveness of advertising policies pursued, since such policies both get the goods into the hands of dealers and out of their hands into those of the ultimate user.

The following information is sought when the Institute evaluates a sales organization:

1. How is the sales personnel selected?
2. What sales-training programs exist, and how do they operate?
3. What is the nature of the distributing organization?
4. What facilities are maintained for quick delivery and speedy repairs or replacement?
5. To what extent, and in what form, is market research conducted?
6. What routine reports are required from each segment of the sales division?
7. How are sales quotas established?
8. How does the company price its goods?
9. What is the company's advertising policy?
10. What structural link exists between advertising, selling and production?

Exceptional sales vigor is evident in the following companies: Grand Union Company; General Electric Company; Procter & Gamble Company; General Mills, Incorporated; Sun Oil Company; Eastman Kodak Company; Carrier Corporation; CIT Financial Corporation; Studebaker Corporation; International Business Machines Corporation; Marathon Corporation; Sylvania Electric Products, Incorporated; and Cluett Peabody & Company.

Executive Evaluation   Excellent management demands that men work together in harmony, each pursuing his own special task within the general effort, conscious that he is participating in a joint endeavor with men who command his respect. This unity of command is the central question to be sought in any management audit. It exists only where a qualified top executive is able to surround himself with other qualified men who will operate with him as co-executives and not as henchmen.

It is essential to learn whether the executive group actually operates as a team, and whether each man is already grooming one or more possible successors to take over his task when the day comes for his retirement. In no case should such possible successors be chosen from among an executive's relatives! Nepotism, indeed, is the antithesis of sound management. It renders a team spirit impossible of achievement and turns a public corporation into a private preserve. Many of our largest enterprises suffer in this respect.

Executive evaluation is by far the most important of the ten functional divisions of the management audit. The other nine categories, in fact, are no more than expressions of the thinking and actions of the executive group. They are examined separately in order that the effective results of the human qualities of the men in management may be measured. Analysis of the individual officers is therefore indispensable to management appraisal.

The attitude of the public towards the individual company is a prime expression of the state of public knowledge regarding the calibre of the men in top management. This means: The good will of the communities in which plants, offices, and sales organizations are located; the expressed confidence of stockholders in the ability and integrity of the officers; the quality of the mutual relations existing between the company and its suppliers and customers; the extent to which relations with the public authorities are honest, forthright and healthful. Good will is earned not by advertising but by the daily actions of men of the proper type conducting the affairs of responsible corporations.

Analysis of the executive personnel requires knowledge regarding:

1. What changes have occurred in executive personnel in recent years and why?
2. Is there, or has there ever been, nepotism in the organization?
3. Are there any rules, written or unwritten, which forbid employment of two or more

members of the same family in executive position?

4. In what way are executives selected?

5. What procedures are followed in training promising executives?

6. Have any training programs been established on the top management level? If so, what are they?

7. In what public activities do the top executives engage?

8. What is the company's attitude towards the importance of public relations regarding the entire executive group?

9. How do executives' salaries compare within the industry?

Companies with especially fine executive personnel characterized by unity of command, sound programs for the training of executives, and with a general spirit of competent harmony which has resulted in an over-all excellence of management performance, include: Procter and Gamble Company; Merck and Company; E. I. Du Pont de Nemours; General Foods Corporation; National Cash Regis-ter Company; Standard Oil Company (New Jersey); B. F. Goodrich Company; General Motors Corporation; Sears, Roebuck & Company; National Gypsum Company; Union Carbide and Carbon Corporation; Electric Boat Company; Gillette Safety Razor Company; J. C. Penny Company; and American Telephone and Telegraph Company.

SUMMARY AND CONCLUSIONS

The foregoing résumé has been presented in order to make both investors and executives more familiar with the Institute's thinking regarding a simplified approach to the Management Audit.

In order to justify the system of corporate enterprise, it must be demonstrable that it is increasing in efficiency, and it must offer sound evidence of its progressive improvement. Progressive development of the profession of management, based upon rational self-analysis, contributes to increasing the strength of private enterprise itself. The investor's greatest safety lies in the comforting knowledge of good management.

81

Outline for a Management Audit*

METROPOLITAN LIFE INSURANCE COMPANY

How productive is your management? Does it measure up to present day requirements?

Most progressive companies make it a point to audit their accounts at least once a year in order to establish the adequacy and accuracy of such accounts and to reveal fiscal weaknesses that may need correction. The periodic inventorying and appraising of physical assets is also an accepted practice.

There is need for the same sort of stock-taking as applied to the management of business. This can be accomplished through the medium of a management audit. Through this device, a business executive undertakes, in effect, to back off and survey his company critically and objectively. A comprehensive management check-list is helpful in this connection.

PROBLEMS OF THE SMALL ORGANIZATION

The smaller organization has essentially the same management problems as a large concern. Naturally, the emphasis on specific problems is different in the small company because of the

* Taken from *Outline for a Management Audit*, A Report for Metropolitan Group Policyholders, Metropolitan Life Insurance Company, New York, 1947.

close personal contact between management and employees and because the executive must necessarily be a jack of all trades. However, these differences are primarily superficial and they should not blind the small company's management to the real nature of their job.

The check list† shown in this report raises a wide variety of questions on basic management problems. The importance of each problem will naturally vary with the individual concern, depending on its size or its field of operations. Some of the questions are more important to large organizations than to small ones, and vice versa. However, all companies, irrespective of their size or industry, will find in these questions an outline of their basic management problems.

To use the check list effectively, attention should be paid to the substance rather than to the exact wording of each question, because the wording may seem to be directed at the problems of the large company. Conversely, the wording will be pointed toward the small company if the problem involved is of greater importance to it.

ORGANIZATION

1. Is your organization set up in accordance with a definite plan, or has it developed in a "hit-or-miss" fashion with little or no recognition of basic functions or logical groupings of activities?

   (a) Have you conducted organization surveys to correct wartime distortions or to adjust to postwar changes in the volume or nature of operations?

2. Are the functions and responsibilities clearly defined for each department and division of your business and for individual executives?

   (a) Are lines of authority clear-cut and direct?

   (b) Does every individual know to whom he reports and who reports to him?

3. Has the organization been put on paper in the form of carefully prepared organization charts or written outlines of duties?

   (a) Is there some provision for keeping these up to date?

4. Has your policy of centralizing the ad-

† The original outline had an interesting check list of questions in the functional fields of finance, procurement, inventories, traffic and transportation, insurance, office management, business research, personnel management, production management, marketing management, and public relations.—Editors

ministration of various functions or activities been such as to get the maximum benefits from the specialization of personnel—at the same time, have you had in mind the possible value of some decentralization of management as a means of executive development and of encouraging initiative?

5. Do you follow the principle of an understudy for every executive position to provide for contingencies and to insure continuity?

   (a) Have you some means of locating and developing potential executive ability?

   (b) Have you some plan for rewarding executives in proportion to results secured?

6. Do you employ committees or some other practical means of coordinating all the different phases or activities of your company so that the organization operates as a team and not as a collection of individuals and independent departments or divisions?

7. Are you making the best use of the "line and staff" organization plan as a means of providing specialized staff assistance at various organization levels?

   (a) Are line and staff relationships and authorities clearly established?

EXECUTIVE CONTROL

1. Are you making the most effective use of control techniques, i.e., the establishment of practical standards or yardsticks, the measurement and reporting of performance, and the initiation of corrective action?

   (a) Does your control procedure serve to spotlight conditions requiring action in time for such action to be taken?

2. Is your accounting system designed to furnish significant control information both by functions and by departments?

3. Do you get current and reliable information on the costs of individual products or services, processes, customers, and localities?

4. Do you operate under a budget?

   (a) Are budget allowances and classifications designed to reflect individual executive responsibilities? Is there provision for frequent comparison of budgeted with actual performance?

5. Have you taken steps to develop or to reinstill a spirit of cost consciousness throughout your organization so that each action will be weighed in terms of the costs involved?

(a) Do you hold regular cost analysis meetings of operating executives and supervisors for this purpose?

6. Have you examined and appraised all your control reports and records from the standpoints of (a) the value, adequacy, and timeliness of the information furnished; (b) economy of executive time; (c) cost of preparation? Do you check this at least once a year?

(a) Do you require that those submitting reports include a brief interpretation of the significant points revealed?

7. Is there provision for acquainting executive and supervisory personnel with the company's basic policies?

82

How to Evaluate a Firm*

ROBERT B. BUCHELE

The sharp drops in earnings and even losses recently suffered by many so-called "growth" companies, whose stocks had been bid so high, have cast doubts upon the adequacy of the established methods which are used by investment specialists to evaluate companies.

Equally dramatic but less evident have been the serious declines of numerous companies shortly after having been rated as "excellently managed" by the best known of the evaluation systems using a list of factors covering numerous aspects of corporate management.

What has happened to render these evaluation systems so inadequate? What lessons can be learned by persons whose work requires them to do overall evaluations of companies—investors, acquisition specialists, consultants, long-range planners, and chief executives? Finally, what are the requirements for a system for evaluating firms that will function reliably under today's conditions?

After all, the decline of even blue chip companies is not a new phenomenon. To quote

* Reprinted by permission of the California Management Review, vol. 5, no. 1, pp. 5–16, Fall, 1962. Mr. Buchele is now lecturer at the University of Hawaii.

Author's note: The author, while retaining full responsibility for the content of this article, wishes to express thanks to Drs. Harold D. Koontz, William B. Wolf, J. F. Weston, and Mr. Ora C. Roehl for suggestions that have been most helpful. R. B. B.

from an unpublished paper recently presented by Ora C. Roehl before a management conference at UCLA:

The Brookings Institution sometime ago made a study of the 100 top businesses in the USA in the early 1900's, and they found that after 40 years only 36 were still among the leaders.

We all look at the Dow-Jones Industrial Average practically every day and we know the companies that are a part of the Average today —from Allied Chemical, Aluminum Company of America, and American Can to U. S. Steel, Westinghouse, and Woolworth. But, as we go back in time a bit, we find names that once were important enough to be a part of the Average and which we have heard of, such as Hudson Motors, Famous Players-Lasky, and Baldwin Locomotive. It is not long, however, before we run into one-time business leaders whose names are strange to us, such as Central Leather, U. S. Cordage Company, Pacific Mail, American Cotton Oil Company, and one with a nostalgic sort of name, The Distilling and Cattle Feeding Company.[1]

What is new, however, is the current pace of such events. Stemming in part from the rise of industrial research expenditures from less than $200 million in 1930 to an estimated $12.4 billion in 1960,[2] the pace of industrial change has been accelerating for many years.

Outline for Evaluation of a Firm

I. PRODUCT LINES AND BASIC
COMPETITIVE POSITION

A. PAST

What strengths and weakness in products (or services) have been dominant in this firm's history—design features, quality-reliability, prices, patents, proprietary position?

B. PRESENT

What share of its market(s) does the firm now hold, and how firmly? Is this share diversified or concentrated as to number of customers? In what phases of their life cycles are the present chief products and what is happening to prices and margins? How do customers and potential customers regard this firm's products? Are the various product lines compatible marketing-wise, engineering-wise, manufacturing-wise? If not, is each product line substantial enough to stand on its own feet?

C. FUTURE

Is the market(s) as a whole expanding or contracting, and at what rate? What is the trend in this firm's share of the market(s)? What competitive trends are developing in numbers of competitors, technology, marketing, pricing? What is its vulnerability to business cycle (or defense spending) changes? Is management capable of effectively integrating market research, R & D, and market development into a development program for a new product or products?

II. R & D AND OPERATING DEPARTMENTS

A. R & D AND ENGINEERING

What is the nature and the depth of its R & D capability? Of engineering capability? What are engineering's main strengths and weaknesses re creativity, quality-reliability, simplicity? Is the R & D effort based on needs defined by market research, and is it an integral part of an effective new product development program? Are R & D efforts well planned, directed, and controlled? What return have R & D dollars paid in profitable new products? Have enough new products been produced? Have schedules been met?

B. MARKETING

Nature of the Marketing Capability—What channels of distribution are used? How much of the total marketing job (research, sales, service, advertising and promotion) is covered? Is this capability correctly tailored to match the nature and diversity of the firm's product lines? Is there a capability for exploiting new products and developing new markets? Quality of the marketing capability

—Is market research capable of providing the factual basis that will keep the firm, especially its new product development and R & D programs, truly customer-oriented? Is there a capability for doing broad economic studies and studies of particular industries that will help management set sound growth and/or diversification strategies?

C. MANUFACTURING

What is the nature of the manufacturing processes, the facilities and the skills—are they appropriate to today's competition? How flexible are they—will they be, or can they be made, appropriate to tomorrow's competition? What is the quality of the manufacturing management in terms of planning and controlling work schedule-wise, cost-wise, and quality-wise? Is there evidence of an industrial engineering capability that steadily improves products and methods? Does manufacturing management effectively perform its part of the process of achieving new products?

D. SUMMARY ON R & D AND
OPERATING DEPARTMENTS

Is this a complete, integrated, balanced operation; or have certain strong personalities emphasized some functions and neglected others? What is the quality of performance of key R & D and operating executives; do they understand the fundamental processes of management, namely planning, controlling organizing, staffing and directing? Are plans and controls in each department inadequate, adequate or overdeveloped into a "paperwork mill?" Is there throughout the departments a habit of steady progress in reducing overhead, lowering breakeven points and improving quality? Are all departments future-minded? Do they cooperate effectively in developing worthy new products geared to meet the customer's future needs?

III. FINANCIAL ANALYSIS AND
FINANCIAL MANAGEMENT

A. FINANCIAL ANALYSIS

What main strengths and weaknesses of the firm emerge from analysis of the trends in the traditional financial data: earnings ratios (to sales, to tangible net worth, to working capital) and earnings-per-share; debt ratios (current and acid tests, to tangible net worth, to working capital, to inventory); inventory turnover; cash flow, and the capitalization structure? What do the trends in the basic financial facts indicate as to the firm's prospects for growth in sales volume and rate of

Outline (Continued)

earnings? Does "quality of earnings" warrant compounding of the earnings rate?

B. FINANCIAL MANAGEMENT

What is the quality of financial management? Is there a sound program for steadily increasing return on investment? Do the long-range financial plans indicate that management understands the cost of capital and how to make money work hard? Have balance sheets and operating statements been realistically projected for a number of years into the future? Is there careful cash planning and strong controls that help the operating departments lower breakeven points? Are capital expenditures inadequate or excessive with respect to insuring future operating efficiency? Are capital investment decisions based on thorough calculations? Does management have the respect of the financial community? Is the firm knowledgeable and aggressive in tax administration?

IV. TOP MANAGEMENT

A. IDENTIFICATION OF TOP MANAGEMENT AND ITS RECORD

What person or group constitutes top management? Has present top management been responsible for profit-and-loss results of the past few years?

B. TOP MANAGEMENT AND THE FUTURE

What are top management's chief characteristics? How adequate or inadequate is this type of management for coping with the challenges of the future? Will the present type and quality of top management continue? Will it deteriorate, will it improve, or will it change its basic character?

C. BOARD OF DIRECTORS

What influence and/or control does the Board of Directors exercise? What are the capabilities of its members? What are their motivations?

V. SUMMARY AND EVALUATION STRATEGY

What other factors can assume major importance in this particular situation? (Use a check list.) Of all the factors studied, which if any, is overriding in this particular situation? Which factors are of major importance by virtue of the fact that they govern other factors? What are the basic facts-of-life about the economics and competition of this industry now and over the next decade? In view of this firm's particular strengths and weaknesses, what are the odds that it will succeed, and at what level of success, in this industry? What are the prospects of its succeeding by diversifying out of its industry?

It is now so rapid that firms can rise or fall more quickly than ever before.

Sophisticated technologies are spreading to many industries; in addition, as we shall see in this article, various management techniques contribute to the quickening pace of change. In consequence, the rapid rate of change now affects a great many American firms rather than just that minority known as "growth" companies.

PRESENT EVALUATION METHODS

Financial Analysis This method typically consists of studying a "spread" of profit and loss figures, operating statements and balance sheet ratios for the past five or ten years. The underlying assumption is that the future performance of a company can be reliably projected from trends in these data. The reasoning is that these data represent the "proof of the pudding." If they're sound, the company as a whole, particularly its top management, must be sound, for a competent top management will keep a firm healthy.

Through the years this method has worked well because the basic assumption has been reasonably valid. Despite the fact that some blue chip companies have failed, it is still reasonably valid for the large firms who are thoroughly entrenched in their markets and who make substantial investments in executive development, in market development, and in any technology that promises to threaten one of their market positions.

However, the assumption is becoming less safe, especially in connection with medium-sized and small firms, as the pace of industrial change steadily accelerates. Thus, a firm whose financial record is unimpressive may be on the verge of a technological breakthrough that will send its profits rocketing ahead: conversely, a company that looks good in financial analyses may be doomed because it is being bypassed technologically or marketing-wise or because rigor mortis has taken over the executive offices.

In practice the financial analysis method is often supplemented by market research in the form of interviews with leading customers, by interviews with the firm's top executives, and by consultation with scientists capable of evaluating technological capabilities and trends. While these supplementary activities help, financial analysis still is neither adequately comprehensive nor adequately oriented to the future.

Thus, this type of market research can yield some insights into the effectiveness of past and present performance but is too superficial to tell much about the future. The interviews with top executives can be more misleading than informative simply because they are conducted by financial people inexperienced in management, marketing, or technology.[3] The use of scientists is a commendable step forward. However, it provides help in only one and possibly two of the many areas essential to a thorough evaluation.

Key Factor Ratings   Systems more comprehensive than the financial analysis method have been developed, mainly by consultants seeking to understand firms' overall strengths and weaknesses in order to be able to prescribe for them. Such systems typically involve ratings based on a series of key factors underlying the financial factors themselves. Little has been published about these systems because the consulting firms regard them as proprietary secrets. One system that has been published and, therefore, is well known is that developed by the American Institute of Management.[4] That this system is not adequately future-oriented is clearly proved by the fact that numerous companies have encountered deep trouble shortly after being rated "excellently managed" by the AIM.[5]

Professor Erwin Schell a decade ago set forth a comprehensive system with some future-oriented elements; however, he recently stated that his system should be revised to give greater emphasis to the future via more attention to the R & D function.[6]

As indicated in the Outline for evaluation which accompanies this article, the evaluation of a firm, as it is at present and as it will be in the future, can be organized around a series of penetrating questions. Thorough study of the areas covered by these questions will yield a picture, oriented to the future, of the strengths and weaknesses of the firm under consideration and a reliable indication of its chances for success in the future.

There are, as the outline shows, four vital areas in a firm about which you should ask questions. They are: its product lines and basic competitive position; its R & D and operating departments; its financial position as revealed by analysis of the traditional financial data plus an estimate of the quality of its financial management; its top management with emphasis not only upon its past record, but also on its adequacy to cope with the future.

When these data have been assembled and summarized, you are in a position to evaluate both the present situation and potential of the firm under study as an investment possibility or as a management problem.

The rest of this article will be devoted to a discussion of these factors one by one. First we shall pose the questions contained in the outline; then we shall discuss the techniques professional analysts use for obtaining such data and determining what it means.

PRODUCT LINES AND COMPETITION

The first things to investigate are a firm's product lines and its basic competitive position. This involves a study of its past, present, and future. Here are the lines your inquiry should take:

Past. What strengths and weaknesses in products (or services) have been dominant in this firm's history—design features, quality-reliability, prices, patents, proprietary position?

Present. What share of its market(s) does the firm now hold, and how firmly? Is this share diversified or concentrated as to number of customers? In what phases of their life cycles are the present chief products and what is happening to prices and margins? How do customers and potential customers regard this firm's products? Are the various product lines compatible marketing-wise, engineering-wise, manufacturing-wise? If not, is each product line substantial enough to stand on its own feet?

Future. Is the market(s) as a whole expanding or contracting, and at what rate? What is the trend in this firm's share of the market(s)? What competitive trends are developing in numbers of competitors, technology, marketing, pricing?

What is the vulnerability to business cycle (or defense spending) changes?

Is there the capability effectively to integrate market research, R & D and market development into a new products development program?

The past-present-future structure furnishes the material needed to determine whether the firm has presently or in-the-pipeline the type of products needed for success in the future.

A key technique here is to determine how much quantitative information the company executives have and, then, to spot-check the quality of that information by the evaluator's own research. The firm that has sound, pertinent market data usually has achieved the first step to success—a clear definition of the job to be done. Conversely, the firm that has only sparse, out-of-date, out-of-focus data and relies heavily on executives' opinions is usually a poor bet for the future. Unsupported opinions, no matter how strongly held or ably stated, can be misleading. Although top management often must rely on such opinions, failure to secure the data that are available is a serious weakness.

LIFE CYCLE CURVES
FOR PRODUCTS MADE

Another device for focusing on the basic facts of life about a product line is the building of S, or life cycle curves. These curves plot sales and/or margins for a product against time. For a given firm such plots picture clearly the life expectancy of products. Composite plots can show the trends in life expectancies. Also, they can indicate developing gaps. When past data are joined to carefully projected estimates of the future, dangerous situations can be revealed. Thus, the firm that is currently highly profitable but has not provided for the future will show virtually all of its products at or near the period of peak profitability.[7]

The question of compatibility of product lines may seem too elementary for mention; however, major mistakes are made in this area, especially by firms headed by scientists. Seeing their own skill as the key one in business, scientists tend to underestimate the importance and difficulty of other management activities. In consequence, they often develop or acquire products that present marketing problems far beyond the financial or managerial capability of the firm.

One science-based and scientist-led company, after an acquisition binge, was attempting to market ten distinct product lines through one centralized marketing organization, all with a total of less than $18 million annual volume. None of the products could individually support a top-flight marketing organization; yet no two of them could be effectively marketed through the same people. The result was disaster.

Integration of market research, R & D and market development into an effective new product development program is one of the newer and more difficult arts of management. Such integration, which is the heart of profit planning, apparently accounted for much of the success of the Bell and Howell Company during the decade of the '50's.[8]

In vivid contrast to the coordinated profit planning of Bell and Howell, is the case of the small glamor firm that "went public" in early 1961 for $1,000,000 and has since seen the price of its stock triple. The scientist-president and his associates have developed a dazzling array of technically ingenious new products; however, they have little data on the market for the products and have not yet started to build an organization for distributing and selling them.

R & D AND OPERATING DEPARTMENTS

Having probed a firm's product lines and competitive position, the second vital area for investigation is its R & D, marketing, and operating divisions. Good questions to guide your analysis are:

R & D and Engineering. What is the nature and the depth of the R & D capability? Of the engineering capability? What are the main strengths and weaknesses re creativity, quality-reliability, simplicity?

Is the R & D effort based on needs defined by market research, and is it an integral part of an effective new product development program? Are R & D efforts well planned, directed and controlled? What return have R & D dollars paid in profitable new products? Have enough new products been produced, and have schedules been met?

A truly basic change in American industry since the start of World War II has been that thousands of companies have R & D programs whereas earlier only a handful of firms did so. The figures cited earlier concerning the growth of R & D expenditures indicate that sophisticated technologies and rapidly changing products and markets characterize not only electronics and defense industries but also such diverse fields as food processing, photography, communications, pharmaceuticals, metallurgy, plastics, and equipments used in industrial automation processes. The consequence is that most firms beyond the "small business" category must have R & D programs; increasingly a firm must take on the characteristics of a "growth" firm in order to survive.

How to Evaluate a Firm's R & D   One of the newest of management activities, R & D management, is one of the hardest to evaluate. For lack of better technique, the vogue has been to assume that the volume of dollars spent on R & D is commensurate with results achieved. However, we now know that there has been great waste, also, there has been deception by firms "padding" their reported R & D expenditures to give the impression of being more R & D oriented than they really are.

A growing literature reports useful techniques for conceiving, planning, controlling and directing R & D programs and for evaluating R & D output.[9] The truth is being established that R & D management is a capability different from and much rarer than the capability of performing straight engineering or scientific work.

The first task of the evaluator is to determine whether the selection of R & D programs is integrated with a sound overall long-range plan and is based on market research findings. The next task is to compare the nature and depth of the R & D capability with the job to be done. Can it cope with the firm's future needs in regard to maintaining and improving market position by an integrated new products program? The third job is to compare cost and output. Techniques for evaluating output include assessing the quantity and quality of patents produced, measurement of the contribution of R & D to increased (or maintained) sales volume and profit margins, and measurement of the contribution to lowered break-even points via improved materials and methods.

Are Its Innovations Well-timed? An evaluator needs to understand the time cycle required for research, development and introduction to application; also, he must be able to relate this understanding to the basic facts about the market being served. Such an evaluator can tell when a firm is proceeding in the vanguard of the competition or when it is jumping on a bandwagon too late—as so many electronics firms did with respect to the transistor bandwagon.

MARKETING

Closely allied with R & D and product innovation are the marketing skills of the firm under analysis. Strengths and weaknesses in this area can be uncovered by digging into the following topics.

Nature of the Marketing Capability. What channels of distribtution are used? How much of the total marketing job (research, sales, service, advertising, and promotion) is covered? Is this capability correctly tailored to match the nature and diversity of the firm's product lines?

Is there a capability for exploiting new products and for developing new markets?

Quality of the Marketing Capability. Is market research capable of providing the factual basis that will keep the firm, especially its new product development and R & D programs, truly customer-oriented? Is there a capability for doing broad economic studies and studies of particular industries that will help management set sound growth and/or diversification strategies?

The evaluator will already have learned much about market research capability in answering the product line questions posed earlier in this article. There it was indicated that the firm that knows the facts about trends in its market and technologies is well on the way to success in the future. This clearly places great responsibility on market research, a field still neglected or abused by many science-based firms, especially those in defense work.

To cope adequately with the challenges of the future requires more than market research in the old narrow concept; rather, it requires an ability at economic analysis of entire industries. Survival and growth in a rapidly changing economy sometimes demands more than a stream of new products; often it requires diversification into substantially different fields that offer greater growth and better profits for a given time period.

Diversification strategy is another subject that is currently being developed.[10] The aircraft industry today presents a case study in which certain firms are prospering because ten years ago they started to diversify while other firms are suffering badly because they failed to do so.

The accelerating rate of change in industry is a process that feeds on itself. Thus, sophisticated methods of market research and planning not only help a firm cope with rapid change but also foster more rapid change.

The evaluator must know enough about quantitative methods of research to be able to distinguish between valid use and abuse of market research. If not so equipped, he is at the mercy of the super-salesman with a smattering of scientific lore who can spin great tales about how a given firm has made a technological breakthrough that soon will have tremendous impact upon the market.

The evaluator must also be able to distinguish between creative market research and pedestrian fact-gathering that plods along a year too late to help management conquer the future. Only when market research secures fresh quantitative data on future markets can management integrate market development with product development.

MANUFACTURING

Next area to be studied is production. Questions to be asked include:

Manufacturing. What is the nature of the manufacturing processes, the facilities and the skills—are they appropriate to today's competition? How flexible are they—will they be or can they be made appropriate to tomorrow's competition?

What is the quality of the manufacturing management in terms of planning and controlling work schedule-wise, cost-wise, and quality-wise? Is there evidence of an industrial engineering capability that steadily improves products and methods? Does manufacturing management effectively perform its part of the process of achieving new products?

The answers to these questions call mainly for conventional type analysis which need not be commented upon here. This is not to say that there are not now, as always, new and better techniques being developed in the manufacturing field. Certainly an alert manufacturing management will use such progressive techniques as "value engineering" to simplify product designs and, thus, reduce costs; and it will use electronic data processing and other modern industrial engineering methods of controlling the work pace and other cost elements.

But, basically, manufacturing management still is, and long has been, evaluated on the basis of performance schedule-wise, cost- and quality-wise, and techniques for such evaluations are among the oldest and best-developed tools of management consultants and others concerned with industrial engineering.

The quickening pace of technological change does, however, require special attention to the ability of the engineering and manufacturing departments to cooperate effectively in bringing new products into production and in utilizing new processes. Also, it requires special caution with respect to firms with heavy investments in inflexible capital equipment because such investments might be susceptible to almost sudden obsolescence.

SUMMARY ON R & D AND OPERATIONS

To make the most of information acquired about a firm's operating departments and R & D, it is well at this point to pull all this sometimes diffuse information together into a sight summary that pulls the whole picture of operations into focus. Questions running along lines such as these help clarify it.

The Overall Picture. Is this a complete, integrated, balanced operation; or have certain strong personalities emphasized some functions and neglected others?

What is the quality of performance of key R & D and operating executives; do they understand the fundamental processes of management, namely planning, controlling, organizing, staffing, and directing? Are plans and controls in each department inadequate, adequate, or over-developed into a "paperwork mill"?

Is there throughout the departments a habit of steady progress in reducing overhead, lowering breakeven points and improving quality?

Are all departments future-minded; do they cooperate effectively in developing worthy new products geared to meet the customer's future needs?

Finance is the third area of a corporation which should be analyzed carefully in appraising its present and future development. In this connection, both the men handling a company's finances and the figures on the balance sheet should be studied. Beginning inquiries could be:

Financial Analysis. What main strength and weaknesses of the firm emerge from analysis of the trends in the traditional financial data: earnings ratios (to sales, to tangible net worth, to working capital) and earnings-per-share; debt ratios (current and acid tests, to tangible net worth, to working capital, to inventory); inventory turnover; cash flow; and the capitalization structure?

What do the trends in the basic financial facts indicate as to the firm's prospects for growth in sales volume and rate of earnings? Does "quality of earnings" warrant compounding of the earnings rate?

Although this article has already pointed out limitations of financial analysis standing alone as a method of evaluating firms, its importance as one of the key elements of an evaluation should never be overlooked. Because financial analysis has been so important for so long, its techniques have been well developed. Therefore, it is not necessary to discuss them here.

One concept concerning "growth" companies, however, does require comment. The technique of evaluating a growth firm on the basis of an assumption that it will "plow back" its earnings and thereby achieve a compounded rate of increase in earnings per share is of questionable validity. By compounding earnings on a straight-line (or uninterrupted) basis, financial analysts arrive at estimates of future earnings that justify stock prices from 40 to 100 times present earnings per share.

NO FIRM PROGRESSES EVENLY

The concept of straight-line progress just doesn't square with the facts of life as observed by students of management. Especially in small and medium-sized companies, progress typically occurs in a saw-tooth, rather than a straight-line pattern. This phenomenon is based partly on the existence of business cycles and partly on the fact the firms are affected by the strengths and limitations of humans in key positions. There are stages in which the typical growing firm requires managerial talents greater than—or, possibly, only different from—those talents essential to its start.

At these critical periods the earnings per share may slow down or even turn into losses. Such events devastate the compounding process; if one compounds a more realistic 5–10 percent rate of growth per year, the result is far less sensational than is secured by compounding a 20–25 percent rate. It is exceedingly rare that a firm achieves the higher percentages for any sustained period; Litton Industries and IBM appear to be the exceptions that prove the rule. The reference to quality of earnings is meant to shed light on the sustainability of the rate of improvements in earnings. Here the evaluator must distinguish between continuous, sustainable improvement and isolated events (such as a single acquisition or securing an especially favorable contract) or cyclical events (a period of high profitability certain to be followed by a corresponding low).

THE MONEY MEN

Figures alone don't tell the complete financial story of a firm. Its money management must be rated and this involves an evaluation of both policies and men, not only those in the financial division but also the men in charge of planning and top management. You need to know their attitudes about

Financial Management. Is there a sound program for steadily increasing return on investment? Do the long-range financial plans indicate that management understands the costs of capital and how to make money work hard? Have balance sheets and operating statements been realistically projected for a number of years into the future?

Is there careful cash planning and strong

controls that help the operating departments lower breakeven points? Are capital expenditures inadequate, adequate, or excessive with respect to insuring future operating efficiency? Are capital investment decisions based on thorough calculations?

Does management have the respect of the financial community?

Is the firm knowedgeable and aggressive in tax administration?

While many financial departments function only as record-keepers and rules-enforcers, some play a truly creative role. Financial management can today contribute as much or more to improvement in earnings per share as can any other part of management.[11] In fact, in recent years bold use of the newer forms of financing have in many cases contributed as much to the rapid rise of companies as have technological innovations. And, alas, bold but unwise financing has ruined many a promising young company.

The questions here are designed to help the evaluator discover whether or not the financial people are vigorously contributing in a number of ways to the steady improvement of earnings currently and in the long run.

RATING TOP MANAGEMENT

All study of management invariably and understandably leads to a searching examination of the top management men. Here there are pitfalls for the unwary. The analyst must first identify the true top management before he can examine their performance record. Things, in terms of who actually runs the show, are not always what they seem on the organization chart. So key topics are:

Top Management and Its Record. What person or group constitutes top management? Has present top management been responsible for profit-and-loss results of the past few years?

The problem is to determine the individual or group of individuals who contribute directly and regularly to those decisions that shape the basic nature of this business and significantly affect profit and loss results. This usually cannot be determined reliably by direct questions to persons in key positions; few men are objective about themselves on these matters.

Watch Them Work   Rare is the top executive who will admit that he is a one-man rule type; rare is the vice-president or department head who will admit that he is a highly-paid errand boy. Accordingly, direct observation of management at work is needed. Some additional information can also be gained through examination of minutes of meetings and files of memos.

After top management has been identified, the evaluator must ask whether this management has had time to prove itself one way or the other. The criterion is whether or not major decisions and programs put forth by this top management have come to fruition. It is not simply a matter of looking at profit and loss figures for a few years. We all know that in certain situations factors other than top management capability (for example, an inherited product line that is unusually strong) can produce good profits for a number of years.

Next comes consideration of:

Top Management and the Future. What are top management's chief characteristics? How adequate or inadequate is this type of management for coping with the challenges of the future?

Will the present type and quality of top management continue, or will it deteriorate, will it improve, or will it change its basic character?

We must ask how and why top management has achieved the results that it has achieved so that we can judge how adequate it will be for meeting tomorrow's challenges. Exploring the how and why gets the evaluator into the subject of types of management and their effects on profitability—the thorniest area of contemporary management theory. Over the past twenty years a tremendous literature has accumulated on such subjects as participative leadership, autocratic vs. bureaucratic vs. democratic types of management, and related subjects.

Some writers have claimed or implied great virtues for participative-democratic methods; others have attacked such methods as wasteful and ineffective, wholly inappropriate in industrial life and have advocated "benevolent autocracy." The confusion recently reached a zenith with the almost simultaneous publication of conflicting views by eminent professors from the same university.[12]

Industrial psychologists and sociologists have provided valuable insights into management practices and their effects upon profitability. While a skilled social scientist could contribute importantly to the evaluation of a firm's top management, there is a more direct way of evaluating top management's capability for coping with future challenges.

The direct method is to determine how top management has in the past coped with the future. This technique is based on the idea that management is essentially the process of planning to achieve certain goals and, then, controlling activities so that the goals are actually attained. It is in the processes of planning and controlling that top management does its major decision-making. Since planning and controlling are the heart of the managerial process, it is in these activities that top management most fully reveals its vital characteristics.

The evaluator can probe deeply into the content of the firm's past and current long-range and short-range plans, into the methods by which the plans are formulated, and into the controls used to bring those plans to fruition. This technique gets away, to a considerable extent, from subjective judgments; it deals with such facts as what was planned, how it was planned and what actually happened.

Fortunately these activities can be studied without great difficulty and by persons who do not have formal training in the behavioral sciences. A simple yet highly informative procedure is to compare succeeding sets of old long-range plans with one another, with present plans and with actual events.

Do Their Plans Work?   First, a firm that is effectively tomorrow-minded will have long-range plans. These may not be neatly bound in a cover labeled "long-range plans"; however, they will exist either in minutes of meetings, in memos, in reports to stockholders or in other places. Second, the old plans will contain evidence as to whether top management truly has studied the future to determine and anticipate the nature of the opportunities and threats that will inevitably arise.

Third, the old plans will contain evidence of the nature and quality of the solutions developed for meeting the challenges of the future— how creative, aggressive and realistic management has been in initiative matters such as selecting R & D programs, establishing diversification strategy and program, developing new markets, planning the organizational changes needed to keep fit for new tasks, and effectively utilizing advanced techniques (e.g., operations research, automation, etc.) when feasible.

Special attention to initiative matters will indicate whether or not top management is creative and aggressive enough to keep up with an accelerating rate of change.

Fourth, comparison of succeeding sets of plans will indicate whether consistent progress has been made or top management is recklessly aggressive in that it undertakes unrealistic, ill-conceived, unachievable plans.

The same technique can be applied to short-range plans such as annual budgets, sales forecasts and special developmental programs of many types. This study will indicate whether or not forecasts are typically accurate, whether or not plans typically are successfully completed, whether or not new products are developed on schedule, and whether or not they are supported by marketing, finance, and management programs ready to go at the right time. Again, as in the case of long-range plans, the inquiry will reveal whether decision-making is mature or immature. Has management made profitability a habit, or just a subject of wishful thinking?

A management that knows how to bring plans to fruition builds into every plan a set of controls designed to give early warning of problems and an indication that corrective action is needed. Examination of the controls and the ways in which they are used will indicate whether or not top management is on top of its problems or vice versa.

Who Makes the Plans?   Investigation of the methods by which plans are formulated and control is exercised will reveal a great deal about whether top management is autocratic, bureaucratic or democratic. This inquiry holds more than academic interest; the extent to which lower levels of management contribute to the formulation of plans and the extent to which they are held accountable for results will tell much about the firm's down-the-line strength.

Executive Turnover   Also, these factors are particularly important indicators of whether top management will retain its vigor will improve or will deteriorate. Thus, they indicate whether or not top management is making sincere efforts to recruit and develop middle management that will become a new and better generation of top management. Other insights into whether management is bringing in too little or too much new blood can be gained by examining age patterns and statistics on turnover in executive ranks, by reviewing formal executive development efforts and by interviews with some of the men.

Yardstick to Gauge Growth Factors   In summary, the technique of probing deeply into the firm's actual plans and controls and methods of planning and control can yield abundant evidence to indicate whether or not top management has the characteristics of a growth firm. These characteristics have been set forth in a major study by Stanford Research Institute of the factors that usually distinguish growth from nongrowth firms. They are:

- Affinity for growth fields.
- Organized programs to seek and promote new opportunities.
- Proven competitive abilities in present lines of business.
- Courageous and energetic managements, willing to make carefully calculated risks.
- Luck.

Incidentally, this study found that high growth companies had twice the earning power of low growth companies, while maintaining four times the growth rate.[13]

THE BOARD OF DIRECTORS

Rounding out the top management of every corporation is an enigmatic, unpublicized group of men about whom a competent analyst should be most curious. They are the Board of Directors. Questions such as these should be asked about them: What influence and/or control does the Board of Directors exercise? What are the capabilities of its members? What are their motivations?

In the author's experience one of the most frequent and serious errors of small and medium-sized firms is failure to have and use effectively a strong Board of Directors. Too often the entrepreneurial types who start firms disdain help until they are in deep trouble.

Especially in firms headed by a scientist or a super-salesman, a strong and active Board can be invaluable in helping make up for the top executives' lack of rounded managerial training and experience. Except in a few unusual situations, a Board must be an "outside," or nonemployee, Board to be strong.

Dummies or Policy Makers   To be active and helpful, an "outside" Board must have some motivation, either financial or the psychic motivation involved in being confronted with real problems and being able to contribute to their solution. Examination of files and minutes of Board meetings will reveal whether or not there is a good flow of information to the outside directors and a contribution by them to the solution of significant problems.

ADDING UP THE FACTS

With all the data in about the four vital areas of a firm, products and competition, operations and R & D, finance, and top management, the analyst ends his task by posing one more set of questions which might be called Summary and Evaluation Strategy. They should run something like this:

What other factors (use a checklist)[14] can assume major importance in this particular situation?

Of all the factors studied, which, if any, is overriding in this particular situation? Which factors are of major importance by virtue of the fact that they govern other factors?

What are the basic facts of life about the economics and competition of this industry now and over the next decade? In view of this firm's particular strengths and weaknesses, what are the odds that it will succeed and at what level of success, in this industry? What are the prospects of its succeeding by diversifying out of its industry?

DETERMINING OTHER VITAL FACTORS

There is a purpose behind every evaluation study. That purpose or the particular nature of the firm and its industry might place importance upon any of an almost infinite number of factors. Accordingly, the evaluator must thoughtfully run through a checklist containing such considerations as: personnel management practices (e.g., labor relations, profit-sharing, compensation levels), valuation questions (e.g., valuation of fixed or real assets or inventory or unique assets), geographical location as related to labor markets, taxes, cost of distribution, seasonality factors, in-process or impending litigation, or any matter footnoted in the financial reports so that the auditing firm is, in effect, warning of an unusual circumstance.

The purpose of a particular evaluation study often will determine which factor, if any, is overriding. Logically, the quality of top management should usually be the overriding factor. By definition a highly competent top management group can solve the other problems such as securing competent scientists and other personnel, developing new products, getting financing, etc. However, there may be an investment or acquisition situation in which the product line, for example, is the overriding factor because it is so obsolete that even the finest management could not effect a recovery within existing time and financial parameters.

Matching Buyer and Acquisition   If the evaluation is being done to help decide the advisability of an acquisition, many additional considerations come into play. The problem is one of matching the acquiring and acquired

firms; many firms have acquired grief rather than growth because they have neglected this point. At one extreme, acquisition of one healthy company by another may be unwise because the two are so different that the acquirer may mismanage the acquired company. At the other extreme, it may be wise for one unhealthy company to acquire another unhealthy one if the strengths of one remedy the weaknesses of the other, and vice versa.

The Character of the Company   The acquirer must precisely define his objectives in acquiring. Also, he must carefully consider the "character," or "climate," of the other firm in relation to his own. The subject of "company character" has not been well developed in management practice or literature.[15] Nevertheless, a consideration of the "character" of the two companies is highly relevant, and the outline presented in this article will help the evaluator consider some of the more obvious elements of "company character" such as the nature of its engineering and manufacturing skills, the type of distribution channels and marketing skills required, the type of managerial leadership practiced and top management's aggressiveness and the quality of its decisions in initiative matters.

In sum, the evaluation of a firm requires a clinical judgment of the highest order. The purposes of the evaluation study set the criteria for the judgment. Except in a few instances in which conditions are highly stable, the day is rapidly passing when simple financial analyses, or even financial analyses supplemented by a few interviews and judgments of scientists will suffice for evaluation of a firm.

REFERENCES

1. Ora C. Roehl, "Evaluating Your Company's Future," unpublished paper presented at the Fourth Annual Management Conference, UCLA Executive Program Association, Los Angeles, Oct. 20, 1960, p. 2.

2. Data from the National Science Foundation, cited in *Research Management,* vol. 3, no. 3, p. 129, Autumn, 1960.

3. Lee Dake explains in detail a case in which a financial analyst and a management consultant arrived at opposite conclusions about a firm's prospects in "Are Analysts' Techniques Adequate for Growth Stocks?" *The Financial Analysts Journal,* vol. 16, no. 6, pp. 45–49, November–December, 1960. Dake's thesis can be confirmed many times over in the present author's experience. Particularly distressing was the case where a persuasive but incompe-

tent chief executive persuaded three investment firms to recommend his stock less than six months before declaration of losses exceeding the firm's tangible net worth!

4. The factors are: (a) Economic Function; (b) Corporate Structure; (c) Health of Earnings; (d) Services to Stockholders; (e) Research and Development; (f) Directorate Analysis; (g) Fiscal Policies; (h) Production Efficiency; (i) Sales Vigor; (j) Executive Evaluation. The factors and their use are explained in detail in a series of ten reports: American Institute of Management, *Management Audit Series,* New York, starting in 1953.

5. Most dramatic was the case of the Douglas Aircraft Company whose "excellently managed" rating for 1957–8–9 was followed by staggering losses in late '59 and '60. Among numerous other examples that can be cited are the 1957 ratings of Olin Mathiesen Chemical Co. and Allis-Chalmers Manufacturing Company, both of whom, soon after receiving "excellently managed" ratings, suffered serious declines that have been openly discussed in business magazines. For the ratings, see *Manual of Excellent Managements,* American Institute of Management, New York, 1957. For accounts of the travails of these firms see *Business Week,* Apr. 15, 1961, pp. 147–149, and Apr. 9, 1960, p. 79.

6. Erwin Schell, "Industrial Administration Through the Eyes of an Investment Company," *Appraising Managerial Assets: Policies, Practices and Organization,"* American Management Association, General Management Series, no. 151, New York, 1950. The new emphasis is suggested in a postscript to a reprint published in 1960 by the Keystone Custodian Funds, Inc., Boston, 1960, p. 13. Professor Schell suggested increased emphasis on tax administration, too. The original factors were: (a) Breadth and variety of viewpoint in administration; (b) Vigor and versatility in operating management; (c) Clarity and definiteness of long-term objectives; (d) Vigilance in matters of organization; (e) Dependence upon far-reaching plans; (f) Maintenance of integrated controls; (g) Upkeep in harmony with an advancing art; (h) Improvement as a normal expectancy; (i) Creativeness through high morale; (j) Effectiveness of managerial attitudes; (k) Resources for consistently distinguished leadership in a specific industry.

7. For an illustration and discussion of use of life-cycle curves, see C. Wilson Randle, "Selecting the Research Program: A Top Management Function," *California Management Review,* vol. 2, no. 2, pp. 10–11, Winter, 1960.

8. The Bell and Howell methods are described in two articles: "How to Coordinate Executives," *Business Week,* Sept. 12, 1953, pp. 130ff., and "How to Plan Profits Five Years Ahead," *Nation's Business,* October, 1955, p. 38.

9. An invaluable review of this literature up to early 1957 is given in Albert H. Rubenstein, "Looking Around: Guide to R & D," *Harvard Business Review,* vol. 35, no. 3, pp. 133ff, May–June, 1957. Among the most pertinent articles since Rubenstein's review are Ora C. Roehl, "The Investment Analyst's Evaluation of Industrial Research Capabilities," *Research Management,* vol. 3, no. 3, pp. 127ff, Autumn, 1960; Maurice Nelles, "Changing the World Changers," paper presented at the Ninth Annual Management Conference, Graduate School of Business Administration, University of Chicago, Mar. 1, 1961; C. Wilson Randle, "Problems of R & D Management," *Harvard Business Review,* vol. 37, no. 1, pp. 128ff, January–February, 1959; James B. Quinn, "How to Evaluate Research Output," *Harvard Business Review,* vol. 38, no. 2, pp. 69ff, March–April, 1960; and "Long-range Planning of Industrial Research," *Harvard Business Review,* vol. 39, no. 4, pp. 88ff, July–August, 1961.

10. H. Igor Ansoff, "Strategies for Diversification," *Harvard Business Review,* September–October, 1957.

11. For an exposition of this thought as applied to large firms, see "The New Power of the Financial Executive," *Fortune,* vol. 65, no. 1, pp. 81ff, January, 1962. See also the new text by J. Fred Weston, *Managerial Finance,* Holt, Rinehart and Winston, Inc., New York, 1962.

12. Rensis Likert, reporting on a decade of social science research into patterns of management makes a case for participative management in *New Patterns of Management,* McGraw-Hill Book Company, New York, 1961. George Odiorne, reporting on studies of successful managements, warns strongly against the views of social scientists and makes a case for the more traditional, somewhat autocratic, business leader in *How Managers Make Things Happen,* Prentice-Hall, Inc., Englewood Cliffs, N.J., 1961. Both authors are professors at the University of Michigan.

13. *Environmental Change and Corporate Strategy,* Stanford Research Institute, Menlo Park, Calif., 1960, p. 8. A more recent report on this continuing research project is Robert B. Young, "Keys to Corporate Growth," *Harvard Business Review,* vol. 39, no. 6, pp. 51–62, November–December, 1961. Young concludes: "In short, the odds for corporate

growth are highest when the top executives of a firm treat their future planning as a practical decision making challenge requiring personal participation, and direct their planning efforts toward the origins of opportunity itself. Such an approach can make the difference between having constantly to adapt to day to day crises and enjoying profitable future growth."

14. For one such checklist, see Robert G. Sproul, Jr., "Sizing Up New Acquisitions," *Management Review,* vol. 49, no. 1, pp. 80–82, February, 1960.

15. A new textbook brings together for the first time the few and scattered writings on the subject of "company character." See William B. Wolf, *The Management of Personnel,* Wadsworth Publishing Company, Inc., San Francisco, 1961, pp. 8–43.